D0475094

STRATEGIC MANAGEMENT OF TECHNOLOGY AND INNOVATION

SECOND EDITION

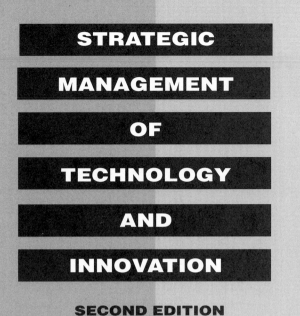

STRATEGIC MANAGEMENT OF TECHNOLOGY AND INNOVATION

SECOND EDITION

Robert A. Burgelman
Stanford University

Modesto A. Maidique
Florida International University

Steven C. Wheelwright
Harvard University

IRWIN

Chicago • Bogotá • Boston • Buenos Aires • Caracas
London • Madrid • Mexico City • Sydney • Toronto

Case material of the Harvard Graduate School of Business Administration is made possible by the cooperation of business firms and other organizations which may wish to remain anonymous by having names, quantities, and other identifying details disguised while maintaining basic relationships. Cases are prepared as the basis for class discussion rather than to illustrate either effective or ineffective handling of administrative situations.

Senior sponsoring editor:	Kurt L. Strand
Senior marketing manager:	Kurt Messersmith
Project editor:	Rebecca Dodson
Production supervisor:	Dina L. Treadaway
Art studio:	Electronic Publishing Services, Inc.
Graphics supervisor:	Charlene Breeden
Compositor:	BookMasters, Inc.
Typeface:	10/12 Times Roman
Printer:	R. R. Donnelly & Sons Company

ISBN 0-256-09128-5

Library of Congress Cataloging-in-Publication Data

Burgelman, Robert A.
Strategic management of technology and innovation / Robert A. Burgelman, Modesto A. Maidique, Steven C. Wheelwright. — 2nd ed.
p. cm.
Includes bibliographical references and index.
ISBN 0-256-09128-5
1. Technological innovations—Management. 2. New products—Management. 3. High technology industries—Management. I. Maidique, Modesto A. II. Wheelwright, Steven C. III. Title.
HD45.B799 1995
658.5′14—dc20 94-44907

Printed in the United States of America
1 2 3 4 5 6 7 8 9 0 DO 2 1 0 9 8 7 6 5

To
Rita, Anna, and Margaret

Preface

Technology and innovation must be managed. That much is generally agreed upon by thoughtful management scholars and practitioners. But can the management of technology and innovation be taught, and if so, how? What concepts, techniques, tools, and management processes facilitate successful technological innovations? The answers to these and several related questions are of great interest to those academics and practitioners who concern themselves with organizations in which technology and innovation are vitally important.

These concerns have been heightened during the past two decades. For more than 30 years following World War II, it appeared that America would reign indefinitely as the world's technological superpower. Although the U.S. is still at the frontier in many key areas of technology, the industrial recovery of Europe and the rise of Japan and other Asian countries as economic and technological superpowers has ended American hegemony. Germany, Japan, Korea, and other European and Asian countries have made major inroads into industries once considered unassailable U.S. strongholds. At first, it seemed that the challenge was mainly in the traditional, capital-intensive, heavy manufacturing industries such as steel and automobiles. But during the 1980s and early 1990s, the challenge broadened to include machine tools, consumer electronics, virtually all aspects of semiconductors, computers and telecommunications, aerospace, and biotechnology. Japanese companies also began to develop the corporate R&D depth and breadth that traditionally had been associated with large U.S. or German companies.

Hayes and Abernathy's 1980 *Harvard Business Review* article, "Are We Managing Our Way to Economic Decline?," signaled the growing awareness that effective management of technological innovation was becoming a high-priority concern for U.S. business. During the 1980s and early 1990s, the importance of technological innovation for competitive advantage, at the level of both the firm and the country, spurred research and the development of related teaching materials. Literally hundreds of universities, through their schools of engineering or business (or both), introduced or substantially expanded the management of technology and innovation as part of their curriculum. This field has indeed become a major topic of broad interest to students, managers, and academics.

Since the late 1980s, the first edition of *Strategic Management of Technology and Innovation* contributed to the development of courses on this subject in many schools. The second edition intends to do the same for the coming years. Many new materials—theory, empirical findings, and cases—have been developed during the period 1988–1994. The second edition reflects the results of many of these efforts.

Overview

The second edition of *Strategic Management of Technology and Innovation* continues to take the perspective of the general manager at the product line, business unit, and corporate levels. The book not only examines each of these levels in some detail, but addresses the interaction between the different levels of general management—for example, the fit between product strategy and business unit strategy, and the link between business and corporate level technology strategy.

The book's new structure reflects a conceptual framework rooted in evolutionary theories of technology, strategy, and organization that have become prominent during the past several years. Each part of the book starts with an introductory chapter laying out an overall framework and offering a brief discussion of key tools and findings from existing literature. The remainder of each part offers a selected handful of seminal readings and case studies. Most of the cases deal with recent events and situations, but some "classics" have been retained because they capture a timeless issue or problem in such a definitive way that the historical date of their writing is irrelevant.

Part I—"Introduction: Integrating Technology and Strategy"—discusses what the general manager needs to know to integrate technology with the firm's strategy and to assess the firm's capacity for innovation. It provides tools for examining the links between technology and firm strategy, and for auditing the firm's innovative capabilities. Part II—"Design and Evolution of Technology Strategy"—discusses the substance of a technology strategy and the key external and internal forces that determine its evolution. In this part, we bring together cases and recent advances in the academic literature on technological evolution, industry and competitive dynamics involving technology, interplays between technology and organizational context, and issues of strategic choice and intent.

Part III—"Enactment of Technology Strategy—Developing the Firm's Innovative Capabilities"—deals with key issues in implementing a technology strategy: internal and external technology sourcing, managing new business, product, and process development, and technical support of customers. The readings and cases in this part examine issues such as managing corporate research, managing strategic research alliances, and managing internal corporate venturing. In Part IV, "Creating and Implementing a Development Strategy," we examine the key stages and tasks in new product development, managing the interfaces between key functional groups in the product development process, the role of the project manager, and the link between product and business strategy. How to augment and develop the firm's innovative capabilities is the unifying thread running through this part of the book.

Part V—"Conclusion: Innovation Challenges in Established Firms"—offers the opportunity for recapitulation and provides an integrated perspective on the innovation challenges faced by the CEO of a high-technology firm.

Acknowledgments

The second edition of *Strategic Management of Technology and Innovation,* like the first, is inspired by the many colleagues whose work has helped shape this dynamic and important field. We will only highlight a handful here, but we continue to be grateful to all who have contributed to this effort. We also want to thank the new scholars who have contributed directly to the materials presented in this second edition for letting us use their work.

We want to express special thanks to Dr. Andrew S. Grove, CEO of Intel Corporation, and to Professor Richard S. Rosenbloom of Harvard Business School. Since 1988, Andy Grove has provided unusual access for Robert Burgelman's research in one of the most important high technology companies of our time. More recently, Andy has become a valued colleague at the Stanford Business School in developing a new course, "Strategy and Action in the Information Processing Industry." Several of the cases and industry notes developed for that course are included here. In 1987, Dick Rosenbloom invited Robert Burgelman to become co-editor of the JAI Press series on *Research on Technological Innovation, Management, and Policy.* "Technology Strategy: An Evolutionary Process Perspective," written together for Volume 4, became the organizing framework for this book.

We also want to express special thanks to Professor Kim Clark and our colleagues at the Harvard Business School for their many research and case publications. Their perspective, insights, and encouragement have done much to improve our work.

Since the 1988 publication of the first edition of *Strategic Management of Technology and Innovation,* Harvard University, Florida International University, and Stanford University have continued to provide generous support for our research and course development. For Robert Burgelman, this support has come from the Strategic Management Program and the 1988–1989 BP America Fellowship of Stanford's Graduate School of Business, and from the 1991–1992 Marvin Bower Fellowship of Harvard Business School; for Mitch Maidique, it has come from the generous support of alumni and friends of Florida International University; and for Steve Wheelwright, it has come from the Division of Research at the Harvard Business School and its many alumni, friends, and corporate sponsors.

We would like to thank the following colleagues who reviewed the first edition of the text:

Dr. John Aje – *University of Maryland,* Mohammad Ala – *California State University in Los Angeles,* Edward J. Cherian – *George Washington University,* Redding H. Thompson – *Rivier College,* Dr. Karl H. Grote – *California State University in Long Beach,* Brad Kleindl – *Missouri Southern State College,* Robert M. Mason – *Case Reserve Western University,* Michael Musi – *Boston University,* V. K. Narayanan – *University of Kansas,* Karol I. Pelc – *Michigan Technological University,* Dr. Catherine L. Propst – *Northwestern University,* William H. Read – *Georgia Institute of Technology,* Michael Shaw – *University of Illinois,* and Jennifer Starr – *Babson College.*

As anyone who has completed a book-length manuscript knows, the final product is a team effort. This book would never have been completed without the help of Kurt Strand, our senior editor at Irwin, and Jean Smith of the Harvard Business School. For more than two years Kurt encouraged us as he inquired about progress on the book, only to find that ongoing research and teaching had caused delay. But he persisted and we are all the better for it. Jean put together all the materials, edited the chapters, and was instrumental in helping us meet the publisher's deadlines. Many thanks to Kurt and Jean.

Thanks also to our secretaries, especially Jiranee Tongudai and Natasha Omdahl, who have provided essential administrative assistance, and to our many research associates who helped with individual cases and notes. These include: George Cogan, Stanford MBA 1989; Bruce Graham, Stanford MBA 1991; Thomas Kurian, Stanford MBA 1994; Dan Steere, Stanford MBA 1993; and Alva Taylor, Ph.D. candidate at Stanford's Graduate School of Business. They have written several new cases and industry notes under Robert Burgelman's direction. In addition, Tom Kosnik, lecturer at Stanford's Department of Industrial Engineering and Engineering Management, wrote a new case on Microsoft under Mitch Maidique's direction.

We are also grateful to the several thousand Stanford and Harvard MBA and engineering students, and the hundreds of participants in executive programs worldwide, who, through their many interactions helped us test and improve the materials in the book.

Finally, a word of thanks to Rita, Anna, and Margaret for their unwavering support throughout this venture.

Robert A. Burgelman

Modesto A. Maidique

Steven C. Wheelwright

Acknowledgments for Case Materials

Angelmar, R.	Advanced Drug Delivery Systems: ALZA and CIBA Geigy (A) ALZA Corporation (A) CIBA-Geigy Limited: Pharmaceutical Division (A);
Bartlett, C. A.	EMI and the CT Scanner (A) and (B)
Bower, J. L.	PC&D, Inc.
Bupp, I. C.	Texas Instruments' "Speak and Spell" Division
Christiansen, E. T.	PC&D, Inc.
Cogan, G. W.	Intel Corporation (A): The DRAM Decision Intel Corporation (C): Strategy for the 1990s
Cross, K.	Microsoft LAN Manager
Crowe, J. M.	Biodel, Inc. (A)
Cunningham, M. W.	Advanced Drug Delivery Systems: ALZA and CIBA-Geigy (A) ALZA Corporation (A) CIBA-Geigy Limited: Pharmaceutical Division (A)
Dheer, S.	EDS: Information Technology Outsourcing
Doz, Y.	Advanced Drug Delivery Systems: ALZA and CIBA Geigy (A) ALZA Corporation (A)
Dugal, S.	Associated Instruments Corporation: Analytic Instruments Division
Freeze, K.	Braun AG: The KF 40 Coffee Machine Banc One Corporation and the Home Information Revolution
Gable, J. S.	Apple Computer (A)
Garvin, D. A.	Allegheny Ludlum Steel (Abridged) Allstate Chemical Company
Gill, G. K.	Campbell Soup Company
Gomes-Casseres, B.	MIPS Computer Systems, Inc.
Grove, A. S.	Telecommunications Industry Note The Wireless Communications Industry: After AT&T-McCaw
Hammermesh, R.	PC&D, Inc.
Huntington, C.	Claire McCloud
Hurstak, J. M.	Reshaping Apple Computer's Destiny 1992
Jakimo, A. L.	Texas Instruments' "Speak and Spell" Division
Kurian, T.	The Operating Systems Software Industry in 1994
Kosnik, T. J.	Medical Equipment (A) Microsoft LAN Manager
Langowitz, N. S.	Plus Development Corporation (A) (Abridged)
Lawrence, P.	Aerospace Systems (A) and (B) (Condensed)
Leonard-Barton, D. A.	Chaparral Steel: Rapid Product and Process Development Monsanto's March into Biotechnology
March, A.	Allstate Chemical Company
McQuade, K.	Mips Computer Systems, Inc.
Pisano, G.	Biotechnology: A Technical Note Monsanto's March into Biotechnology

Porter, M. E.	Bendix Corporation (A)
Preuss, G.	Chaparral Steel: Rapid Product and Process Development
Rosenbloom, R. S.	Advent Corporation (C) Banc One Corporation and the Home Information Revolution
Roth, S. J.	Bendix Corporation (A)
Ruedi, A.	Aerospace Systems (A) and (B) (Condensed)
Saloner, G.	EDS: Information Technology Outsourcing
Seecharan, B. A.	Microsoft LAN Manager
Steere, D.	Intel Corporation (D): Microprocessors at the Crossroads
Taylor, A.	Telecommunications Industry Note The Wireless Communications Industry: After AT&T-McCaw
Tylka, S.	Apple Computer (A)
Viard, B.	EDS: Information Technology Outsourcing
Yoffie, D. B.	Reshaping Apple Computer's Destiny 1992

Contents

PART

I Introduction: Integrating Technology and Strategy

Technology, Innovation, and Strategy: A General Management Perspective

A key purpose of this book is to help the general manager—someone responsible for the overall strategic management of an organization or autonomous business unit—deal with issues of technology and innovation. Established high-technology companies typically spend at least 5 percent of sales on technology and innovation-related activities; start-up companies may spend significantly more. Although most of the companies studied here are considered high-technology, the issues and problems associated with technology and innovation in the environment of the 1990s are part of the general management task in *all* firms.

One key task of the general manager is to acquire, develop, and allocate an organization's resources. Technology is a resource of paramount importance to many organizations; managing this resource for competitive advantage entails integrating it with the firm's strategy. A second key task of the general manager is to develop and exploit the firm's capacity for innovation. This requires that the general manager be able to assess the firm's innovative capabilities and identify how they may be leveraged or improved. This chapter provides a set of tools the general manager can use to accomplish both of these major tasks.

The chapter consists of three sections. In the first, we define a set of key concepts concerning technological innovation and then outline their interrelations. This step is important because strategic management of technology and innovation is a young field and the domains of different, partly overlapping concepts are still somewhat in flux. Though we do not claim that the definitions and interrelations presented here are definitive, they are generally accepted by scholars and practitioners in the field, and they are useful for organizing the discussion of cases and readings that follows. The second section of the chapter discusses the integration of technology with business and corporate strategy. The third section presents a framework for auditing and assessing the firm's innovative capabilities. A brief conclusion follows the third section.

Key Concepts and Their Relationships

Inventions/Discoveries/Technologies

At the origin of the technological innovation process are inventions or discoveries. As Webster points out, "We discover what before existed, though to us unknown; we invent what did not before exist." Inventions and discoveries are the result of creative processes which are often serendipitous and very difficult to predict or plan. For instance, Aspartame, a sweetener used in many food and beverage products, was a chance discovery. Researchers in universities, the government, and industrial labs following the canons of modern science—as well as idiosyncratic tinkers in a garage—play a role in these processes. *Basic* scientific research refers to activities involved in generating new knowledge about physical, biological, and social phenomena. *Applied* scientific research is geared toward solving particular technical problems. The cumulative body of systematic and codified knowledge resulting from scientific research forms the substratum for many, but not all, inventions and discoveries (e.g., the wheel was not the result of scientific research).

The criteria for success regarding inventions and discoveries are technical (is it true/real?) rather than commercial (does it provide a basis for economic rents?). Through *patents*, inventions and discoveries sometimes allow their originators to establish a potential for economic rents with subsequent innovations (see below), but there may be a significant time lag (10 years or more) between doing scientific research and using the inventions and discoveries to create successful innovations (superconductivity and genetic engineering are examples).

Technology refers to the theoretical and practical knowledge, skills, and artifacts that can be used to develop products and services as well as their production and delivery systems. Technology can be embodied in people, materials, cognitive and physical processes, plant, equipment, and tools. Key elements of technology may be implicit, existing only in an embedded form (e.g., trade secrets based on know-how). Craftsmanship and experience usually have a large tacit component, so that important parts of technology may not be expressed or codified in manuals, routines and procedures, recipes, rules of thumb, or other explicit articulations. The criteria for success regarding technology are also technical (Can it do the job?) rather than commercial (Can it do the job profitably?). Technologies are usually the outcome of development activities to put inventions and discoveries to practical use. The invention of the transistor (1947), integrated circuit (1959), and microprocessor (1971), for example, gave rise to successive generations of new technologies in the semiconductor industry that were, in turn, applied in areas such as data processing and telecommunications.

Technological Innovations

Some innovations are technology-based (e.g., disposable diapers, oversized tennis racquets, electronic fuel injection, and personal computers). Other innovations, such as new products or services in retailing and financial services, are facilitated by new technology (e.g., electronic data processing). The criteria for success of technological innovation are commercial rather than technical: a successful innovation is one that returns the original investment in its development plus some additional returns. This requires that a sufficiently large market for the innovation can be developed. Innovations are the outcome of the *innovation process*, which can be defined as the combined activities leading to new, marketable products and services and/or new production and delivery systems.

Different types of innovation have been identified in the literature. *Incremental* innovations involve the adaptation, refinement, and enhancement of existing products and services and/or production and delivery systems—for example, the next generation of a microprocessor. *Radical* innovations involve entirely new product and service categories and/or production and delivery systems (e.g., wireless communications). *Architectural* innovations refer to reconfigurations of the system of components that constitute the product—for example, the effects of miniaturization of key radio components.

Technological Entrepreneurship

Entrepreneurship is a fundamental driver of the technological innovation process. Technological entrepreneurship refers to activities that create new resource combinations to make innovation possible, bringing together the technical and commercial worlds in a profitable way. Administrative capabilities must be deployed both effectively and efficiently. Technological entrepreneurship can involve one individual (*individual* entrepreneurship) or the combined activities of multiple participants in an organization (*corporate* entrepreneurship).

Activities and Outcomes

The discussion of key concepts suggests that it is useful to distinguish between activities and outcomes. Inventions, discoveries, and technologies (outcomes) are the result of tinkering and experimenting, as well as of systematic basic and applied R&D (activities). Technological innovations (outcomes) are the result of product, process, and market development (activities). Technological entrepreneurship involves product, process, and market development

EXHIBIT 1 The Relationships between Key Concepts Concerning Technological Innovation

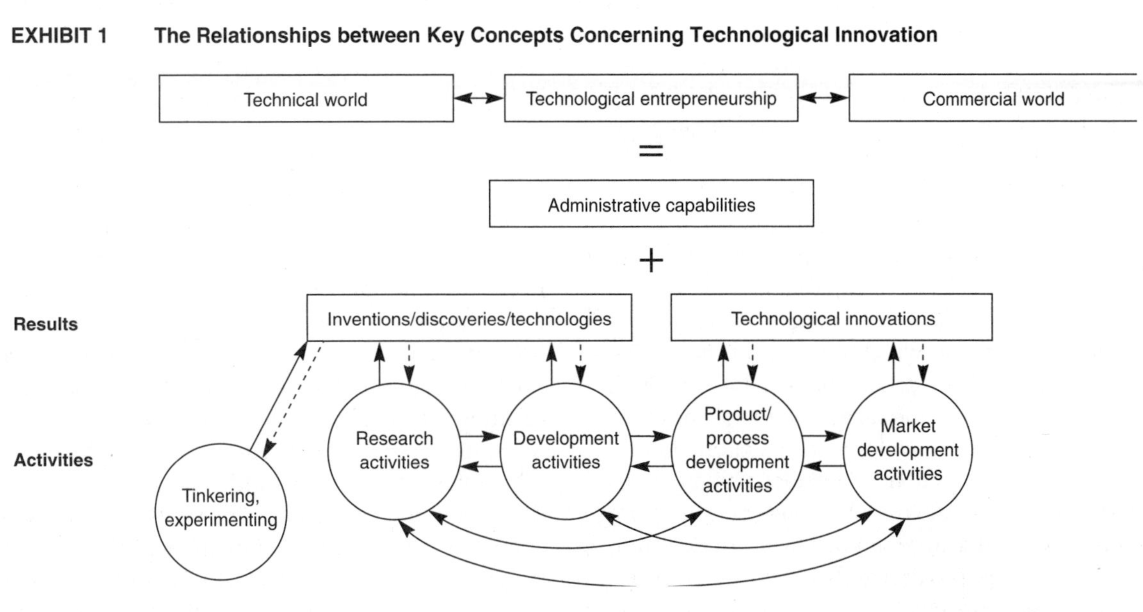

(activities) as well as the development of administrative capabilities.

Interrelations among Key Concepts

Exhibit 1 shows the relationships between key concepts in the technological innovation process. It highlights the activities constituting the process and the outcomes produced. The process depicted in Exhibit 1 can start with market development or technical activities. In reality, the technological innovation process will almost always be iterative and concurrent rather than unidirectional and sequential.

Integrating Technology and Strategy

Perspectives on Strategy

Positive versus normative views. The positive view of strategy is concerned with the firm's actual strategy and how it comes to be. The normative view, on the other hand, is concerned with what the firm's strategy should be.

The positive view of strategy proposes that the firm's strategy reflects top-management beliefs about the basis of the firm's past and current success.[1] These beliefs concern (*a*) core competencies, (*b*) product market areas, (*c*) core values, and (*d*) people, as well as associations between these elements and the firm's success. They can be viewed as the result of organizational learning processes. They drive top management's efforts to establish a strategic process that will take advantage of this organizational learning. Not surprisingly, there is likely to be a good deal of inertia associated with this set of beliefs.[2] Hence, to understand a firm's strategy, it is necessary not only to consider top management statements and assertions about the firm's strategy but also to observe what the firm actually does. Quite often, especially in the dynamic environments associated with high-technology firms, there is a divergence between professed strategy and strategic action.[3]

Product-market versus resource-based views. The product-market view of strategy is primarily concerned with how the firm competes with its products

[1]See, for example, R. A. Burgelman, "Corporate Entrepreneurship and Strategic Management: Insights from a Process Study," *Management Science* 29 (1983), pp. 1349–64.

[2]R. A. Burgelman, "Intraorganizational Ecology of Strategy Making and Organizational Adaptation: Theory and Field Research," *Organization Science* 2 (1991), pp. 239–62.

[3]R. A. Burgelman, "Fading Memories: A Process Theory of Strategic Business Exit in Dynamic Environments," *Administrative Science Quarterly* 39 (1994), pp. 24–56.

and services. The resource-based view of strategy is concerned primarily with how the firm can secure the factors needed to create the core competencies and capabilities that form the basis for establishing and sustaining competitive advantage. Strategy is inherently a function of the quantity and quality of a firm's capabilities. Strategy without capabilities has no force. On the other hand, capabilities without strategy remain aimless. Strategy asks the question, How do competencies and capabilities help create and sustain competitive advantage? Strategy thus articulates the ways in which the opportunities that are created by the firm's capabilities can be exploited.

During the 1980s, normative views of product-market strategy received widespread attention. Porter's "five forces" and "generic strategies" frameworks offered tools for explaining why some industries are inherently more attractive than others, for understanding a firm's strategic position relative to that of its rivals, and for devising strategic actions that can affect the overall industry attractiveness and the strategic position of individual firms.[4] Normative statements about core competence and capabilities-based competition during the early 1990s indicate the growing prominence of the resource-based view of strategy.[5] Current normative work in strategy is oriented toward better integrating the product-market and resource-based views.

Connecting Technology and Strategy

During the 1980s, strategic management scholars began to recognize technology as an important element of business definition and competitive strategy. For instance, Abell identified technology as one of three principal dimensions of business definition, noting "technology adds a dynamic character to the task of business definition, as one technology may more or less rapidly displace another over time."[6] Porter observes that technology is among the most prominent factors that determine the rules of competition.[7] Friar and Horwitch explain the growing prominence of technology as the result of historical forces: disenchantment with strategic planning, the success of high-technology firms in emerging industries, the surge of Japanese competition, a recognition of the competitive significance of manufacturing, and the emergence of an academic interest in technology management.[8]

But what, precisely, does a general manager considering the role of technology in a firm's strategy need to know? According to one school of thought, it is enough to understand the parameters transformed by the technological black box (the computer or instrument in question). That is, it is enough to know *what* the technological device or system does, not *how* it does it. An alternative view argues that unless one understands the functioning of a device and the laws that delineate its limitations, one cannot make effective judgments regarding the shaping of relevant technologies into successful products. The position taken in this book is that general managers need not have backgrounds in science or engineering, but they do need to invest significant effort in learning to understand the technologies important to their business. They must also identify reliable and trustworthy sources of technical advice. Most important, they must be able to frame the key strategic questions in relation to technology. The remainder of this section focuses on these key questions and discusses the tools necessary to examine how a firm's technology and business strategy can be integrated most effectively.

Technology and product-market strategy. A firm's strategy is expressed in the products and services it brings to market. One way to get at the integration of a firm's technology and product-market strategy is to decompose each product or service into its constituting technologies and assess the relative strength—the degree of distinctive competence—the firm has with respect to that technology. Exhibit 2 shows the outline for constructing a technology/product matrix.

Although Exhibit 2 is a first step in analyzing a firm's degree of integration, it is often difficult to specify the various technologies in the matrix at the appropriate level of detail and in their concrete relation to the firm's products. It is obvious that a firm manufacturing and marketing cameras should have

[4]M. E. Porter, *Competitive Advantage* (New York: Free Press, 1985).

[5]C. K. Prahalad and G. Hamel, "The Core Competence of the Corporation," *Harvard Business Review,* May–June 1990; G. Stalk, P. Evans, and L. E. Shulman, "Competing on Capabilities: The New Rules of Corporate Strategy," *Harvard Business Review,* March–April 1992.

[6]D. Abell, *Defining the Business* (Englewood Cliffs, NJ: Prentice Hall, 1980).

[7]M. E. Porter, "The Technological Dimension of Competitive Strategy," *Research on Technological Innovation, Management, and Policy* 1 (1983), pp. 1–33.

[8]J. Friar and M. Horwitch, "The Emergence of Technology Strategy: A New Dimension of Strategic Management," *Technology in Society* 7 (1985), pp. 143–78.

EXHIBIT 2 The Product/Technology Matrix

	Product A	Product B	•••	Product N
Technology 1 Technology 2 • • • Technology K	(*)			

Note: Each entry (*) should establish the firm's relative strength vis-à-vis the state of the art.

SOURCE: Adapted from A. Fusfeld. "How to Put Technology into Corporate Planning." *Technology Review*, May 1978. Reprinted with permission from *Technology Review*, MIT Alumni Association, © 1978.

EXHIBIT 3 Developing the Technology Portfolio

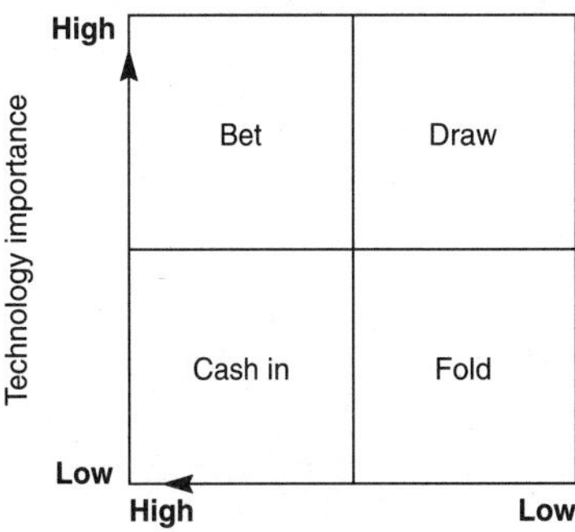

SOURCE: J. M. Harris, R. W. Shaw, Jr., and W. P. Somers, *The Strategic Management of Technology* (New York: Booz Allen Hamilton Inc., 1981).

competencies in optics, for instance. But it is not enough to determine the strength of the firm's capabilities; it is necessary to specify how the firm's strengths in the area of optics help the firm's cameras have higher quality or lower cost.

Technology portfolio. Harris, Shaw, and Somers suggest that once the various technologies have been identified, they can be classified in terms of their importance for competitive advantage.[9] Next, the firm's position relative to its competitors can be assessed. *Technology importance* needs to be expressed in terms of the value added it brings to a particular class of products and the value added it could potentially bring to other product classes for the customer/user. The importance of a particular technology is strongly affected by where it is situated in the technology life cycle (see below). *Relative technology position* should be expressed in reference to competitors in terms of, for example, patent position, know-how and trade secrets, learning curve effects, and key talent. Relative technology position is strongly (but not wholly) affected by the firm's historical and future levels of investment. Exhibit 3 presents a framework based on these two dimensions. Harris, Shaw, and Somers propose that technologies in the "bet" quadrant warrant the firm's full commitment.[10] That is, the firm should be willing to engage in frontier R&D, push the limits of its product development process, and invest in the newest equipment.

Technologies in the "cash in" quadrant should be examined carefully. These technologies may have been very important at one time, but changes in the basis of competition in the industry may have reduced their relative importance. Understanding these changes and why they came about often leads to insight into the firm's strategic situation.[11] Also, while "cash in" might suggest that no further investment in these technologies is warranted, such a move may be premature or misguided. Sometimes parts of these technologies continue to be linked in subtle ways with other technologies judged to be relatively more important.

Technologies in the "draw" quadrant are also positioned ambiguously. A technology may be placed here because of changes in the basis of industry competition. At this point, the firm must decide whether to invest, probably heavily, in the technology so as to reach (at least) parity with its competitors, or to disengage from a particular product or business. Again, it is extremely important to ask why and how this change came about.

Technologies in the "fold" quadrant require that the firm reconsider its investments in them. Inertial forces often lead to continued investment in R&D beyond the level where reasonable returns can be expected. Regular reviews of investments patterns may indicate a need to disengage and redeploy resources.

---

[9]J. M. Harris, R. W. Shaw, Jr., and W. P. Somers, *The Strategic Management of Technology* (New York: Booz Allen Hamilton Inc., 1981).

[10]Ibid.

[11]For example, see Burgelman, "Fading Memories," pp. 24–56.

EXHIBIT 4 Matching Business and Technology Portfolios

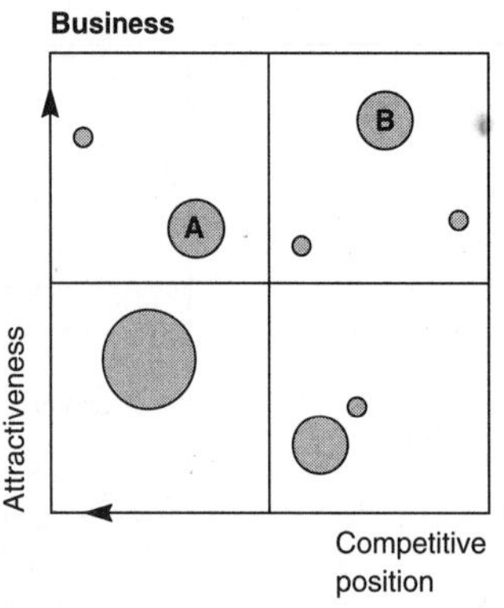

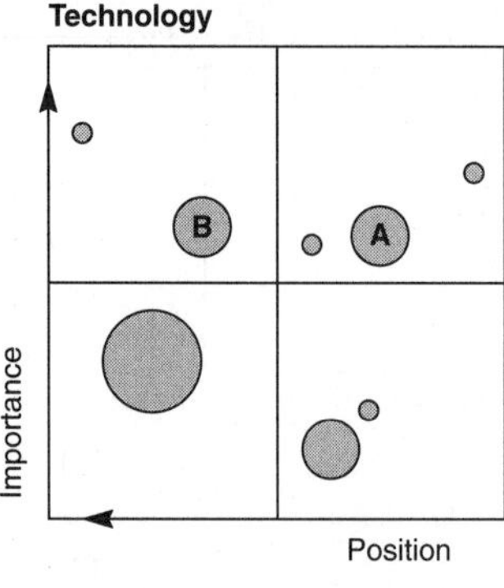

SOURCE: J. M. Harris, R. W. Shaw, Jr., and W. P. Somers, *The Strategic Management of Technology* (New York: Booz Allen Hamilton Inc., 1981).

Technology portfolio and business portfolio. Many companies have multiple businesses in their corporate portfolio, each with its own technologies. Corporate strategy development has been enhanced by portfolio planning techniques, but most have failed to pay explicit attention to technology. One such portfolio planning tool is McKinsey's framework based on *industry attractiveness* and *competitive position* dimensions. Harris, Shaw, and Somers suggest examining the relationship between the traditional portfolio planning matrix and the technology portfolio matrix (see Exhibit 2).[12] This is presented in Exhibit 4.

Such analysis offers the possibility of investigating the match (or mismatch) of a firm's business and technology portfolios and its resulting technology investment priorities. For instance, standard strategic analysis may indicate that a particular business is in a strong competitive position in an attractive industry. However, technological analysis may indicate that the technologies supporting this business, while important for competitive advantage, are actually in a relatively weak position. This would indicate the need to increase investment in technology development.

Technology and the Value Chain

In the broadest sense, the term *technology* encompasses the entire set of technologies employed in the sequence of activities that constitute a firm's value chain.[13] Exhibit 5 shows an example of various technologies in a firm's value chain.

As Porter points out, any of these technologies can affect the industry structure or a firm's differentiation or cost position—and, therefore, its competitive advantage.[14] Hence, it is important for the general manager to track the evolution of all the technologies that affect the firm's value activities. Designing a technology strategy (Part II of this book) requires that the firm decide (*a*) how each technology can be used for competitive advantage, and (*b*) whether a given technology should be developed in-house or procured.

Technological Evolution and Forecasting

Technology life cycle. Technological change is one of the most important forces affecting a firm's competitive position, and research suggests that firms find it difficult to respond to such changes.[15] Integrating technology and strategy should therefore

[12]Harris et al., *The Strategic Management of Technology.*

[13]Porter, *Competitive Advantage.*

[14]Ibid.

[15]A. C. Cooper and D. Schendel, "Strategic Responses to Technological Threats," *Business Horizons,* February 1976, pp. 61–63; M. L. Tushman and A. Anderson, "Technological and Organizational Environments," *Administrative Science Quarterly* 31 (1986), pp. 439–65; R. Henderson and K. B. Clark, "Architectural Innovation: The Reconfiguration of Existing Systems and the Failure of Established Firms," *Administrative Science Quarterly* 35, no. 1 (1990), pp. 9–30; and Burgelman, "Fading Memories," pp. 24–56.

EXHIBIT 5 Representative Technologies in a Firm's Value Chain

Inbound logistics	Operations	Outbound logistics	Marketing sales	Service
Transportation technology	Basic product technology	Transportation technology	Media technology	Diagnostic and testing technology
Material handling technology	Materials technology	Material handling technology	Audio and video recording technology	Communication system technology
Storage and preservation technology	Machine tool technology	Packaging technology	Communication system technology	Information system technology
Communication system technology	Material handling technology	Communication system technology	Information system technology	
Testing technology	Packaging technology	Information system technology		
Information system technology	Maintenance methods			
	Testing technology			
	Building design operation technology			
	Information system technology			

SOURCE: Adapted with permission of the Free Press, a division of Macmillan, Inc., from M. E. Porter, *Competitive Advantage: Creating and Sustaining Superior Performance* (New York: Free Press, 1985). Copyright © 1985 by Michael E. Porter.

be a dynamic process, and it requires that the firm understand the dynamics of the life cycle of the various technologies it employs. Exhibit 6 shows the link between stages in the technology life cycle and the potential for competitive advantage.

Technology forecasting. An important element in integrating technology and strategy is the capacity to perform systematic technological forecasting. Several authors have presented useful techniques, such as technological progress functions (S-curves), trend extrapolation, the Delphi method, and scenario development.[16] Underlying the capacity to forecast—and, perhaps more importantly, to see the relationships between technologically significant events—is the effort to gather data systematically and continuously. Maintaining a log book for this purpose is often an effective way of doing such data collection.

Assessing Innovative Capabilities

General managers are responsible for managing the innovation process. They must make difficult decisions about which innovations will receive managerial attention and resources. Insights into the firm's innovative potential and into the barriers to innovation are necessary to make effective proactive strategic choices. But how can general managers assess the innovation potential of their organizations? The remainder of this chapter offers a framework for doing an *innovative capabilities audit.*[17] Such an audit may help the general manager assess the

[16]See, for example, B. Twiss, *Managing Technological Innovation* (London: Longman, 1980); R. N. Foster, *Innovation: The Attacker's Advantage* (New York: Summit, 1986); and S. C. Wheelwright and S. Makridakis, *Forecasting Methods for Management,* 5th ed. (New York: Wiley-Interscience, 1989).

[17]R. A. Burgelman, T. J. Kosnik, and M. Van den Poel, "Toward an Innovative Capabilities Audit Framework," in R. A. Burgelman and M. A. Maidique, eds., *Strategic Management of Technology and Innovation* (Homewood, IL: Richard D. Irwin, 1988).

EXHIBIT 6 Technology Life Cycle and Competitive Advantages

Stages in Technology Life Cycle	Importance of Technologies for Competitive Advantage
I. Emerging technologies	Have not yet demonstrated potential for changing the basis of competition.
II. Pacing technologies	Have demonstrated their potential for changing the basis of competition.
III. Key technologies	Are embedded in and enable product/process. Have major impact on value-added stream (cost, performance, quality). Allow proprietary/patented positions.
IV. Base technologies	Minor impact on value-added stream; common to all competitors; commodity.

SOURCE: Adapted from Arthur D. Little, "The Strategic Management of Technology," *European Management Forum*, 1981.

potential of existing innovative capabilities and construct a development plan for the future. An audit must address at least three questions:

1. How has the firm been innovative in the areas of product and service offerings and/or production and delivery systems?
2. How good is the fit between the firm's current business and corporate strategies and its innovative capabilities?
3. What are the firm's needs in terms of innovative capabilities to support its long-term business and corporate competitive strategies?

Innovative Capabilities Audit Framework

Innovation depends on technological as well as other critical capabilities in areas such as manufacturing, marketing and distribution, and human resource management. For example, a technology strategy designed to achieve superior product performance must be complemented by a technically trained sales force that can educate the customer regarding the product's performance advantages, and by a high-quality manufacturing system.

Innovative capabilities. Innovative capabilities can be defined as *the comprehensive set of characteristics of an organization that facilitate and support innovation strategies.* Innovative capabilities exist at the business unit and corporate (multibusiness) levels.

- Business unit—a unit for which a particular strategy and resource commitment posture can be defined because it has a distinct set of product markets, competitors, and resources. An innovative capabilities audit identifies the critical variables that influence the innovation strategies at this level.
- Corporate—an audit at this level identifies the critical variables that influence both the relationships between corporate and business unit levels in terms of innovative capabilities and the formulation and implementation of an overall corporate innovation strategy.

Business unit level audit. In general, the innovative strategies at this level with respect to new products and services and/or new production and delivery systems can be characterized in terms of:

- Timing of market entry.
- Technological leadership or followership.
- Scope of innovativeness.
- Rate of innovativeness.

Five important categories of variables influence the innovation strategies of a business:

- Resources available for innovative activity.
- Capacity to understand competitors' strategies and industry evolution with respect to innovation.
- Capacity to understand technological developments relevant to the business unit.
- Structural and cultural context of the business unit affecting internal entrepreneurial behavior.
- Strategic management capacity to deal with internal entrepreneurial initiatives.

These are represented in Exhibit 7.

The first three categories listed above are important inputs for the *formulation* of business unit innovation strategies; the final two, for the *implementation* of business unit innovation strategies. Exhibit 8 lists some of the critical issues for auditing each of the five categories. This list is not exhaus-

EXHIBIT 7 Innovative Capabilities Audit Framework—Business Unit Level

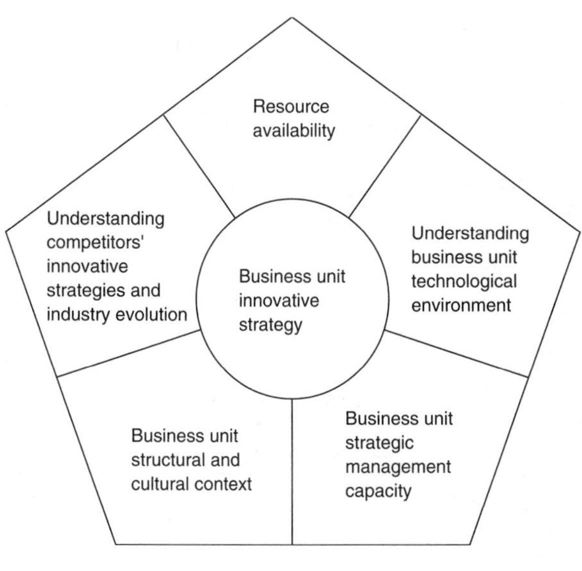

tive; additional items may be added to reflect the particulars of different situations.

The combination of the five categories determines the relative strength of the business unit for formulating and implementing innovation strategies. Thus, the audit should address this as well. For example, a business unit may have ample resources for new product development but lack the strategic management capacity to channel these resources (both within the unit and relative to competitors' moves). Alternatively, the necessary resources and strategic management capacity may bring about new products whose technologies are on the verge of becoming obsolete.

Corporate level audit. The raison d'être of multibusiness firms is based on corporate management's ability to identify and exploit synergies. An audit at the corporate level thus introduces an additional dimension. Here, it is necessary to examine how the corporate innovative capabilities enhance the innovative capabilities at the business unit level. In other words, it is necessary to investigate whether and how the total corporate innovative capabilities are larger than the sum of the business units' innovative capabilities. In general, corporate level innovative capabilities can be characterized in terms of:

- The scope and rate of development of new products and services and/or production and delivery systems that are derived from combining innovative capabilities across existing business units.
- The scope and rate of new business development based on corporate R&D and technology development efforts.
- Timing of entry with respect to the above.

Again, five categories of variables are considered for the corporate level audit, each of which corresponds to a category at the business unit level but with a somewhat different emphasis: the capacity to do more than what the business unit could do on its own. Exhibit 9 represents the five categories of variables:

- Resource availability and allocation (e.g., corporate R&D, cash availability for risky projects).
- The capacity to understand multi-industry competitive strategies and evolution (e.g., corporate strategic planning for innovation).
- The capacity to understand technological developments (e.g., multi-industry scanning and technological forecasting).
- Corporate structural and cultural context.
- Corporate strategic management capacity (e.g., exploitation of synergies in innovation through "horizontal" strategies; internal corporate venturing and acquisition strategies).

Resource availability and corporate level capacities to understand the competitive and technological environments again serve as inputs for corporate strategy formulation. Corporate structural and cultural context as well as corporate strategic management capacity serve as inputs for corporate strategy implementation. Exhibit 10 lists critical issues to be addressed in each category to carry out the corporate level audit. As for the business level audit, the combinatory effects of the five categories of variables on corporate innovation strategies should be assessed.

Audit frames of reference. One frame of reference for interpreting the results of the innovative capabilities audit is historical—how the current situation compares to the past; a second frame of reference concerns the firm's position relative to current competitors. Both allow major variances with respect to desired positions to be identified.

EXHIBIT 8 Innovative Capabilities Audit Framework—Business Level

1. *Resource Availability and Allocation*
   Level of R&D funding and evolution:
      In absolute terms.
      As percentage of sales.
      As percentage of total firm R&D funding.
      As compared to main competitors.
      As compared to leading competitor.
   Breadth and depth of skills at business unit level in R&D, engineering, and market research.
   Distinctive competences in areas of technology relevant to business unit.
   Allocation of R&D to:
      Existing product/market combinations.
      New product development for existing product categories.
      Development of new product categories.
2. *Understanding Competitors' Innovative Strategies and Industry Evolution*
   Intelligence systems and data available.
   Capacity to identify, analyze, and predict competitors' innovative strategies.
   Capacity to identify, analyze, and predict industry evolution.
   Capacity to anticipate facilitating/impeding external forces relevant to business unit's innovative strategies.
3. *Understanding the Business Unit's Technological Environment*
   Capacity for technological forecasting relevant to business unit's technologies.
   Capacity to assess technologies relevant to business unit.
   Capacity to identify technological opportunities for business unit.
4. *Business Unit Structural and Cultural Context*
   Mechanisms for managing R&D efforts.
   Mechanisms for transferring technology from research to development.
   Mechanisms for integrating different functional groups (R&D, engineering, marketing, manufacturing) in the new product development process.
   Mechanisms for funding unplanned new product initiatives.
   Mechanisms for eliciting new ideas from employees.
   Evaluation and reward systems for entrepreneurial behavior.
   Dominant values and definition of success.
5. *Strategic Management Capacity to Deal with Entrepreneurial Behavior*
   Business unit level management capacity to define a substantive development strategy.
   Business unit level management capacity to assess strategic importance of entrepreneurial initiatives.
   Business unit level management capacity to assess relatedness of entrepreneurial initiatives to unit's core capabilities.
   Capacity of business unit level management to coach product champions.
   Quality and availability of product champions in the business unit.

Who should do the audit? General managers will have to rely on others to collect much of the information necessary for the audit and for some of the interpretation as well. They will have to decide how much to rely on help from insiders and outsiders. Insiders are likely to have an advantage in understanding the firm's resource availability and structural and cultural context. Outsiders may provide a more realistic assessment of the firm's strategic management capacity and its ability to understand the competitive and technological environments. The major disadvantage of using insiders is the possibility of a narrow or biased perspective. Outsiders, on the other hand, are more likely to misunderstand internal realities and deliver impractical recommendations.

The audit could be undertaken by the firm's strategic planning department. More valuable insights would probably be generated by setting up an ad hoc audit team with representatives from strategic planning, R&D, new product managers, and key functional managers.

Conclusion

A variety of concepts, tools, perspectives, and roles are important and useful to the management of technology, strategy, and innovation. It is the premise of this book, however, that the *leadership* of general managers is critical to the success of these endeavors. Thus, while much can be done to assist general managers in these tasks, nothing can substitute for or replace their leadership. Throughout the text and cases of subsequent chapters, we will highlight not only analytical and organizational approaches, but also methods and techniques, for asserting and exercising leadership.

EXHIBIT 9 Innovative Capabilities Audit Framework—Corporate Level

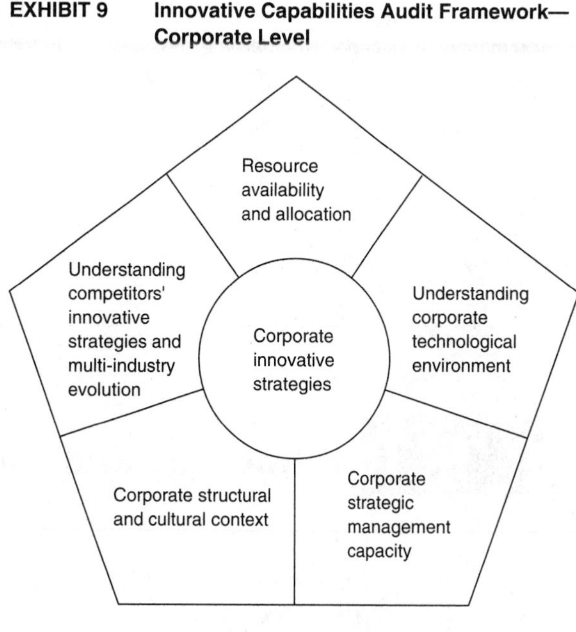

EXHIBIT 10 Innovative Capabilities Audit Framework—Corporate Level

1. *Resource Availability and Allocation*
   Corporate R&D funding level and evolution:
      In absolute terms.
      As percentage of sales.
      As compared to average of main competitors.
      As compared to leading competitor.
   Breadth and depth of skills of corporate level personnel in R&D, engineering, and market research.
   Distinctive competences in areas of technology relevant to multiple business units.
   Corporate R&D allocation to:
      Exploratory research.
      R&D in support of mainstream business.
      R&D in support of new business definition.
      R&D in support of new business development.
2. *Understanding Competitors' Innovative Strategies and Multi-Industry Evolution*
   Intelligence systems and data available.
   Capacity to identify, analyze, and predict competitors' innovative strategies spanning multiple industries.
   Capacity to develop scenarios concerning evolution of interdependencies between multiple industries.
   Capacity to anticipate facilitating/impeding external forces relevant to firm's innovative strategies.
3. *Understanding the Corporate Technological Environment*
   Capacity for technological forecasting in multiple areas.
   Capacity to forecast cross-impacts between areas of technology.
   Capacity to assess technologies in multiple areas.
   Capacity to identify technological opportunities spanning multiple areas.
4. *Corporate Context (Structural and Cultural)*
   Mechanisms to share technologies across business unit boundaries.
   Mechanisms to define new business opportunities across business unit boundaries.
   Internal and external organization designs for managing new ventures.
   Mechanisms to fund unplanned initiatives.
   Evaluation and reward systems for entrepreneurial behavior.
   Movement of personnel between mainstream activities and new ventures.
   Dominant values and definition of success.

EXHIBIT 10 *(continued)*

5. *Strategic Management Capacity to Deal with Entrepreneurial Behavior*
   Top management capacity to define a substantive long-term corporate development strategy.
   Top management capacity to assess strategic importance of entrepreneurial initiatives.
   Top management capacity to assess relatedness of entrepreneurial initiatives to the firm's core capabilities.
   Middle-level management capacity to work with top management to obtain/maintain support for new initiatives (organizational championing).
   Middle-level management capacity to define corporate strategic framework for new initiatives.
   Middle-level management capacity to coach new venture managers.
   New venture managers' capacity to build new organizational capabilities.
   New venture managers' capacity to develop a business strategy for new initiatives.
   Availability of product champions to identify and define new business opportunities outside of mainstream activities.

Technology and the Manager

Case I–1
Claire McCloud

C. Huntington and M. A. Maidique

"Think it over, Claire. You've worked closely with me for two years, and I think you're now ready to take on a division of your own. You're smart, determined, and you've got good business sense.

"We need an executive at the fiber optics division who can solve the present operating problems and at the same time get it established firmly in the fiber optics market. Give it serious thought, Claire, and I'll come by in the morning to hear your decision." With that, Mr. W. H. Walton, "the Colonel," chairman and founder of Walton International, closed the door behind him as he left Claire McCloud's office. As usual, Mr. Walton, a physicist who was unusually proud of his stint as a communications officer in Korea, had made his case forcefully and explicitly.

McCloud sat back to consider Walton's offer. Walton International had had great hopes for the fiber optics business when Optical Wavelength Specialists (OWS) had been acquired three years before in 1976, but the division had not performed as well as had been expected. The fiber optics industry, however, was expected to grow rapidly as it expanded its participation in the telecommunication equipment market and thus it presented a major opportunity for the firm. McCloud also knew that Walton was personally committed to establishing the company's position in the fiber optics industry. If she accepted the job of managing the division, it could be a unique and exciting opportunity. But she wondered if her experience and abilities were suited for the job.

Prior to joining Walton International, McCloud had received a B.A. in economics magna cum laude from Stanford, worked four years as an economist for a large private investment management firm, and spent two years at a well-known eastern business school where she received her M.B.A. degree. During the past two years as the Colonel's assistant, she had gained experience in working with people and in dealing with company problems from the top. She had worked closely with Walton in the step-by-step reorganization of the components division and the instruments division, and had studied and initiated changes in the pension administration policies of the company. Through this involvement, she had become intimately familiar with the aggressive, highly technical top management group of Walton International.

But perhaps what was of most relevance to her current decision was her direct involvement with the fiber optics division. Claire had evaluated several project proposals from the fiber optics division. These proposals had ranged from requests for new capital equipment to a formal proposal for the acquisition of a wire and cable company. While her

Harvard Business School case 9-680-030.

principal contributions in these project evaluations had been largely in the areas of finance and marketing, she felt, thanks to her persistent inquisitiveness, that she had also gained a fairly good understanding of the technical aspects of the fiber optics business from frequent conversations with the fiber optics division technical staff. But she wondered if this level of technical understanding was sufficient for the position Walton had proposed. She also wondered what particular tools she would need to be an effective manager of a high-technology business such as fiber optics. She had the rest of the day to reach a decision.

EXHIBIT 1 Market Segmentation Projection for Fiber Optic Communication Systems, 1987

Estimated Expenditures on Fiber Optics (dollars in millions)

	1987
Commercial telecommunications	$350.0
CCTV and broadcast TV	3.0
Data communications	2.0
Computer applications	75.0
Other (industrial, office equipment, instrumentation)	15.0
Military and aerospace	100.0
Total	$545.0

SOURCE: Frost and Sullivan Report #415.

Fiber Optics[1]

The principle of sending signals by light was first demonstrated in 1880 by Alexander Graham Bell. By 1978, the fiber optics industry was still embryonic but was expected to evolve into one of the most exciting and fruitful growth industries of the 1980s. A conservative estimate by an industry analysis firm placed the market at over $500 million by 1987. A breakdown of one of these projections is given in Exhibit 1. The invention of the laser by Bell Laboratories in 1960 and other recent developments in electronics had paved the way for the application of optical fiber technology to communication equipment. According to many observers, fiber optics had the potential to revolutionize the communications industry. Claire explained the elements of fiber optics technology:

> In principle, the technology offers many advantages over conventional copper cable for voice, data, and video communication. Because of the unique aspects of optical physics, a glass or plastic fiber can transmit light signals much faster and can carry much more information than copper cable. A fiber optic cable is also much smaller, lighter, and more flexible, thus simplifying and reducing the cost of shipping and handling. A further significant but not yet completely realized advantage is that of manufacturing cost; with volume production, fiber optic cable is expected to cost at least 1/10 that of premium coaxial cable and, in addition, requires fewer peripheral structures such as repeaters and grounding equipment that would otherwise add to cost.[2]
>
> Optical systems also offer many advantages that are not attainable in metal or wire cables because of the physical properties of the fiber. For example, they are immune from electrical or electromagnetic interference. They can be made to have total electrical isolation, and are unaffected by extreme weather or temperature conditions. Another advantage is that the system can be upgraded easily, so technological improvements can translate immediately into better performance.

The components of a fiber optic system are described in Exhibit 2 and consist of a power source, a modulator, a light source such as a laser or light-emitting diode (LED), the optical fiber encased in a cable, and a demodulator and amplifier for receiving the signal.[3] The modulator and demodulator are used to modulate the signals transmitted between the fiber optics cable and the copper cable.

By 1978, fiber optic technology had undergone radical changes. Significant improvement had taken place in the four major aspects of system design: (1) information-carrying capacity, (2) the distance over which signals could be carried, (3) reliability, and (4) cost. Information-carrying capacity, measured in bandwidth, had improved significantly and had

[1]This section is based on three main sources: G. R. Elion and H. A. Elion, *Fiber Optics in Communication Systems* (New York: Marcel Dekker, Inc., 1978); "The Fiber Optics Industry in 1978: Competition," Case Clearing House #1-379-139; and "The Fiber Optics Industry in 1978: Products, Technology, and Markets," Case Clearing House #1-379-136.

[2]Repeaters are used to boost the signals on long-length cable runs.

[3]A light-emitting diode (LED) is a semiconductor device that emits light when it is powered by an electric voltage.

EXHIBIT 2 Block Diagram of a Fiber Optic System

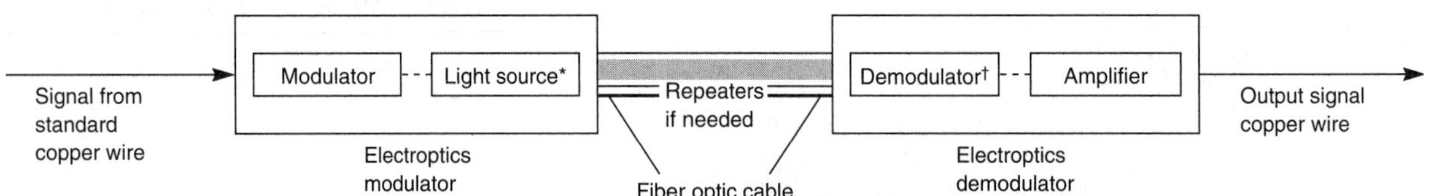

*Typically an LED (light-emitting diode) or laser. At present, LEDs usually employed for lasers are less durable and more expensive. It was expected, however, that lasers would ultimately dominate the fiber optics market due to their greater bandwidth potential.

†Typically accomplished via a standard semiconductor device known as a PIN diode.

SOURCE: Casewriter's drawing.

become extremely competitive with other communications methods by 1978, as shown in Exhibits 3–A and 3–B. While the distance over which fibers could commercially operate was still fairly short—very few systems had been tested at over five kilometers—there had been rapid improvement. Technological developments had focused on reducing attenuation losses (weakening in the light signal as it travels through the fiber). In eight years, from 1970 to 1978, attenuation losses had improved from 20 decibels per kilometer (db/km) in Corning Glass Works' initial low-loss fiber to a fiber with a loss of only 1 db/km. Finally, costs were declining, and by 1978, optical fiber had become cost competitive with conventional cable. Prices of fibers had fallen from $25 per meter for fiber with an attenuation loss of 30 db/km to $1 per meter for fibers with losses of 6 to 10 db/km. Corning projected that fiber prices would eventually reach 15 cents per meter.

By 1978, there were several techniques for fabricating optical fibers. The major processes were double crucible, stratified melt, chemical vapor deposition, rod-in-tube, and direct fiber drawing. All required ultrapurified raw materials. The main differences among the various processes involved the extent to which the process was batch or continuous and the way in which the fiber was drawn. Walton International used the double crucible method, in which the "core" and "cladding" materials are drawn together from separate crucibles in a continuous process. See Exhibit 4 for a simplified diagram of the process. The advantages of this method are that it allows continuous production and provides a superior core/cladding interface. However, it can have the disadvantage of minor variations in the fiber's diameter which can limit its potential for low attenuation. Manufacturing problems were also sometimes experienced in the melt of the core and cladding materials. By 1978, fibers produced by this method had achieved attenuation losses of about 5 db/km.

The fiber fabrication process could be contrasted with the electronics manufacturing process used by OWS for demodulator and modulator instruments. Very few of the components used in assembly of fiber optic instruments were made by Walton Inter-

EXHIBIT 3–A Information-Carrying Capacity of Selected Communications Systems

	Twisted Pair Wire	Coaxial Cable	Radio	TV	Microwave	Fiber Optics
Usable bandwidth (Hz)*	5×10^3	5×10^3	4.2×10^3	4.2×10^6	4.2×10^7	4.2×10^{11}
	5×10^3	2×10^8				
Number of usable voice channels†	0–1	0–10^4	1.0	10^3	10^4	10^8
Number of usable video channels‡	0	0–10	0	1	10	10^5

*The frequency of the signal source determined the nominal frequency. Inefficiencies within the system resulted in a usable bandwidth that was somewhat less than normal frequency.

†Voice channels required 4.2×10^3 Hz per channel.

‡Video channels required 4.2×10^6 Hz per channel.

SOURCE: Industry analyst's estimates. Reprinted with permission from page 15, ICCH #379-136.

EXHIBIT 3–B Coaxial versus Optical Underwater Cable Systems

System Parameter	Coaxial Cable	Optical Cable	Ratio: Coaxial to Optical
Cable diameter (cm)	3.2	1.6	2.0
Cable weight (kg/km)	1,250	625	2.0
Total cable weight (kg)	6×10^6	3×10^6	2.0
Total cable volume (m^3)	4,021	1,005	4.0
Cost of cable ($M)	35	25	1.4
Number of repeaters	150	500	0.3
Cost of each repeater ($K)	60	10	6.0
Cost of all repeaters ($M)	9	5	1.8
Total cable cost ($M)	44	30	1.5
Number of channels	300	600	0.5
Cost per channel ($K)	147	50	2.9

SOURCE: G. R. Elion and H. A. Elion, *Fiber Optics in Communications Systems* (New York: Marcel Dekker, Inc., 1978).

EXHIBIT 4 Double Crucible Fiber Drawing Process

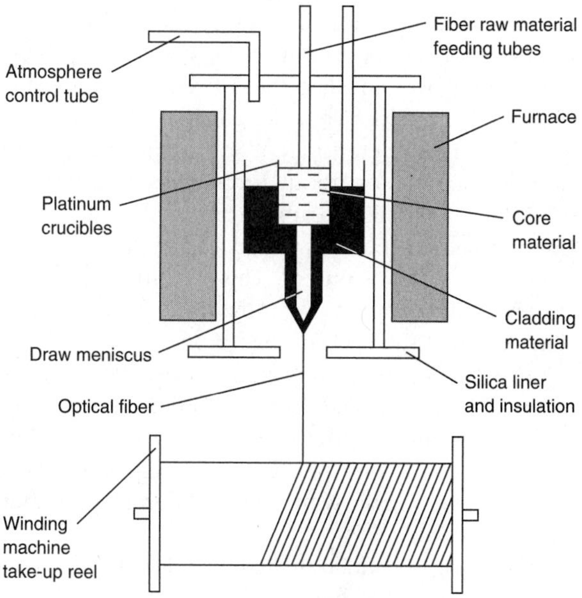

DC starting materials

As_2O_3	Li_2CO_3
B_2O_3	Na_2CO_3
$BaCO_3$	$NaNO_3$
$CaCO_3$	$PtSiO_3$
K_2CO_3	SiO_2
KNO_3	

SOURCE: G R. Elion and H. A. Elion, *Fiber Optics in Communications Systems* (New York: Marcel Dekker, Inc., 1978), p. 23. Used with permission of Marcel Dekker, Inc.

national. Lasers, diodes, transformers, and other components were purchased from other manufacturers. Instruments were assembled in batches of five and carefully tuned and inspected by an individual technician in the last stage of the process.

As fiber optic technology becomes increasingly sophisticated and as production costs decline, the market for optical fiber is expected to expand significantly. Current applications include: telephone loops, trunks, terminals and exchanges; internal and external computer links; cable TV; space vehicles; military and commercial aircraft; ships; submarine cable; security and alarm systems; electronic instrumentation systems; medical systems; satellite ground stations; and industrial automation and process control. Of all these, telecommunications and computer applications were expected to account for as much as three-fourths of the market in the early 1980s.

By 1978, a diverse multitude of players had become involved in producing one or more components, and an even greater number of potential participants were rumored to be waiting in the wings. Corning Glass Works and Bell Laboratories had established themselves as the technological leaders in manufacturing optical fiber, but many smaller companies produced components or complete systems. The participants came from many other industries: electronics, glass, wire and cable, chemicals, and others with peripheral connections to fiber optic technology. The industry, although embryonic, showed great potential. Exhibit 5 provides a partial list of competitors in the industry in 1978.

EXHIBIT 5 Selected Manufacturers of Fiber Optic Products

Optical Fibers and Cables (includes international)

American Optical
Corning Glass
Fiber Optic Cable
General Cable
ITT
Pilkington Brothers
Quartz Products
Siemens
Valtec

Fiber Optic Connectors or Splices

Bell-Northern
Elecro-Fiberoptics
Fujitsu
ITT
Thomson & CSF

LED or Laser Light Sources

AEG-Telefunken
Hewlett-Packard
Hitachi
ITT
Laser Diode Laboratories
National Semiconductor
Tektronics
Texas Instruments
Thomson & CSF

PIN or APD Photodetectors

Bell-Northern
Bell & Howell
EG&G
Ferranti
Fujitsu
General Electric
General Instrument
Hewlett-Packard
Motorola Semiconductor
Plessey
Raytheon
RCA

SOURCE: G. R. Elion and G. A. Elion, *Fiber Optics in Communications Systems.*

The Company

Walton International was established in 1958 by W. H. Walton, shortly after he was honorably discharged from the U.S. Air Force, to supply specialized electronic devices to the U.S. military. By 1978, the company had grown to $300 million in annual revenues and had diversified into supplying a variety of specialized electronic instruments and components to both industrial and military markets. Walton was known to be a technological leader in many of its markets and this leadership had become a source of pride to the Colonel. Several years ago, he had established a corporate R&D lab to supplement R&D programs conducted in the divisions; he claimed that his focus on R&D was one of the reasons behind the company's success. A summary organization chart and financial history of the company are presented in Exhibits 6 and 7.

In 1975, Walton International acquired Optical Wavelength Specialists (OWS) in the belief that it could combine its electronics capabilities with experience in fiber optics technology to gain a foothold in what was thought to be a rapidly growing and potentially lucrative business. At the time, OWS had annual revenues of close to $30 million. OWS's main products were a broad line of fiber optic modulators and demodulators using both LEDs and lasers as optical sources. The Walton International corporate R&D labs had also produced pilot quantities of soda-boro-silicate fiber optic cable.

Since its acquisition, however, the division had not lived up to expectations. Sales had remained relatively flat; over the last three years its leadership position in low-loss short-length fiber manufacture and design had deteriorated. Sources and detectors now accounted for about four-fifths of sales.[4] An additional $3 million came from cable sales. The division had just been awarded a $3 million contract from the U.S. government. This was the first major government contract for advanced sources and detectors that the division had won.

OWS executives were asked to describe the division. All had been with OWS before the acquisition and had remained with the division. OWS's founder, Allan Gray, was one of the few principals in OWS who did not remain with Walton International after the acquisition.

John Lang, production manager for the division and 56 years old, had been with Corning Glass Works before he joined OWS in 1972. He described the situation as follows:

> When Walton acquired us in 1975, most of us figured we would get the best of all worlds—we would get the financing we needed because Walton seemed so committed to the business, and we would get indepen-

[4]A *source* was another term for *modulator.*

EXHIBIT 6 Organization Chart

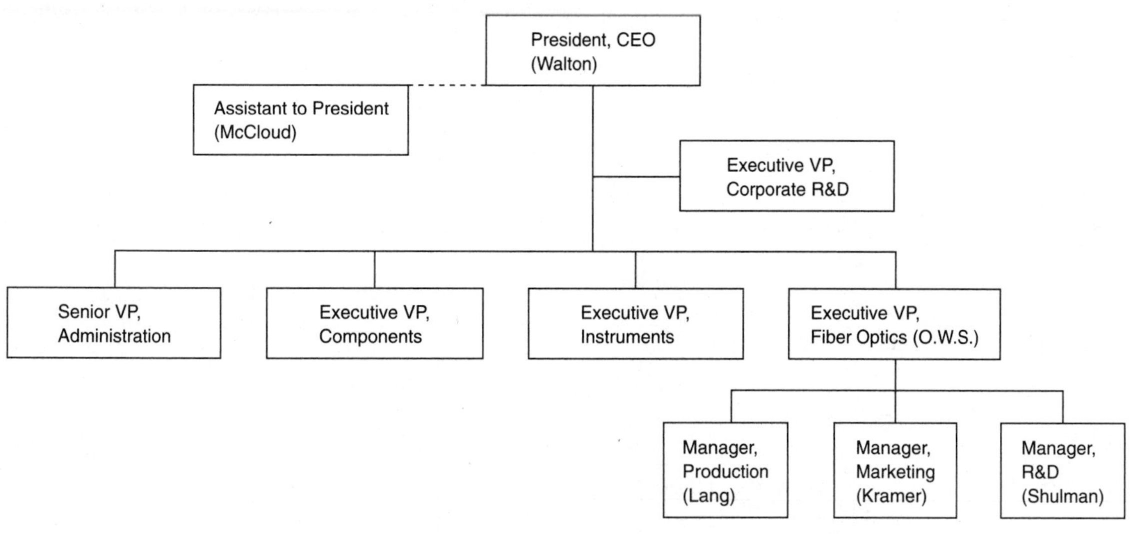

dence in running our own affairs. Well, it didn't work out. We had all the backing we could have wanted from Walton, but he didn't know how to run this kind of business and neither did the guy he sent in as division manager. We wanted to get into higher volume production because we feel we have the know-how and the market for our products, but too many people want their fingers in the pie.

R&D, however, keeps changing the design specs on some of our fiber runs and coming up with so many new ideas—most of which don't work—that I can never get my shop under control. When we were just a small business and there were only a few of us around, everything worked fine.

Now we've got these new sources and detectors which appear to be pretty good products, but combined with the rest of the disorganization around here they just complicate my job.

EXHIBIT 7 Statement of Income (millions of dollars)

	1976	1977	1978
Revenues	$235	$270	$300
Cost of goods	165	190	210
Gross margin	70	80	90
SG&A	31	35	41
Research and development	15	17	19
Profit before tax	24	28	30
Income taxes	12	14	15
Profit after tax	$ 12	$ 14	$ 15

John Kramer, marketing manager and 32 years old, saw the situation in a different light:

> The business is evolving so rapidly now—you blink and someone's made a lower loss fiber or more efficient laser source. . . . The competition is fierce and believe me, it's technology that counts. At present, if you have a couple of first-rate components, you can make money. But five years from now, it may be that you need to have whole systems to sell in order to be considered a viable competitor. Anyway, aside from the long-term situation, what concerns me here is how we seem to be missing the boat on some of this technology.
>
> When Allan [Gray] was here, he knew exactly who was doing what and where R&D should be putting its best efforts. He *should* have known—he was a materials science engineer with a Ph.D. in physics from MIT, a real R&D man. But since 1975, even though we have some good new lines, we seem to lack strong direction. This is unfortunate because the industry is really taking off now.

Dr. Larry Shulman, 33 years old and the manager of R&D, had been acting division manager for three months following his predecessor's unexpected resignation. Dr. Shulman was considered one of the nation's foremost authorities on fiber optic electronic systems. In addition to a Ph.D. in physics from Princeton, he holds an M.S. in electrical engineering from MIT. He also holds 20 patents, about half of them on fiber optic systems. He had joined Walton International from Bell Labs the same year that

Claire McCloud finished her M.B.A. At Bell, he had done research on fiber optic materials and systems. He stated:

> This business depends on its research talent. Without new ideas, a fiber optic company wouldn't last long because of the speed of technological change. Of course, there is also the problem of getting too many ideas, and that must be managed as well. No clear strategy was outlined and no direction was given to the division for R&D. We don't lack bright and talented people here; that's not the problem. We have one of the strongest technical teams in the industry. But R&D must be a first priority for this division, and we have got to organize around it.

The Decision

McCloud knew she had a great deal to consider that afternoon before she could make a decision on whether or not to take the division manager's job. She decided her first step should be to prepare a list of the important issues she felt she had to address.

Her first question concerned the technology itself. What did she have to know about fiber optics to be an effective manager? How much would she have to know to keep current on the advances taking place? She pulled from her files a recent list of papers on the industry (see Exhibit 8). Would the journals listed there keep her adequately informed? Even though she had had little prior training in engineering, physics, or electronics, she had picked up quite a bit of general knowledge on the subject during her two years as Walton's assistant. She also felt familiar with the basic principles of fiber optics. Would this be enough?

What framework would she use to manage the division? What were the unique aspects of a fiber optics business that required a special management framework? In business school, she had developed an overall familiarity with technological innovation and some of the strategies for managing the innovation process; she thought these would give her a start. For example, one decision she felt she would have to make is where the division should position itself technologically in the fiber optics market. Did it have the resources and talent to become a technological leader, and if so, what kind of products should it emphasize—modulators, demodulators, or the basic fibers themselves? What would the organizational and recruitment implications be for being a technological leader? Where could she find the additional technical know-how it required?

This brought her to another question. How should new products be evaluated? R&D clearly had problems right now in its ability to manage new product ideas and evaluate those ideas. What system should

EXHIBIT 8 Walton International: Recent Papers on Fiber Optics

Bodem, F., et al. "Investigation of Various Transmission Properties and Launching Techniques of Plastic Optical Fibers Suitable for Transmission of High Optical Power." *Optical and Quantum Electronics* 7, no. 5 (1975).

Brandt, G. B. "Two Wavelength Measurements of Optical Waveguide Parameters." *Applied Optics* 14, no. 4 (1975).

Eickhoff, W., et al. "Measuring Method for the Refractive Index Profile of Optic Glass Fibers." *Optical and Quantum Electronics* 7, no. 2 (1975).

Ford, S. G., et al. "Principles of Fiber Optical Cable Design." *Proceedings of IEE* 123 (1976).

Inada, K., et al. "Experimental Consideration of the Pulse Spreading of Multimode Optical Fibers." *Electronics Communication Engineers of Japan* 75 (1976).

Justice, B. "Strength Considerations of Optical Wavelength Fibers." *Fiber and Integrated Optics* 1 (1977).

Kapron, F. P. "Maximum Information Capacity of Fiber Optic Waveguides." *Electronic Letters* 13, no. 3 (1977).

Kawana, A., et al. "Fabrication of Low-Loss Single-Mode Fibers." *Electronic Letters* 13, no. 7 (1977).

Kuroha, T., et al. "Optical Fiber Drawing and Its Influence on Fiber Loss." International Conference on Integrated Optics and Optical Fiber Communication, July 1977, Tokyo, Japan.

Lussier, F. M. "Widening Choices in Fiber Optics." *Laser Focus*, June 1977.

Marcatili, E. A. J. "Factors Affecting Practical Attenuation and Dispersion Measurements." Topical Meeting on Optical Fiber Transmission, February 1977, Williamsburg, Virginia.

Marcuse, D. "Scattering and Absorption Losses of Multimode Optical Fiber Lasers." *Bell System Technical Journal* 55, no. 10 (1976).

Maurer, R. C. "Strength of Fiber Optical Waveguides." *Applied Physics Letters* 27 (1975).

Mims, F. M. "Measuring LED Power Distribution." *Electro-Optical Systems Design*, June 1976.

Titchmarsh, J. G. "Fiber Geometry Control with the Double Crucible Technique." Second European Conference on Optical Fiber Communication, September 1976, Paris, France.

she use to choose between proposals with apparently equal financial potential?

A further question was how the division should be organized. Should R&D really be the focal point for this kind of a business as Shulman recommended? Once she had developed a technological strategy, she thought the organization problem would fall into place. Nevertheless, she knew she would still have to choose among a variety of organizational structures. Should she organize functionally in a matrix structure or form new venture groups? How closely should OWS's R&D group work with the corporate R&D office? Her choice should, of course, also be very sensitive to the people currently in the division.

She felt that the people management issue was critical to her framework. How would these individuals be most productive and most satisfied? She knew that it would take delicate leadership to get the division working again as a team. Not the least of her concerns was how a group of technically trained people would accept an economist—and a young one at that—as their boss. (Claire McCloud was 30 at the time of the case.) How closely would she need to work with the vice presidents of R&D, marketing, and production? To what extent should she rely on their judgments? To what extent should she seek the counsel of other technical experts in the organization?

Finally, she would have to plan for her first priorities and would have to anticipate what her first problems would be. She had much more thinking to do before she could give Walton an answer in the morning.

Reading I–1
The Art of High-Technology Management

M. A. Maidique and R. H. Hayes

Over the past 15 years, the world's perception of the competence of U.S. companies in managing technology has come full circle. In 1967, a Frenchman, J.-J. Servan-Schreiber, expressed with alarm in ,his book *The American Challenge* that U.S. technology was far ahead of the rest of the industrialized world.[1] This "technology gap," he argued, was continually widening because of the *superior ability of Americans to organize and manage technological development.*

Today, the situation is perceived to have changed drastically. The concern now is that the gap is reversing: the onslaught of Japanese and/or European challenges is threatening America's technological leadership. Even such informed Americans as Dr. Simon Ramo express great concern. In his book *America's Technology Slip,* Dr. Ramo notes the apparent inability of U.S. companies to compete technologically with their foreign counterparts.[2] Moreover, in the best-seller *The Art of Japanese Management,* the authors use as a basis of comparison two technology-based firms: Matsushita (Japanese) and ITT (American).[3] The Japanese firm is depicted as a model for managers, while the management practices of the U.S. firm are sharply criticized.

Nevertheless, a number of U.S. companies appear to be fending off these foreign challenges successfully. These firms are repeatedly included on lists of "America's best-managed companies." Many of them are competitors in the R&D-intensive industries, a sector of our economy that has come under particular criticism. Ironically, some of them have even served as models for highly successful Japanese and European high-tech firms.

For example, of the 43 companies that Peters and Waterman judged to be excellent in *In Search of Excellence,* almost half were classified as high-technology firms, or as containing a substantial high-technology component.[4] Similarly, of the five U.S.

Reprinted from *Sloan Management Review* 25 (Winter 1984), pp. 18–31, by permission of the publisher.

[1]See J.-J. Servan-Schreiber, *The American Challenge* (New York: Atheneum Publishers, 1968).

[2]See S. Ramo, *America's Technology Slip* (New York: John Wiley & Sons, 1980).

[3]See R. Pascale and A. Athos, *The Art of Japanese Management* (New York: Simon & Schuster, 1981).

[4]See T. J. Peters and R. H. Waterman, Jr., *In Search of Excellence* (New York: Harper and Row, 1982). For purposes of this article, the high-technology industries are defined as those which spend more than 3 percent of sales on R&D. These industries, though otherwise quite different, are all characterized by a rapid rate of change in their products and technologies. Only five U.S. industries meet this criterion: chemicals and pharmaceuticals, machinery (especially computers and office machines), electrical equipment and communications, professional and scientific instruments, and aircraft and missiles. See National Science Foundation, *Science Resources Studies Highlights,* NSF81-331, December 31, 1981, p. 2.

organizations that William Ouchi described as best prepared to meet the Japanese challenge, three (IBM, Hewlett-Packard, and Kodak) were high-technology companies.[5] Indeed, high-technology corporations are among the most admired firms in America. In a *Fortune* study that ranked the corporate reputation of the 200 largest U.S. corporations, IBM and Hewlett-Packard (HP) ranked first and second, respectively.[6] And of the top 10 firms, 9 compete in such high-technology fields as pharmaceuticals, precision instruments, communications, office equipment, computers, jet engines, and electronics.

The above studies reinforce our own findings, which have led us to conclude that U.S. high-technology firms that seek to improve their management practices to succeed against foreign competitors need not look overseas. The firms mentioned above are not unique. On the contrary, they are representative of scores of well-managed small and large U.S. technology-based firms. Moreover, the management practices they have adopted are widely applicable. Thus, perhaps the key to stimulating innovation in our country is not to adopt the managerial practices of the Europeans or the Japanese, but to adapt some of the policies of our *own* successful high-technology firms.

The Study

Over the past two decades, we have been privileged to work with a host of small and large high-technology firms as participants, advisors, and researchers. We and our assistants interviewed formally and informally over 250 executives, including over 30 CEOs, from a wide cross section of high-tech industries—biotechnology, semiconductors, computers, pharmaceuticals, and aerospace. About 100 of these executives were interviewed in 1983 as part of a large-scale study of product innovation in the electronics industry (which was conducted by one of this article's authors and his colleagues).[7] Our research has been guided by a fundamental question: What strategies, policies, practices, and decisions result in successful management of high-technology enterprises? One of our principal findings was that no company has a monopoly on managerial excellence. Even the best run companies make big mistakes, and many smaller, lesser regarded companies are surprisingly sophisticated about the factors that mediate between success and failure.

It also became apparent from our interviews that the driving force behind the successes of many of these companies was strong leadership. All companies need leaders and visionaries, of course, but leadership is particularly essential when the future is blurry and when the world is changing rapidly. Although few high-tech firms can succeed for long without strong leaders, leadership itself is not the subject of this article. Rather, we accept it as given and seek to understand what strategies and management practices can *reinforce* strong leadership.

The companies we studied were of different sizes ($10 million to $30 billion in sales), their technologies were at different stages of maturity, their industry growth rates and product mixes were different, and their managers ranged widely in age. But they all had the same unifying thread: a rapid rate of change in the technological base of their products. This common thread, rapid technological change, implies novel products and functions and thus usually rapid growth. But even when growth is slow or moderate, the destruction of the old capital base by new technology results in the need for rapid redeployment of resources to cope with new product designs and new manufacturing processes. Thus, the two dominant characteristics of the high-technology organizations that we focused on were growth and change.

In part because of this split focus (growth and change), the companies we studied often appeared to display contradictory behavior over time. Despite these differences, in important respects, they were remarkably similar because they all confronted the

[5]See W. Ouchi, *Theory Z: How American Management Can Meet the Japanese Challenge* (New York: John Wiley & Sons, 1980).

[6]See C. E. Makin, "Ranking Corporate Reputations," *Fortune,* January 10, 1983, pp. 34–44. Corporate reputation was subdivided into eight attributes: quality of management, quality of products and services, innovativeness, long-term investment value, financial soundness, ability to develop and help talented people, community and environmental responsibility, and use of corporate assets.

[7]See: M. A. Maidique and B. J. Zirger, "Stanford Innovation Project: A Study of Successful and Unsuccessful Product Innovation in High-Technology Firms," *IEEE Transactions on Engineering Management,* in press; M. A. Maidique, "The Stanford Innovation Project: A Comparative Study of Success and Failure in High-Technology Product Innovation," *Management of Technological Innovation Conference Proceedings* (Worcester Polytechnic Institute, 1983).

same two-headed dilemma: how to unleash the creativity that promotes growth and change without being fragmented by it, and how to control innovation without stifling it. In dealing with this concern, they tended to adopt strikingly similar managerial approaches.

The Paradox: Continuity and Chaos

When we grouped our findings into general themes of success, a significant paradox gradually emerged—which is a product of the unique challenge that high-technology firms face. Some of the behavioral patterns that these companies displayed seemed to favor promoting disorder and informality, while others would have us conclude that it was consistency, continuity, integration, and order that were the keys to success. As we grappled with this apparent paradox, we came to realize that continued success in a high-technology environment requires periodic shifts between chaos and continuity.[8] Our originally static framework, therefore, was gradually replaced by a dynamic framework within whose ebbs and flows lay the secrets of success.

Six Themes of Success

The six themes that we grouped our findings into were: (1) business focus, (2) adaptability, (3) organizational cohesion, (4) entrepreneurial culture, (5) sense of integrity, and (6) hands-on top management. No one firm exhibits excellence in every one of these categories at any one time, nor are the less successful firms totally lacking in all. Nonetheless, outstanding high-technology firms tend to score high in most of the six categories, while less successful ones usually score low in several.[9]

1. Business Focus

Even a superficial analysis of the most successful high-technology firms leads one to conclude that they are highly focused. With few exceptions, the leaders in high-technology fields, such as computers, aerospace, semiconductors, biotechnology, chemicals, pharmaceuticals, electronic instruments, and duplicating machines, realize the great bulk of their sales either from a single product line or from a closely related set of product lines.[10] For example, IBM, Boeing, Intel, and Genentech confine themselves almost entirely to computer products, commercial aircraft, integrated circuits, and genetic engineering, respectively. Similarly, four-fifths of Kodak's and Xerox's sales come from photographic products and duplicating machines, respectively. In general, the smaller the company, the more highly focused it is. Tandon concentrates on disk drives, Tandem on high-reliability computers, Analog Devices on linear integrated circuits, and Cullinet on software products.

Closely related products

This extraordinary concentration does not stop with the dominant product line. When the company grows and establishes a secondary product line, it is usually closely related to the first. Hewlett-Packard, for instance, has two product families, each of which accounts for about half of its sales. Both families—electronic instruments and data processors—are focused on the same technical, scientific, and process control markets. IBM also makes two closely related product lines—data processors (approximately 80 percent of sales) and office equipment—both of which emphasize the business market.

Companies that took the opposite path have not fared well. Two of yesterday's technological leaders, ITT and RCA, have paid dearly for diversifying away from their strengths. Today, both firms are trying to divest many of what were once highly touted acqui-

---

[8]A similar conclusion was reached by Romanelli and Tushman in their study of leadership in the minicomputer industry, which found that successful companies alternated long periods of continuity and inertia with rapid reorientation. See E. Romanelli and M. Tushman, "Executive Leadership and Organizational Outcomes: An Evolutionary Perspective," *Management of Technological Innovation Conference Proceedings* (Worcester Polytechnic Institute, 1983).

[9]One of the authors in this article has employed this framework as a diagnostic tool in audits of high-technology firms. The firm is evaluated along these six dimensions on a 0–10 scale by members of corporate and divisional management, working individually. The results are then used as inputs for conducting a strategic review of the firm.

[10]General Electric evidently has also recognized the value of such concentration. In 1979, Reginald Jones, then GE's CEO, broke up the firm into six independent sectors led by "sector executives." See R. Vancil and P. C. Browne, "General Electric Consumer Products and Services Sector," Harvard Business School Case Services 2-179-070.

sitions. As David Packard, chairman of the board of Hewlett-Packard, once observed, "No company ever died from starvation, but many have died from indigestion."[11]

A communications firm that became the world's largest conglomerate, ITT began to slip in the early 1970s after an acquisition wave orchestrated by Harold Geneen. When Geneen retired in 1977, his successors attempted to redress ITT's lackluster performance through a far-reaching divestment program.[12] So far, 40 companies and other assets worth over $1 billion have been sold off—and ITT watchers believe the program is just getting started. Some analysts believe that ITT will ultimately be restructured into three groups, with the communications/electronics group and engineered products (home of ITT semiconductors) forming the core of a new ITT.

RCA experienced a similar fate to ITT's. When General David Sarnoff, RCA's architect and longtime chairman, retired in 1966, RCA was internationally respected for its pioneering work in television, electronic components, communications, and radar. But by 1980, the three CEOs who followed Sarnoff had turned a technological leader into a conglomerate with flat sales, declining earnings, and a $2.9 billion debt. This disappointing performance led RCA's new CEO, Thorton F. Bradshaw, to decide to return RCA to its high-technology origins.[13] Bradshaw's strategy is to concentrate on RCA's traditional strengths—communications and entertainment—by divesting its other businesses.

Focused R&D

Another policy that strengthens the focus of leading high-technology firms is concentrating R&D on one or two areas. Such a strategy enables these businesses to dominate the research, particularly the more risky, leading-edge explorations. By spending a higher proportion of their sales dollars on R&D than their competitors do, or through their sheer size (as in the case of IBM, Kodak, and Xerox), such companies maintain their technological leadership. It is not unusual for a leading firm's R&D investment to be one and a half to two times the industry's average as a percent of sales (8 to 15 percent) and several times more than any individual competitor on an absolute basis.[14]

Moreover, their commitment to R&D is both enduring and consistent. It is maintained through slack periods and recessions because it is believed to be in the best, long-term interest of the stockholders. As the CEO of Analog Devices, a leading linear integrated circuit manufacturer, explained in a quarterly report which noted that profits had declined 30 percent, "We are sharply constraining the growth of fixed expenses, but we do not feel it is in the best interest of shareholders to cut back further on product development . . . in order to relieve short-term pressure on earnings."[15] Similarly, when sales, as a result of a recession, flattened and profit margins plummeted at Intel, its management invested a record-breaking $130 million in R&D, and another $150 million in plant and equipment.[16]

Consistent priorities

Still another way that a company demonstrates a strong business focus is through a set of priorities and a pattern of behavior that is continually reinforced by top management: for example, planned manufacturing improvement at Texas Instruments (TI), customer service at IBM, the concept of the entrepreneurial product champion at 3M, and the new products at HP. Belief in the competitive effectiveness of their chosen theme runs deep in each of these companies.

A business focus that is maintained over extended periods of time has fundamental consequences. By concentrating on what it does well, a company develops an intimate knowledge of its markets, competitors, technologies, employees, and the future needs and opportunities of its customers.[17]

---

[11]Personal communication, March 4, 1982.

[12]After only 18 months as Geneen's successor as president, Lyman Hamilton was summarily dismissed by Geneen for reversing Geneen's way of doing business. See G. Colvin, "The Re-Geneening of ITT," *Fortune,* January 11, 1982, pp. 34–39.

[13]See "RCA: Still Another Master," *Business Week,* August 17, 1981, pp. 80–86.

[14]See "R&D Scoreboard," *Business Week,* July 6, 1981, pp. 60–75.

[15]See R. Stata, Analog Devices *Quarterly Report,* 1st Quarter, 1981.

[16]See "Why They Are Jumping Ship at Intel," *Business Week,* February 14, 1983, p. 107, and M. Chase, "Problem-Plagued Intel Bets on New Products, IBM's Financial Help," *The Wall Street Journal,* February 4, 1983.

[17]These SAPPHO findings are generally consistent with the results of the Stanford Innovation Project, a major comparative study of U.S. high-technology innovation. See M. A. Maidique, "The Stanford Innovation Project: A Comparative Study of Success and Failure in High-Technology Product Innovation," *Management of Technology Conference Proceedings* (Worcester Polytechnic Institute, 1983).

The Stanford Innovation Project recently completed a three-year study of 224 U.S. high-technology products (half were successes, half were failures) and concluded that a continuous, in-depth, informal interaction with leading customers throughout the product development process was the principal factor behind successful new products. In short, this coupling is the cornerstone of effective high-technology progress. Such an interaction is greatly facilitated by the longstanding and close customer relationships that are fostered by concentrating on closely related product-market choices.[18] "Customer needs," explains Tom Jones, chairman of Northrop Corporation, "must be understood *way ahead of time*" (author's emphasis).[19]

2. Adaptability

Successful firms balance a well-defined business focus with the willingness, and the will, to undertake major and rapid change when necessary. Concentration, in short, does not mean stagnation. Immobility is the most dangerous behavioral pattern a high-technology firm can develop: technology can change rapidly, and with it the markets and customers served. Therefore, a high-technology firm must be able to track and exploit the rapid shifts and twists in market boundaries as they are redefined by new technological, market, and competitive developments.

The cost of strategic stagnation can be great, as General Radio (GR) found out. Once the proud leader of the electronic instruments business, GR almost singlehandedly created many sectors of the market. Its engineering excellence and its progressive human relations policies were models for the industry. But when its founder, Melville Eastham, retired in 1950, GR's strategy ossified. In the next two decades, the company failed to take advantage of two major opportunities for growth that were closely related to the company's strengths: microwave instruments and minicomputers. Meanwhile, its traditional product line withered away. Now all that remains of GR's once dominant instruments line, which is less than 10 percent of sales, is a small assembly area where a handful of technicians assemble batches of the old instruments.

It wasn't until William Thurston, in the wake of mounting losses, assumed the presidency at the end of 1972 that GR began to refocus its engineering creativity and couple it to its new marketing strategies. Using the failure of the old policies as his mandate, Thurston deemphasized the aging product lines, focused GR's attention on automated test equipment, balanced its traditional engineering excellence with an increased sensitivity to market needs, and gave the firm a new name—GenRad. Since then, GenRad has resumed rapid growth and has won a leadership position in the automatic test equipment market.[20]

The GenRad story is a classic example of a firm making a strategic change because it perceived that its existing strategy was not working. But even successful high-technology firms sometimes feel the need to be rejuvenated periodically to avoid technological stagnation. In the mid-1960s, for example, IBM appeared to have little reason for major change. The company had a near monopoly in the computer mainframe industry. Its two principal products—the 1401 at the low end of the market and the 7090 at the high end—accounted for over two-thirds of its industry's sales. Yet, in one move, the company obsoleted both product lines (as well as others) and redefined the rules of competition for decades to come by simultaneously introducing six compatible models of the "System 360," based on proprietary hybrid integrated circuits.[21]

During the same period, GM, whose dominance of the U.S. auto industry approached IBM's dominance of the computer mainframe industry, stoutly resisted such a rejuvenation. Instead, it became more and more centralized and inflexible. Yet, GM was also once a high-technology company. In its early days when Alfred P. Sloan ran the company, engines were viewed as high-technology products. One day, Charles F. Kettering told Sloan he believed the high efficiency of the diesel engine could be engineered into a compact power plant. Sloan's response was: "Very well—we are now in the diesel engine business. You tell us how the engine should run, and I will . . . capitalize the program."[22] Two years later, Kettering achieved a major breakthrough

---

[18]See: Maidique and Zirger, "Stanford Innovation Project." Several other authors have reached similar conclusions. See, for example, Peters and Waterman, *In Search of Excellence.*

[19]Personal communication, May 1982.

[20]See W. R. Thurston, "The Revitalization of GenRad," *Sloan Management Review,* Summer 1981, pp. 53–57.

[21]See T. Wise, "IBM's 5 Billion Dollar Gamble," *Fortune,* September 1966; "A Rocky Road to the Marketplace," *Fortune,* October 1966.

[22]See A. P. Sloan, *My Years with General Motors* (New York: Anchor Books, 1972), p. 401.

in diesel technology. This paved the way for a revolution in the railroad industry and led to GM's preeminence in the diesel locomotive markets.

Organizational flexibility

To undertake such wrenching shifts in direction requires both agility and daring. Organizational agility seems to be associated with organizational flexibility—frequent realignments of people and responsibilities as the firm attempts to maintain its balance on shifting competitive sands. The daring and the willingness to take "you bet your company" kinds of risks is a product of both the inner confidence of its members and a powerful top management—one that either has effective shareholder control or the full support of its board.

3. Organizational Cohesion

The key to success for a high-tech firm is not simply periodic renewal. There must also be cooperation in the translation of new ideas into new products and processes. As Ken Fisher, the architect of Prime Computer's extraordinary growth, puts it: "If you have the driving function, the most important success factor is the ability to integrate. It's also the most difficult part of the task."[23]

To succeed, the energy and creativity of the whole organization must be tapped. Anything that restricts the flow of ideas or undermines the trust, respect, and sense of a commonality of purpose among individuals is a potential danger. This is why high-tech firms fight so vigorously against the usual organizational accoutrements of seniority, rank, and functional specialization. Little attention is given to organizational charts: often they don't exist.

Younger people in a rapidly evolving technological field are often as good a source of new ideas as are older ones—and sometimes even better. In some high-tech firms, in fact, the notion of a "half-life of knowledge" is used; that is, the amount of time that has to elapse before half of what one knows is obsolete. In semiconductor engineering, for example, it is estimated that the half-life of a newly minted Ph.D. is about seven years. Therefore, any practice that relegates younger engineers to secondary, nonpartnership roles is considered counterproductive.

Similarly, product design, marketing, and manufacturing personnel must collaborate in a common cause rather than compete with one another, as happens in many organizations. Any policies that appear to elevate one of these functions above the others—either in prestige or in rewards—can poison the atmosphere for collaboration and cooperation.

A source of division, and one which distracts the attention of people from the needs of the firm to their own aggrandizement, are the executive perks that are found in many mature organizations: pretentious job titles, separate dining rooms and restrooms for executives, larger and more luxurious offices (often separated in some way from the rest of the organization), and even separate or reserved places in the company parking lot all tend to establish distance between managers and doers and substitute artificial goals for the crucial real ones of creating successful new products and customers. The appearance of an executive dining room, in fact, is one of the clearest danger signals.

Good communication

One way to combat the development of such distance is by making top executives more visible and accessible. IBM, for instance, has an open-door policy that encourages managers at different levels of the organization to talk to department heads and vice presidents. According to senior IBM executives, it was not unusual for a project manager to drop in and talk to Frank Cary (IBM's chairman) or John Opel (IBM's president) until Cary's recent retirement. Likewise, an office with transparent walls and no door, such as that of John Young, CEO at HP, encourages communication. In fact, open-style offices are common in many high-tech firms.

A regular feature of 3M's management process is the monthly Technical Forum where technical staff members from the firm exchange views on their respective projects. This emphasis on communication is not restricted to internal operations. Such a firm supports and often sponsors industrywide technical conferences, sabbaticals for staff members, and cooperative projects with technical universities.

Technical Forums serve to compensate partially for the loss of visibility that technologists usually experience when an organization becomes more complex and when production, marketing, and finance staffs swell. So does the concept of the dual-career ladder that is used in most of these firms; that is, a job hierarchy through which technical person-

---

[23]Personal communication, 1980. Mr. Fisher was president and CEO of Prime Computer from 1975 to 1981.

nel can attain the status, compensation, and recognition that is accorded to a division general manager or a corporate vice president. By using this strategy, companies try to retain the spirit of the early days of the industry when scientists played a dominant role, often even serving as members of the board of directors.[24]

Again, a strategic business focus contributes to organizational cohesion. Managers of firms that have a strong theme/culture and that concentrate on closely related markets and technologies generally display a sophisticated understanding of their businesses. Someone who understands where the firm is going and why is more likely to be willing to subordinate the interests of his or her own unit or function in the interest of promoting the common goal.

Job rotation

A policy of conscious job rotation also facilitates this sense of communality. In the small firm, everyone is involved in everyone else's job: specialization tends to creep in as size increases and boundary lines between functions appear. If left unchecked, these boundaries can become rigid and impermeable. Rotating managers in temporary assignments across these boundaries helps keep the lines fluid and informal, however. When a new process is developed at TI, for example, the process developers are sent to the production unit where the process will be implemented. They are allowed to return to their usual posts only after that unit's operations manager is convinced that the process is working properly.

Integration of roles

Other ways that high-tech companies try to prevent organizational, and particularly hierarchical, barriers from rising is through multidisciplinary project teams, special venture groups, and matrixlike organizational structures. Such structures, which require functional specialists and product-market managers to interact in a variety of relatively short-term problem-solving assignments, inject a certain ambiguity into organizational relationships and require each individual to play a variety of organizational roles.

For example, AT&T uses a combination of organizational and physical mechanisms to promote integration. The Advanced Development sections of Bell Labs are physically located on the sites of the Western Electric plants. This location creates an organizational bond between Development and Bell's basic research and an equally important spatial bond between Development and the manufacturing engineering groups at the plants. In this way, communication is encouraged among Development and the other two groups.[25]

Long-term employment

Long-term employment and intensive training are also important integrative mechanisms. Managers and technologists are more likely to develop satisfactory working relationships if they know they will be harnessed to each other for a good part of their working lives. Moreover, their loyalty and commitment to the firm is increased if they know the firm is continuously investing in upgrading their capabilities.

At Tandem, technologists regularly train administrators on the performance and function of the firm's products and, in turn, administrators train the technologists on personnel policies and financial operations.[26] Such a firm also tends to select college graduates who have excellent academic records, which suggest self-discipline and stability, and then encourages them to stay with the firm for most, if not all, of their careers.

4. Entrepreneurial Culture

While continuously striving to pull the organization together, successful high-tech firms also display fierce activism in promoting internal agents of change. Indeed, it has long been recognized that one of the most important characteristics of a successful high-technology firm is an entrepreneurial culture.[27]

Indeed, the ease with which small entrepreneurial firms innovate has always inspired a mixture of puzzlement and jealousy in larger firms. When new ventures and small firms fail, they usually do so

[24]At Genentech, Cetus, Biogen, and Collaborative Research, four of the leading biotechnology firms, a top scientist is also a member of the board of directors.

[25]See, for example, J. A. Morton, *Organizing for Innovation* (New York: McGraw-Hill, 1971).

[26]Jimmy Treybig, president of Tandem Computer, Stanford Executive Institute Presentation, August 1982.

[27]See D. A. Schon, *Technology and Change* (New York: Dell Publishing, 1967), and Peters and Waterman, *In Search of Excellence.*

because of capital shortages and managerial errors.[28] Nonetheless, time and again they develop remarkably innovative products, processes, and services with a speed and efficiency that baffle the managers of large companies. The success of the Apple II, which created a new industry, and Genentech's genetically engineered insulin are of this genre. The explanation for a small entrepreneurial firm's innovativeness is straightforward, yet it is difficult for a large firm to replicate its spirit.

Entrepreneurial characteristics

First, the small firm is typically blessed with excellent communication. Its technical people are in continuous contact (and oftentimes in cramped quarters). They have lunch together, and they call each other outside of working hours. Thus, they come to understand and appreciate the difficulties and challenges facing one another. Sometimes they will change jobs or double up to break a critical bottleneck; often the same person plays multiple roles. This overlapping of responsibilities results in a second blessing: a dissolving of the classic organizational barriers that are major impediments to the innovating process. Third, key decisions can be made immediately by the people who first recognize a problem, not later by top management or by someone who barely understands the issue. Fourth, the concentration of power in the leader/entrepreneurs makes it possible to deploy the firm's resources very rapidly. Lastly, the small firm has access to multiple funding channels, from the family dentist to a formal public offering. In contrast, the manager of an R&D project in a large firm has effectively only one source, the "corporate bank."

Small divisions

In order to re-create the entrepreneurial climate of the small firm, successful large high-technology firms often employ a variety of organizational devices and personnel policies. First, they divide and subdivide. Hewlett-Packard, for example, is subdivided into 50 divisions: the company has a policy of splitting divisions soon after they exceed 1,000 employees. Texas Instruments is subdivided into over 30 divisions and 250 tactical action programs. Until recently, 3M's business was split into 40 divisions. Although these divisions sometimes reach $100 million or more in sales, by Fortune 500 standards they are still relatively small companies.

Variety of funding channels

Second, such high-tech firms employ a variety of funding channels to encourage risk taking. At Texas Instruments, managers have three distinct options in funding a new R&D project. If their proposal is rejected by the centralized strategic planning (OST) system because it is not expected to yield acceptable economic gains, they can seek a "Wild Hare Grant." The Wild Hare program was instituted by Patrick Haggerty, while he was TI's chairman, to ensure that good ideas with long-term potential were not systematically turned down. Alternatively, if the project is outside the mainstream of the OST system, managers or engineers can contact one of dozens of individuals who hold "IDEA" grant purse strings and who can authorize up to $25,000 for prototype development. It was an IDEA grant that resulted in TI's highly successful Speak and Spell learning aid.[29]

3M managers also have three choices: they can request funds from (1) their own division, (2) corporate R&D, or (3) the new ventures division. This willingness to allow a variety of funding channels has an important consequence: it encourages the pursuit of alternative technological approaches, particularly during the early stages of a technology's development, when no one can be sure of the best course to follow.

IBM, for instance, has found that rebellion can be good business. Thomas Watson, Jr., the founder's son and a longtime senior manager, once described the way the disk memory, a core element of modern computers, was developed:

> [It was] not the logical outcome of a decision made by IBM management; [because of budget difficulties] it was developed in one of our laboratories as a bootleg project. A handful of men . . . broke the rules. They risked their jobs to work on a project they believed in.[30]

---

[28]See S. Myers and E. F. Sweezy, "Why Innovations Fail," *Technology Review,* March–April 1978, pp. 40–46.

[29]See: *Texas Instruments* (A), Harvard Business School case 9-476-122; *Texas Instruments Shows U.S. Business How to Survive in the 1980s,* Harvard Business School case 3-579-092; *Texas Instruments "Speak and Spell Product,"* Harvard Business School case 9-679-089, revised 7/79.

[30]Thomas Watson, Jr., address to the Eighth International Congress of Accountants, New York City, September 24, 1962, as quoted by D. A. Shon, "Champions for Radical New Inventions," *Harvard Business Review,* March–April 1963, p. 85.

At Northrop, the head of aircraft design usually has at any one time several projects in progress without the awareness of top management. A lot can happen before the decision reaches even a couple of levels below the chairman. "We like it that way," explains Northrop Chairman Tom Jones.[31]

Tolerance of failure

Moreover, the successful high-technology firms tend to be very tolerant of technological failure. "At HP," Bob Hungate, general manager of the Medical Supplies Division, explains, "it's understood that when you try something new you will sometimes fail."[32] Similarly, at 3M, those who fail to turn their pet project into a commercial success almost always get another chance. Richard Frankel, the president of the Kevex Corporation, a $20 million instrument manufacturer, puts it this way: "You need to encourage people to make mistakes. You have to let them fly in spite of aerodynamic limitations."[33]

Opportunity to pursue outside projects

Finally, these firms provide ample time to pursue speculative projects. Typically, as much as 20 percent of a productive scientist's or engineer's time is "unprogrammed," during which he or she is free to pursue interests that may not lie in the mainstream of the firm. IBM Technical Fellows are given up to five years to work on projects of their own choosing, from high-speed memories to astronomy.

5. Sense of Integrity

While committed to individualism and entrepreneurship, at the same time successful high-tech firms tend to exhibit a commitment to long-term relationships. The firms view themselves as part of an enduring community that includes employees, stockholders, customers, suppliers, and local communities: their objective is to maintain stable associations with all of these interest groups.

Although these firms have clear-cut business objectives, such as growth, profits, and market share, they consider them subordinate to higher order ethical values. Honesty, fairness, and openness—that is, integrity—are not to be sacrificed for short-term gain. Such companies don't knowingly promise what they can't deliver to customers, stockholders, or employees. They don't misrepresent company plans and performance. They tend to be tough but forthright competitors. As Herb Dwight—president of Spectra-Physics, one of the world's leading laser manufacturers—says, "The managers that succeed here go *out of their way* to be ethical."[34] And Alexander d'Arbeloff, cofounder and president of Teradyne, states bluntly, "Integrity comes first. If you don't have that, nothing else matters."[35]

These policies may seem utopian, even puritanical, but in a high-tech firm they also make good business sense. Technological change can be dazzlingly rapid; therefore, uncertainty is high, risks are difficult to assess, and market opportunities and profits are hard to predict. It is almost impossible to get a complex product into production, for example, without solid trust between functions, between workers and managers, and between managers and stockholders (who must be willing to see the company through the possible dips in sales growth and earnings that often accompany major technological shifts). Without integrity, the risks multiply and the probability of failure (in an already difficult enterprise) rises unacceptably. In such a context, Ray Stata, president and CEO of Analog Devices and cofounder of the Massachusetts High-Technology Council, states categorically, "You need an environment of mutual trust."[36]

This commitment to ethical values must start at the top; otherwise, it is ineffective. Most of the CEOs we interviewed considered it to be a cardinal dimension of their role. As Bernie Gordon, president of Analogic, explains, "The things that make leaders are their philosophy, ethics, and psychology."[37] Nowhere is this dimension more important than in dealing with the company's employees. Paul Rizzo, IBM's vice chairman, puts it this way: "At IBM we have a fundamental respect for the individual . . . people must be free to disagree and to be heard. Then, even if they lose, you can still marshal them behind you."[38]

[31]Personal communication, May 1982.

[32]Personal communication, 1980.

[33]Personal communication, April 1983.

[34]Personal communication, 1982.

[35]Personal communication, 1983.

[36]Personal communication, 1980.

[37]Personal communication, 1982.

[38]Personal communication, 1980.

Self-understanding

This sense of integrity manifests itself in a second, not unrelated, way—self-understanding. The pride, almost arrogance, of these firms in their ability to compete in their chosen fields is tempered by a surprising acknowledgment of their limitations. One has only to read Hewlett-Packard's corporate objectives or interview one of its top managers to sense this extraordinary blend of strength and humility. Successful high-tech companies are able to reconcile their dream with what they can realistically achieve. This is one of the reasons why they are extremely reticent to diversify into unknown territories.

6. Hands-On Top Management

Notwithstanding their deep sense of respect and trust for individuals, CEOs of successful high-technology firms are usually actively involved in the innovation process to such an extent that they are sometimes accused of meddling. Tom McAvoy, Corning's president, sifts through hundreds of project proposals each year trying to identify those that can have a "significant strategic impact on the company"—the potential to restructure the company's business. Not surprisingly, most of these projects deal with new technologies. For one or two of the most salient ones, he adopts the role of "field general": he frequently visits the line operations, receives direct updates from those working on the project, and assures himself that the required resources are being provided.[39]

Such direct involvement of the top executive at Corning sounds more characteristic of vibrant entrepreneurial firms, such as Tandon, Activision, and Seagate, but Corning is far from unique. Similar patterns can be identified in many larger high-technology firms. Milt Greenberg, president of GCA, a $180 million semiconductor process equipment manufacturer, stated: "Sometimes you just have to short-circuit the organization to achieve major change."[40] Tom Watson, Jr. (IBM's chairman) and Vince Learson (IBM's president) were doing just that when they met with programmers and designers and other executives in Watson's ski cabin in Vermont to finalize software design concepts for the System 360—at a point in time when IBM was already a $4 billion firm.[41]

Good high-tech managers not only understand how organizations, and in particular engineers, work, they understand the fundamentals of their technology and can interact directly with their people about it. This does not imply that it is necessary for the senior managers of such firms to be technologists (although they usually are in the early stages of growth): neither Watson nor Learson was a technologist. What appears to be more important is the ability to ask lots of questions, even "dumb" questions, and dogged patience in order to understand in-depth such core questions as: (1) how the technology works; (2) its limits, as well as its potential (together with the limits and potential of competitors' technologies); (3) what technical and economic resources these various technologies require; (4) the direction and speed of change; and (5) the available technological options, their cost, probability of failure, and potential benefits if they prove successful.

This depth of understanding is difficult enough to achieve for one set of related technologies and markets; it is virtually impossible for one person to master many different sets. This is another reason why business focus appears to be so important in high-tech firms. It matters little when one or more perceptive scientists or technologists foresees the impact of new technologies on the firm's markets if its top management doesn't internalize these risks and make the major changes in organization and resource allocation that are usually necessitated by a technological transition.

The Paradox of High-Technology Management

The six themes around which we arranged our findings can be organized into two, apparently paradoxical groupings: into one group fall business focus, organizational cohesion, and a sense of integrity; adaptability, entrepreneurial culture, and hands-on management fall into the other group. On the one hand, business focus, organizational cohesion, and integrity imply stability and conservatism. On the other hand, adaptability, entrepreneurial cul-

[39]Personal communication, 1979.

[40]Personal communication, 1980.

[41]See Wise, "IBM's 5 Billion."

ture, and hands-on top management are synonymous with rapid, sometimes precipitous change. The fundamental tension is between order and disorder. Half of the success factors pull in one direction, and the other half tug the other way.

This paradox has frustrated many academicians who seek to identify rational processes and stable cause–effect relationships in high-tech firms and managers. Such relationships are not easily observable unless a certain constancy exists. But in most high-tech firms, the only constant is continual change. As one insightful student of the innovation process phrased it: "Advanced technology requires the collaboration of diverse professions and organizations, often with ambiguous or highly interdependent jurisdictions. In such situations, many of our highly touted rational management techniques break down."[42] One recent researcher, however, proposed a new model of the firm that attempts to rationalize the conflict between stability and change by splitting the strategic process into two loops, one that extends the past, the other that periodically attempts to break with it.[43]

By their very nature, established organizations resist innovation. By defining jobs and responsibilities and arranging them in serial reporting relationships, organizations encourage the performance of a restricted set of tasks in a programmed, predictable way. Not only do formal organizations resist innovation, they often act in ways that stamp it out. Overcoming such behavior—which is analogous to the way the human body mobilizes antibodies to attack foreign cells—is, therefore, a core job of high-tech management.

The Paradoxical Challenge

High-tech firms deal with this challenge in different ways. Texas Instruments, long renowned for the complex, interdependent matrix structure it used in managing dozens of product-customer centers (PCCs), recently consolidated groups of PCCs and made them into more autonomous units. "The manager of a PCC controls the resources and operations" for his or her entire family. "In the simplest terms, the PCC manager is to be an entrepreneur," explained Fred Bucy, TI's president.[44]

Meanwhile, a different trend is evident at 3M, where entrepreneurs have been given a free reign for decades. A recent major reorganization was designed to arrest snowballing diversity by concentrating its sprawling structure of autonomous divisions into four market groups. "We were becoming too fragmented," explained Vincent Ruane, vice president of 3M's Electronics Division.[45]

Similarly, HP recently reorganized into five groups, each with its own strategic responsibilities. Although this simply changes some of its reporting relationships, it does give HP, for the first time, a means for integrating product and market development across generally autonomous units.[46]

These reorganizations do not mean that organizational integration is dead at Texas Instruments, or that 3M's and HP's entrepreneurial cultures are being dismantled. They signify, first, that these firms recognize that both (organizational integration and entrepreneurial cultures) are important and, second, that periodic change is required for environmental adaptability. These three firms are demonstrating remarkable adaptability by reorganizing from a position of relative strength—not, as is far more common, in response to financial difficulties. As Lewis Lehr, 3M's president, explained, "We can change now because we're not in trouble."[47]

Such reversals are essentially antibureaucratic, in the same spirit as Mao's admonition to "let a hundred flowers blossom and a hundred schools of thought contend."[48] At IBM, in 1963, Tom Watson, Jr., temporarily abolished the corporate management committee in an attempt to push decisions downward and thus facilitate the changes necessary for IBM's great leap forward to the System 360.[49] Disorder, slack, and ambiguity are necessary for innovation since they provide the porosity that facilitates

[42]See L. R. Sayles and M. K. Chandler, *Managing Large Systems: Organizations for the Future* (New York: Harper and Row, 1971).

[43]See R. A. Burgelman, "A Model of the Interaction of Strategic Behavior, Corporate Context, and the Concept of Corporate Strategy," *Academy of Management Review* (1983), pp. 61–70.

[44]See S. Zipper, "TI Unscrambling Matrix Management to Cope with Gridlock in Major Profit Centers," *Electronic News,* April 26, 1982, p. 1.

[45]See M. Barnfather, "Can 3M Find Happiness in the 1980s?" *Forbes,* March 11, 1982, pp. 113–16.

[46]See R. Hill, "Does a 'Hands-Off' Company Now Need a 'Hands-On' Style?" *International Management,* July 1983, p. 35.

[47]See Barnfather, "Can 3M Find Happiness?"

[48]S. R. Schram, ed., *Quotations from Chairman Mao Tse Tung* (Bantam Books, 1967), p. 174.

[49]See: D. G. Marquis, "Ways of Organizing Projects," *Innovation,* August 1969, pp. 26–33; T. Levitt, *Marketing for Business Growth* (New York: McGraw-Hill, 1974), in particular, chap. 7.

entrepreneurial behavior—just as do geographically separated, relatively autonomous organizational subunits.

But the corporate management committee is alive and well at IBM today. As it should be. The process of innovation, once begun, is both self-perpetuating and potentially self-destructive: although the top managers of high-tech firms must sometimes espouse organizational disorder, for the most part they must preserve order.

Winnowing Old Products

Not all new product ideas can be pursued. As Charles Ames, former president of Reliance Electric, states, "An enthusiastic inventor is a menace to practical businessmen."[50] Older products, upon which the current success of the firm was built, at some point have to be abandoned: just as the long-term success of the firm requires the planting and nurturing of new products, it also requires the conscious, even ruthless, pruning of other products so that the resources they consume can be used elsewhere.

This attitude demands hard-nosed managers who are continually managing the functional and divisional interfaces of their firms. They cannot be swayed by nostalgia, or by the fear of disappointing the many committed people who are involved in the development and production of discontinued products. They must also overcome the natural resistance of their subordinates, and even their peers, who often have a vested interest in the products that brought them early personal success in the organization.

Yet, firms also need a certain amount of continuity because major change often emerges from the accretion of a number of smaller, less visible improvements. Studies of petroleum refining, rayon, and rail transportation, for example, show that half or more of the productivity gains ultimately achieved within these technologies were the result of the accumulation of minor improvements.[51] Indeed, most engineers, managers, technologists, and manufacturing and marketing specialists work on what Thomas Kuhn might have called "normal innovations,"[52] the little steps that improve or extend existing product lines and processes.

Managing Ambivalently

The successful high-technology firm, then, must be managed ambivalently. A steady commitment to order and organization will produce one-color Model T Fords. Continuous revolution will bar incremental productivity gains. Many companies have found that alternating periods of relaxation and control appear to meet this dual need. Surprisingly, such ambiguity does not necessarily lead to frustration and discontent.[53] In fact, interspersing periods of tension, action, and excitement with periods of reflection, evaluation, and revitalization is the same sort of irregular rhythm that characterizes many favorite pastimes—including sailing, which has been described as "long periods of total boredom punctuated with moments of stark terror."

Knowing when and where to change from one stance to the other and having the power to make the shift are the core of the art of high-technology management. James E. Webb, administrator of the National Aeronautics and Space Administration during the successful Apollo ("man on the moon") program, recalled that "we were required to fly our administrative machine in a turbulent environment, and . . . a certain level of *organizational instability was essential if NASA was not to lose control*" (authors' emphasis).[54]

In summary, the central dilemma of the high-technology firm is that it must succeed in managing two conflicting trends: continuity and rapid change. There are two ways to resolve this dilemma. One is an old idea: managing different parts of the firm differently—some business units for innovation, others for efficiency.

A second way—a way which we believe is more powerful and pervasive—is to manage differently at different times in the evolutionary cycle of the firm.

---

[50]Charles Ames, former CEO of Reliance Electric, cited in "Exxon's $600 Million Mistake," *Fortune,* October 19, 1981.

[51]See, for example, W. J. Abernathy and J. M. Utterback, "Patterns of Industrial Innovation," *Technology Review,* June–July 1978, pp. 40–47.

[52]See T. Kuhn, *The Structure of Scientific Revolutions,* 2d ed. (Chicago: University of Chicago Press, 1967).

[53]After reviewing an early draft of this article, Ray Stata, president, Analog Devices, wrote, "The articulation of dynamic balance, of yin and yang, . . . served as a reminder to me that there isn't one way forever, but a constant adaption to the needs and circumstances of the moment." Ray Stata, personal communication, November 29, 1982.

[54]Quoted in "Some Contributions of James E. Webb to the Theory and Practice of Management," a presentation by Elmer B. Staats before the annual meeting of the Academy of Management on August 11, 1978.

The successful high-technology firm *alternates* periods of consolidation and continuity with sharp reorientations that can lead to dramatic changes in the firm's strategies, structure, controls, and distribution of power, followed by a period of consolidation.[55]

[55]See Romanelli and Tushman, "Executive Leadership."

Thomas Jefferson knew this secret when he wrote 200 years ago, "A little revolution now and then is a good thing."[56]

[56]See J. Bartlett, *Bartlett's Familiar Quotations,* 14th ed. (Boston: Little, Brown), p. 471B.

PART

Design and Evolution of Technology Strategy

Designing and Implementing a Technology Strategy[1]

In today's competitive environment, technology is a resource of primary importance to most organizations. As such, its management must be part of a firm's overall business strategy. Technology strategy encompasses, but extends beyond, R&D strategy.[2] It helps answer questions such as:

1. Which distinctive technological competencies and capabilities are necessary to establish and maintain competitive advantage?
2. Which technologies should be used to implement core product design concepts and how should these technologies be embodied in products?
3. At what level should the organization invest in technology development?
4. Should technologies be sourced internally or externally?
5. When and how should new technology be introduced to the market?
6. How should technology and innovation be organized and managed?

[1]This paper is based, in part, on R. A. Burgelman and R. S. Rosenbloom, "Technology Strategy: An Evolutionary Process Perspective," *Research on Technological Innovation, Management, and Policy* 4 (1989), pp. 1–23.

[2]G. R. Mitchell, "New Approaches for the Strategic Management of Technology," *Technology in Sceiety* 7, no. 2/3 (1986), pp. 132–44, and P. Adler, "Technology Strategy: A Review of the Literatures," *Research on Technological Innovation, Management, and Policy* 4 (1989), pp. 25–152.

EXHIBIT 1 A Capabilities-Based Organizational Learning Framework of Technology Strategy

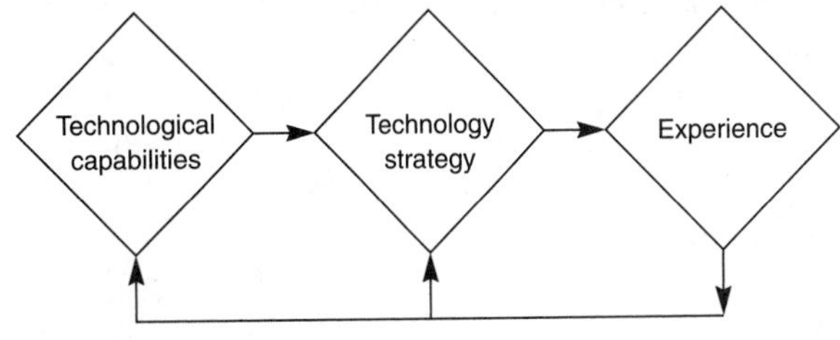

Technology strategy can be conceptualized as an evolutionary organizational learning process, as seen in Exhibit 1, which highlights the links between technical competencies and capabilities, technology strategy, and experience. Technology strategy is a function of the quantity and quality of technical capabilities that feed into it. The experience that results from enacting technology strategy similarly feeds back into technical capabilities and technology strategy, thus continuing the cycle.

The remainder of this chapter consists of five major sections. In the first, we examine technological competencies and capabilities. Next, we discuss the substance of technology strategy—the theoretical dimensions in which technology strategy can be expressed. The third section presents an overview of the internal and external forces that shape the evolution of a firm's technology strategy. The fourth section discusses the role of experience. In the fifth section, we examine the various key tasks through which a firm's technology strategy is implemented and experience is accumulated. A brief conclusion follows the final section.

Technological Competence and Capability

Over time organizations develop competencies closely associated with their ability to cope with environmental demands.[3] McKelvey and Aldrich view distinctive competence as "the combined workplace (technological) and organizational knowledge and skills . . . that together are most salient in determining the ability of an organization to survive" (p. 112).[4] Nelson and Winter, in a similar vein, use the concept of "routines," which they believe play a role similar to genes in biological evolution.[5] Interestingly, research has revealed that distinctive competencies can become a competence trap[6] or core rigidity.[7] Other research has found strong inertial forces associated with distinctive technological competencies, but maintains that strong technological competencies are likely to generate innovations.[8]

In general, a firm's distinctive competence involves the differential skills, complementary assets, and routines used to create sustainable competitive advantage.[9] Prahalad and Hamel, building on the work of Selznick and Andrews, define core competencies as "the collective learning in the organization, especially how to coordinate diverse production skills and integrate multiple streams of technologies" (p. 82).[10] The authors provide criteria for identifying a firm's core competence (pp. 83–84). A core competence should:

1. Provide potential access to a wide variety of markets.
2. Make a significant contribution to the perceived customer benefits of the end product.
3. Be difficult for competitors to imitate.

In this chapter, we focus primarily on a firm's subset of technological competencies, but their relationships with competencies in other key areas (such as marketing) are always to be considered as well.

Stalk, Evans, and Shulman distinguish core competences from strategic capabilities: "whereas core competence emphasizes technological and production expertise at specific points along the value chain, capabilities are more broadly based, encompassing the entire value chain" (p. 66).[11] They define a *capability* as "a set of business processes strategically understood. . . . The key is to connect them to real customer needs" (p. 62). Thus, though distinct, technological competencies and capabilities are complementary concepts.

The Substance of Technology Strategy

There are four substantive dimensions of technology strategy: (1) the deployment of technology in the firm's product-market strategy to position itself in terms of differentiation (perceived value or quality) and delivered cost, and to gain technology-based competitive advantage; (2) the use of technology, more broadly, in the various activities comprised by the firm's value chain; (3) the firm's resource commitment to various areas of technology; and (4) the firm's use of organization design and management techniques to manage the technology function.[12]

---

[3]P. Selznick, *Leadership in Administration* (New York: Harper and Row, 1957).

[4]B. McKelvey and H. E. Aldrich, "Populations, Organizations, and Applied Organizational Science," *Administrative Science Quarterly* 28 (1983), pp. 101–28.

[5]R. R. Nelson and S. G. Winter, *An Evolutionary Theory of Economic Change* (Cambridge, MA: Harvard University Press, 1982).

[6]B. Levitt and J. G. March, "Organizational Learning," *Annual Review of Sociology* 14 (1988).

[7]D. Leonard-Barton, "Core Capabilities and Core Rigidities: A Paradox in Product Development," *Strategic Management Journal* 13 (Summer 1992), pp. 111–26.

[8]R. A. Burgelman, "Fading Memories: A Process Theory of Strategic Business Exit in Dynamic Environments," *Administrative Science Quarterly* 39 (1994), pp. 24–56.

[9]Selznick, *Leadership in Administration;* K. Andrews, *The Concept of Corporate Strategy* (Homewood, IL: Richard D. Irwin, 1981); D. J. Teece, G. Pisano, and A. Shuen, "Firm Capabilities, Resources, and the Concept of Strategy," Working Paper 90-9, Center for Research in Management, University of California at Berkeley, 1990.

[10]C. K. Prahalad and G. Hamel, "The Core Competence of the Corporation," *Harvard Business Review,* May–June 1990, pp. 79–91.

[11]G. Stalk, P. Evans, and L. E. Shulman, "Competing on Capabilities: The New Rules of Corporate Strategy," *Harvard Business Review,* March–April 1992, pp. 57–69.

[12]R. A. Burgelman and R. S. Rosenbloom, "Technology Strategy: An Evolutionary Process Perspective," *Research on Technological Innovation, Management, and Policy* 4 (1989), pp. 1–23;

Competitive Strategy Stance

Technology strategy is a component of more comprehensive business and corporate strategies; as such, a business defines the role technology should play in increasing the differentiation and/or reducing the costs of its products and services.[13] From a competitive strategy point of view, technology can be used defensively to sustain an already achieved advantage in product differentiation or cost, or offensively as an instrument to create new advantage in established lines of business or new products and markets.

Technology choice. Recent work on the distinction between design concepts and their physical implementation[14] and on the distinction between components and architecture in product design and development[15] is useful to establish a framework for technology choice. Henderson and Clark offer the example of a room fan—a system for moving air in a room.[16] Its major components include the motor, the blade, the blade guard, the control system, and the mechanical housing. A component is defined as "a physically distinct portion of the product that embodies a core design concept and performs a well-defined function" (p. 2). Core design concepts correspond to the functions the product design must embody for the manufactured product to meet the needs of its user. For instance, the need for the fan to move corresponds to a core design concept. Core design concepts can be implemented in many ways. For instance, fan movement could be achieved through manual power or electrical motors. Each of these implementations, in turn, refers to an underlying technological knowledge base; designing and building electrical motors, for example, requires knowledge of electrical and mechanical engineering. Each of a product's core concepts thus entails technology choices.

In addition to components, a product also has an architecture which determines how its components fit and work together. The room fan's overall architecture lays out how its various components will work together. Product architectures usually become stable with the emergence of a "dominant design" in the industry.[17] Product architecture also affects technology choice.

Technology choice requires that a firm carefully assess technical as well as market factors and identify an array of targets for technology development. Targeted technology development may range from minor improvements in a mature process to the employment of an emerging technology in the first new product in a new market.[18] The relative irreversibility of investments makes this assessment and identification particularly critical.

Technology leadership. The implications of technological leadership have been explored in earlier writings on technology and strategy.[19] Technological leadership has often been discussed in terms of the timing (relative to rivals) of commercial use of new technology—that is, in terms of product-market strategy. A broader strategic definition, however, views technological leadership in terms of relative advantage in the command of a body of technological competencies and capabilities. This sort of leadership results from commitment to a pioneering role in the development of a technology, as opposed to a more passive monitoring role.[20]

K. D. Hampson, "Technology Strategy and Competitive Performance: A Study of Bridge Construction," unpublished doctoral dissertation, Department of Civil Engineering, Stanford University, 1993.

[13]M E. Porter, "The Technological Dimension of Competitive Strategy," *Research on Technological Innovation, Management, and Policy* 1 (1983), pp. 1–33, and M. E. Porter, *Competitive Advantage* (New York: Free Press, 1985).

[14]K. B. Clark, "The Interaction of Design Hierarchies and Market Concepts in Technological Evolution," *Research Policy* 14 (1985), pp. 235–51.

[15]K. B. Clark, "Managing Technology in International Competition: The Case of Product Development in Response to Foreign Entry," in *International Competitiveness,* ed. M. Spence and H. Hazard (Cambridge, MA: Ballinger Publishing, 1987), pp. 27–74; R. H. Henderson and K. B. Clark, "Architectural Innovation: The Reconfiguration of Existing Product Technologies and the Failure of Established Firms," *Administrative Science Quarterly* 35 (1990), pp. 9–30.

[16]Henderson and Clark, "Architectural Innovation."

[17]W. J. Abernathy and J. Utterback, "Patterns of Industrial Innovation." *Technology Review,* 1978.

[18]R. S. Rosenbloom, "Managing Technology for the Longer Term: A Managerial Perspective," in *The Uneasy Alliance: Managing the Productivity-Technology Dilemma,* ed. K. B. Clark, R. H. Hayes, and C. Lorenz (Boston, MA: Harvard Business School Press, 1985).

[19]H. I. Ansoff and J. M. Stewart, "Strategies for a Technology-Based Business," *Harvard Business Review,* November–December 1967; M. A. Maidique and P. Patch, "Corporate Strategy and Technological Policy," Harvard Business School case 9-679-033.

[20]R. S. Rosenbloom and M. S. Cusumano, "Technological Pioneering: The Birth of the VCR Industry," *California Management Review* 24, no. 4 (Summer 1987), pp. 51–76.

A firm's competitive advantage is most likely to arise from the unique aspects of its technology strategy. Companies that are successful over long periods of time develop technological competencies and capabilities distinct from those of their competitors and not easily replicable. Crown Cork and Seal, Marks and Spencer, and Banc One are examples briefly discussed below. Canon[21] and Wal-Mart[22] are other examples. The capabilities-based strategies of such companies cannot easily be classified simply in terms of differentiation or cost leadership; they combine both.

The competencies and capabilities–based view of technological leadership draws attention to the importance of the accumulation of capabilities.[23] Technological leadership cannot be bought easily in the market or quickly plugged into an organization. A firm must understand the strategic importance of different competencies and capabilities, and be willing to patiently and persistently build them, even though it may sometimes seem cheaper or more efficient in the short term to rely on outsiders for their procurement.

Thinking strategically about technology means raising the question of how a particular technical competence or capability may affect a firm's future degrees of freedom. This involves identifying and tracking key technical parameters and considering their impact on the speed and flexibility of product and process development cycles. It also requires distinguishing carefully between technologies that are common to all players and have little impact on competitive advantage, and those that are proprietary and likely to have a major impact on competitive advantage. Furthermore, it requires paying attention to new technologies that are only beginning to manifest their potential for competitive advantage.[24]

Technology entry timing. When to bring technology to market, of course, remains a key strategic issue. Porter identifies conditions under which pioneering is likely to be rewarded.[25] In his terms, lasting first-mover advantages are associated with:

1. Developing a leadership reputation with customers/users.
2. Preempting an attractive market position.
3. Creating switching costs for customers/users.
4. Accessing effective distribution channels first.
5. Locking in key suppliers.
6. Defining industry standards.
7. Establishing barriers to imitation (e.g., patents).
8. Reaping early profits.

But Porter points to potential first-mover *dis*-advantages:

1. Incurring pioneering costs that benefit followers as well.
2. Experiencing the greatest demand uncertainty.
3. Having to cope with changing customer/user needs.
4. Making irreversible specific capital investments.
5. Experiencing technological discontinuities.
6. Having to cope with unexpected low-cost imitation.

Teece extends Porter's analysis by identifying the importance of *appropriability regimes* and *control of specialized assets*.[26] Appropriability regimes are the first mover's ability to protect proprietary technological advantage, usually through patents, proprietary know-how, and/or trade secrets. The legal battle between Intel and Advanced Micro Devices over access to Intel's microcode for microprocessor development provides an example of the significance of appropriability regimes. An important consideration here is the cost of defending one's proprietary technological position. For instance, the prospect of rapidly escalating legal costs and/or claims on scarce top-management time may sometimes make it difficult for smaller firms to go to court to protect their proprietary position unless violations are very clear.

Control of specialized assets refers to the fact that, in many cases, the first mover may need access to complementary specialized assets owned by others. Gaining access to those assets—through acquisitions or strategic alliances—may absorb a large part of the innovation's rent stream. The alliances between start-up and established firms in the biotechnology indus-

---

[21]Prahalad and Hamel, "The Core Competence of the Corporation," pp. 79–91.

[22]Stalk et al., "Competing on Capabilities," pp. 57–69.

[23]H. Itami, *Mobilizing Invisible Assets* (Cambridge, MA: Harvard University Press, 1987).

[24]A. D. Little, "The Strategic Management of Technology," *European Management Forum,* 1981.

[25]Porter, *Competitive Advantage.*

[26]D. J. Teece, "Profiting from Technological Innovation: Implications for Integration, Collaboration, Licensing, and Public Policy," *Research Policy* 15 (1986), pp. 285–305.

try highlight the importance of complementary assets.[27] Unless companies command strong positions in appropriability regimes and complementary assets, their capacity to exploit potential first-mover advantages remains doubtful.

Technology licensing. Sometimes firms must decide whether to bring technologies to market themselves, or to offer other firms licensing arrangements.[28] Ford and Ryan identify several reasons why companies may be unable to fully exploit technologies through product sales alone.[29] First, not all technologies generated by R&D efforts fit into a firm's line of business and corporate strategies.[30] Second, a company may need to consider licensing its technology to maximize returns on R&D investments, because patents provide only limited protection against imitation by competitors. Third, smaller firms may be unable to exploit their technologies because they lack the necessary cash and/or complementary assets (e.g., manufacturing). Fourth, international market development for the technology may require licensing local firms because of local government regulation. Finally, antitrust legislation may prevent a company from fully exploiting its technological advantages (Kodak, Xerox, and IBM are fairly recent examples). Technology-rich companies should therefore consider developing a special capability for marketing their technologies beyond their own products.

Value Chain Stance

Technology pervades the value chain. A competencies and capabilities–based view goes beyond the strategic use of technology in products and services and takes a competitive stance towards its use in all value chain activities.[31]

[27]G. Pisano and D. J. Teece, "Collaborative Arrangements and Global Technology Strategy: Some Evidence from the Telecommunications Equipment Industry," *Research on Technological Innovation, Management, and Policy* 4 (1989), pp. 227–56.

[28]A. Shepard, "Licensing to Enhance Demand for New Technologies," *The Rand Journal of Economics* 21 (1987), pp. 147–60.

[29]D. Ford and C. Ryan, "Taking Technology to Market," *Harvard Business Review,* March–April 1981.

[30]Also see K. L. R. Pavitt, M. J. Robson, and J. F. Townsend, "Technological Accumulation, Diversification, and Organization of U.K. Companies, 1945–83," *Management Science* 35 (1989), pp. 91–99.

[31]Porter, *Competitive Advantage.*

Scope of technology strategy. Considering technology strategy in relation to the value chain defines its scope: the set of technological capabilities that a firm decides to develop internally. This set of technologies can be called the *core technology.* Core technologies are the areas in which a firm must first assess its distinctive technological competencies, and then decide whether to be a technological leader or follower and when to bring its competencies to market. The scope of technology strategy is especially important in relation to the threat of new entrants in the firm's industry. All else being equal, firms with a broader set of core technologies appear less vulnerable to attacks from new entrants producing and delivering new types of technology-based customer value. Resource constraints, however, will limit how many technologies the firm can opt to develop internally. Thus, it is important to limit the scope of technology strategy to the set of technologies considered to have a material impact on competitive advantage.

The scope of a firm's technology strategy may be determined to a significant extent by its scale and business focus. Businesses built around large, complex systems such as aircraft, automobiles, or telecommunication switches must be able to apply and integrate distinct types of expertise. General Electric, for instance, was reportedly able to bring high-powered mathematical analysis used for military research to bear on the development of computerized tomography (CT) products in its medical equipment division.[32]

Resource Commitment Stance

The third dimension of the substance of technology strategy is the intensity of the firm's resource commitment to technology. The variation among manufacturing firms is pronounced: although many do not spend on R&D, a few commit as much as 10 percent of their revenues. While interindustry differences may explain a large share of this variation, substantial differences in R&D commitment remain between rivals.

Depth of technology strategy. Resource commitments determine the *depth* of the firm's technology strategy, which can be expressed in terms of the

[32]D. Rutenberg, "Umbrella Pricing," working paper, Queens University, 1986.

number of technological options the firm has available. Depth of technology is likely to be correlated with the firm's capacity to anticipate technological developments early on. Greater technological depth may offer the benefit of increased flexibility and the ability to respond to new demands from customers/users.

Management Stance

Recent research[33] based on Burgelman and Rosenbloom's framework[34] suggests that the substance of technology strategy also encompasses a management stance: the choice of a management approach and organization design that are consistent with the stances taken on other substantive dimensions.

Organizational fit. Firms that organize themselves to meet the requirements flowing from their competitive, value chain, and resource commitment stances are more likely to have an effective technology strategy. For instance, a science-based firm that has decided to be a technology leader for the long run probably needs to create a central R&D organization, while a firm that is satisfied with commercially exploiting existing technologies to the fullest may be able to decentralize all R&D activity. Imai et al.[35] describe how Japanese firms use multiple layers of contractors and subcontractors in an external network to foster extreme forms of specialization in particular skills; this, in turn, provides them with flexibility, speed in response, and the potential for cost savings because the highly specialized subcontractors operate on an experience curve even at the level of prototypes.

Evolutionary Forces Shaping Technology Strategy

An evolutionary process perspective raises the question of how a firm's technology strategy actually develops and changes over time. Evolutionary theory applied to social systems focuses on variation-selection-retention mechanisms for explaining dynamic behavior over time.[36] It recognizes the importance of history, irreversibilities, invariance, and inertia in explaining the behavior of organizations. But it also considers the effects of individual and social learning processes.[37] An evolutionary perspective is useful for integrating extant literatures on technology. The study of technological development, for instance, contains many elements that seem compatible with the variation-selection-retention structure of evolutionary theory.[38] While cautioning against the fallacy of unwarranted analogy in applying concepts from biological evolution to cultural (organizational) evolution, Gould's interpretation[39] of the establishment of QWERTY[40] as the dominant, if inferior, approach to laying out keys on typewriter keyboards shows the power of evolutionary reasoning to identify and elucidate interesting phenomena concerning technological evolution.

The evolutionary factors shaping technology strategy comprise internal and external generative and integrative forces. In this section, we explore a simple framework to conceptualize these forces, presented in Exhibit 2.

As seen in Exhibit 2, technology strategy is shaped by the generative forces of technology evolution

[33]Hampson, "Technology Strategy and Competitive Performance."

[34]Burgelman and Rosenbloom, "Technology Strategy," pp. 1–23.

[35]K. Imai, I. Nonaka, and H. Takeuchi, "Managing the New Product Development Process: How Japanese Learn and Unlearn," in *The Uneasy Alliance: Managing the Productivity-Technology Dilemma,* ed. K. B. Clark, R. H. Hayes, and C. Lorenz (Boston, MA: Harvard Business School Press, 1985).

[36]For example: D T. Campbell, "Variation and Selective Retention in Sociocultural Evolution," *General Systems* 14 (1969), pp. 69–85; H. E. Aldrich, *Organizations and Environments* (Englewood Cliffs, NJ: Prentice Hall, 1979); K. Weick, *The Social Psychology of Organizing* (Reading, MA: Addison-Wesley, 1979); R. A. Burgelman, "Corporate Entrepreneurship and Strategic Management: Insights from a Process Study," *Management Science* 29 (1983), pp. 1349–64; R. A. Burgelman, "Intraorganizational Ecology of Strategy Making and Organizational Adaptation: Theory and Field Research," *Organizational Science* 2 (1991), pp. 239–62; A. H. Van de Ven and R. Garud, "A Framework for Understanding the Emergence of New Industries," *Research on Technological Innovation, Management, and Policy* 4 (1989), pp. 195–226.

[37]For example, see R. A. Burgelman, "Strategy-Making as a Social Learning Process: The Case of Internal Corporate Venturing," *Interfaces* 18, no. 3 (May–June 1988), pp. 74–85.

[38]For example: N. Rosenberg, *Inside the Black Box* (Cambridge: Cambridge University Press, 1982); P. Kelly and M. Kranzberg, eds., *Technological Innovation: A Critical Review of Current Knowledge* (San Francisco: San Francisco Press, 1978); W. J. Abernathy, *The Productivity Dilemma: Roadblock to Innovation in the Automobile Industry* (Baltimore: Johns Hopkins University Press, 1978); Clark, "The Interaction of Design Hierarchies"; Henderson and Clark, "Architectural Innovation"; Burgelman, "Fading Memories."

[39]S. J. Gould, "The Panda's Thumb of Technology," *Bully for Brontosaurus: Reflections in Natural History* (New York: W. W Norton & Company, 1991).

[40]P. A. David, "Clio and the Economics of QWERTY," *Administrative Economic Review* 75, no. 2 (May 1985), pp. 332–37.

EXHIBIT 2 Determinants of Technology Strategy

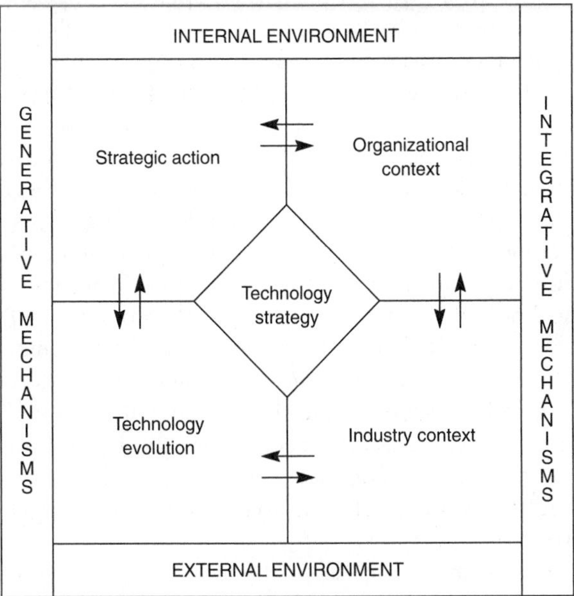

and the firm's strategic action, and by the integrative, or selective, forces of industry context and the firm's organizational context.

Technology Evolution

A firm's technology strategy is rooted in the evolution of its technical capabilities. However, the dynamics of these capabilities, and hence the technology strategy, are not completely endogenous. A firm's technical capabilities are significantly affected by the evolution of broader areas of technology that evolve largely independently. Different aspects of technological evolution have been discussed in the literature:

1. The evolution of technologies along S-curve trajectories.[41]
2. The interplay between product and process technology development within design configurations over the course of a particular technological trajectory.[42]
3. The emergence of new technologies and their trajectories (S-curves).[43]
4. The competence enhancing or destroying consequences of new technologies.[44]
5. Dematurity, or renewed technological innovation in the context of well-established markets, high production volumes, and well-established organizational arrangements.[45]
6. The organizational determinants of technological change.[46]

These are some of the major evolutionary forces associated with technological development that transcend the strategic actions of any given firm.

Industry Context

Important aspects of industry context are (1) the industry structure, which can be understood in terms of five major forces,[47] all of which can be affected in important ways by technology,[48] but the interplay of which, in turn, determines the technological competencies that can form the basis of competitive advantage;[49] (2) the appropriability regime associated with a technological innovation;[50] (3) the complementary assets needed to commercialize a new technology;[51] (4) the emergence of dominant designs;[52] (5) increasing returns to adoption for particular technologies;[53] (6) the emergence of industry

[41]For example: B. Twiss, *Managing Technological Innovation* (London: Longman, 1980); G. Dosi, "Technological Paradigms and Technological Trajectories: A Suggested Interpretation of the Determinants and Directions of Technical Change," *Research Policy* 11 (1982), pp. 147–62.

[42]Abernathy, *The Productivity Dilemma.*

[43]R. N. Foster, *Innovation: The Attacker's Advantage* (New York: Summit, 1986).

[44]W. G. Astley, "The Two Ecologies: Population and Community Perspectives on Organizational Evolution," *Administrative Science Quarterly* 20 (1985), pp. 224–41; W. J. Abernathy, K. B. Clark, and A. M. Kantrow, *Industrial Renaissance* (New York: Basic Books, 1983); M. L. Tushman and P. Anderson, "Technological and Organizational Environments," *Administrative Science Quarterly* 31 (1986), pp. 439–65.

[45]Abernathy, Clark, and Kantrow, *Industrial Renaissance.*

[46]M. L. Tushman and L. Rosenkopf, "Organizational Determinants of Technological Change," *Research in Organizational Behavior* 14 (1992), pp. 311–25.

[47]M. E. Porter, *Competitive Strategy* (New York: Free Press, 1980).

[48]Porter, "The Technological Dimension of Competitive Strategy," pp. 1–33.

[49]Burgelman, "Fading Memories," pp. 24–56.

[50]Teece, "Profiting from Technological Innovation."

[51]Ibid.

[52]Abernathy and Utterback, "Patterns of Industrial Innovation."

[53]W. B. Arthur, "Competing Technologies: An Overview," in *Technical Change and Economic Theory,* ed. G. Dosi et al. (New York: Columbia University Press, 1988); David, "Clio and the Economics of QWERTY."

standards;[54] (7) the social systems aspects of industry development;[55] and (8) the competitive effects of the interplay of social systems characteristics and technological change.[56] These various factors and their interplay affect the likely distribution of profits generated by a technological innovation among the different parties involved, as well as the strategic choices concerning the optimal boundaries of the innovating firm. They also affect the expected locus of technological innovations.[57]

Strategic Action

A firm's strategy captures organizational learning about the basis of its past and current success.[58] Strategic action is, to a large extent, induced by the prevailing concept of strategy. Induced strategic action is likely to manifest a degree of inertia relative to cumulative changes in the external environment.[59] Cooper and Schendel found that established firms, when confronted with the threat of radically new technologies, were likely to increase their efforts to improve existing technology rather than switch to new technology even after the latter had passed the threshold of viability.[60] Abernathy, Clark, and Kantrow[61] point out that "core design concepts" may emerge that "'lock in' or stabilize the domain of relevant technical effort."[62] Henderson and Clark found that firms faced with architectural innovations were often unable to adapt their product development efforts.[63] Burgelman found that inertial forces associated with a firm's distinctive competence impeded adaptation to changes in the basis of competition as a product moved from specialty to commodity.[64]

Firms also exhibit some amount of autonomous strategic action aimed at getting the firm into new areas of business.[65] These initiatives are often rooted in technology development efforts. In the course of their work, for example, technical people may serendipitously discover results that provide a basis for the redirection or replacement of a firm's major technologies. The existence of a corporate R&D capability often provides a substratum for the emergence of such new technical possibilities that extend beyond the scope of the firm's corporate strategy.[66] But, as Itami has observed, "In reality, many firms do not have . . . complete knowledge and discover the full potential of their ability only after the fact" (p. 15).[67]

Hamel and Prahalad, on the other hand, have proposed that global leadership requires "strategic intent" on the part of top management.[68] Top managers with strategic intent had ambitions for their organizations "that were out of all proportion to their resources and capabilities"; they "created an obsession with winning at all levels of their organization and then sustained that obsession over the 10- to 20-year quest for global leadership" (p. 64). This is an inspiring assertion for which the evidence, however, remains somewhat limited.

Organizational Context

Industry context exerts strong external selection pressures on incumbent firms and their strategies.

---

[54]F. Farrell and G. Saloner, "Competition, Compatibility, and Standards: The Economics of Horses, Penguins, and Lemmings," in *Product Standardization and Competitive Strategy,* ed. G. Landis (New York: Elsevier, 1987), pp. 1–21; J. S. Metcalfe and M. Gibbons, "Technology, Variety, and Organization: A Systematic Perspective on the Competitive Process," *Research in Technological Innovation, Management, and Policy* 4 (1989), pp. 153–94.

[55]Van de Ven and Garud, "A Framework for Understanding the Emergence of New Industries."

[56]W. P. Barnett, "The Organizational Ecology of a Technological System," *Administrative Science Quarterly* 35 (1990).

[57]E. A. Von Hippel, *The Source of Innovation* (New York: Oxford University Press, 1988).

[58]Burgelman, "Corporate Entrepreneurship and Strategic Management"; Burgelman, "Intraorganizational Ecology of Strategy Making and Organizational Adaptation"; G. Donaldson and J. W. Lorsch, *Decision Making at the Top* (New York: Basic Books, 1983); Weick, *The Social Psychology of Organizing.*

[59]H. T. Hannan and J. H. Freeman, "Structural Inertia and Organizational Change," *American Sociological Review* 43 (1984), pp. 149–64.

[60]A. C. Cooper and D. Schendel, "Strategic Responses to Technological Threats," *Business Horizons,* February 1976, pp. 61–63.

[61]Abernathy et al., *Industrial Renaissance,* p. 23.

[62]Clark, "The Interaction of Design Hierarchies."

[63]Henderson and Clark, "Architectural Innovation."

[64]Burgelman, "Fading Memories."

[65]For example: E. T. Penrose, *The Theory of the Growth of the Firm* (White Plains, NY: M. E. Sharpe, 1968); Burgelman, "Corporate Entrepreneurship and Strategic Management"; Burgelman, "Intraorganizational Ecology of Strategy Making and Organizational Adaptation."

[66]R. S. Rosenbloom and A. M. Kantrow, "The Nurturing of Corporate Research," *Harvard Business Review,* January–February 1982, pp. 115–23; R. A. Burgelman and L. R. Sayles, *Inside Corporate Innovation* (New York: Free Press, 1986); Pavitt et al., "Technological Accumulation."

[67]H. Itami, "The Case for Unbalanced Growth of the Firm," Research Paper Series 681, Graduate School of Business, Stanford University, Stanford, CA, 1983.

[68]G. Hamel and C. K. Prahalad, "Strategic Intent," *Harvard Business Review,* May–June 1989, pp. 63–76.

However, a key feature of established firms is that they have an organizational context that allows them, to some extent, to substitute internal selection for external selection. Continued survival may very well depend on the effectiveness of the firm's internal selection environment, which affects its capacity to deal with major strategic management challenges: (1) the ability to exploit opportunities associated with the current strategy (induced process), (2) the ability to take advantage of opportunities that emerge spontaneously outside the scope of the current strategy (autonomous process), and (3) the ability to balance challenges (1) and (2) at different times in the firm's development.[69]

Organizational context takes shape over time and reflects the firm's administrative approaches and dominant culture. The dominant culture as it relates to technology differs depending on whether the firm's distinctive competencies are rooted in science (e.g., pharmaceutical firms), engineering (e.g., semiconductor firms), or manufacturing (e.g., Japanese firms); whether the product development process has been driven by technology push, need pull, or a more balanced approach; and so on. Some research suggests that the background and management approaches of the firm's founders have a lasting impact on its organizational context.[70] Other research has shown that product architecture becomes reflected in organization structure and culture and greatly affects communication channels and filters.[71] This, in turn, makes it difficult for organizations to adapt architectural innovations that change the way a product's components are linked while leaving the core design concepts (and thus the basic technological knowledge underlying the components) intact.

Applying the Framework: Some Examples

Several examples can be offered to indicate how the framework (outlined in Exhibit 2) may help gain insight into a firm's technology strategy.

- Crown Cork and Seal (CC&S) has done very well over a 30-year period as a relatively small player in a mature industry. Technology strategy seems to have contributed significantly to Crown's success. CEO John Connelly, who took over the company in 1957, chose to build on Crown's existing skills in metal formation and specialized in "hard-to-hold" applications for tin cans (*competencies/capabilities*). Crown lacked an R&D department, but developed strong links between a highly competent technical sales force and an applications-oriented engineering group so it could provide complete technical solutions for customers' "filling needs" (*competencies/capabilities*). In the face of a major external technological innovation—the two-piece can—initiated by an aluminum company (*technology evolution*), Crown was able to mobilize its own capabilities as well as those of its steel suppliers to quickly adapt the innovation for use with steel. Over several decades, CC&S continued to stick to what it did best (*strategic action*)—manufacturing and selling cans—driven by a strong customer-oriented culture (*organizational context*) while its competitors were directing their attention to diversification and gradually lost interest in the metal can industry (*industry context*). CC&S has continued to refine its skill set (*experience*); it is now the only remaining independent metal can company of the four original major players.
- The success of Marks and Spencer (M&S), a British retailer with a worldwide reputation for quality, is based on a consistent strategy founded on an unswerving commitment to giving the customer "good value for money." The genesis of its technology strategy was the transformation, in 1936, of a small textile testing department into a Merchandise Development Department designed to work closely with vendors to bring about quality improvements. Thirty years later, the M&S technical staff, then numbering more than 200 persons working on food technology as well as on textiles and home goods, allowed M&S to control the cost structure of its suppliers. The development of the technical capability itself was driven by the strong value of excellent supplier relationships held and continuously reinforced by top management.
- Banc One Corporation is a Midwest banking group that consistently ranks among the most profitable U.S. banking operations. In 1958, the new CEO of City National Bank of Columbus, Ohio (CNB), John G. McCoy, persuaded his Board to invest 3 percent of profits each year to support a "research and development" activity. Over the next two decades, CNB, which became the lead bank of Banc One Corporation, developed capabilities that made it a national leader in the application of elec-

---

[69]Burgelman and Sayles, *Inside Corporate Innovation*.

[70]For example, see W. Boeker, "Strategic Change: The Effects of Founding and History," *Academy of Management Journal* 32 (1989), pp. 489–515.

[71]Henderson and Clark, "Architectural Innovation."

tronic information processing technologies to retail banking. It was the first bank to install automatic teller machines and a pioneer in the development of bank credit cards, point-of-sale transaction processing, and home banking. While not all of its innovative ventures succeeded, each contributed to the cumulative development of a deep and powerful technical capability that remains a distinctive element of the bank's highly successful competitive strategy.

The three companies cited above are notable for the consistency of their technology strategy over several decades. The following example illustrates the problems that can arise in a time of changing technology and industry context when a fundamental change in strategy is not matched by corresponding adaptation of the organizational context.

■ The National Cash Register Company (NCR) built a dominant position in worldwide markets for cash registers and accounting machines on the basis of superior technology and an outstanding sales force created by the legendary John H. Patterson. By 1911, NCR had a 95 percent share in cash register sales. Scale economies in manufacturing, sales, and service presented formidable barriers to entry to its markets (*industry context*), preserving its dominance for another 60 years. Highly developed skills in the design and fabrication of complex low-cost machines (*competencies/capabilities*) not only supported the strategy, but also shaped the culture of management, centered in Dayton, where a vast complex housed engineering and fabrication for the traditional product line (*organizational context*). In the 1950s, management began to build new capabilities in electronics (*a revolution, not just evolution, in technology*) and entered the emerging market for electronic data processing (EDP). A new strategic concept tried to position traditional products (registers and accounting machines) as data-entry terminals in EDP systems (*changing strategic behavior*). But a sales force trained to sell stand-alone products of moderate unit cost proved ineffective in selling high-priced total systems. At the same time, the microelectronics revolution destroyed the barriers inherent in NCR's scale and experience in fabricating mechanical equipment. A swarm of entrants found receptive customers for their new electronic registers (*changing industry context*). As market share tumbled and red ink washed over the P&L in 1972, the chief executive was forced out. His successor was an experienced senior NCR manager who had built his career entirely outside of Dayton. He moved swiftly to transform the ranks of top management, decentralize manufacturing (reducing employment in Dayton by 85 percent), and restructure the sales force along new lines. The medicine was bitter, but it worked; within two years, NCR had regained leadership in its main markets, and was more profitable in the late 1970s than it had been at any point in the 1960s.

Experience through Enactment of Technology Strategy

A Note on Performance (Enactment) as Experience

The conventional view of performance in strategy literature is framed in terms of outcomes such as ROE, P/E, market share, and growth. Typically, strategy researchers have tried to establish statistical associations between such outcomes and strategic variables—between measures of product quality and profitability, for example. Although establishing such associations is useful, little insight is gained as to how outcomes come about (e.g., how quality is achieved and how it influences buyer behavior). In the framework represented in Exhibit 1, experience is viewed in terms of performing (enacting) the different tasks involved in carrying out the strategy.

This view of performance is akin to that used in sports. For instance, to help a swimmer reach his or her highest possible performance, it is not enough to measure the time needed to swim a certain distance and communicate that outcome to the swimmer, or to establish that, on average, a certain swimming style will be associated with better times. Sophisticated analysis of every movement of the swimmer traversing the water provides clues on how this swimmer may be able to achieve a better time. Similarly, experience derived from using technology in strategy provides feedback concerning the quantity and quality of the firm's technical competencies and capabilities and the effectiveness of its strategy. The learning and unlearning potentially resulting from this analysis serve, in turn, to leverage, augment, and/or alter the firm's capabilities, strategy, or both.[72]

---

[72]M. A. Maidique and B. J. Zirger, "The New Product Learning Cycle," *Research Policy*, 1984, pp. 1–40; Imai et al., "Managing the New Product Development Process"; Itami, *Mobilizing Invisible Assets;* Burgelman, "Fading Memories."

Technology strategy is realized in practice through the enactment of several key tasks: (1) internal and external technology sourcing, (2) deploying technology in product and process development, and (3) using technology in technical support activities. In turn, performing these activities provides valuable experience that serves to augment and change the firm's technical competencies and capabilities. These activities are briefly described below and are examined in depth in Part II of the book.

Technology Sourcing

Because the sources of technology are inherently varied, so too must be the mechanisms employed to make it accessible within the firm. It is useful to distinguish between internal R&D activity and acquisitive functions that import technology originating outside the firm.

Internal sourcing. Internal sourcing depends on the firm's R&D capability. Each firm's technology strategy finds partial expression in the way it funds, structures, and directs the R&D activities that will create new pathways for technology. Relatively few firms are able to support the kind of science-based R&D that can lead to important new technologies. Most established technology-based firms instead emphasize applied R&D in support of existing and emerging businesses. Cohen and Levinthal found that an internal R&D capability is also an important determinant of the firm's "absorptive capacity," that is, the firm's "ability to recognize the value of new, external information, assimilate it, and apply it to commercial ends" (p. 128).[73] This indicates a close link between internal sourcing of technology and the capacity to use external sources of technology.

External sourcing. Many important technologies used in the value chain are outside of the firm's technological capabilities. While internal sourcing is necessary for most of the firm's core technologies, some may need to be sourced externally through exclusive or preferential licensing contracts or through strategic alliances. How a firm acquires external technologies can reveal a great deal about its underlying technology strategy. To what extent does the firm rely on ongoing alliances, as opposed to discrete transactions? Is the acquisition structured to create the capability for future advances to be made internally, or will it merely reinforce dependence?

Continuous concern with improving all aspects of the value creation and delivery process may guard a firm from quirky moves in external technology sourcing. Viewing the issue of external sourcing from this perspective highlights the importance of managing interdependencies with external capabilities providers. To the extent that a firm engages in strategic alliances, it must establish the requisite capabilities to manage the relationships. For instance, a company may need a strong technical staff to manage its relationship with a supplier. Alternatively, if the strategic alliance is formed to compensate for a technology shortfall, the firm may need to invest in plant and equipment to apply what is learned and begin building the capability inhouse. For example, Japanese electronics firms that acquired technology from abroad during the 1950s and 1960s structured their learning in the ways that made it possible for them to become the leaders in pushing the frontiers of those same technologies in the 1970s and 1980s.[74]

Product and Process Development

Technology strategy is also enacted by deploying technology to develop products and processes. An understanding of what the strategy is can be gained from considering the resources committed, how they are deployed, and how they are directed in product and process development. For instance, how does the organization strike the delicate balance between letting technology drive product development and allowing product development and/or market development to drive technology? While the availability of integrated-circuit technology drove product development in many areas of consumer electronics, for example, notebook computers drove the development of new disk drive technology and semiconductor "Flash" memory.

Wheelwright and Clark suggest three potential benefits associated with product and process development: market position, resource utilization, and organizational renewal and enhancement.[75] They

---

[73]W. M. Cohen and D. A. Levinthal, "Absorptive Capacity: A New Perspective on Learning and Innovation," *Administrative Science Quarterly* 35 (1990), pp. 128–52.

[74]I. L. Doz, G. Hamel, and C. K. Prahalad, "Collaborate with Your Competitors—and Win," *Harvard Business Review,* January–February 1989, pp. 133–39.

[75]S. C. Wheelwright and K. B. Clark, *Revolutionizing Product Development* (New York: Free Press, 1992), pp. 28–29.

point out that the potential benefits are seldom fully realized because most firms lack a development strategy framework to consistently integrate technology strategy with product-market strategy. Beyond product and process development for the firm's mainstream businesses, companies can also develop new competencies and capabilities through corporate entrepreneurship.[76]

Technical Support

The function commonly termed *field service* creates the interface between a firm's technical function and the users of its products or services. Experience in use provides important feedback to enhance the firm's technological capabilities.[77] Airline operations, for example, are an essential source of information about jet engine technology. In some industries, such as electronic instrumentation, important innovations often originate with the users.[78] The technology strategy of a firm, then, finds important expression in the way it carries out this important link to users. Two-way flows of information are relevant: expert knowledge from product developers can enhance the effectiveness of field operations, while feedback from the field informs future development.

Enactment Reveals the Substance of Technology Strategy

Studying the processes involved in performing the key tasks sheds light on how technology strategy relates technical capabilities to competitive advantage and how organizational learning and unlearning actually come about. In other words, enactment reveals the substance of technology strategy. The matrix illustrated in Exhibit 3 presents a framework for mapping the interactions between substance and enactment in technology strategy making.

Two Conjectures

Implicit in the foregoing discussion are two normative conjectures about technology strategy. The first is that the substance of technology strategy should be comprehensive. That is, technology strategy, as it is enacted through the various tasks of acquisition, development, and technical support, should address the four substantive dimensions and do so in ways that are consistent across the dimensions. Second, we suggest that technology strategy should be integrated. That is, each key task should be informed by the position taken on the four substantive dimensions in ways that create consistency across the various tasks.

Conclusion

This chapter argues that an evolutionary process perspective provides a useful framework for thinking about technology strategy and its role in a firm's broader competitive strategy. The essence of this perspective is that technology strategy is built on technical competencies and capabilities and tempered by experience. These three main constructs—technical competencies and capabilities, strategy, and experience—are tightly interwoven. Technical competencies and capabilities give technology strategy its force; technology strategy enacted creates experience that modifies technical competencies and capabilities. Central to this idea is the notion that the reality of a strategy lies in its enactment, not in those pronouncements that appear to assert it. In other words, the substance of technology strategy can be found in its enactment of the various modes by which technology is acquired and deployed—sourcing, development, and support activities. The ways in which these tasks are actually performed and the ways in which their performance contributes, cumulatively, to the augmentation and deepening of competencies and capabilities convey the substance of technology strategy in practice.

A second central idea in this chapter is that the ongoing interactions of technical capabilities–technology strategy–experience occur within a matrix of generative and integrative mechanisms that shape strategy. These mechanisms (Exhibit 2) are both internal and external to the firm. Anecdotal evidence suggests that successful firms operate within some sort of harmonious equilibrium of these forces. Major change in one, as in the emergence of a technological discontinuity, ordinarily must be matched by adaptation in the others. This leads to the final conjecture of this chapter—namely, that it is advantageous to attain a state in which technology strategy is both comprehensive and integrated. By

[76]Burgelman, "Corporate Entrepreneurship and Strategic Management."

[77]Rosenberg, *Inside the Black Box.*

[78]E. A. Von Hippel, "Has a Customer Already Developed Your Next Product?" *Sloan Management Review,* Winter 1978.

EXHIBIT 3 Substance and Enactment in Technology Strategy

	Modes of Experience				
Substance	External Technology Sourcing	Internal Technology Sourcing	Product Development	Process Development	Technical Support
Competitive strategy stance (choice/leadership/ entry timing/licensing)					
Value chain stance (scope)					
Resource commitment stance (depth)					
Management stance (organizational fit)					

comprehensive we mean that it embodies consistent answers to the issues posed by all four substantive dimensions, and by *integrated* we mean that each of the various modes of experience is informed by the technology strategy.

D istinctive Technological Competences and Capabilities

Case II–1
Advent Corporation (C)

R. S. Rosenbloom

Early in November 1970, Henry Kloss was reviewing the progress Advent Corporation had made in the preceding months. The September profit and loss statement had registered a net profit of almost $30,000, against a cumulative loss of nearly $165,000 in the preceding 10 months. The new Advent cassette recorder, Model M200, had just completed its third month on the market. The M200 recorder, with its sophisticated circuitry, was felt to represent real potential as a replacement for the phonograph as the central element in any home entertainment sys-

Harvard Business School case 9-674-027.

tem. With the financial turnaround, Mr. Kloss felt confident that a sales level of $40 million to $50 million was achievable by Advent within five years. His problem was how to organize for continuing innovation.

Introduction

Mr. Kloss was a well-known figure in consumer electronic product design and manufacturing. Prior to Advent, he had participated in the founding and operation of Acoustic Research, Inc. (AR), and later, KLH Corporation. He had been the mind behind the products at KLH, an organization which was renowned for its very-high quality, slightly oddball electronic products. He left KLH in 1967 after 10 years as president.

The formation of AR had originated during the Korean crisis. While stationed in New Jersey, Mr. Kloss was able to attend the City College of New York, where he was a student of Edgar Vilchur. He and Vilchur had mutual interests in an acoustic suspension speaker because of its immense reproductive advantages over conventional mechanical speaker systems and its small size. With Mr. Kloss providing some capital and a "garage," Acoustic Research, Inc., was formed. Financial guidance of the business was provided by Anton (Tony) Hofmann, who was later to become a principal of KLH, and then treasurer of Advent.

Mr. Kloss and other active management sold their share of AR, Inc., after irreparable disagreements with Vilchur over company policies. KLH was initiated shortly thereafter with $60,000 in capital and Mr. Kloss as president, Malcolm Low as manager of sales, and Mr. Hofmann as financial manager. After seven years and a series of innovative audio products that were producing a $4 million level of sales, KLH was sold because of sheer tiredness of the managers and uncertainties associated with KLH's growing size. With the sale, Mr. Kloss agreed to remain as president for three years, and he left in 1967.

Advent Corporation was incorporated by Mr. Kloss in May 1967 for the purpose of manufacturing specialized electronic products for home entertainment use. The actual justification for forming the company was to do work in television, especially to create an organization which would support the R&D and marketing of a large screen (4′ × 6′) color television system. Formal development work on the television system had been suspended in 1970.

With the formation of Advent Corporation, Mr. Kloss embarked on a plan to see what a big company could do. He felt that growth was always a primary goal, always desirable, but that one had to think in terms of what was realizable without beating one's head against the wall. Mr. Kloss sought to retain strong financial control of the company, having sold his share of Acoustic Research, Inc., under duress and his share of KLH Corporation with mixed feelings. He had this to say to the case researchers about financial policies:

> The size one desires is really only limited by the dollars available for working capital. There's a firm intention to reach the middle tens of millions of dollars certainly in less than five years; one anticipates a faster accumulation of staff, faster than the 30 percent one might be able to do from profits, so the question becomes how fast does one dribble out equity if you're not staff limited?

Mr. Kloss continued:

> Eighteen months ago, there was a small private offering of 12 percent of the company in which we offered 20 units consisting of $10,000 in 8 percent convertible debentures, and 300 shares of equity common at $7.50 per share, 10 cents par value. I retained 75 percent control; company directors and others have 13 percent. It was simply that circumstances warranted our doing that. In addition, we have a $1.15 million line of credit, of which $600,000 is revolving and $550,000 open, secured by the directors and pegged to 80 percent of the accounts receivable. I will not offer any further equity until a really big push (for which the sales are guaranteed) requires it, and when a price several times the $7.50 price per share is attainable. Beyond that, we are working hard to slash overhead and to build profits.

Financial data regarding the operations of Advent Corporation are given in Exhibits 1 and 2.

Current Operations

In the fall of 1970, Advent Corporation manufactured and sold five products for home entertainment use: the Advent loudspeaker; the Advent Frequency Balance Control, which allowed the listener to alter the relative musical balance in any audible octave; two models of the Advent Noise Reduction Unit, which allowed virtually hiss-free tape recording and playback; and the new Advent Tape Deck, which also featured noise-free recording and playback. These products, as well as a special recording tape

EXHIBIT 1

Advent Corporation (C)
Balance Sheet
As of September 26, 1970

Assets		
Current assets:		
Cash		$ 64,488.34
Accounts receivable		650,226.68
Less: Reserve for bad debts		(10,000.00)
Advance to employees		(650.00)
Inventory:		
Material	$ 375,486.13	
Labor	37,076.97	
Manufacturing overhead	38,189.91	450,753.01
Prepaid insurance and other assets		10,958.21
Total current assets		1,165,770.24
Property, plant, and equipment	221,030.07	
Less: Accumulated depreciation	(57,524.71)	163,505.36
Deferred financing expense		5,450.00
Advent television system		205,085.92
Total assets		$1,539,811.52
Liabilities		
Current liabilities:		
Accounts payable		$ 347,449.36
Notes payable, bank		666,714.00
Due officers		0.00
Loans, other		50,000.00
Accrued debenture interest		4,002.65
Accrued payroll		17,441.39
Royalties payable		(2,000.00)
Accrued royalty expense		7,584.80
Accrued audit and legal fees		20,628.38
Accrued taxes and fringe benefits		37,083.67
Accrued promotion and discount allowances		65,312.20
Miscellaneous accounts		17,471.29
Total current liabilities		1,231,687.74
Long-term debt:		
8% convertible debentures		200,000.00
Stockholders' equity:		
Common stock (10¢ par value)	$ 45,925.10	
Additional paid-in capital	821,866.29	
Retained earnings deficit to 10/31/69	(595,130.66)	
Deficit 11/1/69 to date	(164,536.95)	
Total stockholders' equity		108,123.78
Total liabilities and stockholders' equity		$1,539,811.52

that Advent sold under license from Du Pont, are described in detail in Exhibit 3, in a piece of Advent promotional literature.

Several specific policies of Advent Corporation served to interlock the company with the consumer electronics market. Most important, perhaps, was product policy. Mr. Kloss felt that there were several repugnant aspects to direct competition with the industry giants such as Zenith, Magnavox, and Motorola. Advent sought to turn to specialized areas of the audio market, the 5 percent or so where no competition existed, where whole new classes of products might be developed. Quality was an important Advent byword; to make the most effi-

EXHIBIT 2

Advent Corporation (C)
Statement of Profit and Loss
As of September 26, 1970

	Current Month Units	Current Month Amount		November 1, 1969, to Date Amount
Gross sales:				
Regular speakers	1,561	$115,222.44		$ 685,003.10
Utility speakers	278	17,838.58		46,653.19
F.B.C.	161	23,148.34		182,995.73
M 100	303	50,481.83		260,995.63
M 101	295	24,139.50		68,485.25
M 101 Advocate	146	11,826.00		13,284.00
M 200	988	170,718.00		245,960.30
CC-1	6	100.02		363.40
WC-1	138	1,603.12		3,371.03
Parts	—	605.00		2,757.16
Crolyn tape	1,824	3,997.44		11,108.20
Total		419,680.27		1,520,976.99
Less: Provision for promotional and quantity discounts		21,489.78		86,385.59
Net sales		398,190.49	(100%)	1,434,591.40
Cost of sales:				
Material		196,431.82		663,770.07
Labor		41,366.25		199,930.01
Manufacturing overhead		45,908.85		232,392.33
Royalties		3,182.88		13,222.26
Total cost of sales		286,889.80	(72%)	1,109,314.67
Gross profit		111,300.69	(28%)	325,276.73
Operating expenses:				
Sales		47,517.13		242,799.78
General and administrative		13,753.68		91,570.51
Research and development		14,371.13		195,877.20
Total operating expenses		75,641.94	(19.0%)	530,247.49
Operating profit (loss)		35,658.75	(9.0%)	(204,970.76)
Other income (expense)		(6,428.79)	(−1.6%)	(34,652.11)
Capitalization of Advent TV system (included in R&D above)				75,085.92
Net profit		$ 29,229.96		$ (164,536.95)

cient piece of equipment at the lowest possible price to the consumer was the primary objective. Such product sanctity was not protected by patent but rather by the product itself, which had a real name, which gathered equity as it was seen and became known, and which hopefully represented the perfect low-price product. Even though the entry fee was low, Advent anticipated specializing upon a base product already determined by the major suppliers (e.g., tape decks), which had an appeal to a broad spectrum of the market.

Production operations of Advent Corporation were closely supervised by Mr. Kloss, although there was a production manager for all but the M200 line. Speakers were manufactured in a separate 12,000-square-foot plant in Cambridge, Massachusetts. Major operations of the company took place in a 20,000-square-foot, three-story building also in Cambridge, which Mr. Kloss leased upon forming the company. A move was being planned to consolidate the operations of the company in the spring of 1971 into a 64,000-square-foot building also in Cambridge, which had already been leased.

Production itself was typical of the small manufacturers in the industry. Approximately 130 production workers formed the products in a specified

EXHIBIT 3 A Progress Report from Advent on Loudspeakers, Cassette Recorders, a New Kind of Tape, and Other Matters

After more than a year in business, we (Advent Corporation) think it's time for an accounting of where we are and why.

We began, you may remember, with the intention of making products that would differ significantly from other people's—products that would fill special needs others weren't filling, explore genuinely new ways of doing things, and keep testing accepted limits of performance and value.*

One of the products we had in mind was a new kind of color television set, a high-performance system with a screen size several times the present limit for home use. We are happy to report that it's coming along nicely (and slowly, as such things do), and that the present prospects for prerecorded video material make it look more appealing than ever.

Audio, however, was where we could do the most the quickest, and our first product was:

The Advent Loudspeaker

Anybody who knew us might have predicted that we would make a loudspeaker system pretty early in the game, but few would have predicted that we'd make just *one,* call it simply The Advent Loudspeaker, and say flatly that it was the best we could offer for a long way into the future.

The reason for that was, and is, that it had become possible to design a speaker system as good as anyone would ever need for home listening—one as good in every measurable and audibly useful way as any speaker system of any size or price—at a cost slightly below what most people consider the "medium price" category. Our prior experience in design and manufacturing techniques convinced us that this could be done, and we did it.

We will be happy to send you full particulars on The Advent Loudspeaker, including its reviews. But we believe its sound will tell you quickly enough why it has become, in its first year, one of our industry's all-time best sellers.

(To avoid surprises in a showroom, we should note that our one speaker system comes in two styles of cabinet: the original walnut model, priced at $125†, and a "utility" version that is actually in a rather handsome vinyl finish that looks like walnut, priced at $105.† Both sound the same.)

All of the first year's reviews of The Advent Loudspeaker finished by saying that it was an auspicious beginning for a company. But it represented only one of our immediate directions. The next was:

The Advent Frequency Balance Control

One of the things to be learned in the design of speaker systems is that "flat" frequency response is in the ear of the beholder and virtually nowhere else. True, there are amplifiers and tuners with straight-line frequency response, but practically everything else—recordings, listening rooms, cartridges, loudspeakers—is anything but flat. Different things sound different, not because of basic differences in quality or performance in many instances, but because a recording engineer, or speaker designer, or room plasterer had a slightly special view of the world.

There is nothing wrong with those differences, in our view. And one of the challenges for a speaker designer is to accept and cope with them by designing for an octave-to-octave musical balance that sounds "right" with the wildest variety of present recording techniques. But there is no single perfect balance, and that lack is a source of discomfort to a number of critical listeners. It causes many listeners with really superb (and really expensive) sound equipment to keep trading for new and more expensive equipment in the hope that it will sound "perfect" for everything from Deutsche Grammophon's conception of the Berlin Philharmonic's sound to Columbia's notions about Blood, Sweat, and Tears.

Anyone who keeps pursuing that ideal, and many who don't, would be well advised to investigate our Frequency Balance Control, a unique device that enables listeners to alter the relative musical balance of any octave in the audible frequency spectrum. It is uniquely flexible and uniquely effective in dealing with sonic differences between recordings, equipment, and even the placement of speakers in a room—and in making things sound subjectively "right" more consistently than could be accomplished any other way.

The FBC, designed around our own experience with subjective judging of sound quality, is worth investigation by anyone who can't just sit back and listen, accepting the bad with the wonderful. At $225‡, it is a far better, more pertinent investment than most changes of components.

One of the special abilities of the FBC is the reclaiming of many recordings from an unlistenable state. The need for another kind of recording reclamation led to another kind of product.

EXHIBIT 3 *(continued)*

The Advent Noise Reduction Units (Models 100 and 101)

Background noise in tape recording—specifically, tape hiss—is a far bigger enemy of sound quality than most listeners realize. One reason it isn't properly identified (and vilified) is that few people have heard tape recordings without it. Lacking the standard of blessed silence is something like never having seen a television picture without "snow." If you don't know it isn't supposed to be there, you just look or listen past it and accept it as part of the medium. But once you see—or hear—things free of interference, life is different.

Getting rid of tape noise is a prime function of the now-famous Dolby® System of noise reduction, which in its professional version is in use in virtually every major recording studio in the world.§ We became interested in the Dolby System not only because it helps rid even the best conventional tape recordings of background noise, but because it had even greater possibilities when applied to low-speed home tape recording. Home recording at 3 ¾ and 1 ⅞ ips has been plagued by the problem of really excessive tape hiss—which manufacturers have chosen either to tolerate or to "reduce" by giving up frequency and dynamic range in recording at those speeds. The Dolby System makes it possible to remove that problem and get first-class performance at the low speeds best suited, from the standpoint both of economy and convenience, to home recording.

So we designed a product that would make the Dolby System available—in a version designed by Dolby Laboratories exclusively for home recording and prerecorded tapes—for use with any good tape recorder. The product was our Model 100 Noise Reduction Unit, a flexible and effective piece of equipment that can make any recorder sound better and can do wonders in opening up the world of low-speed recording to the home user.

The Model 100 combines the Dolby System with a recording control system that supersedes a recorder's own and provides a recording accuracy and simplicity seldom seen in home tape equipment. One crucial advantage of that control system, which provides separate input level controls (with input-mixing) *and* a master record-level control, is that it gets stereo recording balance right and does so easily. Improper balance, almost guaranteed with many tape recorders, is the chief reason for recordings (on even the best recorders) that don't sound like the original. It is, in other words, the chief reason for many people's dissatisfaction with their recorders.

The Model 100, at $250, is a required investment for anyone who takes recording very seriously and measures the results critically. But since some people won't need its tremendous flexibility, we also decided to offer the Model 101—which, at $125, provides identical performance at half the price. To make that possible, we omitted the input-mixing provided with the Model 100, supplied slightly less flexible recording controls (it takes a bit longer to get stereo balance just right), and provided one Dolby circuit per channel instead of two. (As in the professional studio Dolby System, you switch the Model 101's two circuits to function first for stereo recording and then for stereo playback, but not for both at the same time.) The result, again, was performance identical to the more elaborate unit, at a price that makes sense for serious recordists on tight budgets.

While designing the Noise Reduction Units, we became interested in what the Dolby System and other factors might do for a kind of tape recording that no one was taking seriously enough. The result was:

The Advent Tape Deck (Model 200)

We had known before, and confirmed in our work on the Model 100, that tape hiss was the underlying reason for the compromised, AM-radio kind of sound quality that people had come to associate with cassette recording. Because the hiss was present in a quantity that made wide-range recording unpleasant to listen to on cassettes, it had effectively set an upper limit on quality—giving manufacturers little incentive to optimize *any* aspect of cassette recording, including mechanical performance.

We realized that once you used the Dolby System to get rid of the noise, you would then have reason to go on to improve all the performance areas that nobody was really attending to. So, to show just how good cassette recording could be, we optimized everything we could around a good cassette transport, added our Noise Reduction Unit, and held a demonstration for the press. The reaction, even though we couldn't demonstrate everything we wanted to in a rigged-together unit, was that we had proved that cassette performance could be as good as, and in some ways better than, the standard for records.

In the meantime, we worked on our own cassette recorder—which was to include not only the Dolby System and the necessary improvements in all areas of performance, but also the means, not given to our knowledge with any previous cassette recorder, to make really superb recordings. That meant effective and precise controls for setting balance and recording levels, including a VU meter that read both stereo channels simultaneously and indicated the louder of the two at a given moment.

EXHIBIT 3 *(continued)*

We felt that calling the resulting tape machine a cassette recorder wouldn't fully indicate our conviction that it was probably the single best choice among *all* kinds of recorders for most serious listeners who want to tape records and broadcasts. So we called it The Advent Tape Deck (Model 200) and let its being a cassette machine speak for itself. At $260, it is a new kind of tape machine that we hope will prove the key, given "Dolbyized" commercial cassette releases, to making cassettes the medium most serious listeners prefer for most listening.

About midway in our development of The Advent Tape Deck, we became convinced that the Dolby System's contribution to performance would become even greater if it were combined with the use of DuPont's chromium-dioxide tape in cassettes. Lots of people had been talking about DuPont's "Crolyn," but nobody had hard facts on what it could do in cassette recordings.§ So we got samples, experimented with its characteristics, and were convinced that we had to supply a means to use it on our recorder. That meant a special switch on The Advent Tape Deck to provide the right recording and playback characteristics (a good bit different from those of other tape formulations) for its use. It also meant another product:

Advocate Crolyn Tape

Although DuPont's Crolyn tape was being used extensively in critical video recording applications, and justifying its advance press notices, no one had made the leap to marketing it for audio purposes for home use. We decided to do so because we felt that Crolyn was necessary for the very best in potential cassette performance.

We are, then, marketing Crolyn tape under the "Advocate" brand in cassettes. One of our hopes in doing so is to get others to market chromium-dioxide tape as well.

There is no doubt in our mind that it's worth the trouble. Chromium dioxide has the ability to put greater high-frequency energy on tape than other oxide formulations, and is also increasingly sensitive as frequency goes up. Those are ideal characteristics for cassette recording, making possible a still greater signal-to-noise ratio in conjunction with the Dolby System and better overall high-frequency performance than any other tape we know of.

The Advent Packet

At this writing, we can't predict exactly what product is going to follow Advocate Crolyn tape. As you probably have noted by now, we develop products in what might be thought of as organic style, letting each product stand on its own. We don't sit down and decide to manufacture a "line" of speakers or amplifiers or tape recorders.

We are into other things at this point, and hope that they will be firm enough to talk about soon. In the meantime, we invite you to write us at the address below for any information you would like, including a list of Advent dealers. ||

If you like, ask for "The Advent Packet." That will bring you everything we have on all of our products, and will also—unless you specify otherwise—put you in jeopardy of getting future informational mailings from us.

So much for the first year.

---

*Having helped found two successful companies previously, and having prior credit for some of audio's most significant products (including something like half of the loudspeakers in use in music systems and serious radios and phonographs in this country), our president, Henry Kloss, had some pretty firm notions about what he wanted to do now.

†Slightly lower in some parts of the country.

‡Slightly higher in some parts of the country.

§"Dolby" is a trademark of Dolby Laboratories. "Crolyn" is a trademark of Du Pont.

||Advent Corporation, 377 Putnam Ave., Cambridge, Mass. 02139.

sequence of assembly steps that was usually determined by Mr. Kloss. He also carried out "time and motion" studies to determine an appropriate production rate. No significant economies of scale existed in the industry. Mr. Kloss felt very strongly that higher overhead would destroy any advantages to be gained by mechanization. In addition, it seemed that after a quantity order of 100 per week more, no important savings could be gained from higher quantity parts orders. It had been found that direct labor ran about one half of material cost over a wide range of products. With manufacturing overhead being determined as a percent of direct labor, cost of sales could easily be forecast for any given product, and a price determined on the basis of a typical margin percentage. Pricing policy, therefore, was also dependent upon the emphasis on making an excellent low-cost product, and not on selling products at a what-the-market-may-bear level.

Marketing management at Advent was a relatively autonomous activity. Vice president of sales was Mr. Stan Pressman, who had performed similar duties at KLH before coming to Advent. Nationwide distribution was maintained through 150 dealers across the country, who were carefully selected on their ability to sell and service Advent products intensively. Shelf space was originally attained by contacting each dealer personally and promising a succession of useful and high-quality products, with which it would be valuable for the dealer to be associated. The reputation of Mr. Kloss was also emphasized. Finally, exposure to the trade press and to the public had been attained through press conferences designed to place the Advent audio products in sink-or-swim competition with similar offerings then on the market. Response had been overwhelmingly favorable.

Under pressure to reach the marketplace with successful products and to improve profitability, Advent had expanded on a day-to-day functional basis. Emphasis on "continually optimizing its position" rather than responding to a long-range plan had placed substantial importance upon production efficiency and rapid response to daily marketing problems. As a result, current operating managers were expected to monitor the functions of their departments in fine detail.

Innovation at Advent

Both Acoustic Research and KLH had demonstrated the ability to recognize changing product and consumer trends and to respond quickly in a dynamic marketplace. Henry Kloss had been able to achieve similar success during the initial life of Advent. Mr. Kloss was unable to explain why Advent had succeeded in accomplishing responses to market needs in advance of other companies in the industry. He discussed this phenomenon at some length during conversations with the case researchers in his president's office, a room that was bewilderingly cluttered with all sorts of electronic gear. His desk was laden with trade journals and other papers reporting the current developments in home electronics. Only a few feet from his desk was the door that led to the R&D section, which was never seen closed.

Mr. Kloss

Perhaps a recent example will highlight what I mean. Du Pont Company, which is really not concerned with products at all, I mean, their basic formulations are raw materials or processes to make raw materials, recently developed a way of making a material which is simply a process kind of thing. That was chromium dioxide, which can be used in the manufacture of magnetic tape and which results in a really quite important product. But Du Pont stopped short very early in the process. They'll sell you all the chromium dioxide you want. But their involvement with the resulting product (Crolyn tape) was absolutely nil. A lot of time was lost until Advent recognized the product and did something about it. They (Du Pont) had no market for it at all. And they are extremely grateful to us for it now. I really didn't think a big company could be so pleasant to work with.

Casewriter

Are you suggesting that product innovation is primarily characterized by observation that a need or a market exists for that product and then going after it, after that specific product?

Mr. Kloss

Yes. And from the process innovation, which is a new way of making something, or some new combination of things. Often a new process could have a connection with a new product, but it doesn't tell.

All of *our* working has been backwards from the person. Others work hard to find a physical phenomenon, or to develop a new bearing, and then work hard to find a market. This is to work completely in isolation, with no connection to the product at all.

Nobody asked at Du Pont, "In what way can this new process make a higher quality result?" At the same time, we were asking, "In what way can this be used irrespective of presently established systems of using tape—what are the limitations inherent within this tape on its ability to produce music for the listener at home?" And we found that it had a distinct and strong advantage, and this has not even been done by the Du Pont people. You know, it's really hard to believe! I'm not trying to boost Advent, or knock Du Pont, but their detachment from this thing in terms of people was absolutely complete!

Exemplifying the kind of reasoning that went on at Advent prior to a product decision, Mr. Kloss mentioned the following incident:

Somebody came around the other day with a way of making a very high-powered amplifier that requires only a very small size and bulk. Any normal amplifier wastes up to half its power at any one moment in heat loss. There is a way of making an amplifier, which we've known for some time, that is 97 percent efficient—you waste almost no power in the amplifier itself. Now since the size of the amplifier is largely determined by the need to dissipate power, clearly the size here could be reduced. One has known it can be done; it's called Class D circuitry. This size might make possible a whole new class of things; whether we do this in a year or so is uncertain. But it's a possible kind of thing, which we didn't go to invent, and which has been around for years and years and years, but which might become practical to do, if you do the rest of the things to get all the merit out of it, such as creating a small power supply and all, which calls for minor invention on our part. We've had a feeling that exceedingly small kinds of things were worthwhile; when something like this comes up, you notice it more sharply than somebody else, who looks at it only as just a cheaper way of getting a high-power amplifier.

Formal market research at Advent Corporation was never mentioned. Mr. Kloss had the following remarks to offer when the case researchers asked him about it:

Mr. Kloss

Oh! One never does market research! The only test of the market that there will ever be is to fully commit to a product itself; one is never going to make any test marketing or any asking of anything. And it will be done whenever it's the product that will most certainly, most quickly, give a certain amount of money here. It's just a matter of priority of products; one could, within a couple of months' time, make a noise reduction unit and turn it into a product and sell it. That had to be done first.

Casewriter

But with all due respect, you must feel that it will go, that when people see it, they're going to buy it?

Mr. Kloss

Well, yes. But there's no way of proving this before you spend the money to produce it, that I know of.

Casewriter

Experience and intuition tell you that it will go?

Mr. Kloss

This is about, yes, all that one has. Experience that my intuition has been right gives me a little more confidence, maybe.

The Dolbyized Cassette Recorder

Critical to Advent's recovery from unprofitable development operations was the successful manufacture and marketing of the Dolbyized cassette recorder (Advent Tape Deck M200), described briefly in Exhibit 3. The way the idea of noise reduction recording became a product for Advent, and at just the right time, is indicative of the whole Advent innovation process.

Mr. Kloss had noted very early in the company's history that it was possible, in theory, to do something like noise reduction. That is, he noted that at any moment in the recording process, the normal recording methods from basic information theory resulted in great waste. He noted that there ought to be some way of continuously optimizing the recording technique. However, his investigation stopped there. He knew it was possible, but he did not embark then and there upon a process of invention. Instead, Mr. Kloss became sensitized to noticing if somebody else had really done it. All of the Advent products began in familiar fashion. Mr. Kloss commented,

The things that I have done have never started from noticing something was important and then working backwards to the fundamental way to do it. You know, "Gee, it would really be desirable to have instant photographs," and then work hard to do it. I don't know if that's what Land did or not. But that has never been our particular way of doing things. All of the work has been to think about things that would be desirable to do, and then be continuously looking around to see what things are possible to do, perhaps with minor invention on our part, which would satisfy a perceived need in the market and begin to define a product. Only when the need in the marketplace simultaneously matches the knowledge of the technology does one spend more than a few minutes thinking about it.

... So any product I think of for longer than a few minutes is already one that I know can be made. ... You want to constantly have in mind, stored with very short access time, the different technologies. You sort of somehow keep aware of what kind of things can be done. When several of these come together to form a product, that can result in your deciding to make that product. You have to have, at any moment, a moderate-sized number of floating possibilities of things that you can do.

But there's a cost to this floating process of having all these pieces of information available which makes it very hard to expand to a large group of people.

In 1967, Mr. Kloss heard about Ray Dolby, a man who had been making professional noise reduction systems in England and was just starting to sell them in the United States. That was just at the conclusion of Mr. Kloss's presidency at KLH. He negotiated an agreement between Dolby and KLH for KLH to have the rights to incorporate that system in a tape deck. Mr. Kloss agreed to manufacture that tape deck for KLH, to help KLH introduce the Dolby system to the world.

For many reasons, the product, which was envisioned as a $600 reel-to-reel machine with Dolby circuitry, never got made. By May 1969, Mr. Kloss personally had suffered a loss of $265,000, largely through design and production problems. At that time, Advent began manufacturing the Advent loudspeaker to support further development work on the large-screen television. Simultaneously, KLH had renegotiated a manufacturing contract with a Japanese firm, Nakamichi, to build a $250 reel-to-reel machine with Dolby circuitry. Such a product was on-line by the fall of 1969, when Nakamichi offered KLH a similar deal on a cassette recorder with Dolby circuitry. Mr. Kloss described the events that followed:

> Even though KLH had a selling reel-to-reel machine with Dolby, they decided not to make the cassette machine. There were many reasons for this; they were having trouble with the Nakamichi machine they had, they had had gross trouble with my deck, and they had just gotten a new president who was against expansionist moves. So they just backed off the whole thing, just when the right product was there. Advent's contribution to the process was really a floating knowledge of the benefits of chromium dioxide tape, the Dolby circuit, and a manufacturer of heads who knew about Dolby. It was gathering these things together into a product and bringing them to people's attention that Advent accomplished.

Within hours, before the Nakamichi representatives had returned to Japan, Mr. Kloss had negotiated an agreement granting Advent the productive capacity to employ Nakamichi heads in an Advent deck. The Dolby system it uses is described in Exhibit 4. While the new product received numerous adulations in the press, by October 1970 Mr. Kloss felt that the primary shift toward central cassette recording that he had expected with the marketing of the Advent Tape Deck was not occurring as fast as he had hoped. He felt that the primary reason for this deficiency was the inherent difficulty of depending on a dealer organization to push Advent products that incorporated sophisticated innovations, features that had to be understood by the consumer before he made the logical choice of an Advent product. Consequently, he and Mr. Pressman were spending considerable time in attempting to find a solution to this problem, the final step in completing the innovation of the Dolbyized recorder.

Television

Although Mr. Kloss had suspended formal development work on Advent's large-screen color television set, he continued to make minor modifications to it when time was available. Several experimental sets functioned without major problems in the Advent plant and homes of employees, but decisions remained as to the exact design the set would have and the marketing approach to be used. Mr. Kloss estimated that the first production models would be available for sale six to nine months after the "go" decision was made, and that the decision would be made "whenever it's the product that most certainly, most quickly, can give the right amount of money here."

Describing the product's origins, Kloss said:

> I was vaguely interested in TV as an important medium. One reads a magazine article that points out a way to make projection television. All you had to do was read that article and see that it could apply to a screen this size [four and one-half feet by six feet]. And then you quickly ask the question, Is this worthwhile? You make a guess that it might be worthwhile at the right price.

In 1964, Kodak announced the development of a screen which could effectively increase the amount of perceived reflected light by a factor of five over ordinary mat screens. This development suggested that it might be possible to diffuse light from a projection tube over a larger screen of this type and still retain satisfactory brightness. However, Mr. Kloss said that he would have built a high-quality television set even if the large screen had not been possible.

> If there never was a big screen, we'd be in television anyway because you can do a high-quality small set. So our interest in TV is not restricted to the big screen, though it's much more fun because there's no comparison available.

Mr. Kloss believed he could discern in color TV the typical product life cycle of consumer electronics products working to the advantage of new producers with sufficient marketing skill. During

EXHIBIT 4 How the Dolby System Works

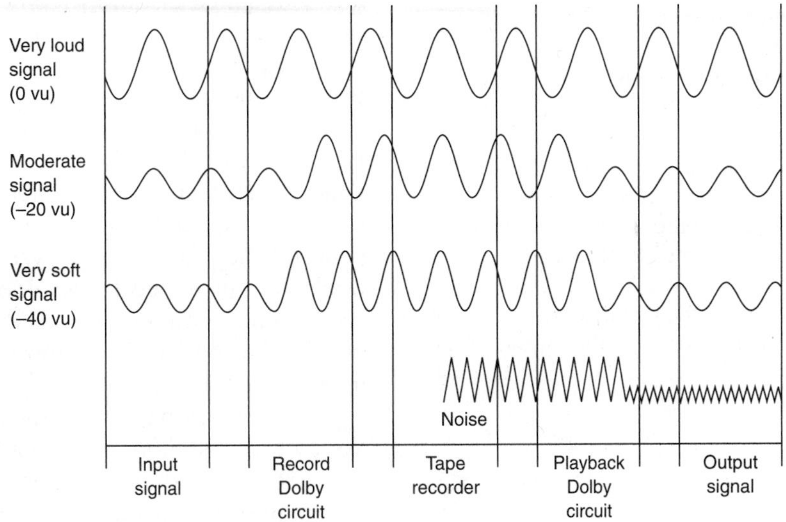

1. The signal being recorded passes through the record Dolby circuit *first.* The Dolby circuit operates on the higher ("hiss") frequencies in a predetermined manner, depending on their loudness level. The loudest signals (0vu) pass unaffected through the circuit. Signals of moderate intensity (−20vu) are boosted moderately, while the very soft signals (−40vu) receive maximum boost.
2. After being thus "Dolbyized," the signal is recorded onto the tape. It is at this point that tape hiss makes its appearance. You can see on the diagram how the record Dolby circuit's action has made the low-level signal louder than usual, relative to the tape hiss.
3. On playback, the signal from the tape is passed through the playback Dolby circuit, which is an exact "mirror-image" of the record Dolby circuit. The playback Dolby *lowers* the previously boosted parts of the signal, by precisely the same amount they had been boosted. The tape hiss—which made its appearance between the record and playback halves of the Dolby System—is automatically lowered at the same time by a very substantial amount, effectively 100 db, or 90 percent. At the same time, because of the precise "mirror-image" playback action, the Dolby System causes no other change in the signal relative to the original source that was recorded.

the late 1950s and early 1960s, color TV quality improved as bugs were worked out of it, but by 1966 short-cut production methods were reducing overall quality. Mr. Kloss observed:

> NTSC [National Television Standards Committee] standards permit a very high quality to be broadcast which is usually badly degraded by a set at home. What you see on a regular picture is not what you would see on a really high-quality set.

Evaluation of demand, though not verbalized, suggested to Mr. Kloss that larger-screen TV was an inherently desirable thing. The evaluation was not, he said, an extrapolation of the popularity of larger screens in ordinary television sets. Nor could he isolate any one other factor which dominated his evaluation except that it was the kind of thing he would like to have in his home. There was no way to extrapolate from sales of expensive large-screen sets. He said:

> There is absolutely no experience on large-screen television for consumer use. . . . Yes, I feel that large-screen TV will be popular but there's no way to prove this until you spend the money to produce it, that I know of.
>
> A lot of people go to the flicks. The whole business is to bring things up close, large, and important. . . . This is doing that and there's that kind of rightness about it. That's about the only defense one has. It just doesn't have any connection with television as one thinks about it. Once you say television, somebody brings to mind almost repugnant kinds of images. They don't do it for books though. You talk about books and they think about great books and the University of Chicago, and this kind of thing. They don't think about the kinds of things they sell down on Washington Street.

> . . . And for big screens, there's no expressed desire for anybody to want a big screen. . . .
>
> Exactly what's happening out in the store, where people are expressing what they want, sure I get some information on that from somebody else. But this sort of shapes the end features of products. People are not out there expressing a new kind of thing that they would like to have—a compacter for kitchen garbage: I've never heard anybody say that they ever wanted something like this. I think maybe some people do; we'll see. . . . The kinds of products that people might want are not limited to what people have said they want or what people, when you knock on their door, say that they will want. In the first case, it's too late if people express the desire for what they want. In the second case, the answers are invalid when you ask about it.

Development

Shortly after organizing Advent Corporation in May 1967, Mr. Kloss began working on the television set. Though he was confident that the idea was technically feasible, there were many questions yet to be answered regarding design. For example:

> The way of finishing mirrors at a very low cost—it's been used in the eyeglass industry; it's not used in making lenses; it's not used in telescopic work. But the technology to make very low-cost kinds of mirrors exists in the trade. And we sort of know that technology is there and go and use it. If it had required our finding a very-low-cost way of making a lens which hadn't been developed yet, I would have cut out from any of our consideration the making of a low-cost projection television. . . . It maybe would have been a very fruitful investigation, but it would have been the kind of thing for which you couldn't be absolutely certain of finding an answer. We've always avoided the kind of investigation where the answer had some reasonable chance of being negative.

The major cost in operating the Advent large-screen TV was expected to be cathode-ray tube replacement. Phosphor life (and therefore tube life) was expected to lie between 700 to 2,500 playing hours. The projection tube had been used in some of the earliest television sets, but the large screen desired would put new demands on it for maximizing total light output. Thus, an RCA commercial projection system with the mirror and corrector lens outside the tube was rejected as too inefficient and troublesome.

Rights to produce the Kodak screen had been given to Advent with no guarantee of the practicality of doing so in a large size. It was concave toward the audience and leaned forward slightly. These two factors required that the screen extend about a foot out from a normal wall. Brightness fell off rapidly as the viewer moved about 70° off an axis perpendicular to the screen. While satisfactory viewing required the room to be no brighter than would be required to read a newspaper with strain, a bright light could be situated to the side of the screen without seriously degrading the image. Mr. Kloss believed the Kodak screen was the best presently available, but hoped to develop a proprietary flat screen which could be patented. It would be composed of many elements which would each direct light in the optical direction.

In a conventional color receiver, the electronics assembly feeds information to a single picture tube which contains three electron guns. The Advent system was based on similar electronic circuitry, but the video image was projected on the screen by three separate cathode-ray tubes, one each for the red, green, and blue color constituents. The Advent tube is diagramed in Exhibit 5. Within each tube, a stream of electrons of varying intensity was beamed toward the positively charged internal anode, coated with a phosphor that generated one of the three colors to be projected. This beam was accelerated, focused, and deflected in a rapid horizontal scan of 15°, with the U.S. standard 525 sweeps for each vertical transit. This stream of electrons hitting the anode recreated the transmitted picture for that color. The internal spherical mirror reflected this image and focused it through the corrector lens on the external screen where the three colors were superimposed.

Tests of experimental models had shown that this system, based on three projection tubes with internal optics, could produce large images of amazingly high quality. Internal optics (mirror and corrector lens within the tube) were superior to external optics which required exact positioning of mirrors, greater light wastage, and attendant problems in keeping the optics clean. Internal optics had been used by the U.S. Navy many years previously and were not patentable. Mr. Kloss commented, "We may very well have been in error in the past in not getting some nominal patents to make it easier to sit down with somebody and sell some of this technology." He did not feel that protection was the primary value in patents "because the reluctance of manufacturers to get into any new field is really quite surprising. It's unfamiliar, sort of strange; they

EXHIBIT 5 Projection Television Tube

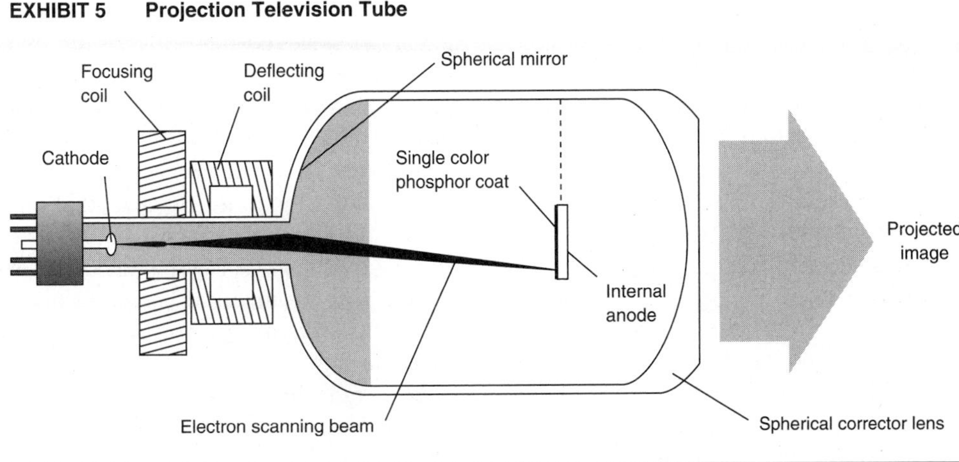

would like to buy it. We wouldn't mind, but it's always a mess to do manufacturing for someone else."

Competition

There were no large-screen TV sets on the market which would compete directly with the Advent set in the home market. The Eidophore system, developed in Switzerland in the early 1950s, used an electron beam physically to change the surface of an oil film. A light projected through this film and onto a screen provided a much brighter and larger picture. The Eidophore set, however, required an operating technician and cost about $40,000 for a monochrome version and over $100,000 for color. General Electric had produced a modified version which was more easily operated and cost about $29,000 in monochrome and $38,000 in color. People who had seen this set reported to Mr. Kloss that its brightness and resolution were inferior to Advent's though he felt that improvement might be obtained by using a higher gain screen.

Very little of the current discussion in trade journals about future trends in television centered on large screens. More was aimed at miniaturized TV or at development of a flat screen which could be installed in a wall. Mr. Kloss commented that "there might be a message there. You talk about desirable things of the future; nobody talks about larger screen television at all." During 1968, Sony Corporation demonstrated an experimental set which was flat and large (eight feet diagonally). This set was essentially a board of 26,000 elements of one red, one blue, and one green light each. This compared with 350,000 elements of phosphor in the typical shadow mask tube and resulted in a picture of noticeably poor resolution. The problems to be solved were to decrease the size of individual lights and obtain more rapid switching of the lights. While many years of development work remained before this set could be competitive, Mr. Kloss felt that the ultimate and best TV of the future would in some way generate light on the screen itself.

Although projection television was well recognized in the industry as a means of obtaining both a large and flat screen, the immediate objection was that it could not be made bright enough for viewing in a lighted room. Several large companies had experimented with it, nonetheless. Mr. Kloss described one such effort in explaining why the large manufacturers were unlikely to provide competition soon after he began production. A large military and consumer electronics firm had shown him a cathode-ray tube under development for projection use. A configuration of optics very similar to Advent's had been adopted, but a maximum falloff in brightness at the edges of the screen of 10 percent to 20 percent had been specified by someone. Conventional knowledge of human eye sensitivity would suggest that humans would be insensitive to falloffs of 200 percent to 300 percent. However, this error caused engineers to design an aspherical corrector lens which would disperse light nearly perfectly on the screen and cost many thousands of dollars. Similar mistakes eventually caused the system to reach a height of nearly six feet and to require a sealed refrigeration unit for cooling. RCA had estimated about a year earlier that it could develop a large-screen TV within several years for from $5 million to $50 million (the exact figure was not recalled). Mr. Kloss believed that a radically improved system could not be designed and built within 5 years and more likely 10 years. Competitive projection systems would probably require two years minimum after the Advent set was introduced.

Production and Costs

Production was expected to be carried out in Advent's new 64,000-square-foot plant. Receiver units were the same as those required in ordinary sets except that less deflection power was needed due to the decreased deflection angle. No decision had yet been made whether to make or buy the receiver units. Projection tubes were expected to cost about $50 each produced on a small scale and involved no unusual technology. Some equipment had already been purchased to produce test models. The cost could probably be reduced to $100 for a set of three tubes on an automated line. Production of the screen involved handwork to sketch and mold a thin aluminum foil, apply backing, and construct a frame and stand.

Mr. Kloss did not envision a highly automated line. He believed from experience at KLH and Acoustics Research that cost penalties would be only 10 percent to 20 percent if as few as 100 sets a week were produced. Electronic components were priced the same to all buyers if ordered in quantities over approximately 1,000, and the inflexibility and high fixed costs of an automated line would prevent great economies of scale. Tooling costs for a line adequate for 100 sets per week would be "many tens of thousands of dollars." Production costs were expected to be similar to those for other Advent products, with direct labor costing about one half as much as materials. Mr. Kloss believed that production costs of shadow mask tubes were about $100 and far outweighed cabinet and receiving equipment costs.

Concessions were made to simplify design, and production of the Advent set included replacement of electrostatic focusing with the less common and more expensive static magnetic focusing. This decision would result in a selling price about $200 higher than it would otherwise be. Similar concessions were expected in screen design.

Distribution and Marketing

Mr. Kloss believed that most of the expected technical problems which could become customer complaints had been effectively ironed out of the TV design. He felt that sales personnel could cause complaints, however, by creating or allowing unreasonable expectations. He said that "the expected kinds of troubles are that we just haven't anticipated somebody's attitude toward this or his expectations. This comes from rather recent learning in noise reduction systems where you have a difficult time explaining to someone."

Although the set would eventually be designed for installation by the customer, the first installations would require a technician:

> It will be exactly equivalent to what the early color sets had with technicians running around. . . . The whole thing was mechanically fragile and fussy. . . . The beginning of any new kind of thing is troublesome. You can't even tell how you finally want to make it until you go through this manufacturing process.

Retail price had originally been estimated at $1,500 to $2,000, but had been revised upward to $2,000 to $2,500 based upon estimated costs and normal margins.

Mr. Kloss expected to engage in enough advertising to identify the product in consumer minds as reasonably priced and to lock in a portion of the market. The only scheme he had which might help lock in the consumer was to give the product a simple name and then not change it. He would "never engage in what might be interpreted as an annual model change." He felt that this strategy had given KLH an advantage over other companies which introduced new products and consequently destroyed their equity in the name.

Mr. Pressman, marketing vice president of Advent, said he had purposely avoided having his attention diverted by the TV, which was still at least several months from introductions. He did feel that video products were exciting and had a greater long-range potential for Advent than audio did. He thought, as well, that 5,000 unit sales a year sounded possible. Though attempts by other video product manufacturers to distribute through audio dealers had proven unsuccessful, he had not eliminated the possibility of trying it again. No opinions regarding advertising and promotional strategies had been formed.

When the Advent large-screen television was conceived, Mr. Kloss envisioned its use in the home as a high-quality display medium and believed that the increasing quantity of broadcast materials would lead to proportionally increased quality programs for which a large screen would be preferred. Video tape recording units being brought out by several manufacturers would permit quality programs to be recorded or purchased, which might encourage more intensive viewing of programs at convenient times on a unit like the Advent TV. However, recorders would have to have sufficient capability to reproduce most of the information content of the signal broadcast so that playback on a large screen would be of adequate quality. Mr. Kloss had no immediate plans to produce complementary products except the improved screen, though he did wish to broaden Advent's product line over the long term.

The possibility of selling the television set to another company was not considered because:

> If a product that I developed and sold to somebody else did not succeed, I would be free to blame somebody else. And that's an unsatisfactory position. I have to have the complete responsibility. I really, honestly wouldn't know whether it was their fault or mine; so I have no way of knowing whether I've done anything worthwhile or not if I don't have complete knowledge of the total process. So to me it would be very unsatisfactory to invent things and sell them to somebody. If they continually and regularly were successful, I'd, after a period of time, be satisfied . . . with my contribution. This probably wouldn't happen.

The Future

Despite several problems with Advent that were apparent in late 1970, the company's future promised to be an exciting one. Mr. Kloss especially looked forward toward making the decisions necessary to reach his stated sales goal, a level of sales which he felt confident of reaching. Specifically, Mr. Kloss felt that a $50 million sales level could be reached within the $2.25 billion audio equipment market and the $2.5 billion television market, without sacrificing Advent's policy of operating within a specialized and protected market niche. Beyond that point, however, it was uncertain whether such a position could be maintained. Mr. Kloss commented,

> If one grows in an established market area, then there can be a succession of products that are based on a careful and sensitive reading of what people in the marketplace express that they want, and what competent engineering can produce, and this may well be an important part of Advent's future. . . . I've no objection to growing in the regular kind of way, and that's the kind of thing that can be happily delegated to somebody else. In fact, to delegate enough of that to make a strong, growing company, and yet continue in the company, would be highly desirable. How strong you have to be before you can have the luxury of doing "me too" kinds of products, though, I don't know.
>
> I think a perfectly honorable way is to continue to grow making products which, on the strength of the market position, are salable. . . . Up until now one has restricted one's attention to things which are fundamentally better and different than anything else. But there is nothing wrong with growing doing ordinary kinds of products. . . . The idea of making products which continually add to the volume of Advent may well be completely done by someone else. I'd be happy to have that done. That would leave me increasingly free to think longer about things which were different in kind, new kinds of products.
>
> There's an ideological inclination to want to make broad-spectrum kinds of products. The interest is to get back to where one was at KLH. The cassette recorder with Dolby, I envision that as not nearly as broad spectrum at the present time as it was planned to be. All the products that would grow out of the fact of the cassette being the primary music listening medium for a lot of people in the home, this isn't happening so fast.

One issue of great concern to Mr. Kloss was the institutionalization of the Advent innovation process. On the one hand, Mr. Kloss felt it would be possible to find a full-time administrator who could work closely with him in handling the company's growing management responsibilities, while he could continue to devote his major efforts to the very enjoyable work of conceiving new products and staying abreast of consumer electronics technology. On the other hand, Mr. Kloss felt that it was possible to institutionalize the product conception function, but he was unsure how best to proceed. In the current situation, he personally perceived market needs, was able to match those needs with the technological state of the art, and was further capable of completing the product conception that fulfilled the market–technology match. As the company grew, Mr. Kloss recognized that some division of these functions would have to take place. Should he separate the more routine R&D functions from the esoteric, or should he attempt to pool the efforts of a large number of people in order to arrive at an effective product conception function? In late 1970, Mr. Kloss could not see how the latter plan might work.

Concerning his role as Advent grew, Mr. Kloss mentioned his admiration for the situation Edwin Land was reputed to have at Polaroid, namely, the situation of ready access to any level of R&D. Mr. Kloss commented, "To contribute to it or direct it without interfering with its normal process. That to me is a really very desirable kind of thing. And it can't frequently be achieved." Mr. Kloss felt that he might be on the way toward such a situation already, toward an Advent that could carry on, increasing a bit in his absence, but to which he could contribute substantially.

Reading II–1
How to Put Technology into Corporate Planning

Alan R. Fusfeld

Every executive knows of corporate successes in which technology has played a dominant role. Almost everyone in venture capital and entrepreneurship has a personal list of these successes to emulate. Dreams of technology turned to profit are nurtured by real-life success—Intel Corporation, Minnesota Mining and Manufacturing (3M), Polaroid, Hewlett-Packard, and Digital Equipment Corporation, to name a few of many.

Despite the obvious role of technology in superlatively successful enterprises, technological issues only occasionally are included explicitly in typical corporate strategy reviews, and only rarely are they among the regular inputs to corporate planning and development.

Technology: The Underutilized Input to Planning

Most executives have limited management experience with technology. They see research and development as a black box: money and manpower resources are put in, but what should come out? How should these resources be directed and managed? And what should be the characteristic delays, success rates, and managerial control variables? General business management lacks an intuitive feel for strategically directing and positioning research and development investments as compared with similar investments in marketing, sales, and manufacturing. The result is that technology issues tend to be downgraded in overall importance to the business. Technology is addressed in strategic plans only implicitly, except in the case of special endeavors which are outside the main lines of production—new and joint business ventures, licensing, and acquisitions. In these, technology cannot be overlooked; it is often a major ingredient and even rationale in a purchase or joint venture plan.

In general, key management decision makers have inadequate background and ability to make judgments and forecasts in the area of technology. Without that ability, their options in utilizing technology in corporate strategy are severely limited.

There are many reasons for this blindness to technology and its management in our traditional administration practices:

- Most managers have been trained and have made their successful contributions in marketing, manufacturing, law, accounting, or some other corporate function. Their limited training in science or engineering is not enough to give them confidence in dealing with technological change.

  For similar reasons, corporate economists fail to recognize the process of technological change in their economic forecasts. They either consider all products as homogeneous or see technological change as a wildcat input to their processes—something that comes from heaven or not at all.

  Market research, too, has drawn very little on the technological field. Market researchers typically focus on short-term perspectives. Good, future-oriented market research should provide information that puts together a corporate strategy involving a realistic contribution from technology.
- We know very little about the process of technological change; the knowledge we have is new (accumulated in the last 10 to 15 years) and has yet to be synthesized.
- Partly due to limited experience, we lack adequate frameworks for viewing technological change. There is nothing comparable in this field to the sim-

---

Reprinted with permission from *Technology Review,* MIT, Alumni Association,

plifying frameworks for strategic business planning which have become prevalent in the last decade. The management of technology is, in fact, the only functional area which is not represented by a discipline within any management school.

- Technological change proceeds slowly: significant change requires 5 to 10 years. This time span meshes poorly with the planning objectives of most American corporations. Although most corporations have five-year plans, 90 percent of their research and development activities are designed to be implemented within three years, and the remaining 10 percent within four years. Most corporations outline their strategic objectives on the short time horizon enforced by their need to manage short-term cash flow needs. That's not a time horizon appropriate for significant technological change.

  Most research and development objectives are biased toward existing needs—such defensive goals as product improvement and cost reduction. This bias toward the use of technology in the support role to implement strategic objectives planned for three or four years in advance is the obvious result when managers lack an intuitive understanding of any larger goal for their research and development investments.

- Most U.S. corporations are organized around the production process. They are not organized to recognize or to reward the uncertainties, risks, and time constraints of the technological innovation process. Not surprising, then, that most significant technological change originates outside of the firm—or even of the industry—that eventually uses it.

In only three areas of strategic corporate planning has technological change been widely—and, in general, wisely—considered in corporate planning. Acquisition has been a major activity of corporate development and diversification in the last half-century, and expected technological change and the acquisition of new technology has usually been an explicit consideration in this area. Technology has also been addressed explicitly in the licensing area, and it is an implicit part of new venture activities. In all these cases, technology is the essential element of the new opportunity.

Putting Technology in Its Place

Put yourself in the place of an executive assigned to set forth a corporate strategy. You must consider many elements—the broad characteristics of the industry, the qualifications of your firm's competitors in it, and your organization's corporate resources—managerial, financial, organizational, research and development, manufacturing, marketing, and distribution.

Technological issues enter as a result of activities both inside and outside the industry. They can affect the whole range of corporate activities: management, materials procurement, manufacturing, marketing, financial results, and future growth through new products and into new markets.

As you begin your analysis of corporate strategy, ask yourself such questions as these:

- How are technological issues recognized by your senior management? As a black box? As an input to long-range planning? For meeting short-term objectives? How explicit is the recognition of technology in each of these roles?
- How has management used technology to implement strategic objectives?
- How has technology been monitored? (One of the simplest and most conventional ways is by simply maintaining a research and development department to keep abreast of the state of the art. Other methods include outside technology boards and liaison activities to keep informed on areas where your own technical resources are limited.)
- How are activities relevant to technology recognized and organized in your enterprise? Where are they located, and how are they rewarded? (The typical corporate reward system is biased to short-term, cash flow performance; these criteria are simply not appropriate to the risks that must be taken in a viable technological development system.)

The Fundamental Units of Technology

To improve your understanding of technology in your corporation, you will need first of all an adequate unit of analysis.

When we talk about technologies, we tend to speak of specific techniques and products—internal combustion engines, refrigeration and air conditioning, and machine tools, for example. But technology flows in and out of such products as these, and they do not provide the fundamental basis by which to measure technological change. The analysis must be on the level of generic technologies. A carburetor, for example, is an application of the generic technology of vaporizing a liquid and mixing it with a gas. The same technology applied in the paint industry might become an automatic paint sprayer or in the aerospace industry a jet backpack. This way of focusing on generic technologies and the variety of technical applications of each is necessary if your planning is to be effective at capturing the implications of technological change that's going to affect a company's general product area. Consider, for example, how Raychem and Hewlett-Packard have succeeded by concentrating on a single generic technology, developing and exploiting it in countless products for many different industries.

Seven Dimensions of Product Acceptability

Having defined the unit of technology for analysis, you now need some basic parameters for explicit analysis of how a given technology is to be applied in your company's products and how effective they will be as a result.

After collecting information from many corporations on the characteristics of successful new products, I have found seven qualities which determine the success of any embodiment of any generic technology by any industry:

- *Functional performance*—an evaluation of the basic function that a device is supposed to perform. For example, the functional performance of a household refrigerator is to remove heat, and engineers evaluate a refrigerator's performance of this basic task in terms of what is called pull-down efficiency.
- *Acquisition cost*—in the example of the refrigerator, the price per cubic foot.
- *Ease-of-use characteristics*—the form of the user's interface with the device; in the example of the refrigerator, magnetic door latches and automatic defrosters contribute to the consumer's acceptance of the technology.
- *Operating cost*—in the case of the refrigerator, the number of kilowatt-hours used per unit of service performed.
- *Reliability*—the question of how often the device or process normally requires service, how free it is from abnormal service requirements, and—ultimately—what its expected useful lifetime is.
- *Serviceability*—the question of how long it takes and how expensive it is to restore a failed device to service.
- *Compatibility*—the way the device or product fits with other devices in the context of the larger system.

These are useful categories for analyzing applications of technologies because they are general, applying to everything from refrigerators to jet engines to medical services; they describe technology in a specific application very quickly and very adequately; they describe the goals of most research and development efforts; and they describe most of the emphasis in advertising and marketing strategies. Without such a set of dimensions, you will find yourself talking about the costs and benefits of potential technological change in haphazard, incomplete ways.

Technology Demand Elasticities

Economists talk about price elasticity for a product, an indication of the role of price in determining demand. In the same way, each of the different dimensions in which technological change can affect the acceptability of a product is subject to evaluation in a fashion analogous to price elasticity. For example, you can analyze the change in demand for a product when its functional performance has been improved, or when its ease of use has been increased or its service requirements lowered. In some cases elasticity will be low, in other cases high. Such data can be measured and used in the same way as the economists obtain and use price elasticity.

Two types of elasticity—absolute and relative—are very important in technology planning. Absolute elasticity represents the responsiveness of total market demand to improvements in function, ease of use, reliability, cost, and the like. Relative elasticity is a similar measure of the tendency for shifts in market share to occur as competitors introduce new products with better performance in one or more of the various dimensions.

To see how these ideas enter into technological planning, consider a piece of medical equipment. In one case the product is destined for emergency-room use in a hospital; in another the same functions are to be performed in an individual doctor's office. Some characteristics will be more important in one market than in the other. Cost and ease of use will be relatively unimportant to the hospital; medical insurance will pay most of the bills, and the machine in the emergency room will be operated by a technician. The individual doctor, who must collect from individual patients and use the machine without a technician's help, will put a higher priority on low cost and ease of operation.

Or consider the example of Black and Decker, a company that once concentrated exclusively on commercial and industrial construction tools. The technological demands and price constraints of that market are different from those of the market for home use, and until Black and Decker recognized the differences and developed its technology accordingly, its penetration of the home tool market was very small.

In short, there are significant differences among customers' preference sets and hence different technological market elasticities. Calculation of technology elasticity results from analyzing statistically different market segments according to priorities in purchase decisions which can be established for each individual class of behavior.

Profiling Technology by Market Segments

You now have determined a unit of technology on which to concentrate, the dimensions in which it is embodied in the market, and the relative demand for those dimensions. The next step is to apply these analyses to compare your company's technology with the needs by market segments, producing a competitive technological profile. Where do competitors' technologies stand in relation to yours in any particular market? Where did they stand a few years ago? And where are they going? Your goal, of course, will be to answer a question such as this: by the time my company's new technology-based product or service is in operation or online, what will the competitive situation be?

The competitive profile helps answer that question by answering some simpler ones: what have the rates of change been in the past? And can you project a continuation of those rates into the future? How fast must one company move to gain ground on the others?

Assessing the Technology and Product Portfolio

To develop an overall technology strategy around your company's existing technical and business strength, draw a chart (such as Exhibit 1) to show the generic technologies in which your company is engaged and the products in which they are applied. Such a chart provides a profile of the portfolio of technologies and products which may be illuminating to a management whose business has grown and developed in an opportunistic way. A similar chart for competitors in your company's product lines will help reveal what competitors are doing and what has been their strategy.

The company represented in Exhibit 2 may have difficulties in the future because it is trying to manage under the same roof different kinds of technology in which the manufacturer has different roles.

Exhibit 2 reveals that particle separation is a primary driving force of this company's corporate strategy, and there is at least the possibility that the company intends to be a leader in that field. The chart also shows that another part of this company is pursuing strategy that emphasizes a product area,

EXHIBIT 1

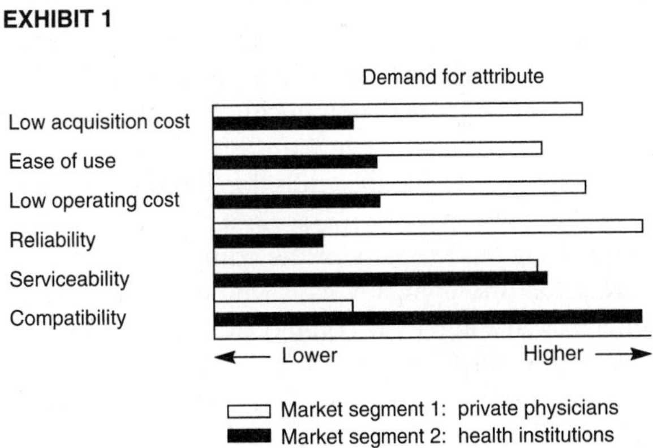

Matching the qualities which technology can impart to a product with the different needs of potential consumers. Cost is relatively unimportant to an institutional buyer of medical equipment—but it is a major consideration of the physician in private practice. Reliability is important to both, but the hospital may have a technician to effect repairs promptly. An analysis such as this demonstrates the different technological market elasticities for the same product in different markets—an important concept in any firm's planning for future investment in technology.

EXHIBIT 2

Generic technologies	Industrial pollution	Commercial filtration	Medical filtration	Construction	Wall/floor coverings	Automotive engines
	Principal product applications					
Particle separation	O	O	O			
Metal fiber formation				O		
Molded material formation					O	
Noise control						O
Static electricity control					O	
Energy conservation					O	

A profile of the generic technologies in relation to the principal products of a hypothetical company. All six of this company's technological interests are good examples of what the author calls generic technologies, and all are sensible responsibilities of a central research and development laboratory. But only one of them is germane to more than one of the company's products; three of them result from the company's interest in the wall/floor coverings industry. Such a chart could be revealing to a management whose business has grown and developed in an opportunistic way. In this case it reveals that this company is actually two companies—one driving the technology of particle separation and one driven by the several technologies involved in floor coverings of several kinds.

picking up all kinds of technologies because of their common applications. This company may be said to have two parts—one technologically driven and one driving technology. Their technological strengths, their laboratories, their organizations, their pursuit of joint ventures and acquisitions programs, and their technology strategy in general are different. Indeed, these two parts of the company are so different that the company as a whole may be weakened by having to accommodate two such very different enterprises in its management structure.

A chart of this kind is the first stage in combining all the ideas previously discussed so that you may understand the role of technology in your company and weigh the investment and strategy options that are open to it. To select a particular strategy, begin by considering the generic technological strengths of your enterprise. You may find that you have no adequate strengths: you may find that your strengths in technology are not complemented by strengths in manufacturing or marketing, for example. Or you may find that your organization is fully prepared to drive a particular technology into many different product applications. Or you may see that your best strategy is to capitalize on similar applications of different technologies. Depending on your analysis, you may want to add by merger a new generic technology in order to extend your applications area one step further, or you may want to offer your technology through merger to some firm which is equipped to capitalize on it through manufacturing and marketing.

In making these decisions, review the profile of your technologies by your market segments. Which technological dimensions of your products are important? Reliability? Function? Ease of use? Operating cost? How much emphasis will you place on reducing acquisition costs? On increasing ease of use? On reducing operating costs? On improving service?

This evaluation of technology dimensions in relation to market needs and competitive thrusts—the elasticity of technology demand—is the part that's missing from most research and development plans. But it provides answers to the crucial questions: What is your basic competitive advantage relative to other people? Why is your product or service going to sell? Why is it going to work in the marketplace?

Answering such questions succinctly and consistently will help many managements increase the strategic use of technology in their corporate planning.

Reading II–2
The Core Competence of the Corporation

C. K. Prahalad and Gary Hamel

The most powerful way to prevail in global competition is still invisible to many companies. During the 1980s, top executives were judged on their ability to restructure, declutter, and delayer their corporations. In the 1990s, they'll be judged on their ability to identify, cultivate, and exploit the core competencies that make growth possible—indeed, they'll have to rethink the concept of the corporation itself.

Consider the last 10 years of GTE and NEC. In the early 1980s, GTE was well positioned to become a major player in the evolving information technology industry. It was active in telecommunications. Its operations spanned a variety of businesses, including telephones, switching and transmission systems, digital PABX, semiconductors, packet switching, satellites, defense systems, and lighting products. And GTE's Entertainment Products Groups, which produced Sylvania color TVs, had a position in related display technologies. In 1980, GTE's sales were $9.98 billion, and net cash flow was $1.73 billion. NEC, in contrast, was much smaller, at $3.8 billion in sales. It had a comparable technological base and computer businesses, but it had no experience as an operating telecommunications company.

Yet look at the positions of GTE and NEC in 1988. GTE's 1988 sales were $16.46 billion, and NEC's sales were considerably higher at $21.89 billion. GTE has, in effect, become a telephone operating company with a position in defense and lighting products. GTE's other businesses are small in global terms. GTE has divested Sylvania TV and Telenet, put switching, transmission, and digital PABX into joint ventures, and closed down semiconductors. As a result, the international position of GTE has eroded. Non-U.S. revenue as a percent of total revenue dropped from 20 percent to 15 percent between 1980 and 1988.

NEC has emerged as the world leader in semiconductors and as a first-tier player in telecommunications products and computers. It has consolidated its position in mainframe computers. It has moved beyond public switching and transmission to include such lifestyle products as mobile telephones, facsimile machines, and laptop computers—bridging the gap between telecommunications and office automation. NEC is the only company in the world to be in the top five in revenue in telecommunications, semiconductors, and mainframes. Why did these two companies, starting with comparable business portfolios, perform so differently? Largely because NEC conceived of itself in terms of *core competencies,* and GTE did not.

Rethinking the Corporation

Once, the diversified corporation could simply point its business units at particular end product markets and admonish them to become world leaders. But with market boundaries changing ever more quickly, targets are elusive and capture is at best temporary. A few companies have proven themselves adept at inventing new markets, quickly entering emerging markets, and dramatically shifting patterns of customer choice in established markets. These are the ones to emulate. The critical task for management is to create an organization capable of infusing products with irresistible functionality or, better yet, creating products that customers need but have not yet even imagined.

This is a deceptively difficult task. Ultimately, it requires radical change in the management of major companies. It means, first of all, that top managements of Western companies must assume responsibility for competitive decline. Everyone knows about high interest rates, Japanese protectionism, outdated antitrust laws, obstreperous unions, and impatient investors. What is harder to see, or harder to acknowledge, is how little added momentum companies actually get from political or macroeconomic relief. Both the theory and practice of Western management have created a drag on our forward motion. It is the principles of management that are in need of reform.

NEC versus GTE, again, is instructive and only one of many such comparative cases we analyzed to understand the changing basis for global leadership. Early in the 1970s, NEC articulated a strategic intent to exploit the convergence of computing and communications, what it called C&C.[1] Success, top management reckoned, would hinge on acquiring *competencies,* particularly in semiconductors. Management adopted an appropriate "strategic architecture," summarized by C&C, and then communicated its intent to the whole organization and the outside world during the mid-1970s.

NEC constituted a C&C Committee of top managers to oversee the development of core products and core competencies. NEC put in place coordination groups and committees that cut across the interests of individual businesses. Consistent with its strategic architecture, NEC shifted enormous resources to strengthen its position in components and central processors. By using collaborative arrangements to multiply internal resources, NEC was able to accumulate a broad array of core competencies.

NEC carefully identified three interrelated streams of technological and market evolution. Top management determined that computing would evolve from large mainframes to distributed processing,

[1]For a fuller discussion, see our article, "Strategic Intent," *Harvard Business Review,* May–June 1989, p. 63.

components from simple ICs (integrated circuits) to VLSI (very-large-scale-integration), and communications from mechanical cross-bar exchange to complex digital systems we now call ISDN (integrated services digital network). As things evolved further, NEC reasoned, the computing, communications, and components businesses would so overlap that it would be very hard to distinguish among them, and that there would be enormous opportunities for any company that had built the competencies needed to serve all three markets.

NEC top management determined that semiconductors would be the company's most important *core product.* It entered into myriad strategic alliances—over 100 as of 1987—aimed at building competencies rapidly and at low cost. In mainframe computers, its most noted relationship was with Honeywell and Bull. Almost all the collaborative arrangements in the semiconductor-component field were oriented toward technology access. As they entered collaborative arrangements, NEC's operating managers understood the rationale for these alliances and the goal of internalizing partner skills. NEC's director of research summed up its competence acquisition during the 1970s and 1980s this way: "From an investment standpoint, it was much quicker and cheaper to use foreign technology. There wasn't a need for us to develop new ideas."

No such clarity of strategic intent and strategic architecture appeared to exist at GTE. Although senior executives discussed the implications of the evolving information technology industry, no commonly accepted view of which competencies would be required to compete in that industry were communicated widely. While significant staff work was done to identify key technologies, senior line managers continued to act as if they were managing independent business units. Decentralization made it difficult to focus on core competencies. Instead, individual businesses became increasingly dependent on outsiders for critical skills, and collaboration became a route to staged exits. Today, with a new management team in place, GTE has repositioned itself to apply its competencies to emerging markets in telecommunications services.

The Roots of Competitive Advantage

The distinction we observed in the way NEC and GTE conceived of themselves—a portfolio of competencies versus a portfolio of businesses—was repeated across many industries. From 1980 to 1988, Canon grew by 264 percent, Honda by 200 percent. Compare that with Xerox and Chrysler. And if Western managers were once anxious about the low cost and high quality of Japanese imports, they are now overwhelmed by the pace at which Japanese rivals are inventing new markets, creating new products, and enhancing them. Canon has given us personal copiers; Honda has moved from motorcycles to four-wheel off-road buggies. Sony developed the 8mm camcorder, Yamaha, the digital piano. Komatsu developed an underwater remote-controlled bulldozer, while Casio's latest gambit is a small-screen color LCD television. Who would have anticipated the evolution of these vanguard markets?

In more established markets, the Japanese challenge has been just as disquieting. Japanese companies are generating a blizzard of features and functional enhancements that bring technological sophistication to everyday products. Japanese car producers have been pioneering four-wheel steering, four-valve-per-cylinder engines, in-car navigation systems, and sophisticated electronic engine-management systems. On the strength of its product features, Canon is now a player in facsimile transmissions machines, desktop laser printers, even semiconductor manufacturing equipment.

In the short run, a company's competitiveness derives from the price/performance attributes of current products. But the survivors of the first wave of global competition, Western and Japanese alike, are all converging on similar and formidable standards for product cost and quality—minimum hurdles for continued competition, but less and less important as sources of differential advantage. In the long run, competitiveness derives from an ability to build, at lower cost and more speedily than competitors, the core competencies that spawn unanticipated products. The real sources of advantage are to be found in management's ability to consolidate corporationwide technologies and production skills into competencies that empower individual businesses to adapt quickly to changing opportunities.

Senior executives who claim that they cannot build core competencies either because they feel the autonomy of business units is sacrosanct or because their feet are held to the quarterly budget fire should think again. The problem in many Western companies is not that their senior executives are any less capable than those in Japan or that Japanese companies possess greater technical capabilities.

Instead, it is their adherence to a concept of the corporation that unnecessarily limits the ability of individual businesses to fully exploit the deep reservoir of technological capability that many American and European companies possess.

The diversified corporation is a large tree. The trunk and major limbs are core products, the smaller branches are business units; the leaves, flowers, and fruit are end products. The root system that provides nourishment, sustenance, and stability is the core competence. You can miss the strength of competitors by looking only at their end products, in the same way you miss the strength of a tree if you look only at its leaves. (See Exhibit 1, "Competencies: The Roots of Competitiveness.")

Core competencies are the collective learning in the organization, especially how to coordinate diverse production skills and integrate multiple streams of technologies. Consider Sony's capacity to miniaturize or Philips's optical-media expertise. The theoretical knowledge to put a radio on a chip does not in itself assure a company the skill to produce a miniature radio no bigger than a business card. To bring off this feat, Casio must harmonize know-how in miniaturization, microprocessor design, material science, and ultrathin precision casing—the same skills it applies in its miniature card calculators, pocket TVs, and digital watches.

If core competence is about harmonizing streams of technology, it is also about the organization of work and the delivery of value. Among Sony's competencies is miniaturization. To bring miniaturization to its products, Sony must ensure that technologists, engineers, and marketers have a shared understanding of customer needs and of technological possibilities. The force of core competence is felt as decisively in services as in manufacturing. Citicorp was ahead of others investing in an operating system that allowed it to participate in world markets 24 hours a day. Its competence in systems has provided the company the means to differentiate itself from many financial service institutions.

Core competence is communication, involvement, and a deep commitment to working across organizational boundaries. It involves many levels of people and all functions. World-class research in, for example, lasers or ceramics can take place in corporate laboratories without having an impact on any of the businesses of the company. The skills that together constitute core competence must coalesce around individuals whose efforts are not so narrowly focused that they cannot recognize the opportunities for blending their functional expertise with those of others in new and interesting ways.

Core competence does not diminish with use. Unlike physical assets, which do deteriorate over time, competencies are enhanced as they are applied and shared. But competencies still need to be nurtured and protected; knowledge fades if it is not used. Competencies are the glue that binds existing businesses. They are also the engine for new business development. Patterns of diversification and market entry may be guided by them, not just by the attractiveness of markets.

Consider 3M's competence with sticky tape. In dreaming up businesses as diverse as Post-it notes, magnetic tape, photographic film, pressure-sensitive tapes, and coated abrasives, the company has brought to bear widely shared competencies in substrates, coatings, and adhesives and devised various ways to combine them. Indeed, 3M has invested consistently in them. What seems to be an extremely diversified portfolio of businesses belies a few shared core competencies.

In contrast, there are major companies that have had the potential to build core competencies but

EXHIBIT 1 Competencies: The Roots of Competitiveness

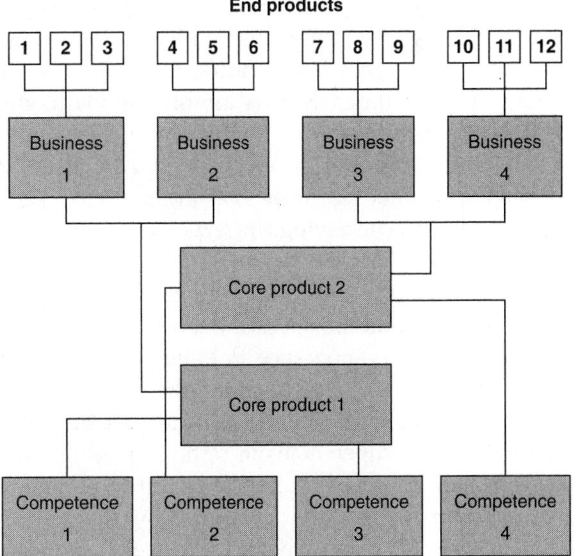

The corporation, like a tree, grows from its roots. Core products are nourished by competencies and engender business units, whose fruits are end products.

failed to do so because top management was unable to conceive of the company as anything other than a collection of discrete businesses. GE sold much of its consumer electronics business to Thomson of France, arguing that it was becoming increasingly difficult to maintain its competitiveness in this sector. That was undoubtedly so, but it is ironic that it sold several key businesses to competitors who were already competence leaders—Black & Decker in small electrical motors, and Thomson, which was eager to build its competence in microelectronics and had learned from the Japanese that a position in consumer electronics was vital to this challenge.

Management trapped in the strategic business unit (SBU) mind-set almost inevitably finds its individual businesses dependent on external sources for critical components, such as motors or compressors. But these are not just components. They are core products that contribute to the competitiveness of a wide range of end products. They are the physical embodiments of core competencies.

How Not to Think of Competence

Since companies are in a race to build the competencies that determine global leadership, successful companies have stopped imagining themselves as bundles of businesses making products. Canon, Honda, Casio, or NEC may seem to preside over portfolios of businesses unrelated in terms of customers, distribution channels, and merchandising strategy. Indeed, they have portfolios that may seem idiosyncratic at times: NEC is the only global company to be among leaders in computing, telecommunications, and semiconductors *and* to have a thriving consumer electronics business.

But looks are deceiving. In NEC, digital technology, especially VLSI and systems integration skills, is fundamental. In the core competencies underlying them, disparate businesses become coherent. It is Honda's core competence in engines and power trains that gives it a distinctive advantage in car, motorcycle, lawn mower, and generator businesses. Canon's core competencies in optics, imaging, and microprocessor controls have enabled it to enter, even dominate, markets as seemingly diverse as copiers, laser printers, cameras, and image scanners. Philips worked for more than 15 years to perfect its optical-media (laser disc) competence, as did JVC in building a leading position in video recording. Other examples of core competencies might include mechantronics (the ability to marry mechanical and electronic engineering), video displays, bioengineering, and microelectronics. In the early stages of its competence building, Philips could not have imagined all the products that would be spawned by its optical-media competence, nor could JVC have anticipated miniature camcorders when it first began exploring videotape technologies.

Unlike the battle for global brand dominance, which is visible in the world's broadcast and print media and is aimed at building global "share of mind," the battle to build world-class competencies is invisible to people who aren't deliberately looking for it. Top management often tracks the cost and quality of competitors' products, yet how many managers untangle the web of alliances their Japanese competitors have constructed to acquire competencies at low cost? In how many Western boardrooms is there an explicit, shared understanding of the competencies the company must build for world leadership? Indeed, how many senior executives discuss the crucial distinction between competitive strategy at the level of a business and competitive strategy at the level of an entire company?

Let us be clear. Cultivating core competence does *not* mean outspending rivals on research and development. In 1983, when Canon surpassed Xerox in worldwide unit market share in the copier business, its R&D budget in reprographics was but a small fraction of Xerox's. Over the past 20 years, NEC has spent less on R&D as a percentage of sales than almost all of its American and European competitors.

Nor does core competence mean shared costs, as when two or more SBUs use a common facility—a plant, service facility, or sales force—or share a common component. The gains of sharing may be substantial, but the search for shared costs is typically a post hoc effort to rationalize production across existing businesses, not a premeditated effort to build the competencies out of which the businesses themselves grow.

Building core competencies is more ambitious and different than integrating vertically, moreover. Managers deciding whether to make or buy will start with end products and look upstream to the efficiencies of the supply chain and downstream toward distribution and customers. They do not take inventory of skills and look forward to applying them in nontraditional ways. (Of course, decisions about competencies *do* provide a logic for vertical integration. Canon is not particularly integrated in its copier business, except in those aspects of the vertical chain that support the competencies it regards as critical.)

Identifying Core Competencies—and Losing Them

At least three tests can be applied to identify core competencies in a company. First, a core competence provides potential access to a wide variety of markets. Competence in display systems, for example, enables a company to participate in such diverse businesses as calculators, miniature TV sets, monitors for laptop computers, and automotive dashboards—which is why Casio's entry into the handheld TV market was predictable. Second, a core competence should make a significant contribution to the perceived customer benefits of the end product. Clearly, Honda's engine expertise fills this bill.

Finally, a core competence should be difficult for competitors to imitate. And it *will* be difficult if it is a complex harmonization of individual technologies and production skills. A rival might acquire some of the technologies that comprise the core competence, but it will find it more difficult to duplicate the more or less comprehensive pattern of internal coordination and learning. JVC's decision in the early 1960s to pursue the development of a videotape competence passed the three tests outlined here. RCA's decision in the late 1970s to develop a stylus-based video turntable system did not.

Few companies are likely to build world leadership in more than five or six fundamental competencies. A company that compiles a list of 20 to 30 capabilities has probably not produced a list of core competencies. Still, it is probably a good discipline to generate a list of this sort and to see aggregate capabilities as building blocks. This tends to prompt the search for licensing deals and alliances through which the company may acquire, at low cost, the missing pieces.

Most Western companies hardly think about competitiveness in these terms at all. It is time to take a tough-minded look at the risks they are running. Companies that judge competitiveness, their own and their competitors', primarily in terms of the price/performance of end products are courting the erosion of core competencies—or making too little effort to enhance them. The embedded skills that give rise to the next generation of competitive products cannot be "rented in" by outsourcing and OEM (original equipment manufacturer) supply relationships. In our view, too many companies have unwittingly surrendered core competencies when they cut internal investment in what they mistakenly thought were just "cost centers" in favor of outside suppliers.

Consider Chrysler. Unlike Honda, it has tended to view engines and power trains as simply one more component. Chrysler is becoming increasingly dependent on Mitsubishi and Hyundai: between 1985 and 1987, the number of outsourced engines went from 252,000 to 382,000. It is difficult to imagine Honda yielding manufacturing responsibility, much less design, of so critical a part of a car's function to an outside company—which is why Honda has made such an enormous commitment to Formula One auto racing. Honda has been able to pool its engine-related technologies; it has parlayed these into a corporationwide competency from which it develops world-beating products, despite R&D budgets smaller than those of GM and Toyota.

Of course, it is perfectly possible for a company to have a competitive product line up but be a laggard in developing core competencies—at least for a while. If a company wanted to enter the copier business today, it would find a dozen Japanese companies more than willing to supply copiers on the basis of an OEM private label. But when fundamental technologies changed or if its supplier decided to enter the market directly and become a competitor, that company's product line, along with all of its investments in marketing and distribution, could be vulnerable. Outsourcing can provide a shortcut to a more competitive product, but it typically contributes little to building the people-embodied skills that are needed to sustain product leadership.

Nor is it possible for a company to have an intelligent alliance or sourcing strategy if it has not made a choice about where it will build competence leadership. Clearly, Japanese companies have benefited from alliances. They've used them to learn from Western partners who were not fully committed to preserving core competencies of their own. As we've argued in these pages before, learning within an alliance takes a positive commitment of resources—travel, a pool of dedicated people, test-bed facilities, time to internalize and test what has been learned.[2] A company may not make this effort if it doesn't have clear goals for competence building.

---

[2]"Collaborate with Your Competitors and Win," *Harvard Business Review,* January–February 1989, p. 133, with Yves L. Doz.

Another way of losing is forgoing opportunities to establish competencies that are evolving in existing businesses. In the 1970s and 1980s, many American and European companies—like GE, Motorola, GTE, Thorn, and GEC—chose to exit the color television business, which they regarded as mature. If by "mature" they meant that they had run out of new product ideas at precisely the moment global rivals had targeted the TV business for entry, then yes, the industry was mature. But it certainly wasn't mature in the sense that all opportunities to enhance and apply video-based competencies had been exhausted.

In ridding themselves of their television businesses, these companies failed to distinguish between divesting the business and destroying their video media-based competencies. They not only got out of the TV business but they also closed the door on a whole stream of future opportunities reliant on video-based competencies. The television industry, considered by many U.S. companies in the 1970s to be unattractive, is today the focus of a fierce public policy debate about the inability of U.S. corporations to benefit from the $20-billion-a-year opportunity that HDTV will represent in the mid- to late 1990s. Ironically, the U.S. government is being asked to fund a massive research project—in effect, to compensate U.S. companies for their failure to preserve critical core competencies when they had the chance.

In contrast, one can see a company like Sony reducing its emphasis on VCRs (where it has not been very successful and where Korean companies now threaten), without reducing its commitment to video-related competencies. Sony's Betamax led to a debacle. But it emerged with its videotape recording competencies intact and is currently challenging Matsushita in the 8mm camcorder market.

There are two clear lessons here. First, the costs of losing a core competence can be only partly calculated in advance. The baby may be thrown out with the bath water in divestment decisions. Second, since core competencies are built through a process of continuous improvement and enhancement that may span a decade or longer, a company that has failed to invest in core competence building will find it very difficult to enter an emerging market, unless, of course, it will be content simply to serve as a distribution channel.

American semiconductor companies like Motorola learned this painful lesson when they elected to forgo direct participation in the 256k generation of DRAM chips. Having skipped this round, Motorola, like most of its American competitors, needed a large infusion of technical help from Japanese partners to rejoin the battle in the 1-megabyte generation. When it comes to core competencies, it is difficult to get off the train, walk to the next station, and then reboard.

From Core Competencies to Core Products

The tangible link between identified core competencies and end products is what we call the core products—the physical embodiments of one or more core competencies. Honda's engines, for example, are core products, linchpins between design and development skills that ultimately lead to a proliferation of end products. Core products are the components or subassemblies that actually contribute to the value of the end products. Thinking in terms of core products forces a company to distinguish between the brand share it achieves in end product markets (for example, 40 percent of the U.S. refrigerator market) and the manufacturing share it achieves in any particular core product (for example, 5 percent of the world share of compressor output).

Canon is reputed to have an 84 percent world manufacturing share in desktop laser printer "engines," even though its brand share in the laser printer business is minuscule. Similarly, Matsushita has a world manufacturing share of about 45 percent in key VCR components, far in excess of its brand share (Panasonic, JVC, and others) of 20 percent. And Matsushita has a commanding core product share in compressors worldwide, estimated at 40 percent, even though its brand share in both the air-conditioning and refrigerator businesses is quite small.

It is essential to make this distinction between core competencies, core products, and end products because global competition is played out by different rules and for different stakes at each level. To build or defend leadership over the long term, a corporation will probably be a winner at each level. At the level of core competence, the goal is to build world leadership in the design and development of a particular class of product functionality—be it compact data storage and retrieval, as with Philips's optical-media competence, or compactness and ease of use, as with Sony's micromotors and microprocessor controls.

To sustain leadership in their chosen core competence areas, these companies *seek to maximize their world manufacturing share in core products.* The manufacture of core products for a wide variety of external (and internal) customers yields the revenue and market feedback that, at least partly, determines the pace at which core competencies can be enhanced and extended. This thinking was behind JVC's decision in the mid-1970s to establish VCR supply relationships with leading national consumer electronics companies in Europe and the United States. In supplying Thomson, Thorn, and Telefunken (all independent companies at that time) as well as U.S. partners, JVC was able to gain the cash and the diversity of market experience that ultimately enabled it to outpace Philips and Sony. (Philips developed videotape competencies in parallel with JVC, but it failed to build a worldwide network of OEM relationships that would have allowed it to accelerate the refinement of its videotape competence through the sale of core products.)

JVC's success has not been lost on Korean companies like Goldstar, Sam Sung, Kia, and Daewoo, which are building core product leadership in areas as diverse as displays, semiconductors, and automotive engines through their OEM-supply contracts with Western companies. Their avowed goal is to capture investment initiative away from potential competitors, often U.S. companies. In doing so, they accelerate their competence-building efforts while "hollowing out" their competitors. By focusing on competence and embedding it in core products, Asian competitors have built up advantages in component markets first and have then leveraged off their superior products to move downstream to build brand share. And they are not likely to remain the low-cost suppliers forever. As their reputation for brand leadership is consolidated, they may well gain price leadership. Honda has proven this with its Acura line, and other Japanese car makers are following suit.

Control over core products is critical for other reasons. A dominant position in core products allows a company to shape the evolution of applications and end markets. Such compact audio disc–related core products as data drivers and lasers have enabled Sony and Philips to influence the evolution of the computer-peripheral business in optical-media storage. As a company multiplies the number of application arenas for its core products, it can consistently reduce the cost, time, and risk in new product development. In short, well-targeted core products can lead to economies of scale *and* scope.

The Tyranny of the SBU

The new terms of competitive engagement cannot be understood using analytical tools devised to manage the diversified corporation of 20 years ago, when competition was primarily domestic (GE versus Westinghouse, General Motors versus Ford) and all the key players were speaking the language of the same business schools and consultancies. Old prescriptions have potentially toxic side effects. The need for new principles is most obvious in companies organized exclusively according to the logic of SBUs. The implications of the two alternative concepts of the corporation are summarized in Exhibit 2, "Two Concepts of the Corporation: SBU or Core Competence."

Obviously, diversified corporations have a portfolio of products and a portfolio of businesses. But we believe in a view of the company as a portfolio of competencies as well. U.S. companies do not lack the technical resources to build competencies, but their top management often lacks the vision to build them and the administrative means for assembling resources spread across multiple businesses. A shift in commitment will inevitably influence patterns of diversification, skill deployment, resource allocation priorities, and approaches to alliances and outsourcing.

We have described the three different planes on which battles for global leadership are waged: core competence, core products, and end products. A corporation has to know whether it is winning or losing on each plane. By sheer weight of investment, a company might be able to beat its rivals to blue-sky technologies yet still lose the race to build core competence leadership. If a company is winning the race to build core competencies (as opposed to building leadership in a few technologies), it will almost certainly outpace rivals in new business development. If a company is winning the race to capture world manufacturing share in core products, it will probably outpace rivals in improving product features and the price/performance ratio.

Determining whether one is winning or losing end product battles is more difficult because measures of product market share do not necessarily reflect various companies' underlying competitiveness. Indeed, companies that attempt to build market share by relying on the competitiveness of others, rather than investing in core competencies and world core-product leadership, may be treading on quicksand. In the race for global brand domi-

EXHIBIT 2 Two Concepts of the Corporation: SBU or Core Competence

	SBU	Core Competence
Basis for competition	Competitiveness of today's products	Interfirm competition to build competencies
Corporate structure	Portfolio of businesses related in product-market terms	Portfolio of competencies, core products, and businesses
Status of the business unit	Autonomy is sacrosanct; the SBU "owns" all resources other than cash	SBU is a potential reservoir of core competencies
Resource allocation	Discrete businesses are the unit of analysis; capital is allocated business by business	Businesses and competencies are the unit of analysis: top management allocates capital and talent
Value added of top management	Optimizing corporate returns through capital allocation trade-offs among businesses	Enunciating strategic architecture and building competencies to secure the future

nance, companies like 3M, Black & Decker, Canon, Honda, NEC, and Citicorp have built global brand umbrellas by proliferating products out of their core competencies. This has allowed their individual businesses to build image, customer loyalty, and access to distribution channels.

When you think about this reconceptualization of the corporation, the primacy of the SBU—an organizational dogma for a generation—is now clearly an anachronism. Where the SBU is an article of faith, resistance to the seductions of decentralization can seem heretical. In many companies, the SBU prism means that only one plane of the global competitive battle, the battle to put competitive products on the shelf *today,* is visible to top management. What are the costs of this distortion?

Underinvestment in developing core competencies and core products

When the organization is conceived of as a multiplicity of SBUs, no single business may feel responsible for maintaining a viable position in core products or be able to justify the investment required to build world leadership in some core competence. In the absence of a more comprehensive view imposed by corporate management, SBU managers will tend to underinvest. Recently, companies such as Kodak and Philips have recognized this as a potential problem and have begun searching for new organizational forms that will allow them to develop and manufacture core products for both internal and external customers.

SBU managers have traditionally conceived of competitors in the same way they've seen themselves. On the whole, they've failed to note the emphasis Asian competitors were placing on building leadership in core products or to understand the critical linkage between world manufacturing leadership and the ability to sustain development pace in core competence. They've failed to pursue OEM-supply opportunities or to look across their various product divisions in an attempt to identify opportunities for coordinated initiatives.

Imprisoned resources

As an SBU evolves, it often develops unique competencies. Typically, the people who embody this competence are seen as the sole property of the business in which they grew up. The manager of another SBU who asks to borrow talented people is likely to get a cold rebuff. SBU managers are not only unwilling to lend their competence carriers, but they may actually hide talent to prevent its redeployment in the pursuit of new opportunities. This may be compared to residents of an underdeveloped country hiding most of their cash under their mattresses. The benefits of competencies, like the benefits of the money supply, depend on the velocity of their circulation as well as on the size of the stock the company holds.

Western companies have traditionally had an advantage in the stock of skills they possess. But have they been able to reconfigure them quickly to respond to new opportunities? Canon, NEC, and Honda have had a lesser stock of the people and technologies that compose core competencies but could move them much quicker from one business unit to another. Corporate R&D spending at Canon is not fully indicative of the size of Canon's core competence stock and tells the casual observer nothing about the velocity with which Canon is able to move core competencies to exploit opportunities.

When competencies become imprisoned, the people who carry the competencies do not get assigned to the most exciting opportunities, and their skills begin to atrophy. Only by fully leveraging core competencies can small companies like Canon afford to compete with industry giants like Xerox. How strange that SBU managers, who are perfectly willing to compete for cash in the capital budgeting process, are unwilling to compete for people—the company's most precious asset. We find it ironic that top management devotes so much attention to the capital budgeting process yet typically has no comparable mechanism for allocating the human skills that embody core competencies. Top managers are seldom able to look four or five levels down into the organization, identify the people who embody critical competencies, and move them across organizational boundaries.

Bounded innovation

If core competencies are not recognized, individual SBUs will pursue only those innovation opportunities that are close at hand—marginal product-line extensions or geographic expansions. Hybrid opportunities like fax machines, laptop computers, hand-held televisions, or portable music keyboards will emerge only when managers take off their SBU blinkers. Remember, Canon appeared to be in the camera business at the time it was preparing to become a world leader in copiers. Conceiving of the corporation in terms of core competencies widens the domain of innovation.

Developing Strategic Architecture

The fragmentation of core competencies becomes inevitable when a diversified company's information systems, patterns of communication, career paths, managerial rewards, and processes of strategy development do not transcend SBU lines. We believe that senior management should spend a significant amount of its time developing a corporationwide strategic architecture that establishes objectives for competence building. A strategic architecture is a road map of the future that identifies which core competencies to build and their constituent technologies.

By providing an impetus for learning from alliances and a focus for internal development efforts, a strategic architecture like NEC's C&C can dramatically reduce the investment needed to secure future market leadership. How can a company make partnerships intelligently without a clear understanding of the core competencies it is trying to build and those it is attempting to prevent from being unintentionally transferred?

Of course, all of this begs the question of what a strategic architecture should look like. The answer will be different for every company. But it is helpful to think again of that tree, of the corporation organized around core products and, ultimately, core competencies. To sink sufficiently strong roots, a company must answer some fundamental questions: How long could we preserve our competitiveness in this business if we did not control this particular core competence? How central is this core competence to perceived customer benefits? What future opportunities would be foreclosed if we were to lose this particular competence?

The architecture provides a logic for product and market diversification, moreover. An SBU manager would be asked: Does the new market opportunity add to the overall goal of becoming the best player in the world? Does it exploit or add to the core competence? At Vickers, for example, diversification options have been judged in the context of becoming the best power and motion control company in the world (see the insert "Vickers Learns the Value of Strategic Architecture").

The strategic architecture should make resource allocation priorities transparent to the entire organization. It provides a template for allocation decisions by top management. It helps lower level managers understand the logic of allocation priorities and disciplines senior management to maintain consistency. In short, it yields a definition of the company and the markets it serves. 3M, Vickers, NEC, Canon, and Honda all qualify on this score. Honda *knew* it was exploiting what it had learned from motorcycles—how to make high-revving,

Vickers Learns the Value of Strategic Architecture

The idea that top management should develop a corporate strategy for acquiring and deploying core competencies is relatively new in most U.S. companies. There are a few exceptions. An early convert was Trinova (previously Libbey Owens Ford), a Toledo-based corporation, which enjoys a worldwide position in power and motion controls and engineered plastics. One of its major divisions is Vickers, a premier supplier of hydraulics components like valves, pumps, actuators, and filtration devices to aerospace, marine, defense, automotive, earth-moving, and industrial markets.

Vickers saw the potential for a transformation of its traditional business with the application of electronics disciplines in combination with its traditional technologies. The goal was "to ensure that change in technology does not displace Vickers from its customers." This, to be sure, was initially a defensive move: Vickers recognized that unless it acquired new skills, it could not protect existing markets or capitalize on new growth opportunities. Managers at Vickers attempted to conceptualize the likely evolution of (*a*) technologies relevant to the power and motion control business, (*b*) functionalities that would satisfy emerging customer needs, and (*c*) new competencies needed to creatively manage the marriage of technology and customer needs.

Despite pressure for short-term earnings, top management looked to a 10- to 15-year time horizon in developing a map of emerging customer needs, changing technologies, and the core competencies that would be necessary to bridge the gap between the two. Its slogan was "Into the 21st Century." (A simplified version of the overall architecture developed is shown here.) Vickers is currently in fluid-power components. The architecture identifies two additional competencies, electric-power components and electronic controls. A systems integration capability that would unite hardware, software, and service was also targeted for development.

The strategic architecture, as illustrated by the Vickers example, is not a forecast of specific products or specific technologies but a broad map of the evolving linkages between customer functionality requirements, potential technologies, and core competencies. It assumes that products and systems cannot be defined with certainty for the future but that preempting competitors in the development of new markets requires an early start to building core competencies. The strategic architecture developed by Vickers, while describing the future in competence terms, also provides the basis for making here-and-now decisions about product priorities, acquisitions, alliances, and recruitment.

Since 1986, Vickers has made more than 10 clearly targeted acquisitions, each one focused on a specific component or technology gap identified in the overall architecture. The architecture is also the basis for internal development of new competencies. Vickers has undertaken, in parallel, a reorganization to enable the integration of electronics and electrical capabilities with mechanical-based competencies. We believe that it will take another two to three years before Vickers reaps the total benefits from developing the strategic architecture, communicating it widely to all its employees, customers, and investors, and building administrative systems consistent with the architecture.

Vickers Map of Competencies

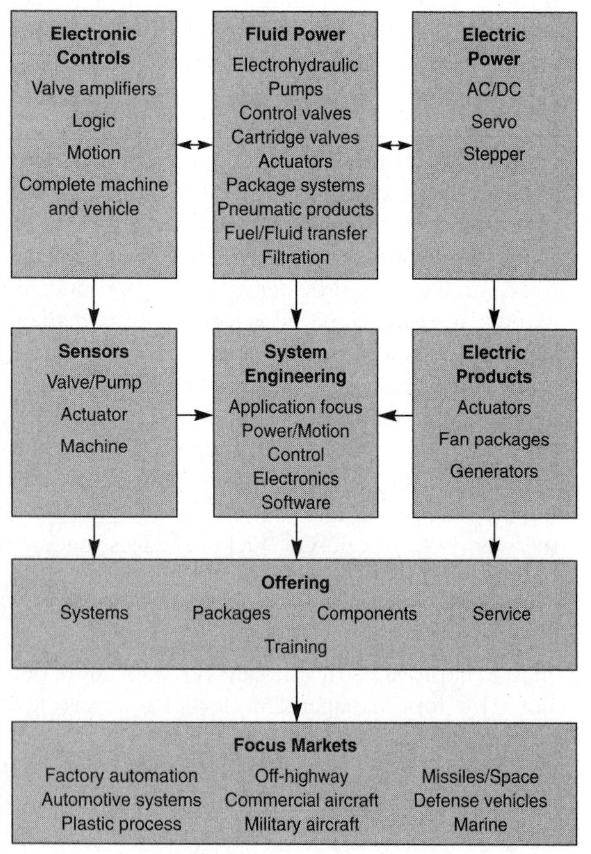

smooth-running, lightweight engines—when it entered the car business. The task of creating a strategic architecture forces the organization to identify and commit to the technical and production linkages across SBUs that will provide a distinct competitive advantage.

It is consistency of resource allocation and the development of an administrative infrastructure appropriate to it that breathes life into a strategic architecture and creates a managerial culture, teamwork, a capacity to change, and a willingness to share resources, to protect proprietary skills, and to think long-term. That is also the reason the specific architecture cannot be copied easily or overnight by competitors. Strategic architecture is a tool for communicating with customers and other external constituents. It reveals the broad direction without giving away every step.

EXHIBIT 3 Core Competencies at Canon

	Precision mechanics	*Fine optics*	*Micro-electronics*
Basic camera	■	□	
Compact fashion camera	■	□	
Electronic camera	■	□	
EOS autofocus camera	■	□	■
Video still camera	■	□	■
Laser beam printer	■	□	■
Color video printer	■		■
Bubble jet printer	■		■
Basic fax	■		■
Laser fax	■		■
Calculator			■
Plain paper copier	■	□	■
Battery PPC	■	□	■
Color copier	■	□	■
Laser copier	■	□	■
Color laser copier	■	□	■
NAVI	■	□	■
Still video system	■	□	■
Laser imager	■	□	■
Cell analyzer	■	□	■
Mask aligners	■		■
Stepper aligners	■		■
Excimer laser aligners	■	□	■

Every Canon product is the result of at least one core competency.

Redeploying to Exploit Competencies

If the company's core competencies are its critical resource and if top management must ensure that competence carriers are not held hostage by some particular business, then it follows that SBUs should bid for core competencies in the same way they bid for capital. We've made this point glancingly. It is important enough to consider more deeply.

Once top management (with the help of divisional and SBU managers) has identified overarching competencies, it must ask businesses to identify the projects and people closely connected with them. Corporate officers should direct an audit of the location, number, and quality of the people who embody competence.

This sends an important signal to middle managers: core competencies are *corporate* resources and may be reallocated by corporate management. An individual business doesn't own anybody. SBUs are entitled to the services of individual employees so long as SBU management can demonstrate that the opportunity it is pursuing yields the highest possible payoff on the investment in their skills. This message is further underlined if each year in the strategic planning or budgeting process, unit managers must justify their hold on the people who carry the company's core competencies.

Elements of Canon's core competence in optics are spread across businesses as diverse as cameras, copiers, and semiconductor lithographic equipment and are shown in Exhibit 3, "Core Competencies at Canon." When Canon identified an opportunity in digital laser printers, it gave SBU managers the right to raid other SBUs to pull together the required pool of talent. When Canon's reprographics products division undertook to develop microprocessor-controlled copiers, it turned to the photo products group, which had developed the world's first microprocessor-controlled camera.

Also, reward systems that focus only on product-line results and career paths that seldom cross SBU boundaries engender patterns of behavior among unit managers that are destructively competitive. At NEC, divisional managers come together to identify next-generation competencies. Together they decide how much investment needs to be made to build up each future competency and the contribution in capital and staff support that each division will need to make. There is also a sense of equitable exchange. One division may make a disproportionate contribution or may benefit less from the progress made, but such short-term inequalities will balance out over the long term.

Incidentally, the positive contribution of the SBU manager should be made visible across the company. An SBU manager is unlikely to surrender key people if only the other business (or the general manager of that business who may be a competitor for promotion) is going to benefit from the redeployment. Cooperative SBU managers should be celebrated as team players. Where priorities are clear, transfers are less likely to be seen as idiosyncratic and politically motivated.

Transfers for the sake of building core competence must be recorded and appreciated in the corporate memory. It is reasonable to expect a business that has surrendered core skills on behalf of corporate opportunities in other areas to lose, for a time, some of its competitiveness. If these losses in performance bring immediate censure, SBUs will be unlikely to assent to skills transfers next time.

Finally, there are ways to wean key employees off the idea that they belong in perpetuity to any particular business. Early in their careers, people may be exposed to a variety of businesses through a carefully planned rotation program. At Canon, critical people move regularly between the camera business and the copier business and between the copier business and the professional optical-products business. In midcareer, periodic assignments to cross-divisional project teams may be necessary, both for diffusing core competencies and for loosening the bonds that might tie an individual to one business even when brighter opportunities beckon elsewhere. Those who embody critical core competencies should know that their careers are tracked and guided by corporate human resource professionals. In the early 1980s at Canon, all engineers under 30 were invited to apply for membership on a seven-person committee that was to spend two years plotting Canon's future direction, including its strategic architecture.

Competence carriers should be regularly brought together from across the corporation to trade notes and ideas. The goal is to build a strong feeling of community among these people. To a great extent, their loyalty should be to the integrity of the core competence area they represent and not just to particular businesses. In traveling regularly, talking frequently to customers, and meeting with peers, competence carriers may be encouraged to discover new market opportunities.

Conclusion

Core competencies are the wellspring of new business development. They should constitute the focus for strategy at the corporate level. Managers have to win manufacturing leadership in core products and capture global share through brand-building programs aimed at exploiting economies of scope. Only if the company is conceived of as a hierarchy of core competencies, core products, and market-focused business units will it be fit to fight.

Nor can top management be just another layer of accounting consolidation, which it often is in a regime of radical decentralization. Top management must add value by enunciating the strategic architecture that guides the competence acquisition process. We believe an obsession with competence building will characterize the global winners of the 1990s. With the decade underway, the time for rethinking the concept of the corporation is already overdue.

Licensing and Marketing Technology

Case II–2
Biodel, Inc. (A)

J. M. Crowe and M. A. Maidique

Dr. Oscar Feldman, founder and president of Biodel, Inc., sat back for a moment and reflected. The year 1979 had recently ended. It had been a constructive 12 months for his small biotechnology company, yet Feldman knew that several difficult strategic choices loomed before him in 1980.

Biodel stood at an enviable crossroad. Feldman was confident that Biodel had distinct competences in its current biotechnologies. These competences currently provided the company with competitive advantages on which the president had resolved to capitalize. Should the company pursue the significant growth prospects in these current technologies—cell biology, molecular biology, and immunodiagnostics? Or should the company expand its technological focus to include genetic engineering, a field poised at the threshold of exciting advances? If Biodel were to pursue genetic engineering, how should it do so?

Finally, Feldman wondered if Biodel had sufficient personnel and funds to pursue an aggressive strategy.

EXHIBIT 1 Financial History

Fiscal Year	Revenues	Net Income	PAT
1962	$ 250,000	$ 5,000	2%
1965	510,000	45,000	9
1968	619,000	31,000	5
1969	647,000	59,000	9
1970	352,000	(32,000)	−8
1971	289,000	(44,000)	−11
1972	394,000	26,000	7
1973	460,000	15,000	3
1974	583,000	49,000	8
1975	748,000	62,000	8
1976	1,011,000	88,000	8.7

Company Background

Oscar Feldman was originally from Scotland, where his father had been a successful businessman. After a McGill chemistry Ph.D. and postdoctoral work at Harvard Medical School, Dr. Feldman taught at Stanford University. His work there centered on applying chemistry to biological and medical problems, including cancer research. During his 11 years at Stanford, Dr. Feldman published almost 100 papers, enjoyed widespread popularity, and established a base of contacts in the academic community which he valued highly.

Biodel was founded in 1962, shortly after Dr. Feldman obtained a contract for research which he felt could be executed more effectively in a commercial setting. The contract required the combination of several disciplines, including chemistry, biochemistry, biology, and enzymology, in order to obtain the best results. In an effort to cover initial working capital and facilities requirements for the start-up, Dr. Feldman raised $50,000 from local businessmen. He considered seeking a larger sum, but decided that he would rather remain the principal shareholder of a smaller enterprise.

Dr. Feldman's initial business objective for Biodel was simply to establish a position of technological leadership in the biomedical industry. A key to his strategy was the leveraging of his academic contacts. Dr. Feldman relied on his contacts at Stanford, for example, to bring on scientists to commence work on Biodel's first contract. He also planned to obtain additional government research contracts. Such contracts would provide Biodel with the financial support necessary to build technological leadership through the development of high-quality facilities and staff. Finally, Dr. Feldman began to assemble a small group of leading academics to advise Biodel. He stated at the time: "It is important to associate with none but the very best minds in the field."

During the start-up phase, Dr. Feldman held several views about his company's long-term strategy. Once Biodel had established itself in the contract research marketplace, he expected that the company would expand its focus. Dr. Feldman's exposure to his father's lumber business had convinced him that earning contract revenues and royalties would not be a sufficient long-term business base for Biodel. He envisioned a time when his company would manufacture and market biomedical products developed through its own research. Dr. Feldman was also wary of Biodel's depending only on a few government agencies for its revenues. Marketing a product, he believed, would endow his company with a broad base of customers.

Despite slow but steady growth throughout the 1960s, Dr. Feldman's fears about dependence on government contracts were eventually realized. (See Exhibit 1.) In the early 1970s, government cutbacks resulted in the loss of Biodel contracts with the Surgeon General, the Quartermaster Corps, and other agencies. At the time, the government had been responsible for 85 percent of Biodel's revenues. Biodel was forced into its first layoff, which troubled Dr. Feldman greatly. He considered the technological expertise of his employees to be one of Biodel's significant assets and regarded layoffs as damaging to the company's long-term potential.

This period of cutbacks and layoffs was a crucial point in the company's history. Biodel faced the threat of bankruptcy. Dr. Feldman later claimed that "it was a good thing I wasn't such a good businessman, otherwise I would have realized that Biodel was insolvent."

Concerns with its long-term survival caused Biodel in the early 1970s to move into the business of scientific research products, an area which Dr. Feldman had not originally anticipated. Biodel's scientific research products, numbering approximately 500, were initially items which the company produced to utilize in its own research efforts. Biodel discovered, however, that biochemists and molecular biologists in other organizations also needed such research products, yet often lacked the technical expertise to make them. Biodel found a ready market for various reagents and synthetic nucleic acids which it had been using internally. Relying on word of mouth as its basic marketing tool, Biodel generated enough demand for its research products to reverse the sharp decline in revenues from lost contracts. The company was so successful in commercializing research products throughout the 1970s that research products constituted approximately 60 percent of the company's revenues by 1980.

In January 1980, Biodel conducted all of its research and development at a 14,000-square-foot leased location in Menlo Park, California. Due to the rapid growth of the late 1970s, quarters in the aging building were becoming cramped and Dr. Feldman knew that he had to start looking for additional space soon.

Technologies and Products

By the end of the 1970s, Biodel had developed special expertise in three areas of biotechnology: molecular biology, cell biology, and immunology. The company conducted research and sold research products to scientists working in each of the three areas.

All of Biodel's researchers were in some way studying cells, which are the basic biological units of life. Each cell possesses the biochemical machinery to grow and reproduce. An important component of this machinery is nucleic acid, a form of which is deoxyribonucleic acid (DNA). DNA is a relatively large molecule which consists of small building blocks called nucleotides. Specific arrangements of nucleotides, called genes, determine the production of specific proteins through a sequence of steps aided by biocatalysts called enzymes. Proteins provide the machinery by which cells utilize nutrients to grow and reproduce.

The techniques of *molecular biology* have played a leading role in determining the molecular structure and function of DNA and relating this structure to the production of proteins. In 1980, Biodel was using the techniques of molecular biology to isolate and prepare biologically active substances, such as nucleic acids and enzymes. The company then marketed the products to other researchers in molecular biology and genetic engineering.

Cell culture technology, a technique of *cell biology,* concerns itself with the growth of mammalian cells. Such cells have stringent nutrition requirements normally supplied by serum, the fluid portion of the blood. In this area, Biodel was primarily involved in manufacturing and marketing cell growth factors, products which could be used, either partially or completely, to replace serum in helping cells to grow. Adequate quantities of uniformly high quality serum (usually derived from horses, pigs, and calves) were proving difficult for researchers to obtain. Thus, Biodel had enjoyed increasing success in the late 1970s in selling its cell growth factors to scientists who could not locate serum for use in their cell proliferation research. By 1980, Biodel's pioneering efforts had paid off. The company dominated the growth factor market with about 60 percent share.

Biodel's third area of special expertise was *immunodiagnostics.* Immunodiagnostics is one field within immunology, which is the study of how organisms protect themselves against infection. When foreign substances (antigens) are introduced into an organism, the organism responds by producing antibodies which bond themselves to the antigens. The presence of a specific antigen in a sample may be measured by adding to the sample a known level of antigen which has been radioactively tagged. The radioactive antigen competes with the sample's antigen for the antibodies in the sample. By measuring the residual radioactive antigen not attached to the antibodies, the level of antigen in the sample can be accurately estimated. Biodel had research expertise and a small product line in radioactive immunodiagnostic products.

Current Organization

Contract Research

During the 1970s, Biodel reported its revenues in two lines: contract research and research products.

(See Exhibit 2.) The contract research activities were projected to generate $1 million in revenues in fiscal 1980. Seventy percent of those revenues related to industrial research, the two prime customers being a large pharmaceutical company and a large chemical company. The government accounted for the remaining 30 percent of the contract research.

The scope of Biodel's contract research included work in the company's three primary areas of expertise (molecular biology, cell biology, and immunology) as well as in fields such as cancer chemotherapy and enzymology. Within those areas, the company offered its customers high-quality technical advice, numerous links to the scientific community, and a highly sophisticated contract research and development service with a record of many successes.

Dr. Feldman marketed Biodel's contract research efforts. He personally secured the contracts through his relationships with scientists in government and industry. Dr. Feldman also supervised the ongoing contract research activities. He managed the activities informally, preferring not to set exceedingly detailed milestones and budgets. He commented: "I consider my researchers to be professionals. I see no need for me to continually monitor them. Scientists are motivated by new technical challenges, not by heavy-handed supervision."

Research Products

Dr. Feldman expected sales of research products to reach $1.5 million in fiscal 1980. Research products consisted of three interrelated product lines corresponding to the company's three areas of scientific expertise: molecular biological products, cell biological products, and immunodiagnostic products. The product lines were generally sold to researchers in universities, private laboratories, and industrial firms. Despite a limited marketing effort, sales had been growing at a 35 percent clip over the last several years.

In the area of molecular biology, Biodel prepared and stocked the largest commercially available selection of synthetic nucleotides. Researchers used nucleotides as substitutes and primers for nucleic

EXHIBIT 2 Selected Financial Data (for fiscal years ending August 31)

	1977	1978	1979	Est. 1980
Revenue:				
Product sales	$ 598,941	$ 738,732	$1,153,749	$1,450,000
Contract revenue	754,207	836,385	730,942	1,000,000
Royalty and license income	—	—	—	50,000
Total revenue	1,353,148	1,575,117	1,884,691	2,500,000
Cost of revenue:				
Cost of product sales	271,225	324,781	489,091	750,000
Cost of contract revenue	550,652	659,480	667,548	800,000
Total cost of revenue	821,877	984,261	1,156,639	1,550,000
Gross profit	531,271	590,856	728,052	950,000
Operating expenses:				
Research and development	146,228	193,285	274,224	200,000
Selling, general, and administrative	205,592	245,475	436,057	650,000
Total operating expenses	351,820	438,760	710,281	850,000
Net interest income	—	—	2,000	—
Income before income taxes	179,451	152,096	19,771	110,000
Income taxes	81,400	56,200	2,000	10,000
Net income	98,051	95,896	17,771	100,000
Net income per common share	.08	.08	.01	.07
Common shares outstanding	1,351,875	1,351,875	1,351,875	1,351,875
Working capital	449,209	485,587	476,698	325,000
Total assets	803,238	875,063	965,559	1,400,000
Long-term debt, including capital lease obligations	127,095	108,414	114,732	30,000
Stockholders' investment	433,233	529,129	546,900	650,000

EXHIBIT 3 Research Product Sales

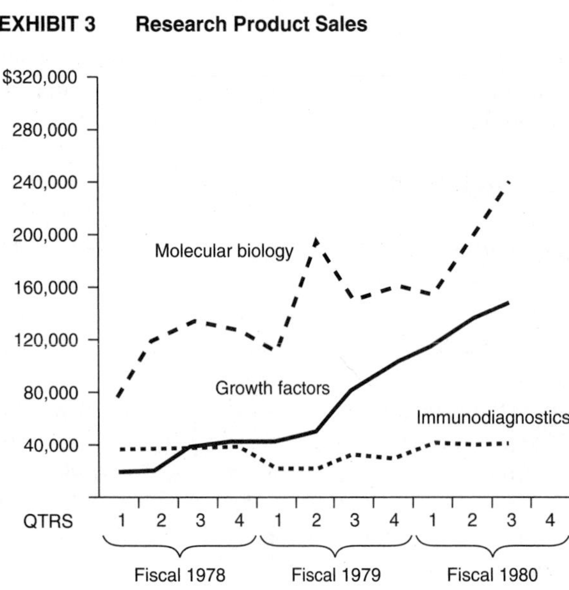

acid enzymes, as reference compounds for sequence analysis in studies of nucleic acids, for the development of new separation techniques, and as tools in recombinant DNA research. Nucleotides accounted for 50 percent of the sales of all research products. (See Exhibit 3.)

Cell growth factors, Biodel's primary product offspring in the cell biology field, generated 40 percent of the research product revenues. Sales of cell growth factors had risen rapidly over the past several years, and Dr. Feldman believed that they represented a fertile area for future growth. There did exist disagreement within the company's management team, however, over the company's current competitive position in cell growth factors. Dr. Feldman considered Biodel to be the technological leader, yet several top employees believed that this assessment might be too optimistic. All did agree, however, that they lacked the necessary market research data to back their conclusions with confidence.

Biodel had been a major factor in the immunodiagnostics market for several years until several large firms aggressively entered the field and slashed the company's market share. The product line had not expanded since that time and constituted 10 percent of the sales of research products in 1980. Further significant growth in radioactive diagnostic products was not considered likely.

Profitability for these research products varied, depending upon the intensity of the product's research and development. Operating profit margins, after charges for product cost, research and development, and marketing, were estimated at 20 percent on the aggregate. Biodel's current accounting system, however, did not provide product-by-product profitability data and aggregate data were clouded by overhead allocations that in the opinion of some managers were arbitrary.

Personnel

Biodel was organized along lines of scientific expertise. (See Exhibit 4.) The three operating groups—molecular biology, cell biology, and immunodiagnostics—were each under the control of a manager who reported directly to Dr. Feldman. All three managers were experienced scientists who were long-time employees of the company. Each manager supervised R&D and production and held some marketing responsibility. The organization within each operating group was highly fluid. Generally, those scientists who completed research on a particular product would then turn to manufacturing the product in small quantities and would also determine which scientists in other organizations would be likely customers for that product.

From the standpoint of staff, Dr. Feldman had kept Biodel a lean organization. Biodel had 55 employees, most of whom were scientists or technicians. The company employed neither a marketing manager nor a research director. Dr. Feldman filled both roles due to his widespread contacts and scientific expertise. All of Biodel's financial functions were handled by an accountant who was also a long-time employee. Insofar as Dr. Feldman perceived major strategic, financial, or administrative issues, he invariably made the decisions himself. He rarely convened staff meetings and did not require regular reports from his subordinates. Dr. Feldman considered his management style well-fitted to Biodel's organization and atmosphere:

> We are a paternalistic company. I believe in management by walking around and talking to people. That's the best way for me to stay on top of what is happening. I don't want our employees tied up in paper shuffling. And anyway, "professional management," goals, budgets, and meetings are not my "schtik."

One employee characterized Biodel's board of directors as "Dr. Feldman and his friends." The board consisted of four members, including Dr. Feldman. A corporate lawyer, age 79, sat on the

EXHIBIT 4 Organization Chart

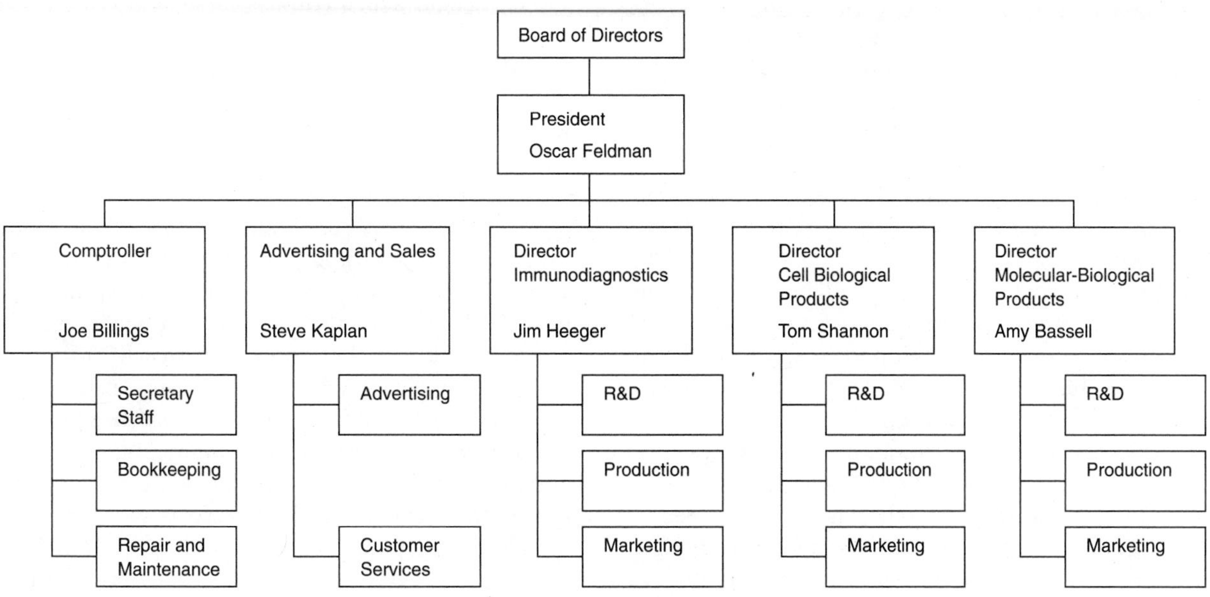

board. He had been involved with the company since its founding. Dr. Feldman had also wanted scientific expertise on the board and had persuaded a gifted Stanford scientist, now retired, to join him. The fourth member was an associate of Dr. Feldman who was an officer of an investment banking firm. The board was convened infrequently, whenever Dr. Feldman felt a need to discuss the company's affairs.

From the standpoint of the researchers, Biodel was an exciting place to work. Dr. Feldman believed that he placed heavy pressure on his researchers and in return offered them projects at the cutting edge of technology. Although Biodel's equipment was not the most sophisticated and the company's quarters were spartan, the work itself was more challenging and fruitful than that of many commercial labs. In fact, employees likened the company's atmosphere to one of an academic facility. They considered the combination of informality and high challenge to be attractive. Turnover among employees, especially the senior technical people, was extremely low. The technical staff expressed pride in the company's work, and one referred to the firm's reputation as the "Cadillac of the industry." Dr. Feldman, who had distinct automotive preferences, preferred to refer to it as the "Mercedes of the industry."

A second reason for the low turnover was Oscar Feldman himself. Dr. Feldman was generally regarded as the hub of Biodel's universe. The senior employees were unanimous in their affection for the president. One of the senior scientists explained the phenomenon as follows:

> Simply put, Oscar is an attractive man. His warmth and effusiveness is infectious. He is so naturally witty and charming that you can't help but enjoy working with him. Oscar gets so enthusiastic about the work that it's contagious.

A senior manager added:

> Oscar is unique. Irrespective of the situation, he never fails to appear distinguished. He wears perfectly tailored suits, drives a stately old convertible, and has impeccable manners. He also looks remarkably trim and healthy for his age. There are not too many people still skiing avidly at age 65. True, sometimes he'll forget a fact or two, but he can also be extraordinarily articulate.

Marketing

Throughout the 1970s, Biodel's marketing effort was an informal mixture of different activities. Research products were sold by mail, with customers typically having heard of the company through word of mouth. Trade shows, advertising, direct mail, and phone solicitation were also employed from time to time. Order processing and shipping were handled informally, without much emphasis on control. Dr. Feldman cited Biodel's customer service as "almost laughable."

In 1979, Dr. Feldman determined that the company needed to market its research products more aggressively and systematically. He decided that he needed someone who had familiarity both with the sales function and with biotechnology. In May 1979, he hired Steve Kaplan, who had been marketing manager at a large pharmaceutical company.

Tension eventually developed between Dr. Feldman and his new manager. Dr. Feldman wanted Kaplan only to organize a sales effort and gather information on customers and competitors. He still felt that he should direct Biodel's marketing strategy himself. Kaplan, on the other hand, perceived a need for focus in the company's marketing strategy. In addition, he concluded that Biodel was understaffed and proceeded to hire additional salespeople, an administrative assistant, an order entry clerk, and a secretary.

The results were mixed. Sales of research products increased 65 percent in the first quarter of fiscal 1980, an achievement for which Kaplan took credit. In addition, the customer service function began to respond more systematically to shipment delays and other problems. On the other hand, marketing costs increased 500 percent, resulting in sharply reduced profits despite the jump in sales. Dr. Feldman began to wonder if his marketing group was too large for Biodel, given its size and stage of development. He also began to question Steve Kaplan's tendency to make solo decisions regarding the company's marketing direction.

Growth Opportunities

While Dr. Feldman was satisfied with the course Biodel had taken over the past 10 years, he knew that important choices remained to be made. Several of his top scientists were excited about two of the company's new product developments in cell biology and immunodiagnostics. At the same time, interest was building rapidly in scientific and financial circles in genetic engineering. The new genetic engineering technology was closely related to Biodel's expertise in molecular biology and could be a natural extension of the company's scientific focus. Each of the growth opportunities looked attractive, and Dr. Feldman wondered how he should decide which path to pursue.

Cell Biology

Based on its experience and expertise in using cell growth factors as components of serum substitutes, Biodel had under development several synthetic serums which were formulated to satisfy the growth requirements of a variety of cell lines in tissue culture. The synthetic serum substitutes would replace natural fetal calf serum, which was currently the most widely used source of growth for cells. Horse serum was second in market importance. The price and quality of fetal calf serum had been unstable over time because the availability of the product depended upon the slaughter of cattle, which tended to be cyclical. Biodel's researchers projected the market for fetal calf serum at about $50 million domestically in 1980 and $80 million worldwide and growing at 15 percent a year. Biodel believed that the market for synthetic serums of uniformly high quality and reliable supply would be even larger. However, these numbers were somewhat speculative, for the firm had not conducted a systematic analysis of the serum market.

Dr. Feldman believed that the company would have a competitive edge in synthetic serums which would be difficult for other firms to overcome. This advantage would allow Biodel to achieve a market share of up to 20 percent of the current market. The serums would be produced by adding to distilled water certain combinations of cell growth factors which would not be easy to break down and analyze. Even if a competitor could break the combinations down, Dr. Feldman believed that developments in this scientific discipline could not be quickly duplicated. It might require several years between the time a firm initially studied an area and the time it commercialized a product. Dr. Feldman was not certain whether other firms were currently pursuing the same course as his company. Finally, Biodel planned to cement its advantage by applying for patent protection, although it was by no means certain that a patent could be obtained.

Tom Shannon, the cell biology manager, felt that Biodel could eventually produce the synthetic serums at costs which would allow it to price the products competitively with fetal calf serum. At this point, Shannon guessed that a $1 to $2 million investment would be needed in manufacturing facilities. Dr. Feldman thought that the company would also need additional management personnel to oversee the venture. Both he and Tom Shannon were unsure as to just how best to market the product and what product introduction and marketing costs would likely be.

Immunodiagnostics

Within immunodiagnostics lay another opportunity for Biodel to enter markets vastly larger than its current customer base in research organizations. The company had under development a new testing technology based on enzyme membranes rather than radioactivity. Jim Heeger, the immunodiagnostic manager, expected that the new product (called DEMA) would have many applications in clinical, medical, environmental, and industrial testing. The product could determine the presence and level of many substances, including hormones, enzymes, drugs, viruses, and bacteria. The tests could include, among others, those for pregnancy, syphilis, hepatitis, cancer, toxins in food, and carcinogens in the environment.

Heeger considered DEMA an alternative to tests based on radioactivity. It appeared to share the high sensitivity of radioactive tests without the drawbacks and hazards associated with radioactivity. In addition, Heeger believed that DEMA tests would be simpler, faster, and less expensive than radioactive tests. Other enzyme-linked immunodiagnostic technologies, such as EMIT and ELISA, were already in existence, but Heeger judged them to be less sensitive and applicable to fewer substances than DEMA. The company had filed for patent protection and had been encouraged to believe by its patent attorneys that a patent for the technology would be forthcoming.

As with synthetic sera, the market for DEMA tests appeared to be vast, perhaps in excess of $100 million. One analyst's estimate placed the potential home market at over $1 billion. Again, however, Dr. Feldman and his subordinates were unsure how to bring the product to the marketplace. Investments in the necessary manufacturing and marketing facilities and personnel could easily total in the millions. Further R&D costs would range from $1 million to $3 million. On the other hand, several large drug companies had expressed an interest in exploring a joint venture or licensing agreement. Under such conditions, license percentages ranged from 4 percent to 7 percent, depending on the fraction of R&D costs funded by the sponsoring firm. Dr. Feldman wanted Biodel to have some manufacturing and marketing capability, but he did not know how much of the marketplace his company could feasibly pursue on its own. One possibility was to have Biodel target the clinical diagnostics market, which was limited and well defined. Medical clinics would be a logical place to introduce the new DEMA technology. On the other hand, drugstore sales of DEMA potentially could generate enormous revenues and would be best pursued in conjunction with a partner that had an established distribution system and brand name. Pharmacies greatly outnumbered clinics, and DEMA would easily have numerous applications in the vast consumer markets.

Genetic Engineering

Dr. Feldman saw genetic engineering as a third opportunity for Biodel's expansion. The company currently had no direct expertise in the field, although it was closely associated with genetic engineering laboratories by virtue of its work as a supplier of molecular biology products. The nucleotides and synthetic genes which Biodel produced and sold were used as support products by genetic engineers. In some cases, Biodel was the sole supplier.

The opportunity for Biodel to move into genetic engineering itself arose through Dr. Feldman's contacts. Dr. Daniel Ballantine, a Berkeley Nobel Laureate and a pioneer in genetic engineering, was a longtime friend of Dr. Feldman and a consultant to Biodel. He had risen to prominence in the 1970s, and for the last two years he had been suggesting to Dr. Feldman that genetic engineering offered Biodel explosive opportunities for growth. Dr. Feldman began to consider seriously his associate's recommendations when he noticed an intensive interest developing in financial circles in the concept of genetic engineering.

The technology of genetic engineering is not complex in theory. To "engineer" a cell to produce a specific product, DNA containing the desired sequence must be isolated. The desired gene is either obtained from a biological source or is synthesized chemically. The gene is then spliced into a carrier molecule, called a vector, to form a recombinant DNA molecule. Control sequences which program the cell to produce the product coded by the gene are introduced into the vector, which itself could be a virus or a plasmid. The vector carries the new gene into the host cell, thereby programming the host cell to manufacture the desired product. The most widely used host cell has been Escherichia coli, or E. coli. (See Appendix A for more detailed technical explanation of the genetic engineering.) More is known about E. coli than about any other bacteria.

While the theory of genetic engineering may be easy to understand, the techniques have been difficult to perform. Procedures for isolating DNA and for utilizing vectors were not discovered until the early 1970s. By the mid-1970s, however, the academic world realized the future of gene splicing and many major universities launched DNA research programs. A critical breakthrough came in 1973 when Stanley Cohen of Stanford and Herb Boyer of the nearby University of California in San Francisco first chemically translated DNA from one species to another by gene splicing. (See Appendix A.) In contrast, the commercialization of the technology began slowly. In 1971, Cetus was the only genetic research firm. Genentech and Bethesda Research Labs were founded in 1976, followed by Genex in 1977, and Biogen in 1978. (See Exhibit 5.) Venture capitalists and large pharmaceutical, chemical, and energy companies provided the financing for the start-up phases of the fledgling firms. The large corporate investors had two goals: (1) to establish a technological window in a potentially revolutionary technology; and (2) to make a profitable investment.

The early investments were already generating large capital gains by 1979. In 1976, Inco purchased $400,000 of Genentech's stock, only to sell it to Lubrizol four years later for $5.2 million. In early 1980, Genentech estimated that the market value of its privately held stock exceeded $100 million—one half of which was owned by the company's officers, directors, and employees. A frenzy was enveloping the whole field of genetic engineering. Investors seemed willing to stake significant sums of money on almost any company that employed well-known scientists with connections to gene splicing. Financial journals continually touted genetic engineering's revolutionary potential to impact the manufacturing processes of products in the chemical, pharmaceutical, and petrochemical industries. *The New York Times* editorialized, "Recombinant DNA technology seems poised at the threshold of advances as important as antibiotics or electronic semiconductors" (January 19, 1980).

Despite the euphoria surrounding genetic engineering, no firm had yet sold a genetically engineered product in mass quantities. Investors were lured by the prospects of production of a host of recombinant products, including pharmaceuticals,

EXHIBIT 5 The Four Pacesetting Genetic Engineering Firms

GENENTECH, INC.:

Headquarters: South San Francisco. Founded in 1976; 110 employees. Has announced more DNA-made products than competitors. Joint ventures with Eli Lilly for human insulin; with A. B. Kabi of Sweden for human growth hormone; with Hoffmann-La Roche for interferon. Half-owned by employees. Lubrizol, a lubricating oil company, holds 20 percent; venture capitalists own the rest.

CETUS CORPORATION:

Headquarters: Berkeley, California. Founded in 1971; 250 employees. Concentrates on industrial and agricultural chemicals, also interferon. Joint ventures with Standard of California for chemicals and fruit sugar; with National Distillers for fuel alcohol. Founders, employees, and private investors own almost 40 percent; Standard California, 24 percent; National Distillers, 16 percent; Standard Indiana, 21 percent.

GENEX CORPORATION:

Headquarters: Rockville, Maryland. Founded in 1977; 50 employees. Concentrates on industrial chemicals. Has interferon research contract with Bristol-Myers; another contract with Koppers, a mining and chemicals company. Management owns about 45 percent; Koppers, 30 percent; InnoVen, a venture capital company backed by Monsanto and Emerson Electric, about 25 percent.

BIOGEN S.A.:

Headquarters: Geneva, Switzerland. Founded in 1978; about a dozen employees, plus others under contract. First to make interferon. Schering-Plough, a New Jersey pharmaceutical company that owns 16 percent, plans to begin pilot production of the antiviral drug using Biogen's process. Inco, formerly International Nickel, owns 24 percent. Remainder held by management and various outside investors.

SOURCE: *The New York Times,* June 29, 1980, section 3, p. 1. Reprinted by permission.

biologicals, chemicals, and fuels. Several firms had announced product capability—Biogen was making interferon; Genentech, interferon and insulin—but observers believed that years would transpire before any genetically engineered product generated significant revenues. The major pharmaceutical and chemical companies had set up their own gene splicing departments, but they, as well as the small firms, had yet to understand the intricacies of production on a mass scale.

Amidst the mounting excitement over gene splicing's long-run potential, Dr. Feldman pondered Biodel's role. While the business of selling support products to the genetic engineering firms was expected to grow at a 30 percent to 50 percent clip over the next several years, it held neither the glamour nor the potential for explosive expansion associated with genetic engineering. One of Biodel's competitors in the molecular biology products industry was quoted as saying: "Our market won't ever compare to the markets for genetically engineered products. After all, it only takes one dollar of our stuff to make a thousand or a million dollars of their stuff." Cetus was the world's biggest user of enzymes in its genetic engineering research, yet it could have bought one year's supply for $12,000. The market for synthetic nucleotides, enzymes, and the like seemed limited.

What Dr. Ballantine offered Biodel was a route to expand into genetic engineering itself. He proposed a novel approach to the problem of growing cells by using yeast organisms as hosts in place of the E. coli predominantly used by other genetic engineering firms. For the past two years, Dr. Ballantine had been collaborating with three other renowned scientists on the development of yeast as the host cell in the genetic engineering process. The four men believed that yeast cells would ultimately prove more attractive than E. coli for industrial applications of genetic engineering. Yeast cells were easier and less costly to grow and it was believed by Biodel scientists that they could be grown to higher yields and thus with lower costs than E. coli. In addition, yeast cells contained biochemical machinery, absent in E. coli, which allowed for the possibility of programming the yeast cells to produce glycoproteins (proteins which contained carbohydrates).

Interferon and urokinase were two examples of glycoproteins which, although currently produced by conventional extraction processes, could potentially be manufactured by yeast cells through genetic engineering techniques. Interferon was a protein which performed a regulatory function in the body: it appeared to inhibit the multiplication of viruses and cancerous tissue cells. Because of the extraordinary difficulty of producing it in large quantities through conventional techniques, interferon was highly valued in medical circles. In 1980, its price exceeded $1 billion per pound. Urokinase was an enzyme produced in the human body as an agent to dissolve blood clots. Sales of urokinase up to 1980 had been limited due to the complication and high cost of conventional extraction processes. Biodel had already had some experience producing urokinase through a tissue culture process and knew that several drug companies were interested in securing a large, stable supply of the enzyme if it could be genetically engineered. In short, Biodel scientists believed that genetic engineers using yeast might have an advantage over researchers using E. coli in producing both interferon and urokinase.

Dr. Ballantine indicated his willingness to convene his three colleagues with Dr. Feldman in order to discuss a possible association with Biodel. Dr. Ballantine and his friends were all experts in yeast genetics. Full professors at the nation's most distinguished university laboratories, the four had been elected to the National Academy of Sciences and had jointly won all of the coveted biochemistry and molecular genetics prizes in American science. Dr. Feldman was excited at the possibility of attracting them to Biodel. He commented:

> As a group, they have talents unsurpassed in genetic engineering. James Finney, Columbia's leading biochemist, possesses one of the most penetrating intellects I've come across. He is a mature scientist with unimpeachable integrity. He's the type of person you'd want at your side when the going gets tough. Ralph Davidson is noted among the scientists at Cal Tech for his brilliant creativity. Despite his quiet nature, he could make invaluable intellectual contributions to our activities. Dennis Bernstein generates more ideas than 10 scientists combined. His work at University of Wisconsin has earned acclaim throughout scientific circles. And of course, we have my good friend Daniel Ballantine. He is simply the best there is. If the four of them worked with us, it would give our company a tremendous edge. If even one of them joined us, we'd have an advantage over Genentech, Cetus, and the rest. However, if we plan to land any or all of them, we will have to make an extraordinary offer.

Indeed, all four individuals were in high demand. They had offers from large chemical and pharmaceutical companies for positions as senior scientists with salaries ranging from $75,000 to $100,000. Smaller biotechnology firms were luring them with stock option packages which included 1 percent to 4 percent of the companies' outstanding stock. Leading universities were proposing prestigious endowed chairs with unparalleled academic freedom and clout. Even venture capital firms had approached them, exploring the possibilities of a start-up. One venture capitalist had asserted that he could raise $5 million on the strength of Dr. Ballantine's reputation alone.

Biodel, however, was not without its attractions. The company could offer the scientists both the freedom to start up their own gene-splicing R&D operation and the expertise in key related areas. Biodel had placed itself at the leading edge of technology and had earned a position of respect in science. The scientists' ideas could be further developed and enhanced through an association with the company. Despite the intangible benefits, however, Dr. Feldman knew that he would also have to structure a lucrative financial package to lure them away, even on a consulting basis, from their well-established academic environments.

Although there was much uncertainty surrounding genetic engineering—estimates varied widely on market sizes and on the time required for successful refinement of production processes—Dr. Feldman hoped that Biodel would be able to quickly generate revenue if it secured the services of the four scientists. He felt that the company could land a gene-splicing research contract from one of several large corporations for $5 to $10 million over a period of five years. From such an arrangement, Biodel could earn as much as a 25 percent margin after deduction for salaries, capital expenditures, and other associated costs. More important, the company would retain licensing rights at agreed-upon rates for potential products. In effect, Biodel would be conducting research at the expense of a commercial sponsor who sought to participate in genetic breakthroughs but who lacked the necessary technical capability.

Actions to Be Taken

Several routes lay open to Biodel at this point. Shannon was pushing to develop synthetic serums. He thought the company would lose any competitive edge it might have in cell biology if it did not bring the serums to market as soon as possible. Heeger, in contrast, pressed for more investment in DEMA. The immunodiagnostics manager argued that DEMA could reach the marketplace in a year if his group could obtain substantial additions in people and facilities. Both managers believed that Biodel could within reason meet whatever goals Dr. Feldman might set simply by pursuing the company's present product opportunities. They saw little reason to look elsewhere. Genetic engineering, on the other hand, represented a potentially lucrative expansion of Biodel's focus and a considerable boost to the company's prestige. Dr. Feldman was fascinated by the idea of having world-famous scientists officially and intimately associated with his firm.

No matter what course Biodel chose, tough financial decisions needed to be made. Development of synthetic serums was projected to cost more than $500,000; development of DEMA was estimated to be several times more expensive. On the advice of a finance professor at the Graduate School of Business at Stanford, Dr. Feldman held informal conversations with local bankers and venture capitalists. He discovered from the bankers that a loan above $500,000 would require his personal guarantee. One bank was willing to supply Biodel with as much as $1 million. In exchange, it wanted two points over the prime rate (currently 17 percent) and covenants restricting further debt, dividend payments, equity issues, and mergers and acquisitions. Venture capitalists generally expressed reluctance to invest in Biodel unless it strengthened its management team. One venture capital firm, however, tentatively offered Dr. Feldman $2 million for 40 percent of the company's equity. On January 1, 1980, Biodel had 1 million shares of common stock outstanding. Upon hearing the proposal, Dr. Feldman exclaimed that his company was worth many times more, prompting the investor to dryly remark that the financial community would not commit large sums of money simply for the potential of developing synthetic serums.

Another issue was the financial package that Biodel might offer to Dr. Ballantine and his cohorts. One alternative was to set up a separate subsidiary of Biodel, with all transactions between the parent and the subsidiary at arm's length. The four scientists would not work directly for the subsidiary, but they would act as an advisory board and recruit other top scientists to work for it. In return, they would receive a consulting fee and restricted stock in the subsidiary, which would vest over a four-year period at 25 percent per year. In this way, the four could maintain their affiliation with their respective universities. The finance professor guessed that a per diem of $500 to $1,000 and ownership of 2 percent to 10 percent of the subsidiary for each of the scientists would be a reasonable range within which Dr. Feldman could make an offer.[1]

A second possibility was to hire one or more of the geneticists as employees of the company itself. Dr. Feldman knew that to employ the scientists directly, he would have to match any salary and equity combination that another company might offer. This would pose a commitment larger than Dr. Feldman was used to for his own employees. Biodel's three managers currently earned salaries under $35,000, and their ownership of the company's stock jointly totaled less than 2 percent. Dr. Feldman owned over 80 percent of the outstanding stock. Friends, business associates, and relatives of Dr. Feldman owned another 10 percent. On the other hand, by hiring directly, Biodel would get at least one top scientist solely committed to the company's efforts and an immediate boost to its reputation. Dr. Feldman believed that one of the geneticists ought to be employed full time if Biodel planned to set up and operate a significant genetic engineering operation. He was not certain, however, of how difficult it would be to entice one of the scientists away from his academic research on a full-time basis.

A third alternative was to retain the scientists as technical consultants. Biodel would pay them a per diem fee of $800 to $1,200 in exchange for guidance on the company's current projects, proposals for new avenues of research, and recruitment of geneticists. In addition, the company would offer incentive agreements which would allot the scientists stock options on the basis of the company's performance. One possible measure of performance was revenue earned from genetic engineering contracts and products. The Stanford finance professor suggested the following proposal: Biodel would grant the scientists, as a group, options to purchase 50,000 shares at 10 cents per share for each incremental $1,000 in annual revenues related to genetic engineering. The grants would be made yearly for the next four years, based on Biodel's genetic engineering revenues in the particular year. Dr. Feldman estimated that over a four-year period, genetic engineering contract revenue could rise to about $5 to $10 million. The options would be exercisable starting one year from the date of grant if, and only if, the scientists were still consulting for the company. In this way, the Stanford professor noted, the scientists would have an incentive to remain with Biodel. They would also be motivated to help the company grow enough to go public, a development which would greatly increase the value of their options. A final advantage of this alternative was that Biodel would be able to avoid a drain on its cash flow stemming from large salaries.

Dr. Feldman felt that he had to make a move. Shannon and Heeger were pressing for more money, more people, and more facilities. Dr. Ballantine warned that his colleagues were being pressured to accept individual offers. It was a time for decisions.

[1]Maximum allowed consulting time at major universities was one day per week.

APPENDIX A
PUTTING DESIGNER GENES TO WORK

Channing Robertson

Over a century ago, the Swiss biochemist Johann Friederich Miescher reported that the contents of nuclei obtained from human cells were rich with organic acids containing nitrogen and phosphate. To this mixture he gave the name nucleic acids. In 1929, the geneticist Muller proposed that every living cell possessed "genes," and that the information required to perform metabolic functions and self-replication was in some way mapped onto genes. In the years that followed, genes and nucleic acids were shown to be one and the same, and in 1953, James Watson, Francis Crick, Rosalind Franklin, and others working in the Cavendish Laboratories at Cambridge University reported the structure of DNA (deoxyribonucleic acid). Of the several nucleic acids, it was this one that represented the data bank, common to all organisms, needed to remember the past and preserve the present. And of utmost importance to species propagation, it was this storehouse of information that must be transmitted to future generations with unfailing accuracy.

Since 1953, much of the molecular information code of DNA has been deciphered and more

Excerpt from Fall/Winter 1981–82 issue. Reprinted by permission of *The Stanford Engineer*.

recently, with code in hand, molecular biologists have been attempting to create new forms of DNA. For billions of years, DNA has been altered in random ways by nature, an event referred to as evolution through mutation and natural selection. Eight years ago, DNA was altered, for the first time, by humans, in a predictable and controlled fashion. Such alterations are now commonplace activities in university, government, and industrial laboratories throughout the world.

Without a doubt, man's ability to reprogram and someday synthesize the master molecule of life, DNA, will affect our society in ways none of us can even imagine. At the very least, I believe it will lead to the development of an entirely new chemical process industry, one based on biological feedstocks that in time will supersede and ultimately replace the fossil materials-based chemicals industry now in existence. For this to happen, engineers and technologists will have to conceive, develop, and put into place processes that accommodate living organisms and biological catalysts in an optimally efficient and economic way for the synthesis of tomorrow's chemicals.

When nature is viewed at its most fundamental levels, one cannot help but be awed by the presence of the underlying symmetry and simplicity. For instance, all of the instructions to propagate every life form known to man reside within the chemical structure of a highly organized linear polymer known as DNA. How is this possible?

On a molecular level, each DNA molecule consists of parallel strands of polymerized sugar residues. Every sugar residue is attached to one of four heterocyclic bases: adenine (A); thymine (T); cytosine (C); or guanine (G). These bases fill the space between the two polymer strands and are juxtaposed according to an inviolate base-pairing rule. Only a T may be associated with an A, and G with a C. As shown in the figure, the molecular order in one strand imposes a complementary molecular order in the opposite strand. The two strands are held together rather loosely by hydrogen bonds (dotted line). As discovered by Crick and Watson, the dual strands are twisted about one another like two intertwined spiral staircases (the double helix) with each turn incorporating 10 base pairs. In a simple bacterial cell, the DNA polymer contains approximately 2.5 million base pairs, whereas animal cell DNA has roughly 5 billion base pairs. To give an idea of the scale involved, imagine if each base (A, T, G, or C) were a model H-O scale railroad car

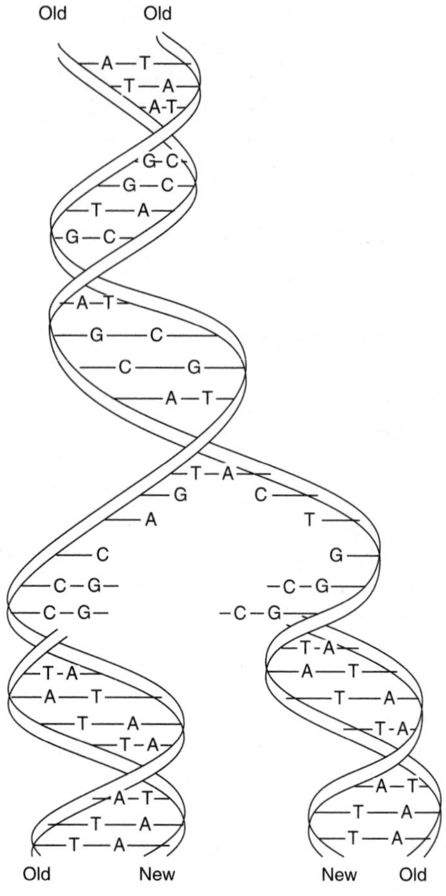

(about three inches long). The two juxtaposed "trains" represented by a bacterial DNA molecule would then be a little over 100 miles in length. This "train" in turn would have to be packed in a space (a bacterium is about 2mm in diameter) approximately four football fields in diameter. In human cells, the equivalent DNA "train" is about 200,000 miles long, about eight times the earth's circumference. This train would have to be confined within a space approximately two thirds of a mile in diameter. In either case, one is impressed by the densities of information packing that nature is able to achieve.

In the vernacular of information processing, nature uses a three-bit per word vocabulary; that is to say, each sequence of three base pairs along the double helix of DNA (called a codon) specifies one of the 20 amino acids that are themselves joined into a linear polymer to form polypeptides and proteins (both are linear amino acid sequences). A sequence of base-pair triplets (or codons) together with start-stop codons is then sufficient to instruct for protein synthesis. This entire sequence of base pairs is called a gene. For instance, the protein insulin is composed of 51 amino acids. Therefore, the insulin gene must be 153 base pairs in length. A few additional base pairs are required to provide start/stop instructions so the organism can identify the insulin gene on its DNA and ascertain its length. Given the number of base pairs in bacteria ($\sim 2.5 \times 10^6$), several thousand protein molecules may be synthesized from the information encoded on bacterial DNA. In animal cells, instructions for several tens of thousands of proteins are contained in the DNA. One might expect this number to be higher in animal cells since there are about 2,000 times more base pairs available than there are in bacteria. A particular distinction between animal cells and bacterial cells is that in the former, only about 10 percent of the base pairs code for proteins. That is to say, 90 percent of the information data bank is blank—perhaps allowing for future programming either by natural or synthetic processes.

To this point, I have discussed only how information is stored by DNA. How is this information passed on to succeeding generations with such precision? Conceptually, when a cell divides to form two progeny, the DNA unzips and complementary base pairs are simultaneously retrieved from the cellular contents. As a result, two identical DNA molecules are synthesized, one being allocated to each of the progeny of cell division. This bifurcation process coupled with complementary base-pairing insures that all the genes are preserved for future generations.

In many ways, DNA recombination occurs all the time in nature. Sexual reproduction is a good example wherein the gene pool of the progeny is contributed to in equal amounts by each parent. Mistakes or errors in DNA replication and in DNA recombination are known to occur. Some may be traced to the presence of toxic chemicals, radiation, and the like, whereas others seem to be chance errors. The result of such mistakes are genetic mutants, and typically they are at an evolutionary disadvantage in competing with nonmutants of their species (recall Darwin's theories on the subject) and in due time most, although not all, are eliminated together with their erroneous genes.

DNA recombination performed as an orderly, conscious, and explicit act was first reported in 1973 by Stanley Cohen of Stanford and Herbert Boyer of the University of California at San Francisco and their colleagues. Using chemical scissors (enzymes known as restriction endonucleases), they cut open a small circular strand of extrachromosomal DNA (known as a plasmid) in a bacterium. Plasmids are small rings (they have roughly 100 times fewer base pairs than does the primary chromosomal DNA) of DNA found in bacteria that are not needed, in principle, for survival, but which impart useful properties to the bacterium, such as antibiotic resistance. They also used the same chemical scissors to cut up a DNA molecule from an unrelated bacterial species. A useful property of the enzyme employed is that it severs any DNA molecule at the same base-pair location (i.e., the G-A bond in a G-A-A-T-T-C sequence). Consequently, when the ruptured plasmid DNA and the fractured foreign DNA were mixed, some of them joined together according to the base-pairing rules discussed earlier. The plasmid chimera was reinserted into its original bacterial species and was replicated during cell division. As a result, the foreign DNA was "cloned" into the unrelated bacterium. As one might imagine, since 1973 numerous techniques have become available to chemically translate DNA from one species to another. The utility of doing so is best understood by example.

Consider the protein hormone insulin. Currently insulin is extracted from the pancreatic glands of cows and pigs. It is a costly and tedious process that results in a product (animal insulin) that is not quite the same as human insulin. Porcine insulin differs in only a single amino acid from that produced in humans, whereas bovine insulin has three overlapping amino acids. Nevertheless, both bovine and porcine insulin work well, in most cases, in humans who suffer from insulin deficiency. There are, however, ways in which one might imagine obtaining human insulin. One approach would be to culture human pancreatic cells in vitro and collect the insulin they manufacture. Unfortunately, large-scale culture of mammalian cells is very difficult to achieve. Yet another approach would be to excise the gene (i.e., sequence of base pairs) that codes for human insulin and insert it into a bacterial plasmid. The bacteria could then be cultured en masse and, provided the human insulin gene was expressed (i.e., that it indeed caused insulin to be synthesized), we would have a bacterial insulin factory. Unfortunately, it is not enough merely to insert the human gene amid the myriad of bacterial genes. It must be placed in such a way that it does not interfere with any of the normal bacterial functions while at the same time it must be duplicated on cell division and also transcribed into its amino acid (protein) analog. These are all exceedingly nontrivial considerations.

In essence, recombinant DNA, molecular cloning, and DNA recombination all refer to the same activity, namely, the insertion of a DNA segment into an intact DNA molecule that is replicated faithfully by the descendants of the organism into which it is placed. This is not unlike coupling a new set of boxcars into the molecular "train" used earlier as an example. Furthermore, the instructions for polypeptide or protein synthesis must be recognized and obeyed by the bacterium.

Given the ability to augment the molecular instruction book for chemicals manufacture by cells, is it reasonable to ask what one might accomplish? Generally speaking, there are two approaches to be taken. Cells (bacterial, animal, or plant) can be made to express a chemical in far greater quantities than they normally would by multiple copying of the gene (or genes) that codes for the chemical. For instance, a particular microbe might produce a useful substance, a protein; however, the rate at which the protein is synthesized may be low. By "stitching" in multiple copies of the organism's gene that codes for the protein, then it would, in principle, be possible to amplify chemical productivity. This procedure would be akin to xeroxing the same page in the microbe's instruction manual many times, yet having them all read more or less simultaneously. The other approach is that of removing the instruction page (the gene) responsible for a particular chemical's synthesis and pasting it in someone else's manual (e.g., an unrelated organism). An example would be the insulin example referred to earlier. In either case, we are talking about synthesizing chemicals already made by cells. By virtue of DNA recombination, the cells will either make the material in more copious quantities (e.g., at higher rates), or else manufacture chemicals they normally (as a result of evolutionary pressures) did not but which instead were produced by some other cell line.

Since almost every chemical substance, or at least the precursor to same, is or can be synthesized by some type of cell, the possibilities for putting this new technology to work are indeed staggering. Already a number of biochemicals have been synthesized using molecular cloning techniques. Among them are: human insulin, human interferons (antiviral proteins), and somatostatin (a brain hormone). The current interest in interferons is particularly keen due in part, I presume, to their current retail value of $20 billion per pound.

In time we will see a host of recombinant products become available. Most of them will fall into one of the following classes: pharmaceuticals and biologicals; fine, intermediate, and bulk chemicals; and fuels. Examples of each include: pharmaceuticals and biologicals—human-growth hormone, antibiotics, nerve-growth hormone, other immune proteins besides the interferons, and vaccines; chemicals—epoxides, oxides, glycols, alcohols, acids, herbicides, pesticides, enzymes, lubricants, and sugars; fuels—alcohols, hydrogen, and methane. The impact of this new technology will also be felt by the farming and food industries. Fertilizers are normally produced from ammonia, which in turn is manufactured using methane, a dwindling resource. Some bacteria are able to form a symbiotic relationship with plants, the result of which is the direct fixation of atmospheric nitrogen to organic nitrogen, thereby obviating the need for externally applied fertilizer. Gene-splicing can, in principle, be employed to genetically alter plants to give them pest resistance and tolerance to drought and to saline soils, or to enhance their photosynthetic efficiency. Cells cloned to manufacture prodigious amounts of protein offer a new source of food and food supplements.

Case II–3
EDS: Information Technology Outsourcing

Sanjeev Dheer, Brian Viard, and Garth Saloner

EDS (Electronic Data Systems) had been the leader in the information technology (IT) outsourcing industry since the 1960s. In an industry which it pioneered and continued to develop, EDS held a commanding market share. In the early 1990s, however, EDS faced new challenges as clients' outsourcing needs were changing, innovations in computing technology were altering the delivery of services, and additional competitors were entering the industry.

The IT Outsourcing Industry

Information Technology

IT referred broadly to the resources a firm applied to process and manage its data. These resources included computing hardware, software, communications (voice, data, and video), and associated personnel. Advances in IT over the past few decades had led to new applications and substantial changes in how businesses employed IT.

The decentralization of companies after World War II increased the need for centralized financial control. The emergence of the mainframe computer as a commercial device in the 1960s allowed companies to process data centrally, and the mainframe became the center of firms' IT operations. IT applications during this time focused on automating highly repetitive tasks, and investment decisions in IT were usually evaluated in terms of reduced labor costs.

In the 1970s, the introduction of the minicomputer allowed firms to develop applications which served specific departments or groups within the firm to supplement the centralized functions running on the mainframe. Data on these two different hardware platforms could be processed independently or shared in so-called distributed networks. The minicomputer also increased usage of IT as firms that could not afford mainframe systems could now invest affordably in IT. During this period, return on IT projects was still equated with savings related to cost reductions; however, accurate measurement was more complicated because more advanced technologies increasingly allowed intellectual rather than mechanical labor to be replaced.

During the 1960s and 1970s when companies' IT operations relied on mainframes and minicomputers, a firm typically housed its computer and communications equipment and related personnel in a data processing center. Users accessed data online by displaying it on computer terminals or by generating printed reports. The data center was also responsible for running various software application programs in "background," which processed and updated data for users.

Personnel in the data center performed such activities as entering commands to start the running of software applications, mounting magnetic tapes for backups, monitoring the computer's performance, and maintaining the computer. Data center personnel usually reported to the firm's management information systems (MIS) department.

Related to the data center operations and also part of the MIS department was the development of new software applications. MIS departments had a staff of analysts and programmers who identified, designed, and developed new software applications to support the firm's activities.

The 1980s introduced the personal computer (PC) and a proliferation of hardware and software standards which began to alter these traditional structures. Due to the availability of inexpensive PCs, departmental managers began developing standalone applications outside the control of the central MIS department. These applications met specific departmental needs but were not coordinated with corporate data. By the end of the decade the installed computer power of PCs exceeded that of the large mainframes of the MIS department. The complexity of managing large-scale systems development projects and integrating disparate systems with varying standards resulted in escalating MIS budgets. Such increases prompted companies to view outsourcing as a source of cost containment and efficiency (Exhibit 1 illustrates the evolution of IT).

Outsourcing Services

Outsourcing provided companies with an alternative to their own in-house IT activities. Outsourcing included consulting, systems development, systems integration, and systems management.

IT consulting services were concerned with identifying a strategy for applying technology to achieve the client's business goals. One of the values of a consulting project was identifying new applications which would improve the competitive position of the client. Before assuming the operations of a client's data center, a provider often performed a consulting study to establish such a strategy. To perform a consulting study it was necessary to have both general business and specific industry knowledge. Consulting projects often led to follow-on work to develop and implement the identified applications.

Systems development involved designing and implementing custom software applications to automate a business process or function. Developing an application consisted of identifying user requirements, coding and testing programs, and incorporating them into the firm's existing applications.

EXHIBIT 1 Evolution of Information Technology

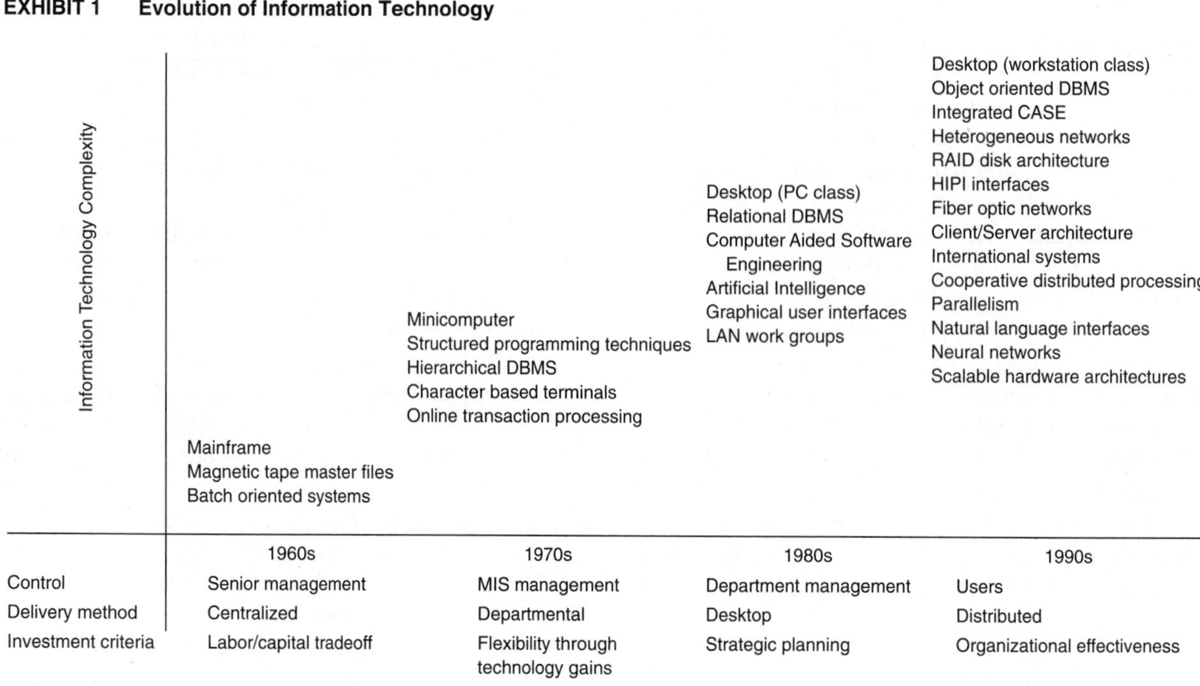

	1960s	1970s	1980s	1990s
Control	Senior management	MIS management	Department management	Users
Delivery method	Centralized	Departmental	Desktop	Distributed
Investment criteria	Labor/capital tradeoff	Flexibility through technology gains	Strategic planning	Organizational effectiveness

Depending on the size of the application, a development project took from a few weeks to several years and required industry and technical knowledge and project management skills.

Systems integration involved modifying or creating interfaces for disparate hardware and software components to make them compatible. Integration differed from development in that it involved combining existing hardware and software technologies rather than creating custom applications. For example, often a company wanted to incorporate a packaged software system into its existing applications, but the two were incompatible, or it wanted to integrate two systems that had been developed separately over time or had been purchased from two separate vendors. Combining the disparate systems involved modifying the existing applications or creating custom interface programs. Systems integration required industry and technical knowledge and project management skills.

The most highly publicized segment of the outsourcing market was systems management outsourcing. *Systems management* referred to the assumption of all or part of clients' IT operations by an external provider. A provider managed and operated a client's data processing center, frequently from their own off-site data centers. The systems management provider managed all elements of the data processing center: hardware, software, communications, and personnel.

The centerpiece of the provider's operation was its technical infrastructure, which included computer hardware, operating systems, peripheral equipment, and telecommunications (such as local area networks and satellite or terrestrial data transmission). This infrastructure was used to run the unique software applications necessary to process data for each client.

The provider could combine up to hundreds of clients' processing needs on the same facilities. Increased capacity utilization allowed investment in productivity-enhancing technology and automation of labor-intensive functions, such as scheduling and submitting computer programs for running, loading magnetic tapes, and monitoring system performance.

A systems management contract usually involved deploying provider personnel to the client's site. In addition to running the client's existing software applications, the on-site personnel handled user inquiries and enhanced existing client applications or created new ones. Except for these employees, the end users could not distinguish systems management services from an internal data center. Terminals were linked to the provider's remote data center and reports were printed on the premises or delivered from a printing facility. The following example demonstrates one approach to providing systems management services.

A systems management contract could be implemented in three major stages. This phased approach was required because of the complexity of managing a data center; however, the sequence of events in implementing these stages varied across providers and clients. During the first stage, the provider assumed all assets and personnel of the client's existing data center and operated the data center at the client site. Client personnel were integrated into the provider organization, although most remained at the client site to provide continuity during the transition of the data center. The provider supplemented this staff with its own technical experts to manage the transition.

In the next stage, the provider transferred the client's applications to its remote data center. This step could require substantial effort because the client's software often had to be modified to be compatible with different hardware platforms at the provider's data center. At this point, the client's staff was available to be integrated into the provider's organization.

In the final stage the provider took additional measures to increase the efficiency of the client's data processing. Efficiency improvements could be as simple as making minor changes to programs to allow them to read data faster or as major as processing portions of the client's data on the provider's own proprietary applications. During the life of the systems management contract, the provider was responsible for maintaining the client's applications. In addition, the provider usually provided a pool of analysts and programmers to make minor modifications to the software. Major modifications or systems enhancements not identified in the original contract could be priced as separate consulting, systems development, or systems integration projects.

Unlike systems management services, consulting, systems development, and systems integration activities were personnel-intensive. Outsourcing providers also offered these services separately from a systems management contract. Traditionally, these discrete services were performed on a fixed-price basis or according to time and materials used. Systems management outsourcing providers faced additional competition when bidding for unbundled services from firms such as American Management Systems in systems development and Booz Allen & Hamilton in consulting. Also, a client often maintained an internal staff to perform these activities after outsourcing its data center.

Clients

Any corporation with an in-house data center was a potential client for outsourcing its systems management activities. Since the early 1960s, thousands of small and medium-sized companies, as well as government agencies, had outsourced their data centers. In the late 1980s several large corporations entered into systems management outsourcing agreements. Because of their greater IT needs, the contracts they entered into were larger and of longer duration than previous contracts. With a value of at least $100 million and a typical duration of 10 years, these contracts were known as *megacontracts* in the industry. The total value of megacontracts had grown from close to zero in 1987 to an estimated value of $8.4 billion in 1991.

While the first commercial megacontracts were signed in the early 1980s, such contracts gained widespread attention with the contract signed by Eastman Kodak in 1989. Kodak outsourced its data processing business to three providers: IBM for its data center operations, Digital Equipment Corporation (DEC) for its telecommunications, and Businessland for maintaining its installed base of personal computers. This contract increased interest in systems management outsourcing among the Fortune 500. Since then, many other large corporations had signed megacontracts (Exhibit 2). One market research firm predicted in 1989 that all Fortune 500 companies would evaluate systems management outsourcing during the 1990s and that 20 percent of them would sign contracts.[1]

Although figures varied by industry, corporations spent up to 4 percent of their revenues on information technology products and services (Exhibit 3). Ideally, the application of IT affected the business performance of the entire organization. If properly applied, IT could be used to enhance the competitive position of the firm by improving the cost structure of the entire firm, improving the quality of the product produced or service performed, and improving the ability to respond to its customers' needs.

---

[1]Yankee Group quoted in *Network World,* July 2, 1990.

EXHIBIT 2 Outsourcing Megacontracts, 1988–1991

End User	Supplier	Estimated Revenue ($m)	Length (years)
1991			
General Dynamics	CSC	$3,000	10
Continental Airlines	EDS	2,100	10
National Car Rental	EDS	500	10
McDonnell Douglas	EDS	n.a.	n.a.
First American Bancshares	Perot	400	10
Continental Bank	IBM, E&Y	400	10
SAAB	EDS	360	10
Signet Bank	EDS	300	10
Zale	IBM	286	10
NCNB	Perot	200	10
United Technologies	IBM	n.a.	n.a.
Supermarkets General	IBM	150	10
FAI Insurance Ltd	PMS	140	10
Comdata	IBM	120	10
Ramada/Howard Johnson's	EDS	100	10
Signetics	EDS	100	10
Robert Plan	Perot	100	10
Greyhound Bus	ACS	80	10
Federal Home Loan Bank S.F.	Systematics	80	n.a.
Total		$8,416	
1990			
First Fidelity	EDS	450	10
Sun Refining/Marketing	Andersen	180	n.a.
Riggs National Bank	IBM	160	10
International Telecharge	ACS	160	10
American Medical International	Perot	115	5
Team Bank	Systematics	100	10
Integra (Union National Bank)	Systematics	100	3
Total		$1,265	
1989			
Eastman Kodak	IBM, DEC, Businessland	500	n.a.
Glendale Fed./Gesco	FIServ	300	n.a.
Great Western Financial	EDS	300	9.5
ICH Insurance	Perot	250	n.a.
Western Union	EDS	250	10
Cummins Engine	EDS	240	10
Meritor Savings Bank	EDS	250	10
Southland	ACS	150	10
Hibernia National Bank	IBM	150	9
First Tennessee National Bank	IBM	150	n.a.
Bank South	IBM	120	10
Columbia Pictures Entertainment	EDS	95	10
Total		$2,755	
1988			
First City Banc	EDS	600	10
Enron	EDS	500	10
Banc One Texas (M Bank)	EDS	275	10
Freeport McMoRan	EDS	200	10
Total		$1,575	

SOURCE: Merrill Lynch, Ledgeway.

EXHIBIT 3 IT Expenditure by Industry, 1988

	Expenditures as Percent of Revenue*	Total Expenditures ($M)
Auto and industrial	3.2	$11,179
Banking and finance	0.6	6,303
Electronics	3.7	7,135
Food and beverage	1.1	1,189
Health care and pharmaceuticals	2.6	1,570
Insurance	1.7	2,545
Metal and metal products	2.2	1,117
Petroleum	1.3	3,670
Process industries	2.1	2,978
Retail	0.8	1,583
Telecommunications	4.0	5,294
Transportation	2.6	1,979

*For banking, assets rather than revenues
SOURCE: Business Research Group

In-house data centers were operated by an MIS department under the leadership of an MIS executive. The MIS executive's responsibilities on a daily basis were to ensure that the computer system was available and responding quickly for online use, that data were processed without error, and that reports were available on time. On a longer-term basis the MIS executive chose software and hardware to support the organization in the future and oversaw any in-house application development. Beginning in the mid-1980s, large corporations often employed a chief information officer (CIO) to oversee the firm's technology strategy, but in smaller firms the MIS executive fulfilled this role. The MIS department was usually treated as a cost center and its costs were allocated as overhead. It normally submitted an annual budget for funds. Special expenditures such as capital equipment purchases or large systems development projects were evaluated separately.

The Systems Management Outsourcing Decision

The decision to outsource a data center was usually made by the chief executive officer (CEO), chief financial officer (CFO), or CIO because it was a business decision rather than a technical one. The decision was complex, with many parameters. Although MIS executives participated in the decision, the relationship between the MIS manager and the provider was sometimes strained because the MIS executive's management of the data center was directly compared to the provider's promised performance. There was less tension for providers who had a strong, preexisting relationship with the MIS executive.

Outsourcing brought two broad categories of benefits to the client. First, cost savings were achieved by consolidating many small data centers of different clients into one, reducing expenditures in overhead, hardware, software, and personnel. Industry analysts estimated that these economies could be reaped up to a data center capacity of about 250 millions of instructions per second (MIPS) in a mainframe environment.[2] Large corporations with efficient operations could reap such economies on their own since their data center capacities exceeded that size. In the past many corporations lacked the experience to run an efficient data center operation, but by the late 1980s most could match the efficiency of an outsourcing provider.

The second source of benefits to the client was the provider's knowledge of IT. Even the very largest corporations could reap these benefits. Because of their size, providers could employ specialists even a large company could not afford. This expertise allowed providers to remain current with rapid changes in technologies and industry practices which would influence clients' investments in IT.

[2]"Consolidating Multiple Data Centers," *I/S Analyzer,* November 1990.

Other criteria were taken into account when deciding whether to outsource. Many executives believed that outsourcing demystified the technical aspects of computing, turning it into a quantifiable business. The strategic importance of the company's IT function affected the decision to outsource. Some firms viewed IT as a core business function and preferred to keep it in-house. Other firms wanted to focus on what they considered to be their core business functions, such as marketing or distribution, and to leave technology decisions to outside experts. Many firms, especially those with severe cash flow constraints, were attracted by the cash infusion, often of several million dollars, that resulted from selling data center assets. In the late 1980s several firms, such as Avon and American Standard, that had to meet interest payments from leveraged buyouts, decided to outsource.

Many potential clients were reluctant to outsource their data center even if they could lower costs or increase performance. Many feared a loss of control from turning over their data center to a third party. Other clients feared the difficulty of reversing an outsourcing contract. Although clients had successfully brought their data center operations back in-house, contracts could be difficult to reverse because the provider had absorbed the client's MIS personnel. Resuming internal operations required rehiring personnel and significant cooperation from the outsourcing provider. Clients also worried that it might be difficult to preserve confidentiality in an outsourcing contract since providers shared personnel across clients. Because of all of these factors, it was essential for a provider to maintain an excellent reputation for being trustworthy.

Some criteria for choosing a provider were common to all potential clients. One important criterion was the provider's reputation for timely and accurate service delivery. Reputations were established through client references or, especially, a preexisting relationship with the provider. Financial stability was also important given the length of outsourcing contracts and the implications if a provider were to lack funds to update old technology or applications or provide ongoing processing services.

Other criteria depended upon the firm's outsourcing needs. Some firms simply wanted a provider to keep their hardware and software running so that their own internal development team could identify and develop new applications. Other firms wanted to work closely with the provider to apply a full range of services in helping them meet their business objectives and highly valued the industry expertise of the provider personnel. These firms tended to be less price-sensitive than those interested in pure data center operations. It was estimated that about half the companies that outsourced viewed it primarily as a way to save money, while others focused more on the provider's service.[3]

Because of significant setup costs, outsourcing tended to be done through multiyear contracts. Although provider practices varied, contracts were usually fixed-price with additional fees based on processing volume, or time and material costs for setup with processing fees based on volume. Service performance parameters specified in the contract typically included terminal response time, online availability, report delivery responsibilities, and backup/recovery requirements. Contracts also clearly specified control and transfer of equipment, space, and personnel.

Market Growth

IT services represented only 18 percent of the $848 billion IT industry in 1990, but was the fastest growing segment. Between 1991 and 1996, the services sector was expected to grow at a rate of 13 percent compared to the industry growth rate of 7 percent.[4]

Worldwide market size estimates for systems management outsourcing varied greatly depending on which services were included, but most analysts agreed it was around $92 billion in 1990.[5] Systems management outsourcing revenues were expected to increase at a rate of 11 percent per year until 1996. This rapid growth was expected for several reasons.

First, MIS directors were facing pressures of tighter budgets and rising user expectations. The historical IT budget increases of 10 percent to 30 percent in the early 1980s had given way to pressure to cut costs. Moreover, many firms were concerned that the large expenditures on IT in the early 1980s had not resulted in substantial productivity gains or increases in market position. Firms wanted to be able to contain and predict their IT costs.

---

[3]"Why Not Farm Out Your Computing," *Fortune*, September 23, 1991.

[4]Based on data by Input Inc. and casewriter estimate.

[5]Based on data by Input Inc. and casewriter estimate. Definition of systems management includes equipment services, processing services, systems operations, and network services.

Second, within MIS departments, systems management outsourcing allowed the staff to focus their energies on developing new applications to improve the company's competitive position rather than on maintaining, or making minor enhancements to, existing applications. On average, 70 to 80 percent of application development personnel in MIS departments were involved in maintenance and enhancement work.[6] Consequently, most MIS departments had an extensive backlog of user requests for new applications.

Third, the increasing complexity of technology and proliferation of standards increased the risk of choosing the wrong technology and the difficulty of staying current with technology. Contracting with an outsourcing provider gave firms access to specialists and state-of-the-art proprietary software. For example, Systematics used its own banking software to run the operations of its client banks.

Suppliers

Outsourcing providers were large users of computing equipment, software, and communications services. For example, EDS was IBM's largest commercial customer for mainframes, and was estimated to purchase about 50 mainframes per year.[7] These large purchases allowed providers to receive discounts not available to other customers. Most independent outsourcing providers used multiple suppliers of hardware to receive the best prices.

The software used by providers was of two kinds. The first consisted of operating systems, database management systems, and communications switching systems which formed a basic platform on which specific applications were run. Software of the first kind was typically licensed from the leading vendors to facilitate compatibility with clients' applications. The second consisted of the applications programs themselves. Applications software was available from multiple software vendors, although functionality differed greatly across packages. Providers also developed their own applications software.

The consolidation of data centers by clients and through systems management outsourcing providers had resulted in a shrinking customer base for software vendors. The licensing fee for a given mainframe capacity was lower than that for equivalent capacity on multiple smaller computers. Many software providers had begun to take a strong stand on the transfer of software licenses in outsourcing contracts. It was believed that some systems management deals were made considerably less attractive because of fees demanded for software license transfers.[8] Several court cases were pending in 1991 involving disputes over these transfers.

No providers were fully vertically integrated in support services. IBM, DEC, and EDS used subcontractors for specific skills when it was more cost-effective in selected locations. EDS, for example, had teamed up with independent providers for hardware support and local network integrators for LAN support services.[9]

Human Resources

Outsourcing providers competed aggressively for a limited pool of highly skilled personnel. In the late 1980s, the demand for qualified new computer personnel exceeded the number of those entering the workforce.

Because it focused exclusively on IT services, an outsourcing provider offered employees better advancement possibilities than clients usually did. Providers also offered employees the opportunity to work with a variety of clients. Although personnel policies varied across firms, providers generally rotated employees through different industry or technical areas during their first few years before having the employee specialize in a technical area or industry area and work for multiple clients applying that specialty.

Training was also critical to ensure that employees were familiar with current technologies and industry trends. Some providers employed an internal development group which developed methodologies and tools which were used across clients and industries.

Marketing

The marketing efforts of outsourcing providers were aimed at identifying and building a relationship with potential clients. Personnel would establish contact with a potential client through trade shows, refer-

---

[6]Chris Disher, of Nolan, Norton & Company, quoted in *I/S Analyzer,* September, 1990.

[7]"Why EDS Loves a Recession," *New York Times,* October 20, 1991.

[8]"Software Licensing and Pricing: The Network Changes the Rules," Yankee Group.

[9]G2 Research report, G2 Research Inc.

rals, or "cold calls." After establishing contact, the salesperson would attempt to build a relationship through consultations about the client's business and technology needs and discussions of the provider's previous work, especially in the potential client's industry. Consequently, previous success stories and client references were critical. Providers often used smaller lead-in projects like a consulting or systems development project to establish a relationship which could lead to a full systems management outsourcing contract.

Proposals could be generated in one of two ways. In some cases the provider took the initiative and wrote the proposal outlining its services and price. In other cases, companies seeking outsourcing first published a request for proposal (RFP), and then the interested providers responded with written proposals.

During the 1980s, several providers, including Andersen Consulting, IBM, and EDS, began nationwide print and media advertising to raise general awareness of their service offerings. However, most marketing was still performed at the industry level.

EXHIBIT 4 Estimated Market Shares of Systems Management Outsourcing Megacontract Providers (1991)

EDS	45%
CSC	23
IBM	13
Andersen	1
Others	18

SOURCE: Casewriter estimates.

Competitors

The market consisted of both full-service and niche outsourcing providers. Full-service providers were large firms with the resources to provide the full range of IT services to the government and large corporations across a variety of industries. Niche providers concentrated on specific industries or services. For example, Policy Management Systems focused on the insurance industry while Systematics served the banking industry. Full-service providers benefited from both expertise within each industry and generic technical expertise which spanned across industries. Niche providers competed based on their extensive expertise in a single industry. The Policy Management Systems' 1989 10-K report stated:

> These [full-service competitors], especially the larger ones, present a significant competitive challenge to the Company's information services business growth, but the Company believes that it can meet this challenge through its knowledge of the insurance industry and its ability to meet the customer's needs.

It was difficult for niche providers to expand into other industries without forming alliances or merging with other providers. Many niche players were forming such alliances with full-service competitors.

Industry analysts focused on the value of megacontracts when determining the relative strength of providers. On an annualized basis the revenues from megacontracts for 1991 were estimated to be $2 billion. Estimates of provider market shares for systems management megacontract revenues varied greatly, but EDS was by far the industry leader with a 45 percent market share (Exhibit 4). However, four other full-service providers that had entered the industry during the last few years, IBM, DEC, Andersen Consulting, and Computer Sciences Corporation (CSC), were increasing their market shares. Approximately 400 niche players comprised the remainder of industry revenues.

The leading competitors in outsourcing are profiled below. Their financial positions are summarized in Exhibit 5.

Computer Sciences Corporation. CSC was founded in 1959 to subcontract programmers to clients on a temporary basis. By the 1980s it had evolved into a full-service provider of IT services. All of CSC's revenues in 1989 came from IT services, the majority from systems integration and development projects. Historically, CSC's revenues had been based on long-term federal government contracts, mainly from the operation of government-owned data centers.

In the late 1980s, CSC decided to pursue the commercial market. It scored a major victory in 1991 when it was awarded a $3 billion outsourcing contract by General Dynamics, the largest contract to that date. The three data centers purchased in the agreement doubled CSC's capacity to service commercial outsourcing contracts. As a result of this contract, CSC's commercial revenues in fiscal year 1992 increased to 41 percent of overall revenues, up from 36 percent the year before.

EXHIBIT 5 Financial Performance of Leading Competitors ($ millions)

	1991	1990	1989	1988	1987	1986	1985	1984	1983	1982
Computer Sciences Corporation										
Sales	$1,738	$1,500	$1,304	$1,152	$1,031	$839	$723	$712	$695	$630
Profit before tax	103	103	84	71	58	43	41	30	33	34
Total assets	1,007	918	715	661	596	468	431	398	354	320
Equity	526	458	389	333	285	214	186	158	139	120
Pretax return on sales (%)	5.9	6.9	6.5	6.2	5.6	5.1	5.7	4.3	4.7	5.3
Return on total assets (%)	6.8	8.0	7.6	6.9	6.1	5.3	6.7	4.9	5.3	5.9
Return on equity (%)	13.2	15.5	14.6	14.1	13.0	12.0	16.1	12.3	13.8	16.1
Electronic Data Systems										
Sales	$7,099	$6,109	$5,467	$4,844	$4,428	$4,366	$3,442	$948	$630	$503
Profit before tax	894	789	680	589	524	464	362	139	101	70
Total assets	5,703	4,565	3,918	3,416	3,107	2,512	1,665	649	406	330
Equity	2,610	2,182	1,764	1,404	1,054	798	531	346	260	205
Pretax return on sales (%)	12.6	12.9	12.4	12.2	11.8	10.6	10.5	14.6	16.0	14.0
Return on total assets (%)	9.6	10.9	11.1	11.2	10.4	10.4	11.4	12.4	14.5	14.2
Return on equity (%)	21.0	22.8	24.7	27.4	30.7	32.7	35.8	23.4	22.6	23.0
International Business Machines										
Sales	$64,792	$69,018	$62,710	$59,681	$55,256	$52,160	$50,056	$45,937	$40,180	$34,364
Profit before tax	121	10,203	6,645	9,033	8,609	8,389	11,619	11,623	9,940	8,222
Total assets	92,473	87,568	77,734	73,037	70,029	63,020	52,634	42,806	37,461	32,541
Equity	37,006	42,832	38,509	39,509	38,263	34,374	31,990	26,489	23,219	19,960
Pretax return on sales (%)	0.2	14.8	10.6	15.1	15.6	16.1	23.2	25.3	24.7	23.9
Return on total assets (%)	−0.6	6.9	4.8	7.5	7.5	7.6	12.5	15.4	14.6	13.5
Return on equity (%)	−1.5	14.8	9.6	14.9	14.5	14.4	22.4	26.5	25.4	23.4
Andersen Consulting* (estimated)										
Sales	$2,260	$1,748	$1,220	$1,199	$749	$546	$344	$282	n/a	n/a
Digital Equipment Corporation										
Sales	$13,911	$12,943	$12,742	$11,475	$9,389	$7,590	$6,686	$5,584	$4,272	$3,881
Profit before tax	(520)	124	1,421	1,741	1,689	857	431	401	411	673
Total assets	11,875	11,655	10,668	10,112	8,407	7,173	6,369	5,593	4,541	4,024
Equity	7,624	8,182	8,036	7,510	6,294	5,728	4,555	3,979	3,541	3,165
Pretax return on sales (%)	−3.7	1.0	11.2	15.2	18.0	11.3	6.4	7.2	9.6	17.3
Return on total assets (%)	−5.2	0.7	10.3	14.1	14.6	9.1	7.5	6.5	6.6	11.2
Return on equity (%)	−7.8	0.9	13.8	18.9	18.9	12	10.5	8.7	8.5	14.3

*Prior to 1990, estimate of data processing revenues for Arthur Andersen & Co.

SOURCE: Annual reports. Datamation for estimate of Andersen Consulting.

CSC's 1991 annual report stated that its goal was to become one of the industry's top three professional services firms. In the same report it outlined its approach to achieving that goal:

> Our extensive experience with systems operations in the federal arena will enable us to gain a larger commercial market share, focusing on vertical industries such as insurance, health care, and financial services where we are well-established providers of systems and services.

To increase its consulting capabilities and contacts with large corporations, CSC had purchased the Index Group, a leading IT consulting firm. Although the Index Group had contacts with many large corporations, it had historically advised MIS departments on improving their internal operations.

CSC's experience in providing IT services to the government provided it with data center operation, project management, and system development skills that were directly transferable to commercial contracts. However, CSC had limited experience in industry practices and identifying the need for and requirements of commercial systems. CSC also was accustomed to bidding for cost-plus government contracts rather than fixed-price commercial contracts.

Andersen Consulting. Arthur Andersen & Co., a Big Six accounting firm, had provided IT services since implementing one of the first commercial computer applications for General Electric in 1954. In October 1988, Arthur Andersen & Co. reorganized, separating its IT service offerings from its tax and audit structure under a separate unit called Andersen Consulting. Andersen Consulting grew dramatically during the 1980s. Its staff grew from 3,600 in 1980 to over 18,000 in 1989 mainly from systems development and integration business.

Although Andersen had provided advice and help to clients in running their data center operations for many years, Andersen did not begin systems management outsourcing until the late 1980s. As of 1991, Andersen had landed only one megacontract but had over 40 smaller contracts. Andersen had its own data centers as well as a worldwide communications network to support outsourcing. Andersen predicted that outsourcing would move from a cost reduction device in the 1980s to a strategic positioning tool in the 1990s provided by value-added service firms, such as Andersen. Andersen stated that its approach to outsourcing was as a business partnership focused on attaining business goals.

Andersen's desire to create an outsourcing business was believed to be motivated by two factors. First, it viewed outsourcing as an attractive business. Second, it found that potential development contracts were being won by providers of the downstream outsourcing services.

Andersen benefited from established relationships with most of the Fortune 500 firms from its audit and consulting experience. Andersen was also considered a leader in IT strategic consulting, providing it with a good understanding of clients' business needs. Some securities and investment analysts believed that firms like Andersen Consulting, with experience in accounting and management consulting, had a better understanding of clients' business than its competitors.[10]

As a partnership, Andersen was more limited in its sources of financing, but in the late 1980s Andersen was raising new capital to finance the hardware and software associated with large systems management contracts. In 1990, Andersen's CEO announced that the company was preparing a credit line of $250 million as a war chest for competing with EDS and IBM for large systems management contracts. It was also reported in 1991 that Andersen had raised more than 5 percent of its current capital through private placements with banks and insurance companies. Andersen was using the funds to support its heavy investment in training and equipment.

It was believed that Andersen was focusing on selected industries and technological environments to increase its share of the outsourcing market. For example, Andersen was targeting clients migrating from a mainframe to a client-server environment and had formed a partnership with Systematics to serve banking clients.

International Business Machines. Founded in the early 1900s, IBM was the largest producer of computers in the world. It sold about 10,000 computer hardware, software, and peripheral products in more than 130 countries.

By the mid-1980s, IBM's superiority in the computer hardware business was being threatened. Advances in semiconductor technology had allowed independent suppliers to produce standardized

---

[10]Stephen McClellan quoted in *Information Week,* April 30, 1990.

computer parts which independent companies could purchase and assemble. This decreased the scale needed to manufacture computers and led to a surge in competition and a significant drop in hardware margins. At the same time competitors began offering so-called open systems, which had operating systems that allowed easier interconnection of different providers' hardware. This was a direct threat to IBM's proprietary systems. Even within its own product line, IBM mainframes were incompatible with its minicomputers. IBM also faced slowing growth in hardware sales, especially mainframes, whose sales were projected to grow at about 2 percent in the early 1990s. Much of this decline in growth was attributable to an increase in processing power in smaller machines which had led to some mainframes being substituted by desktop and minicomputers linked through networks. In order to decrease its reliance on hardware sales, IBM set a goal of generating 50 percent of its revenues from software and services by the year 2000.

On May 15, 1991, IBM announced the formation of a wholly owned subsidiary to handle its outsourcing business, the Integrated Systems Solutions Corporation (ISSC). ISSC inherited some existing outsourcing contracts from its predecessor, the IBM Systems Services Division. The transferring of its outsourcing contracts to a wholly owned subsidiary was done to avoid legal pressure from competing outsourcing providers over an earlier consent decree. These legal challenges had surfaced due to IBM's increasing emphasis on services. In 1956, IBM signed a consent decree not to compete in the service bureau business defined as "the preparation of information and reports for others on a fee basis." The consent decree did allow IBM to compete through an independent subsidiary. Although IBM had limited its range of offerings prior to the formation of ISSC, one market research firm commented that "with the formation of ISSC, concerns about what IBM can or cannot offer have been eliminated."[11]

ISSC's revenues were estimated to be $800 million in 1990.[12] This included systems management contracts as well as disaster/recovery services for 1,000 clients. IBM had signed at least 17 major outsourcing accounts by 1991. IBM also received outsourcing revenues from the Federal Systems Division which included government contracts. In addition, IBM performed significant systems integration work for the government and large commercial customers.

Through ISSC, IBM hoped to shift its revenue base toward software and services in order to increase its margins and take advantage of the faster growth in services revenues. Although IBM was known for its excellent hardware support services (IBM had a representative on-site in most major data centers to assist in running applications on its hardware), it had always been reluctant to explicitly price its services, choosing instead to bundle them with the hardware purchase.

Historically, IBM's contract with a client was usually limited to the MIS department and the running of the data center and did not extend into the user community. In 1989, IBM established an Applications Solutions Division to focus on application and industry-specific solutions in order to establish credibility outside the MIS environment and generate consulting and systems development projects.

ISSC provided the full range of outsourcing activities, including on-site and remote data center operations, consulting, systems development, and systems integration, although it was believed that IBM subcontracted services in some instances. It was believed that the new structure would make IBM more responsive to clients and perhaps give IBM more credibility in presenting itself as vendor-independent.

IBM's applications and systems software revenue increased from 10 percent in 1986 to 14 percent in 1990. However, its service revenue fell from 17 percent to 16 percent during the same time period. The decrease in services revenue was due partially to a decline in hardware-maintenance fees, but was also thought to have resulted from IBM having lowered its prices to compete with other outsourcing firms.

At the same time as the formation of ISSC, IBM had formed a joint venture with Coopers & Lybrand, a Big Six accounting firm, to improve its position in the services business. IBM had also formed a joint venture with AT&T to make its mainframes more compatible with AT&T's networks.

IBM had no direct outsourcing sales force but instead depended on its geographically organized sales force to generate new outsourcing business. Only on potentially large accounts would ISSC

[11]"IBM Subsidizes Outsourcing," Yankee Group, p. 2.

[12]"IBM Spins Off Outsourcing Unit," *Computerworld,* May 20, 1991.

become involved to help the account manager. In the late 1980s IBM began an advertising campaign which emphasized IBM's ability to deliver cost benefits to clients. IBM placed an advertisement in major newspapers with the headline: "The cost crunch. Budgets get cut. Demands don't. If you need help, we have it." The advertisement included an image of a penny.

Digital Equipment Corporation. DEC, also a major computer manufacturer, had pioneered production of the minicomputer. In the late 1980s, DEC, like IBM, suffered from the drop in hardware margins and identified services as a way to supplement its declining hardware margins. The 1991 DEC annual report clearly identified outsourcing as one of DEC's goals:

> Our service organization designs and installs networks, integrates systems, runs complete information shops . . . and provides all the services the customer wants, or needs, after our equipment is shipped. This business is growing and profitable and is key to our success.

In its 1989 annual report DEC claimed to support 8,000 hardware and software products by 800 other manufacturers. DEC had performed significant systems integration work. Systems integration accounted for about 11 percent of DEC's revenues in 1991.

DEC was hiring industry experts to supplement its technical expertise: "If we're asked to help with a banking problem we have former bankers on our staff. If it's a manufacturing problem, we'll assign manufacturing specialists to the job." Many of these specialists had experience in management consulting firms. DEC had organized these industry experts into 17 industry groups, called Application Centers for Technology, in which industry consultants and systems specialists worked together. DEC had also formed an alliance with Deloitte & Touche, a Big Six accounting firm, to jointly pursue the utilities industry. DEC faced the challenge of integrating these newly hired consultants into its sales organization and developing account managers to sell services rather than products.

To date DEC had participated in only one major outsourcing contract, the Kodak deal, in which it managed Kodak's communication systems. Analysts predicted that DEC would target those industries in which it had performed systems integration work and expand into other industries later.

Electronic Data Systems

EDS was the world's largest computer services company with 1991 revenues of $7.1 billion and after-tax earnings of $547 million. About 47 percent of EDS's revenue originated from its parent General Motors (GM), down from 73 percent of total revenue in 1985 (Exhibit 6). EDS employed 70,500 people worldwide and had operations in 30 countries. EDS provided all outsourcing services, including consulting, systems development, systems integration, systems management, and process management. However, systems management and process management services accounted for 70 percent of its revenues (Exhibit 7). EDS planned to continue its rapid growth. Les Alberthal, CEO of EDS, said: "We believe the marketplace we are in can take this company to $25 billion. If you take our base business and grow it at 20 percent compounded annually and keep the GM business flat, you can reach it."[13]

History of EDS

EDS was founded by Ross Perot in 1962 with the belief that computer services would become much more important than computer equipment. In the beginning, EDS operated by renting excess computing capacity on other companies' computers to run its clients' data processing applications. Each night, EDS employees filled the trunks of their cars with forms, tapes, and programs and drove to different locations to process the work. During this period, EDS introduced the long-term fixed-price contract that became one of its standard contracting mechanisms.

In 1963, EDS signed the first outsourcing contract with Frito Lay. This five-year agreement was the forerunner for systems management agreements with predetermined scope of work, delivery time, and pricing. Following the establishment of Medicare and Medicaid in 1965, EDS signed a number of major contracts in the health care industry. In 1965, EDS designed and developed a system to process insurance claims and payments for Texas' Medicare program. Modified versions of this system were then installed in other states in rapid succession.[14]

By 1969 EDS expanded the scope of outsourcing contracts by becoming an independent provider for Blue Shield of Pennsylvania and Blue Shield of Cal-

---

[13]Quoted in *Fortune,* July 10, 1990.

[14]EDS annual report, 1987.

EXHIBIT 6 EDS's Financial Performance, 1986–1991 (in millions except per share data)

	1991	1990	1989	1988	1987	1986
Income Statement						
Revenues:						
Systems and other contracts						
GM and subsidiaries	$3,362.2	3,234.2	2,988.9	2,837.0	2,883.3	3,195.1
Outside customers	3,666.3	2,787.5	2,384.6	1,907.6	1,444.8	1,127.7
Interest and other income	70.5	87.1	93.3	99.5	99.6	43.2
Total revenues	7,099.0	6,108.8	5,466.8	4,844.1	4,427.7	4,366.0
Cost and expenses:						
Cost of revenues	5,415.1	4,639.0	4,168.6	3,749.5	3,452.5	3,463.1
Selling, general, and administrative	761.9	663.0	605.2	500.0	447.0	434.8
Interest	28.3	18.1	12.7	5.2	3.9	4.1
Total cost and expenses	6,205.3	5,320.1	4,786.5	4,254.7	3,903.4	3,902.0
Income before income taxes	893.7	788.7	680.3	589.4	524.3	464.0
Provision for income taxes	330.7	291.8	245.0	205.3	201.2	203.1
Consolidated net income	547.5	496.9	435.3	384.1	323.1	260.9
EPS attributable to GM Class E Stock	1.14	1.04	0.9	0.79	0.66	1.07
Cash dividends per share of GM Class E common stock	0.32	0.28	0.24	0.17	0.13	0.2
Selected Balance Sheet Numbers						
Property and equipment, net	1,551.6	1,197.1	1,083.1	1,076.6	1,106.8	1,125.8
Operating and other assets	2,206.0	1,651.8	1,377.2	1,000.0	422.3	302.6
Current assets	1,945.6	1,716.4	1,457.9	1,339.4	1,577.8	1,083.1
Current liabilities	2,396.7	1,653.9	1,494.5	1,377.2	1,337.7	908.3
Long-term debt	281.9	285.1	326.4	401.9	531.3	633.7
Expenditures on PP&E	673.2	514.8	382.5	300.5	324.8	727.7
Stockholder's equity	2,610.3	2,181.8	1,763.6	1,403.9	1,053.5	798.3
Total assets	5,703.2	4,565.3	3,918.2	3,416.0	3,106.9	2,511.5

Note: In 1991, EDS took a cumulative accounting adjustment of $15.5 million.

SOURCE: EDS annual report.

ifornia (BSC). EDS contracted with BSC to process claims, monitor membership, and perform underwriting, actuarial, and administrative services. This was the first contract in which EDS had assumed responsibility for running the client's entire data center as well as business applications. In this case, EDS broadened its pricing scheme from a fixed charge to charging BSC a fee per claim processed. EDS initially assumed BSC's existing applications but later developed and installed a new system which automated many of the pricing, benefit, and payment functions. The system was improved several times in subsequent years to add functionality. In 1987, EDS consolidated BSC's processing with that of Blue Cross and Blue Shield of Arizona. In 1991, the BSC contract was further extended to the year 2001.

In 1968, EDS went public with annual revenues of $7.7 million and 303 employees. In the ensuing years, EDS expanded its computing facilities through the creation of regional data centers which it called Information Processing Centers (IPCs). These IPCs represented the consolidation of computing facilities to serve multiple clients in a region. In 1982, EDS signed the largest systems integration contract ever awarded, a $650 million contract with the U.S. Army.[15] In 1984, GM acquired EDS for $2.6 billion. As a result of the acquisition, EDS's revenues increased from $1 billion to $3.4 billion overnight. Over the next 18 months EDS's workforce grew threefold from 14,000 to 40,000. The merger received significant media attention partly because of the merger of two markedly different corporate cultures.

A majority of EDS contracts with GM were covered by fixed-price, multiyear agreements.

[15]EDS financial data.

EXHIBIT 7 EDS's Revenues by Industry and Service Line

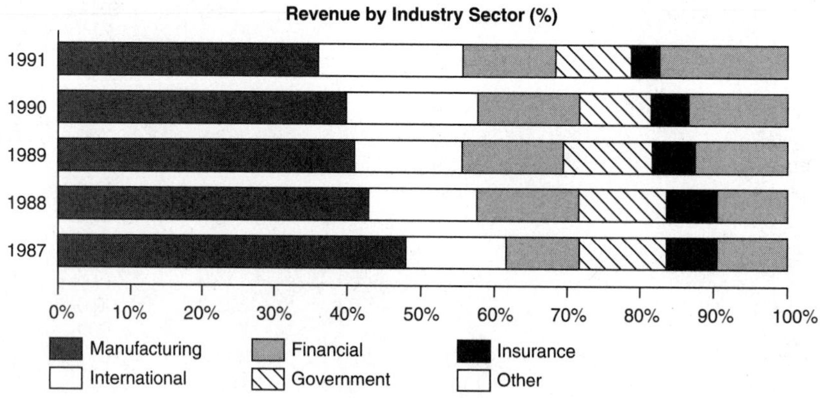

EDS Revenues by Service ($ in millions)

	GM Revenue	Percent of Total GM	Base Revenue	Percent of Total Base	Total Revenue	Percent of Total
1990						
Consulting	$ 90.50	3%	$ 69.20	3%	$ 159.70	3%
Systems development	489.00	15	240.30	9	729.30	12
Systems integration	362.40	11	524.50	19	886.90	15
Systems and process management	2,290.60	71	1,954.90	70	4,245.50	71
Total operating revenue	3,232.50	100	2,788.90	100	6,021.40	100
1991						
Consulting	$ 94.10	3%	$ 106.30	3%	$ 200.40	3%
Systems development	507.70	15	339.10	9	846.80	12
Systems integration	376.50	11	648.00	18	1,024.50	15
Systems and process management	2,383.70	71	2,572.70	70	4,956.40	71
Total operating revenue	3,362.00	100	3,666.10	100	7,028.10	100

SOURCE: EDS.

Although profit margins vary, these contracts, all initially on a cost-plus basis, have been estimated by analysts to carry pre-tax profits between 10 and 12 percent, a few points lower than those on EDS's other business.[16]

In the late 1980s EDS began to sign megacontracts that differed from earlier contracts in size, duration, and the use of new financial engineering techniques. Under some of these contracts EDS would pay money up front to buy the client's computing equipment and hire the client's data processing staff. In a few cases EDS also purchased equity in the client's company. Many of these approaches were quickly adopted by other players in the industry.

EDS and its subsidiaries began signing megacontracts outside the government arena in the early 1980s. One of the first contracts was with Blue Cross and Blue Shield United of Wisconsin. In 1988, EDS won megacontracts with an estimated value of $1.6 billion.[17] One of the most significant contracts was with Enron Corporation, the largest natural gas company in the United States.[18] EDS signed a 10-year contract worth an estimated $500 million to manage Enron's computer and communications facilities.[19]

[16]Stephen McClellan quoted in *Business Week*, December 23, 1991.

[17]"Outsourcing Tidal Wave," Stephen McClellan, Merrill Lynch.

[18]"EDS," The Ledgeway Group.

[19]"Outsourcing Tidal Wave," Stephen McClellan, Merrill Lynch.

EDS paid $6 million for Enron's computers, software, and data transmission network and hired its 550 information services employees at comparable wages and benefits.[20]

Starting in 1988, EDS undertook a number of acquisitions of data processing companies. Analysts believed that these acquisitions were designed to acquire expertise and clients. In 1991, EDS acquired SD-Scicon PLC, a British computer services firm, for $266 million in a takeover bid. SD-Scicon PLC, along with its French subsidiary GFI, was one of the largest European computer services companies. That same year, EDS purchased McDonnell Douglas Systems Integration (MDSI) for $199 million.[21] MDSI provided EDS with additional expertise in aerospace and defense manufacturing, over 600 new clients such as General Electric and Pratt & Whitney, and the leading CAD/CAM product. Together, these businesses were believed to have added $700 million to EDS's 1991 revenues.[22]

Products and Services

EDS was a full-service provider of information services. Exhibit 8 illustrates the range of EDS's services. However, until 1990, consulting services were not marketed separately from systems management and process management services.

EDS's systems management services included data center operations and communication services. EDS provided these services by managing the company's facilities or providing the services from its network of IPCs. EDS's systems management contracts frequently included significant systems development and integration functions as well.

These contracts could evolve in one of several ways. One common path involved EDS signing a systems management contract for running the company's data center with the company's existing applications. EDS would modify the existing application or transfer the applications to its own proprietary systems to provide enhanced performance and functionality. Another method included beginning with an initial systems integration or systems development contract. Under this scenario EDS could contract to develop a new application for a client or combine existing applications with those developed by EDS and third-party providers into an integrated system. Having completed the systems integration part, EDS could be assigned to run and maintain the applications for the client in a systems management contract. In some industries EDS developed a set of proprietary software applications in collaboration with a client, with the understanding that these applications would be used to serve other outsourcing clients in that industry.[23] Analysts believed that EDS had lower costs than its competitors.[24]

Although EDS began to market stand-alone consulting projects in 1990, many were part of a systems management or development contract. EDS had developed a methodology and computerized tools which it applied to consulting projects. Analysts did not expect personnel-intensive activities like consulting or systems development to become a major source of revenue for EDS in the future.[25] However, EDS considered these activities important for new business development.

Process management involved performing a business function rather than a purely technical function. Performance measures for process management services were usually business-based rather than technically based. An example of process management was Cadillac Roadside Service initiated in 1988 by GM. Under this program, Cadillac owners could call a 24-hour telephone service for travel assistance or help with an emergency. The telephone advisors were all employees of EDS Customer Service Technologies, a group that developed and supported customer service, marketing, and sales operations for clients. The customer service unit included nearly 1,000 employees who worked in a range of industries such as manufacturing, energy and chemicals, transportation, and retail.[26]

Most of EDS's services were offered on a fixed-price or per-transaction basis. However, since 1990 EDS had increased its emphasis on value-based (incentive-based) contracts in which EDS made part of its payment contingent on the value created for the client. Value was typically interpreted as an improvement in business performance measured by criteria such as increased profitability, reduced business costs, or improved time to market. Only a few value-based contracts (also known as incentive-based contracts) had been signed.

[20] *Fortune,* September 23, 1991.

[21] EDS annual report, 1991.

[22] Merrill Lynch investor report, September 3, 1991.

[23] EDS annual report, 1989, pp. 4–5.

[24] *New York Times,* October 20, 1991.

[25] "EDS," The Ledgeway Group, p. 10.

[26] "Roadside Service Keeps GM Customers in the Fast Lane," EDS Success Stories series.

EXHIBIT 8 The EDS Business Integration Continuum

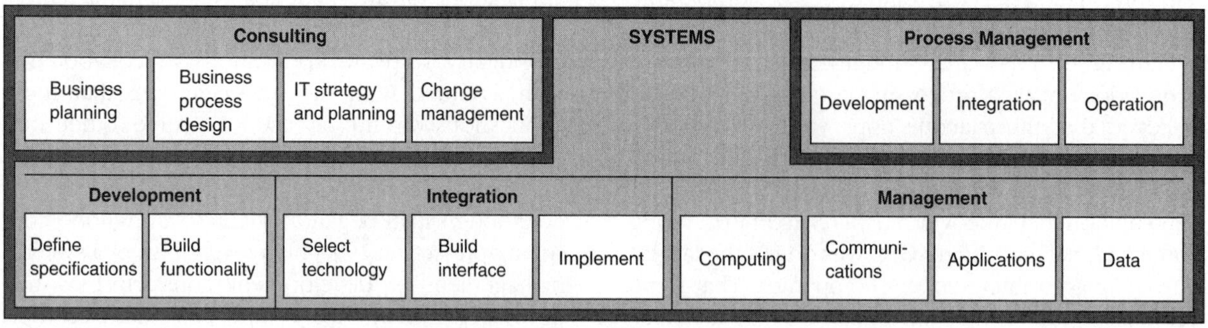

Consulting				SYSTEMS	Process Management		
Business planning	Business process design	IT strategy and planning	Change management		Development	Integration	Operation

Development		Integration			Management			
Define specifications	Build functionality	Select technology	Build interface	Implement	Computing	Communi-cations	Applications	Data

A well-publicized example of a value-based contract was a contract with the Chicago Bureau of Parking Enforcement in 1990 to automate ticket issuance and collection of fines. The City of Chicago had a backlog of 19 million parking tickets representing $420 million in uncollected fines. EDS designed a new system in which parking enforcement aides used hand-held computers to transmit the data directly to EDS computers and print the ticket on the scene. According to news reports EDS won this contract over IBM, Unisys, and Lockheed because of its ability to assemble the most suitable hardware and software providers and to deliver the product on time.[27] The new system significantly reduced lost tickets by printing them on adhesive paper which would not blow away and eliminated a substantial data-entry backlog by eliminating the need to manually enter ticket data in the computer. After implementing the system, ticket collection increased from 10 percent of tickets issued to 65 percent in less than 18 months.[28] EDS's payment was estimated to consist of a base charge of $40 million and a percentage of the face value of delinquent tickets collected under the new system.[29]

Organizational Structure

In 1979, EDS was organized in three industry groups: Finance and Insurance, Commercial, and Government.[30] This broad industry grouping was maintained and refined in the ensuing years. In 1989, EDS reorganized itself into 38 strategic business units (SBUs) and 49 strategic support units (SSUs) (Exhibit 9). The SBUs were aligned with industries, while the SSUs provided cross-industry support services. Under this structure each SBU was accountable for its own strategy and profits.[31] The SSUs provided technical support to the SBUs in such areas as telecommunications services, IPC operations, technical products, and research and development. The SBU presidents reported to the Leadership Council, the highest management organization in the company. The Leadership Council spent 70 percent of its time developing corporate strategy and the remaining time on the oversight of specific SBUs.[32]

Technical Infrastructure

In the last three decades, EDS had built a vast and sophisticated technical infrastructure consisting of 18 IPCs connected by a global communications network. The IPCs were large computer data centers with computing capacities ranging from 136 MIPs to a combined capacity of multiple IPCs in Plano, Texas, of 2,267 MIPS. The company's total computing capacity exceeded 260,000 MIPS, with 87 percent represented by desktop computers. IPCs were connected worldwide by EDSNET, EDS's communications network. EDSNET was one of the world's largest private digital communications networks with integrated voice, data, and video capabilities. The Information Management Center (IMC), located in Plano, Texas, was the hub for EDSNET, controlling more than 8 million long-distance phone calls and 284 million data transactions worldwide each month (Exhibit 10). The

[27]"EDS Win Tied to Partners," *Computer Systems News,* October 1, 1990.

[28]*Business Week,* December 23, 1991 and EDS.

[29]"Crossing State Lines," *Computer Systems News,* November 26, 1990.

[30]EDS organizational data.

[31]*Business Week,* December 23, 1991.

[32]"EDS," The Ledgeway Group.

EXHIBIT 9 EDS Organization Structure

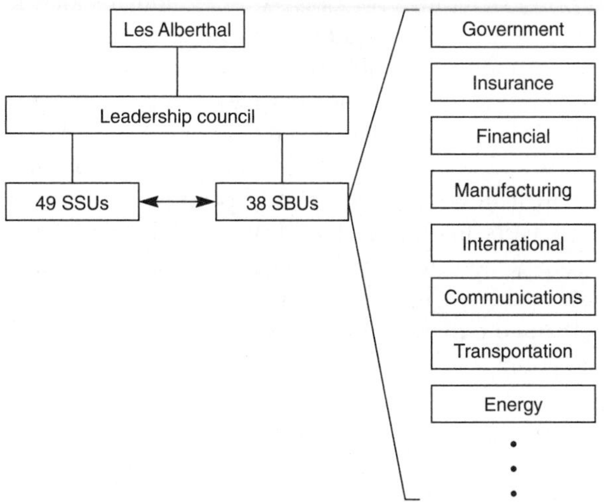

EXHIBIT 10 EDS Information Management Center

EDS' futuristic Information Management Center in Plano, Texas, serves as the network command site for managing the company's global communications in more than 30 countries.

IMC used artificial intelligence tools to monitor network performance continuously. The IMC was equipped with tight security, sophisticated environmental controls, and advanced disaster recovery systems. In addition to IPCs, EDS had four print centers around the country employing over 500 professionals trained in various printing technologies.[33]

Sales and Marketing

Each SBU was responsible for its own marketing and sales activities, including planning, promotion, and research. The sales function was performed by each SBU sales staff, which sold EDS services to over 7,000 clients worldwide. Whenever possible, EDS directed its sales efforts at the CEO, CFO, or CIO of the client company.

The sales process was usually complicated and lengthy and involved developing a good understanding of the client's business needs as well as their technical infrastructure. The account manager who would serve the client was often included in this process to provide additional expertise or provide for continuity if a contract were signed. A crucial task performed by the sales staff was to assess EDS's risk in signing a fixed-price, multiyear contract. After a contract was signed account managers were physically located on the premises of the clients that they served. When necessary they would bring in technical and industry experts from within EDS. The account manager also had responsibility for new business development. Most account managers were technical people promoted from within EDS. In 1985, EDS instituted a new program to recruit personnel exclusively for sales positions, especially individuals with previous selling experience. New recruits attended a nine-month sales development program in selling IT services.

In 1990, EDS created a corporate marketing department. Previously some of these functions had been performed informally by EDS senior managers. Part of corporate marketing's responsibility was to develop a cohesive marketing strategy and corporate message. The corporate marketing department had developed a message that EDS provided value through outsourcing. The message was designed to shift the focus from outsourcing as a means of reducing IT costs, which represented 1 to 2 percent of a firm's costs, to IT's potential for creating business value for the company. Since its inception, the corporate marketing department had spent considerable time in disseminating this message to industry analysts externally and to EDS staff.

Historically, EDS had maintained a low profile in the media. In 1989, EDS hired a market research firm to survey its reputation in the market. Les Alberthal reported on the study results: "The good news came back that we didn't have a bad image. The bad news was that we didn't have much of an image at all."[34]

---

[33]Ibid.

[34]"Sharper Image: EDS in the '90s," *Computerworld,* October 1, 1990.

In 1991, EDS initiated an advertising campaign in leading business publications and on television. The campaign was intended to communicate EDS's ability to help its clients take advantage of change. In 1992, the second phase of the campaign was launched, describing client success stories which demonstrated how EDS helped clients compete more effectively (Exhibit 11).[35]

Human Resources

EDS typically acquired people through recruiting and by assimilating client staff after a systems management contract. Entry-level technical people were trained internally in a three-year Systems Engineering Development (SED) program. Many EDS managers, including the CEO, were graduates of the company's SED program. Overall, EDS spent over $150 million annually on employee training.

On average, EDS officers had spent an average of 17 years with the company and more than a third had been with the company throughout their entire careers.[36] EDS typically promoted its senior managers internally. To advance, members of the management team were required to have worked in multiple industries and internationally and obtained experience in internal operations and staff positions.

[35]EDS organizational data.

[36]EDS annual report, 1987.

EXHIBIT 11 EDS Advertisement

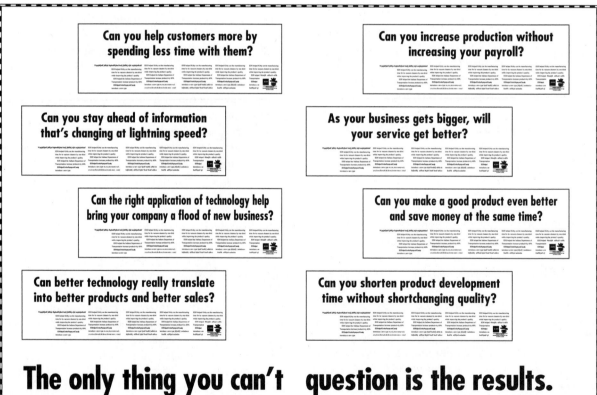

Can you help customers more by spending less time with them?

Can you increase production without increasing your payroll?

Can you stay ahead of information that's changing at lightning speed?

As your business gets bigger, will your service get better?

Can the right application of technology help bring your company a flood of new business?

Can you make a good product even better and save money at the same time?

Can better technology really translate into better products and better sales?

Can you shorten product development time without shortchanging quality?

The only thing you can't question is the results.

EDS helped Kirby cut the manufacturing time for its vacuum cleaners by one-third while improving the product's quality.

EDS helped the Indiana Department of Transportation increase productivity 60%.

EDS helped Omaha Property and Casualty introduce a new type of insurance months ahead of its competitors. The new insurance quickly turned into a $75 million business.

EDS helped Neodata triple its size and become a leader in direct marketing services.

In case after cash, for companies large and small all around the world. EDS has demonstrated how information technology can contribute to a company's success in dozens of measurable ways.

Increasing productivity. Boosting quality. Controlling costs. Improving the bottom line. Increasing speed to market. Delivering the kind of results that give EDS customers a distinct competitive advantage. EDS is the world leader in applying information technology. To find out how we could help you, contact Barry W. Sullivan, EDS, 7171 Forest Lane, N38, Dallas, TX 75230. Or call (214) 490-2000, extension 238.

EDS

Barcelona '92

OFFICIAL RESULTS INFORMATION SYSTEMS OF THE OLYMPIC GAMES

Purchasing

EDS was the largest commercial buyer of computing equipment in the United States and IBM's largest commercial purchaser of mainframe computers. EDS also bought about $1 billion of PC and network hardware for itself and its clients from over 6,000 providers.[37] For large projects, EDS was usually designated the project manager and would use as many as 100 subcontractors.[38] In 1989, EDS, in partnership with Hitachi Ltd., purchased a 20 percent stake in National Advanced Systems Corporation, a seller of IBM-compatible mainframes. The company was renamed Hitachi Data Systems (HDS). According to press reports, EDS expected to enhance its ability to acquire compatible products from multiple vendors and to influence the direction of future products from its vendors.

Future Strategy

In charting their strategy for the 1990s, EDS senior managers were acutely aware that the industry that they had helped pioneer in the 1960s had changed radically in the last three decades. To achieve its growth objectives, EDS would have to consider the rapid advances in IT, the changes in clients' outsourcing needs, and the marked increase in the number of competitors.

Reading II–3
Taking Technology to Market

David Ford and Chris Ryan

Corporate management of technology requires careful planning of the relationships among a company's technologies, its markets, and its development activities. It requires coordination of R&D activities to ensure an optimum research level—depending on a company's available resources, competitive pressures, and market requirements. And it requires systematic linkage between a company's product and process technologies: the products developed must also be produced efficiently.

Current management wisdom says that a company invests its skills and resources in developing products or services that are of value to its customers. However, we argue that to maximize the rate of return on its technology investment, a company must plan for the fullest market exploitation of all its technologies. These technologies may, but need not necessarily, be incorporated into that company's own products or services. In fact, the growth of low-cost Third World producers will make it increasingly difficult for Western companies to exploit fully their technologies through their own production alone.

Thus, a company's marketing strategy may—and probably should—provide for the sale of technologies for a lump sum or a royalty. (By *sale,* we mean either the direct sale of a technology or the sale of a license to use it.)

The marketing literature, however, provides little help for the manager who wishes to exploit fully his or her company's technologies. Many critical questions remain unanswered, among them:

- What problems are involved in selling a technology?
- Is a company that sells a technology giving away its "seed corn" and thus prejudicing its future?
- How, to whom, and when should a technology be sold?
- What is the relationship between the sale of a technology and the sale of a product based on that technology?

In this article, we draw on our own research to examine these important questions within the conceptual framework of the technology life cycle (TLC), which traces the evolution of a technology from the idea stage through development to exploitation by direct sale. In particular, we examine the relationships between product and technology sales and describe the important choices and strategies open to management throughout the TLC. Specifically, we examine the value of shifting from managing a product portfolio to managing a portfolio of technologies. We also consider the impact of the TLC positions of technologies in the portfolio and the significance of a company's level of dependence on individual technologies.

---

[37] *New York Times* for number of mainframes; *PC Week* for number of PCs and vendors.

[38] "EDS," The Ledgeway Group.

Reprinted by permission of *Harvard Business Review,* March–April 1981, vol. 59, no 2.

Why Sell Technologies?

Let us look at some of the reasons that even a successful company cannot fully exploit its technologies through product sales alone:

1. The ever-increasing costs and risks of R&D, especially of basic research, mean that companies must be certain to get the most out of the technologies they develop—including those that do not have immediate relevance to their own lines of business. For example, General Electric (GE) in the United States developed a microorganism that destroys spilled oil by digesting it. However, after winning a well-publicized patent case in the U.S. Supreme Court, GE is now offering this technology for sale because it does not fit into the company's major lines of business.

2. Some technologies may not fit into a company's overall strategy. Their application may be in markets that are too small or undesirable, or a company may have ethical objections to their use. Technologies may even cease to fit with a corporate strategy after they have been in use for some time. For example, GE sold off its mature Fluidics technology (which uses pressure changes in gas streams for measurement purposes and has wide application in textiles and metalworking) because it no longer fitted the company's major strengths or strategy.

3. Producers of products based on new technologies frequently rely on patents as a protection against competitive pressures, but patent rights offer only limited protection. After all, most technology can be copied by other producers, given time. These producers have cost advantages in not having to amortize the high R&D costs incurred by the originator. And Third World producers, in particular, have the benefits of lower labor costs. The recent battle between Eastman Kodak and Polaroid over instant-picture technology is an extreme case of heavy reliance on patents that were unable to prevent competitive entry into a market.

4. Similarly, a company may refuse to sell a technology to an overseas producer because it fears competition at home or in other markets. If, however, a competitor agrees to sell that technology, then the first company will face the same competition without any compensating royalty payments or any control over the technology's diffusion.

5. A company may develop a new technology and then, because of financial woes or restrictions on its own production capabilities, may not be able to exploit it fully in the market. Sinclair Radionics, a small British company in the consumer electronics industry, claims to have made a breakthrough in the technology of flat-screen color TVs. The screens, measuring several feet in length and width and three-quarters of an inch in thickness, would render obsolete hundreds of millions of dollars of investment in conventional cathode-ray tube plants. The first company to succeed in producing them at a competitive cost would have a decisive advantage in a market worth more than $20 billion a year. But Sinclair's past marketing problems have made it impossible for the company to find further risk capital. Thus, it has sought joint venture arrangements with large multinational electronics companies as a way of combining resources.

6. A company may not be able to capture through its own production all the world markets for a given technology. For one thing, sophisticated import restrictions on direct sales of manufactured products are common in Third World countries. For example, American Motors—which produces jeeps through subsidiaries in South Korea, India, and Australia and through license agreements in the Philippines, Pakistan, Sri Lanka, Thailand, and Bangladesh—is trying to penetrate the Chinese market. It is doing this through a license arrangement with the Beijing Automotive Industrial Corporation. Beijing has produced a line of four-wheel drive vehicles since 1964 and now wants to acquire the technology to produce certain jeep models in an existing plant.

7. Finally, a company may be restricted in its direct exploitation of technology by antitrust legislation. One well-documented example is the Federal Trade Commission's complaint against Xerox. The FTC charged Xerox with using its patent position to acquire a complete monopoly over the paper copier market. The proceedings were terminated in 1975 when the court entered a consent decree under which Xerox offered its competitors nonexclusive licenses on a number of its patents at either no royalty or a minimal royalty.

The Technology Life Cycle

Given these restrictions on the direct embodiment of technology in products, a company that wants to get the most out of its technology must plan carefully to realize the full market value of that technology at all stages of its TLC evolution.

EXHIBIT 1 The Technology Life Cycle

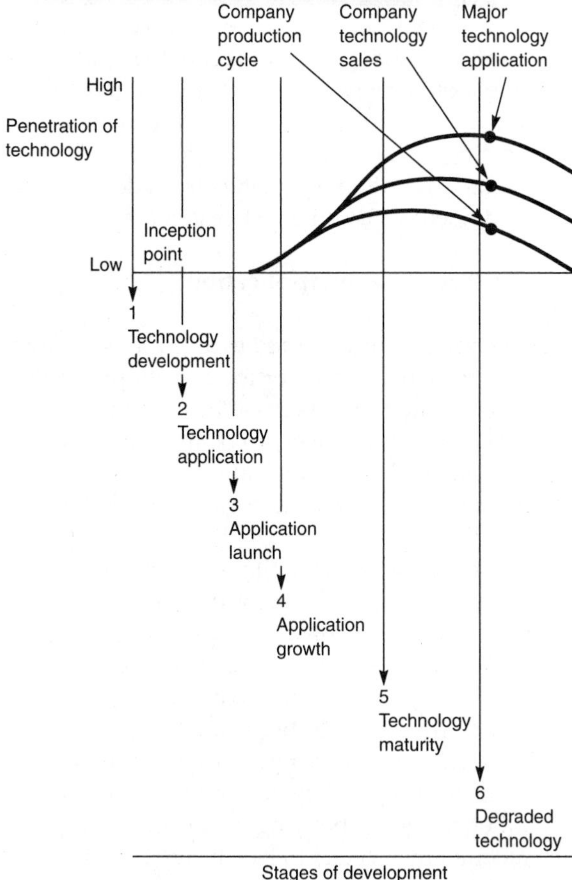

In developing the concept of the TLC from the more familiar notion of the product life cycle,[1] we examined technology development, application, and degradation in such diverse industries as electronics components, consumer electronics, automobiles, shoe manufacturing, construction, mining equipment, and air conditioning.

Exhibit 1 shows the complete TLC for a major technology application. It is equivalent to the product life cycle for an entire industry for a generic product. Included are the proportion of the total use of the technology accounted for by the originator's technology sales and the product or, more accurately, the *production* life cycle of the original manufacturer.

[1]Theodore Levitt, "Exploit the Product Life Cycle," *Harvard Business Review,* November–December 1965, p. 81. See also Rolando Polli and Victor Cook, "Validity of the Product Life Cycle," *The Journal of Business* 42, no. 4 (October 1969), p. 385.

We now turn to the particular issues in marketing and selling a technology that face an originating company in each of the stages of the TLC.

Stage 1: Technology Development

This stage begins long before any production, when research indicates a potentially valuable technology. The major issue the company faces here is whether further development of the technology should take place. Normally, development continues if:

- The technology has an obvious application in a readily identifiable market that fits with the company's overall strategy.
- The company has the financial resources to develop the technology, and the technology is compatible with that company's production and marketing skills.
- The projected rate of return on development is favorable when compared with alternative investments.

The situation is often less clear-cut. The technology may have several potential—but unclear and possibly unrelated—applications. Say a pharmaceutical company were to make a breakthrough in the technology surrounding the complex group of chemicals known as prostaglandins, which have wide applications in medicine, agriculture, and bioengineering. Early on, it might not be clear which application had the most potential or was most capable of realization. And even if the best application were readily identifiable, it might not match the company's strategy or resources.

Under these circumstances, the company would face more complex questions:

- Should it find a partner with whom to develop the technology further, especially if related technologies or additional financial resources were required?
- Should it try to sell the technology if it did not have immediate application within present markets or strategy?

Technology sales at GE

GE in the United States has formalized the latter approach by packaging for sale technologies that are too small or that lie outside its areas of interest. Since 1968, it has sold surplus technologies through a technology marketing operation, which is staffed by five technically trained people with experience in business planning, product sales, product planning, or market research, as well as by a licensing counsel. In each case, the technology marketing operation, after being approached by the operating division involved, seeks potential buyers on the basis of the data file that it maintains on known customer needs, which it cross-references with GE technologies available for sale.

This operation is also responsible for *Selected Business Ventures,* a monthly publication based on potentially useful and salable technologies. Ninety-eight percent of the ideas in it do not emanate from GE but are collected by it for the 400 to 600 companies that subscribe to the publication. In addition, the unit updates and sells to subscribers technical manuals, such as those on heat transfer and fluid flow, developed by the company. It does not, however, involve itself in major licensing decisions, which remain the responsibility of the individual product divisions.

Benefits of hanging on

Even if a company wished to sell a technology this early in the TLC, it might have difficulty doing so; potential applications or the costs of developing marketable applications might be too uncertain. There is, however, an alternative at this stage that companies frequently ignore: their technology might be marketable but not in its present form. If developed further and incorporated into a product, it might then be salable to other companies. Frequently, technologies are ditched when they do not immediately fit into a company's product strategy, despite the fact that further development might lead to a marketable technology for someone else. Of course, this alternative also preserves a company's own option to produce products based on the technology.

Importance of staffing

Companies face still another major issue in this early stage of the TLC: they must have staff who are as sophisticated in the marketing of technologies as in the marketing of products. Unfortunately, this is rarely the case.

The people who make decisions early on about a technology's future are frequently nonmarketing staff. Decisions to kill development of a technology often take place before a company's marketing staff are involved. On the other hand, when marketers are involved, they will more likely see the future of a technology solely in terms of its translation into a company's own products. They are often unable either to think about selling a technology or to analyze the potential market for a technology. More important, the market for a new technology may lie among a company's product competitors, and marketing staff may often have difficulty in dealing with these competitors as potential customers.

Stage 2: Technology Application

After a company has decided to apply a technology to a new product—whether for its own production or for production by others—it incurs its first major costs. These costs are likely to be the primary factor in the company's decision either to continue with development or to sell the technology during this stage.

Few stockholders of a public corporation will tamely allow the development of technologies that even at the outset involve both high costs and high risks.[2] For instance, the Pilkington Company's successful development of the float glass process was brought to fruition only because of the support of the privately held company's board and because of the determination of the entrepreneur involved.

Further, when embodying technology in a product, a company is likely to face heavy costs in other areas—for example, in developing associated process and product technologies. The company may find it necessary to buy into these associated technologies either by licensing or on a risk-bearing basis. Perhaps the largest recent example is the design for the European A300 Airbus, whose initial success led to the production consortium that included such companies as British Aerospace.

At this stage of the TLC, regardless of the high costs involved or the possibility of buying into related technologies, a company must not base its development decisions on the projected returns from product sales alone. Instead, it should consider potential returns from the technology as a whole—including product sales, license revenues, and perhaps turnkey deals.

Burroughs, for example, has put its computer technology to work in a network that allows some

---

[2]See L. Nabseth and G. F. Ray, *The Diffusion of New Industrial Processes* (Cambridge, England: Cambridge University Press, 1974), p. 200.

700 of the world's largest banks to make transactions anywhere in the world in a matter of seconds. The banks run the network as a nonprofit organization, but it is staffed by Burroughs' people using Burroughs' equipment. A similar computer system, Ethernet, is being launched by Xerox in conjunction with Digital Equipment and Intel. This system allows participating companies to set up total communications networks within single buildings or closely built clusters of buildings. The three companies have made a special point of allowing other manufacturers to license their network system—in this case, as a way of encouraging use of their protocols and equipment.

Sell or license?

Possible applications of a technology become clearer and financing is more likely to be forthcoming when the technology has progressed beyond the idea stage to the point of practical demonstration. Similarly, potential licensees are likely to become more interested in a technology after it has been brought to the prototype or preproduction stage.

Nevertheless, decisions on the sale of technology at the end of stage 2 are primarily determined by the development costs incurred and by the projected initial revenues from licenses or product sales or both.

Dolby Laboratories provides an example of the problems created by high development costs and the need to ensure an adequate return. Ray Dolby initially saw his company as a research laboratory that would sell its noise reduction technology for tape equipment to the professional electronics industry. He wished to sell to this market first to gain a quality reputation among recording engineers. But, having invested $25,000 of personal savings and loans from friends, he quickly found that to survive he needed the income which could come only from product sales. Thus, he decided to make and sell noise reduction units initially for the professional music recording market.

The professional market in the electronics field is small, and any attempt to exploit it through the licensing of technology would not have provided sufficient revenue to justify Dolby's initial investment. On the other hand, the smallness of the market made it possible for a new company such as Dolby's to exploit the technology without major investment capital and without attracting overwhelming competition from large rivals. Once Dolby established the reputation of his technology, he had a strong marketing position when he later introduced the technology into the mass market for consumer tape-recording equipment.

Unfortunately, there are no universally applicable rules of thumb for making sound decisions about the sale or production of a technology at this stage. Too many variables enter into the equation: initial development costs, a company's cash position, its other development activities and their requirements, the technology's potential market, the possibilities of market segmentation, and—perhaps most important—the extent to which a technology is perceived as *essential* to a company's present or future activities.

Stage 3: Application Launch

The application launch stage of the TLC corresponds to the first, or "performance maximizing," phase of Abernathy and Utterback,[3] during which a company is likely to be developing its technology further—either through product modification or through application to different or perhaps wider product areas. But if a technology has been developed to the point of product launch without the involvement of potential buyers, decisions on its exploitation become more complex. The originating company, having faced both the high costs of development and of product launch, now confronts a number of issues that work *against* its recovery of some of those costs through license arrangements.

First, there may not be enough companies around with the skill to employ the new technology properly. The hasty sale of licenses could easily damage the reputation of the technology. This factor weighed heavily, for example, in the considerations of the Pilkington Company in exploiting the technology for glass-reinforced concrete.

Pilkington bought the license for this technology from the British Building Research Council with the aim of selling it to individual construction companies. Thus, Pilkington served as middleman between a research-oriented development company and the market because of its experience in license deals and its understanding of glass technology. However, the license process proved very lengthy, for Pilkington found it necessary to restrict the number of buyers by rigorous company appraisal and

---

[3]William J. Abernathy and J. M. Utterback, "A Dynamic Model of Process and Product Innovation," *Omega* 3, no. 6 (1975), p. 639.

product inspection in order to maintain high product quality.

Sale of a technology during stage 3 may also be delayed by the long lead times involved in customer purchase of a relatively unproved technology. The purchase may depend on government backing for the buyer, which in turn may depend on a country's industrial policy. In addition, the sale of a technology may be held up or prevented by government restrictions on the seller, especially where the technology has strategic or military implications—as, for example, in such fields as computer networks, high-energy lasers, wide-bodied aircraft, and diffusion bonding. In the United States, the Technology Transfer Ban Act, updated in 1978, prohibits the sale to any communist country—or to any country that fails to impose restrictions on such a sale—of any significant or critical technology or product with a potential military or crime control application.

Consider, as well, how a sale of technology affects those technologists who are responsible for development within the purchasing company. They may see a purchase as an indication of failure and therefore may try to delay the decision to buy a technology while pressing for funds to develop their own. The "not invented here" syndrome is rife, although it may be more prevalent in some countries than in others. In Japan, for example, the ratio of license revenues to license payments has remained fairly constant at around 1 to 8; in West Germany, the ratio is 1 to 2.5. By contrast, the ratio in the United Kingdom is approximately 1 to 1; in the United States, 10 to 1.

The final market factor working against technology sales at this stage is that customer purchase usually requires major changes in the purchaser's way of doing things. A company may be unwilling to undertake these changes until a technology is proved through more extensive product application or until its own technology is seen to be clearly inadequate.

On the other hand, the originating company itself may now wish to delay the sale of a technology, thinking that its potential value will increase with greater market acceptance. The company may also feel the need to recoup its development costs while taking advantage of the opportunity to skim the market as a monopoly supplier of a possible major technology. Further, it may wish to control the use of the technology in order to use its own production facilities to capacity.

The Swedish ASEA Company, for instance, provides electric locomotives for U.S. railroads. Although the technology involved in electric locomotive construction is relatively well known, the ASEA locomotives have a sophisticated electronic control system that makes them especially attractive to American railroads. Hence, the electric locomotive as a product is literally the vehicle for a technology sale. By tying the technology sale to its own product, ASEA hopes to maximize its revenues at this stage of the TLC.

Stage 4: Application Growth

Until this point in the TLC, the major issue restricting technology sales has been development costs. It is this fourth stage that Abernathy and Utterback call the stage of "sales maximization."[4] As an originating company begins to reap the rewards of increasing product sales, a number of strong reasons *for* technology sales begin to surface. The arguments made within the company, however, are likely to be in favor of delaying any sale. Thus, the crucial issue here is *timing*.

Growth in customer demand usually coincides with great interest in a technology by the developer's competitors. These competitors may well wish to avoid the high costs of developing their own alternative versions of products based on the technology. Therefore, the market value of the technology is probably now at its maximum. Nonetheless, the originating company's success in its own product sales, together with the discomfort of its competitors, is often a persuasive argument against selling the technology. In fact, a decision to sell during stage 4 is one of the most difficult that a company can make.

A technology sale is thus often delayed until later in the TLC when the value of the technology has decreased, both because of lessened customer interest and because of the development of alternative and perhaps improved technologies by competitors. This is often a mistake. A cold assessment of market potential could lead many companies to sell their technologies at the very moment that their own sales are increasing and before their markets are saturated. Such an assessment should include consideration of:

---

[4]Ibid., p. 643.

1. Market size. A decision to sell a technology through geographically selective license arrangements can lead to increased revenues based on wider application of the technology. More generally, a company faced with booming or novel market demand for an innovative technology may not be able to generate cash quickly enough to exploit the technology fully through its own production.

2. Technological leadership. The willingness of a company to share a technology much in demand can reduce its competitors' incentive to engage in their own technological development. The originator, by investing its additional revenues in further R&D, can better maintain its leadership position. Of course, such an approach must rest on a careful strategic assessment of whether the company's strengths are more in the creation of new ideas or in the reduction of old ideas to practical implementation.[5]

3. Standardization. The issue of government and industry standards is often vital in the growth phase of the TLC. The originator of a technology has a clear early advantage: the first product on the market *is* the standard. However, by stage 4 some of the company's competitors may develop alternative technologies and, if they have production advantages, may soon flood the market with their own products.

The active sale of licenses by the originating company will help ensure that its technology is incorporated into the production of as many companies as possible. Different technologies are often incompatible, and thus the first company to have its technology widely adopted may well set the technology standard for all. For example, Philips N.V. successfully achieved such standardization in the market for pocket dictating machine cassettes. Although Philips does not produce all the cassettes for all the machines in the world, most are produced according to its design and are subject to a royalty payment to Philips.

Another example is Ray Dolby's strategy for exploiting his noise reduction technology in the tape-recorder market. Dolby sold his technology to professional users in the form of equipment only (Dolby units) but has not allowed other professional equipment manufacturers to use his technology in their products. The market was small enough for him to do this without provoking competition.

Had he tried the same strategy in the consumer cassette market, which is vast in scale, he would immediately have invited rivalry. His decision there was to offer his technology to all manufacturers on a license basis and to require that licensees display the Dolby name and logo on the front of their equipment. In return for their license fees, manufacturers can submit their new products to Dolby for detailed criticism and advice, and improvements in the Dolby circuitry are made available to them without charge.[6] Even so, standardization has been difficult to achieve. Philips produced and promoted a rival technology system and only later was won over to become a licensee of Dolby.

Exhibit 2 summarizes the crucial factors in stage 4 of the TLC. In general, the best strategy is to seek both wide application and standardization of a technology while discouraging other companies from producing substitute technologies. Technology sales have an important part to play. Delay in sales here can mean that the value of the technology decreases, leaving the company to exploit the technology by other means after it has passed its peak value.

EXHIBIT 2 The Critical Timing Decision during Stage Four

Factors *for* Early Sale	Factors *against* Early Sale
Difficulty of developing new market alone	Low value of technology until proved
Lack of process or support technologies in company	High initial investment by developer
Cash shortage	Need to use production facilities
Importance of achieving standardization	High value added in production
Wide potential application for technology	

[5]H. Igor Ansoff and John M. Stewart, "Strategies for a Technology-Based Business," *Harvard Business Review,* November–December 1967, p. 71.

[6]See the *Financial Times,* September 11, 1979.

Stage 5: Technology Maturity

By the time a technology reaches maturity, it will have been modified and improved, not only by the originator but also by competing companies. No longer is timing of technology sales crucial. Instead, the originating company will be concerned with its production costs, the involvement with buyers that technology sales would now bring, and the relationship between those sales and its own production.

The originator's production will level off or decline as the overall market for products based on the technology stabilizes. The only fresh markets for the technology will now be found in less advanced countries, which are eager to substitute their own production for imports.

Technology transfer to a Third World country often takes place on the basis of standard turnkey deals. However, a number of developing countries have tied the technology seller into ever more complicated arrangements. For example, the Algerians have increasingly sought to transfer technology through *clef en main, produit en main,* and *marché en main* purchases (literally, "key in hand," "product in hand," and "market in hand").

In the *clef en main* arrangement, the technology seller's involvement continues past the point of completing a production facility to training of staff. *Produit en main* transactions are not complete until the facility is fully on stream and has delivered products for an extended time. In the *marché en main* arrangement, the technology seller provides both *produit en main* services and a guaranteed market.

Dangers of technology transfer

During stage 5, which corresponds to Abernathy and Utterback's "cost reduction" phase,[7] the originating company must reduce costs to compete in its own markets. Hence, any decision to transfer technology to a low-cost producer must take into account the effects of that transfer on the company's own manufacturing plans. No producer wants to stumble by accident into the kind of competition Fiat now faces in its Western European car markets from its licensees in the Soviet Union and Poland.

In general, developing countries, like those of the Eastern bloc, wish to add value to their natural resources by buying sophisticated process technologies. Brazil, for example, wants to sell steel, not iron ore, and may be able to export steel relatively cheaply because it possesses key raw materials. This need to turn raw materials into finished or semifinished products is good news for companies like Davy International of the United Kingdom, which now has a big Brazilian steel plant under way. But the buy-back and barter arrangements on which such deals often rest make it essential that a technology seller consider the effects of those arrangements on its own plants, work force, and other product areas.

Stage 6: Degraded Technology

The final stage of the TLC occurs when a technology has reached the point of virtually universal exploitation. By this time, license agreements will probably have expired, and the technology will be so well known as to be of little commercial value for direct sale.

However, many older technologies may still have market value in Third World countries. For example, some Middle Eastern countries had to import from Western Europe prefabricated ventilating ducts, which were essentially large boxes of air that were expensive to transport. But imports ceased when old-fashioned spot-welding technology was sold to the importing countries. Similarly, a small British company sold the technology for manufacturing simple wooden school furniture to another Middle Eastern country.

Cyril Hobbs, managing director of R&D at Laing Construction Group (a U.K. company), believes that what these

> countries are looking for is basic standard technology. The question is how to identify what to us is old hat but may be just what other countries need. Here it [is] useful to have an outsider looking in. . . . I'm constantly explaining that I'm not selling Britain's seed corn just because technology is involved. We're selling yesterday's and today's know-how to the developing countries . . . it will take most of them 20 years to absorb what we're throwing at them now.[8]

Technology middlemen

Many transactions, including the two just described, are arranged by one of the growing number of technology middlemen, who are in business to bring together potential buyers and sellers of technology.

---

[7]Abernathy and Utterback, "Dynamic Model," p. 644.

[8]*London Sunday Times,* May 16, 1976.

The number of companies or individuals acting as intermediaries in technology transactions has grown considerably in recent years. They usually operate for a fee paid by the technology seller based on a percentage of royalty or lump-sum revenue.

A member company of the British Technology Transfer Group, which was set up as a nonprofit body by 10 companies that had a wide variety of skills of particular interest to less developed countries, confirms the value of these intermediaries:

> When we were trying to sell our expertise in the Middle East, we found out how difficult it was as an individual company, however well known we were in the U.K. You have two different levels of selling. First you have to convince the technical experts, then they have to persuade the nontechnical people in charge of the purse strings. If you can say you are part of an organization recognized by the British Overseas Trade Board, that is a reference straightaway.[9]

In Conclusion

Fifteen years ago, Theodore Levitt's article on the product life cycle suggested that a company's basic technology should be embodied in a range of products.[10] We argue here that the full exploitation of a company's technology should include not only product applications but also technology sales. The complete marketing of a technology requires at least the following prerequisites:

- *Development of a coherent strategy for a full portfolio of technologies.* Just as a company analyzes its product portfolio according to the position of its products in their life cycle, so it should pay attention to the TLC positions of its existing product and process technologies. Are its products, although selling well, based on a technology that is now widely available to other, perhaps lower cost, competitors? Is the company heavily dependent on a single main technology or on vulnerable sources of raw materials?

  One British company, a market leader in specialized industrial pumps, reinforced its position with a series of new product introductions, each incorporating refinements on previous products. However, all the company's products were based on a single main technology that was increasingly available to other lower cost producers. Analysis of the situation led the company to rethink its overall strategy. First, it embarked on a program of license and buy-back arrangements to exploit more fully its existing technology; and second, it changed the direction of its R&D activity away from past over-reliance on a single, widely available technology.

- *Decisions on acquisition or divestment of individual technologies.* TLC planning involves at the outset clear *marketing* decisions about the whole course of a technology's development. The possibility of license or sale must be built into development plans, which need constant review both before and after application launch.
- *Awareness of the value of developing technology primarily for direct sale without incorporation into products.* This can occur in the case of technologies which do not fit into a company's main strategy or for which the company lacks the required production or marketing resources. It is likely that there will be a growth in the number of companies whose sole aim is the development of technologies to the application launch stage for subsequent sale to other companies.
- *Clear understanding of the relationship between the sale of a technology through license and the sale of products based on that technology.* All too frequently, the licensing of a technology is delayed until the company's product sales and, thus, the market value of the technology start to decline. Full exploitation of a technology frequently involves *earlier* rather than *later* license or sale.
- *Recognition that a technology buyer often has a better idea of its needs and opportunities than a technology seller.* Most companies find it easier to analyze an inadequacy in their own technology when they know of a product or process innovation elsewhere in use than to assess the value of their own potentially marketable technologies or the appropriate customers, prices, and overall strategies for them.
- *Reliance on technology marketers.* All too frequently, technology sales are the part-time responsibility of top management. The marketing of a technology during all the stages of its TLC requires specialized decisions usually beyond the expertise of top corporate managers and of conventional product marketers. Our research suggests that this marketing function be separated both from a company's overall strategic planners and from its regular marketing staff. Only after these specialists have carried out detailed analyses of a technology and its potential markets should their work be integrated with that of general strategic planners.

---

[9] Ibid., January 30, 1977.

[10] Levitt, "Exploit," p. 81.

Technological Evolution

Case II–4
EMI and the CT Scanner (A)

Christopher A. Bartlett

In early 1972 there was considerable disagreement among top management at EMI Ltd., the U.K.-based music, electronics, and leisure company. The subject of the controversy was the CT scanner, a new medical diagnostic imaging device that had been developed by the group's Central Research Laboratory (CRL). At issue was the decision to enter this new business, thereby launching a diversification move that many felt was necessary if the company was to continue to prosper.

Complicating the problem was the fact that this revolutionary new product would not only take EMI into the fast-changing and highly competitive medical equipment business, but would also require the company to establish operations in North America, a market in which it had no prior experience. In March 1972 EMI's board was considering an investment proposal for £6 million to build CT scanner manufacturing facilities in the United Kingdom.

Development of the CT Scanner

Company Background and History

EMI Ltd. traces its origins back to 1898, when the Gramophone Company was founded to import records and gramophones from the United States. It soon established its own manufacturing and recording capabilities, and after a 1931 merger with its major rival, the Columbia Gramophone Company, emerged as the Electric and Musical Industries, Ltd. EMI Ltd. quickly earned a reputation as an aggressive technological innovator, developing the automatic record changer, stereophonic records, magnetic recording tape, and the pioneer commercial television system adopted by the BBC in 1937.

Beginning in 1939, EMI's R&D capabilities were redirected by the war effort toward the development of fuses, airborne radar, and other sophisticated electronic devices.

The company emerged from the war with an electronics business, largely geared to defense-related products, as well as its traditional entertainment businesses. The transition to peacetime was particularly difficult for the electronics division, and its poor performance led to attempts to pursue new industrial and consumer applications. EMI did some exciting pioneering work, and for a while held hopes of being Britain's leading computer company.

Market leadership in major electronics applications remained elusive, however, while the music business boomed. The 1955 acquisition of Capitol Records in the United States, and the subsequent success of the Beatles and other recording groups under contract to EMI, put the company in a very strong financial position as it entered the 1970s. In 1970 the company had earned £21 million before tax on sales of £215 million, and although extraordinary losses halved those profits in 1971, the company was optimistic for a return to previous profit levels in 1972 (see Exhibit 1).

Around that time, a change in top management signaled a change in corporate strategy. John Read, an accountant by training and previously sales director for Ford of Great Britain, was appointed chief executive officer after only four years in the company. Read recognized the risky, even fickle, nature of the music business, which accounted for two-thirds of EMI's sales and profits. In an effort to change the company's strategic balance, he began to divert some of its substantial cash flow into numerous acquisitions and internal developments.

To encourage internal innovation, Read established a research fund that was to be used to finance innovative developments outside the company's immediate interests. Among the first projects financed was one proposed by Godfrey Hounsfield, a research scientist in EMI's Central Research Laboratories (CRL). Hounsfield's proposal opened up an

Harvard Business School case 383–194.

EXHIBIT 1 EMI Limited: Profit and Loss Statement, 1969–1971 (£ in thousands)

Years Ended June 30	1969	1970	1971
Sales			
Music	£110,554	£129,439	£128,359
Leisure	20,960	32,651	35,798
Television	4,640	10,625	13,593
Electronics	40,170	42,571	52,819
Total	176,324	215,286	230,569
Profit (loss) before Interest and Taxation			
Music	13,293	16,427	1,970
Leisure	1,691	3,875	4,146
Television	733	992	3,833
Electronics	3,741	3,283	3,090
Subtotal	19,458	24,577	13,039
Property	—	(20)	939
Total	19,458	24,557	13,978
Sales			
United Kingdom	63,144	89,069	103,824
Europe	25,987	27,017	39,673
North America	65,528	74,622	58,989
Other countries	21,665	24,578	28,083
Total	176,324	215,286	230,569
Profit (loss) before Interest and Taxation			
United Kingdom	8,301	10,465	13,113
Europe	3,176	3,230	3,113
North America	5,525	7,627	(5,754)
Other countries	2,456	3,235	3,506
Subtotal	19,458	24,557	13,978
Net interest payable	(1,857)	(3,599)	(5,010)
Total	£17,601	£20,958	£8,968
As a percentage of net assets	15.8%	17.3%	7.4%
Taxation	£8,407	£10,443	£3,541
As a percentage of profit	47.8%	49.8%	39.5%
Profit after Taxation	£9,194	£10,515	£5,427
As a percentage of net assets	8.3%	8.7%	4.5%

opportunity for the company to diversify in the fast-growing medical electronics field.

CT Scanning: The Concept

In simple terms, Hounsfield's research proposal was to study the possibility of creating a three-dimensional image of an object by taking multiple X-ray measurements of the object from different angles, then using a computer to reconstruct a picture from the data contained in hundreds of overlapping and intersecting X-ray slices. The concept became known as computerized tomography (CT).[1]

Although computerized tomography represented a conceptual breakthrough, the technologies it harnessed were quite well known and understood. Essentially, it linked X-ray, data processing, and

[1]Sometimes called CAT scanning, for computerized axial tomography.

EXHIBIT 2 Schematic Drawing of Scanner System

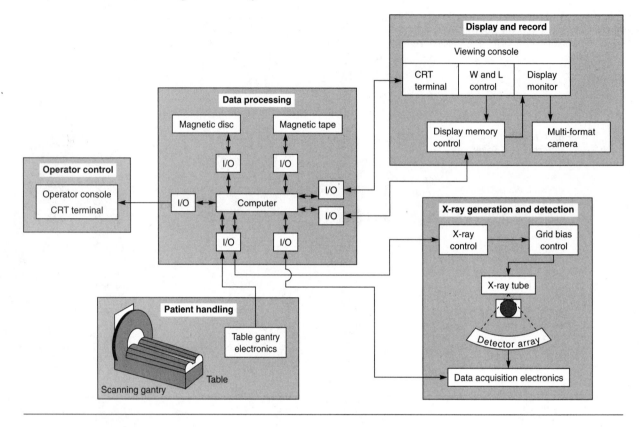

cathode ray tube display technologies in a complex and precise manner. The real development challenge consisted of integrating the mechanical, electronic, and radiographic components into an accurate, reliable, and sensitive system. Exhibit 2 provides a schematic representation of the EMI scanner, illustrating the linkage of the three technologies, as well as the patient handling table and X-ray gantry.

Progress was rapid, and clinical trials of the CT scanner were under way by late 1970. To capture the image of multiple slices of the brain, the scanner went through a translate-rotate sequence, as illustrated in Exhibit 3. The X-ray source and detector, located on opposite sides of the patient's head, were mounted on a gantry. After each scan, or "translation," had generated an X-ray image comprising 160 data points, the gantry would rotate 1° and another scan would be made.

This procedure would continue through 180 translations and rotations, storing a total of almost 30,000 data points. Since the detected intensity of

EXHIBIT 3 Translate-Rotate CT Scanning

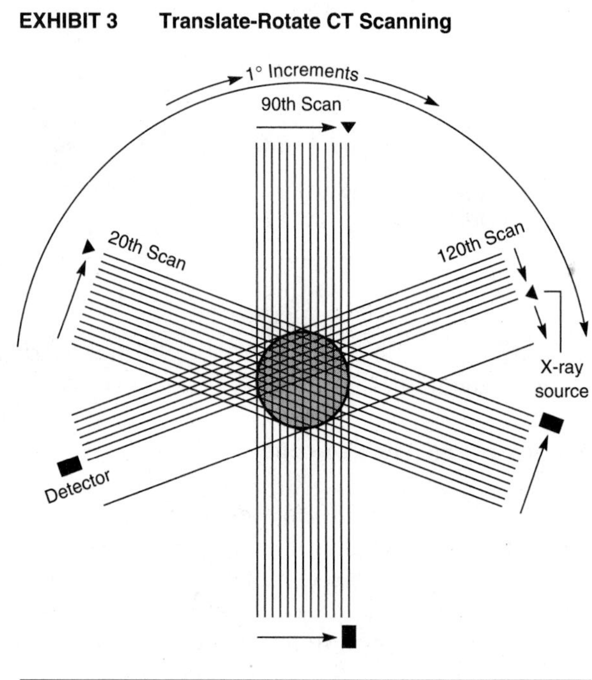

an X-ray varies with the material through which it passes, the data could be reconstructed by the computer into a three-dimensional image of the object that distinguishes bone, tissue, water, fat, and so on.

At about the time of the CT clinical trials, Dr. John Powell, formerly managing director of Texas Instruments' English subsidiary, joined EMI as technical director. He soon became convinced that the poor profitability of the nonmilitary electronics business was due to the diffusion of the company's 2,500-person R&D capability over too many diverse small-volume lines. In his words, "EMI was devoted to too many products and dedicated to too few."

Because the CT scanner project built on the company's substantial and well-established electronics capability, Powell believed it gave EMI an important opportunity to enter an exciting new field. He felt that this was exactly the type of effort in which the company should be prepared to invest several million pounds.

Diagnostic Imaging Industry

During the first half of this century, diagnostic information about internal organs and functions was provided almost exclusively by conventional X-ray examination, but in the 1960s and 1970s, several new imaging techniques emerged. When the CT scanner was announced, three other important technologies existed: X-ray, nuclear, and ultrasound.

EMI management believed its CT scanner would displace existing diagnostic imaging equipment in only a few applications, specifically head and brain imaging.

X-ray

In 1895 Wilhelm Roentgen discovered that rays generated by a cathode ray tube could penetrate solid objects and create an image on film. Over the next 40 to 50 years, X-ray equipment was installed in almost every health care facility in the world. Despite its several limitations (primarily due to the fact that detail was obscured when three-dimensional features were superimposed on a two-dimensional image), X-rays were universally used. In 1966 a Surgeon General's report estimated that between one-third and one-half of all crucial medical decisions in the United States depended on interpretation of X-ray films. That country alone had more than 80,000 X-ray installations in operation, performing almost 150 million procedures in 1970.

The X-ray market was dominated by five major global companies. Siemens of West Germany was estimated to have 22 percent of the world market, N.V. Philips of the Netherlands had 18 percent, and Compagnie Generale de Radiologie (CGE), subsidiary of the French giant Thomson Brandt, held 16 percent. Although General Electric had an estimated 30 percent of the large U.S. market, its weak position abroad gave it only 15 percent of the world market. The fifth largest company was Picker, with 20 percent of the U.S. market, but less than 12 percent worldwide.

The size of the U.S. market for X-ray equipment was estimated at $350 million in 1972, with an additional $350 million in X-ray supplies. The United States was thought to represent 35–40 percent of the world market. Despite the maturity of the product, the X-ray market was growing by almost 10 percent annually in dollar terms during the early 1970s.

A conventional X-ray system represented a major capital expenditure for a hospital, with the average system costing more than $100,000 in 1973.

Nuclear Imaging

In the mid-1960s a nuclear diagnostic imaging procedure was developed. Radioisotopes with a short radioactive life were projected into the body, detected and monitored on a screen, then recorded on film or stored on a tape. Still in an early stage of development, this technology was used to complement or, in some instances, replace a conventional X-ray diagnosis. Both static and dynamic images could be obtained.

Following the pioneering development of this field by Nuclear-Chicago, which sold the first nuclear gamma camera in 1962, several other small competitors had entered the field, notably Ohio Nuclear. By the late 1960s larger companies such as Picker were getting involved, and in 1971 GE's Medical Systems Division announced plans to enter the nuclear medicine field.

As new competitors, large and small, entered the market, competition became more aggressive. The average nuclear camera and data processing system sold for about $75,000. By 1973, shipments of nuclear imaging equipment into the U.S. market were estimated to be over $50 million.

Ultrasound

Ultrasound has been used in medical diagnosis since the 1950s, and the technology advanced significantly in the early 1970s, permitting better-defined images. The technique involves transmitting sonic waves and picking up the echoes, which when converted to electric energy could create images. Air and bone often provide an acoustic barrier, limiting the use of this technique. But because the patient was not exposed to radiation, it was widely used as a diagnostic tool in obstetrics and gynecology.

In 1973 the ultrasound market was very small, and only a few small companies were reported in the field. Picker, however, was rumored to be doing research in the area. The cost of the equipment was expected to be less than half that of a nuclear camera and support system, and perhaps a third to a quarter that of an X-ray machine.

U.S. Market Potential

Because of its size, sophistication, progressiveness, and access to funds, the U.S. medical market clearly represented the major opportunity for a new device such as the CT scanner. EMI management was uncertain about the sales potential for their new product, however.

As of 1972, there were around 7,000 hospitals in the United States, ranging from tiny rural hospitals with fewer than 10 beds to giant teaching institutions with 1,000 beds or more.

	Number of Hospitals		
Size (number of beds)	Short-Term	Long-Term (chronic)	Total
Less than 100	3,110	375	3,485
100–299	1,904	385	2,289
300–499	574	141	715
More than 500	537	91	628
Total	6,125	992	7,117

Since the price of the EMI Scanner was expected to be around $400,000, only the largest and financially strongest short-term institutions would be able to afford one. But the company was encouraged by the enthusiasm of the physicians who had seen and worked with the scanner. In the opinion of one leading American neurologist, at least 170 machines would be required by major U.S. hospitals. Indeed, he speculated, the time might come when a neurologist would feel ethically compelled to order a CT scan before making a diagnosis.

During the 1960s the radiology departments in many hospitals were recognized as important money-making operations. Increasingly, radiologists were able to commission equipment manufacturers to build specially designed (often esoteric) X-ray systems and applications. As their budgets expanded, the size of the U.S. X-ray market grew from $50 million in 1958 to $350 million in 1972.

Of the 15,000 radiologists in the United States, 60 percent were primarily based in offices and 40 percent in hospitals. Little penetration of private clinics was foreseen for the CT scanner. Apart from these broad statistics, EMI had little ability to forecast the potential of the U.S. market for scanners.

EMI's Investment Decision

Conflicting Management Views

By late 1971 it was clear that the clinical trials were successful and EMI management had to decide whether to make the investment required to develop the CT scanner business. One group of senior managers felt that direct EMI participation was undesirable for three reasons. First, EMI lacked medical product experience. In the early 1970s EMI offered only two very small medical products, a patient-monitoring device and an infrared thermography device, which together represented less than 0.5 percent of the company's sales.

Second, they argued that the manufacturing process would be quite different from EMI's experience. Most of its electronics work had been in the job shop mode required in producing small numbers of highly specialized defense products on cost-plus government contracts. In scanner production, most of the components were purchased from subcontractors and had to be integrated into a functioning system.

Finally, many believed that without a working knowledge of the North American market, where most of the demand for scanners was expected to be, EMI might find it very difficult to build an effective operation from scratch.

Among the strongest opponents of EMI's self-development of this new business was one of the scanner's earliest sponsors, Dr. Broadway, head of the Central Research Laboratory. He emphasized that EMI's potential competitors in the field had considerably greater technical capabilities and resources.

As the major proponent, John Powell needed convincing market information to counter the critics. In early 1972 he asked some of the senior managers how many scanners they thought the company would sell in its first 12 months. Their first estimate was five. Powell told them to think again. They came back with a figure of 12, and were again sent back to reconsider. Finally, with an estimate of 50, Powell felt he could go to bat for the £6 million investment, since at this sales level he could project handsome profits from year one. He then prepared an argument that justified the scanner's fit with EMI's overall objectives, and outlined a basic strategy for the business.

Powell argued that self-development of the CT scanner represented just the sort of vehicle EMI had been seeking to provide some focus to its development effort. By definition, diversification away from existing product-market areas would move the company into somewhat unfamiliar territory, but he firmly believed that the financial and strategic payoffs would be huge. The product offered access to global markets and an entry into the lucrative medical equipment field. He felt the company's objective should be "to achieve a substantial share of the world medical electronics business not only in diagnostic imaging, but also through the extension of its technologies into computerized patient planning and radiation therapy."

Powell claimed that the expertise developed by Hounsfield and his team, coupled with protection from patents, would give EMI three or four years, and maybe many more, to establish a solid market position. He argued that investments should be made quickly and boldly to maximize the market share of the EMI scanner before competitors entered. Other options, such as licensing, would impede the development of the scanner. If the licensees were the major X-ray equipment suppliers, they might not promote the scanner aggressively since it would cannibalize their sales of X-ray equipment and consumables. Smaller companies would lack EMI's sense of commitment and urgency. Besides, licensing would not provide EMI with the major strategic diversification it was seeking. It would be, in Powell's words, "selling our birthright."

The Proposed Strategy

Because the CT scanner incorporated a complex integration of some technologies in which EMI had only limited expertise, Powell proposed that the manufacturing strategy should rely heavily on outside sources of those components rather than trying to develop the expertise internally. This approach would not only minimize risk, but would also make it possible to implement a manufacturing program rapidly.

He proposed the concept of developing various "centers of excellence" both inside and outside the company, making each responsible for the continued superiority of the subsystem it manufactured. For example, within the EMI U.K. organization a unit called SE Labs, which manufactured instruments and displays, would become the center of excellence for the scanner's viewing console and display control. Pantak, an EMI unit with a capability in X-ray tube assembly, would become the center of excellence for X-ray generation and detection subsystem. An outside vendor with which the company had worked in developing the scanner would be the center of excellence for data processing. Finally, a newly created division would be responsible for coordinating these subsystem manufacturers, integrating the various components, and assembling the final scanner at a company facility in the town of Hayes, not far from the CRL site.

Powell emphasized that the low initial investment was possible because most of the components and subsystems were purchased from contractors and vendors. Even internal centers of excellence such as SE Labs and Pantak assembled their subsystems from purchased components. Overall, outside vendors accounted for 75–80 percent of the scanner's manufacturing cost. Although Powell felt his arrangement greatly reduced EMI's risk, the £6 million investment was a substantial one for the company, representing about half the funds available for capital investment over the coming year. (See Exhibit 4 for a balance sheet and Exhibit 5 for a projected funds flow.)

The technology strategy was to keep CRL as the company's center of excellence for design and software expertise, and to use the substantial profits Powell was projecting from even the earliest sales to maintain technological leadership position.

EXHIBIT 4 EMI Group Consolidated Balance Sheet, 1972 (£ thousands)

Employment of Capital		
Goodwill		80,814
Fixed assets		104,174
Other investments		14,354
Current assets:		
Inventories	45,508	
Films, programs, and rights	7,712	
Accounts receivable	82,483	
Liquid funds	20,086	
	155,789	
Less:		
Current liabilities:		
Accounts payable	96,942	
Bank borrowings	14,168	
Taxes payable	17,174	
Dividends declared	4,202	
	132,486	
Net current assets		23,303
Total		222,645
Capital Employed		
Share capital		40,937
Reserves		90,239
Minority shareholders' interests		14,992
Loan capital		76,011
Deferred taxes		466
Total		222,645

EXHIBIT 5 EMI Group Projected Funds Flow, 1972 (£ thousands)

Sources of Funds	
Profit before tax	18.3
Depreciation	6.7
Sale of fixed assets	5.5
Sale of investments	5.4
Loan capital	0.3
Decrease in working capital	4.5
Total	40.7
Uses of Funds	
Tax payments	5.9
Dividends paid	5.6
Fixed asset additions	13.0
Repayment of loan capital	3.4
Reduction in short-term borrowings	12.8
Total	40.7

Powell would personally head up a team to develop a marketing strategy. Clearly, the United States had to be the main focus of EMI's marketing activity. Its neuroradiologists were regarded as world leaders and tended to welcome technological innovation. Furthermore, its institutions were more commercial in their outlook than those in other countries and tended to have more available funds. Powell planned to set up a U.S. sales subsidiary as soon as possible, recruiting sales and service personnel familiar with the North American health care market. Given the interest shown to date in the EMI scanner, he did not think there would be much difficulty in gaining the attention and interest of the medical community. Getting the $400,000 orders, however, would be more of a challenge. In simple terms, Powell's sales strategy was to get machines into a few prestigious reference hospitals, then build from that base.

The Decision

In March 1972 EMI's chief executive, John Read, considered Powell's proposal in preparation for a board meeting. Was this the diversification opportunity he had been hoping for? What were the risks? Could they be managed? How? If he decided to back the proposal, what kind of an implementation program would be necessary to ensure its eventual success?

EMI and the CT Scanner (B)

Christopher A. Bartlett

It looked as if 1977 would be a very good year for EMI Medical Inc., a North American subsidiary of EMI Ltd. EMI's CT scanner had met with enormous success in the American market. In the three years since the scanner's introduction, EMI medical electronics sales had grown to £42 million. Although this figure represented only 6 percent of total sales, the new business contributed pretax profits of £12.5 million, almost 20 percent of the corporate total (see Exhibit 6). EMI Medical Inc. was thought to have sold almost three-quarters of all scanners worldwide. And with an order backlog of more than 300 units, the future looked rosy.

Despite this formidable success, senior management in both the subsidiary and the parent company were concerned about several developments. First, this fast-growth field had attracted more than a dozen new entrants in the past two years, and technological advances were occurring rapidly. Second, the growing political debate over hospital cost containment often focused on $500,000 CT scanners as an example of questionable hospital spending. Finally, EMI was beginning to feel some internal organizational strains.

Entry Decision

Product Launch

Following months of debate within EMI's top management, the decision to go ahead with the EMI scanner project was assured when John Read, the company CEO, gave his support to John Powell's proposal. In April 1972 a formal press announcement was greeted by a response that could only be described as overwhelming. EMI was flooded with inquiries from the medical and financial communities, and from most of the large diagnostic imaging companies, which wanted to license the technology, enter into joint ventures, or at least distribute the product. The response was that EMI had decided to enter the business directly itself.

Powell's manufacturing strategy was immediately put into operation. Manufacturing facilities were developed and supply contracts drawn up with the objective of beginning shipments within 12 months.

In May, Godfrey Hounsfield, the brilliant EMI scientist who had developed the scanner, was dispatched to the United States, accompanied by a leading English neurologist. The American specialists with whom they spoke confirmed that the scanner had great medical importance. Interest was running high in the medical community.

In December EMI mounted a display at the annual meeting of the Radiology Society of North America (RSNA). The exhibit was the highlight of the show, and boosted management's confidence enough that it decided to establish a U.S. sales company to penetrate the American medical market.

U.S. Market Entry

In June 1973, with an impressive pile of sales leads and inquiries, a small sales office was established in Reston, Virginia, home of the newly appointed U.S. sales branch manager, Gus Pyber. Earlier that month the first North American head scanner had been installed at the prestigious Mayo Clinic, with a second machine promised to the Massachusetts General Hospital for trials. The new sales force had little difficulty getting into the offices of leading radiologists and neurologists.

By the end of the year, however, Pyber had been fired in a dispute over appropriate expense levels, and James Gallagher, a former marketing manager with a major drug company, was hired to replace him. One of Gallagher's first steps was to convince the company that the Chicago area was a superior location for the U.S. office. It allowed better servicing of a national market, was a major center for medical electronics companies, and had more convenient linkages with London. This last point was

Harvard Business School case 383–195.

EXHIBIT 6 EMI Limited: Profit and Loss Statement, 1969–1976 (£ thousands)

Years Ended June 30	1969	1970	1971	1972	1973	1974	1975	1976
Sales								
Music	£110,554	£129,439	£128,359	£137,755	£169,898	£213,569	£258,343	£344,743
Leisure	20,960	32,651	35,798	37,917	45,226	53,591	66,566	81,428
Television	4,640	10,625	13,593	17,165	22,011	22,814	29,107	38,224
Electronics (nonmedical)	40,170	42,571	52,819	58,215	83,516	104,811	128,644	164,943
Medical electronics	—	—	—	—	321	5,076	20,406	42,104
Total	176,324	215,286	230,569	251,052	320,972	399,861	503,066	671,442
Profit (loss) before Interest and Taxation								
Music	13,293	16,427	1,970	9,333	16,606	26,199	19,762	27,251
Leisure	1,691	3,875	4,146	4,983	4,255	2,639	5,981	5,619
Television	733	992	3,833	5,001	6,104	4,465	2,982	5,646
Electronics (nonmedical)	3,741	3,283	3,090	1,353	5,264	5,835	5,378	13,937
Medical electronics	—	—	—	—	(67)	1,242	9,230	12,502
Subtotal	19,458	24,577	13,039	20,670	32,162	40,380	43,333	64,955
Property	—	(20)	939	2,118	1,842	402	(103)	—
Total	19,458	24,557	13,978	22,788	34,004	40,782	43,230	64,955
Sales								
United Kingdom	63,144	89,069	103,824	113,925	142,945	165,641	198,153	241,972
Europe	25,987	27,017	39,673	52,541	82,405	105,251	134,450	170,385
North America	65,528	74,622	58,989	53,151	55,143	67,141	78,154	128,798
Other countries	21,665	24,578	28,083	31,435	40,479	61,828	92,309	130,287
Total	176,324	215,286	230,569	251,052	320,972	399,861	503,066	671,442
Profit (loss) before Interest and Taxation								
United Kingdom	8,301	10,465	13,113	15,447	19,287	16,784	16,494	21,802
Europe	3,176	3,230	3,113	3,133	6,133	9,043	9,679	14,521
North America	5,525	7,627	(5,754)	1,091	3,555	6,412	7,065	13,067
Other countries	2,456	3,235	3,506	3,117	5,029	8,543	9,992	15,565
Subtotal	19,458	24,557	13,978	22,788	34,004	40,782	43,230	64,955
Net interest payable	(1,857)	(3,599)	(5,010)	(4,452)	(6,386)	(5,690)	(8,258)	(5,604)
Total	£17,601	£20,958	£8,968	£18,336	£27,618	£35,092	£34,972	£59,351
As a percentage of net assets	15.8%	17.3%	7.4%	14.4%	18.9%	22.8%	21.2%	31.2%
Taxation	£8,407	£10,443	£3,541	£8,575	£13,227	£18,666	£19,549	£31,224
As a percentage of profit	47.8%	49.8%	39.5%	46.8%	47.9%	53.2%	55.9%	52.6%
Profit after Taxation	£9,194	£10,515	£5,427	£9,761	£14,391	£16,426	£15,423	£28,127
As a percentage of net assets	8.3%	8.7%	4.5%	7.7%	9.8%	10.7%	9.3%	14.8%

important since all major strategic and policy decisions were being made directly by John Powell in London.

During 1974 Gallagher concentrated on recruiting and developing his three-person sales force and two-person service organization. The cost of maintaining each salesperson on the road was estimated at $50,000, while a service employee's salary and expenses at that time were around $35,000 annually. Scanners were being produced at a rate of only three or four machines a month, and Gallagher saw little point in developing a huge sales force to sell a product with limited supply and unlimited customer interest.

In this seller's market the company developed some policies that were new to the industry. Most notably, they required that the customer deposit one-third of the purchase price with the order to guarantee a place in the production schedule. Sales leads and inquiries were followed up when the sales force could get to them, and the general attitude of the company seemed to have a somewhat take-it-or-leave-it tone. It was in this period that EMI developed a reputation for arrogance in some parts of the medical profession.

Nonetheless, by June 1974 the company had delivered 35 scanners at $390,000 each and had another 60 orders in hand.

Developing Challenges

Competition

Toward the end of 1974, the first competitive scanners were announced. Unlike the EMI scanner, the new machines were designed to scan the body rather than the head. The Acta-Scanner had been developed at Georgetown University's Medical Center and was manufactured by a small Maryland company called Digital Information Sciences Corporation (DISCO). Technologically, it offered little advance over the EMI scanner except for one important feature. Its gantry design would accommodate a body rather than a head. Although specifications on scan time and image composition were identical to those of the EMI scanner, the $298,000 price tag gave the Acta-Scanner a big advantage, particularly with smaller hospitals and private practitioners.

The DeltaScan offered by Ohio Nuclear (ON) represented an even more formidable challenge. This head and body scanner had 256 × 256 pixels[1] compared with EMI's 160 × 160, and promised a 2½-minute scan rather than the 4½-minute scan offered by EMI. ON presented these superior features on a unit priced at $385,000—$5,000 below the EMI scanner.

Many managers at EMI were surprised by the speed with which these products had appeared, barely two years after the EMI scanner was exhibited at the RSNA meeting in Chicago and 18 months after the first machine was installed in the Mayo Clinic. The source of the challenge was also interesting. DISCO was a tiny private company, and ON contributed only 20 percent of its parent Technicare's 1974 sales of $50 million.

To some, the biggest surprise was how closely these competitive machines resembled EMI's own scanner. The complex wall of patents had not provided an enduring defense. ON tackled the issue directly in its 1975 annual report. After announcing that $882,200 had been spent in Technicare's R&D center to develop DeltaScan, the report stated:

> Patents have not played a significant role in the development of Ohio Nuclear's product line, and it is not believed that the validity or invalidity of any patents known to exist is material to its current market position. However, the technologies on which its products are based are sufficiently complex and application of patent law sufficiently indefinite that this belief is not free from all doubt.

The challenge represented by these new competitive products caused EMI to speed up the announcement of the body scanner Hounsfield had been working on. The new CT 5000 model incorporated a second-generation technology in which multiple beams of radiation were shot at multiple detectors, rather than the single pencil beam and the single detector of the original scanner (see Exhibit 7). This technique allowed the gantry to rotate 10° rather than 1° after each translation, cutting scan time from 4½ minutes to 20 seconds. In addition, the multiple-beam emission also permitted a finer image resolution by increasing the number of pixels from 160 × 160 to 320 × 320. Priced over $500,000, the CT 5000 received a standing ovation when Hounsfield demonstrated it at the radiological meetings held in Bermuda in May 1975.

---

[1]Pixels were the picture element cells that made up the image. The more elements in the matrix of cells that composed the image, the greater the theoretical resolution.

EXHIBIT 7 Three Generations of CT Scanning Technology

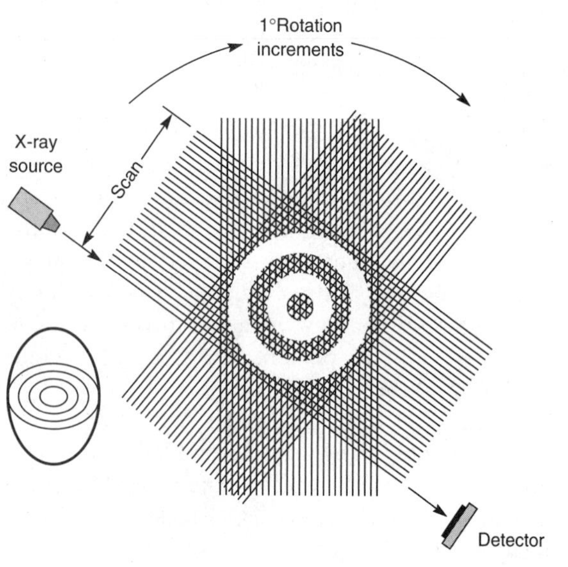

First generation CT scanning rectilinear pencil beam

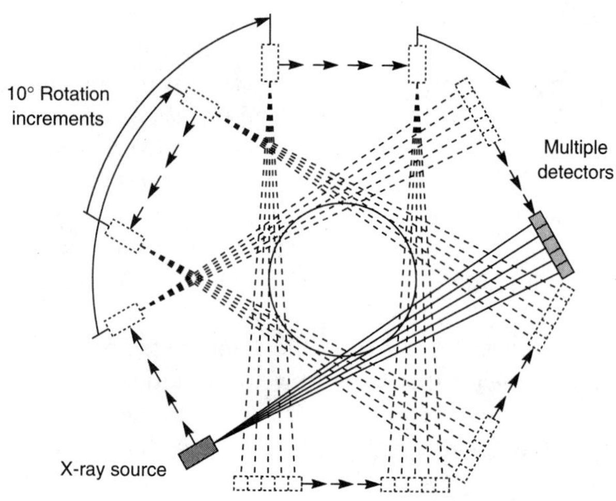

Second generation CT scanning rectilinear multiple pencil beam and multiple detectors

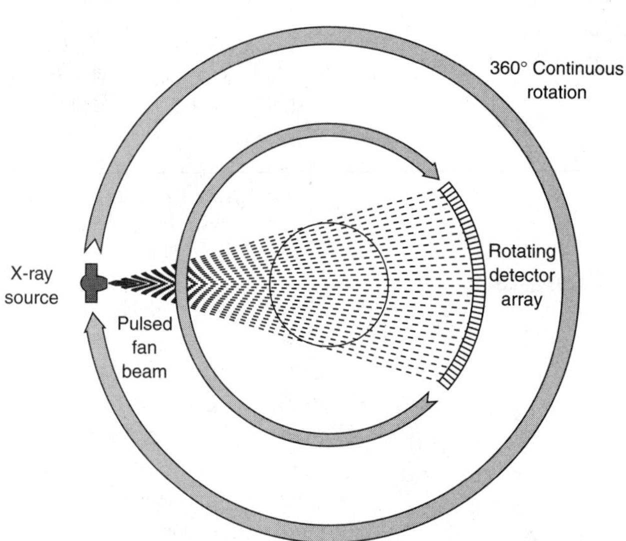

Third generation CT scanning continuously rotating pulse fan X-ray beam

Despite EMI's reassertion of its leadership position, aggressive competitive activity continued. In March 1975, Pfizer Inc., the $1.5 billion drug giant, announced it had acquired the manufacturing and marketing rights for the Acta-Scanner.

By June 1975, managers at EMI estimated competitors' cumulative orders as follows:

	Total Shipped	On Order
EMI	122	110
Ohio Nuclear	2	50 (est.)
Pfizer	0	20 (est.)

EMI was then operating at an annual production rate of 150 units, and ON had announced plans to double capacity to 12 units per month by early 1976. Pfizer's capacity plans were unknown.

The most dramatic competitive revelation came at the annual RSNA meeting in December 1975, when six new competitors displayed CT scanners. Although none of the newcomers offered immediate delivery, all were booking orders with delivery dates up to 12 months out on the basis of their spec sheets and prototype or mock-up equipment exhibits.

Some of the new entrants (Syntex, Artronix, and Neuroscan) were smaller companies, but others (General Electric, Picker, and Varian) were major medical electronics competitors. Perhaps most impressive was a General Electric CT/T scanner, which took the infant technology into its third generation (see Exhibit 7). By using a 30°-wide pulsed fan X-ray beam, the GE scanner could avoid the time-consuming "translate-rotate" sequence of the first- and second-generation scanners. A single continuous 360° sweep could be completed in 4.8 seconds, and the resulting image was reconstructed by the computer in a 320 × 320 pixel matrix on a cathode ray tube. The unit was priced at $615,000. Clinical trials were scheduled for January, and shipment of production units was being quoted for mid-1976.

The arrival of GE on the horizon signaled the beginning of a new competitive game. With a 300-person sales force and a service network of 1,200, GE clearly had marketing muscle. The company had reputedly spent $15 million developing its third-generation scanner and was continuing to spend at a rate of $5 million annually to keep ahead technologically.

During 1975 one industry source estimated that about 150 new scanners were installed in the United States and more than twice as many orders were entered. (Orders were firm, since most were secured with hefty front-end deposits.) Overall, orders were split rather evenly between brain and body scanners. EMI was thought to have accounted for more than 50 percent of orders taken in 1975, ON for almost 30 percent.

Market Size and Growth

Accurate assessments of market size, growth rate, and competitors' shares were difficult to obtain. The following represents a sample of the widely varying forecasts made in late 1975:

> Wall Street was clearly enamored with the industry prospects (Technicare's stock price rose from 5 to 22 in six months), and analysts were predicting an annual market potential of $500 million to $1 billion by 1980.[2]
>
> A market analysis by Frost and Sullivan, however, predicted a U.S. market of only $120 million by 1980, with 10 years of cumulative sales only reaching $1 billion by 1984 (2,500 units at $400,000).[3]
>
> Some leading radiologists suggested that CT scanners could be standard equipment in all short-term hospitals with 200 beds or more by 1985.
>
> Technicare's president, R. T. Grimm, forecast a worldwide market of over $700 million by 1980, of which $400 million would be in the United States.
>
> Despite the technical limitations of its first-generation product, Pfizer said it expected to sell more than 1,500 units of its Acta-Scanner over the next five years.

Within EMI, market forecasts had changed considerably. By late 1975 the estimate of the U.S. market had been boosted to 350 units a year, of which EMI hoped to retain a 50 percent share. Management was acutely aware of the difficulty of forecasting in such a turbulent environment, however.

International Expansion

New competitors also challenged EMI's positions in markets outside the United States. Siemens, the $7 billion West German company, became ON's international distributor. The distribution agreement appeared to be one of short-term convenience for both parties, since Siemens acknowledged that it was developing its own CT scanner. Philips, too, had announced its intention to enter the field.

Internationally, EMI had maintained its basic strategy of going direct to the national market rather than working through local partners or distributors. Although all European sales had originally been handled out of the U.K. office, it quickly became evident that local servicing staffs were generally required. Soon separate subsidiaries were established in most continental European countries, typically with a couple of salespeople and three or four service personnel. Elsewhere in the world, salespeople were often attached to EMI's existing music organization in a particular country (e.g., in South Africa, Australia, and Latin America). In Japan, however, EMI signed a distribution agreement with Toshiba, which in Octo-

[2]"Heard on the Street," *The Wall Street Journal,* November 21, 1975, p. 47.

[3]Frost and Sullivan, *Advanced Medical Imaging Equipment Market,* May 1975.

ber 1975 submitted the largest single order to date: a request for 33 scanners.

EMI in 1976: Strategy and Challenges

By 1976 the CT scanner business was evolving rapidly, but EMI had done extremely well financially (see Exhibit 6). Although smaller competitors had challenged EMI somewhat earlier than might have been expected, none of the big diagnostic imaging companies had brought its scanner to market, even four years after the original EMI scanner announcement. Technology was evolving rapidly, but the expertise of Hounsfield and his CRL group and the aggressive reinvestment of much of the early profits in R&D had given EMI a strong technological position. And although market size and growth were highly uncertain, the potential was unquestionably much larger than EMI had forecast in its early plans. In all, EMI was well established, with a strong and growing sales volume and a good technical reputation. The company was undoubtedly the industry leader.

Nonetheless, the company would face a new set of strategic tasks in the years ahead.

Strategic Priorities

EMI's first sales priority was to protect its highly visible and prestigious customer base from competitors. When its second-generation scanner was introduced in mid-1975, EMI promised to upgrade without charge the first-generation equipment already purchased by its established customers. Although each of these 120 upgrades was estimated to cost EMI $60,000 in components and installation costs, the U.S. sales organization felt that the expense was essential to maintain the confidence and good faith of this important core of customers.

To maintain its leadership image, the U.S. company also expanded its service organization substantially. Beginning in early 1976 new regional and district sales and service offices were opened, aiming to provide customers with the best service in the industry. A typical annual service contract cost the hospital $40,000 per scanner. At year's end the company boasted 20 service centers with 150 service engineers—a ratio that represented one service representative for every two or three machines installed. The sales force had grown to 20 and had become much more attuned to the customer.

Another important task was to improve delivery performance. The interval between order and promised delivery had been lengthening; meanwhile, promised delivery dates were often missed. By late 1975 a 6-month promise frequently converted into a 12- or 15-month actual delivery time. Fortunately for EMI, all CT manufacturers were in backorder and were offering extended delivery dates. However, EMI's poor performance in meeting promised dates was hurting its reputation. The company responded by substantially expanding its production facilities. By mid-1976 there were six manufacturing locations in the United Kingdom, yet because of continuing problems with components suppliers, combined capacity for head and body scanners was estimated at less than 20 units a month.

Organizational and Personnel Issues

As the U.S. sales organization became increasingly frustrated, it began urging top management to manufacture scanners in North America. Believing that the product had reached the necessary level of maturity, Powell judged that the time was ripe to establish a U.S. plant to handle at least final assembly and test operations. A Northbrook, Illinois, site was chosen.

Powell had become EMI's managing director and was more determined than ever to make the new medical electronics business a success. A capable manager was desperately needed to head the business, particularly in view of the rapid developments in the critical North American market. Consequently, Powell was delighted when Normand Provost, who had been his boss at Texas Instruments, contacted him at the Bermuda radiological meeting in March 1975. He was hired with the hope that he could build a stronger, more integrated U.S. company.

With the Northbrook plant scheduled to begin operations by mid-1976, Normand Provost began hiring skilled production personnel. He also envisioned a Northbrook product development center, to allow EMI to draw on U.S. technical expertise and experience in solid-state electronics and data processing. The company began seeking people with strong technological and scientific backgrounds.

Having hired Provost, Powell made several important organizational changes aimed at facilitating the medical electronics business's growth and development. In the United Kingdom, he announced the cre-

EXHIBIT 8 EMI Medical Electronics Organization, 1976

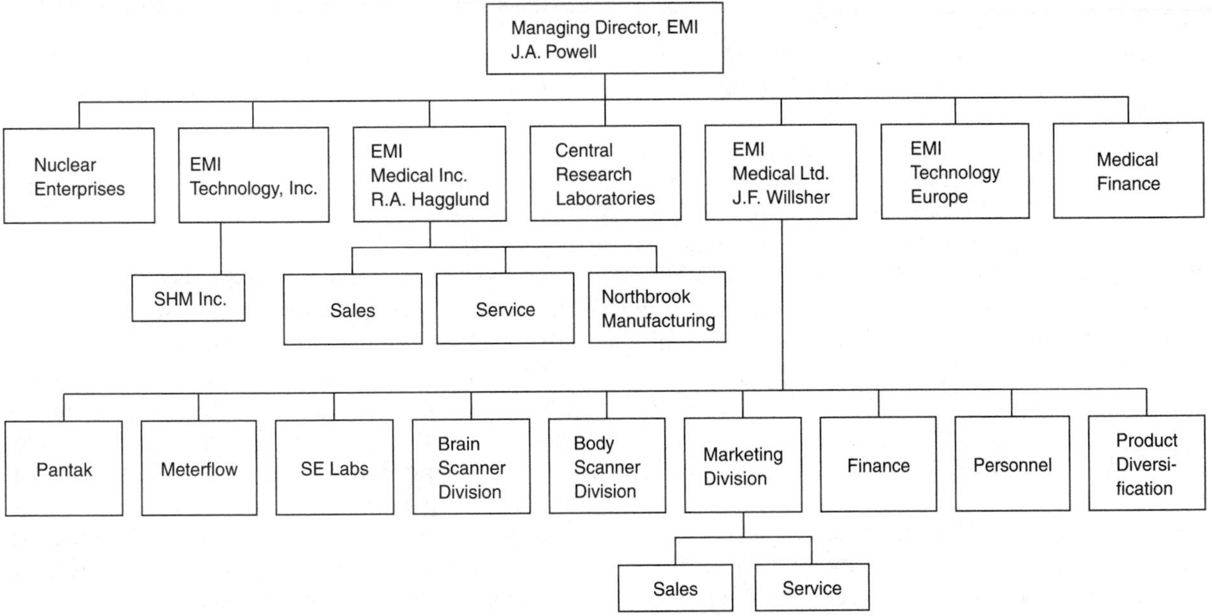

[a]Only the medical business responsibilities reporting to John Powell are shown. In addition, he had overall responsibility for EMI's other businesses (music, industrial electronics, etc.).

ation of a separate medical electronics group. The various operating companies—EMI Medical Ltd. (previously known as the X-Ray Systems Division), Pantak (EMI) Ltd., SE Labs (EMI) Ltd., and EMI Meterflow Ltd.—could now be grouped under a single executive, John Willsher (see Exhibit 8). At last, a more integrated scanner business seemed to be emerging organizationally.

The U.S. sales subsidiary was folded into a new company, EMI Medical Inc., but continued to operate as a separate entity. The intention was to develop this company as an integrated diversified medical electronics operation. Jim Gallagher, the general manager of the U.S. operations, was fired, and Bob Hagglund became president of EMI Medical Inc. Although Gallagher had been an effective salesman, Powell thought the company needed a more rounded general manager in its next phase of expansion. Hagglund, previously executive vice president of G. D. Searle's diagnostic business, seemed to have the broader background and outlook required to manage a larger integrated operation. He reported through Provost back to Powell in the United Kingdom.

Although Provost's initial assignment was to establish the new manufacturing and research facilities in the United States, it was widely assumed within EMI that he was being groomed to take responsibility for the company's medical electronics businesses worldwide. In April 1976, however, while visiting London to discuss progress, Provost died of a heart attack. As a result, the U.S. and U.K. organizations reported separately to Powell.

Product Diversification

Since EMI wished to use the scanner as a means to become a major force in medical electronics, Powell argued that some bold external moves were needed to protect the company's leadership position. In March 1976 EMI acquired for $2 million (£1.1 million) SHM Nuclear Corporation, an innovative but somewhat shaky California-based company that had developed linear accelerators for cancer therapy and computerized radiotherapy planning systems. Although the SHM product line needed substantial further development, the hope was that linking such systems to the CT scanner would permit a synchronized location and treatment of cancer.

Six months later EMI paid £6.5 million to acquire an additional 60 percent of Nuclear Enterprises Ltd., an Edinburgh-based supplier of ultrasound equipment. In the 1976 annual report, Sir John Read, now EMI's chairman, reaffirmed his support for Powell's strategy: "We have every reason to believe that this new grouping of scientific and technological resources will prove of national benefit in securing a growing share of worldwide markets for high-technology products."

Future Prospects

At the close of 1976 EMI's medical electronics business was exceeding all expectations. In just three years sales of electronics products had risen from £84 million to £207 million; a large part of this increase was due to the scanner. Even more impressive, profits of the electronics line had risen from £5.2 million in 1972–1973 to £26.4 million in 1975–1976, jumping from 16 percent to 40 percent of the corporate total.

Rather than dwindling, interest in scanners seemed to be increasing. Although the company had sold around 450 scanners over the past three years (over 300 in the United States alone), its order backlog was estimated to be 300 units. At the December 1976 RSNA meeting, 120 of the 280 papers presented were related to CT scanning.

In reviewing the medical electronics business that he had built, Powell was generally pleased with how the company had met the challenges of pioneering a new industry segment. There were, however, several developments that promised to require considerable attention over the next few years. First, Powell felt that competitive activity would continue to present a challenge; second, some changes in the U.S. regulatory environment concerned him; and finally, he knew that the recent organization changes had created some strains.

Competitive Problems

By the end of 1976, EMI had delivered 450 of the 650-odd scanners installed worldwide, yet its market share had dropped to 56 percent in 1975–1976 (198 of 352 scanners sold in that June-to-June period were EMI's). Despite its premium pricing strategy and its delivery problems, the company gained some consolation from conceding less than half the total market to the combined competitive field. Management also felt some sense of security in the 300 orders awaiting delivery. Nonetheless, Sir John Read expressed concern. "We are well aware of the developing competition," he noted. "Our research programme is being fully sustained to ensure our continued leadership."

In mid-1976 the company announced its intention "to protect its inventions and assert its patent strength," and subsequently filed suit against Ohio Nuclear claiming patent infringement. EMI, however, simultaneously issued a statement proclaiming that "it was the company's wish to make its pioneering scanner patents available to all under suitable licensing arrangements."

In December 1976 at the annual RSNA meeting, 16 competitors exhibited scanners. The year's new entrants (including CGR, the French X-ray giant; Hitachi from Japan; and G.D. Searle, the U.S. drug and hospital equipment company) were not yet making deliveries, however. The industry's potential production capacity was estimated to be over 900 units annually.

GE's much-publicized entry was already six months behind its announced delivery date, but rumors abounded that production shipments of GE's third-generation scanner were about to begin. EMI Medical Inc. anxiously awaited the event. (A summary of major competitors and their situations as of 1976 appears in Exhibit 9).

Regulatory Problems

By mid-1976 indications suggested that the government might try to exert tighter control over hospital spending in general and purchase of CT scanners in particular.

The rapidly escalating cost of health care had been a political issue for years, and the National Health Planning and Resources Development Act of 1974 required states to control the development of costly or unnecessary health services through a procedure known as the Certificate of Need (CON). If they wished to qualify for Medicare or Medicaid reimbursements, health care facilities had to submit documentation to their state's department of health to justify major capital expenditures (typically over $100,000).

EXHIBIT 9 Selected Competitive Data

Company	Product Line	Price ($000)	Delivery (months)	Company Strengths/Weaknesses
EMI	2d generation Head and body 20 sec. scan Multiple models for various applications 320 × 320 pixels	$395 (head) $550 (body) 20% deposit	10	Original innovator—some base in ultrasound $10 million per annum in R&D $1.2B sales: $85M in medical Strong service base Modular product line Strong customer base
Ohio Nuclear	2d generation Head and body 20 sec. scan 256 × 256 pixels	$385 (head) $525 (body) 20% deposit	10	Rapid follower R&D increased to $8M–$10M per annum Technicare sales $100M; scanners 50% Had nuclear; acquired ultrasound co. Strong marketing
Pfizer	1st generation (announced 2d generation) Head and body 30+ sec. scan	$295 (head) $475 (body) $25K deposit	9	Acquired technology—slow developing Company sales $1.6B; scanners 2% No other diagnostic imaging
General Electric	3d generation Head and body 3 sec. scan 320 × 320 pixels	$315 (head) $595 (body) $15K with order $75K on mfg. start	15	Strong R&D capability Leader in diagnostic imaging (X-ray, nuclear, entering ultrasound) $16B sales: Medical Systems $400M Very strong sales and service base
Picker	Hybrid 3d generation (announced) Body only 20 sec. (est.) Expected on market mid-1977	$550	10–12	Good design and development skills Late entrant—but strong performance expected Leader in X-ray, nuclear, and ultrasound Strong marketing and service base $300M sales

Before 1976 the CON procedure had generally been a mere administrative impediment to the process of selling a scanner, delaying but not preventing the authorization of funds. By 1976, however, the cost of medical care represented 8 percent of the gross national product and Jimmy Carter made control of the "skyrocketing costs of health care" a major campaign issue. One of the most frequently cited examples of waste was the proliferation of CT scanners. It was argued that this $500,000 device had become a symbol of prestige and sophistication in the medical community so that every institution wanted its own scanner, even if a neighboring facility had one that was grossly underutilized.

Responding to heightened public awareness, five states declared a moratorium on the purchase of new scanners, including California, which had accounted for over 20 percent of total U.S. scanner placements to date. In November Jimmy Carter was elected president.

Organizational Problems

Perhaps most troublesome to Powell were the organizational problems. Tensions within the EMI organization had been developing for some time, centering on the issues of manufacturing and product design. Managers in the U.S. company felt that they had little control over manufacturing schedules and little input into product design, even though they were responsible for 80 percent of corporate scanner sales. In their view, the company's market position was being eroded by the worsening manufacturing delivery performance from the United Kingdom, while its longer-term prospects were threatened by the competitive challenges to EMI's technological leadership.

Although the Northbrook plant had been completed in late 1976, U.S. managers were still not satisfied that they had the necessary control over production. Arguing that the quality of subassemblies and components shipped from the United Kingdom was deteriorating and delivery promises were becoming even more unreliable, they began investigating alternative supply sources in the United States.

U.K.-based manufacturing managers felt that much of the responsibility for backlogs lay with the product engineers and the sales organizations. Their unreliable sales forecasts and constantly changing design specifications had severely disrupted production schedules. The worst bottlenecks involved outside suppliers and subcontractors that were unable to gear up and down overnight. Complete systems could be held up for weeks or months awaiting one simple component.

As the Northbrook plant became increasingly independent, U.S. managers sensed that the U.K. plants felt less responsibility for them. In tight supply situations they felt there was a tendency to ship to European or other export customers first. Some U.S. managers also believed that components were increasingly shipped from U.K. plants without the rigid final checks they normally received. The assumption was that the U.S. plant could do its own quality control. The English group strongly denied both these assertions.

Nonetheless, Bob Hagglund soon began urging Powell to let EMI Medical Inc. become a more independent manufacturing operation rather than simply a final assembly plant for U.K. components. This prospect disturbed John Willsher, managing director of EMI Medical Ltd., who argued that dividing manufacturing operations could mean duplicating overhead and spreading existing expertise too thin. Others felt that the "bootleg development" of alternate supply sources showed a disrespect for the "center of excellence" concept and could easily compromise the ability of Pantak (X-ray technology) and SE Labs (displays) to remain at the forefront of technology.

Product development issues also created some organizational tension. The U.S. sales organization knew that GE's impressive new third-generation "fan beam" scanner would soon be ready for delivery, and found customers hesitant to commit to EMI's new CT 5005 until the GE product came out. For months telexes had been flowing from Northbrook to EMI's Central Research Laboratories asking if drastic reductions in scan time might be possible to meet the GE threat.

Meanwhile, scientists at CRL felt that U.S. CT competition was developing into a specifications war based on the wrong issue, scan time. Shorter elapsed times meant less image blurring, but in the trade-off between scan time and picture resolution, EMI engineers had preferred to concentrate on better-quality images. They felt that the 20-second scan offered by EMI scanners was practical since a patient could typically hold his or her breath that long while being diagnosed.

CRL staff were exploring some entirely new imaging concepts and hoped to have a completed new scanning technology ready to market in three or four years. Although he was optimistic that it could provide a major breakthrough, Hounsfield could not guarantee that a commercially viable product would result from this research. He told Powell, however, that CRL had conducted experiments with the fan beam concept in the early 1970s, but had been unable to produce good-quality images. He argued that it was prohibitively costly to use sodium iodide detectors similar to those in existing scanners in the large numbers necessary to pick up a broad scan; to use other materials, such as xenon gas, would lead to quality and stability problems, in Hounsfield's view. Since GE and others offering third-generation equipment had not yet delivered commercial machines, he felt little incentive to redirect his staff to these areas that he had already researched and rejected.

There were many other demands on the time and attention of Hounsfield and his staff, all seemingly important for the company. They were in constant demand by technicians to deal with major problems that nobody else could solve. Salespeople wanted Hounsfield to talk to their largest and most prestigious customers, since such a visit often swung an important sale. Hounsfield and his staff also helped with internal training on all new products. The scientific community wanted them to present papers and give lectures. And increasingly Hounsfield found himself in a public relations role, accepting honors from all over the globe. EMI's reputation flourished and its image as the leader in the field was reinforced.

When it appeared that CRL was unwilling or unable to make the product changes the U.S. organization felt it needed, Hagglund made the bold proposal that the newly established research laboratories in Northbrook take responsibility for developing a three- to five-second scan, fan-beam-type scanner. Powell agreed to study the suggestion, but was finding it difficult to evaluate the relative merits of the U.S. subsidiary's views and the CRL scientists' opinions.

At year's end Powell had still been unable to find anybody to take charge of the worldwide medical electronics business. By default, the main decision-making forum became the Medical Group Review Committee (MGRC), a group of key line and staff managers that met, monthly at first, to help establish and review strategic decisions.

Among the issues discussed by this committee were the manufacturing and product development decisions that had produced tensions between the U.S. and U.K. managers. Powell had hoped that the MGRC would help build communications and consensus among his managers, but it soon became evident that this goal was unrealistic. In the words of one manager close to the events, "The problem was that there was no mutual respect between managers with similar responsibilities. Medical Ltd. was resentful of Medical Inc.'s push for greater independence, and were not going to go out of their way to help the Americans succeed."

As the business grew larger and more complex, Powell's ability to act as both corporate CEO and head of the worldwide medical business diminished. Increasingly, he was forced to rely on the MGRC to address operating problems as well as strategic issues. The coordination problem became so complex that by early 1977 there were four subcommittees of the MGRC, each with representatives of the U.S. and U.K. organizations, and each meeting monthly on one side of the Atlantic or the other. Committees included Manufacturing and Operations, Product Planning and Resources, Marketing and Sales Programs, and Service and Spares.

Powell's Problems

As the new year opened, John Powell reviewed EMI's medical electronics business. How well was it positioned? Where were the major threats and opportunities? What were the key issues he should deal with in 1977? Which should he tackle first, and how? These were the issues he turned over in his mind as he prepared to note down his plans for 1977.

Reading II–4
Technological Forecasting for Decision Making

B. C. Twiss

Thus in policy research we are not only concerned with anticipating future events and attempting to make the

---

Managing Technological Innovation, 2d ed. (New York: Longman, 1980), pp. 206–34. Reprinted with permission.

desirable ones more likely and the undesirable less likely. We are also trying to put policymakers in a position to deal with whatever future actually arises, to be able to alleviate the bad and exploit the good.

Herman Kahn

The Need to Forecast

All we know for certain about the future is that it will be different from the present. Thus the products, organizations, skills, and attitudes, which today serve a business well, may have little relevance to the conditions of tomorrow. If a business is to survive it must change. And the changes must be timely and appropriate to meet the needs of the future. The difficulty arises in prognosticating what these needs will be. Nevertheless, an attempt must be made to do so and, however imperfect forecasts may be, managers cannot afford to make decisions affecting the future of their organization without examining any clues they can find to the best of their ability.

Forecasts are important inputs to the process of strategy formulation and planning. They have been used to gain a better understanding of the threats and opportunities likely to be faced by established products and markets and, consequently, of the nature and magnitude of the changes needed. Thus, anticipation enables the business to be steered into the future in a purposeful fashion, in contrast to belated reaction to critical events. Nowadays, technical lead times are often so long that a market can be lost before a proper response is made. While this approach may be satisfactory conceptually, it is of little value unless one can make sufficiently accurate forecasts to aid the practical manager in decision making. During recent years, numerous techniques for technological forecasting have been developed with the object of enabling the manager to obtain the maximum use from the information available.

Since technology is responsible for many of the most important changes in our society, forecasting future advances in technology and their impact can be as vital for top management in the formulation of corporate strategy as it is for the technologist reviewing his R&D program. For technological changes may sometimes result in a major redefinition of an industry or market. We have seen, for example, that the producer of metal cans may find its major threats coming not from direct competitors in can manufacture, but from other packaging technologies such as glass, plastics, or paper, or from different forms of preservation such as freeze drying. However, the area of consideration might need to be widened even further to take in factors such as: the size of the future market for convenience goods upon which the relative económic merits of alternative packaging technologies may depend, the availability and future costs of packaging materials, customer tastes in convenience products, health and hygiene standards, and a multitude of similar items. Similarly, the manufacturer of razor blades, whilst aware of the direct alternative of the electric razor, may eventually suffer more dangerous competition from the development of effective depilatory creams. But in order to assess this threat, it is necessary not only to forecast the technological possibility of a satisfactory product being developed, but also to predict whether it would be socially acceptable to the market.

It follows that the field of investigation has to be very extensive if some important indication is not to be missed and it must include a wide range of social, economic, and political as well as technological factors. While sometimes identification of the threat or opportunity may be sufficient, more frequently the real implication can only be properly evaluated by a detailed study. When it is realized that each factor is associated with a high degree of uncertainty, the task of the forecaster might seem well nigh impossible. Yet, however daunting the difficulties may appear, the manager cannot avoid making decisions which will be proved good or bad by future events. He must take a view of the future. If forecasting techniques can enable the manager to obtain a more accurate picture of the future and in consequence improve his decision making, the effort devoted to it is justified. This can be the only real justification for forecasting.

In any consideration of forecasting, it is important not to lose sight of the high degree of uncertainty in the outcome. The future will never be predictable. Forecasting can assist in the formation of managerial judgment but will never replace it. Many of the critics of forecasting condemn it for its failures, of which there are abundant examples. Perhaps the forecasters themselves are largely to blame for encouraging others to place more reliance on their forecasts than they merit. We must learn to accept that many forecasts will remain poor, but appreciate that if conducted conscientiously, they will lead to fewer errors and the avoidance of some of the most costly mistakes.

With this perspective in mind, it can be seen that there are limitations which must set some bounds to the resources devoted to forecasting. For like any other managerial activity, the investment of time and resources can only be justified in terms of the benefit expected to derive from it. This criterion must be used to prevent excessive expenditure on forecasts which do not aid decision making, however interesting they may be in themselves. As Drucker comments:

> Decisions exist only in the present. The question that faces the long-range planner is not what we should do tomorrow, it is: What do we have to do today to be ready for an uncertain tomorrow? The question is not what will happen in the future. It is what futuristics do we have to factor into our present thinking and doing; what time spans do we have to consider, and how do we converge them to a simultaneous decision in the present?[1]

In some industries, today's decisions cover a long time scale. This is true of fuel, power generation, and communications where the effects of what is decided now will still be felt several decades hence. In the case of a power station—for example, in the choice of the reactor system for a nuclear plant—the design and construction stages may take 5 to 6 years, to be followed by an operating life of 20 years or more. Although the importance of the more distant dates loses significance because of financial discounting, it may still be necessary to make forecasts for a period of 20 or more years.

By contrast, the planning horizons for most companies are much shorter—on the order of 5 to 10 years. It is still important to forecast, for many significant changes can occur in a decade. Thus the only meaningful determinant of the time period for which forecasts are necessary would appear to be the planning horizon of the company. This is a function of the rate at which the company's activities can be made to respond to changes rather than the rate at which the environment itself is changing.

Hall, of International Computers Ltd., writes:

> In the field of product development, however, close control is necessary to ensure commercial viability, control of costs, and particularly of time scales. In this area, we can in the computer field respond to outside stimuli within about five years for any normal project and seven years for the very largest. . . . The practical range of technological forecasting required, therefore, and on which whole attention needs to be focused, is about five to seven years, this corresponding both to our response time and to the generation period of computer development.[2]

Summarizing, we can see that forecasting can assist business decision making in the following ways:

1. Wide-ranging surveillance of the total environment to identify developments, both within and outside the business's normal sphere of activity, which could influence the industry's future and, in particular, the company's own products and markets.

2. Estimating the time scale for important events in relation to the company's decision making and planning horizons. This gives an indication of the urgency for action.

3. The provision of more refined information following a detailed forecast in cases where an initial analysis finds evidence of the possibility of a major threat or opportunity in the near future, but where this evidence is insufficient to justify action, or continued monitoring of trends which, while not expected to lead to the necessity for immediate action, are, nevertheless, likely to become important at some time in the future and must consequently be kept under review.

4. Major reorientation of company policy to avoid situations which appear to pose a threat or to seek new opportunities by:

a. Redefinition of the industry or the company's business objectives in the light of new technological competition.

b. Modification of the corporate strategy.

c. Modification of the R&D strategy.

5. Improving operational decision making, particularly in relation to:

a. The R&D portfolio.

b. R&D project selection.

c. Resource allocation between technologies.

d. Investment in plant and equipment, including laboratory equipment.

e. Recruitment policy.

---

[1]P. F. Drucker, *Technology, Management, and Society* (London: Heinemann, 1970).

[2]P. D. Hall, "Technological Forecasting for Computer Systems," *Proceedings of National Conference on Technological Forecasting*, University of Bradford, 1968.

Level of Investment in Technological Forecasting

There is a common assumption that technological forecasting (TF) is for the larger companies, since only they can afford to undertake the exhaustive process of data collection and analysis required by the more sophisticated techniques. Technological forecasters often point to the dangers of forecasts based on inadequate analysis and argue that useful results can only be expected when information is meticulously gathered and carefully analyzed. This view is supported by Nicholson, who states:

> The useful analysis of present information to predict the future is likely to be more than a spare-time occupation for research or marketing staff. There needs to be a nucleus of planning staff who are familiar with the subject and who can act as a focus. Specialist staff can then be brought in temporarily to form teams for particular studies as required. In current practice, these teams are attached either to the headquarters of a company or to the central R&D department. Scientists and engineers have, to date, predominated in such activities, but economists, and hopefully sociologists, should be able to play a considerable part. In forecasting, one needs a wide range of thought processes brought to bear as well as a variety of methods.[3]

TF, then, appears to be an expensive activity employing a multidisciplinary team in detailed analysis. Without doubt, effort on this scale is normally essential if the most accurate forecasts are to be prepared. But this is a counsel of perfection. Small companies equally face an uncertain future and need to build some form of forecasting into their decision making even if it is based only on the judgment of the chief executive. If the CEO's judgment can be assisted by simple forecasting techniques, then they should be used, even though it is realized that more accurate forecasts might have resulted from the investment of greater effort in sophisticated techniques. The question should not be whether or not to forecast, but:

- To what extent is it necessary to forecast?
- Which are the most appropriate techniques to use, given the limitations of what can be afforded?

When attention is focused on need rather than the ability to pay, it can be seen that the importance of forecasting is much more a matter of the business environment than the size of the company. The large firm in a mature industry is unlikely to be overtaken suddenly by a technological development which will have a catastrophic effect. For such a company, TF can be confined to monitoring the environment to give early warning of the occasional advance; only then does it need more detailed forecasts. It was not, for example, St. Gobain's ignorance of the float glass process which led to its late investment in the new technology, but its lack of adequate response to the threat. TF might have helped the company's understanding, but its effect upon the decision-making process is likely to have been negligible.

By contrast, one can see how TF could have been applied both by IBM and its competitors when the IBM 360 series was being evaluated. Computer technology was advancing rapidly and forecasts showed a very close correlation between a computer's performance and the date of its introduction.[4] The rate of technological change in an industry should therefore be a much better criterion than size of company as a determinant of the need for TF, although as we have seen earlier, the speed at which a company can react to change is also important.

The obscurity of the precise nature of a threat also has an important bearing on the degree of detail required in a TF. Sometimes the threat is obvious, as in the case of the manufacturer of lead additives for petrol—the only area of doubt is in the time scale of antipollution legislation. On the other hand, the maker of lead acid batteries has a much more complex problem to resolve. Firstly, he has to consider whether the conventional reciprocating petrol engine will be totally banned, or whether the petroleum or motor industry will find an acceptable solution to exhaust pollution. If banned, it might be replaced by the Wankel engine, gas turbine, steam, or electric propulsion. Even if his analysis shows a high probability of electric traction being widely adopted, he will be aware that major motor manu-

---

[3]R. L. R. Nicholson, *Technological Forecasting as a Management Technique* (London: HMSO, 1968).

[4]R. U. Ayres, "Envelope Curve Forecasting," in *Technological Forecasting for Industry and Government,* ed. James R. Bright (Englewood Cliffs, NJ: Prentice Hall, 1968). Ayres shows a remarkably high degree of correlation between computer performance measured as

$$\frac{\text{capacity (bits)}}{\text{add time (secs)}}$$

and date for the period 1945–70. Hall has applied the Delphi technique to forecasting computer applications for up to 40 years from 1968. (Hall, "Technological Forecasting for Computer Systems.")

facturers are engaged in research into new forms of electric power storage. It is, therefore, not immediately obvious whether he is facing a threat or an opportunity. In this situation, detailed technological forecasting could be of invaluable assistance.

An offensive R&D strategy exposes a company to much greater risks than a defensive strategy, particularly in relation to the state of the technological art and timing. Greater steps into the unknown are involved. In this situation, opportunities are being sought, rather than the avoidance of threats. Thus, a company adopting an offensive strategy should devote correspondingly more resources to TF.

In summary, we can conclude that:

1. All companies should undertake some form of technological forecasting.

2. The amount of effort devoted to TF should take into account:

a. The rate of change in the environment.

b. The planning horizon determined by the technological and marketing lead times for new products or processes.

c. The complexity of the underlying problems.

d. The R&D strategy.

e. The size of the company only in so far as the availability of resources limits the choice of techniques which can be afforded.

The Definition of Technological Forecasting

Although there is nothing new in attempting to forecast the future trends of technology, it is only during the last decade or so that the range of techniques known collectively as technological forecasting has been developed. They differ from informal methods in their systematic analysis of data within a formalized structure. The main features of what we know as TF can be seen by examining several definitions.

Prehoda defines TF as:

> The description or prediction of a foreseeable technological innovation, specific scientific refinement, or likely scientific discovery, that promises to serve some useful function, with some indication of the most probable time of occurrence.[5]

Or Bright:

> Forecasting means systems of logical analysis that lead to common quantitative conclusions (or a limited range of possibilities) about technological attributes and parameters, as well as technical economic attributes. Such forecasts differ from opinion in that they rest upon an explicit set of quantitative relationships and stated assumptions, and they are produced by a logic that yields relatively consistent results.[6]

Or Cetron, who adds: "A prediction, with a level of confidence, of a technological achievement in a given time frame with a specified level of support."[7]

Let us now look at some of the phrases used in these definitions to obtain a clearer picture of the underlying basis for the techniques of TF.

Foreseeable

This reservation is not so restrictive as might be thought, for although it is true that forecasting is not an occult science, the fact emerges from the accumulated body of forecasting knowledge that unexpected breakthroughs are much rarer than commonly supposed. The much quoted example of penicillin is the exception rather than the rule. Most of the innovations of the next 20 years will be based upon scientific and technological knowledge existing now. The difficulty lies in identifying what is of real significance. With hindsight, what today appears obscure will tomorrow seem remarkably clear. The role of TF is to evaluate today's knowledge systematically, thereby identifying what is achievable and, more particularly, how one technological advance, perhaps in conjunction with another, could fulfil a human need.

Specific scientific refinement

Most writers lay heavy stress upon the need to focus attention upon a specific development or discovery. The complex interplay of environmental factors escalates a detailed forecast rapidly even when the subject of the exercise is defined in specific terms. Without this restriction, the study would quickly get out of hand. Admittedly the scenarios for the year 2000 of the think tank investigators such as Kahn

[5] R. W. Prehoda, *Designing the Future—The Role of Technological Forecasting* (London: Chilton Books, 1967).

[6] J. R. Bright, ed., *Technological Forecasting for Industry and Government: Methods and Applications* (Englewood Cliffs, NJ: Prentice Hall, 1968).

[7] M. J. Cetron, *Technological Forecasting—A Practical Approach* (London: Gordon and Breach, 1969).

explore every aspect of human activity, but these are far removed from the practical consideration of industrial forecasters, who are concerned with decision making in respect of specific threats, opportunities, or innovations.[8]

Nevertheless, we have seen already that the initial screening of the environment should be wide-ranging; otherwise, there is a danger of becoming distracted by detailed forecasting of the wrong phenomenon. Thus, while accepting that detailed forecasts must be focused upon a specific development, they must be preceded by a much broader investigation to ensure that the effort is being allocated to the right task.

That promises to serve some useful function

The importance of a market orientation in successful technological innovation has already been stressed. As a corollary, one might assume that technological progress will respond to market needs. But is this so? It is certainly not true of science where progress stems from the desire of scientists to push back the frontiers of knowledge. Technology, however, is different. It advances through industrial investment motivated by the desire to reap specific benefits, financial in the case of business, though they may be social or political where government expenditure is involved. Thus, it is the market which ultimately determines the pace of progress.

Corroborative evidence comes from an extensive study of the growth and application of technology carried out in respect of defense projects in the United States under the title of "Project Hindsight." Isenson, reporting on this project, writes, "The first conclusion of the study is that real needs result in accelerated technological growth. Conversely, in the absence of real needs, technological growth is inhibited."[9]

The importance of practical objectives for technological advance is self-evident. Nevertheless, it is easy for technological forecasters, wrapped up in the elegance of their techniques, to lose sight of this simple truth. There is a clear distinction to be drawn between *what could happen,* because of human capabilities, and *what is likely to occur,* because of what we want.

Quantitative conclusions, levels of confidence, a given time frame

Since the purpose of a forecast is to provide a useful basis for decision making, it must be expressed in terms the manager can apply. Vague qualitative statements are of little use. Managers require specific quantitative information with an indication of its reliability. The uncertainties inherent in any forecast must also be reflected in its presentation.

Whereas the statement "The computer will eventually eliminate the need for cheques in financial transactions" is unhelpful since it is unquantified, the alternative "By 1990, 80 percent of the financial transactions currently carried out by cheque will be replaced by the computer" is misleading, because although quantified, it gives no indication of the uncertainties involved. This second statement needs to be associated with a probability distribution, albeit subjective, relating the time of occurrence of the event to the probability of it happening by that date.

Specific level of support

We have already noted that technology advances in response to a market need. The rate of progress, however, depends upon the scale of effort devoted to it, in itself a function of the importance attached to the need. In many cases, the need will be stimulated by events largely unconnected with technology. One example is provided by the programme to land a man on the moon's surface. The prime objective was national prestige rather than the furtherance of science. For the origins one must look to the "space race" between the United States and Russia. Thus international technopolitical competition created conditions enabling the U.S. government to provide NASA with funds on a massive scale. Although technological feasibility was a precondition for success, the date when the mission could be accomplished was closely geared to the level of financial support.

Similarly, the development of motor car antipollution devices is not the result of direct pressure from individual owners unwilling to poison their fellow citizens; it is the outcome of social pressure

---

[8] H. Kahn and A. J. Weiner, *The Year 2000: A Framework for Speculation on the Next Thirty-Three Years* (New York: Macmillan, 1967).

[9] C. W. Sherwin and R. S. Isenson, *First Interim Report on Project Hindsight,* Office of the Director of Defense Research and Engineering Clearing House for Scientific and Technological Information, no. AD. 642-400, 1966. See also Bright, *Technological Forecasting for Industry and Government.*

which subsequently manifests itself in political action resulting in legislation. This determines the scale of the motor manufacturer's investment in the development of antipollution equipment. Another example is found in the development of, and investment in, automation equipment where the supply and cost of labour provides the incentive rather than the availability of suitable technologies.

Exhibit 1 shows this interlinking chain of events. The timing of a specific innovation depends upon the investment available for the development and the technological complexity. But the level of financial support or investment is in turn determined by the importance of the need as perceived by those people responsible for making available the resources; usually this will be corporate management, though it may also be the government or another sponsoring organization. However, it is a convergence of environmental pressures which gives rise to the need and their strength which determines its importance. Thus, it follows that technological forecasting must look behind the need at the whole of the environment if any useful attempt is to be made to gauge the likely level of support and consequently the timing of an innovation. Furthermore, technology cannot be looked at in isolation, since it is necessary to forecast the interaction of these economic, political, social, industrial, and technological forces.

Produced by a logic that yields relatively consistent results

This phrase goes to the heart of the matter. For TF is a logical, systematic examination of data which substantially eliminates human judgment from the processing of the information. Judgment enters in the selection of the area to be examined (e.g., technological parameter), the collation of data, and the interpretation of the results. The stage in the middle, the application of the technique, should, however, be little affected by opinion—two people using the same technique on identical data should produce forecasts different only in detail.

EXHIBIT 1 Technological Forecasting and the Innovation Chain

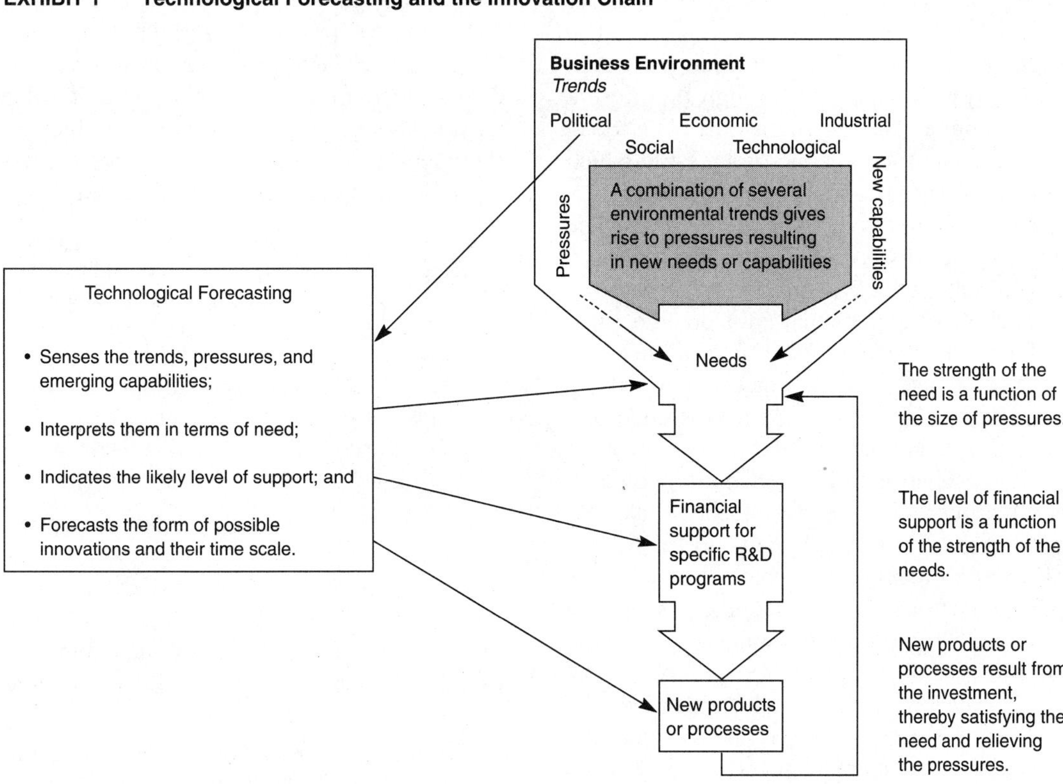

Inputs to the Forecasting System

Like any other procedure for systematic analysis, forecasting can only be as accurate as the information fed into it. The inadequacy of the input data cannot be compensated, though it might easily be hidden, by highly sophisticated quantitative analysis. And what we have at our disposal is limited to:

1. Information from the past.
2. Knowledge of the present.
3. The ability of the human intellect—logical thought process, insight, and judgment.

These are the only resources to be marshaled and interpreted within a forecasting system. Discussion of TF inevitably centers on the detail of the techniques themselves, but this must not be allowed to distract attention from the two factors that determine the usefulness of the results—the quality of the input data and the caliber of the minds applied to the task.

Classification of Forecasting Techniques

The techniques of TF are commonly classified under the headings of "exploratory" or "normative." The term *exploratory* covers those techniques based upon an extension of the past through the present and into the future. They look forward from today taking into account the dynamic progression which brought us to today's position.

A normative approach starts from the future. The mind is projected forward by postulating a desired or possible state of events represented by the accomplishment of a particular mission, the satisfaction of a need, or state of technological development. It is then necessary to trace backwards to determine the steps necessary to reach the end point and assess the probability of their achievement. In the elaborate scenarios developed by the research of think tanks such as the Hudson Institute, alternative futures for the whole of mankind are developed. These workers claim that the scenarios present a choice from which mankind can select the most desirable of the alternative futures enabling the formulation of policies and the allocation of resources to travel the path to reach the desired end. However, these prognostications are beyond the concern of the industrial manager whose objectives are specific and limited. Nevertheless, they do underline that there is always a choice to be made.

In a practical forecasting exercise, it is usually necessary to employ a combination of techniques, some of which may be exploratory and some normative. For in dealing with great uncertainty, it is essential to examine every clue from as many angles as possible.

Too much stress must not be placed on "making the future happen." It is rare that one company or series of decisions has a profound influence on the future of technology, although the consequences of a decision may be of great significance for the company concerned. If one firm does not proceed with a potential innovation, there is a high probability that another will do so within a short space of time. The history of technology contains many examples where similar innovations occurred almost simultaneously in several places. This is not chance, but the result of a combination of the advances in several technologies necessary for the achievement of an innovation. It was not, for example, the discovery of the principle of the gas turbine, which had been known for many years, that made possible its practical realization in the late 1930s, but the availability of high-temperature materials. Project Hindsight provides further evidence and concludes, "Engineering design of improved military weapon systems consists primarily of skillfully selecting and integrating a large number of innovations from diverse technological areas so as to produce systematically the high performance achieved." This statement is supported by evidence from several examples investigated during the research program:

> As an example, transistor technology is credited with being responsible for size reduction in electronic equipment; however, without the development of such ancillary technologies as tantalytic capacitors, high-core permeability chokes and transformers, printed circuits, dip soldering, nickel cadmium batteries, and silicon cell power supplies, the electronic equipment chassis would be only marginally (perhaps 10 percent) smaller than a vacuum tube version.[10]

Thus, if a forecasting exercise is to give useful guidance to decision makers regarding a specific innovation, it must take into account not only a wide range of technological advances but also their mutual interactions. Furthermore, timing is of the essence. Before a certain date, the convergence of

---

[10]R. S. Isenson, "Technological Forecasting Lessons from Project Hindsight," in *Technological Forecasting for Industry and Government: Methods and Applications,* ed. J. R. Bright (Englewood Cliffs, NJ: Prentice Hall, 1968).

technological capabilities is insufficient to support the innovation. Once that stage has been reached, competitive forces are likely to ensure a limited time advantage to the company that seizes the initiative. TF can assist in deciding when to start. But the competitive edge so gained will be quickly eroded by an R&D program poorly conceived or conducted without vigor.

Most businesses are living in the type of environment we have just examined, where opportunities will emerge from marginal improvements in a number of advancing and converging technologies. In this situation, exploratory techniques of TF are likely to be the most helpful.

Mission-oriented programs are rarer. Frequently, they result from socially or politically motivated needs and are likely to involve major investments. The end point of the project will be postulated—landing a man on the moon, low toxicity motor car exhausts, a supersonic airliner, or an antiballistic missile system. Normative techniques, usually in conjunction with exploratory methods, can be of assistance here in forecasting the likely time of achieving the desired outcome with different levels of support, evaluating the alternative paths and selecting the best, and estimating the probabilities that each component of the overall program will be satisfied within a given time scale.

EXHIBIT 2 History of a Developing Technology Where Rate of Advance Does Not Follow a Regular Path

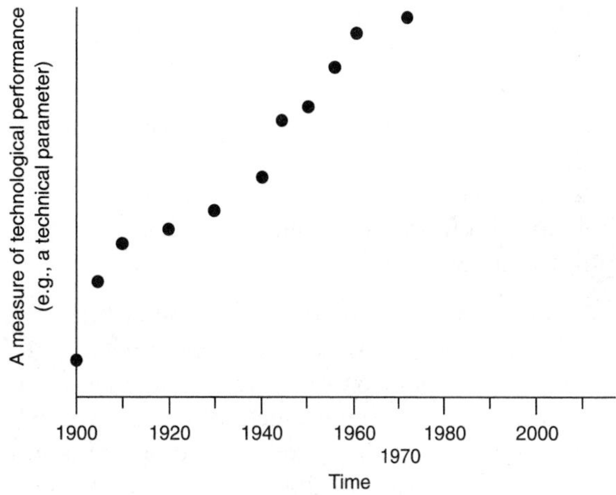

Note: 1. Although there has been an advance of performance with time, it has not followed a regular pattern. With this information it is not possible to fit a curve to give a meaningful forecast for the future.

2. If technological parameters followed such an erratic path, forecasting would not be possible. Fortunately this is rarely the case.

The Paths of Technological Progress

If technological progress consisted of a succession of random events (Exhibit 2) where it was not possible to establish any relationship between the rate of technological advance and time, any attempt to forecast would be impossible. Fortunately, however, analysis of historical data from a considerable number of phenomena shows that progress is not random and discontinuous, but follows a regular pattern when a selected attribute, such as functional performance (e.g., aircraft speed), a technical parameter (e.g., the tensile strength to density ratio for a material), or economic performance (e.g., cost per kwhr for electrical generation) is plotted against time. Characteristically, one finds an S-curve pattern (Exhibit 3).

EXHIBIT 3 The S-Curve

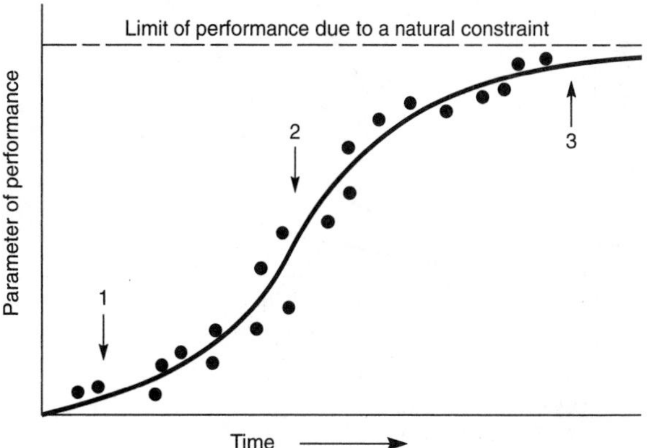

1 Period of slow initial growth.

2 Rapid exponential growth.

3 Growth slows as performance approaches a natural physical limit asymptotically.

The S-curve is similar to a product life cycle in that we observe a slow initial growth, followed by a rapid rise of approximately exponential growth, which slows down as it approaches asymptotically an upper limit normally set by some physical property.

Two important guidelines for R&D management can be inferred from observation of the shape of the S-curve:

1. The human intellect, with its linear thought patterns, may seriously underestimate the rapidity of the potential progress when establishing design specifications during the exponential midphase.
2. The decreasing managerial returns which may be expected from investment in a technology as its physical limit is approached.

It must not be assumed, however, that there is a predetermined path which progress inevitably follows. No progress occurs without human investment decisions. Thus, although a technology follows an S-curve, the actual path it takes will be one of a family of such curves. If the stimulus to invest in reaching a higher performance is low, the curve described is likely to be one of the form OB (Exhibit 4). By contrast, OC_2 exhibits the much greater rate of progress to be found when market needs have led to a high expenditure in R&D. It is also possible to modify the shape of the curve: for example, a technology having reached the point A_1 on curve OA, at time t_1 may receive a stimulus from a needs-oriented mission which causes it to follow the path $A_1C_1C_2$; there is, of course, a limit to the maximum slope of the curve set by the size of the resources available or the rate at which they can be usefully employed. From the viewpoint of a forecaster at time t_1 attempting to predict the future with the knowledge that progress to date has followed the path OA_2, the indications are that the curve A_1A_2 has a high probability of describing the immediate future, unless he or she can positively identify some factor likely to cause a discontinuity producing a departure along a different path. In practice, such occurrences are infrequent.

An approaching physical limit does not remove the need to forecast. For it is at such a time that a new technology may emerge. This new technology will have a different physical limit and a potential for further progress in performance. Eventually it is likely to supplant the existing technology in a wide range of applications, particularly when they call for high performance. This situation frequently gives rise to a succession of S-curves (Exhibit 5) which can be contained within an "envelope" curve, also of the familiar S-shape. Ayres has plotted the efficiency of the external combustion engine from the time of

EXHIBIT 4 Possible Paths of Progress

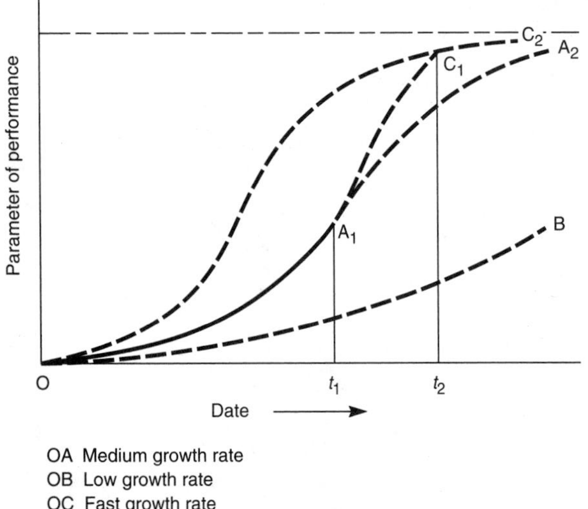

The rate of growth is largely determined by the technological effort devoted to it. A technology which has advanced along OA_1 to time t_1 may be expected to progress along A_1A *unless* an identifiable outside factor causes an acceleration along A_1C_1.

EXHIBIT 5 Effect of an Emergent New Technology on an Established Technology

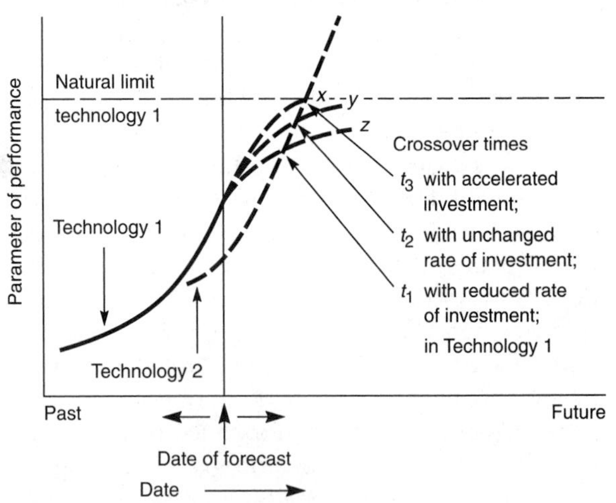

An emerging technology 2 is likely to replace the existing technology 1. The question is, when? What effect will the threat from 2 have on investment in 1? And how will this influence the date of substitution of 2 for 1?

Savery (1698) and Newcommen (1712) to the high pressure turbines of the present day, spanning seven different technological approaches.[11] In every case, he observes the same pattern. For example, between 1820 and 1850, the efficiency of the Cornish type engine rose rapidly from less than 5 percent to over 15 percent. Between 1850 and 1880, progress was slow until the triple expansion engine appeared on the scene, raising the efficiency to 22 percent by 1910, at which date the Parsons Turbine brought about another rapid rise. In the total period of 270 years, efficiencies have risen from virtually zero to over 50 percent and the "envelope" curve describing them has closely followed the S-shape. On the much shorter time scale of 30 years, Ayres has plotted computer performance on semilog paper, showing a remarkably close straight line relationship between computer performance and time spanning four technologies—valves, transistors, hybrids, and integrated circuits.

As would be expected from the S-curve, an emergent new technology at first grows slowly. This is because its early performance is likely to be inferior to the highly developed existing technology. But when the performance of the two technologies approaches the same level, the greater potential of the newcomer attracts increasing investment, particularly once it has taken the lead when it begins to grow exponentially.

No natural law governs the emergence of a new technology. There is a physical limit even to the discovery of new technologies as evidenced by the flattening of the "envelope" curve. This phenomenon does, however, present the R&D manager with some particularly tricky judgments. The experience of history suggests that a slowing down or the approach of a natural limit should be an alert to the possible appearance of something new. But the correct reaction to the identification of a substitute technology is not straightforward.

The initial expectation is that R&D effort will be transferred and that attempts to approach closer to the upper performance limit of the established technology will be reduced. However, in practice, the reaction may be the reverse. A great deal of capital is invested in the existing system. The threat may call for a defensive response and an increased rather than reduced investment when some development potential remains. This can be seen in Exhibit 5 where an established technology (1) is threatened by progress in technology (2). Extrapolating the past trends suggests a crossover point at time t_2 where T represents the present. But in spite of the approaching natural limit for (1) it is still possible to invest more heavily in it to follow the path TX rather than TY, thereby delaying the crossover point to time t_3. In the perspective of history, the delay represented by t_2–t_3 is insignificant, but it may be of great importance to the short-term strategy of a business heavily invested in (1). This effect is often observed in practice. A good example is provided by the substitution of nuclear for conventional fuels in electric power generation. The forecasts of the economic crossover point for these two systems made 20 years ago have been shown to be grossly optimistic. One important reason for this has been an unexpected improvement in the performance of conventional power stations stimulated by the threat of nuclear power.

We can see that study of the past progress of technology confirms the existence of regular patterns, and provides a framework within which forecasting can be undertaken. It also indicates the types of information that the R&D manager would like to extract from forecasts, as:

1. The performance levels likely to be reached within his decision-making horizons in the absence of any new stimuli.
2. The identification of stimuli which may change the level of technological support and the effect this would have on the rate of progress.
3. The approach of a natural or physical limit for a technological parameter and its impact on the rate of progress.
4. The emergence of new technologies and the identification of crossover points:
   a. Without additional investment in the established technology.
   b. With changed levels of investment.
5. The determination of performance milestones in several technologies the achievement of which would together make feasible a specific innovation.

The Techniques of Technological Forecasting

It is beyond the scope of this chapter to explain in detail the many techniques for technological forecasting now available and fully described in the lit-

[11]Ayres, "Envelope Curve Forecasting."

erature.[12] The following brief descriptions of a few of the most widely used techniques will not attempt to provide the reader with a working basis for their practical application; they are intended to show how the principles described previously can be applied and some of the major problems likely to be encountered. But it is worth reiterating that the techniques are not an end in themselves, and their successful application must rest heavily upon the technological experience and insights of the managers using them.

Trend Extrapolation

The extrapolation of past trends into the future is a technique economic forecasters have used for many years. At first sight, this seems to present the easy exercise of applying a mathematical curve-fitting technique to past data and extrapolating into the future. However, the technological forecaster will encounter many practical difficulties and traps into which he may fall. Considerable judgment is required both in the choice and use of data.

Selection of the appropriate parameters or attributes to plot is critically important. The wrong choice will lead to the wrong conclusion. Bright, for example, suggests that one reason for the late entry of U.S. aeroengine manufacturers into gas turbines for civil air transport was their preoccupation with specific fuel consumption as the criterion of aeroengine performance. Consideration of the performance of the aircraft system in terms of passenger miles per unit of cost would have shown the potential of the gas-turbine powered aircraft in spite of the high specific fuel consumption of the power units. With the benefit of hindsight, it is easy to see how this error could occur. For several decades, the development of propeller-driven aircraft powered by piston engines had been progressing along one S-curve. Marginal improvements in engine fuel consumption which did not significantly modify the system were the main concern. Thus, the thinking of the aeroengine manufacturers was focused on their own technology. But the emergence of the gas turbine called for a reexamination of the engine in relation to the total system of which it formed only a part. The technological orientation of the traditional aeroengine manufacturers caused them to lose sight of the needs of the market for the system in which their product was embodied.

Although it is desirable for the parameter being plotted to be an independent variable, this is not always possible. Lenz quotes the example of aircraft passenger capacity, passenger miles, load factor, and total aircraft miles flown.[13] These are clearly independent. Whereas the graphs for passenger miles and seating capacity follow a rising pattern, that for aircraft miles flown begins to fall after about 1965 because of the impact of increased aircraft size. This fall is unlikely to be predicted from consideration of this factor in isolation and the simple fitting of a curve to past data. It is incorrect, therefore, to select aircraft miles flown as a parameter for trend extrapolation; it should be derived from extrapolation of the other factors. For example:

$$\text{Aircraft miles flown} = \frac{\text{Passenger miles}}{\text{Aircraft seating capacity} \times \text{Load factor}}$$

This again underlines the dangers of attempting to forecast mechanically without a proper understanding of the underlying technologies and their interrelationships.

One of the most frequent sources of difficulty arises from the absence or inadequacy of data upon which to base the forecast. Whereas the economic forecaster has at his disposal a wealth of relatively reliable statistics, systematically gathered, this is rarely the case with historical technological data. Furthermore, the data available to the economist—population and demographic information, GNP figures, income distribution, and the like—is unambiguous and requires the minimum of judgment in selection. The technological forecaster attempting to establish the trend for, say, aeroengine-specific fuel consumption faces a much more difficult problem. Where does one find the data from the past? What do we mean by the term—is it the maximum achieved on the test bed? In the latest military application? Or in civil use? Unless such questions are resolved satisfactorily, the data plotted will not be strictly comparable. In any case, the forecaster will be lucky if the data eventually unearthed do not present a difficult curve-fitting problem. Thus, the forecaster

[12]E. Jantsch, *Technological Forecasting in Perspective,* Organization for Economic Cooperation and Development (OECD), 1967. Also, H. Jones and B. C. Twiss, *Forecasting Technology for Planning Decisions* (New York: Macmillan, 1978).

[13]R. C. Lenz, "Forecasts of Exploding Technologies by Trend Extrapolation," in Bright, *Technological Forecasting for Industry and Government.*

would be wise to make several projections, perhaps using different curve-fitting techniques, although he or she should avoid the temptation of offering so wide a range of possibilities that, while providing the forecaster with an alibi for the future, he or she gives the decision maker little useful guidance.

The inadequacy of data about the past available today indicates a first priority when initiating TF within a company. A system for collecting, interpreting, and recording contemporary data should be established to provide future forecasters with an improved data base. In this way, forecasting accuracy can be steadily improved.

In spite of the difficulties of accurate trend extrapolation, it provides one of the most useful and widely used techniques. However, confidence will diminish with the time period of the forecast and this technique is consequently of greatest value in the short term, say 5 to 15 years. In this period, the accuracy of the forecast is likely to fall within limits imposed by the quality of the input data, unless some distorting factor, a new technology, or a mission-oriented program emerges.

Precursor Trends—Curve Matching

Most industrial R&D is conducted in areas where the commercial application of a new technology or innovation has been preceded by its use where special attributes have outweighed the possible shortcomings. Thus, in scientific research or military applications, high cost or doubtful reliability may be less important than performance. Aerospace and electronics are two industries where this is particularly true.

The trends for both the first application and the commercial adoption are likely to follow each other, but with a regular lag (Exhibit 6). Lenz has shown that the trend line for the speed of transport aircraft has lagged behind that for combat aircraft by a period which has slowly extended from 9 years in 1930 to 11 years by 1970. The value of this knowledge to the commercial aerospace forecaster is obvious. If one can identify a precursor application which follows a regular trend behind which one's own application follows, then there is a good indication of when today's advanced technologies are likely to appear in commercial products. The example of aircraft speed also shows how careful one has to be in attempting to use past data to forecast the future. Whereas the correlation was good up to the mid-1960s, we may query whether it will still hold

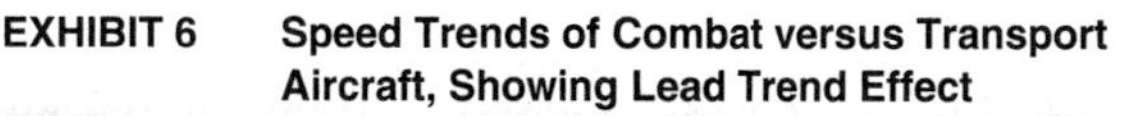

EXHIBIT 6 Speed Trends of Combat versus Transport Aircraft, Showing Lead Trend Effect

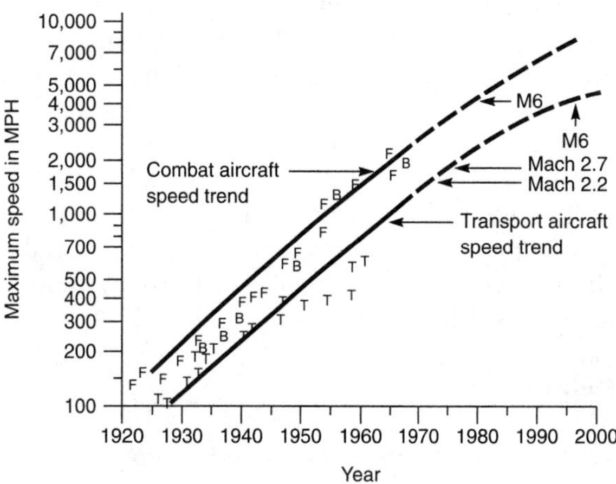

SOURCE: Ralph C. Lenz, "Forecasts of Exploding Technologies by Trend Extrapolation."

for the future. This arises from two factors. Firstly, the importance to passengers of reduced air travel times as a proportion of actual travel time is decreasing. There is, of course, a natural limit of zero travel time. But more importantly, the size of the investment required to develop supersonic airlines is so large that it has been removed from the realm of industrial commercial decision making to that of politics and governments. This change of the industrial environment may well cause a departure from the trend line produced from past data.

In the frequency of radio transmissions, three stages of development can be traced—research, amateur and military, and commercial applications. In all three, a good correlation has been observed from the time of Marconi's first propagation experiment to the present day, the time lag between research and commercial use being about 30 years, with the military/amateur application appearing about halfway through this period.

This discovery of a precursor relationship gives the forecaster additional confidence for he has two "fixes" for a point in the future, that obtained from extrapolating the curve for his own application, and a cross-reference from the precursor. It may also provide him with a useful clue to the date when a new substituting technology (e.g., the laser), at present in use in the research laboratory, is likely to achieve commercial exploitation.

Technological Substitution

Frequently a new technology substitutes for an existing technology. Study of a large number of historical examples indicates that the growth pattern follows the S-shaped curve of Exhibit 3. Fisher and Pry have shown that when the proportion of the new product has reached about 5 percent, the dynamics of the substitution process are likely to be well established. Thus, the remainder of the curve may be predicted with reasonable confidence in the absence of any discontinuities which may modify the rate of substitution.

Delphi

The opinion of experts can give important insights into the future, particularly in the identification of potential innovations likely to disturb the path of progress away from the extrapolated trend. Traditionally, expert opinion has been brought to bear through the medium of committee meetings. The Delphi technique was developed by Helmer at the Rand Corporation to overcome the weaknesses of the committee by using the individual judgments of a panel of experts working systematically and in combination, divorced from the distortions introduced by their personalities.

The committee method suffers from a variety of shortcomings. In the first place, geographical dispersion and the full diaries of prominent experts severely limit the membership and opportunities to bring them together. Once assembled, the committee process may not lead to a conclusion representing the unbiased views of all its members. Some people who are persuasive or articulate in discussion have a greater influence because of these characteristics rather than the strength of their case.

Other members may obtain a better hearing because of a position of authority or a high scientific reputation. Furthermore, there is a natural reluctance to change publicly a view which has previously been expressed strongly.

Another major weakness of the committee is the "bandwagon" effect produced by the disinclination of an individual to disagree with a majority view, in spite of one's own judgment. This phenomenon is illustrated with great force in the work of the psychologist Asch.[14] In a series of experiments, all but one of a group of students were briefed to support an erroneous view unbeknown to the remaining member. He described one of his experiments in which the subjects were shown two cards, one bearing a standard line, and the other three lines of which only one was the same length as the standard. When asked to select which of these three was the same length as the standard, Asch found that, "whereas in ordinary circumstances, individuals matching the lines will make mistakes less than 1 percent of the time, under group pressure, the minority subjects swing to acceptance of the misleading majority's wrong judgment in 36.8 percent of the selections." When such distortions can be created in a straightforward situation, one can appreciate the possible influence of this effect where there is genuine uncertainty as is inevitable when considering the future. Nevertheless, the minority view might well be valid and its expression should not be suppressed.

Delphi attempts to eliminate these problems by using a questionnaire technique circulated to a panel of experts who are not aware of the identity of their fellow members. The procedure is as follows:

1. *Round 1:* Circulate the questionnaire by post to the panel.
2. *Round 2:* After analysis of the Round 1 replies, recirculate, stating the median and interquartile range of the replies. Respondents are asked to reconsider their answers and those whose replies fall outside the interquartile range are invited to state their reasons—these may result from lack of knowledge, or more importantly, from some specialist information unknown to the other members.
3. *Round 3:* Analysis of replies from Round 2 are recirculated, together with the reasons proferred in support of the extreme positions, in the light of which the panel members are asked once more to reconsider their replies.
4. Further rounds for additional clarification may be employed if thought necessary.

Selection of the panel members is a task of the utmost importance, for the value of the forecast is a function of the caliber and expertise of the individual contributors as well as the appropriateness and comprehensiveness of the areas of knowledge they represent. Questionnaire formulation also requires considerable skill to ensure the right questions are

[14] S. E. Asch, "Opinions and Social Pressures," *Scientific American,* November 1955. Reprinted in *Readings in Managerial Psychology,* eds. H. J. Leavitt and L. R. Pondy (Chicago: University of Chicago Press, 1964).

EXHIBIT 7 Part of Delphi Forecast for Computer Systems—International Computer, Ltd.

Use

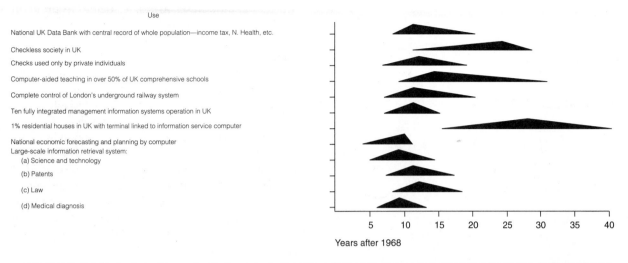

National UK Data Bank with central record of whole population—income tax, N. Health, etc.

Checkless society in UK

Checks used only by private individuals

Computer-aided teaching in over 50% of UK comprehensive schools

Complete control of London's underground railway system

Ten fully integrated management information systems operation in UK

1% residential houses in UK with terminal linked to information service computer

National economic forecasting and planning by computer

Large-scale information retrieval system:

(a) Science and technology

(b) Patents

(c) Law

(d) Medical diagnosis

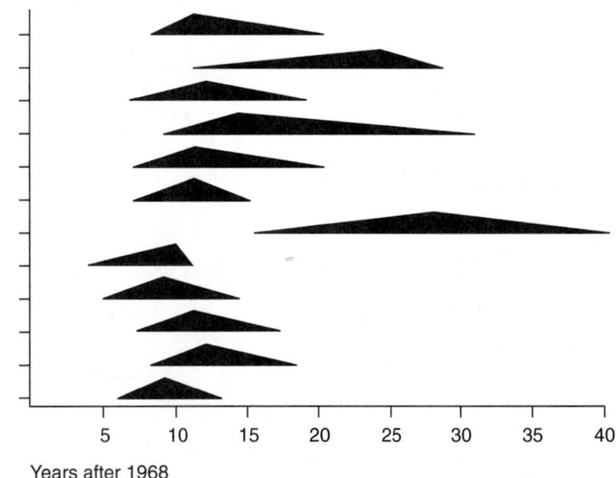

SOURCE: P. D. Hall, "Technological Forecasting for Computer Systems." Proc. National Conference on Technological Forecasting, University of Bradford, 1968.

asked and that they are framed in specific, quantified, and unambiguous terms.

Delphi is most widely used for longer range forecasts. Exhibit 7 is part of a typical Delphi presentation for the computer industry. Another interesting published study has been conducted by Smith, Kline, and French Laboratories, into future developments in medicine.[15]

The evidence supports the contention that Delphi studies result in a gain of consensus either by the rejection of extreme positions or by shifting the median as a consequence of specialist knowledge introduced by one or more members of the panel. But how accurate are the resulting forecasts? The technique is of too recent origin to provide a great deal of validation. There are some indications, however, that there may be a tendency to err in an optimistic direction in the short term due to an underestimation of development times. By contrast, long-term forecasts may well be pessimistic because of the mind's inability to appreciate fully the effects of exponential growth.

Rand Corporation has, however, conducted experiments to validate the methodology. These show clearly that when experts have been asked about current phenomena where it is possible to establish a factual answer, consensus grows as the study progresses, and moves toward the correct answer. This suggests possible applications outside TF such as in cost estimation and R&D project selection.

Scenarios

Scenario writing has become most widely known through the work of American think tanks such as the Hudson Institute. The scenarios describe a possible future situation based upon a wide-ranging environmental analysis. Frequently several scenarios or alternative futures are prepared supported by detailed research using a wide variety of TF techniques. Scenario writing is based upon the recognition that it is not always possible to choose between alternative sets of assumptions.

In recent years, interest in scenario writing has increased at both the national and industrial level. Energy forecasting is a field where this approach has been used extensively.[16] A number of practical techniques for industrial scenario writing have been

[15]A. D. Bender et al. "Delphi Study Examines Developments in Medicine," *Futures,* June 1969.

[16]*Energy Research and Development in the UK.* Energy Paper No. 11, HMSO, 1976. Also, P. Chapman, *Fuel's Paradise: Energy Options for Britain* (New York: Penguin Books, 1975).

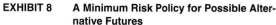

EXHIBIT 8 A Minimum Risk Policy for Possible Alternative Futures

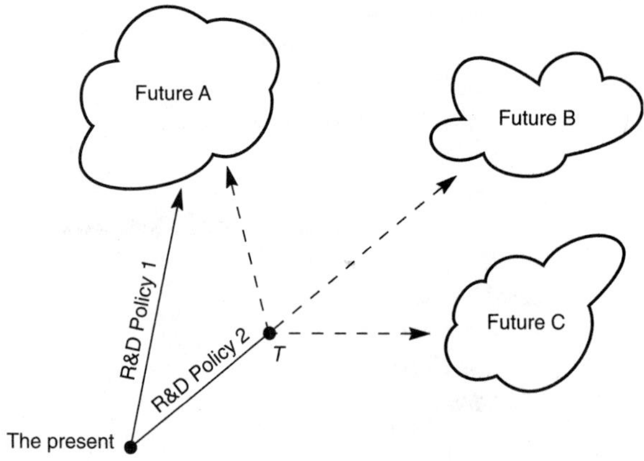

Futures A, B, and C are three scenarios of alternative futures. The forecast may result in R&D action as follows:

Policy 1 Future A is considered so probable that decisions are made assuming the forecast is correct.

Policy 2 A minimum risk policy permitting an advance to *T*, without precluding any of the scenarios. At time *T* a decision cannot be deferred any longer. In this way the decision has been delayed to the latest possible date.

developed to enable the consideration of the mutual interactions of a wide range of environmental factors both upon themselves and upon an organization's strategic objectives.[17] Thus, this is an approach which extends beyond top management to review their strategic assumptions and the consequences flowing from them.

The use of scenarios in decision making is illustrated diagrammatically in Exhibit 8. Three alternative futures have been identified: A, B, and C. Although it is possible to attach probabilities to the likelihood of occurrence of each of the alternatives, they are not likely to be very reliable. It may, of course, emerge that all the evidence points in one direction with a high probability of the future being similar to that described by Scenario A. In this case, the long-term R&D programs (Policy 1) could be based on this assumption. Policy 1 might, however, be such that it has no relevance to Futures B or C. In the more likely case when it is not possible to choose clearly between A, B, or C, a program (Policy 2) which keeps the options open is likely to be the best compromise. At a later date, the program can be reoriented in the light of future events. Thus, a minimum risk strategy can be adopted as a conscious act of policy.

Most writers stress the interaction between the decisions resulting from forecasts and the determination of the future. If Scenario A is thought to be likely, then following Policy 1 as a result of the forecast could make it a self-fulfilling prophecy. Such freedom to shape the future is open to few companies. But one can see how scenarios could be used to shape the government policy. If, for example, Scenario C described a highly undesirable future for humankind, then, given the correct political conditions, government policies could ensure that the path leading to it is sealed off.

Relevance Trees

The purpose of a relevance tree is to determine and evaluate systematically the alternative paths by which a normative objective or mission could be achieved. How this is done can best be seen by examining the abbreviated version illustrated in Exhibit 9.

The objective (O) is the starting point—let us say a pollution-free road transport system. At the next level, the problem can be broken down into alternative solution concepts A, B, C, etc. (e.g., electric car, Wankel Engine, "clean" petrol piston engine), or by functions to be performed (e.g., for a moon landing there would be launch, midcourse flight and control, lunar landing, lunar take-off, earth reentry). For a particular solution, a variety of systems will be necessary (e.g., fuel systems, combustion, and exhaust), each of which in turn may be satisfied in a variety of ways involving alternative subsystems (e.g., mechanical, electrical, or catalytic exhaust cleaners).

Thus, starting from the desired end result, it is possible to examine exhaustively all the alternative paths by which it can be reached, working backwards through a hierarchy ending with detailed and limited R&D project objectives. The next stage is to investigate each step in greater depth including feasibility, resources required, probability of success, and time scale. This involves the employment of other TF techniques such as Delphi and trend extrapolation.

Relevance trees can be useful to the R&D manager in:

[17] Jones and Twiss, *Forecasting Technology*. Also, C. A. R. MacNulty, "Scenario Development for Corporate Planning," *Futures*, April 1977.

EXHIBIT 9 Relevance Tree

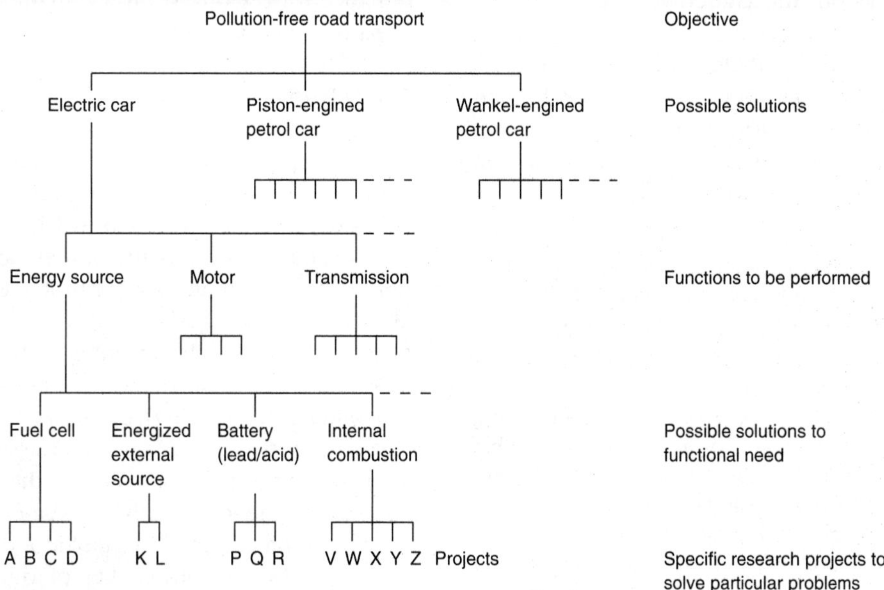

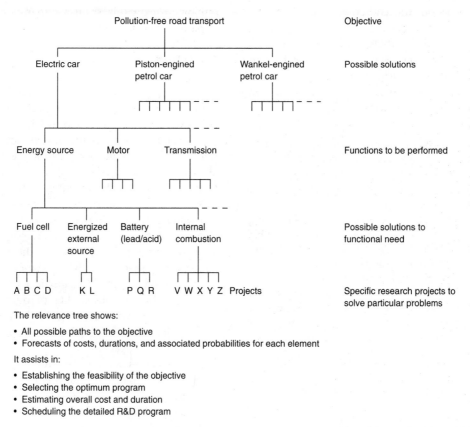

The relevance tree shows:

- All possible paths to the objective
- Forecasts of costs, durations, and associated probabilities for each element

It assists in:

- Establishing the feasibility of the objective
- Selecting the optimum program
- Estimating overall cost and duration
- Scheduling the detailed R&D program

1. Establishing the feasibility of a technological mission. If no feasible path can be found, the mission cannot be achieved with the technological capability of the present or the foreseeable future.
2. Determining the optimum R&D program, that is, the paths to be followed up the hierarchy. This could vary with the program objective. Early achievement of the objective may call for a different program (i.e., path) from that for minimum cost.
3. Selecting and planning the initiation of detailed research projects.

This technique can lead to highly complex and sophisticated computer-based approaches. In the Honeywell Pattern program, all military and aerospace activities in which the company was or could be involved were covered. The cost of setting up this program has been estimated at $250,000 to $300,000 with a further annual running cost of $50,000. Relevance trees have also been used by the British Post Office R&D department for relating the choice of projects to the organization's objectives.[18] The scale of effort involved in Pattern should not, however, deter the industrial R&D manager with limited resources at his disposal. The basic relevance tree methodology in a much simplified form can still be a useful planning tool.

Technology Monitoring

We have noted previously that innovation frequently depends upon the convergence of advances in several technologies and, furthermore, that the period between the emergence of a technological advance or a new technology and its practical application may span a number of years. Well-informed judgment and insight are also important. Most managers receive their information inputs haphazardly

[18]H. Beastall, "The Relevance Tree in Post Office R&D," *R&D Management* 1, no. 2 (1971).

from reading, discussions, conferences, and so on. If judgment is to be based upon good and comprehensive information, the gathering of these inputs should be organized, so far as possible. Those of potential future value should be stored to enable retrieval without relying upon the vagaries of human memory, and their significance noted.

Bright has proposed monitoring the environment on a systematic basis. He writes:

> Note that monitoring includes much more than simply "scanning." It includes search, consideration of alternative possibilities and their effects, and a conclusion based on evaluation of progress and its implications. The feasibility of monitoring rests on the fact that it takes a long time for a technology to emerge from the minds of men into economic reality, with its resulting social impacts. There are always some identifiable points, events, relationships, and other types of "signals" along the way that can be used in an analytical framework. If a manager can detect these signals, he should be able to follow the progress of the innovation relative to time, cost, performance, obstacles, possible impacts, and other considerations. Then he will have two more important inputs to his decisions:
>
> (*a*) Awareness of new technology and its progress; and
> (*b*) Some thoughtful speculation about its possible impact.[19]

The monitoring process is based upon a journal in which significant events are recorded. Bright suggests four column headings: Date; Event and Technical Economic Data; Possible Significance; and Things to Consider. The events may be likened to the pieces of a jigsaw. Over a period of time, the number of pieces we have increases. Not all may be useful, but by careful selection and assembly, a picture of one part of the future may slowly emerge. Sometimes a vital piece may be missing; this could lead to the deduction—"if advance X were made, then innovation Y would be possible," with the corollary "we must monitor the environment carefully for signs of X being achieved since we shall then know that Y is feasible." The reporting of X might appear first in an obscure scientific paper in any part of the world.

The attraction of monitoring is that it can be performed by any individual manager for his or her own information. It is surprising how much one person can glean from systematically processing the information received daily. The richness of the information and the deductions are obviously enhanced if organized on a departmental or interdepartmental basis.

Cross-Impact Analysis

The techniques we have discussed so far have centered on forecasting the future behavior of specific attributes or likely events in isolation, although we have seen that in fact many of them are interdependent not only within the technological sphere but also between technology and other environmental factors. Gordon of the Institute of the Future classifies these interconnective modes as *enhancing* (enabling or provoking) or *inhibiting* (denigrating or antagonistic). Thus, our forecasts for automotive antipollution legislation enhance the probability of the development of catalytic exhaust cleaners, but the development of noncatalytic exhaust cleaners would inhibit the probability of developments of new processes for purifying platinum, the future demand for which is closely related to the potential demand for catalysts.

The cross-impact analysis technique has been devised to permit these interrelationships to be recognized and reflected in the forecasts. The procedure adopted by the Institute of the Future is briefly as follows:

a. Establish the principal possible events associated with the problem under consideration.

b. Assign to each of these events individual probabilities, for example, by using Delphi or trend extrapolation.

c. Determine the interactions between events in terms of their interconnective mode and strength, identifying in some cases predecessor–successor relationships.

d. After programming into a computer, select an event from the predecessor group. Use random numbers to determine whether an event occurred, in which case adjust the other items accordingly. Repeat this process for all items.

e. Repeat stage (*d*) up to 1,000 times.

Organization for Technological Forecasting

Projects such as PATTERN presuppose a heavy investment of organizational and financial resources

[19]J. R. Bright, "Evaluating Signals of Technological Change," *Harvard Business Review,* January–February 1970.

in TF. For the majority of companies, however, the employment of more than two or three full-time technological forecasters is the exception. In most of the companies where the techniques have been studied, the involvement has been largely confined to a part-time activity of a few interested staff in the R&D department.

The best person to make a forecast is the manager who has to make a decision which is future related. Usually, however, he or she will need assistance in two areas:

1. The provision of data.
2. The application of TF techniques.

Much of the data required for TF is of the type which is needed in several areas of the company (e.g., economic and statistical data, market research) and is most conveniently collected and stored centrally within the organization, perhaps in the economics or corporate planning section. Other data which is of a specialist nature, of interest only to the departments preparing the particular forecast, needs to be collected at the departmental level. The value of such data storage grows with time since early efforts at TF are frequently frustrated by the absence of information. Thus, the first and critical step in adopting TF is to lay the foundation for future forecasting by organizing the collection and recording of data.

Few managers have been trained in TF and it is impracticable to provide the training for all those who might be called upon to make forecasts. There is thus need for consultancy advice from a small staff who are well versed in the techniques and can advise the manager in the preparation of his or her forecasts and warn the manager of the many pitfalls. Nevertheless, it is better that the individual manager makes his or her own forecast, with assistance, rather than the removal of forecasting to a central service department remote from the problem area.

Current Status of Technological Forecasting

Most of the initiatives in TF originally came from the United States, where several major companies invested heavily in it. There is some doubt whether the results justified the substantial investments.

In Europe, the rate of adoption has been much slower. The fuel crises of recent years have given a stimulus to industrial concern with the future and a growth in forecasting activity. It is possible to identify two levels of support; the first is concerned primarily with R&D planning decisions whereas the second focuses on corporate strategic issues. The latter is often referred to as "futures studies" rather than as forecasting. There is also a recognition that the future is more uncertain now than it was in the recent past and, furthermore, it is more likely to experience discontinuities. Thus, we are witnessing a growth in the use of scenarios and such techniques as trend-impact analysis.[20]

A major cause for the low rate of acceptance is likely to be reluctance to invest the large resources, which the literature suggests are necessary, in an untried technique. This has not encouraged more modest attempts. Nevertheless, as the pace of technological progress continues to increase, so will the need to forecast. Thus, we may expect to see a growth in the use of TF. But this growth is likely to be hindered by exaggerated claims for what it can achieve.

Summary

Since the benefits from R&D decisions are gained in the future, it is incumbent upon the R&D manager to satisfy himself or herself, so far as is possible, that the results of the investments are relevant to the market needs and the competitive technologies at the time they reach fruition. Thus, all R&D decision makers must take a conscious view of the future. Forecasts are needed which take full account of the information available and the techniques of TF. It was seen, however, that the effort devoted to TF should be related to the characteristics of the industry, the company, and the decisions to be made, rather than to the size of the company.

Technological forecasting cannot enable decision makers to predict the future with certainty. But it can assist them in refining their judgments. The value of the forecasts was seen to be highly dependent upon the quality of the informational inputs to the forecasting process and the caliber of the minds applied to it. Sophisticated forecasting techniques can only be aids to this process, and care should be taken to guard against TF's absorbing greater resources than can be justified in economic terms.

---

[20] J. Fowles, ed. *Handbook of Futures Research* (Westport, CT: Greenwood Press, 1978). Also, H. A. Linstone and W. H. Simmonds, *Futures Research: New Directions* (Reading, MA: Addison-Wesley Publishing, 1977).

The principles underlying technological forecasting were discussed and brief descriptions given of how they are applied in some of the most commonly used techniques—trend extrapolation, precursor trend curve matching, Delphi, scenarios, relevance trees, technology monitoring, and cross-impact analysis.

Whilst the practical application of TF is still limited, it was concluded that its use is likely to become more widespread once a better understanding is gained of what it can contribute to R&D decision making and, perhaps more important, what it cannot be expected to do. No R&D manager can afford to ignore TF, but enthusiasm for the techniques must be tempered by the realization that they alone will never remove completely the uncertainties inseparable from any consideration of the future.

Additional References

Arnfield, R. V., ed. *Technological Forecasting*. Edinburgh: Edinburgh University Press, 1969.

Currill, D. L., "Technological Forecasting in Six Major UK Companies." *Long-Range Planning,* March 1972.

Jantsch, E. *Technological Planning and Social Futures*. Cassell/Associated Business Programmes, 1972.

Linstone, H. A., and M. Turoff. *The Delphi Method: Techniques and Applications*. Reading, Mass.: Addison-Wesley Publishing, 1975.

Martino, J. P. *Technological Forecasting for Decision Making*. New York: Elsevier-North Holland Publishing, 1972.

Morrell, J. *Management Decisions and the Role of Forecasting*. London: Pelican Books, 1972.

Twiss, B. C. "Economic Perspectives of Technological Progress: New Dimensions for Forecasting Technology." *Futures,* February 1976.

Twiss, B. C. "The Production Manager's Need for Technological Forecasting." *Production Engineer,* August 1972.

Reading II–5
Patterns of Industrial Innovation

William J. Abernathy and James M. Utterback

How does a company's innovation—and its response to innovative ideas—change as the company grows and matures? Are there circumstances in which a pattern generally associated with successful innovation is in fact more likely to be associated with failure? Under what circumstances will newly available technology, rather than the market, be the critical stimulus for change? When is concentration on incremental innovation and productivity gains likely to be of maximum value to a firm? In what situations does this strategy instead cause instability and potential for crisis in an organization?

Intrigued by questions such as these, we have examined how the kinds of innovations attempted by productive units apparently change as these units evolve. Our goal was a model relating patterns of innovation within a unit to that unit's competitive strategy, production capabilities, and organizational characteristics.

This article summarizes our work and presents the basic characteristics of the model to which it has led us. We conclude that a productive unit's capacity for and methods of innovation depend critically on its stage of evolution from a small technology-based enterprise to a major high-volume producer. Many characteristics of innovation and the innovative process correlate with such an historical analysis, and on the basis of our model we can now attempt answers to questions such as those above.

A Spectrum of Innovators

Past studies of innovation imply that any innovating unit sees most of its innovations as new products. But that observation masks an essential difference: what constitutes a product innovation by a small, technology-based unit is often the process equipment adopted by a large unit to improve its high-volume production of a standard product. We argue that these two units—the small, entrepreneurial organization and the larger unit producing standard products in high volume—are at opposite ends of a spectrum, in a sense forming boundary conditions in the evolution of a unit and in the character of its innovation of product and process technologies.

One distinctive pattern of technological innovation is evident in the case of established, high-volume products such as incandescent light bulbs, paper, steel, standard chemicals, and internal-combustion engines, for examples.

The markets for such goods are well defined; the product characteristics are well understood and often standardized; unit profit margins are typically low; production technology is efficient, equipment intensive, and specialized to a particular product; and competition is primarily on the basis of price. Change is costly in such highly integrated systems because an alteration in any one attribute or process has ramifications for many others.

In this environment innovation is typically incremental in nature, and it has a gradual, cumulative effect on productivity. For example, Samuel Hollander has shown that more than half of the reduction in the cost of producing rayon in plants of E. I. du Pont de Nemours and Company has been the result of gradual process improvements which could not be identified as formal projects or changes. A similar study by John Enos shows that accumulating incremental developments in petroleum refining processes resulted in productivity gains which often eclipsed the gain from the original innovation. Incremental innovations, such as the use of larger railroad cars and unit trains, have resulted in dramatic reductions in the cost of moving large quantities of materials by rail.

In all these examples, major systems innovations have been followed by countless minor product and systems improvements, and the latter account for more than half of the total ultimate economic gain due to their much greater number. While cost reduction seems to have been the major incentive for most of these innovations, major advances in performance have also resulted from such small engineering and production adjustments.

Such incremental innovation typically results in an increasingly specialized system in which economies of scale in production and the development of mass markets are extremely important. The productive unit loses its flexibility, becoming increasingly dependent on high-volume production to cover its fixed costs and increasingly vulnerable to changed demand and technical obsolescence.

Major new products do not seem to be consistent with this pattern of incremental change. New products which require reorientation of corporate goals or production facilities tend to originate outside organizations devoted to a "specific" production system; or, if originated within, to be rejected by them.

A more fluid pattern of product change is associated with the identification of an emerging need or a new way to meet an existing need; it is an entrepreneurial act. Many studies suggest that such new product innovations share common traits. They occur in disproportionate numbers in companies and units located in or near affluent markets with strong science-based universities or other research institutions and entrepreneurially oriented financial institutions. Their competitive advantage over predecessor products is based on superior functional performance rather than lower initial cost, and so these radical innovations tend to offer higher unit profit margins.

When a major product innovation first appears, performance criteria are typically vague and little understood. Because they have a more intimate understanding of performance requirements, users may play a major role in suggesting the ultimate form of the innovation as well as the need. For example, Kenneth Knight shows that three-quarters of the computer models which emerged between 1944 and 1950, usually those produced as one or two of a kind, were developed by users.

It is reasonable that the diversity and uncertainty of performance requirements for new products give an advantage in their innovation to small, adaptable organizations with flexible technical approaches and good external communications, and historical evidence supports that hypothesis. For example, John Tilton argues that new enterprises led in the application of semiconductor technology, often transferring into practice technology from more established firms and laboratories. He argues that economies of scale have not been of prime importance because products have changed so rapidly that production technology designed for a particular product is rapidly made obsolete. And R. O. Schlaifer and S. D. Heron have argued that a diverse and responsive group of enterprises struggling against established units to enter the industry contributed greatly to the early advances in jet aircraft engines.

A Transition from Radical to Evolutionary Innovation

These two patterns of innovation may be taken to represent extreme types—in one case involving incremental change to a rigid, efficient production system specifically designed to produce a standardized product, and in the other case involving radical innovation with product characteristics in flux. In fact, they are not rigid, independent categories. Several examples will make it clear that organizations currently considered in the "specific" category—

where incremental innovation is now motivated by cost reduction—were at their origin small, "fluid" units intent on new product innovation.

John Tilton's study of developments in the semiconductor industry from 1950 through 1968 indicates that the rate of major innovation has decreased and that the type of innovation shifted. Eight of the 13 product innovations he considers to have been most important during that period occurred within the first 7 years, while the industry was making less than 5 percent of its total 18-year sales. Two types of enterprise can be identified in this early period of the new industry—established units that came into semiconductors from vested positions in vacuum tube markets, and new entries such as Fairchild Semiconductor, IBM, and Texas Instruments, Inc. The established units responded to competition from the newcomers by emphasizing process innovations. Meanwhile, the latter sought entry and strength through product innovation. The three very successful new entrants just listed were responsible for half of the major product innovations and only one of the nine process innovations which Dr. Tilton identified in that 18-year period, while three principal established units (divisions of General Electric, Philco, and RCA) made only one-quarter of the product innovations but three of the nine major process innovations in the same period. In this case, process innovation did not prove to be an effective competitive stance; by 1966, the three established units together held only 18 percent of the market while the three new units held 42 percent. Since 1968, however, the basis of competition in the industry has changed; as costs and productivity have become more important, the rate of major product innovation has decreased, and effective process innovation has become an important factor in competitive success. For example, by 1973 Texas Instruments, which had been a flexible, new entrant in the industry two decades earlier and had contributed no major process innovations prior to 1968, was planning a single machine that would produce 4 percent of world requirements for its integrated-circuit unit.

Like the transistor in the electronics industry, the DC-3 stands out as a major change in the aircraft and airlines industries. Almarin Phillips has shown that the DC-3 was in fact a cumulation of prior innovations. It was not the largest, or fastest, or longest-range aircraft; it was the most economical large, fast plane able to fly long distances. All the features which made this design so completely successful had been introduced and proven in prior aircraft. And the DC-3 was essentially the first commercial product of an entering firm (the C-1 and DC-2 were produced by Douglas only in small numbers).

Just as the transistor put the electronics industry on a new plateau, so the DC-3 changed the character of innovation in the aircraft industry for the next 15 years. No major innovations were introduced into commercial aircraft design from 1936 until new jet-powered aircraft appeared in the 1950s. Instead, there were simply many refinements to the DC-3 concept—stretching the design and adding appointments; and during the period of these incremental changes, airline operating cost per passenger-mile dropped an additional 50 percent.

The electric light bulb also has a history of a long series of evolutionary improvements which started with a few major innovations and ended in a highly standardized commoditylike product. By 1909, the initial tungsten filament and vacuum bulb innovations were in place; from then until 1955 there came a series of incremental changes—better metal alloys for the filament, the use of "getters" to assist in exhausting the bulb, coiling the filaments, "frosting" the glass, and many more. In the same period, the price of a 60-watt bulb decreased (even with no inflation adjustment) from $1.60 to 20 cents each, the lumens output increased by 175 percent, the direct labor content was reduced more than an order of magnitude, from 3 to 0.18 minutes per bulb, and the production process evolved from a flexible job-shop configuration, involving more than 11 separate operations and a heavy reliance on the skills of manual labor, to a single machine attended by a few workers.

Product and process evolved in a similar fashion in the automobile industry. During a four-year period before Henry Ford produced the renowned Model T, his company developed, produced, and sold five different engines, ranging from two to six cylinders. These were made in a factory that was flexibly organized much as a job shop, relying on trade craftsmen working with general-purpose machine tools not nearly so advanced as the best then available. Each engine tested a new concept. Out of this experience came a dominant design—the Model T; and within 15 years, 2 million engines of this single basic design were being produced each year (about 15 million all told) in a facility then recognized as the most efficient and highly integrated in the world. During that 15-year period, there were incremental—but no fundamental—innovations in the Ford product.

In yet another case, Robert Buzzell and Robert Nourse, tracing innovations in processed foods, show that new products such as soluble coffees, frozen vegetables, dry pet foods, cold breakfast cereals, canned foods, and precooked rice came first from individuals and small organizations where research was in progress or which relied heavily upon information from users. As each product won acceptance, its productive unit increased in size and concentrated its innovation on improving manufacturing, marketing, and distribution methods which extended rather than replaced the basic technologies. The major source of the latter ideas is now each firm's own research and development organization.

The shift from radical to evolutionary product innovation is a common thread in these examples. It is related to the development of a dominant product design, and it is accompanied by heightened price competition and increased emphasis on process innovation. Small-scale units that are flexible and highly reliant on manual labor and craft skills utilizing general-purpose equipment develop into units that rely on automated, equipment-intensive, high-volume processes. We conclude that changes in innovative pattern, production process, and scale and kind of production capacity all occur together in a consistent, predictable way.

Though many observers emphasize new product innovation, process and incremental innovations may have equal or even greater commercial importance. A high rate of productivity improvement is associated with process improvement in every case we have studied. The cost of incandescent light bulbs, for example, has fallen more than 80 percent since their introduction. Airline operating costs were cut by half through the development and improvement of the DC-3. Semiconductor prices have been falling by 20 to 30 percent with each doubling of cumulative production. The introduction of the Model T Ford resulted in a price reduction from $3,000 to less than $1,000 (in 1958 dollars). Similar dramatic reductions have been achieved in the costs of computer core memory and television picture tubes.

Managing Technological Innovation

If it is true that the nature and goals of an industrial unit's innovations change as that unit matures from pioneering to large-scale producer, what does this imply for the management of technology?

We believe that some significant managerial concepts emerge from our analysis—or model, if you will—of the characteristics of innovation as production processes and primary competitive issues differ. As a unit moves toward large-scale production, the goals of its innovations change from ill-defined and uncertain targets to well-articulated design objectives. In the early stages, there is a proliferation of product performance requirements and design criteria which frequently cannot be stated quantitatively, and their relative importance or ranking may be quite unstable. It is precisely under such conditions, where performance requirements are ambiguous, that users are most likely to produce an innovation and where manufacturers are least likely to do so. One way of viewing regulatory constraints such as those governing auto emissions or safety is that they add new performance dimensions to be resolved by the engineer—and so may lead to more innovative design improvements. They are also likely to open market opportunities for innovative change of the kind characteristic of fluid enterprises in areas such as instrumentation, components, process equipment, and so on.

The stimulus for innovation changes as a unit matures. In the initial fluid stage, market needs are ill-defined and can be stated only with broad uncertainty, and the relevant technologies are as yet little explored. So there are two sources of ambiguity about the relevance of any particular program of research and development—target uncertainty and technical uncertainty. Confronted with both types of uncertainty, the decision maker has little incentive for major investments in formal research and development.

As the enterprise develops, however, uncertainty about markets and appropriate targets is reduced, and larger research and development investments are justified. At some point before the increasing specialization of the unit makes the cost of implementing technological innovations prohibitively high and before increasing cost competition erodes profit with which to fund large indirect expenses, the benefits of research and development efforts would reach a maximum. Technological opportunities for improvements and additions to existing product lines will then be clear, and a strong commitment to research and development will be characteristic of productive units in the middle stages of development. Such firms will be seen as "science based" because they invest heavily in formal research and engineering departments, with emphasis on process innovation and product differentiation through functional improvements.

Although data on research and development expenditures are not readily available on the basis of productive units, divisions, or lines of business, an informal review of the activities of corporations with large investments in research and development shows that they tend to support business lines that fall neither near the fluid nor the specific conditions but are in the technologically active middle range. Such productive units tend to be large, to be integrated, and to have a large share of their markets.

A small, fluid entrepreneurial unit requires general-purpose process equipment which, typically, is purchased. As it develops, such a unit is expected to originate some process-equipment innovations for its own use; and when it is fully matured, its entire processes are likely to be designed as integrated systems specific to particular products. Since the mature firm is now fully specialized, all its major process innovations are likely to originate outside the unit.

But note that the supplier companies will now see themselves as making product—not process—innovations. From a different perspective, George Stigler finds stages of development—similar to those we describe—in firms that supply production-process equipment. They differ in the market structure they face, in the specialization of their production processes, and in the responsibilities they must accept in innovating to satisfy their own needs for process technology and materials.

The organization's methods of coordination and control change with the increasing standardization of its products and production processes. As task uncertainty confronts a productive unit early in its development, the unit must emphasize its capacity to process information by investing in vertical and lateral information systems and in liaison and project groups. Later, these may be extended to the creation of formal planning groups, organizational manifestations of movement from a product-oriented to a transitional state; controls for regulating process functions and management controls such as job procedures, job descriptions, and systems analyses are also extended to become a more pervasive feature of the production network.

As a productive unit achieves standardized products and confronts only incremental change, one would expect it to deal with complexity by reducing the need for information processing. The level at which technological change takes place helps to determine the extent to which organizational dislocations take place. Each of these hypotheses helps to explain the firm's impetus to divide into homogeneous productive units as its products and process technology evolve.

The hypothesized changes in control and coordination imply that the structure of the organization will also change as it matures, becoming more formal and having a greater number of levels of authority. The evidence is strong that such structural change is a characteristic of many enterprises and of units within them.

Fostering Innovation by Understanding Transition

Assuming the validity of this model for the development of the innovative capacities of a productive unit, how can it be applied to further our capacity for new products and to improve our productivity?

We predict that units in different stages of evolution will respond to differing stimuli and undertake different types of innovation. This idea can readily be extended to the question of barriers to innovation, and probably to patterns of success and failure in innovation for units in different situations. The unmet conditions for transition can be viewed as specific barriers which must be overcome if transition is to take place.

We would expect new, fluid units to view as barriers any factors that impede product standardization and market aggregation, while firms in the opposite category tend to rank uncertainty over government regulation or vulnerability of existing investments as more important disruptive factors. Those who would promote innovation and productivity in U.S. industry may find this suggestive.

We believe the most useful insights provided by the model apply to production processes in which features of the products can be varied. The most interesting applications are to situations where product innovation is competitively important and difficult to manage; the model helps to identify the full range of other issues with which the firm is simultaneously confronted in a period of growth and change.

EXHIBIT 1

The changing character of innovation, and its changing role in corporate advance. Seeking to understand the variables that determine successful strategies for innovation, the authors focus on three stages in the evolution of a successful enterprise: its period of flexibility, in which the enterprise seeks to capitalize on its advantages where they offer greatest advantages; its intermediate years, in which major products are used more widely; and its full maturity, when prosperity is assured by leadership in several principal products and technologies.

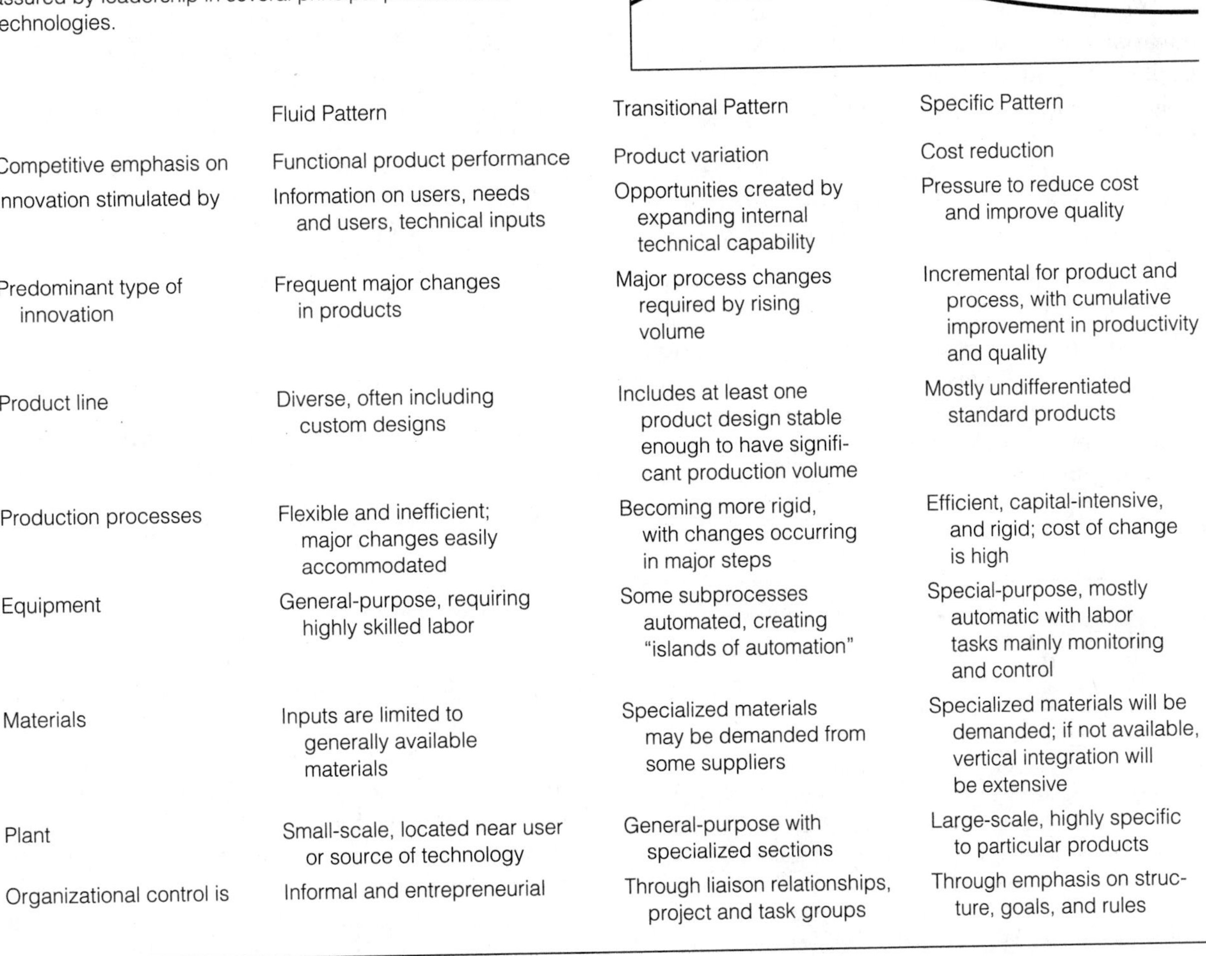

	Fluid Pattern	Transitional Pattern	Specific Pattern
Competitive emphasis on	Functional product performance	Product variation	Cost reduction
Innovation stimulated by	Information on users, needs and users, technical inputs	Opportunities created by expanding internal technical capability	Pressure to reduce cost and improve quality
Predominant type of innovation	Frequent major changes in products	Major process changes required by rising volume	Incremental for product and process, with cumulative improvement in productivity and quality
Product line	Diverse, often including custom designs	Includes at least one product design stable enough to have significant production volume	Mostly undifferentiated standard products
Production processes	Flexible and inefficient; major changes easily accommodated	Becoming more rigid, with changes occurring in major steps	Efficient, capital-intensive, and rigid; cost of change is high
Equipment	General-purpose, requiring highly skilled labor	Some subprocesses automated, creating "islands of automation"	Special-purpose, mostly automatic with labor tasks mainly monitoring and control
Materials	Inputs are limited to generally available materials	Specialized materials may be demanded from some suppliers	Specialized materials will be demanded; if not available, vertical integration will be extensive
Plant	Small-scale, located near user or source of technology	General-purpose with specialized sections	Large-scale, highly specific to particular products
Organizational control is	Informal and entrepreneurial	Through liaison relationships, project and task groups	Through emphasis on structure, goals, and rules

Consistency of Management Action

Many examples of unsuccessful innovations point to a common explanation of failure: certain conditions necessary to support a sought-after technical advance were not present. In such cases, our model may be helpful because it describes conditions that normally support advances at each stage of development; accordingly, if we can compare existing conditions with those prescribed by the model, we may discover how to increase innovative success. For example, we may ask of the model such questions as these about different, apparently independent, managerial actions:

- Can a firm increase the variety and diversity of its product line while simultaneously realizing the highest possible level of efficiency?
- Is a high rate of product innovation consistent with an effort to substantially reduce costs through extensive backward integration?
- Is government policy to maintain diversified markets for technologically active industries consistent with a policy that seeks a high rate of effective product innovation?
- Would a firm's action to restructure its work environment for employees so that tasks are more challenging and less repetitive be compatible with a policy of mechanization designed to reduce the need for labor?
- Can the government stimulate productivity by forcing a young industry to standardize its products before a dominant design has been realized?

The model prompts an answer of no to each of these questions; each question suggests actions which the model tells us are mutually inconsistent. We believe that as these ideas are further developed, they can be equally effective in helping to answer many far more subtle questions about the environment for innovation, productivity, and growth.

The Unit of Analysis

As we show in this article, innovation within an established industry is often limited to incremental improvements of both products and processes. Major product change is often introduced from outside an established industry and is viewed as disruptive; its source is typically the start-up of a new, small firm, invasion of markets by leading firms in other industries, or government sponsorship of change either as an initial purchaser or through direct regulation.

These circumstances mean that the standard units of analysis of industry—firm and product type—are of little use in understanding innovation. Technological change causes these terms to change their meaning, and the very shape of the production process is altered.

Thus the questions raised in this article require that a product line and its associated production process be taken together as the unit of analysis. This we term a *productive unit.* For a simple firm or a firm devoted to a single product, the productive unit and the firm would be one and the same. In the case of a diversified firm, a productive unit would usually report to a single operating manager and normally be a separate operating division. The extreme of a highly fragmented production process might mean that several separate firms taken together would be a productive unit.

For example, analysis of change in the textile industry requires that productive units in the chemical, plastics, paper, and equipment industries be included. Analysis involving the electronics industry requires a review of the changing role of component, circuit, and software producers as they become more crucial to change in the final assembled product. Major change at one level works its way up and down the chain, because of the interdependence of product and process change within and among productive units. Knowledge of the production process as a system of linked productive units is a prerequisite to understanding innovation in an industrial context.

Case II–5
Banc One Corporation and the Home Information Revolution

Karen J. Freeze and Richard S. Rosenbloom

Introduction

In February 1982, John F. Fisher pondered how to spend $2 million Banc One Corporation had budgeted for research and development over the next year. As senior vice president and head of research and development for the innovative bank holding company whose character he had helped form, he was responsible for proposing where that money should go. Although Banc One was consistently among the top four most profitable bank holding companies in the country, it was still relatively small, with only $39 million in earnings for fiscal 1981; hence $2 million was no trivial allotment. "I've got a big chip to play," Fisher remarked, "but only one. And as long as I don't throw it away on the wrong game, I can always play."

Only a year before, Bank One of Columbus, Ohio, Banc One's lead bank, had conducted a

---

Harvard Business School case 9-682-091, revised March 1988.

widely publicized, three-month experiment in home banking. Fisher, whom a colleague described as "not interested in anything that works today," had been dreaming for years of bringing the bank and its range of financial services directly to people in their homes. The experiment and its promising results were Banc One's first step in turning that dream into reality.

Fisher envisioned home banking as part of a larger home information service based on videotex technology, still in its infancy. He was considering such questions as: How can Banc One help move videotex from experiments to commercial application? How can we encourage the development of hardware (the "home information appliance") suitable for a mass market and of software (many kinds of information services) customers are willing to pay for? Whom do we encourage in the race to develop a viable system for transmitting information? Ultimately, how should Banc One position itself in this sophisticated technological development so that it will be the bank—or one among a few banks nationwide—to process "any transaction a consumer makes that has to be paid for"?

Fisher knew that Banc One's top management was prepared to move boldly. Considering Banc One's resources, he had sketched out three possible approaches:

1. To pioneer, perhaps in collaboration with a few other banks, in the establishment of a nationwide transaction processing service to support home banking.
2. To wait until someone else invented the business, then take a franchise, as they had done with BankAmericard (now VISA).
3. To provide home banking and, in cooperation with other software companies, other videotex services exclusively to Banc One's customers.

With $2 million, Fisher could buy "a sophisticated software system" for home banking and the beginnings of a processing capability in a single-site processing center. But whatever commitment Banc One made, Fisher anticipated that it would take 18 months to two years to "arrive at day one" and $1 million to $2 million more over the following two to three years before the operation might expect a positive cash flow.

Banc One Corporation

At the end of 1981 Banc One Corporation had 22 affiliates with 155 offices in 24 of the 88 counties of Ohio. With a total of $3.6 billion in assets ($2.9 billion in deposits), it was the 3rd largest bank holding company in Ohio and (a year earlier) the 77th largest in the United States (see Exhibits 1, 2, and 3

EXHIBIT 1 Financial Indicators, 1968–1981 ($ millions)

Year	Number of Banks	Total Assets	First Bank of Columbus[a] Assets	Return on Assets	Total Deposits	Net (operating income)
1968	2	$ 480.5	$ 424.0	1.06%	$ 431.1	$ 4.7
1969	4	562.0	435.0	1.16	490.5	5.4
1970	6	694.0	479.0	1.19	599.7	8.0
1971	9	879.2	513.5	1.08	758.0	9.6
1972	13	1,200.3	597.6	1.08	1,020.7	11.8
1973	13	1,331.4	659.8	1.16	1,118.5	14.2
1974	15	1,474.0	656.1	1.12	1,246.4	15.8
1975	16	1,538.2	659.8	1.15	1,357.5	16.8
1976	16	1,727.2	745.0	1.21	1,492.3	19.3
1977	16	1,950.6	870.1	1.26	1,620.4	22.2
1978	17	2,197.4	1,004.9	1.31	1,856.0	25.5
1979	18	2,523.7	1,145.6	1.30	2,121.0	29.8
1980	21	2,823.7	1,230.2	1.27	2,321.0	32.8
1981	22	3,638.9	1,433.0	1.27	2,874.0	38.6

[a]City National Bank until 1979.

EXHIBIT 2 Consolidated Statement of Income and Balance Sheet

Consolidated Statement of Income ($000)

	1981	1980
Total interest income	$ 376,786	$ 272,442
Total interest expense	246,185	164,165
Net interest income	130,601	108,277
Net interest income after provision for loan and lease losses	118,171	98,494
Total other income	37,739	27,776
Total other expenses	115,909	90,152
Income before federal income taxes and loss on sale of securities	40,001	36,118
Income before loss on sale of securities	39,031	33,409
Net income	38,583	32,849

Consolidated Balance Sheet—December 31, 1980 and 1981 ($000)

Assets	1981	1980
Cash and due from banks	$ 327,666	$ 275,735
Deposits in other banks, interest bearing	362,468	30,500
Securities (mostly government)	674,326	705,191
Federal funds sold and repurchase agreements	36,123	51,785
Net loans	1,938,700	1,549,674
Investment in financing leases	82,045	61,973
Bank premises and equipment	93,292	66,533
Other	124,239	82,337
Total assets	3,638,859	2,823,728
Liabilities		
Deposits:		
Demand	770,310	702,435
Savings	199,251	135,398
Time	409,568	381,993
Total deposits	2,874,238	2,320,934
Short-term borrowings	384,178	207,308
Other borrowings	18,412	10,795
Total liabilities	3,390,587	2,620,875
Total stockholders' equity	248,272	202,853
Total liabilities and stockholders' equity	$3,638,859	$2,823,728

for financial indicators). Founded in 1967 from the merger of two banks as "the uncommon partnership," it emphasized the individuality and independence of its member banks. Nevertheless, many of its strategies reflected patterns established earlier by its lead bank, until 1979 called City National Bank of Columbus.

History

City National Bank (CNB) could trace its heritage back 128 years, but its modern history began when John G. McCoy assumed its presidency upon his father's death in 1958. His father, John H. McCoy, had been head of the bank since 1935 and had brought its deposits from $40 million to $140 million. The elder McCoy sent his son to Harvard Business School, then Stanford, where he received an M.B.A. in 1937. Beginning at the bank upon graduation, the younger McCoy became a vice president in 1946 and a board member in 1949. When he inherited the bank in 1958 at the age of 45, he made two fundamental decisions: to run a "Tiffany bank rather than a Woolworth's" and, to achieve that goal,

EXHIBIT 3 **A Comparison with the 100 Largest Banks and Other Large Ohio Banks**

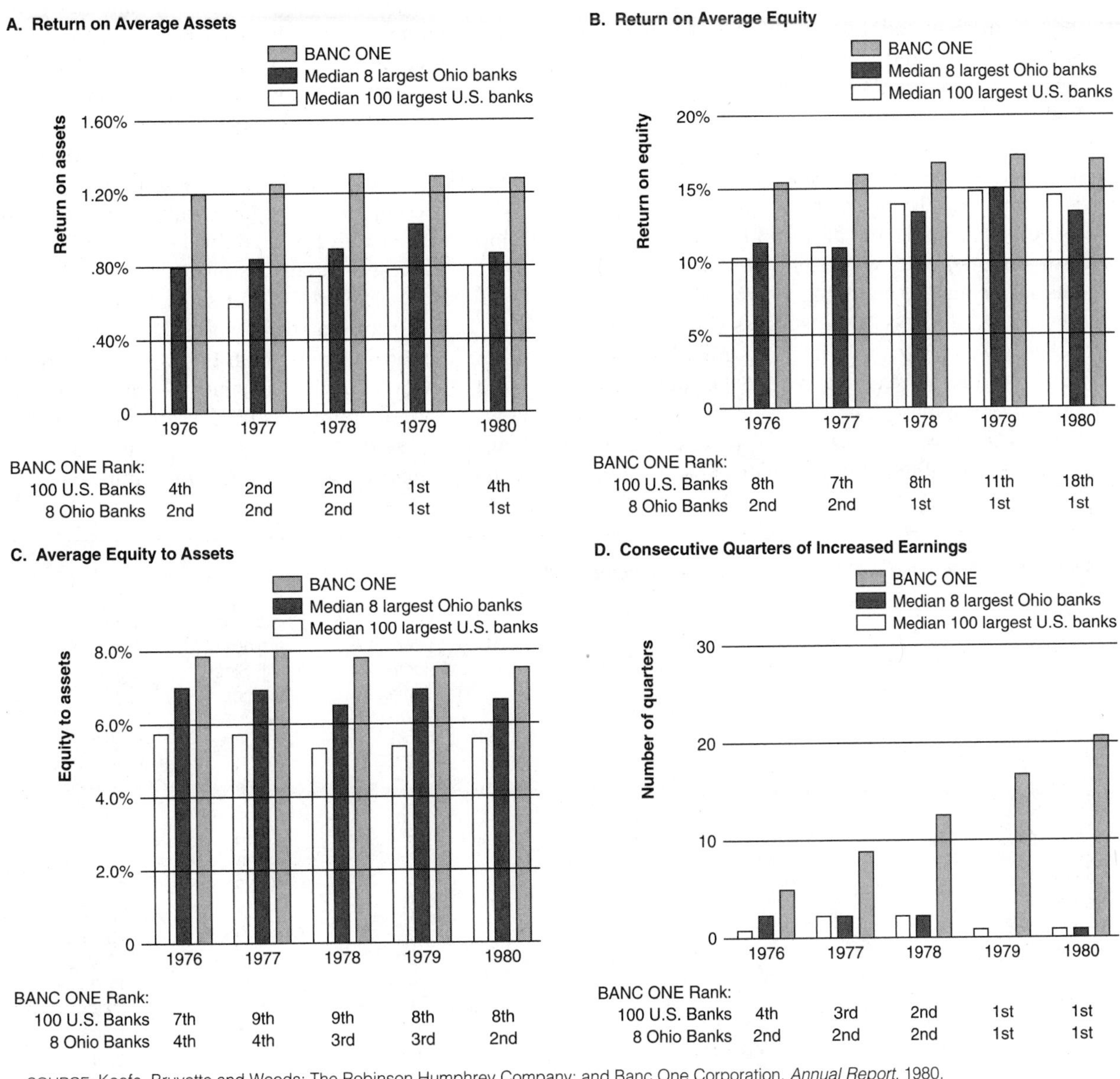

SOURCE: Keefe, Bruyette and Woods; The Robinson Humphrey Company; and Banc One Corporation, *Annual Report,* 1980.

"to hire the best people and then delegate; there wasn't any use of putting you in if you were the finest in the world, and then telling you how to do it." For this his father offered no model; he had made every decision in the bank himself.

McCoy's guiding principle was to "provide financial services to people," who McCoy believed tended to choose a bank "because of one word: convenience." To help implement that principle in his first year, he hired banking statesman Everett Reese as chairman and young radio adman John Fisher as head of a newly created advertising department. Reese, president of the American Banker's Association in 1953–1954, had come to Columbus at age 62 from Newark, Ohio, where his bank had hired Fisher to do commercials. When

Reese moved to Columbus, he wanted to bring Fisher's creative talents to the task of turning around City National. McCoy concurred, hired Fisher, commissioned him to "find out what the customer wants," and forbade him to learn how to open an account or make a loan.

Soon in charge of marketing and public relations, Fisher became involved in the community, creating a new image for CNB with slogans like "The good neighbor bank," "The loaningest bank in town," and "The best all around bank all around town." The first slogan endured and was embodied in advertisements in all media, including a prizewinning outdoor ad in 1961. CNB's success in attracting depositors was reflected in its rapid growth. In less than a decade it reached over $400 million in deposits. (See Exhibit 1.)

Limited in growth by Ohio law to one county, CNB merged in 1968 with a smaller bank, Farmers Savings and Trust ($55.2 million in deposits) to form a holding company, the First Banc Group (FBG). The spelling of *Banc* was dictated by another Ohio law prohibiting nonbank institutions from including the designation *bank* in their names. The First Banc Group adopted "The uncommon partnership" as its slogan and proceeded to sell the benefits of membership by disclaiming any intention to "take over" other banks and by pointing to bottom-line results. Exhibit 3 compares Banc One with other banks in Ohio and the nation, and Exhibit 4 gives 1981 results for the holding company's affiliates.

A decade old in 1977 and still growing rapidly, First Banc Group had 16 members and $1,951 million in aggregate assets. With FBG's next decade in mind, McCoy and his colleagues—including CNB's new president, John B. McCoy (John G.'s son)—began to consider the implications of federal limits to the company's growth. With the entire banking

EXHIBIT 4 Operating Highlights of Banc One Affiliates, 1981

Bank One of:	Banking Offices	Assets Year-End 1981 ($ millions)	1981	Year Prior to Affiliation	Compound Earnings Growth Since Affiliation	Average Equity to Deposits 1981
Columbus	38	$1,433	1.12%	1.05%	10.53%	8.65%
Ashland	3	43	1.45	.89	16.04	10.04
Athens	4	77	1.47	1.29	8.61	10.09
Cambridge	4	83	1.29	1.30	9.37	10.93
Coshocton	4	119	1.79	1.13	12.86	10.74
Dover	5	123	1.85	.60	19.35	9.46
Fairborn	3	53	2.13	1.43	35.22	12.45
Fremont	3	56	1.29	.77	13.12	9.57
Kenton	2	29	1.60	.82	60.29	8.41
Mansfield	8	164	1.74	.93	13.42	10.46
Marion	4	75	1.93	.79	48.87	11.25
Medina	3	35	.79	.58	12.30	9.61
Middletown	6	131	1.79	1.20	13.61	10.66
Milford	11	139	1.62	1.00	18.09	10.44
Mt. Sterling	1	23	1.86	.88	24.02	9.60
Northeastern Ohio[a]	24	452	1.99	1.06		8.66
Pomeroy	3	41	1.88	1.37	34.20	9.60
Portsmouth	7	154	1.40	.82	13.92	10.30
Ravenna	7	127	1.23	.99	9.93	10.29
Sidney	7	105	1.07	1.08	10.74	8.47
Wapakoneta	4	95	1.11	.58	17.34	9.17
Wooster	4	71	1.95	1.03	15.94	10.42
Total banks	155	$3,628	1.39%			9.51%
Average bank Unweighted			1.56%	.98%	19.89%	9.97%

[a]Affiliated September 1, 1981.

SOURCE: Banc One Corporation, *Annual Report*, 1981.

industry in upheaval as it faced challenges from other financial institutions, McCoy and others expected the law against interstate banking to be revised. Anticipating that event, First Banc Group sought a new name unique in the country and decided upon Banc One, which it registered in every state. In 1979 the name change was announced; henceforth, the holding company would be known as Banc One, and each branch as Bank One, followed by its location. Thus, City National Bank became Bank One of Columbus.

Electronic Banking at Banc One

Although McCoy's basic philosophy of better banking service to more people was not unique to City National, his methods of achieving his goal while keeping the bank profitable were uncommon. Shortly after assuming the presidency, he instituted research and development at the bank:

> I asked the board of directors—my father's friends, not mine—to approve setting aside 3 percent of earnings annually for research and they said, "We're a bank. Why do we need research?" And I said, "I don't know. That's what I want to find out."

The board approved the request ("We weren't making $1 million a year, so $30,000 wasn't much") and McCoy began to explore how technology might help CNB be more efficient. In 1961 CNB printed its checks with computer readable codes and began construction of a 20,000-square-foot processing plant, which opened in 1962 with the latest in computer equipment. Two years later CNB opened an ultramodern main office in a new high-rise, in which it could expand upward as needed. The facilities were complete with the latest automatic equipment, a centrex phone system, and, for the front lines, 9-to-5 customer hours.

Financial Card Services

While developing electronic means for executing traditional tasks more efficiently, City National sought to apply this technology in new ways. California's Bank of America had been using a plastic card, called the BankAmericard (BAC, now VISA), since 1958. Fashioned after the charge cards issued by major oil companies and department stores, the BankAmericard was serving a rapidly growing network of small merchants in California. In the early 1960s too, Carte Blanche and Diner's Club cards were beginning to give big hotels an advantage over smaller competitors, represented by the American Hotel Association (AHA). In 1961, the president of the AHA approached McCoy with the idea of establishing a card for his membership. CNB financed the card, but with the limited technology of the time, it was not profitable.

In early 1966 City National was mobilized by a threat from New York: Diner's Club and Carte Blanche were planning to extend their card markets into Ohio. To cut them off at the border, CNB needed a card of its own. McCoy tried to talk Bank of America into franchising its card; the California giant told him that "City National was too small" to handle a credit card. In the end, McCoy chuckled, "they gave it to us because we were their friends, not because they thought it would work."

McCoy's strategy for City National's BankAmericard was straightforward and consistent with his basic philosophy: service and profit. "We knew we'd succeed, because we were willing to put brains into it." Fisher launched a massive advertising campaign focusing on the convenience the BankAmericard would offer during the coming Christmas shopping season. Before its inaugural day of December 1, 1966, CNB issued 100,000 cards, 60,000 to "grade A" names bought from the Credit Bureau, and 40,000 to its own customers. It also signed up 800 merchants, expanding the number to 2,000 within a year.

Within a few months it was clear not only that BankAmericard would be a much bigger business than anticipated for CNB, but that CNB was developing a processing expertise that could be sold to other, smaller banks without increasing CNB's role as a creditor. But that would require a substantial investment in a much larger processing facility with new hardware and software. As Fisher later recalled, "Thirty guys from operations, DP guys, were sitting there telling me we were doing so well right now—why rock the boat?" But McCoy and Reese agreed with Fisher that the only way to expand the card base was to let other banks in—for a fee. In August 1967 they began processing for other banks, and soon afterward broke ground on a two-story processing plant, which opened in the spring of 1969 with 350 employees. By the end of 1969, over 200 banks in Ohio, Kentucky, and West Virginia offered a BankAmericard processed by CNB; the card no longer carried CNB's name, but was called the Ohio BankAmericard. Later in 1969 Mastercharge (now

Mastercard) came to town, expanding the market for both cards. "Before Mastercharge," remarked Fisher, "we had 100 percent of 10 percent; now we had 50 percent of 50 percent—a smaller share but of a much bigger pie."

By 1968, abuses of plastic credit were becoming evident, and CNB was a leader in measures to counter such abuse. McCoy's bank was the first to put color Polaroid pictures of cardholders on the back of the card for positive ID; it also took initiative in educating consumers about using credit cards responsibly. The latter effort won CNB recognition from Ralph Nader, who was engaged in attacking card issuers for seducing consumers into unmanageable debt.

By 1971, CNB ranked among the top 10 plastic card processors nationwide. Credit card systems had blanketed the country rapidly, serving 50 million card holders in three years. As Fisher pointed out, "By 1971 it was all over; if you weren't in the processing business by then, it was too late."

In 1975 CNB was the first bank to introduce BAC's debit card, ENTREE, which was essentially a reusable check.[1] Although a transaction with a debit card looked to the user and the merchant like one with a credit card, the effect on the user's bank account was different. With a debit card the account was debited as soon as the transaction arrived at the bank; with a credit card charges were held until a monthly billing date. In introducing the debit card, the bank's target was the so-called convenience user, who charged purchases not so much for deferred payment, but as a substitute for cash. Since the bank made money only from the interest on overdue payments, customers who paid their BAC bills on time were a losing business. From the customer's point of view, however, the debit card offered no advantages as long as the regular BAC was free of service charges. Thus, until 1980 when it began charging a yearly fee for BAC (VISA), CNB had limited success with the debit card.

Serving Nonbanks Too

In 1977 City National's card processing business—second in size only to Bank of America's—was a decade old and the most profitable part of the bank. Renamed "Financial Card Services" (FCS) and ready for further expansion, it took a major and controversial step and began processing check and credit card transactions for Merrill Lynch's Cash Management Account (CMA). (Exhibit 5 illustrates the relationship between Bank One and Merrill Lynch.) CNB won the contract against much larger competitors not only because of its expertise but because, according to a Merrill Lynch representative, "It was creative. We were concerned that bigger banks might not see this as important enough to use their best people." When McCoy contemplated whether City National Bank should be performing such a service for a brokerage house, increasingly a competitor to the banking industry, he decided that "if we didn't do it, someone else would."

The Merrill Lynch contract brought CNB national attention. Writing checks or charging purchases on funds held by one's broker was novel in 1977, and, more important for visibility, Merrill Lynch's CMA clients nationwide had checking accounts and BankAmericards from CNB, soon to be Bank One of Columbus.

Within four years, Bank One's success with Merrill Lynch's CMA had attracted several of the largest brokerage houses, which were scrambling to devise similar services.[2] Because of its lead in the processing business, Bank One was able to compete with firms like American Express by offering such advantages as a proprietary security system to minimize illegal use of plastic cards and credit information. In 1981, processing for 168 other organizations—banks, brokers, credit unions, and so forth—brought in an estimated $14 million in fees; $21 million in fees was anticipated for 1982. Bank officers expected such rapid growth to continue, as new account segments like catalog retailers and insurance companies joined up to offer their customers VISA accounts processed by Bank One's FCS.

In mid-1980 the bank purchased 58 acres of land in Columbus and in September 1981 moved into the first of several buildings (called the Bank One Center) planned for the expansion of its Financial Card Services in the 1980s. Anticipating the future, it installed a computing capacity considerably beyond its current needs. Its staff, like Fisher and others at Banc One, was working closely with IBM and other manufacturers on ways to automate still further and

[1]When BAC became VISA, the ENTREE name was dropped, and the debit card became simply another kind of VISA card.

[2]Including: Dean Witter Reynolds, Inc.; A. G. Edwards and Sons, Inc.; Charles Schwab and Co.; Thomson McKinnon Securities, Inc.; and Bache Halsey Stuart Shields.

EXHIBIT 5

THE NEW YORK TIMES, MONDAY, MAY 18, 1981

The New York Times

Merrill Lynch's C.M.A. Boom

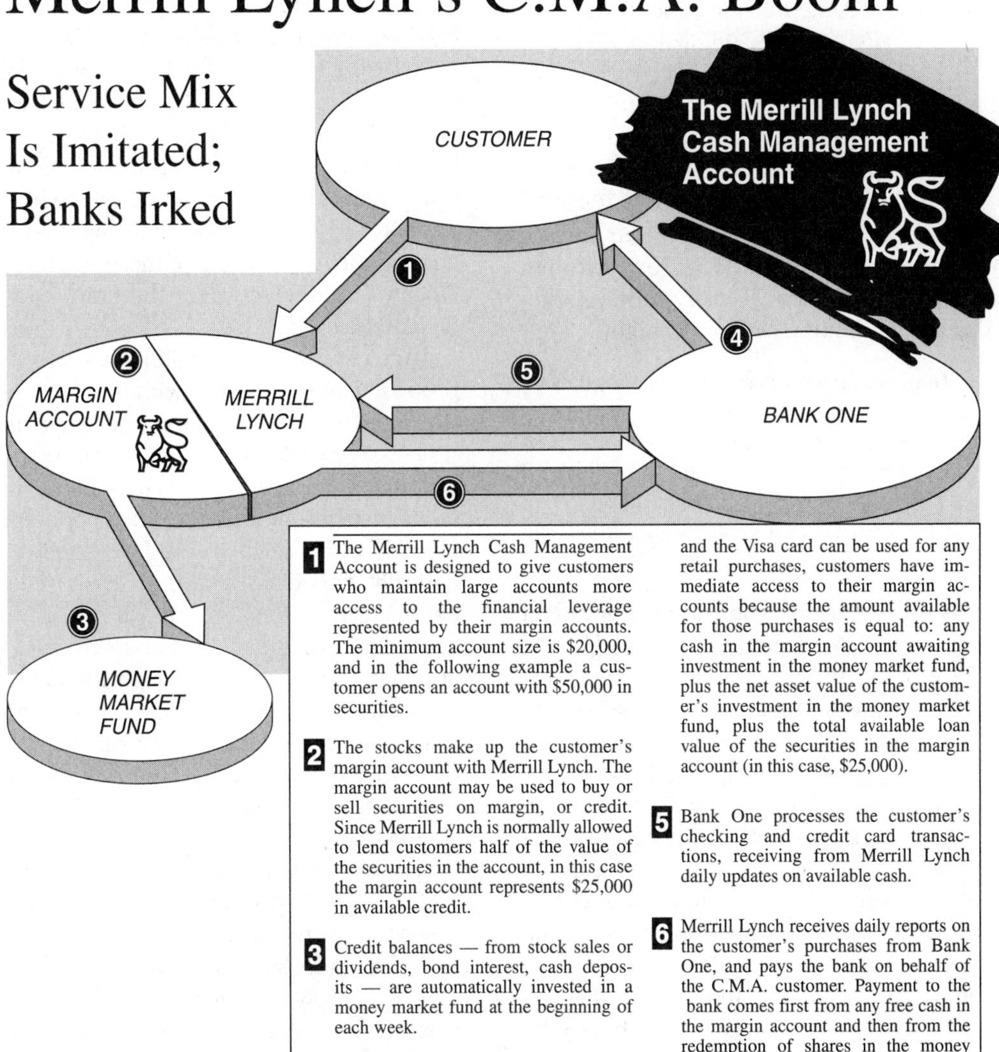

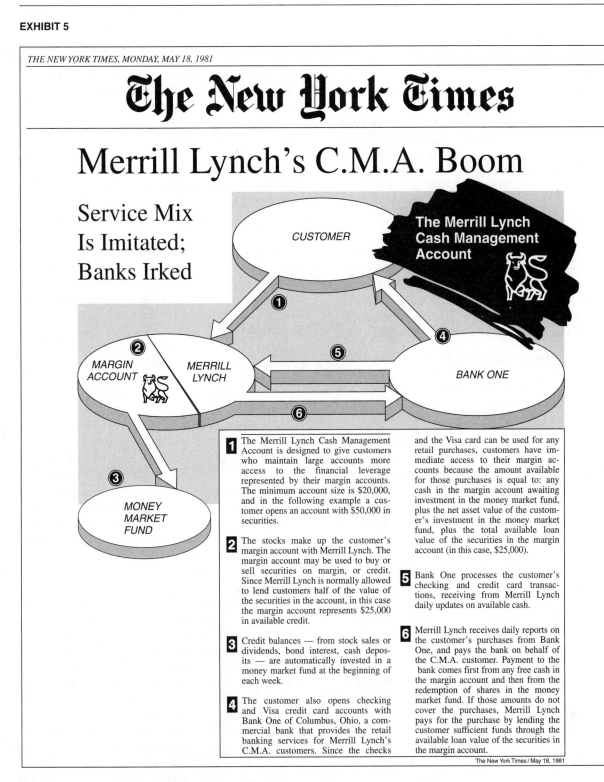

1 The Merrill Lynch Cash Management Account is designed to give customers who maintain large accounts more access to the financial leverage represented by their margin accounts. The minimum account size is $20,000, and in the following example a customer opens an account with $50,000 in securities.

2 The stocks make up the customer's margin account with Merrill Lynch. The margin account may be used to buy or sell securities on margin, or credit. Since Merrill Lynch is normally allowed to lend customers half of the value of the securities in the account, in this case the margin account represents $25,000 in available credit.

3 Credit balances — from stock sales or dividends, bond interest, cash deposits — are automatically invested in a money market fund at the beginning of each week.

4 The customer also opens checking and Visa credit card accounts with Bank One of Columbus, Ohio, a commercial bank that provides the retail banking services for Merrill Lynch's C.M.A. customers. Since the checks and the Visa card can be used for any retail purchases, customers have immediate access to their margin accounts because the amount available for those purchases is equal to: any cash in the margin account awaiting investment in the money market fund, plus the net asset value of the customer's investment in the money market fund, plus the total available loan value of the securities in the margin account (in this case, $25,000).

5 Bank One processes the customer's checking and credit card transactions, receiving from Merrill Lynch daily updates on available cash.

6 Merrill Lynch receives daily reports on the customer's purchases from Bank One, and pays the bank on behalf of the C.M.A. customer. Payment to the bank comes first from any free cash in the margin account and then from the redemption of shares in the money market fund. If those amounts do not cover the purchases, Merrill Lynch pays for the purchase by lending the customer sufficient funds through the available loan value of the securities in the margin account.

The New York Times/May 18, 1981

on developing a more refined image processing capability.[3]

Moving Banking Out of the Bank

City National Bank did not limit the diffusion of its expertise in electronics to the development of plastic card processing. That specialized business remained CNB's most profitable and fastest-growing department, generating a cash flow Fisher could count on for further R&D. But the processing business did not obscure McCoy's original concern: to provide convenient service to the retail customers of all First Banc Group's members.

To find ways to embody that concern was largely John Fisher's responsibility. Since arriving in 1959, he had continually asked three questions: What do the customers want? Can we do it at a profit? Can we do it before the other guys do it? McCoy gave him free rein in "trying to invent what it is the market needs" because "his batting average is high":

> The great thing about John Fisher is that he not only has a creative mind, he has the ability to get down to the bottom line. Back in the days when he was running the advertising, we would give him a budget and at the end of the year he would get right down to that budget. That is unusual in a creative guy, don't you think?

Despite his success at CNB (he was vice president by 1964 at the age of 35), Fisher was attracted by the "romantic lure of the West," as he put it, and went to Colorado in 1969 to set up a Mastercharge system for 250 banks statewide. But the Colorado banks were not receptive to his more radical notions ("I just couldn't get those guys to move"), so after 18 months he returned to Columbus as vice president for research at the holding company. There, in the "marketing environment" of "creative pragmatists" who "look at reality, then do something about it," he believed he could implement his ideas.

These ideas centered on the automation of banking services beyond the technology available to the teller. Given the advancing technology in the bank, tellers could no longer be untrained high school graduates; thus, the cost of the customer–teller interface was rapidly increasing. By the end of the 1960s it was clear that ways had to be found to enable the customers to make their own routine banking transactions. Moreover, the costs of check and other forms of paper processing were escalating toward a prohibitive level; only through electronic transactions could banking services remain affordable.

During his stay in Colorado, Fisher had established contacts with hardware manufacturers such as IBM and Docutel, contacts he would henceforth nurture by providing design engineers with blueprints of his vision for the future of banking. In return, he was privy to the latest technological embodiments of that vision. Thus, on Columbus Day 1970, CNB was the first bank anywhere to install automatic cash dispensing machines in its lobby. "We didn't know at the time what the results would be," Fisher recalled, "displacing tellers or increasing our market share—but we wanted to find out." Customers adapted quickly to this first attempt at automation; the success of these machines, made by Docutel, set the stage for the ubiquitous ATM of a decade later.

Attracted by CNB's willingness to pioneer, IBM proposed an experiment with IBM-built point of sale (POS) terminals. The nine-month experiment, called "POST 1," took place in an affluent suburb of Columbus from late 1971 to mid-1972. The terminals were installed at the checkout counters of supermarkets and other stores and were activated by magnetically encoded BankAmericards. The test drew national attention and a flurry of articles and speeches on the "checkless/cashless society" it apparently presaged. Although the experiment was moderately successful from the customers' viewpoint, the procedure did not offer cost advantages over the standard BankAmericard service for the merchant or enough profit for IBM, so the idea was shelved.

Self-service banking efforts continued, however, and in 1973 CNB installed the first 24-hour drive-in cash-dispensing machines in the country. Their overwhelming success led to the outfitting of an almost entirely automated branch a short distance from CNB's head office. Here 12 automatic teller machines (ATMs) greatly outnumbered four human tellers. That move proved premature, however, and 4 of the 12 machines were subsequently removed.

Despite mixed success with self-service innovations, Fisher persisted, and in 1976 CNB was ready to try yet another service: check and credit-card verification machines in stores. Activated by BankAmericards or special "CheckOK" cards, 60 of these POS terminals were installed in Columbus

---

[3]FCS was looking for a machine that could process everything on a check or VISA slip digitally, including the user's signature and the payee line on the check.

stores. As the first of their kind, they had loopholes for abuse that did not get plugged up before CNB lost nearly $400,000 and decided to disband the service. Unlike later systems, these terminals (called Financial Transaction Centers) had a high limit—$800 at first—and did not require the use of a Personal Identification Number (PIN); hence, stolen BankAmericards could easily be used to steal thousands of dollars daily. Such abuse was easy because the terminals were entirely customer operated, unsupervised by store personnel.[4]

Well-cushioned by its card processing business and led by an undaunted Fisher, CNB proceeded to figure out other ways to make banking easier and more attractive to the customer and less expensive for the bank. In 1978 CNB built its first "Autobank," an 80-square-foot, self-contained branch with a teller and a 24-hour ATM. This concept proved so successful that by the end of 1981 nine Autobanks had sprouted up throughout Bank One's territory. Seven could be built for the cost of one full-service branch. If POS terminals had thus far failed, the ATMs had taken off: Bank One of Columbus alone had installed 45 of them. Some 26,000 had emerged from bank walls nationwide, and the average cost of an ATM transaction had shrunk to 75 percent of a transaction performed by a human teller.[5] In mid-1982 Banc One was preparing to test an inexpensive, single-function ATM, a cash-dispenser, that could be installed in such places as airports and major hotels around the country.[6]

Taking the Bank Home: Home Banking Services

In the mid-1970s, with basic bank services available around the corner and around the clock, Fisher began contemplating the next step: banking right in the customer's home. Familiar with the technology of the early 1970s—both what was then available and what would be available a few years hence—Fisher sought ways to experiment with the concept of home banking, long before such a service would be cost-effective. Information technology was moving so rapidly, with the cable TV industry taking off and home computers imminent, that he wanted Banc One to position itself early.

In the late 1960s and early 1970s companies had been experimenting with technologies by which data could be transmitted to a television receiver in the home. In 1975 IBM asked Banc One to participate in a study of home banking with five other unnamed organizations. The study, called The Network Company, concluded that a switching network between homes and service providers would have to be invented and that the biggest profits in the future home information business would accrue to that network, not to the hardware manufacturer. It therefore ended its study without further plans for IBM's participation in the industry at that time.

About the same time, a perfect opportunity to experiment with home information services seemed imminent. Golfer Jack Nicklaus planned to build Muirfield Village, a self-contained little suburb just outside Columbus. Fisher's dream was that each new home would be wired for interactive television while being built. His skills of persuasion notwithstanding, the developers did not concur and he had to drop the idea of a "wired city."

In Britain and France, experiments with home information services—collectively called videotext at first—got underway between 1975 and 1977. They could be classified into two categories: one-way information transfer, or "teletext," and interactive systems called viewdata. Whereas the technology for teletext was straightforward, viewdata, now generally called videotex (without the *t*), required a way for the viewer to communicate with the program—to make a deposit, pay a bill, inquire about the location of a library book, or make a catalogue purchase. The French government had decided in 1978 that it would be cost-effective to supply telephone subscribers with a videotex terminal called Antiope—without charge—instead of a printed telephone directory. Fisher visited France for the first time in 1978 and returned home convinced that videotex would come to the United States much sooner and develop much faster than generally expected. Exhibit 6, showing screens from a late 1980 experiment by AT&T and Knight-Ridder, illustrates what videotex might bring into the home only three years later.

The city of Columbus itself, because of its location and social composition, had long been a test ground for new products, public opinion surveys, and network program ratings. In connection with that role, Warner Communications and American Express

---

[4]Fisher observed that abuse was not the only problem; the experiment was not carried further because rapidly developing electronic cash registers were coming to perform many of the tasks the POS terminal had been intended for.

[5]Assuming monthly volume of 4,000 transactions per machine.

[6]Manufacturers in the United States included Diebold, Docutel, IBM, and Burroughs.

EXHIBIT 6

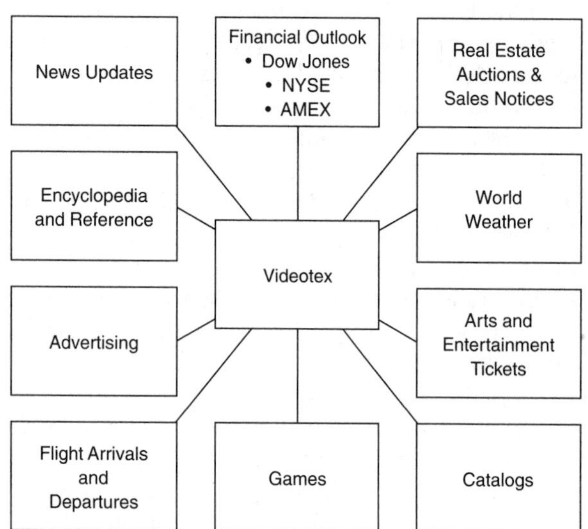

Adapted from the June 29, 1981 issue of *Business Week* by special permission.

developed in 1978 a semi-interactive cable television network called Qube, which enabled subscribers to "talk back" to their television sets. Using a keypad, they could vote electronically on various issues and avail themselves of several other services. By 1981, Qube had been installed in nearly 30,000 Columbus homes. Soon after Qube arrived, Fisher began discussing with Warner-Amex the possibility of using it for home banking. His efforts received considerable press attention, but little progress resulted. Fisher subsequently decided that the limits of cable—both in the households served and in the technology—made it unsuitable at that time and that the telephone would be a more effective vehicle for a home banking experiment.

While contemplating the technology involved, Fisher tried to imagine what would make home banking successful. Why would customers want to bank at home? What would motivate them to purchase the necessary hardware? How much would they pay for the service? Although answers to these questions were one objective of the experiment, Fisher realized that its success would rest largely on his ability to anticipate them. Most fundamentally, Fisher decided that people would pay for home banking only as part of a larger system of home services. The $150 worth of attachments to the television set or the $300 self-contained "home information appliance" of the future had to make available an array of services—shopping, library information, up-to-the-minute news reports, a telephone directory, travel information, and so on—along with home banking. Thus, a fair test had to include other services as well as home banking.

The Online Computer Library Center of Columbus (OCLC, Inc.), established in 1971, was a computer network, a "bibliographic utility" that provided 2,500 member libraries with online access to titles acquired by each library since the mid-1970s.[7] OCLC's research division had been contemplating how to extend a similar but local service to users at home. When Fisher heard of OCLC's interest, he suggested to the latter that the two companies might collaborate.

Channel 2000

By 1979 developments external to banking—escalation in the price of gas and postage—had increased the attractiveness of banking in the home by improving its economics. Fisher believed that the time was right for a full-scale test of home banking services and proposed to OCLC that they run a test together. In January 1980, Bank One of Columbus and OCLC, in cooperation with Franklin County and Columbus libraries, announced that Channel 2000, a videotex experiment that would incorporate what was expected to be the first home banking test in the country, would commence that fall.

Three tasks lay ahead: (1) designing and procuring the hardware, (2) designing the software, and (3) choosing the participants. OCLC took on the first task. Users had keypads hooked up to their ordinary television receivers through decoders (or modems) and "wires all over the place." Since the equipment was rather delicate, it did not stand up well to pets or children tripping over wires or knocking decoders off a table; the resulting problems proved annoying to some users. At the other end, the equipment was equally primitive; although users' terminals were hooked up with computers (in the bank and at OCLC), human intervention was required to complete all transactions; in the bank that was accomplished each morning by two bank tellers. In general, however, the components' lack of sophistication did not stand in the way of the experiment's

[7]OCLC was originally the Ohio College Library Center, established in 1967.

primary purpose, which was to test the visibility and possible configuration of home banking and other videotex services.

OCLC's research department designed software enabling participants to access the videocard catalogs of the public libraries of Columbus and Franklin County and select books to be mailed to their homes, to locate and read any of 32,000 articles from the Academic American Encyclopedia, to call up information on public and legislative affairs in Ohio and on local educational events and entertainment in Columbus, to use programs for math and reading for children, and to access the Deaf Community Bulletin Board.

Bank One set about designing its software in the summer of 1980. David Ortega, a newly hired Harvard Business School graduate (1980), was given the option of working on Channel 2000. With an undergraduate background in accounting and computer science, Ortega had the necessary expertise and took Channel 2000 as his first assignment in the bank. "It was exciting," he later reflected. "The great thing about this place is that they give you an idea and let you run with it." Ortega first began with note cards, trying to simulate what users would see, what buttons they would press, and what would come on the screen next. After a few days of frustrating efforts, he moved to an Apple computer, on which he designed the program.

Channel 2000 tested two separate programs for bill paying. The first was only semielectronic because the customer still received bills in the mail and simply paid them through Channel 2000. With the second program, the merchants sent bills directly to the bank and the customer saw them for the first time on the screen. The object of the latter program was to lay the groundwork for electronic bill paying whereby a merchant could send a bill electronically through a computer tied directly to the bank, rather than through the mail. Other banking services offered by Channel 2000 included account information, current and previous months' bank statements, and a display of current interest rates for various types of accounts and mortgages.

The number of participants was set at 200, half chosen by OCLC, half by Bank One. The bank chose its 100 from bank customers, mostly volunteers, and OCLC hired a market research firm, Design Research Corporation, to choose more scientifically a mix of participants from throughout Columbus. Of the 100 it chose, 30 turned out to be Bank One customers.

The Channel 2000 experiment provided a fund of data on home information services. The most important finding for Bank One, according to Ortega, was that "people wanted it." They didn't want to give up the service when the experiment was over. Moreover, most said they would be willing to pay a moderate service charge per month to use such a system. Among unexpected observations was that older people seemed to adapt more quickly and eagerly to the system than younger people. A common complaint was that the system tied up the telephone; Fisher pointed out that AT&T had already developed a dual-channel technology that would remedy that problem by the late 1980s without the expense of a second phone line. Otherwise the phone system had performed well. In fact, by January 1982, with AT&T free to invest in research in a more intense and accelerated fashion, Fisher could say, "We're betting on Ma Bell" as the provider of the communications system for home videotex services.

Banc One in Its Competitive Context

Banc One Corporation was a little fish among giant fish in a big pond. Its challenge was to maintain and enhance the special qualities that could continue to prevent the big fish from swallowing it up.

Banc One's Competitors in Home Banking

Banc One's competitors included other banks, nonbank financial institutions, and other processing companies. Among other banks eager to get a piece of the home banking action were Chemical Bank, Citibank, Bank of America, and Southeast First National Bank of Miami. (Exhibit 7 ranks Banc One and these competitors in terms of assets and provides data on profitability.) Southeast had run an experiment in Coral Gables, Florida, concurrent with Channel 2000. Chemical Bank had recently completed a home banking experiment and planned to schedule another. The others had also undertaken small tests or were about to do so. Exhibit 8 provides data on home banking experiments—their participants, scope, and technologies.

The larger brokerage firms, like Merrill Lynch, also had good reasons to think about participating in videotex. Some had already developed software for limited use by their branches throughout the

EXHIBIT 7 Banc One's Competitors: Financial Indicators, 1980 ($ million)

Bank Holding Co. (lead bank)	National Rank[a]	Assets[a,b]	Net Income[a,b]	Return on Equity (4-Year Average) (Median 13.8)[b]	Return on Assets (Median 0.9)[a]
Citicorp (Citibank, New York)	1	$114,920	$507.0	15.2	0.4
Bankamerica Corp. (Bank of America, San Francisco)	2	111,617	645.0	18.3	0.6
Chase Manhattan Corp. (Chase Manhattan Bank)	3	76,190	364.7	12.3	0.5
Manufacturers Hanover Corp., New York (Manufacturers Hanover Trust Co.)	4	55,522	230.2	14.5	0.4
Chemical New York Corp. (Chemical Bank, New York)	7	41,342	175.2	12.7	0.4
Western Bancorp. (United California Bank)	9	32,100	233.4	17.7	0.7
First National Boston (First National Bank, Boston)	17	15,948	103.1	15.6	0.6
First Bank System, Inc., Miami (First National Bank of Miami)	20	13,475	111.6	15.4	0.9
Southeast Banking Corp., Miami (Southeast First National Bank)	32	5,854	47.9	12.8	0.8
Banc One Corporation (Bank One of Columbus)	77	2,824	33.4	17.6	1.2

[a]*Moody's Bank and Finance Manual,* 1981, pp. a5–a6.
[b]"1981 Annual Banking Survey," *Forbes,* April 13, 1981, pp. 136–39.

country; it was but one step further to serve a broader base of clients in their homes. Other plastic card processors, like Bank of America and American Express, could also presume to have ambitions, like Banc One, of capturing a big share of the financial transaction part of any videotex system. The processing business in 1981 was highly fragmented, with more than 100 competitors; the largest processor was American Express's subsidiary, First Data Resources, which had only 12 to 14 percent of the market. Whether and how future consolidations would take place to make home banking a profitable segment of processing was entirely unclear.

In contemplating Banc One's competitors in the home banking business, McCoy expressed a concern that the "alley cats" not make it a brawl. "A key problem is how you price it. If the alley cats come in and price it unrealistically, then nobody will make any money." In McCoy's view, the "gentlemen" banks would at least make it a fair game.

Participants in the Videotex Industry

Banc One and its competitors could not develop their strategies without considering the other participants in the much broader videotex industry of which home banking would be a part. These included: (1) the hardware manufacturers, (2) the communications system providers, (3) the central switching computers, or computer networks, and (4) the providers of various home information services. Exhibit 9 lists companies already participating in videotex, and Exhibit 10 shows Fisher's schematic vision of the industry.

1. *Hardware manufacturers:* Until mid-1982, tests of home banking and other videotex services had been conducted mostly with components—television receivers, keypads, and modems (or decoders, or couplers)—hooked to a computer via the telephone or coaxial cable. But other configurations were on the horizon, embodied in designs by

EXHIBIT 8 Pioneers in Home Banking

Date	Company	Location	Link	Type of Terminal	Number of Households
Fall 1980 (3 mos.)	Bank One of Columbus, Ohio	Columbus, Ohio	Phone	TV/keypad/decoder	200
1980–1981 (14 mos.)	Southeast First National Bank of Miami with AT&T and Knight-Ridder	Coral Gables, Florida	Phone	TV adapted by AT&T	200
October 1980	United American Bank with United American Service Corp. and Radio Shack	Knoxville, Tennessee	Phone	Radio Shack TSR-80	400
Fall 1981	First Interstate, Los Angeles with Tymeshare, Inc. and Radio Shack	San Fernando Valley, California	Cable	Atari and TSR-80	200
1981	Citibank	Queens, New York	Phone	Proprietary terminal	100
1981	Chemical Bank	New York City	Phone	Atari Computer	200
1982 (6 mos.)	Bank of America with Times Mirror and Infomart	Orange County, California	Cable and phone	Various terminals	350
1982	First Bank System, Minnesota	Fargo, North Dakota, and Twin Cities, Minnesota	Phone	Antiope terminal	270–280
1982	Chemical Bank	New York City	Phone	Atari	
1983	Southeast First National Bank and Knight-Ridder	Miami, Florida	Phone	AT&T terminal	5,000
1983	Six or more California banks, including California First and United California, plus Cox Cable and HomeServe	San Diego, California	Cable	Keypad/TV	
1983	Cox Cable, HomeServe, Homebanc	Omaha, Nebraska	Cable	Keypad/TV	

EXHIBIT 9 U.S. Companies and Videotex, 1981

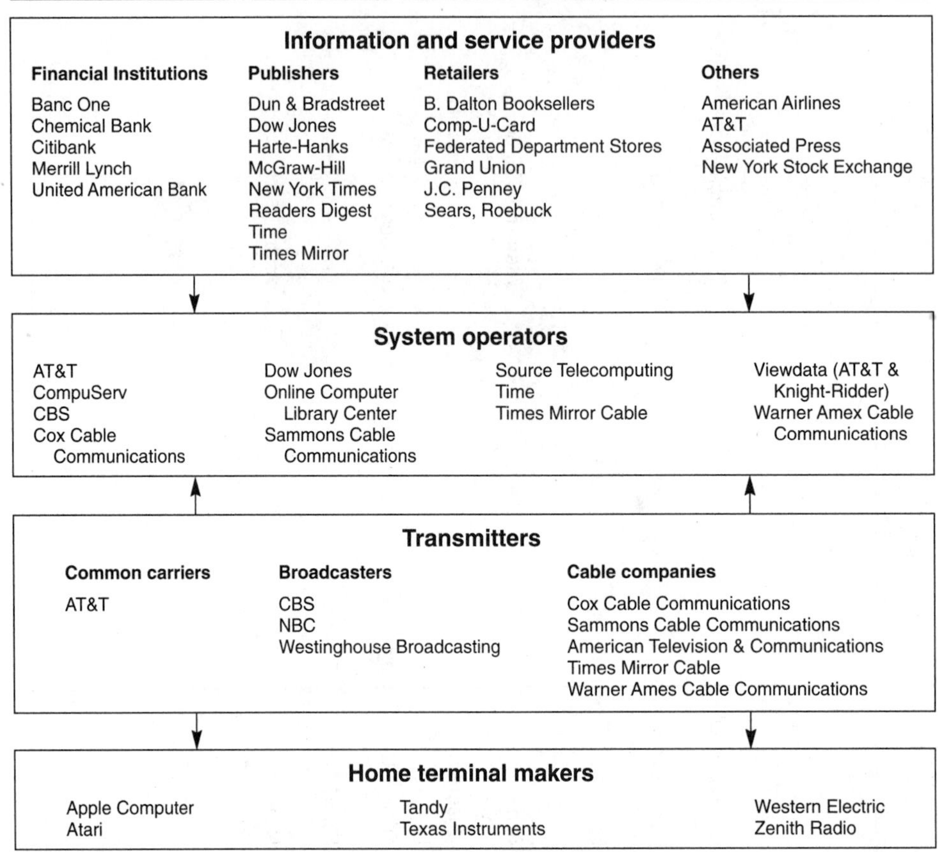

companies worldwide. In 1982 Radio Shack was already marketing a videotex terminal for $400; it had a keyboard and modem in one unit. The French terminal was a self-contained home information appliance with a nine-inch screen; it was to be used for tests in the United States. In 1982, Texas Instruments had designed a self-contained unit with a five-inch, high-resolution screen. The British and Canadians, with several years' more experience than their U.S. counterparts, also wanted a piece of the action. Japanese companies too were apparently eager to enter the business, though by March 1982 none had demonstrated any terminals. Home computers like the Apple could also be used to receive videotex. Fisher was urging IBM and others to get into the game and come up with a suitable, salable product. To this end he continually shared with those companies ideas generated at Banc One, including the results of Channel 2000.

The marketing of these home terminals was another question. Would they be distributed through outlets like Radio Shack and department stores, or would they be bought or rented from manufacturers' outlets like AT&T's phone stores?

2. *Communications system providers:* Although Fisher believed that telephone lines would be the medium of communication for videotex, cable was still in the running. AT&T's commitment was unwavering: tests of an electronic telephone directory in Texas, Florida, and New Jersey were among several

EXHIBIT 10 In-Home Banking Network

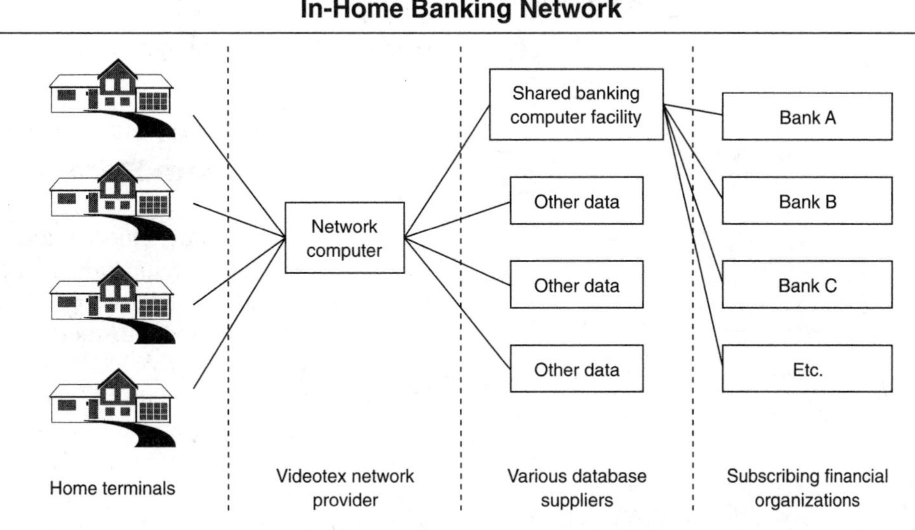

related experiments the mammoth company was undertaking. But in 1982 the information-carrying capacity of phone lines was limited; not only were transactions via telephone relatively slow, but displays on the screen were limited to primitive graphics. AT&T promised dramatic improvements no later than the end of the decade with packet switching, digitalization, and dual-channel phone lines. Warner-Amex, the leader in interactive cable, believed cable superior in potential to whatever AT&T could devise; after all, moving graphics or a Sears Catalog in all its detail could be transmitted easily via cable. Nevertheless, of 20 million cable subscribers at the end of 1981, only 60,000 had interactive service. Although more two-way cable was being installed, even optimists predicted only 30 million homes with two-way cable by 1991. In either case, the technology was developing so fast that it was difficult in early 1982 to predict which would prove most cost-effective, either in initial equipment cost or in distribution. It was also conceivable that the two systems might coexist, either independently or interdependently (as in a cable-in, phone-out system). In Fisher's view, it was crucial that Bank One be ready for both: "The only thing we are committed to is a display 20 lines deep and 40 characters wide."

3. *Computer networks:* Whatever the technology of the communications system, users would need to dial up a computer that could connect them with the videotex service they wished to use—banking, shopping, library research, stock reports, phone directory, want ads, or whatever. As Exhibit 10 shows, Banc One envisioned a small number of central switching computers, or "network computers," owned by AT&T, CBS, Knight-Ridder, Times Mirror, and others. These networks might also provide some of the services, but for the most part they would charge a fee to other service providers on a per transaction basis or a fixed fee or both.

4. *Videotex service providers:* Several software houses, providing various home information data bases, were already in operation—like CompuServe, a multiservice provider, and Comp-u-Star, a "Teleshopping" service. Although they were available to only a minuscule number of consumers in 1982, they were ready to take off once the hardware became available at a reasonable cost. Banks and other financial institutions were developing the software for the financial services component of the system.

Banc One's Strategy

In Fisher's vision, the central computer switching networks would subcontract the huge financial services component of videotex to processors like Banc One. His original intention had been that Banc One would be the major (and perhaps exclusive) processor for one major network nationwide. By the end

EXHIBIT 11

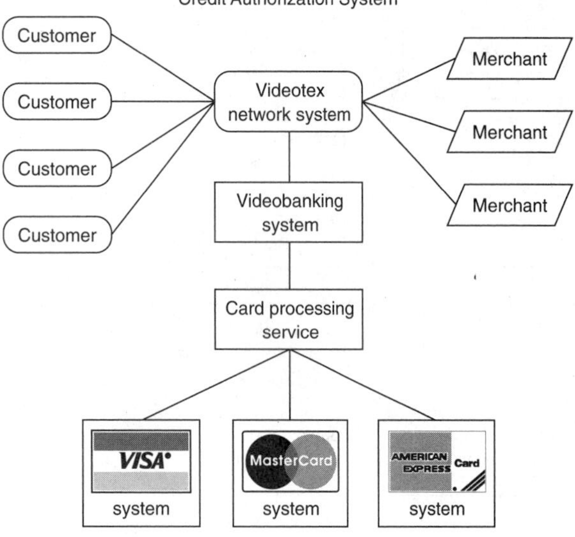

of 1981, however, it was clear to Fisher that Banc One's competitors were not about to let that happen. Fisher had tried to involve Banc One in an experiment in Florida that would have tested this vision. He presented the idea to the management of Knight-Ridder/AT&T, the joint venture undertaking the experiment, only to see Knight-Ridder give the idea—and the contract—to Southeast First National Bank of Miami.

With their sheer size and resources, the giant banks had the power to swallow up Banc One at will—to "buy us out," as McCoy put it. To preempt their next moves, Fisher decided to stimulate a joint venture, which he dubbed Videobanking, Inc.,[8] with at least one giant and several other banks to develop the financial transactions component of videotex. (Exhibits 11 and 12 show the structure he envisioned.) Chemical Bank was the first giant on Fisher's list, but it expected to be a much bigger player in videotex and home banking than it would be as part of Fisher's joint venture scheme. Thus, it gave Fisher's proposal a cool reception and proceeded to budget $6 million to $8 million for yet another home banking experiment itself. Fisher believed that money alone would not give Chemical Bank the expertise to succeed. Citicorp was the next giant on Fisher's list. It had never worked with other banks on anything, and it was not clear that the benefits of a joint venture in this new industry would persuade it to change that pattern.

Where Does Banc One Go from Here?

In contemplating Banc One's future, McCoy had stated outright that all Banc One needed to succeed was "people and capital." People like Fisher and "other guys just as good in their areas as Johnny Fisher is in his" had provided the bank with the imagination, creativity, and boldness leading to its current success. Profits from its processing business had enabled it to pioneer at every stage in banking innovation of the past two decades. But videotex was a venture of quite different dimensions. To be a nationwide player in a business of videotex's scope required financial resources consonant with Banc One's ambitions. In that light, Fisher's "big chip" was meager indeed.

In 1981 McCoy had designated his successor, going outside the bank to hire John Havens as Banc One's chairman in 1981. Havens was a native of Columbus whose success in real estate and banking ventures convinced McCoy that he had the persistence, business savvy, and deal-making skills Banc One needed to grow—to extend its capital base—in the 1980s. "We're going to be doing lots of things in the future," McCoy declared, "and I want an entrepreneur to run this shop." Indeed, in the year since Havens took office and began leading the campaign for new members, Banc One had risen from sixth in size among bank holding companies in Ohio to third; Havens expected it to be second or first within another year. With the greater assets this entailed, Banc One could think credibly of even greater investments in its future.

As far as other talent was concerned, McCoy continued to recruit aggressively at major business schools and elsewhere. He still had to overcome the bank's location in Columbus, but he liked to remind visitors:

> Nobody thought a great football team could come from Green Bay, Wisconsin. Who'd want to go there, with the worst weather in the world? Then someone had the idea of hiring the greatest coach in the world, and then he would get the greatest center, the greatest guard, greatest tackle, greatest end, greatest quarterback, and

---

[8]Banc One has registered the name and associated trademark of Videobanking as it appears in Exhibits 11 and 12.

EXHIBIT 12

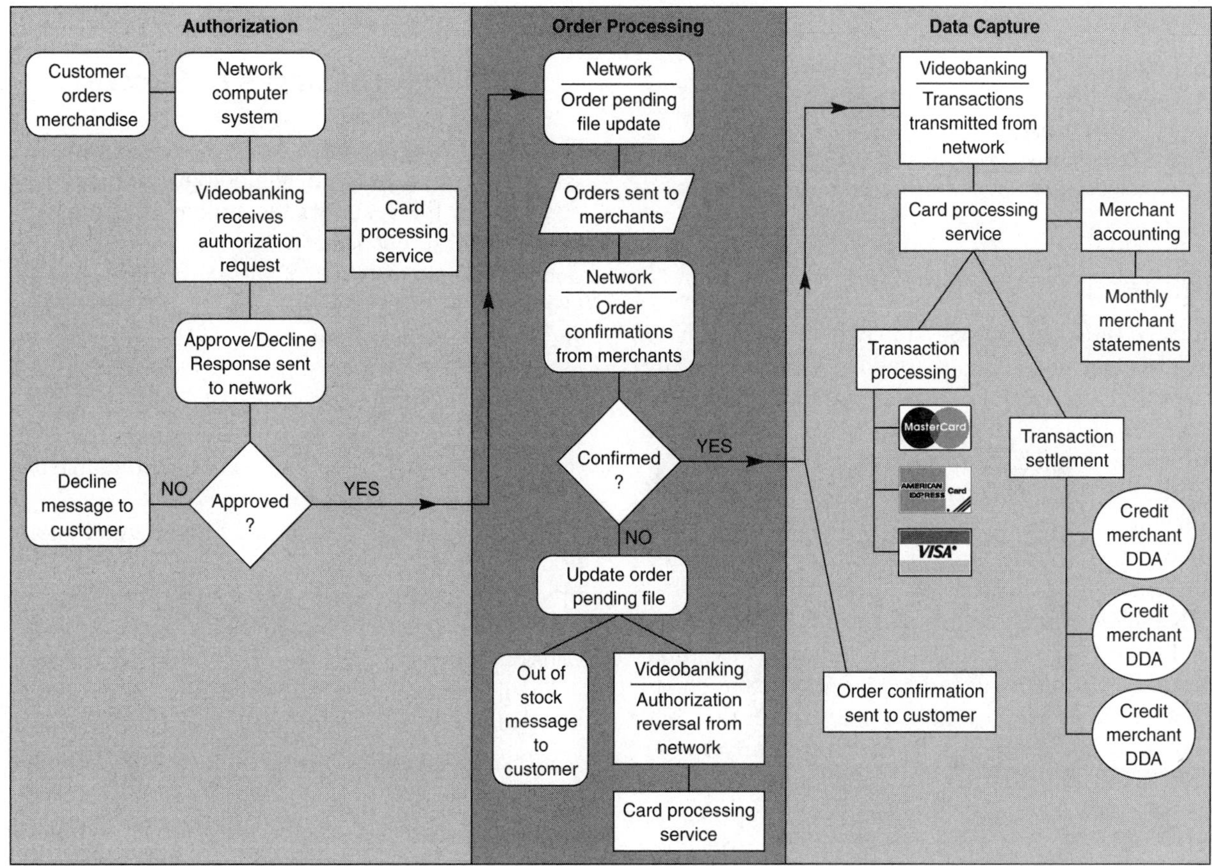

on down the line. Teach the fundamentals and they will win. This is all we ever tried to do. Why does a great bank have to be in New York or San Francisco?

Fisher's Big Chip

In the immediate future, Banc One had to decide how best to invest in the development of home banking over the next year or two and with whom to cooperate in the process, while maintaining a competitive lead and profitable niche. Three options seemed most promising to John Fisher:

1. *Videobanking, Inc.*[9] If Banc One could not copy the strategy it had followed in the late 1960s with its card processing business, developing the software for a nationwide processing system of its own, then it might be the leader in a nationwide joint venture. But to do so credibly, Fisher believed he would need to sign on one of the biggest banks in the country.

2. *A franchise of someone else's system:* Banc One had gone far with its original BAC franchise from Bank of America in 1966; perhaps it should do the same with videotex. In the meantime, while waiting for a system to develop, Banc One could concentrate on its card business and ATM development, both of which were essential for further research in any direction.

3. *Home banking in Columbus.* Banc One could develop home banking for its own customers and cooperate with home information software compa-

[9]See footnote 8.

nies in making these services available locally. If it created a viable system before other banks in the country did, it would still have something to sell.

We conclude that we can in fact identify management criteria which effectively discriminate between profitable and unprofitable new technologies, and that these criteria have utility in appraising technological innovation in a wide variety of cases.

Reading II–6
Management Criteria for Effective Innovation

George R. White

Early in the corporate era, it may have been easy to believe that technological stability was the normal condition and technological innovation the occasional, fortuitous balm for problems to which we otherwise could have adapted. But since World War II, innovation has been the norm; technology-based innovations, coming in rapid sequence, have been seen as the crucial source of prosperity, the panacea for all business problems.

Now we know that this panacea is not necessarily benign. The U.S. electronics industry was in far better condition in the early 1950s, before the emergence of the transistor, than it is now with the consumer business largely penetrated by Japan. On the other hand, it is also true that a previous modest participant in electronics, the Motorola Corporation, used the transistor to expand its position in consumer electronics and then, by integration backwards, gained a significant new role as a component supplier.

When compared to those available in finance, marketing, and production, the tools available to management for assessing and directing technological innovation are rudimentary. Intrigued by this fact, Margaret B. W. Graham and I determined to study in detail two fully completed, well-documented innovations—the transistor in consumer electronics and the jet engine in subsonic jet transports. We postulated that the criteria for success in these cases could be applied to predicting the future outcomes in two immature innovations—the supersonic transport and computerized automobiles.

Technology Review. February 1978, pp. 21–28. Reprinted with permission from *Technology Review,* MIT Alumni Association,

The Determinants of Success

We began by predicting that determinants of success could be found in both technology and business contexts. In the realm of technology, the determinants would surely depend on some appraisal of the quality and significance of the innovative concept itself: it must be new, and it must also be good. But such an innovative concept alone does not assure technical potency; there must be an embodiment for the new device, a product or system which is waiting for it. The embodiment surrounding an inventive concept has a major effect on how profitable the new technology proves to be.

Even with technical potency, a high rate of adoption and great profitability are not assured. The operational consequences of the new technology on manufacturing, marketing, and distribution must be considered.

Finally, market dynamics are extremely important—and often complex. Many industries have several dependent stages of intermediate demand; for example, transistor manufacturers sell to radio manufacturers, and radio manufacturers in turn sell to consumers. It is not enough to study the transistor market; analysis of final consumer demand is essential to understanding the outcome of transistor technology.

Balancing Old and New Constraints

Three questions turn out to be crucial in determining the technical potential of any inventive concept:

What fundamental technical constraints limiting the prior art are lifted? This is the key technical challenge: identify the core physical constraints underlying the previous technologies that have been lifted by the new invention, and assess the significance of lifting those constraints. Consider an example from the field of aircraft engines. In the piston engine, the upper limit in compression ratio is set by the detonation of the fuel charge in the cylinder. A turbine engine has no such limit; it is possible to have a higher compression ratio in a turbine engine than in a piston engine, and today's successful turbine engines do have those higher compression ratios.

What new technical constraints are inherent in the new art? The first question had to do with the credit side, and this question determines the debit side—that is, what fundamental constraints limit the effectiveness of the innovation. In jet engines, for example, the wake efficiency or the Froude efficiency of an aircraft propulsion system depends on the ratio of the velocity of the rearward stream of air to the forward velocity of the aircraft; the lower that ratio, the more efficient the propulsion. A propeller, moving a large amount of cold air slowly, has a higher wake efficiency than a jet engine moving a small amount of hot air rapidly, so a new constraint exists.

How favorable is relief of the former weighed against the stringencies of the latter? The net of the first two questions with respect to any inventive concept is a qualitative technical balance. The comparisons cannot be quantitative because they are not necessarily of similar characteristics; so this is highly judgmental balance, but it can be technically quite meaningful.

Putting Innovations in Context

The second stage of applying these management criteria is to analyze the embodiment in which the new technology will go to market. Here again the analysis takes the form of answering three questions:

Is the end product enhanced by additional technology and components required to make use of the innovation? This question calls for an analysis of the changes which must be made to a product if the innovation is to be used in it. A good example occurs in radios. Every radio must have a power supply, an R-F section, an I-F section, and an audio section. The transistor penetrated the automobile radio as a replacement for the output power tube, but the R-F and I-F sections of the radio were unaffected by the presence of a germanium power transistor instead of an output power pentode; however, because the output stage no longer required 300-volt B+ plate potential, it was possible to eliminate the unreliable vibrator power supplies as soon as R-F and I-F tubes requiring only 12-volt B+ potential were developed. These hybrid radios were much more reliable, but they could not have succeeded without the 12-volt tube development.

Is the inventive concept itself diluted or enhanced by the embodiment required? Now analyze the effect on the innovation itself of the changes required for its use in the product. There are favorable cases where the additional art surrounding the new invention enhances its value; that is a very happy situation. But there are many cases where the embodiment surrounding the new art dilutes it.

Does the additional embodiment offer opportunity for further inventive enhancement? Once more a balance is needed, this time between the value added to a product and that subtracted from it by the requirements of the innovation. Does it add more punch, or does the new innovation on balance decrease the acceptability of the product into which it is incorporated?

A Balance Sheet on Financing Business Operations

The answers to these two sets of questions establish the technical potency of a new innovation, but they offer no criteria in the business context from which to judge such things as profit potential. Three questions are also involved here:

What previously emplaced business operations are displaced or weakened by the new innovation? Assess the potential changes in existing business that will be brought about by the innovation. In the case of the entry of the transistor into electronics, the impact on the dealer service network is a perfect example. All tube sets were guaranteed to have tube failures and to require tube replacement. That phenomenon simply does not exist in transistor devices, and the dealer service network predictably declined in importance as transistors were introduced.

What new business operations are needed or wisely provided to support the new innovation? Assess the nature and cost of new business operations required by adoption of the new technology. The Japanese penetration of the U.S. consumer electronics market provides an example; it was simultaneously an innovation in distribution and retail marketing. Trading companies were now the distributors, and retail sales by stores, department stores, and discount houses replaced the previous pattern of selling which focused on the brand-franchise dealer.

How favorable is cessation of the former practices weighed against provision of the latter? Draw the trial balance again; we claim that this analysis can yield a qualitative business balance stemming from the new invention.

What Will Sell and What Won't

Finally, we determine a set of criteria having to do with market dynamics, on the basis of three questions:

Does the product incorporating the new technology provide enhanced effectiveness in the marketplace serving the final user? The Pilkington Float Glass Process represents a substantially more effective way of making plate glass by casting the glass against molten tin instead of grinding the surfaces; there are dramatic cost savings. But smooth glass is smooth glass, and there is no increased effectiveness resulting from its use in windows. The process is a perfect example of an innovation which made no change at all in the marketplace; it does not, unlike many others, yield economic payback because of market expansion due to enhanced effectiveness.

Does the operation reduce the cost of delivering the product or service? Taken together, this question and the one above are really the scissors of supply and demand, the first dealing with demand, the second with supply. If the answer to both of these questions is no, we can forget the whole thing; and if it is yes, then there need be little market uncertainty. The challenging case is where one of these is positive and the second is not.

Does latent demand expansion or price elasticity expansion determine the characteristics of the new markets? When the factor driving a market area is lower price per unit, market expansion by hundreds of percent is hard to obtain; major expansion in revenue is much more likely when the change in the market is driven by a dramatic change in product effectiveness. This final question, of course, determines the quantitative business balance.

In these criteria, we have avoided terms such as *return on investment* and *return on assets managed*. Our view is that these issues are overwhelmed whenever a new inventive concept can be placed in a beneficial embodiment which will enhance its value in a major latent market with lowered operational costs. If evaluations of an innovation must be based on assumptions of narrow differences in return on investment, they are quite possibly based on fallacy. What we propose is a logic structure to identify a small class of innovations of great promise whose success will transcend the cash value of any normal investment.

Putting the Determinants to the Test of History

Some examples from our work show how this logic structure might have served as a meaningful discriminant between successful and unsuccessful innovations in the past.

The Japanese Portable Radio Game

Consider first three aspects of the changes in the consumer electronics market wrought by the transistor. Transistor radios made their first strong showing in the U.S. portable radio market in 1956; prior to that time all portables had been tube sets. In 1956, the center of gravity of the U.S. market (according to listings in *Consumer Reports*) was in personal-size transistorized portable radios weighing an average of 20 ounces and costing an average of $57; eight models were available. This was a substantial innovation; the dominant radio in the previous year's market had been a tube-based portable weighing about six pounds. No Japanese sets were in the U.S. market in 1956.

By 1959, the U.S. industry had responded fully to the transistor as it was then applied; there were 25 portable models in the 20-ounce size, and prices were down slightly.

But in 1959, there was also a new market never populated before, filled by 11 different Japanese miniature portable sets weighing about 10 ounces (less than half as much as the smallest U.S. radios then available) and costing 10 percent less than the 20-ounce U.S. radios. The Japanese had made a dramatic innovation in the size and weight of personal portable radios and thus had opened up a new market not serviced by the U.S. industry.

The Japanese did not do this by innovating in transistors; they did it by other innovations through which they reduced the sizes of tuning capacitors, loudspeakers, battery supplies, and antennas. It was the transistor innovation supported by these additional innovations that allowed the Japanese to open up this exclusive new pocket-radio market and begin their successful penetration into U.S. consumer electronics. In fact, the U.S. industry's innovation based on the transistor was an incomplete innovation; it had not taken advantage of the embodiment surrounding the transistor as the Japanese had done.

By 1962, the market outcomes were clear. In 1955, the U.S. market for portables was 2 million sets, all tubes, and all made in the United States. By 1962, the Japanese had captured 58 percent of the market, and they had in fact captured 68 percent of the market growth made possible by the transistor.

Auto Radios and TV: Who Needs Transistors?

Compare this history with that of the second transistor innovation, which was in auto radios.

In 1955, the only auto radios were tube sets; they used high-voltage R-F, I-F, and output tubes, and of course they required vibrator power supplies.

In 1956 came a new type of auto radio with no vibrator power supply, no step-up transformer, and no high B+ potential. Germanium output transistors allowed low power drain; they were driven directly by the negative-ground 12-volt power supply of the automobile battery. In addition, an embodiment innovation provided 12-volt B+ tubes to handle R-F and I-F.

Only one year later, the first all-transistor auto radio, completely transistorized in R-F and I-F and with low-drain output transistors, all running directly on the battery supply, became available.

On average the tube sets of 1955 cost $45, the hybrid sets cost $8 more (a modest step-up), and the completely transistorized sets of 1957 cost $125, a luxury prestige item in the Cadillac Eldorado but otherwise priced out of the market.

The production of auto radios follows very closely the production of automobiles. In the mid-1950s, 67 percent of new cars went to market with radios. Since then this figure has increased steadily—no sudden changes in auto radio use have been associated with the new technologies—until now it is almost 100 percent. There were 6.86 million auto radios made in 1955 and only 6.43 million in 1960; these figures reflect almost exactly the volume of new-car demand. In this period, the transition from tube sets to the tube-plus-output-transistor hybrid set was essentially completed (fully transistorized radios were still not sold in any meaningful quantity). Yet there was no expansion at all in this market.

Turn now to color television consoles, the last of three transistor substitution innovations we have studied. All consoles marketed from 1955 through 1967 used tubes. The first transistorized console was available in 1968, but only in 1974 (almost two decades after the first transistor portable was sold) did transistorized color sets become the industry standard. Since portability and maintenance cost are dominated by the vacuum cathode-ray tube, transistor penetration was very slow.

Summing a Transistorized Balance

Portable radios, automobile radios, and color television consoles represent three different transistor innovations which were technically very similar in circuit design and in cost. Yet the business outcomes were dramatically different. Our criteria applied to this field reveal the differences in technology and its business context that led to these strikingly different outcomes.

Recall that our criteria reflected first a balancing of constraints removed against new constraints added by an innovation. In the case of portable radios, transistors meant that weight, size, and frequency of repair were all improved dramatically. For auto radios, the vibrator failure mode (which provided 60 to 80 percent of the maintenance engagement) was eliminated and with it the problem of battery drain when the radio was used without the engine running. Frequency of repair was generally reduced. In television, transistors served only to reduce the frequency of repair. As we progress from auto radios to television, the value of constraints lifted by the transistor declines.

New technology always has new problems. The audio fidelity of the little portable radios was poor, and that is a fundamental constraint. Similarly, the capture value of the tiny ferrite antennas was not as good as that of the bigger antennas. There were no particular penalties in auto radios or in television.

Drawing a technical balance on the value of these inventions, we conclude that the portable radios presented a vast increase in portability—from six to eight pounds down to shirt-pocket size. The auto radios offered a major increase in reliability. Transistorized television sets only had a slight increase in reliability going for them. We conclude that the portable radio had dramatic new value, the auto radio had substantial new value in its hybrid mode, and the television set had very little new value.

Next, what additional technology was required in the embodiments in which transistors were placed to realize their full potential? Small tuning capacitors, loudspeakers, antennas, and batteries were crucial to the reduced size of the portable radios. If these had not been included, the value of the transistor innovation would have been diluted, since in fact tubes were not the fundamental limit on the size of portable radios. As the Japanese demonstrated—to the detriment of their American competitors—only if you spent extra money to miniaturize all the other components could you fully capitalize on the transistor invention itself.

On auto radios, the additional innovation required for auto radios were the 12-volt tubes for R-F and I-F sections, and these were rapidly achieved. This allowed elimination of the vibrator; without that, the transistor innovation would have been diluted and transistorized auto radios might not have been successful.

An interesting situation prevails in television. As far as we can imagine now, a television set requires a cathode-type picture tube. Even after 20 years of looking, we find the prospects dim for a cheap, all-solid-state display. Therefore, we are nailed to the low reliability, high repair cost, and large size of present picture tubes. There is essentially no opportunity for incremental enhancement in the embodiment surrounding the transistors.

As we compare these different applications of the transistor on the basis of these criteria statements, we can understand why the portable radio transition was complete and rapid, why the auto radio transition was quite rapid for one portion (hybrid) and quite slow for the other portion (fully transistorized), and why the color television transition was quite slow. (See Exhibit 1.)

EXHIBIT 1

	Effects of the Advent of the Transistor on:		
	Portable Radios	Auto Radios	Television
Inventive concept			
Constraints lifted	Weight, size, and frequency of repair.	Vibrator failure, battery drain, and frequency of repair.	Frequency of repair.
New constraints	Low sensitivity, low fidelity.	None.	None.
Advantage	Vast increase in portability.	Major increase in reliability.	Slight increase in reliability.
Embodiment merit			
Additional components	Condenser, speaker, antenna, and battery.	12-volt R-F/I-F tubes.	Cathode-ray tube.
Dilution or enhancement	Dilution of size and weight gains.	Dilution if vibrator required.	Dilution, since no rewards of small size or low weight
Additional opportunity	Enhancement if above are miniaturized.	Enhancement if 12-volt tubes eliminate vibrator.	No enhancement; elimination of CRT seems impossible.
Operational practice			
Displaced business operations	Dealer service no longer very important.	Service less important.	Service slightly easier.
New business operations	Low transport and inventory cost encourage wide distribution network	New field of transistor and electronic manufacture opened.	None.
Advantage	Low-cost mass marketing opens new market to imports.	Radio makers integrate backward to transistors, auto makers to radios.	Slight if any.
Market dynamics			
Enhanced effectiveness to final user	Great increase only in portability.	Slight.	None.
Reduced cost	Higher cost in early years.	Only slightly higher cost, due to vibrator savings.	Much higher cost in early years.
Expansion of substitution market	Expansion in miniature size only.	Substitution.	Substitution.

Assessing the impact of the transistor on consumer electronics. The author proposes that analysis of these 12 aspects of the changes wrought by the transistor demonstrates why its penetration was so instant and its revolution so complete in the portable radio industry, its penetration equally complete but its revolution insignificant in auto radios, and its penetration small and slow in the television industry.

On the operational side, the transistor led to some business innovations. In Japan, a wholly new concept of low-cost mass marketing followed the design of nine-ounce radios.

The fundamental change in a key component of auto radios—the output tube became a germanium output transistor—was adopted throughout the industry and led to a new business opportunity. The Motorola Corporation, a radio manufacturer which never made tubes in its life, was effectively able to integrate backwards and started making germanium power output transistors—first for use in its own production of auto radios and also in its military equipment and later as components for sale to others. Thus this change in technology allowed Motorola to expand its role and penetration in the industry. The transistorized television set, having only slight advantages, offered no new business opportunities; essentially it is a null case.

The application of transistors to the portable radio definitely increased the effectiveness of the product to the final user; it now became a go-with-you-anywhere radio rather than a carry-it-and-set-it-down radio. The combination of the transistor and the further innovation surrounding it led to a new product that claimed a new latent market never populated before, rather than a substitution market. In contrast, the enhanced effectiveness of the transistorized auto radio to the final user was quite slight—a little bit of reliability, a little bit of battery drain. It was a substitution market; in fact, the total demand did not increase at all. There simply was one radio (approximately) for every new car sold. The television case is our null case; nothing happened.

The Battle of the Turbines

Here is a brief review of how our criteria illuminate the different outcomes in the case of turbine aircraft. Here we are dealing with three fundamentally different types of aircraft—the wide-bodied jets (707 and DC-8), the Lockheed Electra, and the Boeing 727. The first jets, as well as the first Electras, entered service in 1958. By 1961, the Big Five U.S. airlines (these firms provided 75 percent of U.S. passenger miles in the late 1950s, and they were historically the airlines which first bought new equipment) had 177 big jets; by 1969 they were using 500 such aircraft. The Lockheed Electra went from an initial 1961 fleet of 72 down to only 28 aircraft in 1969. The 727, which was not even in the first round of purchases, turned out to be the single most effective jet aircraft; by 1969, 400 of them were in service in the United States.

The inventions on which these aircraft were based were largely similar—the substitution of rotating compressors and high-temperature gas turbines for reciprocating pistons. But these aircraft are very different in their ensemble of other elements beyond turbine engines—embodiment merit, according to the terminology of this article. To achieve the full potential for higher speed inherent in the turbine, the 707 and DC-8 used swept wings, at 35° and 30°, respectively. This was possible because Boeing and Douglas engineers solved (each in slightly different fashion) the problem of controlling a phenomenon called Dutch roll, which affected stability. The outcome was that the 707 and DC-8 were fundamentally faster than the British Comet, which was designed with a 20° wing sweep to avoid the stability problem. Thus the opportunity came not in jet engines but in solving aerodynamic problems brought into relevance by jets.

Lockheed engineers were trapped with a dilemma in designing the Electra. They concluded that they were better off moving a large mass of cold air slowly than a small mass of hot air rapidly, because of the runway length requirements of the latter. So they stuck with propellers. But propellers in fact have an ultimate speed limit, since their tips cannot easily go faster than the speed of sound, and this in turn constrains the aircraft to a top speed nearly 200 miles slower than that of a turbojet such as the 707. The Electra designers chose the old, familiar art of propellers, where no risk was entailed but no new enhancement was possible.

The 727, the third member of our jet set, has been successful because of two additional embodiment innovations—fanjet engines and high-wing-lift devices. In order to use the short runways of intermediate-range airports, the 727 had to obtain much more take-off thrust and much more lift from the wing in landing than had been possible before; yet it also required a small wing for cruising at high speed. This was achieved by using fanjet engines (with cold air flow around the hot turbine exhaust) in the rear of the aircraft so that the wing was clean, and by using triple-slotted flaps with leading edge slats which provided the equivalent of a variable-configuration wing. The innovation was effective; the 727 ended up with short-field capability that matches that of propeller aircraft, yet it cruises at speeds typical of all jets.

Market dynamics are the next criterion of importance. The 707 and DC-8 presented a great advantage in comfort and speed; they flew higher and faster than any aircraft before, and it was simply more pleasant to travel. In addition, because of their high speed and capacity, they cost less per seat mile to operate than long-range piston planes. So the best of all possible worlds was obtained: demand was higher and cost was lower. These aircraft led to a strong market expansion for air travel.

The Electra offered only modest improvements. Some of the vibration coming from piston engines had disappeared, but Electras could not fly as high or as fast as the jets. Operating cost per seat mile excluding depreciation was less than that of medium-range piston aircraft, but this meant a market based on substitution (slowly penetrating by doing the same function against depreciated equipment), not one based on expansion (rapidly penetrating on the basis of payback from new customers).

Finally, the 727 had the speed and comfort of the big jets and costs roughly equal to the Electra, and it could fly in and out of the smaller airports. As soon as the 727 was available, all of the intermediate-range traffic, piston or Electra, went to it. (See Exhibit 2.)

Forecasting Future Innovation

Now that we have seen how the innovation criteria apply to the transistor case and to the case of jet aircraft, it is appropriate to make some general statements about their application to two prospective innovations, microprocessors for automobiles and supersonic transport aircraft.

Automotive Microprocessors: Everything Up

Microprocessors promise flexibility and precision of control and operation of automotive engines that are simply not available in mechanical control systems, and this is the heart of the technical advantage.

At the level of embodiment, we find that the sensors and actuators, not the computer chips, are the most crucial components requiring further development. An automobile is an analog mechanical environment; a microprocessor is a digital electronic environment. We need either sensors, actuators, and/or analog-to-digital converters, and these are the key embodiment elements. We also know that they represent the dominant portions of system cost and are the dominant determinants of system performance. If these can be made right, there will be

EXHIBIT 2

	707/DC-8	Electra	727
Embodiment merit			
Additional components	Swept wings required.	Propellers required.	High-lift wing devices needed.
Dilution or enhancement	Slight roll control problem.	Speed and maintenance constraint.	Clean wing with triple-slotted flaps from rear engine.
Additional opportunity	Speed advance over Comet due to high sweep angle.	None.	Short-field capability matches that of propeller aircraft.
Market dynamics			
Final user effectiveness	Great advance in speed and comfort.	Only modest gain over piston engine in speed and vibration.	Great advance in speed and comfort.
Cost reduction	Net cost less than long-range piston.	Cost much less than piston planes.	Costs roughly equal to Electra.
Expansion or substitution market	Strong expansion.	Substitution for piston craft.	Substitution for Electra and piston craft.

The battle of the turbine-powered transports. Only 6 of the author's 12 criteria are needed to demonstrate the superiority of pure jets in the marketplace—why the 707, DC-8, and 727-type aircraft became the standard for U.S. air travel in the 1970s. He believes the same kind of analysis can be used to show why innovations leading to a supersonic transport aircraft have much less potential in the U.S. market.

regulatory benefits, better driveability (which to the auto industry means desire to buy cars), and long-life, stable performance; automobiles will stay in tune and their control and performance functions will not deteriorate over the life of the car.

These will be major new design, manufacturing, and marketing opportunities, and our operational practice criteria are useful in seeing how to make a business operation out of these possibilities. Absolutely, one would expect that firms such as Bendix or TRW (with aerospace and electronic skills and a large presence in the auto industry) could take advantage of this opportunity to expand backwards (as Motorola did with auto radios) into special electronic precision sensors and actuators, seizing a key part of this technical ensemble for a long-term, stable market. We also have the possibility of car manufacturers expanding their domain of technical activities.

The market that is implied by these prospects for computerized automobiles is absolutely unique. It has been decreed by the U.S. government. Microprocessors and related control systems do not have to be evaluated against the cost of today's mechanical alternatives; they offer the most promising way we can yet envision to meet emission and economy standards mandated for motor vehicles in the 1980s. There is a billion-dollar value to manufacturers in avoiding the fines for high fuel consumption or the preemption of marketability if new automobiles fail to meet pollution standards set by federal law. The value to the auto industry hinges not on new revenue gain—because all the industry can hope to do is continue to sell high-value cars—but rather on the avoidance of loss.

The Fundamental Problem of the S.S.T.

To evaluate prospects for a supersonic transport, one can go through the same four-point check sequence on criteria. The key inventive concept, the thing that is fundamentally new on supersonic transports, is supersonic aerodynamics, the increase of aerodynamic drag at supersonic speed. Two different aerodynamic structures to deal with this problem have been examined in the United States. One (which is now a failed concept for transports) is the swing wing; the other, which survived until the entire transport project was shelved, is a wing swept back at an angle sharper than the Mach cone so the wing is subsonic while the airplane is supersonic.

This is a good concept. But it cannot deal with the fact that aircraft flying faster than the speed of sound always leave a sonic boom below, and the energy required to overcome that lost in the sonic boom results in high fuel consumption. So there is a good concept, but it has some debits.

Now we go to the embodiment criteria. The key regulatory decision was that sonic booms would not be allowed over the United States. So American supersonic aircraft must be efficient at subsonic cruise over the United States as well as at supersonic cruise over areas where boom is permitted. This requires what are called variable configuration engines, operating in bypass mode below the speed of sound and as straight jets above—a corollary innovation. The sharply swept wings present some unique control and stability problems; they lack the inherent stability of conventional wings, behaving much like classroom paper airplanes. There must be active controls, called "fly-by-wire." This is not hard, but creating reliable "fly-by-wire" equipment that will last for the 20-year life of an airplane presents a significant challenge.

A supersonic aircraft requires structures that go beyond those we have had before, because supersonic flight causes thermal as well as aerodynamic loads. The required composite materials represent a new art which now must be mastered.

Finally, we have a question about pollution: we absolutely know that oxides of nitrogen behave differently in the meteorological system at 65,000 feet than at 25,000 feet. The problem is that we do not know how they behave. If these oxides lead to depletion of the ozone layer, we will have somehow to change engine combustion.

If we understand all these embodiments surrounding the supersonic wing innovations, we can proceed to the issues of operational practice. The key problem here is that the U.S. domestic market has underwritten the basic costs of all major air transport innovations since the DC-3. It will not do so for the supersonic transport; long-range aircraft earn value only in international travel. Our airlines and our manufacturers need to understand what it means to be primarily international; pooling of traffic and manufacturing consortia are probable.

The market outcome is not clear. Is it an expansion market or a substitution market? We already have very effective long-range aircraft; if the only problem were to fly 4,000 to 5,000 miles, supersonic travel would be a substitution market, and the economics would not be optimistic. On the other hand, if the value of time saved is substantial, it is conceivable that supersonic travel could result in market expansion.

Having followed this procedure of drawing orderly balances in the areas of inventive concepts, embodiment merit, operational practices, and market outcomes, I have concluded that though no single constraint prohibits supersonic transports from being commercially successful, the broad array of concerns says that the mere passage of time will not assure an S.S.T. There must be some urgent national mission to override some of the constraints to their emergence.

We believe our procedure for evaluating the viability and likely outcomes of an innovation can largely account for the differentiated outcomes in high-technology businesses—businesses that are as far removed from each other as transistor radios and jet transports. When these criteria are applied to important potential future innovations, they indicate plausibility for a computerized car, given a reasonable regulatory atmosphere, and they indicate implausibility for many years for a U.S. supersonic transport. We are convinced that a similar analysis can be useful in indicating the likely future course of other projected innovations.

Reading II–7
Organizational Determinants of Technological Change: Toward a Sociology of Technological Evolution

Michael L. Tushman and Lori Rosenkopf

Abstract

This paper employs organization literature and concepts to help understand the path of technological progress. Our premise is that since technological progress is underdetermined by factors internal to the technology, it is the interaction of technical options with organization and interorganization dynamics that shapes the actual path of technological progress. Rather than reviewing technology as an autonomous force or as driven by an elite set of organizations, we argue that technologies evolve through the combination of random events, the direct action of organizations shaping industry standards, and the invisible hand of multiple competing organizations in a technological community. We suggest that the greater a product's technical uncertainty, the greater the intrusion of nontechnical factors in the product's evolution. Two fundamental factors shape technological uncertainty: the stage of the technology's evolutionary cycle and the technological complexity of the product itself. During periods of technological ferment, uncertainty is substantial. During these periods, organizational and interorganizational processes emerge to close on industry standards. Technological uncertainty is, however, minimized during periods of incremental technical change. We also suggest that technology can be described as systems ranging from nonassembled closed systems to complex, open systems. The more complex a product, the greater the number of subsystems, interfaces, dimensions of merit, and linking requirements. The more complex and/or open the product, the greater the technical uncertainty and the greater the intrusion of organizational dynamics in technological evolution. Technological cycles and complexity together affect the relative importance of organizational processes in shaping the path of technological change. As technology is an ever more important determinant of organization outcomes, the time is ripe to open up the black box of technological evolution; to use organization theory and research to understand the social, political, and organizational roots of technological change.

Research in Organizational Behavior 14, pp. 311–47.

Organization theory has long considered technology and technological change as influential determinants of organizational phenomena.[1] There is extensive literature on the effects of technology on organizations at the individual,[2] organization,[3]

---

[1]C. Perrow, "A Framework for Comparative Organizational Analysis," *American Sociological Review* 32 (1967), pp. 194–208; J. Thompson, *Organizations in Action* (New York: McGraw-Hill, 1967); J. Woodward, *Industrial Organization* (London: Oxford University Press, 1965).

[2]C. Hulin and M. Roznowski, "Organizational Technologies: Effects on Organizations' Characteristics and Individuals' Responses," in *Research in Organizational Behavior,* vol 7, ed. L. Cummings and B. Staw (Greenwich, CT: JAI Press, 1985).

[3]M. Burkhardt and D. Brass, "Changing Patterns or Patterns of Change: The Effects of a Change in Technology on Social Network Structure and Power," *Administrative Science Quarterly* 35 (1990), pp. 104–27.

population,[4] and community[5] levels of analysis. While we have extensive knowledge of the effects of technology on organizations, we know very little about the determinants of technology.[6] Technology is treated as a black box—as either a contextual fact or as an outcome of stochastic processes driven by unpredictable individual genius.[7] This primitive view of technology minimizes the impacts that organizations have on technological progress and, in turn, stunts theory and research on innovation processes within organizations, industries, and communities.[8]

This paper's purpose is to get inside the black box of technological change. Our premise is that technological progress is underdetermined by factors internal to the technology. It is the interaction of technical options with organization and interorganization dynamics that shapes the actual path of technological progress. We borrow from sociology, history of technology, economics, and organization theory to build a community-level model of technological progress and a systems perspective on technology. We explore the relative impacts of chance and individual genius, as well as organization and interorganization action in shaping technological change. We find that at critical junctures, organization action (and inaction) dramatically affects the shape and direction of technological change. This approach to technological change suggests that technological evolution is driven by a combination of technical, economic, social, political, and organizational processes and, as such, deserves more sustained attention from organizational scholars.

Both scientific progress and technological progress are affected by social and organizational dynamics. Historians and sociologists of science and technology find that the conduct of scientific and technological progress is not coldly rational, but is infused with value.[9] Science is driven by core norms and values that are carried, interpreted, and defined by the community of scientific practitioners. Discipline-oriented scientists define locally agreed-on status distinctions, problem areas, methodologies, and legitimate solutions.[10]

Social dynamics are accentuated in technological change because of the underlying nature of technology. Unlike science, technology almost always involves interdependence between disciplines.[11] For example, where physics is executed by interactions among physicists, jet engines require interactions between aerodynamic, metallurgical, combustion, and mechanical engineers. The conduct of technological evolution involves more uncertainty and dissensus as there are normative and knowledge-based differences across engineering and scientific functions.

Further, the nature of satisficing is different between science and technology. Where science is focused on understanding some phenomena, technology is focused on doing a task in a given context.[12] Where criteria for satisficing in science are defined within disciplines, technology must satisfy cross-disciplinary performance and sociopolitical contextual criteria. Thus those engineers developing digital switches must satisfy electrical, mechanical, and computer science constraints, constraints embedded in the telephone network, and sociopolitical constraints in the community. As the network of interdependencies is more complex in technology than in science, technological progress involves a greater array of uncertainties than progress in science. These complex uncertainties associated with technological progress can only be adjudicated by

---

[4]M. Tushman and P. Anderson, "Technological Discontinuities and Organizational Environments," *Administrative Science Quarterly* 31 (1986), pp. 439–65.

[5]G. Astley, "The Two Ecologies: Population and Community Perspectives on Organizational Evolution," *Administrative Science Quarterly* 30 (1985), pp. 224–41.

[6]M. Tushman and R. Nelson, "Introduction: Technology, Organizations and Innovation," *Administrative Science Quarterly* 35 (1990), pp. 1–8.

[7]B. Arthur, "Self-Reinforcing Mechanisms in Economics," in *Economy as an Evolving Complex System,* ed. P. Anderson et al. (Reading, MA: Addison-Wesley, 1988).

[8]G. Astley and C. Fombrum, "Technological Innovation and Industrial Structure," *Advances in Strategic Management* 1 (1983), pp. 205–29. Note: Throughout this paper, we use the term *community* to refer to the collection of organizations that have a stake in technological development. These organizations include private or public organizations, professional associations, and governmental bodies.

[9]E. Constant, "The Social Locus of Technological Practice: Community, System or Organization," in *The Social Construction of Technological Systems,* ed. W. Bijker, T. Hughes, and T. Punch (Cambridge, MA: MIT Press, 1987).

[10]D. Crane, *Invisible Colleges: Diffusion of Scientific Knowledge* (Chicago: University of Chicago Press, 1972); T. Kuhn, *The Structure of Scientific Revolutions* (Chicago: University of Chicago Press, 1962); R. Merton, *The Sociology of Science* (Chicago: University of Chicago Press, 1973).

[11]R. Laudan, ed., *The Nature of Technological Knowledge* (Boston: D. Reidel, 1984).

[12]Constant, "The Social Focus of Technological Practice"; E. Constant, "Cause or Consequence: Science, Technology and Regulatory Change in the Oil Industry," *Journal of Business History* (1989), pp. 426–55.

social, political, and organizational dynamics at the community level. Given the underlying nature of technology, technological progress can be seen as driven by interdisciplinary and interorganizational community dynamics and by the systemic nature of the technology itself.

This paper is organized into four sections. The first section provides several examples of the phenomenon of technological change and the intrusion of nontechnical factors in technological evolution. The second section explores technology as an outcome of community dynamics. We build a model of technical change that is driven by sociocultural processes of variation, selection, and retention. Technical change is driven by both random technological jolts and by social, political, and organizational action in adjudicating between alternative technical regimes. Selection of an industry standard, in turn, anchors a period of incremental technical progress. This period of incremental, puzzle-solving, technical progress enhances the community's competence within the technical paradigm but stunts openness to technical approaches outside the paradigm.

The third section explores technology as systems composed of component and linking technologies. Technological progress occurs at the subsystem and system levels of analysis and is shaped by both technical capabilities and by the actions of technical practitioners constrained by suppliers, customers, and the larger socioeconomic community. The more complex the system, the greater the technical uncertainties, and the greater the impact of sociopolitical processes in shaping technical advance. Thus, while the technical system itself may suggest logical evolutionary paths, as the system gains complexity, nontechnical forces weigh more heavily on the process of technological evolution.

In the final section, we synthesize our community and systems perspectives on technological evolution. If the evolution of technological systems is fundamentally underdetermined by technical forces, then it is the interaction of community dynamics with technological systems that should interest students of organizations and technology. By viewing the process of technological change as determined through the interaction of communities and technical systems, we can begin to identify hierarchies of actors shaping technological evolution and, in turn, deepen our understanding of the sociology of technological evolution.

On the Nature of Technological Evolution

Consider these examples of technological evolution:

1. In cement manufacture, there were four revolutionary technological advances between 1890 and 1980.[13] In each case, new technology substituted for the prior technology and resulted in new industry standards within eight years. Similarly, in container glass, there were four technological discontinuities between 1893 and 1950. As in cement, in each case the new technology substituted for the prior technology and resulted in new industry standards within 15 years of the discontinuity.[14] In each industry, competence-destroying discontinuities were initiated by new entrants while competence-enhancing discontinuities were initiated by a combination of veterans and new entrants. In the American photographic industry, technological progress between 1839 and 1925 was characterized by four technological discontinuities which demarked different periods of incremental technical change. In these industries, the breakthrough technology quickly substituted for the prior film technology, and was initiated by firms outside the existing film industry.[15]

2. In the diagnostic imaging industry there were at least four competing technologies between 1963 and 1973 (X-ray, nuclear, sound, computer tomography). In this product class there was technological uncertainty within and between each diagnostic mode.[16] Within ultrasound alone, no clear technical regime dominated relevant dimensions of merit. In the absence of a technologically dominant regime, negotiations between powerful producers and users led to the emergence of CT scanners as the dominant technological form through the early 1970s.[17]

At the turn of the century, the choice between gas, electric and steam technologies for automobile

---

[13]P. Anderson and M. Tushman, "Technological Discontinuities and Dominant Designs: A Cyclical Model of Technological Change," *Administrative Science Quarterly* 35 (1990), pp. 604–33.

[14]Ibid.

[15]R. Jenkins, *Images and Enterprise* (Baltimore, MD: The Johns Hopkins University Press, 1975).

[16]W. Mitchell, "Whether and Why? Probability and Timing of Incumbents' Entry in Subfields," *Administrative Science Quarterly* 32 (1989), pp. 208–30.

[17]E. Yoxen, "Seeing with Sound: A Study of the Development of Medical Imaging," in *Social Construction of Technological Systems,* ed. W. Bijker, T. Hughes, and T. Punch (Cambridge, MA: MIT Press, 1987).

engines could not be driven by technical criteria since each technology dominated on different dimensions of merit (e.g., cost, safety, range, noise, power, etc.).[18] Internal combustion engines became the industry standard only after Ford invested in mass production technology and mass distribution administrative systems.[19] Similarly, even though cast-iron stoves dominated openhearth stoves along every technological dimension of merit (e.g., fuel efficiency, comfort, safety, and cleanliness), they were dominated by openhearth stoves until process innovation reduced the price per unit.[20]

In the technological competition between the QWERTY and DVORAK typewriter keyboards, the technologically inferior technology (QWERTY) dominated partly due to chance events and partly due to technical constraints in the typewriter as a technical system.[21] Finally, technological competition between alternative machine tool technologies and alternative inertial guidance systems could not be settled on technical grounds. In both industries, collaboration between the Air Force, MIT, and a few powerful organizations led to the emergence of industry standards.[22]

3. In 1904, during a major fire in Baltimore, Maryland, reinforcements were called from Washington, D.C., New York, and Philadelphia. While there was plenty of water, reinforcements were of no use since screw couplings for "foreign" fire hoses would not fit Baltimore hydrants.[23] Similarly, interstate railway commerce was severely restricted as long as each state had different gauge track.[24] While there were clearly no technologically determined best fitting couplings or railway gauge, for these systems to operate effectively, sociopolitical processes must decide between alternative interface standards and technologies.

Similarly, in communication, radio, TV, or in information systems, there are myriad competing technical subsystems and linking technologies whose differences are not amenable to simple technical analyses. Given these substantial technical uncertainties, technical decisions are driven by sociopolitical dynamics shaped by technological constraints.[25] Indeed, in the battle of alternative power systems in the late nineteenth century, neither AC nor DC dominated each other on technical grounds. While individual, political, and organizational factors led to AC in the United States, similar social and political dynamics led to DC being the standard in England through World War I.[26]

These technological histories demonstrate three aspects of the phenomenon of technological evolution. Evidence from the cement, glass, and photography industries suggests that technical progress is characterized by incremental change punctuated by discontinuous advance. In these industries, the new technologies rapidly replaced prior technological regimes. Furthermore, while technological discontinuities transform industries, the technological breakthroughs are most frequently driven by organizations outside the existing technical order.

In the second collection of examples, technological competition among diagnostic imaging systems, automobile engines, stoves, typewriter keyboards, machine tooling technologies, and inertial guidance systems suggests that while it is possible for technical advance to be driven by clear technical dominance, it is much more common that no technological variant is dominant over all dimensions of merit. In these technically underdetermined cases, economic, social, political, and organizational processes determine which technical options survive.

The third collection of historical phenomena highlights the role of sociopolitical influences on technical evolution for complex technological systems. Complex systems, whether for firefighting, transportation, communication, or transmission, require

---

[18]W. Abernathy, *The Productivity Dilemma* (Baltimore, MD: The Johns Hopkins University Press, 1978).

[19]D. Hounshell, *From the American System to Mass Production* (Baltimore, MD: The Johns Hopkins University Press, 1984).

[20]R. Cowan, "The Consumption Junction: Research Strategies for the Social Construction of Technology," in *Social Construction of Technological Systems,* ed. W. Bijker, T. Hughes, and T. Punch (Cambridge, MA: MIT Press, 1987).

[21]P. David, "Clio and the Economics of QWERTY," *Economic History* 75 (1985), pp. 227–32.

[22]D. MacKenzie, "Missile Accuracy: A Case Study in the Social Processes of Technological Change," in *Social Construction of Technological Systems,* ed. W. Bijker, T. Hughes, and T. Punch (Cambridge, MA: MIT Press, 1987); D. F. Noble, *Forces of Production* (New York: Alfred A. Knopf, 1984).

[23]D. Hemenway, *Industry Wide Voluntary Product Standards* (Cambridge, MA: Ballinger, 1975).

[24]A. Chandler, *The Visible Hand* (Cambridge, MA: Harvard University Press, 1977).

[25]P. David, "Some New Standards for the Economics of Standardization in the Information Age," in *Economic Policy and Technological Performance,* ed. P. Dasgupta and P. Stoneman (Cambridge: Cambridge University Press, 1987).

[26]T. Hughes, *Networks of Power* (Baltimore, MD: The Johns Hopkins University Press, 1983).

consensus by multiple actors so that technological subsystems are compatible. The more complex the technology, the more important linking technologies become. For complex technical systems, sociopolitical and interorganizational processes emerge to shape technical progress.

A Cyclical Model of Technological Change: Technology as Community

Building on work in sociology, history, economics, and industrial engineering, Anderson and Tushman[27] argue that technological change can be characterized by sociocultural evolutionary processes of variation, selection, and retention.[28] Variation is driven by stochastic technological breakthroughs. Technological discontinuities initiate substantial technological rivalry between alternative technological regimes. Because technical rivalry is often not settled by technical logic, social and organizational dynamics select from among technological opportunities, single industry standards, or dominant designs. Positively selected variants then evolve through retention periods marked by incremental technical change and increased interdependence and enhanced competence within and between communities of practitioners.[29] These periods of incremental technical change may be broken by subsequent technological breakthroughs.[30]

A technology cycle has four components: technological discontinuities, eras of ferment, dominant designs, and eras of incremental change. Technological discontinuities and dominant designs are events that mark the transitions between eras of ferment and eras of incremental change, as illustrated in Exhibit 1. Technological advance is, then, driven by the combination of chance events (variation), direct social and political action of organizations in selecting between rival technical regimes (artificial selection), as well as by incremental, competence-enhancing, puzzle-solving actions of many organizations learning-by-doing (retention). This retention stage provides a context for the subsequent technological discontinuity. We briefly examine each ele-

EXHIBIT 1 A Technology Cycle

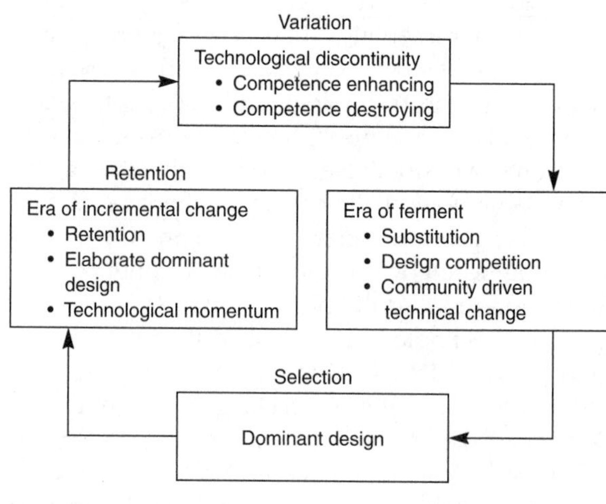

ment of this technology cycle, stressing the roles of social, political, and organizational actors in the course of technological evolution.

Technological Discontinuities

Technological discontinuities are those rare, unpredictable innovations which advance a relevant technological frontier by an order-of-magnitude *and* which involve fundamentally different product or process design.[31] Product discontinuities are fundamentally different product forms which command a decisive cost, performance, or quality advantage over prior product forms (e.g., jet engines, diesel locomotives, quartz oscillation, electronic typing). Process discontinuities are fundamentally different ways of making a product which are reflected in order-of-magnitude improvements in the cost of quality of the product (e.g., Bessemer steel, float glass).

Not all technological discontinuities are alike. Tushman and Anderson[32] characterize technological discontinuities as competence destroying or enhancing. Competence-destroying discontinuities are based on fundamentally different technological knowledge or concepts and, as such, obsolete expertise required to master existing technology.

---

[27]"Technological Discontinuities and Dominant Designs."

[28]G. Basalla, *The Evolution of Technology* (Cambridge: Cambridge University Press, 1988); D. T. Campbell, "Variation and Selective Retention in Sociocultural Evolution," *General Systems* 14 (1969), pp. 69–85.

[29]Constant, "The Social Focus of Technological Practice."

[30]Jenkins, *Images and Enterprise.*

[31]Anderson and Tushman, "Technological Discontinuities and Dominant Designs."

[32]"Technological Discontinuities and Organizational Environments."

For example, mechanical watch-making skills were rendered irrelevant by quartz movements. Similarly, drawing-machine know-how was not transferable to the float-glass process in glass manufacture. Competence-enhancing discontinuities, on the other hand, build on existing know-how. In watch technology, for example, automatic mechanical movements represented a fundamentally different way of providing energy to the spring, but built on prior mechanical competence. Competence-enhancing innovations introduce a new technical order while building on, not obsolescing, the existing technical regime.

Eras of Ferment—Community-Driven Technologies

Technological discontinuities open eras of ferment, as radical technical advances increase variation in a product class. Technological discontinuities usher in an era of experimentation as organizations struggle to absorb (or destroy) the innovative technology. This era of ferment is characterized by two distinct processes: competition between old and new technological regimes, and competition within new technical regimes. This period of substantial product class variation and, in turn, uncertainty, is closed by the emergence of a dominant design.[33]

Eras of ferment are characterized by substantial uncertainty as rival technologies and communities compete for dominance. Competition between old and new technologies is fierce; older technological orders seldom vanish quietly.[34] The response of the existing community of practitioners is often to increase the innovativeness and efficiency of the existing technical regime. For example, mechanical typewriters, piston jets, spark gap radio transmission, gas lighting, and mechanical watches all experienced sharp performance advances in response to technological threat.[35] Given the innovative response of practitioners rooted in the existing technical order, technological discontinuities do not always dominate (e.g., bubble memory, wankel engines, quadraphonic sound systems).[36]

Concurrent with competition between technical orders is the process of design competition within a technological order. Several, often incompatible, versions of the breakthrough appear both because the technology is not well understood and because each pioneering firm has an incentive to differentiate its variant from rivals. For example, in electric power generation, AC systems competed with DC systems. Indeed, even within AC systems there was competition among alternative frequencies.[37] Similarly, in medical imaging, there was technical competition between and within fundamentally different imaging technologies (i.e., nuclear, ultrasound, X-ray).[38]

During eras of ferment, substitution processes and design competition are associated with substantial technical and market uncertainty.[39] Technological variants compete along functional dimensions of merit. Competition exists both for which dimensions of merit are important and how each technology fares along these functional parameters. For example, in the opening of the automobile product class, electric, internal combustion, and steam powered automobiles competed against each other (and against the bicycle and carriage) on safety, range, noise, economy, power, and convenience dimensions of merit.[40] Similarly, in watch manufacture in the 1960s, quartz, tuning fork, and escapement mechanisms competed with each other on size, stability, durability, complexity, and frequency dimensions of merit.[41]

During eras of ferment, critical dimensions of merit are unclear because users themselves are not certain of the product's critical characteristics.[42] For example, early in CT scanners, doctors were not clear on the relative priorities of scan time versus

---

[33]Anderson and Tushman, "Technological Discontinuities and Dominant Designs"; J. Utterback and L. Kim, "Invasion of a Stable Business by Radical Innovation," in *The Management of Productivity and Technology in Manufacturing,* ed. P. Kleindorfer (New York: Plenum, 1985).

[34]R. Foster, *Innovation* (New York: Summit Books, 1986).

[35]H. Aitken, *The Continuous Wave* (Princeton, NJ: Princeton University Press, 1985); J. Bright, *The Electric-Lamp Industry* (New York: Macmillan, 1949); A. Cooper and D. Schendel, "Strategic Responses to Technological Threat," *Business Horizons* (1976), pp. 61–69; Hughes, *Networks of Power;* D. Landes, *Revolution in Time* (Cambridge, MA: Harvard University Press, 1983).

[36]S. Postrel, "Competing Networks and Proprietary Standards," *Journal of Industrial Economics* 29 (1990), pp. 169–85.

[37]David, "Some New Standards"; Hughes, *Networks of Power.*

[38]See Yoxen, "Seeing with Sound."

[39]K. Clark, "The Interaction of Design Hierarchies and Market Concepts in Technological Evolution," *Research Policy* 14 (1985), pp. 235–51.

[40]F. Leslie, *Automobiles of 1904* (Maynard, MA: Chandler Press, 1904).

[41]Landes, *Revolution in Time.*

[42]W. Teubal, "Market Research and Product Summation," *Business Horizons* 21 (1979), pp. 22–26.

resolution.[43] Further, during this period of design competition, it is not clear which technology will dominate on a single (typically a new) dimension of merit, but lag considerably behind the technical frontier on other critical dimensions of merit.[44] Substitute technologies will dominate existing technologies only if they add an important functional parameter and do as well on existing parameters, or if they dominate existing parameters. However, during eras of ferment, neither dimensions of merit nor subsequent technical performance are clear.

The degree of uncertainty during eras of ferment may be contingent on the type of discontinuity. When a technology builds on a completely new knowledge base, it may take longer for technical and market forces to sort out rival designs than for competence-enhancing technical change. Similarly, firms and/or communities of organizations confronted with the choice of abandoning existing know-how in the face of competence-destroying technical change will defend older technology more stubbornly, prolonging uncertainty about whether the new technology will become dominant.[45]

Dominant Designs—Community-Driven Technological Selection

For variation and selection to cumulate in an evolutionary process, there must be a retention mechanism; a successful variation must be preserved and propagated.[46] A dominant design is the second watershed event in a technology cycle, demarking the end of the era of ferment. A dominant design is a single architecture that establishes dominance in a product class.[47] Once a dominant design emerges, future technological progress (until the next discontinuity) consists of incremental improvements elaborating the standard. For example, in the early automobile and airplane industries, technological variation between fundamentally different product designs remained high until standard designs emerged to usher in periods of incremental technical change (i.e., the internal combustion engine, open automobile, and the DC-3 airplane).[48]

Dominant designs emerge across diverse product classes.[49] Whether in sewing machines or rifles,[50] VCRs,[51] bicycles,[52] synthetic dyes,[53] radio transmission and receiving,[54] reprographic machines,[55] or photolithography,[56] single designs emerge to dominate rival designs. These designs remain dominant until the next technological discontinuity. While only known in retrospect, dominant designs reduce variation and, in turn, uncertainty in the product class.[57]

Once dominant designs emerge, technological uncertainty decreases. Uncertainty associated with substitute or design competition decreases as critical dimensions of merit are settled and critical technical problems (or reverse salients) get defined.[58] For example, by 1972, quartz movements dominated both the tuning fork and escapement movements for watches. Technical problem solving then focused on the size, cost, and stability of quartz oscillation and on linking quartz technology to other watch subsystems. Similarly, only after VHS dominated beta format for cassette recorders did intensive effort begin to increase the resolution and quality of VHS technology.[59]

---

[43]Yoxen, "Seeing with Sound."

[44]Utterback and Kim, "Invasion of a Stable Business by Radical Innovation."

[45]Anderson and Tushman, "Technological Discontinuities and Dominant Designs."

[46]Campbell, "Variation and Selective Retention in Sociocultural Evolution."

[47]Abernathy, *The Productivity Dilemma;* D. Sahal, *Patterns of Technological Innovation* (Reading, MA: Addison-Wesley, 1981).

[48]Abernathy, *The Productivity Dilemma;* R. E. Miller and D. Sawers, *The Technical Development of Modern Aviation* (London: Routledge & Kegan Paul, 1968).

[49]Sahal, *Patterns of Technological Innovation;* J. Utterback and W. Abernathy, "A Dynamic Model of Process and Product Innovation," *Omega* 33 (1975), pp. 639–56.

[50]Hounshell, *From the American System to Mass Production.*

[51]R. Rosenbloom and M. Cusumano, "Technological Pioneering and Competitive Advantage: The VCR Industry," *California Management Review* 29 (1987).

[52]W. Bijker, T. Hughes, and T. Punch, *The Social Construction of Technological Systems* (Cambridge, MA: MIT Press, 1987).

[53]H. Van den Belt and A. Rip, "The Nelson-Winter-Dosi Model and Synthethic Dye Chemistry," in *The Social Construction of Technological Systems,* ed. W. Bijker, T. Hughes, and T. Punch (Cambridge, MA: MIT Press, 1987).

[54]Aitken, *The Continuous Wave.*

[55]J. Dessaur, *My Years with Xerox* (New York: Manor Books, 1975).

[56]R. Henderson and K. Clark, "Architectural Innovation: The Reconfiguration of Existing Product Technologies and the Failure of Established Firms," *Administrative Science Quarterly* 35 (1990), pp. 9–30.

[57]Anderson and Tushman, "Technological Discontinuities and Dominant Designs."

[58]Hughes, *Networks of Power.*

[59]Rosenbloom and Cusumano, "Technological Pioneering and Competitive Advantage."

After dominant designs emerge, technical uncertainty decreases and the nature of technical change shifts from variation to incremental change. Technical clarity and convergence on a set of technical parameters permit firms to design standardized and interchangeable parts and to optimize organizational processes for volume and efficiency.[60] Practitioner communities develop industrywide procedures, traditions, and problem-solving modes that permit focused, incremental technical puzzle solving.[61] Dominant designs permit more stable and reliable relations with suppliers, vendors, and customers. From customers' perspectives, dominant designs reduce product class confusion and promise dramatic decreases in product cost. Finally, if the product is part of a larger system, industry standards permit system-side compatibility and integration.[62]

A dominant design emerges in several ways. For simple or nonassembled products, dominant designs emerge from technological logic. For example, suspension preheating cement manufacture became the industry standard because it was a significantly more fuel efficient method of producing high volumes of cement.[63] For more complex products, however, single sets of technologies are rarely optimal. Under conditions of technical ambiguity, dominant designs emerge from sociopolitical processes within and between competing technical communities and their contexts. For more complex products or processes, satisficing replaces optimizing in the closing on industry standards.

De facto standards emerge when users prefer one design over others. David's[64] descriptions of the QWERTY typewriter keyboard and the battle between AC and DC power systems indicates that dominant designs sometimes emerge from market demand which is affected by the combination of technological possibilities and economic, organizational, and governmental factors. Similarly, the Apple II personal computer or the VHS format in VCRs were not necessarily the best products of the day (measured purely by technical performance), but they contained a package of features that found favor in the market.[65] Though the DC-3 embodied many ideas previously introduced on other aircraft, it offered a unique combination of features that made it the most popular propeller-driven aircraft of all time.[66]

Dominant designs may also arise in other ways. The market power of a dominant producer may swing enough weight behind a particular design to make it a standard, as in the case of the IBM 370 series mainframe and the IBM personal computer,[67] or AT&T's Touchtone standard.[68] A powerful user may mandate a standard, as the U.S. Air Force imposed numerical control on the programmable machine tool industry.[69] An industry committee may establish a durable standard, as in the case of computer communications protocols[70] and operating systems,[71] or a group of firms may form an alliance around a standard, as in the case of shared bank card systems.[72] Government regulation often compels the adoption of standards, as in the case of television standards;[73] some have suggested that governments may employ standards as specific policy instruments capable of erecting barriers to trade.[74]

The crucial point is that with the exception of the most simple products, the emergence of dominant designs is not a function of economic or technolog-

---

[60]Hounshell, *From the American System to Mass Production*.

[61]Constant, "The Social Locus of Technological Practice."

[62]David, "Some New Standards for the Economics of Standardization in the Information Age."

[63]Anderson and Tushman, "Technological Discontinuities and Dominant Designs."

[64]"Clio and the Economics of QWERTY" and "Some New Standards for the Economics of Standardization in the Information Age."

[65]P. Freiberger and M. Swaine, *Fire in the Valley: The Making of the Personal Computer* (Berkeley, CA: Osborne/McGraw-Hill, 1984).

[66]Miller and Sawers, *The Technical Development of Modern Aviation*.

[67]R. DeLamarter, *Big Blue: IBM's Use and Abuse of Power* (New York: Dodd, Mead & Company, 1986).

[68]G. Brock, *The Telecommunications Industry* (Cambridge, MA: Harvard University Press, 1981).

[69]Noble, *Forces of Production*.

[70]J. Farrell and G. Saloner, "Coordination through Committees and Markets," *Rand Journal of Economics* 16 (1985), pp. 71–83.

[71]H. L. Gabel, "Open Standards in the European Computer Industry: The Case of X/OPEN," in *Product Standardization and Competitive Strategy*, ed. H. L. Gabel (Amsterdam: North Holland, 1987).

[72]A. Phillips, "The Role of Standardization in Shared Bank Card Systems," in *Product Standardization and Competitive Strategy*, ed. H. L. Gabel (Amsterdam: North Holland, 1987), pp. 263–82.

[73]J. Pelkmans and R. Beuter, "Standardization and Competitiveness: Private and Public Strategies in the E.C. Color TV Industry," in *Product Standardization and Competitive Strategy*, ed. H. L. Gabel (Amsterdam: North Holland, 1987), pp. 29–46.

[74]D. LeCraw, "Japanese Standards: A Barrier to Trade?" in *Product Standardization and Competitive Strategy*, ed. H. L. Gabel (Amsterdam: North Holland, 1987), pp. 29–46; D. Teece, "Profiting from Technological Innovation: Implications for Integration, Collaboration, Licensing, and Public Policy," *Research Policy* 15 (1986), pp. 285–305.

ical determinism; they do not appear because there is one best way to implement a product or process.[75] Rival designs are often technologically superior on one or more key performance dimensions. For example, the IBM PC was not the fastest personal computer, Matsushita's VHS format did not offer the sharpest videocassette reproduction, and Westinghouse's AC power systems were not the most efficient. Indeed, dominant designs may not be particularly innovative; they often incorporate features pioneered elsewhere.[76]

If dominant designs do not arise from inexorable technical or economic logic, how do they evolve? We argue that because a single technological order rarely dominates alternative technologies across critical dimensions of merit, community level sociopolitical processes adjudicate among feasible technical/economic options. The closing on critical dimensions of merit is shaped by a process of compromise and accommodation between suppliers, vendors, customers, and governments.[77] For example, David[78] and Frost and Egri[79] describe the collusion, compromise, accommodation, and coalitions between divergent interest groups in the competition between QWERTY and DVORAK typewriter keyboards. Similarly, Noble[80] and Hughes[81] describe activities of champions, networks of coalitions and interest groups, and the use of language and negotiation tactics to shape standards in the machine tool and power system industries.

Dominant designs, then, emerge not from technical logic, but from a negotiated logic enlivened by actors with interests in competing technical regimes. Social logic drives technical progress as suppliers, customers, or governments react to the uncertainty and inefficiencies associated with eras of ferment. Where technological discontinuities may be driven by random events or strokes of genius (e.g., Fessenden's discovery of the alternator for continuous wave transmission in radio), dominant designs are driven by the visible hand of organizations interacting with other organizations and practitioner communities to shape dimensions of merit and industry standards to maximize local needs.[82]

Dominant designs emerge from these interorganizational dynamics at the product class level. These industry standards cannot be known in advance since they are an outcome of sociopolitical processes within the product class. For a particular organization, betting on a particular industry standard involves substantial risk (witness Sony's bet on beta technology or RCA's bet on videodiscs). During the era of ferment, organizations must develop not only technical competence, but also interorganizational network skills to forge alliances in order to shape critical dimensions of merit and critical industry problems.[83] The concept of dominant design, then, brings technological evolution squarely into organization and interorganization realms. Actions of individuals, organizations, and networks of organizations shape dominant designs which, in turn, close the era of ferment. These socially driven outcomes directly affect the time path of technical change until the next technological discontinuity.

Era of Incremental Change—Technology-Driven Communities

After a dominant design emerges, product dimensions of merit are settled and critical technical problems are defined.[84] For example, once internal combustion engines dominated battery and steam engines in automobiles, technological progress shifted to safety, distance, and reliability of internal combustion driven autos. After dominant designs emerge, technical progress is driven by numerous incremental innovations.[85] These innovations elaborate and extend the dominant design. As in normal science,[86] normal technological progress involves puzzle-solving about a given set

[75]For example, W. Cohen and R. Levin, "Empirical Studies of Innovation and Market Structure," in *Handbook of Industrial Organization,* vol. 11, ed. R. Schmalensee, and D. Willig (New York: Elsevier, 1989), pp. 1060–1107.

[76]Miller and Sawers, *The Technical Development of Modern Aviation.*

[77]For example, Constant, "Cause or Consequence."

[78]"Clio and the Economics of QWERTY."

[79]P. Frost and C. Egri, "The Political Process of Innovation," in *Research in Organizational Behavior,* vol. 13, ed. L. Cummings and B. Staw (Greenwich, CT: JAI Press, 1990).

[80]*Forces of Production.*

[81]*Networks of Power.*

[82]Abernathy, *The Productivity Dilemma;* Aitken, *The Continuous Wave;* Noble, *Forces of Production.*

[83]Astley and Fombrum, "Technological Innovation and Industrial Structure" MacKenzie, "Missile Accuracy."

[84]Hughes, *Networks of Power.*

[85]S. Hollander, *Sources of Efficiency* (Cambridge, MA: MIT Press, 1965); S. Myers and D. G. Marquis, *Successful Industrial Innovations* (Washington, DC: National Science Foundation, 1969).

[86]Kuhn, *The Structure of Scientific Revolutions.*

of technological premises (see also Nelson and Winter's[87] and Dosi's[88] work on technological trajectories). After dominant designs emerge, technical uncertainty in a product class decreases and the basis of competition shifts from product to process innovation.[89]

Within technical communities, social structures arise which reinforce this period of incremental, order-creating, technical change. Critical problems are defined, legitimate procedures are established, and community norms and values emerge from interaction between interdependent actors.[90] During periods of incremental change, informal know-how trading occurs between competitors.[91] Practice traditions are socially constructed and, unlike scientific progress, cross disciplinary boundaries. For example, Constant describes the evolution of practice traditions in the turbojet industry as evolving through interactions among combustion, mechanical, aerospace, and metallurgical engineers.[92]

Over time, periods of normal technology development build ever more interlinked competencies between technological communities and related suppliers, vendors, and customers. As competencies are deepened about given technical premises and as routinized problem-solving modes become institutionalized, technological mind-sets and momentum build in a product class.[93] While technical progress may be substantial, the community of practitioners look more and more inward, and problem solving becomes more routinized and rigid as the era of incremental change unfolds.[94] These interlocked and rigid processes are located within the community of practitioners and competing organizations.[95] Where dominant designs are established by the visible hand of a few powerful organizations competing for dominance, in the era of incremental change, technological progress is driven by the invisible hand of a multitude of organizations competing within sharp technical, social, and normative constraints.[96]

Eras of incremental change persist until they are ended by subsequent technological discontinuities.[97] Technological discontinuities directly challenge technical premises that underlie the prior period of incremental change. For example, tuning-fork and quartz oscillation both challenged fundamental assumptions about frequency and stability of oscillation in watch manufacture.[98] However, these technological threats are met with resistance by technological momentum within the community of practitioners and within competing organizations, especially because any discontinuity is originally associated with substantial uncertainty, ambiguity, and implementation costs.

The response of veteran firms and communities to external threat is often increased commitment to the status quo.[99] Because technology has social and community effects, threatened technical communities resist technological change by both increased persistence in the prior technical regime and by increased political action (see Frost & Egri[100] for a thorough discussion of these political processes). For example, in the watch, steel, and power industries, new technologies were resisted by enhanced technical efforts in the soon to be obsolete technology and by increased political efforts.[101] Given technical momentum generated by normal technological progress, existing technical communities and/or organizations virtually never give birth to radically new, competence-destroying technologies. The locus of technological discontinuity occurs from out-

---

[87]R. Nelson and S. Winter, *An Evolutionary Theory of Economic Change* (Cambridge, MA: Belknap Press, 1982).

[88]G. Dosi, *Technical Change and Industrial Transformation* (New York: St. Martin's Press, 1984).

[89]Abernathy, *The Productivity Dilemma;* W. Abernathy and K. Clark, "Innovation: Mapping the Winds of Creative Destruction," *Research Policy* 14 (1985), pp. 3–22.

[90]A. Van de Ven and R. Garud, "A Framework for Understanding the Emergence of New Industries," in *Research and Technological Innovation, Management, and Policy,* vol. 4, ed. A. Van de Ven and S. Poole (New York: Harper & Row, 1989).

[91]E. Von Hipple, "Cooperation Between Rivals: Informal Know-how Trading," *Research Policy,* 16 (1987), pp. 291–302.

[92]E. Constant, *The Origins of the Turbojet Revolution* (Baltimore, MD: The Johns Hopkins University Press, 1980).

[93]Hughes, *Networks of Power;* Jenkins, *Images and Enterprise.*

[94]W. Dutton and A. Thomas, "Relating Technological Change and Learning by Doing," in *Research on Technological Innovation,* ed. R. Rosenbloom (Greenwich, CT: JAI Press, 1985), pp. 187–224; Myers and Marquis, *Successful Industrial Innovations.*

[95]W. Cohen and D. Levinthal, "Absorptive Capacity: A New Perspective on Learning and Innovation." *Administrative Science Quarterly* 35 (1990), pp. 128–52.

[96]Van de Ven and Garud, "A Framework for Understanding the Emergence of New Industries."

[97]Anderson and Tushman, "Technological Discontinuities and Dominant Designs"; Tushman and Anderson, "Technological Discontinuities and Organizational Environments."

[98]Landes, *Revolution in Time.*

[99]Cooper and Schendel, "Strategic Response to Technological Threat"; Foster, *Innovation.*

[100]"The Political Process of Innovation."

[101]Constant, "Cause or Consequence"; M. Horwitch, *Clipped Wings* (Cambridge, MA: MIT Press, 1982); Landes, *Revolution in Time.*

side the existing technical community and from outside veteran organizations.[102] During eras of incremental change, then, community and organizational norms and processes drive incremental, normal technical progress, but drive out variance required for breakthrough technical advance.

Normal technical progress builds interdependent competencies within a product class as well as shared norms and values within the practitioner community. Given inertial processes within the era of incremental change, subsequent technological discontinuities are resisted by technological, social, and political processes as veteran organizations and communities defend the existing paradigm. Given the conservative nature of technical communities, technological discontinuities are often initiated from outside the community. This community perspective on technological change puts a premium on social and organizational dynamics in shaping dominant designs and associated incremental change, and in resisting discontinuous technical advance.

Technology as Systems in Context

Technology is developed to solve problems in a particular context.[103] Except for the most primitive products, technological artifacts are composed of more basic subsystems which must, in turn, be linked together. Technological design involves both subsystem developments and integration across subsystems.[104] In this section, we build on the idea of technology as systems in context, linking characteristics of systems and contexts to sociopolitical dynamics.

Conceptualizing technology as systems permits detailed understanding of technological evolution at both the subsystem and system levels of analysis. Technological cycles of variation, selection, and retention apply both at the subsystem and system levels of analysis (e.g., at the oscillation and watch levels of analysis). Further, the interaction of subsystems leads to emergent system-level concepts of interfaces, linkage requirements, subsystem hierarchies, and critical system problems.

Understanding products as technical systems permits greater understanding of the conditions under which social/political processes affect technical progress. The greater the number of subsystems and the greater the number of interface and interdependence demands, the greater the number of dimensions of merit that must be adjudicated. The more complex the system, the more political, social, and community dynamics operate to resolve trade-offs between alternative technical choices. Similarly, the more central the technical subsystem, the greater its impact on the overall system. Change in central subsystems will involve more sociopolitical dynamics than change in peripheral subsystems.[105]

In this section, we develop a typology of products ranging from simple to complex. We distinguish four types of products: (1) nonassembled products, (2) simple assembled products, (3) closed systems, and (4) open systems. We focus on product technology but examine associated process technology for simpler products. With this complexity-based typology, we link technological complexity to the relative importance of sociopolitical factors in shaping technological progress.

Nonassembled Products

Products like aluminum, cement, flat glass, paper, gears, fibers, petroleum, springs, and steel have no separable components. The technological essence of these products stems from the manufacturing process and the raw materials that enter this process. Produced through chemical, thermal, or machining processes, nonassembled products are made through a set of sequentially interlinked steps or subprocesses. Linking mechanisms transport the product through the different subprocesses. Raw materials pass through each subsystem in a specific order to produce the finished product. For example, aluminum manufacture is composed of distinct subprocesses of mining, refining, smelting, and fabrication. Each of these subprocesses has its own set of processes.[106] (See Exhibit 2.)

---

[102]For example: Cooper and Schendel, *Strategic Responses to Technological Threat;* Tushman and Anderson, "Technological Discontinuities and Organizational Environments."

[103]C. Alexander, *Notes on a Synthesis of Form* (Cambridge, MA: Harvard University Press, 1964).

[104]Clark, "The Interaction of Design Hierarchies and Market Concepts in Technological Evolution"; Constant, "The Social Focus of Technological Practice."

[105]Clark, "The Interaction of Design Hierarchies and Market Concepts in Technological Evolution."

[106]G. Smith, *From Monopoly to Competition: Transformation of ALCOA* (Cambridge, MA: Cambridge University Press, 1988).

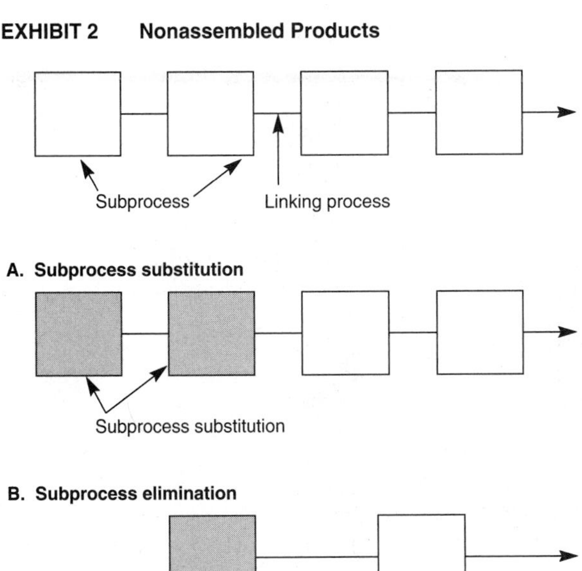

EXHIBIT 2 Nonassembled Products

For nonassembled products, technological progress occurs either in process or materials. For process technology, either the replacement or elimination of subprocesses increases process speed and/or efficiency. For example, in glass manufacture in the late 19th century, artisans blew glass in large cylinders, and assistants cut these cylinders and then flattened and polished the pieces of glass. In 1903, the Lubbers machine substituted for artisans blowing glass. These machines could blow glass rapidly and inexpensively and contributed to great increases in the volume and efficiency of glass production.[107] (See Exhibit 2A.)

Float glass technology revolutionized glass production by producing polished, smooth flat glass from molten glass passed across a bath of molten alloy. Float glass eliminated three steps from the prior glass production process and resulted in extraordinary production efficiencies (see Exhibit 2B).[108] Similar examples of either subsystem substitution or elimination of subprocesses occur in steel,[109] petroleum,[110] cement,[111] aluminum,[112] and textile fibers.[113]

For nonassembled products, dimensions of merit are quality or efficiency related and can be easily measured (e.g., price/unit, price/performance). Substitute subsystems and simpler processes clearly dominate prior production modes on relevant dimensions of merit (e.g., Lubbers machine or float process in glass manufacture). For example, no amount of increase in human glass blowing efficiency could ever compete with machine glass blowing, even as no amount of improving cutting, grinding, and polishing of flat glass could ever compete with the float process.

Substitute processes may trigger design competition between rival designs.[114] For example, in glass bottle manufacture, the Owens machine stimulated multiple, rival designs. This design competition converged on the 10-arm Owens machine which became the dominant design in bottle manufacture until gob-fed machinery substituted for the Owens process.[115] For nonassembled products, because the dimensions of merit are so unequivocal, the choice between alternative processes is driven by the interaction of professionals in a single professional community (e.g., steel, cement, fiber) with managers in competing organizations. Given the clarity of dimensions of merit and the relative ease in measurement, the amount of sociopolitical dynamics is minimal in shaping technological progress for nonassembled products.[116] (See Exhibit 3.)

Simple Assembled Products

Classes of products such as stoves, hoses, cans, skis, containers, guns, escapements, and balance wheels are made up of distinct subsystems that are combined or fit together. These subsystems together define the product. Like nonassembled products,

---

107W. Scoville, *Revolution in Glass-Making* (Cambridge, MA: Harvard University Press, 1948).

108Anderson and Tushman, "Technological Discontinuities and Dominant Designs"; Emhart Corporation, *The Big Picture: Proceedings of Executive Seminar Presented by Hartford Division, Emhart Corporation,* Technical Publication TP-1071B, Emhart Corporation, Farmington, CT, 1974.

109Tarman, 1972.

110Z. Yin and J. Dutton, "Systems Learning and Technological Change in 20th Century Petroleum Refining," working paper, New York University, 1986.

111R. Lesley, *A History of the United States Portland Cement Industry* (Chicago: Portland Cement Association, 1924).

112Smith, *From Monopoly to Competition.*

113Hollander, *Sources of Efficiency.*

114Anderson and Tushman, "Technological Discontinuities and Dominant Designs."

115P. Davis, *The Development of the American Glass Industry* (Cambridge, MA: Harvard University Press, 1949).

116Hollander, *Sources of Efficiency.*

EXHIBIT 3 Technological Complexity and the Relative Influence of Social, Political, Organizational Dynamics

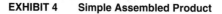

Technological Complexity	Driver of Technological Progress	Basis of Design Dominance	Arbiter of Dominant Design	Influence of Social, Political, Organization Dynamics
■ Nonassembled products ■ Simple assembled products	■ Subprocess replacement or elimination ■ Materials substitution ■ Product substitution	Technical superiority of easily measured dimensions of merit	Single or focused practitioner community	Minimal
■ Closed assembled system	■ Subsystem substitution or dominant design ■ Core subsystem evolution ■ Linking technology	Competition among alternative designs with diverse dimensions of merit	Heterogeneous professional, organizational communities	High
■ Open systems	■ Core subsystem substitution/dominant design ■ Linking and/or interface technologies	Competition among alternative component and interface designs with diverse dimensions of merit	Multiple, diverse organizational, professional, governmental communities	Pervasive

simple assembled products are made through a set of interlinked steps that are sequentially ordered. For example, in gun manufacture during the nineteenth century, locks, stocks, and barrels were distinct subsystems which were hand-fitted together to produce the gun.[117] Similarly, aluminum cans (a replacement for steel cans) were joined together to produce the finished can.[118] (See Exhibit 4.)

For simple assembled products, technical progress occurs either through process, material, and/or product substitution. The most primitive form of technological progress is process innovation. The use of standardized or interchangeable parts in gun manufacture permitted more efficient production of the component pieces of the gun (locks, stocks, barrels) and eliminated costly and inefficient hand fitting of the component.[119] Similarly, as in nonassembled products, process innovations that result in fewer subsystems permit greater speed and volume production. For example, the development of the two-piece aluminum cans sharply increased the price-performance ratio of the product (see Exhibit 4).

Distinct from process innovation, sharp technical progress is also associated with product substitution via either alternative materials or product forms. Substitute materials can drastically alter price/performance characteristics of simple assembled products. For example, alternate materials have

EXHIBIT 4 Simple Assembled Product

A. Process innovation

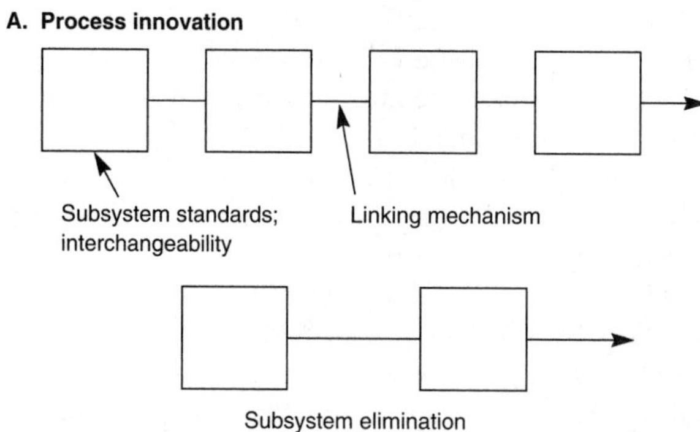

B. Materials substitution

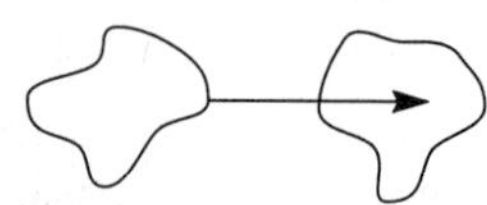

C. Product substitution

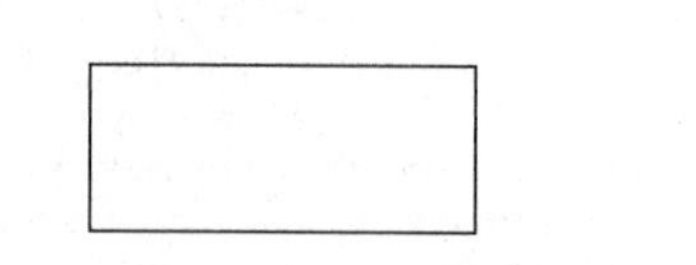

[117]Hounshell, *From the American System to Mass Production.*
[118]Smith, *From Monopoly to Competition.*
[119]Hounshell, *From the American System to Mass Production.*

transformed many simple assembled product classes, including: escapements (jeweled → pin lever), skis (wood → metal → fiberglass), containers (steel → glass → aluminum → plastic). Finally, new product forms may substitute for the simple product itself. For example, disposable diapers, quartz oscillation, and batteries each substituted for the prior product form (cloth diapers, escapements, and springs, respectively).

For simple assembled products, as with nonassembled products, dimensions of merit are clear and easily measured (e.g., price/unit or price/performance). Substitute products and/or production processes clearly dominate prior product and process forms. Substitute products and production processes trigger an increase in product and process variation in a product class as old and new product forms compete for dominance.[120] As dimensions of merit are clear for simple assembled products, technical considerations dominate organizational considerations in closing on dominant designs. Industry standards are driven by technical and engineering considerations as articulated by professionals in a given practitioner community in interaction with organizational considerations (see Exhibit 3).

EXHIBIT 5 Assembled Systems

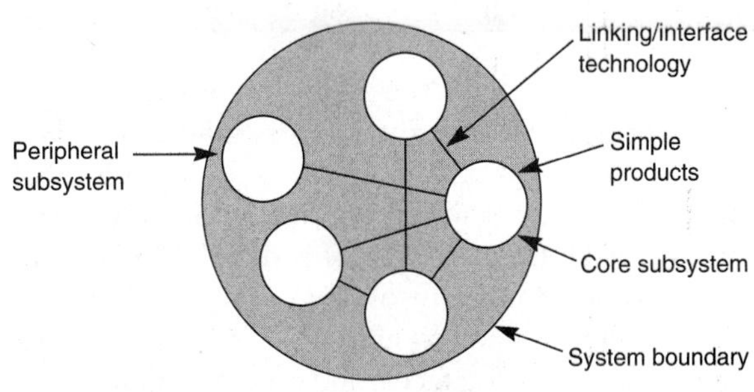

Open assembled system

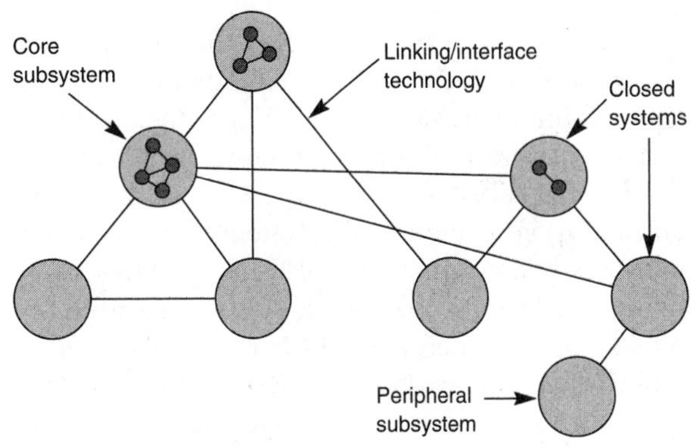

Assembled Systems

Classes of products like watches, automobiles, televisions, airplanes, telephone networks, railroad systems, and power systems are made up of distinct subsystems that interact with each other. Assembled systems are, therefore, more complex than nonassembled or simple assembled products since the individual subsystems must be linked together via interface and linkage technologies.[121] Further, because of complex interdependencies in assembled systems, some subsystems will be more central to the product, while others will be more peripheral.

There are two distinct classes of assembled systems. Closed systems are bounded where open systems are unbounded. In closed systems, the set of subsystems has a clear boundary; the system is enclosed (e.g., watch, bicycle, VCR, automobile, airplane). In open systems, component subsystems (often assembled closed systems) are dispersed and are not enclosed (e.g., telephone, railroad, power systems). Closed assembled systems are produced by single organizations (or units of multidivisional firms), while open systems are produced by networks of organizations (see Exhibit 5). We discuss the relative importance of sociopolitical and organizational dynamics in the technical progress of both types of assembled systems.

Closed systems are composed of a set of component subsystems or simple products that are linked together through linkage and interface technologies.[122] Because there are multiple subsystems, closed assembled systems are characterized by multiple dimensions of merit. For example, CT scanners can be described by their speed, resolution, size, scanning mode, and cost.[123] Technical progress occurs at the subsystem, linkage, and interface levels of analysis. Each subsystem of a closed system has its own unidimensional time path of technical progress which is driven by process or product

[120]Anderson and Tushman, "Technological Discontinuities and Dominant Designs"; Utterback and Kim, "Invasion of a Stable Business by Radical Innovation."

[121]Henderson and Clark, "Architectural Innovation."

[122]Ibid.

[123]Yoxen, "Seeing with Sound."

innovation and by shifts in materials. For example, any watch is composed of five generic subsystems—energy, oscillation, transmission, face, and casing. Each of these simple subsystems has its own history of technical progress (i.e., substitutions and dominant designs, product and process innovation) and can be measured on clearly defined dimensions of merit (durability, stability, oscillation rate, etc.). The product itself (i.e., the watch) is defined by its subsystems and linking technology. For example, by 1950, watches were composed of springs, escapements, gears, analog faces, and precious metal cases and were evaluated by their accuracy, thinness, durability, and cost.[124]

Closed systems have a set of technological issues that emerge at the system level of analysis—hierarchy, critical problems and system dominant design. Unlike simple or nonassembled products, not all subsystems are of equal importance in closed systems. Some subsystems have more internal linkages and are more central to the system than those less interdependent subsystems. Closed systems can be hierarchically ordered—some subsystems are core while others are peripheral.[125] For example, in automobiles, the engine is a core subsystem in that the body, brakes, steering and ignition are all dependent on the engine's characteristics (see Exhibit 5). Thus, technological changes in core subsystems are likely to effect complementary changes in interdependent subsystems.

The set of subsystems will together define system-level critical problems—technical problems that emerge from the interaction of the subsystems. For example, in automobiles, after internal combustion engines dominated battery and steam powered engines, critical technical problems shifted from the engine to the brake, steering, and body subsystems.[126] In turbojet development, Constant defined functional failures and presumptive anomalies as system-level phenomena that arose out of interactions between subsystem technologies (e.g., compressor and turbine components).[127]

For closed assembled systems, technical progress occurs at the subsystem and linkage levels of analysis. Technical progress at the subsystem level may shift the relative hierarchy of components and the nature of critical technical problems. For example, between 1955 and 1975 each subsystem of a watch was transformed—batteries replaced springs, quartz oscillation replaced escapements and tuning forks, electronic transmission replaced gears, and plastic casing replaced precious metals. By 1975, each watch subsystem evolved through its own technology cycle of substitution and design competition to new dominant design. During this period, the hierarchy of components and critical system problems shifted. For example, the emergence of quartz oscillation shifted critical technological problems away from oscillation (the dominant technical problem for centuries) towards transmission and display.[128] Similarly, Henderson and Clark's[129] description of the photolithography industry demonstrates the shift in critical systems problems from subsystems to their linking technologies.

Just as simple products evolve dominant designs, so too do closed assembled products. For closed systems products, dominant designs are composed of a standard set of component and linking subsystems. Closing on a dominant design ushers in a period of incremental technical change at the component and interface levels of analysis. This incremental progress is shaped by critical systemwide technical problems. For example, by 1920 the dominant design for watches was the mechanical, lever-escapement, spring-driven watch. Technical progress through the 1950s focused on incremental improvements to ensure even more accurate, durable, and thin watches. As discussed earlier, dominant designs are found across diverse closed systems product classes (bicycles, machine tools, radio, reprographic machines, automobiles, TVs, VCRs, etc.). Because of the centrality of core subsystems, dominant designs of closed systems may shift when the technology of a core component shifts. For example, the shift to quartz as an oscillation standard in watches drove the shift to a new watch standard by 1974 (i.e., battery-powered, quartz, electronic watch).

Dominant designs emerge from technical competition between alternative designs. Whereas dimensions of merit are unidimensional for simple assembled products, there are diverse and multiple dimensions of merit for closed assembled systems (e.g., resolution, speed, safety, and cost in CT scanners). These multiple dimensions of merit cannot be

[124] Landes, *Revolution in Time.*

[125] Clark, "The Interaction of Design Hierarchies and Market Concepts in Technological Evolution"; Henderson and Clark, "Architectural Innovation."

[126] Abernathy, *The Productivity Dilemma.*

[127] Constant, *The Origins of the Turbojet Revolution.*

[128] Landes, *Revolution in Time.*

[129] "Architectural Innovation."

adjudicated by technical logic. Indeed, as closed systems are made up of diverse technologies, heterogeneous technical professionals will themselves disagree on appropriate industry standards.[130] The closing on a dominant design for closed assembled systems is, then, driven by sociopolitical processes constrained by technical boundaries. The more complex the product, the greater the number of incompatible dimensions of merit, the greater the impact of social dynamics in shaping dominant designs. For example, Noble[131] provides detail on collusion, bargaining, and coalitional behavior as diverse interest groups worked to shape numerical control as the industry standard in machine tools over record-playback technology.[132]

Once a dominant design is selected, however, a diverse community of practitioners develops increasingly interlinked competence and inertia. These emergent community and organizational processes work to resist subsequent competence-destroying technical changes. This resistance to competence-destroying technical change is substantial since roots of the inertia are spread throughout a wide and diverse network of practitioners, suppliers, customers, and vendors.[133] This technological momentum (and resultant resistance to fundamental change) emerges out of the internal logic of the product as a hierarchical technical system, and from emergent processes within organizations and in the community of practitioners.[134] The resistance to the DVORAK keyboard is an extreme example of communitywide resistance to a superior subsystem technology in the typewriter/word processing product classes.[135]

Open systems, the most complex form of technological systems, are composed of a set of closed systems that are linked together through interface technologies. Unlike closed systems that are linked together through interface systems, the product is not self-contained, but is a function of networked components working together over a distance (e.g., television, radio, power, telephone, computer, railroads). Whereas closed systems are produced by single organizations, open systems must cope with technological interdependencies and economies of scale via multiple organizations operating at a distance.[136]

Open systems have some characteristics that are similar to closed systems. The set of closed subsystems is linked together through linkage and interface technologies. Because there are multiple subsystems, open systems are characterized by multiple dimensions of merit. For example, in the late 19th century, AC and DC power systems could be compared on safety, flexibility, distance, and efficiency dimensions.[137] Technical progress occurs at the subsystem (i.e., closed system) and interface levels. As with closed systems, an open system is defined by its subsystem and linkage mechanisms at a point in time. Thus by the 1920s, radio systems were composed of vacuum tube transmitters, receivers, and amplifiers.[138] Each closed subsystem and linkage technology evolves through its own technology cycle of discontinuous change, product variation, dominant design, and incremental change. Thus in radio, the signal generator itself evolved through three discontinuous technical changes from 1900 to 1920.

As with closed systems, open systems also have emergent technical issues that arise from the interdependence between subsystems. Not all subsystems are of equal importance. Those subsystems with greater linkages to other subsystems are more central to the system than those subsystems that are peripheral. For example, in both telephone and radio systems, the mode of transmission was the core subsystem in that all other subsystems depended on transmission technology.[139] Similarly in power systems, the power generation subsystem (e.g., DC, AC, nuclear) affects every other network subsystem.[140] Finally, given the distributed nature of open systems, linking and interface technologies assume significant importance over and above subsystems.[141]

---

[130]Yoxen, "Seeing with Sound."

[131]*Forces of Production.*

[132]See also Frost and Egri, "The Political Process of Innovation."

[133]For example, Constant, "The Social Focus of Technological Practice."

[134]For instance: Aitken, *The Continuous Wave;* Jenkins, *Images and Enterprise.*

[135]David, "Clio and the Economics of QWERTY"; Frost and Egri, "The Political Process of Innovation."

[136]Astley and Fombrum, "Technological Innovation and Industrial Structure"; David, "Some New Standards for the Economics of Standardization in the Information Age."

[137]Hughes, *Networks of Power.*

[138]Aitken, *The Continuous Wave.*

[139]Ibid.; N. Wasserman, *From Invention to Innovation: Long Distance Telephone Transmission* (Baltimore, MD: The Johns Hopkins University Press, 1985).

[140]P. David and J. Bunn, "The Economics of Gateway Technologies and Network Evolution," *Information Economics and Policy* 3 (1988), pp. 165–202.

[141]David, "Some New Standards for the Economics of Standardization in the Information Age."

The set of subsystems together defines system-level critical problems. Uneven growth of subsystems affects the overall network. These network problems define critical technical agendas for practitioner communities.[142] Similarly, interactions between subsystem technologies produce either system failures or potential failures. These real or presumptive failures also focus systemwide problem solving.[143] For example, after AC dominated DC in power generation, a range of subsidiary AC technical problems became the focus of power system practitioners (e.g., surge-proof transformers, fuses, insulation).[144] Critical system problems and the technical hierarchy may shift as the network evolves. For example, once local telephone technology stabilized at the turn of the century, long-distance transmission emerged as a central, systemwide problem.[145]

Even though open systems are more complex than closed systems, open systems also evolve through periods of systemwide variation leading to a dominant design. Dominant designs are composed of a standard set of subsystems and linking mechanisms. For example, in power systems, the competition between AC and DC systems resulted in the closing on AC as the standard in the United States, but DC in England.[146] Similarly, in radio transmission, competition between spark and continuous wave technology led to the convergence on wave-based radio systems.[147] As with closed systems, convergence on industry standards ushers in a period of incremental, puzzle-solving, technical change at the subsystem, linkage, and interface levels of analysis.

Closing on a dominant design for open systems is an inherently political and social process. Competing systems dominate each other on different dimensions of merit. Given technological uncertainties, the closing on industry standards is driven by sociopolitical dynamics between different sets of organizations that represent competing technological systems.[148] As open systems often have national consequences, governments (or governmental units) are often involved in closing on standards for network systems (e.g., the Navy in radio systems or the FCC in TV). Because open systems have substantial technological, interorganizational, community, and governmental interfaces, sociopolitical dynamics play a more important role in closing on network standards than they do for closed systems or simple products. For example, Hughes[149] and Constant[150] illustrate the actions of system champions, bargaining, sabotage, and complex interest group negotiations that led to the emergence of power system and petroleum system standards in the United States.

Once an open system closes on a dominant design, a period of incremental technical change ensues. The network of organizations, the community of practitioners, suppliers, governmental units, and customers develops ever more interlinked relations and enhanced competence. This period of puzzle solving and normal technical progress builds technical and social momentum. Machines, devices, structures, and procedures become so interlinked that the technical system builds technical inertia.[151] Further, the community of practitioners across multiple organizations and disciplines develops a well-ordered internally focused society with its own local problems, norms, values, and status hierarchy.[152] The technical and social systems required to produce reliable and standard products from a multitude of organizations and professional groups bring with them technical and social inertia which resists all but competence-enhancing technical change.[153]

As distributed networks, open systems are composed of multiple closed systems connected by linkage and interface technologies. To achieve scale economies and to effectively utilize the network, standard linking technologies across the entire network are crucial.[154] In open systems, linking technologies are always a core technical subsystem. For example, in computer systems, incompatible languages and interface standards hindered the development of fully integrated networks.[155] Where

[142]See W. Barnett, "The Organizational Ecology of a Technological System," *Administrative Science Quarterly* 35 (1990), pp. 31–60; W. Barnett and G. Carroll. "Competition and Mutualism among Early Telephone Companies," *Administrative Science Quarterly* 32 (1987), pp. 400–21.

[143]Hughes, *Networks of Power;* G. Smith, *The Anatomy of a Business Decision* (Baltimore, MD: The Johns Hopkins Press, 1985).

[144]See Hughes, *Networks of Power.*

[145]Smith, *The Anatomy of a Business Decision.*

[146]Hughes, *Networks of Power.*

[147]Aitken, *The Continuous Wave.*

[148]Hughes, *Networks of Power.*

[149]Ibid.

[150]"Causes or Consequence."

[151]Hughes, *Networks of Power.*

[152]Aitken, *The Continuous Wave;* Laudan, *The Nature of Technological Knowledge.*

[153]Constant, "Causes or Consequence."

[154]J. Farrell and G. Saloner, "Standardization, Compatibility, and Innovation," *Rand Journal of Economics* 16 (1985), pp. 71–83.

[155]Brock, 1975.

linking in closed systems is driven by intrafirm logic, in open systems, linking standards are inherently interorganizational phenomena.[156]

In open systems, network interface standards evolve at multiple levels of analysis.[157] System standards evolve to define fundamental units of measure (e.g., time, distance, currency, language, frequencies), minimal system attributes (e.g., safety, quality), and interface standards (e.g., design interfaces, communication protocols or codes). These system interface and linkage standards permit scale economies and orderly system development. Without system standards, confusion stunts the system's ability to develop.[158] For example, computer networks in the 1960s were paralyzed as there were over 50 different types of tape drives, each with multiple formats and tape width.[159] While system-linking standards have competitive benefits, permit variety in the system through mixing and matching subsystems, and are associated with cost savings, these standards can also get locked in by technical and social inertia.[160]

As illustrated by the Baltimore fire hoses, there are rarely technically optimal linking and interface technologies. Since these technologies are often technically indeterminate, only sociopolitical dynamics between multiple organizations, professional societies, and governmental agencies can adjudicate between rival technical options. These standards may emerge from governmental regulation (e.g., radio, TV), international committees (fax, ISDN telephone protocols), mutual agreement between industry leaders (e.g., operating system consortia led by AT&T and IBM), or through market power (AT&T's telephone standards). As with the emergence of dominant designs at the component level, linkage standards also emerge in open systems. These linkage standards emerge from sociopolitical dynamics shaped by technical constraints.

Open systems are the most complex form of product technology. Open systems involve multiple closed systems, multiple practitioner communities, and networks of organizations. With all this social and technical complexity, open systems must evolve dominant designs and standards at the component and linkage levels of analysis. As technology rarely provides optimal choices, the choice from among a feasible set of technical options is driven by sociopolitical processes between organizations, technical practitioners, governmental units, and communities. Once open systems close on standards, technical and social momentum drive ever more incremental, competence-enhancing change and resist competence-destroying technical change. The more complex the system, the more complex the social and technical uncertainty, the greater the intrusion of social and political processes on the nature of technological progress (see Exhibit 3).

Towards a Sociology of Technological Evolution

Under what conditions do organization dynamics affect the path of technical progress? Rather than viewing technology as an autonomous force acting on organizations[161] or as a predictable outcome of an elite set of organizations,[162] we find that technologies evolve through the combination of random and chance events, the direct action of organizations shaping industry standards, and the invisible hand of multiple competing organizations in a technological community. Our purpose has been to illustrate the conditions under which social, political, and organizational dynamics affect technological progress and, in turn, to stimulate theory and research on the organizational determinants of technological progress.

Roots of the nontechnical determinants of technological advance lie in the fundamental nature of technology itself. Unlike science, technology is developed to solve a problem in a particular context (versus universal understanding of a particular phenomenon). Unlike scientific progress, technological progress involves practitioners from multiple disciplines working to solve problems that are, in turn, shaped by contextual constraints. In tech-

---

[156]Astley and Fombrum, "Technological Innovation and Industrial Structure."

[157]David, "Some New Standards for the Economics of Standardization in the Information Age."

[158]Barnett, "The Organizational Ecology of a Technological System."

[159]Brock, *The Telecommunications Industry*.

[160]Farrell and Saloner, "Standardization, Compatibility and Innovation" and "Coordination through Committees and Markets."

[161]S. Barley, "The Alignment of Technology and Structure through Roles and Networks," *Administrative Science Quarterly* 24 (1990), pp. 286–308; R. Blauner, *Alienation and Freedom* (Chicago: University of Chicago Press, 1964); J. Ellul, *The Technological Society* (New York: J. Wilkinson, 1964).

[162]For example, Noble, *Forces of Production*.

nological development, uncertainty resides in the technologies utilized and in the interaction of these technologies in context. These uncertainties affect the choice of dimensions of merit upon which to evaluate technological options. Except for the most simple technologies, no technological package dominates all dimensions of merit. Trade-offs must be made between alternative dimensions of merit and, in turn, between alternative technological options.

In science, the locus of decision making is within the disciplinary community. In technology, however, the locus of technical decision making is between multiple disciplines, whose actors reside in competing organizations constrained by community and governmental demands. As networks of interdependence are more complex in technology than science, and because dimensions of merit are more heterogeneous in technology than science, technological progress involves compromise, accommodation, and political dynamics between organizations, professional communities, customers, and sometimes governmental units. In the context of technologically underdetermined systems, it is only through social, political, and organizational dynamics that technical trade-offs and decisions can be made.[163]

In this section we integrate the community and systems perspectives on technology to investigate the relative influence of sociopolitical dynamics versus straightforward technical logic. The nature of technology and its evolution suggest that the prominence of nontechnical processes will vary with the stage of the technology cycle, the complexity of the technological system, and the centrality of the technological subsystem.

Sociopolitical Dynamics and the Technology Cycle

During periods of technological uncertainty, nontechnical dynamics adjudicate between dimensions of merit and technological options. Technological uncertainty is rooted in the nature of technology cycles and in the characteristics of technology as systems. Technology evolves through cycles of variation, selection, and retention. Chance and individual genius drive technological breakthrough which ushers in a period of uncertainty as rival technologies compete, and variations of the substitute technology vie for dominance. These rival technologies compete on different dimensions of merit. As a single technology rarely dominates all relevant dimensions of merit, the emergence of a dominant design is driven by sociopolitical dynamics constrained by technology. These social dynamics are played out between competing organizations, practitioner communities, suppliers, vendors, and customers.

Dominant designs set clear dimensions of merit and technological premises. Dominant designs initiate eras of incremental, puzzle-solving technical progress. Technological uncertainty is reduced as competing organizations, practitioner communities, suppliers, and customers develop ever more interlinked and enhanced competencies. During eras of incremental change, technical progress is driven by a logic internal to the technology and by institutional momentum in the community of practitioners. This technical and social momentum admits only competence-enhancing change. Those technological breakthroughs based on alternative premises are actively resisted both technically and politically.

Organizational and interorganizational processes directly shape the selection of product class standards and subsequent incremental technical change and, in turn, perpetuate the selected technology's premises and buffer the core technology from change. Social, political, and organizational dynamics, then, are maximized during periods of uncertainty in a technology cycle—during eras of ferment, in closing on a dominant design, and during periods of technological discontinuity (see Exhibit 6).

Sociopolitical Dynamics and System Complexity

Technology as systems focuses on differences in technical complexity across products. The more complex the product, the more subsystems, the greater the number of internal and external interfaces, the greater the technical and contextual uncertainty. The greater these uncertainties, the greater the intrusion of sociopolitical dynamics in the technology's evolution. Social dynamics are not important for nonassembled or for simple assembled products. For these classes of products, dimensions of merit are unambiguous, subsystems (or processes) are either physically or sequentially linked, and technical progress is carried out by practitioners in a single

---

[163]Constant, "Cause or Consequence"; Frost and Egri, "The Political Process of Innovation"; Hughes, *Networks of Power;* Noble, *Forces of Production.*

EXHIBIT 6 Technology as Community

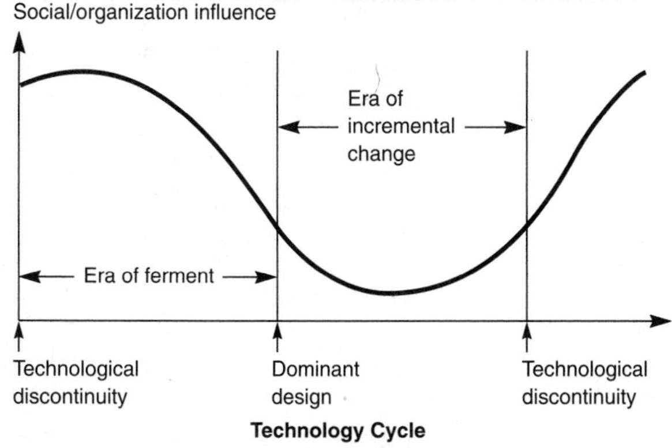

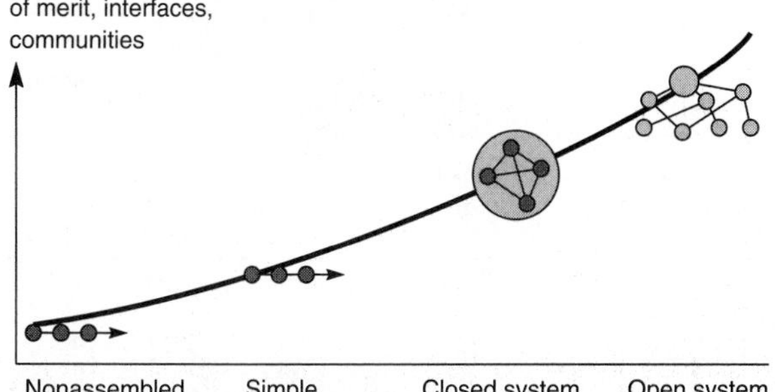

discipline. For these simple products, differences between alternative technological options can be resolved through technical logic.

Closed assembled systems are composed of multiple simple products that must interact with each other. Closed systems are characterized by multiple dimensions of merit—dimensions of the subsystems and of linking technologies. Moving toward a dominant design for closed systems involves selecting relevant dimensions of merit and choosing between alternative technological packages. As no single technological configuration dominates across dimensions of merit, sociopolitical dynamics adjudicate between technical options. These social dynamics involve interactions between competing organizations, professional communities, and influential suppliers and customers. These political processes are also heightened when technological discontinuities threaten core subsystems within closed systems.

Open systems are composed of multiple closed systems and complex linking technologies. Where closed systems are bounded and produced by single organizations, open systems are unbounded, distributed networks whose products are produced by sets of organizations. Open systems are the most complex technological form in terms of subsystems and linking technologies, and in terms of linkages with multiple professional organizations and communities affected by the technology. Open systems, then, have all the technical-context uncertainties associated with closed systems plus those involved with the complex linkage technologies. Given these pervasive technical and contextual uncertainties, sociopolitical dynamics are accentuated in open systems. These dynamics occur at the organizational, interorganizational, disciplinary, and community levels of analysis and are maximized during eras of ferment and when technological breakthroughs affect either core subsystems or linking technologies (see Exhibit 6).

Sociopolitical Dynamics and Subsystem Centrality

Moving from the system to the subsystem level of analysis, there is variation in the extent of sociopolitical dynamics for technological change in core versus peripheral subsystems. Core subsystems are strongly linked to many components of the system. Change in these components requires concurrent or complementary change in peripheral components. Thus, the process of technological change in core subsystems involves the organizations and communities for peripheral subsystems as well as those for the core subsystems. With more constituencies holding a stake in technological outcomes for core subsystems, nontechnical dynamics will be accentuated when core subsystems are threatened.

Integrating Community and Systems Perspectives

Understanding technology cycles and technology as community directs attention to when sociopolitical dynamics have an impact on technological progress. Social logic is least important for nonassembled products. Even during eras of ferment or at technological discontinuities, dimensions of merit are clear and the community of practitioners uses technical logic to resolve differences between alternative technologies. For nonassembled products, technology drives organizations.

On the other hand, sociopolitical dynamics are maximized for open systems either during eras of ferment or when technological discontinuities affect core or linking subsystems (see Exhibit 7). These sociopolitical dynamics operate across a wide network of competing organizations, suppliers, professional organizations, and communities, all of whom have substantial stakes in the technology's evolution. For open systems, nontechnical dynamics drive technological progress within the feasible set of technological options. The relative importance of sociopolitical forces versus technical logic increases from simple assembled products, to closed systems to open systems, and as the product evolves through eras of ferment closing on a dominant design and at those subsequent technological discontinuities that affect core subsystems (see Exhibit 7).

Sociopolitical dynamics are minimal for peripheral subsystems across all types of products, and are minimal during eras of incremental change. During eras of incremental change, technological dimensions of merit and technical premises are fixed, and competing organizations and practitioner communities evolve well-ordered social systems. During these periods, incremental technological change is driven by logic internal to the technology and by well-developed norms and values in the practitioner communities. The more complex the technology, the more pervasive this technical and social momentum. Where sociopolitical processes directly shape technology during eras of ferment and at technological discontinuities, during eras of incremental technical change, technological progress is driven by technical logic. Only during periods of incremental technical change does technical logic dominate nontechnical logic in shaping technological progress and, in turn, organization outcomes (see Exhibit 7).

EXHIBIT 7 Toward a Sociology of Technology

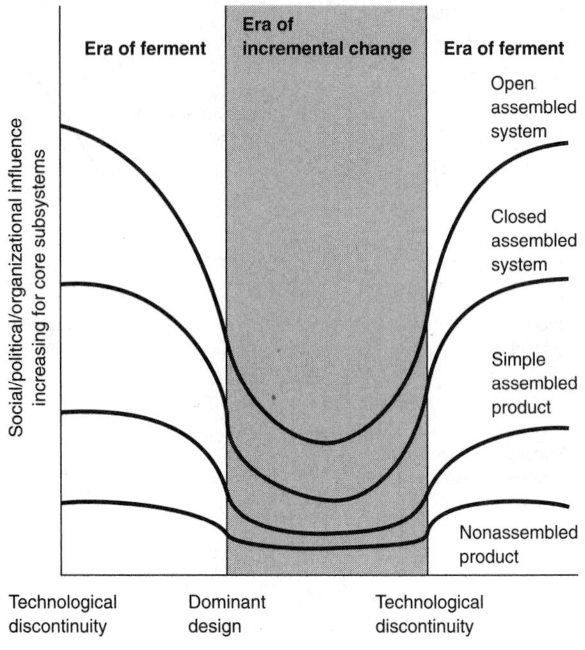

Conclusion

Our objective has been to bring the study of technological evolution more centrally into the realm of organization analysis. Except for the most simple products, at critical junctures in technological evolution choices among technological options cannot be made solely with reference to technology; products are often technologically underdetermined. This paper has explored when and under what conditions social, political, and organizational dynamics affect technological progress. We need to expand upon these ideas and better understand the mechanism by which organizational action affects technical change. We need to know more about how interactions between competing organizations, professional societies, suppliers, customers, and governmental units shape technological evolution. Research on technological progress must be able to span individual, organization, and interorganization levels of analysis.

To better understand the nontechnical determinants of technological change, research must focus more attention on those junctures where sociopolitical dynamics are accentuated. Future research could explore the selection of dominant designs and the impact of technological discontinuities in closed or open systems. Any research on organizational impacts on technical progress must move to the interorganization and community levels of analysis. Research could explore roles of individuals and teams in forging coalitions to shape technological progress or the role of practitioner communities and organizations in shaping (or resisting) technical change. Whatever the research question, research on technological evolution must capture the interplay of individuals, organizations, networks of organizations, and chance in shaping technological evolution.[164]

Because technology is inherently underspecified, sociopolitical processes have an important impact on technological evolution. As technology has pervasive impacts on organizations, it is vital that we better understand when, under what conditions, and the explicit mechanisms by which organizations affect technological progress. This research area calls for research that crosses levels of analysis, and methodologies that can capture organization and interorganization phenomena. The time is ripe to open up the black box of technological change,[165] and to use organizational theory and research to understand technology's social, political, and organizational roots.

[164]See also Frost and Egri, "The Political Process of Innovation."

[165]N. Rosenberg, *Inside the Black Box: Technology and Economics* (Cambridge: Cambridge University Press, 1982).

Industry Context

Case II–6
Telecommunications Industry Note

Alva H. Taylor, Robert A. Burgelman, and Andrew S. Grove

The purpose of this note is to provide an introductory outline of the major concepts and facts of the U.S. telecommunications industry. Covered in this primer are descriptions of the wireline industry (traditional telephone service), wireless industry (currently made up of cellular service), and the cable industry. The wireline sector alone generates approximately $155 billion in annual revenues.[1] This note is an entry point for those unfamiliar with the telecommunications industry, and a refresher for those with telecommunications background.

Wireline Service

Prior to 1984, almost all U.S. telephone service was provided by American Telephone and Telegraph's (AT&T) operation of the Bell System (a small portion of telephone service in isolated areas such as Hawaii was provided by independent companies such as GTE). From the early 1900s the Bell System acted as a virtual monopoly. The first measure of competition was introduced with the Carterfone case in 1968 when the FCC required that all terminal equipment be connected to the telephone network through standard plugs and jacks, and technical information be provided to independent suppliers on the same terms as subsidiaries of telephone companies. The decisions allowed equipment vendors to compete with AT&T. The second major introduction of competition stemmed from MCI's efforts to gain entry into the long-distance telephone market. In 1963 MCI was formed to offer limited microwave service between St. Louis and Chicago and in 1969 the Federal Communications Commission (FCC) approved the application.[2] In 1974 MCI filed an antitrust suit against AT&T, and in 1982 the antitrust suit was settled, with AT&T retaining Long Lines, Western Electric, and Bell Laboratories, but divesting the 22 Bell Operating Companies (BOCs).

In 1984 the Department of Justice's Modified Final Judgment organized the 22 BOCs into 7 Regional BOCs (RBOCs). The seven RBOCs are Ameritech, Bell Atlantic, BellSouth, NYNEX, Pacific Telesis, Southwestern Bell, and US West. The RBOCs were restricted from manufacturing telecommunications equipment (though they could manufacture and sell

[1]This revenue figure and the other revenue estimates discussed in the wireline section of this note are from Northern Business Information, a research subsidiary of McGraw-Hill.

[2]The Federal Communications Commission is the governmental body which regulates the telecommunications industry. Due to its importance to national security, reliance on public right-of-ways, and impact on the public good, the telecommunications industry is regulated by this independent commission.

overseas as long as it was separate from domestic business), offering long-distance services, and offering information services. AT&T was restricted from owning any portion of the RBOCs, and was required to purchase local service access. In most cases the local access was purchased from the RBOCs at a standard rate that the RBOCs had to offer to all carriers (long-distance carriers pay 40 to 50 percent of their revenues to RBOCs for local access). The agreement also drew the geographical boundaries for local-access transport areas (LATAs). Local-exchange carriers (LECs)—primarily RBOCs, GTE, and a large number of smaller independents—are able to offer intraLATA service, while the interexchange, or long-distance, carriers (e.g., AT&T, MCI, Sprint) can offer interLATA service.

The long-distance portion of the industry is expected to generate 1993 revenues of $59.1 billion, representing a 4.8 percent growth rate over 1992. AT&T generates 66 percent of the revenues in the long-distance sector, MCI 15 percent, Sprint 9 percent, while over 800 other carriers generate the remaining 10 percent. The local-exchange portion of the wireline telephone industry is estimated to generate 1993 revenues of $96.6 billion, representing a 3 percent growth rate over 1992.

The structure of a typical call is for it to be made via a telephone where the transmission is carried over a dedicated subscriber line to a local-exchange switch. If it is a local call the call is then "switched," or routed, to the proper local subscriber line and completed. If the call is a long-distance[3] call, the local switch routes the call to the interexchange switch for long-distance transmission, where it is then routed by the long-distance carrier to the appropriate local-exchange switch and finally connected to the proper subscriber line and telephone.

Much of the current telecommunications infrastructure (the physical transmission apparatus) is made of underground fiber optic cable connecting the switches, and a combination of copper and fiber serving the subscribers' residences and businesses.

Wireless Service

Cellular technology was commercially implemented in 1984. The cellular telephone business is essentially a regulated duopoly, as the FCC divided the United States into 734 markets and grants two licenses per market to operate cellular systems. One license is provided to the local-exchange wireline carrier (the A block) while the second license (the B block) was sold via auction by the FCC. The acquired licenses give the carrier the right to use the designated spectrum. The number of cellular subscribers has risen from 91,000 users in 1984 to approximately 11 million users in 1993.[4] Estimated 1993 revenues are $13.5 billion (including paging revenues of approximately $700 million), representing a growth rate of 13 percent over 1992. Currently, some metropolitan markets have cellular subscriber penetration rates of 7 percent, but most cellular systems have a penetration rate of 2 percent. McCaw Cellular services the largest number of customers at 61 million, followed closely by GTE Mobilenet at 54 million, BellSouth Cellular at 39.1 million, Bell Atlantic Mobile at 34.7 million, and Pac Tel Cellular at 33.0 million. Subscriber increase has been steady but is costly as acquisition expenses (made up of commissions and residuals paid to independent dealers) averaged approximately $400 per new subscriber.

Current wireless service is provided by dividing geographical areas into "cells," each equipped with a receiver, signaling equipment, and a low power transmitter. Close placement of the cells allows reuse of frequencies, increasing the volume of calls that can be handled over that of previous mobile telephone systems. A cellular telephone system has a mobile transmission switching office (MTSO), which monitors the strength of the signal of a subscriber's telephone, and when the strength falls below a certain level, the MTSO automatically passes, or "hands-off," the call to the next cell.

There are several developments in the wireless industry segment. The most widely discussed development is the advent of personal communication services (PCSs). The FCC allocated radio spectrum for the development of a family of portable communications services which could provide service to individuals or businesses and be integrated with a variety of competing networks. The wide-ranging technologies grouped under PCS includes personal communication networks (PCNs), telepoint, and User-PCS. The overall concept behind PCS is that the communication service will be centered on the individual, where the individual can have a single phone number which travels with him or her regard-

[3]In this document for ease of reading we refer to interLATA traffic as long-distance and intraLATA traffic as local exchange or local service. Discussions needing precise technical delineation would use the LATA distinctions.

[4]NATA, Telephony, and the U.S.I.T.C.

less of location. PCNs use smaller transmission cells (microcells) than current cellular, enabling use of smaller, lighter phones, and increased traffic capacity. Telepoint service provides cordless pay phone service to customer-owned handsets within a limited range of base stations in public places. User-PCS refers to transmission over a spectrum designed for general public use (requiring no license) and includes user-owned wireless service such as wireless local-area networks (WLANs), portable information devices, and even smaller transmission cells that provide cellular service to buildings and business complexes such as hospitals.

Cable Service

Cable companies provide a wide variety of television programming, primarily video entertainment and informational programming, to subscribers who pay a monthly service fee. The television and radio signals are received via satellite or off-air delivery by antennas and microwave relay stations, and they are modulated, amplified, and distributed over a network of coaxial or fiber optic cable to the subscribers' television sets. Since cable systems use local streets and rights of way, they are subject to state and local legislation. Rate regulation is carried out by the local cities and the FCC. Cable systems are typically constructed and operated pursuant to nonexclusive franchises awarded by local municipalities for a specified period of time. Although licenses have been nonexclusive, municipalities have started awarding multiple cable system licenses for the same geographical locations only recently.

Cable systems were initially developed to service communities where television transmission was poor due to topography or remoteness from broadcast towers. The systems have grown to provide multiple channel packages consisting of basic programming, including broadcast local programs, superstations, and governmental and education access; premium nonbroadcast programming such as ESPN, MTV, or HBO; and displays of information such as time, news, weather, and stock market reports. In 1992, basic cable reached approximately 70 percent of U.S. households with pay cable reaching 35 percent. Approximately 35 percent of the industry subscribers are serviced by at least 54-channel capacity.[5]

[5]Continental Cable annual report.

Revenues are derived from subscribers' initial connection charges and monthly fees (the highest source of revenues), advertising spots on advertiser-supported programming and home shopping services (which pay the companies a share of revenues from the sales of products in the system's service areas), and pay-per-view or pay-per-program sales. Revenue growth for the cable systems in the 1980s occurred through the raising of subscription rates and the construction and operation of new cable systems. As the unserviced portion of the country has diminished, and regulation of rates has been reintroduced, growth in the 1990s occurs through increased marketing and service extensions within existing cable networks. The cable companies usually pay the program provider a monthly fee per subscriber (the most typical arrangement), or a percentage of the gross receipts for the programming on its basic and premium services.

There are two dominant FCC rulings which impact the cable industry. The 1984 Cable Act limits cross-ownership of cable systems by prohibiting local telephone exchange companies from providing video programming directly to subscribers, except in rural areas or by special waiver, and prohibiting cross-ownership of cable systems and broadcast stations in the same service area. The 1984 act also requires cable systems to reserve a percentage of activated channels for use by unaffiliated third parties, and requires the cable operator to provide channel capacity, equipment, and facilities for public, educational, and governmental access. It limited the maximum fee the cable operator paid to the franchise authorities (the local regulatory body) to 5 percent of revenues. In October 1992, the FCC enacted the 1992 Cable Act, which expanded the federal and local regulation of cable. The provisions in the act increase local and federal control over rates of both basic and premium cable, allow broadcast stations to negotiate with cable operators for payments as a consent to carry the broadcast signals, and require allocation of one-third of channel capacity for carriage of both commercial and noncommercial stations.

While many of the existing cable systems have been laid using coaxial cable, most new systems and most rebuilding of existing systems are using a combination of fiber optic and coaxial cable. The fiber optic cable is capable of carrying hundreds of video, data, and voice channels, and new digital compression technology is being developed which will allow cable to offer 500-channel systems. The cable industry is developing an infrastructure that can provide similar transmission technology for voice, data, and video as that provided by the traditional wireline and wireless telephone communication providers. Proposed new services include interactive television, data services, remote utility monitoring, and personal communication network (PCN) telephone services. Currently, cable operators are prohibited from providing telephone services, but are vigorous in the legislative arena to gain approval to provide this additional service.

Digital Technology

Much of the current local-exchange telecommunications service is provided via analog transmission. In both the traditional telecommunications and the cable sector, market participants are investing vast amounts in upgrading their systems to offer digital service. Most of today's telephone lines were built with copper cable for transmitting the human voice, but do not have the capacity for a large volume of video. Long-line and local-exchange carriers are upgrading their systems to fiber optic technology. One bottleneck for this effort is the inability of the current companies to rapidly write down the existing copper cable (an estimated $60 billion) and analog switching equipment.[6]

While there is consensus that a digital infrastructure is most desirable, one impediment for the transfer and use of the digital communications is that the companies must find a feasible financial plan to fund the upgrades. A second impediment is the lack of digital standards. In the wireline sector there is a move to integrated services digital network (ISDN), allowing digital transmission over copper wire, with support for competing asynchronous transfer mode (ATM) technology. In the wireless segment there is the competition between the existing Time Division Multiple Access (TDMA) digital technology and Code Division Multiple Access (CDMA), under development. Additional wireless data services face competition between proprietary systems and open systems using Cellular Digital Packet Data (CDPD) transmission. Cable companies are experimenting with differing compression technologies to allow information to be compressed and transmitted along their cable systems.

[6] *Business Week*, September 16, 1991.

Future Considerations

The sectors of the telecommunications industry face different constraints and restrictions on the key dimensions of information transmission capacity and access. The constraints are both regulatory and physical. Exhibit 1 provides a summary of these constraints. Due to the differing characteristics, the means for revenue expansion differ across the industry segments.

Application Uncertainty

The telecommunications sectors also face a proliferation of possible applications for transmission capability. The possible applications include those in the entertainment industry (interactive television, programs on demand, interactive games, 500-channel cable), business applications (video teleconferencing, PCS, WLANs, increased cellular phone use, real-time processing and tracking), and home use (shopping, education, banking, news services, financial planning, and stock trading). Investments are being made in each of these industries. While the future dominant application has yet to be determined, most participants are betting that the most active near-term applications will be home shopping and video on demand.

Industry Convergence

At the center of the convergence of the entertainment, computing, and telecommunications industries sectors is digital technology. Digital technology allows easier transmission of information across mediums that were previously incompatible due to the idiosyncrasies of their analog transmission. A major future player in this industry may be the computer industry as it has well-established experience and competencies in applying and developing digital information transfer. The cable industry's probable importance to the telecommunications industry is increasing as new participants in the industry look for ways to decrease the infrastructure cost in reaching consumers and see the installed-cable infrastructure as a way of lowering capital costs. Additionally, as entertainment applications appear to be a key use of future telecommunications, the cable industry's ties and experience in handling entertainment programming become more valuable. However, cable companies are generally weak in

EXHIBIT 1 Telecommunications Industry Characteristics (within current boundaries)

	Transmission Vehicle	Capacity Constraint	Access	Expansion
Long-distance carriers	■ Wireline infrastructure —Copper cable —Fiber optic cable	■ Line availability ■ Switching equipment availability ■ Bandwidth for video	■ Prohibited from local wireline service	■ Service expansion —800, 900 numbers —Watts lines ■ LD use increase ■ Cellular local access
Local-exchange carriers	■ Wireline infrastructure —Copper cable —Fiber optic cable	■ Line availability ■ Switching equipment availability ■ Bandwidth for video	■ Prohibited from long-distance service ■ Geographically constrained ■ Connects directly to the home	■ Service expansion —Call waiting —Voice mail ■ Population growth
Current cellular carriers	■ Allocated radio bandwidth ■ Analog and digital radios	■ Channels per bandwidth	■ Limited to two carriers per MSA	■ Increased subscribers ■ Increased cellular phone use ■ Acquisition of other cellular companies
Personal communication service	■ Allocated radio bandwidth	■ Channels per bandwidth —Increased density over current cellular	■ Limited to licenses extended by the FCC	■ License acquisition ■ Development and subscriber sign-up
Cable operators	■ Cable infrastructure —Coaxial cable —Fiber optic cable	■ Two way interactivity ■ Channels per cable	■ Nonexclusive franchise granted by local municipality	■ Increased subscribers ■ Pay-per-view ■ Acquisition of other cable companies ■ Increased programming services

handling transaction-based services, which is a strength of the telecommunications companies.

In addition to technological issues, the regulatory climate is also encouraging convergence. The FCC recently ruled that local exchange carriers can begin to offer video dialtone service. In addition the FCC has revised its affiliation restrictions on telephone company (telco) cable ownership to allow programming from telcos. These rulings, plus additional recommendations by the FCC to relax the restrictions on LECs, offer an opportunity for the RBOCs to gain a presence in the growing entertainment market, and to escape the geographical constraints of their local-exchange service. Similar relaxation of service provision restrictions is taking place throughout the industry, slowly reducing the regulatory barriers between the different industry segments.

Case II–7
The Wireless Communications Industry: After AT&T-McCaw

Alva H. Taylor, Robert A. Burgelman, and Andrew S. Grove

Wireless communications has grown from limited radio dispatch in the 1960s and 1970s to impending nationwide cellular telephony in the 90s. This industry segment is expected to have 1993 revenues of $13.5 billion and projected service and equipment revenues of $40 billion by the year 2000.[1] On November 4, 1993, American Telephone and Telegraph (AT&T) generated a jolt to the industry with its agreement to buy one-third of McCaw Cellular Communications Inc.—the largest cellular carrier. Subsequently, the company decided to up the stakes by acquiring and gaining complete control of McCaw. This move increased speculation of the role of the wireless segment in the overall telecommunications industry, as well as its role in the touted convergence between the telecommunications, multimedia, and computer sectors.

The questions remain: How important is wireless communication to the participants in the telecommunications industry? And how important will it be to the anticipated industry convergence?

Wireless Industry History

Mobile radio systems have been in use since the 1920s by police departments, fire departments, trucking companies, and taxis, but cost and capacity limitations restricted their use to organizations with critical needs to communicate with mobile operations. In 1970, AT&T submitted to the FCC a plan that included the concept known as cellular telephony that had been conceived by its Bell Labs back in 1947. Rather than using one powerful transmitter as in mobile telephony, cellular telephony uses a network of low-power transmitters to send messages within an area. The advent of cellular telephony transformed wireless transmission from a closed network used by business entities to a communications medium available to individuals. Ameritech offered the first cellular system, introduced in Chicago in 1984, followed by a second system in the Baltimore-Washington area.

The active start of the U.S. wireless industry coincided with the breakup of the Bell System. Many of the regulatory decisions concerning wireless came during the breakup period. "Given the overriding, overwhelming importance of divestiture, no one really had much energy to look at cellular. Cellular was just a wayside, a back eddy that happened to be there at an inconvenient time" says Herschel Shosteck, a telecommunications consultant based in Maryland. Initially AT&T stood to gain all of the cellular business, but lagging regulatory business allowed the radio common carriers (RCCs) to gain access. Cellular was originally intended to be structured as just another form of telephone service. Said Craig McCaw, CEO of McCaw Cellular in 1993, "The regulatory process of cellular was too long, but people forget that had licenses been issued sooner, there would have been only one license per market. And it would have been AT&T."

The FCC decided to split each cellular market between wireline and nonwireline, and the nation was divided into relatively small markets—306 metropolitan statistical areas (MSAs) and 428 rural service areas (RSAs). The wireline market, or B block,

[1] U.S. International Trade Commission, "Global Competitiveness of U.S. Advanced-Technology Industries: Cellular Communications," Investigation No. 332–329.

of each of the segments was awarded to the existing wireline operator, while the A block was to be issued to an unaffiliated wireless operator. The initial award of nonwireline licenses was to be made based on comparative hearings, but the hearings were time-consuming and generated few applicants as small concerns did not feel they could stand up under comparative scrutiny to the major corporations. In 1984 Congress authorized the FCC to award licenses based on a lottery system. While this system speeded up the process, it also led to speculation as the number of applications (or ticket holders) rose from 3 to over 600 in some markets. In the smaller markets almost 90 percent of the lottery winners resold their licenses (originally costing $10,000) to experienced carriers at windfall profits. The high prices companies had to pay to get the licenses, coupled with the cost of building the cellular infrastructure from the ground up, led to large start-up costs and huge debt loads by the initial carriers. Service in the smaller markets began in 1987.

U.S. subscribers have grown from 100,000 in 1984, to 3.5 million in 1989, to approximately 11 million in 1993. Cellular telephones have reached 10 million customers at about the same rate as the VCR (9 years), and faster than the facsimile (22 years), cable television (25 years), landline telephones (36 years), and the pager (41 years).[2] Cellular phones penetrated 8 percent of households 10 years after initial introduction, a greater penetration than telephone answering machines, and slightly behind VCR's.

Current Cellular

The prevailing wireless transmission application is wireless voice transmission through analog cellular telephony. Current cellular transmissions operate in the following manner: upon dialing a telephone number and initiating the "send" signal, individual calls radiate from the user's cellular telephone via its antenna to a base station (or cell site) which is equipped with a low-power radio receiver/transmitter. At the base station the calling traffic is combined and conveyed to the mobile telephone switching office (MTSO) and then to the conventional worldwide telephone network serving homes and offices (as illustrated in Exhibit 1). Each base station or cell defines a geographical calling area. Cells range from one to twenty miles in diameter, with cells in major cities generally less than one mile apart. Currently there are more than 10,000 cells in the United States. As the caller moves from one geographical area to another the call is automatically transferred to the local cell site. Each cellular MTSO supports several cell sites, and it may take hundreds of cell sites to complete a network's coverage of a given geographical area—thus requiring a fairly complex set of connections for one call to be successful.

There are three basic types of cellular phones: car phones, transportables, and portables. Car phones are permanently installed in a vehicle and cost approximately $200. Transportables are phones approximately the size of a home slim-line phone, and are usually carried in their own carrying bag or pouch (hence the term "bag phone") and also cost around $200. Portables are much smaller and fit into a suit pocket or briefcase and cost approximately $300. Prices among cellular phones vary widely based on sales offers and discounts offered by subscriber services attempting to generate cellular traffic. Due to greater transmitter power (6 watts versus 3 watts), car phones and transportables have greater broadcast ranges.

Each cell of a cellular system contains low-power transmitters, receivers, antennas, processing equipment, power amplifiers, and backup power equipment. The cellular switch performs the automated routing, locates the mobile phone unit, confirms operability, directs the change of frequency when coverage area changes, and performs billing and other administrative functions. The equipment necessary for a single cell to cover a typical geographical area costs approximately $250,000. Even without sophisticated switching technology, it costs approximately $100,000 to install a 100-phone wireless PBX system in a typical office complex.[3]

One change current cellular transmission is undergoing is the advent of digital service. Digital signals convert sound to a series of zeros and ones for transmission, while an analog transmission signal is a wave covering the continuous spectrum from zero to one. Since digital information is restricted to zeros and ones, errors are less likely to occur, which results in cleaner, static-free sound, and 3 to 10 times more information can be transmitted over the same bandwidth. However there is no established digital standard, with the major com-

---

[2]The Cellular Telecommunications Industry Association.

[3]*Business Week*, August 30, 1993.

EXHIBIT 1

HOW IT WORKS

Cellular Connections

Cellular calls may seem effortless (at least when they go through), but behind them is a complex high-tech network. Dial someone from a street corner or your car, and the call moves through a radio highway of inconspicuous transmission towers, monitored and steered by advanced digital switches and computers.

1. A call from a cellular phone moves as radio waves to the transmitting-receiving tower, or cell site, that provides service in its area, or cell.
2. From the cell site, the call moves through wires or microwaves to the mobile telephone switching office, or MTSO.
3. The MTSO routes the call on the next leg of its journey, generally connecting it to the regular local phone exchange.
4. From the local exchange, the call becomes a conventional phone call.
5. For a call to a cellular phone, the MTSO transmits the number dialed to all its cells. Once it finds the phone, it steers the call to it through the nearest cell.
6. For calls to or from phones on the move, the MTSO's computers sense when a phone's signal is becoming weak and needs to be "handed off" to an adjacent cell. The computers then figure out to which cell the call should be switched, and find an open frequency for it in the new cell.

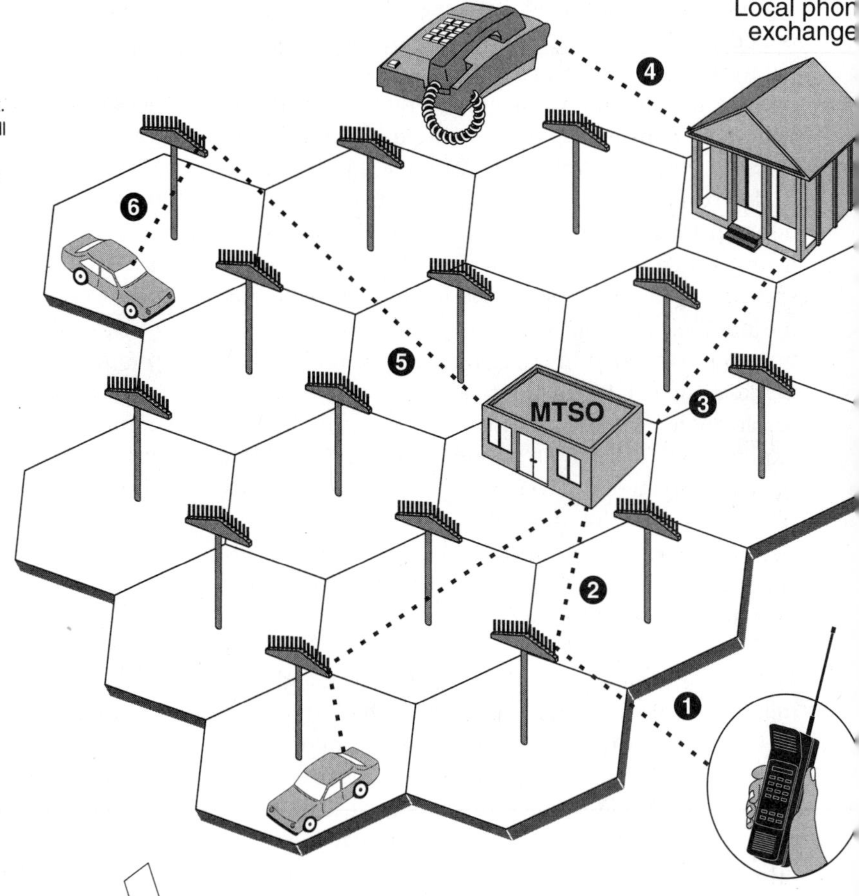

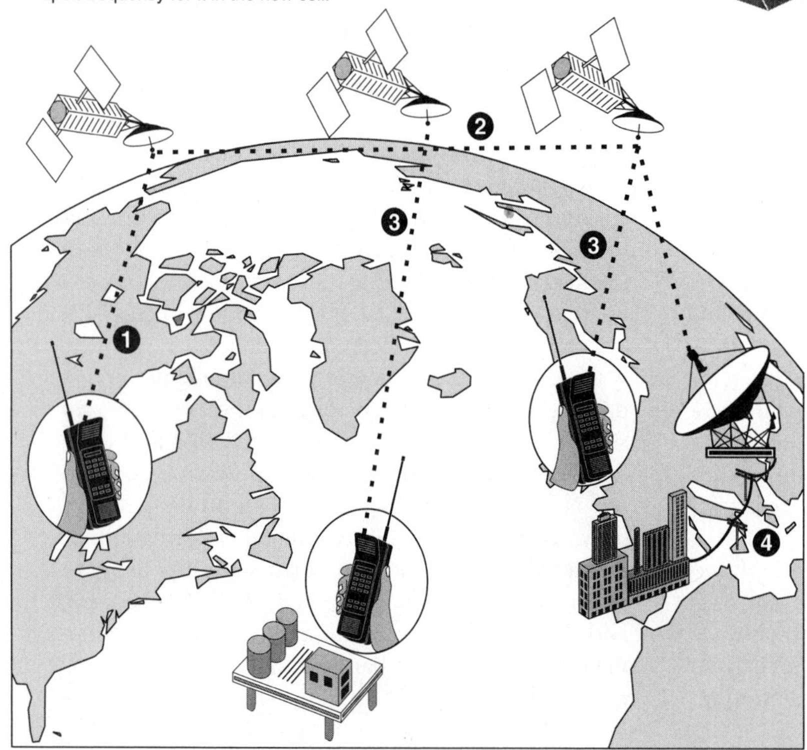

Sky Phones

Several companies plan to use satellites to help calls ho over vast regions such as mountains, deserts, and ocea that aren't served by cellular systems. Satellite phones w also help international travelers stay in wireless contact where local cellular technology isn't compatible with thei phones from home.

1. In one type of system being developed, high-powered portable phones will connect directly to satellites in low orbits.
2. The satellites will switch the signals among themselves as needed and then bounce them back to Earth.
3. Calls to people with the same type of phones or the right kind of pagers will be transmitted directly to them from the satellites.
4. Other calls will move from the satellites through ground stations, and then into the wired phone network, to reach their destinations.

SOURCE: *The Wall Street Journal.*

peting technologies being noncompatible. Consumers will need special digital phones to use the digital systems, and the phones will be configured to be used with only one of the digital transmission standards. Even when systems are able to transmit digitally, the analog service will not disappear; analog services are expected to account for between 60 and 70 percent of industry revenues through 1998.[4]

The major participants in the wireless telecommunications industry can be separated into service providers and equipment manufacturers (both network equipment manufacturers and transmission origination equipment manufacturers). Service provision of wireless communications, prior to the active mergers and partnership activity starting in the early 1990s, could be split between the traditional wireline service providers, which are firms that also offer telecommunication services over wireline networks, and the "pure-play" service providers, firms that exclusively operate mobile communication networks. Under the pure-play providers, there are the open-service providers that acquired the A licenses and provide general service, and the proprietary service providers (specialized mobile radio–SMR operators) that have grown from the fleet dispatch services of the 1970s and continue to provide specialized business communication services. The equipment-manufacturing effort is divided between the switching equipment and the terminal equipment. In the network equipment segment, the major manufacturers of the cellular switches also are the major manufacturers of the radio base stations (see Exhibit 2 for an illustration of the main wireless service and equipment providers).

Cellular Market Growth and Characteristics

About 9,500 new cellular subscribers sign up daily; the average subscriber bill has fallen from an average of approximately $200 a month in 1984, to $103 a month in 1991, to approximately $70 per month in 1993, with an average call length of three minutes. Portable calls were the shortest, averaging only 85 seconds per call.[5] Forecasted growth in the market places the total number of U.S. subscribers between 16 million and 25 million by the year 1995, and 40 million by the year 2000. Revenues in the industry are expected to grow to between $18 billion and $20 billion by 1996 and then drop due to the pressure of competition in the industry.[6]

Cellular markets are defined by the population served. Exhibit 3 gives the cellular market share by company, and the providers to the top populated cities in the United States. As the exhibit shows, McCaw Cellular is the leading cellular communications provider, closely followed by GTE Mobile Network. McCaw has a presence in 6 of the top 10 population centers, while no other carrier has a presence in more than 3. Market penetration of the cellular carriers is low. While a few dense metropolitan markets have penetration as high as 7 percent, most cellular systems have a penetration rate of subscribers per total population of less than 2 percent. It is expected that larger markets will register penetration levels of 18 to 20 percent within two years.

Cellular service is primarily sold through independent dealers, with dealer sales accounting for an estimated 60 percent of sales. A local dealer is given authorization to sell a carrier's service. A commission is paid to the dealer for new activation and the dealer also collects residuals based on subscriber usage level. This method is an expensive manner of acquiring customers, but initially these incentives were necessary when cellular use was uncommon. While the cellular companies have been successful at lowering the commissions paid, acquisition costs are still substantial. In 1992 acquisition cost averaged $600 (includes all marketing and selling expenses); in 1993 the acquisition cost fell to near $400 per new subscriber. Given the regulatory requirement of two service providers per market, cellular companies also fall victim to "churn," or frequent switching between service providers. Sources of churn can be a switch to the competitor; voluntary deactivation due to cost, moving, and usage level; and involuntary deactivation due to missed payments. Average churn rates range from 2 to 3.5 percent. Given the high cost of signing users, gaining casual users who are sporadic cellular users may cost the carriers as much to acquire as the revenue they produce.

Cellular providers also have started direct sales staffs for corporate accounts, with direct sales to corporate, medium-to-small businesses, and high-usage individuals accounting for about 30 percent of cellular service sales. It often requires six months of effort to land a direct account. Retail outlets such

[4]BIS Strategic Decision.
[5]*USA Today*.

[6]BIS Strategic Decisions.

EXHIBIT 2 Wireless Industry Participants

A. Wireless Source Providers

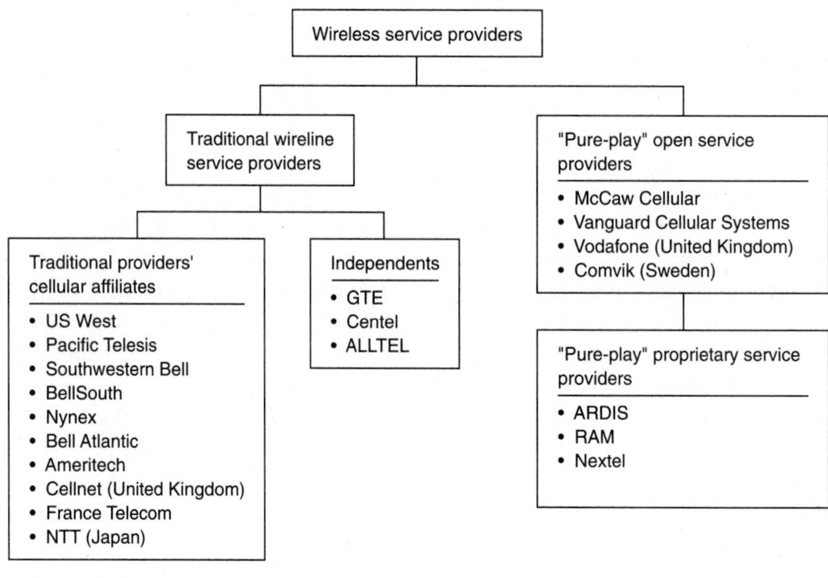

SOURCE: USITC staff.

B. Wireless Equipment Manufacturers

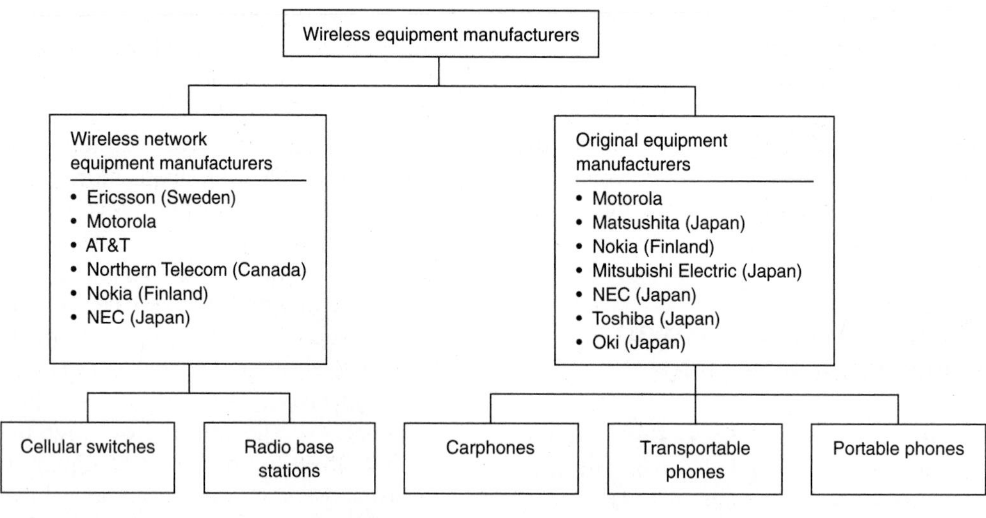

as electronic superstores and mass merchandisers make up the third largest service channel, but still represent less than 10 percent of the service provider revenue. The electronic superstores have started to take advantage of their growing importance by demanding commissions of up to $200 per customer (up from $50 per customer in 1991), while commissions for mass merchandisers are substantially lower. In most cases, the superstores will align themselves with one service provider and sign customers exclusively to that carrier. Exhibit 4 shows the growth of subscribers, revenues, cell sites, capital outlay, and systems of the cellular industry.

EXHIBIT 3 1993 Cellular Market Share by Population and U.S. Cellular Markets Ranked by Population

Company	Population Size Served
McCaw	61.0 million
GTE Mobilenet	54.2 million
Bell South Cellular	39.1 million
Bell Atlantic Mobile	34.7 million
Pac Tel Cellular	33.0 million

SOURCE: Cellular Telephone Industry of America.

City	Population (1992 estimate in millions)
■ New York LIN Broadcasting (52% owned by McCaw) NYNEX Mobile Communications	14.97
■ Los Angeles BellSouth Cellular (40% owned by LIN) Pac Tel Cellular	14.59
■ Chicago Southwestern Bell Mobile Ameritech Mobile Communications	7.36
■ Philadelphia Comcast Cellular (49% owned by LIN) Bell Atlantic Mobile	4.90
■ Detroit Cellular Communications/Pac Tel (50–50 partnership with McCaw) Ameritech Mobile Communications	4.55
■ Dallas LIN Broadcasting (52% owned by McCaw) Southwestern Bell Mobile Systems	4.22
■ Boston Southwestern Bell Mobile Systems NYNEX Mobile Communications	4.02
■ Washington, D.C. Southwestern Bell Mobile Systems Bell Atlantic Mobile	3.82
■ San Francisco Pac Tel Cellular (50% owned by McCaw) GTE Mobilenet	3.76
■ Houston LIN Broadcasting (52% owned by McCaw) GTE Mobilenet	3.64

SOURCES: Donnelley Marketing Information Services; Paine Webber, Cellular Telecommunications Industry Association.

Emerging Wireless Transmission Technologies

In addition to current cellular telephony, there are three major emerging transmission technologies which will compete against current cellular transmission for wireless transmission traffic: personal communication services, satellite communications, and specialized mobile radio (SMR). SMR operators generally provide dispatch and private radio systems. These carriers use proprietary systems to provide specialized wireless communication services. Currently, these systems are used for applications such as local-area dispatch and fleet management systems. However, a few, such as Ardis and RAM Mobile Data, have accumulated enough licenses to

EXHIBIT 4 Cellular Telecommunications Industry Association Midyear Data Survey

Date	Subscribers	Six-Month Revenues	Roamer Services	Cell Sites	Employees	Cumulative Capital Investment	No. of Systems	Average Monthly Bill	Average Call Length (in minutes)
6/85	203,600	$ 176,231,000		599	1,697	$ 588,751,000	65		
12/85	340,213	$ 306,197,000		913	2,727	$ 911,167,000	102		
6/86	500,000	$ 360,197,000		1,194	3,556	$ 1,140,163,000	129		
12/86	681,825	$ 462,467,000		1,531	4,334	$ 1,436,753,000	166		
6/87	883,778	$ 479,514,000		1,732	5,656	$ 1,724,348,000	206		
12/87	1,230,855	$ 672,005,000		2,305	7,147	$ 2,234,635,000	312	$96.83	2.33
6/88	1,608,697	$ 886,075,000		2,789	9,154	$ 2,589,589,000	420	$95.00	2.25
12/88	2,069,441	$1,073,473,000	$ 89,331,000	3,209	11,400	$ 3,274,105,000	517	$98.02	2.26
6/89	2,691,793	$1,406,463,000	$121,368,000	3,577	13,719	$ 3,675,473,000	559	$85.52	2.35
12/89	3,508,944	$1,934,132,000	$173,199,000	4,169	15,927	$ 4,480,141,752	584	$89.30	2.48
6/90	4,368,686	$2,126,362,000	$192,350,000	4,768	18,973	$ 5,211,765,025	592	$83.94	2.32
12/90	5,283,055	$2,422,458,000	$263,660,000	5,616	21,382	$ 6,281,596,000	751	$80.90	2.20
6/91	6,390,053	$2,653,505,000	$302,329,000	6,685	25,545	$ 7,429,739,000	1,029	$74.56	2.37
12/91	7,557,148	$3,055,017,000	$401,325,000	7,847	26,327	$ 8,671,544,000	1,252	$72.74	2.38
6/92	8,892,535	$3,633,285,000	$436,725,000	8,901	30,595	$ 9,276,139,000	1,483	$68.51	2.38
12/92	11,032,753	$4,189,441,000	$537,146,000	10,307	34,348	$11,262,070,000	1,506	$68.68	2.58
6/93	13,067,318	$4,819,259,000	$587,347,000	11,551	36,501	$12,775,967,000	1,523	$67.31	2.38

build nationwide data networks, and the FCC has granted NexTel (previously named Fleet Call) a waiver to provide telephone service in the future.

PCS is a generic term describing mobile or portable services to individuals or businesses that operate similarly to current cellular systems. The PCS family of services includes personal communication networks (PCNs) and unlicensed PCSs. The linking concept behind the family of services is that the communication service revolves around the individual, whether in the home, office, or traveling—with the communication number staying the same for the individual regardless of location. The FCC has proposed to allocate bandwidth for PCS systems, but unlike the small revenues generated by the cellular licenses, the government hopes to make as much as $8 billion from the auction of PCS licenses nationwide. Estimates suggest it will cost $8 billion to $10 billion to serve 75 percent of the population, contrasted to the estimated $11 billion having been spent on current cellular.

The most visible part of PCS is PCN, a technology which consists of a large number of low-power microcell transmitters that increase system capacity by allowing increased frequency reuse. PCN systems use less power, allowing handsets to run on smaller batteries, allowing for reductions in size, weight, and cost of handsets. The smaller cells also give PCNs greater capacity, which would mean that increased volume could lead to lower costs per call and lower transmission prices. In an attempt to cut the infrastructure costs required for the dense equipment network, tests are being conducted to offer PCS over cable plant. U.S. cable companies are currently testing the concept, hoping that by piggybacking on the cable infrastructure that already exists to serve the entertainment industry, the costs associated with implementing PCS will be lowered.

Unlicensed PCS refers to user-PCS devices owned and operated by end users on their own premises, without the need for FCC licensing or call charges. Using very small microcells, called picocells, and a wireless PBX, calls can be switched back and forth between phone desks and portables. Target markets for these business PCSs are hospitals, hotels, factories, and other businesses with highly mobile staff.

Satellite systems are another transmission mechanism which is being developed to offer wireless communications services. In the satellite system, the transmission is routed to a satellite dish where it is relayed to an orbiting satellite and reflected to a satellite dish in the connecting region and routed to its destination. The system requires a network of orbiting satellites which are able to cover the geographical region where service is being provided. The new satellite systems would beam signals to portable phones, computers, and pagers anywhere on earth. Satellite plans differ in the ambitiousness of their wireless vision. Most systems plan to interconnect to local exchanges globally in order to connect to current land line services. More ambitious systems hope to support true personal communications systems without relying on either the local interchange companies or the long-distance companies by having the call transmitted directly to a satellite uplink and to the orbiting satellite for routing. In either case, an individual would have a number that dials their PCS without regard to where the call is coming from or where the PCS is located.

In addition to the initial capital costs, maintenance costs will remain high as the satellites would have to be kept in low-flying orbits, requiring replacement every few years when they crash due to atmospheric drag. There is also some concern that the satellite phones will be more expensive than cellular phones—an expected $2,500 phone and $3 per minute to use versus $100 and 20 to 95 cents a minute charge for current cellular use. Satellite systems target domestic (e.g., rural locations) and global markets which do not have an extensive land-based communications infrastructure. Despite the huge funding requirements, several prospective satellite systems are in development.

Exhibit 5 provides current and estimated future growth of wireless subscribers by service type, and shows projected wireless data device growth and anticipated future events.

Regulatory Environment

The regulatory environment has greatly shaped the telecommunications industry, and continues to do so. Prior to the breakup of the AT&T monopoly, U.S. telecommunications was highly regulated but stable as the government and AT&T negotiated service, rates, and margins. The 1984 divestiture decree specified that long-line carriers (e.g., AT&T, MCI, and GTE Sprint) are prohibited from offering local-exchange service (provided by the regional Bell operating companies—RBOCs). The long-line carriers are also prohibited from acquiring any portion of companies offering local-exchange service. The RBOCs are prohibited from providing long-distance

EXHIBIT 5

Projected U.S. Subscribers by Service Type

	1993	1994	1995	1996	1997	1998	Growth
Voice services:							
Cellular	14,163	17,350	20,965	25,182	29,917	35,500	20.20%
SMR	1,620	1,750	1,890	2,040	2,200	2,380	8.00
Data services:							
Cellular	600	1,150	1,535	1,818	2,083	2,500	33.00%
Paging	17,655	21,250	25,500	30,600	36,720	44,064	20.20
Mobile data networks	300	500	800	1,000	1,200	1,400	38.00
Satellite phone services	50	60	72	86	120	160	26.20
Total	34,388	42,060	50,762	60,726	72,240	$86,004	20.10%

SOURCE: *The Wall Street Journal,* Link Resources Corp.

Wireless Data Device Estimates and Expected Major Milestones

	Installed Base		
Year	PDAs	Other Wireless Data Devices	Expected Events
1993	52,000	364,000	Data only networks, Ardis & Ram, start to upgrade service; first PDAs—Newton, Simon, Zoomer—are introduced.
1994	170,000	685,000	Radio modems and cellular phones on small slip-in cards are introduced for PDAs and portable computers; Motorola, Compaq, Sony ship more advanced PDAs; two new data networks—SMR and CDPD—are introduced; FCC awards licenses for personal communications services.
1995	368,000	1,245,000	Regional personal communications systems for data and voice are established; companies complete national messaging network and national SMR network; Philips, Matsushita, others introduce PDAs.
1996	895,000	1,198,000	CDPD becomes a seamless national network, promoting transmission of voice and data on single devices, hundreds of services become available on intelligent networks through easy-to-use software applications; demand for wireless data devices soars.
1997	1,808,000	2,967,000	Handheld wireless data devices become a mass market.
1998	3,224,000	4,278,000	

SOURCE: *The Wall Street Journal,* BIS Strategic Decisions

service and from manufacturing telecommunications equipment. However, the RBOCs can market and distribute telecommunications equipment under the agreement. The Baby Bells cannot charge the long distance carriers differing rates for local exchange service. The exchange charges represent an expense of 40 to 50 percent of the long-distance carriers' revenues. The long-line carriers must provide long-distance access to all users, with maximum rates determined by established tariff rates which designate the maximum allowable charge rates for the time and traffic type of the transmission.

The FCC also has begun to open up competition in local telephone service. The commissioners voted to allow local-exchange service competitors (called competitive access providers—CAPs) to provide local transmission and to link with established local networks. The independent local companies, like MFS Communications and Teleport Communications, serve mainly large corporations and are expected to go after the access fees paid by the long-distance carriers for the local access. Residential customers will be largely unaffected by this ruling. For cellular service the FCC has established a system of limited competition with the A and B carrier structure in each designated market. Starting with the Carterfone case in 1968, the FCC has introduced competition into the supply of equipment to telephone customers, and has required that all terminal equipment be connected to the telephone network through standard plugs and jacks and that technical information be provided to independent suppliers on the same terms as those given to subsidiaries of telephone companies. These decisions allowed equipment vendors to compete effectively, and have contributed to the declines of market share, including AT&T's share of telecommunication equipment sales, which decreased from almost 100 percent prior to the 1980s to 60 percent in the early 1980s, with a current share of approximately 36 percent for handsets, 25 percent for key systems, and 20 percent for PBXs.

Background of the AT&T and McCaw Deal

In late 1990 Harold Eastman, director at McCaw Cellular, made a call to Robert Allen, CEO of AT&T, to inquire about the possibility of a partnership between McCaw Cellular and AT&T. Preliminary discussions were started, only to be put on hold as AT&T's efforts focused on the acquisition of NCR. AT&T's negotiations with McCaw were restarted in late 1991. The negotiations stalled again in the spring of 1992 when AT&T balked at contributing substantial sums of money, as well as providing McCaw with the use of its name, without gaining control over McCaw. AT&T was willing to provide a small sum of money without gaining control, or to provide a large sum of money and gain immediate control. Neither one of these alternatives was attractive to McCaw at the time.

Alex J. Mendl, chief financial officer at AT&T, suggested a two-stage agreement whereby AT&T would purchase the option of gaining control of McCaw at a later date if an urgent need arose. Craig McCaw, CEO of McCaw, agreed to the idea given that AT&T was willing to set the hurdle for gaining control prohibitively high to prevent AT&T from acquiring control easily. After much negotiation, the terms were agreed upon and made public on November 4, 1992. The original deal called for AT&T to pay $3.72 billion for one-third of new McCaw shares, and $100 million up front to purchase the option to pay an additional $600 million to gain control of McCaw. On August 16, AT&T announced that rather than undertaking the incremental deal, it would be acquiring McCaw outright for $12.6 billion in new stock, in addition to assuming $4.9 billion in McCaw debt.

With McCaw's customer base at approximately 61 million, it is estimated that the deal results in AT&T's paying over $280 per potential cellular user (or almost $8,000 per current McCaw cellular subscriber). The price per person in the area, or pop, paid by AT&T approached the peak paid in the late 1980s when McCaw purchased premium properties in New York City and Los Angeles for a $350 pop. Prices had dropped in the early 90's as Contel paid a $215 pop for eastern presence, Pacific Telesis paid a $190 pop in Cleveland and Cincinnati, and Crowley Cellular Telecommunications paid a $165 pop for Illinois properties.

McCaw Cellular is the leading cellular carrier with a subscriber base of 2.2 million, and growth of 500,000 customers in 1992. However, the expansions of its cellular network and the purchase of users resulted in a company with heavy debt and strong cash needs. The company had used large amounts of debt to purchase cellular licenses and in its 1989 acquisition of LIN Broadcasting, which held cellular licenses in New York, Los Angeles, Houston, and Dallas. The company needed to reduce its debt load and to acquire capital for improving its digital technology, acquiring more network cells, and improving general service to its rapidly expanding customer base (see Exhibit 6 for selected financial statements for McCaw Cellular, AT&T, and other selected long-line RBOCs and pure-play cellular companies).

EXHIBIT 6 **Financial Information for Selected RBOCs and Pure-Play Cellular Carriers (dollars in millions except for per share figures)**

	Bell Atlantic			Bell South			Pacific Telesis		
	1992	1991	1990	1992	1991	1990	1992	1991	1990
Operating revenues									
Network and related services:									
Local service	$4,892	$4,758	$4,617	$6,236	$5,846	$5,665	$3,378	$3,364	$3,109
Network access	$2,953	$2,922	$2,970	$3,818	$3,725	$3,754	$2,285	$2,276	$2,235
Toll	$1,556	$1,539	$1,544	$1,249	$1,374	$1,565	$2,086	$2,177	$2,235
Directory Advertising	$1,659	$1,559	$1,579	$1,460	$1,426	$1,394	$994	$990	$972
Wireless communications	$518	$428	$388	$1,196	$775	$557	$838	$700	$599
Other services	$1,069	$1,252	$1,423	$1,244	$1,300	$1,410	$354	$395	$448
Total operating revenues	$12,647	$12,498	$12,520	$15,202	$14,445	$14,345	$9,935	$9,902	$9,598
Operating expenses:									
Cost of services and products	$7,723	$7,634	$7,495	$5,681	$5,739	$5,797	$5,949	$5,913	$5,574
Depreciation	$2,417	$2,339	$2,411	$3,032	$2,965	$2,901	$1,854	($1)	$1,868
Selling, general, and administration				$3,327	$2,931	$2,621			
Total operating expenses	$10,140	$9,973	$9,906	$12,040	$11,635	$11,319	$7,803	$5,912	$7,442
Operating income	$2,506	$2,525	$2,614	$3,161	$2,809	$3,027	$2,132	$2,114	$2,227
Interest income (expense)	$695	$807	$741	$746	$802	$774	($509)	($585)	($649)
Other income, net	$214	$176	$27	$178	$253	$157	$136	$113	$71
Provision for income taxes	$646	$665	$670	$934	$753	$778	$617	$627	$619
Extraordinary loss	($42)	—	—	($41)	—	—			
Accounting change	—	($1,554)	—	—	($35)	—			
Net income	$1,341	($324)	$1,230	$1,618	$1,472	$1,632	$1,142	$1,015	$1,030
Other financial information:									
EPS (before extraord. losses)	$3.23	$2.91	$2.92	$3.30	$3.04	$3.38	2.83	2.58	2.59
Debt ratio	56.30%	59.50%	57.50%	39.00%	41.30%	40.70%	43.50%	45.20%	46.20%
Return to equity	17.40%	−4.40%	14.40%	11.90%	11.30%	12.80%	3.60%	14.20%	13.70%

	McCaw			Vanguard Cellular		
	1992	1991	1990	1992	1991	1990
Operating revenues:						
Cellular revenues	$1,743	$1,366	$1,037	$90	$69	$64
Total operating revenues	$1,743	$1,366	$1,037	$90	$69	$64
Operating expenses:						
Operating costs	$1,079	$888	$715	$29	$31	$28
Selling general, and administration	$20	$17	$21	$46	$43	$46
Depreciation and amortization	$384	$345	$254	$22	$19	$14
Total operating expenses	$1,483	$1,250	$990	$97	$93	$88
Operating income	$260	$116	$47	($7)	($24)	($24)
Other income (expenses):						
Interest income/expense (net)	($472)	($548)	($451)	($16)	($19)	($20)
Gain (loss) on dispositions	$3	$249	$1,173	($3)	$1	$17
Other income/expense (net)	$40	$29	$0	$0	$1	$0
Total other expenses	($429)	($270)	$722	($19)	($17)	($3)
Net income	($169)	($154)	$769	($26)	($41)	($27)
Other financial information:						
EPS (before extraordinary items)	($2.03)	($2.04)	$1.92	($1.08)	($1.44)	($1.42)

EXHIBIT 6 *(concluded)*

	AT&T 1992	AT&T 1991	AT&T 1990
Operating revenues:			
Telecommunications services	$39,580	$38,805	$38,263
Telecom. products and system:			
Telecommunications network products and systems	$7,711	$7,490	$7,303
Computer products and systems	$3,433	$3,667	$4,120
Communications products	$3,098	$2,852	$2,837
Microelectric products	$2,231	$1,932	$1,864
Total telecommunication network products and systems	$16,473	$15,941	$16,124
Rentals and other services	$6,957	$6,959	$6,993
Financial services and leasing	$1,894	$1,384	$811
Total operating revenues	$64,904	$63,089	$62,191
Operating expenses:			
Access and interconnection costs	$18,132	$18,395	$18,572
Other telecom. service costs	$7,135	$6,881	$7,061
Network products and system costs	$9,846	$9,134	$9,228
Rental costs	$3,287	$3,344	$3,377
Financial service costs	$1,310	$1,071	$645
Total operating expenses	$39,710	$38,825	$38,883
Operating income	$25,194	$24,264	$23,308
Other expenses:			
Selling, general, and administration	$15,950	$16,220	$14,782
R&D expenses	$2,911	$3,114	$2,935
Provision for business restructuring	$64	$3,572	$95
Total other expenses	$18,925	$22,906	$17,812
Net income	$6,269	$1,358	$5,469
Other financial information:			
EPS (before extraordinary items)	$2.86	$0.40	$2.42
Debt ratio	46.10%	48.90%	47.60%
Return to equity	21.10%	3.10%	19.70%

SOURCE: Company 10K and annual reports.

	MCI 1992	MCI 1991	MCI 1990
Operating revenues:			
Telecommunication services	$10,562	$9,491	$8,454
	—	—	—
	—	—	—
	—	—	—
	—	—	—
	—	—	—
	—	—	—
	—	—	—
Total operating revenues	$10,562	$9,491	$8,454
Operating expenses:			
Telecommunications expense	$5,684	$5,112	$4,462
	—	—	—
	—	—	—
	—	—	—
	—	—	—
Total operating expenses	$5,684	$5,112	$4,462
Operating income	$4,878	$4,379	$3,992
Other expenses:			
Sales, operation, and general	$2,794	$2,512	$2,079
Depreciation	$873	$776	$743
Network digitization	—	—	$550
Interest expense	$248	$243	$180
Total other expenses	$3,915	$3,531	$3,552
Net income	$963	$848	$440
Other financial information:			
EPS (before extraordinary items)	$2.21	$2.01	$1.06
Debt ratio	39.00%	41.30%	40.70%
Return to equity	11.90%	11.30%	12.80%

	Sprint (including acquisition of Centel) 1992	1991	1990
Operating revenues:			
Long-distance services	$5,658	$5,388	$5,065
Local communication services	$3,862	$3,754	$3,674
Wireless services	$ 322	$ 242	$ 182
Other businesses	$ 863		
Intercompany revenues	($ 285)	($ 276)	($ 262)
	—	—	—
	—	—	—
	—	—	—
	—	—	—
	—	—	—
Total operating revenues	$10,420	$9,933	$9,470
Operating expenses:			
Long-distance access charges	$2,575	$2,457	$2,357
Other long-distance expenses	$3,083	$2,636	$2,560
Local service expenses	$3,023	$2,914	$2,804
Wireless services	$325	$253	$208
Other operating expenses	$201	$488	$496
Total operating expenses	$9,207	$8,748	$8,425
Operating income	$1,213	$1,185	$1,045
Other income (expenses):			
Interest expense	($511)	($548)	($533)
Gain from dispositions and sales	$81	$75	($18)
Other income (expense), net	($5)	($36)	$13
Total other expenses	($435)	($509)	($538)
Net income	$778	$676	$508
Other financial information:			
EPS (before extraordinary items)	$1.46	$1.41	$1.08

The words of Robert Allen, AT&T's chairman, provide a picture of the vision AT&T has been ardently championing: "Wireless communications is a business we invented, and it's a growing business. We know how to build the systems to make it work—we sell those—and we know how to build devices to put on the end of it. We know how to make the network work on a nationwide seamless basis. That was Craig McCaw's vision, and that's our joint vision together."[7] By using its long distance system and network intelligence, coupled with the McCaw cellular capabilities, AT&T is moving toward being able to provide that service.

Even without the seamless vision, AT&T acquisition makes sense from both a defensive and offensive position. Heavy communication users constitute the bulk of cellular subscribers, and also generate heavy long distance traffic. Most of McCaw's subscribers are in major cities and about two thirds of all domestic long distance calls originate or terminate in the top 25 U.S. cities. Defensively, it makes sense for AT&T to get in front of this long distance traffic pattern and subscriber base, or risk losing it to a competitor like MCI acting as the long distance carrier for a company like McCaw. Offensively, the move makes sense because it enables AT&T to potentially elude the local access charges, as well as creating a captive market for the extensive equipment needs projected by McCaw to upgrade and expand its system.

AT&T's purchase of McCaw was just one part, albeit a major one, of its acquisition strategy over the past five years (see Exhibit 7 for a summary of AT&T's recent acquisitions). The company has made over 20 acquisitions in that time frame, with the acquisitions of McCaw and EO Inc./Go Corporation having the most direct relationship to the wireless industry. The acquisition of EO/Go fits into the seamless vision as these companies hope to be able to offer equipment that combines the messaging, paging, data transfer, and voice communication that currently is provided by separate devices. AT&T also expects to profit on the equipment end as it has developed a chip, called Hobbit, that will work with the new communicators. In addition to EO/Go, three of Japan's leading consumer electronics firms (Matsushita, NEC, and Toshiba Corp.) have agreed to use the Hobbit chip in their personal communicators, and NEC will build Hobbit under license from AT&T.

AT&T has been placing bets on almost every segment of both the wireline and wireless telecommunications area. The one area it has shown little interest in is the content side of telecommunications. As Robert Allen stated:

> We don't have any knowledge of the content area. It is not a core competency of ours. We are trying to build relationships with content people, but as a network provider, as a host technology platform to allow them to get their products to whatever customers they want to reach. So content is not an issue for us, it is not an interest of ours, and we don't have any talents there. It is just not in our culture, they are just a different breed of people to deal with.

Response from the RBOCs

The announced partnership was not taken lightly by AT&T's competitors. The regional Bell operating companies (RBOCs) called for an investigation by the FCC of the proposed agreement. The companies argued that this violated the prohibition against AT&T reentering the local exchange business. The partnership skirts that limit because the conditions tendered on the 1984 breakup of AT&T did not explicitly include wireless communications traffic. In their statement the Bells contended that the alliance "would create a dominant nationwide vertically integrated telecommunications service company." The Baby Bells also argue that given the efforts by AT&T, they should be allowed to offer long-distance service (which is currently prohibited under the same breakup agreement).

AT&T's response was that it was not interested in the RBOCs' local exchange business, or as Craig McCaw stated: "We're not trying to take their gold; we're trying to mine platinum. Why fight over their low-margin, local-exchange business; we're after the value-added, high-margin mobile services that will give people communications flexibility."

The breakup of the Bell system set up a delicate balance between AT&T and the Baby Bells—they are each other's largest customers. Under the agreement, the Baby Bells cannot charge companies differing rates for local-exchange service due to volume. The RBOCs gain about one-third of their revenues from access charges from the long-distance carriers. With the potential for wireless transmission to bypass the local exchange requirement, and the growth of the unregulated competitive access providers in the high-traffic, high-revenue

[7]From an interview in *Upside,* 1993.

EXHIBIT 7 American Telephone & Telegraph Co. Alliances

The Following is a Partial List of Recent AT&T Acquisition, Investment, and Partnership Activity
By John Ochwat

Acquisitions

McCaw Cellular Communications Corp. If approved, AT&T's acquisition of McCaw would be the fifth largest takeover in U.S. history. AT&T would gain a number of benefits from the deal, including a better avenue for pursuing wireless communications (which would subsequently benefit its efforts at marketing its personal communicators), and cost reductions if cellular customers bypass the Baby Bells and make long-distance calls directly.

NCR Corp. AT&T's takeover of NCR in 1990 worked toward a couple of goals: one was to link AT&T's experience in networks with NCR's worldwide installed base of cash registers and ATMs; the other was to buy entry into the computer business, NCR's core business. Reportedly, NCR and AT&T have launched more than 250 R&D projects, in a variety of areas.

Paradyne AT&T acquired Paradyne, a data communications equipment company, in 1989.

Eaton Financial Also in 1989, AT&T acquired Eaton Financial, an equipment financing unit.

Teradata Corp. AT&T acquired Teradata, a massively parallel computer manufacturer, for $500 million in 1992.

Shayne Communications In April 1993, AT&T acquired Shayne, a U.K.-based manufacturer of cordless telephones.

EO Inc./Go Corp. AT&T previously had a stake in both of these companies, but has since bought majority control and merged them into a single company. EO makes pen-based personal communicators, and Go is the developer of PenPoint, a mobile operating system for personal communicators. By merging the two, AT&T hopes to license the combined technologies as an open platform for other developers working on personal communicators.

Equity Investments

General Magic Inc. Equity partner AT&T is building an enhanced network service based on General Magic's Telescript communications language. AT&T is also an equity partner in GM to build personal communicators with interactive network technology. In addition, GM will likely work with EO and Go on network technology for personal communicators.

The 3DO Co. AT&T owns a 6% stake in 3DO and licenses the hardware of 3DO's Interactive Multiplayer. AT&T plans to manufacture and market an interactive version of the player.

Compagnie Industriali Riunite In 1989 AT&T gave up on its investment in Olivetti, and exchanged it for 17% of C.I.R., its parent company.

Italtel In 1989 AT&T exchanged $135 million and a 20% stake in AT&T Network Systems International for 20% of Italtel, an Italian communications equipment maker.

Spectrum Holobyte In an early foray into computer games, AT&T invested in virtual reality developer Spectrum Holobyte in 1992.

Sierra Network In late July, AT&T acquired a 20% stake in Sierra Network, a wholly owned subsidiary of Sierra On-Line Inc. Sierra Network is an online service that provides interactive computer games and entertainment to subscribers.

PF Magic AT&T took an undisclosed stake in this entertainment software company, based in San Francisco. AT&T will market a device developed by PF Magic which allows people to play video games over telephone lines.

Knowledge Adventure Inc. In August 1993, AT&T invested in Knowledge Adventure, a multimedia educational software company based in La Crescenta, California.

Partnerships

Zenith Electronics Corp. AT&T is partnering with Zenith to develop video compression technology, primarily for HDTV.

Viacom Inc. Viacom is going to provide technology (mainly ATM switches) for AT&T's test of interactive consumer video services via Viacom's two-way cable system in Castro Valley, California.

TCI and US West This viewer-controlled cable television venture will test consumer demand for interactive television services being conducted in Englewood, Colorado.

General Instrument Corp. General Instrument customized the settop boxes for the Englewood, Colorado, trial.

Sega Corp. In early July, AT&T entered into a joint venture with Sega that will enable players to compete against opponents over AT&T's phone lines.

Compression Labs Inc. AT&T is partnering with Compression Labs to develop a settop box to deliver movies and assorted video services to televisions over phone lines.

Bell Atlantic AT&T will supply asymmetrical digital subscriber line (ADSL) technology for a Bell Atlantic test of video over twisted-copper lines. The partnership will also conduct a test of voice, video, and data transmissions using ADSL technology.

Southwestern Bell AT&T and Southwestern Bell will research "The Intelligent Home" of the future, which includes a prototype ISDN Personal Video System from AT&T.

GTE Corp. AT&T will develop digital switching technology with GTE and supply GTE with ATM switching technology for a video and data services trial in the Dallas–Fort Worth area.

US West The partnership will test a distance learning network based on AT&T's ATM technology.

SOURCE: *Upside Magazine*

EXHIBIT 8

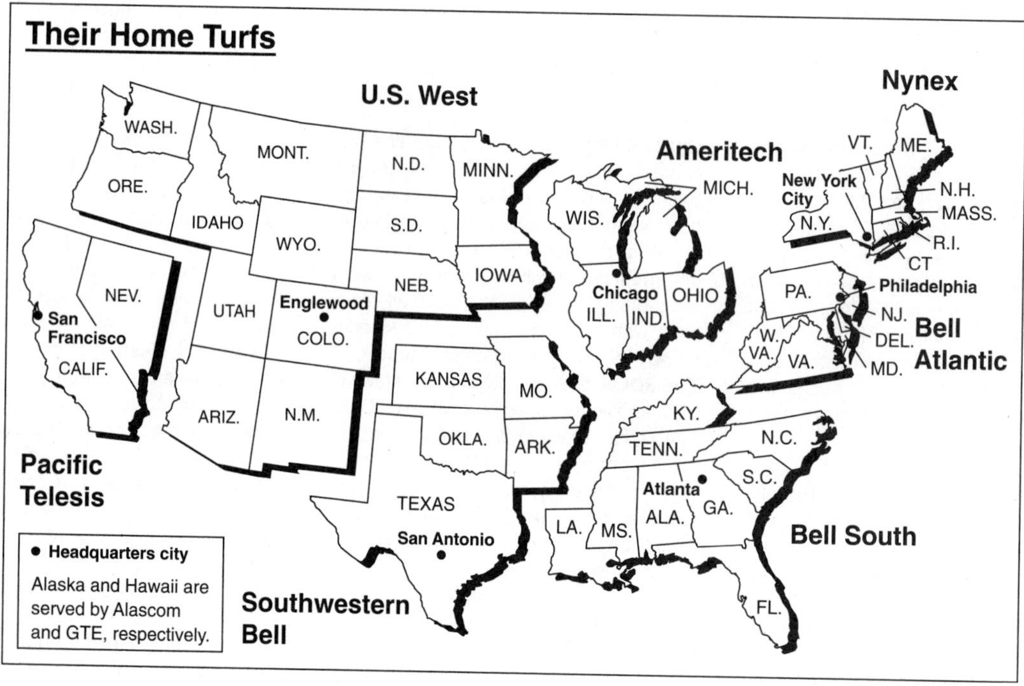

SOURCE: *The New York Times.*

markets, the RBOCs look to generate revenues from other sources (see Exhibit 8 for the geographical areas for which the RBOCs provide local-access service). Wireless transmission is seen as one opportunity to do this, and the Baby Bells have been aggressive in extending their cellular markets, both domestically and internationally. One of the most aggressive of the RBOCs has been Bell Atlantic.

Bell Atlantic has 229 wireless cell sites (adding 33 in the last year), and expects to have 60 microcells in operation by the end of the year (based on a first trial using Union Station in Washington, D.C.). The company has 40 Mobile Phone Center stores, and agreements with 750 retail outlets to sell their products and services. Its cellular phone company, Bell Atlantic Mobile, services 15 states and more than 850,000 customers. Bell Atlantic has also formed a new company—Bell Atlantic Personal Communications—headed by the former FCC chairman Mark Fowler, to search out promising personal communications wireless opportunities.[8]

[8]Personal communication from Irving B. Taylor Jr., area manager, Bell Atlantic.

To extend its wireless prospects, Bell Atlantic acquired a 42 percent interest in Iusacell S.A. de C.V. (Iusacell), the second largest telecommunications provider in Mexico, agreeing to invest up to $1.04 billion. Iusacell is privately owned and provides cellular service to four of Mexico's nine cellular regions, covering 70 percent of the country's 89 million customers, including Mexico City. The Iusacell system currently has over 100,000 wireless subscribers. Mexico's cellular customers average over 200 minutes per month per customer in 1992; due to limited terrestrial based line availability (less than 8 lines per 100 people), the customers are more likely to use their cellular phone as the principal communications service.

Bell Atlantic is also a participant in the Mobilink Alliance (announced March 1, 1993). The alliance is made up of 15 cellular operators, including 6 of the 7 Baby Bells, and its stated purpose is to create a nationwide cellular network, ending the need for the use of a special code or other methodology when a receiver is outside of the home service area. Using new call-switching software, member companies will alert the system of user locations, and calls will be transferred anywhere along the Mobilink system. The members offer cellular service that covers 83 percent of the population in the United States and Canada, and operates in 161 of the 200 top markets.

While the talks concerning the alliance were said to predate the AT&T–McCaw agreement, members make no secret that one of the prime goals of the alliance is to counter that deal. McCaw's Cellular One service is usually used by the A-side carriers, while the members of the Mobilink alliance are generally the B-side carriers. However, some of the cellular companies are in both camps. For example, Pacific Telesis Group owns cellular systems jointly with McCaw and does business under the Cellular One banner. US West owns cellular systems outside its local territory and will find itself competing against the Mobilink name used by the local phone company's cellular system. Wholehearted competition may be tempered by the cross alliances in place.

In addition to its wireless activity, Bell Atlantic launched an attempt to gain new markets through a $12 billion acquisition of the cable company Tele-Communications Inc. (TCI). TCI is the largest U.S. cable carrier, with 10 million customers in 49 states, and is in 57 of the top 100 U.S. markets. While the primary driver behind the planned acquisition was the acquisition of entertainment and multimedia access, some speculated that Bell Atlantic also hoped to use the cable infrastructure to implement a PCS system cost-efficiently and to use wireless as a means to provide revenues to buffer the high cost of installing the digital video to the home systems that are being proposed by the cable companies. The potential TCI–Bell Atlantic deal was announced in October 1993, and was killed in February 1994. Both companies offered various reasons for the collapse of the deal. Among the explanations were the decline in Bell Atlantic's stock price (from $68.825 at the time of the deal to the low 50s at the time the deal was called off), cultural differences (between the more structured former monopoly Bell Atlantic and the more entrepreneurial TCI), and the 7 percent decrease of cable subscriber rates by the FCC, which decreased the cash flow prospects of TCI by approximately 15 percent (or $144 million a year). Due to the changing fortunes of both companies, the deal had been renegotiated four times, with increasing complexities of stock swaps and dividend formulas, until it finally fell through.

The failure of the TCI–Bell Atlantic deal has created a more cautious merger and acquisition environment in the telecommunications arena. However, RBOCs are continuing to make significant investments in the cellular industry. At the same time the TCI–Bell Atlantic deal was being called off, Southwestern Bell agreed to acquire Associated Communications Corp.'s domestic cellular business for $552 million in stock. The acquisition gives Southwestern Bell access to upstate New York markets. See Exhibit 9 for a summary of RBOC offensive and defensive efforts in the telecommunications sector.

Nonvoice Wireless Transmission[9]

The immediate major impact of the AT&T acquisition of McCaw centers on the wireline and wireless voice transmission segment, but an equally important segment which may be impacted is data and nonvoice information. The wireless data transmission segment is still in its infancy with less than 1 percent of users presently transmitting data over cellular circuits. However, data usage growth is expected to exceed that of pure voice service. If wireless data revenues grow at a rate similar to cellular voice transmission, the wireless data segment would generate approximately $3 billion in revenues by 1997. In the wireline area data already accounts for one-half of the transmitted bits in the network, and 20 percent of the profits, with data income growing six times as fast as voice.[10] Wireless data consumers are expected to pay monthly transmission fees of $15 to $30 per month, plus application, software, and hardware purchases to support the data transmission. In 1992 mobile data users (70,000 users) averaged $150 revenues per month, while fixed wireless data users (13,000 users) averaged $40 revenues per month. Fixed users are point-of-sales devices and vending machines equipped with "management information systems," and mobile users include field sales, professional business users, and fleet communication.

Two different types of transmission participants providing public wireless networks allow laptops and other computers to communicate over the airwaves. The first are the proprietary systems—like Ardis, run by Motorola and IBM, or RAM Mobile Data Network, run by RAM Broadcasting and BellSouth—that use SMR technology for transmission.

[9]This section benefited greatly from the insights of Les Vadasz, senior vice president, Intel Corporation.

[10]George Gilder, "The Death of Telephony," *The Economist.*

EXHIBIT 9 The Baby Bells: What They're Doing, Where They're Going

Ameritech

Recent deals None.
Attack capability None yet.
Defense strategy for home turf Cutting costs, spending heavily on fiber optics to support core telephone business. Wants to enter video business, but hasn't decided yet on time frame or strategy.
Outlook Very vulnerable. Its big urban territories are already under attack, and it has no cable partners with which to fire back.

Bell Atlantic

Recent deals Buying Tele-Communications Inc. in $26 billion stock deal. Also spent $1 billion for 46% of Iusacell Group, Mexico's second-largest cellular company.
Attack capability Excluding cable systems within its own region, which will not be acquired, it will have more than 400 cable systems in every state except Alaska and extensive ownership of popular cable programming. Spending roughly $5 billion over five years to upgrade systems for two-way voice and data services.
Defense strategy Has been spending more than $2.2 billion annually on new technology; hopes to deliver video services through 20 top markets in five years.
Outlook Unmatched ability to raid other Bell territories. But dense and affluent markets in its region will come under attack as well.

Bell South

Recent deals Acquiring minority stake for $1.5 billion in QVC homeshopping network, which is seeking to buy Paramount Communications. Bought 22.5% of Prime Management, a cable company with 500,000 customers in Las Vegas, Houston and Chicago. Owns cellular properties in Latin America.
Attack capability Very limited. QVC and Paramount would provide programming.
Defense strategy No video strategy yet, but heavy spending on fiber optics in key cities to shore up telephone market for business customers.
Outlook Steady but unspectacular growth in region. Limited competition, due to heavy rural concentrations. Not much growth from invading other regions.

NYNEX

Recent deals Investing $1.2 billion for noncontrolling stake in Viacom Inc., the cable company.
Attack capability Limited. Viacom owns cable systems with 1 million subscribers and popular programming, not enough to make a dent in other territories.
Defense strategy Not yet announced. Expected to speed up spending on fiber optics and digital switching, but seeks state regulatory changes first.
Outlook Extremely vulnerable. Heavy competition looming; no major cable partner; high costs within region. But cable TV investments in Britain and Asia could bring hope.

Pacific Telesis

Recent deals None in cable. Spinning off its cellular properties as a separate company.
Attack capability None.
Defense strategy Fortress strategy. Spending extra $400 million annually to provide video services and defend key urban markets like Los Angeles, San Francisco, and San Diego.
Outlook Uncertain. Big California titles to come under heavy attack. Company still lacks a programming partner within region, and no ability to grab market share in other Bell territories.

Southwestern Bell

Recent deals Buying cable systems outside Washington for $650 million. Has bought numerous cellular systems outside its home base and a 10 percent stake in a Mexican phone company. Now third-largest cellular carrier in country.
Attack capability Limited, but believed on prowl for deals with Cox Enterprises and Cablevision Systems, the fourth- and fifth-largest cable TV operators, respectively.
Defense strategy Conservative, betting that large rural areas are insulated from imminent competition. Relatively slow fiber-optic installation, mainly directed at needs of big business.
Outlook Promising. Cellular purchases doing well, allowing company to rely less on traditional core telephone business. Competition on its home ground will be less acute, because so much territory is sparsely populated.

US West

Recent deals Invested $2.5 billion for 25.5% stake in Time Warner cable systems—the largest collection of cable systems after T.C.I. The two companies will invest $5 billion over five years to upgrade systems reaching 85% of customers.
Attack capability Formidable. Cable systems primarily clustered around urban markets, including 15 of top 50 metropolitan areas.
Defense strategy Recently announced a 25-year plan to extend fiber-optic network throughout its region, adding $500 million a year to its capital budget to wire 500,000 customers annually. Moving to shore up Denver and other cities first against expected competition from Bell Atlantic/T.C.I. and others.
Outlook Strong ability to raid other Bell territories. Heavy rural concentrations make much of region unattractive to new competitors, though Denver and Seattle are vulnerable.

SOURCE: *The New York Times.*

The second is the Cellular Digital Packet Data (CDPD), an open data transmission network which uses idle cellular channels to send packets of data without affecting voice quality. The proprietary SMR systems require proprietary send/receive equipment that broadcast data only over their networks. CDPD allows the addition of data transmission capability over the cellular network with low cost additions to the current cellular network.

From the viewpoint of computer users and developers, the implementation of wireless transmission was done in the opposite manner to meet their needs. The plethora of standards, analog transmission, geographical demarcation, and bandwidth limitations all hinder the attractiveness of wireless transmission among the computer segment. A wish list of wireless characteristics from the computer user perspective would include nationwide roaming (no change of frequency or equipment needed regardless of geographical location), one consistent nationwide transmission standard, in-building and out-building communication using the same frequency, all-digital network, transparent linkages between current E-mail and other internal communications with wireless transmissions, bandwidth on demand, and the ability to do file and video transfer and transmission. The current wireless options do not meet the bulk of computer users' needs. The current cellular transmission—based on analog technology—does not meet the reliability and speed requirements of computer data transmission.

With its acquisition of McCaw, AT&T acquires a principal proponent of CDPD. CDPD offers an intriguing solution, with the potential weakness that it relies on the availability of idle cellular bandwidth to send its packets of data. Given that much of the current cellular effort is to combat channel congestion, it is yet to be seen if this will work effectively in major traffic areas like the large metropolitan cities. However, if CDPD does work, it offers a relatively cost-effective way to offer data transmission with no additional bandwidth or capacity needed (eliminating the need for additional allocations by the FCC), and it is an inexpensive add-on to the current cellular network.

The PCS solution presents another unstandardized access method. PCN service under PCS, other than the advantages of digital technology from the start, provides little additional service to the computer user from current cellular. User-PCS (unlicensed PCS) does offer limited applicability to small-scale locations. The future use of microcells and picocells to cover buildings and building complexes in the PCS bandwidth will allow WLANs to offer shared computing, shared note taking, and mobile data entry in retail and industrial environments. These products will have to compete against wired LANs, which have an inherent advantage in that wire is cheaper, is less sensitive, and has greater capacity. However, one problem that may arise is that many buildings have such wire congestion that additional wire solutions may not be feasible.

Probably the biggest competitor to CDPD will be specialized mobile radio. SMR exhibits some advantages: it can offer nationwide roaming capability (currently offered by RAM Mobile Data Network, and in development to be offered by Ardis), has a consistent standard for the subscribed network, and is digital. SMR is constrained because it lacks the base station density that PCS-style systems would have, requiring more power for the transmissions. Importantly, SMR is the one wireless option in which the providers have experience transmitting data—via their current systems to report vending machine information, point of sale terminals, delivery person data updates, and restaurant systems. The data transmission options outside of CDPD, unlicensed PCS, and SMR (e.g., satellite data transmission) are still too untested to be incorporated into development efforts by software and hardware firms.

Despite the inherent problems, computer use offers an intriguing avenue of growth for wireless providers. With the expansion of current cellular via PCS, PCN, SMR, and satellite transmission, the availability of wireless voice service may outstrip demand. Wireless computer networks provide the promise of an untapped valuable resource, as well as an unsaturated market. The potential for people to be able to access remote databases more readily than they can reach their own hard disks or CD-ROM drives could have far-reaching impact on how information is processed and used. With reliable remote access, users can carry around in their hands a device that will provide them with the processing power and data storage capability of the largest and most powerful computer that they can connect—essentially free CPU and data storage. Thus, the option with the most current problems in providing wireless service—linking computers rather than people—may also be the most explosive in revenue growth and in the potential impact on how people do business. A major hurdle in making this a reality is that the computer sector would want a nationwide undifferentiated communications service (e.g., same standards, transmission frequencies, equipment necessary)—essentially a genetic transmission pipeline through which they decide which data should be transmitted and in what form. However, telecommunications companies want differentiated service, where they are value-added carriers and can lock customers into their particular transmission vehicle.

Motorola's Contrasting Vision

Motorola has an enviable position in the wireless equipment market. It is the dominant player in the paging, cellular phone, and noncomputer microprocessor segments. The company is Number 2 in cellular switching equipment provision with an approximately 22 percent market share behind AT&T, but relatively new entrants such as Ericsson and Northern Telecom have been gaining market share, primarily at the expense of Motorola. Cellular handset receivers and the microprocessing chips that they use account for 30 percent of Motorola's $14 billion sales and 35 percent of earnings (see Exhibit 10 for details of Motorola's revenues by segment and cellular equipment market share).[11] However, competition has been pushing the price of phones down 25 percent every year.

In contrast to the direction that AT&T has taken in its wireless strategy, Motorola has decided to place its bet on satellite cellular transmission. The company is gambling on the demand and feasibility of a global PCS system with the development of a low-orbit satellite system called Iridium. Iridium will use satellites to send signals directly to or from any telephone to a small handheld unit manufactured by Motorola. The system will be seamless, without boundaries, and it will provide true global cellular service. Motorola has spent eight years and over $100 million developing Iridium, the low-orbit sys-

[11]"Pre-emptive Strike," *Financial World,* September 14, 1993.

EXHIBIT 10 Vendor Market Share Data (1992) MSA Market 1-306

Vendor	Number of Wireless Markets	Number of Nonwireless Markets	Total Markets	Total Wireless Markets	Total Nonwireless Pops	Total Pops
AT&T	138	61	199	122,563,575	36,238,260	158,801,835
Motorola	79	52	131	44,975,710	37,708,405	82,684,115
Northern Telecom	48	73	121	15,730,054	25,914,574	41,644,628
Ericsson	0	83	83	0	86,528,688	86,528,688
Novatel	19	14	33	4,284,850	2,003,555	6,288,405
Astronet	14	9	23	4,352,460	1,499,079	5,851,539
NEC	5	1	6	124,286	747,830	872,116
Plexsys	1	0	1	128,287	0	128,287
Total	304	293	597	192,159,222	190,640,391	382,799,613

Total MSA Pops by Vendor

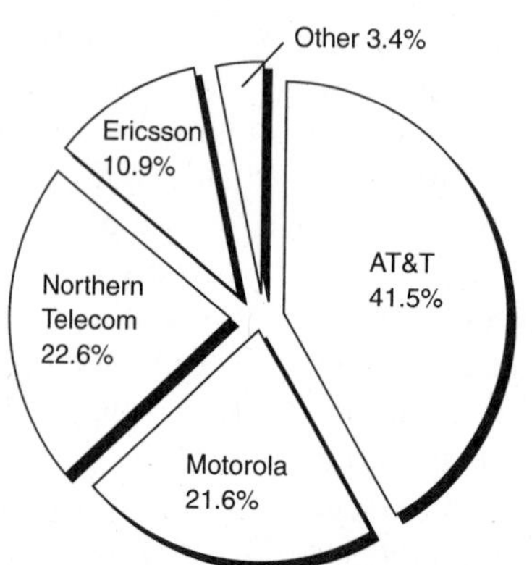

tem of 66 satellites scheduled to offer wireless phone service by 1998, and will spend approximately $240 million through project completion. The total project is expected to cost $3.4 billion, and Motorola has garnered $800 million of first-round financing from over a dozen companies, including Sprint, BCE Canada, Italy's telephone holding company Stet, and a Japanese group including Daini Denden, Mitsubishi, and Kyocera. After the first round, Motorola will own 34 percent of the project, and by the time the full $3.4 billion is raised their ownership will fall to 15 percent. In addition, Motorola will get a five-year, $3 billion maintenance contract. An Iridium-handled call will cost approximately $3 a minute and the handset will initially cost $3,000. The satellite effort hopes to have a million subscribers by the year 2002, and attract 2 percent of the projected worldwide wireless customer market of 200 million. Currently there are 28 million wireless subscribers worldwide. Iridium's plan depends on the needs of global executives who require instant worldwide access.

If Motorola is successful in its Iridium gambit, it will be able to provide a seamless wireless transmission vehicle for both voice and data transmission. Coupled with its expertise in paging and microprocessor technology and production, the company might be able to offer wireless information transmission products that meet many of the wish-list items of the computer industry segment. One caution is that even if the effort is successful, developers may still be hesitant because users would be locked into Motorola technology.

In addition to its satellite push, Motorola has also been active in the SMR segment of the wireless industry. Motorola has been swapping its radio-service licenses and networks for a minority stake in SMR providers. The company exchanged rights to provide wireless phone and data services in 21 states in exchange for a 20 percent stake in Nextel (the 20 percent is worth approximately $1.8 billion). Motorola made similar agreements with other SMR providers such as Dial Page and CenCall Communications in which the company swapped 42 percent of its dispatch licenses for approximately $1.2 billion in stock. Motorola took a 30 percent stake in CenCall and a 34 percent stake in Dial Page. Nextel has spent more than $1 billion in late 1993 buying dispatch services around the country, and now holds licenses in each of the 10 largest metropolitan areas in the nation. Motorola will also provide Nextel with $260 million in new financing.

Going Forward

The major companies in the telecommunications industry—AT&T, Motorola, and the RBOCs—all seem to have differing strategies for gaining a role in future wireless transmission. While the three industry players may have similar views on what is technically possible, they differ in current position, number of installed wireless bases, relative profitability, importance to the core business, and reason for participation in this industry segment. The transmission of voice is the dominant application of wireless, but data transmission and the bundling of wireless capability with other services may loom larger in the future.

Reading II–8
Profiting from Technological Innovation: Implications for Integration, Collaboration, Licensing, and Public Policy

*David J. Teece**

This paper attempts to explain why innovating firms often fail to obtain significant economic returns from an innovation, while customers, imitators, and other industry participants benefit. Business strategy—particularly as it relates to the firm's decision to integrate and collaborate—is shown to be an important factor. The paper demonstrates that when imitation is easy, markets don't work well, and the profits from innovation may accrue to the owners of certain complementary assets, rather than to the developers

---

*I thank Raphael Amit, Harvey Brooks, Chris Chapin, Therese Flaherty, Richard Gilbert, Heather Haveman, Mel Horwitch, David Hulbert, Carl Jacobsen, Michael Porter, Gary Pisano, Richard Rumelt, Raymond Vernon and Sidney Winter for helpful discussions relating to the subject matter of this paper. Three anonymous referees also provided valuable criticisms. I gratefully acknowledge the financial support of the National Science Foundation under grant no. SRS-8410556 to the Center for Research in Management, University of California–Berkeley. Earlier versions of this paper were presented at a National Academy of Engineering Symposium titled "World Technologies and National Sovereignty," February 1986, and at a conference on innovation at the University of Venice, March 1986.

Research Policy 15 (1986), pp. 285–305.

of the intellectual property. This speaks to the need, in certain cases, for the innovating firm to establish a prior position in these complementary assets. The paper also indicates that innovators with new products and processes which provide value to consumers may sometimes be so ill positioned in the market that they necessarily will fail. The analysis provides a theoretical foundation for the proposition that manufacturing often matters, particularly to innovating nations. Innovating firms without the requisite manufacturing and related capacities may die, even though they are the best at innovation. Implications for trade policy and domestic economic policy are examined.

EXHIBIT 1 Explaining the Distribution of the Profits from Innovation

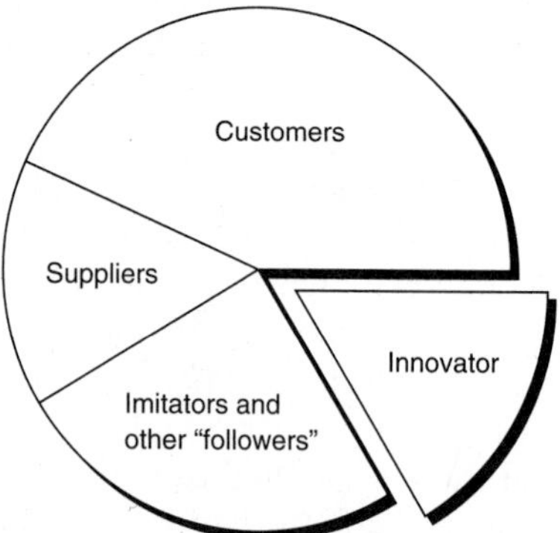

What determines the share of profits captured by the innovator?

Introduction

It is quite common for innovators—those firms which are first to commercialize a new product or process in the market—to lament the fact that competitors/imitators have profited more from the innovation than the firm first to commercialize it! Since it is often held that being first to market is a source of strategic advantage, the clear existence and persistence of this phenomenon may appear perplexing if not troubling. The aim of this article is to explain why a fast second or even a slow third might outperform the innovator. The message is particularly pertinent to those science- and engineering-driven companies that harbor the mistaken illusion that developing new products which meet customer needs will ensure fabulous success. It may possibly do so for the product, but not for the innovator.

In this paper, a framework is offered which identifies the factors which determine who wins from innovation: the firm which is first to market, follower firms, or firms that have related capabilities that the innovator needs. The follower firms may or may not be imitators in the narrow sense of the term, although they sometimes are. The framework appears to have utility for explaining the share of the profits from innovation accruing to the innovator compared to its followers and suppliers (see Exhibit 1), as well as for explaining a variety of interfirm activities such as joint ventures, coproduction agreements, cross distribution arrangements, and technology licensing. Implications for strategic management, public policy, and international trade and investment are then discussed.

The Phenomenon

Exhibit 2 presents a simplified taxonomy of the possible outcomes from innovation. Quadrant 1 represents positive outcomes for the innovator. A first-to-market advantage is translated into a sustained competitive advantage which either creates a new earnings stream or enhances an existing one. Quadrant 4 and its corollary quadrant 2 are the ones which are the focus of this paper.

The EMI CAT scanner is a classic case of the phenomenon to be investigated.[1] By the early 1970s, the U.K. firm Electrical Musical Industries (EMI) Ltd. was in a variety of product lines including phonographic records, movies, and advanced electronics. EMI had developed high-resolution TVs in the 1930s, pioneered airborne radar during World War II, and developed the United Kingdom's first all solid-state computers in 1952.

In the late 1960s Godfrey Houndsfield, an EMI senior research engineer, engaged in pattern recognition research which resulted in his displaying a scan of a pig's brain. Subsequent clinical work established that computerized axial tomography (CAT) was viable for generating cross-sectional views of the human body, the greatest advance in radiology since the discovery of X rays in 1895.

[1]The EMI story is summarized in Michael Martin, *Managing Technological Innovation and Entrepreneurship* Reston Publishing Company, (Reston, VA, 1984).

EXHIBIT 2 Taxonomy of Outcomes from the Innovation Process

	Innovator	Follower-Imitator
Win	1 • Pilkington (Float Glass) • G.D. Searle (NutraSweet) • DuPont (Teflon)	2 • IBM (personal computer) • Matsushita (VHS video recorders) • Seiko (quartz watch)
Lose	4 • RC Cola (diet cola) • EMI (scanner) • Bowmar (pocket calculator) • Xerox (office computer) • DeHavilland (Comet)	3 • Kodak (instant photography) • Northrup (F20) • DEC (personal computer)

While EMI was initially successful with its CAT scanner, within 6 years of its introduction into the United States in 1973 the company had lost market leadership, and by the eighth year had dropped out of the CT scanner business. Other companies successfully dominated the market, though they were late entrants, and are still profiting in the business today.

Other examples include RC Cola, a small beverage company that was the first to introduce cola in a can, and the first to introduce diet cola. Both Coca Cola and Pepsi followed almost immediately and deprived RC of any significant advantage from its innovation. Bowmar, which introduced the pocket calculator, was not able to withstand competition from Texas Instruments, Hewlett Packard, and others, and went out of business. Xerox failed to succeed with its entry into the office computer business, even though Apple succeeded with the MacIntosh which contained many of Xerox's key product ideas, such as the mouse and icons. The de Havilland Comet saga has some of the same features. The Comet I jet was introduced into the commercial airline business two years or so before Boeing introduced the 707, but de Havilland failed to capitalize on its substantial early advantage. MITS introduced the first personal computer, the Altair, experienced a burst of sales, then slid quietly into oblivion.

If there are innovators who lose, there must be followers/imitators who win. A classic example is IBM with its PC, a great success since the time it was introduced in 1981. Neither the architecture nor components embedded in the IBM PC were considered advanced when introduced; nor was the way the technology was packaged a significant departure from then-current practice. Yet the IBM PC was fabulously successful and established MS-DOS as the leading operating system for 16-bit PCs. By the end of 1984, IBM had shipped over 500,000 PCs, and many considered that it had irreversibly eclipsed Apple in the PC industry.

Profiting from Innovation: Basic Building Blocks

In order to develop a coherent framework within which to explain the distribution of outcomes illustrated in Exhibit 2, three fundamental building blocks must first be put in place: the appropriability regime, complementary assets, and the dominant design paradigm.

Regimes of Appropriability

A regime of appropriability refers to the environmental factors, excluding firm and market structure, that govern an innovator's ability to capture the profits generated by an innovation. The most important dimensions of such a regime are the nature of the technology and the efficacy of legal mechanisms of protection (Exhibit 3).

It has long been known that patents do not work in practice as they do in theory. Rarely, if ever, do patents confer perfect appropriability, although they do afford considerable protection on new chemical products and rather simple mechanical inventions. Many patents can be "invented around" at modest costs. They are especially ineffective at protecting process innovations. Often patents provide little protection because the legal requirements for upholding their validity or for proving their infringement are high.

In some industries, particularly where the innovation is embedded in processes, trade secrets are a viable alternative to patents. Trade secret protection

EXHIBIT 3 Appropriability Regime: Key Dimensions

- Legal instruments
  - —Patents
  - —Copyrights
  - —Trade secrets
- Nature of technology
  - —Product
  - —Process
  - —Tacit
  - —Codified

is possible, however, only if a firm can put its product before the public and still keep the underlying technology secret. Usually only chemical formulas and industrial-commercial processes (e.g., cosmetics and recipes) can be protected as trade secrets after they're out on the market.

The degree to which knowledge is tacit or codified also affects ease of imitation. Codified knowledge is easier to transmit and receive, and is more exposed to industrial espionage and the like. Tacit knowledge by definition is difficult to articulate, and so transfer is hard unless those who possess the know-how in question can demonstrate it to others.[2] Survey research indicates that methods of appropriability vary markedly across industries, and probably within industries as well.[3]

The property rights environment within which a firm operates can thus be classified according to the nature of the technology and the efficacy of the legal system to assign and protect intellectual property. While a gross simplification, a dichotomy can be drawn between environments in which the appropriability regime is "tight" (technology is relatively easy to protect) and "weak" (technology is almost impossible to protect). Examples of the former include the formula for Coca Cola syrup; an example of the latter would be the Simplex algorithm in linear programming.

The Dominant Design Paradigm

It is commonly recognized that there are two stages in the evolutionary developments of a given branch of a science: the preparadigmatic stage when there is no single, generally accepted conceptual treatment of the phenomenon in a field of study, and the paradigmatic stage which begins when a body of theory appears to have passed the canons of scientific acceptability. The emergence of a dominant paradigm signals scientific maturity and the acceptance of agreed upon standards by which what has been referred to as normal scientific research can proceed. These standards remain in force unless or until the paradigm is overturned. Revolutionary science is what overturns normal science, as when Copernicus's theories of astronomy overturned Ptolemy's in the 17th century.

Abernathy and Utterback[4] and Dosi[5] have provided a treatment of the technological evolution of an industry which appears to parallel Kuhnian notions of scientific evolution.[6] In the early stages of industry development, product designs are fluid, manufacturing processes are loosely and adaptively organized, and generalized capital is used in production. Competition amongst firms manifests itself in competition amongst designs, which are markedly different from each other. This might be called the preparadigmatic stage of an industry.

At some point in time, and after considerable trial and error in the marketplace, one design or a narrow class of designs begins to emerge as the more promising. Such a design must be able to meet a whole set of user needs in a relatively complete fashion. The Model T Ford, the IBM 360, and the Douglas DC-3 are examples of dominant designs in the automobile, computer, and aircraft industry, respectively.

Once a dominant design emerges, competition shifts to price and away from design. Competitive success then shifts to a whole new set of variables. Scale and learning become much more important, and specialized capital gets deployed as incumbents seek to lower unit costs through exploiting economies of scale and learning. Reduced uncertainty over product design provides an opportunity to amortize specialized long-lived investments.

Innovation is not necessarily halted once the dominant design emerges; as Clark[7] points out, it can occur lower down in the design hierarchy. For instance, a "v" cylinder configuration emerged in automobile engine blocks during the 1930s with the emergence of the Ford V-8 engine. Niches were quickly found for it. Moreover, once the product design stabilizes, there is likely to be a surge of process innovation as producers attempt to lower production costs for the new product (see Exhibit 4).

The Abernathy–Utterback framework does not characterize all industries. It seems more suited to

[2]D. J. Teece, "The Market for Know-how and the Efficient International Transfer of Technology," *Annals of the American Academy of Political and Social Science,* November 1981.

[3]R. Levin, A. Klevorick, N. Nelson, and S. Winter, "Survey Research on R&D Appropriability and Technological Opportunity," unpublished manuscript, Yale University, 1984.

[4]W. J. Abernathy and J. M. Utterback, "Patterns of Industrial Innovation," *Technology Review* 80(7) (January/July 1978), 40–47.

[5]G. Dosi, "Technological Paradigms and Technological Trajectories," *Research Policy* 11 (1982), 147–62.

[6]Thomas Kuhn, *The Structure of Scientific Revolutions,* 2nd ed. (University of Chicago Press, Chicago, 1970).

[7]Kim B. Clark, "The Interaction of Design Hierarchies and Market Concepts in Technological Evolution," *Research Policy* 14 (1985), 235–51.

EXHIBIT 4 Innovation over the Product/Industry Life Cycle

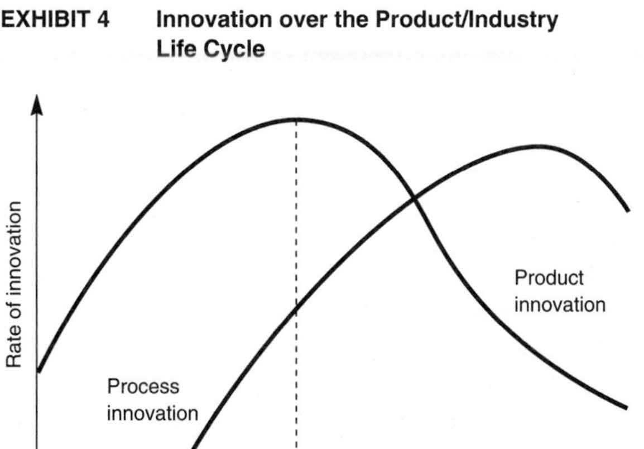

mass markets where consumer tastes are relatively homogeneous. It would appear to be less characteristic of small niche markets where the absence of scale and learning economies attaches much less of a penalty to multiple designs. In these instances, generalized equipment will be employed in production.

The existence of a dominant design watershed is of great significance to the distribution of profits between innovator and follower. The innovator may have been responsible for the fundamental scientific breakthroughs as well as the basic design of the new product. However, if imitation is relatively easy, imitators may enter the fray, modifying the product in important ways, yet relying on the fundamental designs pioneered by the innovator. When the game of musical chairs stops and a dominant design emerges, the innovator might well end up positioned disadvantageously relative to a follower. Hence, when imitation is possible and occurs coupled with design modification before the emergence of a dominant design, followers have a good chance of having their modified product anointed as the industry standard, often to the great disadvantage of the innovator.

Complementary Assets

Let the unit of analysis be an innovation. An innovation consists of certain technical knowledge about how to do things better than the existing state of the art. Assume that the know-how in question is partly codified and partly tacit. In order for such know-how to generate profits, it must be sold or utilized in some fashion in the market.

In almost all cases, the successful commercialization of an innovation requires that the know-how in question be utilized in conjunction with other capabilities or assets. Services such as marketing, competitive manufacturing, and after-sales support are almost always needed. These services are often obtained from complementary assets which are specialized. For example, the commercialization of a new drug is likely to require the dissemination of information over a specialized information channel. In some cases, as when the innovation is systemic, the complementary assets may be other parts of a system. For instance, computer hardware typically requires specialized software, both for the operating system and for applications. Even when an innovation is autonomous, as with plug-compatible components, certain complementary capabilities or assets will be needed for successful commercialization. Exhibit 5 summarizes this schematically.

Whether the assets required for least-cost production and distribution are specialized to the innovation turns out to be important in the development presented below. Accordingly, the nature of complementary assets is explained in some detail. Exhibit 6 differentiates between complementary assets which are generic, specialized, and cospecialized.

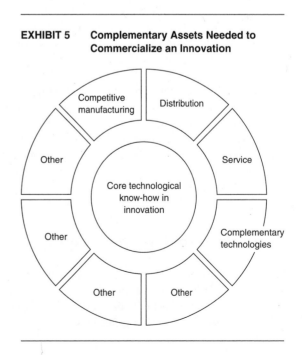

EXHIBIT 5 Complementary Assets Needed to Commercialize an Innovation

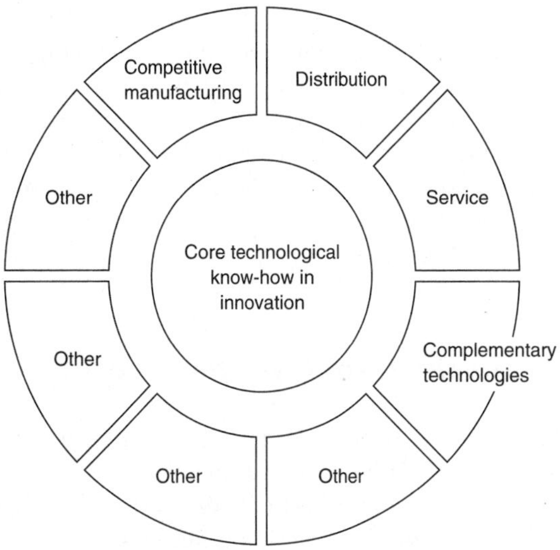

Competitive manufacturing
Distribution
Other
Service
Core technological know-how in innovation
Other
Complementary technologies
Other
Other

EXHIBIT 6 Complementary Assets: Generic, Specialized, and Cospecialized

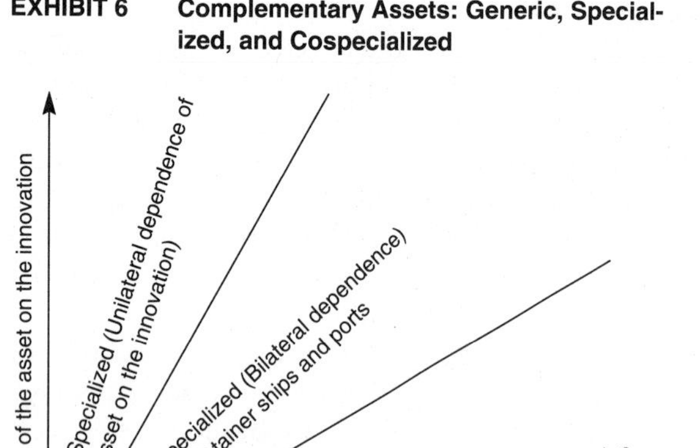

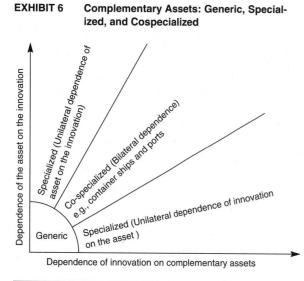

Generic assets are general-purpose assets which do not need to be tailored to the innovation in question. Specialized assets are those where there is unilateral dependence between the innovation and the complementary asset. Cospecialized assets are those for which there is a bilateral dependence. For instance, specialized repair facilities were needed to support the introduction of the rotary engine by Mazda. These assets are cospecialized because of the mutual dependence of the innovation on the repair facility. Containerization similarly required the deployment of some cospecialized assets in ocean shipping and terminals. However, the dependence of trucking on containerized shipping was less than that of containerized shipping on trucking, as trucks can convert from containers to flat beds at low cost. An example of a generic asset would be the manufacturing facilities needed to make running shoes. Generalized equipment can be employed in the main, exceptions being the molds for the soles.

Implications for Profitability

These three concepts can now be related in a way which will shed light on the imitation process, and the distribution of profits between innovator and follower. We begin by examining tight appropriability regimes.

Tight Appropriability Regimes

In those few instances where the innovator has an iron clad patent or copyright protection, or where the nature of the product is such that trade secrets effectively deny imitators access to the relevant knowledge, the innovator is almost assured of translating its innovation into market value for some period of time. Even if the innovator does not possess the desirable endowment of complementary costs, iron clad protection of intellectual property will afford the innovator the time to access these assets. If these assets are generic, contractual relation may well suffice, and the innovator may simply license its technology. Specialized R&D firms are viable in such an environment. Universal Oil Products, an R&D firm developing refining processes for the petroleum industry, was one such case in point. If, however, the complementary assets are specialized or cospecialized, contractual relationships are exposed to hazards, because one or both parties will have to commit capital to certain irreversible investments which will be valueless if the relationship between innovator and licensee breaks down. Accordingly, the innovator may find it prudent to expand its boundaries by integrating into specialized and cospecialized assets. Fortunately, the factors which make for difficult imitation will enable the innovator to build or acquire those complementary assets without competing with innovators for their control.

Competition from imitators is muted in this type of regime, which sometimes characterizes the petrochemical industry. In this industry, the protection offered by patents is fairly easily enforced. One factor assisting the licensee in this regard is that most petrochemical processes are designed around a specific variety of catalysts which can be kept proprietary. An agreement not to analyze the catalyst can be extracted from licensees, affording extra protection. However, even if such requirements are violated by licensees, the innovator is still well positioned, as the most important properties of a catalyst are related to its physical structure, and the process for generating this structure cannot be deduced from structural analysis alone. Every reaction technology a company acquires is thus accompanied by an ongoing dependence on the innovating company for the catalyst appropriate to the plant design. Failure to comply with various elements of the licensing contract can thus result in a cutoff in the supply of the catalyst, and possibly facility closure.

Similarly, if the innovator comes to market in the preparadigmatic phase with a sound product concept but the wrong design, a tight appropriability regime will afford the innovator the time needed to perform the trials needed to get the design right. As discussed earlier, the best initial design concepts often turn out to be hopelessly wrong, but if the innovator possesses an impenetrable thicket of patents, or has technology which is simply difficult to copy, then the market may well afford the innovator the necessary time to ascertain the right design before being eclipsed by imitators.

Weak Appropriability

Tight appropriability is the exception rather than the rule. Accordingly, innovators must turn to business strategy if they are to keep imitators/followers at bay. The nature of the competitive process will vary according to whether the industry is in the paradigmatic or preparadigmatic phase.

Preparadigmatic phase

In the preparadigmatic phase, the innovator must be careful to let the basic design "float" until sufficient evidence has accumulated that a design has been delivered which is likely to become the industry standard. In some industries there may be little opportunity for product modification. In microelectronics, for example, designs become locked in when the circuitry is chosen. Product modification is limited to "debugging" and software modification. An innovator must begin the design process anew if the product doesn't fit the market well. In some respects, however, selecting designs is dictated by the need to meet certain compatibility standards so that new hardware can interface with existing applications software. In one sense, therefore, the design issue for the microprocessor industry today is relatively straightforward: deliver greater power and speed while meeting the computer industry standards of the existing software base. However, from time to time windows of opportunity emerge for the introduction of entirely new families of microprocessors which will define a new industry and software standard. In these instances, basic design parameters are less well defined, and can be permitted to float until market acceptance is apparent.

The early history of the automobile industry exemplifies exceedingly well the importance for subsequent success of selecting the right design in the preparadigmatic stages. None of the early producers of steam cars survived the early shakeout when the closed body internal combustion engine automobile emerged as the dominant design. The steam car, nevertheless, had numerous early virtues, such as reliability, which the internal combustion engine autos could not deliver.

The British fiasco with the Comet I is also instructive. De Havilland had picked an early design with both technical and commercial flaws. By moving into production, significant irreversibilities and loss of reputation hobbled de Havilland to such a degree that it was unable to convert to the Boeing design which subsequently emerged as dominant. It wasn't even able to occupy second place, which went instead to Douglas.

As a general principle, it appears that innovators in weak appropriability regimes need to be intimately coupled to the market so that user needs can fully impact designs. When multiple parallel and sequential prototyping is feasible, it has clear advantages. Generally, such an approach is simply prohibitively costly. When development costs for a large commercial aircraft exceed one billion dollars, variations on a theme are all that is possible.

Hence, the probability that an innovator—defined here as a firm that is first to commercialize a new product design concept—will enter the paradigmatic phase possessing the dominant design is problematic. The probabilities will be higher the lower the relative cost of prototyping, and the more tightly coupled the firm is to the market. The latter is a function of organizational design, and can be influenced by managerial choices. The former is embedded in the technology, and cannot be influenced, except in minor ways, by managerial decisions. Hence, in industries with large developmental and prototyping costs—and hence significant irreversibilities—and where innovation of the product concept is easy, then one would expect that the probability that the innovator would emerge as the winner or amongst the winners at the end of the preparadigmatic stage is low.

Paradigmatic stage

In the preparadigmatic phase, complementary assets do not loom large. Rivalry is focused on trying to identify the design which will be dominant. Production volumes are low, and there is little to be gained in deploying specialized assets, as scale economies are unavailable, and price is not a principal competitive factor. However, as the leading design or designs begin to be revealed by the market, volumes increase and opportunities for economies of scale will induce firms to begin gearing up for mass production by acquiring specialized tooling and equipment, and possibly specialized distribution as well. Since these investments involve significant irreversibilities, producers are likely to proceed with caution. Islands of specialized capital will begin to appear in an industry, which otherwise features a sea of general-purpose manufacturing equipment.

However, as the terms of competition begin to change, and prices become increasingly unimportant, access to complementary assets becomes absolutely critical. Since the core technology is easy to imitate, by assumption, commercial success swings upon the terms and conditions upon which the required complementary assets can be accessed.

It is at this point that specialized and cospecialized assets become critically important. Generalized equipment and skills, almost by definition, are always available in an industry, and even if they are not, they do not involve significant irreversibilities. Accordingly, firms have easy access to this type of capital, and even if there is insufficient capacity available in the relevant assets, it can easily be put in place as it involves few risks. Specialized assets, on the other hand, involve significant irreversibilities and cannot be easily accessed by contract, as the risks are significant for the party making the dedicated investment. The firms which control the cospecialized assets, such as distribution channels, specialized manufacturing capacity, and so on, are clearly advantageously positioned relative to an innovator. Indeed, in rare instances where incumbent firms possess an airtight monopoly over specialized assets, and the innovator is in a regime of weak appropriability, all of the profits to the innovation could conceivably accrue to the firms possessing the specialized assets, which should be able to get the upper hand.

Even when the innovator is not confronted by situations where competitors or potential competitors control key assets, the innovator may still be disadvantaged. For instance, the technology embedded in cardiac pacemakers was easy to imitate, and so competitive outcomes quickly came to be determined by who had easiest access to the complementary assets, in this case specialized marketing. A similar situation has recently arisen in the United States with respect to personal computers. As an industry participant recently observed:

> There are a huge numbers of computer manufacturers, companies that make peripherals (e.g. printers, hard disk drives, floppy disk drives), and software companies. They are all trying to get marketing distributors because they cannot afford to call on all of the U.S. companies directly. They need to go through retail distribution channels, such as Businessland, in order to reach the marketplace. The problem today, however, is that many of these companies are not able to get shelf space and thus are having a very difficult time marketing their products. The point of distribution is where the profit and the power are in the marketplace today.[8]

Channel Strategy Issues

The above analysis indicates how access to complementary assets, such as manufacturing and distribution, on competitive teams is critical if the innovator is to avoid handing over the lion's share of the profits to imitators, and/or to the owners of the complementary assets that are specialized or cospecialized to the innovation. It is now necessary to delve deeper into the appropriate control structure that the innovator ideally ought to establish over these critical assets.

There are a myriad of possible channels which could be employed. At one extreme the innovator could integrate into all of the necessary complementary assets, as illustrated in Exhibit 7, or just a few of them, as illustrated in Exhibit 8. Complete integration (Exhibit 7) is likely to be unnecessary as well as prohibitively expensive. It is well to recognize that the variety of assets and competences which need to be accessed is likely to be quite large, even for only modestly complex technologies. To produce a personal computer, for instance, a company needs access to expertise in semiconductor technology, display technology, disk drive technology, networking technology, keyboard technology, and several others. No company can keep pace in all of these areas by itself.

At the other extreme, the innovator could attempt to access these assets through straightforward contractual relationships (e.g. component supply contracts, fabrication contracts, service contracts). In many instances such contracts may suffice, although

---

[8]David A. Norman, "Impact of Entrepreneurship and Innovations on the Distribution of Personal Computers," in *The Positive Sum Strategy,* ed. R. Landau and N. Rosenberg (National Academy Press, Washington, DC, 1986).

EXHIBIT 7 Complementary Assets Internalized for Innovation: Hypothetical Case #1 (Innovator Integrated into All Complementary Assets)

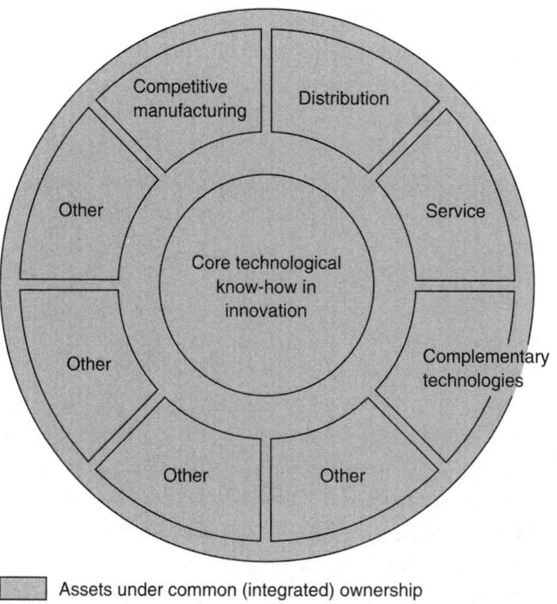

EXHIBIT 8 Complementary Assets Internalized for Innovation: Hypothetical Case #2 (Innovator Subcontracts for Manufacturing and Service)

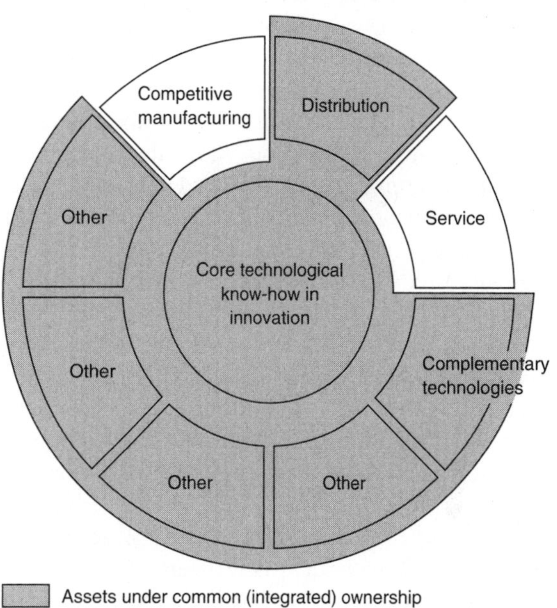

it sometimes exposes the innovator to various hazards and dependencies that it may well wish to avoid. In between the fully integrated and full contractual extremes, there are a myriad of intermediate forms and channels available. An analysis of the properties of the two extreme forms is presented below. A brief synopsis of mixed modes then follows.

Contractual Modes

The advantages of a contractual solution—whereby the innovator signs a contract, such as a license, with independent suppliers, manufacturers or distributors—are obvious. The innovator will not have to make the upfront capital expenditures needed to build or buy the assets in question. This reduces risks as well as cash requirements.

Contracting rather than integrating is likely to be the optimal strategy when the innovator's appropriability regime is tight and the complementary assets are available in competitive supply (i.e., there is adequate capacity and a choice of sources).

Both conditions apply in petrochemicals for instance, so an innovator doesn't need to be integrated to be successful. Consider, first, the appropriability regime. As discussed earlier, the protection offered by patents is fairly easily enforced, particularly for process technology, in the petrochemical industry. Given the advantageous feedstock prices available in hydrocarbon-rich petrochemical exporters, and the appropriability regime characteristic of this industry, there is no incentive or advantage in owning the complementary assets (production facilities) as they are not typically highly specialized to the innovation. Union Carbide appears to realize this, and has recently adjusted its strategy accordingly. Essentially, Carbide is placing its existing technology into a new subsidiary, Engineering and Hydrocarbons Service. The company is engaging in licensing and offers engineering, construction, and management services to customers who want to take their feedstocks and integrate them forward into petrochemicals. But Carbide itself appears to be backing away from an integration strategy.

Chemical and petrochemical product innovations are not quite so easy to protect, which should raise new challenges to innovating firms in the developed nations as they attempt to shift out of commodity petrochemicals. There are already numerous examples of new products that made it to the marketplace, filled a customer need, but never generated competitive returns to the innovator because of imitation. For example, in the 1960s Dow decided to start manufacturing rigid polyurethene foam. However, it was imitated very quickly by numerous small firms which had lower costs.[9] The absence of low-cost manufacturing capability left Dow vulnerable.

Contractual relationships can bring added credibility to the innovator, especially if the innovator is relatively unknown when the contractual partner is established and viable. Indeed, arm's-length contracting which embodies more than a simple buy–sell agreement is becoming so common, and is so multifaceted, that the term *strategic partnering* has been devised to describe it. Even large companies such as IBM are now engaging in it. For IBM, partnering buys access to new technologies enabling the company to "learn things we couldn't have learned without many years of trial and error."[10] IBM's arrangement with Microsoft to use the latter's MS-DOS operating system software on the IBM PC facilitated the timely introduction of IBM's personal computer into the market.

Smaller, less-integrated companies are often eager to sign on with established companies because of the name recognition and reputation spillovers. For instance, Cipher Data Products, Inc., contracted with IBM to develop a low-priced version of IBM's 3480 0.5-inch streaming cartridge drive, which is likely to become the industry standard. As Cipher management points out, "One of the biggest advantages to dealing with IBM is that, once you've created a product that meets the high quality standards necessary to sell into the IBM world, you can sell into any arena."[11] Similarly, IBM's contract with Microsoft "meant instant credibility" to Microsoft.[12]

It is most important to recognize, however, that strategic (contractual) partnering, which is currently very fashionable, is exposed to certain hazards, particularly for the innovator, when the innovator is trying to use contracts to access specialized capabilities. First, it may be difficult to induce suppliers to make costly irreversible commitments which depend for their success on the success of the innovation. To expect suppliers, manufacturers, and distributors to do so is to invite them to take risks along with the innovator. The problem which this poses for the innovator is similar to the problems associated with attracting venture capital. The innovator must persuade its prospective partner that the risk is a good one. The situation is one open to opportunistic abuses on both sides. The innovator has incentives to overstate the value of the innovation, while the supplier has incentives to "run with the technology" should the innovation be a success.

Instances of both parties making irreversible capital commitments nevertheless exist. Apple's Laserwriter—a high-resolution laser printer which allows PC users to produce near-typeset-quality text and art-department graphics—is a case in point. Apple persuaded Canon to participate in the development of the Laserwriter by providing subsystems from its copiers—but only after Apple contracted to pay for a certain number of copier engines and cases. In short, Apple accepted a good deal of the financial risk in order to induce Canon to assist in the development and production of the Laserwriter. The arrangement appears to have been prudent, yet there were clearly hazards for both sides. It is difficult to write, execute, and enforce complex development contracts, particularly when the design of the new product is still floating. Apple was exposed to the risk that its coinnovator Canon would fail to deliver, and Canon was exposed to the risk that the Apple design and marketing effort would not succeed. Still, Apple's alternatives may have been rather limited, inasmuch as it didn't command the requisite technology to go it alone.

In short, the current euphoria over strategic partnering may be partially misplaced. The advantages are being stressed,[13] without a balanced presentation of costs and risks. Briefly, there is the risk that the partner won't perform according to the innovator's perception of what the contract requires; there is the added danger that the partner may imitate the innovator's technology and attempt to compete with the innovator. This latter possibility is particu-

---

[9]Executive V.P. Union Carbide, Robert D. Kennedy, quoted in *Chemical Week,* Nov. 16, 1983, p. 48.

[10]Comment attributed to Peter Olson III, IBM's director of business development, as reported in "The Strategy Behind IBM's Strategic Alliances," *Electronic Business,* October 1 (1985), p. 126.

[11]Comment attributed to Norman Farquhar, Cipher's vice president for strategic development, as reported in *Electronic Business,* October 1 (1985), p. 128.

[12]Regis McKenna, "Market Positioning in High Technology," *California Management Review* 27 (3) (Spring 1985), p. 94.

[13]For example, McKenna, "Marketing Position in High Technology."

larly acute if the provider of the complementary asset is uniquely situated with respect to the complementary asset in question and has the capacity to imitate the technology, which the innovator is unable to protect. The innovator will then find that it has created a competitor who is better positioned than the innovator to take advantage of the market opportunity at hand. *Business Week* has expressed concerns along these lines in its discussion of the "Hollow Corporation."[14]

It is important to bear in mind, however, that contractual or partnering strategies in certain cases are ideal. If the innovator's technology is well protected, and if what the partner has to provide is a "generic" capacity available from many potential partners, then the innovator will be able to maintain the upper hand while avoiding the costs of duplicating downstream capacity. Even if the partner fails to perform, adequate alternatives exist (by assumption, the partners' capacities are commonly available) so the innovator's efforts to successfully commercialize its technology ought to proceed profitably.

Integration Modes

Integration, which by definition involves ownership, is distinguished from pure contractual modes in that it typically facilitates incentive alignment and control. If an innovator owns rather than rents the complementary assets needed to commercialize, then it is in a position to capture spillover benefits stemming from increased demand for the complementary assets caused by the innovation.

Indeed, an innovator might be in the position, at least before its innovation is announced, to buy up capacity in the complementary assets, possibly to its great subsequent advantage. If future markets exist, simply taking forward positions in the complementary assets may suffice to capture much of the spillovers.

Even after the innovation is announced, the innovator might still be able to build or buy complementary capacities at competitive prices if the innovation has iron clad legal protection (i.e., if the innovation is in a tight appropriability regime). However, if the innovation is not tightly protected and once out is easy to imitate, then securing control of complementary capacities is likely to be the key success factor, particularly if those capacities are in fixed supply—so called bottlenecks. Distribution and specialized manufacturing competences often become bottlenecks.

As a practical matter, however, an innovator may not have the time to acquire or build the complementary assets that ideally it would like to control. This is particularly true when imitation is easy, so that timing becomes critical. Additionally, the innovator may simply not have the financial resources to proceed. The implications of timing and cash constraints are summarized in Exhibit 9.

Accordingly, in weak appropriability regimes innovators need to rank complementary assets as to their importance. If the complementary assets are critical, ownership is warranted, although if the firm is cash constrained, a minority position may well represent a sensible trade-off.

Needless to say, when imitation is easy, strategic moves to build or buy complementary assets which

EXHIBIT 9 Specialized Complementary Assets and Weak Appropriability: Integration Calculus

Time Required to Position (Relative to Competitors)

Investment required	Long	Short
Minor	OK if timing not critical	Full steam ahead
Major	Forget it	OK if cost position tolerable

Optimum Investment for Business in Question

How critical to success?	Minor	Major
Critical	Internalize (majority ownership)	Internalize (but if cash constrained, take minority position)
Not critical	Discretionary	Do not internalize (contract out)

[14]See *Business Week*, March 3 (1986), pp. 57–59. *Business Week* uses the term to describe a corporation which lacks in-house manufacturing capability.

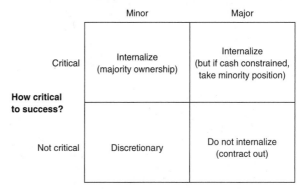

are specialized must occur with due reference to the moves of competitors. There is no point moving to build a specialized asset, for instance, if one's imitators can do it faster and cheaper.

It is hopefully self-evident that if the innovator is already a large enterprise with many of the relevant complementary assets under its control, integration is unlikely to be the issue that it might otherwise be, as the innovating firm will already control many of the relevant specialized and cospecialized assets. However, in industries experiencing rapid technological change, technologies advance so rapidly that it is unlikely that a single company has the full range of expertise needed to bring advanced products to market opportunely and cost-effectively. Hence, the integration issue is not just a small-firm issue.

Integration versus Contract Strategies: An Analytic Summary

Exhibit 10 summarizes some of the relevant considerations in the form of a decision flowchart. It indicates that a profit-seeking innovator, confronted by weak intellectual property protection and the need to access specialized complementary assets and/or capabilities, is forced to expand its activities through integration if it is to prevail over imitators. Put differently, innovators who develop new products that possess poor intellectual property protection but which require specialized complementary capacities are more likely to parlay their technology into a commercial advantage, rather than see it prevail in the hands of imitators.

Exhibit 10 makes it apparent that the difficult strategic decisions arise in situations where the appropriability regime is weak and where specialized assets are critical to profitable commercialization. These situations, which in reality are very common, require that a fine-grained competitor analysis be part of the innovator's strategic assessment of its opportunities and threats. This is carried a step further in Exhibit 11, which looks only at situations where commercialization requires certain specialized capabilities. It indicates the appropriate strategies for the innovators and predicts the outcomes to be expected for the various players.

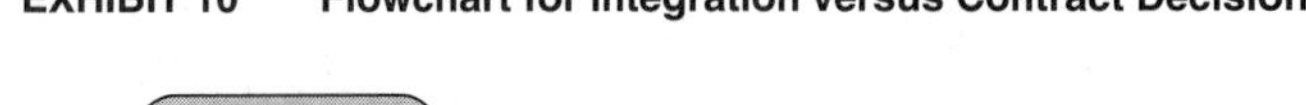
EXHIBIT 10 Flowchart for Integration versus Contract Decision

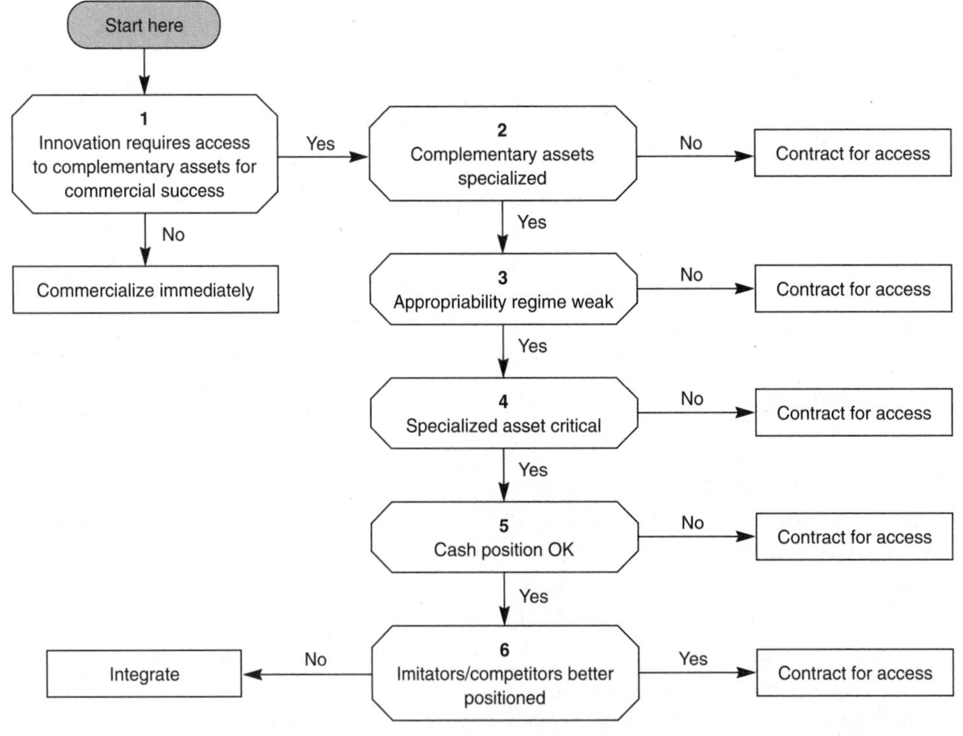

EXHIBIT 11 Contract and Integration Strategies and Outcomes for Innovators: Specialized-Asset Case

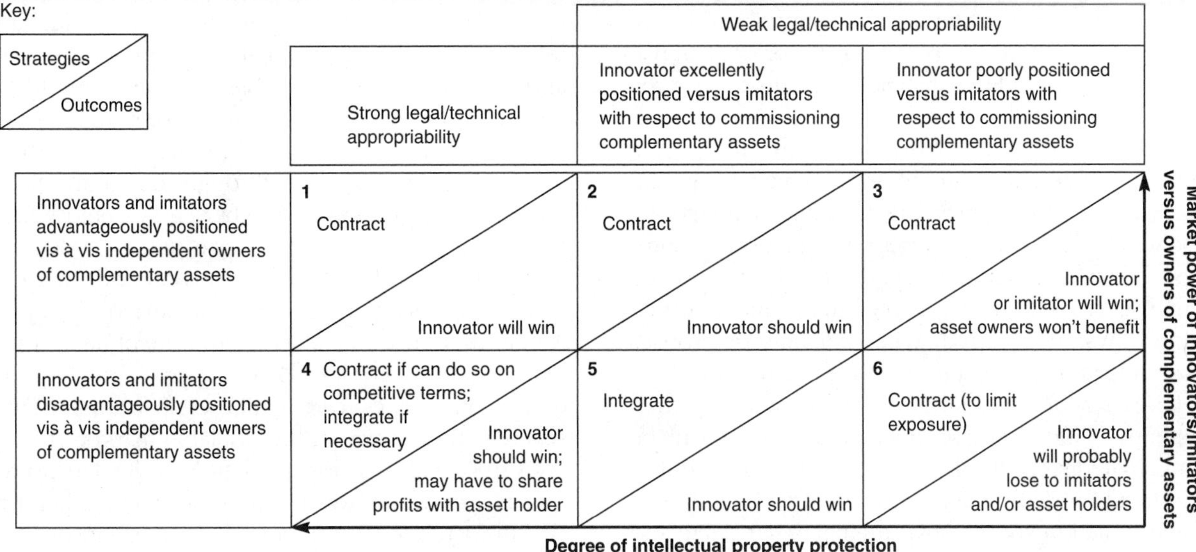

Three classes of players are of interest: innovators, imitators, and the owners of cospecialized assets (e.g., distributors). All three can potentially benefit or lose from the innovation process. The latter can potentially benefit from the additional business which the innovation may direct in the asset owner's direction. Should the asset turn out to be a bottleneck with respect to commercializing the innovation, the owner of the bottleneck facilities is obviously in a position to extract profits from the innovator and/or imitators.

The vertical axis in Exhibit 11 measures how those who possess the technology (the innovator or possibly its imitators) are positioned vis-à-vis those firms that possess required specialized assets. The horizontal axis measures the *tightness* of the appropriability regime, tight regimes being evidenced by ironclad legal protection coupled with technology that is simply difficult to copy; weak regimes offer little in the way of legal protection and the essence of the technology, once released, is transparent to the imitator. Weak regimes are further subdivided according to how the innovator and imitators are positioned vis-à-vis each other. This is likely to be a function of factors such as lead time and prior positioning in the requisite complementary assets.

Exhibit 11 makes it apparent that even when firms pursue the optimal strategy, other industry participants may take the jackpot. This possibility is unlikely when the intellectual property in question is tightly protected. The only serious threat to the innovator is where a specialized complementary asset is completely locked up, a possibility recognized in cell 4. This can rarely be done without the cooperation of government. But it frequently occurs, as when a foreign government closes off access to a foreign market, forcing the innovators to license to foreign firms, but with the government effectively cartelizing the potential licensees. With weak intellectual property protection, however, it is quite clear that the innovator will often lose out to imitators and/or asset holders, even when the innovator is pursuing the appropriate strategy (cell 6). Clearly, incorrect strategies can compound problems. For instance, if innovators integrate when they should contract, a heavy commitment of resources will be incurred for little if any strategic benefit, thereby exposing the innovator to even greater losses than would otherwise be the case. On the other hand, if an innovator tries to contract for the supply of a critical capability when it should build the capability itself, it may well find it has nurtured an imitator better able to serve the market than the innovator itself.

Mixed Modes

The real world rarely provides extreme or pure cases. Decisions to integrate or license involve trade-offs, compromises, and mixed approaches. It is not surprising, therefore, that the real world is characterized by mixed modes of organization, involving judicious blends of integration and contracting. Sometimes mixed modes represent transitional phases. For instance, because of the convergence of computer and telecommunication technology, firms in each industry are discovering that they often lack the requisite technical capabilities in the other. Since the technological interdependence of the two requires collaboration amongst those who design different parts of the system, intense cross-boundary coordination and information flows are required. When separate enterprises are involved, agreement must be reached on complex protocol issues amongst parties who see their interests differently. Contractual difficulties can be anticipated since the selection of common technical protocols amongst the parties will often be followed by transaction-specific investments in hardware and software. There is little doubt that this was the motivation behind IBM's purchase of 15 percent of PBX manufacturer Rolm in 1983, a position that was expanded to 100 percent in 1984. IBM's stake in Intel, which began with a 12 percent purchase in 1982, is most probably not a transitional phase leading to 100 percent purchase, because both companies realized that the two corporate cultures are not very compatible, and IBM may not be as impressed with Intel's technology as it once was.

The CAT Scanner, the IBM PC, and NutraSweet: Insights from the Framework

EMI's failure to reap significant returns from the CAT scanner can be explained in large measure by reference to the concepts developed above. The scanner which EMI developed was of a technical sophistication much higher than would normally be found in a hospital, requiring a high level of training, support, and servicing. EMI had none of these capabilities, could not easily contract for them, and was slow to realize their importance. It most probably could have formed a partnership with a company like Siemens to access the requisite capabilities. Its failure to do so was a strategic error compounded by the very limited intellectual property protection which the law afforded the scanner. Although subsequent court decisions have upheld some of EMI's patent claims, once the product was in the market it could be reverse engineered and its essential features copied. Two competitors, GE and Technicare, already possessed the complementary capabilities that the scanner required, and they were also technologically capable. In addition, both were experienced marketers of medical equipment, and had reputations for quality, reliability, and service. GE and Technicare were thus able to commit their R&D resources to developing a competitive scanner, borrowing ideas from EMI's scanner, which they undoubtedly had access to through cooperative hospitals, and improving on it where they could while they rushed to market. GE began taking orders in 1976 and soon after made inroads on EMI. In 1977 concern for rising health care costs caused the Carter Administration to introduce "certificate of need" regulation, which required HEW's approval on expenditures on big ticket items like CAT scanners. This severely cut the size of the available market.

By 1978 EMI had lost market share leadership to Technicare, which was in turn quickly overtaken by GE. In October 1979, Godfrey Houndsfield of EMI shared the Nobel prize for invention of the CT scanner. Despite this honor and the public recognition of its role in bringing this medical breakthrough to the world, the collapse of its scanner business forced EMI in the same year into the arms of a rescuer, Thorn Electrical Industries, Ltd. GE subsequently acquired what was EMI's scanner business from Thorn for what amounted to a pittance.[15] Though royalties continued to flow to EMI, the company had failed to capture the lion's share of the profits generated by the innovation it had pioneered and successfully commercialized.

If EMI illustrates how a company with outstanding technology and an excellent product can fail to profit from innovation while the imitators succeeded, the story of the IBM PC indicates how a new product representing a very modest technological advance can yield remarkable returns to the developer.

The IBM PC, introduced in 1981, was a success despite the fact that the architecture was ordinary and the components standard. Philip Estridge's design team in Boca Raton, Florida, decided to use existing technology to produce a solid, reliable micro rather than state of the art. With a one-year mandate to develop a PC, Estridge's team could do little else.

However, the IBM PC did use what at the time was a new 16-bit microprocessor (the Intel 8088) and a new disk operating system (DOS) adapted for

[15]See "GE Gobbles a Rival in CT Scanners," *Business Week,* May 19, 1980.

IBM by Microsoft. Other than the microprocessor and the operating system, the IBM PC incorporated existing micro "standards" and used off-the-shelf parts from outside vendors. IBM did write its own BIOS (Basic Input/Output System) which is embedded in ROM, but this was a relatively straightforward programming exercise.

The key to the PC's success was not the technology. It was the set of complementary assets which IBM either had or quickly assembled around the PC. In order to expand the market for PCs, there was a clear need for an expandable, flexible microcomputer system with extensive applications software. IBM could have based its PC system on its own patented hardware and copyrighted software. Such an approach would cause complementary products to be cospecialized, forcing IBM to develop peripherals and a comprehensive library of software in a very short time. Instead, IBM adopted what might be called an "induced contractual" approach. By adopting an open system architecture, as Apple had done, and by making the operating system information publicly available, a spectacular output of third-part software was induced. IBM estimated that by mid-1983, at least 3,000 hardware and software products were available for the PC.[16] Put differently, IBM pulled together the complementary assets, particularly software, which success required, without even using contracts, let alone integration. This was despite the fact that the software developers were creating assets that were in part cospecialized with the IBM PC, at least in the first instance.

A number of special factors made this seem a reasonable risk to the software writers. A critical one was IBM's name and commitment to the project. The reputation behind the letters I.B.M. is perhaps the greatest cospecialized asset the company possesses. The name implied that the product would be marketed and serviced in the IBM tradition. It guaranteed that MS-DOS would become an industry standard, so that the software business would not be solely dependent on IBM, because emulators were sure to enter. It guaranteed access to retail distribution outlets on competitive terms. The consequences were that IBM was able to take a product which represented at best a modest technological accomplishment, and turn it into a fabulous commercial success. The case demonstrates the role that complementary assets play in determining outcomes.

[16]F. Gens and C. Christiansen, "Could 1,000,000 IBM PC Users Be Wrong?," *Byte,* November 1983, p. 88.

The spectacular success and profitability of G.D. Searle's NutraSweet is an uncommon story which is also consistent with the above framework. In 1982, Searle reported combined sales of $74 million for NutraSweet and its table top version, Equal. In 1983, this surged to $336 million. In 1985, NutraSweet sales exceeded $700 million[17] and Equal had captured 50 percent of the U.S. sugar substitute market and was number one in five other countries.

NutraSweet, which is Searle's tradename for aspartame, has achieved rapid acceptance in each of its FDA-approved categories because of its good taste and ability to substitute directly for sugar in many applications. However, Searle's earnings from NutraSweet and the absence of a strategic challenge can be traced in part to Searle's clever strategy.

It appears that Searle has managed to establish an exceptionally tight appropriability regime around NutraSweet—one that may well continue for some time after the patent has expired. No competitor appears to have successfully "invented around" the Searle patent and commercialized an alternative, no doubt in part because the FDA approval process would have to begin anew for an imitator who was not violating Searle's patents. A competitor who tried to replicate the aspartame molecule with minor modification to circumvent the patent would probably be forced to replicate the hundreds of tests and experiments which proved aspartame's safety. Without patent protection, FDA approval would provide no shield against imitators coming to market with an identical chemical and who could establish to the FDA that it is the same compound that had already been approved. Without FDA approval, on the other hand, the patent protection would be worthless, for the product would not be sold for human consumption.

Searle has aggressively pushed to strengthen its patent protection. The company was granted U.S. patent protection in 1970. It has also obtained patent protection in Japan, Canada, Australia, U.K., France, Germany, and a number of other countries. However, most of these patents carry a 17-year life. Since the product was only approved for human consumption in 1982, the 17-year patent life was effectively reduced to five. Recognizing the obvious importance of its patent, Searle pressed for and obtained special legislation in November 1984 extending the patent protection on aspartame for another 5 years. The United Kingdom provided a

[17]See *Monsanto Annual Report, 1985..*

similar extension. In almost every other nation, however, 1987 will mark the expiration of the patent.

When the patent expires, however, Searle will still have several valuable assets to help keep imitators at bay. Searle has gone to great lengths to create and promulgate the use of its NutraSweet name and a distinctive "Swirl" logo on all goods licensed to use the ingredient. The company has also developed the "Equal" tradename for a table top version of the sweetener. Trademark law in the U.S. provides protection against unfair competition in branded products for as long as the owner of the mark continues to use it. Both the NutraSweet and Equal trademarks will become essential assets when the patents on aspartame expire. Searle may well have convinced consumers that the only real form of sweetener is NutraSweet/Equal. Consumers know most other artificial sweeteners by their generic names—saccharin and cyclamates.

Clearly, Searle is trying to build a position in complementary assets to prepare for the competition which will surely arise. Searle's joint venture with Ajinomoto ensures them access to that company's many years of experience in the production of biochemical agents. Much of this knowledge is associated with techniques for distillation and synthesis of the delicate hydrocarbon compounds that are the ingredients of NutraSweet, and is therefore more tacit than codified. Searle has begun to put these techniques to use in its own $160 million Georgia production facility. It can be expected that Searle will use trade secrets to the maximum to keep this know-how proprietary.

By the time its patent expires, Searle's extensive research into production techniques for L-phenylalanine, and its eight years of experience in the Georgia plant, should give it a significant cost advantage over potential aspartame competitors. Trade secret protection, unlike patents, has no fixed lifetime and may well sustain Searle's position for years to come.

Moreover, Searle has wisely avoided renewing contracts with suppliers when they have expired.[18] Had Searle subcontracted manufacturing for NutraSweet, it would have created a manufacturer who would then be in a position to enter the aspartame market itself, or to team up with a marketer of artificial sweeteners. But by keeping manufacturing in-house, and by developing a valuable trade name, Searle has a good chance of protecting its market position from dramatic inroads once patents expire. Clearly, Searle seems to be astutely aware of the importance of maintaining a "tight appropriability regime" and using cospecialized assets strategically.

[18]Purification Engineering, which had spent $5 million to build a phenylalanine production facility, was told in January 1985 that their contract would not be renewed. In May, Genex, which claimed to have invested $25 million, was given the same message. See "A Bad Aftertaste," *Business Week*, July 15, 1985.

Implications for R&D Strategy, Industry Structure, and Trade Policy

Allocating R&D Resources

The analysis so far assumes that the firm has developed an innovation for which a market exists. It indicates the strategies which the firm must follow to maximize its share of industry profits relative to imitators and other competitors. There is no guarantee of success even if optimal strategies are followed.

The innovator can improve its total return to R&D, however, by adjusting its R&D investment portfolio to maximize the probability that technological discoveries will emerge that are either easy to protect with existing intellectual property law, or which require for commercialization cospecialized assets already within the firm's repertoire of capabilities. Put differently, if an innovating firm does not target its R&D resources towards new products and processes which it can commercialize advantageously relative to potential imitators and/or followers, then it is unlikely to profit from its investment in R&D. In this sense, a firm's history—and the assets it already has in place—ought to condition its R&D investment decisions. Clearly, an innovating firm with considerable assets already in place is free to strike out in new directions, so long as in doing so it is cognizant of the kinds of capabilities required to successfully commercialize the innovation. It is therefore rather clear that the R&D investment decision cannot be divorced from the strategic analysis of markets and industries, and the firm's position within them.

Small-Firm versus Large-Firm Comparisons

Business commentators often remark that many small entrepreneurial firms which generate new, commercially valuable technology fail while large multinational firms, often with a less meritorious record with respect to innovation, survive and prosper. One set of reasons for this phenomenon is now clear. Large firms are more likely to possess the relevant specialized and cospecialized assets within their boundaries at the time of new product introduction. They can therefore do a better job of milking their technology, however meager, to maximum advantage. Small domestic firms are less likely to have the relevant specialized and cospecialized assets within their boundaries and so will have to incur the expense either of trying to build them, or of trying to develop coalitions with competitors/owners of the specialized assets.

Regimes of Appropriability and Industry Structure

In industries where legal methods of protection are effective, or where new products are just hard to copy, the strategic necessity for innovating firms to integrate into cospecialized assets would appear to be less compelling than in industries where legal protection is weak. In cases where legal protection is weak or nonexistent, the control of cospecialized assets will be needed for long-run survival.

In this regard, it is instructive to examine the U.S. drug industry.[19] Beginning in the 1940s, the U.S. Patent Office began, for the first time, to grant patents on certain natural substances that involved difficult extraction procedures. Thus, in 1948 Merck received a patent on streptomycin, which was a natural substance. However, it was not the extraction process but the drug itself which received the patent. Hence, patents were important to the drug industry in terms of what could be patented (drugs), but they did not prevent imitation.[20] Sometimes just changing one molecule will enable a company to come up with a different substance which does not violate the patent. Had patents been more all-inclusive—and I am not suggesting they should—licensing would have been an effective mechanism for Merck to extract profits from its innovation. As it turns out, the emergence of close substitutes, coupled with FDA regulation which had the de facto effect of reducing the elasticity of demand for drugs, placed high rewards on a product differentiation strategy. This required extensive marketing, including a sales force that could directly contact doctors, who were the purchasers of drugs through their ability to create prescriptions.[21] The result was exclusive production (i.e., the earlier industry practice of licensing was dropped) and forward integration into marketing (the relevant cospecialized asset).

Generally, if legal protection of the innovator's profits is secure, innovating firms can select their boundaries based simply on their ability to identify user needs and respond to those through research and development. The weaker the legal methods of protection, the greater the incentive to integrate into the relevant cospecialized assets. Hence, as industries in which legal protection is weak begin to mature, integration into innovation-specific cospecialized assets will occur. Often this will take the form of backward, forward, and lateral integration. (Conglomerate integration is not part of this phenomenon.) For example, IBM's purchase of Rolm can be seen as a response to the impact of technological change on the identity of the cospecialized assets relevant to IBM's future growth.

Industry Maturity, New Entry, and History

As technologically progressive industries mature, and a greater proportion of the relevant cospecialized assets are brought in under the corporate umbrellas of incumbents, new entry becomes more difficult. Moreover, when it does occur it is more likely to involve coalition formation very early on. Incumbents will for sure own the cospecialized assets, and new entrants will find it necessary to forge links with them. Here lies the explanation for the sudden surge in strategic partnering now occurring internationally, and particularly in the computer and telecommunications industry. Note that it should not be interpreted in anticompetitive terms. Given existing industry structure, coalitions ought to be seen not as attempts to stifle competition, but as mechanisms for lowering entry requirements for innovators.

In industries in which technological change of a particular kind has occurred, which required

---

[19]P. Temin, "Technology, Regulation, and Market Structure in the Modern Pharmaceutical Industry," *The Bell Journal of Economics,* Autumn 1979, pp. 429–46.

[20]Ibid., p. 436.

[21]In the period before FDA regulation, all drugs other than narcotics were available over-the-counter. Since the end user could purchase drugs directly, sales were price sensitive. Once prescriptions were required, this price sensitivity collapsed; the doctors not only did not have to pay for the drugs, but in most cases they were unaware of the prices of the drugs they were prescribing.

deployment of specialized and/or cospecialized assets at the time, a configuration of firm boundaries may well have arisen which no longer has compelling efficiencies. Considerations which once dictated integration may no longer hold, yet there may not be strong forces leading to divestiture. Hence existing firm boundaries may in some industries—especially those where the technological trajectory and attendant specialized asset requirements has changed—be rather fragile. In short, history matters in terms of understanding the structure of the modern business enterprise. Existing firm boundaries cannot always be assumed to have obvious rationales in terms of today's requirements.

The Importance of Manufacturing to International Competitiveness

Practically all forms of technological know-how must be embedded in goods and services to yield value to the consumer. An important policy for the innovating nation is whether the identity of the firms and nations performing this function matter.

In a world of tight appropriability and zero transactions cost—the world of neoclassical trade theory—it is a matter of indifference whether an innovating firm has an in-house manufacturing capability, domestic, or foreign. It can simply engage in arm's-length contracting (patent licensing, know-how licensing, co-production, etc.) for the sale of the output of the activity in which it has a comparative advantage (in this case R&D) and will maximize returns by specializing in what it does best.

However, in a regime of weak appropriability, and especially where the requisite manufacturing assets are specialized to the innovation, which is often the case, participation in manufacturing may be necessary if an innovator is to appropriate the rents from its innovation. Hence, if an innovator's manufacturing costs are higher than those of its imitators, the innovator may well end up ceding the lion's share of profits to the imitator.

In a weak appropriability regime, low-cost imitator-manufacturers may end up capturing all of the profits from innovation. In a weak appropriability regime where specialized manufacturing capabilities are required to produce new products, an innovator with a manufacturing disadvantage may find that its advantage at early stage research and development will have no commercial value. This will eventually cripple the innovator, unless it is assisted by governmental processes. For example, it appears that one of the reasons why U.S. color TV manufacturers did not capture the lion's share of the profits from innovation, for which RCA was primarily responsible, was that RCA and its American licensees were not competitive at manufacturing. In this context, concerns that the decline of manufacturing threatens the entire economy appear to be well founded.

A related implication is that as the technology gap closes, the basis of competition in an industry will shift to the cospecialized assets. This appears to be what is happening in microprocessors. Intel is no longer out ahead technologically. As Gordon Moore, CEO of Intel points out, "Take the top 10 [semiconductor] companies in the world . . . and it is hard to tell at any time who is ahead of whom. . . . It is clear that we have to be pretty damn close to the Japanese from a manufacturing standpoint to compete."[22] It is not just that strength in one area is necessary to compensate for weakness in another. As technology becomes more public and less proprietary through easier imitation, then strength in manufacturing and other capabilities is necessary to derive advantage from whatever technological advantages an innovator may possess.

Put differently, the notion that the United States can adopt a "designer role" in international commerce, while letting independent firms in other countries such as Japan, Korea, Taiwan, or Mexico do the manufacturing, is unlikely to be viable as a long-run strategy. This is because profits will accrue primarily to the low-cost manufacturers (by providing a larger sales base over which they can exploit their special skills). Where imitation is easy, and even where it is not, there are obvious problems in transacting in the market for know-how, problems which are described in more detail elsewhere.[23] In particular, there are difficulties in pricing an intangible asset whose true performance features are difficult to ascertain ex ante.

The trend in international business towards what Miles and Snow[24] call *dynamic networks*—characterized by vertical disintegration and contracting—

---

[22]"Institutionalizing the Revolution," *Forbes,* June 16, 1986, p. 35.

[23]Teece, "The Market for Know-how and the Efficient International Transfer of Technology."

[24]R. E. Miles and C. C. Snow, "Network Organizations: New Concepts for New Forms," *California Management Review,* Spring 1986, pp. 62–73.

ought thus be viewed with concern. (*Business Week*, March 3, 1986, has referred to the same phenomenon as the Hollow Corporation.) Dynamic networks may not so much reflect innovative organizational forms, but the disassembly of the modern corporation because of deterioration in national capacities, manufacturing in particular, which are complementary to technological innovation. Dynamic networks may therefore signal not so much the rejuvenation of American enterprise, but its piecemeal demise.

How Trade and Investment Barriers Can Impact Innovators' Profits

In regimes of weak appropriability, governments can move to shift the distribution of the gains from innovation away from foreign innovators and towards domestic firms by denying innovators ownership of specialized assets. The foreign firm, which by assumption is an innovator, will be left with the option of selling its intangible assets in the market for know-how if both trade and investment are foreclosed by government policy. This option may appear better than the alternative (no remuneration at all from the market in question). Licensing may then appear profitable, but only because access to the complementary assets is blocked by government.

Thus when an innovating firm generating profits needs to access complementary assets abroad, host governments, by limiting access, can sometimes milk the innovators for a share of the profits, particularly that portion which originates from sales in the host country. However, the ability of host governments to do so depends importantly on the criticality of the host country's assets to the innovator. If the cost and infrastructure characteristics of the host country are such that it is the world's lowest cost manufacturing site, and if domestic industry is competitive, then by acting as a de facto monopolist, the host country government ought to be able to adjust the terms of access to the complementary assets so as to appropriate a greater share of the profits generated by the innovation.[25]

If, on the other hand, the host country offers no unique complementary assets except access to its own market, restrictive practices by the government will only redistribute profits with respect to domestic rather than worldwide sales.

Implications for the International Distribution of the Benefits From Innovation

The above analysis makes it transparent that innovators who do not have access to the relevant specialized and cospecialized assets may end up ceding profits to imitators and other competitors, or simply to the owners of the specialized or cospecialized assets.

Even when the specialized assets are possessed by the innovating firm, they may be located abroad. Foreign factors of production are thus likely to benefit from research and development activities occurring across borders. There is little doubt, for instance, that the inability of many American multinationals to sustain competitive manufacturing in the United States is resulting in declining returns to U.S. labor. Stockholders and top management probably do as well if not better when a multinational accesses cospecialized assets in the firm's foreign subsidiaries; however, if there is unemployment in the factors of production supporting the specialized and cospecialized assets in question, then the foreign factors of production will benefit from innovation originating beyond national borders. This speaks to the importance to innovating nations of maintaining competence and competitiveness in the assets which complement technological innovation, manufacturing being a case in point. It also speaks to the importance to innovating nations of enhancing the protection afforded worldwide to intellectual property.

However, it must be recognized that there are inherent limits to the legal protection of intellectual property, and that business and national strategy are therefore likely to be the critical factors in determining how the gains from innovation are shared worldwide. By making the correct strategic decision, innovating firms can move to protect the interests of stockholders; however, to ensure that domestic rather than foreign cospecialized assets capture the lion's share of the externalities spilling over to complementary assets, the supporting infrastructure for those complementary assets must not be allowed to decay. In short, if a nation has prowess at innovation, then in the absence of iron-clad protection for intellectual property, it must maintain well-developed

[25]If the host country market structure is monopolistic in the first instance, private actors might be able to achieve the same benefit. What government can do is to force collusion of domestic enterprises to their mutual benefit.

complementary assets if it is to capture the spillover benefits from innovation.

Conclusion

The above analysis has attempted to synthesize from recent research in industrial organization and strategic management a framework within which to analyze the distribution of the profits from innovation. The framework indicates that the boundaries of the firm are an important strategic variable for innovating firms. The ownership of complementary assets, particularly when they are specialized and/or cospecialized, help establish who wins and who loses from innovation. Imitators can often outperform innovators if they are better positioned with respect to critical complementary assets. Hence, public policy aimed at promoting innovation must focus not only on R&D, but also on complementary assets, as well as the underlying infrastructure. If government decides to stimulate innovation, it would seem important to clear away barriers which impede the development of complementary assets which tend to be specialized or cospecialized to innovation. To fail to do so will cause an unnecessarily large portion of the profits from innovation to flow to imitators and other competitors. If these firms lie beyond one's national borders, there are obvious implications for the internal distribution of income.

When applied to world markets, results similar to those obtained from the "new trade theory" are suggested by the framework. In particular, tariffs and other restrictions on trade can in some cases injure innovating firms while simultaneously benefiting protected firms when they are imitators. However, the propositions suggested by the framework are particularized to appropriability regimes, suggesting that economywide conclusions will be illusive. The policy conclusions derivable for commodity petrochemicals, for instance, are likely to be different from those that would be arrived at for semiconductors.

The approach also suggests that the product life cycle model of international trade will play itself out very differently in different industries and markets, in part according to appropriability regimes and the nature of the assets which need to be employed to convert a technological success into a commercial one. Whatever its limitations, the approach establishes that it is not so much the structure of markets but the structure of firms, particularly the scope of their boundaries, coupled with national policies with respect to the development of complementary assets, which determines the distribution of the profits amongst innovators and imitator/followers.

Reading II–9
Telephone Companies

William P. Barnett

Since the breakup of the Bell System and the deregulation of telecommunications in the United States, we have seen thousands of companies entering the industry. The actions of the U.S. Department of Justice and Judge Harold Green triggered an explosion of strategic activity, with telephone equipment manufacturers, long-distance service providers, so-called interconnect firms that connect subscribers to the telephone system, and cellular companies all parceling out the industry's sectors as the traditional operating companies see their domain changing substantially. But this surge of new organizing is only half of the story. Exhibit 1 describes the development of the interconnect (or CPES—customer premises equipment and service) sector from 1981 through 1986, and shows that market exit rates have been high across the sector's strategic groups even as this part of the industry has expanded.

Many are surprised to learn that such volatility is not new to the U.S. telephone industry. From the first commercial application of the telephone in 1877 until FCC regulation began in 1933, over 30,000 companies populated this industry in the United States. Some were large, viable rivals to Bell, and even the many small companies were formidable when taken collectively—controlling over half the U.S. telephone market in their heyday. However, even as the so-called independent telephone movement seemed to be succeeding, thousands of these companies failed. For instance, Exhibit 2 shows foundings and failures among all telephone companies that operated in the state of Pennsylvania over the early competitive period—a volatile pattern seen throughout the nation at the time. Thus instability is not new to the U.S. telephone industry. Rather, today's upheavals are in some ways a return to the patterns of the industry's first half-century.

Organizations in Industry, ed. G. Carroll and M. Hannan (New York: Oxford University Press, 1995).

EXHIBIT 1 The Development of the CPES Market in the United States, 1981–1986

	1981	1982	1983	1984	1985	1986	81–86
All firms							
Total number nationally	490	635	777	870	858	856	1,117
Number of state-level operations	641	836	977	1091	1259	1245	1,577
Exits from state markets	10	53	35	52	112	119	381
Percentage exiting from state markets	.016	.063	.036	.048	.089	.096	.242
Single-state CPES firms							
Total number nationally	444	585	723	809	788	783	1,037
Number of state-level operations	444	585	723	809	788	783	1,037
Exits from state markets	10	38	28	47	74	69	266
Percentage exiting from state markets	.023	.065	.039	.059	.094	.088	.257
Multistate CPES firms							
Total number nationally	31	33	36	40	41	41	45
Number of state-level operations	77	88	92	113	205	200	235
Exits from state markets	0	8	2	5	11	14	40
Percentage exiting from state markets	0	.091	.022	.044	.054	.070	.170
Integrated manufacturers							
Total number nationally	11	13	14	16	18	21	24
Number of state-level operations	75	107	105	109	165	160	200
Exits from state markets	0	6	5	0	26	31	68
Percentage exiting from state markets	0	.056	.048	0	.158	.194	.340
Utility affiliates							
Total number nationally	4	4	4	5	11	11	11
Number of state-level operations	45	56	57	60	101	102	105
Exits from state markets	0	1	0	0	1	5	7
Percentage exiting from state markets	0	.018	0	0	.010	.049	.067

Why has the organization of this industry been so volatile? We will try to answer this question by looking historically at the evolution of the industry. Compared to the methods typically used when teaching organizational strategy, this approach is not sexy. For example, the CEOs of these organizations cannot be interviewed because they all are dead. And, obviously, students cannot contemplate working in long-gone organizations. We can, however, use the benefit of hindsight to understand the actual, possibly unanticipated results of strategies that seemed like rational moves at the time. In short, we can learn.

As we look back on the evolution of the telephone industry, I will be reporting facts and regularities that come from a study conducted by me and several of my colleagues. This study drew on four data sources; each source shed light on specific aspects of the industry's evolution:

1. We found qualitative institutional information in archival documents—especially those in the AT&T archives—describing the strategies and motives of many individual companies, government regulators, and other social actors.

2. We collected a nationwide data set covering the more than 30,000 independent telephone companies that operated in the contiguous United States from 1902 until 1942. These data allowed both cross-sectional and temporal statistical comparisons to see the effects of different regulatory policies on the telephone company population.

3. We collected a more detailed sample, including the life histories of the 298 telephone companies that operated in southeast Iowa at any time from the turn of the century until 1933. These data allowed the investigation of industry evolution in rural areas.

4. Another detailed sample included the life histories of the 707 companies that operated at any time in Pennsylvania from the invention of the telephone until 1933. The Pennsylvania sample permitted inquiry into the industry's evolution in more urban areas, as well as a look at the interactions between large and small companies.

Here, I describe only the results of the study, without elaborate theorizing or technical details. Those interested in more in-depth reports should read the work listed in the bibliography. To keep the chap-

EXHIBIT 2

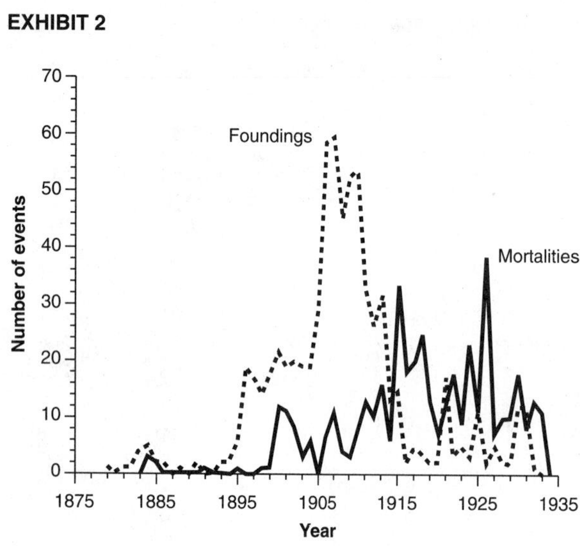

ter straightforward, I will review the dynamics of the industry's evolution by time period. This kind of approach often is misused, implying a life cycle or some other stage-wise inevitability in industrial evolution. No such implication is intended here. In fact, many of the regularities reported for one or another time period likely occurred at other times as well.

1861–1894: From Invention to Litigation

The late 19th century was a time when curious tinkerers and scientists alike experimented with what electricity could do. Some investigated the transmission of sound, leading to innovations such as the telegraph, the phonograph, and the telephone. The earliest reference I have found to an electronic telephone was the invention of Phillip Reis in Germany in 1861, but interest in telephony was widespread among electricity buffs all over Europe and America. The high-tech dreamers of those times no doubt saw a vision of isolated farmers able to call for supplies, or even of business deals closed from miles away. Yet none of the dozens of early telephone designs were commercially viable. Not until the development of the liquid transmitter was the telephone's sound quality sufficient to sustain organizations specializing in telephone service.

So it was that when Elisha Gray and Alexander Bell each separately invented liquid transmitters in 1875, Bell's earlier arrival at the patent office was pivotal. The Bell patents acted as a *segregating mechanism*—a barrier that protected Bell from thousands of other potential entrepreneurs as it began the first commercial telephone company in 1877. Widespread interest in telephone technology continued to grow, however, so that during the period of the Bell patents—1876 to 1894—hundreds of new telephone companies were founded anyway. While the Bell company was reluctant to expand beyond the most lucrative business markets, the independent companies wasted no time, attempting to organize in small and large communities across the nation. When it came to taking legal action, however, the Bell company was fast to act; Bell brought more than 600 patent suits over the period, in most cases driving these rivals out of business.[1]

Judged in terms of its effects on market power, Bell's litigation strategy was successful. Only about 100 independent companies were in operation by the time the most important Bell patents expired in 1893–94, and the monopoly power enjoyed over that period made Bell very profitable. Judged in terms of its effects on legitimacy, however, the strategy backfired. "The monopoly," as it became known, had built a reputation as a ruthless, arrogant trust. To those with populist sentiments, Bell was an archetype of how a large-scale organization runs afoul of the national interest. In this light, those who would build competing telephone organizations were seen as "telephone pioneers," a name that reflected the legitimacy conferred on anyone with the salt to take on Bell.

Meanwhile, by the 1890s the social requirements for building telephone organizations were well developed in the United States. Knowledge of telephone technology was relatively widespread (although equipment was often in short supply). More important, the quarter million telephone instruments in place in the U.S. by the 1890s showed a broad acceptance of the technology—if not the company that had monopolized it. What was once a novelty gadget had become a tool for doing business or being sociable.[2]

[1]C. F. Phillips, Jr., *The Regulation of Public Utilities: Theory and Practice* (Arlington, Virginia: Public Utilities Reports, Inc., 1985).

[2]C. S. Fischer, *American Calling: A Social History of the Telephone to 1940* (Berkeley: University of California Press, 1992).

In general, this sort of increasing legitimacy stimulates an increase in the numbers of organizations in an industry. In telephony, however, Bell's patents and its litigation strategy limited this proliferation, so that increasing legitimacy only ripened the industry's potential. When the Bell patents expired, then, the way was clear for the independent telephone movement to grow.

1894–1913: Organizational Proliferation

From the hundred or so companies that operated when the Bell patents expired in 1894, the industry exploded to number more than 9,000 organizations by 1902. The numbers of companies grew more slowly after that, peaking at well more than 10,000 in operation by 1912. Seen through the lens of economics, this clearly was an aberration. After all, the telephone industry is a natural monopoly where average costs decrease with scale without limit. Suffering severe cost disadvantages, these small companies should soon have failed. In fact, most of these companies did fail after only a few short years on average. They were poorly organized and technically primitive—far less likely to offer long-distance service than were the larger, firmly established survivors of the Bell patent era. Most did not and often could not issue stock to raise capital. In fact, only a small minority were explicitly organized for the purpose of making profits. Each of these factors made the average independent company very likely to fail.

Viewed in terms of the organizational population, however, a different picture appears. Through this lens *population dynamics*—the comings and goings of organizations—catches our attention. As quickly as these organizations failed, new ones were founded to take their places. Just as small and primitive, these successors also were likely to fail when considered individually. But through this process of replenishment, the independents were a robust organizational population, despite being individually insignificant and fragile. Consequently, this organizational population expanded collectively to control over half the U.S. telephone market by 1903, and clearly dominated the industry in some states.

Nonetheless, it is hard to believe that this was an efficient way to organize the telephone system. Why didn't competitive selection processes consolidate the independent movement into one or a few large companies? This question directs us to look for segregating mechanisms that would have retarded competition. In this case political boundaries maintained a large population of smaller organizations, each specialized to one or a few local political areas such as towns or counties. This occurred because local governmental units were the first political actors to regulate telephony. They issued permits and franchise rights to telephone companies, and otherwise settled jurisdictional disputes among rival firms. Furthermore, telephone entrepreneurs typically defined their own service territories by the taken-for-granted boundaries implied by county borders—a normative segregating mechanism. All in all, this meant that political boundaries retarded competition, so that the industry was organized by many more companies than efficiency alone might dictate. For instance, the Pittsburgh & Allegheny Telephone Company was the largest independent company in the Pittsburgh, Pennsylvania area in 1910—but it shared the region's independent markets with 11 other companies, each specializing to some of the 120 distinct political units in the vicinity. This pattern occurred throughout the United States, so that a good predictor of the number of telephone companies in a state was its number of incorporated places as illustrated in Exhibit 3.

Finding so many different organizations leads naturally to another question: What were the *organi-*

EXHIBIT 3

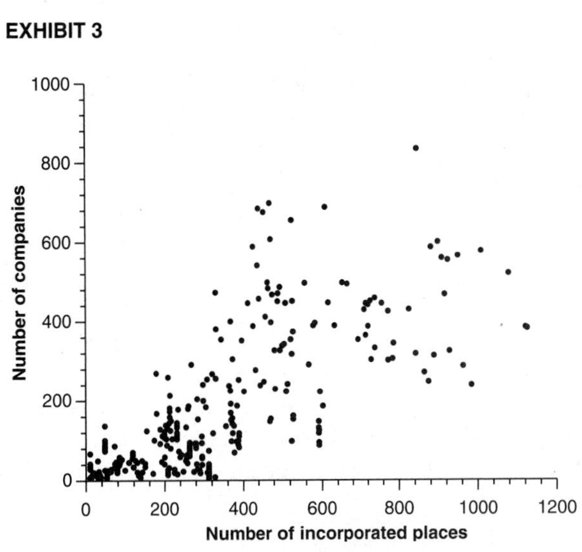

zational forms that developed in the industry? The idea here is that while all organizations are idiosyncratic in many ways, it is helpful to categorize organizations into groupings according to general similarities that make them operate alike in similar part of the environment. In this case, two general organizational forms appeared among the thousands of early independent companies: cooperatively run *mutual companies,* including a large number of lines run by farmers, and for-profit *commercial firms.* The mutual companies usually operated in rural areas, benefitting from the loyalty and volunteerism of locals who were often suspicious of large companies, especially Bell.[3] For example, in 1900 residents in and around Marengo and Ladora, two towns in rural southeastern Iowa, could solicit telephone service from several commercial telephone companies in Iowa County. However, over 100 residents instead purchased shares in a new cooperative venture, the Iowa County Mutual Telephone Company. Staying in rural areas where distrust of commercial ventures was strong, the company supported only about five telephones per pole mile. Yet by relying largely on voluntary labor and the capital of members, it grew modestly and continued to operate in the area for years to come.

By comparison, commercial telephone firms usually located in more densely populated areas and were professionally managed. The Marengo Telephone Company was founded in 1901, one year after Iowa County Mutual and in the same general area. Although it began with only 90 subscribers, the Marengo company grew rapidly by serving townsfolk, with a system supporting double the number of instruments per pole mile than Iowa County Mutual. In this way, the mutual and commercial forms operated in distinct *niches* for which each was particularly well-suited.

Once one attends to differences between organizational forms, other patterns become easier to see, since different organizational forms tend to pursue different *strategies.* In this case, mutual companies were not well-suited to growth, since they lacked professional management and the more sophisticated technical know-how growth would require. But they were quick to establish. Thus, this form expanded its service by proliferating in numbers—an appropriate strategy given the scattered, disparate nature of the rural communities that comprised the mutuals' niche. Meanwhile, the commercial firms tended to grow in size individually—again, a fit strategy considering the more populated areas they inhabited.

All this talk of niches would be fine for many other kinds of organizations, one might say, but how could telephone companies provide service when they were limited to particular communities? After all, a telephone system that does not reach out of town would not be of much use. The answer, it turns out, was that the independents often connected their lines to one another, forming loosely organized networks of interconnected systems. Typically, several mutual companies would connect to a commercial firm, which in turn would be connected to other commercials and possibly to a long-distance network—or maybe to Bell.[4]

For any individual telephone company, connecting to neighboring companies was done on a case-by-case basis rather than as part of some grand strategy. Consequently, these networks were poorly coordinated, leaving islands of isolated subscribers disconnected from the wider world—a situation often made worse when feuding companies reneged on connection arrangements. Yet in the aggregate, the thousands of effective connections among companies turned out to be of great strategic importance. Because of these connections, the fates of companies within common networks became linked in a positive way, so that an organization's viability was increased as its partners expanded and prospered. This kind of relationship, known as *mutualism,* can be thought of as the opposite of competition.

Viewed from the organization level, mutualism usually is seen as something that benefits individual companies: linked organizations are better off than unlinked organizations. Ecologists take mutualism a step further, however, noting that it gives rise to *organizational communities*—collectives of organizations that share a common fate because they work together. Organizational communities are important strategically because they shift the level where natural selection occurs. Individual companies within such communities become less vulnerable to exogenous factors, since mutualism helps them survive hard times. Instead, selection shifts more to the community level—so that success or failure occurs not so much for isolated organizations as for entire net-

[3]R. Atwood, "Telephony and its Cultural Meanings in Southeastern Iowa, 1900–1917," unpublished Ph.D. dissertation, University of Iowa, 1984.

[4]Ibid.

works. Consequently, whether an individual company succeeded or failed increasingly depended on whether it was part of a larger network of companies that, in turn, succeeded or failed in competition with other such networks. In this light, it is no coincidence that the Marengo Telephone Company and the Iowa County Mutual Telephone Company, along with several dozen other companies, all were founded at about the same time and place and continued to survive alongside one another. They were separate companies, but as an organizational community they shared a common fate.

It is important to keep in mind that these organizational communities were not understood to be formal alliances among large numbers of companies. Indeed, archival records suggest that those who managed these companies typically were aware only of the few firms to which they connected directly, not the hundreds of other companies that may also have been within their wider networks. Neither, then, would they have been aware of community-level regularities in performance. Rather, patterns of success and failure probably appeared chaotic to those in the trenches, where managers of independent companies usually saw neighboring companies as rivals—working with one another out of necessity while squabbling more often than not.[5] It is only with the bird's-eye view of the analyst that we detect patterns at the community level that likely seemed random to any particular strategist.

Meanwhile, the Bell System did not sit by while its market share plummeted. To the contrary, Bell responded by refusing to sell equipment to the independents at any price. (In rural areas, in fact, it was not unusual to see fence wire used for telephone lines!) As fast as it could, Bell moved into direct price competition with the independents wherever it stood even a remote chance of regaining market share, and practically any tactic was considered fair game if it would beat the independents. This meant acquiring pesky rivals, of course, but even included such tactics as operating "independent" companies that were secretly owned by Bell.[6]

Although these tactics slowed the independents' surge, they forced Bell to operate unprofitably in many areas while serving to reinforce Bell's onerous reputation. So it was that when J. P. Morgan led a group of bankers to take over the Bell System in 1907, Theodore Vail—once the mastermind behind the initial Bell expansion—was returned to Bell's helm. Vail immediately changed Bell's strategy to one of "systems awareness" in which Bell aggressively acquired large, independent companies. Meanwhile, Bell also shifted its treatment of small independent companies—connecting with and supporting them in order to place the large independents in a competitive squeeze.

Altogether, the period up to 1913 saw the development of a collectively formidable, although fragmented, independent telephone movement facing an aggressive, predatory Bell System. With this stage set, changes then unfolded very quickly over the next few years—but in some entirely unexpected ways.

1913–1921: Collective Stagnation

It is difficult, in hindsight, to see the independents as anything but underdogs in their battle with Bell. As the struggle climaxed, however, several forces were pushing strongly in favor of the independents. Distress over Bell's predatory behavior spread from the populists to the growing progressive political movement of the times. More generally, concern was widespread that the U.S. telephone system was becoming impossibly fragmented. Consequently, from 1904 to 1919, 34 states passed laws requiring neighboring companies to connect their lines. We found that these laws increased mutualism among the independent companies, while reducing the strength of competition from Bell. Meanwhile, the federal government also reacted to the anti-Bell wave, with the Department of Justice preparing to investigate possible antitrust violations by the company. To head off this investigation, Bell agreed in 1913 to what would become known as the Kingsbury Commitment with the U.S. Attorney General. In this, Bell agreed to stop acquiring directly competing independent companies, and to allow toll connections to the independents at a reasonable rate. All in all, by 1913 the independent movement was supported by a range of powerful institutional measures.

Around the same time, technologies appeared that also increased the potential for coordination among the independents. The first independent companies used so-called magneto instruments. This name refers to the hand-cranked magneto that supplied ringing current, but the more important characteristic of these instruments was the use of a separate battery in each instrument to power sound

[5]Ibid.

[6]Fischer, *America Calling*.

transmission. Because of this decentralized power supply, systems using these instruments suffered serious problems of incompatibility and poor maintenance. By 1915, however, independent companies were adopting the so-called common-battery power technology, which featured an organizationally controlled power source housed in a central office or switchboard. By ensuring proper maintenance and a uniform standard in power supply, the common battery helped greatly in the coordination of the independent movement. Meanwhile, a technology known as *line loading* also was spreading among the independents. This technology increased the range of a telephone central office from 30 to 300 miles, permitting the development of long-distance companies within the independent movement.

These technical developments dramatically increased the potential for mutualism among the independent companies. Smaller, single-exchange systems and the larger, multiexchange systems worked together as complements—at least so long as they all adopted common-battery systems. As a result, these organizations increased one another's growth rates while decreasing one another's failure rates. Thus the new technologies gave the loose affiliations of commercial and mutual companies the potential to compose smoothly functioning, viable networks capable of large-scale operation.

It is important to emphasize the community-level logic here. These technologies did not aid the independents by making individual companies technically superior so that they could break from their fellow independents and compete on their own. In fact, we found that head-on competition among the most technically sophisticated independents did more harm than good to these companies. On the one hand, having the most sophisticated technologies would reduce a company's failure rate by 94 percent, but head-on competition from other sophisticated companies more than offset this advantage—with the net effect of actually doubling failure rates on average. Rather, the benefits from these technologies came from allowing organizations to coordinate their systems with one another—a gain not so much for any single company as for entire networks of standardized, complementary organizations.

Despite the institutional supports and technical developments, however, the independent telephone movement stopped growing after about 1913—losing ground in terms of the numbers of companies as well as market share. Why? The answer, it appears, is found in the very same forces that were expected to bring success to the independents. The evidence suggests that both the institutional and technical developments of the time seriously (albeit unintendedly) harmed the independent movement.

On the institutional side, after celebrating Bell's retreat under the Kingsbury Commitment, the independent companies then turned their attention to competing ferociously with one another. Our results show that this increase in competition was strong—powerful enough to turn what was a mutualistic relationship among the independents into a competitive one. This is a specific example of a more general process known as *competitive release,* where organizations relieved of rivalry from one source increase the strength of their competition with others. Given that the independents relied—even if unknowingly—on collective success, this competitive release was extremely damaging to the movement.

If that was not bad enough, the movement also became seriously fragmented technologically during this period. This may seem surprising, given all that was just said about new technical developments that could aid coordination. Most students, implicitly thinking like economists, naturally would assume that the various organizations involved would behave rationally and adopt the technologies that would bring them success. Ecologists are more skeptical about making such a jump from a normative prescription to an expectation about what really goes on in organizational life. In the case of the telephone industry, this skepticism seems to have been borne out for two reasons.

First, although many companies did attempt to change technologies—adopting line loading and common battery power—this attempt to change often caused them to fail. This result is a specific case of a more general process, where change disrupts reliable organizational functioning. According to *structural-inertia* theory, changing organizations must develop new capabilities, new roles for members to fill, new routines to coordinate behavior, new formal and informal structural arrangements, and new ties to different suppliers and other social actors in the environment. In sum, by changing, these telephone companies became as vulnerable to failure as a new firm. For example, the Blairsville

EXHIBIT 4

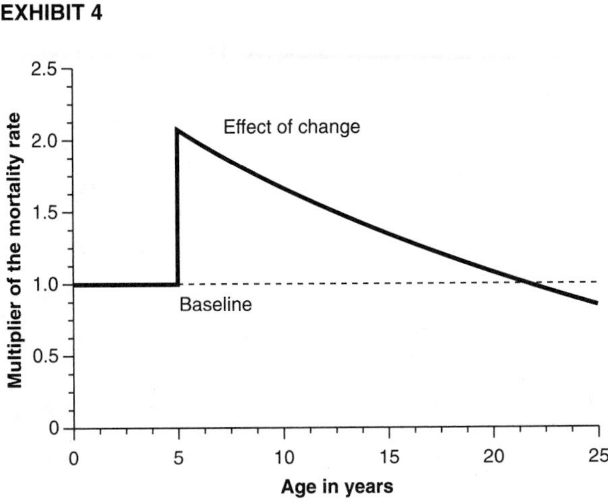

telephone company in Pennsylvania was founded in 1896, and it had grown to nearly 1,000 subscribers by 1925. It then made an apparently sensible strategic move, adopting common-battery technology. The adjustment to the new technology proved to be too difficult, however, and within two years the Blairsville telephone company failed. More broadly, the study found that these companies doubled their failure rates, on average, due to the disruption caused when they adopted more advanced technologies. Exhibit 4 illustrates this result in terms of the multiplicative effect that change had on failure rates. It also illustrates, however, that these organizations recovered from the shock of having changed technologies—if they did not die first—after about 16 years on average. It took that long to restore these organizations to the level of functioning and institutional support that they knew before the change.

Second, despite these new technologies, large numbers of primitive, magneto companies entered the industry during this period. It would be difficult to make sense of this if we think of these foundings as the calculated acts of fully rational entrepreneurs. However, if we view the entrepreneur as constrained by existing social and economic conditions, this new surge of magneto firms is less surprising. The new technologies and the know-how to operate them were not commonplace, nor was the needed financial support in many areas. Thus telephone entrepreneurs, no doubt encouraged by Bell's surrender under Kingsbury, mustered whatever primitive resources were available and entered the industry. With the flood of these magneto companies, the independent movement became increasingly fragmented. Although individually harmless, these small, often incompatible companies collectively crippled the movement—increasing failure rates and decreasing growth rates for all independent companies. In fact, these effects were so powerful that they more than offset the benefits that had been gained by those parts of the movement that had adopted the new technologies.

While the independent movement was collectively stagnating, Bell was busily expanding into latent markets all over the United States. As Bell grew it occupied more and more of the potential telephone market, reducing the growth rate of the independent movement. At the same time, Bell took a highly visible role as a patriotic institution during World War I—a move that built public confidence in Bell at the same time the independents were being blamed for ongoing problems with the coordination of the nation's telephone system. Fairly or unfairly, the independents were then roundly blamed when telephone rates skyrocketed at the end of the war as price controls were lifted. (The industry was nominally nationalized in 1918–19, but this amounted to little more than price regulation.) With the winds of public support blowing in its favor, Bell was freed from its Kingsbury Commitment by the Willis-Graham act of 1921. What was to have been the heyday of the independent telephone movement ended dismally, with Bell again on the offensive.

1921–1933: Concentration

After 1921, the independent movement continued to lose market share, and the number of companies fell as the independent market became more concentrated. These trends, it turns out, resulted in part from the aging of the independent telephone population. By the 1920s independent telephone companies were, on average, older than at any time in the past. With age, organizational growth rates tend to fall (other things being equal), since both an organization's internal potential and external opportunities for growth are depleted over time.

Furthermore, increasing ages imply that the existing organizations of the 20s were survivors—they were the ones that endured even as their fellow companies were being selected against. This meant, then, that the telephone companies of the 1920s were stronger competitors on average. As such, they were more capable of harming one another than had been the case in earlier eras. Consequently, the 1920s saw founding rates fall, failure rates increase, and growth rates flatten—a pattern that seems to result generally when organizational populations mature.

Bell's expansion remained steady and rapid in the 1920s. Although Bell and most other companies declined slightly in size at the onset of the depression, Bell clearly had risen to its position of dominance in the industry by 1933, when active national regulation began under the FCC. Through several decades of relative stability, Bell would then be known as the nation's telephone company, even as several thousand independent telephone companies continued to exist as regulated monopolists in various locations throughout the United States.

Conclusion

Nowadays the U.S. telecommunications industry again is an arena where new firms and new strategies are experimenting, succeeding, and failing. Although it is still too early to know how the current era will evolve, students may find it valuable to conduct an ecological analysis of the modern telecommunications industry or one of its major sectors using the ideas developed in this and other papers.[7] In doing so, it may help to structure your investigation by asking: What are the segregating mechanisms that shape competition in the industry or sector? What organizational forms have appeared? What are their strategies? Where are their niches? Are any organizational forms complementary, so that you would expect to see mutualism between them? Do organizational communities exist? Are any forms sufficiently protected from competition that you expect to see competitive release? What strategic changes are firms attempting? What will happen to these changing organizations? As you ask these questions, make predictions about how the population dynamics of the industry would look if you were right. Seek out data about the industry to see whether your analysis appears to be correct.

---

[7]See, for example, W. P. Barnett, "Strategic Deterrence Among Multipoint Competitors," *Industrial and Corporate Change* 2 (1993), pp. 249–78.

Additional References

Barnett, W. P. "The Organizational Ecology of a Technological System." *Administrative Science Quarterly* 35 (1990), pp. 31–60.

Barnett, W. P. "The Liability of Collective Action: Growth and Change Among Early American Telephone Companies." In *Evolutionary Dynamics of Organizations,* ed. Baum and J. Singh. New York: Oxford, 1993.

Barnett, W. P. "The Dynamics of Competitive Intensity." Working paper, Graduate School of Business, Stanford University, 1993.

Barnett, W. P., and T. L. Amburgey. "Do Larger Organizations Generate Stronger Competition?" In *Organizational Evolution: New Directions,* ed. J. Singh. Beverly Hills: Sage, 1990.

Barnett, W. P., and G. R. Carroll. "Competition and Mutualism among Early Telephone Companies." *Administrative Science Quarterly* 32 (1987), pp. 400–421.

Barnett, W. P., and G. R. Carroll. "How Institutional Constraints Affected the Organization of Early American Telephony." *Journal of Law, Economics and Organization* 9 (1993), pp. 98–126.

Brock, G. W. *The Telecommunications Industry.* Cambridge: Harvard University Press, 1981.

Brooks, J. *Telephone: The First Hundred Years.* New York: Harper & Row, 1976.

Danielian, N. R. *AT&T: The Story of Industrial Conquest.* New York: Vanguard, 1939.

DuMoncel, T. A. L. *The Telephone, Microphone and the Phonograph.* New York: Arno Press, 1879, 1974 tr.

Federal Communications Commission. *Proposed Report: Telephone Investigation.* Washington: U.S. Government Printing Office, 1938.

Fischer, C. S., and G. R. Carroll. "Telephone and Automobile Diffusion in the United States, 1902–1937," *American Journal of Sociology* 93 (1988), pp. 1153–78.

Gabel, R. "The Early Competitive Era in Telephone Communications, 1893–1920." *Law and Contemporary Problems* 34 (1969), pp. 340–59.

MacMeal, H. B. *The Story of Independent Telephony.* Chicago: Independent Pioneer Telephone Association, 1934.

Schlesinger, L. A.; D. Dyer; T. N. Clough; and D. Landau. *Chronicles of Corporate Change: Management Lessons From AT&T and Its Offspring.* Lexington, MA: Lexington Books, 1987.

Wasserman, N. *From Invention to Innovation: Long Distance Telephone Transmission at the Turn of the Century.* Baltimore: Johns Hopkins University Press, 1985.

Case II–8 Mips Computer Systems (A)

Krista McQuade and Benjamin Gomes-Casseres

Our mission is to make the MIPS architecture pervasive worldwide.

—Mips Annual Report, 1990

On April 9, 1991, 20 computer hardware and software firms announced the formation of an industry alliance centering around a new, and as yet untried, microprocessor from Mips Computer Systems. Due out at the end of 1991, the R4000 microprocessor from Mips was chosen as part of an attempt by some of the industry's leading firms to establish hardware and software standards in the divided market for personal computers (PCs) and workstations. Uniting such firms as Compaq Computer, Microsoft, and Digital Equipment Corporation behind the Mips chip, the Advanced Computing Environment (ACE) consortium had the potential to affect significantly the position of industry leaders Sun Microsystems, Motorola, Intel, Hewlett-Packard, and IBM. For Mips, the newest player in the industry, it meant a major endorsement of its technology.

Headquartered in Sunnyvale, California, Mips designed and developed high-performance reduced instruction set computing (RISC) chips and systems. In 1985, Mips was the first company to bring a viable RISC design to the marketplace; by the late 1980s, the struggle for dominance in the RISC-based segment of the marketplace involved all the major computer companies and semiconductor firms worldwide. A lot was at stake; it was estimated that RISC chips had the potential to capture as much as 95 percent of the global workstation market by 1993, and also significantly affect the much larger markets for PCs and minicomputers.

In 1990, Mips had sales of just over $152 million and 775 employees worldwide; it was among the smallest players in the industry. Its size, however, belied a larger market effect. Since 1987, the company had promoted its technology worldwide through a network of alliances with semiconductor manufacturers and large systems developers. In addition, it provided technology licenses to dozens of original equipment manufacturers (OEMs) and value-added resellers (VARs). Mips chairman and CEO Robert Miller, who came to Mips from minicomputer maker Data General in 1987 and then led the start-up company out of the red, set his sights high:

> There have only been three successful standard architectures[1] in the computer industry: the IBM 360 in mainframes, the DEC VAX in minicomputers, and the Intel X86 in personal computers. Each company has made a ton of money. At Data General I used to argue that it was too late to stop VAX from being the standard. Instead, we had to be on the forefront of the next wave. That is what we are doing at Mips and why we need to make the Mips architecture pervasive worldwide.

RISC Technology

RISC technology was essentially a streamlined approach to microprocessor design. Traditional microprocessor design, called complex instruction set computing (CISC), was based on the theory that the more complex the instruction set embedded in the chip's design, the more efficiently the computer operated. RISC challenged this premise, claiming that, in practice, only 20 percent of conventional instructions were called upon to perform 80 percent of a computer's functions. RISC designers set out to increase processing speeds by reducing and simplifying the instruction set. In RISC, many of the more complex commands and functions included in conventional designs were transferred to the compiler[2] and the application software.

Besides seeing advantages in performance, RISC designers thought that there were cost and time-to-market advantages to their approach. With simpler instruction sets, RISC chips were implemented using less circuitry. This typically resulted in a shorter

Harvard Business School Case 9-792-055, revised December 1992.

[1]Computer *architectures* generally referred to the technical design of components, such as the microprocessors, as well as to the way in which components were linked to make the whole system. *Standard* architectures were those with substantial, or dominant, shares of the relevant market.

[2]Compilers translate language commands into machine-readable instructions. In RISC designs, the speed and efficiency of program execution was substantially determined by the quality of the compiler.

design and initial testing phase, as well as in lower manufacturing costs. Just as in CISC, however, the viable manufacture of RISC chips required a high level of capital investment and volume production. Throughout the 1980s, a debate had raged about the technology's commercial potential.

Although RISC technology was invented at IBM in 1975, 10 years later not one major chip manufacturer or computer firm had introduced a RISC-based product. Ridge Computer Systems and Pyramid Computer had both introduced early RISC designs,[3] but had been unsuccessful in converting many customers to their technologies. Major U.S. chip manufacturers Intel and Motorola were slow in developing chips with the new technology, due to the firms' reluctance to cannibalize their existing CISC-based product lines. Hewlett-Packard (HP), DEC, and IBM had all established RISC R&D programs; however, a lack of confidence in the market's acceptance of RISC kept these projects on wait-and-see status. The major drawback to RISC was that software developed for traditional CISC systems was incompatible with RISC systems. IBM was said to have dropped its early RISC program in the late 1970s because it estimated that writing programs to attract customers to RISC would require 1,000 employee-years.[4] This lack of application software, many believed, would keep RISC a theoretical concept, or at best a niche technology.

Mips was instrumental in changing the industry's opinion of RISC technology. In 1985, Mips brought a RISC chip to the marketplace that represented a 10-fold increase in processing power at a fraction of the price of a CISC chip. This demonstration of RISC's commercial feasibility caused other firms to launch full-blown RISC development programs, and by 1991 seven different RISC architectures competed in the marketplace. The major designers of RISC microprocessors in 1991 were Sun Microsystems, Mips, Hewlett-Packard, and IBM.

RISC in the Marketplace

One of the advantages of RISC processors was that their architecture was "scalable," meaning that it could be used in large and small computer systems. Unlike the IBM 360 architecture, for example, RISC architectures could be used in PCs, workstations, minicomputers, mainframes, and even in supercomputers. RISC processors first became widely used in workstations, and in the early 1990s were still largely confined to this segment and certain minicomputer segments. One reason for the early application of RISC in workstations was the price–performance advantages of RISC. Other reasons were the rapid growth of the workstation segment and the existence of well-established standards in PCs, minicomputers, and mainframes.

RISC's future success in penetrating any of these markets depended on the establishment of an operating system standard.[5] Nearly every RISC architecture on the marketplace in 1991 used Unix, an operating system originally developed by AT&T that was prevalent mainly in the workstation segment of the industry. In 1990, nearly half of all workstations used Unix; by 1994, this percentage was expected to rise to 80 percent. In the market for personal computers, however, Unix was not popular. In part, this was because there were many versions of Unix; hundreds of versions had been developed since the 1970s, when AT&T began to license this operating system. Furthermore, most Unix systems were difficult to use.

In an attempt to clear up the confusion, Sun Microsystems collaborated with AT&T in May 1988 to combine two versions of Unix that were popular in the workstation industry. Fearing that Sun would gain an advantage in the marketplace through early access to new AT&T versions, a group of competitors aligned themselves to form the Open Software Foundation (OSF). OSF established its own version of Unix, which it called OSF/1, to compete against the AT&T/Sun version. By 1991, OSF numbered over 200 members, including DEC, IBM, HP, Groupe Bull, Nixdorf, and Siemens. In December 1988, AT&T and Sun formed their own broad industry alliance—Unix International—in response to the

[3]These early RISC products were not considered "pure" RISC. That is, although their design incorporated some RISC principles, some complex instructions were left in the design to avoid the complicated problems of redesigning system and compiler software.

[4]IBM reentered the RISC field in 1986, as discussed below.

[5]An operating system was the software code that controlled the computer and provided interface between application software, the user, and the microprocessor. DOS and Unix were both operating systems common in desktop computers. Traditionally, computer companies had attempted to protect their markets by developing proprietary operating systems and software to match. IBM's 370 operating system had long dominated the market for mainframes, for example, while DEC's VMS held the majority of the minicomputer market. Open systems, in contrast, allowed hardware and software made by different companies to be used, and promised greater competition between vendors.

EXHIBIT 1 Worldwide Market Shares of Leading PC and Workstation Vendors in 1990

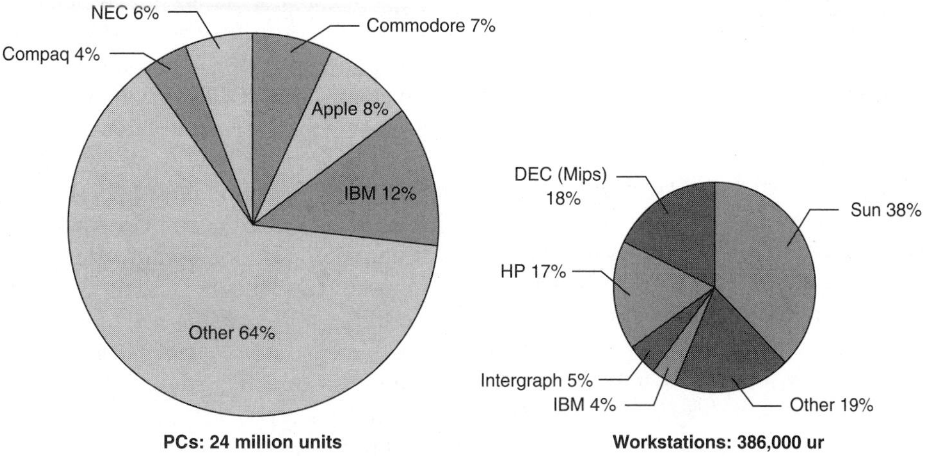

NEC 6%
Commodore 7%
Compaq 4%
Apple 8%
IBM 12%
Other 64%

PCs: 24 million units

DEC (Mips) 18%
Sun 38%
HP 17%
Intergraph 5%
IBM 4%
Other 19%

Workstations: 386,000 ur

SOURCE: Compiled from Dataquest information appearing in *Electronics,* November 1991, p. 59.

OSF. Key members included Intel, Motorola, Unisys, NCR, Fujitsu, and Control Data.

Workstations. In 1991, the greatest penetration of RISC-based computer systems was in the workstation segment of the marketplace. Originally purchased for computationally intensive scientific and engineering applications, workstations were gaining popularity during the late 1980s in commercial markets such as electronic publishing and business graphics. In 1989, revenues from sales for commercial applications represented just over 7 percent of total workstation revenues, and industry analysts expected this to rise to one-third by 1994. Potentially, commercial applications represented a much larger market for workstations than technical applications. In 1991, the workstation market was dominated by four vendors—Sun Microsystems, HP/Apollo,[6] IBM, and DEC. Thirteen other firms manufactured workstations, including niche players such as Silicon Graphics (3-D graphics) and Intergraph (military applications). Still, the whole workstation market was smaller than the PC market (see Exhibit 1).

Workstations were the fastest growing segment of the computer industry; between 1990 and 1994, workstation revenues were expected to grow at a compound annual rate of 53 percent. In 1990, sales of U.S.-based vendors hit $8.5 billion, up from $6.8 billion in 1989, and $4.5 billion in 1988. But experts disagreed about the potential for growth of RISC workstations; in 1990, their forecasts for 1993 of the proportion of RISC in total workstations sold ranged from 95 percent to less than 50 percent.

One reason for this wide variance was uncertainty about how established CISC customers and producers would react over the long term. Despite 50 to 75 percent annual gains in performance expected from RISC architectures, compared to 30 percent annual gains for CISC, not all end users would find switching feasible or desirable. Some large CISC customers, such as banks, department stores, and airlines, had invested billions of dollars in software over the years. For smaller customers, the selection of third-party software available was much greater for CISC than for RISC, making a strong case for staying with the former. In addition, faced with the RISC threat, CISC developers were increasing the performance of their chips and lowering prices. Paired with CISC's overwhelming advantage in software applications, improved price/performance from CISC put it in a position to compete with RISC. Intel's 80586 chip, due out in 1992, would combine RISC principles for improved performance with the original Intel design, and so would be compatible with existing software designed for the X86 family.

Several trends were expected to increase the demand for RISC and Unix. First, increasingly complex applications such as 3D graphics and large database management required increased amounts

[6]In 1989, HP acquired Apollo, one of the pioneers in the workstation segment.

of processing power, and RISC offered significant performance boosts without large increases in price. Second, a market had developed for network computing, providing connectivity between incompatible computer systems so that a variety of users—workstations, personal computers, and terminals, for example—could access specific services at the same time. These network computing environments also required increased processing power. Third, customers' demand to protect their investment in software and gain independence from proprietary operating systems led to an increasing acceptance of Unix as an industry standard. Unix was well-suited to RISC implementations, and Unix and RISC together could operate across the entire spectrum of computing, from desktop workstations to mainframes.

International markets. Although all of the major workstation manufacturers were based in the United States, firms in both Europe and the Far East were entering the workstation business. U.S. firms, for their part, were also continuing to expand their international operations. In 1990, non-U.S. markets surpassed the U.S. market for the first time. Technical workstations, however, were still most popular in the United States. In Europe, commercial workstation applications were widespread, perhaps due to the popularity of Unix in that market. Many European producers embraced Unix in an effort to increase their independence from the operating systems controlled by IBM, DEC, and other U.S. leaders. Unix represented one-third of the total European computer market in 1989, and was expected to grow 40 percent per year into the 1990s.

RISC technology was also dominated by U.S. firms in 1991—not one European or Pacific Rim firm had introduced a RISC design other than one developed by U.S. vendors. Instead, these firms were licensing RISC technology from U.S. firms in large numbers. Mips had been the most successful in attracting companies to its RISC technology in Europe, with the giant German firm Siemens-Nixdorf Informationsystems and French Groupe Bull as its flagship licensees. In Asia, Mips, Sun, and HP competed for distribution channels. Toshiba, Fujitsu, and Daewoo had lined up behind Sun; NEC and Sony, behind Mips; and Samsung and Hitachi, behind HP. While the U.S. firms welcomed foreign licensees, critics decried how easy it was for foreign firms to gain access to advanced microprocessor technology developed in the United States.

Company Background

Mips began as a Stanford University research project led by three professors, who went on to found the company in 1984. They obtained $22 million in financing from a Silicon Valley venture capital firm and concentrated on research and product development during the first two years. Mips developed the first commercially available RISC microprocessor (the R2000), RISC compiler software, and a RISC-based computer system; volume shipment of its chips and systems began in the last quarter of 1986. At this time, the production of chips and boards was contracted out, while Mips's manufacturing department assembled complete computer systems. A small sales force sold Mips products directly to the end user.

But by early 1987, despite several design wins,[7] Mips had accumulated a deficit of $16 million, and less than $1 million of the original venture capital was left. The company was in precarious financial shape (see Exhibits 2 and 3). Although its leadership in RISC technology was widely acknowledged, customers were hesitant to invest in a new technology when they could not be sure that the young company would survive. Also, Mips had no clear strategic vision. Robert Miller recalled: "When I was senior VP at Data General, Mips tried to convince us to adopt their microprocessor. We didn't do so, in part because Mips did not pass the strategy test. They had no clear idea of where they wanted the company to go and how to get there."

Mips's Strategic Turnaround

Miller was trained in electrical engineering and worked 15 years at IBM before joining Data General in 1981. He was highly regarded in the industry as a savvy and experienced manager. In time, he hired equally seasoned executives for his team (see Exhibit 4). Observers were soon calling Mips the million-dollar company with a billion-dollar management.

Miller's first concern at Mips was to return the company to secure financial footing. First, he led a crash effort to reduce cash outflows. In the three months before his arrival, the company had spent $3 million; in the two-and-a-half months after that, it

[7] The selection of a particular technology for a new product line was termed a *design win* for that technology. In the computer industry, this was a widely used measure of the success of a new technology.

EXHIBIT 2 Mips Income Statement, 1985–1991 (in thousands except per share data)

	1985	1986	1987	1988	1989	1990	1991 (Q1+Q2)	1991 (Q3)
Revenues	0	$ 7,882	$ 13,902	$ 39,383	$101,862	$152,347	$88,502	$ 32,727
of which:								
Product	—	7,882	13,902	32,032	70,032	105,703	60,681	29,514
Technology	—	—	—	7,383	31,830	46,044	27,821	3,213
of which								
U.S.A.	—	7,882	13,485	35,144	79,994	124,407		
Europe	—	—	417	4,239	13,789	22,288		
Pacific Rim	—	—	—	—	8,082	5,652		
Costs and Expenses								
Cost of revenue	—	3,986	7,554	16,069	41,877	67,331	43,678	20,213
SG&A	2,684	5,848	8,223	15,123	33,349	53,166	29,329	13,871
R&D	3,593	7,334	8,801	12,910	18,982	27,828	17,285	8,749
Restructuring costs	—	—	—	—	—	—	—	25,500
Total costs and expenses	6,277	17,078	24,578	44,102	94,208	148,325	90,292	68,333
Operating income	−6,277	−9,196	−10,676	−4,719	7,654	4,022	−1,790	−35,606
Interest income	290	171	176	1,977	2,091	6,219	1,840	597
Income before taxes	−5,987	−9,025	−10,500	−2,742	9,745	10,241	50	−35,009
Provision for income taxes	—	—	—	240	2,749	3,127	23	2,287
Net income from continuing operations	−5,987	−9,025	−10,500	−2,982	6,996	7,114	27	−37,296
Discontinued operations	—	—	—	−736	−4,065	—	—	—
Net income	$-5,987	$−9,025	$−10,500	$−3,718	$ 2,931	$ 7,114	$ 27	$−37,296
Per share information ($)								
Income from continuing operations	−1.06	−1.03	−.92	−.19	.36	.28	.00	−1.55
Net income	−1.06	−1.03	−.92	−.24	.15	.28		

Memo Items on Technology Revenues (end of year; in millions $)

	1985	1986	1987	1988	1989	1990	1991 (Q1+Q2)	1991 (Q3)
Technology revenues reported above			—	7.4	31.8	46.6	27.8	3.2
Accumulated deferred income[a]			4.8	14.4	17.0	8.5	11.7	−12.8
Identifiable sources of technology revenues:[b]								
Kubota:								
Up-front fee			2.4					
Received			2.4			[c]		
DEC:								
Up-front fee				15.0				
Received				11.7	3.3			
NEC and Siemens together:								
Up-front fee					21.5			
Received					17.0	4.5		
Nonmonetary transactions[d]						6.5		

[a]Technology fees received, but not yet reported. See balance sheet note (a).

[b]Identified in Mips annual and press reports. Financial details of licenses to Bull, Sony, and others have been identified. Up-front license fees from LSI, IDT, and Performance Semiconductor (1987) were reported to be insignificant.

[c]Mips reported that a new license and manufacturing agreement with Kubota in the third quarter had a significant impact on technology revenues.

[d]Three separate agreements where technology and services were acquired by Mips in exchange for architecture licenses, which Mips ordinarily sells. These transactions were reported as technology revenue and as purchased assets.

SOURCE: Mips annual reports, IPO Prospectus, and 1991 unaudited quarterly reports.

EXHIBIT 3 Mips Balance Sheets, 1985–1991 (end of year; in thousands)

	1985	1986	1987	1988	1989	1990	1991 (Q1+Q2)	1991 (Q3)
Assets								
Current assets:								
Cash and cash equivalents			}$30,584	} $38,292	} $ 91,732	$ 42,005	$ 31,449	} 52,394
Short-term investments						18,303	26,103	
Accounts receivable			4,379	10,753	26,820	40,108	47,965	41,276
Inventories			1,704	10,028	17,888	33,050	27,098	25,396
Prepaid expenses and other			676	2,220	1,773	4,458	4,620	5,908
Total current assets			37,343	61,293	138,213	137,924	137,235	124,974
Property and equipment, net			5,406	8,700	17,954	34,134	32,495	29,478
Other assets			2,313	4,907	9,777	21,131	26,517	5,730
Total assets	6,390	16,659	45,062	74,900	165,944	193,189	196,247	170,182
Liabilities								
Current liabilities:								
Accounts and notes payable			3,076	9,776	12,048	16,548	12,654	14,030
Accrued compensation			461	1,550	3,122	6,051	7,131	} 22,502
Other liabilities			2,599	1,712	4,979	8,901	7,238	
Total current liabilities			6,136	13,038	20,149	31,500	27,023	36,532
Deferred revenue[a]			4,834	14,430	16,990	8,540	11,701	} 12,772
Long-term convertible debt	672	2,101	378	—	1,500	1,521	1,567	
Other			—	2,630	2,630	—	—	—
Total liabilities	$1,997	$ 9,098	$11,348	$30,098	$ 38,639	$ 41,561	$ 40,291	$ 49,304
Shareholders' Equity								
Total equity	$4,393	$ 7,561	$33,714	$44,802	$127,305	$151,628	$155,956	$120,878

[a]Deferred revenue is up-front technology licensing fees that have been received, but that have not yet been recognized as income.

SOURCE: Mips annual reports, IPO Prospectus, and 1991 unaudited quarterly reports.

spent only about $150,000. He then raised $14 million from the venture capital community, half of it from existing Mips investors.

Next, the question of the company's strategic direction was addressed in a four-day, off-site meeting of top executives. What emerged was a plan to change Mips's basic business approach. Miller explained: "Mips had wanted to build semiconductors. It thought it could compete with the likes of Intel and Motorola, but it could not. It was paying foundries on a wafer-by-wafer basis to produce its chips, but with its small volume, it was getting second-hand treatment." Instead, Miller proposed to license Mips's technology to leading semiconductor firms who could manufacture Mips chips using leading process technology, and help market the product. By the end of 1987, he had succeeded in signing on three small California firms—LSI Logic, Integrated Device Technology, and Performance Semiconductor.

Mips executives also agreed to build up a systems business to complement technology revenues. Remaining simply a design house for RISC technology, they thought, would not provide the marketing clout needed to convince software developers to write applications. The company thus began forming alliances with computer companies that had strong marketing and service capabilities. The companies acted as resellers for Mips systems products, either licensing its technology for use in their own systems, or purchasing computer systems products from Mips.

In September 1988, Mips entered into a key alliance with DEC. The minicomputer maker paid $15 million for access to all current and future Mips architectures, designs, and related systems software.

EXHIBIT 4 Mips Organizational Chart, December 1991

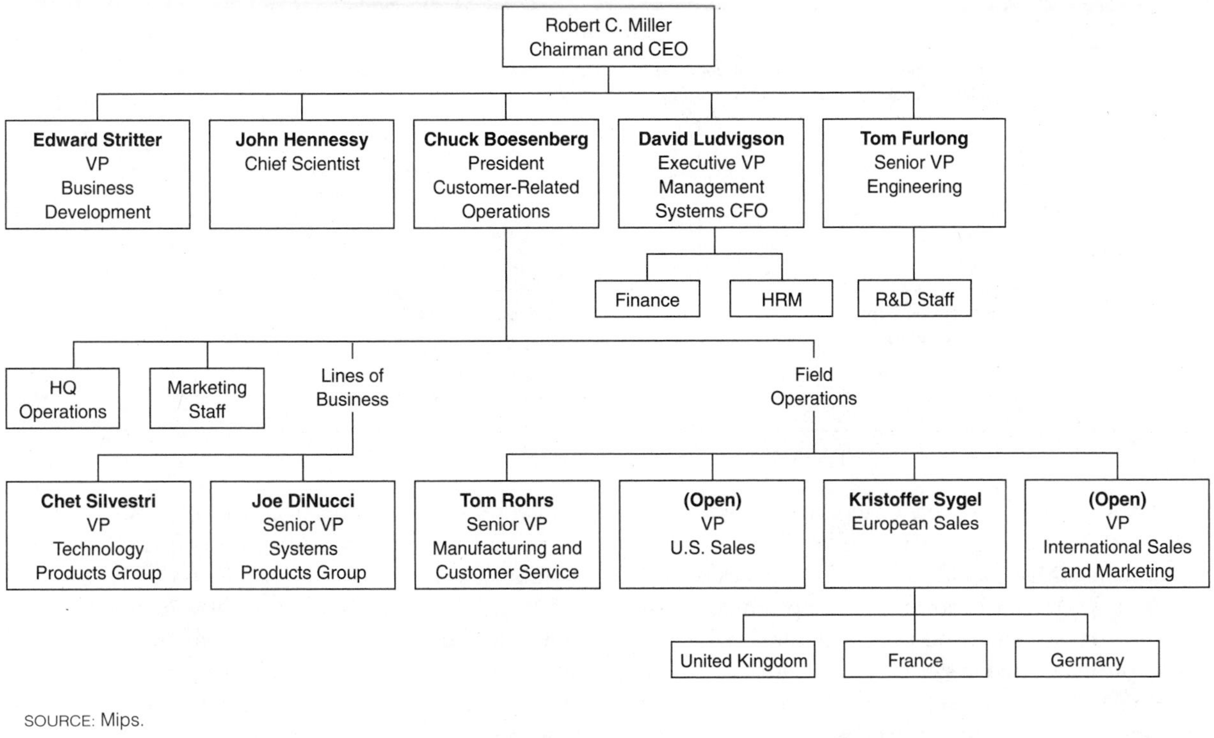

SOURCE: Mips.

It also invested an additional $10 million for a 5 percent equity stake in Mips, with the option to purchase another 15 percent and the right to elect one of Mips's six board members. In addition to strengthening the company's financial footing, the DEC alliance provided credibility in the industry for Mips technology, and helped Mips sign agreements with other major firms, such as NEC and Siemens (see below). It also provided access to DEC's strong engineering customer base. In the fall of 1988, DEC announced plans to design its new generation of workstations around the Mips RISC chip. It was the first time that DEC had gone to outside technology for its products. DEC did so because its own proprietary RISC project—code-named Prism—was running behind schedule. This internal project was canceled when DEC decided to use the Mips chip.

Early on, Mips recognized the importance of a strong international presence. "Companies like to buy locally," explained Miller. "The computer industry is a global business supported by domestic suppliers." In addition, the best technology, process manufacturing, and marketing capabilities for semiconductors were often located abroad. In order to succeed at attracting regional system vendors and OEMs, Mips's strategists thought, an indigenous supply of chips was critical. In addition, the company benefitted from reseller alliances with international firms. Still, Mips's early offers of partnerships were turned down, as the foreign firms found a relationship with Mips too risky. After Mips signed DEC in 1988, however, there was more interest than Miller could accommodate.

On the strength of the company's new strategy, its growing network of alliances, and its improving financial situation, Miller took Mips public in December 1989. The public was offered 24 percent of the company's stock at a price of $17.50 per share. The offer was oversubscribed and Mips's share price rose rapidly after that to a peak of $24 in April 1990.

Mips Business Model in 1991

By 1991, Mips had established itself as a one-stop shop for RISC technology, designing RISC microprocessors, compiler and operating system software, board products, and RISC systems (see Exhibit 5).

EXHIBIT 5 Mips's Business Approach

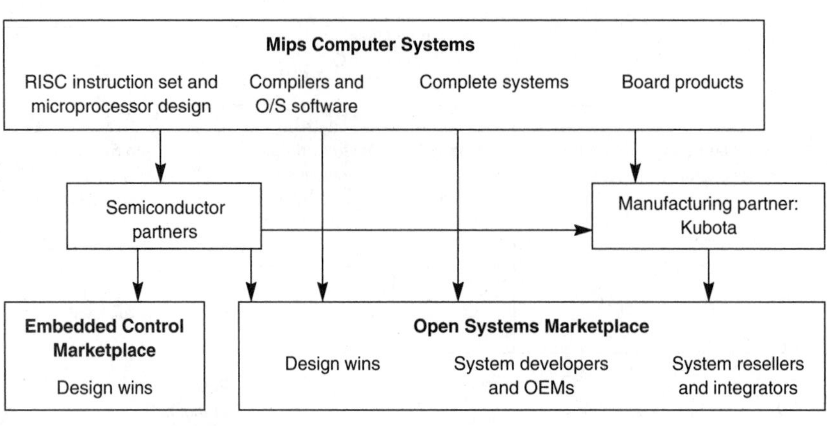

All of Mips's products were based on a single, compatible RISC architecture. Chip and software designs were licensed for production to six semiconductor partners, who in turn marketed these products. Mips licensed its system products (including software, board products, and systems architecture) to system developers, OEMs, resellers, and integrators and also sold them directly. Chester Silvestri, Mips vice president for technology products, summed up this business model:

> The foundation of our strategy is that one customer can buy at any level of integration. We attract them at either part of the food chain. Sometimes they begin with a chip and move up, or they begin with a box and move down to the boards. Once we begin a relationship, we build a business strategy around selling to them at all levels.

By 1991, Mips had introduced three generations of 32-bit RISC microprocessors—the R2000 (1985), R3000 (1988), and R6000 (1990)—and one 64-bit one, the R4000 (1991). With each introduction, Mips set performance records in the industry. In addition, Mips had brought seven systems products to the marketplace by 1991. Manufacturing of these products was limited, consisting mainly of box assembly and testing. The manufacture of boards was contracted out. Only approximately $1 million had been invested in manufacturing since the company's inception. Seventy-five percent of manufacturing costs were for material costs and components. The manufacturing division employed only 100 people.

Mips did not develop application software; its customers either developed their own, adapted popular software, or purchased from third parties. In 1988, Mips had invested in a separate software business, Synthesis Software Solutions, in order to acquire, port, and distribute third-party software for Mips systems. It sought out software of interest to two or more of its customers and tried to arrange joint ventures to split the cost of porting it to Mips systems. But the plan did not work well, and Synthesis was dissolved in 1989. Mips then began to sign independent software developers to pursue specific applications, such as database management and desktop publishing. By the end of 1990, RISCware—the name Mips gave to software available to its systems—numbered nearly 1,000, compared to 2,000 software packages available for Sun's RISC design.

Mips sold its last microprocessor in the first quarter of 1988. From then on its revenues were divided between the sales of systems products and income from technology licenses. There were significant differences between these two businesses. Technology revenues were a mix of initial licensing fees and continuing royalties; while initial fees had outweighed royalties in 1989 and 1990, the company expected that from 1991 on, royalties would make up the larger percentage share. Systems sales had average gross margins of 45 percent, while gross margins from technology licensing were closer to 85 percent. Mips predicted that 10 percent of its systems sales would eventually come from software sales and customer service. Twenty percent of R&D expenditures was dedicated to semiconductor design, 20 percent to operating system software and basic chip software, 30 percent to system software, and 30 percent to system hardware. Mips's long-term business model aimed for revenues split 80 percent to 20 percent between systems and technology licensing, giving the company overall gross margins of 50 to 55 percent.

In 1990, 72 percent of Mips product sales were for commercial applications. The company believed that it was better positioned than its competitors to take advantage of the expected swelling of demand in commercial segments; only 9 percent of Sun's sales, for example, came from this segment.

Mips's Alliance Strategy

"Making Mips architecture pervasive," explained Miller, "means seeing that it is implemented across companies, across applications, and across geography." Since 1987, the formation of partnerships and alliances worldwide had been the key element in Mips's strategy to achieve market pervasiveness (see Exhibits 6 and 7). Mips president Chuck Boesenberg, whom Miller hired from Apple, explained that there were important differences in the Mips relationship with its semiconductor partners and the system resellers:

> I think we're getting a bit too schmaltzy in American business in using words like partners and alliances. What we do with our semiconductor partners is provide them with the design in return for a royalty, and leave it to them to do the manufacturing and marketing. They can't survive without us, nor we without them; there is a great amount of mutual dependence.

EXHIBIT 6 Main Alliances of Mips in 1991

Type	North America	Europe	Far East
	Technology Licensing Partners		
Semiconductor partners	LSI Logic Integrated Device Performance Semiconductor DEC[a]	Siemens	NEC
Other semiconductor			Sony Toshiba NKK Daewoo
Manufacturing license			Kubota Computer
	Systems Resellers		
OEMs[b]	Control Data	Groupe Bull	Daewoo
Technology	Evans & Sutherland Prime Computer Pyramid Technology Tandem Computer Wang Laboratories	IN2 (Siemens) Siemens-Nixdorf Olivetti	Kubota Computer Sumitomo Electric
VARs	American Airlines Bachal Telematique Computer Dynamics Dynix Corporation Falcon Microsystems Gain Communications	TIS Metrologic S.A.	Hitachi-Zosen Systems
Distributors	Comperex Texas Instruments		Kubota Computer
Systems Integrators	Bolt Beranek & Newman Sylvest Management Sys.	GEI Rechnersysteme	

[a]DEC had a license to manufacture Mips processors for its internal use, but had not exercised it as of 1991.
[b]OEM resellers also have software licenses from Mips.

SOURCE: Mips Computer Systems.

EXHIBIT 7 Major RISC Alliances of Mips, Sun, HP, and IBM: 1987–1991

		Mips	Sun	HP	IBM
1987	Q1				
	Q2	Joint R&D with Prime and SiGraphics			
	Q3		License to Fujitsu, Cypress, and Bipolar		
	Q4	License to LSI Logic and Performance	Equity investment from AT&T		
1988	Q1	License to Integrated Device Tech.	Joint R&D with Unisys License to LSI Logic		
	Q2	Equity investment from Kubota	Design win ICL License to TI		
	Q3	Equity investment from DEC	OEM sales to Toshiba Design win TI and Solbourne		
	Q4		OEM sales and license to Seiko	Stop joint R&D with IBM	Stop joint R&D with HP
1989	Q1	License to Siemens and NEC			
	Q2	OEM sales to Pyramid	Joint R&D with Toshiba Design win Tatung and other Taiwan firm	License to and joint R&D with Hitachi License and OEM sales to Samsung	
	Q3	License to Bipolar	License to Philips		
	Q4	OEM sales to Bull, Nixdorf and CDC; license to Sony	Design win Goldstar		
1990	Q1	Manufacturing license to Kubota	Design win Hyundai		License from SiGraphics
	Q2		Design win Twinhead		
	Q3	Design win Prime	Cross-license to IBM		Cross-license to Sun
	Q4	Design win AT&T and Daewoo	Marketing deal with Compuadd Design win Matsushita and Taiwan firm		
1991	Q1	OEM Wang	Design win Tandon		
	Q2	Consortium with ACE, with Compaq, DEC, 18 others		Consortium with Hitachi, Samsung, and Sequioa	OEM sales to Wang
	Q3	License to Toshiba			Joint venture with Apple and license to Motorola

SOURCE: Press reports, compiled by casewriter.

Our OEM resellers are more like customers. We sell them a board or complete system and then we each go our own way. We depend on them to market the product, not to build it.

Kubota

Mips did not seek out its first license. Only a few months after his arrival at Mips, Miller was approached by Kubota Ltd., a $5.2 billion Japanese agricultural equipment manufacturer that was interested in diversifying into new technologies. Kubota had already provided financing to several other U.S. firms, among them California start-up Ardent Computer Corporation. Ardent planned to build a line of supercomputers around the Mips RISC chip, and Kubota thus had a direct stake in the survival of Mips. In an agreement signed in September 1987, Kubota purchased a 20 percent equity stake in Mips, worth $20 million. For an additional $5 million, Kubota helped to fund a high-end systems development program at Mips in return for the exclusive right to sell that product in the Far East. Kubota also agreed to build a $100 million computer factory in Japan. Mips, in turn, agreed to restrictions on its ability to grant additional manufacturing licenses in the territory covered by the agreement, and agreed to source a certain percentage of its sales to OEMs through Kubota.

In time, Kubota purchased further, nonexclusive manufacturing rights to other Mips products, and Mips appointed the company a distributor of certain semiconductor products in its territory. The company also began to purchase some components directly from Mips—those that were hard to source in Japan, although no finished boards. In 1991, one product made up 90 percent of Kubota's manufacturing for Mips, while Kubota products represented 20 to 25 percent of Mips's revenues.

Semiconductor Partners

Mips's semiconductor partner strategy was formed when Mips switched from being a chip manufacturer to a chip design house. The first three small U.S. licenses were signed soon after management's off-site strategy meeting in 1987, when it decided to seek a maximum of six partners. Mips would promise these firms that no other semiconductor partners would be added until 1992. Miller explained that Mips "had as an ideal to sign one of the top three semiconductor firms in the United States, one of the top three in Japan, and one of the top three in Europe." (See Exhibit 8 for rankings of global semiconductor firms.) Three other U.S. firms—Motorola, Advanced Micro Devices (AMD), and National Semiconductor—were approached by Mips, but refused. Motorola and AMD were unwilling to give up their own RISC development efforts, which was a Mips requirement, while National Semiconductor would not agree to marketing and sales obligations.

In September 1988, DEC became the fourth licensee of Mips semiconductor technology when it signed the equity deal with Mips, although as of 1991 DEC was not manufacturing the chip. For the two remaining slots, Mips sought international partners. Siemens A.G., of West Germany, had had its own RISC project going, but the Mips chip would allow them to reduce to one-quarter the time-to-market with a RISC chip. Also, since Siemens was DEC's largest supplier of semiconductors in Europe, DEC Europe welcomed the deal. NEC, the largest semiconductor manufacturer in the world, signed on in Japan. Through a former agreement with Intel, NEC had experience making and selling microprocessors, and the company was willing to commit exclusively to Mips's RISC. "Because of the NEC connection, we are almost bigger than life in Japan," added Boesenberg.

The terms of these semiconductor licenses, which Mips called Level III licenses, were similar to second-source agreements, with the exception that Mips would not be a competitor. The firms were granted licenses to Mips's second-generation RISC chip, the R3000. Mips provided each firm with the RISC instruction set and VLSI[8] design, or layout, for this chip, as well as licenses to all applicable system software. The licensees, for their part, agreed to an up-front payment of about $10 million, and royalties of approximately 5 percent based on the selling price of each unit sold. Mips believed that the up-front payment was close to the actual cost for the technology being transferred. Mips provided exact technical specifications for the R3000, and tested all products for pin-compatibility.[9] Mips's seal of approval assured customers that chips from different manufacturers were fully interchangeable. The licenses lasted 5 to 10 years, during which time Mips guaranteed that it would provide access to new generations of its technology, each time for an additional up-front fee. Beyond 10 years, the licensees had complete rights to continue to use the architecture covered by the license in perpetuity, but there was no guarantee of access to future technology.

Bob Miller explained that although Sun Microsystems also licensed its SPARC chip widely, its approach differed from that of Mips:

> Mips completely designs its microprocessor, down to the mask level. So when we sign our semiconductor partners, we give them everything, and they can be in production faster than licensees of other designs. Sun provides only the instruction set and licensees have to do all of the designing themselves; as a result, it can take them up to two years to reach the production phase. For this reason, Mips can command much higher up-front fees and royalty payments.[10] Furthermore, SPARC chips made by different firms are not pin-compatible.

---

[8]VLSI stood for very large scale integration.

[9]Pin compatibility meant that the functions of each of the pin connectors of a chip were identical, regardless of manufacturer. The chips were thus functionally and physically completely interchangeable in computer systems.

[10]In 1991, Sun licensed SPARC for $15,000, with no royalties.

EXHIBIT 8 Rankings of World's Top Semiconductor Vendors in 1989–90

A. Ranked by Share of Whole Semiconductor Market

Rank	Company	1990 Share of World Market	RISC Ally
1	NEC	8.4%	Mips
2	Toshiba	8.4	Sun[a]
3	Hitachi	6.7	HP
4	Motorola	6.4	IBM
5	Intel	5.5	
6	Fujita	5.0	Sun
7	Texas Instruments	4.4	Sun
8	Mitsubishi	4.0	
9	Philips	3.5	Sun
10	Matsushita	3.3	Sun
11	National Semiconductor	3.0	
12	SGS-Thomson	2.5	
13	Sanyo	2.4	
14	Sharp	2.3	
15	Samsung	2.3	HP
16	Siemens	2.1	Mips
17	Sony	2.0	Mips
18	Oki	1.9	
19	AMD	1.8	
20	AT&T	1.5	Sun

B. Ranked by Share of the Microprocessor Market

Rank	Company	1990 Share of World Market	RISC Ally
1	Intel	53.2%	
2	Motorola	13.3	IBM
3	AMD	5.1	
4	Hitachi	3.6	HP
5	NEC	3.5	Mips
6	National Semiconductor	2.7	
7	SGS-Thomson	2.3	
8	Toshiba	2.1	Sun[a]

Note: Total market size for all semiconductors (Table A) was approximately $58 billion in 1990. The world microprocessor market was about $6 billion.

[a]In the fall of 1991 Toshiba also became a Mips licensee.

SOURCE: Dataquest.

However, Mips's dependence on its allies was not without risks. The R6000 chip, which was of a different type than the R2000, R3000, and R4000, had been licensed only to Bipolar Technologies, a small U.S. firm. Problems with supply cost, reliability, and quantities resulted in substantial delays in commercializing the product. While it was announced and demonstrated in the fourth quarter of 1989, the product was not shipped in large volumes until 1991. This delay, in turn, affected Mips's sales of R6000-based systems. Aside from this dependence, managing the interests of five semiconductor partners could be challenging, as Bob Miller explained:

> The key ingredient to our semiconductor partnership is perseverance. Keeping five companies on the same strategic path can be difficult; it takes diplomacy, time, and energy at the senior level. Chuck Boesenberg and

I spend a lot of our time resolving issues to keep us all in the same line.

Other Technology Licensees

By 1991 Mips had also created two other types of semiconductor licenses, which allowed it to continue to promote its technology without creating competition for its first six semiconductor partners. Level I semiconductor licensees had access to the Mips instruction set for internal use only—for example, for research purposes to build systems around the Mips chip—but could not sell chips. Level II semiconductor licensees were allowed access to the Mips instruction set without the VLSI design, in order to build their own version of the Mips chip. These chips could be used for special "embedded control" applications, which were estimated to account for half the total market for RISC chips. For embedded control applications the microprocessor was slightly redesigned and built into a system other than a general purpose computer. In 1990, for example, Sony became a Level II licensee from Mips to use modified versions of Mips chips in an array of consumer products.

Finally, Mips also created licensing agreements for its operating systems (RISC/os) and compiler software. Mips allowed licensees to modify the software for their products and applications, and in turn, license these to third parties. As before, however, third parties needed to execute a licensing agreement with Mips for the original software. Mips believed that by optimizing all of a RISC system's components—chip, operating system, and compiler software—and licensing it all, its architecture would maintain technological superiority in the marketplace.

Alliances for Marketing System Products

Mips's distribution strategy for system products grew out of the realization that Mips could not single-handedly create the volume that would make Mips a major player in the RISC marketplace. In 1989, the company began to develop sales relationships with OEMs, distributors, value-added resellers (VARs), and systems integrators. Many of Mips's largest OEM customers were ailing makers of minicomputers, the segment of the market most directly threatened by the rise of RISC workstations. The company avoided competition with these parties by deemphasizing its direct sales efforts. In 1990, Mips's direct customer contact was mainly with advanced technical end users, such as universities.

Systems were marketed under Mips's brand label and under the brand labels of the company's OEM customer. Prime Computer, Control Data, Wang, Bull, Nixdorf, and others purchased system products manufactured by Mips, packaged in various configurations. This approach gave the systems vendors a range of options. They could purchase complete Mips systems, add their company logo, and achieve quick time-to-market advantages. Or they could purchase products at the chip, board, or subsystem level and add their own value to the design before selling them to end users and resellers. Finally, they could design their own products using a combination of these integration options. Boesenberg explained how varied and dynamic these OEM relationships could be:

> We often begin working with an OEM to fill a gap in their product line, say, by providing workstations to complement their minicomputers. In time, the more successful they are in reselling our systems, the more likely they are to want to design and build them from the microprocessor up, with the result that our sales to them would decline. So our challenge is to keep replenishing these OEMs with new products.

VARs, typically, would purchase complete system products from Mips, and then bundle them with their own application software; they often specialized in specific vertical markets. Since these VARs did not build systems, they were not likely to replace Mips machines with their own. Systems integrators, still another type of reseller, purchased products from Mips, and incorporated them into customer-specific systems and networks. They provided custom end user system design and management. Distributors were mainly used for sales to end users, often in international markets where Mips had no direct sales presence.

From 1988 to 1991, Mips's system products were sold increasingly through VAR channels. At the end of 1988, for example, Mips reseller contracts were divided nearly equally between VARs, OEMs, and systems integrators/distributors. By the end of 1990, however, Mips had signed 136 VARs, compared to 34 OEMs and 27 systems integrators. Mips, like its competitors, looked increasingly to new channels, as competition in the RISC/Unix market heated up. In 1990, nearly 250 computer dealers started to carry workstation products of Mips and others.

Mips's Main Competitors

Mips had four main competitors in 1991: the three companies that had developed commercially successful RISC processors (Sun, HP, and IBM)[11] and Intel, which dominated the desktop market with its CISC processors. Among these competitors, Mips was the only one exclusively selling RISC systems, but not the only one using alliances to spread its technology worldwide (see Exhibit 6). In addition, while in 1991 DEC was still an important Mips ally, the company was rumored to be planning the introduction of its own RISC processor in 1992.

Sun Microsystems

Sun Microsystems, like Mips, was formed out of computer science research at Stanford University. Sun's strategy was to manufacture computers based on open standards and purchasing readily available components. Sun started in the workstation business using off-the-shelf Motorola CISC processors. Through aggressive selling and championing of the open systems concept, the company's sales soared—in 1987 its revenues passed then market leader Apollo (which also used Motorola chips), and by 1990 Sun held over 30 percent of the workstation market.

In 1987, Sun entered the market for RISC-based workstations with the Sun-4, based on the company's proprietary RISC architecture, SPARC. Sun's first licensee was Solbourne Computers, a small U.S. firm controlled by Japan's Matsushita. By 1991, Solbourne had produced a SPARC clone and was competing against Sun in the marketplace. Other major licensees were Unisys, AT&T, Xerox, Prime Computer, ICL, Philips, Fujitsu, Toshiba, and Matsushita itself. As of March 1991, a total of 30 vendors had announced SPARC-based systems. Still, in 1990, Sun itself supplied 95 percent of the SPARC systems sold. In 1991 *Unix World* characterized Sun's alliance strategy as follows:

> [Sun] has tried to set an industry microprocessor standard and let companies clone the technology, but so far there's only one winner: Sun. Despite Sun's posturing as an "open systems company," the company has made progress difficult for SPARC-compatible vendors. . . . Earlier this year, Sun issued an edict to its VARs barring them from selling Sun clones. It also lowered its prices to undercut the least expensive SPARC clone machines. Sun's paranoia about the potential success of SPARC-compatible vendors is jeopardizing the very market Sun is trying to create, say analysts.[12]

Hewlett-Packard

Although HP's traditional strength lay in minicomputers, decreasing sales in this market led the company to turn toward higher-growth segments of the industry. In 1985, it entered workstations using Motorola chips, with systems that complemented its minicomputer lines. In 1989 it acquired ailing workstation leader Apollo Computer for $500 million; this propelled HP into second place in the industry, and first place among suppliers of Motorola-based workstations.

HP's first RISC machine was a minicomputer, based on the company's proprietary Precision Architecture (PA-RISC). This was followed by its first RISC workstation, introduced in February 1991. Introduced at a price that undercut Sun's comparable RISC workstation and marketed with aggressive advertising, this machine claimed to offer twice the performance, for half the price. This machine turned out to be a hot seller and helped drive HP's excellent financial results in 1991, one of the few bright spots in the performance of global computer firms in that year. By 1991, HP had also completed the merger with Apollo, having moved the former Apollo customers to the PA-RISC architecture, which by then had become the company's core architecture.

Compared to Sun and Mips, HP had formed few international alliances in the RISC field, but it did joint research with Hitachi and licensed Samsung to make low-end PA-RISC workstations. Observers expected HP to become more aggressive in pushing its PA-RISC architecture.

IBM

In 1991, IBM, too, was poised to become a major competitor in the RISC workstation marketplace. Its first RISC workstation line—the RT family—was introduced in 1986 based on its proprietary RISC architecture. Widely considered overpriced and

---

[11]A fourth company, Intergraph, also had a proprietary RISC design on the market, but it focused almost exclusively on the military market.

[12]Gary Andrew Poole, "Sun in Their Eyes," *Unix World,* October 1991, p. 79.

underpowered, the RT line was not successful. In 1990, however, the company entered the fray in a big way with its RS/6000 line of Unix RISC workstations. The performance of these machines temporarily leapfrogged Sun's entire RISC product line. Twenty-five thousand units were sold in the first six months of production, and the line accounted for some $750 million of IBM's $1 billion in workstation sales that year. With its vast market power and pool of application software, IBM was a serious threat to its smaller competitors.

In October 1991, IBM announced a major alliance with Apple and Motorola that included collaboration in the RISC field. IBM and Apple agreed to develop a new operating system that would function, among others, on a future generation of IBM's RISC processor. The RS/6000 processor actually consisted of seven chips used together, and was therefore much more expensive than the single-chip designs of Mips and Sun. As part of the new alliance, IBM agreed to redesign its RISC processor to fit onto one chip, and granted Motorola a license to manufacture the new chip. Motorola had been the CISC supplier for all Apple computers, and had not developed a widely used RISC chip. IBM and Motorola announced that they intended to license the new RS/6000 chip widely.

Intel

Even though RISC was rapidly penetrating the Unix workstation market, Intel's X86 CISC architecture continued to dominate the personal computer world. The company had not developed a commercially successful RISC chip, although it had a special-purpose RISC processor and planned to incorporate RISC principles in its design for the 80586, due out in 1992. In 1991 Intel redoubled its development efforts on the 80586. Because Intel-based PCs dominated the desktop, Intel's executives did not seem overly concerned about the threat posed by the new RISC competitors. As Intel chairman Gordon Moore explained:

> As to the people ganging up on us—the Mips thing, for example—one thing you have to look at is the relative market size you are serving. We'll ship more 486 processors this quarter than all the RISC processors in all the designs shipped from the beginning of time.[13]

[13]Samuel Weber, "Waging War on Intel: The RISC Crowd Moves In," *Electronics,* November, 1991, p. 58.

DEC

Probably the biggest wild card for Mips was DEC's decision around 1990 to revive its project for a proprietary RISC chip, this time under the code-name Alpha. By the end of 1991, it was expected that DEC would come out with this new chip within a year, and would use it as the core of its new minicomputer lines. DEC intended to port its VMS operating system to run on Alpha, and in time would help its customers migrate from the old VAX architecture to the new RISC-based systems. But it was unclear what DEC would do about its involvement with Mips. Since 1988, it had used Mips chips successfully in its line of Unix workstations. There was a possibility that the company would continue to use the Mips architecture for its low-end machines and would move to the more expensive Alpha architecture for its high-end systems.

The ACE Consortium

Late in 1990, Compaq Computer, the third largest PC maker behind IBM and Apple, announced that it was investigating the possibility of a new RISC-based high-end PC line. It was rumored that Compaq's search had been narrowed to Mips and Sun. Working in Mips's favor was a previously announced alliance with software developer Microsoft Corporation. Microsoft had agreed to adapt its Windows operating environment to run on Mips's RISC architecture.

By February 1991, it was clear that an alliance was forming around Mips's R4000 chip. Under development since 1989, the R4000 was expected to be available by late 1991. Led by Compaq, the alliance announced support for two hardware platforms—Mips's R4000 RISC chip and the Intel X86 microprocessors that dominated the PC market—as well as two operating systems—a unified version of Unix, based on a version from the Santa Cruz Operation, and the Windows New Technology (NT) from Microsoft. In this way, alliance members hoped to create new hardware and software standards for desktop and laptop computers, as well as capitalize on the huge installed base of Windows application programs, which would be recompiled to run on Windows NT, even though they would not exploit its most advanced features. By the time the alliance was formalized in April, over 21 firms had joined. Key members included DEC, Control Data, Silicon

Graphics, Prime, Wang, and Pyramid Technology of the United States; Olivetti, Siemens-Nixdorf, and Bull/Zenith of Europe; and NEC, Sony, Sumitomo, and NKK of Japan. Robert Miller summed up the challenge for Mips: "At the end of the day, the winner—a relative term anyway—will be the one who gets the customers' desktops converted. Our new mission is to provide as much enabling technology to the ACE members as possible."

ACE membership continued to grow rapidly to over 60 in July and almost 200 in October. Many of these new members were foreign clone makers and small software firms. But on October 15 Mips announced a new semiconductor partner—Toshiba. Like the other semiconductor partners, Mips licensed Toshiba to make, sell, and develop Mips R3000 and R4000 chips, and incorporate these into its systems. The signing of Toshiba was particularly noteworthy because the company had been one of the first licensees of Sun's SPARC technology. The status of Toshiba's relationship to Sun remained unclear.

The Future of Mips and ACE

While ACE and the Mips architecture seemed to be gaining momentum in the second half of 1991, Mips's financial prospects began to look less promising. The company incurred a loss of $597,000 in the second quarter of 1991, which compared unfavorably with the $624,000 profit in the first quarter, and the $4 million profit of the second quarter of the previous year. Mips executives attributed this trend to the general slowdown in computer sales and to the changing mix of Mips's product line, which showed technology revenues declining relative to product revenues. Furthermore, Miller warned that significant restructuring of the company's operations was needed to reduce costs and address ACE's goals and the needs of its members. He said that "the company expects to incur significant costs related to these actions."

The third quarter of 1991 was not kind to Mips and ACE. "Mips Computer has a beautiful future behind it," wrote *Business Week* in October, in an article that reported an expected loss of $15 million for the quarter. By then, investors had already driven Mips stock down to $11 per share, from $21 in March 1991.

Part of the blame for the loss lay with disrupted relations with resellers that followed Mips's decision to phase out high-end systems in favor of ACE-compliant desktop systems. Groupe Bull was among the resellers reportedly unhappy with this shift, as was Wang, which became a reseller of IBM workstations. It began to look as if Bull, too, might follow that route: in December the company was considering adopting IBM's RS/6000 or HP's PA-RISC to replace Mips.

The ACE consortium began to exhibit other cracks. DEC was reported to be close to introducing the Alpha chip, and consortium members forced the group to accept a second version of Unix, which competed with the Santa Cruz version. Furthermore, the early momentum behind ACE spurred competitors to action. As IBM, Apple, and Motorola began to work together, Sun began offering a version of its Solaris operating system for Intel-based computers, and Compaq was reportedly one of the PC makers considering breaking ranks and offering Solaris as an option. Intel, for its part, reported good progress on its 80586 chip.

When Mips announced its third quarter results (Exhibits 2 and 3), they were even worse than *Business Week* had projected. Revenues fell 27 percent from the second quarter, and the company incurred a net loss of $37.3 million, which included a $25.5 special charge for corporate restructuring. The drop in revenues was largely attributable to a decline in technology income from $11.6 million in the second quarter to $3.2 in the third. "Our technology revenue is influenced significantly by new technology-licensing agreements, which are often the result of long sales cycles," explained CFO David Ludvigson. He expected that new licensing programs in the fourth quarter would increase technology revenue.

The one-time restructuring charge included severance costs related to a 10 percent reduction in employment; write-downs of capitalized software, inventory, and equipment; and a provision for idle factory costs. Mips expected that the 1991 cash impacts of this charge would be minimal, and that the restructuring would reduce operating costs. Miller added: "Mips remains a strong company. We have substantial capital resources and remain a leader in our core technologies."

As the year drew to a close, observers wondered what would become of Mips and of ACE. Whatever the answer to this question, it was bound to have implications for firms joining the popular trend to stake their future on inter-firm alliances and industry consortia. Were these strategies the road to riches or to ruin? And was Mips's management of its alliance network an example to follow or to shun?

Case II–9
The Operating System Software Industry in 1994

Thomas Kurian and Robert A. Burgelman

In 1994, the operating system (OS) market was poised to undergo dramatic changes. Throughout the 1980s it had been dominated by Microsoft, first with its Disk Operating System (MS-DOS) and then Microsoft Windows. During 1993 alone, Microsoft shipped nearly 14 million units of DOS and 12 million units of Windows, accounting for nearly 85 percent of all personal computers shipped. Despite Microsoft's strong market presence, the convergence of several new technologies and the demand from corporate customers for more powerful and flexible systems threatened to introduce fundamental changes in the industry. Competitors, such as Novell and IBM, who had successfully defended specific niches in the OS market, had begun to introduce exciting new products ahead of Microsoft. Simultaneously, Microsoft's new operating system, Windows NT, had met with a decidedly tepid response in the market. Industry observers wondered how the operating system market might change in the next five years.

History of the Operating System Industry*

Functional Role of the Operating System

Operating systems are an important element of modern computers. From a functional standpoint, OSs play two important roles, as "resource managers" and as "abstract machines" (see Exhibit 1). As a resource manager, the OS manages the resources of a computer system, allocating them to different end users and applications according to their needs. This role is becoming increasingly complex as computers begin to interoperate with other machines in complicated, networked architectures. In its abstract machine role, the OS plays an intermediary role serving as an easy-to-interact-with interface between the underlying computer hardware and programmers and users. By creating this abstract machine with which users can interface easily, the OS enables users to use the computer's resources more easily and effectively. Abstract machines also allow programmers to extend the functionality incorporated in a computer's hardware.

During the 1940s and 1950s, computers supported only a single user at any one time. In this single-user environment, most of the systems were batch processing systems servicing individual jobs that had been submitted as decks of punched cards. All the OS needed to do was to pull a job off the queue and execute the steps that had been prescribed in the deck of cards. As advances in hardware in the late 1960s allowed more sophisticated computers to support multiple users simultaneously, the role of the OS began to change. Competition between end users and software programs for the computer's limited resources and facilities became fierce. A significant portion of the OS's time was spent on "time sharing"—an extension of its resource management role. At roughly the same time, mainframe OSs also began to extend the centralized resources provided by the mainframe's hardware to create for each end user an independent "virtual" machine that appeared to have a complete suite of resources. The most popular OSs in this generation were primarily International Business Machines' (IBM) CMS and CICS systems.

With the advent of minicomputers in the early 1970s, Digital Equipment Corporation's (DEC) VAX computers and their VMS OSs became very widely used, particularly in educational, industrial, and commercial environments. Throughout the 1980s, two fundamental shifts characterized the OS market. The first and most important was the advent of the personal computer (PC). Created in 1978 by Apple Computer and followed shortly thereafter by IBM, the personal computer revolutionized the computer industry. End users, excited by the PC's flexibility, ease of use, and low price, purchased an estimated 50 million PCs during the decade. The primary PC OSs were Microsoft Corporation's MS-DOS and Windows systems, which dominated the IBM-compatible segment of the market; Apple's machines used a proprietary OS and accounted for between 10 and 15 percent of the total market.

At roughly the same time, another class of machines—the workstation—was emerging as the computer of choice among more sophisticated computer users. While the first workstation was created by Apollo Computers, the market soon came to be

*See the glossary for a definition of selected technical terms.

EXHIBIT 1 Functional Role of Operating System

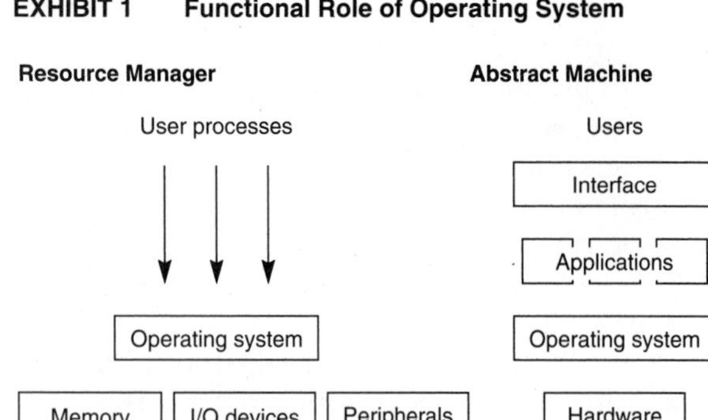

EXHIBIT 2 Classification of Operating Systems

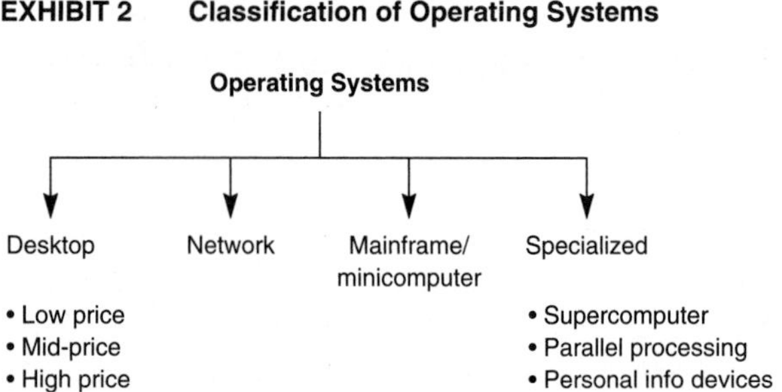

dominated by Sun Microsystems. To rapidly build its market share in the workstation business, Hewlett-Packard had acquired Apollo Computers to become the second largest player in the business. IBM's RS/6000 line of workstations had also become a strong competitor in the workstation market by the early 1990s. While workstations were first used by scientists and educators, the power of their hardware, larger disk storage, and higher resolution graphics monitors facilitated their rapid penetration into several commercial markets. The primary OS for workstations was UNIX, a system that had become extremely popular in the scientific community following its creation in 1974 at AT&T Bell Laboratories.

As users began to link personal computers and workstations together to form networks, another segment of the OS market emerged. Network OSs, typically, reside on one host machine (called the server) and process requests from multiple machines that are linked to the host (called clients). Novell, a company based in Provo, Utah, was the first to deliver a robust OS—Netware—that could perform the elementary functions in early, fairly primitive networks. By working cooperatively with other hardware and software vendors and constantly improving its products, Novell had captured nearly 70 percent of its niche by 1993.

Types of Operating Systems

OSs can broadly be classified into four main classes (see Exhibit 2): desktop OSs, network OSs, mainframe and minicomputer systems, and specialized niche OSs.

Desktop OSs. Desktop OSs run stand-alone desktop PCs and workstations. This segment can be further divided into three subsegments based on price-performance and volume of systems:

1. The *low price segment* consists of products with suggested retail prices less than $200 per copy. It is dominated by MS-DOS and Windows and constitutes about 75 percent of all desktop machines sold. The other competitors in this segment include IBM's OS/2, Apple Computer's System 7 and System 8, and Novell's DR-DOS products. The majority of these systems were installed on low-priced personal computers used for general productivity applications such as spreadsheets and word processors. The low-price segment was by far the largest segment of the OS market with nearly 24 million units shipped in 1993—14 million DOS units, of which 12 million had Windows, 3 million had OS/2 units, and 7 million had Apple System 7 units.[1] This translated into a market of approximately $1.2 billion to $2.4 billion.[2]

2. The *high price segment* of the desktop market is dominated by variants of the UNIX OS which typically retail for more than $800 per copy. The major competitors in this segment are proprietary versions of Unix—IBM's AIX, Hewlett-Packard's HP-UX, the Santa Cruz Operation's SCO Open Desktop, and Sun Microsystems' Solaris. Steve Jobs's NeXT had also introduced a Unix derivative OS—NeXTStep. These higher-priced systems are primarily used for robust, mission critical, horizontal or vertical corporate applications run typically on a workstation or a high-end PC. This segment was significantly smaller—only 10 percent of the size of the low-

[1]Since operating systems are shipped bundled with hardware, it is difficult to impute a specific price for the OS. Using an imputed Windows price of $50 (for an upgrade) to $120 (for a new unit), the market can be valued at between $1.2 billion and $2.4 billion.

[2]"1993 Software Market Share Report," *Dataquest.*

priced segment. Of the nearly 2.5 million units shipped in this segment during 1993, Sun had 36 percent of the market, HP 24 percent, and IBM 20 percent.[3]

3. During 1993, a *a mid-price segment* had begun to emerge between the high-price and low-price segments. These products were typically priced between $300 and $500 retail. The major entrants in this segment were Microsoft's new Windows NT OS, and Novell's Unix product, Unixware. OS vendors viewed this segment as a way to differentiate their new products and segment their customer base. Vendors in the low-price segment, such as Microsoft, saw it as an opportunity to extract value for the added functionality incorporated in their new products while gradually migrating customers from their existing systems. Competitors in the high-price segment, particularly the Unix vendors, faced with the growing threat from Windows NT and OS/2, saw it as an opportunity to deliver cheaper versions of their systems to run on higher-volume platforms without cannibalizing their higher-end products. This segment had shown much slower growth primarily because the OSs were newly released, not very robust, and lacked many third-party applications. During 1993, fewer than 300,000 units were shipped in this segment.

Network OSs. As desktop computers became increasingly connected as client–server networks, this segment began to show rapid growth. The segment was dominated by Novell's Netware products; other competitors included Microsoft's NT Advanced Server and Lan Manager products, and IBM's Lan Server (a derivative of Lan Manager). Some networks also used versions of Unix.

Mainframe and minicomputer OSs. While this segment had begun to show steady declines during the late 1980s and early 1990s, it was still extremely popular. The two main segments within this class were mainframe OSs, such as IBM's CICS and CMS systems, and minicomputer systems such as DEC's VMS system. As competition to mainframes and minis stiffened from workstations and PCs clustered in client-server networks, the total number of mainframes and minicomputers sold had declined sharply, falling by more than 40% between 1990 and 1993 alone. Fewer than 10,000 units were sold during 1993.

[3]Ibid.

Market niches. Cray dominated the supercomputer market with its proprietary hardware and software. Parallel processing companies such as n-Cube and Thinking Machines delivered their own proprietary OSs which were customized to exploit the power of their hardware. Fewer than 5,000 parallel processing machines were sold each year. Small companies, such as Geoworks and General Magic, offered software to operate the emerging class of personal information devices.

Economics of OS Business

Driven both by technological advances and by constantly changing customer needs, the economics of the OS business continued to shift. Five fundamental characteristics underpin the economics of the business.

Economies of scale in product development. The fundamental factor driving the OS business is the enormous economies of scale associated with the product. Each OS requires a very large up front investment in product development, resulting in heavy fixed costs (see Exhibit 3). These development expenses can be borne only by a limited number of players in the market and serve as a barrier to smaller entrants.

Having developed the product, however, additional costs were small. Variable costs included manufacturing costs for documentation and products, the cost of training users and developers on the use of the system, and the cost of supporting customers. With the availability of CD-ROMs, costs for producing documentation and "manufacturing" the product were nearly $5 to $15 per copy. These represented less than 4 percent of the retail price ($150–$500) for the Windows OS.[4] Training costs represent only a very small fraction of total costs—Microsoft reports between 1 and 2 percent of total revenues are spent on training. Most major systems vendors, including Microsoft, provided only limited training free of cost. Support costs tend to have a fixed component and a variable component. In setting up a telephone response center to provide customer support for a new product, vendors do incur significant capital expenditures. (Microsoft is reported to have spent upwards of $20 million

[4]The Gartner Group, "Survey of Emerging Software Distribution Channels," December 1993.

EXHIBIT 3 Operating System Development Costs

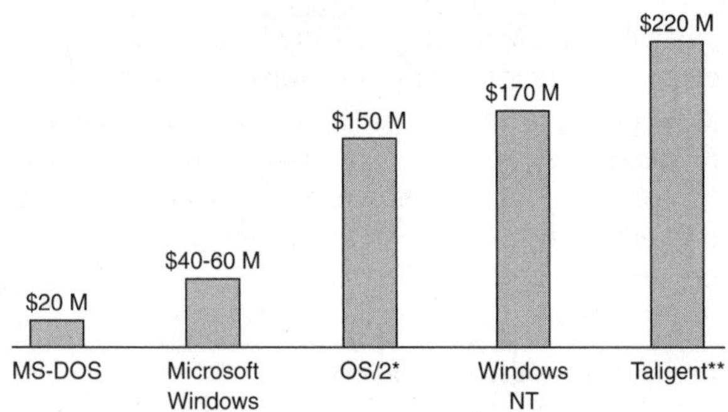

* IBM has spent over $4 billion on the OS/2 project to date. $150 million represents the development cost alone for the first release of OS/2.

** Taligent's costs represents expenditures through December 1993; product was not expected to ship until 2Q 1994.

developing a corporate response center for its Windows NT OS.)[5] Variable support costs come mainly from the additional support operators required as customers are added.

Two factors mitigate these costs. Fully loaded costs for a customer support engineer are significantly lower than the costs of a software developer—Apple Computer, for example, estimates the fully loaded cost of a support engineer to be $125,000 per year as compared to nearly $200,000 for a software developer.[6] Most vendors treat support as an important profit center and charge customers for additional services over a fairly limited basic service package.

Development costs for new operating systems have increased sharply over the years. The operating system purchase decision is a highly risk averse choice and customers are very reluctant to switch from their existing systems to try a new system. As a result, OS vendors find it necessary to incorporate significant incremental functionality compared to existing systems in order to encourage customer trial. This has raised the cost of developing new systems. Moreover, the added functionality has dramatically increased the complexity of the new systems. As a result, very few companies have the internal expertise to develop and deliver a bug-free operating system. Both these trends are expected to accelerate in the future, further limiting the number of vendors who can develop and market new OSs.

Long product life cycle. Since an OS takes typically between four and five years to develop, it has a fairly long product life cycle. The prolonged product life cycle complicates the development process in two ways: first, it makes it difficult to develop products to a specific set of customer needs which have been identified in detail before the development process is started. This requires fairly significant shifts in product development priorities as customer needs change, and the applications software market changes, typically raising total development costs. Second, due to the extended development process, it is difficult to line up third-party support from hardware vendors, resellers, and ISVs at the start of the development process. Third parties typically take a wait-and-see approach to different OS platforms, preferring to get a market response to the product before making a commitment to it as a strategic platform. Therefore, developing an OS is a very risky venture requiring substantial resource commitments while betting on customer and third-party support.

Long payback period. The economics of the business are further complicated by the long payback period for the products. Three factors lengthen the payback period. First, the long product development cycle extends the time for initial product release. Second, the customers purchasing OSs are highly risk averse, and are unwilling to cut over to a new system until they are certain that it enables a substantial number of new applications. Enabling many new types of applications requires building significant commitment to the platform among ISVs, a slow process. Third, customers are also unwilling to make a commitment to a new system until they are convinced that the platform is stable, and most of the software bugs have been worked out of the system. The vast majority of customers typically delay purchasing the product until at least the third release, further extending the payback period. These three factors together lengthen the payback period, making it difficult for many competitors to afford the significant resource expenditures required to develop a competitive OS product.

Distribution economics vary by channel. Distribution channel economics are a large part of the total cost to the customer. OS vendors primarily use two-tier, indirect distribution channels. The three most important channels are: (1) bundled with hardware and sold by computer makers (OEMs),

[5]"Windows NT—Developing a New Operating System," *The Wall Street Journal,* July 27, 1993.

[6]Apple Computer, Finance Department.

EXHIBIT 4 Economics of OEM Channel

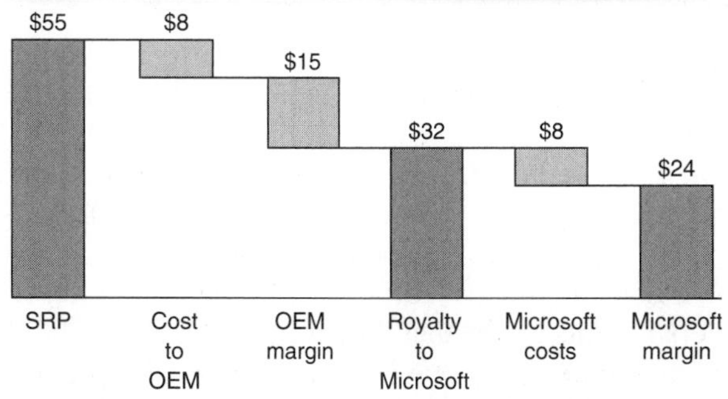

EXHIBIT 5 Economics of Retail Channel

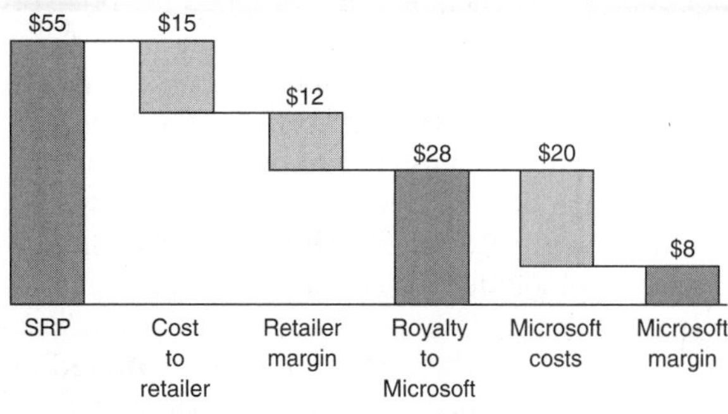

(2) bundled with applications and sold via resellers (VARs, SIs, ISVs), and (3) as standalone products through retail channels (Egghead, BusinessLand). The OEM channel offers far higher margins than the other channels due to the low costs involved at both tiers (see Exhibit 4). By preloading the OS on a PC or workstation, the OEM eliminates incremental distribution costs and keeps sales and marketing expenses to the minimum. In turn, the OS vendor bears very little incremental expense to support an OEM (limited selling and marketing cost; almost no distribution and manufacturing cost since the vendor ships the OEM a single master copy of the software for the OEM to duplicate).[7] As a result, gross margins from the OEM channel to the OS vendor are very high compared with other channels (see Exhibit 5). Further, the OEM channel shows the least variability in unit shipments and represents a stable source of royalties to the OS vendor. Therefore, OS vendors that control the OEM channel can derive sustainable competitive advantage relative to their rivals.

Upgrade economics. The OS business is fundamentally attractive due to the enormous and steady cashflows generated by the upgrade business. The development cost associated with the production of an OS upgrade is very small compared with the new OS. Also, an OS vendor has very low customer churn (loss of installed base of customers) due to high customer switching costs. Switching costs are high because it requires changing the complete application suite in addition to the OS, retraining users unfamiliar with a new system, and, frequently, purchasing new hardware since the system requirements (disk space, RAM, bus performance, etc.) of OSs differ considerably. Finally, having purchased an OS, customers tend to purchase most new upgrades. Over the last five years, estimates indicate that roughly 32 percent of Microsoft's customer base upgraded on interim releases (the "dot" releases) while nearly 75 percent upgraded on major releases. The numbers were even higher for Unix with nearly 70 percent purchasing both interim releases and major releases. Customers choose to upgrade either to be able to use the most current versions of the applications developed for the system, or to ensure that they continue to receive customer service and support from the systems vendor. The upgrade stream of cashflows makes it extremely attractive for vendors to widely proliferate a new OS by pricing it aggressively and then recovering their investments from the upgrade stream. Rick Sherlund, of Goldman Sachs, estimates the potential revenue stream of Microsoft's Chicago product (the next upgrade to Windows) to be between $700 million and $1.5 billion over the next three years.[8]

Misperceptions of the nature of the business have frequently led even large systems vendors with significant industry expertise to make strategic mistakes. The most prevalent misperception was that price could be used to encourage customers to switch from their existing OS. When an OS is released, the vendors have already spent a lot of money for product development. Vendors tend to consider their development expenses as sunk costs and frequently price their product to cover their variable costs. Additionally, vendors recognize the

[7]Dell Computer Corporation annual report, 1993, was used to determine the cost of OEM channel.

[8]"Analyst Report on Microsoft," Goldman Sachs and Co., February 1993.

upgrade nature of the business and tend to pursue penetration pricing strategies. Beginning in 1993, prices began to plummet. IBM dropped the price of OS/2 from $495 to $99 and typically sells it after discounts for less than $50 per copy.[9] Microsoft responded, pricing Windows NT at $295, considerably below the $795 to $895 prices for Unix, its primary competitor.[10] While vendors aggressively compete on price, data collected from various industry surveys indicate that customers do not perceive price to be a very important factor in their purchase decision. Hence, while price should be lowered to the point where price is no longer a barrier to customer purchase, further price reductions have proved counterproductive and destroyed margins.

Wide gap between winners and losers. New OS products can either be priced at the low end of the market or at the high end. OS vendors therefore face a dilemma when bringing new products to market—how should they price their new products? With the continued commoditization of PC hardware and the associated decline in prices and margins, OEMs are reluctant to burden their machines with high-priced OSs. Therefore, pricing an OS too high can limit it to very high-end systems and preclude its establishing a broad horizontal standard.

The vendor can price the OS in the low-price band and bet on generating a large installed base and a substantial upgrade revenue stream. Should the vendor fail to achieve significant market penetration, it becomes trapped in a vicious "low-price, low-volume" cycle. It cannot afford to lower prices significantly since it is already cash thin, and still lower prices may not generate incremental volume. Additionally, it cannot raise prices easily—since the product is not competitive at a low price, raising price is likely to further worsen its competitive position. These factors therefore create a wide gap between winners and losers. Winners, such as Microsoft, generate enormous cash flows and enjoy very high market valuations. Losers could spend large amounts of capital and fail to gain any share. It is estimated that IBM spent nearly $4 billion between 1985 and 1993 on the OS/2 product alone.[11]

[9]IBM Personal Systems Division, Boca Raton, Florida.

[10]"Windows NT Released," *Information Week*, July 27, 1993.

[11]IBM Personal Systems Division, Boca Raton, Florida. This includes payments to OEMs to test OS/2 on their systems. OEMs typically test Windows only at their own expense.

Trends in the Operating System Industry in 1994

Despite Microsoft's dominance of the OS market in 1993, many observers had begun to predict significant changes in the market during the early 1990s. On the one hand, many corporate customers felt that existing OSs severely constrained their ability to create solutions to their business needs in a timely manner. Frequently corporate information systems departments found that they wasted a large fraction of their time and money creating marginal elements of a business solution (particularly sophisticated graphical user interfaces) rather than solving the real problem. Moreover, whenever they were able to deliver a solution, it was frequently at substantial cost and schedule overruns. Often the business problem had completely changed by the time they had delivered the solution.

Third-party solution providers—value added resellers (VARs) and system integrators (SIs)—faced a different problem. Since the cost of developing a business solution working around the constraints created by existing OSs was substantial, they found themselves limited to fairly large vertical and horizontal markets. As many new players entered these markets with generic applications, competition had intensified considerably and profitability declined sharply. What VARs and SIs needed was an OS and a set of tools that allowed them to rapidly build customized solutions to target smaller, more profitable market niches. Seeking to eliminate many of these obstacles, a large number of corporate customers had begun to indicate in the early 1990s a willingness to experiment with new software technologies. Many observers felt that several emerging technologies, particularly object orientation, held considerable promise.

At the same time as these changes were transforming the market, several major technological trends had begun to shape the future direction of the computer industry.

Shift to 32-bit and 64-bit operating systems. In 1994, existing 16-bit DOS and Windows OSs dominated the desktop personal computer market. With the availability of new 32-bit CISC and RISC microprocessors from a variety of providers, customers are beginning to demand solutions that will exploit the capability of the hardware advances. OSs must provide the enabling technology—32-bit (and soon 64-bit) OSs—that will allow applications providers to create solutions that leverage the advances in hardware technology.

Shift to distributed computing environments. The shift to open systems has led to the emergence of distributed computing environments consisting of heterogeneous systems from multiple vendors networked together in client–server and peer-to-peer models. The demand for distributed computing systems is expected to grow even more rapidly as corporations continue to undergo rapid "right sizing."

Emergence of object technology. Object-oriented technology is based on a software design and programming methodology created at AT&T Bell Laboratories that enables the creation of reusable modules of software code that can be easily combined together to form a complete application. Early tests of object-oriented systems, although limited by the primitive state of the technology, have demonstrated the orders-of-magnitude improvements in programming time and cost that these systems can deliver. By 1994, object-oriented systems had become widely recognized as the predominant enabling technology that will allow applications developers to deliver faster, cheaper, more easily extensible, and more customized solutions to customers. Object technology is also recognized as a primary enabling technology for transparent customer access to complex, distributed computing environments.

The convergence of these three trends will open the door for the emergence of a new computing paradigm—a distributed object environment—in the mid 1990s. As Microsoft struggles to transition its very large installed base of customers from their existing DOS- and Window-based systems, many vendors recognize that this change offers them a "window of opportunity" to establish a new standard in the marketplace. All the major players in the OS market have begun to rush next generation OS products to the market. These products will enter the market at a significant point in the history of personal computing.

Establishing an OS Standard

A peculiar feature of the OS business is the strength of established standards and the difficulty entrants encounter in dislodging an entrenched incumbent. To understand why the effects of standards are so strong in the industry, it is necessary to consider each of three players in the industry—customers, applications suppliers (ISVs, VARs), and hardware manufacturers (OEMs).

Customers choose an OS by the number of applications it offers and their usefulness in meeting a specific need. Two kinds of applications are necessary to win widespread acceptance of a product—a minimum set of general productivity horizontal applications, such as spreadsheets and word processors, are a "ticket to play" without which customers will not even consider the product. These ticket-to-play packages are referred to as *ante* applications. In addition to this minimal set, an OS must differentiate itself from the competition by offering additional value added vertical and horizontal solutions. This creates two barriers to customers switching to a new OS. First, since the existing standard offers a stable environment for the customer, changing it will require taking significant technological risks with the changeout, and incurring additional costs in retraining users. Second, the new system also has far fewer applications than the entrenched standard. As a result, customers are extremely reluctant to change their systems. They do so only when they recognize their existing system does not meet their needs or a new system offers substantial performance advantages.

Applications developers take their cue from customers. They primarily target their application development efforts at the dominant standard since that platform offers them access to the widest customer base, both in terms of new units shipped and size of the installed base. This creates a "virtuous cycle" for an established standard, further heightening barriers to entry for a new OS vendor (see Exhibit 6).

Hardware manufacturers offer customers a range of OS choices in order to maximize the number of PCs and workstations they sell. OEMs serve to heighten entry barriers to entrants in three ways. First, since there are significant economy-of-scale advantages that lower the cost of distributing the dominant standard relative to an entrant's product, OEMs offer the standard at a much lower price than the entrant's product. Second, most OEMs will not even consider offering a new entrant's product until it can demonstrate volumes in the range of 200,000 units per year. Since OEMs constitute the highest volume distribution channel for OSs, this creates a

EXHIBIT 6 Establishing an OS Standard

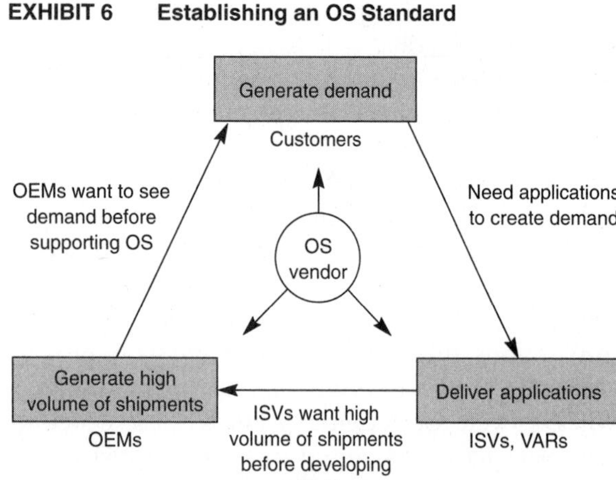

catch-22 for new entrants. Finally, most OEMs now offer convenient ready-to-run packages with the OS preloaded on the machine. These packages have attracted a growing number of customers to purchase a larger share of their software through the OEM channel. This fact, coupled with the OEM channel's attractive economics, makes it difficult for entrants who do not have access to this distribution channel to dislodge the standard.

In addition to these market-related factors, OS vendors must also take into account several product-related factors to win customer acceptance for their new operating systems. Customers have made considerable investments in their existing systems and applications. In order to encourage customer trial, vendors need to ensure that their new systems run a large number of applications from the existing system—backward compatibility with existing standards. This is typically done using an emulation package. Simply providing an emulator is, however, insufficient. On the one hand, customers complain that the emulator for Windows provided by Windows NT is extremely slow. On the other hand, too good an emulator will make customers purchase the new system primarily to run the old standard under emulation mode. Nearly 40 percent of OS/2's installed base primarily uses OS/2 as an emulator for Windows.

Another issue that confronts vendors is how much functionality to add in the system: Too little and customers do not find it attractive enough to switch; too much and the system becomes so big that it can run only on very high-end systems.

Vendors must also decide how they intend to deliver the new operating system. Since the new system does not have any new applications, simply putting the product on the hard disk of a PC does not ensure that customers will use it. Vendors have adopted different methods to launch their new systems. Microsoft launched Windows by bundling it for free with Excel, its fast-selling spreadsheet. Customers purchased Excel and received Windows transparently with it. Once Windows had a large installed base, ISVs wrote new applications for it allowing Microsoft to split the product from Excel over time.

Vendors must also establish close relationships with third parties—VARs, SIs, ISVs, and hardware OEMs—to create a new standard. One of Microsoft's greatest assets has been its established relations with each of these groups through its DOS and Windows products. In particular, small ISVs are particularly loyal to Microsoft and its dominant standard—by targeting a single operating system they can reach nearly all end users.

Major Competitors and Their Strategies

As competitors sought to stake their positions in the emerging market, they recognized that there would be two key elements to their product strategy—delivering a competitive suite of products, and providing the smoothest migration path from existing systems to their new platforms. In the long run, vendors also felt that they needed to provide two types of OSs: desktop OSs to run on client machines, and network OSs to run on servers. Not only would these products need to interoperate with each other, but in order to be widely accepted, vendors needed to ensure that they would interoperate efficiently with OSs from a variety of vendors. The transition period is likely to occur over a fairly extended period of time, since new hardware advances will only gradually be introduced to the market, and customers tend to be fairly averse to making large-scale changeouts of their existing systems.

During this transition period, each vendor will need to develop and communicate a complete product strategy that includes parts of several elements. First, a suite of OS products consisting of a high-volume desktop OS for the mass market, a high-end desktop OS targeted primarily at introducing new technologies to early adopter corporate customers, and a network OS. While OS vendors had initially focused on specializing in one of these segments, driven by pressure from Microsoft, the market leader, all the vendors had begun to evaluate developing more complete product lines. Second, in order to capture applications developers and encourage them to target new applications to a vendor's OS (and not a competitor's product), OS vendors need to define a set of interfaces, called application programming interfaces (APIs), which applications programmers can target when they write new software packages. Not only does this play a role in developing a captive developer base, but it also adds an important time-to-market element in vendors' strategies allowing them to preannounce a significant suite of applications before they release a new OS to the market. Third, while introducing elements of object technology into their product offering, vendors must maintain backward compatibility with existing procedure-based systems.

Microsoft

Microsoft dominated the desktop operating system market in 1994. Microsoft had built its operating system business by developing Microsoft Disk Operating System (MS-DOS), the product that would become a standard in the IBM-compatible segment of the PC market. Microsoft extended MS-DOS by adding a graphical user interface–based extension called Windows that further entrenched its position as the market leader in the OS business. Extending from this core business, the company had successfully built a very broad product line and dominated several segments of the applications market, including both word processors and spreadsheets. Revenues continued to accelerate and profit margins remained high (see Exhibit 7). The applications software business had surpassed the OS business in 1992 as the primary source of Microsoft's revenues.[12] In addition, the company had begun to broaden its position into other emerging markets, including multimedia, consumer software, educational software, and products related to the information highway (see Exhibit 8).

Microsoft's operating system business

While the OS business has declined as a portion of Microsoft's revenues, it continues to remain strategically important to the company for a variety of reasons.

Due to Microsoft's control of the highly attractive OEM channel, its OS business enjoyed extremely attractive economics. The OS business enjoyed gross margins of over 80 percent and net contribution margins close to 67 percent.[13] While the OS business as a whole accounted for only 34 percent of Microsoft's total revenues in 1993, it accounted for nearly 55 percent of the total contribution. These gross margins have increased gradually over the last five years as Microsoft raised Windows' prices once it became widely established as a standard.[14] Moreover, the OS business has continued to produce robust growth, accounting for nearly 50 percent of Microsoft's total market capitalization of nearly $24 billion in August 1993.

Microsoft's OS business also represented a very steady source of cash flows to the company. The gradual increase in gross margins over the previous three years and limited customer switching from its large installed base had provided Microsoft with a very stable source of cash flows. Moreover, its two major OS products—DOS and Windows—were in the highly profitable upgrade phase of their product life cycle. Microsoft was supporting a very small team of software developers who were producing upgrades to these products; each upgrade in turn generated close to $200 million in revenues.[15] The importance of this stable source of cash flows had grown dramatically as Microsoft's other cash flow generating business—applications software—faced growing price pressures and declining margins in the face of aggressive price competition.

Microsoft has exploited the synergies from its presence in both the OS market and the applications market in developing its product line strategy. It has bundled new OSs with its best-selling applications to build a captive customer base for the OS. Its application business derives tremendous time-to-market advantages relative to rivals by knowing what features will be incorporated in new versions of DOS and Windows. For example, the early versions of its Microsoft Windows product were sold bundled at no extra charge to customers with its more successful Microsoft Excel product. The success of Excel, which was the first graphical user interface (GUI) capable

[12]Sherlund, "Analyst Report on Microsoft."

[13]Ibid.

[14]Microsoft raised the price of Windows 3.1 from $99 in 1991 to $149 in 1993.

[15]Sherlund, "Analyst Report on Microsoft."

EXHIBIT 7 Microsoft Financials

	Millions of Dollars (except EPS)				
	1989	1990	1991	1992	1993
Net revenues	804	1,183	1,843	2,759	3,753
Net income	171	279	463	708	953
EPS	0.67	1.04	1.64	2.41	3.15
Return on net revenues	21%	24%	25%	26%	25%
Cash	301	449	686	1,345	2,290
Total assets	721	1,105	1,644	2,640	3,805
Stockholders' equity	562	919	1,351	2,193	3,242

spreadsheet for IBM-compatible personal computers, created a large installed base of Windows users, thereby paving the way for other Windows-based Microsoft applications. By being the first major ISV to move all its applications to the Windows 3.1 platform, Microsoft was able to beat its major competitors—Lotus and WordPerfect—to market on that platform. When Windows 3.1 volumes increased dramatically, Microsoft captured the dominant share in most of the major horizontal applications segments. Microsoft's success with Windows offers it another benefit—concerned that a failure to match Microsoft's time-to-market on new OS platforms could produce similar results to Windows, ISVs have now become more proactive in seeking to port their applications to new Microsoft platforms. This allows Microsoft to generate a large number of applications for its platforms much faster than rival OS vendors, a critical factor in winning customer adoption.

Microsoft's OS business continues to remain the primary source of its strong relationships with a variety of resellers—hardware manufacturers (OEMs), system integrators (SIs), independent software vendors (ISVs), and value-added resellers (VARs). As it seeks to enter new markets, Microsoft has sought to build on these reseller relationships.

EXHIBIT 8 Microsoft Revenue Composition

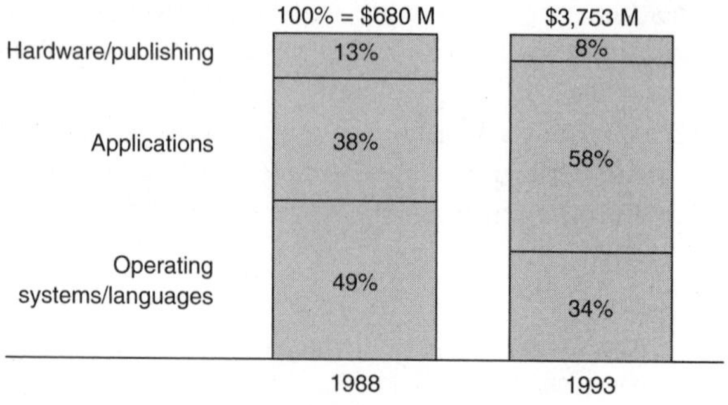

	1988 (100% = $680 M)	1993 ($3,753 M)
Hardware/publishing	13%	8%
Applications	38%	58%
Operating systems/languages	49%	34%

Recognizing that corporate customers had begun to demand greater OS functionality than Windows 3.1 provides, and faced with the need to generate additional revenues, Microsoft plans to bring a number of OS products to market during the next few years. Each new platform is targeted at a specific segment of the market. Windows 3.1 and Chicago are the primary Microsoft OSs targeted at the high-volume client desktop market. Windows NT is the OS it is targeting at high-end PC users and workstation customers. NT will over time be evolved into Microsoft's strategic object-oriented platform—Cairo. Microsoft has also developed a version of Windows NT, the NT Advanced Server, to attack Novell and IBM in the fast-growing server market. Estimates of the release dates for these products from various analysts are indicated in Exhibit 9.

Windows 3.1

Microsoft has pursued a three-pronged product strategy to build and continue to reinforce Windows 3.1's position as the predominant OS for desktop and portable personal computers. It has engaged in massive marketing campaigns—including media, OEM deals, and road shows—to horizontal and vertical industry segments in order to push its Windows vision. Windows—not DOS—applications now drive the applications market, giving Microsoft an advantage over major applications competitors. Also, Windows' success has accelerated the demand for high-powered 80386- and 80486-based desktop and portable systems.[16]

[16] *Microsoft's Networking Strategy,* Harvard Business School Case, 1993, pp. 14–15.

EXHIBIT 9 Microsoft Product Line

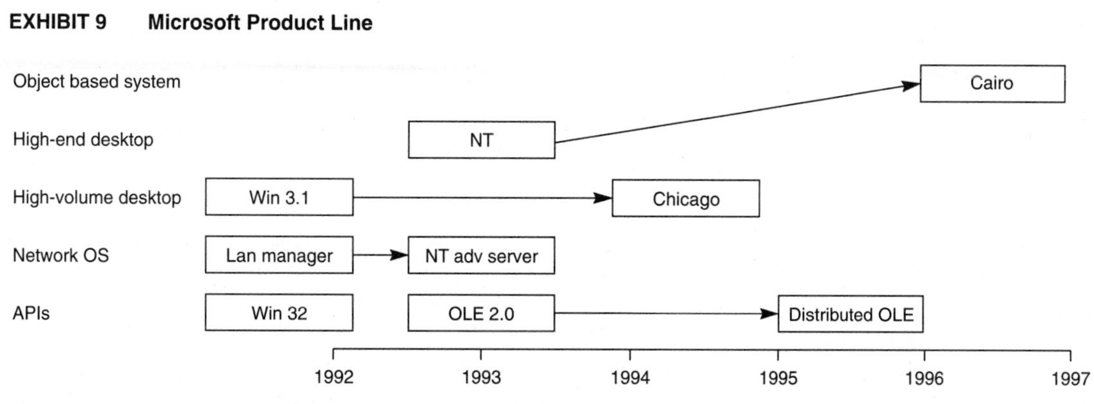

As a result, Microsoft has built a very strong relationship with Intel. Finally, having established Windows 3.1 as a standard in the market, Microsoft has gradually raised retail prices on the product from $99 per copy to $149 per copy. Simultaneously, however, it has aggressively cut royalties to OEMs, encouraging them to bundle Windows with their hardware as ready-to-run packages. This strategy has proved particularly effective in locking competitor products such as OS/2 and DR-DOS into higher-cost retail distribution channels.

Chicago

Microsoft is positioning Chicago as its high-volume, 32-bit successor to Windows 3.1. Similar to Windows 3.1, Chicago is designed for the mainstream Windows desktop (i.e., 386 or above with 4 MB RAM). It is expected to improve upon Windows 3.1 in several respects.[17] First, it will deliver significantly enhanced setup and configuration features. Second, it is a completely self-contained OS and does not use or require a version of MS-DOS. Third, it will run all existing MS-DOS and Windows 16-bit applications as well as 32-bit Windows applications using subsets of the full Win 32 application programming interface (API). Chicago is also expected to add several 32-bit features designed to deliver more responsive and reliable multitasking to mainstream Windows desktops. Industry analysts expect Microsoft to begin a very rapid cutover of its installed base of DOS and Windows 3.1 customers to Chicago once it is released. By consolidating customers onto the single Chicago software base, Microsoft eliminates the need to maintain and enhance two separate code bases. From a cost standpoint, Chicago is therefore very attractive. Chicago represents two substantial revenue streams to Microsoft—upgrade revenues to the OS alone have been estimated by Rick Sherlund, of Goldman Sachs, to be over $500 million. Additionally, Chicago will result in a major incremental upgrade revenue stream for Microsoft applications such as Word and Excel. Microsoft CEO Bill Gates has indicated that Chicago will be offered at an upgrade price between $49 and $99 per copy.

However, Microsoft faces several risks in bringing Chicago to market. While the product is currently in alpha testing, Microsoft has already published the Chicago API to encourage ISVs to begin developing applications to the platform. While Microsoft has already announced the Win 32C API to allow ISVs to begin writing applications targeted to run on Chicago, the API still remains a "virtual" API, and major ISVs are waiting for the release of the product before expending major resources behind it. Also, Microsoft's positioning of Chicago vis-à-vis its Windows 3.1 and Windows NT OSs has changed. Chicago has now been positioned as the volume 32-bit desktop successor to Windows 3.1, while Windows NT has been targeted toward corporate mission-critical applications. This has created considerable confusion among early adopter corporate customers. Finally, Chicago's hardware requirements are certain to be significantly larger than a large percentage of the installed base of DOS and Windows systems. It is still unclear exactly how Microsoft intends to upgrade the installed base of

[17]Microsoft Corporation product literature, December 1993

customers (e.g., ship them a hardware card with the required RAM upgrade and Chicago preloaded).

Windows NT

Microsoft released Windows NT on July 24, 1993.[18] Windows NT represented the first complete OS development effort that Microsoft had conducted—MS-DOS had been purchased from another vendor due to time constraints—and Windows represented primarily the addition of a graphical user interface to existing DOS systems. Partly to freeze the market, Bill Gates had preannounced Windows NT to the market as early as 1990. A herculean four-year product development effort led by David Cutler, the architect responsible for the VMS OS at DEC, had produced a sophisticated system with several million lines of code. Following the product's release, early consumer feedback had been tepid—many customers felt that Windows NT's price–performance was not attractive enough to warrant their swapping out their existing systems for it. Bill Gates had therefore repositioned NT away from the high-volume desktop toward a more high-end, strategic platform for early adopter customers. Despite favorable reactions from the trade press, Microsoft continued to face several problems in establishing NT in the industry.

Microsoft has generated considerable publicity and attention for Windows NT. However, NT is still in its first release and faces several performance issues: (1) Windows 3.1 applications running via adapters on Windows NT have demonstrated performance hits of nearly 30 percent. Customers may be reluctant to migrate to NT given these performance impacts.[19] (2) Windows NT beta test sites indicate that successive beta versions of the product demand growing memory requirements limiting the class of systems on which the product can be run. Currently, versions of NT cannot be run on anything smaller than a 486-class machine with at least 16 megabytes of memory in order to access the minimal functionality set. These specifications would necessitate widespread hardware upgrades in order to run NT on the desktop. (3) The NT Advanced Server product—the application server version of Windows NT—continues to face backward compatibility issues with Netware, the current standard for network OSs. Unless Microsoft resolves these issues, the product could face problems in receiving customer acceptance.[20]

Microsoft also faces considerable problems reaching the target customers for Windows NT. High-end PC and workstation customers, who are the early adopters for advanced operating systems, are primarily large corporate customers who are served most effectively by direct sales forces. In attempting to penetrate this market, Microsoft faces competition from major systems vendors, including IBM and Hewlett-Packard, who have strong ties with the corporate market through their direct sales forces, and from Novell, which has built a formidable presence in the reseller channel. Microsoft has decided to pursue indirect VAR and SI channels to access corporate customers for Windows NT, and has begun to establish several reseller programs to build its presence in these channels.

Due to the performance issues that have hindered Windows NT adoption, Microsoft has also constantly shifted its focus and marketing message for Windows NT. While NT was initially positioned as the successor to Windows 3.1, Microsoft has now shifted NT to corporate mission-critical applications.

While Microsoft released Windows NT to the market in July 1993, it was well behind earlier announced product release schedules. The schedule slippage has offered a window of opportunity for IBM's competitive OS/2 v 2.1 to generate positive attention from the trade press and members of the developer community.[21] While Windows NT will eventually gain some share of the 32-bit OS market, customers are likely to adopt far more gradually than originally expected. Microsoft has, therefore, tried to downplay the industry's expectations for early high-volume shipments.

Object linking and embedding 2.0

As OS vendors compete for market leadership in the emerging 32-bit market, they have also recognized the importance of applications and solutions to the success of their OS offering. An important element in their strategies to capture developer mindshare has been their offering of integrated middleware APIs for application developers to target. Currently, three major products are competing in this seg-

[18] "Windows NT Released," *Information Week,* July 27, 1993.

[19] "OS/2 v 2.1 vs Windows NT—Comparing the New 32-bit Operating Systems," *InfoWorld,* September 1993.

[20] Ibid.

[21] "Windows NT behind Schedule," *Unixworld,* March 1993.

ment—Microsoft's OLE, Novell's Appware, and Apple's Open Doc.

Microsoft's Object Linking and Embedding (OLE) technology is designed to let applications share functionality through live data exchange and embedded data.[22] Embedded objects are packaged statically within the source application, called the client; linked objects launch the server applications when instructed to by the client application. OLE 2.0 includes visual editing and the ability to drag and drop objects across applications. OLE Automation, another key part of OLE 2.0, will enable cross-application communication by allowing an object to expose its commands and data to another object or program. Microsoft has positioned OLE 2.0 as a migration path toward its future OS, Cairo.[23]

However, OLE 2.0's success is by no means certain and several major issues need to be resolved. Since Microsoft views OLE as a convergence point for its widely proliferated procedural Win 16 APIs and its next-generation object-based APIS, it has attempted to incorporate a large amount of functionality into OLE. This has led to an explosion in the complexity of the product with over 500 APIs currently published. Many ISVs have indicated reluctance to support OLE due to the costs associated with learning the product. Moreover, embedding OLE 2.0 in applications has proved complicated and the results have proved inadequate. [24] Microsoft has also not provided significant networking functionality with OLE 2.0 since it would further expand the complexity of the API and considerably delay time to market.[25] The lack of networking functionality has significantly delayed adoption of OLE 2.0 in the critical market for client–server applications. Microsoft is planning to incorporate distributed capabilities in its next release of the Object Linking and Embedding technology, Distributed OLE. Finally, Windows Open Systems Architecture (WOSA), Microsoft's strategic effort to define a set of APIs that will make its proprietary Windows platform more open and thereby more competitive in the client–server market, is not currently integrated with its OLE effort. As a result, cross-platform alternatives to OLE, particularly Apple's OpenDoc, have raised considerable interest from the developer community.

[22]Microsoft Corporation product literature, 1993.

[23]Microsoft Corporation, *Proceedings from the OLE 2.0 Conference,* 1993.

[24]Ibid.

[25]Microsoft Corporation product literature, 1993.

Cairo

Cairo is Microsoft's next version of Windows NT representing Microsoft's attempt to migrate the NT platform toward object orientation. The product will be based on Distributed OLE, OLE 3.0, and Win 32 and essentially consists of an object file system, distributed OLE, and a distributed file structure layered over a Windows NT kernel (see Exhibit 10).[26]

Cairo's success is predicated upon the confluence of several factors, many of which continue to remain uncertain. Since the product, essentially, represents the confluence of Windows NT's Win 32 APIs and Distributed OLE, the critical factors driving Cairo's success will be the widespread acceptance of Windows NT and OLE 2.0 by the marketplace. Both these products continue to face several risks.

Also, Cairo's product technology is as yet unproven. Cairo will be based on a combination of procedural Win 32 APIs and object-based OLE 2.0

[26]"What is Cairo? A Developer's Perspective," *Microsoft News,* June 21, 1993.

EXHIBIT 10 Microsoft Migration Path

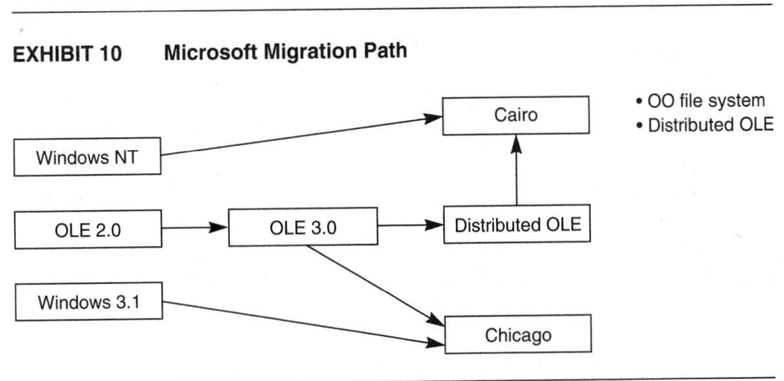

APIs. The merging of procedure-based technologies with the cleaner, more robust object-oriented technology could potentially result in a complex inextensible system that will be unable to provide developers the enabling technology they require. Also, Cairo will primarily use OLE 3.0 and Distributed OLE objects. OLE was designed to encapsulate present-day large applications as embedded pieces of code, and does not address issues such as reuse, ease of development, programmer productivity, and reduction in development complexity.[27] Microsoft's evolutionary approach may, therefore, fail initially to deliver many of the benefits that make object-oriented technology attractive. Finally, to fully exploit the power of object technology, developers require objects which can be reused easily. An essential requirement for object reuse is "inheritance." OLE objects which are not completely object oriented do not support inheritance.

It remains to be seen whether Microsoft's evolutionary approach toward object orientation will be technically feasible when a completely new paradigm shift may be required.

International Business Machines (IBM)

With 1993 revenues of $62 billion, International Business Machines continued to remain the largest computer company in the world (see Exhibit 11). Despite its size and presence in almost all segments of the computer industry, IBM had gone through a period of wrenching restructuring in the 1990s as its highly profitable mainframe business was rapidly eroded by competition from low-cost PCs and workstations. Facing severe competitive pressure in the PC business that it had helped create, IBM had focused its efforts on regaining market share in two segments of the business—microprocessors, with its PowerPC technology, and operating systems. In 1993, IBM had revenues of $11 billion from all its software businesses with operating systems alone contributing nearly 40 percent of the total (see Exhibit 12). However, IBM's operating system revenues were primarily from the declining mainframe and minicomputer businesses, and had consistently faced problems penetrating the key PC and workstation markets (see Exhibit 13).

OS/2

To recapture share in the operating system business, IBM is pursuing several initiatives in each of the key market segments. While Microsoft has established a very strong presence in the desktop personal computer market, IBM's OS/2 product enjoys a substantial presence in the corporate market and has built a loyal following of corporate developers. IBM shipped nearly 5 million units of OS/2 in 1993. IBM still needed to resolve several critical issues with OS/2. Some of its largest corporate customers had begun to switch from OS/2 to other platforms, particularly Windows, frustrated by the lack of commercially available software applications for OS/2. Others were concerned that with the release of Chicago, much of the value that differentiated OS/2 in the market would be eliminated. As a result, several CIOs (chief information officers) had expressed concern about standardizing their corporations on OS/2. Finally, despite the large number of OS/2

[27] Craig Brockschmidt, "OLE 2.0—A Review of the Fundamentals," August 1993.

EXHIBIT 11 IBM Financials

	Millions of Dollars (except EPS)				
	1989	1990	1991	1992	1993
Revenues	62,710	69,018	64,766	64,523	62,716
Hardware sales	41,586	43,959	37,093	33,755	30,591
Software	8,424	9,952	10,398	11,103	10,953
Services and maintenance	9,858	11,322	12,996	14,987	17,006
Rentals and financing	2,842	3,785	4,179	4,678	4,166
Costs and expenses	27,701	30,723	32,073	35,069	38,568
Gross profit	35,009	38,295	32,693	29,454	24,148
Net income	3,758	6,020	(2,861)	(4,965)	(8,101)
EPS	6.47	10.51	(5.01)	(8.70)	(14.22)

EXHIBIT 12 IBM's Software Business

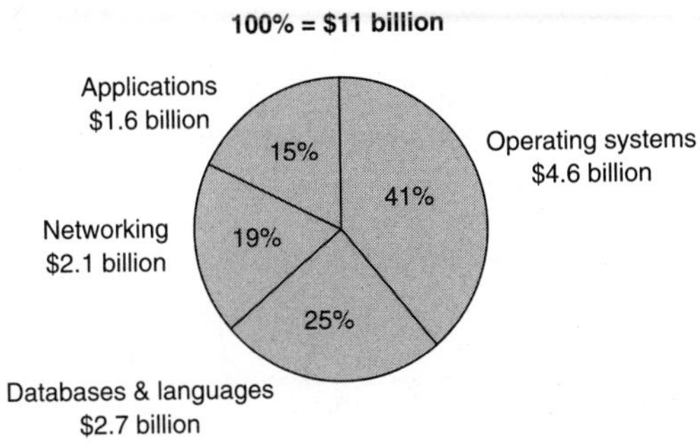

units that IBM shipped, several end users were primarily using OS/2 as an emulator for Windows. This not only hurt IBM's positioning of OS/2 but it further expanded the base of Windows users and strengthened Microsoft's marketing message. IBM's efforts were further complicated by the fact that different parts of the company felt more or less loyal to OS/2. Hardware business units felt their charter was to sell more PCs and felt no particular loyalty to OS/2, preferring to bundle Windows with their units. This made it difficult for IBM to win support for OS/2 from other hardware vendors.

In the near term, IBM will position OS/2 v 2.1 as a 32-bit, multithreaded, multitasking OS competing against Microsoft's Windows NT and Windows products.[28] When Microsoft releases its Chicago product, OS/2 will primarily compete with Chicago to capture existing DOS/Windows users who are transitioning to a 32-bit operating system. Exploiting

[28]IBM Personal Systems Division, Boca Raton, Florida.

EXHIBIT 13 IBM's Operating System Business

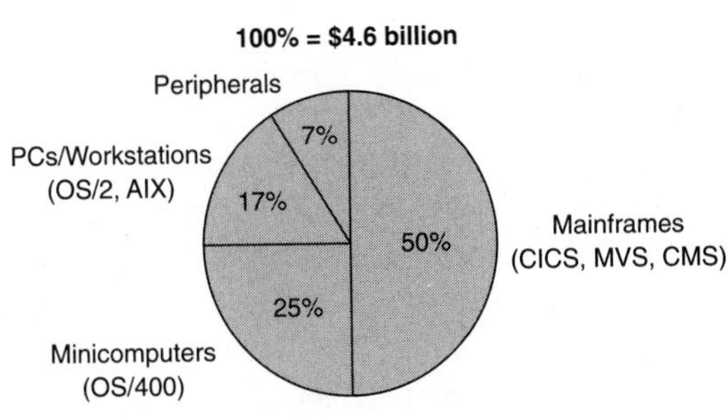

the window of opportunity offered by the schedule slippage of Windows NT, IBM had unveiled an aggressive marketing campaign aimed at solidifying ISV and corporate support behind OS/2 as the premier client–server platform.

AIX

While it has positioned OS/2 to compete with Chicago as the high-volume desktop OS, IBM continues to evolve its strategy vis-à-vis Windows NT in the high-end PC and workstation segment. Currently its most attractive product offering in that segment is the RS/6000 workstation running AIX (IBM's version of the Unix OS). Released as late as 1989, several years behind industry leaders Sun and Hewlett-Packard, these workstations have already captured 18 percent of the highly competitive workstation market and are gaining market share at the expense of smaller competitors.[29] Industry analysts and executives at IBM's Personal Systems Division indicate that IBM's strategy would be two-pronged. First, continue to promote AIX as a stable, robust platform of choice to VARs to develop high value-added vertical and horizontal market solutions. Second, offer a tiered high-end version of OS/2 to customers as an option primarily to increase the volume deployment of OS/2 and thereby increase its attractiveness as a target platform for ISVs and other application developers.

OS/2 Lan Server

To complement OS/2 and AIX as its client desktop offering, IBM offers two server products—Lan Server and Lan Manager, an extension of Microsoft's Lan Manager product. Recent releases of both products have received widespread praise for their technical robustness and sophistication. OS/2 Lan Server had built up a large installed base and captured a loyal base of customers in the fast-growing server market. In 1993, it was the second largest network OS, behind Novell's Netware. The server market had, until recently, not been a major focus of IBM's marketing efforts and Lan Server will likely retain a secondary market presence behind Novell's Netware. IBM may refocus its efforts on this segment when faced with competition from Microsoft's NT Advanced Server.

[29]"IBM's Growing Strength in the Unix Market," *Unixworld*, May 21, 1993

Workplace OS strategy

Beginning in 1995, IBM will offer OS/2 and Unix offerings (AIX) on a microkernel-based OS called Workplace OS.[30] The Workplace OS concept represents three significant advances over existing OSs. First, the Workplace OS aims to offer cross-platform portability for applications based on OS/2, DOS, Windows, AIX, and NFL through a microkernel designed to share low-level functionality across various OS layers.[31] On the one hand, application developers will be able to continue to program in the environment and using the APIs of their choice—the microkernel will then allow their applications to interoperate with other OSs. Second, existing OS standards—DOS, Windows, Unix—will all run as "multiple personalities" under the Workplace OS umbrella. The Workplace OS will therefore substantially enhance the degree of choice offered to customers. Third, the Workplace OS will incorporate the advanced object-oriented technology currently being developed by Taligent, an Apple–IBM joint venture. In the long term, Taligent's Pink Operating System will become a personality on the Workplace OS platform. Following the release of Chicago by Microsoft, the Workplace OS will primarily compete with Windows NT, Cairo, and Chicago.

Unix Vendors

Unix has traditionally held a substantial market share in the client–server, multiuser, and distributed computing markets. It has also established a strong presence as a development platform among ISVs, SIs, VARs, and corporate developers. Currently, close to 1,000,000 Unix units are deployed a year with nearly a third (300,000+) serving as developer platforms. Despite its large share in these markets, applications developers have traditionally faced difficulties targeting Unix platforms due to the many varieties of Unix (with different APIs) in the market. With Microsoft's entry into these markets with its Windows NT product, several major vendors are leading the effort to converge Unix, including IBM, HP, SunSoft, Univel, and the SVR4 licensees.[32]

Unix vendors have begun to undertake several initiatives. They have attempted to coalesce their efforts to present a united front against Microsoft. The most important initiative they have undertaken is the Cooperative Open Systems Environment (COSE) which is chartered with creating a standard set of system functions, APIs, and user interface that applications developers can target.[33] Also, several Unix vendors have ported or are considering porting Unix to run on high-volume platforms, particularly Intel, and pursuing the appropriate high-volume distribution channels. SCO, Univel, Solaris, and NeXT are some of the Unix vendors who have begun this process.[34] Finally, coupled with their strategy to convert their products to high-volume run-times, many PC Unix vendors, such as Santa Cruz Operation (SCO) and Univel, have begun unbundling tools and networking support from run-times. They have pursued this strategy for two reasons. First, by unbundling these pieces, they can reduce the size of the OS "footprint" (memory and hard disk requirements), thereby allowing them to target high-volume low-end PCs. Second, by selling these tools and networking as add-on products, they hope to generate significant incremental revenues.

Unix vendors, however, do face a difficult transition in the market. Customers continue to remain skeptical about efforts to coalesce Unix through COSE. By unbundling tools and run-times, Unix vendors have created a product that has failed to capture share from Windows 3.1 while remaining unattractive to traditional Unix users. Aggressive price-cutting efforts led by Univel have failed to capture share from Windows 3.1 but have destroyed the economics of the PC Unix marketplace.

Apple

Apple continues to evolve its strategy in the desktop and server markets in order to position itself to compete against Microsoft. Currently, Apple's focus appears to be in two areas (see Exhibit 14).

Mac OS

System 7 is Apple's most current release of its proprietary Macintosh OS. Apple will continue to evolve System 7 through system extensions, such as QuickTime and the Open Collaboration Environment (OCE), on the way to System 8.

---

[30]IBM Personal Systems Division, "What Is the Workplace OS?" *OS/2 Users Group Magazine,* September 1, 1993.

[31]Ibid.

[32]"COSE—Can It Unify Unix?" *Unixworld,* July 20, 1993.

[33]Ibid.

[34]"PC Unix Vendors Face Difficult Future," *Unixworld,* August 2, 1993.

EXHIBIT 14 Migration Paths of Other OS Vendors

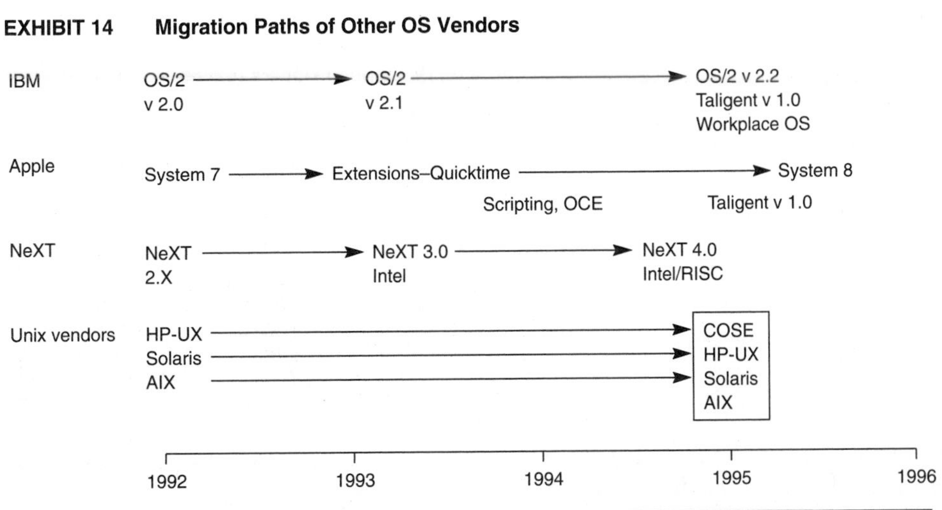

Taligent

Apple continues to evolve its strategy to pursue major corporate accounts through its enterprise system offering. Apple's version of Unix—AUX (PowerOpen) product—could be positioned as a robust OS product for the enterprise market.[35] By early 1994, Apple has begun to position Taligent's object-oriented technology running on a microkernel-based version of AUX as its strategic OS in the enterprise market.[36]

Open Doc

Open Doc is Apple's cross-platform open compound-document architecture, which is intended to redefine the relationship between documents, applications, and users.[37] It is designed to bring about a gradual shift from the application-centered approach that characterizes desktop computing today to a more document-centered approach. It is expected to provide application developers and users a high degree of customization, allowing developers to turn their monolithic applications into packages of focused tools, called parts editors, which can be used to quickly customize applications. Open Doc uses the Bento file format and will interwork with OLE 2.0. Apple has positioned Open Doc as a key element of its strategy to port key Macintosh technologies, tools, and services to Windows, Unix, and other platforms.

Pursuant with that strategy, Apple has committed to releasing Open Doc simultaneously for both Windows and Macintosh platforms, and is evaluating several flavors of Unix. Apple has also positioned Open Doc as an open alternative to OLE 2.0. Unlike Microsoft, Apple has committed to making its Open Doc specification and source code available without restriction to all developers. Furthermore, Apple has announced that it intends to make its Open Doc specification comply with OLE 2.0 allowing Open Doc objects to interoperate with OLE 2.0 objects. Finally, Apple has successfully recruited other vendors to support Open Doc, including IBM. Elements of Taligent's object-oriented technology will also be incorporated into Open Doc.

Apple seems to face a very difficult transition period. On the one hand, its failure to make its proprietary system software and graphical user interface available on the more popular IBM-compatible machines has allowed Microsoft to capture a dominant market position. While it has finally made successive generations of its products available on multiple platforms, the market is now largely Microsoft-centric and Apple's announcements have met with lukewarm responses. As it sought to once again reestablish its pre-eminent position in the PC marketplace, Apple's problems were further compounded by its dire financial position. The widespread acceptance of Microsoft Windows had diluted Apple's product differentiation—ease of

---

[35]Apple Computer, interviews conducted October 1993.

[36]"Apple—What Future for Pink?" *MacWorld,* November 11, 1993.

[37]Apple Computer, Open Doc product literature.

EXHIBIT 15 Apple Computer Financials

	Millions of Dollars (except EPS)				
	1989	1990	1991	1992	1993
Revenues	5,284	5,558	6,308	7,086	7,976
Costs and expenses	4,649	4,846	5,861	6,280	7,866
Operating Income	634	712	447	806	140
Net income	454	475	309	530	87
EPS	3.53	3.77	2.58	4.33	0.73
Cash and short-term investments	808	997	892	1,435	892
Total assets	2,743	2,975	3,493	4,223	5,171
Stockholders' equity	1,485	1,446	1,766	2,187	2,026

use—and had led to a collapse in the price and gross margin of its products. Apple needed to change its cost structure, which had been designed around a fat 30 percent margin on PCs, to operate on the slim 6 to 7 percent that its most cost-effective competitors were operating on (see Exhibit 15).

Novell

In 1993, Novell enjoyed the dominant position in the network OS market with over 70,000 major installations of its popular Netware product, the most widely used file-and-print server in the industry.[38] Faced with a grave threat from the aggressively priced NT Advanced Server, Novell has launched several initiatives to counter Microsoft's momentum. During the 1980s, Novell had focused exclusively on the network OS business, preferring to work cooperatively with third parties in other markets. This cooperative strategy had been a large element of its marketing message to VARs, SIs, and ISVs. During 1993, Novell shifted away from its traditional focus and had made several acquisitions to broaden its product line and compete directly with Microsoft in all major market segments. It entered the applications market by acquiring WordPerfect's word processing package and Borland's spreadsheet. It acquired Unix System Laboratories from AT&T and offered its own version of Unix as a desktop OS. Finally, in an attempt to broaden Netware from a file-and-print server, Novell launched Appware. Partly due to the difficulties associated with merging the acquired companies and schedule slippages of new releases of Netware, Novell had begun to demonstrate slower revenue growth and falling profitability (see Exhibit 16).

Appware

Novell recognized that its primary competitive advantage relative to Microsoft in the server market is its large installed base of systems and its very strong presence in the reseller channel—Novell has

[38]IDC Corporation, *Annual Survey of the Desktop PC Market*, 1993, pp. 115–17.

EXHIBIT 16 Novell Financials

	Millions of Dollars (except EPS)				
	1989	1990	1991	1992	1993
Revenues	421	498	640	933	1,122
Gross profit	270	365	516	749	898
Operating income	71	134	226	355	74
Net income	48	94	162	249	(35)
EPS	0.18	0.34	0.55	0.81	(0.11)
Cash and short-term investments	129	254	347	545	664
Total assets	346	494	726	1,096	1,343
Stockholders' equity	236	398	598	937	996

over 25,000 resellers supporting its Netware product compared to only 300 to date for NT Advanced Server. Additionally, the key factor in generating demand for a particular network OS is the ability to deliver high value-added solutions developed to the OS platform. In order to slow NT's momentum, Novell recognized that it must develop a captive base of applications developers (ISVs and VARs) and lock in its resellers who will develop and deliver superior solutions to customers. Novell, therefore, recently announced Appware,[39] a middleware platform that will help developers write applications across heterogeneous server and client systems. Appware essentially defines a set of APIs that allow software developers to write applications that will target a broad set of clients connected to Netware servers.

Appware offers two benefits to developers—first, by allowing developers to write client applications to a single set of APIs which will then work through the Appware Foundation Layer with a variety of back-end servers, and second, by not attempting to introduce a fundamentally new API with Appware—developers can continue to program to existing Win 32 APIs or Macintosh APIs, which will then be made portable by Appware to run on other platforms. Appware comprises a set of APIs which provide complementary networking functionalities that are not incorporated in the base Windows APIs.

By providing Appware, therefore, Novell envisions an environment in which customers develop applications for multiple clients using Appware. These applications will then interwork with servers running Netware, thereby generating demand for Netware. Additionally, Novell claims that the new platform will cut network application development times by as much as 90 percent. Market reaction has been tempered by Novell's refusal to offer specific time frames for extending the platform beyond its proprietary systems to other popular network service systems, including potentially Microsoft's NT Directory Service and Apple's Open Collaborative Environment (OCE).

DR-DOS

Novell also continues to position its DR-DOS product, a DOS version that Novell acquired from Digital Research, as a viable alternative to DOS 6.0 in the desktop personal computer market.

[39]"Appware—Novell Announces Cross Platform Development Environment," *Infoworld,* August, 1993.

Unixware

An element of its strategy has been its attempt to work with a coalition of Unix vendors to evolve a common Unix standard. Novell could then couple Unix with its Netware product as a viable alternative to Windows NT. As a step toward this goal, Novell recently acquired Unix System Laboratories, a former AT&T subsidiary, and has recently released Unixware.

Novell, however, faces numerous obstacles in maintaining its position in the new market segments it has entered. It will face difficulties in countering Windows NT's momentum if Unix vendors are slow to coalesce through COSE. Its Unixware product, a combination of its Netware file-and-print server with Unix System Laboratories' version of Unix, has faced difficulty in establishing itself in the marketplace. Finally, its desktop products will face difficulty in breaking Microsoft's lock on the OEM channel and may not make any significant inroads into the entrenched base of DOS and Windows users.

NeXT

NeXT Computer Inc.'s NeXTSTEP was the first commercially available OS that demonstrated the power of object-oriented technology to the broad market. NeXTSTEP essentially consists of the Mach OS, which is compatible with Unix 4.3 BSD, and a powerful object-oriented graphical user interface, based on Display Postscript technology. In addition to standard Unix features such as pre-emptive multitasking, the OS provides multiple threads, memory mapping, and message-based interprocess communication.[40] NeXT continues to evolve its OS strategy.

To establish NeXTSTEP as a widely available standard in the marketplace, NeXT needed to port the OS from its proprietary hardware platform to high-volume platforms, particularly Intel. With the June 1993 release of NeXTSTEP for Intel 3.1, NeXT began to take steps in this direction. With subsequent releases, NeXT will also consider porting its system to other high-volume RISC platforms.[41]

NeXT also needs to develop channel partners who will push its system into the market. NeXT had gradually begun to sign up systems vendors,

[40]NeXT Computer, NeXTSTEP Operating System, product literature.

[41]Unixworld, NeXTStep released on Intel, June 31, 1993.

including Hewlett-Packard, but has still been unable to build a substantial presence in the PC marketplace.

Finally, NeXT has built considerable strength in specific vertical markets, where it has been viewed as a platform on which to rapidly prototype and build custom vertical applications. NeXTSTEP has particularly built a strong presence in the financial services and securities trading markets, where NeXT and Hewlett-Packard jointly market the product.

NeXT, however, faces several issues in maintaining a long-term presence in the market. Despite gradually building its presence in the market, NeXT has still been unable to gain substantial share of the OEM or reseller channels that will be necessary to establish it as a standard in the market. Further, due to the high royalty burden that NeXTSTEP carries, NeXT has been constrained to price its product significantly higher than competitor products such as Windows NT and OS/2. This has limited its ability to penetrate lower-priced systems and channels.

Future of the Industry

As competitors struggled to comprehend the structural shifts taking place in the OS market and to stake out their positions in the market, they needed to be aware of the changes occurring in the related markets. Most important was the microprocessor market which had until 1994 been dominated by Intel's x86 line. Driven by the huge demand for PCs during the 1980s, Intel had established itself as an entrenched standard in much the same way as Microsoft. Despite its large cash reserves, its large installed base, and huge economies of scale advantages relative to rivals, Intel for the first time faced two significant threats to its dominance—first, the PowerPC RISC microprocessor, developed jointly by Apple, IBM, and Motorola; second, beginning with Windows NT, Microsoft had begun to port new versions of its operating systems to other microprocessors, reducing the barriers for customers to switch to these new platforms. Other OS vendors recognized that while Intel would probably continue to control the largest share of the market for the foreseeable future, OSs in the future would need to be portable across hardware platforms.

In addition, Microsoft's rivals needed to decide whether they would confront it individually or through a consortium of industry participants. There were advantages and disadvantages to both these approaches. Only the largest hardware manufacturers, such as IBM, possessed the financial resources to face Microsoft alone. The PC manufacturing industry was too fragmented for any one supplier to successfully push a standard on the market. Moreover, in attempting to establish a standard, hardware vendors like IBM found it very difficult to win the support of other OEMs. As a result, individual OEMs found it very difficult to win widespread acceptance for their operating systems.

As an alternative approach, IBM and Apple had attempted to knit together a consortium of hardware vendors to mount a credible offensive against Microsoft. This strategy had also proved difficult. Most large-system vendors had their own proprietary OSs that they would need to sacrifice when they migrated to a system developed by a consortium. While the top management in these companies recognized the need to set aside their proprietary systems, their strategic vision was often thwarted by middle managers who felt threatened by the loss of control to an outside organization. These organizational tensions had hampered coalition efforts to push new standards on the market.

Faced with these factors, competitors needed to quickly resolve a variety of issues: What was their overall product strategy? Should they compete in all three segments of the market or focus only on a niche? Did they have the financial and organizational resources to compete in all three segments? If they focused on a segment, should they choose a specific partner in the other segments or make their product interoperate with all other products? Why would customers switch from their existing systems to new products? How could they induce "fence sitters" to try the new systems? What distribution channels could they use to reach customers? How much functionality should they incorporate in their product?

Glossary

Application Programming Interface (API): A clearly defined interface that allows applications programmers to communicate with the operating system.

Bento file format: A proprietary file format defined by Apple that supports distributed objects and is a defined standard in Open Doc. The Bento file format allows Open Doc to support OLE objects.

Client–server. Client-server is an information system architecture by which data is primarily stored on a central computer called the server and can be accessed from multiple clients. The client-server architecture contrasts with a peer-to-peer architecture in which there is no single centralized server machine.

Footprint: The configuration of an operating system defined in terms of the hardware system on which it can be operated (e.g., RAM, memory, hard disk capacity).

Inheritance: A feature of object-oriented technology whereby an object defined as a subtype or subclass of another object class inherits all the characteristics of the latter in a "parent-child" relationship.

Microkernel: A core set of operating system functions that are defined in a consistent manner across multiple hardware systems. This allows the operating system that is built on top of the microkernel to be easily ported across multiple hardware systems.

Multitasking: An operating system's ability to handle multiple tasks at one time. Preemptive multitasking and sequential tasking are two different approaches to providing multitasking capability.

Multithreaded: An operating system's ability to handle multiple threads simultaneously, each thread itself handling multiple processes at one time.

Object orientation, object-oriented technology: A programming methodology by which software programs are decomposed into discrete objects that can be developed independent of each other and communicate through well-defined interfaces. Object orientation allows programmers to assemble predefined (prefabricated) objects together very quickly, enabling greater reuse of code.

OLE: Microsoft Object Linking and Embedding technology that defines a set of objects that can be embedded within applications and allows them to be linked together. It represents Microsoft's first step toward providing object-oriented capability in its operating systems.

Open Doc: Apple Computer's response to Microsoft's OLE also defines a set of object APIs that programmers can target to embed object capabilities within their applications.

Reuse: A software development methodology that aims to speed up the development process by enabling programmers to reuse already existing code. Object-oriented programming enables reuse by allowing programmers to assemble prefabricated objects and allowing for inheritance of features.

RISC: Reduced instruction set computing is a technology developed by IBM that simplifies the operations executed by a microprocessor to a limited set that can be executed very fast and efficiently. All other operations are defined in terms of this core set of operations.

WOSA: Windows Open Systems Architecture is a set of APIs defined by Microsoft to make the Windows architecture more open. WOSA is aimed at making Windows the centerpiece of client-server architectures and consists of a set of client APIs and server APIs. WOSA allows different types of clients to communicate efficiently with different types of servers through its clearly defined interfaces.

Reading II–10
Competition, Compatibility, and Standards

Joseph Farrell and Garth Saloner

Compatibility issues have long been important in industrial economies: railroad gauges are an early example, and the use of interchangeable parts was an important step in the industrial revolution. With the rapid growth of importance of the computer and telecommunications industries (and especially with their recent convergence), compatibility has become more important than ever. Remarkably, the subject has until very recently received little attention from academic economists. In this paper, we survey some important economic questions in compatibility and standardization.[1]

Compatibility and Standardization

Compatibility

Compatibility is the result of coordinated product design. We call products compatible when their design is coordinated in some way, enabling them to work together.

We can distinguish three classes of compatibility. First is physical compatibility: physical objects are designed to fit together physically or electromagnetically. Examples include hydrants and hoses,[2] peripheral and CPU equipment for computers,[3]

Source: *Product Standardization and Competitive Strategy,* ed. H. Landis Gable (Amsterdam: Elsevier Science Publishers B.V., 1987).

[1]We do not consider quality standards, but restrict attention to compatibility.

[2]D. Hemenway, *Industrywide Voluntary Product Standards* (Ballinger, Cambridge, MA, 1975); A. Nesmith, "A Long, Arduous March toward Standardization," *Smithsonian,* March 1985, pp. 176–94.

[3]H. L. Gabel, "Open Standards in the European Computer Industry: The Case of X/OPEN."

stereo components, auto encryption of cable TV, HBO's choice of an encryption standard effectively (and rapidly) determined the marked standard.[4] In other cases, a de facto standard emerges as one of a number of competing standards wins the bandwagon competition: Swann[5] describes this process in microprocessor design. After the first entrants into an industry have broadly spanned the product space, later arrivals begin to imitate the successful products. When there are agglomeration economies, this process is not self-limiting; rather, it snowballs.

The leader may or may not welcome being followed; this depends on how much being followed enhances its standard versus how much profit it loses. In some cases, a vendor may choose to give up proprietary control of a technology, or license it cheaply (as with the Ethernet local-area-network standard) in order to make it more credible as a market standard; here, imitation enhances the value of the product, and so the "price" may rise. This contrasts with the case under the assumption of diminishing returns, in which imitation not only reduces the leader's market share in its product but also (by increasing supply) reduces the price of the product.

Fourth, there may be direct government regulation, for instance the FCC's 1949 mandatory choice of the CBS color television standard.

Fifth, the international standardization commissions, such as the CCITT (for telephone protocols), the CCIR (for broadcast standards), and the ISO, work to achieve international compatibility. These commissions suffer from two interrelated problems (present, in less extreme form, in all voluntary standards organizations). First, they are slow: often, many months pass between meetings of the relevant committees, and even once the committee makes its recommendation there are further processes to go through. Because of this,[6] firms and countries often begin working on their prototype technologies before a standard is officially set. Once some costs are sunk, the firms have an incentive to fight hard for their standard to be adopted, even if objectively it may not be the best. Interacting with these difficulties are all the problems of democratic organizations, and of organizations without direct enforcement power. Television standards differ across the world because of these problems.[7]

Of course, the standardization processes described above are neither mutually exclusive nor independent. For instance, the same firms that are involved in voluntary standards boards may also simultaneously try to create de facto standards. In some cases, this might create incentives for a de facto standard setter to sabotage the work of the standards board, in order to avoid the creation of a rival to its de facto standard; alternatively it may be able to combine market forces and political action to choose a standard.

Benefits of Compatibility

We describe here four types of benefit from compatibility: network externalities, competitive effects, variety or mix-and-match benefits, and cost savings.

Network Externalities

One major source of compatibility benefits is the fact that we are often linked in physical or conceptual "networks" whose value depends on their size in a direct way. Perhaps the most obvious examples are electronic communications networks[8] such as telephone networks and computer networks. But language itself can be seen as another example: the repeated attempts to develop a *lingua franca* (whether by selecting a dominant natural language, such as Latin, French or English, or by creating an artificial one such as Esperanto) pay tribute to the potential benefits of compatibility.

Competitive Effects

When competing products are compatible, they compete more on price and less on design. This makes the market more of a "commodity" market,[9] and it is

[4]S. Besen and L. Johnson, "Compatibility Standards and Competition: Lessons from AM Stereo and TV Stereo," mimeo, Rand Corporation, April 1986; "Compatibility Standards, Competition and Innovation in the Telecommunications Industry," mimeo, Rand Corporation, 1986.

[5]G. Swann, "Industry Standard Microprocessors and the Strategy of Second-Source Production."

[6]It might not be helpful to speed up the process to a realistic (or desirable) degree: one view is that firms and nations are engaged in a "race to sink costs" and will do so as fast and as prematurely as is necessary to preempt their rivals.

[7]R. Crane, *The Politics of International Standards: France and the Color TV War* (Ablex Publishing, Norwood, NJ, 1979); J. Pelkmans and R. Beuter, "Standardization and Competitiveness: Private and Public Strategies in the EC Color TV Industry," in H. Landis Gabel, ed., *Product Standardization and Competitive Strategy* (North-Holland, Amsterdam, 1987).

[8]J. Rohlfs, "A Theory of Interdependent Demand for a Communications Service," *Bell Journal of Economics* 5, 1974, pp. 16–37.

[9]The same is true of quality standards, which reduce the role of reputation and of advertising. See C. Shapiro, "Premiums for High Quality Products as Rents to Reputation," *Quarterly Journal*

natural to think that this enhances price competition, which is in itself a good thing for economic efficiency. Moreover, some aspects of compatibility may encourage entry; for instance, it is possible to enter the market for computer printers without having to develop and market an entire line of computers.

However, there may also be adverse competitive effects from compatibility. We return to this subject below.

Variety

While compatibility requirements can limit variety, as discussed for instance in Farrell and Saloner,[10] compatibility can also increase available variety, by allowing mix-and-match purchases, as Matutes and Regibeau point out.[11] For example, the buyer of a stereo system can combine any amplifier and any turntable. By contrast, because the body-lens interface is not standardized across vendors, camera buyers are limited in their combinations of bodies and lenses.

Evidently, the value of this benefit depends on the value of variety in each component (do people's preferences differ?) and also on the absence of perfect correlation between buyers' preferences over the components (if everyone who wanted a brand-X turntable also wanted a brand-X amplifier, there would be no mix-and-match gains).

Cost Savings

By allowing greater scale economies (e.g., by enabling different manufacturers to exploit economies of scale in using a common supplier), and by allowing the use of interchangeable parts, standardization reduces production costs.[12]

A complementary product may be more readily or more cheaply available as more people have the original product—an example is the provision of software for personal computers. The importance of ready availability of a repair network for a product is another example. This network externality was behind much of the success of the Singer sewing machine company in the late 1870s.[13]

Standardization also saves on the costs of learning how to use a good. Thus, typewriter keyboards are standardized[14] because it is desirable for users to be able to "carry" their skills from one machine to another. This can have subtle implications. For instance, Brock[15] discusses how pressure for standardization of the programming language COBOL increased when machine time became cheaper relative to programmer time, making it less important to design programs that run efficiently and more important to make it easier to write or transfer programs.

The Policy Importance of Economies of Scale

The benefits discussed above encourage users and vendors to do the same as others do. This advantage to going along with the crowd is a form of demand-side economy of scale. When there are economies of scale, textbook economic analysis, based on diminishing returns, can be misleading. For instance, when two product designs compete in the conventional framework, there is a stable outcome in which typically both are produced in optimal proportions, and these proportions can effectively track any changes in tastes or in technology, whether predictable or not. With agglomeration economies, by contrast, the typical outcome is for one good or the other to take over the market, and which one wins may depend excessively on historical accident or early preferences[16] or on strategic considerations.[17]

---

of Economics, 1983; R. Grant, "The Effects of Product Standardization on Competition: Octane Grading of Petrol in the UK," in H. Landis Gabel, ed., *Product Standardization and Competitive Strategy* (North-Holland, Amsterdam, 1987).

[10]"Standardization and Variety," *Economics Letters* 20 (1986), pp. 71–74.

[11]"Compatibility and Multiproduct Firms: The Symmetric Case," mimeo, INSEAD, 1986.

[12]This is a staple of economic history; see, for instance, D. Landes, *The Unbound Prometheus: Technological Change 1750 to the Present* (Cambridge University Press, 1969), and *Revolution in Time* (Harvard University Press, 1983); D. Hemenway, *Industry-wide Voluntary Product Standards.* Cost reductions may be valued by users or by makers (or both), depending on the incidence of cost savings, which is a matter of market structure. In a perfectly competitive market, all cost savings that reduce marginal costs are passed on to buyers, but cost savings that reduce fixed costs are not. In imperfectly competitive markets, some cost savings may enhance the profits of sellers.

[13]A. Chandler, *The Visible Hand* (Harvard University Press, Cambridge, 1977).

[14]P. David, "Clio and the Economics of QWERTY," *American Economic Review* 75 (May 1985), pp. 332–36.

[15]"Competition, Standards and Self-Regulation in the Computer Industry," in R. Caves and M. Roberts, eds., *Regulating the Product: Quality and Variety* (Ballinger, Cambridge, MA, 1975).

[16]B. Arthur, "On Competing Technologies and Historical Small Events: The Dynamics of Choice under Increasing Returns," mimeo, Stanford, 1981.

[17]M. Katz and C. Shapiro, "Technology Adoption in the Presence of Network Externalities," mimeo, Princeton University, 1986; and "Product Compatibility Choice in a Market with Technological Progress," mimeo, Princeton University, 1986.

As we will see below, conventional wisdom about the possibility of predation is also misleading in our context, and issues of lock-in become important.[18] Overall, we must be careful in applying views formed by thinking about price-taking competitive economies to economic problems in which economies of scale are central.

Does Standardization Enhance Competition?

A common view is that incompatibility restricts competition via product differentiation. In this view, under incompatibility, each vendor has a monopoly on its part of the market.

It is true that this view ignores competition between systems. If the entire system is purchased at one time, then such between-systems competition may make within-system competition unnecessary.[19] However, if buyers do not buy entire systems at once, and if sellers do not commit themselves to prices on the later-purchased components, then the ex-ante competition between systems need not adequately substitute for the ex-post competition within systems.[20] Buyers become, to some extent, captives of the vendor from whom they began buying. Where such issues of lock-in arise, standardization can commit producers to compete in an aftermarket for spare or replacement parts, complementary inputs, or peripheral devices.

Without standardization, we will see some monopoly power in the aftermarket, perhaps partly compensated by fierce competition in the original market, as vendors compete to lock-in buyers.

Often, the aftermarket (e.g., replacement fenders for a car model) is a natural monopoly, and the original manufacturer (car maker) has an advantage in taking the market (because it makes the original fenders). Absent standardization, this is a possible source of after-sale profits; indeed, in the auto industry, it is notorious that spare parts have a much higher profit margin than cars do. But often such pricing policies are inefficient (e.g., because buyers will inefficiently substitute away from the complementary input), and if that is anticipated, it may be profitable for the seller to commit to low or reasonable prices for afterparts. Standardization will achieve this.

We will briefly discuss two other competitive benefits of standardization. First, market compatibility protects buyers against the threat of being orphaned in a losing technology. If it is feared that a supplier may go bankrupt, or suffer a crippling strike, buyers will worry about support for their purchases.[21] Standardization avoids this problem, and thus enhances competition, since a seller no longer need be seen as both financially secure and committed to the industry in order to sell a product. Sometimes buyers insist on "second-sourcing" to protect themselves against these problems. This is equivalent to guaranteeing (limited) standardization of their selected technology.[22]

Second, standardization can help in, or help replace, regulation. Long-distance telecommunications have been (partly) deregulated in the United States by the requirement that local telephone companies interconnect with non-AT&T long-distance carriers (the OCCs). Mark Fowler, chairman of the U.S. Federal Communications Commission (FCC), has recently suggested that some aspects of local telephone services could also be deregulated if switching protocols were standardized and suitable provision were made for interconnections between rival part-networks in the local exchange. The traditional view of the telephone service as a natural monopoly is based on the inefficiency of having duplicate networks. This assumes that competing telephone companies would not have interconnection (a form of compatibility). While this may be a plausible result of unregulated competition,[23] it is possible that requiring interconnection would make it unnecessary to regulate some other aspects of competition.

---

[18]This is not the only way in which nonconvexities can arise; see P. David, "New Technology Diffusion, Public Policy, and Industrial Competitiveness," Center for Economic Policy Research, Stanford, 1985, p. 46.

[19]For an exposition of this view, see F. Fisher, "Diagnosing Monopoly," *Quarterly Review of Economics and Business* 19 (1979).

[20]P. Klemperer, "Collusion via Switching Costs: How Frequent Flyer Programs, Trading Stamps, and Technology Choice Aid Collusion," research paper no. 786, Stanford University, May 1984; J. Farrell, "Competition and Lock-In," mimeo, GTE Labs, 1985; J. Farrell and C. Shapiro, "Dynamic Competition with Lock-In," forthcoming, 1986.

[21]See, for instance, Hemenway's discussion (note 2) of the auto parts industry before the ASME achieved standardization. If a seller is large enough, it may be presumed that someone would take over these support services, but it is typically not the large sellers that suffer from this fear.

[22]M. Porter, *Competitive Strategy* (The Free Press, NY 1985), p. 209.

[23]For a history, see G. Brock, *The Telecommunications Industry* (Harvard University Press: Cambridge, MA, 1981).

In contrast to these competitive benefits, compatibility may have adverse effects on competition. First, the mix-and-match effect of compatibility means that sellers sell their brand of each component only to those buyers who most value it. In some circumstances this can lead to higher equilibrium prices, and some buyers may be worse off.[24]

Second, if competing standards are "sponsored," or proprietary, their sponsors may compete fiercely to have them adopted as the de facto standard. In early periods, this competition may be very good for buyers; but once one standard has won, the proprietary de facto standard may become a source of monopoly power. Katz and Shapiro analyze these problems.[25]

Compatibility and Innovation

In recent decades, technological progress has been especially impressive in two industries—telecommunications and computers—in which questions of compatibility are of paramount importance. Because options and needs change so fast, and because the standardization process is in any case imperfect, it is important that we should not be inefficiently locked into old choices. Of course, since the old choice is likely to be embodied in costly physical and human capital, we would not want to switch to a new standard every week, but sometimes a change is worthwhile. The optimal decision must depend on the gross benefits from switching (how much better is the new standard?), on the costs (replacement of physical capital, disruption of complementary markets, retraining costs), and on the extent to which there might be an even better alternative available soon. Evidently, we cannot expect any single agency to have all this information, especially since there are often incentives for those who do know things to misrepresent and exaggerate if asked to reveal them. In practice, of course, the problem is often "left to the market." How well does "the market" cope?

Suppose that there is a status-quo standard, and a new, possibly better technology appears on the scene. In Farrell and Saloner[26] we showed that sometimes the market will not switch even though it should. We called this effect *excess inertia*. We also discussed the opposite phenomenon of wrongly abandoning a technology, which we called *excess momentum*. These inefficiencies can arise either from problems of coordination and communication, or from the importance of installed base.

Coordination Problems

To illustrate how coordination problems can result in inefficient adoption decisions, we use a zoological analogy. In movies of the old West, cowboys who camped for the night where there were no trees to which to tie their horses would often tie the horses to one another. Even though the horses as a group were free to go wherever they wanted, they would not go far—whereas a single horse left free overnight would. The horses' difficulty in coordinating just where they would move at any instant prevented them from moving effectively. The fact that it is not only horses who have this problem is shown whenever a group of more than half a dozen people walk from office to restaurant: progress is far slower than with a smaller group.

In much the same way, it can happen that an industry may get stuck on an old and inferior technology, even when all participants might prefer to move to a new technology. This happens because the group is tied together by reluctance to sacrifice the benefits of being compatible.

To formalize this, consider a model in which each of a number of users chooses (in predetermined order) to switch to a new technology or to stay with the old. Because of network externalities or other benefits of standardization, we assume that whatever choice a user makes, it will prefer others to make the same choice. Assuming that agents have complete information[27] we showed[28] that if all users would be better off with the new technology, then they will all switch (in the unique perfect Nash equilibrium). If their preferences differ, then the early movers have considerable power to determine the outcome, because of the bandwagon effect. This result (which we called *the New Hampshire Theorem*

[24]Matutes and Regibeau, "Compatibility and Multiproduct Firms."

[25]Katz and Shapiro, "Technology Adoption in the Presence of Network Externalities," and "Product Compatibility Choice in a Market with Technological Progress."

[26]J. Farrell and G. Saloner, "Standardization, Compatibility and Innovation," *Rand Journal of Economics* 16 (Spring 1985), pp. 70–83; and J. Farrell and G. Saloner, "Installed Base and Compatibility: Innovation, Product Preannouncement, and Predation," mimeo, GTE Labs and MIT, 1986.

[27]This term means that each decision maker knows the preferences of all others, and everyone knows that, and so on.

[28]Farrell and Saloner, "Standardization, Compatibility, and Innovation."

from the timing of political primaries in the United States) comes from our assumption that a user has only one chance to switch; thus, the early movers are Stackelberg leaders. More realistically, whatever makes a user able to commit itself early to a decision on standards will give it power.

However, when we allowed for the fact that preferences are not perfectly known, and studied a model in which each user could choose to switch or not at each period, we showed that there can be what we called *symmetric excess inertia:* all prefer the new technology, but none switch. With incomplete information about others' preferences, no user can be sure that it would be followed in a switch to the new standard. This uncertainty can lead all the users to remain with the status quo even when they do all in fact favor switching, because they are unwilling to risk switching without being followed.

Nonbinding communication about preferences and intentions eliminates the above possibility: each agent will tell the others that it would like a joint switch, and we will be back in the complete-information case. But communication actually exacerbates the asymmetric problem (i.e., the case in which one user would be much better off if both switched, but the other would be somewhat worse off). The reason for this is that a discouraging message will prove more discouraging than it should if, in fact, the opponent of switching is only somewhat opposed. Thus, there can be excess inertia here too. Similarly, excess momentum is possible; all users may switch, even though it would be more efficient not to do so.

Thus, only a user with a strong preference for the new standard will be an early adopter and if there are no early adopters, then the standard will never be adopted. Excess inertia arises when not enough users are willing to go out on a limb by adopting the new technology. This is most likely when network externalities are strong and there is a great deal of uncertainty about whether a lead would be followed. In practice, there are also questions of delay in following a lead, which we now discuss.

Installed Base Problems

In the model just described, time did not play an essential role (except that decisions were sequential). In particular, any transient incompatibility resulting from adoption of the new standard was ignored. In fact, however, there are generally real delays in achieving compatibility on a new standard after compatibility on an old one has been abandoned. These delays can create inefficiencies that are absent in the previous model. We studied this problem in two related models in a 1986 paper.

In the first model, we suppose for simplicity that old users do not switch to the new standard, and that the new network must be built up by the adoption decisions of new users. Because new users arrive at a finite rate, this imposes delays in achieving a satisfactory network.

The incompatibility costs of these delays are borne disproportionately by the first users to adopt the new standard. Because of this, they may be unwilling to adopt it, even when (in the long run) it is socially desirable that they do so: this is excess inertia. Moreover, if the first users who could adopt the new standard choose instead to swell the installed base on the old, then a fortiori we cannot expect that later arrivals will start the new-standard bandwagon, for the old network is now larger (and thus more attractive) than ever. Thus, these early choosers have a great deal of power; it is their preferences, their expectations, and their choices that determine the outcome.

We see therefore how these pivotal users may be unwilling to switch to a new standard when, from a social point of view, they should. In other cases, however, these pivotal users may find the new standard attractive and adopt it, thus stranding the earlier users who are committed to the old standard. These earlier users may lack a voice in this decision, and so there can be excess momentum.

The new standard is less likely to succeed the more important the transient incompatibility costs, and the larger the installed base. If one standard is proprietary, its sponsor may be able to take actions to affect the likelihood of adoption of the new standard. Some of these actions may be socially undesirable, and may have conventionally anticompetitive features.

There may, for instance, be anticompetitive product preannouncements (as alleged in the Justice Department suit against IBM). In a standard economic framework, it is hard to see how product preannouncements can be anticompetitive. One would expect[29] that an announcement of a superior product would be socially beneficial (though detrimental to competitors) while an announcement of an

[29]F. Fisher, J. McGowan, and J. Greenwood, *Folded, Spindled and Mutilated: Economic Analysis and the IBM Case* (MIT Press, Cambridge, 1983).

inferior product would have no effect. However, both these views can be misleading if network externalities and installed base are important. In these circumstances, it is possible that if a new technology does not begin to sell by some critical date, the old standard will have an invulnerable advantage because the market will refuse to adopt anything incompatible with the large installed base. Preannouncements of new products complying with old standards may erode this time limitation for companies producing to the new standard.

In such cases, announcing the future availability of a product can encourage some potential users to wait for it, and can thus ensure its success when otherwise it would have failed. While this may be a good thing, it can also be socially undesirable and can be predatory in the sense that the firm that undertakes the action is sacrificing short-run profits in order to cause the exit or failure of a rival, and when it succeeds in doing so it enhances its future profits.

The importance of installed base can also provide an incentive for predatory pricing. If a seller with market power is threatened by a new incompatible entry, it may be worth its while to reduce its prices temporarily in order to make its installed base large enough for its market position to become invulnerable, at which time it can raise its prices again without inducing entry. We also observe that standard tests for predation may fail to detect this particular type.

In our second model, by contrast, we assume that there are no new users, and that the new network is built up through old users' switching. We suppose that a user who switches is not immediately followed by the others; more precisely, we suppose that switching is only convenient for a given user at certain times, which arrive stochastically. For instance, it may only consider a switch when some costly capital good needs replacing anyway.

The fact that it would not immediately be followed makes each user more reluctant to switch first than it otherwise would be; it may rather prefer to wait for another user to switch first, even if it would be better off switching first than not switching at all. (This we have dubbed the *penguin effect:* penguins gather on the edges of ice floes, each trying to jostle the others in first, because although all are hungry for fish, each fears there may be a predator lurking nearby.) However, if being temporarily stranded on the old standard is undesirable, then this excess inertia may disappear and even be reversed: in fact it is possible to get a preemptive equilibrium in which each user is poised to switch first only because it fears that otherwise another would do so.

Katz and Shapiro[30] study the problem of technology choice when installed base is important and there is sponsorship of one or both technologies, so that sellers may engage in strategic pricing or cross-subsidization between early and late users. They show that the market outcome may involve standardization on the wrong standard, or standardization when it would be preferable to have none. In their model, there is a tendency towards excess momentum, in the sense that the technology that will be cheaper in the future is too likely to prevail over that which is better today.

A striking result that emerges from these analyses is that excess momentum can arise in all models in which excess inertia is possible, and indeed sometimes when excess inertia is impossible, as in Katz and Shapiro. The externality in excess momentum is the stranding effect; early adopters may be left high and dry by later users who do not take their predecessors' preferences into account. Moreover, the fear of such stranding may deter early potential users from adopting the technology at all. (For instance, this is plausibly the case at present with local area networks.)

This suggests that some form of commitment to an early, even if arbitrary, choice of standard may be desirable. An alternative suggestion might be that the capital goods that embody an early and tentative standard should be leased rather than sold; this at least relieves early adopters of the capital risk in the physical plant (although they cannot avoid investing in some human capital). By putting this risk onto the vendor, who may have some control over whether there is a switch, we may internalize at least part of the stranding externality. If buyers are aware of this problem, as they often are, the vendor may find it profitable to offer to lease, even if it may subsequently have to take back old-fashioned machines at a loss. We see this strategy adopted in the market for AM stereo broadcast equipment,[31] where broadcasters are in any case moving very slowly in adopting stereo technology, partly because of compatibility problems.

---

[30]"Product Compatibility Choice in a Market with Technological Progress."

[31]Besen and Johnson, "Compatibility Standards and Competition," and "Compatibility Standards, Competition, and Innovation in the Telecommunications Industry."

Timing of Standardization

Much discussion of standardization concerns *whether* to standardize and, if so, on *what standard*. A third important problem that has received much less attention is *when* to standardize.

Cognate with all the advantages of compatibility are advantages of early standardization. First, early standardization yields a longer and earlier flow of benefits from compatibility. But there are other advantages too. For instance, users may wait to adopt a product until there is a standard; thus, early standardization hastens the growth of the market. Another strategic consideration is that delay in standardization encourages vendors of incompatible products to develop their installed bases and to sink costs in developing their technologies. In this way they become entrenched in their different product designs, and thus *delayed standardization is difficult standardization*.

The benefits of early standardization have tempted people to identify early standardization with successful standardization. But this may be quite wrong. There are also good reasons to wait. When we do not know for sure which standard will be the best in the long run, and information is coming in on that question, a later decision will on average be a better decision. The technology that would be chosen today may not turn out to be the best tomorrow. Choosing today sacrifices the option value of waiting to see. This is especially important where a choice is largely irrevocable, as it will be if the physical and learning costs of changing the network are large. Moreover, if there is excess inertia in switching standards ex post, then a choice is hard to revoke even if the costs would not be very great.

There is thus a difficult trade-off to be made in choosing the timing of standardization. A great deal of information is required to make the correct choice. For instance, we must know what the important attributes of a standard are and how they compare in importance in users' preferences. We must know the "scores" of each possible standard on these attributes, not only now but also in probabilistic terms in the future. Costs, current and future, need to be worked out. How important is it to allow for compatibility with each possible change that might be needed later? Currently undeveloped technologies are also relevant: their prospects for success and for making a significant improvement on the current technologies must be accurately assessed. Clearly, no agency can have all this information, especially since there are often powerful incentives for those who do have information to misreport it. This may be the reason for the widespread view that the choice is perhaps best "left to the market," but in our view that is not necessarily a good solution.

While the market is capable of aggregating preferences and information in some contexts, the main intellectual foundations of the laissez-faire approach depend on assumptions of diminishing returns. In this problem, as we have pointed out above, there are many aspects of increasing returns, and we can make no presumptions about the efficiency of market performance.

There are at least two kinds of bias in market solutions to this problem. First, the power to determine what gets adopted is often effectively vested in a few market participants: sometimes because they are large, and sometimes because they are early. These few powerful participants may not be especially well informed, and even if they are, their preferences may differ from those of the other participants. Second, a vendor's incentives to standardize early versus late depend on the extent to which it appropriates the benefits from early standardization compared to the extent to which it appropriates the benefits from waiting. For example, a vendor may be able to appropriate (in enhanced profits) a considerable fraction of the benefits from early standardization, but may be unable to capture the benefits from waiting. In this case, it would tend to standardize too soon. Or it could equally go the other way. While market structure, among other things, is probably relevant here, we have no reason to expect that competitive or unconcentrated industries will do well on this score: attributing problems of market standardization to conventional imperfections of market structure is a mistake.

While the market always produces some outcome and often produces a de facto standard, we should not confuse this with success. The story of the QWERTY typewriter keyboard, related by David,[32] is an instructive lesson. Lemmings would be well advised to look before they leap.

Industrial Policy

Since the benefits from compatibility are not limited by national boundaries, and since compatibility

[32]"Clio and the Economics of QWERTY."

choices affect the nature of competition, standardization has consequences for international trade. We briefly describe two aspects of this. The interested reader should consult Crane.[33]

First, the economies of scale on the demand side can act in the same way as supply-side scale economies. When there is a dynamic element, as when the network externalities are embodied in installed base, an early start or a protected market could in principle lead to lasting competitive advantage. For a treatment of this problem (in the case of learning-by-doing) see Krugman.[34]

Second, international standard-setting is often a two-stage affair. National interests are represented in international committees. As a result, the more entrenched a nation is in one standard, the more power it has in getting its standard adopted (though it also loses more if it loses). This may encourage premature standardization at the national level and may give a strategic advantage to countries with central direction of standardization activities.

Conclusion

Standardization is extremely important in modern economies, especially in the information processing industries. While it has many benefits, it may also have serious social costs. There has been little economic analysis of the policy problems.

Conclusions reached by traditional economic reasoning, in which convexity and diminishing returns are generally assumed, are likely to be misleading when bandwagon effects, windows of opportunity for entry, and installed-base problems are important. We have seen that the analysis of such staples of industrial organization as pricing, predation, innovation, and variety is very different when compatibility is important.

There is no easy prescription for microeconomic policy in markets in which network externalities play an important part. In this paper and in our other work, we have identified some of the factors that should be kept in mind, and we have shown how certain standard lessons of economics must be treated cautiously. Further work on the subject is needed.

---

[33] *The Politics of International Standards.*

[34] P. R. Krugman, "Import Protection as Export Promotion: International Competition in the Presence of Oligopolies and Economics of Scale," in H. Kierzkowski, ed., *Monopolistic Competition and International Trade* (New York: Oxford, 1984).

Additional References

Adams, W. and J. Brock. "Integrated Monopoly and Market Power: System Selling, Compatibility Standards, and Market Control." *Quarterly Review of Economics and Business* 22 (Winter 1982), pp. 29–42.

Berg, S. "Duopoly Compatibility Standards with Partial Cooperation and Stackelberg Leadership." Mimeo, University of Florida, 1984.

Berg, S. "A Duopoly Model of Technological Externalities and Compatibility Standards." Mimeo, University of Florida, 1985.

Berg, S. "Public Policy and Corporate Strategies in the AM Stereo Market," in H. Landis Gabel, ed., *Product Standardization and Competitive Strategy* (North-Holland, Amsterdam, 1987).

Braunstein, Y. M., and L. J. White. "Setting Technical Compatibility Standards: An Economic Analysis." *The Antitrust Bulletin* 30 (1985), p. 337.

Carlton, D. W., and J. M. Klamer. "The Need for Coordination among Firms, with Special Reference to Network Industries." *University of Chicago Law Review* 50 (1983), p. 446.

Dybvig, P., and C. Spatt. "Adoption Externalities as Public Goods." *Journal of Public Economics* 20 (1983), pp. 231–48.

Farrell, J., and G. Saloner. "Economic Issues in Standardization," in J. Miller ed., *Telecommunications and Equity: Proceedings of the Fourteenth Telecommunications Policy Research Conference* (North-Holland, Amsterdam, 1986).

Federal Trade Commission. "Standards and Certification: Final Staff Report," April 1983.

Hanson, W. "Bandwagons and Orphans: Dynamic Pricing of Competing Technological Systems Subject to Decreasing Costs." Mimeo, University of Chicago, 1985.

Hergert, M. "Technical Standards and Competition in the Microcomputer Industry," in H. Landis Gabel, ed., *Product Standardization and Competitive Strategy* (North-Holland, Amsterdam, 1987).

Irmer, T. "International Standardization in Telecommunications—Conflicting Forces in a Changing World." Comments on "Product Standardization as a Tool of Competitive Strategy." Symposium at INSEAD, June 1986.

Katz, M., and C. Shapiro. "Network Externalities, Competition and Compatibility." *American Economic Review* 75 (May 1985), pp. 424–40.

Kindleberger, C. "Standards as Public, Collective, and Private Goods." *Kyklos* 36 (1983), pp. 377–97.

Kudrle, R. T. "Regulation and Self-Regulation in the Farm Machinery Industry." In R. Caves, ed., *Regulating the Product.*

Link, A. "Market Structure and Voluntary Product Standards." *Applied Economics,* 1983, pp. 393–401.

Oren, S., and S. Smith. "Critical Mass and Tariff Structures in Electronic Communications Markets." *Bell Journal of Economics* 12 (1981), pp. 467–86.

Phillips, A. "The Role of Standardization in Shared Bank Card Systems," in H. Landis Gabel, ed., *Product Standardization and Competitive Strategy* (North-Holland, Amsterdam, 1987).

Putnam, Hayes. "Impacts of Voluntary Standards on Industrial Innovation and Growth." U.S. National Bureau of Standards, Bartlett, Inc., 1981.

Sirbu, M., and K. Hughes. "Standardization of Local Area Networks." Mimeo, Carnegie-Mellon, 1986.

Sirbu, M., and L. Zwimpfer. "Computer Communications Standards: The Case of X.25." *IEEE Communications*, March 1985.

Sirbu, M., and S. Stewart. "Market Structure and the Emergence of Standards: A Test in the Modem Market." Mimeo, MIT, April 1985.

Reading II–11
*Competing Technologies: An Overview**

W. Brian Arthur

Every steam carriage which passes along the street justifies the confidence placed in it; and unless the objectionable feature of the petrol carriage can be removed, it is bound to be driven from the road, to give place to its less objectionable rival, the steam-driven vehicle of the day.

William Fletcher (1904), *Steam Carriages and Traction Engines,* p. xi.

Introduction

When a new engineering or economic possibility comes along, usually there are several ways to carry it through. In the 1890s the motor carriage could be powered by steam, or by gasoline, or by electric batteries. In more modern times nuclear power can be generated by light-water, or gas-cooled, or heavy-water, or sodium-cooled reactors. Solar energy can be generated by crystalline-silicon or amorphous-silicon technologies. An AIDS vaccine may eventually become possible by cell-type modification methods, or by chemical synthesis, or by anti-idiotype methods. Video recording can be carried out by Sony Betamax® or by VHS technologies.

In each case we can think of these methods or technologies as "competing" for a "market" of adopters.[1] They may compete unconsciously and *passively,* like species compete biologically, if adoptions of one technology displace or preclude adoptions of its rivals. Or they may compete consciously and *strategically* if they are products that can be priced and manipulated. (In this latter case, following nomenclature introduced in Arthur,[2] we will say they are *sponsored.*)

What makes competition between technologies interesting is that usually technologies become more attractive—more developed, more widespread, more useful—the more they are adopted. Thus competition between technologies usually becomes competition between bandwagons, and adoption markets display both a corresponding instability and a high degree of unpredictability.

Increased attractiveness caused by adoption, or what I will call increasing returns to adoption, can arise from several sources; but five are particularly important:

1. *Learning by using.*[3] Often the more a technology is adopted, the more it is used and the more is learned about it; therefore, the more it is developed and improved. A new airliner design, like the DC-8, for example, gains considerably in payload, passenger capacity, engine efficiency and aerodynamics, as it achieves actual airline adoption and use.

2. *Network externalities.*[4] Often a technology offers advantages to "going along" with other adopters of it—to belonging to a network of users. The video technology VHS is an example. The more other users there are, the more likely it is that the VHS adopter benefits from a greater availability and variety of VHS-recorded products.

*I am grateful to Paul David, Giovanni Dosi, Frank Englmann, Christopher Freeman, Richard Nelson, Nathan Rosenberg, Gerald Silverberg and Luc Soete for comments on this paper, and to participants at the May 1987 IFIAS meeting on Technical Change and Economic Theory, Maastricht, The Netherlands. In G. Dosi, ed., *Technical Change and Economic Theory* (New York: Columbia University Press, 1987), pp. 590–607.

[1]W. B. Arthur, "Competing Technologies and Lock-in by Historical Events: The Dynamics of Allocation under Increasing Returns," Paper WP-83–90, International Institute for Applied Systems Analysis, Laxenburg, Austria, 1983.

[2]W. B. Arthur, "Information, Imitation and the Emergence of Technological Structures," mimeo, Stanford University, 1985.

[3]N. Rosenberg, *Inside the Black Box: Technology and Economics* (Cambridge, England: Cambridge University Press, 1982).

[4]M. Katz and C. Shapiro, "Network Externalities, Competition, and Compatibility," *American Economic Review* 75 (1985), pp. 424–40.

3. *Scale economies in production*. Often, where a technology is embodied in a product, like the polariod technology, the cost of the product falls as increased numbers of units of it are produced. Thus the technology can become more attractive in price as adoption increases.

4. *Informational increasing returns*. Often a technology that is more adopted enjoys the advantage of being better known and better understood. For the risk-averse, adopting it becomes more attractive if it is more widespread.

5. *Technological interrelatedness*.[5] Often, as a technology becomes more adopted, a number of other subtechnologies and products become part of its infrastructure. For example, the gasoline technology has a huge infrastructure of refineries, filling stations, and auto parts that rely on it. This puts it at an advantage in the sense that other technologies, if less adopted, may lack the requisite infrastructure or may require a partial dismantling of the more widespread technology's in-place infrastructure.

Of course, with any particular technology, several of these benefits to increased adoption may be mixed in and present together. Rarely do we have a pure source of increasing returns to adoption.

Whatever the source, if increasing returns to adoption are indeed present, they determine the character of competition between technologies. If one technology gets ahead by good fortune, it gains an advantage. It can then attract further adopters who might otherwise have gone along with one of its rivals, with the result that the adoption market may tip in its favor and may end up dominated by it.[6] Given other circumstances, of course, a different technology might have been favored early on, and *it* might have come to dominate the market. Thus in competitions between technologies with increasing returns, ordinarily there is more than one possible outcome. In economic terms there are multiple equilibria. To ascertain how the *actual* outcome is selected from these multiple candidate outcomes, we need to keep track of how adoptions of rival technologies build up (together with the small events that might influence these) and how they eventually sway and tip the market. We need, in other words, to follow the dynamics of adoption.

Where competing technologies possess increasing returns, a number of very natural questions arise:

1. How can we model the adoption process when there is competition between increasing-return technologies and hence indeterminacy in the outcome?
2. What analytical techniques can be brought to bear on this increasing-return allocation problem? In particular, what techniques can help us determine the possible outcomes of the adoption process?
3. When technologies compete, under what circumstances *must* one technology—albeit an indeterminate one at the outset—achieve a monopoly and eventually take 100 percent of the adoption market? Under what circumstances will the market eventually be shared?
4. How does the "competing standards" case differ from the competing technologies one?
5. What difference does it make to have different sources of increasing returns: network externalities rather than learning effects, for example?
6. What policy issues arise in the competing technology case?
7. What major research questions remain to be answered?

In this paper I will provide an overview of my work on the competing technology problem, highlighting in particular the dynamic approach. Where possible I will connect my approach and results with those of others and I will mention open research problems. I begin with a review of the basic competing technologies model and then go on to discuss some of the questions raised above.

Lock-in by Small Events: A Review of the Basic Model

As one possible, simple model of competition between technologies with increasing returns,[7] imagine two unsponsored technologies, A and B, competing passively for a market of potential adopters who are replacing an old, inferior technology. As adoptions of A (or B) increase, learning-by-using takes place and improved versions of A (or B) become available, with correspondingly higher payoffs or returns to those adopting them. Each agent—

---

[5] M. Frankel, "Obsolescence and Technological Change in a Maturing Economy," *American Economic Review* 45 (1955), pp. 296–319.

[6] Arthur, "Competing Technologies and Lock-in by Historical Events."

[7] Ibid.

EXHIBIT 1 Returns to Adopting *A* or *B*, Given Previous Adoptions

Previous Adoptions	0	10	20	30	40	50	60	70	80	90	100
Technology *A*	10	11	12	13	14	15	16	17	18	19	20
Technology *B*	4	7	10	13	16	19	22	25	28	31	34

each potential adopter—must choose either *A* or *B* when its time comes to replace the old technology. Once an agent chooses it sticks to its choice. The versions of *A* or *B* are fixed when adopted, so that agents are not affected by the choices of future adopters.

Suppose for a moment, in a preliminary version of this model, all agents are alike. And suppose that returns to adopting *A* or *B* rise with prior adoptions as in Exhibit 1. The dynamics of this preliminary model are trivial but instructive. The first agent chooses the higher-payoff technology—*A* in this table. This bids the payoff of *A* upward, so that the next agent a fortiori chooses *A*. *A* continues to be chosen, with the result that the adoption process is locked in to *A* from the start. Notice that *B* cannot get a footing, even though if adopted it would eventually prove superior.

Already in this simple preliminary model, we see two properties that constantly recur with competing technologies: *potential inefficiency* in the sense that the technology that takes the market need not be the one with the longer-term higher payoff to adopters; and *inflexibility*, or lock-in, in the sense that the left-behind technology would need to bridge a widening gap if it is to be chosen by adopters at all.

Although there are examples of technologies that lock out all rivals from the start, this preliminary model is still not very satisfactory. The outcome is either predetermined by whichever technology is initially superior or, if both are evenly matched, the outcome is razor-edged. In reality, adopters are not all alike and, at the outset of most competitions, some would naturally prefer technology *A*, and some technology *B*. If this were the case, the order in which early adopter types arrived would then become crucial, for it would decide how the market might tip.

Consider now a full model that shows this. We now allow two types of adopters, *R* and *S*, with natural preferences for *A* and *B*, respectively, and with payoffs as in Exhibit 2. Suppose each potential-adopter type is equally prevalent, but that the actual arrivals of *R* and *S* agents are subject to small unknown events outside the model, so to speak. Then all we can say is that it is equally likely that an *R* or an *S* will arrive next to make their choice. Initially at least, if an *R*-agent arrives at the adoption window to make its choice, it will adopt *A*; if an *S*-agent arrives, it will adopt *B*. Thus the difference in adoptions between *A* and *B* moves up or down by one unit depending on whether the next adopter is an *R* or an *S*; that is, it moves up or down with probability one-half. This process is a simple gambler's coin-toss random walk. There is only one complication. If by chance a large number of *R*-types cumulates in the line of choosers, *A* will then be heavily adopted and hence improved in payoff. In fact, if *A* gains a sufficient lead over *B* in adoptions, it will pay *S*-types choosing to switch to *A*. Then both *R*- and *S*-types will be adopting *A*, and only *A*, from then on. The adoption process will then become locked in to technology *A*. Similarly, if a sufficient number of *S*-types had by chance arrived to adopt *B* over *A*, *B* would improve sufficiently to cause *R*-types to switch to *B*. The process would instead lock in to *B* (see Exhibit 3). Our random walk is really a random walk with absorbing barriers on each side, the barriers corresponding to the lead in adoption it takes for each agent-type to switch its choice.

EXHIBIT 2 Returns to Adopting *A* or *B*, given n_A and n_B Previous Adopters of *A* and *B*

	Technology A	Technology B
R-agent	$a_R + rn_A$	$b_R + rn_B$
S-agent	$a_S + sn_A$	$b_S + sn_B$

Note: The model assumes that $a_R > b_R$ and that $b_S > a_S$. Both *r* and *s* are positive.

EXHIBIT 3 Difference in Adoptions: Random Walk with Absorbing Barriers

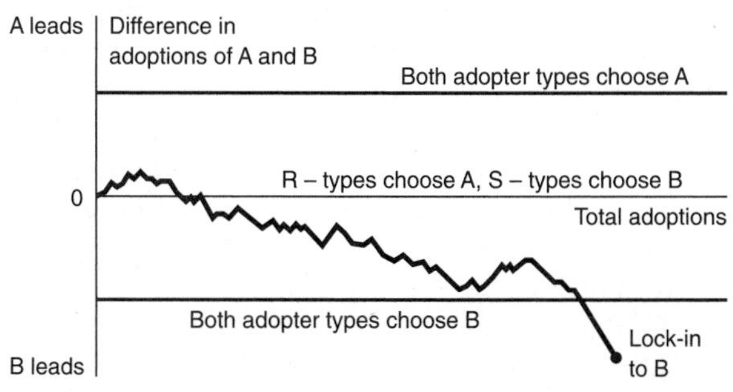

All this is fine. We can now use the well-worked-out theory of random walks to find out what happens to the adoption process in the long run. The important fact about a random walk with absorbing barriers is that absorption occurs eventually with certainty. Thus in the model I have described, the economy *must* lock in to monopoly of one of the two technologies, *A* or *B*, but *which* technology is not predictable in advance. Also, the order of choice of agent is not averaged away. On the contrary, it decides the eventual market outcome. Thus, the process is *non-ergodic*—or more informally we can say that it is *path-dependent* in the sense that the outcome depends on the way in which adoptions build up, that is, on the path the process takes. As before, the process becomes inflexible; once lock-in occurs the dominant technology continues to be chosen; hence it continues to improve, so that an ever larger boost to the payoff of the excluded technology would be needed to resuscitate it. Further, it is easy to construct examples in which this greedy algorithm of each agent's taking the technology that pays off best at its time of choice may miss higher rewards to the future adoption and development of the excluded technology. As in the preliminary model, economic efficiency is not guaranteed.

This model, like all theoretical models, is obviously stylized. But it does capture an important general characteristic of competition between technologies with increasing returns. Where the competition is not dead at the outset, with a single technology dominating from the start, the adoption process is inherently unstable, and it can be swayed by the cumulation of small historical events, or small heterogeneities, or small differences in timing. Thus low-level events, stemming from the inevitable graininess present in the economy, can act to drive the process into the gravitational orbit of one of the two (or, with several technologies competing, many) possible outcomes. What we have in this simple model is order (the eventual adoption-share outcome) emerging from fluctuation (the inherent randomness in the arrival sequence). In modern terminology, our competing-technologies adoption process is therefore a *self-organizing process.*[8]

Of course, it could be objected that at some level—in some all-knowing Laplacian world—the arrival sequence in our model is foreordained, and that therefore the outcome that this sequence implies is foreordained, and that therefore our technology competition is determinate and predictable. Ultimately this comes down to a question of modelling strategy. Where increasing returns are present, different patterns of small events—whether known or not—can lead to very different outcomes. If they are unknown at the outset, if for practical purposes they lie beneath the resolution of our model, we must treat them as random; so that unless we believe we know all events that can affect the buildup of adoptions and can therefore include them explicitly, models of technological competition must typically include a random component. In the model above, randomness was introduced by lack of knowledge of the arrival sequence of the adopters. But in other models it could have different sources. Randomness might, for example, enter in a homogeneous adopter-type model because technological improvements occur in part by unpredictable breakthroughs. The subject is new enough that even obvious extensions like this have not yet been studied. There may be a wide class of competing-technology models, but we would expect to see much the same properties as we found above upheld: inflexibility or lock-in of outcome, nonpredictability, possible inefficiency, and non-ergodicity or path-dependence.

Do real-world competitions between technologies show these properties? Does the economy sometimes lock in to an inferior technology because of small, historical events? It appears that it does. Light-water reactors at present account for close to 100 percent of all U.S. nuclear power installations and about 80 percent of the world market. They were originally adapted from a highly compact unit designed to pro-

[8]I. Prigogine, "Order through Fluctuation: Self-Organization and Social System," in *Evolution and Consciousness,* ed. E. Jantsch and C. H. Waddington (New York, Addison-Wesley, 1976).

pel the first American nuclear submarine, the U.S.S. *Nautilus*, launched in 1954.[9] A series of circumstances—among them the U.S. Navy's role in early construction contracts, political expediency within the National Security Council, the behavior of key personages like Admiral Rickover, and the Euratom Program—acted to favor light water, so that learning and construction experience gained with light water early on locked the market in by the mid-1960s.[10] And yet the engineering literature consistently argues that, given equal development, the gas-cooled design would have been superior.[11]

Similarly, gasoline now dominates as the power source for automobiles. It may well be the superior alternative, but certainly in 1895 it was held to be the least promising option. It was hard to obtain in the right grade, it was dangerous, and it required more numerous and more sophisticated moving parts than steam. Throughout the period 1890–1920, developers, with predilections depending on their previous engineering experience, produced constantly improving versions of the steam, gasoline, and electric automobiles. But a series of circumstances—among them, in the North American case, unlikely ones like a 1895 horseless carriage competition which appears to have influenced Ransom Olds in his decision to switch from steam to gasoline, and an outbreak in 1914 of hoof-and-mouth disease that shut down horse troughs where steam cars drew water—gave gasoline enough of a lead that it subsequently proved unassailable.[12] Whether steam and electric cars, given equal development, could have been superior is not clear, but this question remains under constant debate in the engineering literature.[13]

Is lock-in to a possibly inferior technology permanent? Theoretically it is, where the source of increasing returns is learning by using, at least until yet newer technologies come along to render the dominant one obsolete. But lock-in need not be permanent if network externalities are the source. Here, if a technology's advantage is mainly that most adopters are going along with it, a coordinated changeover to a superior collective choice can provide escape. In an important paper, Farrell and Saloner[14] showed that as long as agents know other agents' preferences, each will decide independently to switch if a superior alternative is available. But where they are uncertain of others' preferences and intentions, there can be excess inertia: each agent would benefit from holding the other technology but individually none dares change in case others do not follow.

Whatever the source of increasing returns in competitions between technologies, the presence of lock-in and sudden release causes the economy to lose a certain smoothness of motion.

Technology Structure: The Path-Dependent Strong Law of Large Numbers

In the discussion so far, we have derived some basic ideas and properties of technology competition from a dynamic model with a very particular linear-returns-from-learning mechanism. We would like to be able to handle competing-technology problems with more general assumptions and returns-to-adoption mechanisms. In particular we are interested in qualitative questions such as whether, and under what circumstances, an adoption market must end up dominated by a single technology.

In thinking about the type of analytical framework we would need for more general versions of the problem, it seems important to preserve two properties: (1) that choices between alternative technologies are affected by the numbers of each alternative present in the adoption market at the time of choice; equivalently, that choices are affected by current market shares; (2) that small events outside the model may influence the process, so that a certain amount of randomness must be allowed for. Thus the state of the market may not determine the next choice, but rather the probability of each alternative being chosen.

---

[9]A. M. Weinberg, "Power Reactors," *Scientific American* 191 (1954), pp. 33–39.

[10]R. Cowan, "Backing the Wrong Horse: Sequential Technology Choice under Increasing Returns," doctoral dissertation, Stanford University, 1987.

[11]H. M. Agnew, "Gas-Cooled Nuclear Power Reactors," *Scientific American* 244 (1981), pp. 55–63.

[12]C. McLaughlin, "The Stanley Steamer: A Study in Unsuccessful Innovation," *Explorations in Entrepreneurial History* 7 (1954), pp. 37–47; W. B. Arthur, "Competing Technologies and Economic Prediction," *Options* (1984), International Institute for Applied Systems Analysis, Laxenburg, Austria.

[13]R. L. Burton, "Recent Advances in Vehicular Steam Engine Efficiency," Society of Automotive Engineers, Preprint 760340, 1976; W. C. Strack, "Condensers and Boilers for Steam-powered Cars," NASA Technical Note TN D-5813, Washington, DC, 1970.

[14]J. Farrell and G. Saloner, "Standardization, Compatibility and Innovation," *Rand Journal of Economics* 16 (1985), pp. 70–83.

Consider a dynamical system that abstracts and allows for these two properties. I will call it an *allocation process.* At each time that a choice occurs, a unit addition or allocation is made to one of K categories, with probabilities $p_1(x)$, $p_2(x) \ldots$, $p_K(x)$, respectively, where this vector of probabilities p is a function of x, the vector giving the proportion of units currently in categories 1 to K (out of the total number n so far in all categories). In our competing technologies problem, this corresponds to a choice of one technology from K competing alternatives, each time of choice, with probabilities that depend upon the numbers of each alternative already adopted and therefore upon current adoption shares.[15] (For a given problem, if we know the source of randomness and the payoff-returns at each state of the market, we can, in principle at least, derive these probabilities as a function of adoption shares.)

Our question is: what happens to the long-run proportions (or adoption shares) in such a dynamical system? What long-run technological structures can emerge? The standard probability-theory tool for this type of problem is the Strong Law of Large Numbers, which makes statements about long-run proportions in processes where increments are added at successive times. For example, if we successively add a unit to the category Heads with probability 1/2 in tossing a coin, the standard Strong Law tells us that the proportion of Heads must settle to 0.5. But we cannot use the standard Strong Law in our process. We do not have the required *independent* increments. Instead we have increments—unit adoptions or allocations to technologies 1 through K—which occur with probabilities influenced by past increments. We have a "coin" whose probability of Heads changes with the proportion of Heads tossed previously.

We can still generate a Strong Law for our dependent-increment process. Suppose we consider the mapping from present proportions, or adoption shares, to the probability of adoption, as with the two examples in Exhibit 4, where $K = 2$. We can see that where the probability of adoption A is higher than its market share, there would be a tendency in the allocation (or adoption) process for A to increase in proportion; and where it is lower, there would be

EXHIBIT 4 Probability of Adoption as a Function of Adoption Share

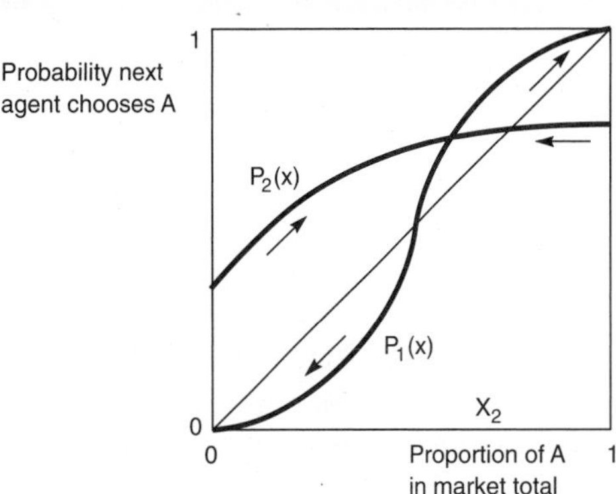

a tendency for it to decrease. If the proportions or shares in each category settle down as total allocations increase, then they should settle down at a fixed point of this mapping. In 1983 Arthur, Ermoliev, and Kaniovski proved that (under certain technical conditions) indeed this conjecture is true.[16] Allocation processes indeed settle down in the long run, with probability one, to an unchanging vector of proportions (adoption shares) represented by one of the fixed points of the mapping from proportions (or adoption shares) to the probability of adoption. They converge to a vector of adoption shares x where $x = p(x)$. Not all fixed points are eligible. Only "attracting," or stable, fixed points (ones that expected motions lead toward) can emerge as the long-run outcomes. (Thus in Exhibit 4 the possible

[15]If these probabilities depend on *numbers adopted* rather than directly on market shares we can write them as $p_1(nx)$, $p_2(nx)$, $p_K(nx)$. This becomes equivalent to a probability function p_n that depends on time n as well as adoption share x.

[16]Hill, Lane and Sudderth proved a version of this theorem in 1980 for the case $K = 2$ and p unchanging with time n. The informally stated version in the text holds for $K \geq 2$ and for time-varying functions p_n provided they converge to a limiting function p. See: W. B. Arthur, Y. M. Ermoliev, and Y. M. Kaniovski, "On Generalized Urn Schemes of the Polya Kind" (in Russian), *Kibernetika* 19 (1983), pp. 49–56; English trans. in *Cybernetics* 19, pp. 61–71; "Strong Laws for a Class of Path-Dependent Urn Processes," in *Proceedings of the International Conference on Stochastic Optimization,* Kiev 1984, ed. Arkin et al. (Berlin: Springer, 1984); "Path-Dependent Processes and the Emergence of Macro-Structure," *European Journal of Operational Research* 30 (1987), pp. 294–303. Technically, the sequence of Borel functions p_n needs to converge to p at a rate faster than $1/n$ converges to zero; the set of fixed points of p needs to have a finite number of connected components; and for $K > 2$ convergence to a point rather than to a cycle or more complex attractor requires the deterministic dynamics formed by the expected motion of the process to be a gradient system. The 1986 paper is perhaps the best introduction to this theorem.

long-run shares are 0 and 1 for the function p_1 and x_2 for the function p_2.) Of course, where there are multiple fixed points, *which* one is chosen depends on the path taken by the process: it depends upon the cumulation of the random events that occur along the way. This very general Strong Law for dependent-increment processes (which, following convention, I shall label AEK) generalizes the conventional Strong Law of Large Numbers.

The *allocation process* framework, with its corresponding Strong Law, applies to a wide variety of self-organizing or autocatalytic problems in economics and physics.[17] For our competing-technology purposes, however, we now have a powerful piece of machinery that enables us to investigate the possible long-run adoption outcomes under different adoption-market mechanisms. For a particular problem we would proceed in three steps:

1. Detail the particular mechanisms at work in the adoption process, paying special attention to returns functions, heterogeneities, and sources of randomness.
2. Use this knowledge to derive the probabilities of choice of each technology explicitly as a function of current adoption shares.
3. Use the AEK Strong Law to derive actual long-run possible adoption shares as the stable fixed points of the adoption-share-to-probability mapping.

A number of studies now use this technique.[18] The "informational increasing returns" model of Arthur[19] is an example. In this model risk-averse potential adopters are uncertain about the actual payoff of two fixed payoff technologies they can choose from. They gather information by polling some random sample of previous adopters. (Neither learning-by-using nor network effects are present.) Increasing returns come about because, if adopters of *A* are more numerous, the next chooser will likely sample more *A*'s than *B*'s, and will therefore be better informed on *A*. Being risk-averse, it will therefore choose *A*, with a probability that increases with *A*'s proportion of x of the market. Application of the AEK Strong Law to a rigorous model of this mechanism yields precise circumstances under which informational-increasing returns allow stable fixed points only at the points $x = 0$ and $x = 1$. That is, it yields circumstances under which information-increasing returns alone cause eventual monopoly of *A* or of *B* with probability 1.

EXHIBIT 5 Payoffs to Adoption of *A* and *B* under a Continuum of Adopter Types

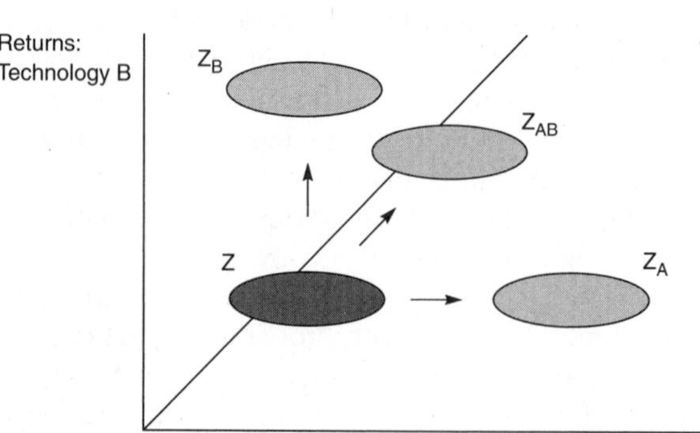

Note: At the outset, adopter payoffs lie in set *Z*. Adoptions of technolgy *A* only shift this set horizontally to the right as in Z_A. Adoptions of *B* only shift it vertically as in Z_B. Adoptions of *A* and *B* shift it diagonally as in Z_{AB}.

When Is Technological Monopoly Inevitable?

Is it inevitable that one technology must eventually shut out the others when there are increasing returns to adoption? The answer is no. Consider a more general version of the heterogeneous-adopter–unknown-arrival-sequence model, in which there is now a continuum of agent types rather than just two. We can now think of agents—potential adopters—as distributed over adoption payoffs as in Exhibit 5. An adopter is chosen at random from this probability distribution each time a choice is to be made; and the distribution itself shifts either to the right or upward as returns to *A* or *B* increase with an adoption of either *A* or *B*, respectively. Monopoly—lock-in to a single technology—corresponds to the distribution of payoffs getting driven over the 45°

[17] Arthur, Ermoliev, and Kaniovski, "Strong Laws for a Class of Path-Dependent Urn Processes," and "Path-Dependent Processes and the Emergence of Macro-Structure"; W. B. Arthur, "Industry Location and the Importance of History," Center for Economic Policy Research, Paper 84, Stanford, 1986; "Urban Systems and Historical Path-Dependence," in *Urban Systems and Infrastructure,* ed. R. Herman and J. Ausube, NAS/NAE Volume, 1987.

[18] See, for example P. David, "Some New Standards for the Economics of Standardization in the Information Age," Paper 79, Center for Economic Policy Research, Stanford, 1986.

[19] Arthur, "Information, Imitation and the Emergence of Technological Structures."

line in this two-technology case. (We assume the distribution of adopter payoffs has "bounded support"—i.e., it does not tail off to infinity in any direction.) Where *K* technologies compete, we can use the AEK Strong Law to show that where there is no ceiling to the increasing returns (so that returns increase without bound as adoptions increase), then sooner or later one technology *must* by the cumulation of chance achieve sufficient adoption advantage to drive the distribution of adopters "over the line." With unbounded increasing returns eventual monopoly by a single technology is indeed inevitable.[20]

But where returns to adoption increase but are bounded, as when learning effects eventually become exhausted, monopoly is no longer inevitable. The reason is interesting. In this case, certain sequences of adopter types could bid the returns to both technologies upward more or less in concert. These technologies could then reach their "increasing returns ceilings" together, with adopter-type-payoffs still straddled across the 45° line (as with Z_{AB} in Exhibit 5), and thus with the adoption market shared from then on. But other adopter-arrival sequences may push the payoff distribution across the line early on. Thus with increasing returns to adoption that are bounded, the general finding is that some "event histories" dynamically will lead to a shared market; other event histories lead to monopoly.[21]

Exact conditions for monopoly in the strategic-competition case where technologies exist as sponsored products are not yet known. Hanson[22] explored a version of this IBM-versus-Apple problem, building on the basic linear-increasing-returns model above. He assumed that firms could price technologies and thereby manipulate adoption payoffs in a market where heterogeneous adopters arrived at random. Hanson was able to show in this stochastic-duopoly problem that firms would price low early on to gain adoptions, possibly even taking losses in an arm-wrestling match for market share. If both firms were evenly matched enough to stay in the market under these circumstances, then sooner or later the cumulation of chance events might allow one firm sufficient adoption advantage to tip the market in its favor. It would then have sufficient advantage to be able to raise its price and take monopoly profits, while keeping the other firm on the contestable margin of the market. Using AEK, Hanson was able to detail certain conditions under which monopoly by a single-technology-product would be inevitable. It is clear, however, that conditions can be constructed where the markets can also end up shared. For example, when increasing returns are bounded, and firms discount future income heavily so that they are mainly interested in present sales, neither firm may wish to price low early on. Neither might then eventually win the natural customers of the other and the result would be a shared market.

[20]Arthur, "Industry Location and the Importance of History."

[21]Ibid.

[22]W. Hanson, "Bandwagons and Orphans: Dynamic Pricing of Competing Systems Subject to Decreasing Costs," doctoral dissertation, Stanford, 1985.

Competing Standards and the Role of Expectations

The term *standard* has two meanings in the technology literature: that of a convention or code of practice, such as distributing alternating current at 110 volts or transmitting it at 60 hertz; and that of the technology or method or code that comes to dominate—that becomes "standard." Standards in the first sense—conventions—can compete much the same as method-technologies do, for a market of adherents, or users, or adopters. Competing standards raise somewhat different issues from competing technologies.[23] I will treat standards here only in so far as they overlap with our dynamics-of-adoption problem.

With standards, learning, information, and production externalities are less important, and the main sources of increasing returns are network externalities and possibly technological interrelatedness. Both sources confer benefits if *future* adopters go along with one's choice. This introduces something not yet considered in our discussion—*expectations.*

Katz and Shapiro, in an important paper,[24] consider a static version of the problem of competing "networks" of different standards, in which "network externalities" accrue to increased network

[23]See David, "Some New Standards for the Economics of Standardization in the Information Age." Also see J. Farrell and G. Saloner, "Installed Base and Compatibility," *American Economics Review* 76 (1986), pp. 940–55; "Standardization and Variety," *Economic Letters* (1986), pp. 71–74; and Standardization Compatibility, and Innovation."

[24]"Network Externalities, Competition, and Compatibility."

size. The networks are provided by firms which must determine network size in advance. It pays firms to provide large networks if potential adopters expect these networks to be large and thereby commit their choice to them. Therefore if, prior to adoption, sufficient numbers of agents believe that network *A* will have a large share of adopters, it will; but if sufficient numbers believe *B* will have a large share, *it* will. Katz and Shapiro showed that there could be multiple "fulfilled-expectation equilibria," that is, multiple sets of eventual network adoption shares that fulfill prior expectations.

In this simple but important model, expectations are given and fixed before the adoption process takes place. More realistically, if adoption were not instantaneous, potential adopters might change or modify their expectations as the fortunes of alternatives changed during the adoption process itself. One possible formulation[25] is to assume that agents form expectations in the shape of beliefs about the adoption process they are in. That is, they form probabilities on the future states of the adoption process—probabilities that are conditioned on the numbers of current adoptions of the competing alternatives. Thus these probabilities, or beliefs, change and respond as the adoption market changes. (We would have a *fulfilled-equilibrium-stochastic-process* if the *actual* adoption process that results from agents acting on these beliefs turns out to have conditional probabilities that are identical to the *believed* process.) In this model, if one standard, or technology, gets ahead by chance adoptions, its increased probability of doing well in the adoption market will further enhance expectations of its success. Analysis here confirms the basic Katz and Shapiro finding. Adaptive or dynamic expectations act to destabilize further an already unstable situation: lock-in to monopoly positions now occurs more easily.

Policy Issues

We have seen that in uncontrolled competitions between technologies with learning effects, or network externalities, or other sources of increasing returns to adoption, there is no guarantee that the fittest technology—the one with superior, long-run potential—will survive. There are therefore grounds for intervention.

Where a central authority with full information on future returns to alternative adoption paths knows which technology has superior long-run potential, it can of course attempt to tilt the market in favor of this technology. Timing is, of course, crucial here:[26] in Paul David's phrase there are only "narrow windows" in which policy would be effective.[27]

More often, though, it will not be clear in advance which technologies have most potential promise. The authorities then face the difficult problem of choosing which infant technologies to subsidize or bet on. This yields a version of the multiarm bandit problem (in which a gambler plays several arms of a multiarm bandit slot machine, trying to ascertain which has the highest probability of producing jackpots). Cowan[28] has shown that, where central authorities subsidize increasing-return technologies on the basis of their current estimates of future potential, locking into inferior technologies is less likely than in the uncontrolled adoption case. But it is still possible. An early run of bad luck with a potentially superior technology may cause the central authority, perfectly rationally, to abandon it. Even with central control, escape from inferior technological paths is not guaranteed. This finding is important for projects like the U.S. Strategic Defense Initiative, where ground-based excimer lasers, particule-beam weapons, X-ray lasers, homing vehicles, and other devices compete for government subsidy on the basis of expected long-run promise. Where each of these improves with development, it is likely that lock-in to one will occur; however, it may not be lock-in to the one with superior long-run potential.

It may sometimes be desirable as a policy option to keep more than one technology alive, to avoid monopoly problems (if the technology is marketed), or to retain "requisite variety" as a hedge against shifts in the economic environment or against future "Chernobyl" revelations that the technology is unsafe. The question of using well-timed subsidies to prevent the adoption process tipping and shutting out technologies has not yet been looked at. But its

[25] W. B. Arthur, "Competing Technologies and Lock-in by Historical Events: The Dynamics of Allocation under Increasing Returns," revised from 1983 paper as Center for Economic Policy Research, Paper 43, Stanford, 1985.

[26] Arthur, "Competing Technologies and Lock-in by Historical Events."

[27] "Some New Standards for the Economics of Standardization in the Information Age."

[28] "Backing the Wrong Horse."

structure—that of artificially stabilizing a naturally unstable dynamical process—is a standard one in stochastic feedback control theory.

Some Research Questions

Several open or only partially resolved research questions have already been mentioned. Besides these, there are at least three major classes of problems that I believe would benefit from future study:

1. *Recontracting models.* Where the source of increasing returns is learning-by-using, results would change little if adopters could reenter the queue and change their choice at a future date. What counts with learning is the previous number of adoptions of a technology, not the fact that an agent is choosing a second time.[29] Where the source is network externalities, results *would* change substantially. In this case, with agents changing their preferences occasionally as well as striving to go along with the more prevalent alternative, recontracting or changing choice would take place as adoptions built up and might continue even when the market was at its full, saturated size. We would then have something akin to a stochastic version of the Farrell and Saloner model.[30] The important difference from our earlier models is that with "deaths" as well as "births" of adoptions allowed, increments to market-share position would tend to be of constant order of magnitude. Adoption processes with recontracting would therefore tend to show convergence in distribution rather than strong convergence, with punctuated equilibria possible in the shape of long sojourns near or at monopoly of one technology coupled with intermittent changeover to monopoly by a different technology. This type of structure has counterparts in genetics, sociology and in far-from-equilibrium thermodynamics.[31] But it has not yet been studied in the technology context.

2. *Empirical studies.* So far we have two excellent historical studies on the set of events and varied sources of increasing returns that led to dominance of the QWERTY typewriter keyboard[32] and the dominance of alternating current.[33] For most present-day uses, alternating current indeed appears to be superior to the alternative, direct current. The QWERTY keyboard, however, may be slightly inferior to the alternative Dvorak keyboard. Norman and Rumelhard[34] find Dvorak faster by 5 percent. Missing as yet, however, are detailed empirical studies of the actual choice-by-choice dynamics of technological competitions. For prominent competitions such as that between nuclear reactors it might be possible to put together a complete account of the adoption sequence and the events that accompanied it. This would allow identification and parameter estimation of the stochastic dynamics of an *actual* rather than a theoretical case.

3. *Spatial technological competition.* One of the striking features of the classical technology diffusion literature[35] is its concern with the spatial dimension—with the fact that a technology diffuses geographically as well as temporally. In the *competing* technologies problem, geographical diffusion would of course also be present. The spatial dimension would become particularly important if returns to adoption were affected by neighbors' choices. This was the case historically in competitions between railroad gauges[36] where it was advantageous to adopt a gauge that neighboring railroads were using. The dynamics of spatial-technology competitions have not been explored yet. But they would resemble those of the well-known Ising model in physics and voter models in probability theory, where dipoles and voters respectively are influenced by the states of their nearest neighbors.[37] Here geographical clusters of localities locked in to different technologies might emerge, with long-run adoption structure depending crucially on the particular spatial increasing-returns mechanism at work.

---

[29]Agent arrivals, if second-time choosers, might, however, be dependent on the previous arrival sequence.

[30]"Standardization, Compatibility, and Innovation."

[31]H. Haken, *Synergetics* (Berlin: Springer, 1978); W. Weidlich and G. Haag, *Concepts and Models of a Quantitative Sociology* (Berlin: Springer, 1983).

[32]P. David, "Clio and the Economics of QWERTY," *American Economic Review, Proceedings* 75 (1985), pp. 332–37.

[33]P. David and J. Bunn, "The Battle of the Systems and the Evolutionary Dynamics of Network Technology Rivalries," Stanford, mimeo, 1987.

[34]D. Norman and D. Rumelhart, "Studies of Typing from the LNR Research Group," in *Cognitive Aspects of Skilled Typewriting,* ed. W. Cooper (Berlin: Springer, 1983).

[35]Z. Griliches, "Hybrid Corn: An Exploration in the Economics of Technological Change," *Econometrica* 25 (1957), pp. 501–22; P. David, "Clio and the Economics of QWERTY."

[36]D. Puffert, "Network Externalities and Technological Preference in the Selection of Railway Gauges," doctoral dissertation, Stanford, 1988.

[37]T. Liggett, "Interacting Markov Processes," in *Lecture Notes in Biomath 38* (Berlin: Springer, 1979).

Conclusion

In the classical literature on the economics of technology, a new and superior technology competes to replace an old and inferior one. In this new literature, two or more superior technologies compete with *each other*, possibly to replace an outmoded one. Competition assumes a stronger form. In the competing-technologies problem, the theory that emerges is a theory of nonconvex allocation. There are multiple equilibria—multiple possible long-run adoption-share outcomes. The cumulation of small random events drives the adoption process into the domain of one of these outcomes, not necessarily the most desirable one. And the increasing-returns advantage that accrues to the technology that achieves dominance keeps it locked in to its dominant position.

I have indicated that competing technologies are examples of self-organizing, order-through-fluctuation systems. They are also examples of evolutionary systems, although the mechanisms are quite different from the ones in Nelson and Winter.[38] Where competing technologies possess increasing returns to adoption, one technology can exercise competitive exclusion on the others; if it has a large proportion of natural adopters it will have a selectional advantage, and the importance of early events results in a founder effect mechanism akin to that in genetics.

The dynamical picture of the long-term economy that results is less like that of a sphere smoothly rolling on a flat surface, with its point of contact with the ground unique and ever changing, and more like that of a polypod lurching down a slope. Where technologies compete, patterns—technology adoption structures—lock in. But as time passes and new technological competitions come about, the old patterns are changed, shaken up, and reformed, and in due course a new one is locked in.

To the extent that this happens, there may be theoretical limits as well as practical ones to the predictability of the economic future.

---

[38]R. Nelson and S. Winter, *An Evolutionary Theory of Economic Change* (Harvard, MA: The Belknap Press of Harvard University Press, 1982).

Organizational Context

Case II–10
Intel Corporation (A): The DRAM Decision

George W. Cogan and Robert A. Burgelman

Introduction

In November 1984, *Andy Grove*,[1] Intel's chief operating officer, stood in his office cubicle gazing out at Silicon Valley and thought about his company's future. The semiconductor industry which Intel had helped create 16 years earlier had entered what looked to be a prolonged cyclical downturn. Some operations had already been trimmed, but Grove believed the company would have to react again soon (see company financial data in Exhibit 2). The recession hit the company's Memory Components Division particularly hard. For much of the previous five years, memory components had been suffering under competitive pressure from the Japanese.

Since 1980, Intel had been losing its market position in *dynamic random-access memories* (*DRAMs*) as the industry average selling price per chip had declined much more rapidly than the 20 to 30 percent per year which was customary. The Japanese had taken the lead in unit sales of the latest generation of DRAMs, the 256-*kilobit* (256K) version, but Intel was fighting back with a program to leapfrog the Japanese in the product's next generation. Its

---

[1]Note: All italicized names appear with biographies in Exhibit 1; all italicized words appear with definitions in the technical appendix.

EXHIBIT 1 Biographies of Key Intel Personnel

Jack Carsten joined Intel from Texas Instruments and has held various high level management positions since then. In 1985 he was senior vice president and general manager of the Components Group.
Dennis Carter is a Harvard MBA with an engineering background. He has worked in several areas of the company and is currently assistant to the president.
Sun Lin Chou received his BS and MS degrees in Electrical Engineering from MIT and his PhD in electrical engineering from Stanford University. He joined Intel in 1971 and has managed the DRAM technology development group in Oregon since then.
Dov Frohman joined Intel from Fairchild in 1969. He was responsible for the invention of the EPROM. He currently manages Intel's design group in Israel.
Edward Gelbach joined Intel from Texas Instruments in 1969. He is currently senior vice president of sales.
Andrew Grove was born in Budapest. He received his BS from CCNY, and his PhD from Berkeley. After working at Fairchild Camera and Instrument for five years, he joined Intel in 1968. He has been president and chief operating officer since 1979.
Ted Hoff joined Intel as a designer in 1969. He headed the group that invented the microprocessor. Hoff left Intel in 1983.
Gordon Moore was born in San Francisco. He received his BS in chemistry from Berkeley, and his PhD in chemistry and physics from the California Institute of Technology. He worked as a member of the technical staff at Shockley Semiconductor from 1956 to 1987, and he founded Fairchild. He founded Intel in 1968 and is currently the chairman and CEO.
Robert Noyce was born in Burlington, Iowa. He received his BS from Grinell College and his PhD from MIT. He was a research engineer at Philco from 1953 to 1956, a research engineer at Shockley Transistor, and a founder and director of Fairchild Camera and Instrument. He is credited with coinventing (with Kilby at TI) the integrated circuit. He founded Intel and currently serves as vice chairman of the board of directors.
Bob Reed received his bachelor's degree from Middlebury College and his MBA from the University of Chicago. He joined Intel in 1974. He was appointed chief financial officer in 1984.
Ron Smith received his bachelor's degree in physics from Gettysburgh College and his MS and PhD degrees in physics from University of Minnesota. He joined Intel in 1978 as a device physicist in the Static Logic Technology Development Group. In 1985, he was manager of that group.
Dean Toombs joined Intel from Texas Instruments in 1983 with the express purpose of running the Memory Components Division.
Leslie Vadasz joined Intel in 1968 and has held a variety of senior management positions since then. He is currently senior vice president and director of the Corporate Strategic Staff.
Ron Whittier holds a PhD in chemical engineering from Stanford University. He joined Intel in 1970. From 1975 until 1983, he managed the memory products division. In 1983, he became vice president and director of Business Development and Marketing Communications.
Albert Yu was born in Shanghai and holds a PhD in electrical engineering from Stanford University. He jointed Intel in 1975.

$50 million 1 *megabit* (1 meg = 4 × 256K) research project was soon to produce working prototypes. Intel managers estimated they were ahead of the Japanese in the 1-meg device. Still, a debate was growing within the company about whether Intel could continue to compete in the commodity market of DRAMs. Grove was formulating his personal position on the matter.

It seemed clear that if Intel chose to continue with the DRAM product line, it would have to commit to at least one $150 million state-of-the-art *Class 10 production facility*. On the other hand, Intel's other businesses were much more profitable than memories; in an ROI framework, the microprocessor business deserved the majority of Intel's corporate resources. It was difficult for both Grove and *Gordon Moore*, Intel's chief executive officer, to imagine an Intel without DRAMs. The memory business had made Intel, and was still by far the largest market segment in integrated circuits. Not the least of Grove's worries was how the investment community would react to Intel's decision to cede such a large market segment to the Japanese.

Company Background

Early History

On August 2, 1968, the *Palo Alto Times* announced that *Bob Noyce* and *Gordon Moore* had left Fairchild to form a new company. Andy Grove, who had been Moore's assistant director of research at Fairchild, also left to complete what the company's historians have called the triumvirate. The three were key technologists in the emerging solid state electronics industry. Noyce had invented the integrated circuit (simultaneously with Jack Kilby at Texas Instruments), and Intel was the first company to specialize in making large-scale integrated circuits.

In mid 1969, Intel introduced its first product, a *bipolar static random-access memory (SRAM)* with a

EXHIBIT 2 Selected Intel Corporation Financial Data

					(Year ended December 31)				
	1976	1977	1978	1979	1980	1981	1982	1983	1984
Sales	226	283	400	663	854	788	900	1,122	1,629
COGS	117	144	196	313	399	458	542	624	883
Gross margin	109	139	204	350	455	330	358	498	746
R&D	21	28	41	67	96	116	131	142	180
SG&A	37	48	76	131	175	184	198	217	315
Operating profit	51	63	87	152	184	30	29	139	251
Interest and other			(1)	(3)	2	10	2	40	47
Profit before tax	51	63	86	149	186	40	31	179	298
Income tax	26	31	42	71	89	13		63	100
Net income	25	32	44	78	97	27	31	116	198
Depreciation	10	16	24	40	49	66	83	103	114
Capital invest	32	97	104	97	152	157	138	145	388
					(December 31)				
	1976	1977	1978	1979	1980	1981	1982	1983	1984
Cash and ST invest	26	39	28	34	127	115	85	389	230
Working capital	93	81	67	115	299	287	306	608	568
Fixed assets	30	80	160	217	321	412	462	504	778
Total assets	156	221	356	500	767	871	1,056	1,680	2,029
LT debt	0	0	0	0	150	150	197	127	146
Equity	109	149	205	303	432	488	552	1,122*	1,360
Employees	7,300	8,100	10,900	14,300	15,900	16,800	19,400	21,500	25,400
ROS	11.1%	11.3%	11.0%	11.8%	11.4%	3.4%	3.4%	10.3%	12.2%
ROA**	24.3%	20.5%	19.9%	21.9%	19.4%	3.5%	3.6%	11.0%	11.8%
ROE**	33.8%	29.4%	29.5%	38.0%	32.0%	6.3%	6.4%	21.0%	17.6%

Note: The first and second quarters of 1985 showed revenue of $375 million and $360 million and profit of $9 million and $11 million, respectively. The first and second quarters of 1984 showed revenue of $372 million and $410 million and profit of $54 million and $50 million, respectively.
*Includes $250 million proceeds from sale of 11% stake to IBM.
**Based on beginning-of-year asset (equity) values.

SOURCE: Intel annual reports.

64-bit storage capacity. The chip itself was less than a quarter of an inch on a side and contained nearly 400 *transistors*. While the SRAM had some small markets, Intel had set its sights on the growing computer memory business, then dominated by *magnetic core* technology. To attack the magnetic core business required at least a 10-fold reduction in cost per bit.

The Intel managers decided early on to pursue a new process technology in addition to the relatively proven bipolar process. The *metal-oxide-semiconductor* (MOS) process promised to lead to increased transistor density while simultaneously reducing the number of fabrication steps required to make a working chip. The process had been published in scientific journals, but serious manufacturability questions remained. MOS transistors consumed only a fraction of the power of a traditional bipolar transistor and thus could be more densely packed on the chip. But they were also very sensitive to trace amounts of impurities in processing, raising the question of whether their performance characteristics would remain stable over time.

Les Vadasz headed the MOS team of several engineers. In contrast to the bipolar effort, the MOS effort moved slowly. The primary problem was to develop a stable transistor *threshold voltage*. After a year of frustration and setbacks, Vadasz's team produced the first commercially available MOS SRAM, the 256-bit "1101." The successful processing sequence had several proprietary aspects which put Intel in the forefront of semiconductor technology development. Vadasz commented that at this early stage of development, the processing sequences had proprietary aspects, but were not always well understood.

Since the market for SRAMs was young, Intel had difficulty selling the new device. But the successful MOS process was immediately applied to the existing market for *shift registers* among mainframe computer makers. Shift register sales provided the company with a war chest of cash needed to weather its first semiconductor recession of 1970–1971.

Development of DRAM

Another technical innovation followed the 1101. Intel worked closely with Honeywell engineers to design and develop the first DRAM in 1970, the 1-kilobit "1103." While the SRAM required six MOS transistors per memory cell, the DRAM required only three transistors. With fewer elements in each memory cell, the 1103 contained more storage capacity in the same silicon area. While the new design allowed increased memory cell density, it also required a significant amount of external circuitry for *access* and *refresh*. An advertisement placed in computer trade journals in early 1971 announced: "THE END. CORES LOSE PRICE WAR TO NEW CHIP."

In spite of the price/performance advantage, customers had to be taught how to use the new device and convinced of its reliability. *Ed Gelbach,* VP of sales, remembered 1971:

> We could never find a customer that used them and yet we were shipping literally hundreds of thousands of them. They were all testing them and putting them in boards . . . but it seemed like none of the customers ever shipped machines with the part. My recurring nightmare was that all of those chips would be returned over a single weekend.

In order to speed the adoption of DRAMs, Intel started the Memory Systems Operations (MSO) which assembled 1103 chips along with the required peripheral controller circuitry for OEM sale into the computer maker market. Soon MSO was responsible for about 30 percent of Intel's business. By 1972, the 1103 was the largest selling integrated circuit in the world and accounted for over 90 percent of Intel's $23.4 million in revenue.

Gordon Moore called the 1103 "the most-difficult-to-use semiconductor product ever invented." Ironically, that may have helped its market success:

> There was a lot of resistance to semiconductor technology on the part of the core memory engineers. Core was a very difficult technology and required a great deal of engineering support. The engineers didn't embrace the 1103 until they realized that it too was a difficult technology and wouldn't make their skills irrelevant.

New DRAM Generations

From its early days, Intel was fighting a battle with processing yields. The early 1103's were produced on 2-inch-diameter silicon wafers, each containing about 250 devices. Of the 250, early 1103 runs produced an average of 25 fully functional devices, or an overall yield of 10 percent. *Ron Whittier,* general manager of the Memories Components Division from 1975 until 1983, said that throughout a product's life cycle, wafer yields increased continually as process improvements were developed. The productivity of the factory was also increased by changing the size of the wafer whenever silicon manufacturers developed techniques to grow larger silicone ingots and equipment manufacturers developed machines which could handle larger wafers. In 1972, *Albert Yu* headed a team which converted the bipolar process from 2-inch to 3-inch wafers, effectively doubling capacity.

In the early days, Vadasz recalled, MSO developed another strategy for increasing yield. Since it only took one defective memory cell (out of 1024 in the 1103) to make a chip dysfunctional, it seemed inefficient to throw away all defectives. MSO's scheme was to compensate for a defective memory cell using creative peripheral logic circuitry. The peripheral circuitry was designed to bypass the defective cells within each memory chip so that rejected 1103s could still be used. Since the scheme required extra 1103s in each system, Intel referred to the concept as redundancy.

Soon after Intel's early success, competitors entered the market for DRAMs and began to erode Intel's MOS process technology lead. By the mid 1970s, Intel was one of several companies vying to be the first at introducing the new generation of DRAM memories. Every three years, a new generation with four times as much capacity as its predecessor was developed (See Exhibit 3).

EXHIBIT 3 Product Introduction Timelines

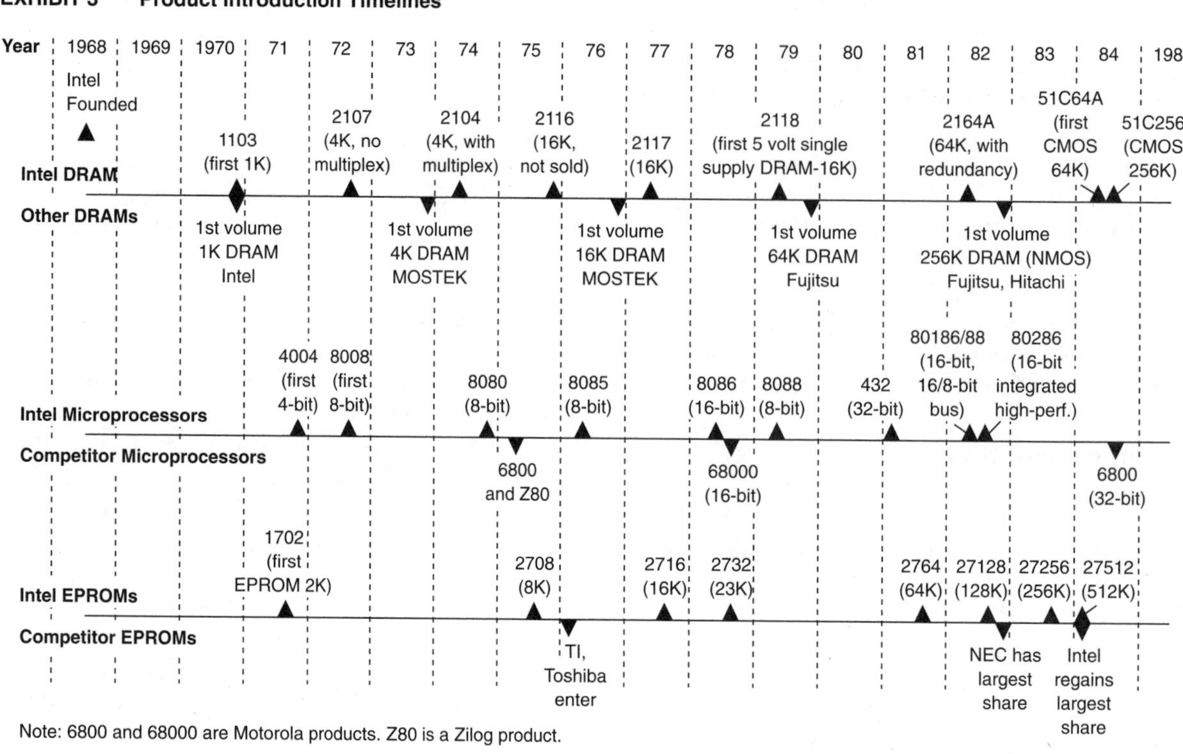

Note: 6800 and 68000 are Motorola products. Z80 is a Zilog product.

SOURCE: Intel documents, Dataquest.

Vadasz recalled that even at the 4K and 16K level, Intel was struggling to keep up with its competitors. During the formative years of the DRAM market, the chip design was in rapid flux. A start-up company, MOSTEK, was able to take market share from Intel in the 4K generation by incorporating the peripheral circuitry required to manage the memory on the chip itself. Vadasz recalled: "The first DRAMs were not very user-friendly, and MOSTEK came out with a better product." MOSTEK introduced the concept of on-chip *multiplexing,* which allowed a smaller number of output pins to address the entire memory. Multiplexing started a trend in DRAMs towards user-friendliness.[2]

Vadasz commented:

> Even though you have invented the product, sometimes it is easier for new entrants to seize an opportunity and beat you to the punch. They are not encumbered by the same things you are. . . . The real problem in technological innovation is in anticipating the relevant issues. Once a technological "box" has been defined, it is easy for a team of great engineers to optimize everything in that box. Choosing the box is the hard part.

Intel's first 4K DRAM was redesigned to include the internal multiplexing logic. *Sun Lin Chou,* who was involved in the 4K DRAM development, said that in the revised version, Intel also implemented a one-transistor DRAM cell, which became the industry standard. While more challenging from a process technology standpoint, the reduction in the number of transistors allowed for a smaller chip size. The revised 4K version sold well, but time was short before the next generation.

Dennis Carter described Intel's early strategy as "staying ahead of the experience curve using process technology."[3] According to Sun Lin Chou, a

---

[2]Eventually Intel sold MSO since the value added had been integrated onto the chip itself and the majority of MSO's customers had learned how to use DRAMs.

[3]The experience curve referred to the declining nature of industrywide manufacturing costs over time due to experience. The semiconductor industry had a 70 percent experience curve (costs reduced by 30 percent for each doubling in cumulative

successful DRAM company participates in the early phase of each generation when low competitor yields and high demand support high prices.

> In fact, for the first two years, the demand for DRAMs to the first market entrant is semi-infinite. As soon as the leading vendor makes a new DRAM, he can crank his capacity to the maximum and he will be guaranteed of selling all his output. This is not true for more complex products such as a logic product with a new function where the customers have to first learn how to use it.

Each new generation required a quadrupling of the number of transistors contained on a chip. The driving force behind increased density was the ability to define patterns of ever narrower dimensions (functional equivalent of wires and components in a circuit) on the silicon wafer, to invent creative ways of reducing the required number and size of components per memory cell, and to make larger chips without defects. Each new generation reduced the minimum linewidth by a factor of about 0.7, from 5 μm at the 4K generation. The minimum linewidth was controlled primarily by the accuracy of the photolithography process, while the maximum chip size was determined by the ability to control the number of random defects on the wafer.[4]

While competition was tough even at the 4K level, a series of process innovations kept Intel amongst the memory leaders through the 16K DRAM generation (see Exhibit 3). Gordon Moore developed the strategy of using DRAMs as a technology driver. The latest process technology was developed using DRAMs and later transferred to other products. Early on in the company's development, Intel managers decided to merge the research and manufacturing functions. Gordon Moore had been dissatisfied with the linkage between research and manufacturing at Fairchild. As a result, he had insisted that Intel perform all process research directly on the production line. Moore commented:

> Our strategy optimizes our ability to make fast incremental process technology improvements. We don't have a central corporate research lab. We tend to evaluate other research advances in light of how they will affect our businesses. For instance, while Texas Instruments has been funding a research effort in *gallium arsenide,* we have been watching gallium arsenide develop for the past 20 years. We're still silicon believers.

During the 1970s, Intel competed by developing new processes which were used to enhance product features or to enable new product families beyond memories. The *HMOS* (high-performance MOS) process enabled Intel to introduce the first 5-volt-single-power-supply 16K DRAM in 1979. Earlier offerings, including Intel's two previous 16K DRAMs (2116 and 2117), required that the user supply three separate voltages to the chip. The new product, the 2118, greatly simplified the user's design and production tasks. While Intel had lost market share with the 2116 and 2117, it was all alone with the 5-volt device and captured a price premium of double the industry average for three-power-supply 16K DRAMs in 1979 (see Exhibit 4). The DRAM technology development group focused a significant amount of its resources on developing Intel's third 16K DRAM offering while competitors concentrated on the 64K generation.

Intel management decided to focus on the single-power-supply 16K DRAM for two primary reasons: they projected a relatively long life cycle for the 16K generation due to the technical challenge in achieving the 64K generation, and they believed the one-power-supply process would eventually dominate the memory industry. They considered it too risky to tackle both the 64K DRAM generation and the single-power-supply technology in the same product.

The drive towards smaller and smaller geometries was achieved through improvements in both processing methodology and processing machinery. Dennis Carter explained that in the early years some processing steps were considered black magic and defined a company's competitive edge. As time went on, the movement of engineers between chip companies and the involvement of suppliers and equipment manufacturers in process development efforts led to a general leveling of process capability amongst Silicon Valley firms. Sun Lin Chou commented about the trends in processing:

> Process technology and equipment have become so complex and expensive to develop that no vendor can hope to do better than [its] competitors in every process step. The key to innovation is to be on par with your competitors on every process step, but to select

---

volume). Companies who were not ahead of the curve for a particular product or generation suffered erosion of margins or market share.

[4]The size of the chip defines the area of the wafer which each process-induced defect can potentially damage. If the chip size is too large, yields are unacceptably low unless the defect level can be simultaneously reduced.

EXHIBIT 4 **Market Information for DRAMs and Microprocessors**

Product	1974	1975	1976	1977	1978	1979	1980	1981	1982	1983	1984
					Worldwide Unit Shipments of DRAMS (in thousands)						
4K	615	5,290	28,010	57,415	77,190	70,010	31,165	13,040	4,635	2,400	2,250
16K 3PS*			50	2,008	20,785	69,868	182,955	215,760	263,050	239,210	120,690
16K 5V*						150	1,115	5,713	23,240	57,400	40,600
64K					1	36	441	12,631	103,965	371,340	851,600
256K									10	1,700	37,980
					Worldwide Yearly Average Selling Prices of DRAMs ($/unit)						
4K	17.00	6.24	4.35	2.65	1.82	1.92	1.94	1.26	1.62	2.72	3.00
16K 3PS*			46.39	18.63	8.53	6.03	4.77	2.06	1.24	1.05	1.09
16K 5V*						17.67	7.38	3.84	2.23	1.98	2.07
64K					150.00	110.14	46.26	11.00	5.42	3.86	3.16
256K									150.00	47.66	17.90
Total Market	10,455	33,010	124,163	189,559	317,932	562,339	961,785	621,775	950,506	1,885,745	3,593,242
					Intel DRAM Market Share						
4K	82.9%	45.6%	18.7%	18.1%	14.3%	8.7%	3.2%				
16K 3PS*			37.0%	27.9%	11.5%	4.4%	2.1%	2.4%	2.3%	1.9%	1.4%
16K 5V*						100.0%	94.0%	66.5%	33.1%	11.7%	12.3%
64K							0.7%	0.2%	1.5%	3.5%	1.7%
256K											0.1%
Estimated Revenue**	8,667	15,052	23,643	37,976	40,479	32,882	28,139	25,534	33,109	68,238	58,607

*16K 3PS refers to the industry-standard, three-power-supply DRAM. The 16K 5V model requires only one power supply.

**Sales of 1K DRAMs were negligible by 1977. Estimates are created by assuming Intel prices at average selling price. Casewriter estimates that by 1984 Intel DRAM sales were closer to $100 million. Losses to gross income due to DRAMs in 1984 were estimated by the casewriter to be between $20 million and $30 million.

EXHIBIT 4 *(continued)*

Microprocessor Sales History by Architecture†

Architecture (% units sold)	1976	1977	1978	1979	1980	1981	1982	1983	1984
8-bit:									
Zilog (Z80)	2.2%	5.8%	12.4%	17.0%	21.1%	22.7%	23.4%	37.4%	35.1%
Intel (8080, 8088)	22.8%	36.6%	34.6%	38.9%	27.1%	19.7%	19.1%	22.3%	33.5%
Motorola (6800, 650X, 680X)	15.0%	13.0%	17.2%	20.8%	18.8%	21.1%	17.9%	14.8%	14.0%
Others	60.0%	44.6%	35.8%	23.3%	33.0%	36.5%	39.6%	25.5%	17.4%
Total 8-bit (million units)	n/a	n/a	n/a	12.5	22.4	33.8	47.9	67.8	75.1
Average selling price	n/a	n/a	n/a	$6.03	$4.60	$3.32	$3.18	$3.25	$4.06
16-bit:									
Zilog (Z8000)				1.4%	4.5%	3.4%	5.1%	5.8%	6.2%
Intel (80186/286,8086)			6.7%	14.0%	28.9%	31.7%	26.6%	32.1%	59.1%
Motorola (68000)						3.9%	5.8%	10.8%	20.2%
Others			93.3%	84.6%	66.6%	61.0%	62.5%	51.3%	14.5%
Total 16-bit (million units)	n/a	n/a	n/a	0.5	0.8	1.8	4.1	7.1	10.0
Average selling price	n/a	n/a	n/a	$30.29	$38.00	$16.96	$15.29	$14.25	$28.90

†Architecture refers to company who originated design, not to manufacturer. For example, while Intel's designs captured 33.5% and 59.1% of the 8 and 16-bit segments, Intel's actual unit sales of microprocessors accounted for only 14.5% of total market sales in 1984. Licensing agreements with other vendors account for the remainder. Next to Intel, NEC was the second largest unit shipper of microprocessors at 13.5% of total units. Motorola captured fifth place behind Zilog (8.9%) and AMD (7.4%) with 7.3% of microprocessor unit sales in 1984.

SOURCE: Dataquest.

one or two or three process features with the highest leverage and focus your efforts to gain leadership there. In DRAMs we focus on high-quality thin *dielectrics*.

The Invention of the EPROM

Albert Yu, vice president of development and general manager of the components division, said he usually associates the invention of any important product with one person. The EPROM (electrically programmable read-only memory) was invented by *Dov Frohman*. Yu said Frohman not only invented the product, but he also described the physical effect, saw that it could be applied to a memory device, designed the first part, and fabricated the first device.

Frohman's story has become legendary at Intel. As a recent hire from Fairchild in 1969, Frohman was assigned to help understand and remedy a strange phenomenon which was causing reliability problems with the MOS process. The problem involved the silicon gate structure. Frohman saw that the phenomenon could be explained by the existence of an unintentional *floating gate* within the MOS device. He realized that if a floating gate were intentionally constructed, a new type of programmable memory which would permanently store information could be built.

Frohman designed the first test devices and assembled a demonstration for Gordon Moore. According to Frohman:

> We put together a 16-bit array with primitive transistor packages sticking out of the 16 sockets, an oscilloscope and pulse generator, and we carted all this into Gordon's office. There were red bulbs to indicate the bits. This was all new to us, and we were thrashing around. We showed Gordon that by pushing the button you could program the device, and we demonstrated that it would hold a charge.

Later, it was discovered that ultraviolet light could be used to erase the memory. Moore committed the company to the production of the EPROM even though no one could tell where the device would have applications. Recalled Moore:

> It was just another kind of memory at the time, and people saw it as a research and development device. Today, the likelihood of someone killing an effort like this one is very high, because we require a well-defined application to a market from the outset. This is especially so because we are not lacking in opportunities. There is still a lot of evolution left in the current technology. If you consider the possibilities for reducing line width, you can see another 12 years of evolution along the same curve.

The Invention of the Microprocessor

Ted Hoff invented the microprocessor. Intel had been hired by the Japanese firm Busicom to design and build a set of chips for a number of different calculators. Busicom had envisioned a set of around 15 chips designed to perform advanced calculator functions. Hoff suggested building a simpler set of just a few general purpose chips which could be programmed to carry out each of the calculators' instructions.

He was the architect of the chip set which Federico Faggin and a team of designers implemented. The set included four chips: a central processing unit (CPU) called the 4004, a read-only memory (ROM) with custom instructions for calculator operation, a random-access memory (RAM), and a shift register for input/output buffering. It took nearly a year to convince Busicom that the novel approach would work, but by early 1970, Intel signed a $60,000 contract which gave Busicom proprietary rights to the design. The CPU chip, 4004, was eventually called a microprocessor.

While Intel produced chips for Busicom which were successfully made into 100,000 calculators,[5] a debate within the company developed about whether Intel should try to renegotiate the rights to the chip design. Hoff believed that Intel could use the devices as a general-purpose solution in many applications ranging from cash registers to street lights, and he lobbied heavily within the company.

Eventually, Intel decided to offer reduced pricing to Busicom in exchange for noncalculator rights to the design. Ed Gelbach remembered the management decision: "Originally, I think we saw it as a way to sell more memories and we were willing to make the investment on that basis." Busicom, in financial trouble, readily agreed to the proposal.

The 4004 was introduced in 1971. It contained 2,300 MOS transistors and could execute 60,000 instructions per second. Its performance was not as good as custom-designed logic, but Intel believed

---

[5]The casewriter noticed a Busicom calculator on Gordon Moore's desk. Moore also wore an Intel digital watch, which he called his $15 million watch, referring to Intel's ill-fated venture into the watch business. He said: "If anyone comes to me with an idea for a consumer product, all I have to do is look at my watch to get the answer. . ."

there was a significant market for it. Early on, it became apparent that Intel would have to educate its customers in order to sell the 4004. As a result, Gelbach's group developed the first of Intel's development aides, which were programming tools for the customer. By 1973 revenues from design aides exceeded microprocessor sales.

In tandem with the 4-bit 4004, Intel developed an 8-bit microprocessor, the 8008, which was introduced in April 1972. The 8008 was designed with a computer terminal company in mind, but was rejected by the company because it was too slow and required 20 support chips for operation.

In the meantime, Intel's advancements in static and dynamic RAMs had provided a new process technology which promised increased transistor switching speed. Intel had created an *NMOS* process, which was applied to the 8008. In addition, much of the functionality of the support chips was integrated into the new microprocessor, the 8080. As a result of process technology, the 8080 could execute 290,000 instructions per second. In addition, the 8080 required only six support chips for operation.

The introduction of the 8080 in April 1974 heralded the beginning of a new age in computing. The market for microprocessors exploded as new uses were developed. Intel was one year ahead of Motorola's introduction of the 6800 and eventually took nearly the entire 8-bit market. Even though the 6800 used an architecture more familiar to programmers, Intel offered more effective development aids and support systems. Several integrated circuit companies were licensed to produce the 8080 so that customers were assured of a second source of supply. Ed Gelbach remembered the mid-1970s as the good old days. At an initial selling price of $360 per chip, Intel paid for the 8080 research and development in the first five months of shipments.

Motorola and Zilog[6] continued to apply pressure in the 8-bit microprocessor marketplace (see Exhibit 4). But Intel's 16-bit microprocessor, the 8086, again was first to market by about one year when it was introduced in June 1978. Intel management decided that upward compatibility would be a critical feature of the 16-bit chip. While the 8086 could operate software developed originally for the 8080, it employed a new architecture which required new software for full exploitation. An 8-bit *bus* version of the new architecture, the 8088, was also introduced. For two years, Intel did not meet its sales forecasts for the 8086 family as customers purchased only sample quantities and worked on a new generation of software. In the meantime, Motorola introduced its own 16-bit microprocessor, the 68000, and appeared to be gaining momentum in the field.[7]

Recognizing that the 68000 represented a critical threat that could lock Intel out of the 16-bit market and potentially the next generation as well, Intel created a task force to attack the 68000. The project was called operation CRUSH. The project leader said: "We set out to generate 100,000 sales leads and get that down to 10,000 qualified leads resulting in 2,000 design wins in 1980." SWAT teams of engineering, applications, and marketing people were mobilized to travel anywhere in the world whenever a design win was threatened.

The CRUSH campaign emphasized Intel's systems approach, and produced 2,500 design wins in the first year. The most notable win was IBM's decision to use the 8088 in their first personal computer in 1981. IBM planned an open-architecture personal computer, and Intel's 8086 family defined the software standard. Intel sales representatives knew they won the IBM account several months before it was made public when the IBM Boca Raton office started placing orders for Intel's ICE-88 development systems. In 1981, 13 percent of Intel's sales were to IBM.

The project to develop the next microprocessor generation began in 1978. The 80186 and 80286 were designed to be upwardly compatible with the 8086, and to offer increased integration, internal memory management, and advanced software protection (security) capability. The 80286 was designed to operate with as few as four support chips. The 286 team developed product features through extensive field interviews, and created a list of over 50 potential applications ranging from business systems to industrial automation. Ironically, the applications list did not include personal computers, which later became the single largest application.

The 80286 was the most ambitious design effort ever undertaken at Intel. The chip contained 130,000 transistors (versus 29,000 for the 8086). Intel's computerized design tools were stretched to their limit. Four separate computer systems had to be used just to store the design. Design verification (a tool which checks that mask design correctly

[6]Zilog had been formed as a start-up by three Intel design engineers. Andy Grove commented that the loss of those engineers set back Intel's microprocessor program by as much as one year.

[7]Motorola won the Apple computer account with the 68000. The 68000 architecture remains Apple's standard.

reflects schematic design) took four days of continuous computer operation. Several crises arose throughout the development period.

The 286 logic design supervisor recalled:

> At least once a year we went through a crisis that made us wonder whether we would get there or not. One was the chip size crisis. At one point, it looked like the chip would be as big as 340 mils on a side. That was so big that people outside the design team would roll on the floor laughing. They kind of enjoyed our misery. Chip designers love to hear that someone else's chip is too big, but when it happens to you, it's really serious stuff.

The design team of 24 people worked feverishly for three years to develop the first prototype. That device was fabricated in 1982 at Fab 3 in Livermore but did not operate with high enough speed. Gradually, all the bugs were worked out, and only one hurdle remained: developing the methodology to test the chips as they came off the line. Production was ready to start making the 80286 six months before the testing procedure could be developed. Intel had to develop computer tools in order to design the tests. The chip was introduced in 1983, 18 months later than originally planned.

In the meantime, Motorola was gaining momentum. Dennis Carter, who worked on marketing the 80286, said:

> The 68000 came out after the 8086 and it was having some success in the marketplace, but we weren't particularly concerned because we knew the 186 and 286 were on the horizon. We believed we would announce the 286, and everyone would flock to our door. But when we introduced it, the world perceived the 286 not as a powerful monster machine, but as a slight continuation of the 8086. It also seemed that a lot of start-ups were using Motorola, and that was real scary, because that's one indication of where the future is going to be.

Project CHECKMATE paralleled the earlier project CRUSH in concept. CHECKMATE task force members gave a series of seminars 200 different times to 20,000 engineers around the world. Rather than emphasizing performance specifications which Motorola could also use to advantage, the seminar stressed features which had been included at the request of the marketplace in 1978, such as *virtual memory addressing* and *multitasking*. Carter recalled:

> As a result, the design wins completely turned around. When we went into CHECKMATE, some market segments were three or four to one in favor of Motorola. By the time we finished, it had turned around the other way.

Synergies Between EPROMs and Microprocessors

No one foresaw that microprocessors would create a booming market for EPROMs. The original four-chip design for the 4004 was general purpose except for the ROM chip, which had to be customized (at the factory) for each application.

Although it was developed separately, the EPROM substituted for the ROM and provided two advantages: the designer of a custom product could develop and revise the ROM-resident microprocessor programs quickly, and smaller applications which could not afford the expense of a custom ROM could substitute off-the-shelf EPROMS. Ed Gelbach commented:

> It made sense to be able to reprogram the microprocessor instead of buying fixed ROMs for it. You could change your system overnight or every five minutes with EPROM.

Intel had a competitive advantage in the EPROM process, and retained a majority market share until the late 1970s. Competitors had trouble imitating Intel's "floating gate" process. *Ron Smith,* manager of Static/Logic Technology Development said:

> If a device physicist were confronted with the EPROM out of the blue, he might be able to prove it won't work. The EPROM process has as much art as science in it, not only in the wafer fab, but in the packaging, testing, and reliability engineering.

In 1977, Intel introduced the 16K EPROM, 2716, which was compatible with any microprocessor system. All alone with the floating-gate process, Intel enjoyed a boom in EPROM sales for two years.

By 1981, the industry faced a cyclical downturn, and Intel's virtual monopoly on the EPROM market was challenged by several competitors, including the Japanese. The industry average selling prices for the 16K EPROM dropped by 75 percent in 1980. Intel management responded by accelerating the introduction of the 64K EPROM.

In the midst of a semiconductor recession, Intel decided to retrofit the brand new Fab 6 at Chandler, Arizona, with a new photolithography technology: *Stepper alignment*. Fab 6 had just come online and was idle (see Exhibit 5 for more detail on Intel facilities). The gamble was significant: "new process, new product, new plant, and new people." The 64K

EXHIBIT 5 Intel Facilities in 1984

Intel's Wafer Foundaries

Fab Area	Location	Year First Opened	Original Wafer Size	Current Wafer Size	Technology Development	Primary Production Focus
Ex Fab1	Mountain View,	Purchased 1968	1″	Closed		
Fab 1	CA	1977	3″	4″	EPROM	Small number of EPROMs
Fab 2	Santa Clara, CA	1971	4″	4″	No	Logic
Fab 3	Santa Clara, CA	1973	3″	4″	Logic, SRAM	Logic and SRAM (was DRAM)
Fab 4	Livermore, CA	1979	4″	4″	No	Microcontrollers and EPROM
Fab 5	Aloha, OR	1979	4″	4″	DRAM	Pilot and DRAM
Fab 6	Aloha, OR	1980	4″	4″ and 6″	No	Logic, EPROM, Microcontrollers
Fab 7*	Chandler, AZ	1983	5″	6″	No	EPROM only
Fab 8	Albuquerque, NM	Scheduled 1985	6″	6″	No	EPROM
Fab 9	Jerusalem, Israel	Scheduled 1986	6″ plan		No	Under construction
Fab 10**	Rio Rancho, NM	Held at shell				
Fab 11**	Rio Rancho, NM	Held at shell				

*First 6″ fab area in world. Original 5″ facility used DRAMs for shakeout. 1981–82 recession delayed production and allowed installation of 6″ equipment. Process transfer to 6″ wafers was unexpectedly difficult and took over one year.

**These fab areas could be loaded with facilities and equipment and started in about two years

Intel's Other Worldwide Facilities (excluding 50 sales offices)

Location	Date Started	Product Focus	Operation
Penang, Malaysia	1972	Broad	Component assembly and test
Manila, Philippines	1974	Broad	Component assembly and test
Haifa, Israel	1974	Logic	Design center
Barbados, West Indies	1977	Broad	Components assembly
Tsukuba, Japan	1981	Logic	Design center
Las Piedras, Puerto Rico	1981	Systems, DRAMs	Systems assembly, component test
Singapore	1984	Systems	Systems assembly

SOURCE: Intel documents.

EPROM (2764) team met very aggressive yield goals, and Intel was again leading the world in EPROM sales. By mid 1981, Fab 6 had produced hundreds of thousands of 2764s, and output was doubling every quarter.

Technology Development

The 2764 had been used by Intel's Santa Clara Technology Development Group to develop stepper alignment. Steppers allowed smaller feature definition and smaller die size,[8] but the capital equipment was an order of magnitude more expensive than conventional projection aligners. Because of the trend towards more expensive equipment and the growing need for a new generation of equipment for each generation of product, Intel modified its traditional philosophy of developing processes on fabrication lines.

From early on, Intel had divided its technology development into the three groups which represented the three major process areas: EPROM, DRAM, and logic. Competition between the groups for scarce resources in the Santa Clara facility had led to the decision to separate the groups geographically. By 1984, the three separate technology development groups were in three cities: EPROMs in Santa Clara, California; microprocessors and SRAMs in Livermore, California;[9] and DRAMs in Aloha, Oregon. While

[8]Smaller die size leads to higher yield and lower manufacturing costs. If die size is reduced by 25 percent, manufacturing costs are typically reduced by at least 25 percent.

[9]The Livermore site was also a production facility in 1984.

EXHIBIT 6 Technology Development Groups

	DRAM	EPROM	Logic/SRAM
Location	Portland, OR	Santa Clara, CA	Livermore, CA
Product focus	Moderate, undertakes some basic research	Strong, little basic research; EPROM and EEPROM development.	Strong
Process/design interface	Design engineers highly specialized in DRAMs with device physics focus. Process and design development are highly interactive and in parallel.	Process and design less tightly coupled.	Process and design loosely coupled. Design engineers focus on circuit design. Process engineers focus on shrinking linewidth technologies.
Key distinctive technical competence	Thin dielectrics and pushing photolithography limits. Tend to lead Intel in geometry reduction. DRAMS are seen as technology driver. Currently the only group with a 1-micron technology	Problems specific to EPROM and EEPROM. Expertise in developing polysilicon and passivation processes. Also focused on pushing technology to 1 micron.	Processes to shrink existing products and increase yields. Currently developing new process for 386 microprocessor. Developing expertise in double layer metalization.
Number of personnel	120	120	120
1985 budget allocation*	$65 million	$65 million	$65 million
Other comments	DRAM technology development group considered by many to be the most competent group. Major effort in 1-meg DRAM development. Facility has low turnover.	Relatively high turnover to competing companies in Silicon Valley. Has successfully maintained Intel lead in EPROM technology.	Technology development takes place in facility used for production of logic products. Major project in developing 386 process.

*Casewriter's estimate.

development of each technology was independent, management insisted on equipment standardization. Periodically, the groups got together, pooled information on equipment options, and agreed to purchase the same equipment.

Gordon Moore commented that resource allocation did not necessarily parallel the market fortunes of the process families:

> Allocation of resources to the different technology development groups is centralized by Andy and me. We want to maintain commonality. Also, we are old semiconductor guys. Ideally, one of the groups starts a new technology and the others follow. But for stepper technology this was not true; they all did it simultaneously.

The three groups each developed a distinctive style and distinctive competences which related to their product responsibilities (see Exhibit 6). The Santa Clara group was responsible for the EPROM and *EEPROM* (electrically erasable programmable read-only memory) products. They focused on the processing steps most critical to EPROMs, for example, the double polysilicon process used to create the floating gate. Similarly, the Livermore group concentrated on processes critical to logic devices.

The DRAM technology development group led the company in linewidth reduction. For example, the DRAM group was developing a 1-μm process while the logic group was developing a 1.5-μm process. Two key factors made DRAMs suitable as a technology driver: large demand for the latest DRAM generation (early high-volume manufacturing experience), and simplicity of integrating design and testing with process development.

Process specialization in all three technology areas limited the direct transferability of processing modules from one area to another, but DRAMs still provided a convenient vehicle for leading-edge process learning, and the DRAM group was highly regarded. Ron Whittier said:

> In 1984, the memory technology development group represented Intel's best corporate resource for process development. People like Sun Lin Chou are a scarce resource in a technology-driven company. Sun Lin's group understands and executes process development better than any other group at Intel.

Dean Toombs described the DRAM group as different from the others because of the relationship between design and process engineers:

> The DRAM designer is a specialist and more a device physicist than other designers. He focuses on the memory cell and has to understand where every electron in the structure is. There is more of a connection between the designer and the process engineer. The design and the process are developed together. In contrast, a logic designer is not as concerned with the details of a transistor's operation. The process is critical, but not as interactive with the design.

EXHIBIT 7 Composition of Revenues

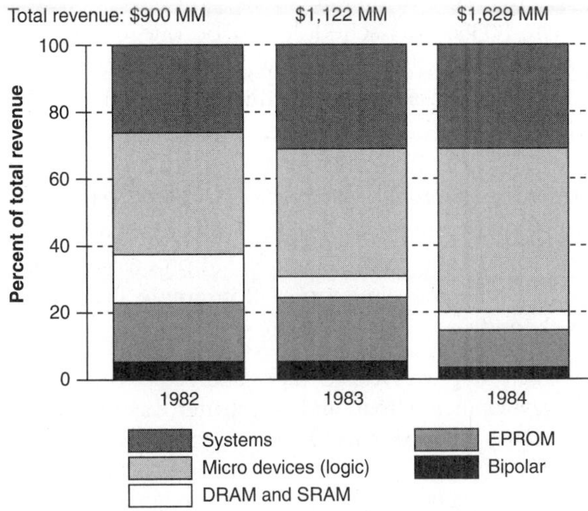

SOURCE: Dataquest.

Intel Product Line and Situation in Late 1984

By the end of 1984, logic products (including microprocessors, *microcontrollers*, and peripherals) were the dominant source of Intel's revenue (see Exhibit 7). The company offered over 70 peripheral chips which worked in tandem with its microprocessor lines. The 80186 and 80286 were tremendously successful. In addition to the IBM PC business, Intel had locked up the IBM PC clone business with customers such as Compaq, who purchased microprocessors either from Intel or from one of its licensed second sources such as Advanced Micro Devices. The only serious 16-bit architectural competitor was Motorola,[10] although *Electronic News* had reported that 10 companies, including NEC, Hitachi, Mitsubishi, Fujitsu, and Zilog, were developing proprietary 32-bit products, and National Semiconductor had already introduced its 32-bit offering. NEC's proprietary design effort was particularly interesting since NEC also supported Intel's microprocessor line as a second source.[11]

Intel had also developed a line of microcontrollers which integrated logic and memory (both SRAM and EPROM) to provide a self-sufficient, one-chip computer. One Intel manager suggested that integration of EPROM technology with logic was an effort to lift EPROMs from a commodity status. The microcontroller business had products in the 4-, 8-, and 16-bit market segments, which were used to control everything from house fans to complex satellites and had prices ranging from one thousand to several thousand dollars per chip.

Scheduled for introduction in late 1985 was the successor to the 286, the 32-bit 80386™ microprocessor.[12] According to one Intel manager, "Once again, Intel was betting the company on a new product." With 270,000 transistors, the 386 was even more complex than the 286. Intel had invested heavily in computerized design and simulation tools which made the design task run more smoothly. In 1984, Intel believed it had the best chip design capability in the world. However, Motorola had devel-

[10] Motorola's 68000 has a 16-bit bus, but actually uses a 32-bit internal architecture.

[11] *Electronic News,* February 18, 1985. The article also reports that Fujitsu did not confirm rumors that it had a proprietary 32-bit design. Instead, Fujitsu indicated its development efforts were still centered on second source agreements with Intel.

[12] 386 is a trademark of the Intel Corporation.

oped a strong 32-bit product, the 68020,[13] and was already in the marketplace winning designs, locking customers into its architecture.

The 80386 was scheduled to be one of the first products made with the new *complementary MOS (CMOS)* process (the 80C51 microcontroller and the 51C64 DRAM had both used versions of CMOS). It was also the first microprocessor to use stepper alignment, *double metalization,* and *plasma etching.* Development of the 386™ process was taking place in parallel with a new SRAM process at Livermore under the direction of Ron Smith. Ron Smith explained:

> Our group was called the Static Logic Technology Development Group and our charter was to develop *scaling improvements*[14] for the logic and SRAM lines. SRAMs were to lead the company in scaling. We saw the SRAMs not only as a product line but as a vehicle for microprocessor development. The SRAM is an indispensable tool in developing any new process. It is much easier to debug a process using memory components, because they are easier to test. That's why Intel traditionally uses memory products to develop a new technology.

In 1984, the Livermore group was developing two distinct processes, since the performance requirements for SRAMs and microprocessors differed. Although Intel had a good position in the low-volume, high-speed SRAM segment, it did not participate in the largest SRAM segment, which demanded higher density (more storage capacity).[15] The high-volume SRAM segment demanded a new four-transistor cell design and process. By contrast, the high-speed SRAM and the new 80386™ microprocessor both demanded a six-transistor CMOS design.

The high-volume SRAM process required a complex *polysilicon resistor* technology which was giving Smith's group difficulty. Smith described the environment as it had evolved in mid-1985:

> Eventually, we decided to drop the poly resistor process and go with a six-transistor CMOS SRAM product so that we could focus our attention on the 386 development. Basically, we sacrificed the high-volume SRAM for the 386™.
>
> To get an idea of the complexity of the 386™ development, compare it to the 286. The 286 team really comprised only six people. When it came time to develop the 386™, we had to come up with a double metalization process while at the same time reducing line widths to 1.5 μm (from 2 μm) and implementing the CMOS process. The 386™ process team had about 60 people: specialists in plasma etching, stepper alignment, chemical etching, and diffusion. If you compare the mask design for the 286 with the 386, you'll be able to tell how much area we saved by going to a double-layer metal. Lots of the 286 area was taken up with the routing of metal.

Gordon Moore described a linkage between market and technology development which may have contributed to the loss of a competitive SRAM product.

> Product designers want to see their product in high volume. So, it is important to have volume in a product line to get high-quality designers on board. For instance, SRAMs received less attention for that reason than I wish they had. We had a strong position in high-speed SRAMs, but we gave it up without really making a conscious decision.

The systems business at Intel had continued to grow with the company and by the end of 1984 represented the same 30 percent of revenue that MSO had represented in 1973. While a great deal of the systems business comprised development products aimed at microprocessor and microcontroller users, Intel also had vertically integrated into software development systems and single-board computers so that it could offer its customers options at several levels of integration.

Manufacturing and Process Fungibility

While tolerating some process proliferation within plants, Intel took great pains to standardize each facility as it expanded its manufacturing base. In 1973, Grove was pictured in a snapshot at his desk with a foot-long mock chip package. On its side was printed the McDonald's Golden Arches logo with "McIntel" substituted. Each Intel chip would "look and taste the same no matter which facility produced it."

As larger-diameter silicon wafers became available, Intel developed a process on one line and then transferred the technology to its other facilities. For example, a process for 4-inch-diameter wafers was first developed at Fab 3 in Livermore, California, by a team of three people. The team leader then super-

---

[13]Introduced in sample quantities in September 1984.

[14]Scaling improvements allowed Intel to reduce the chip size of existing products without expensive redesign. The reduced chip size led to reduced manufacturing costs.

[15]Intel's overall SRAM position had diminished significantly over the years as Japanese manufacturers gained market share.

vised the start-up of Fab 5 in Aloha, Oregon, which was dedicated to 4-inch wafers. In 1983, after delaying start-up due to the 1981–82 recession, Intel was the first semiconductor company to use 6-inch wafers at Fab 7, Rio Rancho, New Mexico (see Exhibit 8).

By 1984, Intel had seven fab areas in the United States, all within a two-hour flight of headquarters in Santa Clara. Due to more stringent manufacturing standards, the cost of a fab area had risen dramatically since the 1970s. A new fab area fully equipped cost between $150 million and $200 million and took about two years to construct. The first overseas fab area had just opened in Jerusalem, Israel. *Jack Carsten,* senior vice president and general manager of the Components Group, commented in retrospect on the decision to locate in Israel:

> Around the time we were deciding to put up a fab in Israel, I supported the idea of building a fab area in Japan. I had actually obtained leases on Japanese soil so that Intel could locate its first overseas fab area in Japan. That plant would have provided some insulation from currency fluctuations, but the Israel plant had tremendous government subsidies and a good labor market. A Japanese plant would have also put us into the pipeline of Japanese equipment vendors, and linked us into the Zaibatsu network. We could have tapped the expertise of Japanese DRAM technology development, silicon makers, mask makers, and the infrastructural support. This is what Texas Instruments did, because they had a commitment to local manufacturing. Eventually, we chose Jerusalem, largely because of the subsidies. This is not to say that the Israel facility is bad. It is a fine facility, but it certainly can't offer currency hedging against the Japanese yen.

Nearly all (97 percent) manufacturing capacity was devoted to MOS devices. Within MOS, the majority of processing was NMOS, but there was a trend towards increased CMOS. Each production facility was more or less dedicated to a particular process family (DRAM, Logic, or EPROM), although some facilities manufactured more than one family. Within each family, some process sequences were sometimes customized to accommodate particular product performance needs. While the equipment within any fab area was similar, different fab areas had different generations of equipment, and some processes required more of a particular machine for line balancing. Gordon Moore commented on the proliferation of process technologies:

> Over time, there has been a tendency to get more and more processes, and that complicates manufacturing allocations. In the past, we solved the problem by brutally getting out of businesses. But the customers didn't like that. For instance, we abdicated share in microcontrollers because we had to clean out somewhere to do other things.

While each facility could not produce every family of products, there was some fungibility between products and facilities. In times when demand was strong and capacity constrained sales, Intel division managers would get together monthly to decide how to load the factories. The chief financial officer, *Bob Reed,* described the process as being one that maximized margin per manufacturing activity:

> Basically, there are three main process areas: fabrication, assembly, and test. Assembly is usually not a constraining factor—you can ramp it up as fast as you need to. Similarly, test can be ramped up in the short term. Fabrication (the front end of the process) is usually the bottleneck in times of tight capacity—it takes long lead times to increase capacity. Since fabrication is the constraining resource, fabrication is the key variable for assigning cost to products.
>
> Each process sequence (EPROM, Logic, or DRAM) is assigned a total amount of manufacturing activity based on the number of steps it requires. Total company manufacturing costs are then allocated to products on the basis of manufacturing activity. For each product, the overall yield (number of good die at final test versus total number of die on starting wafer) is applied as a divisor to the process cost to arrive at a total cost per good part. The sales price per part is then used to calculate margin per part, and margin per activity (see Exhibit 8).

According to Reed, sometimes the numbers told a compelling story about the DRAM business. The difference between margin/activity for DRAMs and for the highest margin products could be an order of magnitude. Ron Whittier, general manager of the Memory Components Division from 1975 until 1983, felt that the system for plant allocation was a very good one:

> Some companies really went too far by selling capacity to the highest bidder within the company. At Intel, a minimum production allocation would be assigned based on how much we needed to produce to maintain our long term market position. Basically, we used our independent distributors as buffers. In times when DRAM production was pressured by other products, we tapered sales to independent distributors while maintaining sales to large account customers.

Grove commented that since the distributors never accounted for more than 20 to 30 percent of

EXHIBIT 8 Sample of Cost Accounting Data for Selected Intel Products in 1984

Product	Process	Raw Wafer Cost	Number of Mask Layers	Number of Activities	Cost per Activity	Line Yield	Cost per Wafer	Die per 6″ Wafer	Wafer Sort Yield	Total Cost per Die	Package/ Test Cost per Die	Yield at Test	Total Cost per Chip	Average Selling Price	Contribution Margin per Chip
64K DRAM	NMOS DRAM	60	8	30	72.00	90%	2,467	1900	90%	1.44	0.45	90%	2.103	2.05	−2%
64K DRAM	CMOS DRAM	100	10	38	72.00	84%	3,376	1806	85%	2.20	0.45	90%	2.944	3.08	4%
256K DRAM	CMOS DRAM	100	10	38	72.00	83%	3,417	922	60%	6.18	0.65	90%	7.585	16.27	53%
64K EPROM	NMOS EPROM	60	12	48	72.00	79%	4,451	1582	75%	3.75	2.65	90%	7.112	8.15	13%
256K EPROM	NMOS EPROM	60	12	48	72.00	78%	4,508	756	60%	9.94	2.45	90%	13.764	21.00	34%
80286	LOGIC	60	10	40	72.00	90%	3,267	172	70%	27.13	2.00	85%	34.273	250.00	86%
80386 (samples)	1.5 μm LOGIC	100	13	50	72.00	90%	4,111	131	30%	104.61	15.00	85%	140.716	900.00	84%

Key:
Raw wafer cost: Raw wafer cost differs depending on whether or not process is CMOS.
Number of mask layers: Refers to the number of times the wafer goes through the photolithography step.
Number of activities: Basic unit of manufacturing for cost accounting purposes. Refers to the number of times the wafer is physically altered in the process.
Cost per activity: An average of worldwide manufacturing costs, including depreciation, materials, labor, and other facilities costs.
Line yield: Ratio of wafers started to wafers completed.
Die per 6″ wafer: Number of devices on a 6″ wafer (function of die size).
Wafer sort yield: Number of good die divided by total die after all processing is completed and before wafer is sawed and devices are packaged.
Total cost per die: Cost per wafer divided by number of good die per wafer at wafer sort test.
Package/test cost: Cost of packaging and testing one device.
Yield at test: Number of devices entering packaging divided by number of devices which pass final test.
Total cost per chip: Total cost per die plus packaging and testing costs all divided by yield at test.

SOURCE: Casewriter estimates.

Intel's DRAM business, they could not really account for the leveling in Intel's DRAM sales (see Exhibit 4).

Whittier also noted that DRAMs had at one time been the single largest product line and thus could not easily be entirely displaced by other products unless total capacity was decreased. The finance group thought of DRAMs as a "low ROI, high beta" product line. Bob Reed insisted that the DRAM manager sign a symbolic check equal to the margin foregone whenever high-margin products were bumped by DRAMs.

Ed Gelbach explained why Intel had stayed with the DRAM even though it looked less profitable than other products:

> I was in favor of keeping DRAMs from a marketing strategy standpoint. A full line supplier has a basic advantage in any sales situation. When you're competing with full-line suppliers, it helps to be able to offer a comparable line. Since customers often pay particular attention to their highest-dollar-volume vendor, it also pays to offer the commodity product since it is generally purchased in high volume. A more subtle reason boils down to reputation. Intel had been known to drop unprofitable products, sometimes leaving customers high and dry.
>
> In board meetings, the question of DRAMs would often come up. I would support them from a market perspective, and Gordon [Moore] would support them because they were our technology driver. Andy [Grove] kept quiet on the subject. Even though it wasn't profitable, the board agreed to stay in it on the face of our arguments.

Environmental Forces

Bob Reed realized the entire U.S. semiconductor industry was in trouble even during the boom year of 1984.

> Even though ROS for the industry was relatively high in 1984, asset turns were decreasing and ROA was low. The business had become too capital intensive. An astute observer could see that the U.S. industry as configured couldn't provide its investors with an adequate return when a new plant cost $150 million and took at least two years to build. Intel was virtually alone with a respectable ROE.

In 1985, the semiconductor industry was expected to enter into another in a series of cyclical down turns which seemed to occur every five years. The cause of the cyclical recessions was a classic case of oversupply and softening demand. Since 1980, a large amount of worldwide semiconductor fabrication capacity had been added, and the learning curve effect (increase in yields, decrease in chip size, etc.) added another 30 percent per year to worldwide capacity.

In the previous recession, Intel had been one of a few companies not to cut back its production workforce. While Intel did not have a no-layoff policy, during the 1981–82 recession, Andy Grove had instituted the "125 percent solution." In that program all salaried employees were asked to work an additional 10 hours per week without additional compensation to accelerate product introductions. When the 1980 recession proved to be longer than expected, Intel instituted a 10 percent pay cut in addition to the 125 percent solution.

Intel had several groups of competitors (see Exhibit 9). The first were other U.S. full-line digital design and supply houses such as Motorola, National Semiconductor, and Texas Instruments (TI). Motorola had made the transition from a tube manufacturer in the 1950s to a diversified semiconductor and electronic systems manufacturer in the 1980s. It offered a full line of products competitive with Intel's, including DRAMs, microcontrollers, and microprocessors and was Intel's only serious challenger in microprocessor architecture. TI, while not renowned for its microprocessors, also had a complete product line, including a facility in Japan which was fabricating DRAMs.

The second category of competitor focused on process technology as opposed to design. That group was represented by AMD. While AMD produced a full line of component products, a significant portion was manufactured under license from Intel and others.

The third group included foreign competition, particularly Japanese. Japanese competitors included Hitachi, Fujitsu, NEC, Toshiba, and others. They had concentrated primarily on DRAM and SRAM products, although each also had a significant share of the EPROM market and served as second sources to U.S. microprocessor and microcontroller suppliers. Intel had second-source agreements for its microprocessor line with Fujitsu and NEC.

Several U.S. DRAM makers had accused Japanese manufacturers of dumping DRAMs at prices below cost throughout the early 1980s.

Industry observers saw that Japanese firms under the direction of MITI had targeted semiconductors as a strategic industry and were investing for the long term. In the years between 1980 and 1984, U.S.

EXHIBIT 9 Selected Competitor Data for 1984

FY 1984 (in millions of dollars)	Intel	National Semiconductor	Texas Instruments	Advanced Micro Devices	Motorola	Hitachi	Toshiba	NEC	Fujitsu
Semiconductor sales	$1,201	$1,213	$2,484	$ 515	$2,319	$2,051	$1,516	$2,251	$1,190
Total sales	1,629	1,655	5,741	583	5,534	18,528	11,003	7,476	5,401
COGS	883	1,146	4,190	276	3,206	13,632	8,182	5,117	3,346
R&D	180	158	367	101	411	898	597	391	(incl.)
SG&A	315	247	491	108	1,064	3,367	2,758	1,443	1,453
Other	(48)	1	168		387		(1,106)	673	335
Profit	299	103	525	98	466	631	572	367	523
Profit after tax	198	64	316	71	387	709	250	189	297
Depreciation	113	115	422	43	353		627		374
Capital expenditure	388	278	705	129	783		1,192	883	747
Total assets	2,029	1,156	3,423	512	4,194	7,997			5,699
LT debt	146	24	380	27	531	1,379	1,830	1,524	915
Total equity	1,360	619	1,540	278	2,278	6,118	2,191	1,728	1,935

Semiconductor Market Share in 1984	Bipolar Digital	EPROM	DRAM and SRAM	MOS Micro-component	MOS Logic	Linear	Discrete	Opto-electronic	Total (in millions)
AMD	5.4%	10.5%	0.5%	1.8%	0.1%	0.4%			$515
Fairchild	8.6%		0.1%	0.5%	0.7%	2.9%	1.3%	0.3%	665
Fujitsu	6.4%	11.1%	7.8%	3.7%	3.0%	0.8%	0.8%	4.3%	1,190
Hitachi	4.7%	17.4%	15.1%	3.7%	2.2%	3.7%	8.6%	4.3%	2,051
Intel	0.7%	16.0%	3.4%	23.0%	1.2%				1,201
Mitsubishi	2.6%	13.3%	4.0%	4.8%	0.4%	2.1%	3.7%	1.1%	964
Mostek			7.1%	1.7%	1.8%				467
Motorola	9.5%	1.1%	6.1%	9.0%	10.4%	5.5%	12.2%	1.6%	2,319
National	6.1%	4.2%	1.1%	3.6%	5.9%	8.9%	0.9%	1.2%	1,213
NEC	2.6%	5.8%	13.0%	12.7%	8.3%	5.9%	7.6%	2.8%	2,251
Philips	12.3%		0.7%	3.2%	3.7%	4.8%	4.4%	1.5%	1,325
TI	22.5%	10.5%	10.8%	3.6%	2.9%	8.4%	1.2%	4.1%	2,484
Toshiba	0.8%	3.6%	7.1%	2.2%	8.7%	4.7%	8.4%	8.8%	1,516
Others	14.4%	6.5%	21.3%	21.9%	50.3%	51.8%	50.9%	70.1%	10,900
Total market (in millions of dollars)	$4,783	$1,319	$4,906	$3,229	$3,493	$4,888	$4,986	$1,221	$29,061

Key:
MOS microcomponent: microprocessors, peripherals, and microcontrollers.
MOS logic: gate arrays, custom logic, application-specific ICs.
Linear: operational amplifiers, comparators, and other analog devices.
Discrete: single transistors, diodes, and thyristors.
Optoelectronic: LEDs, semiconductor lasers, and solar cells.

SOURCE: Dataquest and annual reports.

firms invested a total of 22 percent of sales in new plant and equipment while Japanese firms invested 40 percent. The result was that by 1983, Japanese total investment in semiconductors exceeded U.S. investment. Production yields of Japanese semiconductor companies exceeded those of U.S. producers by as much as 40%.[16]

DRAMs were not the only product under siege by the Japanese. *The Wall Street Journal* published a story in June 1984 which reported on a memo sent by Hitachi to its U.S. EPROM distributors. The memo said: "Quote 10% below their price; if they requote, go 10% again, don't quit until you win."[17]

Intel had been wary of Japanese semiconductor companies for some time and had sued NEC in 1982 when it alleged NEC copied its 8086 product without license. Peter Stoll, an 8086 designer at Intel, realized his chip had been copied when he discovered that NEC's 16-bit microprocessor had two transistors which were disconnected from the rest of the circuit at exactly the same place where he had disconnected them in a late revision of the Intel mask set.[18] This was considered evidence that NEC copied the chip without even understanding its design.

Bob Reed emphasized the importance of Intel's ability to protect its intellectual property:

> If our primary value added is in our design capability, we've got to protect that with vigilance. We have a strict policy of pursuing anyone or any company that appropriates our intellectual property—design or process.

In this highly competitive environment, managers at Intel and other companies often had to consider the problem of spin-off companies. Key engineers had sometimes left Intel to form their own companies with venture capital help. Their departure would stall research at a minimum and, according to Gordon Moore, could be seen as diluting the U.S. industry's ability to compete. Spin-offs were sometimes accused of taking technology with them.[19]

---

[16]"While the best U.S. companies obtained yields of 50–60 percent, the best Japanese were getting 80–90 percent." From Clyde Prestowitz, *Trading Places,* 1988, p. 46

[17]*The Wall Street Journal,* June 5, 1985.

[18]Clyde Prestowitz, *Trading Places,* 1988, p. 48.

[19]Intel had sued SEEQ for taking a technology for Electrically Erasable PROMS (EEPROMs). Excel, a spin-off from SEEQ was later sued by SEEQ. Note: Intel continued to pursue its own EEPROM process, but eventually decided not to participate in that market because it was too small. A second engineering team left Intel on friendly terms to found Xicor. In 1985, Xicor and Intel were negotiating a joint research project.

DRAM Situation in 1984

Loss of Leadership Position

By the end of 1984, Intel had lost significant market share in DRAMs (see Exhibits 4 and 9). The first real difficulties had come with the 64K generation. In 1980, Intel's 5-volt 16K DRAM was still a market success due to process innovations, and work was continuing on the 64K generation. DRAMs traditionally led the company in new technology development, and the 64K DRAM was no exception.

Ron Whittier said that to make the 64K version, the memory cell size was reduced, but the actual die size still had to be increased significantly. The DRAM group calculated that given current defect levels in manufacturing, the required die size would be too big. Based on the number of defects per square centimeter normally experienced in fabrication, the projected yield on the 64K DRAM would be too low to be acceptable. In order to boost yield, the group decided to build in redundancy at the chip level.

Whittier described the redundancy technology:

> Essentially, you have a row-and-column addressing system on a memory chip. The periphery of the chip contains logic and refresh circuitry necessary to control and update the DRAM. In the 64K version, Intel added an extra column of memory elements so that in the event of a process-induced defect, the auxiliary column could be activated. There was a physical switch, or "fuse," built in to each column which could be addressed by the tester machinery. When a bad element was detected, current would be passed through the switch and would blow a "fuse," inactivating the defective column and kicking in the auxiliary column. In this fashion, a defective memory chip could be "reprogrammed" before shipment, and overall yield could be improved.

Dean Toombs, general manager of the memory components division after 1983, had worked on DRAMs at Texas Instruments (TI) before coming to Intel. Toombs said the discussion on redundancy was industrywide. At TI, engineers had concluded that at the 64K generation redundancy would not be economical and had deferred the discussion until the next generation. For the 64K generation, TI ultimately chose to focus on reducing the defect level in manufacturing.

Intel's redundancy program started out successfully. Two 64K DRAM projects were carried out in tandem, one nonredundant and the other redundant. Prior to production commitment, the redundant design was a clear winner, with yields over twice that of the nonredundant design.

Success quickly turned to failure as a subtle but fatal defect in the redundant technology showed up late in development. The fuse technology was less than perfect. The polysilicon fuse would blow during testing as designed, but a mysterious regrowth phenomenon was detected during accelerated aging tests. Sun Lin Chou commented:

> The failing fuse problem was simply a case of not having done enough engineering early on. We just didn't fully characterize the process technology and the fusing mechanism.

The result was that the switch eliminating the defective column of memory cells was not permanent. In some cases, the device would revert to its original configuration after being in the field for some time—meaning the defective cell would again become a part of the memory. Errors would occur in which the device alternated randomly between the two states, meaning that at any given time the location of data stored in the memory became uncertain. In either case, the failures were not acceptable, and Intel could not develop a quick fix.

In the meantime, Japanese competitors were throwing capacity at 64K DRAMs and improving the underlying defect density problem which Intel's redundancy program had meant to address. Between July 1981, and August 1982, Japanese capacity for 64K DRAM production increased from 9 million to 66 million devices per year.[20] Whittier took a one-week trip to see Intel sales engineers[21] and explain that Intel's 64K DRAM would be late:

> The sales force was very disappointed in the company's performance. Any sales force wants a commodity line. It's an easy sell and sometimes it's a big sell. That trip was perhaps the most difficult time in my whole career. When I announced we would be late with the product, the implication was that Intel would not be a factor in the 64K generation.

While the development team eventually fixed the fuse problem and was the first to introduce a redundant 64K DRAM, the 2164, its introduction was too late to achieve significant market penetration.

---

[20]Clyde Prestowitz, *Trading Places,* 1988, p. 44.

[21]Intel sales engineers sold Intel's entire product line, but were supported by applications engineers in a ratio of one engineer to every two sales representatives.

Attempts to Regain Leadership Position

Having assessed that they were behind in the 64K DRAM product generation, the DRAM group took another gamble. The development effort was shifted from NMOS to CMOS. The advantage of CMOS circuitry was lower power consumption and faster access time. Intel defined a set of targeted applications for the CMOS DRAM technology.[22] Whittier's strategy was to introduce the CMOS 64K and 256K DRAMs in 1984. The notion was that by creating a niche market with premium pricing, Intel could maintain a presence in the DRAM market while accelerating forward into a leadership position at the 1-meg generation.

Dean Toombs said that by the time he took over the Memory Components Division in 1983, things were "clicking along." Demand was in an upswing, and Intel seemed to have a technology strategy which could lead to dominance in the 1-meg DRAM market. Many of the 2164 sales in 1983 went to IBM, and in addition Intel sold IBM the 2164 production and design technology. Toombs recalled that in late 1983 and early 1984, the silicon cycle was on an upswing and memory product demand was at an all-time high. The memory components division's bookings exceeded its billings.

During the boom of late 1983 and early 1984, all of Intel's factories were running at capacity. Allocation of production capacity between products was necessary. The question facing the memory components division was how to effect the transition from NMOS to CMOS. Toombs said the "hard decision" was made to completely phase out the NMOS line. All DRAM fabrication was consolidated in Oregon's Fab 5. Toombs suggested that the decision to "go CMOS" was consistent with Intel's general philosophy: to exploit new technology and create a lead against competitors based on proprietary knowledge.

The development of the CMOS 64K and 256K DRAMs took place in a facility adjacent to the Oregon production facility. While the development was not on the production line, there was a fairly smooth transition into manufacturing. The CMOS technology was more complex, requiring 11 to 12 masking steps versus 8 to 9 steps for NMOS. This resulted in a higher manufacturing cost for the CMOS process (see Exhibit 8).

---

[22]One such application was laptop computers, which place a premium on low-power consumption chips.

The CMOS DRAM products were introduced in 1984 and priced at about one and a half to two times the prevailing NMOS price. Intel management developed a niche strategy: differentiate the product from other offerings and sell it on features. In addition to the CMOS feature, Intel offered an alternative memory organization which provided performance advantages in some applications. Intel sampled the products broadly to many customers and made many design wins, particularly in situations where other DRAMs had inadequate performance. The 256K chip was well-designed and executed. Sun Lin Chou commented:

> The 256K CMOS DRAM was the first DRAM product which did not have to go through some sort of design or process revision before or after going to market. With this product, we felt we were regaining our lead in DRAM technology after three generations.

The CMOS DRAMs started as a winning product family. Unfortunately, the market softened as 1984 went along. The price of NMOS DRAMs fell by 40 percent in one three-month period from May to August 1984. In the scramble and upheaval of the semiconductor market, Toombs said that Intel's differentiation message got lost. All suppliers were pushing products into the market, and Intel's superior product specifications seemed like just another ploy to get volume.

By late 1984, Intel's ability to make profits and, more importantly, to project future profits in DRAMs was limited. Said Toombs: "In a commodity marketplace, your staying power is a function of the size of your manufacturing base." According to Toombs, by late 1984, Intel was down to less than 4 percent of the 256K DRAM market and had lost its position entirely in 64K DRAMs.

On the other hand, the technical strategy seemed to work, since the first prototype of the 1-meg DRAM was expected in March 1985. However, as Sun Lin Chou indicated, Intel's technology strategy for the 1-meg DRAM had been different from that of previous generations:

> Our advanced capability in thin dielectric has allowed us to focus on reducing the minimum feature size to one micron instead of changing the entire cell design. Some memory leaders have chosen to scrap the traditional capacitor design, and are trying to move to a smaller "trench" capacitor which requires an entirely new generation of equipment and processing. While they are still at 1.2 to 1.5 microns, we've pushed the photolithography technology further. We may have to go to the trench capacitor in the next generation [4 megabit], but by then we will be able to take advantage of their learning.

Toombs believed that the DRAM technology development group had provided Intel with a unique product capability:

> The 1-meg DRAM will be a technically outstanding product, at least one and a half to two years ahead of any competition in application of CMOS. But the handwriting is on the wall. In order to make the DRAM business go, major capital investment is required and the payback just isn't there. The issue for 1985 is how to survive.

Jack Carsten believed it was critical for Intel to stay in the DRAM business. But in case the company was no longer willing to dedicate facilities to DRAMs, he felt a technology transfer deal should be made with a Korean chip manufacturer:

> The play I am proposing is to stop manufacture of the DRAMs, and to form an alliance with a large Korean company who has state-of-the-art capacity installed. We now have a functional 1-meg DRAM. Basically, Intel could support the business through an R&D alliance and be the technology leader.
>
> To be fair, you have to realize that the Koreans have state-of-the-art equipment, but are not yet expert at using it.[23] In order to make the technology transfer work, we would have to transfer 20 or so of our crack engineers to teach the Koreans how to make the 1-meg DRAM. Apart from the technology risk, there is the risk that we would create a new competitor. History is rife with examples of how technology transfers have backfired, and we've certainly been burned before. But, maybe there's some truth to the logic that the enemy of your enemy is your friend.

Options for DRAM

Grove could see several distinct options for the DRAM business: (1) drop it all together, (2) stay in the business as a niche player, (3) license the tech-

[23]Note: In February 1985, Intel was to enter into an agreement with a Korean firm to transfer technology for two Intel parts. The technology had been developed at Intel to introduce the 8048 microcontroller (same generation as the 8085 microprocessor) and the 2764 EPROM (see Exhibit 3 for timeline). While those processes required 3- to 4-micron geometries, the 1-meg DRAM product required 1-micron geometries. The Korean company had annual semiconductor sales of about $10 million in 1984.

nology to another company, or (4) invest in DRAM capability at the 1-meg level and commit to a low-margin business.

As he reflected on the situation, he thought about how Intel had arrived at its current position:

> At the 16K level, we were leading in both EPROM and DRAM products, but capacity was tight. We reduced our committment to DRAMs in what was, in effect, a capital appropriations decision. Margins and customer dependence were both important in causing us to shift our focus to EPROMs.
>
> Then came the lackluster 64K design. We stumbled and it was a burning embarrassment. Our market position was at 2 to 3 percent. You just can't win like that.
>
> Gordon [Moore] is probably right when he says the only difference between DRAMs and EPROMs is that EPROMs never missed a turn. If you miss a turn, the game is over.
>
> The bright side is that we might have lost a lot more if our 64K generation had been a success. Texas Instruments is probably losing more than five times what we are.
>
> We have been trying to find a clever way to stay in this business without betting everything we have, but maybe there is none.
>
> The key question is, Should we really commit to being a leader? Can we be? What is the cost if we try? What is the cost if we don't?

TECHNICAL APPENDIX

Access: In this context, access refers to the circuitry which allows the DRAM user to read and write to specific locations of memory. Access time is a critical performance feature of DRAMs and refers to the amount of time it takes to read or write a bit of memory. Often DRAMs offer two different access modes, one that is bit by bit, and one that writes or reads large amounts of data. The bit-by-bit rate is typically slower.

Bus: Refers to the communication backbone of the microprocessor. An 8-bit bus can transfer 8 bits of data at a time between the microprocessor and the outside world (memory or other peripherals). The 8-bit-bus version of the 8086 actually has a 16-bit internal bus. Each cycle within the chip can handle two cycles of data input.

Bipolar: Refers to a generic type of transistor and to the family of processes used to make it. The bipolar transistor consumes more power than the MOS transistor, but can be made to switch faster. Excessive power consumption limits the density of bipolar products. The bipolar process is a relatively complex semiconductor process.

Capacitor: A circuit element (transistors, resistors, capacitors) which consists of two metallike layers separated by a thin insulating film. In a typical integrated circuit the silicon substrate (wafer) acts as the first metallike layer. The silicon surface is oxidized to form the insulating layer (silicon dioxide) and then a polysilicon layer is deposited over the oxide to form the second metallike layer. In the context of DRAMs, the capacitor acts as an information storage device. When a positive charge is placed on one surface of a capacitor, a negative charge is induced on the opposite surface. The capacitor holds the charge for a limited period of time, and the presence of the charge indicates a bit (binary digit) of information. The ability of the capacitor to store charge is related to its area and the thickness of the insulating film. The thinner the insulator and the larger the surface area, the more charge a capacitor can store. (See *trench etched capacitor* for more information.)

Chip: Chip refers to the actual integrated circuit which is cut from the wafer after fabrication. Typical chips are 100–400 mils on a side and can contain several hundred thousand transistors. The chip is put into a package where microscopic wires are attached to the die and brought out of the package in larger pins which can be soldered into a printed circuit board.

Class 10 production facility: Semiconductor fabrication plants are perhaps the cleanest areas ever created. Airborne particulates such as dandruff, pollen, and other forms of dust are a major source of semiconductor manufacturing yield problems. One particle of dust settled on a silicon wafer is enough to ruin an entire chip. The class number of a facility refers to the amount of particulate in the air. Class X means that 1 cubic foot of air on average will contain X or fewer particles. A class 10 fabrication facility is designed with advanced air-filtering designed to eliminate turbulence. Operators wear specialized clothing and enter clean rooms only through air showers which remove contamination. To give a sense of the cleanliness, a typical hospital operating room is between class 1,000 and 10,000.

Complementary MOS (CMOS): Refers to a semiconductor process which can produce a specific configuration of transistors which include both NMOS and PMOS devices. A group of six transistors fabricated in CMOS form the fundamental building block for Intel's latest generation of logic circuitry. The six-transistor cell is a bistable cell which is either in the on or off state. CMOS has the advantage of very low power consumption, since none of the transistors ever draws current except during the time when the six-transistor cell changes states from on to off. Laptop computers use exclusively CMOS integrated circuits.

Die: See *chip*.

Dielectrics: Refers to insulating materials. In semiconductor processing they include silicon dioxide, silicon nitride, silicon oxynitride, and others. Dielectrics are used in several areas of integrated circuits. In DRAMs they are used for storage capacitors. In MOS transistors, they form the gate insulator.

Double metalization: Until the 80386, all of Intel's circuits employed only one layer of metalization. The design of logic circuitry (where interconnection between groups of transistors appears to be random) is greatly simplified by adding a second layer of metal. Although the processing sequence is complicated, double-layer metalization allows chip size to be reduced.

Dynamic random-access memory (DRAM): A variety of RAM which maximizes utilization of silicon "real estate" and minimizes power consumption per storage bit. Each bit of information is stored as a charge on a capacitor driven by one transistor. Since the charge dissipates rapidly even when power is constantly supplied to the device, the information within each memory location must be rewritten (refreshed) hundreds of times a second. While the refresh function was originally taken care of by external circuitry, the latest DRAM chips have onboard refresh circuitry. DRAMs are available in 8K, 16K, 64K, 256K, and most recently in 1-meg sizes. K stands for kilobit and refers to the chip's storage capacity. See *kilobit* definition.

Electrically erasable programmable read-only memory (EEPROM): A variety of ROM which can be erased and programmed at the user's factory. The device is similar to the EPROM except it can be erased electrically (without ultraviolet light).

Electrically programmable read-only memory (EPROM): A variety of ROM which can be erased and programmed at the user's factory. The classical EPROM comes with a quartz window in its package so that ultraviolet light can be used to erase its contents. Then each memory location can be programmed to permanently contain desired information. In applications where low volume or time constraints prevent the fabrication of a custom ROM, or where the user may intend to make future modifications to its nonvolatile memory, EPROM devices are used. Sometimes EPROMs are supplied without quartz windows (cheaper). Since ultraviolet light cannot get in to erase these devices, they are programmable only once.

Floating gate: This is the structure in an EPROM device which allows a memory cell to be programmed and later erased. The floating gate can be charged by applying a relatively high voltage to the region surrounding it. Electrical traps in the floating gate store electrons which reach the floating gate. The trapped electrons can be sensed by surrounding structures. When ultraviolet light is directed at the floating gate, the light has sufficient energy to excite the trapped electrons out of the floating gate, and the memory is erased. See *EPROM* definition.

Gallium arsenide: A semiconductor material with properties considered by many to be superior to silicon's. The fastest switching transistors are made with gallium arsenide. Difficulty and expense in device fabrication, as well as constant silicon device improvement, have led to a relatively small market for gallium arsenide products.

Gate oxide: This is a critical part of the MOS transistor which is typically formed by oxidizing the surface of a silicon wafer (to make silicon dioxide) in a high-temperature (1000° C) furnace. The gate itself is typically formed out of a deposited layer of polycrystalline silicon. See definitions for *threshold drift* and *MOS*.

HMOS: An Intel acronym standing for high-performance MOS. HMOS is an NMOS process, with small geometries. See *NMOS* definition.

Kilobit (1K): 2^{10} or 1024 bits. Each DRAM generation has four times as much capacity as its predecessor. Since computers operate in binary code, the actual memory contents are multiples of 2. Thus, the 1K generation has 2^{10} bits, the 4K generation has 2^{12} bits, the 16K generation has 2^{14} bits, the 64K generation has 2^{16} bits, and so on.

Magnetic core: A form of random-access computer memory utilizing ferrite cores to store information. This technology was made obsolete by silicon devices.

Megabit (1 meg): 2^{20} or 1,048,576 bits. See definitions for *kilobit* and *DRAM*.

Metal oxide semiconductor (MOS): Refers to a generic type of transistor (see definition of *transistor*) and to the family of processes used to make it. The switch in an MOS transistor is caused by the action of the metal (or polycrystalline silicon) gate on the "channel." MOS transistors come in two polarities: n-channel (NMOS) or p-channel (PMOS). To turn on a p-channel device, a negative voltage is put on the gate. The charge on the gate induces an opposite charge in the channel which completes the circuit between the source and the drain. When the voltage is removed, the channel no longer conducts. The n-channel device turns on with a positive voltage applied to the gate. The MOS process typically requires fewer processing steps than the bipolar process. The turn-on speed on MOS devices is controlled by fundamental physics (the mobility of electrons and positive charges in silicon) and the geometry of the device (as devices get smaller, they get faster).

Multiplexing: A generic term used in many areas of electronics. In the case of the 4K and later DRAM generations, multiplexing refers to a scheme adopted to economize on the number of output pins required to address each memory location. Instead of using one pin for each column and each row in the matrix of memory cells, multiplexing allows the 4K memory to be addressed with just 12 pins (it contains 2^{12} bits).

Multitasking: Refers to a microprocessor's ability to manage more than one task simultaneously. Multitasking is not simply a software feature. The ability to employ multitasking is embedded in the chip's architecture.

NMOS: See *MOS*. Several generations of logic were built on NMOS circuitry. A cell of six NMOS transistors replaced Intel's traditional PMOS logic family. NMOS transistors are faster than PMOS devices due to fundamental physical properties.

Plasma etching: A process which is used to define patterns on the silicon wafer during the fabrication process. Until the early 1980s, all etching was done with wet chemicals. Plasma etching improves control and linewidth accuracy. It takes place in a partial vacuum chamber. Gaseous chemicals are introduced into the wafer chamber and ionized using radio frequency power. The ionic species selectively etch different materials used to build the integrated circuit. Plasma chemistry is a new discipline which has been brought to bear on semiconductor processing in order to achieve smaller linewidths and better etching control.

Polycrystalline silicon (poly, polysilicon): A material which can be used as a conductor. In the wafer fabrication process, polycrystalline silicon is deposited on the wafer surface (usually in a low-pressure, high-temperature process) and etched in patterns to form connections between transistors. It is also used to form the gate structure of a transistor (the gate turns the transistor on or off), the floating gate of an EPROM cell (stores the state of the EPROM cell), and one side of the storage capacitor which makes up a DRAM cell. Its main advantage as a material in processing is that it serves as a conductor while also being able to withstand high-temperature processing. While other conductive materials (such as aluminum) cannot withstand the high temperatures required by wafer processing and must be applied only at the end of the process, poly can be applied in the middle of the process and subsequently be covered by other layers.

Polysilicon resistor: By varying the conditions under which polysilicon is deposited on a wafer, lines of polysilicon can be used to form resistor elements. The poly resistor process was difficult for Intel to execute.

Random access memory (RAM): Formerly called direct-access memory. Family of information storage devices in which specific memory locations can be accessed (to retrieve or store information) in any sequence. This is distinct from sequential-access memory, in which data must be retrieved or stored in a specific order or sequence (example: magnetic tape memory, CCD memory, bubble memory). RAM is usually volatile memory. Thus, a constant power supply is required in order to retain stored information. Several processing technologies have been used to produce the two generic varieties of RAM, DRAM and SRAM.

Read-only memory (ROM): A variety of memory which contains a fixed set of information which cannot be altered, often referred to as nonvolatile memory. Within a typical computer system, ROM contains a sequence of data which has been embedded in the chip at the factory. Thus, ROM chips are custom-made for each application. Only one masking layer in a 10-layer fabrication process needs to be altered to change the information stored in a ROM.

Refresh: Since a dynamic RAM will hold data only for a fraction of a second before it is lost (the charge on the capacitor holds only for a fraction of a second before it leaks away), a useful DRAM must contain circuitry which can continually read and update the contents of each memory location. This circuitry is referred to as refresh circuitry.

Scaling improvements: Scaling improvements refer to the general process of decreasing linewidths in integrated circuits. In the early 80s, Intel's static/logic group focused on taking existing products and shrinking them to improve yield and increase manufacturing capacity. Devices would be shrunk proportionally (nearly), so that chip design would not have to be changed significantly.

Shift registers: A common type of sequential-access memory used in computer systems to manipulate strings of data.

Static random-access memory (SRAM): A RAM memory device which does not require refreshing as long as power is constantly applied. Each memory cell includes either four transistors and two resistors or six transistors. In comparison with DRAMs, fewer memory cells can be packed into the same area. SRAM memory can be made with faster access times than DRAM. The process for SRAM more closely resembles the process for logic devices. As a result, the on-chip memory contained in microprocessors is often SRAM.

Stepper alignment: The latest generation of photolithography processing is carried out on stepper aligners. The photolithography step has two key goals: to align the current mask layer to all previous layers and to transfer the narrowest possible line widths to the wafer. With traditional projection alignment, the pattern for the entire wafer is exposed at the same time. As wafer diameters increase and minimum geometries decrease, the alignment task becomes more difficult. The slightest thermal expansion or warpage will cause the devices on the edge of the wafer to be misaligned even when those in the center are aligned. Stepper aligners expose patterns across the wafer in several steps so that the run-off at the wafer edges can be minimized. At each step, the mask and the wafer are realigned. Stepper aligners are very sophisticated optical and mechanical devices, costing upwards of $1 million per unit.

Threshold drift: Refers to a phenomenon which causes the turn-on voltage of an MOS transistor to change over time. A certain critical voltage must be applied to the gate of an MOS transistor in order to turn it on. If the oxide insulator which separates the gate from the channel is not free of mobile ionic contamination, the threshold or turn on voltage will drift or change over time making the device useless. One source of mobile ionic contamination is common table salt.

Transistor: First invented at Bell Labs in 1948, the transistor is a solid-state device which can be thought of as an electrical switch. It is a three-terminal device: voltage applied to one terminal opens and closes the circuit between the other two terminals. Transistors are the fundamental building block for electronic and logic circuitry. Configurations of transistors can execute logic functions. The first transistors replaced vacuum tubes and were fabricated one at a time by fusing three material layers together in a "sandwich" structure. Bob Noyce (Intel) and Jack Kilby (TI) invented the "planar transistor," which allows fabrication and interconnection of many transistors on one substrate. While many variations exist, two basic types of transistors dominate the current market: bipolar and MOS (or FET) transistors.

Trench etched capacitor: A traditional capacitor is formed on the surface of the silicon wafer (see *capacitor* definition) and occupies a significant portion of a DRAM cell's area. A trench etched capacitor conserves silicon surface area because it is oriented perpendicular to the wafer surface. Vertical trenches are formed using a relatively new technique called reactive ion etching in which the wafer is exposed to a plasma in a strong electric field. Some manufacturers have chosen to adopt the trench structure in order to produce the 1-meg generation of DRAMs. (Note that another method of maintaining storage capacity while reducing area is to reduce the insulator thickness. This has been the traditional method, but has become more difficult in recent generations. Thin oxide capability is considered a key technological advantage. Current oxide [insulator] thicknesses are about 100 angstroms [one-hundred-millionth of a meter], considered to be near the limit of current manufacturing methods.)

Virtual memory addressing: This microprocessor feature allows the microprocessor to handle many users at the same time without confusing each user's tasks. More specifically, it refers to the microprocessor's ability to use its own protocol to keep track of memory locations regardless of the physical configuration of memory. For example, Intel's 80286 can assign up to one gigabyte of virtual memory addresses to different users. Those virtual memory addresses are then mapped into the physical memory addresses.

Wafer: A slice of silicon which serves as the substrate for integrated circuits. Each wafer contains up to several thousand chips. The first silicon wafers used in production were 2 inches in diameter. Most recently almost all of Intel's fabrication takes place on 6-inch-diameter wafers. In some processing steps such as diffusion, wafers are processed in batches of 25 to 50. Other processing steps such as photolithography take place on individual wafers, one at a time. As processing technology has become more and more complex and wafer size has increased, additional steps have been carried out on individual wafers as opposed to batches.

Reading II–12
Fading Memories: A Process Theory of Strategic Business Exit in Dynamic Environments

Robert A. Burgelman

Introduction

Why do some firms continue to survive while others do not? Arguments based on the study of evolutionary processes applied at the firm level posit that long-term survival depends, in part, on the firm's ability to use intraorganizational ecological processes to cope with external selection pressures.[1] Intraorganizational ecological processes allow firms to generate new businesses based on distinctive competencies and, through internal selection and retention processes, to change the mix of businesses in which they compete. Intraorganizational ecological processes thus allow firms to reduce their dependency on the vagaries of the competitive environment associated with any given business. But this also raises the question of how firms strategically exit from some existing businesses and how they redeploy or shed competencies associated with these.

Not much systematic research has focused on the intraorganizational processes leading to business exit. Organizational theorists have offered insights into the processes associated with organizational

---

 Administrative Science Quarterly 39 (1994), pp. 24– .

[1]R. A. Burgelman, "Intraorganizational Ecology of Strategy Making and Organizational Adaptation: Theory and Field Research," *Organization Science* 2 (1991), pp. 239–62; A. H. Van de Ven, "Suggestions for Studying Strategy Process: A Research Note," *Strategic Management Journal* 13 (Special Issue: Summer 1992), pp. 169–88.

decline,[2] permanently failing organizations,[3] and disbandings[4] but have not documented the processes leading to strategic business exit. Research in industrial organization economics has discussed exit primarily in the context of declining industries and has focused on capacity divestment decisions, using stylized models of competitive interaction[5] or cross-sectional research.[6] Strategic management research has focused on business exit primarily in the context of product-market positioning,[7] portfolio planning, or corporate restructuring.[8]

Focusing on the intraorganizational processes associated with strategic business exit offers the opportunity to examine from the inside out how the dynamics of firm-level distinctive competence match, or fail to match, the dynamics of the basis of competition in the industry. The issue of dynamically matching firm-level distinctive competence and industry-level sources of competitive advantage is particularly salient for firms facing technological change that is competence destroying[9] or that affects the relative importance of different technical competencies within the firm.[10] More generally, the issue is important for all firms facing structural industry change that causes shifts in the basis of competition.

Theory about the matching of firm-level distinctive competence and industry-level sources of competitive advantage remains underdeveloped in strategic management. Received theory has a prescriptive adaptive orientation and pays little attention to the possibility that the processes involved may be coevolutionary, at least in part. Building on Barnard[11] and Selznick[12], Andrews[13] has argued that the task of top management is to match distinctive competence with business opportunities. In the same line of thought, Prahalad and Hamel[14] have explained the success of companies such as Canon, NEC, and Ericsson in terms of the development of core competence. Their explanation depends to a large extent on strategic intent based on the chief executive officer's (CEO's) superior foresight. Such post hoc vision or grand strategy explanations beg important questions, from the perspective of an evolutionary theory of the firm.[15] This sort of explanation also does not sufficiently take into account the fact that strategy making in large, complex firms simultaneously involves multiple levels of management.[16]

---

[2]R. I. Sutton, "Organizational Decline Processes: A Social Psychological Perspective," in B. M. Staw and L. L. Cummings (eds.), *Research in Organizational Behavior*, vol. 12 (Greenwich, CT: JAI Press), pp. 205–53.

[3]M. W. Meyer and L. G. Zucker, *Permanently Failing Organizations* (Newbury Park, CA: Sage, 1989.)

[4]M. T. Hannan and J. H. Freeman, *Organizational Ecology* (Cambridge, MA: Harvard University Press, 1989).

[5]P. Ghemawat and B. Nalebuff, "Exit," *Rand Journal of Economics* 16 (1985), pp. 184–94; "The Devolution of Declining Industries," *Quarterly Journal of Economics* 79 (1990), pp. 167–86.

[6]K. R. Harrigan, "Deterrents to Divestiture," *Academy of Management Journal* 24 (1981), pp. 306–23; C. F. W. Baden-Fuller, "Exit from Declining Industries and the Case of Steel Castings," *Economic Journal* 99 (1989), pp. 949–61; M. B. Lieberman, "Divestment in Declining Industries: Shakeout or 'Stakeout'?" working paper, Graduate School of Business, Stanford University, 1989.

[7]For example: M. E. Porter, *Competitive Strategy* (New York: Free Press, 1980).

[8]For example: C. S. Gilmour, "The Divestment Decision Process," unpublished doctoral dissertation, Harvard Business School, 1973; C. C. Snow and D. C. Hambrick, "Measuring Organizational Strategies: Some Theoretical and Methodological Problems," *Academy of Management Review* 5 (1980), pp. 527–38; J. L. Bower, *When Markets Quake* (Boston: Harvard Business School Press, 1986).

[9]M. E. Tushman and P. Anderson, "Technological Discontinuities and Organizational Environments," *Administrative Science Quarterly* 31 (1986), pp. 439–65.

[10]R. M. Henderson and K. B. Clark, "Architectural Innovation: The Reconfiguration of Existing Product Technologies and the Failure of Established Firms," *Administrative Science Quarterly* 35 (1990), pp. 9–30.

[11]C. Barnard, *The Functions of the Executive* (Cambridge, MA: Harvard University Press, 1938).

[12]P. Selznick, *Leadership in Administration* (New York: Harper and Row, 1957).

[13]K. R. Andrews, *The Concept of Corporate Strategy* (Homewood, IL: Irwin, 1980).

[14]C. K. Prahalad and G. Hamel, "The Core Competence of the Corporation," *Harvard Business Review* 68, pp. 79–91.

[15]For example: S. Winter, "Survival, Selection, and Inheritance in Evolutionary Theories of Organization," in *Organizational Evolution: New Directions,* ed. J. V. Singh (Newbury Park, CA: Sage, 1990), pp. 268–97; Burgelman, "Intraorganizational Ecology of Strategy Making and Organizational Adaption"; R. R. Nelson, "Why Do Firms Differ, and How Does It Matter?" *Strategic Management Journal* 12 (Special Issue, Winter 1991), pp. 61–74; Van de Ven, "Suggestions for Studying Strategy Process."

[16]For example: J. L. Bower and I. Doz, "Strategy Formulation: A Social and Political Process," in *Strategic Management: A New View of Business Policy and Strategic Planning,* ed. D. E. Schendel and C. W. Hofer (Boston: Little Brown, 1979), pp. 152–65; R. A. Burgelman, "A Process Model of Internal Corporate Venturing in the Diversified Major Firm," *Administrative Science Quarterly* 28 (1983), pp. 223–44.

This paper reports longitudinal field research on the processes leading to strategic business exit. The paper documents the processes leading Intel Corporation to exit from dynamic random access memory (DRAM) design and manufacturing in 1984–1985, to halt capacity expansion for erasable programmable read only memory (EPROM) manufacturing in 1991, and to transform itself from a "memory" company into a "microcomputer" company. The paper examines why Intel's distinctive competence was deployed and developed in ways that diverged from the evolving basis of competition in the DRAM industry and why it took top management several years to come to the conclusion that Intel's strategic position in the DRAM business was no longer viable and that exit was necessary. It also examines why middle-level managers were able to shift scarce manufacturing resources gradually from the DRAM business to new, more profitable opportunities in the microprocessor business without a preceding reconsideration of the official corporate strategy. Finally, the paper elucidates further the role played by internal selection processes in maintaining Intel's ability to make viable strategic decisions while its official corporate strategy was in flux.

Method

This study is part of an ongoing research project that tracks the evolution of Intel Corporation's corporate strategy. Intel was founded by Robert Noyce and Gordon Moore, who left Fairchild in the summer of 1968. Andy Grove, who had been Moore's assistant director of research at Fairchild, also left to join Intel, completing what the company's historians have called the triumvirate. Intel was the first company to specialize in making large-scale integrated circuit memory products. The company's strategy in 1968 was to build semiconductor memory products for mainframe computers in competition with the "core memory" standard of the day. In 1991, Intel was a leading microcomputer company that had survived for more than 20 years as an independent company in an extremely dynamic industry. The firm grew from $1 million in sales in 1968 to $4.8 billion in 1991. Profits rose from a loss of $2 million in 1969 to over $800 million in 1991.

Research Design

The research was based on a longitudinal, two-stage, nested case study design within one corporate setting.[17] Archival and interview data were collected on the evolution of two semiconductor memory businesses—DRAM and EPROM—and the microprocessor business at Intel. These cases were selected for theoretical reasons as an intentional sample.[18] The selection criterion was strategic importance to the firm. DRAMs were the business that had made Intel successful during the 1970s. EPROMs, during the mid-1980s, still accounted for about 15 percent of Intel's business. Microprocessors had become Intel's largest source of revenue by 1982 and grew rapidly during the mid-1980s.

The research was carried out in two stages. The first stage, from fall 1988 through spring 1989, focused on the decision to exit DRAMs during 1984–1985. The second stage of the research, from fall 1990 through spring 1991, focused on the implementation of the DRAM exit decision. It sought to document the difficulties that Intel encountered in getting the organization to stop all activity in DRAMs. During this stage of the research, Intel top management also made important decisions regarding EPROMs and microprocessors.

Data Collection

Interview and archival data were collected. All data collection was longitudinal. For DRAM, data were historical, covering the period 1971–1985. For EPROMs and microprocessors, historical data were combined with current data obtained during the research period.

Interview data. Twenty-seven key Intel managers were formally interviewed, many of them

---

[17]R. K. Yin, *Case Study Research: Applied Social Research Methods Series, vol. 5* (Beverly Hills, CA: Sage, 1984); D. Leonard Barton, "A Dual Methodology for Case Studies: Synergistic Use of a Longitudinal Single Site with Replicated Multiple Sites," *Organization Science* 1 (1990), pp. 248–66.

[18]B. G. Glaser and A. L. Strauss, *The Discovery of Grounded Theory* (Chicago: Aldine, 1967); K. M. Eisenhardt, "Building Theories from Case Study Research," *Academy of Management Review* 14 (1989), pp. 532–50.

repeatedly, yielding close to 200 pages of written interview notes. Seventeen of these managers were interviewed during the first stage of the research. Some top managers who had previously left the company were included as well. Managers from different levels, different functional groups, and different businesses who had been involved in or affected by the decision were asked to discuss the causes of Intel's exit decision. Ten additional managers, most of whom were at lower and middle levels in the organization in the mid-1980s, were formally interviewed during the second stage of the research. These interviews provided a more detailed account of how the DRAM exit decision was perceived and experienced by front-line managers. Many of the managers previously interviewed were contacted again to clarify differences and discrepancies. Throughout the research period, informal discussions with current and former Intel employees were used to corroborate data obtained from the formal interviews. The head of R&D of one of the leading Japanese photolithography equipment suppliers was also interviewed. This company had an important impact on the evolution of the DRAM industry, and the interviewee had significant experience with DRAMs in another major U.S. semiconductor company earlier in his career. Exhibit 1 lists the managers who were formally interviewed, with the job they held in 1984–1986 and the number of times they were interviewed.

The interviews lasted between one and two hours and were open-ended. Follow-up interviews were semistructured, for clarification about key events, people, and issues that had been identified. Key events centered primarily around the introduction of successive generations of products in each of the businesses, because these introductions drove and were driven by the competitive dynamics in the industry. Key people were individuals or groups from different functional areas or different hierarchical levels who made critical decisions or made proposals that, while not necessarily implemented, triggered high-level reconsideration of strategic issues. Key issues included the importance of DRAMs as a technology driver at Intel, the importance of DRAMs in Intel's product market strategy, the allocation of scarce manufacturing capacity, the allocation of R&D resources to different businesses, the integration of process technology development and manufacturing, the retention and deployment of key talent, and, more generally, Intel's ability to compete in commodity businesses. No tape recorder was used, but the interviewers made extensive notes. I conducted 15 of the interviews with a research associate. Transcripts of the research associate's notes, when compared with mine, showed consistent agreement on the substantive content of the interview. This provided some confidence that the data were valid and reliable.

Archival data. Archival data, such as documents describing the company's history, annual reports, and reports to financial analysts, were obtained from Intel. The company also provided a statement on the evolution of Intel's approach to the development of computer-aided design tools throughout the 1980s, written specifically for this research. Additional archival data were obtained from Dataquest and from written materials, such as industry publications and financial analysts' reports and business press articles about Intel and the semiconductor industry. These archival data made it possible to construct a quantitative picture of the evolution of the semiconductor industry and Intel's evolving strategic position in major segments. The archival data could be juxtaposed to the interview data to check for potential systematic biases in retrospective accounts of past strategy.[19] Discrepancies between interview data and archival data discovered in the course of the research raised a number of questions that guided further data collection and analysis. Jelinek and Schoonhoven's study[20] of the innovation process at Intel was a fortuitous source of additional data as well as a validity check for the new data collected in this study. Data collection was concluded when a level of saturation was reached.[21]

Limitations

The study is subject to the general limitations associated with field research but also has some specific limitations. First, the research concerns a single and successful corporation in the semiconductor industry that is still run by some of its founders. While it

[19]B. R. Golden, "The Past Is the Past—Or Is It? The Use of Retrospective Accounts as Indicators of Past Strategy," *Academy of Management Journal* 35 (1992), pp. 848–60.

[20]M. Jelinek and C. B. Schoonhoven, *The Innovation Marathon* (Cambridge, MA: Basil Blackwell, 1990).

[21]Glaser and Strauss, *The Discovery of Grounded Theory.*

EXHIBIT 1 Interviewees

Job in 1984–86 Period (except as stated)	Number of Interviews
1. Chief executive officer.	2
2. Chief operating officer.	4
3. Chief financial officer.	1
4. Senior VP and general manager (GM), Components Division.	2
5. Senior VP and GM, Systems Division.	2
6. Director, Assembly/Test.	3
7. Director, Technology Development (TD).	3
8. Director, Memory Components Division (early 1980s).	2
9. Director, Memory Components Division (July 1983 to early 1985).	1
10. Head, DRAM Memory Operations; supervised design, marketing/sales, and customer support.	1
11. Head, Fabrication Facility (Fab) 5 TD (DRAM).	3
12. Head, Fab 3TD (Logic/SRAM).	1
13. Head, Fabs 4,5,8 Manufacturing.	1
14. Head, Fab 5 Manufacturing.	1
15. Project manager, Fab 5TD—1 micron DRAM.	1
16. Supervisor, Fab 3, of TD and manufacturing group leaders; brought in to make TD and manufacturing integrate efforts for the 1.5 micron 80386 microprocessor.	1
17. Fab 3 Manufacturing (group leader).	1
18. Fab 3 Manufacturing group leader; associated with Component Contracting in 1991.	1
19. Head, Component Contracting in 1991.	1
20. DRAM designer.	1
21. Responsible for closing Barbados assembly and Puerto Rico test facilities in 1986.	1
22. General manager, Application Specific Integrated Circuits in the Microcomputer Division in 1988.	1
23. Development manager, Microcomputer Division in 1988.	1
24. Responsible for Intel's Computer-Aided Design Group throughout the 1980s.	1
25. Product development manager for the i860 (RISC) microprocessor in 1988.	1
26. Manager assigned to study and make strategic recommendations for Intel's memory businesses in the mid 1980s.	1
27. Personal assistant to Andy Grove in 1988.	2
28. Senior VP and chief technical officer, Nikon Precision Inc. in 1991.	2

would be useful to study a larger sample that includes failing organizations, few in-depth studies of strategy-making processes of semiconductor firms exist. By concentrating on one organization with more than 20 years of continuity in leadership, the researchers had access to sources with intimate knowledge of the details of the firm's evolution and could examine in depth how the organization had dealt with potential failure. Having excellent access made it possible for the researchers to put themselves into "the manager's temporal and contextual frame of reference."[22] Excellent access also made it possible to reconstruct the strategic business exit with input from people at the different levels of management involved in the process. This provided a basis for triangulation and may alleviate some of the concerns associated with retrospective data.[23] Second, the semiconductor industry is extremely cyclical and expansive[24] and of the high-velocity

[22]Van de Ven, "Suggestions for Studying Strategy Process," p. 181.

[23]For example: Golden, "The Past Is the Past—Or Is It?"

[24]D. W. Webbink, *The Semiconductor Industry: A Survey of Structure, Conduct and Performance*, Staff Report to the Federal Trade Commission, Washington, DC, 1977; J. W. Brittain and J. H. Freeman, "Organizational Proliferation and Density Dependent Selection: Organizational Evolution in the Semiconductor Industry," in *The Organizational Life Cycle,* ed. J. B. Kimberly and R. H. Miles (San Francisco: Jossey-Bass, 1980), pp. 291–338; Jelinek and Schoonhoven, *The Innovation Marathon*; K. M. Eisenhardt and C. B. Schoonhoven, "Organizational Growth: Linking Founding Team, Strategy, Environment, and Growth among U.S. Semiconductor Ventures, 1978–1988," *Administrative Science Quarterly* 35 (1990), pp. 504–29.

type.[25] Hence, some of the phenomena documented in this study may not be generalizable to companies operating in less rapidly changing environments.[26]

Conceptual Framework

Stages of strategic business exit. Data analysis and conceptualization were iterative.[27] The analysis of DRAM case data suggested that the exit process comprised several partly overlapping stages that bracketed key events: (1) Intel's initial success in the DRAM industry, (2) the emergence of external competition and Intel's competitive responses, (3) internal competition for resources between Intel's memory and microprocessor businesses, (4) growing doubts among Intel's top management about the viability of the DRAM business, (5) Intel's strategic decision to exit from DRAMs and its implementation, and (6) articulation of new official corporate strategy and internal "creative destruction" of obsolete routines associated with Intel's early success. Cross-case analysis suggested that the stages were roughly the same for DRAMs and EPROMs but that the time taken by each stage was generally longer for EPROMs.

Questions raised in data collection. Several questions emerged in the course of the longitudinal data collection and were brought into sharper focus by the stages framework. The first question—Why did Intel, the first successful mover in DRAMs, fail to capitalize on and defend its early lead?—focused attention on the changing industry structure and Intel's evolving strategy in DRAMs. It required examining why Intel, a company well suited to developing, marketing, and profiting from innovative products, would not or could not effectively compete in commodity businesses. This, in turn, required examining how inertial forces associated with Intel's distinctive competence affected its competitive responses.

The second question—How did it happen that the bulk of Intel's business had shifted away from DRAMs and DRAM market share was allowed to dwindle while top management, even in 1984, was still thinking of DRAMs as a strategic business for the company?—directed attention to sources of inertia in official corporate strategy and to actions by middle-level managers that were not in line with the professed corporate strategy of Intel, the "memory company." It also directed attention to the fact that top management viewed DRAMs not only as a product but also as a core technology of the firm. The third question—How was it possible that middle-level managers could take actions that were not in line with the official corporate strategy?—directed attention to the role played by Intel's internal selection environment, constituted, in part, by its organization structure, its resource allocation process, and its culture of constructive confrontation. The fourth question—If not planned by top management, how did microprocessors and EPROMs come about at Intel in the first place?—focused attention on the evolution of Intel's distinctive competence, which produced unanticipated innovations, and on the role played by top management in the internal selection processes in supporting these innovations.

The fifth question—If Intel exited from DRAMs because they had become a commodity business, how would that affect the future of EPROMs, which had also become a commodity business by 1988?—was answered during the second stage of the research (1990–1991): Intel decided to halt expansion of manufacturing capacity in EPROMs in 1991. This question focused attention on the organizational learning processes associated with strategic business exit. Finally, the sixth question—Why did it take Intel's top management almost a year to complete the exit from DRAMs after the November 1984 decision not to market 1-meg(abit) DRAMs?—helped determine that Intel was not simply "harvesting" the DRAM business and helped clarify further the intricacies top management faced in determining which key elements of distinctive competence associated with DRAMs to retain and how to do so.

Forces driving strategic business exit. Addressing these questions suggested that the stages in

---

[25]K. M. Eisenhardt, "Making Fast Strategic Decisions in High Velocity Environments," *Academy of Management Journal* 32 (1989), pp. 543–76.

[26]J. R. Williams, "How Sustainable Is Your Competitive Advantage?" *California Management Review* 34 (1992), pp. 29–51.

[27]Glaser and Strauss, *The Discovery of Grounded Theory*; Burgelman, "A Process Model of Internal Corporate Venturing in the Diversified Major Firm"; Eisenhardt, "Building Theories from Case Study Research."

the strategic business exit process could be explained in terms of interplays between dynamic, mostly exogenous industry-level forces and dynamic, mostly endogenous firm-level forces. Five categories of forces were identified: (1) The *basis of competitive advantage* in the semiconductor memory business was determined by evolving industry-level forces, including those identified by Porter,[28] as well as the emergence of dominant designs[29] and changing appropriability regimes.[30] (2) *Distinctive competence* concerned the differentiated skills, complementary assets, and routines Intel evolved to create sustainable competitive advantage in the memory and microprocessor businesses.[31] (3) *Official corporate strategy* reflected top management's beliefs about the basis of the firm's past and current success.[32] Key beliefs concerned the core business of the firm (Intel the "memory company") and the relative importance of particular technological competencies for competitive advantage (DRAMs as "technology driver"). (4) *Strategic action* was what Intel actually did. In principle, official corporate strategy and strategic action should be closely related; however, strategic action depended on initiatives taken by middle-level managers who responded more to external and internal selection pressures than to official corporate strategy.[33]

EXHIBIT 2 Forces Driving the Strategic Business-Exit Process

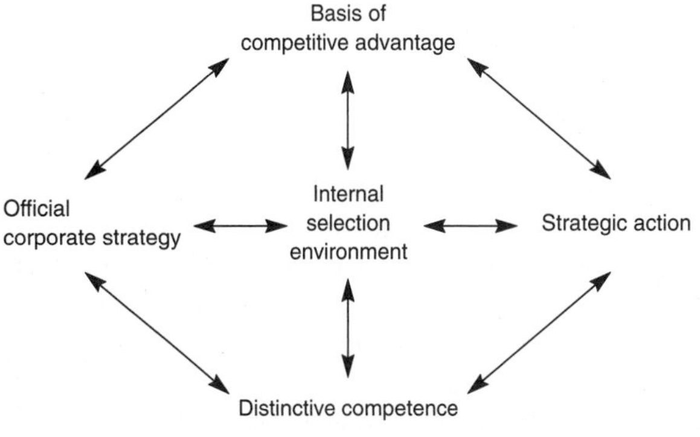

(5) Intel's *internal selection environment* mediated the link between corporate strategy and strategic action as well as the coevolution of industry-level sources of competitive advantage and firm-level sources of distinctive competence. It encompassed the structural and strategic contexts shaping the strategic actions of middle-level managers.[34] The conceptual framework constituted by these five categories of forces and their interplays are illustrated in Exhibit 2 and served to organize the discussion of the key findings.

Discussion: Process Theory of Strategic Business Exit

The conceptual framework and findings reported in the preceding sections (not published here) serve as building blocks for the construction of a grounded process theory of strategic business exit.[35] They yield several testable theoretical propositions concerning forms of internal inertia and the role of inter-

[28]*Competitive Strategy*.

[29]J. M. Utterback and W. Abernathy, "A Dynamic Model of Process and Product Innovation," *Omega* 33 (1975), pp. 639–56.

[30]D. J. Teece, "Profiting from Technological Innovation: Implications for Integration, Collaboration, Licensing, and Public Policy," *Research Policy* 15 (1986), pp. 285–305.

[31]P. Selznick, *Leadership in Administration*; D. J. Teece, G. Pisano, and A. Shuen, "Firm Capabilities, Resources, and the Concept of Strategy." Working Paper #90–9, University of California at Berkeley, Center for Research in Management, 1990.

[32]Burgelman, "A Process Model of Internal Corporate Venturing in the Diversified Major Firm," and "Intraorganizational Ecology of Strategy Making and Organizational Adaption"; G. Donaldson and J. W. Lorsch, *Decision Making at the Top* (New York: Basic Books, 1983); K. E. Weick, "Substitutes for Corporate Strategy," in *The Competitive Challenge,* ed. D. J. Teece (Cambridge, MA: Ballinger, 1987), pp. 221–33.

[33]For example: H. Mintzberg, "Patterns in Strategy Formation," *Management Science* 24 (1978), pp. 934–48; J. B. Quinn, *Strategies for Change* (Homewood, IL: Irwin, 1980); Burgelman, "A Process Model of Internal Corporate Venturing in the Diversified Major Firm" and "Intraorganizational Ecology of Strategy Making and Organizational Adaption"; H. Mintzberg and A. McHugh, "Strategy Formation in an Adhocracy, *Administrative Science Quarterly* 30 (1985), pp. 160–97.

[34]J. L. Bower, *Managing the Resource Allocation Process* (Boston: Harvard Business School Press, 1970); Burgelman, "A Process Model of Internal Corporate Venturing in the Diversified Major Firm."

[35]Glaser and Strauss, *The Discovery of Grounded Theory*; Mohr, *Explaining Organizational Behavior* (San Francisco: Jossey Bass, 1982), p. 95.

nal selection in strategic business exit that contribute to the development of a dynamic theory of the role of strategy in firm evolution.[36]

Forms of Internal Inertia

Relative inertia in distinctive technological competence. Earlier research has found inertial tendencies in the strategic responses of firms faced with radical[37] or architectural[38] technological innovation that led to their having to exit certain businesses or, in some cases, to their demise. The present study suggests that inertial tendencies may also drive the strategic responses of firms facing industry-level changes that move patterns of technological innovation from "fluid" to "specific,"[39] leading to forced exit. Intel continued to rely on process technology (TD) competence to compete even though the basis of competitive advantage in the DRAM industry had shifted toward large-scale precision manufacturing. Inertia in Intel's technological competence deployment did not preclude it from trying to adapt, but it influenced the trajectory of adaptive efforts. Inertial forces led to adaptive efforts based on TD advances that were, in four successive DRAM generations, too early in relation to industry dynamics. Dwindling market share eventually forced Intel to exit from the DRAM business. The study of strategic business exit thus suggests the need to consider inertial forces that make it difficult for firms to continue matching distinctive technological competence with the evolving basis of competition in the industry.[40] More formally:

> **Proposition 1a:** The stronger a firm's distinctive technological competence, the stronger the firm's tendency to continue to rely on it in the face of industry-level changes in the basis of competitive advantage.

Proposition 1a is consistent with earlier findings showing that core competence may become a competence trap[41] or core rigidity,[42] but this study also confirms that the productive potential of a firm's technological competencies may extend beyond the boundaries set by its product-market strategy at any given time.[43] Through the autonomous strategic initiatives of middle-level managers, technological competencies may engender unanticipated innovations that are outside the scope of the official corporate strategy.[44] This study suggests that such innovations may trigger coevolutionary processes that change the mix of the firm's distinctive technological competencies and its product-market strategy. Inertia looked at with dismay from current product-market positioning or portfolio-planning perspectives may thus sometimes be looked at more favorably from a resource or competence-based perspective.[45] More formally:

> **Proposition 1b:** The stronger the firm's technological competence, the higher the probability that it will generate unanticipated innovations that, if successful, will change the firm's mix of distinctive competence and product-market position.

Proposition 1b does not imply that unanticipated technological innovations are viable, nor that the firm will necessarily pursue them. But it does suggest the need to reexamine the processes driving technological leaders and first movers.[46] It seems quite possible that such competitive stances—often associated with "technology push"—may originate from inertial forces associated with the firm's dis-

---

[36]For example, M. E. Porter, "Towards a Dynamic Theory of Strategy," *Strategic Management Journal* 12 (Special Issue, Winter 1991), pp. 95–118.

[37]A. C. Cooper and D. E. Schendel, "Strategic Responses to Technological Threats," *Business Horizons* 19 (1976), pp. 61–73; Tushman and Anderson, "Technological Discontinuities and Organizational Environments."

[38]Henderson and Clark, "Architectural Innovation."

[39]Utterback and Abernathy, "A Dynamic Model of Process and Product Innovation."

[40]Andrews, *The Concept of Corporate Strategy.*

[41]B. Levitt and J. G. March, "Organizational Learning," in *Annual Review of Sociology,* vol. 14, ed. W. R. Scott (Palo Alto, CA: Annual Reviews, 1988), pp. 319–40.

[42]D. Leonard-Barton, "Core Capabilities and Core Rigidities: A Paradox in Managing New Product Development," *Strategic Management Journal* 13 (Special Issue, Summer 1992), pp. 111–26.

[43]For example: K. L. R. Pavitt, M. J. Robson, and J. F. Townsend, "Technological Accumulation, Diversification, and Organization of U.K. Companies, 1945–83," *Management Science* 35 (1989), pp. 81–99.

[44]Burgelman, "A Process Model of Internal Corporate Venturing in the Diversified Major Firm" and "Intraorganizational Ecology of Strategy Making and Organizational Adaption."

[45]For example: E. T. Penrose, *The Theory of the Growth of the Firm* (Oxford: Basil Blackwell, 1968); B. Wernerfelt, "A Resource-Based View of the Firm," *Strategic Management Journal* 5 (1984), pp. 171–80; J. B. Barney, "Strategic Factor Markets: Expectations, Luck, and Business Strategy," *Management Science* 32 (1986), 1231–41.

[46]For example: M. E. Porter, "The Technological Dimension of Competitive Strategy," in *Research on Technological Innovation,*

tinctive technological competence as well as from official corporate strategy.

Inertia of official corporate strategy relative to strategic action. A second form of relative inertia was associated with Intel's official corporate strategy. While Intel is widely regarded as one of the most innovative and adroitly managed high-technology firms, the DRAM exit story suggests that even extraordinarily capable and technically sophisticated top managers, such as Gordon Moore and Andy Grove, do not always have the foresight of the mythical Olympian CEO making strategy. Rational justification, emotional attachment, and bounded rationality, mixed with valid concerns about protecting a core technology of the firm, made it very difficult for Intel's top management to exit from DRAMs. At the same time, actions by some middle-level managers responding to external and internal selection pressures had already begun to dissolve the strategic context of DRAMs and undermine the reality of "Intel the memory company." Incremental shifts in the allocation of scarce manufacturing resources from DRAMs to microprocessors and technological trade-offs favoring microprocessors over DRAMs happened before the official corporate strategy was restated. The study of strategic business exit thus confirms that strategic actions often diverge from statements of strategy,[47] that resource allocation and official strategy are not necessarily tightly linked,[48] and that strategic actions of complex firms involve multiple levels of management simultaneously.[49] In addition, the findings suggest that these middle-level actions provide potentially important signals about the evolution of external selection pressures, especially in dynamic environments. More formally:

Proposition 2: In dynamic environments, actions of middle-level managers that diverge from official corporate strategy may signal important changes in external selection pressures.

The Role of Internal Selection

Prevents escalation of commitment. To some extent, Intel was lucky that there was some fungibility between products and fabs, which reduced exit barriers,[50] and that the maximize-margin-per-wafer-start rule prevented escalation of commitment[51] to the DRAM business during the period that Intel's official corporate strategy was in flux. This type of short-term-oriented rule, in isolation, might equally well have thwarted development of new technologies or strategic thrusts, but this rule was only one element of the internal selection environment created by top management. The maximize-margin-per-wafer-start rule required product divisions to compete for shared manufacturing resources and forced open debates concerning resource allocation. The criteria governing these debates were constructive confrontation based on knowledge rather than hierarchical position and economic performance in the market place rather than success in internal politicking. These criteria ensured that the internal selection processes accurately reflected the competitive pressures faced by different businesses in their external environment. They became the focal point[52] around which the organization came together and prevented the coevolution of its distinctive competence and the basis of competition in the DRAM industry before the official strategic decision to exit from DRAMs had been made.

Once established by top management, the internal selection environment constrained the purposeful behavior of individual participants.[53] It was difficult,

Management, and Policy, ed. R. S. Rosenbloom (Greenwich, CT: JAI Press, 1983), pp. 1–33; Teece, "Profiting from Technological Innovation"; R. A. Burgelman and R. S. Rosenbloom, "Technology Strategy: An Evolutionary Process Perspective," in *Research on Technological Innovation, Management, and Policy,* vol. 4, ed. R. S. Rosenbloom and R. A. Burgelman (Greenwich, CT: JAI Press, 1989), pp. 1–28; M. B. Lieberman and D. B. Montgomery, "First-mover Advantages," *Strategic Management Journal* 9 (1989), pp. 41–58.

[47]C. Argyris and D. A. Schon, *Organizational Learning: A Theory of Action Perspective* (Reading, MA: Addison-Wesley, 1978); Mintzberg, "Patterns in Strategy Formation."

[48]Bower, *Managing the Resource Allocation Process.*

[49]Burgelman, "A Process Model of Internal Corporate Venturing in the Diversified Major Firm."

[50]Porter, *Competitive Strategy.*

[51]B. Staw, L. E. Sandelands, and J. E. Dutton, "Threat-Rigidity Effects in Organizational Behavior: A Multilevel Analysis," *Administrative Science Quarterly* 26 (1981), pp. 147–60.

[52]T. C. Schelling, *The Strategy of Conflict* (Cambridge, MA: Harvard University Press, 1960); C. Camerer and A. Vepsalainen, "The Economic Efficiency of Corporate Culture," *Strategic Management Journal* 9 (1988), pp. 155–26; D. M. Kreps, "Corporate Culture and Economic Theory," in *Rational Perspectives on Positive Political Economy,* ed. J. Alte and K. Shepsle (Cambridge, MA: Cambridge University Press, 1990).

[53]J. S. Coleman, "Social Theory, Social Research, and a Theory of Action," *American Journal of Sociology* 91 (1986), pp. 1309–35.

even for the top managers themselves, to deviate from the criteria constituting the internal selection environment. As DRAMs began to lose out in the resource allocation process, middle-level managers of the DRAM business attempted to change Intel's structural context and lobbied for their own manufacturing resources to compete better as a commodity business. But they could not escape thorough debate and could not win their case. Even though top management continued to invest heavily in DRAM TD, it did not interfere with the manufacturing capacity allocations that were decided at lower levels in the organization. Eventually, CEO Gordon Moore and other top managers accepted the results of the internal selection processes. More formally:

> **Proposition 3:** Firms whose internal selection criteria accurately reflect external selection pressures are more likely to strategically exit from some businesses than firms whose internal selection criteria do not accurately reflect external selection pressures.

Proposition 3 implies that the firm's internal selection environment may be more important for adaptation than its official corporate strategy[54] and may be a source of sustained competitive advantage.[55] It establishes a seemingly simple criterion for adaptation that, as the recent troubles of IBM, Apple, NeXT, and other companies indicate, is surprisingly difficult to satisfy over long periods of time.

Links competence with opportunity. The dissolution of the strategic context of DRAMs was facilitated by the emergence of new distinctive competence-based business opportunities within Intel. Internal entrepreneurial initiatives brought competition for resources within the boundaries of the firm and forced it to make strategic choices. By favoring microprocessors over memories, the internal selection environment reinforced the coevolution of distinctive competence and the basis of competition in the microprocessor industry before the new strategy of Intel the microcomputer company was in place. The strategic choices shifted resources away from the memory business to the microprocessor business, thus causing strategic renewal. Strategic renewal, in turn, made it easier to exit from the memory business. More formally:

> **Proposition 4:** Firms that have new businesses competing with existing businesses for relatively scarce resources are more likely to make a strategic exit from existing businesses than are firms that are not confronted with such strategic choices.

Proposition 4 is consistent with earlier research on the restructuring of the global petrochemical industry[56] and the steel castings industry in the United Kingdom[57] that suggested that financially strong and diversified companies are often the first to exit. Also, diversification through internal entrepreneurship may motivate firms to evaluate the opportunity cost of existing businesses.[58] Gilmour[59] has documented how one firm's acquisition of another created new resource demands that made top management aware of the relatively low profitability of the existing business and thereby activated the divestment process.

Depends on strategic recognition capacity. To some extent, Intel was also lucky in having a distinctive competence base capable of generating new, high-growth business opportunities that provided alternatives to the DRAM business. But Intel's top management needed to be able to recognize their importance and support them in-house. Gordon Moore allowed Dov Frohman to pursue the EPROM development before there was a clear market need for it. Top management responded to Ted Hoff's championing by buying back the rights to the microprocessor before microprocessors were established in the market.

Later on, while top management had not yet redefined Intel's corporate strategy in terms of the microcomputer company, it resisted the efforts of some middle-level managers to redefine the strategic con-

---

[54]Burgelman, "Intraorganizational Ecology of Strategy Making and Organizational Adaption."

[55]J. B. Barney, "Organizational Culture: Can It Be a Source of Sustained Competitive Advantage?" *Academy of Management Review* 11 (1986), pp. 656–65.

[56]Bower, *When Markets Quake,* p. 10.

[57]Baden-Fuller, "Exit from Declining Industries and the Case of Steel Castings."

[58]R. A. Burgelman, "Corporate Entrepreneurship and Strategic Management: Insights from a Process Study," *Management Science* 29 (1983), pp. 1349–64.

[59]Gilmour, "The Divestment Decision Process."

text of DRAMs within Intel and to commit the company to competing on the terms required by a commodity business. Top management recognized that Intel was neither oriented toward nor equipped for competing in a commodity business. Thus, determining the strategic context for microprocessors (a new business) and dissolving the strategic context for memories (an existing business) depended critically on top management's ability to see the broader strategic implications for the firm of strategic actions taken by middle-level managers, in the former case, before the new official strategy of Intel the microcomputer company had been formally stated; in the latter case, before the exit from memories had been formally decided. Such strategic recognition[60] implies the possibility of self-reflexive evaluation of means and ends in the light of changing circumstances but without having to resort to foresight or grand strategy. It also does not assume that top management is necessarily the prime mover in strategy. Rather, it is predicated on strategic initiatives of middle-level managers that top management can assess and support or not support. Strategic recognition augments the adaptive value of the internal selection environment. More formally:

> **Proposition 5:** Firms that have top managers with strong strategic recognition capacity are more likely to make strategic exits from businesses than firms that have top managers with weak strategic recognition capacity.

For proposition 5 not to be a tautology, strategic recognition capacity must, of course, be established independent of a given strategic exit decision. A top manager's strategic recognition capacity could be measured, for instance, by his or her record in supporting and rejecting previous middle-level managerial initiatives.

Produces organizational learning. The dissolution of the strategic context for DRAMs concluded with retroactive rationalization efforts by top management. The exit decision had required top management to examine DRAMs strategically, from a distinctive-competence perspective as well as from product-market and financial-results perspectives. Retroactive rationalization affirmed that the outcomes of the strategic exit were beneficial from the firm's point of view and explicated why that was the case. Top management now took the explicit position that strategic exit was a natural part of competing in high-velocity environments. Once top management had brought the official corporate strategy back in line with the realities of viable strategic actions by middle-level managers, the strategic learning process continued. Top management was now ready to examine the other semiconductor memory businesses in light of the new official corporate strategy of Intel as a microcomputer company. It was ready to set the stage for the strategic exit from EPROM manufacturing, thereby further freeing up resources for the microprocessor business. Exiting from memories had required top management to consider why staying in the microprocessor business was more attractive. More formally:

> **Proposition 6:** Firms that have strategically exited from a business are likely to have a better understanding of the links between their distinctive competence and the basis of competition in the industries in which they remain active than are firms that have not strategically exited from a business.

Alternative Conjectures

But what would have happened if Intel's top managers had understood more quickly that DRAMs had become unviable and had actively sought to diversify their business portfolio? Would they have done better? Or suppose Intel had more closely tracked the evolving basis of competitive advantage in the DRAM industry. Would it have done better? These questions cannot be answered definitively in the context of this study because it was not possible to set up an experiment. But they raise important issues concerning alternative concepts of corporate strategy and forms of adaptation. From a portfolio-planning perspective, the delay in exiting the DRAM business could be viewed as a manifestation of crippling inertia, but such a perspective does not consider the implications of exit for the firm's distinctive compe-

[60]Burgelman, "Corporate Entrepreneurship and Strategic Management"; A. H. Van de Ven, "Central Problems in the Management of Innovation," *Management Science* 32 (1986), pp. 590–607.

tencies. While the study confirms that business exit is viewed by top management as an investment decision,[61] it also suggests that top management is concerned with identifying the elements of distinctive competence associated with the failing business that have the potential to be transferred to new businesses. As noted earlier, this requires time and a capacity for recognizing the substantive aspects of competencies as well as appreciating the financial performance characteristics of different businesses. The conjecture supported by previous research[62] is that Intel would probably have done worse if it had simply divested the DRAM business and entered new businesses through acquisition. Intel would have dissolved the strategic context for DRAMs too soon and thereby failed to capitalize on the full potential of its distinctive competencies in DRAMs. Some of these competencies could be effectively deployed in the microprocessor business, which represented an opportunity for strategic renewal for Intel. Hence, the time involved in dissolving the strategic context for DRAMs helped prevent strategic change that might have been too rapid.[63]

Adaptation through strategic renewal is quite different from adaptation through tracking the basis for competitive advantage in the industry. Intel did not closely track the basis of competitive advantage in the DRAM industry. If Intel's top managers had chosen to follow the logic of competitive advantage in the DRAM business, they would have had to commit hundreds of millions of dollars to a commodity market characterized by relatively low and highly volatile margins. Again, the conjecture is that Intel probably would have done less well.

Implications and Conclusion

This study found that strategic business exit has implications for the firm's distinctive competencies as well as for its product-market position. The findings support the view that top managers must learn to understand the linkage between a firm's businesses in terms of distinctive competencies[64] and suggest that strategic business exits may help the learning process. The study also found that Intel was able to transform itself from a memory company into a microcomputer company, in part because it was able to generate product-market alternatives offering top management strategic choices.[65] This suggests that top managers should nurture the development of the technological competence base of the firm and be ready to tranfer key competencies to new product-market activities before these product-market activities have become powerful in the firm. Furthermore, the study found that Intel was able to transform itself because top management had evolved an internal selection environment that was more adaptively robust than the official corporate strategy. The implication of evolving such an internal selection environment is that strategic actions by middle-level managers will sometimes diverge from official corporate strategy and may signal important environmental changes. Top managers must guard against approaches that will mask or eliminate disharmony without addressing the underlying divergences that cause it. They must develop a capacity for strategic recognition to guide the organization while a new strategic direction is taking shape and be able to decide when is the right time to bring official strategy and strategic action back in line with each other. Finally, the findings indicate that strategic business exit is not equivalent to failure and that new leadership does not necessarily imply new leaders. Andy Grove understood that Gordon Moore and he could walk through the revolving door, retake charge, and do the difficult job of exiting from DRAMs themselves.

While conclusions drawn from one case study require healthy caution, the process theory of strategic business exit presented in this paper provides insight into the organizational capability needed for long-term survival. Dynamic competence that generates new variations, internal selection that correctly reflects external selection pressures, and top management's capacity for recognizing and retaining viable strategic initiatives

---

[61]Baden-Fuller, "Exit from Declining Industries and the Case of Steel Castings," p. 956.

[62]M. E. Porter, "From Corporate Strategy to Competitive Advantage," *Harvard Business Review* 65 (1987) pp. 43–59.

[63]For example: Levitt and March, "Organizational Learning"; D. C. Hambrick and R. A. D'Aveni, "Large Corporate Failures as Downward Spirals," *Administrative Science Quarterly* 33 (1988), pp. 1–23.

[64]Prahalad and Hamel, "The Core Competence of the Corporation."

[65]Eisenhardt, "Making Fast Strategic Decisions in High Velocity Environments."

are key components of such organizational capability. Strategy making supported by this organizational capability results in the timely expansion and contraction of internal support for different businesses. This, in turn, leads to the firm's entering into and exiting from businesses on the basis of its distinctive competence as it evolves. This paper thus contributes to theory about the role of strategy in firm evolution. The theoretical framework, grounded in the study of strategic business exit, identifies key forces whose interplays determine, in part, why some firms are more likely to survive than others. This framework may be used as a tool to explore more generally how coevolution and adaptation at the firm level come about, without having to assume that top managers have extraordinary foresight and a grand strategy.

Case II–11
Bendix Corporation (A)

Steven J. Roth and Michael E. Porter

In early 1976, Douglas Crane, president of Bendix Corporation's Automotive Group, was pondering whether Bendix should go ahead with plans to construct a $10 million manufacturing facility for the production of injectors for electronic fuel injection systems, another step in Bendix's entry into the electronic engine controls business. It was raining as he reviewed the progress of the entry to date:

> Bendix's entry into the electronic engine controls business has so far contributed to three executives losing their jobs and badly hurt another man's career. Now we are at the threshold of embarking on another step that in many ways is more difficult than the ones we have taken before, and which further commits us to this market before it really even exists.

The proposed injector manufacturing facility was another piece of the electronic fuel injection puzzle that had begun many years previously in the Automotive Group. Bendix Corporation had a large stake in the automotive business, with automotive accounting for over 50 percent of Bendix's sales in 1975 and Bendix holding a position as the largest independent supplier of motor vehicle components in North America. Electronic fuel injection was thought to have the potential of becoming a billion dollar total market, up from almost nothing in 1975, and success in the business could mean substantial new sales and profit growth for Bendix's oldest and largest business group. However, the puzzle leading to success in electronic fuel injection was not yet complete.

Background

Bendix was incorporated in the early 1900s in South Bend, Indiana, to serve the growing automobile manufacturing industry with starter motors, brake linings, air filters, and other products for the original equipment market. In the 1920s Bendix relocated to its present headquarters near Detroit, Michigan, and expanded its line of automobile products to include brake system hardware, brake linings, fuel pumps, fuel filters, air filters, and related products for use in automobiles, trucks, tractors, and other vehicles.

By early 1976, Bendix served four basic markets: automotive (52 percent of sales), aerospace and electronics (26 percent of sales), shelter and housing (14 percent of sales), and industrial and energy (8 percent of sales). Bendix had been referred to as one of the best-managed companies in the United States. From fiscal 1970 to fiscal 1975 sales increased from $1.7 billion to $2.6 billion for a compound annual increase of 10 percent, while profits increased at a compound rate of 22 percent per year.[1] This performance was achieved despite a severe recession in 1974 and 1975, price controls in the early 1970s, and a generally high rate of inflation during most of the period. Many observers ascribed a part of Bendix's above-average performance through difficult times to its chief executive officer, W. Michael Blumenthal, who had come to Bendix in 1968 and become president in 1970. It was under Mr. Blumenthal's leadership that Bendix expanded into its four basic businesses to achieve balanced

---

[1]Bendix operated on a fiscal year ending September 30.

growth through involvement in countercyclical areas. Exhibits 1 and 2 summarize Bendix's financial performance.

Bendix was organized into five operating units: automotive, the Fram Corporation (wholly owned by Bendix), aerospace, industrial and energy, and international; each was headed by a group president. The first four were product-oriented groups, while the International Group sold the range of Bendix products overseas. Group presidents reported to an Office of the Chief Executive (OCE), which included Blumenthal and three executive vice presidents. Each group was divided into business units headed by group vice presidents, and further divided into divisions under division general managers.

The Bendix Automotive Business

The Automotive Group and the Fram Corporation each sold product lines to the original equipment market (OEM) and aftermarket in North America, primarily the United States and Canada. Automotive sales to foreign markets were the responsibility of the International Group, which was divided on a country basis. The North American portion of Bendix's $1.3 billion worldwide automotive business in 1975 represented about $700 million. Bendix's automotive operations served the car, light truck, heavy truck and off-the-road construction equipment segments of the automotive market. The car segment was the largest, accounting for over 75 percent of Bendix's sales, while the off-the-road segment had experienced the most rapid growth during the early 1970s.

The Automotive Group produced a wide variety of products, including drum and disc brakes, brake linings and other friction materials, vacuum and hydraulic power brakes for both cars and trucks, air brake compressors, wheel and master brake cylinders, actuating controls for trucks and tractor trailers, power steering assemblies, valves, starter drives, air pumps, carburetors, fuel pumps, and several electronic metering and control systems.[2] The Fram Corporation produced filters, air cleaner assemblies, fans, and windshield wiper arms and blades. Fram also produced spark plugs and vacuum and mechanical controls under the Autolite brand name after purchasing the Autolite Division from the Ford Motor Company in late 1973.

Bendix's automotive products were sold both to manufacturers of original equipment (OEMs) and to wholesale distributors for sale in the replacement market, or aftermarket. On a worldwide basis, sales to OEMs accounted for about two-thirds of automotives sales with the replacement business making up the remainder. In the North American market, sales in the replacement market were slightly more important. OEM sales were made to a rather limited number of customers, with only six companies—General Motors, Ford, Chrysler, AMC, Peugeot, and Renault—accounting for about 40 percent of Bendix's worldwide automotive sales (or 60 percent of OEM sales).

The Automotive Group's strategy had been to attempt to become a major supplier (typically a market share of 25 percent) in each of its product areas, and Bendix was the largest independent parts supplier to the North American market in early 1976. It had developed an excellent reputation as a technologically advanced and reliable supplier of parts for the industry. Bendix sought to remain at the leading edge of automotive technology, encompassing new products, new materials, new engine configurations, and new personal transportation modes should they appear. The Automotive Group's goals were to expand its penetration both in North America and abroad to become a world leader in the automotive industry. In addition, it sought to expand its penetration in the aftermarket.

The Automotive Group competed with a wide range of competitors, including several comparably large auto parts suppliers; TRW, Rockwell International, Eaton and Dana; a group of second-tier firms such as Midland Ross and Skelley-Globe; a large number of smaller regional companies; and the in-house component manufacturing divisions of the major auto companies themselves. Overseas Bendix competed with a similar array of firms, with major international competitors including Robert Bosch, Lucas Industries, ITT Teves, Ferodo, Mintex, several Japanese firms, as well as the overseas units of TRW and Rockwell. Bosch was perhaps Bendix's most significant overseas competitor, and was in a

[2]The metering and control systems were not electronically sophisticated.

EXHIBIT 1 Condensed Income Statement (millions of dollars)

	1975*	1974	1973	1972	1971	1970
Sales						
Automotive	$1,333.0	$1,254.8	$1,077.4	$ 839.2	$ 764.4	$ 718.1
Aerospace	715.2	630.8	608.7	570.8	552.0	638.6
Shelter	330.4	383.1	377.0	214.7	169.1	148.4
Industrial/energy	246.7	226.0	169.7	154.1	111.0	150.3
Other	(17.7)	(13.8)	(3.3)	(9.9)	16.3	24.7
Total sales	$2,607.6	$2,480.9	$2,229.5	$1,768.9	$1,612.8	$1,680.1
Income before interest and tax						
Automotive	117.2	123.8	125.9	97.7	73.6	66.3
Aerospace	48.6	34.8	20.5	31.8	29.3	23.3
Shelter	5.3	18.1	20.7	13.3	7.5	5.4
Industrial/energy	34.8	25.1	5.1	1.9	(3.5)	5.7
Total profit before interest and tax	$ 205.9	$ 201.8	$ 172.2	$ 144.7	$ 106.9	$ 100.7
Cost of sales	2,053.3	1,952.3	1,771.7	1,378.7	1,271.7	1,171.8
Selling, general and administrative	315.6	291.2	255.2	216.6	200.3	176.1
Depreciation and amortization	49.3	51.6	49.0	45.6	44.2	32.1
Interest	42.8	45.0	30.1	23.4	24.1	20.6
Other	22.5	16.3	5.6	4.3	3.7	0.9
Net income after taxes	$ 79.8	$ 75.8	$ 69.3	$ 56.0	$ 42.1	$ 32.3

*Bendix's fiscal year ended September 30.

SOURCE: Form 10Ks and annual reports.

number of overlapping product areas with Bendix. A companion case, "Note on Supplying the Automobile Industry,"[3] describes the automotive parts business and gives profiles of some of the leading competitors.

History of Bendix's Involvement in Electronic Fuel Injection

In 1951 Robert Sutton, a Bendix engineer working in an aerospace division, whom one manager referred to as "an airplane buff," devised a system which would permit airplanes to fly upside down. At this time it was not possible for airplanes to fly upside down for extended periods of time because their engines used gravity to feed gasoline into the cylinders. If exactly the right amount of gasoline could be force-fed directly into the cylinder through an injector, the problem would be solved. After some tinkering, a workable electronic fuel injection system was developed based on the then state-of-the-art electronics technology—the vacuum tube.

Bendix patented the idea in 1951 at a cost of $500, but very little was subsequently done with the invention with respect to aircraft because of the delicacy and unreliability of vacuum tube technology. A number of engineers in the automotive area saw an application for electronic fuel injection in automobiles, but this proved not to be feasible since the cost of fuel injection was high relative to existing carburetor systems, and vacuum tubes were unable to operate in the difficult internal environment of the

[3]HBS Case Services #9–378–219.

EXHIBIT 2 Condensed Balance Sheet (millions of dollars)

	1975	1974	1973	1972	1971	1970
Assets						
Cash and securities	$ 71.2	$ 46.2	$ 44.3	$ 35.1	$ 50.7	$ 57.7
Receivables	392.7	361.9	340.3	289.8	261.9	275.2
Inventories	537.9	574.4	487.9	421.2	423.6	409.2
Other	17.9	17.2	19.4	17.3	14.7	16.8
Total current assets	1,019.7	997.7	891.9	763.4	750.9	758.9
Property, plant, and equipment	423.0	445.5	418.2	380.5	355.6	324.2
Investments	28.5	29.6	28.5	27.8	21.3	19.5
Goodwill	87.4	94.6	78.1	53.3	54.2	50.9
Other	9.0	9.7	10.3	10.2	17.3	14.7
Total assets	$1,567.6	$1,579.1	$1,427.0	$1,235.2	$1,199.3	$1,168.2
Liabilities						
Notes payable	$ 90.5	$ 181.5	$ 133.6	$ 105.0	$ 147.3	$ 118.1
Accounts payable	221.6	217.5	173.0	116.8	103.4	97.3
Accruals and other	193.7	178.5	158.7	144.0	113.7	115.7
Total current liabilities	505.8	577.5	465.3	365.8	369.8	331.1
Long-term debt	285.8	235.0	248.7	195.7	185.0	189.2
Deferred taxes	19.4	26.8	24.2	19.2	21.5	19.4
Minority interest	25.0	58.3	53.2	50.2	48.8	72.7
Stockholders' equity	731.6	681.5	635.6	604.3	574.2	555.8
Total liabilities	$1,567.6	$1,579.1	$1,427.0	$1,235.2	$1,119.3	$1,168.2

SOURCE: Annual reports.

internal combustion engine.[4] One Bendix manager recalled the situation at the time:

> We were very pleased with ourselves. We ran around, showed everybody our invention, went to all the trade shows, did a lot of talking; everyone was very impressed and thought it had a great future, except nobody placed any orders.

The new invention sat on the shelf for approximately 10 years. One or two individuals, working primarily on their own time, tinkered with the project. Despite the lack of activity, Bendix had been awarded a broad, "ironclad" patent on the idea, covering all aspects of shooting combustible material into a cylinder for burning. The patent effectively meant that no one else could manufacture any kind of fuel injection system without Bendix's permission.

In the early 1960s, responsibility for the project was officially transferred from the aerospace division to the carburetor division in Elmira, New York. The transfer was effected because management believed that the automotive industry presented a larger potential market for the product than aerospace, and Elmira's general manager, Jack Campbell, was a strong believer in the potential of the idea. Campbell saw electronic fuel injection as a concept involving Bendix in the frontier of fuel management technology, and he assigned several engineers to work on the project despite the lack of a formal research and development budget for it. This work was to set the stage for the transformation of the long-orphaned project into a full-fledged business opportunity.

[4]The internal combustion engine was known as a very hostile environment for electronics, with fumes, vibration, and heat levels of 200° Fahrenheit.

The Electronic Fuel Injection System

Electronic fuel injection (EFI) performed the same role in the internal combustion engine as the traditional carburetor. The primary function of both was to mix air and fuel in the correct proportions for the most economical fuel consumption consistent with the desired performance characteristics of the automobile, and then feed the mixture into the cylinders for burning.[5] The carburetor, a mechanical device for introducing fuel into the engine, controlled flow of fuel through detecting the flow of air through a tube called the Venturi, except during transient conditions such as starting a cold engine and acceleration when accessory devices supplied a fuel mixture with a higher gasoline-to-air ratio. Carburetor systems cost in the range of $55 to $75 in early 1976.

An EFI system, on the other hand, used sophisticated electronic circuitry to determine the best fuel-air mixture. An EFI system cost approximately $250–$300 in 1976, and consisted of the following components, as illustrated in Exhibit 3:

- *Electronic control unit* (ECU)—the electronic brain of the system. The ECU's job was to continuously evaluate such external data as altitude, temperature, and humidity, and engine parameters such as driving speed, the level of oxygen in the exhaust gases, and engine temperature to determine the optimal air to fuel mixture. Early ECUs consisted of a combination of analog and digital electronic circuitry, though ECUs were expected to soon become all digital and incorporate microprocessors as part of their circuitry.
- *Injectors*—injectors were precision electrical spray nozzles that released an exact quantity of fuel into the airstream passing into each cylinder. In 1976 EFI systems had one injector per cylinder.
- *Sensors and actuators*—these devices either fed data to the ECU or carried out the ECU's instructions. Sensors were used for such tasks as measuring the temperature of the engine coolant, the amount of oxygen in the exhaust and the position of the throttle. Early EFI systems did not have oxygen sensors, but these were expected to be added in the near future. Actuators were used to adjust fuel pressure, manipulate the engine's idle speed, and so forth. Technically, the injector was an actuator, though it was usually treated separately.

The two other EFI components were similar to those used by carburetor systems:

- *Fuel pump*—the pump performed exactly the same function that it did in a conventional carburetor system, forcing the fuel from the fuel tank to the injector.
- *Throttle body*—the device which regulated the amount of air ingested by the engine. This component was not exactly the same as in a conventional carburetor system, but it was similar and not very complex to produce.

The operation of an EFI system was different from that of the conventional carburetor. EFI was self-regulating and would automatically adjust the air-fuel mixture to an optimal level and remain in tune regardless of the driving habits of the owner, length of the trip, terrain, or state of wear of the vehicle.[6] A conventionally carbureted vehicle could only be adjusted for one state of operation—for example, a carburetor adjusted efficiently at sea level would often appear sluggish at higher elevations because of the difference in oxygen levels.

This difference resulted in a number of improvements in engine performance with EFI. First, the engine would start up quickly and perform smoothly under almost any weather conditions. Test cars had been subjected to sustained conditions of extreme heat and cold and a wide variety of humidity conditions and then started without difficulty. Second, EFI needed little or no adjustment by a mechanic, and was subject to very little wear as it was used. Third, EFI was able to sense how efficiently the engine was using gasoline and adjust the fuel mixture accordingly. This was done through use of an oxygen sensor to measure the oxygen content in the engine exhaust, adjusting the fuel mixture to achieve the optimal state where no oxygen was left in the exhaust gases.

EFI's ability to continuously monitor such variables as exhaust oxygen content meant that EFI was able to significantly reduce emissions of nitrous oxide (NO_x). The carburetor could only correct the

---

[5]An automobile's performance was measured by the vehicle's ability to accelerate to cruising speed, pass other cars on the highway, and to respond to the driver's commands.

[6]Such a system was referred to as a closed-loop system.

EXHIBIT 3 A Typical Electronic Fuel Injection System

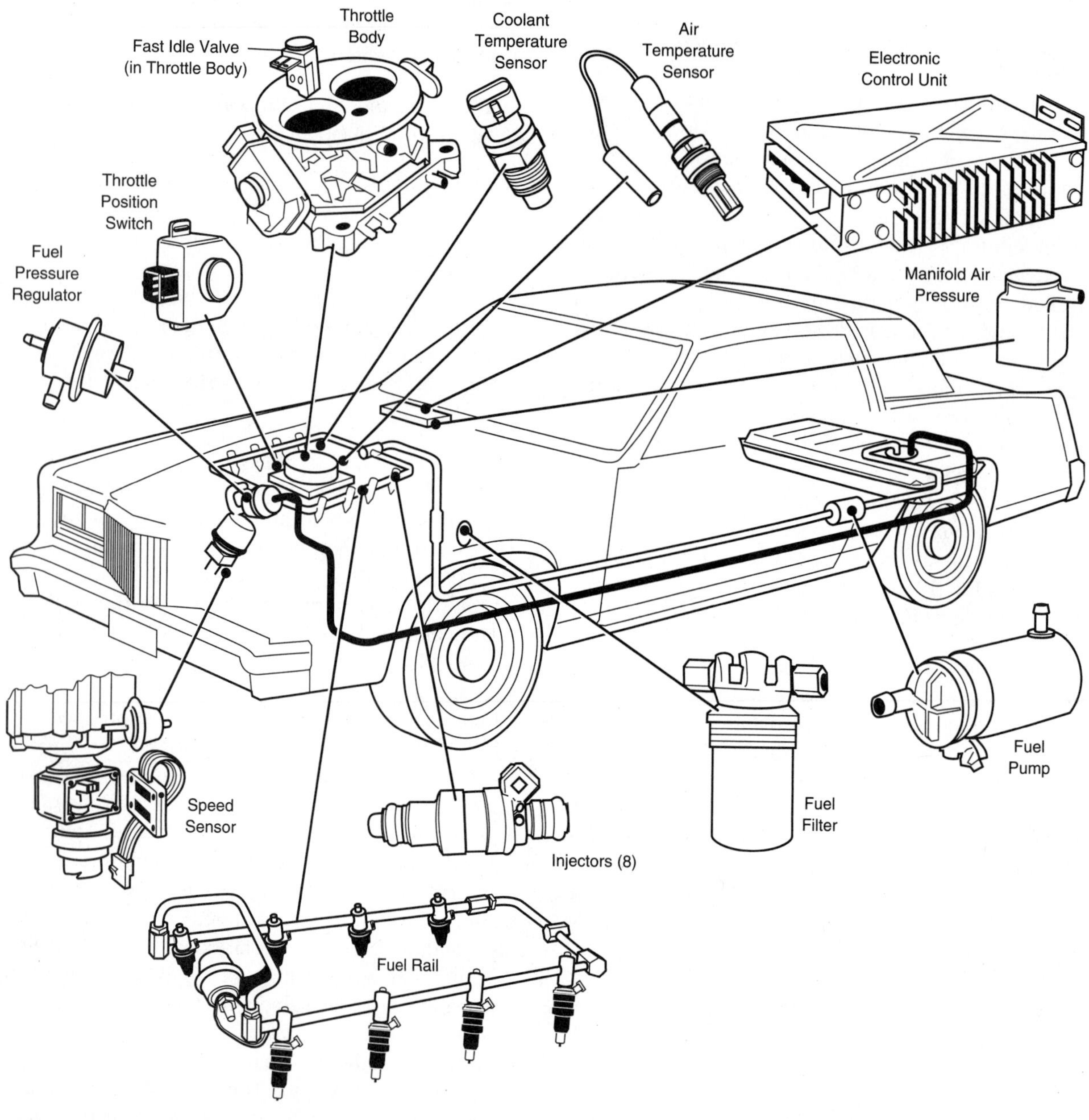

fuel mixture based on one parameter—air flow—and even this ability would often fall out of adjustment. Thus, EFI could significantly reduce engine emissions while maintaining the driveability of the vehicle. Precise control of the air-fuel mixture was also necessary in order to realize the emissions-reducing capabilities of a three-way catalyst. This new catalyst was effective in reducing the level of NO_x emitted, as well as reducing the emitted hydrocarbons and carbon monoxide. A conventional mechanical carburetor could not keep the air-fuel mixture within a narrow enough range to utilize the benefits of a three-way catalyst and could not maintain the driveability of an emission-controlled engine.

An intermediate system between EFI and conventional carburetors was *mechanical fuel injection,* sometimes called Continuous Injection. Continuous Injection utilized injectors to shoot the fuel directly into the cylinder, but computed the correct air-fuel mixture through conventional mechanical means using a vane deflected by inlet air flow. Mechanical fuel injection offered some performance advantages over the carburetor, but it was subject to wear, could get out of adjustment and was quite difficult to adjust properly, and was less self-correcting for differences in climate, terrain, and driving conditions. Mechanical fuel injection systems and electronic fuel injection systems cost about the same in early 1976, though the cost of electronic systems was expected to fall in relative terms.

The Bosch Licensing Agreement

From 1951 until 1967, despite Campbell's belief in the product, Bendix's fuel injection system had gained very limited acceptance and was used only on some expensive European passenger cars and on special high-performance racing machines. The few systems in use had been mechanically rather than electronically controlled, and no company had any extensive expertise in high-volume manufacturing of fuel injection system components. Bendix, the world patent holder, had not invested in any in-house manufacturing capability at all and was licensing its patent to the few firms who were using injectors.

In early 1967, the name of the game changed when Robert Bosch Corporation approached Bendix to negotiate a license agreement under which it could manufacture fuel injection systems on a large-scale basis. Bosch had obtained a contract from the Volkswagen Corporation (VW), a major West German producer of automobiles, to supply a fuel injection system for its 1968 models. VW wanted to use a fuel injection system to achieve greater horsepower and improved engine performance on its small cars without increasing engine displacement, which in Europe was the basis on which automobiles were taxed.

VW's decision to use fuel injection rather than a conventional carburetor system represented a major innovation in the automotive industry. Carburetor technology was very well known and had been in use, in some form, from the earliest days of mass-produced automobiles. The last real innovations in automobile technology had been the introduction of the automatic transmission in the late 1940s, and more recently, disc brakes in the mid-1960s. Therefore, VW's move was certain to attract much attention in the trade press and the industry in general. VW's decision was in part possible because of the configuration of the European automobile industry, which differed in some respects from that of the United States. European auto manufacturers were smaller than the major U.S. companies and relied heavily on independent companies for their parts needs—firms such as VW tended to be less vertically integrated than the major U.S. automakers. This allowed European producers to implement changes in their manufacturing processes faster than their U.S. counterparts, who had many billions of dollars invested in specialized plant, equipment, and tools.

Bosch was planning to use both electronic and mechanical fuel injection systems rather than solely EFI because of the expense of the still cumbersome electronic components, the need to bring the system into production very rapidly, and Bosch's special expertise in mechanically controlled devices. While mechanical systems did not have the electronic circuitry allowing continual adjustment for changes in external and internal factors, Bosch still needed Bendix's permission to manufacture a mechanical system.

Bendix granted Bosch a license in late 1967, and Bosch constructed ECU- and injector-manufacturing facilities in 1968. The agreement netted Bendix a royalty fee for each system produced by Bosch and placed certain restrictions on where and to whom Bosch could make and sell its systems. Bendix could not make EFI for sale in Bosch's markets until the expiration of the agreement in 1978, and the agreement also gave both Bendix and Bosch the right to share in technological developments and visit each other's facilities. However, some at Bendix, notably Jack Campbell, were disturbed that one of Bendix's most active and capable competitors should be capitalizing on a Bendix innovation.

Indeed, under the licensing agreement Bosch had capitalized very nicely on fuel injection systems in the European car market by 1976. Bosch's system did well because the car's weight, economy, and performance requirements were substantially more important in Europe than in the United States. In addition to taxation based on the size of the engine, gasoline had been selling at two to three times U.S. prices in Europe for some time. By the mid-1970s, Bosch supplied mechanical fuel injection systems to nearly all of the major European OEMs, and sold electronic fuel injection systems to VW, BMW, and Porsche. It was estimated that Bosch had sold a cumulative volume of approximately 3 million mechanical and electronic systems by 1976, with an average of approximately five injectors per system.

In the early 1970s, Bosch licensed (with Bendix's permission) a major Japanese auto parts manufacturer, Diesel Kiki, to manufacture EFI for Japanese automobile manufacturers. Bosch and Bendix jointly licensed another Japanese manufacturer, Nippondenso, shortly thereafter. Diesel Kiki was part of the Nissan Group (Datsun) and Nippondenso was part of Toyota. Bosch provided assistance in constructing injector and ECU manufacturing facilities, which were completed in 1973 using the latest available technology. Both firms had produced in excess of 50,000 electronic fuel injection systems in 1975 and this number was expected to grow.

External Changes in the U.S. Market

Fuel injection had languished in the United States despite these inroads in Europe and Japan. However, as Bendix's deal with Bosch was being signed, external changes were occurring that would have a significant impact on the feasibility of the electronic fuel injection system for automobiles in the United States.

Antipollution Regulations

In the late 1960s, the public began to show mounting concern for the quality of its environment; one highly visible component was air cleanliness. The first concrete steps taken by government towards air pollution control were in California, in response to growing public fears about the heavy smog in the Los Angeles basin. The automobile was identified as a major source of Los Angeles's air pollution and of air pollution in urban population centers generally, and in 1970 California passed the first automobile pollution control law which specified the maximum permissible amounts of engine pollutants that could leave the exhaust.

The impact of the California regulations was to force the auto companies to engineer two versions of their product, one for the California market and one for the United States in general. To meet the new standards auto companies relied on essentially off-the-shelf technology that they had been experimenting with for several years, consisting of refinements to the carburetor, the addition of an exhaust gas recirculation valve to the engine, and the addition of an air pump to force extra air into the exhaust manifold, thereby improving the cleanliness of the exhaust. The effect of these changes was to make automobiles more expensive and more difficult to adjust by other than a well-trained mechanic, and to degrade their performance. The initial emissions-controlled cars were harder to start in hot or cold weather, underpowered when going up hills and accelerating onto highways, and less efficient in their use of gasoline.

By the presidential elections of 1972, air pollution had become one of the most significant topics of national debate, and national legislation in the form of the Clean Air Act was passed in 1972 over the strenuous objections of the automobile industry. The act extended the existing California regulations nationwide, and went on to reduce maximum permissible pollution levels in steps toward final target levels which were scheduled to be required on 1978 model cars (see Exhibit 4). Stiff penalties were provided for failing to meet the standards. The first real test for the automobile industry was to come in late 1976 when the designs for 1978 models would be frozen to permit retooling. While interim 1976 and 1977 standards could be met with relatively little difficulty, the act stipulated major reductions in all major classifications of engine pollutants in 1978. There were significant uncertainties in early 1976 about whether the strict 1978 standards would be upheld by Congress or delayed.

The Arab Oil Embargo

Shortly after the Clean Air Act, another event shook the industry—the 1973 Arab oil embargo. The resulting gas shortages and higher gasoline prices turned the American public's attention toward the more fuel-efficient foreign cars, whose share had grown to account for 20 percent of the U.S. auto market by

1976. The concern for fuel economy was reinforced by the federal government, which passed the Energy Policy and Conservation Act in December 1975. The act mandated minimum miles per gallon averages for each auto company's fleet of cars. The mileage standards were scheduled to increase from 18 miles per gallon for 1978 models to 27.5 miles per gallon for 1985 (see Exhibit 4). The auto companies' overall averages on 1976 models were less than 14 miles per gallon. In addition, several industry observers were concerned that this legislation could become the same kind of highly political topic that pollution standards had been, with mileage standards and implementation time frames just as easily changed as the pollution maximums had been.

What made these new pollution and mileage standards even more vexing to the industry was their effect on automobile performance, and the fact that they were in part contradictory. The public's conception of a good automobile did not include hard starting, sluggish acceleration, and frequent engine adjustments. Further, reducing air pollution to meet the pollution standards meant sacrifices in fuel economy, unless new technologies could be employed. However, the dual requirements of improved mileage and reduced pollution had to be dealt with by the automakers and dealt with very quickly indeed.

The Electronics Revolution

The late 1960s and early 1970s were also a time of great change for the electronics industry. The vacuum tube had given way to the transistor, the integrated circuit and, by 1974, the microprocessor, and technological change in electronic circuitry showed few signs of abating. The technological development meant several things to the future of electronic fuel injection and electronic control of the engine generally. First, it substantially lowered the price of the system itself because the new components could perform many times the number of operations per dollar cost than could the older components, and electronic component prices were expected to continue declining. Another major improvement was in the reliability of electronic devices. The new components had no moving parts to wear out, gave off almost no heat of their own, and were very small, which made them relatively easy to shield from the engine's vibration. In addition, the service and repair of an electronic control unit was made easier since entire ECU modules could be removed and new ones replaced in a matter of minutes. Finally, the advances in electronics technology had increased the range of the ECU in providing the best balance between fuel economy, emissions, and performance through continuous adjustment of the mixture of fuel and air. The newest generation of components, the microprocessor, could respond to a wider range of variables than ever before and monitor these variables more frequently.

Electronic Engine Control

Until recently EFI had been viewed as a distinct business in and of itself, but the advent of the microprocessor caused Bendix and others in the industry to widen their view from EFI to the broader concept of "electronic engine controls." The process by which the fuel mixture was fed into the cylinders was but one process a microprocessor could control and manage. Douglas Crane, Bendix Automotive Group president, expressed his opinion about the place of EFI in the future engine controls business:

> There are really three separate games going on in electronic engine control. The first is the EFI system itself, which regulates the flow of fuel into the engine. The second concerns the timing of the spark ignition which provides the energy to burn the fuel. The last deals with managing the exhaust gas recirculation flow, a common technique for decreasing the level of NO_x emissions.
>
> All three affect gas mileage and engine emissions, and control over all three engine functions will clearly be necessary if the automakers are to possibly meet the 1985 mileage/emission standards being contemplated by the federal government.

One approach being investigated was the use of a central microcomputer to manage all engine functions. Dr. John Weil, Bendix's chief of research and development, commented on another view of how future electronic control systems might develop:

> We can foresee a system of microcomputers designed to control different aspects of the car's performance, which, while not linked together through a main computer, would function by sharing information. For example, one computer system could control the engine; another computer system could control the brakes; a third could control the passenger's environment. All would communicate with each other, yet each would be able to operate independently. It's not difficult to imagine that within 10 years all mechanical functions on a car would be controlled

EXHIBIT 4 Existing and Proposed Statutory Requirements for Automobile Emission and Fuel Economy

I. Emissions Maximums*
(grams of pollutant per mile)

Model Year	Statutory Authority	Hydrocarbons (HC)	Carbon Monoxide (CO)	Nitrous Oxide (NO_x)
Effective for 1976	Federal	1.5	15.0	3.1
	California	.9	9.0	2.0
Effective for 1977	Federal	1.5	15.0	2.0
	California	.41	9.0	1.5
Statutory for 1978	Federal	.41	3.4	0.4
	California	.41	3.4	0.4
Senate/House compromise proposal for 1981	Federal	.41	3.4	1.0

II. Fuel Economy Standards**

Model Year	Minimum Fleet Average Miles per Gallon
1978	18
1979	19
1980	20
1981	21.5
1982	23.0
1983	24.5
1984	26.0
1985	27.5***

*Statutory requirements under the Muskie Bill enacted in 1974.

**Statutory requirements under the Energy Policy and Conservation Act of 1975.

***Under the act the Secretary of Transportation was given discretion to reduce the 1985 requirements to 26.0 miles per gallon, or effectively extend the 1984 requirements indefinitely.

SOURCE: Company documents.

electronically as the price of electronic components decreases and the need for reliability and efficiency increases.

Proponents of the single on-board computer approach cited lower costs, greater accuracy in the control process, and easier maintenance in the field. Proponents of the multiple system approach, on the other hand, argued that redundant systems provided an extra margin of safety in the event of a failure, would be easier to implement since each system could be tested and refined independently, and would increase the overall flexibility in the system to respond to additional electronic control needs in the future. This flexibility caused some to judge the multiple system approach to actually be less expensive over the long run.

Douglas Crane commented on possible industry direction over the next several years as it sought to deal with statutory requirements that were not yet finalized:

All the major automobile companies have very active electronic engine management R&D programs. You will see every car make use a different approach to try and solve the problem, particularly in view of the uncertainty over future emission standards. In fact, I would not be at all surprised to see different divisions of General Motors go down separate paths. Some will move to an all-electronic system as fast as they can while others will try to graft electronics on to the carburetor to protect their sizable investment in plant, equipment, and tooling.

For example, Chrysler made a lot out of its "lean burn" engine—which is really just a form of electronic

> spark control—but the problem is much broader than just spark control alone. Ford's electronic engine control (EEC) system is another development effort aimed at centralized microcomputer management of the engine.

Experimentation with approaches to electronic control had already begun in the industry. Standalone subsystems in electronic ignition timing and control of exhaust gases had been announced by Ford and Chrysler, while electronic subsystems for fuel cutoff and transmission shift scheduling were expected to be introduced.

For the long term, to meet the very rigorous 1985 federal mileage and pollution requirements some observers foresaw the possibility of more fundamental changes in the automobile engine. Crane commented:

> For the last 2 or 3 miles per gallon it might be necessary to have to go to improved diesels or some other technology than we have today. The diesel engine gets 25 percent better mileage, but it is hard starting, noisy, gives off exhaust odors, and costs \$250–\$500 more than gasoline engines. In addition, diesels have a tough time with the NO_x standards. The Senate/House compromise version of the pollution bill has raised the No_x minimums, which many believe was done to allow diesels a chance.

European producers already offered diesel models, though they had gained only limited acceptance in the United States, and several American manufacturers planned experiments with diesel options on their cars. However, even the most bullish forecasts gave diesel only a 10 to 20 percent market penetration by 1985, with only 50,000 to 100,000 units annually through 1980.

The Seville Contract

The Bosch licensing agreement coupled with these environmental changes caused Jack Campbell and his group to be even more determined to find some way to capitalize on Bendix's invention of the fuel injection concept. However, while Bosch was working with VW to perfect its fuel injection system, Bendix was maintaining a very conservative attitude toward new investment in EFI. Bendix's corporate posture was to restrict new investment in research and development and specialized plant and equipment for EFI to the level of its licensing fees from Bosch. One manager commented on the company's treatment of EFI:

> We didn't honestly believe that something as different as EFI was practical in the U.S. auto market. In addition, the people directly responsible for automotive operations were wary of becoming involved in a new technology, especially one that included electronics as a primary component. No one was willing to kill the concept given what Bosch was doing with it in Europe, but no one was willing to back it as an investment, either. Therefore, EFI languished for several years.

Bendix did try to extend the basic patent with new breakthroughs and modifications to the existing system, but these efforts were not particularly successful and the basic EFI patent was due to expire in 1978.

Campbell decided the best way to break into the U.S. auto market with EFI was to begin with the most expensive cars. His reasoning was that EFI was still substantially more expensive than conventional carburetors (then \$500 versus \$55) despite the dramatic cost reductions due to improved technology. On the top-of-the-line Cadillacs, Lincoln Continentals, and Chrysler Imperials (all of which sold for over \$10,000), however, the added cost of EFI would be a relatively smaller item, and the auto companies might be interested in the operational advantages of the system as a marketing device.

Campbell chose to start with the Lincoln-Mercury Division of Ford because his Bendix division was already doing business with Ford in car radios, air pumps, and other products. In the spring of 1971, Campbell was able to interest Ford in trying the EFI on the Continental Mark IV, but was unable to obtain clearance from Automotive Group management to commit funds to the project. Campbell commented on the situation as it existed within Bendix:

> Each week we had a new dog and pony show. Every time I wanted to do something, the people above me wanted to monitor it. Every time I wanted to spend money, they wanted to slow it down. I spent more time selling inside the company than outside the company. They were afraid of what would happen if we became heavily involved with Ford or General Motors. I don't believe that I would have had that much trouble getting the product started if they would have left me alone and let me get the job done.

Automotive Group top management, all of whom had been with Bendix for many years and risen through the ranks in engineering/manufacturing or accounting, were skeptical of a story they had heard before. EFI had been discussed for over 10 years and never amounted to anything, and Jack Campbell was in telling his story once again. They finally agreed to develop a system with Ford, but on the condition that Ford pay for the entire $3 million to $4 million in estimated up-front development cost. Other companies had approached Ford without making such demands, and Ford decided to conduct its development effort without Bendix. Ford began working on electronic engine control with Motorola, Essex, Toshiba, and Ford's own Electrical and Electronics Division.

The Cadillac Division of General Motors presented Campbell's next market opportunity. In the early 1970s Cadillac had decided to produce a new smaller 8-cylinder luxury car called the Seville. It was to be positioned in the auto market to compete with Mercedes Benz, which had been making inroads into Cadillac's traditional marketplace. The Seville was to be the first of a new line of small luxury cars within the Cadillac Division. Bob Lund, then the general manager of the Cadillac Division, saw EFI as providing Seville with excellent performance and start-up qualities with only a marginal increase in the overall cost of the car (which was approximately $13,000 fully equipped). Taking the initiative, Lund approached Campbell directly to arrange a meeting at Cadillac's headquarters. Lund had met Campbell previously and was aware that Campbell was anxious to obtain a contract for the EFI and that he had been negotiating with Ford for some time.

The meeting went exceedingly well from Campbell's perspective. Lund had already made up his mind about the desirability of EFI as standard equipment on the Seville and was anxious to get Bendix moving. Lund agreed to pay for all of Bendix's start-up cost on a dollar-for-dollar basis, give Bendix a five-year contract with guaranteed production volumes, and make the contract profitable for Bendix to undertake. In return, Bendix would agree to full and open sharing of their technology and patents with Cadillac. However, securing management approval proved to be more difficult than Campbell anticipated.

Management of Bendix's Automotive Group remained skeptical about start-up ventures and new technologies, particularly this one. They were reluctant to sell the idea to top corporate management and did not believe that Bendix could successfully complete an electronically related venture that involved a brand new product line and might involve a new manufacturing facility and a new manufacturing process. In an effort to break the bottleneck, Campbell arranged a meeting between Lund and Blumenthal. Lund was eager to get the EFI project started in time to meet the Seville's production schedule, which anticipated getting out the new car in record time for an entirely new model. If the agreement could not be reached then Cadillac would have to rely on a conventional carburetor system to avoid holding up the production schedule. Lund agreed to give Bendix a five-year contract for 100 percent of the Seville's production volume, or the first 300,000 systems Cadillac bought, whichever was greater. However, just before the contract was to be signed Blumenthal demurred; he wanted to deal directly with GM's president.

Blumenthal was aware that a division of GM could be overruled by the corporate office when it came to contract and pricing negotiations with outside suppliers, and wanted to be absolutely certain that GM's top management was firmly behind Cadillac's decision to use EFI. After some discussion Lund agreed to the request and referred the matter to Edward Cole, GM's president. Shortly thereafter Bendix got the terms it requested and the contract was signed in December 1973; however, Blumenthal was still somewhat apprehensive about dealing with GM. Only one division of a U.S. car manufacturer had made a tangible commitment to EFI, and one Bendix manager commented that after the contract was finally signed Blumenthal remarked, "GM will get us before this is all over."

Meeting the Seville EFI Contract

After signing the agreement with General Motors, Bendix faced the task of beginning to supply Cadillac with an expected 60,000 EFI systems per year within 18 months despite the lack of any in-house manufacturing capability, a legacy of the conservative investment policy followed with respect to the new product. Bendix also lacked substantial experience in high-volume manufacturing of this type of sophisticated electronic component, since most of Bendix's electronics manufacturing had been in the aerospace divisions (small lot sizes) and in comparatively low-complexity car radios.

Since Bendix did not have time to build an injector plant of its own, which required a lead time of two years, it had anticipated buying the injectors it needed from Bosch under a cross-licensing arrangement. However, Bosch found that it did not have enough excess capacity to meet all of Bendix's requirements and was unwilling to build another injector plant without a long-term contract from Bendix. Bendix decided instead to buy a portion of its needs from Bosch, and purchase the rest from Nippondenso and Diesel Kiki, Bendix's and Bosch's Japanese licensees in EFI. Jack Campbell, given responsibility for the project, also hurriedly sought other subcontractors who could supply other EFI components, since normal lead times for ordering manufacturing equipment were 18 to 24 months. Satisfactory sources for the various sensors, actuators, and other EFI components were secured.

ECU Manufacturing

While most of the EFI components were to be subcontracted, it was decided that Bendix would manufacture ECUs itself at its former radio plant in Newport News, Virginia, now producing air pumps for Ford. This plant had considerable excess space which made it an attractive location for the new Seville business, and since radios and the ECU were both electronic in nature it was hoped that some synergy might be present.

For a company already involved in high-volume electronic manufacturing, ECU (electronic control unit) capacity could be put online in six to nine months as an addition to an existing facility, and required little specialized equipment that was not used in other forms of electronics manufacturing. For Bendix, without such experience, an investment of about $2 million would be required, primarily for sophisticated electronic test equipment that an established firm in electronics manufacturing would have. Bendix planned to purchase electronic components from outside suppliers, and already had the capability to design its own circuits and produce its own etched circuit boards internally.

Bendix management chose Robert Hoge to manage the launching of ECU production in Newport News. Hoge recalled his surprise at getting the assignment:

> I was managing a brake products plant in Canada, doing very well. My background as an electronics engineer and an MIT graduate fellow led my superiors to come to me and urge me to take this new position. Although neither I nor anyone else on my proposed team knew very much about electronics manufacturing, they were persuasive and I felt a sense of obligation to give it a try.

In practice, the manufacture of radios, a well-known and relatively unsophisticated technology, could not be compared with the care and precision needed to produce an ECU. The ECU was a very complex component which required highly trained personnel and a dust- and fume-free manufacturing environment. Like with most electronic assemblies, there was a significant learning curve involved in ECU manufacturing, particularly on the first 75,000 units.

The Newport News plant proved a less than ideal home for the new venture. Since no electronics production had taken place in the plant for over two years, the best electrical engineers and manufacturing specialists had left. The current air pump manufacturing process was a noisy and dirty operation which was to go on side by side with ECU production. Hoge received little cooperation from the Newport News plant manager who seemed more concerned with the air pump business than with the ECU start-up, and did little to help Hoge get established or provide staff support. An inadequate budget had been allocated by this plant manager for refacilitizing the ECU portion of the plant, and some needed expensive electronic test equipment went unpurchased. Borrowed staff from Bendix's aerospace operations were utilized.

To complicate matters even further, no one at Bendix had ever produced an ECU and the original specifications for the component were not based on real production experience. They proved to be infeasible. Hoge reflected on what happened:

> The project quickly started going bad. We were missing deadlines, equipment was not being delivered on time; my people were giving estimates for time and dollars that I had no way of evaluating properly. Therefore, I committed myself and our group to making deliveries and meeting production schedules which were basically impossible. The pressure from the Cadillac Division to fulfill our contract was very high. Cadillac needed these components as part of their scheduled and highly publicized start-up production of the Seville, and Bendix had encouraged Cadillac not to develop an alternate carburetor system for the Seville. If we could not fulfill our obligation we could have a very difficult time with the rest of our GM business. So

> there was tremendous pressure, both from within Bendix Corporation and from General Motors, to do something about the project. Unfortunately, I was the something they did something about.

A management shakeup resulted in Hoge being relieved. But the pressure extended further, and the president of the Automotive Group asked to be demoted and reassigned to the brake products business. The request was accepted and other early retirements followed—top management's feelings about Bendix's inability to manage a start-up in a high-technology manufacturing process had unfortunately been reinforced.

Faced with a management vacuum in Automotive, Blumenthal recruited Douglas Crane to be the group president for Automotive in May 1975. Crane had been group vice president in charge of worldwide industrial operations at AMF, and previously senior group vice president in charge of aerospace, automotive, and recreational vehicle parts production and steel fabrication at the Wickes Corporation. Crane quickly became personally involved in the management of the project:

> When I arrived I asked to have all our microprocessor experts meet in my office. A little later *he* walked in, though it did not seem funny at the time. I went to see Blumenthal and told him that we had a very serious problem. He told me to do whatever was necessary to solve the problem.
>
> I assumed direct control of the Newport News plant and for all practical purposes was the group vice president as well as the group president. I recruited several good electronics people from companies like General Electric, Texas Instruments, and Rockwell, and tripled the size of our engineering department in a year. I also brought in some manufacturing talent with experience in electronics manufacturing and recruited Charles Flannagan, who was head of Texas Instruments' electronic controls group, to manage the EFI business.
>
> Some of the problems were a function of the old management's attitude toward the ECU project. The idea of spending $1 million on a piece of electronic test equipment would send them into shock.

Crane recalled the final weeks before the first deliveries of ECUs were due:

> We had 30 or 40 engineers down there with soldering guns making ECUs, and we were flying them to Cadillac in Jetstars. I didn't quite get to the soldering gun stage myself, but almost.

Bendix met its delivery schedule to Cadillac, and by early 1976 the ECU manufacturing process was operating smoothly though it was currently undergoing modifications to accept newer microprocessors as the brain of the system.[7] The ECU had already been redesigned several times since the original versions were produced.

Sensors and Actuators

Each Bendix EFI system required a variety of sensors and actuators. Most sensors and actuators were relatively low-cost items ($1–$10), and many involved no special technological difficulties, though there was more than one technological approach to performing the sensing function in some cases. However, manifold pressure sensors and oxygen sensors, both important to the developing technology in EFI, were technologically sophisticated, especially oxygen sensors whose technology was considered a "black art." Oxygen sensors were similar to spark plugs in both appearance and manufacturing technology. Participation in the spark plug business was almost a necessity for entry into oxygen sensors, and as much as 85 percent of the manufacturing equipment was common.

Initially, Bendix purchased its sensors and actuators from outside suppliers, primarily Bosch. However, Bendix had plans to add the capability to produce them internally through the Autolite Division, making Bendix the only source of oxygen sensors besides Bosch, which had been making them for some time.[8] Bendix was also planning to manufacture temperature and manifold pressure sensors inside, through incremental investments in existing manufacturing facilities. The time and investment requirements for beginning production of these devices were significantly less than that for injectors.

The Proposed Injector Plant

By early 1976 the Seville was selling very well and the electronic fuel injection system was thought to

---

[7]This was not to say there were no operating problems for the equipment once installed in the car. Stories (unverified) circulated of ECUs burning out as cars passed under power lines, leaving the car and its occupants stranded.

[8]The major U.S. manufacturers of spark plugs were Autolite, Champion, and the A.C. division of General Motors. Both Champion and A.C. were working on the development of oxygen sensors.

be contributing to this, which raised the question of what Bendix's next step in EFI should be. The immediate decision facing Bendix was whether or not to build its own injector manufacturing facility. Bendix was currently purchasing injectors from its licensees—Bosch, Nippondenso, and Diesel Kiki—at a cost penalty of $1 to $2 per injector because of the need to import them from abroad.

Injector manufacturing was a very-capital-intensive process utilizing high-precision, high-volume turning and grinding equipment. Walter Schauer, the Bendix manager in charge of planning for the facility, described injector manufacturing technology:

> On a scale of 1 to 10, this is definitely a 10-level technology. To give you an idea of the reliability of the product, if a car engine is designed to travel 150,000 miles before breaking down, the electronic fuel injection system will have gone through 150 million cycles by the end of that time. In addition, fuel flow tolerances of less than 1 percent to 1½ percent are required for the system to operate efficiently. Even slight pressure fluctuations can cause fuel flow problems which will result in poor performance.
>
> There are several very critical grinding operations which require tolerances of 1 to 1½ microns. This kind of grinding operation is done by perhaps five companies in the entire world and only a dozen companies manufacture equipment that can possibly do the job. This equipment has been undergoing improvements in the last decade in its ability to meet these tolerances at high volumes.

Labor content in the injector manufacturing process was relatively small, though there was significant labor content in final assembly and testing. This led to a learning curve for injector manufacturing that was expected to flatten after the production of 500,000 to 1,000,000 units. The minimum efficient size of an injector facility was approximately 1 million units per year, requiring an investment of $8 million to $10 million and a two-year lead time from go ahead to production. An additional comparable increment of capacity could be added to an existing injector facility for approximately one-half the original investment with 18 months' lead time.

The technology for manufacturing injectors had undergone very close scrutiny by Bendix for an extended period. In December 1974 Bendix made a detailed study of Bosch's manufacturing process (which it was allowed to do under its licensing agreements) that formed the basis for Bendix's own manufacturing feasibility study. Schauer had also recently spent several months in Germany studying Bosch's manufacturing process, and Bendix's planned facility would incorporate improvements in equipment that had occurred since Bosch's facility was constructed. Bendix' proposed facility was to have 1.2 million units of annual capacity.

Exhibit 5 gives Bendix's financial projections for the proposed injector manufacturing business, as well as financial projections for the other major components of the EFI system.

The Market for Electronic Fuel Injection in 1976

The rate of development of the market for electronic fuel injection remained uncertain in 1976. The auto companies, except for Cadillac-Seville, had been carrying on work in EFI and electronic engine controls on a reserve basis. However, GM, Ford, and Chrysler were accelerating their in-house research programs in electronic closed-loop systems, and all had announced the intention of beginning internal manufacture of electronic control units for automobiles. Both Ford and GM were already involved in electronics manufacturing and envisioned additional applications for the ECU on the automobile.

The development of EFI was dependent on the cost of the system relative to the conventional carburetor, on the ability of the auto manufacturers to improve their existing carburetor and ignition systems, and on the government's actions with respect to future mileage and emissions legislation. From 1974 to 1976 the auto companies had been able to do surprising things with their carburetor systems. Carburetor precision had been improved by the addition of electronic subsystems which modulated the air-fuel ratio and by mechanical improvements. An industry participant commented on the companies' achievements:

> When you consider that the auto companies probably have billions of dollars invested in plant and tooling for the manufacture of carburetors, it is no surprise that they are pulling out all the stops they can in R&D to prolong the life of the carburetor. However, the modifications also make the carburetor system more expensive and more complex to adjust and repair. It's still unclear how far they can take carburetor technology.

EXHIBIT 5 Financial Projections for Electronic Fuel Injection (dollars in thousands)

	1975 (estimated actual)	1976	1977	1978	1979	1980	1981
ECU:							
Net sales	$4,115	$8,407	$10,268	$17,282	$29,806	$50,934	$59,624
Gross profit:	(1,446)	1,956	1,756	4,615	8,177	11,344	14,274
Percentage of sales	(35.14)%	23.2%	17.1%	26.7%	27.4%	22.3%	23.9%
Profit before tax:	(2,671)	(2,299)	(3,478)	(1,214)	1,631	3,515	5,694
Percentage of sales	(64.91)%	(27.3)%	(33.9)%	(7.0)%	5.5%	6.9%	9.5%
Investment base:	4,157	5,450	6,836	6,518	8,157	12,028	13,444
ROI percentage*	(31.95)%	(19.8)%	(23.6)%	(7.6)%	12.5%	17.3%	24.1%
Approximate number of units**	50,000	65,000	90,000	150,000	500,000	750,000	800,000
Injectors:							
Net sales			$8,070	$13,667	$17,111	$28,907	$31,680
Gross profit:			2,173	8,689	8,396	7,256	8,237
Percentage of sales			26.9%	63.5%	49.1%	25.1%	26.0%
Profit before tax:		$(306)	(1,914)	5,347	4,550	2,371	2,830
Percentage of sales			(23.7)%	39.1%	26.6%	8.2%	8.9%
Investment base:		1,150	7,663	10,224	10,882	20,734	30,790
ROI percentage*			(10.9)%	29.2%	23.8%	8.0%	6.9%
Approximate number of units		520,000	720,000	1,600,000	2,800,000	5,300,000	5,600,000
Sensors:							
Net sales			$1,129	$2,013	$9,218	$22,646	$26,058
Gross profit:			205	704	2,828	6,733	6,963
Percentage of sales			18.2%	34.9%	34.4%	29.7%	26.7%
Profit before tax:			(2,881)	(2,511)	564	3,170	3,127
Percentage of sales			(255.2)%	(124.7)%	6.9%	14.0%	12.0%
Investment base:			535	1,682	4,175	7,608	7,098
ROI percentage*			(278.0)%	(75.6)%	8.2%	23.7%	25.0%
Approximate number of units		185,000	270,000	1,320,000	4,100,000	11,800,000	13,000,000
EFI mechanical hardware:* **							
Net sales	$9,817	$13,681	$6,900	$9,797	$754	$1,008	$1,202
Gross profit:	3,410	2,378	1,789	1,026	203	336	401
Percentage of sales	34.74%	17.4%	25.9%	10.4%	26.9%	33.3%	33.3%
Profit before tax:	(369)	(1,480)	152	(757)	141	284	344
Percentage of sales	(3.76)%	(10.8)%	2.2%	(7.7)%	18.7%	28.2%	28.6%
Investment base:	6,667	4,141	1,975	1,012	183	210	231
ROI percentage*	(.47)%	(16.5)%	6.1%	(36.7)%	42.1%	72.3%	79.2%
Total EFI:							
Net sales	$13,932	$22,088	$26,367	$42,759	$55,889	$102,495	$118,564
Gross profit:	1,964	4,334	5,923	15,034	19,604	25,669	29,875
Percentage of sales	14.10%	19.62%	22.46%	35.16%	35.08%	25.0%	25.2%
Profit before tax:	(2,986)	(4,085)	(8,121)	865	6,886	9,340	11,995
Percentage of sales	(21.43)%	(18.49)%	(30.80)%	2.02%	12.32%	9.1%	10.1%
Investment base:	10,824	10,741	17,009	19,456	23,397	40,580	51,563
ROI percentage*	(12.3)%	(17.7)%	(22.7)%	4.4%	17.4%	14.0%	14.2%

*Bendix computed ROI by adding back to profit before taxes an assessed corporate capital charge equal to 4% of the investment base. Then corporate taxes (48%) are subtracted to yield profit after taxes. Profit after tax divided by the investment base equals ROI.
**Bendix planned to sell ECUs for other uses besides fuel control. The figures given are unit sales for fuel control.
***Includes sensors and injectors in 1975 and 1976.

SOURCE: Company documents and casewriter compilations. Certain figures have been altered, though integrity of the figures has been preserved.

The cost of carburetors had been inching up with these improvements, and Bendix estimated that the cost of carburetors would rise to the $86 to $90 range by 1981. Bendix management believed that the auto companies would pay a premium for non-carburetor fuel controls if they provided a benefit in meeting emissions and fuel economy standards, the premium depending on the size of the car. It was estimated that the cost of electronic fuel injection systems would have to fall to approximately $100 to achieve meaningful market penetration of the small-car (less than 111-inch wheel base) market, $150 for the medium-car (112 inch to 118 inch) market and $200 for the full size car market.[9]

Bendix expected that technological change and increases in production volume would bring down the cost of EFI. Exhibit 6 gives Bendix's projections of EFI costs, which Bendix management estimated to have an uncertainty of +15 percent. The expected major reductions in the cost of the ECU embodied in Exhibit 6 were due to the rapid technological progress in electronics that was decreasing the cost per function. Another significant part of the cost reduction in EFI was to come from a decrease in the number of injectors used in the system, as discussed by Dr. Weil:

> At this point we're using an eight-injector system, working towards what could be a two-injector system for eight-cylinder engines and a one-injector system for four-cylinder engines. If we can reduce the number of injectors needed from eight to two or from four to one, we will substantially reduce the cost of the system as a whole. There will be certain performance trade-offs that have to be made as a result, but it will definitely bring the cost of our system more in line with the cost of a conventional carburetor system.

As Bendix contemplated building an injector manufacturing facility, improvements in injector design were already on the drawing boards. Bendix management estimated that improvements in injector design might ultimately require investments of several million dollars in retooling costs for injector manufacturing, though they would not require complete reequipping of an injector plant.

Diesel Fuel Injection Systems

Fuel injection systems for diesel engines had been in use for some time, and were produced by a number of U.S. and foreign companies. While diesel systems were quite different from gasoline systems, there were some commonalities which might affect

[9]EFI would eventually have an aftermarket, primarily for replacement injectors. Give system reliability, however, this market could take as long as five years to develop and its size was extremely uncertain without actual field experience.

EXHIBIT 6 Projected Costs to Automobile Company of an Eight-Injector Electronic Fuel Injection System

	1976	1979	1981
Throttle body	$ 16.58	$ 16.83	$ 15.45
Fast-idle valve	8.06	1.70	1.70
Fuel pressure regulator	5.38	2.00	2.00
Eight fuel injectors	98.65	61.50	51.50
Fuel filter	1.50	.35	.35
Fuel rails	19.06	17.00	15.00
Coolant temperature sensor	3.93	2.10	2.00
Air temperature sensor	3.97	2.10	2.00
Throttle position sensor	6.39	4.00	3.00
Fuel pump	36.37	27.00	24.50
ECU	127.96	75.00	56.00
Total	$327.85	$209.58	$183.50

SOURCE: Bendix Corporation projections and casewriter computations.

the development of both. The diesel fuel injection market is briefly profiled in Appendix A.

Legislative Uncertainties

In 1976, the year in which car designs had to be finalized for the 1978 models, the auto companies and Congress were involved in a heated public debate about the ability of the industry to meet the 1978 emissions standards. While emissions standards for 1976 and 1977 had been met, the companies were arguing that meeting the 1978 standards was impossible with existing technology. The federal government was insisting just as vehemently that it could be done with the best technology available. Meeting the 1978 standards in the short run required three-way catalysts and electronic engine controls and Bendix believed that if the 1978 standards were maintained, electronic fuel injection would be nearly mandatory for all cars over 3,000 pounds (112-inch wheel base or higher). However, if the standards were relaxed for one to three years—the consensus of industry predictions—then carburetor systems could continue to be used during that period or longer. Douglas Crane commented on the situation:

> The auto companies really can't meet the standards given the currently available and implementable technology. I'm fairly certain that the government is going to alter the legislation to whatever Detroit's best effort really is. Clearly, they are not going to shut down the auto industry, and that is exactly what would happen if they tried to enforce the 1978 standards right now.

Over the longer run, the need for electronic fuel injection would be influenced by the rate at which government standards were enforced and the ability of the industry to adopt alternative solutions to the dual mileage/emissions problem. With respect to the mileage standards, most industry executives agreed that fleet averages of 22 to 24 mpg could be achieved with already known methods, primarily by reducing the size of the car and engine. After all, European cars had achieved high gasoline mileages for many years. The industry could manufacture only cars that were less than 3,000 pounds (in the present compact range); however, electronic engine controls including EFI would be needed on the larger cars (over 3,000 pounds) to meet the 26 to 27.5 mpg standards for fleet averages combined with the tougher 1978 emission standards. Fleets with nearly all cars less than 3,000 pounds would signal the end of the American family car with capacity for more than 4 passengers, and it appeared that neither the federal government nor the public was prepared to accept this outcome. Bendix had estimated, however, that 58 percent of North American cars would be small cars weighing less than 3,000 pounds by 1981, up from 40 percent in 1975. For cars of less than 3,000 pounds, technological advances might allow the meeting of statutory requirements without EFI, though EFI would improve performance and driveability.

The shape of government emissions standards remained uncertain. In early 1976 it was increasingly evident that Congress would reaffirm the original statutory levels for hydrocarbon (HC) and carbon monoxide (CO), but might back off from the stringent nitrous oxide (NO_x) standard of 0.4 grams per mile. Industry observers were predicting that final NO_x standards in the 1.0 to 2.0 grams per mile range were now likely to go into effect around 1982. NO_x levels at 2.0 grams per mile or below would require sophisticated engine controls if fuel economy and driveability were also to be attained.

APPENDIX A: DIESEL ENGINE FUEL INJECTION

Fuel injection systems had been developed for diesel engines, the engine increasingly installed in trucks, heavy equipment, and to a limited degree in automobiles. Fuel injection systems for diesel and gasoline engines were different in a number of respects. Diesel engines were ignited by creating high pressure on the fuel-air mixture, and not by a timed spark. This meant that cylinder pressures were much higher in diesel engines, as was the delivery pressure of fuel from the fuel injectors. In addition, diesel injectors were not actuated directly by electronic circuitry but rather by a mechanical governor.

Despite these differences, the basic technology and manufacturing process for diesel injectors were similar to that of injectors for gasoline engines. It was estimated by industry sources that a firm already producing in one area could halve the time it took to get into the other compared to a completely new entrant, and that approximately one-half of the production equipment was common to the manufacturing processes for gasoline and diesel injectors.

The producers of diesel injection systems in the United States were Ambac Industries, the Hartford Division of Stanadyne, Robert Bosch, and many of the major diesel engine manufacturers, including General Motors' Diesel Equipment Division. Overseas the major competitors were Bosch, Cav-Lucas, Diesel Kiki, and Nippondenso. In 1974 Bosch began construction of a plant in Charleston, South Carolina, to produce diesel injection equipment for sale in the North American market. Bosch was acknowledged as the world leader in diesel injection.

Ambac Industries

Ambac Industries had corporate sales of $188 million in 1975, of which $56 million were in diesel and fluid power products. The American Bosch Division of Ambac manufactured diesel fuel injection systems (pumps, nozzle holders, and spray nozzles) and diesel engine accessories, such as pumps and governors. In addition to giving technical and engineering assistance to various manufacturers, this division designed and adapted fuel injection equipment to the special needs of particular engines. The division had specialized in the manufacture of a multiplunger pump for heavy duty trucks and a single plunger pump for farm and construction equipment and for medium and light trucks.

The division had a research laboratory for research and development work on fuel-handling systems for various kinds of engines. The division was presently engaged in the development and testing of advanced fuel injection systems for substantially improving fuel economy and meeting future emission levels. It had received a research and development contract from Ford Motor Company and was continuing development of a gasoline fuel injection system for the Ford PROCO (programmed combustion) engine. This was just one of the many engine options Ford was exploring and, while it is a technically excellent product, Ford had not as yet made a decision on PROCO.

Lucas Industries

Lucas Industries was a leading world manufacturer of electric, hydraulic, and mechanical equipment used by internal combustion, diesel, and gas turbine engines, road and rail vehicles, and ships and aircraft, in addition to manufacturing a wide range of industrial products. Corporate sales in 1975 were £455 million, and 80 percent of sales and 90 percent of earnings came from vehicle components. Eighty percent of sales were in the United Kingdom and Europe.

Lucas was perhaps the largest supplier of diesel injection equipment in Europe and was aggressively expanding its position:

> The large increase in the cost of oil has led to more attention being paid to the fuel used per passenger mile and this has meant that much of our earlier work on engine management is now coming to fruition. The growth in the demand for diesel engines fully justifies the major efforts we have undertaken to maintain our lead in this field. . . . The research and development work on electronic systems continues to be very important. We are particularly concerned with improving the inherent reliability of these systems which are used to an increasing extent in the fields of engine management, wheel slide protection, alternators, etc. (Source: Lucas annual report).

Stanadyne, Inc.

Stanadyne was engaged in the following business areas: plumbing products, fasteners and sawblades, ferrous materials, valve train products, and contract components and assemblies. Corporate sales in 1975 were $189 million, of which diesel fuel injection equipment was 17 percent. The Hartford division manufactured and sold diesel fuel injection pumps under the Roosa Master trade name, nozzles under the Pencil Nozzle trade name, filters under the Master Filter trade name, and air starters under the Start Master trade name to diesel engine manufacturers primarily for use in agricultural machinery, roadbuilding equipment, generator sets, on-the-road vehicles and trucks, and marine and stationary engines.

The company announced in January of 1976 that it had received a letter of intent from one of the major automobile manufacturers to purchase the company's diesel fuel injection equipment for use on an eight-cylinder diesel engine under development for light trucks and passenger cars.

Reading II–13
Corporate Entrepreneurship and Strategic Management: Insights from a Process Study

Robert A. Burgelman

In recent years, empirical studies of the strategic management process have provided a number of new insights. These studies have found that strategy formulation and implementation are intrinsically intertwined, incrementally evolving processes,[1] that intended strategies are often different from realized strategies,[2] and that different organizational contexts are associated with different strategic processes.[3] Previous studies have also recognized the multilayered nature of the strategic process in large, complex organizations: the fact that it involves the interlocking strategic activities of managers at different levels in the organization.[4]

Relatively little is known, however, about the process through which large, complex firms engage in corporate entrepreneurship. Corporate entrepreneurship in this reading refers to the process whereby firms engage in diversification through internal development. Such diversification requires new resource combinations to extend the firm's activities in areas unrelated, or marginally related, to its current domain of competence and corresponding opportunity set. In the Schumpeterian[5] sense, diversification through internal development is the corporate analog to the process of individual entrepreneurship. Corporate entrepreneurship, typically, is the result of the interlocking entrepreneurial activities of multiple participants.

This paper purports to extend the theory of strategic management by providing a conceptual integration of the literature on entrepreneurship in organizations and on the strategic process. The basis for this integration is a model of the strategic process, recently developed by Burgelman.[6] The line of argument underlying the proposed integration is as follows. Large, diversified organizations need both order and diversity in strategy for their continued survival. The role of entrepreneurial activity is to provide the required diversity. Whereas order in strategy can be achieved through planning and structuring, diversity in strategy depends on experimentation and selection. The task of strategic management is to maintain an appropriate balance between these fundamentally different processes. These insights have implications for the design of organizational arrangements and for the development of strategic managerial skills.

This reading is organized into four sections. First, the concept of corporate entrepreneurship is elucidated using a newly developed model of the strategic process. The latter is briefly linked to recent insights from the theory of self-organizing systems. The second section relates findings of previous empirical studies of entrepreneurship in organizations to the new theoretical framework. Current approaches to the design and management of entrepreneurial systems, advocated in the literature, are examined in the third section. The final section explores some of the implications of corporate entrepreneurship as a process of experimentation and selection.

Strategic Behavior and Corporate Entrepreneurship

Recently, Burgelman has proposed an inductively derived model of the dynamic interactions between different categories of strategic behavior, corporate

Management Science 29, no. 12 (1983), pp. 1349–64. Support from the Strategic Management Program of the Graduate School of Business, Stanford University, is gratefully acknowledged.

[1]E. A. Murray, "Strategic Choice: A Negotiated Outcome," *Management Science* 24, no. 9 (May 1978), pp. 960–71; J. B. Quinn, "Strategy Formation: A Process Viewpoint," paper presented at TIMS/ORSA Meeting, May 4, 1980.

[2]G. T. Allison, *Essence of Decision* (Boston: Little Brown, 1970); H. Mintzberg, "Patterns in Strategy Formation," *Management Science* 24, no. 9 (May 1978), pp. 934–48.

[3]D. Miller and P. H. Friesen, "Innovation in Conservative and Entrepreneurial Firms: Two Models of Strategic Momentum," *Strategic Management Journal* 3 (1982), pp. 1–25; F. T. Paini and C. R. Anderson, "Contingencies Affecting Strategy Formulation and Effectiveness: An Empirical Study," *Management Studies* 14 (May 1977), pp. 147–58.

[4]J. L. Bower and I. Doz, "Strategy Formulation: A Social and Political View," in *Strategic Management,* ed. D. E. Schendel and C. W. Hofer (Boston, MA: Little Brown, 1973).

[5]J. A. Schumpeter, *The Theory of Economic Development* (Cambridge, MA: Harvard University Press, 1934).

[6]R. A. Burgelman, "A Model of the Interaction of Strategic Behavior, Corporate Context, and the Concept of Strategy," *Academy of Management Review* 8 (1983), pp. 61–70.

context processes, and a firm's concept of strategy.[7] This model, represented in Exhibit 1, can be used to elucidate the nature and the role of corporate entrepreneurship.

The reasoning embedded in this model can be summarized as follows. The current *concept of strategy* represents the more or less explicit articulation of the firm's theory about the basis for its past and current successes and failures. It provides a more or less shared frame of reference for the strategic actors in the organization, and provides the basis for corporate objective setting in its business portfolio and resource allocation.

The concept of strategy thus induces most but not all strategic activity in the firm. *Induced* strategic behavior fits in the existing categories used in the firm's strategic planning, and takes place in relationship to its familiar external environments. To the current concept of strategy corresponds a *structural context* aimed at keeping strategic behavior at operational levels in line with the current concept of strategy. Structural context refers to the various administrative mechanisms which top management can manipulate to influence the perceived interests of the strategic actors at the operational and middle levels in the organization. It intervenes in the relationship between induced strategic behavior and the concept of strategy, and operates as a selection mechanism—a diversity reduction mechanism—on the stream of induced strategic behavior. "Errors" in induced strategic behavior are eliminated by the structure, and the system continues to operate consistent with its current strategy. Corporate entrepreneurship is unlikely to take place through the induced strategic behavior loop. Incremental innovation can occur, but no radically new combinations of productive resources are likely to be generated in this loop.

For reasons discussed in the next section, firms also are likely to generate a certain amount of *autonomous* strategic behavior. While purposeful from the perspective of the actors who engage in it, autonomous strategic behavior does not fit in the existing categories used in the strategic planning of the firm: it falls outside of its current concept of strategy. Through such strategic behavior, new environmental segments are enacted and the firm's environment redefined. From the perspective of the firm, autonomous strategic behavior provides the

EXHIBIT 1 **A Model of the Interaction of Strategic Behavior, Corporate Context, and the Concept of Strategy.**

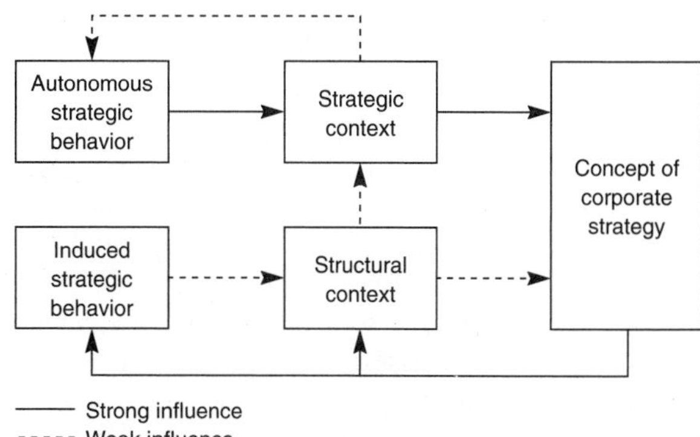

SOURCE: Robert A. Burgelman, "A Model of the Interaction of Strategic Behavior, Corporate Context, and the Concept of Strategy," *Academy of Management Review* 8 (1983), pp. 61–70.

raw material—the requisite diversity—for strategic renewal. As such, autonomous strategic behavior is conceptually equivalent to entrepreneurial activity—generating *new* combinations of productive resources—in the firm. It provides the basis for radical innovation from the perspective of the firm. In this reading, corporate entrepreneurship will be identified with the autonomous strategic behavior loop in the model.

Autonomous strategic behavior takes shape outside of the current structural context; yet, to be successful, it needs eventually to be accepted by the organization and to be integrated into its concept of strategy. The process through which these two conflicting conditions can be satisfied has been identified as the process of *strategic context* determination. Strategic context refers to the political mechanisms through which middle managers question the current concept of strategy and provide top management with the opportunity to rationalize, retroactively, successful autonomous strategic behavior. Strategic context determination intervenes in the relationship between autonomous strategic behavior and the concept of strategy. Through the activation of this process, the effects of the structural context can be circumvented, and successful autonomous strategic behavior can become integrated in the concept of strategy through the process of retroactive rationalization. This, in turn, changes the basis for the further inducement of strategic behavior. The model thus

[7]Ibid.

indicates how diversity becomes transformed into new order.

Strategic Behavior and Self-Organization

Interestingly enough, the idea of diversity as the basis for continued order, embedded in the model of the strategic process discussed here, has a parallel in recent developments concerning self-organization in the physical sciences. Prigogine has developed models in chemistry concerning far-from-equilibrium thermodynamic processes in which "'mutations' and 'innovations' occur stochastically and are integrated into the system by the deterministic relations prevailing at the moment. Thus, we have in this perspective the constant generation of 'new types' and 'new ideas' that may be incorporated in the structure of the system, causing its continued evolution."[8]

In the same line of thought, Sahal has pointed to the paradoxical situation that systems are self-organizing *because of* rather than in spite of disturbances.[9] Homeorhesis, "the capacity of a system not merely to return to its state prior to the occurrence of the disturbances, but to seek out new development pathways through successive instabilities,"[10] is quite different from the more familiar concept of homeostasis, "the capacity to return to a steady state after a temporary disturbance."[11]

Using the mathematical concepts of information theory, Sahal has demonstrated that long-term and short-term regulation of a system must satisfy different conditions. Short-term regulation requires an increase in diversity. Long-term regulation requires a decrease in diversity, but this decrease cannot fall below a certain minimum specified by the short-term requirements.[12] In terms of the model presented here, the induced strategic behavior loop—the lower loop in Exhibit 1—can be viewed as the homeostatic process of the organization. The autonomous strategic behavior loop—the upper loop in Exhibit 1—corresponds to the homeorhetic process of the organization, that is, the process through which new pathways for the organization's development are provided. It is the latter which concerns us in the remainder of this paper.

Entrepreneurship and Organization

The identification of the autonomous strategic behavior loop is the result of grounded theorizing[13] efforts based on a field study of the internal corporate venturing (ICV) process in the large, diversified firm.[14] Such ICV efforts constitute one of the major manifestations of corporate entrepreneurship.[15] This study has produced a detailed, multilayered process model documenting the interlocking key activities of managers from different hierarchical levels in the organization in the ICV process.[16] Such a model depicts the autonomous strategic behavior loop in large, complex organizations as one of "mosaic" building—with different pieces of the mosaic put in place at different levels simultaneously—rather than one of simple, sequential development. It reveals the relationship between strategizing and structuring at the corporate level, and the strategic behavior—initially seeming almost insignificant—of operational participants in and around concrete projects. This, in turn, sheds more light on the less obvious frictions and problems deeply embedded in the strategic process in large, complex organizations.

This process model approach allows us to subsume previous research findings concerning diversification through internal development in large, complex firms. These indicate, indeed, that the strategic process involved in such corporate efforts depends on the interaction of cognitive processes and concrete actions of general managers at multiple levels in the organization,[17] and suggest the

[8]I. Prigogine, *From Being to Becoming* (San Francisco, CA: W. M. Freeman, 1980), p. 128.

[9]D. Sahal, "A Unified Theory of Self-Organization," *Journal of Cybernetics* 9 (1979), pp. 127–42.

[10]Ibid., p. 130.

[11]Ibid.

[12]Sahal, "A Unified Theory of Self-Organization."

[13]B. J. Glaser and L. J. Strauss, *The Discovery of Grounded Theory* (Chicago, IL: Aldine, 1967).

[14]R. A. Burgelman, "Managing Innovating Systems: A Study of the Process of Internal Corporate Venturing," unpublished doctoral dissertation, Columbia University, New York, 1980.

[15]E. B. Roberts, "New Ventures for Corporate Growth," *Harvard Business Review* 57 (July–August 1980), pp. 134–42.

[16]R. A. Burgelman, "A Process Model of Internal Corporate Venturing in the Diversified Major Firm," *Administrative Science Quarterly* 28 (1983), pp. 223–44.

[17]E. W. Trevelyan, "The Strategic Process in Large, Complex Organizations: A Pilot Study of New Business Development," unpublished doctoral dissertation, Harvard University, Boston, MA, 1974.

importance of the middle level "manager champion" in addition to the more familiar operational level "product champion" role in the implementation of a new business idea.[18]

The identification of the interlocking activities constituting the autonomous strategic behavior loop by means of the process model also provides further insight in the vicious circles, paradoxes, dilemmas, and creative tensions encountered by entrepreneurial activities in organizations. Important ones were already identified by Kimberly[19] in a field study of the process of birth and early development of a new, innovative medical school in the context of an established university. Features of the new organization that were required for success in the entrepreneurial stage created problems for its continued success in the later stage of institutionalization. Kimberly has documented the role of the individual entrepreneur as the motor of the organizational innovation. However, the study suggests that neither the entrepreneurial participant nor the organization has a clear idea of the ramifications of the innovation, and it illustrates the difficulty of changing the established organizational context to accommodate the innovation.

These earlier findings would seem to be consistent with the idea of autonomous strategic behavior at levels below top management as the driving force for strategic change. But, even though the theory of self-organizing systems provides a rationale for the need for diversity, that is, for autonomous strategic behavior in organizations, it is not yet clear why such behavior should emerge on the part of operational-level participants, and why top management should tolerate it.

Opportunities for Internal Entrepreneurship

From the perspective of strategically inclined, operational-level participants, the organization constitutes an opportunity structure. Expansion of current business and diversification through internal development are the major ways in which the opportunity-seeking behavior of such participants can exert itself. Such opportunity-seeking behavior results from what Penrose has called the pool of unused resources existing at any given moment in the firm's development.[20] She notes that "both an automatic increase in knowledge and an incentive to reach for new knowledge are, as it were, 'built into' the very nature of the firms possessing entrepreneurial resources of even average initiative."[21] This leads to an internal impulse for growth, distinct from external environmental changes in opportunities.[22]

Kirzner also has expressed forcefully that the corporate form of business organization is an "ingenious, unplanned device that eases the access of entrepreneurial talent to sources of large-scale financing"; and "the executives, to the limited extent that they do possess discretionary freedom of action, are able to act as entrepreneurs and implement their ideas without themselves becoming owners at all."[23] He emphasizes the importance of "alertness" to opportunities as the foundation for all entrepreneurial activity, internal as well as external.

In terms of the model presented here, since the current concept of strategy and the associated induced strategic behavior loop are unlikely to exhaust the potential opportunity set perceived by the operational-level participants, autonomous strategic behavior is very likely to manifest itself.

Recently, Teece has provided an excellent review of the reasons why such entrepreneurial activity will lead to diversification, and why, in fact, it is likely to seek its economic returns in the existing firm rather than through the formation of a new one, or through independent market transactions.[24] On the one hand, many of the capabilities of the firm are fungible and can be applied to different productive activities. On the other hand, much of the firm's knowledge, especially the more complex and newer capabilities, has not been codified, and

---

[18]I. Kusiatin, "The Process and Capacity for Diversification Through Internal Development," unpublished doctoral dissertation, Harvard University, Boston, MA, 1976; M. A. Maidique, "Entrepreneurs, Champions, and Technological Innovation," *Sloan Management Review* (Winter 1980), pp. 59–76.

[19]J. R. Kimberly, "Issues in the Creation of Organizations: Initiation, Innovation, and Institutionalization," *Academy of Management Journal* 22 (1979), pp. 437–57.

[20]E. Penrose, *The Theory of the Growth of the Firm* (Oxford, England: Blackwell, 1968).

[21]Ibid., p. 78.

[22]A. D. Chandler, *Strategy and Structure* (Cambridge, MA: MIT Press, 1962).

[23]I. M. Kirzner, *Perception, Opportunity, and Profit* (Chicago: University of Chicago Press, 1979).

[24]D. J. Teece, "Towards an Economic Theory of the Multi-Product Firm," *Journal of Economic Behavior and Organization* 3 (1982), pp. 39–63.

remains "tacit."[25] Also, this "organizational technology" is distinct from the summation of the individual participants' knowledge and skills, and they often cannot completely identify and separate their own part in it.

This line of argument provides a basis for distinguishing more clearly between external and internal entrepreneurship. External entrepreneurship is a first-order phenomenon. It consists in the individual entrepreneur's process of combining resources dispersed in the environment with his or her own very unique resources to create a new combination that is basically independent of all other resource combinations. Internal entrepreneurship, on the other hand, involves new resource combinations which remain, to some extent, nested in the larger resource combination constituted by the firm, and thus also retain at least a potential degree of dependence on it. In fact, it could be argued that the lack of any significant potential degree of dependence between an internally developed new resource combination and the firm should lead to a spin off.

The existence of these partial dependencies, current or potential, is precisely at the origin of some of the vicious circles, dilemmas, paradoxes, and creative tensions found in studies of corporate entrepreneurship discussed earlier. Such dependencies also create "information impactedness"[26] problems, which make it difficult to communicate clearly what the new business opportunity is, and how it will evolve, to outsiders. This would seem to constitute an important theoretical reason why the venture capitalist's approach, if adopted by large, complex firms, is unlikely to resolve their corporate entrepreneurship problems. It also explains in part the important role of "uncertainty absorption"[27] played by middle-level managers in the strategic context determination process.

To the extent that the content of the opportunity set associated with the unused entrepreneurial resources cannot be known in advance of their application, it would seem that the process of corporate entrepreneurship can hardly be subsumed under the traditional strategic planning approaches. In the final section, the implications of this line of thought will be further explored. At this point, it suffices to realize there exists a theoretical foundation for the existence of autonomous strategic behavior in large, complex firms. Why particular individuals choose advancement opportunities in the autonomous, rather than in the induced, strategic behavior loop may be explained by their particular capabilities relative to the recognized core capabilities of the organization, as much as by their particular personal inclinations. Further research may establish the relative importance of these and other factors.

The Organization's Need for Entrepreneurship

Why does top management tolerate autonomous strategic behavior? One reason would seem to be that such strategic behavior provides the means for extending the frontiers of the corporate capabilities and for the discovery of additional synergies in the large, relatively unique resource combination constituted by such firms. In other words, autonomous strategic behavior provides a means for elaborating and exploring the firm's organizational technology. This, in turn, may lead to the enactment of new environmental niches and the extension of the firm's environmental support base, or at least to maintaining the capabilities necessary to pursue different avenues for corporate development in the future. As a corollary of this, it may be useful to determine more clearly which avenues *not* to pursue.[28]

Entrepreneurial activity may be necessary to avoid increasing competitive pressures, to enter or leave strategic groups, or just to mix up the competitive strategy assessments of major competitors. Peterson and Berger have provided documentation of corporate entrepreneurship as a means for coping with competitive threats.[29] Firms in the music

[25]M. Polanyi, *Personal Knowledge* (Chicago, IL: University of Chicago Press, 1958).

[26]O. E. Williamson, *Markets and Hierarchies* (New York: The Free Press, 1975).

[27]J. G. March and H. A. Simon, *Organizations* (New York: Wiley, 1958).

[28]There may be a systematic bias toward underestimating the true benefits of entrepreneurial activities for the organization, even if they turn out to be failures. The focus is usually on the financial cost of such failures, without correction for the hidden benefits which result in terms of organizational learning, and/ororganizational mobilization. Further research on how to identify and measure such side benefits may reduce this bias.

[29]R. A. Peterson and D. G. Berger, "Entrepreneurship in Organizations: Evidence from the Popular Music Industry," *Administrative Science Quarterly* 16 (1971), pp. 97–106.

industry used entrepreneurial actors (primarily the "producers" of records) to help them absorb the negative consequences of environmental turbulence. To protect themselves, in turn, from the liabilities attached to the use of entrepreneurial actors, they engaged in four major tactics. They limited the direction of each entrepreneurial actor, they maximized the number of entrepreneurial decisions while minimizing the investment in each, they monitored rapidly the market success of each entrepreneurial decision, and they rapidly rewarded or fired the entrepreneurial actors based on their success in the turbulent environment.[30]

Dynamics similar to those documented by Peterson and Berger were found in the ICV study.[31] The firm studied oscillated in its emphasis on new venture activity. Periods of high emphasis seemed to correspond to top management perceiving the opportunity cost of current mainstream business as high. In other words, when things were going well in the mainstream areas of business, only lip service was paid to diversification. When prospects looked not so good, top management seemed to be ready, as one manager put it, "to jump into just anything."

Even though it may seem counterintuitive to propose that companies will be more likely to attempt to diversify when current business is not going too well, other pieces of data exist which suggest that the firms studied are not unique in this respect. In the case of DuPont, for instance, Fast reports the explanation for the decline in support for new venture activities toward the end of the 1960s, provided by a member of the Executive Committee: "You simply don't diversify when you are short of capital *unless your existing businesses are in trouble*, and ours were not."[32] And, in a similar vein, Jelinek reports the following observation made by a manager at Texas Instruments: "In the downturn times, it seemed like the corporation always identified some long-term thrusts to pour money into."[33]

[30]R. A. Peterson, "Entrepreneurship and Organization," in *Handbook of Organizational Design*, ed. P. Nystrom and W. Starbuck (New York: Oxford University Press, 1981).

[31]Burgelman, "Managing Innovating Systems."

[32]N. D. Fast, *The Rise and Fall of Corporate New Venture Divisions* (Ann Arbor, MI: University of Michigan Research Press, 1979), p. 83.

[33]M. Jelinek, "Texas Instruments (A)," Harvard Case Services, Harvard Business School, Boston, MA, 1976, p. 12.

In sum, corporate entrepreneurship would seem to depend both on the capabilities of operational-level participants to exploit entrepreneurial opportunities and on the perception of corporate management that there is a need for entrepreneurship at the particular moment in its development. From the perspective of top management, corporate entrepreneurship is not likely to be a regular concern, or an end in itself. Rather, it is a kind of "insurance" against external disturbances or a "safety valve" for internal tensions resulting from pressures to create opportunities for growth.

Fluctuations in Corporate Entrepreneurship

In situations where both entrepreneurial initiative and top management's desire for it are simultaneously present or absent, no special problems for corporate entrepreneurship would seem to arise. Paradoxical situations may arise, however, if entrepreneurial initiatives emerge but top management has no interest in them, or if top management's interest is not matched by a significant number of entrepreneurial initiatives. In the study of ICV,[34] the former of these paradoxical situations created "orphan" or "misfit" type projects, not able to get management's attention. The latter situation led to pursuing unviable projects which then turned into "failures."

Slack in R & D resources was considered an important factor in the emergence of ICV initiatives.[35] Here, *slack* can be defined in general as the existence of resource levels above those needed for sustaining the induced strategic behavior loop. Assuming a positive relationship between slack and entrepreneurial initiative at operational levels,[36] and assuming a significant time lag in the adjustment of slack at the operational level to the perceptions of top management concerning the prospects of current business, a classification of generic situations can be derived which subsumes the observed paradoxical situations. Exhibit 2 represents this classification.

This classification identifies likely determinants of the relative emphasis in the short run on autonomous strategic behavior by the firm. Other

[34]Burgelman, "Managing Innovating Systems."

[35]Ibid.

[36]G. Zaltman, R. Duncan, and J. Holbek, *Innovations and Organizations* (New York: Wiley, 1973).

EXHIBIT 2 Some Generic Situations Concerning the State of Corporate Entrepreneurship in Large, Complex Organizations

		Top management's perception of the opportunity cost of current business: Low	Top management's perception of the opportunity cost of current business: High
Slack available at operational level	Low	Top management does not want, and operational participants do not provide, many entrepreneurial projects. Result: Minimum emphasis on autonomous strategic behavior loop.	Top management wants, but operational participants do not provide, many entrepreneurial projects. Result: Force the autonomous strategic behavior loop. Jump into just any projects available. Projects end up as "failures."
	High	Top management does not want, but operational participants do provide, many entrepreneurial projects. Result: Suppression of the autonomous strategic behavior loop. New projects end up as "orphans" or "misfits."	Top management wants, and operational participants provide, many entrepreneurial projects. Result: Maximum emphasis on the autonomous strategic behavior loop.

classification efforts have suggested more stable types in the long run.

Corporate Entrepreneurship and Organizational Types

The integration of corporate entrepreneurship and strategic management can, indeed, be related to typologies of organizations and of strategic processes proposed by Miles and Snow[37] and Mintzberg,[38] respectively. Miles and Snow have suggested four empirically derived types of organizations. "Defenders" have narrow product-market domains. Their top managers are highly expert in this limited domain of activity and do not search for opportunities outside of it. They focus on improving the efficiency of their existing operation. "Prospectors" search almost continually for new opportunities and experiment regularly with potential responses to emerging environmental trends. They are creators of change for their competition. Their emphasis on innovation, however, prevents them from being completely efficient. "Reactors" are unable to respond effectively to environmental change. They lack a consistent strategy-structure relationship. They make adjustments only when forced by environmental pressures. Finally, "analyzers" typically operate in two types of product-market domains: one rapidly changing, the other relatively stable. Their top management must be capable of dealing with strategy in different modes.

Mintzberg[39] has proposed a typology of strategic processes which would seem to parallel Miles and Snow's organizational typology. Defenders can be characterized by a "planning" mode, prospectors are likely to use an "entrepreneurial" mode, and reactors are likely to be characterized by an "adapting" mode. This typology has no analog for the analyzer type, but, being a hybrid, it can be viewed in Mintzberg's terms as a mixture of the planning and entrepreneurial modes.

These typologies, as well as the simple dichotomy between "entrepreneurial" and "conservative" firms recently proposed by Miller and Friesen,[40] can be derived from the model presented in this paper. Different firms are characterized by different combinations of autonomous and induced strategic behavior, and the typologies are only special cases of this. This is illustrated in Exhibit 3.

The model and the theory of self-organizing systems could be used to raise questions about the long-term viability of each of these types. Also, it is

[37]R. E. Miles and C. C. Snow, *Organizational Strategy, Structure and Process* (New York: McGraw-Hill, 1978).

[38]H. Mintzberg, "Strategy-Making in Three Modes," *California Management Review* 16, no. 1 (1973), pp. 44–53.

[39]Ibid.

[40]"Innovation in Conservative and Entrepreneurial Firms."

EXHIBIT 3 A Reinterpretation of the Typologies of Miles and Snow and of Mintzberg

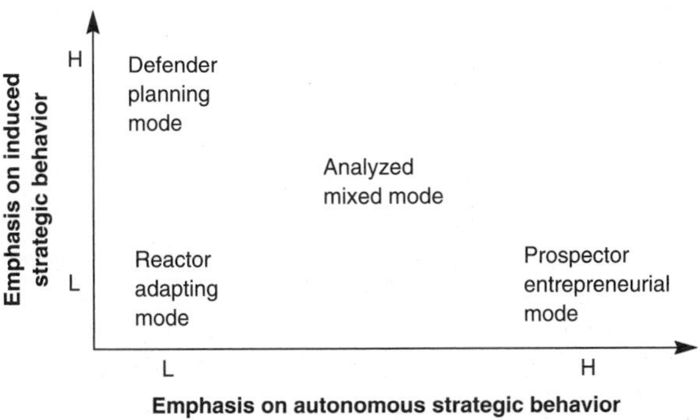

interesting to note that, conceptually, the strategic management problem of finding the optimal level of corporate entrepreneurship could possibly be formulated in terms of a constrained optimization model. If one refers to the theory of self-organizing systems mentioned earlier, this could take the form of maximizing autonomous strategic behavior subject to long-term regulation constraints, or minimizing autonomous strategic behavior subject to short-term regulation constraints. Constructing a realistic model could be very difficult and would require much further research. As Caves recently has pointed out, however, such theoretical efforts may provide a fruitful meeting ground for researchers in economics and organization theory.[41]

Designing and Managing Entrepreneurial Systems

The limited theoretical integration of corporate entrepreneurship and strategic management is clearly reflected in the wide range of recommendations currently proposed in the literature for designing and managing entrepreneurship in organizations. This section examines first various well-publicized approaches in the light of the preceding analysis. In the final section, some new ones are proposed which would seem to follow from the new conceptualization of the strategic process underlying the preceding analysis.

Institutionalizing Innovation

Based on a study of Texas Instruments Corporation (TI), Jelinek has articulated the theory that organizations can institutionalize successfully a process for generating entrepreneurial activity on a continuous basis.[42] "Organizational learning" is a central concept in this theory. Jelinek argues that organizational learning is different from individual learning and from mere adaptation. It refers to a set of administrative systems and a codification process through which discoveries can become accessible to participants other than the inventors, new solutions can become applied to new situations, and new patterns can become adopted by participants who were not involved in their original development. Such administrative systems and codification procedures exist in a hierarchy of increasing complexity.[43] At the peak of this hierarchy are paradigm-regenerating systems and procedures which allow the organization to program its own radical change. Jelinek suggests that the various administrative mechanisms existing at TI, notably the well-known Objectives-Strategies-Tactics (OST) system and its supplements, exemplify such paradigm-regenerating devices.

While the present paper was in progress, Texas Instruments decided to eliminate the complex, matrixed structures involved in OST.[44] This would seem to constitute some counterevidence for the "institutionalization" approach, unless one wants to stretch the argument to claim that OST had these self-destructive changes already built-in. More powerful, theory-based reasons can be provided to question the validity of the institutionalization approach. Administrative systems, it would seem, embody the results of *past* learning. They lead to the more or less explicit articulation of a paradigm which constitutes a common frame of reference for the organizational participants. The concept of strategy in Exhibit 1, discussed earlier, would seem to be the analog to this. Administrative systems and their associated par-

[41]R. E. Caves, "Industrial Organization, Corporate Strategy, and Structure," *Journal of Economic Literature* 18 (March 1980), pp. 64–72.

[42]M. Jelinek, *Institutionalizing Innovation* (New York: Praeger, 1979).

[43]G. Bateson, *Steps Toward an Ecology of Mind* (New York: Ballantine, 1972).

[44]Caves, "Industrial Organization, Corporate Strategy, and Structure."

adigm lead to the reduction of diversity in behavior. They reduce error with respect to particular classes of strategic problems. They make incremental learning likely in known directions, but by the same token may impede learning in *new* directions. From the perspective of the model presented in Exhibit 1, Jelinek thus seems to have described the induced strategic behavior loop. Only as long as the incremental opportunities in existing areas of business are relatively large will this approach generate significant innovations for the organization. This would also seem to be consistent with Haspeslagh's study on the use of SBU systems, which suggests that sophisticated strategic planning is not helpful for managing new business development.[45] Finally, the institutionalization approach can be viewed as an effort to effect the "routinization of charisma"[46] of the original strategic vision of the founders of the organization. Haggerty's own reflections on the origin and purpose of the TI systems would seem to bear this out.[47] The current changes at TI may suggest that the usefulness of this original vision may have run its course.

Importing the Logic of Individual Entrepreneurship

In contrast to the institutionalization approach where entrepreneurial individuals have become ancillary to the entrepreneurship-generating administrative systems, Quinn has advocated an approach in which individual entrepreneurs remain central.[48] Grounded in a large variety of case studies, he has identified a number of critical characteristics of the system of individual entrepreneurship in the capitalist societies. He concluded that "large existing institutions should try to learn from such experience and adapt the best characteristics of this remarkable system."[49] Quinn recommends that the planning-budgeting process should be converted from its primary role of resource rationing to one in which opportunity seeking becomes important too, and views portfolio planning as a helpful tool for this purpose. Control and motivation systems must be redesigned to support entrepreneurial goals. Entrepreneurial teams should be given the opportunity to engage in "skunk work" outside of the formal procedural structures. Entrepreneurial talent must be recruited, which, in turn, requires a revamping of selection procedures and criteria. Finally, the organization must learn to be content with "winning a few"—the 1 in 20 rule—and should try to achieve this through the entrepreneurs' careful building of credibility for their activities. A widely publicized McKinsey study suggests that successful companies have implemented many of Quinn's recommendations. Such companies have strong cultures supporting clear strategic goals concerning entrepreneurial activity. Examples are IBM, 3M, Hewlett-Packard, and again, TI.[50]

Quinn's recommendations imply that the entrepreneurial process is one that can be planned, albeit with less narrowly determined action parameters and more flexible criteria for support. Such a planning process, together with the appropriate determination of the rest of the structural context, is expected to produce an array of entrepreneurial possibilities which remain consistent with the current strategy or, at the limit, with changes in strategy already envisioned by top management. In fact, as Quinn points out, "The process must start at the very top of the organization."[51] Such an approach would thus seem to be again more descriptive of the induced strategic behavior loop than of the autonomous strategic behavior loop. Again, this may work well in firms that have one major technology base for their businesses. 3M, for instance, has about 90 percent of its businesses based on the mature coating and bonding technology. It has continued to be innovative in new product development for its mainstream businesses. However, these innovations have been incremental in nature. The difficulties encountered by 3M in becoming a major player in the emerging office-of-the-future industry would seem to suggest that the traditional approach to entrepreneurship works less

[45]P. Haspeslagh, "Portfolio Planning: Uses and Limits," *Harvard Business Review* 59 (January–February 1982), pp. 58–73.

[46]M. Weber, *The Theory of Social and Economic Organization* (New York: Free Press, 1964).

[47]P. E. Haggerty, "The Corporation and Innovation," *Strategic Management Journal* 2 (1981), pp. 97–118.

[48]J. B. Quinn, "Technological Innovation, Entrepreneurship, and Strategy," *Sloan Management Review* (Spring 1979), pp. 19–30.

[49]Ibid., p. 22.

[50]T. Peters, "Putting Excellence into Management," *Business Week* (July 21, 1980).

[51]Quinn, "Technological Innovation, Entrepreneurship, and Strategy."

well in areas requiring radical, rather than incremental, innovation.[52]

Corporate Entrepreneurship as Experimentation and Selection

Current approaches to the design and management of entrepreneurial systems seem to assume, at least implicitly, that the strategic choices involved in corporate entrepreneurship in large, complex firms can reflect top management's strategic vision *ex ante.* A key proposition of this paper is that corporate entrepreneurship can reflect this vision only *ex post,* because it is governed by a process of experimentation and selection spread over multiple, generic levels of management in the firm.

This somewhat limited role of top management in large, complex firms should not be surprising. To some extent, this is the result of the economic gravity of the very large operating system of such firms, which attracts the full attention of top management. Furthermore, top management is thoroughly familiar with the business strategies of the operating system, but lacks familiarity with the new resource combinations proposed by the entrepreneurial actors. Thus, not only are suchproposals relatively small, they are also relatively difficult to understand and evaluate for top management. Adopting an experimentation and selection approach to deal with entrepreneurial activity may, in fact, be quite rational from their perspective.

Managing an Experimentation-and-Selection Process

If top management of large, complex firms cannot specify the content, or even the precise direction, of entrepreneurial activity in advance, it *can* determine the overall level—how much—of entrepreneurial activity. To establish an optimal range for this type of activity in the light of the assessment of short- and long-term system regulation requirements is a key top-management task. Top management needs to make a firm commitment to support this level of activity independent of fluctuations in nonrelevant variables (e.g., variation in sales volume due to the business cycle). One danger, indeed, of an experimentation-and-selection approach is its tendency to oscillate widely, with concomitant high casualty rates among the entrepreneurial members. The study of ICV[53] and the studies of Peterson and Berger[54], and Kimberly[55] suggest that entrepreneurial individuals absorb a significant part of the cost of the organization's attempts to maintain viability. The organization's ability to make them do so would seem to support the proposition that entrepreneurial initiative is abundant, and that the level of corporate entrepreneurial activity is a function of demand rather than supply for it.[56] Yet, even though entrepreneurial energy may be abundant, positive feedback mechanisms can endanger the continuity in the stream of autonomous strategic behavior. This is especially the case when corporate entrepreneurship remains ancillary and sporadic, rather than an integral and continuous strategic concern of top management. The "safety valve" or "insurance" approach is probably not a very productive one for a firm in the long run, and almost certainly not for the development of its entrepreneurs. This would seem especially the case in times where outside avenues for career advancement for unsuccessful internal entrepreneurs are limited.

Autonomous strategic behavior emerges, by definition, spontaneously. Corporate management thus need not encourage entrepreneurship; it need only make sure not to suppress it. In fact, "encouraging" entrepreneurship may create games and lead to misguided opportunism. From the perspective of top management, guarding the firm against narrowly self-centered opportunism is a special problem in relationship to autonomous strategic behavior.[57] Such opportunism is, indeed, more likely under conditions where corporate support must be based on faith rather than on experience. This reinforces the crucial role of cognizant middle-level managers in selecting and supporting bona fide entrepreneurial actors and their projects.

Not capable to exert direct control over the autonomous strategic behavior originating at the operational level, top management can nevertheless attempt to influence the process through which it gets selected. To contrive a selective internal environment, top management almost automati-

---

[52] "3M Looks Beyond Luck and Fast Profits," *Business Week* (February 23, 1981).

[53] Burgelman, "Managing Innovating Systems"; Fast, *The Rise and Fall of Corporate New Venture Divisions.*

[54] "Entrepreneurship in Organizations."

[55] "Issues in the Creation of Organizations."

[56] Peterson, "Entrepreneurship and Organization."

[57] Williamson, *Markets and Hierarchies.*

cally focuses on manipulating the current structural context. The entrepreneurial activities documented by Peterson and Berger, for instance, were relatively simple compared to the unrelated diversification efforts documented in the study of ICV, and could be more readily monitored and controlled by top management. Still, the study suggests that top management's influence in the entrepreneurial process was exerted through manipulating the structural context in which the entrepreneurs operated, rather than through involvement in the substantive decision-making process. To the extent that the entrepreneurial activity is more complex, it can be expected that the manipulation of the structural context will be less effective, which is exactly what was found in the study of ICV, and which provides the rationale for the activation of the strategic context determination process. Only manipulating the structural context constitutes a rather crude and ineffective approach because the current structural context reflects the current concept of strategy, and autonomous strategic behavior necessarily falls outside the scope of the latter. Through successful autonomous strategic behavior, the firm's current concept of strategy, as well as the corresponding structural context, becomes partially and temporarily suspended. During this fluid period, the strategic context determination process is crucial, and, as noted earlier, middle-level managers play a major role in this.

Managing the Strategic Context

More research is needed to provide the basis for discussing how the strategic context determination process can be managed. A key ingredient in a firm's capacity to do so, however, would seem to be the availability of middle-level managers who can conceptualize strategies for new areas of business based on the results of autonomous strategic initiatives at the operational level. Top management must be willing to let such managers question the current concept of strategy. This may require that top management itself comprises people who have demonstrated these important middle-level skills earlier in their career. Too often, it seems, the road to the top in large, complex firms is the one where entrepreneurial responsibilities can altogether be avoided.[58] A better understanding of the entrepreneurial process at the corporate level may reduce the size of the oscillations in commitment to corporate entrepreneurship, as well as provide better and earlier evaluation of the merits of particular entrepreneurial projects.

To deal effectively with corporate entrepreneurship, top management needs flexibility and tolerance for ambiguity in its strategic vision. March has discussed a "technology of foolishness," which would seem to fit almost perfectly with the experimentation-and-selection approach.[59] Corporate entrepreneurship requires top management to shift focus from what will "always" or "never" be the domain of competence and the opportunity set of the firm, to one of leeway for new areas of corporate development "for the time being" or "maybe in the future." Top management does not need to communicate this because communication creates commitment, and corporate entrepreneurship requires its commitment only at the last possible moment. Not unlike DeCastro in Kidder's popular description of corporate entrepreneurial activity, top management needs to be aware that to deal with autonomous strategic behavior, "the only good strategy is the one that nobody else understands."[60] In fact, top management cannot understand the strategy completely either, but should be capable of sustaining a higher rate of progress in understanding as it unfolds, and a higher level of understanding in terms of the wider system ramifications as they become clear. Thus, corporate entrepreneurship can reflect top management's vision *ex post*.

Organization Design for Corporate Entrepreneurship

Autonomous strategic behavior cannot be planned. Still, once recognized and deemed supportable, it needs a "home," so to speak, for its further nurturing and development. This is the realm of organization design. Administrative linkages (reporting relationships, planning-budgeting jurisdiction, and the like), as well as operational linkages (lateral, work related, and professional), need to be

---

[58]Participants in the ICV study observed that managers who were early on in their career identified as "stars" had no incentive for seeking out positions in new business development, and were most likely to be assigned running large dollar volume type businesses, which are usually the least risky.

[59]J. G. March, "The Technology of Foolishness," in *Ambiguity and Choice in Organizations,* ed. J. G. March and P. Olsen (Bergen: Universitetsforlaget, 1976).

[60]T. Kidder, *The Soul of a New Machine* (Boston: Little Brown, 1981), p. 113.

designed to optimize the development process and/or to maximize the amount of organizational learning.

It is beyond the scope of this paper to examine the array of design options available to top management. In view of the preceding discussion, however, it would seem appropriate to suggest that the envisaged *strategic importance* over time to the firm and the degree of *relatedness to the firm's current capabilities and skills* are two important determinants of the appropriate administrative and operational linkages. Options like spin-off, external venture organization, separate internal venture organization, and innovating system fully integrated with the current operating system of the firm can be examined by top management in the light of this.

Given the high probability of failure among entrepreneurial participants, top management also will have to find ways of devising a reasonably foolproof safety net for such participants. At the same time, given the very high payoff for the firm of successful radical innovation, top management will have to devise ways of rewarding the accomplishments of entrepreneurial participants in a way commensurate with the risks they take. Further theoretical and empirical research is needed to establish more clearly what the risks precisely are, what the net costs or benefits are for an individual to work as an entrepreneur for a corporation as compared to working for himself or herself, and what constitutes the individual decision process that leads to one or the other involves.

Conclusion

Entrepreneurial and administrated ("bureaucratic") economic activity have long been considered essentially opposite forms with little if any connection. Schumpeter had already noted that successful entrepreneurial activity leads to organization building and to entrepreneurs becoming "managers."[61] Interesting bodies of literature in these two areas have been developed in isolation from each other.

Based on the observation that organizations must support a degree of entrepreneurial activity within them if they want to continue to be viable, the present paper has attempted a conceptual integration through the idea of "corporate entrepreneurship." This has been facilitated by the existence of a new model of the strategic process which allows for entrepreneurial activity—diversity—to be transformed into new organizational activity.

The conceptual integration proposed in this article is only a first step. Many research questions remain. It seems appropriate to conclude this paper by restating some of them. Research is needed to provide better understanding of the short-term and long-term regulation requirements for different types of organizations, and to relate this to the level of their entrepreneurial activity. Theoretical models and empirical research are needed to improve our understanding of the differences in strategic calculus of internal and external entrepreneurs. Such efforts could also shed more light on the symmetry-asymmetry of the relations, in terms of costs and benefits, between the corporate resource provider and its entrepreneurial agents. The nature of contrived experimentation-and-selection processes needs further elucidation. Finally, the conditions under which different organization designs are appropriate for different types of corporate entrepreneurship need further study.

Progress in understanding the process of corporate entrepreneurship may help the development of new managerial approaches and innovative administrative arrangements to facilitate the collaboration between entrepreneurial individuals and the organizations in which they are willing to exert their entrepreneurships.

[61] *The Theory of Economic Development.*

Reading II–14
Technological Discontinuities and Organizational Environments

Michael L. Tushman and Philip Anderson

Since Barnard's[1] and Selznick's[2] seminal work, one of the richest streams of research in organizational

 Administrative Science Quarterly 31 (1986), pp. 439–65.

[1] C. Barnard, *The Functions of the Executive* (Cambridge, MA: Harvard University Press, 1938).

[2] P. Selznick, *TVA and the Grass Roots: A Study of Politics and Organization* (Berkeley, CA: University of California Press, 1949).

theory has centered on organization–environment relations.[3] Recent work on organizational life cycles,[4] organizational adaptation,[5] population dynamics,[6] executive succession,[7] and strategy[8] hinges on environment-organization linkages. Environments pose constraints and opportunities for organizational action.[9]

If organizational outcomes are critically influenced by the context within which they occur, then better understanding of organizational dynamics requires that we more fully understand determinants of environmental change. While there has been substantial research on environmental conditions and organizational relations,[10] relatively little research has examined how competitive environments change over time. While it is agreed that environmental conditions are shaped by competitive, legal, political, and technological factors,[11] and the interplay between them,[12] there is little data on how these factors change over time or how they affect environmental conditions.

This reading focuses on technology as a central force in shaping environmental conditions. As technological factors shape appropriate organizational forms,[13] fundamental technological change affects the rise and fall of populations within organizational communities.[14] Basic technological innovation affects not only a given population, but also those populations within technologically interdependent communities. For example, major changes in semiconductor technology affected semiconductor firms as well as computer and automotive firms. Technology is, then, an important source of environmental variation and hence a critical factor affecting population dynamics.

This reading specifically investigates patterns of technological change and their impact on environmental conditions. Building on a considerable body of research on technological change, we argue and empirically demonstrate that patterned changes in technology dramatically affect environmental conditions. There exist measurable patterns of technological change that generate consistent patterns of environmental change over time across three diverse industries. While technology is but one force driving the course of environmental evolution, it is a key building block to better understand how environments and ultimately organizations evolve over time.

Technology and Technological Discontinuities

Technology can be defined as those tools, devices, and knowledge that mediate between inputs and outputs (process technology) and/or that create new products or services (product technology).[15] Technological change has an unequivocal impact on economic growth[16] and on the development of

[3]For a review see W. Starbuck, "Organizations and Their Environments" in *Handbook of Organizational and Industrial Psychology,* ed. M. D. Dunnette (New York: Wiley, 1983), pp. 1069–1123.

[4]D. Miller and P. Friesen, *Organizations: A Quantum View* (Englewood Cliffs, NJ: Prentice Hall, 1984); M. Tushman and E. Romanelli, "Organizational Evolution: A Metamorphosis Model of Convergence and Reorientation," in *Research in Organizational Behavior,* vol. 7, ed. L. L. Cummings and B. M. Staw (Greenwich, CT: JAI Press, 1985), pp. 171–222.

[5]H. Aldrich and E. R. Auster, "Even Dwarfs Started Small: Liabilities of Age and Size and Their Strategic Implications," in *Research in Organizational Behavior,* vol. 8, ed. L. L. Cummings and B. M. Staw (Greenwich, CT: JAI Press, 1986), pp. 165–98.

[6]J. Freeman, "Organizational Life Cycles and Natural Selection Processes," in *Research in Organizational Behavior,* vol. 4, ed. L. L. Cummings and B. M. Staw (Greenwich, CT: JAI Press, 1982), pp. 1–32.

[7]G. R. Carroll, "Dynamics of Publisher Succession in Newspaper Organizations," *Administrative Science Quarterly* 29 (1984), 93–113.

[8]For example, K. Harrigan, *Strategies for Vertical Integration* (Lexington, MA: D.C. Heath, Lexington Books, 1983).

[9]L. G. Hrebiniak and W. F. Joyce, "Organizational Adaptation: Strategic Choice and Environmental Determinism," *Administrative Science Quarterly* 30 (1985), pp. 336–49.

[10]See review in H. K. Downey and R. D. Ireland, "Quantitative versus Qualitative: Environmental Assessment in Organizational Studies," *Administrative Science Quarterly* 24 (1979), pp. 630–37.

[11]For example: Starbuck, "Organizations and their Environments" E. Romanelli and M. L. Tushman, "Inertia, Environments and Strategic Choice: A Quasi-Experimental Design for Comparative-Longitudinal Research," *Management Science* 32 (1986), pp. 608–21.

[12]M. Horwitch, *Clipped Wings: A Study of the Supersonic Transport* (Cambridge, MA: MIT Press, 1982); D. Noble, *Forces of Production: A Social History of Industrial Automation* (New York: Knopf, 1984).

[13]B. McKelvey, *Organizational Systematics—Taxonomy, Evolution, Classification* (Berkeley, CA: University of California Press, 1982).

[14]W. L. Astley, "The Two Ecologies: Population and Community Perspectives on Organizational Evolution," *Administrative Science Quarterly* 30 (1985), pp. 224–41.

[15]N. Rosenberg, *Technology and American Economic Growth* (Armonk, NY: M.E. Sharpe, 1972).

[16]R. M. Solow, "Technical Change and the Aggregate Production Function," *Review of Economics and Statistics* 39 (1957), pp. 312–20; B. Klein, *Wages and Business Cycles: A Dynamic Theory* (New York: Pergamon Press, 1984).

industries.[17] The impact of technology and technological change on environmental conditions is, however, less clear.

For over 30 years, technology and workflows have been central topics in organizational theory.[18] Most studies of technology in organizational theory, however, have been either cross sectional in design,[19] have taken place in technologically stable settings (e.g., public and not-for-profit settings), or simply have treated technology as a constant.[20] Since technology has been taken as a given, there has been a conspicuous lack of clarity concerning how and why technologies change and how technological change affects environmental and/or organizational evolution. An exception is the work of Brittain and Freeman.[21]

There is a substantial literature on technological evolution and change.[22] Some suggest that technological change is inherently a chance or spontaneous event driven by technological genius, as did Taton[23] in his discussion of penicillin and radioactivity, and Schumpeter.[24] Others, like Gilfillan,[25] who described the multiple independent discoveries of sail for ships, suggest that technological change is a function of historical necessity; still others view technological progress as a function of economic demand and growth.[26] An analysis of many different technologies over years of evolution strongly indicates that none of these perspectives alone captures the complexity of technological change. Technology seems to evolve in response to the interplay of history, individuals, and market demand. Technological change is a function of both variety and chance as well as structure and patterns.[27]

Case studies across a range of industries indicate that technological progress constitutes an evolutionary system punctuated by discontinuous change. Major product breakthroughs (e.g., jets or xerography) or process technological breakthroughs (e.g., float glass) are relatively rare and tend to be driven by individual genius (e.g., C. Carlson and xerography; A. Pilkington and float glass). These relatively rare discontinuities trigger a period of technological ferment. As a new product class opens (or following substitution of one product or process for a previous one), the rate of product variation is substantial as alternative product forms compete for dominance. An example is the competition between electric, wood, and internal combustion engines in automobiles or the competition between incompatible videocassette or microcomputer technologies. This technological experimentation and competition persists within a product class until a dominant design emerges as a synthesis of a number of proven concepts.[28]

A dominant design reflects the emergence of product-class standards and ends the period of technological ferment. Alternative designs are largely crowded out of the product class, and technological development focuses on elaborating a widely accepted product or process; the dominant design becomes a guidepost for further product or process change.[29] Dominant designs and associated shifts in product or process change have been found across industries. The Model T, the DC-3, the Fordson tractor, the Smith Model 5 typewriter and the PDP-11 minicomputer were dominant designs that dramatically shaped the evolution of their respective product classes.

---

[17]P. Lawrence and D. Dyer, *Renewing American Industry* (New York: Free Press, 1983).

[18]For example: D. Gerwin, "Relationships between Structure and Technology," in *Handbook of Organizational Design* vol. 2, ed. P. Nystrum and W. Starbuck (New York: Oxford University Press, 1980), pp. 3–31.

[19]For example: J. Woodward, *Industrial Organization: Theory and Practice* (Oxford: Oxford University Press, 1965).

[20]Astley, "The Two Ecologies."

[21]J. Brittain and J. Freeman, "Organizational Proliferation and Density-Dependent Selection," in *The Organizational Life Cycle,* ed. J. R. Kimberly and R. Miles (San Francisco: Jossey-Bass, 1980), pp. 291–338.

[22]For example: G. Mensch, *Stalemate in Technology: Innovations Overcome the Depression* (Cambridge, MA: Ballinger, 1979); D. Sahal, *Patterns of Technological Innovation* (Reading, MA: Addison-Wesley, 1981); J. Dutton and A. Thomas, "Relating Technological Change and Learning by Doing," in *Research on Technological Innovation, Management, and Policy* vol. 2, ed. R. D. Rosenbloom (Greenwich, CT: JAI Press, 1985), pp. 187–224.

[23]R. Taton, *Reason and Chance in Scientific Discovery* (New York: Philosophical Library, 1958).

[24]J. Schumpeter, *History of Economic Analysis* (New York: Oxford University Press, 1961).

[25]S. C. Gilfillan, *Inventing the Ship* (Chicago: Follett, 1935).

[26]J. Schmookler, *Invention and Economic Growth* (Cambridge, MA: Harvard University Press, 1966); R. Merton, *Social Theory and Social Structure* (New York: Free Press, 1968).

[27]E. E. Morison, *Men, Machines, and Modern Times* (Cambridge, MA: MIT Press, 1966); Sahal, *Patterns of Technological Innovation.*

[28]J. Utterback and W. Abernathy, "A Dynamic Model of Process and Product Innovation," *Omega* 33 (1975), pp. 639–56; W. Abernathy, *The Productivity Dilemma* (Baltimore, MD: Johns Hopkins University Press, 1978).

[29]Sahal, *Patterns of Technological Innovation;* W. Abernathy and K. B. Clark, "Innovation: Mapping the Winds of Creative Destruction," *Research Policy* 14 (1985), pp. 3–22.

Once a dominant design emerges, technological progress is driven by numerous incremental, improvement innovations.[30] For example, while the basic technology underlying xerography has not changed since Carlson's Model 914, the cumulative effect of numerous incremental changes on this dominant design has dramatically improved the speed, quality, and cost per unit of reprographic products.[31] A similar effect was documented by Yin and Dutton,[32] who described the enormous performance benefits of incremental process improvement in oil refining.

Incremental technological progress, unlike the initial breakthrough, occurs through the interaction of many organizations stimulated by the prospect of economic returns. This is evident in Hollander's[33] discussion of rayon, Tilton's[34] study of semiconductors, and Rosenbloom and Abernathy's[35] study of VCR technology. These incremental technological improvements enhance and extend the underlying technology and thus reinforce an established technical order.

Technological change is a bit-by-bit, cumulative process until it is punctuated by a major advance. Such discontinuities offer sharp price/performance improvements over existing technologies. Major technological innovations represent technical advance so significant that no increase in scale, efficiency, or design can make older technologies competitive with the new technology.[36] Product discontinuities are reflected in the emergence of new product classes (e.g., airlines, automobiles, plain-paper copiers), in product substitution (e.g., transistors versus vacuum tubes; diesel versus steam locomotives), or in fundamental product improvements (e.g., jets versus turbojets; LSI versus VSLI semiconductor technology). Process discontinuities are reflected either in process substitution (e.g., mechanical ice making versus natural ice harvesting; thermal versus catalytic cracking in crude oil refining; artificial versus natural gems) or in process innovations that result in radical improvements in industry-specific dimensions of merit (e.g., Dundee kiln in cement; Lubbers machinery in glass).

These major technological shifts can be classified as *competence-destroying* or *competence-enhancing*[37] because they either destroy or enhance the competence of existing firms in an industry. The former require new skills, abilities, and knowledge in both the development and production of the product. The hallmark of competence-destroying discontinuities is that mastery of the new technology fundamentally alters the set of relevant competences within a product class. For example, the knowledge and skills required to make glass using the float-glass method are quite different from those required to master other glass-making technologies. Diesel locomotives required new skills and knowledge that steam-engine manufacturers did not typically possess. Similarly, automatically controlled machine tools required wholesale changes in engineering, mechanical, and data processing skills. These new technical and engineering requirements were well beyond and qualitatively different from those skills necessary to manufacture conventional paper-punched machine tools.[38]

A competence-destroying product discontinuity either creates a new product class (e.g., xerography or automobiles) or substitutes for an existing product (e.g., diesel versus steam locomotive; transistors versus vacuum tubes). Competence-destroying process discontinuities represent a new way of making a given product. For example, the float-glass process in glass manufacture substituted for continuous grinding and polishing; mechanical ice making substituted for natural ice harvesting; planar processes substituted for the single-wafer process in semiconductors. In each case, the product remained essentially unchanged while the process by which it was made was fundamentally altered. Competence-destroying process breakthroughs may involve combining previously discrete steps into a more

[30]S. Myers and D. G. Marquis, *Successful Industrial Innovations* (Washington, DC: National Science Foundation, 1969); Dutton and Thomas, "Relating Technological Change and Learning by Doing."

[31]J. H. Dessauer, *My Years with Xerox* (New York: Manor Books, 1975).

[32]Z. Yin and J. M. Dutton, "Systems Learning and Technological Change: The Evolution of 20th Century U.S. Domestic Petroleum-Refining Processes," working paper, New York University Graduate School of Business Administration, 1986.

[33]S. Hollander, *The Sources of Increased Efficiency* (Cambridge, MA: MIT Press, 1965).

[34]J. W. Tilton, *International Diffusion of Technology: The Case of Semiconductors* (Washington, DC: Brookings Institution, 1971).

[35]R. Rosenbloom and W. Abernathy, "The Climate for Innovation in Industry: The Role of Management Attitudes and Practices in Consumer Electronics," *Research Policy* 11 (1982), pp. 209–25.

[36]Mensch, *Stalemate in Technology;* Sahal, *Patterns of Technological Innovation.*

[37]See also Abernathy and Clark, "Innovation."

[38]Noble, *Forces of Production.*

continuous flow (e.g., float glass) or may involve a completely different process (e.g., man-made gems).

Competence-destroying discontinuities are so fundamentally different from previously dominant technologies that the skills and knowledge base required to operate the core technology shift. Such major changes in skills, distinctive competence, and production processes are associated with major changes in the distribution of power and control within firms and industries.[39] For example, the ascendance of automatically controlled machine tooling increased the power of industrial engineers within the machine-tool industry,[40] while the diffusion of high-volume production processes led to the rise of professional managers within more formally structured organizations.[41]

Competence-enhancing discontinuities are order-of-magnitude improvements in price/performance that build on existing know-how within a product class. Such innovations substitute for older technologies, yet do not render obsolete skills required to master the old technologies. Competence-enhancing product discontinuities represent an order-of-magnitude improvement over prior products yet build on existing know-how. For example, IBM's 360 series was a major improvement in price, performance, and features over prior models yet was developed through the synthesis of familiar technologies.[42] Similarly, the introduction of fan jets or of the screw propeller dramatically improved the speed of jets and ocean-going steamships, and aircraft producers and boatyards were able to take advantage of existing knowledge and skills and rapidly absorb these complementary technologies.[43]

Competence-enhancing process discontinuities are process innovations that result in an order-of-magnitude increase in the efficiency of producing a given product. For example, the Edison kiln was a major process innovation in cement manufacture that permitted enormous increases in production capacity yet built on existing skills in the cement industry.[44] Similarly, major process advances in semiconductor integration and in strip steel and glass production eliminated barriers to future growth in their product classes. These advances built on existing knowledge and skills and provided the core for subsequent incremental improvements.[45]

Exhibit 1 gives a typology of technological changes with examples of competence-destroying and competence-enhancing product and process technologies.

Both technological discontinuities and dominant designs are only known in retrospect—technological superiority is no guarantee of success. The dominance of a substitute product (e.g., Wankel engines, supersonic jets, or bubble memory), substitute process (e.g., continuous casting), or a dominant design (e.g., VHS versus beta videocassette systems) is a function of technological, market, legal, and social factors that cannot be fully known in advance. For example, the choice by vacuum tube makers such as RCA, GE, and Philco to concentrate on a dominant design for electron tubes in the early transistor days turned out, in retrospect, to have been an error.[46] Similarly, choices of standard record speeds, widths of railroad track, automatically controlled machine tool technologies, or automated office equipment standards are often less a function of technical merit than of market or political power.[47]

A number of product-class case studies indicate that technology progresses in stages through relatively long periods of incremental, competence-enhancing change elaborating a particular dominant design. These periods of increasing consolidation and learning-by-doing may be punctuated by competence-destroying technological discontinuities (i.e., product or process substitution) or by further competence-enhancing technological advance (e.g., revitalizing a given product or process with complementary technologies). Technological discontinuities trigger a period of technological ferment culminating in a dominant design and, in turn, leading to the next period of incremental, competence-enhancing, technological change. Thus, we hypothesize:

[39]A. D. Chandler, Jr., *The Visible Hand: The Managerial Revolution in American Business* (Cambridge, MA: Belknap Press, 1977; S. R. Barley, "Technology as an Occasion for Structuring: Evidence from Observations of CT Scanners and the Social Order of Radiology Departments," *Administrative Science Quarterly* 31 (1986), pp. 78-108.

[40]Noble, *Forces of Production*.

[41]Chandler, *The Visible Hand*.

[42]E. W. Pugh, *Memories That Shaped an Industry: Decisions Leading to the IBM System 360* (Cambridge, MA: MIT Press, 1984).

[43]R. E. G. Davies, *Airlines of the United States Since 1914* (London: Putnam, 1972).

[44]R. Lesley, *A History of the United States Portland Cement Industry* (Chicago: Portland Cement Association, 1924).

[45]Dutton and Thomas, "Relating Technological Change and Learning by Doing."

[46]Tilton, *International Diffusion of Technology*.

[47]Noble, *Forces of Production*.

EXHIBIT 1 A Typology of Product and Process Technological Changes

Technological Changes	
Competence-Destroying	Competence-Enhancing
Product	
New product class: Airlines (1924) Cement (1872) Plain-paper copying (1959)	*Major product improvements* Jet→turbofan LSI→VSLI semiconductors Mechanical→electric typewriters Continuous aim cannons Nonreturnable→returnable bottles Thin-walled iron cylinder block engine
Product substitution: Vacuum tubes→transistors Steam→diesel locomotives Piston→jet engines Records→compact disks Punched paper→automatic control machine tooling Discrete→integrated circuits Open→closed steel auto bodies	*Incremental product changes:* *Dominant designs** PDP-11, VHS technology IBM 360, DC-3 Numerical control machine tools
Process	
Process substitution: Natural→mechanical ice Natural→industrial gems Open hearth→basic oxygen furnace Individual wafer→planar process Continuous grinding→float glass Thermal cracking→catalytic cracking Vertical→rotary kiln Blown→drawn window glass	*Major process improvements:* Edison kiln Resistive metal deposition (semiconductors) Gob feeder (glass containers) Catalytic cracking→catalytic reforming *Incremental process improvements:* Learning by doing; numerous process improvements

*Some dominant designs are incremental improvements (e.g., PDP-11), while others are major improvements (e.g., DC-3, IBM 360).

Hypothesis 1: Technological change within a product class will be characterized by long periods of incremental change punctuated by discontinuities.

Hypothesis 1a: Technological discontinuities are either competence enhancing (build on existing skills and know-how) or competence destroying (require fundamentally new skills and competences).

Competence-destroying and competence-enhancing discontinuities dramatically alter previously attainable price/performance relationships within a product class. Both create technological uncertainty as firms struggle to master an untested and incompletely understood product or process. Existing firms within an industry are in the best position to initiate and exploit new possibilities opened up by a discontinuity if it builds on competence they already possess. Competence-enhancing discontinuities tend to consolidate industry leadership; the rich are likely to get richer.

Competence-destroying discontinuities, in contrast, disrupt industry structure.[48] Skills that brought product-class leaders to preeminence are rendered largely obsolete; new firms founded to exploit the new technology will gain market share at the expense of organizations that, bound by traditions, sunk costs, and internal political constraints, remain committed to outmoded technology.[49] We thus hypothesize:

Hypothesis 2: The locus of innovation will differ for competence-destroying and competence-enhancing

[48]Mensch, *Stalemate in Technology.*

[49]Tilton, *International Diffusion of Technology;* M. Hannan and J. Freeman, "The Population Ecology of Organizations," *American Journal of Sociology* 82 (1977), pp. 929–64.

technological changes. Competence-destroying discontinuities will be initiated by new entrants, while competence-enhancing discontinuities will be initiated by existing firms.

Technological Discontinuities and Organizational Environments

To determine the extent to which technological discontinuities affect environmental conditions, we build on Dess and Beard's[50] review of environmental dimensions and examine two critical characteristics of organizational environments: uncertainty and munificence. Uncertainty refers to the extent to which future states of the environment can be anticipated or accurately predicted.[51] Munificence refers to the extent to which an environment can support growth. Environments with greater munificence impose fewer constraints on organizations than those environments with resource constraints.

Both competence-enhancing and competence-destroying technological discontinuities generate uncertainty as firms struggle to master an incompletely understood product or process. Technological breakthroughs trigger a period of technological ferment as new technologies are tried, established price/performance ratios are upset, and new markets open. During these periods of technological upheaval, it becomes substantially more difficult to forecast demand and prices. Technological discontinuities, then, will be associated with increases in environmental uncertainty:

> **Hypothesis 3:** Competitive uncertainty will be higher after a technological discontinuity than before the discontinuity.

Technological discontinuities drive sharp decreases in price/performance or input-output ratios. These factors, in turn, fuel demand in a product class. The role of technological progress in stimulating demand is well documented.[52] As both competence-enhancing and competence-destroying discontinuities reflect major price/performance improvements, both will be associated with increased demand and environmental munificence:

> **Hypothesis 4:** Environmental munificence will be higher after a technological discontinuity than before the discontinuity.

Environments can also be described in terms of different competitive conditions.[53] Important dimensions of competitive conditions include entry-exit patterns and degree of order within a product class. Orderliness within a product class can be assessed by interfirm sales variability. Those environments with substantial net entry and substantial interfirm sales variability will be very different competitive arenas than those environments in which exits dominate and there is minimal interfirm sales variability.

Competence-destroying technological discontinuities have quite different effects on competitive conditions than do competence-enhancing discontinuities. Competence-enhancing advances permit existing firms to exploit their competence and expertise and thereby gain competitive advantage over smaller or newer firms. Competence-enhancing discontinuities consolidate leadership in a product class; the rich get richer as liabilities of newness plague new entrants. These order-creating breakthroughs increase barriers to entry and minimum scale requirements. These processes will be reflected in relatively fewer entries relative to exits and a decrease in interfirm sales variability—those remaining firms will share more equally in product-class sales growth.

Competence-destroying discontinuities break the existing order. Barriers to entry are lowered; new firms enter previously impenetrable markets by exploiting the new technology.[54] These discontinuities favor new entrants at the expense of entrenched defenders. New entrants take advantage of fundamentally different skills and expertise and gain sales at the expense of formerly dominant firms burdened with the legacy (i.e., skills, abilities, and expertise) of prior technologies and ways of operating.[55] Competence-destroying discontinuities will be associated with increased entry-to-exit ratios and an increase in interfirm sales variability:

---

[50]G. G. Dess and D. W. Beard, "Dimensions of Organizational Task Environments," *Administrative Science Quarterly* 29 (1984), pp. 52–73.

[51]J. Pfeffer and G. Salancik, *The External Control of Organizations* (New York: Harper & Row, 1978).

[52]For example, Solow, "Technological Change and the Aggregate Production Function"; Mensch, *Stalemate in Technology*.

[53]F. Scherer, *Industrial Market Structure and Economic Performance* (Boston: Houghton Mifflin, 1980).

[54]Astley, "The Two Ecologies"; Abernathy and Clark, "Innovation."

[55]Astley, "The Two Ecologies"; Tushman and Romanelli, "Organizational Evolution."

Hypothesis 5: Competence-enhancing discontinuities will be associated with decreased entry-to-exit ratios and decreased interfirm sales variability. These patterns will be reversed for competence-destroying discontinuities.

If competence-destroying discontinuities do not emerge to alter a product class, successive competence-enhancing discontinuities will result in increased environmental orderliness and consolidation. Each competence-enhancing breakthrough builds on prior advances and further raises barriers to entry and minimum scale requirements. As product classes mature, the underlying resource base becomes ever more limited by physical and resource constraints. Successive competence-enhancing discontinuities will have smaller impacts on uncertainty and munificence as successive advances further exploit a limited technology and market-resource base:

Hypothesis 6: Successive competence-enhancing discontinuities will be associated with smaller increases in uncertainty and munificence.

Environmental changes induced by a technological discontinuity present a unique opportunity or threat for individual organizations.[56] Technological discontinuities alter the competitive environment and reward those innovative firms that are first to recognize and exploit technological opportunities. The superiority of a new technology presents organizations with a stark choice: adapt or face decline. Those firms that are among the first to adopt the new product or process proceed down the learning curve ahead of those that follow. The benefits of volume and experience provide early movers with a competitive edge not easily erased.[57] Therefore, we hypothesize:

Hypothesis 7: Those organizations that initiate major technological innovations will have higher growth rates than other firms in the product class.

Research Design and Measures

Three product classes were selected for study: domestic scheduled passenger airline transport, Portland cement manufacture, and minicomputer manufacture (excluding firms that merely add peripherals and/or software to another firm's minicomputer and resell the system). These three product classes represent assembled products, nonassembled products, and services; this product-class diversity increases the generalizability of our results. These industries were also selected because most participants historically had been undiversified, so environmental conditions outside the industry had little effect on these firms. Data on each product class were gathered from the year of the niche's inception (1872 for cement, 1924 for airlines, and 1956 for minicomputers) through 1980.

The three populations studied included all U.S. firms that produced cement, flew airplane passengers, or produced minicomputers. These industries were chosen partly because archival sources exist permitting a complete census of population members over time. Two outstanding books[58] chronicle the history of the cement and airline industries and include meticulously researched profiles of early entrants into those product classes. In the airline industry, the Civil Aeronautics Board (CAB) lists of entries and exits after 1938 are definitive, due to licensing requirements. In cement, the very high degree of agreement among two trade journals and two industry directories from 1900 on suggests substantially all firms that ever produced cement are included. Similarly, in minicomputers, the very high degree of agreement among trade journals, an exhaustive annual industry directory in *Computers and Automation,* and International Data Corporation (IDC) product listings indicate that virtually all firms that ever produced a minicomputer are included. All sources included very small firms that survived only briefly; any firms that might have been overlooked in this study have never received published mention in three industries thoroughly covered by numerous archival sources.

Technological change. A thorough review of books and trade publications permitted the identification of price/performance changes and key technological events within the three product classes. Technological change was measured by examining key performance parameters for all new kilns, airplanes, or minicomputers introduced in each year

[56]Tushman and Romanelli, "Organizational Evolution."

[57]M. Porter, *Competitive Advantage: Creating and Sustaining Superior Performance* (New York: Free Press, 1985); I. MacMillan and M. L. McCaffrey, "Strategy for Financial Services: Cashing in on Competitive Inertia," *Journal of Business Strategy* 4 (1984), pp. 58–73.

[58]Lesley, *A History of the United States Portland Cement Industry.*

of the industry's existence. For cement and airlines, percentage improvement in the state of the art was calculated by dividing the seat-mile-per-year or barrel-per-day capacity of the most capable plane or largest kiln in existence in a given year by the same capacity figure for the most capable plane or largest kiln in existence the previous year. This review of new equipment also permitted the identification of initiators and early adopters of significant innovations. Technological discontinuities were relatively easy to identify because a few innovations so markedly advanced the state of the art that they clearly stand out from less dramatic improvements.

The key performance parameter in cement production is kiln capacity in barrels of cement per day. For every new kiln, this capacity is reported by the manufacturer and is widely published in trade journals and industry directories. For airlines, the key economic factor is the number of passenger-seat-miles per year a plane can fly, calculated by multiplying the number of seats normally in an aircraft model by the number of miles per year it can fly at normal operating speeds for the average number of flight hours per year it proved able to log. These figures are reported in Davies (*Airlines of the United States Since 1914*) for all aircraft models flown by U.S. airliners. In minicomputers, a key performance parameter is the amount of time required for the central processing unit to complete one cycle; this is the primary determinant of computer speed and throughput capability. Both *Computers and Automation,* a leading trade journal and industry directory, and the International Data Corporation (IDC), a leading computer-industry research firm, report cycle time for all minicomputers.

Uncertainty. Uncertainty is typically measured as a function of variance measures.[59] Because environmental uncertainty refers to the extent to which future states of the environment cannot be predicted accurately, we measured uncertainty in terms of forecasting error—the ability of industry analysts to predict industry outcomes. Published forecasts for every SIC code are collected and indexed in *Predicasts Forecasts.* For each of the three niches, published one-year demand growth forecasts were collected and compared to actual historical results. Forecast error is defined as:

$$\frac{([\text{Forecast demand growth} - \text{Actual demand growth}] \times 100)}{(\text{Actual demand growth})}$$

To measure environmental uncertainty, the mean forecast error for the five-year period before each technological discontinuity was compared to the mean forecast error for the five-year period following the discontinuity. The choice of five-year periods is arbitrary. Major technological changes do not have an overnight impact; it takes several years for their effect on uncertainty and munificence to appear. Yet in the longer run, extraneous events create demand fluctuations whose noise can drown out the patterns generated by major technological advances. Since the industries selected included discontinuities 7 and 10 years apart, 5 years was selected as the maximum practicable period of observation that would not create serious overlap problems between the era following one discontinuity and the era preceding another.

Munificence. Munificence was measured in terms of demand, the basic resource available to niche participants. Annual sales growth in units was obtained from the CAB and Bureau of Mines for the airline and cement niches, respectively. Minicomputer sales data were obtained from the International Data Corporation and from *Computers and Automation.* Since sales figures grow as a result of both inflation and growth in the economy as a whole, these factors were eliminated by dividing demand figures by an index of real GNP growth. Mean demand growth was calculated for five-year periods before and after each technological discontinuity.

Two possible objections may be raised to comparing the means of five-year periods preceding and following a discontinuity. First, if there is a strong upward trend in the time series, then for practically any year chosen, demand in the five succeeding years will be significantly higher than demand in the five preceding years. If this is so, there is nothing special about the eras surrounding a technological discontinuity. On the other hand, it may be that the findings are very sensitive to the exact year chosen to mark the discontinuity. If results are significant comparing, for example, 1960–1964 with 1965–1969, but not significant if the comparison is between 1959–1963 and 1964–1968, or between 1961–1965 and 1966–1970, then the finding is not robust.

---

[59]Dess and Beard, "Dimensions of Organizational Task Environments."

Accordingly, the difference-of-means test was performed for every possible combination of two adjacent five-year periods for each industry. In each industry, it was found that eras of significant before and after demand shift are rare. Sixteen of 96 possible comparisons were significant at the .05 level in the cement industry (17 percent), 17 of 45 possible comparisons of airline demand (38 percent), and 2 of 7 possible comparisons of minicomputer demand (28 percent). This suggests that technological discontinuities are not the only events that seem to be associated with sharp increases in demand. However, neither do such shifts occur frequently or at random. In each case, a difference of one year either way in identifying the discontinuity would have made no difference; the demand shift is not particularly sensitive to the specific year chosen as the discontinuity.

At a few comparatively rare periods in the history of an industry, then, one can locate a demand breakpoint, an era of two or three years during which average demand for the five years following any of these critical years significantly exceeds the average demand in the five years preceding the chosen year. Some of these critical eras are not associated with technological discontinuities. Without exception, every technological discontinuity is associated with such a demand shift.

Entry and exit. Entry and exit data were gathered from industry directories and books chronicling the histories of each product class. An entry was recorded in the year when a firm first began cement production, an airline flew its first passenger-mile, or a firm produced its first minicomputer. An exit was recorded when a firm ceased producing cement, flying passengers, or producing at least one minicomputer. Bankruptcy was recorded as an exit only if production ceased. An exit was recorded whenever a firm was acquired; an entry was recorded only if the acquiring firm did not already produce cement, fly passengers, or produce minicomputers. An entrant was classified as new if the company sold no products prior to its entry into the industry or as an existing firm if it sold at least one product before entering the industry. Entry and exit statistics are not calculated for the airline industry from 1938 through 1979, because entries were forbidden by the CAB, and exits depended more on regulatory action than on market forces. Exhibit 2 provides measures, data sources, and summary data for each variable.

Early adopters. To test hypothesis 7, that those firms initiating technological discontinuities would have higher growth rates than other firms in the product class, we examined the growth rates of the first four adopters. Data were available for airlines after 1955 and for minicomputers. The number of early adopters chosen was arbitrary. Four were selected to provide a group large enough for a mean to be meaningful, yet small enough to argue reasonably that the firms considered were quicker to adopt the innovation than the rest of the industry.

Results

Hypothesis 1 suggested that technological evolution would be characterized by periods of incremental change punctuated by either competence-destroying or competence-enhancing discontinuities. Hypothesis 2 argued that competence-destroying advances would be initiated by new entrants, while competence-enhancing advances would be initiated by existing firm. Exhibit 3 summarizes the key technological discontinuities for each niche, while Exhibits 4–6 provide more detailed data on key performance dimensions over time.

The cement, airline, and minicomputer niches opened in 1872, 1924, and 1956, respectively. After the three niche openings, there were six competence-enhancing technological discontinuities and two competence-destroying discontinuities (see Exhibit 3). Each discontinuity had a marked effect on a key measure of cost or performance, far greater than the impact of other, more incremental technological events.[60]

Exhibit 4 documents the three significant technological changes that have punctuated the history of the Portland cement industry. Portland cement, invented in Europe, was first made in this country about 1872, but early attempts to compete with established European brands were largely failures. Two events effectively established the domestic industry. The development of the rotary kiln made the manufacture of large volumes of cement with little labor practicable, and the invention in 1896

[60]Other industries may not exhibit such marked differences and eventually a coefficient of technological progress could be developed to help distinguish incremental from discontinuous change; one approach might be to pool annual percentage improvements and select those more than two standard deviations above the mean.

EXHIBIT 2 Summary of Variables, Measures, and Data Sources

Variable	Industry	Measure	Data Source	*N*	Range	Mean	SD
Technological change	Cement	Percentage improvement in barrel/day production capacity of largest kiln.	Published specifications of new kilns in *Rock Products.*	90	0–320%		
	Airlines	Percentage improvement in seat-miles per year capacity of most capable plane flown.	Davies.*	54	0–248%		
	Mini-computers	Central processor unit speed.	Published specifications in *Computers and Automation.*	24	.2–9000		
Locus of innovation	Cement	Proportion of new firms among earliest to adopt an innovation.	Reports on new kilns in *Rock Products* and trade directories.	4	.1–1.0		
	Airlines		Davies,* CAB annual studies of airplane purchases.	4	0–.9		
	Mini-computers		Published specifications in *Computers and Automation.*	3	0–.5		
Uncertainty	Cement	Mean percentage error of one-year demand growth forecasts.	*Predicasts Forecasts.*	28	5.2–266.9	52.0	61.6
	Airlines			88	.1-381.4	59.2	58.4
	Mini-computers			36	3.5–811	138.1	167.1
Munificence	Cement	Annual cement consumption (tons).	U.S. Bureau of Mines.	101	8–85513	30296	27103
	Airlines	Annual passenger-seat-miles (mil.).	Civil Aeronautics Board.	52	.1–156.6	34.6	46.1
	Mini-computers	Annual minicomputer sales (000 units).	International Data Corporation.	16	.1–168	47.3	49.6
Entries	Cement	Number of firms producing for first time (mean, range and SD are entries per year, *N* is number of entries).	*Cement Industry Trade Directory; Rock Products.*	281	0–24	2.8	4.2
	Airlines		Davies,* CAB annual reports.	147	1–33	11.3	9.8
	Mini-computers		*Computers and Automation;* International Data Corporation.	173	3–30	10.8	7.3
Exits	Cement	Number of firms acquired or no longer producing (mean, SD and range are exits per year, *N* is number of exits).	*Cement Industry Trade Directory; Rock Products.*	218	0–23	2.2	3.9
	Airlines		Davies,* CAB annual reports.	126	1–28	9.7	8.2
	Mini-computers		*Computers and Automation;* International Data Corporation.	82	0–14	5.1	4.2
Interfirm sales variance	Airlines	Unweighted variance in five-year sales growth percentage among all firms in the industry.	Same as munificence measure.	4	2.0–13.4	5.5	4.6
	Mini-computers		Same as munificence measure.	4	2.6–21.3	11.2	8.6
Firm growth rate	Airlines	Firm sales at end of five-year era divided by sales at beginning of five-year era.	CAB annual reports.	46	−269–346	61.4	79.9
	Mini-computers		International Data Corporation.	67	−96–11900	635.6	1561.6

*R.E.G. Davies, *Airlines of the United States Since 1914* (London: Putnam), 1972.

EXHIBIT 3 Significant Technological Discontinuities

Industry	Year	Event	Importance	Type of Discontinuity	Locus of Innovation: New Firms	Locus of Innovation: Existing Firms	Probability
Cement	1872	First production of Portland cement in the United States.	Discovery of proper raw materials and importation of knowledge opens new industry.	Niche opening	10 of 10	1 of 10	
	1896	Patent for process burning powdered coal as fuel.	Permits economical use of efficient rotary kilns.	Competence-destroying	4 of 5	1 of 5	.333
	1909	Edison patents long kiln (150 ft.).	Higher output with less cost.	Competence-enhancing	1 of 6	5 of 6	.001*
	1966	Dundee Cement installs huge kiln, far larger than any previous.	Use of process control permits operation of very efficient kilns.	Competence-enhancing	1 of 8	7 of 8	.000*
Airlines	1924	First airline.	Mail contracts make transport feasible.	Niche opening	9 of 10	1 of 10	
	1936	DC3 airplane.	First large and fast enough to carry passengers economically.	Competence-enhancing	0 of 4	4 of 4	.005*
	1959	First jet airplane in commercial use.	Speed changes economics of flying.	Competence-enhancing	0 of 4	4 of 4	.005*
	1969	Widebody jets debut.	Much greater capacity and efficiency.	Competence-enhancing	0 of 4	4 of 4	.005*
Minicomputer manufacture	1956	Burroughs E-101	First computer under $50,000.	Niche opening	1 of 8	7 of 8	
	1965	Digital Equipment Corp. PDP-8.	First integrated-circuit minicomputer.	Competence-destroying	3 of 6	3 of 6	.019*
	1971	Data General Supernova SC.	Semiconductor memory much faster than core.	Competence-enhancing	0 of 7	7 of 7	.533

Note: Fisher's exact test compares the pool of firms that are among the first to enter the niche with the pool of firms that introduce or are among the first to adopt a major technological innovation. The null hypothesis is that the proportion of new firms is the same in each sample; probability is the probability of obtaining the observed proportions if the null hypothesis is correct.
*$p<.01$.

of a method for creating a continuous flame fed by powdered coal meant that a high-quality, uniform cement could be made without expensive hand-stoking.

During the following decade, rotary kilns 60 feet in length were standard. In 1909, Thomas Edison patented a technique for making kilns over 150 feet in length, enormously increasing the production capacity of a kiln, and the industry rapidly adopted the new "long kiln." Subsequent progress, though, was gradual; kiln capacity increased greatly over a period of decades, but in a series of incremental advances. In 1960, the industry began experimenting with computerized control of kilns. The introduction of computers permitted the construction of huge kilns, much larger than any that had preceded them. The experimental models of the early 1960s culminated in the enormous Dundee kiln in 1967; previously kilns of such capacity could not have been used because their huge size and weight made them impossible to regulate.

The revolution that brought powdered coal and rotary kilns to the industry was competence-destroying, rendering almost completely obsolete the know-how required to operate wood-fired vertical kilns. A totally new set of competences was

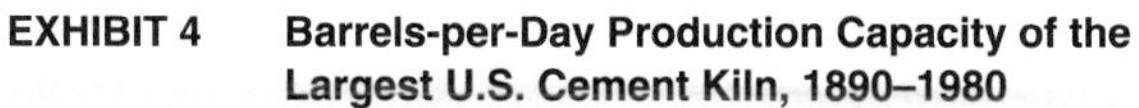
EXHIBIT 4 Barrels-per-Day Production Capacity of the Largest U.S. Cement Kiln, 1890–1980

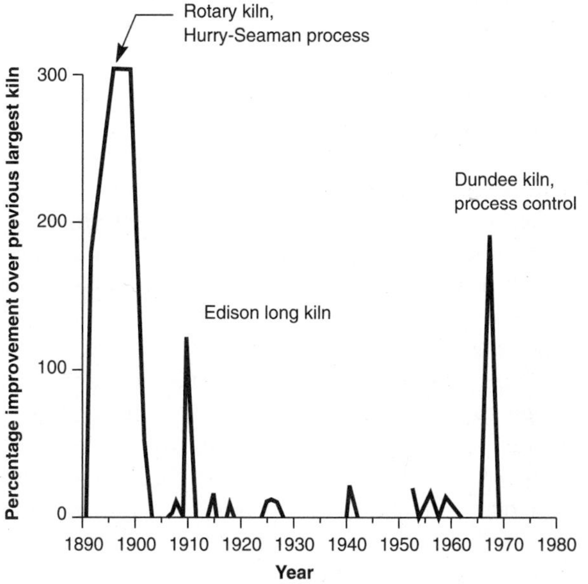

required to make cement, and most vertical kiln operators went out of business. The Edison and Dundee kilns were competence-enhancing innovations; each markedly extended the capability of coal-fired rotary kiln technology. A large investment in new kilns and process-control equipment was required, but existing cement-making techniques were not made obsolete, and the leading firms in the industry proved most able to make the necessary capital expenditures.

New developments in aircraft construction have been the major technological breakthroughs that have affected the economics of the airline industry, as illustrated in Exhibit 5. Numerous flimsy, slow aircraft were flown until the early 1930s, when a flurry of development produced the Boeing 247, Douglas DC-2, and Douglas DC-3 in a span of three years, each a significant improvement on its immediate predecessor. The DC-3, which incorporated some 25 major improvements in aircraft design,[61] superseded all other models to become so dominant that by the outbreak of World War II, 80 percent of U.S. airliners in service were DC-3s. Further aircraft improvements were incremental until 1959, when the debut of jet aircraft, with their considerably greater speed and size, again changed the economics of the airline industry. The final breakthrough event was the introduction in 1969 of the Boeing 747, beginning an era dominated by wide-body jets.

All three of these major advances were competence-enhancing from the perspective of the air carriers (though not from the perspective of aircraft manufacturers). Each advance generated significant economies of scale; airlines could carry many more passengers with each plane than was possible before. Though new skills were required to

[61]Davies, *Airlines of the United States Since 1914.*

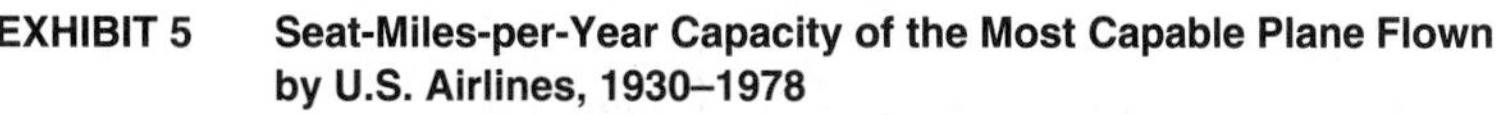
EXHIBIT 5 Seat-Miles-per-Year Capacity of the Most Capable Plane Flown by U.S. Airlines, 1930–1978

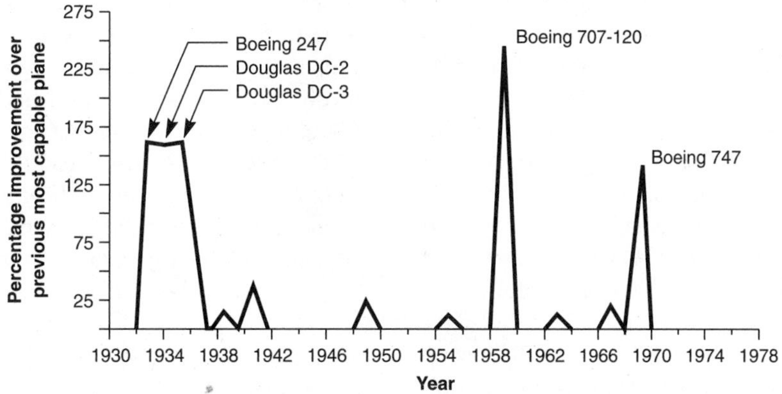

EXHIBIT 6 Central-Processor-Unit Cycle Time of the Fastest Minicomputer in Production, 1956–1980

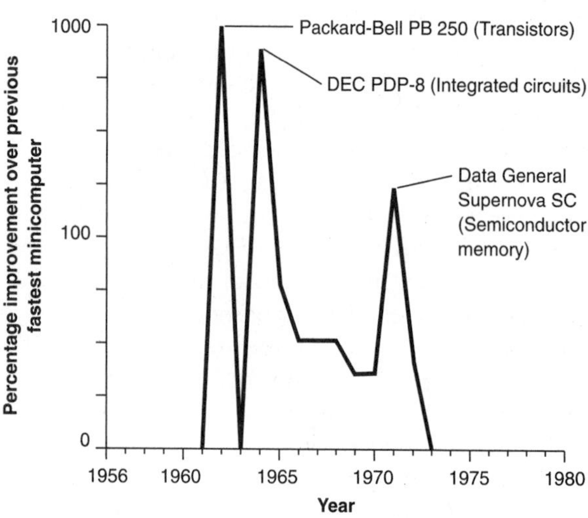

fly and maintain the new machines, airlines were able to build on their existing competences and take advantage of increased scale economies permitted with new aircraft.

In contrast to cement and airlines, in the minicomputer industry established firms built the first inexpensive computers (usually as an extension of their accounting machine lines). These early minicomputers were based on vacuum tubes and/or transistor technology. The first transistor minicomputer was far faster than its vacuum-tube predecessors, but transistor architecture was replaced by integrated circuitry within two years and thus never diffused widely. Sales were meager until integrated-circuit minicomputers were introduced by a combination of new and older firms. Exhibit 6 depicts the enormous impact of transistors, immediately followed by integrated circuitry, on computer performance. Integrated circuitry increased minicomputer speed more than 100 times between 1963 and 1965, while size and assembly complexity also decreased substantially. Integrated circuits permitted the construction of compact machines at a greatly reduced cost by eliminating most of the wiring associated with transistors. Integrated circuit technology was competence-destroying, since expertise in designing, programming, and assembling transistor-based computers was not especially transferable to the design and manufacture of integrated circuit machines.[62]

The introduction of semiconductor memory in 1971 caused another abrupt performance improvement (see Exhibit 6) but did not challenge the fundamental competence of existing minicomputer firms; most companies were able to offer customers versions of their existing models equipped with either magnetic core or semiconductor memory. The effect of semiconductor memory was to increase order in the product class as existing firms were able easily to incorporate this innovation into their existing expertise. For memory manufacturers, however, semiconductor memory was a competence-destroying discontinuity.

These patterns of incremental technological progress punctuated by discontinuities strongly support hypothesis 1. As suggested in hypothesis 2, the locus of technological innovation for competence-enhancing breakthroughs significantly differs from that of competence-destroying discontinuities. The first cement and airline firms were overwhelmingly new start-ups, not existing companies entering a new industry (Exhibit 3). No product classes existed in 1872 or 1924 whose competences were transferable to cement manufacture or flying airplanes. In contrast, early minicomputers were made by existing accounting machine and electronics manufacturers, who found that existing know-how was readily transferable to the first small, crude computers. New industries can be started either by new organizations or by established ones from other industries; a key variable seems to be whether analogous product classes with transferable competences exist when a new product class emerges.

Patterns in the locus of innovation for discontinuities subsequent to product-class openings are remarkably consistent. The two competence-destroying discontinuities were largely pioneered by new firms (i.e., 7 of 11), while the six competence-enhancing discontinuities were almost exclusively introduced by established industry members (i.e., 35 of 37 firms were existing firms; Fisher's exact test; $p = .0002$). Across these three industries, competence-destroying breakthroughs are significantly more likely to be initiated by new firms, while competence-enhancing breakthroughs are significantly more likely to be initiated by existing firms. Simi-

[62]K. Fishman, *The Computer Establishment* (New York: Harper & Row, 1981).

EXHIBIT 7 Forecast Error over Time†

Industry	Era	Mean Forecast Error	t(1)	D.f.	t(2)	D.f.
Airlines	1955–1959	16.15%	1.78*	18		
	1960–1964	77.81%				
Airlines	1965–1969	18.52%	4.35**	66	1.91*	54
	1970–1974	49.13%				
Cement	1963–1967	38.31%	1.85*	26		
	1968–1972	80.26%				
Minicomputers	1967–1971	146.31%	−.14	34		
	1972–1976	136.12%				

*$p < .05$; **$p < .01$.
†t(1) compares mean forecast error of the first period to the mean forecast error of the second period; t(2) compares 1960–1964 with 1970–1974.

larly, within each industry, Fisher's exact tests indicate that the proportion of new firms that initiate competence-destroying discontinuities is significantly greater than the proportion of new firms initiating competence-enhancing discontinuities (see last column in Exhibit 3).

Hypothesis 3 suggested that environmental uncertainty would be significantly higher after a technological discontinuity than before it. Since the forecasts we used to test this hypothesis are not available before 1950, only four of the eight technological discontinuities could be tested. In three of the four cases examined, mean forecast error after the discontinuity was significantly higher ($p < .05$) than before the discontinuity (see Exhibit 7). Except for the period following the introduction of semiconductor memory in minicomputers, the ability of experienced industry observers to predict demand one year in advance was significantly poorer following technological disruption than before.[63] In the semiconductor case, forecast errors were very high both before and after the discontinuity.

Hypothesis 4 suggested that environmental munificence would be higher after a technological discontinuity than before it. The results in Exhibit 8 strongly support the hypothesis. In every case, demand growth following the discontinuity was significantly higher than it was immediately prior to the discontinuity. Further, these demand data indicate the enormous impact of initial discontinuities on product-class demand. Initial discontinuities were associated with, on average, a 529 percent increase

EXHIBIT 8 Demand before and after Technological Discontinuity

Industry	Era	Mean Annual Demand	t†
Cement	1892–1896	168	−3.16**
	1897–1901	1,249	
	1905–1909	9,271	−6.35**
	1910–1914	15,612	
	1963–1967	63,348	−2.16*
	1968–1972	77,122	
Airlines	1932–1936	2,326	−3.01**
	1937–1941	8,019	
	1955–1959	244,625	−3.68**
	1960–1964	355,678	
	1965–1969	742,838	−4.42**
	1970–1974	1,165,943	
Minicomputers	1960–1964	435	−1.96*
	1965–1969	2,181	
	1967–1971	7,274	−4.60*
	1972–1976	47,149	

*$p < .05$; **$p < .01$.
†t-statistic compares mean demand of first period with mean demand of second period. In each case, there are 8 degrees of freedom.

[63]Since data on published forecasts, annual growth in demand, and entry and exit data are available for the three populations, sampling error is not an issue; one could simply report the differences between populations. However, the critical question here is whether consistent differences between pre- and post-discontinuity environments can be discerned. The significance tests show that the probability is small that chance processes could have produced the reported differences between pre- and post-discontinuity eras (H. Blalock, *Social Statistics,* rev. 2d ed. (New York: McGraw-Hill, 1973).

EXHIBIT 9 Entry-to-Exit Ratio before and after Discontinuity

Industry	Era	Entry-to-Exit Ratio*	Discontinuity Type
Cement	1872–1896	3.25	Niche opening
	1892–1896	46.00	Competence-destroying
	1897–1901	12.00	
	1905–1909	1.489	Competence-enhancing
	1910–1914	.814	
	1963–1967	1.250	Competence-enhancing
	1968–1972	.160	
Airlines	1913–1930	1.730	Niche opening
	1930–1934	.820	Competence-enhancing†
	1935–1939	.714	
Minicomputers	1956–1960	Not finite‡	Niche opening
	1960–1964	5.500	Competence-destroying
	1965–1969	2.917	
	1967–1971	4.933	Competence-enhancing
	1972–1976	2.708	

*The difference between the prediscontinuity entry-to-exit ratios and the corresponding postdiscontinuity entry-to-exit ratios, while consistent, do not reach statistical significance, due to the large variance between individual years.

†Airline data for subsequent periods were not reported, because entry and exit were regulated.

‡Six entries, no exits.

in product-class demand. Subsequent discontinuities spark smaller (though still relatively large) increases in demand (226 percent, on average). Technological discontinuities were, then, associated with significantly higher demand after each discontinuity; this effect, though significant in each case, was smaller over successive discontinuities (except for minicomputers, where demand increased substantially after both technological discontinuities).

Hypothesis 5 argued that competence-enhancing discontinuities would be associated with decreased entry-to-exit ratios and decreased interfirm sales variability. Opposite effects were hypothesized for competence-destroying discontinuities. Entry-to-exit ratios were calculated for five years before and after each discontinuity (except for the 1938–1979 period in airlines). Results in Exhibit 9 are partially supportive of hypothesis 5. The ratio of entries to exits was higher in each of the five years before a competence-enhancing discontinuity than during the five subsequent years. None of the differences is statistically significant, though prediscontinuity entry-to-exit ratios range from 1.15 to over 7 times greater than postdiscontinuity entry-to-exit ratios. Entry-to-exit ratios prevailing before a discontinuity are markedly shifted in favor of exits following competence-enhancing discontinuities.

It was expected that entry-to-exit ratios would rise following the two competence-destroying discontinuities; the opposite was observed. Entry-to-exit ratios were quite high following these competence-destroying innovations but were smaller than the extremely large entry-to-exit ratios prevailing just before the discontinuity. Many firms entered and few departed the cement and minicomputer niches in the 1892–1896 and 1960–1964 periods, respectively. Both of these eras were themselves periods of technological ferment in emerging product classes—rotary kilns began to replace vertical kilns in the early 1890s, and transistors began to replace vacuum tubes in the early 1960s. It may be that the rush of new firms to enter emerging product classes confounds the effects of competence-destroying discontinuities.

Entry-to-exit patterns are consistent across these three divergent industries. Entries dominate exits early on, reflecting the rush of new entrants. After competence-enhancing discontinuities in cement and airlines, exits dominate entries, reflecting industry consolidation. In minicomputers, while entry-to-

EXHIBIT 10 Interfirm Sales Variability before and after Discontinuity

Industry	Era	Discontinuity Type	Interfirm Variance	F†	D.f.
Airlines	1955–1959	Competence-enhancing	79.24	2.726*	12,12
	1960–1964		29.07		
	1965–1969	Competence-enhancing	103.63	4.096**	11,11
	1970–1974		25.30		
Minicomputers	1960–1964	Competence-destroying	5,599.32	−17.480**	8,11
	1965–1969		97,873.25		
	1967–1971	Competence-enhancing	86.26	9.960**	9,35
	1972–1976		8.65		

*$p < .05$; **$p < .01$.
†The F-statistic compares the ratio of interfirm sales variance before the discontinuity to interfirm sales variance after the discontinuity.

exit ratios decrease over time, entries dominate exits throughout this 20-year period.

Hypothesis 5 also suggested that competence-enhancing discontinuities would decrease interfirm sales variability as those remaining firms adopt industry standards in both products and processes. Small firms drop out of the industry, entry barriers are raised, and firms exploiting similar existing competences experience relatively similar outcomes. Following competence-destroying discontinuities, though, we expected marked variability in sales growth as firms compete with each other on fundamentally different bases; some firms' sales grow explosively while others experience dramatic sales decline.

The results in Exhibit 10 for airlines and minicomputers support this prediction. In minicomputers, integrated circuits triggered explosive growth in the product class and increased interfirm sales variability. Following the other three competence-enhancing discontinuities, though, interfirm sales variability decreased significantly; niche occupants experienced similar results as they built on their existing competences to exploit demand growth.

Hypothesis 6 suggested that successive competence-enhancing discontinuities would be associated with relatively smaller effects on uncertainty and munificence. Because forecast data are not available before 1950, this hypothesis could only be partially tested in the case of uncertainty. As predicted, the mean forecast error in airlines for the 1960–1964 period is higher than that for the 1970–1974 period ($t = 1.91$; $p < .05$; see Exhibit 7). Hypotheses 6 receives stronger support with respect to munificence. In cement and airlines, mean growth rates in demand are smaller for each successive competence-enhancing discontinuity. These differences are significant for two of the three comparisons (see Exhibit 11). These data suggest that as technology matures, successive competence-enhancing discontinuities increase both uncertainty and munificence, but not as much as those discontinuities that preceded them in establishing the product class. These data, as well as those entry-to-exit data in Exhibit 9, suggest that successive competence-enhancing advances result in increased product-class maturity, reflected in decreased uncertainty, decreased demand growth-rates, and increased product-class consolidation.

EXHIBIT 11 Demand Patterns Following Successive Competence-Enhancing Discontinuities

Industry	Era	Mean Growth*	t(1)	D.f.
Cement	1910–1914	48.3%	12.03**	8
	1968–1972	8.4%		
Airlines	1937–1941	161.5%		
	1960–1964	33.4%	30.79**	8
	1970–1974	32.3%	.75	8

**$p < .01$.
*Mean growth is the average annual *percentage* gain in sales for the industry (in contrast to Exhibit 8, which measures demand in units). The t-statistic compares consecutive post-discontinuity periods; for instance, a comparison of mean percentage growth for 1910–1914 with mean percentage growth for 1968–1972 yields a t-statistic of 12.03, failing to support the null hypothesis that there is no difference in percentage growth rates between successive post-discontinuity eras.

EXHIBIT 12 Relative Sales Growth of First Four Adopters of a Major Innovation

Industry	Innovation†	Era	Mean Sales Growth First Four Adopters	Growth All Others	t‡	D.f.
Airlines	Jet aircraft	1955–1959	38.1%	22.2%	1.268	10
		1960–1964	44.3%	12.3%	2.121**	10
	Widebody jets	1965–1969	101.1%	19.2%	2.487*	9
		1970–1974	16.1%	1.0%	2.642*	9
Minicomputer	Integrated circuits	1960–1964	Not available (new firms)			
		1965–1969	339.2%	179.6%	.44	10
	Semiconductor memory	1967–1971	Not available (new firms)			
		1972–1976	238.0%	188.4%	.14	34

*$p < .05$; **$p < .06$.

†The first four adopters in each case are: *Jet aircraft*: American, TWA, United, Eastern; *Widebody jet*: American, TWA, Continental, United; *Integrated circuits*: Digital Equipment, Computer Control Co., Scientific Data Systems, Systems Engineering Laboratories; *Semiconductors*: Data General, Digital Computer Controls, Interdata, Microdata.

‡The *t*-test compares the mean annual percentage growth rates of the four firms who first introduced or adopted each innovation with the mean annual percentage growth rates of all other firms in the industry. Two periods do not yield interpretable statistics because annual growth for new firms cannot be calculated when the base year contains zero sales.

Hypothesis 7 argued that those firms initiating technological discontinuities would have higher growth rates than other firms in the product class. Exhibit 12 compares five-year growth rates for the four early adopters to all other firms before and after technological discontinuities. As hypothesized in each of the four comparisons, early adopters experienced more growth than other firms. Early adopters had significantly higher five-year growth rates than other firms in the airline industry. For jets, early adopters had growth rates similar to others before the discontinuity, while for widebody jets, the early adopters had higher sales growth before and after the discontinuity (see Exhibit 12). In minicomputers, early adopters had annual percentage growth rates that were 105 percentage points higher, on average, than other firms. Technological discontinuities are, then, sources of opportunities (or threats) for firms. While dominant technologies cannot be known in advance, those firms that recognize and quickly adopt a technological breakthrough grow more rapidly than others.

Discussion

The purpose of this reading has been to explore technological evolution and to investigate its impact on environmental conditions. A better understanding of technological evolution may increase our understanding of a range of phenomena at the population level (e.g., structural evolution, population dynamics, strategic groups) as well as the organizational level of analysis (e.g., organizational adaptation, executive succession patterns, executive demographics, and political dynamics).[64]

Longitudinal data across three diverse industries indicate that technology evolves through relatively long periods of incremental change punctuated by relatively rare innovations that radically improve the state of the art. Such discontinuities occurred only eight times in the 190 total years observed across three industries. Yet in each product class, these technological shifts stand out clearly and significantly altered competitive environments.

The effect of major technological change on the two fundamental dimensions of uncertainty and munificence is unambiguous. Environmental conditions following a discontinuity are sharply different from those that prevailed before the technical breakthrough: the advance makes available new resources to fuel growth within the niche and renders observers far less able to predict the extent of future resource availability. Major technical change opens new worlds for a product class but requires niche occupants to deal with a considerable amount of ambiguity and uncertainty as they struggle to comprehend and master both the new technology and the new competitive environment.

[64]Astley, "The Two Ecologies"; Tushman and Romanelli, "Organizational Evolution."

It is also clear that technological discontinuities are not all alike. Competence-enhancing discontinuities significantly advance the state of the art yet build on, or permit the transfer of, existing know-how and knowledge. Competence-destroying discontinuities, on the other hand, significantly advance the technological frontier, but with a knowledge, skill, and competence base that is inconsistent with prior know-how. While competence-enhancing discontinuities build on existing experience, competence-destroying discontinuities require fundamentally new skills and technological competence.

The locus of innovation and the environmental consequences of competence-destroying versus competence-enhancing discontinuities are quite different. Competence-enhancing breakthroughs are overwhelmingly initiated by existing, successful firms. Competence-enhancing discontinuities result in great product-class consolidation, reflected in relatively smaller entry-to-exit ratios and decreased interfirm sales variability. As competence-enhancing discontinuities build on existing know-how, it appears that the rich get richer, while new firms face liabilities of newness.[65] Product-class conditions become ever more consolidated over successive order-creating discontinuities.

Competence-destroying discontinuities are more rare than competence-enhancing technological advances. Competence-destroying breakthroughs are watershed events in the life of a product class; they open up new branches in the course of industrial evolution.[66] These discontinuities are initiated by new firms and open up the product class to waves of new entrants unconstrained by prior technologies and organizational inertia. While liabilities of newness plague new firms confronting competence-enhancing breakthroughs, liabilities of age and tradition constrain existing, successful firms in the face of competence-destroying discontinuities. Although the data were limited, they appear to show that competence-destroying discontinuities seem to break the grip of established firms in a product class. Interfirm sales variability jumped after integrated circuits were introduced in minicomputers, as new firms and established firms pursued different strategies, with markedly different results. Similarly in cement, new firms initiated rotary kilns and went on to dominate the industry.

These patterns are seen most vividly in minicomputer manufacture. The first inexpensive computers were built by established office-equipment firms (e.g., Monroe), electronics firms (e.g., Packard-Bell), and computer firms (e.g., Burroughs). This new product class continued unchanged until the advent of integrated circuits. Without exception, established firms floundered in the face of a technology based on active components. Integrated circuits rendered obsolete much of the engineering knowledge embodied in the first minicomputers. Office-equipment and the existing computer firms were unable to produce a successful model embodying semiconductor technology. Only the few firms explicitly founded to make minicomputers (e.g., DEC) were able to make the transition. By 1965, almost every firm that produced early minicomputers had exited the product class.

Technological discontinuities, whether competence-destroying or competence-enhancing, appear to afford a rare opportunity for competitive advantage for firms willing to risk early adoption. In all four cases, early adopters of major innovations had greater five-year growth rates than the rest of the product class. While these data are not unequivocal, firms that recognize and seize opportunities presented by major advances gain first-mover advantages. Those firms that do not adopt the innovation early or, worse, increase investment in obsolete technology, risk failing, because product-class conditions change so dramatically after the discontinuity.

Technological advance seems to be an important determinant of market as well as intraorganizational power. Competence-enhancing discontinuities are order creating in that they build on existing product-class know-how. These breakthroughs increase the market power of existing firms as barriers to entry are raised and dependence on buyers and suppliers decreases in the face of larger and more dominant producers. Competence-destroying technological advances, on the other hand, destroy order in a product class. These discontinuities create fundamental technological uncertainty as incompatible technologies compete for dominance. New firms, unconstrained by prior competence and history, take advantage of technological opportunities and the lethargy of organizations burdened with the consequences of prior success. Given the enormous impact of technological advance on product-class order, future research could explore

---

[65]A. Stinchcombe, "Social Structure and Organization," in *Handbook of Organizations,* ed. J. G. March (Chicago: Rand McNally, 1965), pp. 142–93.

[66]Astley, "The Two Ecologies."

the politics of technological change as interest groups attempt to shape technological progress to suit their own competences.[67]

Within the firm, technological discontinuities affect the distribution of power and, in turn, decision-making processes. Those who control technological advances (whether competence destroying or enhancing) will gain power at others' expense.[68] Because technological dominance is rarely known in advance, the control of technological assumptions and the locus of technological decisions will be an important arena for intraorganizational political processes. Shaping technological advance may be a critical organizational issue, since technology affects both intra- and interorganizational bases of power.

Because technology affects organizational adaptation, organizations may be able to use investment in R&D and technological innovation to shape environmental conditions in their favor. While technological dominance cannot be predicted at the outset (e.g., Wankel engines, bubble memory), organizations that create technological variation, or are able to adopt technological change quickly, maximize their probability of being able to move with a changing technological frontier. Organizations that do not contribute to or keep up with multiple technological bases may lose their ability to be aware of and deal with technological evolution.[69]

The patterns of technological change are similar across these three diverse industries. It appears that new product classes are associated with a wave of new entrants, relatively few exits, and substantial technological experimentation. Competence-destroying discontinuties occurred early in both cement and minicomputer manufacture. After competence-destroying breakthroughs, successive competence-enhancing discontinuities resulted in an ever more consolidated and mature product class. While we have no data, subsequent competence-destroying discontinuities may, in turn, break up a mature product class and restart the product class's evolutionary clock (e.g., microcomputers versus minicomputers or compact disks versus records).

Competence-destroying discontinuities initiate a period of technological ferment, as alternative technologies compete for dominance. This period of technological competition lasts until a dominant design emerges as a synthesis of prior technological experimentation (e.g., Dundee kiln, DC-3, PDP-11). Dominant designs reflect a consolidation of industry standards. These designs crowd out alternative designs and become guideposts for incremental product as well as major process change.[70] Thus, quite apart from major technological advance, the establishment of a dominant design may also be an important lever in shaping environmental conditions and organizational fate.

Conclusion

While these data indicate that technological discontinuities exist and that these discontinuities have important effects on environmental conditions, the data are not conclusive. Though the data are consistent across three diverse industries, the number of cases is relatively small, and some of the tests were limited by data availability. Future research needs to focus more closely on patterns of technological change. If technology is an important determinant of competitive conditions, we need to know more about differences between competence-destroying and competence-enhancing technological advances, what distinguishes between incremental improvements and dramatic advances, what are dominant designs and how they occur, and what are the impacts of competence-destroying advances in mature product classes.

Both product and process innovation are important. While the data here are only suggestive, it may be that different kinds of innovation are relatively more important in different product classes. For nonassembled products (e.g., cement, glass, oil), major process innovations may be relatively more important than product innovations. For assembled products (e.g., minicomputers, VCRs, scientific instruments), major product improvements or substitutions may be relatively more important than process innovations. Future research might explore the differential importance of major product and process innovations by different product-class type.

The effects of nontechnological discontinuities must also be examined to understand more fully how competitive environments change. Technological change does not occur in a vacuum. It frequently

[67]For example: Noble, *Forces of Production*.

[68]Morison, *Men, Machines, and Modern Times*; A. Pettigrew, *Politics of Organizational Decision-Making* (London: Tavistock, 1973).

[69]Dutton and Thomas, "Relating Technological Change and Learning by Doing."

[70]Utterback and Abernathy, "A Dynamic Model of Process and Product Innovation."

sparks a response from the legal, political, or social environments. For example, bioengineering, automatic control machinery, nuclear power, and supersonic transportation each has been directly affected by a complex set of interactions among technological and political, social, and legal considerations.[71] Further, periods of incremental technological change and standardization may become turbulent for nontechnological reasons (e.g., airline deregulation or the outlawing of basing-point pricing in cement). More complete analyses of the technology-environment linkages must also take into account the linkages between technological change and these other important social, political, and legal forces.

Technological change clearly affects organizational environments. Beyond exploring more deeply the nature of technological change, future research could also explore the linkage between technological evolution and population phenomena, such as structural evolution, mortality rates, or strategic groups, as well as organizational issues, such as adaptation, succession, and political processes. These results suggest that technology is not a static environmental resource. Rather, technology advances through the competition between alternative technologies promoted by rivalrous organizations. At the organization level, technological action, such as investment in R&D and internal venturing, may be a powerful lever in directly shaping environmental conditions and, in turn, organizational adaptation.

Reading II–15
Architectural Innovation: The Reconfiguration of Existing Product Technologies and the Failure of Established Firms

Rebecca M. Henderson and Kim B. Clark

The distinction between refining and improving an existing design and introducing a new concept that departs in a significant way from past practice is one of the central notions in the existing literature on technical innovation.[1] Incremental innovation introduces relatively minor changes to the existing product, exploits the potential of the established design, and often reinforces the dominance of established firms.[2] Although it draws from no dramatically new science, it often calls for considerable skill and ingenuity and, over time, has very significant economic consequences.[3] Radical innovation, in contrast, is based on a different set of engineering and scientific principles and often opens up whole new markets and potential applications.[4] Radical innovation often creates great difficulties for established firms[5] and can be the basis for the successful entry of new firms or even the redefinition of an industry.

Radical and incremental innovations have such different competitive consequences because they require quite different organizational capabilities. Organizational capabilities are difficult to create and costly to adjust.[6] Incremental innovation reinforces

[71]Horwitch, *Clipped Wings;* W. G. Astley and C. Fombrun, "Technological Innovation and Industrial Structure: The Case of Telecommunications," in *Advances in Strategic Management,* vol. 1, ed. R. Lamb (Greenwich, CT: JAI Press, 1983), pp. 205–29; Noble, *Forces of Production.*

[1]E. Mansfield, *Industrial Research and Technical Innovation* (New York: Norton, 1968); M. Moch and E.V. Morse, "Size, Centralization and Organizational Adoption of Innovations," *American Sociological Review* 42 (1977), pp. 716–25; C. Freeman, *The Economics of Industrial Innovation,* 2d ed. (Cambridge, MA: MIT Press, 1982).

[2]R. Nelson and S. Winter, *An Evolutionary Theory of Economic Change* (Cambridge, MA: Harvard University Press, 1982); J.E. Ettlie, W.P. Bridges, and R.D. O'Keefe, "Organizational Strategy and Structural Differences for Radical vs. Incremental Innovation," *Management Science* 30 (1984), pp. 682–95; R.D. Dewar and J.E. Dutton, "The Adoption of Radical and Incremental Innovations: An Empirical Analysis," *Management Science* 32 (1986), pp. 1422–33; M.L. Tushman and P. Anderson, "Technological Discontinuities and Organizational Environments," *Administrative Science Quarterly* 31 (1986), pp. 439–65.

[3]S. Hollander, *The Sources of Increased Efficiency: A Study of Du Pont Rayon Plants* (Cambridge, MA: MIT Press, 1965).

[4]G.G. Dess and D. Beard, "Dimensions of Organizational Task Environments," *Administrative Science Quarterly* 29 (1984), pp. 52–73; Ettlie et al., "Organizational Strategy and Structural Differences for Radical vs. Incremental Innovation"; Dewar and Dutton, "The Adoption of Radical and Incremental Innovations."

[5]A.C. Cooper and D. Schendel, "Strategic Response to Technological Threats," *Business Horizons* 19 (1976), pp. 61–69; R.L. Daft, "Bureaucratic versus Nonbureaucratic Structure and the Process of Innovation and Change," in *Research in the Sociology of Organizations,* vol. 1, ed. S.B. Bacharach (Greenwich, CT: JAI Press, 1982), pp. 129–66; R. Rothwell, "The Role of Small Firms in the Emergence of New Technologies," in *Design, Innovation and Long Cycles in Economic Development,* ed. C. Freeman (London: Francis Pinter, 1986), pp. 251–48; Tushman and Anderson, "Technological Discontinuities and Organizational Environments."

[6]Nelson and Winter, *An Evolutionary Theory of Economic Change;* M.T. Hannan and J. Freeman, "Structural Inertia and Organizational Change," *American Sociological Review* 49 (1984), pp. 149–64.

the capabilities of established organizations, while radical innovation forces them to ask a new set of questions, to draw on new technical and commercial skills, and to employ new problem-solving approaches.[7]

The distinction between radical and incremental innovation has produced important insights, but it is fundamentally incomplete. There is growing evidence that there are numerous technical innovations that involve apparently modest changes to the existing technology but that have quite dramatic competitive consequences.[8] The case of Xerox and small copiers and the case of RCA and the American radio receiver market are two examples.

Xerox, the pioneer of plain-paper copiers, was confronted in the mid-1970s with competitors offering copiers that were much smaller and more reliable than the traditional product. The new products required little new scientific or engineering knowledge, but despite the fact that Xerox had invented the core technologies and had enormous experience in the industry, it took the company almost eight years of missteps and false starts to introduce a competitive product into the market. In that time Xerox lost half of its market share and suffered serious financial problems.[9]

In the mid-1950s engineers at RCA's corporate research and development center developed a prototype of a portable, transistorized radio receiver. The new product used technology in which RCA was accomplished (transistors, radio circuits, speakers, tuning devices), but RCA saw little reason to pursue such an apparently inferior technology. In contrast, Sony, a small, relatively new company, used the small transistorized radio to gain entry into the U.S. market. Even after Sony's success was apparent, RCA remained a follower in the market as Sony introduced successive models with improved sound quality and FM capability. The irony of the situation was not lost on the R&D engineers: for many years Sony's radios were produced with technology licensed from RCA, yet RCA had great difficulty matching Sony's product in the marketplace.[10]

Existing models that rely on the simple distinction between radical and incremental innovation provide little insight into the reasons why such apparently minor or straightforward innovations should have such consequences. In this reading, we develop and apply a model that grew out of research in the automotive, machine tool, and ceramics industries that helps to explain how minor innovations can have great competitive consequences.

Conceptual Framework

Component and Architectural Knowledge

In this paper, we focus on the problem of product development, taking as the unit of analysis a manufactured product sold to an end user and designed, engineered, and manufactured by a single product-development organization. We define innovations that change the way in which the components of a product are linked together, while leaving the core design concepts (and thus the basic knowledge underlying the components) untouched, as *architectural* innovation.[11] This is the kind of innovation that confronted Xerox and RCA. It destroys the usefulness of a firm's architectural knowledge but preserves the usefulness of its knowledge about the product's components.

This distinction between the product as a whole—the system—and the product in its parts—the components—has a long history in the design literature.[12] For example, a room fan's major components include the blade, the motor that drives it, the blade guard, the control system, and the mechanical housing. The overall architecture of the product lays out how the components will work together. Taken together, a fan's architecture and its components create a system for moving air in a room.

A component is defined here as a physically distinct portion of the product that embodies a core

---

[7]T. Burns and G. Stalker, *The Management of Innovation* (London: Tavistock, 1966); J. Hage, *Theories of Organization* (New York: Wiley Interscience, 1980); Ettlie et al., "Organizational Strategy and Structural Differences for Radical vs. Incremental Innovation"; Tushman and Anderson, "Technological Discontinuities and Organizational Environments."

[8]K.B. Clark, "Managing Technology in International Competition: The Case of Product Development in Response to Foreign Entry," in *International Competitiveness,* ed. M. Spence and H. Hazard (Cambridge, MA: Ballinger, 1987), pp. 27–74.

[9]Ibid.

[10]Ibid.

[11]In earlier drafts of this paper we referred to this type of innovation as *generational.* We are indebted to Professor Michael Tushman for his suggestion of the term *architectural.*

[12]D.L. Marples, "The Decisions of Engineering Design," *IEEE Transactions on Engineering Management* EM.8 (June 1961), pp. 55–71; C. Alexander, *Notes on the Synthesis of Form* (Cambridge, MA: Harvard University Press, 1964).

design concept[13] and performs a well-defined function. In the fan, a particular motor is a component of the design that delivers power to turn the fan. There are several design concepts one could use to deliver power. The choice of one of them—the decision to use an electric motor, for example—establishes a core concept of the design. The actual component—the electric motor—is then a physical implementation of this design concept.

The distinction between the product as a system and the product as a set of components underscores the idea that successful product development requires two types of knowledge. First, it requires component knowledge, or knowledge about each of the core design concepts and the way in which they are implemented in a particular component. Second, it requires architectural knowledge, or knowledge about the ways in which the components are integrated and linked together into a coherent whole. The distinction between architectural and component knowledge, or between the components themselves and the links between them, is a source of insight into the ways in which innovations differ from each other.

Types of Technological Change

The notion that there are different kinds of innovation, with different competitive effects, has been an important theme in the literature on technological innovation since Schumpeter.[14] Following Schumpeter's emphasis on creative destruction, the literature has characterized different kinds of innovations in terms of their impact on the established capabilities of the firm. This idea is used in Exhibit 1, which classifies innovations along two dimensions. The horizontal dimension captures an innovation's impact on components, while the vertical captures its impact on the linkages between components.[15] There are, of course, other ways to characterize different kinds of innovation. But given the focus here on innovation and the development of new products, the framework outlined in Exhibit 1 is useful because it focuses on the impact of an innovation

EXHIBIT 1 A Framework for Defining Innovation

Linkage between Core Concepts and Components	Core Concepts: Reinforced	Core Concepts: Overturned
Unchanged	Incremental innovation	Modular innovation
Changed	Architectural innovation	Radical innovation

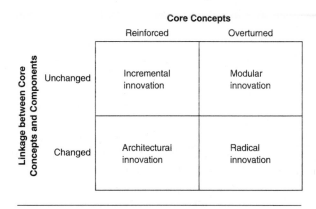

on the usefulness of the existing architectural and component knowledge of the firm.

Framed in this way, radical and incremental innovation are extreme points along both dimensions. Radical innovation establishes a new dominant design and, hence, a new set of core design concepts embodied in components that are linked together in a new architecture. Incremental innovation refines and extends an established design. Improvement occurs in individual components, but the underlying core design concepts, and the links between them, remain the same.

Exhibit 1 shows two further types of innovation: innovation that changes only the core design concepts of a technology and innovation that changes only the relationships between them. The former is a modular innovation, such as the replacement of analog with digital telephones. To the degree that one can simply replace an analog dialing device with a digital one, it is an innovation that changes a core design concept without changing the product's architecture. Our concern, however, is with the last type of innovation shown in the matrix: innovation that changes a product's architecture but leaves the components, and the core design concepts that they embody, unchanged.

The essence of an architectural innovation is the reconfiguration of an established system to link together existing components in a new way. This does not mean that the components themselves are untouched by architectural innovation. Architectural innovation is often triggered by a change in a component—perhaps size or some other subsidiary parameter of its design—that creates new interactions and new linkages with other components in

[13] K.B. Clark, "The Interaction of Design Hierarchies and Market Concepts in Technological Evolution," *Research Policy* 14 (1985), pp. 235–251.

[14] J.A. Schumpeter, *Capitalism, Socialism and Democracy* (Cambridge, MA: Harvard University Press, 1942).

[15] We are indebted to one of the anonymous *ASQ* reviewers for the suggestion that we use this matrix.

the established product. The important point is that the core design concept behind each component—as well as the associated scientific and engineering knowledge—remains the same.

We can illustrate the application of this framework with the example of the room air fan. If the established technology is that of large, electrically powered fans, mounted in the ceiling, with the motor hidden from view and insulated to dampen the noise, improvements in blade design or in the power of the motor would be incremental innovations. A move to central air conditioning would be a radical innovation. New components associated with compressors, refrigerants, and their associated controls would add whole new technical disciplines and new interrelationships. For the maker of large, ceiling-mounted room fans, however, the introduction of a portable fan would be an architectural innovation. While the primary components would be largely the same (e.g., blade, motor, control system), the architecture of the product would be quite different. There would be significant changes in the interactions between components. The smaller size and the colocation of the motor and the blade in the room would focus attention on new types of interaction between the motor size, the blade dimensions, and the amount of air that the fan could circulate, while shrinking the size of the apparatus would probably introduce new interactions between the performance of the blade and the weight of the housing.

The distinctions between radical, incremental, and architectural innovations are matters of degree. The intention here is not to defend the boundaries of a particular definition, particularly since there are several other dimensions on which it may be useful to define radical and incremental innovation. The use of the term *architectural innovation* is designed to draw attention to innovations that use many existing core design concepts in a new architecture and that therefore have a more significant impact on the relationships between components than on the technologies of the components themselves. The matrix in Exhibit 1 is designed to suggest that a given innovation may be less radical or more architectural, not to suggest that the world can be neatly divided into four quadrants.

These distinctions are important because they give us insight into why established firms often have a surprising degree of difficulty in adapting to architectural innovation. Incremental innovation tends to reinforce the competitive positions of established firms, since it builds on their core competencies[16] or is "competence enhancing."[17] In the terms of the framework developed here, it builds on the existing architectural and component knowledge of an organization. In contrast, radical innovation creates unmistakable challenges for established firms, since it destroys the usefulness of their existing capabilities. In our terms, it destroys the usefulness of both architectural and component knowledge.[18]

Architectural innovation presents established firms with a more subtle challenge. Much of what the firm knows is useful and needs to be applied in the new product, but some of what it knows is not only not useful but may actually handicap the firm. Recognizing what is useful and what is not, and acquiring and applying new knowledge when necessary, may be quite difficult for an established firm because of the way knowledge—particularly architectural knowledge—is organized and managed.

The Evolution of Component and Architectural Knowledge

Two concepts are important to understanding the ways in which component and architectural knowledge are managed inside an organization. The first is that of a dominant design. Work by Abernathy and Utterback,[19] Rosenberg,[20] Clark,[21] and Sahal[22] and evidence from studies of several industries show that product technologies do not emerge fully developed at the outset of their commercial lives.[23] Technical evolution is usually characterized by periods of great experimentation followed by the acceptance of a dominant design. The second concept is that organizations build knowledge and capability

[16]W.J. Abernathy and K.B. Clark, "Innovation: Mapping the Winds of Creative Destruction," *Research Policy* 14 (1985), pp. 3–22.

[17]Tushman and Anderson, "Technological Discontinuities and Organizational Environments."

[18]Cooper and Schendel, "Strategic Response to Technological Threats"; Daft, "Bureaucratic versus Nonbureaucratic Structure and the Process of Innovation and Change"; Tushman and Anderson, "Technological Discontinuities and Organizational Environments."

[19]W.J. Abernathy and J. Utterback, "Patterns of Industrial Innovation," *Technology Review* (June–July 1978), pp. 40–47.

[20]N. Rosenberg, *Inside the Black Box: Technology and Economics* (Cambridge: Cambridge University Press, 1982).

[21]"The Interaction of Design Hierarchies and Market Concepts in Technological Evolution."

[22]D. Sahal, "Technological Guideposts and Innovation Avenues," *Research Policy* 14 (1986), pp. 61–82.

[23]E. Mansfield, *The Production and Application of New Industrial Technology* (New York: Norton, 1977).

around the recurrent tasks that they perform.[24] Thus one cannot understand the development of an organization's innovative capability or of its knowledge without understanding the way in which they are shaped by the organization's experience with an evolving technology.

The emergence of a new technology is usually a period of considerable confusion. There is little agreement about what the major subsystems of the product should be or how they should be put together. There is a great deal of experimentation.[25] For example, in the early days of the automobile industry, cars were built with gasoline, electric, or steam engines, with steering wheels or tillers, and with wooden or metal bodies.[26]

These periods of experimentation are brought to an end by the emergence of a dominant design.[27] A dominant design is characterized both by a set of core design concepts that correspond to the major functions performed by the product[28] and that are embodied in components and by a product architecture that defines the ways in which these components are integrated.[29] It is equivalent to the general acceptance of a particular product architecture and is characteristic of technical evolution in a very wide range of industries.[30] A dominant design often emerges in response to the opportunity to obtain economies of scale or to take advantage of externalities.[31] For example, the dominant design for the car encompassed not only the fact that it used a gasoline engine to provide motive force but also that it was connected to the wheels through a transmission and a drive train and was mounted on a frame rather than on the axles. A dominant design incorporates a range of basic choices about the design that are not revisited in every subsequent design. Once the dominant automobile design had been accepted, engineers did not reevaluate the decision to use a gasoline engine each time they developed a new design. Once any dominant design is established, the initial set of components is refined and elaborated, and progress takes the shape of improvements in the components within the framework of a stable architecture.

This evolutionary process had profound implications for the types of knowledge that an organization developing a new product requires, since an organization's knowledge and its information-processing capabilities are shaped by the nature of the tasks and the competitive environment that it faces.[32]

In the early stages of a technology's history, before the emergence of a dominant design, organizations competing to design successful products experiment with many different technologies. Since success in the market turns on the synthesis of unfamiliar technologies in creative new designs, organizations must actively develop both knowledge about alternative components and knowledge of how these components can be integrated. With the emergence of a dominant design, which signals the general acceptance of a single architecture, firms cease to invest in learning about alternative configurations of the established set of components. New component knowledge becomes more valuable to a firm than new architectural knowledge because competition between designs revolves around refinements in particular components. Successful organizations therefore switch their limited attention from learning a little about many different possible designs to learning a great deal about the dominant design. Once gasoline-powered cars had emerged as the technology of choice, competitive pressures in the industry strongly encouraged organizations to learn more about gasoline-fired engines. Pursuing refinements in steam- or electric-powered cars

---

[24]R.M. Cyert and J.G. March, *A Behavioral Theory of the Firm* (Englewood Cliffs, NJ: Prentice Hall, 1963); Nelson and Winter, *An Evolutionary Theory of Economic Change.*

[25]Burns and Stalker, *The Management of Innovation;* Clark, "The Interaction of Design Hierarchies and Market Concepts in Technological Evolution."

[26]W.J. Abernathy, *The Productivity Dilemma: Roadblock to Innovation in the Automobile Industry* (Baltimore: Johns Hopkins University Press, 1978).

[27]Abernathy and Utterback, "Patterns of Industrial Innovation"; Sahal, "Technological Guideposts and Innovation Avenues."

[28]Marples, "The Decisions of Engineering Design"; Alexander, *Notes on the Synthesis of Form;* Clark, "The Interaction of Design Hierarchies and Market Concepts in Technological Evolution."

[29]Clark, "The Interaction of Design Hierarchies and Market Concepts in Technological Evolution"; Sahal, "Technological Guideposts and Innovation Avenues."

[30]Clark, "The Interaction of Design Hierarchies and Market Concepts in Technological Evolution."

[31]R.L. Daft and K.E. Weick, "Towards a Model of Organizations as Interpretation Systems," *Academy of Management Review* 9 (1984), pp. 284–95; B. Arthur, "Competing Technologies: An Overview," in *Technical Change and Economic Theory,* ed. G. Dosi et al. (New York: Columbia University Press, 1988), pp. 590–607.

[32]For simplicity, we will assume here that organizations can be assumed to act as boundedly rational entities, in the tradition of K. Arrow, *The Limits of Organization* (New York: Norton, 1974); Nelson and Winter, *An Evolutionary Theory of Economic Change.*

became much less attractive. The focus of active problem solving becomes the elaboration and refinement of knowledge about existing components within a framework of stable architectural knowledge.[33]

Since in an industry characterized by a dominant design, architectural knowledge is stable, it tends to become embedded in the practices and procedures of the organization. Several authors have noted the importance of various institutional devices like frameworks and routines in completing recurring tasks in an organization.[34] The focus in this paper, however, is on the role of communication channels, information filters, and problem-solving strategies in managing architectural knowledge.

Channels, filters, and strategies. An organization's communication channels, both those that are implicit in its formal organization (A reports to B) and those that are informal ("I always call Fred because he knows about X"), develop around those interactions within the organization that are critical to its task.[35] These are also the interactions that are critical to effective design. They are the relationships around which the organization builds architectural knowledge. Thus, an organization's communication channels will come to embody its architectural knowledge of the linkages between components that are critical to effective design. For example, as a dominant design for room fans emerges, an effective organization in the industry will organize itself around its conception of the product's primary components, since these are the key subtasks of the organization's design problem.[36] The organization may create a fan-blade group, a motor group, and so on. The communication channels that are created between these groups will reflect the organization's knowledge of the critical interactions between them. The fact that those working on the motor and the fan blade report to the same supervisor and meet weekly is an embodiment of the organization's architectural knowledge about the relationship between the motor and the fan blade.

The information filters of an organization also embody its architectural knowledge. An organization is constantly barraged with information. As the task that it faces stabilizes and becomes less ambiguous, the organization develops filters that allow it to identify immediately what is most crucial in its information stream.[37] The emergence of a dominant design and its gradual elaboration molds the organization's filters so that they come to embody parts of its knowledge of the key relationships between the components of the technology. For instance, the relationships between the designers of motors and controllers for a room fan are likely to change over time as they are able to express the nature of the critical interaction between the motor and the controller in an increasingly precise way that allows them to ignore irrelevant information. The controller designers may discover that they need to know a great deal about the torque and power of the motor but almost nothing about the materials from which it is made. They will create information filters that reflect this knowledge.

As a product evolves, information filters and communication channels develop and help engineers to work efficiently, but the evolution of the product also means that engineers face recurring kinds of problems. Over time, engineers acquire a store of knowledge about solutions to the specific kinds of problems that have arisen in previous projects. When confronted with such a problem, the engineer does not reexamine all possible alternatives but, rather, focuses first on those that he or she has found to be helpful in solving previous problems. In effect, an organization's problem-solving strategies summarize what it has learned about fruitful ways to solve problems in its immediate environment.[38] Designers may use strategies of this sort in solving problems within components, but problem-solving strategies also reflect architectural knowledge, since they are likely to express part of an organization's knowledge about the component linkages that are

[33]G. Dosi, "Technological Paradigms and Technological Trajectories: A Suggested Interpretation of the Determinants and Directions of Technical Change," *Research Policy* 11 (1982), pp. 147–62; Clark, "The Interaction of Design Hierarchies and Market Concepts in Technological Evolution."

[34]J. Galbraith, *Designing Complex Organizations* (Reading, MA: Addison-Wesley, 1973); Nelson and Winter, *An Evolutionary Theory of Economic Change;* Daft and Weick, "Towards a Model of Organizations as Interpretation Systems."

[35]Galbraith, *Designing Complex Organizations;* Arrow, *The Limits of Organization.*

[36]H. Mintzberg, *The Structuring of Organizations* (Englewood Cliffs, NJ: Prentice Hall, 1979); E. von Hippel, "Task Partitioning: An Innovation Process Variable," *Research Policy* (1990).

[37]Arrow, *The Limits of Organization;* Daft and Weick, "Towards a Model of Organizations as Interpretation Systems."

[38]J.G. March and H.A. Simon, *Organizations* (New York: Wiley, 1958); M.A. Lyles and I.I. Mitroff, "Organizational Problem Formulation: An Empirical Study," *Administrative Science Quarterly* 25 (1980), pp. 102–19; Nelson and Winter, *An Evolutionary Theory of Economic Change.*

crucial to the solution of routine problems. An organization designing fans might learn over time that the most effective way to design a quieter fan is to focus on the interactions between the motor and the housing.

The strategies designers use, their channels for communications, and their information filters emerge in an organization to help it cope with complexity. They are efficient precisely because they do not have to be actively created each time a need for them arises. Further, as they become familiar and effective, using them becomes natural. Like riding a bicycle, using a strategy, working in a channel, or employing a filter does not require detailed analysis and conscious, deliberate execution. Thus, the operation of channels, filters, and strategies may become implicit in the organization.

Since architectural knowledge is stable once a dominant design has been accepted, it can be encoded in these forms and thus becomes implicit. Organizations that are actively engaged in incremental innovation, which occurs within the context of stable architectural knowledge, are thus likely to manage much of their architectural knowledge implicitly by embedding it in their communication channels, information filters, and problem-solving strategies. Component knowledge, in contrast, is more likely to be managed explicitly because it is a constant source of incremental innovation.

Problems Created by Architectural Innovation

Differences in the way in which architectural and component knowledge are managed within an experienced organization give us insight into why architectural innovation often creates problems for established firms. These problems have two sources. First, established organizations require significant time (and resources) to identify a particular innovation as architectural, since architectural innovation can often initially be accommodated within old frameworks. Radical innovation tends to be obviously radical—the need for new modes of learning and new skills becomes quickly apparent. But information that might warn the organization that a particular innovation is architectural may be screened out by the information filters and communication channels that embody old architectural knowledge. Since radical innovation changes the core design concepts of the product, it is immediately obvious that knowledge about how the old components interact with each other is obsolete. The introduction of new linkages, however, is much harder to spot. Since the core concepts of the design remain untouched, the organization may mistakenly believe that it understands the new technology. In the case of the fan company, the motor and the fan-blade designers will continue to talk to each other. The fact that they may be talking about the wrong things may only become apparent after there are significant failures or unexpected problems with the design.

The development of the jet aircraft industry provides an example of the impact of unexpected architectural innovation. The jet engine initially appeared to have important but straightforward implications for airframe technology. Established firms in the industry understood that they would need to develop jet engine expertise but failed to understand the ways in which its introduction would change the interactions between the engine and the rest of the plane in complex and subtle ways.[39] This failure was one of the factors that led to Boeing's rise to leadership in the industry.

This effect is analogous to the tendency of individuals to continue to rely on beliefs about the world that a rational evaluation of new information should lead them to discard.[40] Researchers have commented extensively on the ways in which organizations facing threats may continue to rely on their old frameworks—or in our terms on their old architectural knowledge—and hence misunderstand the nature of a threat. They shoehorn the bad news, or the unexpected new information, back into the patterns with which they are familiar.[41]

Once an organization has recognized the nature of an architectural innovation, it faces a second major source of problems: the need to build and to apply new architectural knowledge effectively. Simply recognizing that a new technology is architectural in character does not give an established organization

---

[39]R. Miller and D. Sawyers, *The Technical Development of Modern Aviation* (New York: Praeger, 1968); J.P. Gardiner, "Design Trajectories for Airplanes and Automobiles during the Past Fifty Years," in *Design, Innovation and Long Cycles in Economic Development,* ed. C. Freeman (London: Francis Pinter, 1986), pp. 121–41.

[40]D. Kahneman, P. Slovic, and A. Tversky, *Judgment under Uncertainty: Heuristics and Biases* (Cambridge: Cambridge University Press, 1982).

[41]Lyles and Mitroff, "Organizational Problem Formulation"; J.E. Dutton and S.E. Jackson, "Categorizing Strategic Issues: Links to Organizational Action," *Academy of Management Review* 12 (1987), pp. 76–90; S.E. Jackson and J.E. Dutton, "Discerning Threats and Opportunities," *Administrative Science Quarterly* 33 (1988), pp. 370–87.

the architectural knowledge that it needs. It must first switch to a new mode of learning and then invest time and resources in learning about the new architecture.[42] It is handicapped in its attempts to do this, both by the difficulty all organizations experience in switching from one mode of learning to another and by the fact that it must build new architectural knowledge in a context in which some of its old architectural knowledge may be irrelevant.

An established organization setting out to build new architectural knowledge must change its orientation from one of refinement within a stable architecture to one of active search for new solutions within a constantly changing context. As long as the dominant design remains stable, an organization can segment and specialize its knowledge and rely on standard operating procedures to design and develop products. Architectural innovation, in contrast, places a premium on exploration in design and the assimilation of new knowledge. Many organizations encounter difficulties in their attempts to make this type of transition.[43] New entrants, with smaller commitments to older ways of learning about the environment and organizing their knowledge, often find it easier to build the organizational flexibility that abandoning old architectural knowledge and building new requires.

Once an organization has succeeded in reorientating itself, the building of new architectural knowledge still takes time and resources. This learning may be quite subtle and difficult. New entrants to the industry must also build the architectural knowledge necessary to exploit an architectural innovation, but since they have no existing assets, they can optimize their organization and information-processing structures to exploit the potential of a new design. Established firms are faced with an awkward problem. Because their architectural knowledge is embedded in channels, filters, and strategies, the discovery process and the process of creating new information (and rooting out the old) usually takes time. The organization may be tempted to modify the channels, filters, and strategies that already exist rather than to incur the significant fixed costs and considerable organizational friction required to build new sets from scratch.[44] But it may be difficult to identify precisely which filters, channels, and problem-solving strategies need to be modified, and the attempt to build a new product with old (albeit modified) organizational tools can create significant problems.

The problems created by an architectural innovation are evident in the introduction of high-strength-low-alloy (HSLA) steel in automobile bodies in the 1970s. The new materials allowed body panels to be thinner and lighter but opened up a whole new set of interactions that were not contained in existing channels and strategies. One automaker's body-engineering group, using traditional methods, designed an HSLA hood for the engine compartment. The hoods, however, resonated and oscillated with engine vibrations during testing. On further investigation, it became apparent that the traditional methods for designing hoods worked just fine with traditional materials, although no one knew quite why. The knowledge embedded in established problem-solving strategies and communication channels was sufficient to achieve effective designs with established materials, but the new material created new interactions and required the engineers to build new knowledge about them.

Architectural innovation may thus have very significant competitive implications. Established organizations may invest heavily in the new innovation, interpreting it as an incremental extension of the existing technology or underestimating its impact on their embedded architectural knowledge. But new entrants to the industry may exploit its potential much more effectively, since they are not handicapped by a legacy of embedded and partially irrelevant architectural knowledge. We explore the validity of our framework through a brief summary of the competitive and technical history of the semiconductor photolithographic alignment equipment industry. Photolithographic aligners are sophisticated pieces of capital equipment used in the manufacture of integrated circuits. Their performance has improved dramatically over the last 25 years, and although the core technologies have changed only marginally since the technique was first invented, the industry has been characterized by great turbulence. Changes in market leadership have been frequent, the entry of new firms has occurred throughout the industry's history, and incumbents

[42] M.R. Louis and R.I. Sutton, "Switching Cognitive Gears: From Habits of Mind to Active Thinking," working paper, School of Industrial Engineering, Stanford University, 1989.

[43] C. Argyris and D. Schön, *Organizational Learning* (Reading, MA: Addison-Wesley, 1978); K.E. Weick, "Cognitive Processes in Organizations," in *Research in Organizational Behavior* vol. 1, ed. B.M. Staw and L.L. Cummings (Greenwich, CT: JAI Press, 1979), pp. 41–47; Louis and Sutton, "Switching Cognitive Gears."

[44] Arrow, *The Limits of Organization*.

have often suffered sharp declines in market share following the introduction of equipment incorporating seemingly minor innovation. We believe that these events are explained by the intrusion of architectural innovation into the industry, and we use three episodes in the industry's history—particularly Canon's introduction of the proximity aligner and Kasper's response to it—to illustrate this idea in detail.

Innovation in Photolithographic Alignment Equipment

Data

The data were collected during a two-year, field-based study of the photolithographic alignment equipment industry. The study was initially designed to serve as an exploration of the validity of the concept of architectural innovation, a concept originally developed by one of the authors during the course of his experience with the automobile and ceramics industry.[45]

The core of the data is a panel data set consisting of research and development costs and sales revenue by product for every product development project conducted between 1962, when work on the first commercial product began, and 1986. This data is supplemented by a detailed managerial and technical history of each project. The data were collected through research in both primary and secondary sources. The secondary sources, including trade journals, scientific journals, and consulting reports, were used to identify the companies that had been active in the industry and the products that they had introduced and to build up a preliminary picture of the industry's technical history.

Data were then collected about each product-development project by contacting directly at least one of the members of the product-development team and requesting an interview. Interviews were conducted over a 14-month period, from March 1987 to May 1988. During the course of the research, over a hundred people were interviewed. As far as possible, the interviewees included the senior design engineer for each project and a senior marketing executive from each firm. Other industry observers and participants, including chief executives, university scientists, skilled design engineers, and service managers were also interviewed. Interview data were supplemented whenever possible through the use of internal firm records. The majority of the interviews were semistructured and lasted about two hours. Respondents were asked to describe the technical, commercial, and managerial history of the product-development projects with which they were familiar and to discuss the technical and commercial success of the products that grew out of them.

In order to validate the data that were collected during this process, a brief history of product development for each equipment vendor was circulated to all the individuals who had been interviewed and to others who knew a firm's history well, and the accuracy of this account was discussed over the telephone in supplementary interviews. The same validation procedure was followed in the construction of the technical history of the industry. A technical history was constructed using interview data, published product literature, and the scientific press. This history was circulated to key individuals who had a detailed knowledge of the technical history of the industry, who corrected it as appropriate.

We chose to study the semiconductor photolithographic alignment equipment industry for two reasons. The first is that it is very different from the industries in which our framework was first formulated, since it is characterized by much smaller firms and a much faster rate of technological innovation. The second is that it provides several examples of the impact of architectural innovation on the competitive position of established firms. Photolithographic equipment has been shaken by four waves of architectural innovation, each of which resulted in a new entrant capturing the leadership of the industry. In order to ground the discussion of architectural innovation we provide a brief description of photolithographic technology.

The Technology

Photolithographic aligners are used to manufacture solid-state semiconductor devices. The production of semiconductors requires the transfer of small, intricate patterns to the surface of a wafer of semiconductor material such as silicon, and this process of transfer is known as lithography. The surface of the wafer is coated with a light-sensitive chemical, or "resist." The pattern that is to be transferred to the wafer surface is drawn onto a mask and the mask is

[45]Clark, "Managing Technology in International Competition."

EXHIBIT 2 Schematic Representation of the Lithographic Process

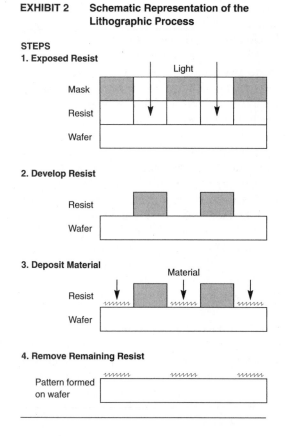

STEPS

1. Exposed Resist

Light

Mask

Resist

Wafer

2. Develop Resist

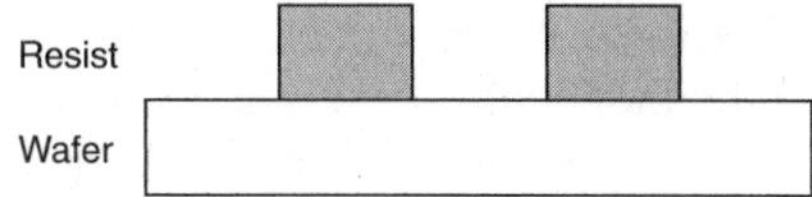

3. Deposit Material

Material

Resist

Wafer

4. Remove Remaining Resist

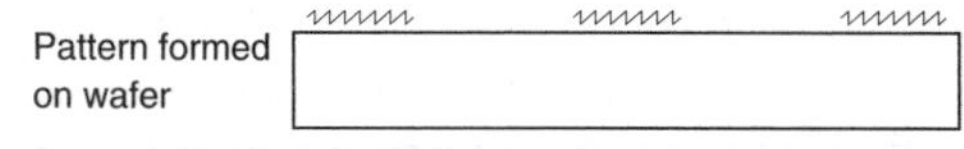

EXHIBIT 3 Schematic Diagram of a Contact Aligner

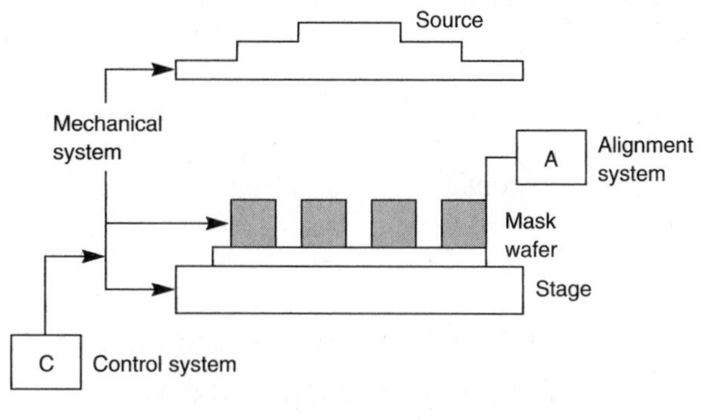

used to block light as it falls onto the resist, so that only those portions of the resist defined by the mask are exposed to light. The light chemically transforms the resist so that it can be stripped away. The resulting pattern is then used as the basis for either the deposition of material onto the wafer surface or for the etching of the existing material on the surface of the wafer. The process may be repeated as many as twenty times during the manufacture of a semiconductor device, and each layer must be located precisely with respect to the previous layer.[46] Exhibit 2 gives a very simplified representation of this complex process.

A photolithographic aligner is used to position the mask relative to the wafer, to hold the two in place during exposure, and to expose the resist. Exhibit 3 shows a schematic diagram of a contact aligner, the first generation of alignment equipment developed. Improvement in alignment technology has meant improvement in minimum feature size, the size of the smallest pattern that can be produced on the wafer surface, yield, the percentage of wafers successfully processed, and throughput, the number of wafers the aligner can handle in a given time.

Contact aligners were the first photolithographic aligners to be used commercially. They use the mask's shadow to transfer the mask pattern to the wafer surface. The mask and the wafer are held in contact with each other, and light shining through the gaps in the mask falls on to the wafer surface. Contact aligners are simple and quick to use, but the need to bring the mask and the wafer into direct contact can damage the mask or contaminate the wafer. The first proximity aligner was introduced in 1973 to solve these problems.

In a proximity aligner the mask is held a small distance away from (in proximity to) the wafer surface, as shown in the simplified drawing in Exhibit 4. The separation of the mask and the wafer means that

EXHIBIT 4 Schematic Diagram of a Proximity Aligner

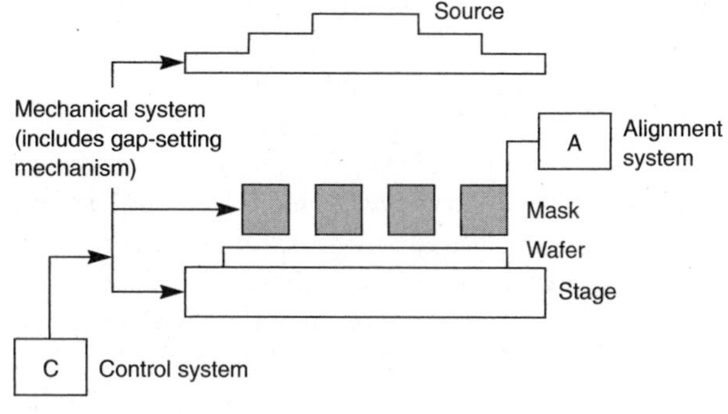

[46]R.K. Watts and N.G. Einspruch, eds., *Lithography for VLSI, VLSI Electronics—Microstructure Science* (New York: Academic Press, 1987).

they are less likely to be damaged during exposure, but since the mask and wafer are separated from each other, light coming through the mask spreads out before it reaches the resist, and the mask's shadow is less well defined than it is in the case of a contact aligner. As a result, users switching to proximity aligners traded off some minimum feature size capability for increased yield.

The basic set of core design concepts that underlie optical photolithography—the use of a visible light source to transmit the image of the mask to the wafer, a lens or other device to focus the image of the mask on the wafer, an alignment system that uses visible light, and a mechanical system that holds the mask and the wafer in place—have remained unchanged since the technology was first developed, although aligner performance has improved dramatically. The minimum-feature-size capability of the first aligners was about 15 to 20 microns. Modern aligners are sometimes specified to have minimum feature sizes of less than half a micron.

Radical alternatives, making use of quite different core concepts, have been explored in the laboratory but have yet to be widely introduced into full-scale production. Aligners using x-rays and ion beams as sources have been developed, as have direct-write electron beam aligners, in which a focused beam of electrons is used to write directly on the wafer.[47] These technologies are clearly radical. Not only do they rely on quite different core concepts for the source, but they also use quite different mask, alignment, and lens technologies.

A constant stream of incremental innovation has been critical to optical photolithography's continuing success. The technology of each component has been significantly improved. Modern light sources are significantly more powerful and more uniform, and modern alignment systems are much more accurate. In addition, the technology has seen four waves of architectural innovation: the move from contact to proximity alignment, from proximity to scanning projection alignment, and from scanners to first- and then second-generation "steppers." Exhibit 5 summarizes the changes in the technology introduced by each generation. In each case the core technologies of optical lithography remained largely untouched, and much of the technical knowledge gained in building a previous generation could be transferred to the next. Yet, in each case, the industry leader was unable to make the transition.

Exhibit 6 shows share of deflated cumulative sales, 1962–1986, by generation of equipment for the leading firms. The first commercially successful aligner was introduced by Kulicke and Soffa in 1965. They were extremely successful and held nearly 100 percent of the (very small) market for the next nine years, but by 1974 Cobilt and Kasper had replaced them. In 1974 Perkin-Elmer entered the market with the scanning projection aligner and rapidly became the largest firm in the industry. GCA, in turn, replaced Perkin-Elmer through its introduction of the stepper, only to be supplanted by Nikon, which introduced the second-generation stepper.

In nearly every case, the established firm invested heavily in the next generation of equipment, only to meet with very little success. Our analysis of the industry's history suggests that a reliance on architectural knowledge derived from experience with the previous generation blinded the incumbent firms to critical aspects of the new technology. They thus underestimated its potential or built equipment that was markedly inferior to the equipment introduced by entrants.

The Kasper Saga

The case of Kasper Instruments and its response to Canon's introduction of the proximity printer illustrates some of the problems encountered by established firms. Kasper Instruments was founded in 1968 and by 1973 was a small but profitable firm supplying approximately half of the market for contact aligners. In 1973 Kasper introduced the first contact aligner to be equipped with proximity capability. Although nearly half of all the aligners that the firm sold from 1974 onward had this capability, Kasper aligners were only rarely used in proximity mode, and sales declined steadily until the company left the industry in 1981. The widespread use of proximity aligners only occurred with the introduction and general adoption of Canon's proximity aligner in the late 1970s.

Clearly, the introduction of the proximity aligner is not a radical advance. The conceptual change involved was minor, and most proximity aligners can also be used as contact aligners. However, in a proximity aligner, a quite different set of relation-

---

[47]T.H.P. Chang, M. Hatzakis, A.D. Wilson, and A.N. Broers, "Electron-Beam Lithography Draws a Finer Line," *Electronics* (May 1977), pp. 89–98; W.L. Brown, T. Venkatesan, and A. Wagner, "Ion Beam Lithography," *Solid State Technology* (August 1981), pp. 60–67; P. Burggraaf, "X-Ray Lithography: Optical's Heir," *Semiconductor International* (September 1983), pp. 60–67.

EXHIBIT 5 A Summary of Architectural Innovation in Photolithographic Alignment Technology

	Major Changes	
Equipment	Technology	Critical Relationships between Components
Proximity aligner	Mask and wafer separated during exposure.	Accuracy and stability of gap are a function of links between gap-setting mechanism and other components.
Scanning projection	Image of mask projected onto wafer by scanning reflective optics.	Interactions between lens and other components are critical to successful performance.
First-generation stepper	Image of mask projected through refractive lens. Image "stepped" across wafer.	Relationship between lens field size and source energy becomes significant determinant of throughput. Depth-of-focus characteristics—driven by relationship between source wavelength and lens numerical aperture—become critical. Interactions between stage and alignment system are critical.
Second-generation stepper	Introduction of "site-by-site" alignment, larger 5 × lenses.	Throughput now driven by calibration and stepper stability. Relationship between lens and mechanical system becomes crucial means of controlling distortion.

SOURCE: Field interviews, internal firm records; see R.M. Henderson. "The Failure of Established Firms in the Face of Technical Change: A Study of Photolithographic Alignment Equipment," unpublished PhD dissertation, Harvard University, 1988.

EXHIBIT 6 Share of Deflated Cumulative Sales (%) 1962–1986, by Generation, for the Leading Optical Photolithographic Alignment Equipment Manufacturers*

	Alignment Equipment				
Firm	Contact	Proximity	Scanners	Step and Repeat (1)	Step and Repeat (2)
Cobilt	44		<1		
Kasper	17	8		7	
Canon		67	21	9	
Perkin-Elmer			78	10	<1
GCA				55	12
Nikon					70
Total	61	75	99+	81	82+

*This measure is distorted by the fact that all of these products are still being sold. For second-generation step and repeat aligners this problem is particularly severe, since in 1986 this equipment was still in the early stages of its life cycle.

SOURCE: Internal firm records, Dataquest, VLSI Research Inc.

ships between components is critical to successful performance. The introduction of the proximity aligner was thus an architectural innovation. In particular, in a proximity aligner, the relationships between the gap-setting mechanism and the other components of the aligner are significantly different.

In both contact and proximity aligners, the mask and the wafer surface must be parallel to each other during exposure if the quality of the final image on the wafer is to be adequate. This is relatively straightforward in a contact aligner, since the mask and the wafer are in direct contact with each other during exposure. The gap-setting mechanism is used only to separate the mask and the wafer during alignment. Its stability and accuracy have very little impact on the aligner's performance. In a proximity aligner, however, the accuracy and precision of the gap-setting mechanism are critical to the aligner's performance. The gap between the mask and the wafer must be precise and consistent across the mask and wafer surfaces if the aligner is to perform well. Thus, the gap-setting mechanism must locate the mask at exactly the right point above the wafer by dead reckoning and must then ensure that the mask is held exactly parallel to the wafer. Since the accuracy and stability of the mechanism is as much a function of the way in which it is integrated with the other components as it is of its own design, the relationships between the gap-setting mechanism and the other components of the aligner must change if the aligner is to perform well. Thus, the successful design of a proximity aligner requires both the acquisition of some new component knowledge—how to build a more accurate and more stable gap-setting mechanism—and the acquisition of new architectural knowledge.

Kasper's failure to understand the challenge posed by the proximity aligner is especially puzzling given its established position in the market and its depth of experience in photolithography. There were several highly skilled and imaginative designers at Kasper during the early 1970s. The group designed a steady stream of contact aligners, each incorporating significant incremental improvements. From 1968 to 1973, the minimum-feature-size capability of its contact aligners improved from fifteen to five microns.

But Kasper's very success in designing contact aligners was a major contributor to its inability to design a proximity aligner that could perform as successfully as Canon's. Canon's aligner was superficially very similar to Kasper's. It incorporated the same components and performed the same functions, but it performed them much more effectively because it incorporated a much more sophisticated understanding of the technical interrelationships that are fundamental to successful proximity alignment. Kasper failed to develop the particular component knowledge that would have enabled it to match Canon's design. More importantly, the architectural knowledge that Kasper had developed through its experience with the contact aligner had the effect of focusing its attention away from the new problems whose solution was critical to the design of a successful proximity aligner.

Kasper conceived of the proximity aligner as a modified contact aligner. Like the incremental improvements to the contact aligner before it, design of the proximity aligner was managed as a routine extension to the product line. The gap-setting mechanism that was used in the contact aligner to align the mask and wafer with each other was slightly modified, and the new aligner was offered on the market. As a result, Kasper's proximity aligner did not perform well. The gap-setting mechanism was not sufficiently accurate or stable to ensure adequate performance, and the aligner was rarely used in its proximity mode. Kasper's failure to understand the obsolescence of its architectural knowledge is demonstrated graphically by two incidents.

The first is the firm's interpretation of early complaints about the accuracy of its gap-setting mechanism. In proximity alignment, misalignment of the mask and the wafer can be caused both by inaccuracies or instability in the gap-setting mechanism and by distortions introduced during processing. Kasper attributed many of the problems that users of its proximity equipment were experiencing to processing error, since it believed that processing error had been the primary source of problems with its contact aligner. The firm "knew" that its gap-setting mechanism was entirely adequate and, as a result, devoted very little time to improving its performance. In retrospect, this may seem like a wanton misuse of information, but it represented no more than a continued reliance on an information filter that had served the firm well historically.

The second illustration is provided by Kasper's response to Canon's initial introduction of a proximity aligner. The Canon aligner was evaluated by a team at Kasper and pronounced to be a copy of a Kasper machine. Kasper evaluated it against the criteria that it used for evaluating its own aligners—criteria that had been developed during its experience with contact aligners. The technical features that made Canon's aligner a significant advance, particularly the redesigned gap mechanism, were not observed because they were not considered important. The Canon aligner was pronounced to be "merely a copy" of the Kasper aligner.

Kasper's subsequent commercial failure was triggered by several factors. The company had problems designing an automatic alignment system of sufficient accuracy and in managing a high-volume manufacturing facility. It also suffered through several rapid changes of top management during the late 1970s. But the obsolescence of architectural knowledge brought about by the introduction of architectural innovation was a critical factor in its decline.

Kasper's failure stemmed primarily from failures of recognition: the knowledge that it had developed through its experience with the contact aligner made it difficult for the company to understand the ways in which Canon's proximity aligner was superior to its own. Similar problems with recognition show up in all four episodes of architectural innovation in the industry's history. The case of Perkin-Elmer and stepper technology is a case in point. By the late 1970s Perkin-Elmer had achieved market leadership with its scanning projection aligners, but the company failed to maintain that leadership when stepper technology came to dominate the industry in the early 1980s. When evaluating the two technologies, Perkin-Elmer engineers accurately forecast the progress of individual components in the two systems but failed to see how new interactions in component development—including better resist systems and improvements in lens design—would give stepper technology a decisive advantage.

GCA, the company that took leadership from Perkin-Elmer, was itself supplanted by Nikon, which introduced a second-generation stepper. Part of the problem for GCA was recognition, but much of its failure to master the new stepper technology lay in problems in implementation. Echoing Kasper, GCA first pronounced the Nikon stepper a "copy" of the GCA design. Even after GCA had fully recognized the threat posed by the second-generation stepper, its historical experience handicapped the company in its attempts to develop a competitive machine. GCA's engineers were organized by component, and cross-department communication channels were all structured around the architecture of the first-generation system. While GCA engineers were able to push the limits of the component technology, they had great difficulty understanding what Nikon had done to achieve its superior performance.

Nikon had changed aspects of the design—particularly the ways in which the optical system was integrated with the rest of the aligner—of which GCA's engineers had only limited understanding. Moreover, because these changes dealt with component interactions, there were few engineers responsible for developing this understanding. As a result, GCA's second-generation machines did not deliver the kind of performance that the market demanded. Like Kasper and Perkin-Elmer before them, GCA's sales languished and they lost market leadership. In all three cases, other factors also played a role in the firm's dramatic loss of market share, but a failure to respond effectively to architectural innovation was of critical importance.

Discussion and Conclusions

We have assumed that organizations are boundedly rational and, hence, that their knowledge and information processing structures come to mirror the internal structure of the product they are designing. This is clearly an approximation. It would be interesting to explore the ways in which the formulation of architectural and component knowledge is affected by factors such as the firm's history and culture. Similarly, we have assumed that architectural knowledge embedded in routines and channels becomes inert and hard to change. Future research designed to investigate information filters, problem-solving strategies, and communication channels in more detail could explore the extent to which this can be avoided.

The ideas developed here could also be linked to those of authors such as Abernathy and Clark,[48] who have drawn a distinction between innovation that challenges the technical capabilities of an organization and innovation that challenges the organization's knowledge of the market and of customer needs. Research could also examine the extent to which these insights are applicable to problems of process innovation and process development.

The empirical side of this paper could also be developed. While the idea of architectural innovation provides intriguing insights into the evolution of semiconductor photolithographic alignment equipment, further research could explore the extent to which it is a useful tool for understanding the impact of innovation in other industries.

The concept of architectural innovation and the related concepts of component and architectural knowledge have a number of important implications. These ideas not only give us a richer characterization of different types of innovation, but they open up new areas in understanding the connections between innovation and organizational capability. The paper suggests, for example, that we need to deepen our understanding of the traditional distinction between innovation that enhances and innovation that destroys competence within the firm, since the essence of architectural innovation is

---

[48]"Innovation."

that it both enhances and destroys competence, often in subtle ways.

An architectural innovation's effect depends in a direct way on the nature of organizational learning. This paper not only underscores the role of organizational learning in innovation but suggests a new perspective on the problem. Given the evolutionary character of development and the prevalence of dominant designs, there appears to be a tendency for active learning among engineers to focus on improvements in performance within a stable product architecture. In this context, learning means learning about components and the core concepts that underlie them. Given the way knowledge tends to be organized within the firm, learning about changes in the architecture of the product is unlikely to occur naturally. Learning about changes in architecture—about new interactions across components (and often across functional boundaries)—may therefore require explicit management and attention. But it may also be that learning about new architectures requires a different kind of organization and people with different skills. An organization that is structured to learn quickly and effectively about new component technology may be ineffective in learning about changes in product architecture. What drives effective learning about new architectures and how learning about components may be related to it are issues worth much further research.

These ideas also provide an intriguing perspective from which to understand the current fashion for cross-functional teams and more open organizational environments. These mechanisms may be responses to a perception of the danger of allowing architectural knowledge to become embedded within tacit or informal linkages.

To the degree that other tasks performed by organizations can also be described as a series of interlinked components within a relatively stable framework, the idea of architectural innovation yields insights into problems that reach beyond product development and design. To the degree that manufacturing, marketing, and finance rely on communication channels, information filters, and problem-solving strategies to integrate their work together, architectural innovation at the firm level may also be a significant issue.

Finally, an understanding of architectural innovation would be useful to discussions of the effect of technology on competitive strategy. Since architectural innovation has the potential to offer firms the opportunity to gain significant advantage over well-entrenched, dominant firms, we might expect less-entrenched competitor firms to search actively for opportunities to introduce changes in product architecture in an industry. The evidence developed here and in other studies suggests that architectural innovation is quite prevalent. As an interpretive lens, architectural innovation may therefore prove quite useful in understanding technically based rivalry in a variety of industries.

Strategic Action

Case II–12
Biotechnology: A Technical Note

Gary Pisano

Historical Background

Biotechnology is a body of knowledge and a set of techniques for using live organisms such as bacteria, yeast, fungi, plant cells, and animal cells in production processes. While the term *biotechnology* was not coined until the mid-1970s, the basic technology has been used since the Stone Age. The first biotechnologists were Neolithic men and women who fermented raw grain into cereals. By 6000 B.C., yeasts were used to produce beer by fermentation. By 4000 B.C., Egyptians discovered how yeast could be used to bake leavened bread. Wine, which also dates back to the ancient world, is another early product of biotechnology. During the early part of the 20th century, Alexander Fleming discovered the

Harvard Business School case 9-690-010, revised March 1992.

first biotechnology-based pharmaceutical, penicillin, an antibiotic produced by the mold *Penicillium*. The breeding and growing of plants and animals are also considered part of the traditional sphere of biotechnology.

The commercial potential of biotechnology was greatly expanded by a series of scientific advances that culminated in the development of genetic engineering during the mid-1970s. Genes, made up of DNA, influence the characteristics of a cell by instructing it which proteins to make and how to make them. Genetic engineering methodologies deliberately change the cell's genetic structure in order to alter its characteristics in some desired fashion. For example, by inserting genes for insulin production into a bacterial cell, the cell can be induced to produce ("express") insulin. By inserting the appropriate set of genes, cells can be "engineered" to produce other proteins as well. Until the advent of genetic engineering, biotechnologists were limited to using only those organisms and cells that already existed. New cells were discovered by physically searching for them in ponds, soil, and other natural habitats. Occasionally, researchers would get lucky and find a cell with useful characteristics. Biotechnologists could also get a new type of cell when an existing cell line mutated. With genetic engineering, biotechnologists no longer have to rely on luck to provide them with new cells.

The two basic methods of genetic engineering discovered during the 1970s were *recombinant DNA* (*r-DNA*) and *hybridoma* (or *monoclonal antibody*) *technology*. These methods and their commercial applications are discussed below.

Recombinant DNA

In 1973, Herbert Boyer, of Stanford University, and Stanley Cohen, of the University of California, San Francisco, developed a technique for implanting the genes of one organism into the genetic structure of another. This technique is known as *recombinant DNA* (*r-DNA*). The first step in genetic engineering via r-DNA is to isolate the gene responsible for producing the protein of interest. Given the enormous number of genes contained in a cell, finding the one responsible for making a particular protein is a complex process. DNA must be extracted, purified, cut, and sorted. Once the specific gene has been found and copied, or cloned, it is inserted into another cell (the host) which may be a bacteria, yeast, plant, or mammalian cell. The host cell containing the inserted gene is now capable of synthesizing a specific protein. The host cell, now genetically engineered, becomes, in essence, a factory. As a living cell, it will reproduce itself and pass on its new production capability to its offspring. In order to produce large quantities of the protein, it is necessary to design a process to facilitate the growth of the cells. Decisions such as what to feed the cells, how much oxygen to supply them, and what temperature to grow them at are absolutely critical for successful large-scale processing. The cells are typically grown in vessels known as bioreactors or fermenters under carefully controlled conditions. A process must also be designed for harvesting and purifying the desired protein from the medium in which the cells are grown.

At this point, it is reasonable to ask: why go through all this trouble to make a particular protein? Are there no alternative chemical methods? The answer to the first question is that proteins have potential commercial value in a wide range of products and processes. Unfortunately, most proteins are simply too large and too complex to be synthesized with traditional chemical methods. In the past, the difficulty of protein synthesis has greatly limited the commercial use of proteins as drugs, diagnostics, and other specialty chemicals. Genetic engineering makes it possible to produce some proteins with significant commercial value. It is for this reason that r-DNA techniques stimulated a wave of commercial interest in the biotechnology field. Applications of r-DNA are discussed below.

Plant Genetics

Plant genetics is concerned with the genetic manipulation of plant cells in order to induce a plant to develop specific characteristics. Generally, researchers are interested in creating resistance to specific diseases, chemicals (e.g., herbicides), or environmental conditions (e.g., frost). Monsanto, for example, has been trying to develop crop plants that are resistant to its Round-up® herbicide so that Round-up® can be used to destroy weeds without damaging the plants. Recently, researchers have also been looking at ways to genetically engineer plants to produce protein pharmaceutical products. Other applications of plant genetic engineering are aimed at improving the food or fiber content of a plant.

Innovation in this area requires competence in genetic engineering as well as a deep understanding of plant genetics. Prior to genetic engineering, the major way to control plant characteristics was through careful cross-breeding. However, unless one found a mutant plant, it was extremely difficult to introduce new characteristics into the plant population. Plant biotechnology has been subject to some environmental controversy because one way to alter the genetic structure of plants is to expose them to a virus which carries the desired gene.

Proteins as Drugs

Biomedical research has long suggested that a number of proteins may have potential therapeutic effects. For example, research in the 1960s suggested that interferon might have beneficial effects in fighting certain cancers and viral diseases. Proteins like interferon, however, are so complex that they cannot be produced synthetically. Only a living cell can make them. Unfortunately, many of the proteins presumed to have therapeutic effects are produced by the body in minute quantities. It was therefore virtually impossible for researchers to collect enough protein material even for experimentation, let alone mass production.

The same methods are also applicable for the production of proteins which may be used to treat animal diseases. In some cases, researchers are attempting to develop a protein therapeutic to treat a particular animal malady. In other cases, a protein is being sought which can alter the animal's physical characteristics (e.g., growth hormones to increase the size of cows, pigs, and chickens). Monsanto's first biotechnological product, expected to reach the market in the early 1990s, is in this area. Monsanto licensed bovine somatotropin, a growth hormone produced from a genetically engineered microorganism, from Genentech. This hormone increases milk production in dairy cows.

One of the critical technical and commercial problems with using proteins as drugs is that because proteins are large molecules, they cannot pass through the digestive system into the bloodstream. The body's digestive system breaks them down and thus destroys the molecule itself. With the current state of the art, most protein-based drugs must be injected directly into the bloodstream and cannot be ingested orally.

Proteins as Biomedical Research Materials

All diseases are biochemical processes. Every biochemical process is catalyzed by specific proteins called enzymes. Thus, certain diseases may be treatable by blocking the action of these catalytic enzymes. For example, one of the world's most popular antiulcer drugs works by inhibiting a protein which stimulates the secretion of gastric acid. This process is analogous to making a key to fit a particular lock. If the enzyme represents the lock, the drug researcher wants to make a key, which will fit it perfectly. Once the drug (the "key") locks into the enzyme (the "lock"), the enzyme cannot be activated by another molecule. Trying to develop a drug from an understanding of a disease's particular biochemistry is sometimes called rational drug design.

In the past, one of the barriers to rational drug design has been the inability of researchers to study the protein enzymes whose action they were trying to inhibit. As noted earlier, some proteins are very complex and rare molecules. As a result, researchers could not develop a sufficiently precise model of the enzyme to design a specific key. With genetic engineering, however, researchers now have a method for making such complex molecules. Many drug companies view this as the chief application of genetic engineering to drug design. It is interesting to note that the drugs which are designed from this process are ultimately synthesized from traditional chemical means. Many pharmaceutical companies therefore prefer this application of genetic engineering because it allows them to build on their in-house expertise in chemically synthesized drugs. Since the chemically synthesized compounds they design to block the enzymes are not themselves complex proteins, they can be ingested orally.

Proteins as Specialty Chemicals

There are many proteins called specialty chemicals used in foods and in industrial production processes. As noted above, biotechnology provides a method for producing these proteins.

Hybridoma Technology

Hybridoma technology is the other basic method of genetic engineering. It was invented in 1975 by Caesar Milstein and Georges Kohler, of the Molecular Biology Laboratories of Britain's Medical Research Council. They fused antibody-producing lymphocyte cells with malignant myeloma (bone cancer) cells. The resulting hybrid-myeloma (or hybridoma) cells could produce specific antibodies (like its lymphocyte parent) and could rapidly proliferate (like its myeloma parent). This discovery provided an entirely new method of antibody production.

Antibodies are produced by the body's lymphocyte cells in response to antigens, which can be bacteria, viruses, and other foreign substances. Each antigen triggers the production of a specific type of antibody. Traditionally, antibodies were produced by injecting an animal with a virus or bacteria. The animal's immune system would, in response, produce antibodies against the intruder. Blood would then be taken from the animal and purified to extract the requisite antibodies. Unfortunately, it was impossible to completely isolate the specific antibody. The blood serum always contains some other antibodies as well, and these impurities could be problematic in therapeutic applications.

With hybridoma technology, the specific lymphocyte cells responsible for producing the specific antibody are fused with the myeloma cell. The lymphocyte cell will only produce a single type of antibody or what is called a *monoclonal antibody*. Three major applications of monoclonal antibodies are currently being developed and commercialized:

1. *Diagnostics*. Since a monoclonal antibody (MAb) will seek out and attach itself to one specific type of antigen, MAbs can be used to detect the presence of specific disease antigens.
2. *Therapeutics*. Likewise, MAbs can also be used to deliver therapeutic compound to the disease site. MAbs are potentially valuable in cancer treatment because there are many powerful anti-cancer drugs which bind indiscriminately to both cancerous and healthy cells.
3. *Industrial processes*. In some biological and chemical production processes, it is very difficult to separate the desired product from the undesirable by-products (waste). MAbs that can attach to the desired product may be helpful in separation.

Case II–13
Monsanto's March into Biotechnology (A)[1]

Dorothy Leonard-Barton and Gary Pisano

> *We were going to become a world force in biotechnology in applying molecular biology to industry in 5 or 10 years. I didn't know if that would occur through making new plastics or making new drugs or making new plants or improving the growth of animals—or what. But I had a vision that we would be outstanding and we would hire outstanding people.*
>
> —Howard Schneiderman

In late 1985, Howard Schneiderman, Monsanto's senior vice president for research and development, faced a number of major decisions. The past six years had seen Monsanto's in-house research and development activity in molecular biology grow from a skunkworks into a world class research capability (see Exhibit 1 for an overview of biotechnology). Now, however, there were those in the company who believed that Monsanto could execute its strategy of moving into high-value-added chemical and biological products better by licensing biotechnologies and by contracting for biotechnology R&D than through extensive internal research. Indeed, Monsanto's first commercial biotechnology product, which was expected to be available on the market in the late 1980s, was developed from technology that had been licensed from the genetic engineering firm Genentech. Even if Monsanto were to continue building internal biotechnology R&D capabilities, there was considerable debate about the proper locus and focus of such activities. Biotechnology R&D was currently centralized at the corporation's Chesterfield Village research campus. With an eye on reducing corporate overhead and on shifting biotechnology R&D from a technology focus to a market focus, some managers within the company were arguing that biotechnology research should be organized according to markets, to correspond with

---

 Harvard Business School Case 9-960-009, revised October 1993.

[1]A few dates have been altered, compressing events in time, so as to create a better teaching vehicle.

EXHIBIT 1 An Overview of Biotechnology

Biotechnology is a body of knowledge and techniques for using live organisms in production processes. It has been used since the Stone Age to make various fermented products like bread or wine from live yeast, bacteria, and fungi. During the first three quarters of the 20th century, biotechnology was used to produce certain foods, beverages, and a limited number of pharmaceuticals (e.g., penicillin), and in the breeding and growing of plants and animals.

Over the past 15 years, biotechnology has been revolutionized by genetic engineering, a set of techniques for selectively altering the genetic structure of plant, bacteria, yeast, and animal cells. Because genes influence the characteristics of cells, a researcher can change a cell in some desired way by selectively altering its genetic component.

Plant agriculture is using biotechnological and genetic engineering methods to develop new types of plants or plants with specific desirable characteristics (such as resistance to cold weather). Before genetic engineering, plant breeders could only develop new plant characteristics by selective breeding.

Because genes control the production of proteins in cells, genetic engineering can also be used to produce proteins which cannot be synthesized through traditional chemical methods. Traditional chemical synthesis is applicable for small molecules. However, proteins are very large molecules and thus normally require genetically engineered cells for production. Once a cell is programmed to produce ("express") a specific protein, it essentially becomes a miniature factory. To produce a protein in any type of quantity, the cell must be placed in a solution of nutrients and kept under carefully controlled conditions so that it can replicate. The process of growing cells and harvesting the protein they produce is known as fermentation or cell culturing. One of the first commercial applications of genetic engineering was the implantation of the human genes for insulin into a bacteria cell; the bacteria cell was then capable of producing insulin. This technology has been particularly important for producing proteins which have been suspected of having therapeutic effects but which are extremely difficult and costly to isolate and purify in quantities sufficient for further development and testing. Genetically engineered cells can produce proteins for a wide variety of applications, including drugs, research materials, diagnostics, specialty chemicals, and food.

the operating divisions that would eventually commercialize the products.

This debate was further stimulated by Monsanto's recent acquisition of G. D. Searle, a $2.8 billion drug company with the strong distribution capabilities that Monsanto would need to compete in pharmaceuticals. The acquisition was requiring some reorganization of research capabilities throughout Monsanto, not only because of the potential for a shift in research emphasis towards drugs, but also because of some redundancies in the biotechnology research conducted at the two companies. Finally, Howard Schneiderman realized that if he was to retire in several years as planned, he must think seriously about grooming a successor. Would it be important to recruit someone to head up research in the coming years who had strong scientific abilities and an academic standing comparable to his own? Or would the future of research at Monsanto be different enough from the past to require different skills? It would certainly be much easier today to attract an academic or business superstar than it had been in 1979, when an executive search firm sought him out at the behest of Monsanto's then-chairman, John Hanley, to head up Monsanto's research.

Monsanto—1979

The Monsanto Company originated in 1901 when John F. Queeny, a chemicals salesman, began producing saccharin, a synthetic sweetener. In the ensuing decades, Monsanto moved into raw materials production and by the 1950s became a multinational, integrated chemical manufacturer. The company was one of the world's largest high-volume, low-margin commodity chemical producers, although it had little proprietary product technology. Exhibit 2 lists the company's product lines in the 1970s. During the late 1970s, most commodity chemical producers, buffeted by unprecedented competition from overseas and new environmental regulations in the United States, began to move toward higher-margin, patent-protected specialty products. Monsanto experienced the same volatility in profits, because the energy crisis sharply increased the costs of the petrochemical raw materials upon which so many of its products were based. Late 1979 quarterly earnings dropped a precipitous 88 percent.

To facilitate diversification, Monsanto set up a venture capital firm, Innoven II, which, according to *Chemical Week* (December 14, 1983), "aggressively

EXHIBIT 2 Monsanto Product Lines in the 1970s

Commodities	Proprietary Products
Ammonium nitrate	Proprietary herbicides
Styrene	Plant-growth regulators
Phenol	Electronic-grade silicon
Acetic acid	Rubber chemicals:
Ethylene	• Plasticizers
Methanol	• Animal feed ingredients
Maleic anhydride	Food ingredients
Phosphorous and derivatives	Pollution-control equipment
Caustic potash	Proprietary plastics
Sulfuric acid and oleum	Specialty resins for coatings
Acrylonitrile	ASTROTURF synthetic surfaces
Adipic acid	Proprietary synthetic fibers
Detergent builders	Fire-resistant additives for plastics and foams
Plasticizers	
Water-treatment chemicals	
Blow-molded plastic containers	
Polyethylene film	
Polyester fiber	
Heat-transfer fluids	
Process-control equipment	
Parathion insecticides	
Analgesics	
Crude oil	
Natural gas	

Note: The products in the left-hand column are not protected by patents and are marketed primarily on the basis of lowest delivered price. The higher-margin products, in the right-hand column, while generally protected by patents, nevertheless represented a small proportion of the company's total sales.

invested in a portfolio of small entrepreneurial companies focused on agribusiness . . . and life sciences, electronic chemicals, process control and instrumentation" as well as biotechnology (specifically Genentech, Genex, and Collagen). Innoven "received a constant stream of proposals from innovators and entrepreneurs. By coinvesting and sharing information with other venture capitalists, Monsanto learned a great deal about the markets and top talent in the company's field of interest." Concurrently, Monsanto began building up a large production capability in silicon, anticipating the explosion of the semiconductor market.

Ernie Jaworski's Skunkworks

John Hanley's interest in biotechnology dated back to his early days as a new Monsanto CEO when he had helped Ernie Jaworski start a small "skunkworks" biotechnology operation in the midst of conventional chemical research projects in Monsanto's Agriculture Company. A PhD biochemist, Jaworski had maintained strong links with the academic research community after coming to Monsanto in 1952. Symposia he organized had kept him abreast of developments in plant genetics. As a result of these symposia, he foresaw enormous potential benefits for Monsanto's traditionally strong agricultural business if crop plants could be genetically altered either to resist herbicides that would kill the weeds around them, or to resist pests rather than being chemically treated with pesticides. The first possibility was especially appealing because rendering plants herbicide-resistant would extend the market for one of Monsanto's prime agricultural products, Roundup® herbicide. Currently, Roundup® could be applied only before crop growth or on weeds near a crop, but could not be applied directly to growing crops because it killed such crops along with the weeds (with the exception of orchard crops like pecan trees).

In 1973, Jaworski went before Monsanto's board of directors to request money for cellular research.

Once the general manager of the Agriculture Company agreed to fund the project, Jaworski set up his program and staffed it with about 35 scientists. Although the focus of the program was on creating plants with innate herbicide resistance, Jaworski saw this research as a door to more ambitious work in genetics and the creation of whole plants from cells. Until Howard Schneiderman was hired, however, the infant cell biology research program was continuously at risk, competing for funds against agricultural projects with much greater likelihood of near-term payback. Moreover, it could not achieve the critical mass of scientists necessary for a top-notch scientific endeavor.

Recruitment of Howard Schneiderman

At the time he was approached by a headhunter, Howard Schneiderman was Dean of Biological Sciences at the University of California at Irvine. He was not interested in moving, yet one meeting with Jack Hanley changed his mind. As Schneiderman recalled:

> Hanley posed a question to me: "We're about to make a big investment in a silicon plant in the United States. Is silicon the material of choice for the semiconductors of the future?"
>
> I asked: "How long will you give me to answer that—one day, one week, a month?"
>
> "Play it by ear," Hanley responded.
>
> Well, if I had one day, I would call up the top biologist at the Massachusetts Institute of Technology, whom I know, and I would ask to be introduced in a telephone conference call to the top materials scientist at MIT. Then I'd pose the question to that person and ask him to think about it. I'd tell him: "I'd be happy to give you $2,000 for an answer, and I'll call you back tomorrow." I figured that guy would get on the telephone, and he would ask colleagues, and in 24 hours, I could give Hanley a reasonable answer, although it wouldn't be perfect.
>
> If I had a week, I'd get people together through my contacts at the National Academy of Sciences and MIT and Caltech and Stanford. Smart people know smart people, and if I spoke to the best biologist I knew, or the top physicists at Cornell where I had been a professor at one time, they would point me in the right direction.
>
> Hanley asked me a bunch of similar questions, and then he said: "Schneiderman, last year we spent $150 million in research. We probably should have spent $250 million. Do you have any good ideas?"
>
> What researcher who has spent years worried about small budgets could resist the question of whether he had $100 million worth of ideas? Of course, Hanley could have been just talking. But he wasn't. Soon after he hired me, he put up another $150 million to build the new Life Science Center in Chesterfield Village, even though we didn't have a single product yet. He said, "I'm sure we will. But we won't if we don't have a place to do research—good enough to attract top people."

Building the Staff

In the fall of 1979, when Schneiderman was brought in, Ernie Jaworski transferred his cellular biology research group from the Agriculture Company to Corporate Research. He and Schneiderman began the task of building a world-class molecular biology program. In addition to Jaworski's existing group, Schneiderman identified a number of "brilliant, flexible chemists" who willingly applied their expertise to biochemistry. Schneiderman gave Jaworski carte blanche for outside recruiting, and Jaworski enthusiastically set about utilizing his numerous contacts with experts in the field. Schneiderman in turn had been given an almost completely free hand to recruit other accomplished scientists. As he recalled, "The Executive V.P. of Monsanto, Louis Fernandez, would ask just one question whenever I said I wanted to hire someone: 'What would this person be doing Monday morning?' " As intended, the question forced Schneiderman to think in pragmatic, industrial terms. CEO Hanley's vision was for Monsanto to become a world force in biotechnology in 5 to 10 years by creating outstanding applications of molecular biology to industrial problems.

Recruiting in the early days was not easy. Other established scientists could have been attracted to Schneiderman's position but saw little advantage in coming to Monsanto just as a team member, however highly salaried the available position might be. In addition, although Schneiderman's presence presaged a good program, younger scientists feared that industry jobs were vulnerable to changes in economic conditions and hence less secure than university positions. During the 1970s, the same downturn in the chemicals industry that led Monsanto management to consider diversifying into biotechnology had necessitated the layoff of about 2,000 employees. Most of the downsizing was accomplished through generous and carefully orchestrated early retirement programs.

Monsanto also invested in reskilling some of its personnel for totally different careers. More than one chemical engineer was able to return to school at Monsanto's expense to gain new skills in biochemical engineering.

None of this changed the fact, however, that business factors had forced Monsanto to restructure, and some academics feared it could happen again. One isolated incident involving about 30 researchers obscured accounts of the humane, often innovative downsizing programs. An overzealous manager, focused on protecting proprietary company materials, had had some researchers abruptly escorted to the door by security personnel, without prior warning that their jobs were terminated. This tale of uncharacteristic brutality reverberated through the academic communities, causing some professors to warn their graduate students against joining Monsanto.

Molecular biologists were scarce: Monsanto had to compete for university-trained scientists with new start-up ventures such as Biogen and Genentech which could offer attractive stock options. However, unlike most other companies and university laboratories, Monsanto could offer its researchers opportunities to devise long-term projects, such as a 14-year project to design new kinds of plants that could resist insects, herbicides, and diseases. Schneiderman made a point of assuring new hires that they could continue to explore cutting-edge issues, to publish, to attend conferences, and even to take sabbaticals to learn new skills. He firmly believed that "we need good science to make really innovative and durable products."

Alliances

Monsanto gradually built up internal capability by attracting young researchers. Schneiderman realized, however, that Monsanto would not grow quickly enough to prove the utility of biotechnology if he relied on in-house capacity alone. "We decided we would get technology and products from wherever we could. There was no problem of NIH (not-invented-here)." Within three months of joining Monsanto, Schneiderman signed a licensing agreement with Genentech. Jaworski already knew this start-up company well: he had tried to interest Monsanto in Genentech at its very inception in 1975 when its founders were seeking venture capital. At the time, Monsanto was uninterested, but by 1979, Genentech had developed a human growth protein which enabled children with extremely stunted growth to achieve a more average stature. In the 1960s, Monsanto scientists had extracted a growth hormone from the pituitary glands of pigs and cows. Because the technology for making proteins was in its infancy at that point, further research was not pursued. Genentech's technology, along with the hiring of a researcher with expertise in the growth hormone field, revived Monsanto's interest in the bovine (cow) and porcine (pig) growth hormones. Jaworski was convinced that Genentech could help speed Monsanto's progress towards commercialization of cow and pig growth hormones.

In 1979, Monsanto and Genentech reached a development and licensing agreement for animal growth hormones. Monsanto agreed to fund a portion of Genentech's animal growth hormone R&D expenses, in return for which Monsanto received the rights to license certain growth hormone producing microorganisms under development by Genentech, paying royalties to Genentech for the sales of those products. In 1983, Genentech delivered a vial of bovine somatotropin (BST) to Monsanto. After preliminary safety and efficacy tests, Monsanto decided to go ahead with development and exercised its right to use the BST-producing microorganisms in a large-scale process, whose development was an extremely complicated project in what one scientist called a "very artsy-craftsy field of science." Few organizations had ever produced large quantities of a genetically engineered protein before.

Schneiderman also looked to universities as sources of knowledge and new technology, focusing much of his efforts on building a strong alliance with nearby Washington University in St. Louis. Schneiderman believed that alliance with universities would ensure that Monsanto was positioned at the cutting edge of research, particularly in the life science: "When you face problems of the difficulty we are trying to solve, we just need the best brains in the world wherever they are, Washington University or overseas in Cologne; we will seek collaborators. Maybe it will be just collaboration for the sake of science; maybe there will be royalties or a consulting arrangement."

A prior arrangement in the form of a $50 million grant to Harvard Medical School had not been satisfactory because the Harvard researchers had been unwilling to share any of the results of their research with Monsanto personnel before it was available through open publication. The informally worded

Harvard agreement, intended to provide a window into new technology, turned out to be a closed door to Monsanto. Determined to make alliances that would be more useful to Monsanto, Schneiderman took care to structure the Washington University relationships so that both parties would profit. It called for Monsanto to invest $23.5 million over five years to establish a program at the Medical School to discover, study, and isolate proteins and peptides regulating cellular functions.

The research would be performed at the university in collaboration with Monsanto scientists when appropriate. Any scientist at the Medical School could apply for a grant, just as they would to the U.S. government's National Institutes of Health. Funding was available both for exploratory research and for studies that could lead to product development. A few Monsanto scientists had adjunct professorships and laboratories at the university as well.

New grant applications would be reviewed by a committee made up of five university Medical School professors and five scientists from Monsanto. Should research develop into a successful product, royalties would be paid to the university. The university decided on the following distribution of royalties: 20 percent would go to the Medical School, 40 percent to the university department originating the discovery, and 40 percent to the departmental laboratory that made the discovery. The individual scientist at the university would not receive royalties. All research would be open, with each scientist able to publish findings, although Monsanto was allowed a 30-day period in which to review an early draft for possible patent positions. All patents would be held by the university, with Monsanto having first rights of refusal for licensing. The agreement was to be reviewed every three years by a panel of prestigious scientists from outside of St. Louis, chaired by a Nobel Prize winner. The Monsanto funding represented about 5 percent of Washington University's total gifts, grants, and so on, in the biomedical field.

The Potential of Biotechnology for Monsanto

Several features of biotechnology were potentially important to a company like Monsanto (see Exhibit 3 for the distribution of firms pursuing specific applications of biotechnology).

Plant Agriculture

Biotechnology, especially genetic engineering, could lead to new crops that would be insect resis-

EXHIBIT 3 Distribution of Firms Pursuing Specific Applications of Biotechnology

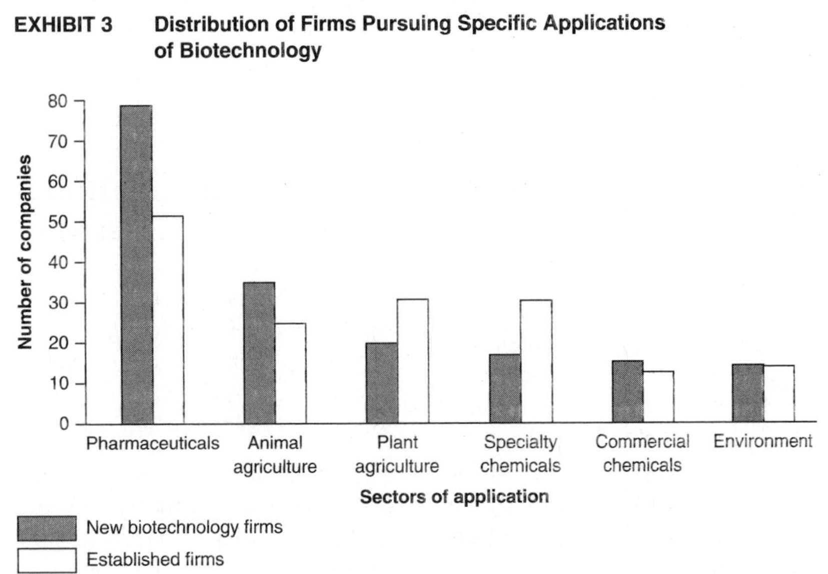

SOURCE: U.S. Congress Office of Technology Assessment, *Commercial Biotechnology: An International Analysis* (Washington, DC: U.S. Government Printing Office, 1984).

tant and never require insecticide sprays, disease resistant and never need fungicide sprays, or resistant to an environmentally friendly herbicide like glyphosate (Roundup®), which could then replace many other less desirable herbicides. However, no one had ever made a business of genetically engineering crop seeds before. Monsanto would either have to license the technology to seed companies, acquire such companies, or set up their own. All three possibilities were accompanied by some risk. Licensing appeared to be the most appealing option, but would require extensive work with the seed companies since Monsanto's bottom line for the seed business would depend upon the performance of those companies. Not only would Monsanto need to transfer the considerable technical know-how required to produce the seed in large quantities, but would also need to train the company personnel to effectively sell this very different kind of seed. The environmental and financial advantages of a seed crop that did not have to be chemically treated six times a year were considerable. However, some farmers were still leery of bioengineering processes and therefore marketing would have to be accompanied by more than the usual amount of consumer education. Furthermore, as in the case of all licensing agreements, Monsanto might not be able to appropriate all the benefits from the invention.

Acquiring or setting up a seed company was problematic because of the myriad ancillary businesses that were required. Seed companies had experimental farms, huge inventories, dispersed warehouses, and elaborate distribution networks. Therefore, any venture into the seed business would require significant investments of management attention and capital.

Animal Agriculture

The application of bioengineering to animal agriculture held ripe possibilities because not only could the company produce therapeutic proteins to prevent or treat various animal diseases, but it was now possible for the first time to enhance natural animal characteristics through such growth proteins as bovine and porcine somatotropin. Bovine somatotropin would increase the efficiency with which dairy cows convert feed into milk by 10 to 25 percent. Tests of porcine somatotropin showed it could speed the growth of pigs to marketable size by about two-and-a-half weeks, yielding 30 percent leaner meat. Such products would run a triple gauntlet in reaching the market. As in the case of other products affecting food, FDA approval would be necessary. This approval process was familiar to Monsanto. Less predictable would be the response from the dairy and pork farmers themselves, since the growth hormones could change the current industry economics and potentially drive prices down. Finally, although studies showed that growth hormone from cows would be inactive in humans and that 90 percent of the hormone would be destroyed in pasteurization, antibiotechnology activists might nonetheless arouse consumer concerns about the use of hormones in the production of something as basic as milk. Furthermore, selling these products directly to farmers would require a new distribution system, which was complicated by the limited and fragile shelf life of the growth hormones; Monsanto currently sold mostly through distributors, and to crop farmers rather than animal husbandry businesses.

Pharmaceuticals

Biotechnology could produce proteins in quantity for use directly as drugs (such as human insulin or interferon). Most such proteins could not be ingested but had to be injected, but research was underway in many laboratories to solve that limitation. Proteins could also be produced for use in designing new drugs. The exploitation of this third possibility would require the acquisition of an established pharmaceutical company, and such an acquisition had been under consideration since the early 1970s.

Formal Creation of Health Sciences at Monsanto

In 1982, Monsanto created the Health Care Division to provide a focus for internal research and development in pharmaceutical products, and to bring technology much closer to the marketplace. The division was established with two purposes in mind:

1. To prepare the way for acquisition of a pharmaceutical company by developing some internal capabilities that would make Monsanto more attractive to prospective acquisition candidates.
2. To provide a focus for developing strategies for how Monsanto was going to develop an important and profitable pharmaceutical company.

This division, which contained about 170 people at its maximum, was an integral part of Schneiderman's strategy:

> I am convinced that unless you build internal capabilities, you don't know the right price for technology that you acquire from the outside. You don't know whether a discovery is significant and durable or whether it is ephemeral. You don't know what the best procedure is, where the bottlenecks are. I think you have to have terrific internal capability to make such judgments. Now that's not a universally held opinion. Some companies have bought other companies and have essentially tried to assimilate them—with varied degrees of success. We are building our technology internally, and I think that way is working for us. The research is part of the company—not separate. There is no "we" versus "they." Everything is "we."

Acquisition of Searle

As early as the mid-1970s, John Hanley, then Monsanto's CEO, had determined that the firm should acquire a pharmaceutical company to support its diversification into therapeutic drugs, but a suitable match was not found until after he turned the reins over to Richard Mahoney. The goal was to build a $2 billion drug company by the early 1990s; anything smaller would not be a real player in the industry. In the mid 1980s, Mahoney bid for the ethical drug business of G. D. Searle, but the owners insisted on a package deal that included their profitable NutraSweet operation. Since the patent on aspartame, the sugar substitute marketed as NutraSweet, was due to expire in 1992, Mahoney initially balked. He eventually gave in and paid $2.7 billion, which was 5.5 times book value and 19 times earnings for what the press at the time frequently described as a "lackluster" pharmaceutical firm. The major value Searle brought to Monsanto was access to the highly profitable drug business through an already established distribution system. In addition to causing an initial downgrading in Monsanto's credit rating—due to $1.2 billion of new long-term debt—the acquisition, not unexpectedly, posed some management challenges. A number of Searle executives resigned, leaving that organization in much uncertainty.

Researchers throughout Searle faced an especially uncertain future. Even after Searle's consumer products division was sold and the NutraSweet division was made a separate company, nearly two thousand people at Searle were still engaged in research and development activities. Searle also had a biotechnology center at High Wycombe in England where a new $15 million biotechnology pilot plant had recently been built. Forty-five of High Wycombe's 350 scientists used this plant for small, preclinical development. Searle had inadvertently become one of the very earliest industrial biotechnology explorers when a group of researchers at High Wycombe had started a small program in 1973. By 1985, the small group had gained much experience, but their work was largely redundant with Monsanto's in St. Louis. Schneiderman thus faced the problem of deciding how to handle the redundancies. The High Wycombe physical plant itself was a problem, because no other biotechnology research organization was likely to want to buy the facility. Each biotechnology venture was taking its individual approach to production and therefore equipment was still quite customized. A far more pressing matter was what to do about the 350 scientists and technicians if the facility were closed: while a few were approaching retirement and would want to take advantage of the kind of retirement package that had been offered in the United States during downsizing, and while a few others would be willing to relocate to St. Louis, Schneiderman had to face the possibility that several prominent specialists, particularly in the field of fermentation, would almost certainly leave the company.

In addition to High Wycombe, there was Searle's Sophia-Antipolis facility in France, where animal safety testing and dosage level formulation took place, and a facility in Belgium, where about 65 people worked on preclinical development of drugs, of whom several were at the top of their fields. Some at Monsanto argued that a certain amount of redundancy should be encouraged in research so that an optimal approach could be identified. Moreover, the research presence in Europe was very desirable because regulations governing testing and dosage differed there. If all the European facilities were closed, not only would much intellectual capital be lost to Monsanto, but so also would presence in Europe and the concomitant representation of the European marketplace during drug development. Although the scheduled advent in 1992 of a combined European community was still several years in the future, some Monsanto researchers warned that it would be short-sighted to close down High Wycombe. Still, R&D funding was limited and hard choices had to be made.

Deciding How to Organize R&D

The Searle acquisition also reopened an issue that still provoked debate several years after the initial establishment of Monsanto's Life Sciences Center in Chesterfield Village: should research in biotechnology be organized according to discipline (molecular biology and chemistry) or according to markets served (agriculture and pharmaceuticals)? However they were organized, the researchers could not all be colocated because of physical constraints on the land available to Monsanto for R&D facilities, either in Chesterfield Village or at Corporate Headquarters, 10 miles away.

There were arguments to support organizing research either way. Operating line managers, many of whom had worked most of their adult life in the chemical industry, favored organizing according to markets. They pointed out that most of the major chemical companies had recently moved towards decentralization in order to focus their research efforts on particular markets. While a few companies in commodity chemicals maintained centralized research facilities focusing on process innovations that would drive down costs, most chemical companies were focusing on specialty chemicals for niche markets, and that product-focus motivated the shift to market-focused research as well.

Multifunctional teams focused on a common objective, they argued, were more likely to produce products that will have a significant impact in the marketplace. Industrial research should have an area of focus relevant to the business—or else the research yield would be very low. Focusing research by market area, they emphasized, did not mean focus as narrow as on a specific product.

Another advantage to cross-disciplinary teams would be a common interface with government regulatory agencies. Team members could develop important personal communication ties into the agencies that would enable the teams to anticipate possible changes in regulation and select appropriate, acceptable scientific tests to meet environmental and health standards. Team members would also have in common regulated procedures for developing new products.

Corporate researchers, who tended to favor organizing by research discipline, pointed out that biotechnology was a far less mature field than chemistry and that copying the structure of research in chemical companies was likely to prove disastrous for the fledgling molecular research. Dispersing the molecular scientists among several market-focused efforts might lead to some advances in products in the short term, but that hope rested on the assumption that individual scientists could make large strides in an emerging science and at the same time apply their new insights towards specific product targets. The more likely outcome of such a division, they argued, would be to diffuse and dilute scientific effort, sacrificing the development of a long-term scientific capability on the altar of short-term goals.

To be a world leader, Monsanto must do great science. "Out of great science," Schneiderman maintained, "will come unique insights that will lead to product opportunity." For example, Schneiderman pointed to research on differences in the dialect of genetic code used by plants versus animals as a piece of extremely "esoteric" research. Yet such basic scientific knowledge, developed at Monsanto, was now supporting the development of a crop that could produce an insect-destroying protein (i.e., a crop with a built-in pesticide). While in the future, Monsanto might wish to reorganize, Schneiderman believed that at this time, when the company was venturing into a totally new area of science, it was important to keep the scientists together so that there would be the critical mass necessary for good scientific work.

The acquisition of Searle threw this debate, which had been initially settled by a division in corporate research along disciplinary lines—such as biology or chemistry—into high gear again for several reasons. First, all the staff operations were undergoing scrutiny, to see where money might be saved and to determine which such functions were contributing to Monsanto's bottom line. Strong arguments were made that all research should be parceled out to operating divisions: this would have created market focus at the expense of a central research capability. Corporate Research had as yet produced no biotechnology products and the ones under development from the Genentech technology (BST and PST) were several years away from commercialization. Secondly, through Searle, Monsanto now had a distribution system clamoring for new products, and market-focused research had better potential to optimize the distribution network in the short-run. Finally, the acquisition meant a larger portfolio of research projects to be funded, and therefore long-term biotechnology projects faced even more competition than before.

Of all these issues, the one most threatening to the existence of Corporate Research was the first—that corporate downsizing might well include doing away with centralized research. As Hilliard Williams, director of Central Research Technology, observed:

> Consultants' advice as well as internal analysis convinced Monsanto that it had much too much corporate overhead. So there was a real drive to break the company up into manageable, free-standing units with autonomy and control over their own destiny and all the resources that they needed, and to get rid of those resources that the operating units didn't need or want. Corporate research underwent the same microscopic scrutiny as everyone else and we had to justify our existence in everything that we did.

Mahoney believed in getting personally involved in the decisions that had to be made if the company was to achieve his goals of 10 percent annual growth rates and 20 percent returns on shareholder's equity. *Management Today* quoted him as saying: "I see and participate in the R&D selection process—I have to," he said. "I've seen a lot of money go down rat holes. You have to be ruthless with R&D." Williams and Schneiderman decided to "offer up for dismemberment those parts of corporate research that were not top priority" but to protect the biotechnology and crucial chemistry projects. The researchers in conventional chemistry, such as polymer chemistry, were dispersed to operating units and the total size of the group was reduced by about 50 percent. The number of patent lawyers was also reduced somewhat. A small-scale production plant, used primarily by the Agricultural Company for pilot runs of new chemical products, was transferred to the Agricultural Company.

Technology Strategy for Pharmaceuticals

The acquisition of Searle also triggered debate among Monsanto and Searle researchers about the appropriate role of biotechnology in the company's drug development efforts. Drugs could be very broadly classified into two basic types: large-molecule and small-molecule compounds. Historically, most drugs had been small-molecule entities. Small-molecule drugs could be synthesized through traditional chemical methods and could be ingested orally by the patient. Large-molecule compounds or protein-based drugs were far too complex to be synthesized through chemical methods; most, therefore, had to be produced from genetically engineered cells. Thus, it was not until advances in biotechnology made possible the efficient production of proteins that drug researchers began to search for protein-based drugs. During the late 1970s and 1980s, many new biotechnology firms such as Genentech were formed specifically to develop potentially therapeutic proteins.

During the late 1980s, many drug companies realized that biotechnology could be an important tool in the discovery of small-molecule drugs. Traditionally, drug research and discovery was a highly empirical process involving a large dose of trial and error. A large pharmaceutical company would screen thousands of chemical compounds every year in search of certain therapeutic properties. Every once in a while, a compound would be found that had desirable therapeutic effects without serious side effects.

For many years, drug researchers had hoped to make drug discovery more rational. Biomedical research had revealed that many diseases occurred when certain of the body's cells either overproduced or underproduced certain chemicals. Thus, a rational way to develop a drug for ulcers was to develop a chemical that could bind to stomach cells and switch off their production of digestive acids. The site on the cell where the chemical would bind was called the receptor. To develop a chemical that fit the cell's receptor, researchers needed to isolate and model the three-dimensional structure of receptors. Receptors were complex proteins, and one barrier to rational drug design in the past has been the lack of a method to produce the receptor proteins of interest. With biotechnology, drug companies had a critical new tool for producing the receptor proteins required for drug research: biotechnology would be used, not to produce the drugs themselves, but rather to create the critical research materials needed to design safe and effective small-molecule compounds.

To date, most of Monsanto's and Searle's biopharmaceutical research had pursued the earlier approach of making proteins to be used directly as drugs. A serious obstacle to this approach appeared to be that proteins needed to be injected, since the digestive system rendered them useless if they were ingested. Given that injections implied disbursement through medical facilities rather than through drug stores, some people argued that research on such products was unlikely to contribute significantly to the bottom line, since the target population for such injectable treatments was significantly lower than that for traditional drugs. For example, Genentech's TPA was used to break up a life-threatening blood clot, and the company could therefore charge several thousand dollars a treatment when it was administered by medical personnel. However, products that were intended to be administered over a longer period of time—for example, antiulcer treatments—needed to be available as a pill or liquid, and some people at Monsanto believed that its therapeutic product possibilities lay in this region.

Another important consideration was that proteins as products might be difficult to protect with patents. Indeed, the entire field of patenting proteins was so new that there was not a body of case law to which one could refer. A clever molecular biologist could make variants that were functionally similar but that did not infringe on the original product patent. The time window between commercialization and a viable imitation was likely to be too short to recover the enormous research investments. In contrast, the second application of biotechnology, as a research tool, appeared promising. Such applications built more directly on Monsanto's and Searle's previous capabilities in chemistry. Perhaps the greatest risk in pursuing this route lay in the potential for reducing the biotechnology function to a mere supplier of receptors for use in drug design, a course of action that could cause Monsanto to lose the best people in its powerful biotechnology group. Some felt the acquisition of Searle could push the biotechnology research too far in this direction. The challenge would lie in keeping biotechnology on the cutting edge of science, where six years of intensive work and investment had placed Monsanto.

Either route would require extensive collaboration between the cell and molecular biologists, located primarily in St. Louis, and the drug designers, located primarily in Skokie, Illinois, some 300 miles away. Even Monsanto's pockets were not deep enough to support major thrusts in all directions at once. Some choices must be made.

Schneiderman's Successor

Schneiderman had several criteria in mind as he considered his successor. Among these was his belief that the senior vice president of research had to be someone who could not be intimidated. "If you are intimidated, you are dead—particularly if you don't have a practical concrete bottom line of sales and profits every year but instead are a loss center, with costs increasing every year."

While some felt that the biotechnology program at Monsanto had matured enough over half a decade that there were some internal candidates to succeed Schneiderman, the most obvious one, Ernest Jaworski, was himself nearing retirement. With a precedent of reaching outside the company for top scientific skills, Monsanto also had the option of hiring one of the several outside expert consultants who had reviewed the internal research over a period of years. A number of these were considered as possible successors to Schneiderman, among them a PhD pharmacologist, Philip Needleman. Professor and chairman of pharmacology at Washington University School of Medicine, Needleman could bring a highly pragmatic approach to the job because of his experience with pharmacology. (Pharmacology, the study of and the discovery of drugs that affect human beings, is a scientific discipline that involves both basic and applied research.) Also, he was a superb scientist. For 25 years he had successfully competed for the scientifically rigorous National Institutes of Health grants and, like Schneiderman, he was a member of the National Academy of Sciences. He was also 12 years younger than Schneiderman and could be with Monsanto for at least a decade.

Needleman had made no secret of his views about research: "I have discovered a lot of things that could be drugs; I have always been interested in the chemical manipulation of biology. Academia is pretty good training for directing research at Monsanto because there is this drive for excellence in science in both places." If selected for the job, Needleman intended to continue to rely upon the universities (rather than licensing from other companies) as prime sources for cutting edge technology:

> The most important external vehicle for Monsanto's discovery base is the university affiliations they have developed. The university professors have no development costs. All their government grants are pure discovery money. So bang for buck, you have access to some of the finest minds. Monsanto's investment in the university research provides a scientific base, a lead for new discoveries far in excess of the cost of the investment. The university ties extend Monsanto's discovery activities. There is no small time player if you are going to biotechnology. Either you can clone the genes, have mammalian cell culture, can build vectors, do all the sequencing—or you are a bit player.

The Future of Biotechnology Research at Monsanto

Whoever took over the position would face enormous challenges to keep the R&D budget in biotechnology at levels comparable to those in the past (Exhibit 4 lists the 1982 biotechnology R&D budgets for leading U.S. and foreign companies; Monsanto's 1985 sales and R&D investments by line of business are shown in Exhibit 5). While CEO Mahoney was on record as supporting the biotechnology push, he was himself being pressured to show some concrete results. After six years of research, Monsanto still had not one biotechnology product on the market—and didn't expect to have one for at least four or five more years.

Wall Street was less than impressed. In 1983, Monsanto shares had traded at about 13 times earnings—close to overall average for the time and somewhat above the industry average of 12 times. However, in early 1985, investors had traded Monsanto shares at a steep discount to rivals DuPont and Dow Chemical. Moreover, some investors made pessimistic comparisons between biotechnology and Monsanto's extremely ambitious foray into silicon manufacture. In 1985, silicon production at Monsanto ran at 20 percent of capacity, way below the break-even point of 50 percent, and there were estimates that the company had lost at least $100 million in the past five years. Mahoney referred to silicon production as "always a bridesmaid," meaning it never really succeeded. Some skeptics believed his optimism about biotechnology in 1985 could be similarly misplaced.

However, Monsanto was not alone in foreseeing enormous potential in biotechnology. Not only were there hundreds of small firms springing up around the world, but a number of well-established firms were making sizable investments as well. Even some traditional competitors such as American Cyanamid, Dow, DuPont, and Sandoz were building in-house biotechnology capabilities in plant-related research and were forging alliances

EXHIBIT 4 Biotechnology R&D Budgets for Leading U.S. and Foreign Companies, 1982[a]

Company	Biotechnology R&D Budget (millions of dollars)
Hoechst (Federal Republic of Germany)	$4.2[b]
Schering A.G. (Federal Republic of Germany)	4.2
Hoffman-La Roche (Switzerland)	59.0
Schering-Plough (United States)	60.0
Eli Lilly (United States)	60.0
Monsanto (United States)	62.0
DuPont (United States)	120.0
Genentech (United States)	32.0
Cetus (United States)	26.0
Genex (United States)	8.3
Biogen (United States)	8.7
Hybritech (United States)	5.0
Sumitomo (Japan)	+6.0
Ajinomoto (Japan)	+6.0
Suntory (Japan)	+6.0
Takeda (Japan)	+6.0
Elf-Aquitaine (France)	+6.0

[a]Biotechnology R&D figures for British companies not available.
[b]1983 figure.

SOURCE: Office of Technology Assessment, *Commercial Biotechnology: An International Analysis* (Washington, DC: U.S. Government Printing Office, 1984).

EXHIBIT 5 Monsanto Sales and R&D by Line of Business (in millions of dollars)

Sector	1985 Sales	1985 R&D
Agricultural products:		
Crop chemicals	$1,073	$110
Animal sciences	79	32
Total	$1,152	$142
Chemicals:		
Detergents and phosphates	550	—
Engineered products	251	—
Manmade fibers	1,080	—
Plastics	804	—
Resin products	637	—
Rubber chemicals and instruments	283	—
Specialty chemicals	446	—
Total	$4,051	128
Electronic materials	137	16
Fisher controls	652	20
NutraSweet	317[a]	11
Pharmaceuticals	262[a]	96
Oil and gas	172	31
Corporate	4	26
Total consolidated	$6,747	$470

[a]G. D. Searle & Co. and The NutraSweet Company are included for the five-month period August–December 1985.

SOURCE: Compiled from the *Monsanto Corporate Book*, 1988.

with small firms to develop drugs with novel characteristics. So were the Japanese. Monsanto could not afford to be left behind.

Reading II–16
Strategic Intent

Gary Hamel and C. K. Prahalad

Today managers in many industries are working hard to match the competitive advantages of their new global rivals. They are moving manufacturing offshore in search of lower labor costs, rationalizing product lines to capture global scale economies, instituting quality circles and just-in-time production, and adopting Japanese human resource practices. When competitiveness still seems out of reach, they form strategic alliances—often with the very companies that upset the competitive balance in the first place.

Important as these initiatives are, few of them go beyond mere imitation. Too many companies are expending enormous energy simply to reproduce the cost and quality advantages their global competitors already enjoy. Imitation may be the sincerest form of flattery, but it will not lead to competitive revitalization. Strategies based on imitation are transparent to competitors who have already mastered them. Moreover, successful competitors rarely stand still. So it is not surprising that many executives feel trapped in a seemingly endless game of catch-up—regularly surprised by the new accomplishments of their rivals.

For these executives and their companies, regaining competitiveness will mean rethinking many of the basic concepts of strategy.[1] As "strategy" has blossomed, the competitiveness of Western companies has withered. This may be coincidence, but we think not. We believe that the application of concepts such as "strategic fit" (between resources and opportunities), "generic strategies" (low cost versus differentiation versus focus), and the "strategy hierarchy" (goals, strategies, and tactics) has often abetted the process of competitiveness decline. The new global competitors approach strategy from a perspective that is fundamentally different from that which underpins Western management thought. Against such competitors, marginal adjustments to current orthodoxies are no more likely to produce competitive revitalization than are marginal improvements in operating efficiency. (The box insert, "Remaking Strategy," describes our research and summarizes the two contrasting approaches to strategy we see in large, multinational companies.)

Few Western companies have an enviable track record anticipating the moves of new global competitors. Why? The explanation begins with the way most companies have approached competitor analysis. Typically, competitor analysis focuses on the existing resources (human, technical, and financial) of present competitors. The only companies seen as a threat are those with the resources to erode margins and market share in the next planning period. Resourcefulness, the pace at which new competitive advantages are being built, rarely enters in.

In this respect, traditional competitor analysis is like a snapshot of a moving car. By itself, the photograph yields little information about the car's speed or direction—whether the driver is out for a quiet Sunday drive or warming up for the Grand Prix. Yet many managers have learned through painful experience that a business's initial resource endowment (whether bountiful or meager) is an unreliable predictor of future global success.

Think back. In 1970, few Japanese companies possessed the resource base, manufacturing volume, or technical prowess of U.S. and European industry leaders. Komatsu was less than 35 percent as large as Caterpillar (measured by sales), was scarcely represented outside Japan, and relied on just one product line—small bulldozers—for most of its revenue. Honda was smaller than American Motors and had not yet begun to export cars to the United States. Canon's first halting steps in the reprographics business looked pitifully small compared with the $4 billion Xerox powerhouse.

If Western managers had extended their competitor analysis to include these companies, it would merely have underlined how dramatic the resource discrepancies between them were. Yet by 1985, Komatsu was a $2.8 billion company with a product scope encompassing a broad range of earth-moving equipment, industrial robots, and semiconductors.

---

[1]Among the first to apply the concept of strategy to management were H. Igor Ansoff in *Corporate Strategy: An Analytic Approach to Business Policy for Growth and Expansion* (New York: McGraw-Hill, 1965) and Kenneth R. Andrews in *The Concept of Corporate Strategy* (Homewood, Ill.: Dow Jones-Irwin, 1971).

Harvard Business Review, May–June 1989, pp. 63–76.

Remaking Strategy

Over the last 10 years, our research on global competition, international alliances, and multinational management has brought us into close contact with senior managers in America, Europe, and Japan. As we tried to unravel the reasons for success and surrender in global markets, we became more and more suspicious that executives in Western and Far Eastern companies often operated with very different conceptions of competitive strategy. Understanding these differences, we thought, might help explain the conduct and outcome of competitive battles as well as supplement traditional explanations for Japan's ascendance and the West's decline.

We began by mapping the implicit strategy models of managers who had participated in our research. Then we built detailed histories of selected competitive battles. We searched for evidence of divergent views of strategy, competitive advantage, and the role of top management.

Two contrasting models of strategy emerged. One, which most Western managers will recognize, centers on the problem of maintaining strategic fit. The other centers on the problems of leveraging resources. The two are not mutually exclusive, but they represent a significant difference in emphasis—an emphasis that deeply affects how competitive battles get played out over time.

Both models recognize the problem of competing in a hostile environment with limited resources. But while the emphasis in the first is on trimming ambitions to match available resources, the emphasis in the second is on leveraging resources to reach seemingly unattainable goals.

Both models recognize that relative competitive advantage determines relative profitability. The first emphasizes the search for advantages that are inherently sustainable, the second emphasizes the need to accelerate organizational learning to outpace competitors in building new advantages.

Both models recognize the difficulty of competing against larger competitors. But while the first leads to a search for niches (or simply dissuades the company from challenging an entrenched competitor), the second produces a quest for new rules that can devalue the incumbent's advantages.

Both models recognize that balance in the scope of an organization's activities reduces risk. The first seeks to reduce financial risk by building a balanced portfolio of cash-generating and cash-consuming businesses. The second seeks to reduce competitive risk by ensuring a well-balanced and sufficiently broad portfolio of advantages.

Both models recognize the need to disaggregate the organization in a way that allows top management to differentiate among the investment needs of various planning units. In the first model, resources are allocated to product-market units in which relatedness is defined by common products, channels, and customers. Each business is assumed to own all the critical skills it needs to execute its strategy successfully. In the second, investments are made in core competences (microprocessor controls or electronic imaging, for example) as well as in product-market units. By tracking these investments across businesses, top management works to assure that the plans of individual strategic units don't undermine future developments by default.

Both models recognize the need for consistency in action across organizational levels. In the first, consistency between corporate and business levels is largely a matter of conforming to financial objectives. Consistency between business and functional levels comes by tightly restricting the means the business uses to achieve its strategy—establishing standard operating procedures, defining the served market, adhering to accepted industry practices. In the second model, business-corporate consistency comes from allegiance to a particular strategic intent. Business-functional consistency comes from allegiance to intermediate-term goals, or challenges, with lower level employees encouraged to invent how those goals will be achieved.

Honda manufactured almost as many cars worldwide in 1987 as Chrysler. Canon had matched Xerox's global unit market share.

The lesson is clear: assessing the current tactical advantages of known competitors will not help you understand the resolution, stamina, and inventiveness of potential competitors. Sun-tzu, a Chinese military strategist, made the point 3,000 years ago: "All men can see the tactics whereby I conquer," he wrote, "but what none can see is the strategy out of which great victory is evolved."

Companies that have risen to global leadership over the past 20 years invariably began with ambitions that were out of all proportion to their resources and capabilities. But they created an obsession with winning at all levels of the organization and then sustained that obsession over the 10- to 20-year quest for global leadership. We term this obsession *strategic intent.*

One the one hand, strategic intent envisions a desired leadership position and establishes the criterion the organization will use to chart its progress. Komatsu set out to "Encircle Caterpillar." Canon sought to "Beat Xerox." Honda strove to become a second Ford—an automotive pioneer. All are expressions of strategic intent.

At the same time, strategic intent is more than simply unfettered ambition. (Many companies possess an ambitious strategic intent yet fall short of their goals). The concept also encompasses an active management process that includes: focusing the organization's attention on the essence of winning, motivating people by communicating the value of the target, leaving room for individual and team contributions, sustaining enthusiasm by providing new operational definitions as circumstances change, and using intent consistently to guide resource allocations.

Strategic intent captures the essence of winning. The Apollo program—landing a man on the moon ahead of the Soviets—was as competitively focused as Komatsu's drive against Caterpillar. The space program became the scorecard for America's technology race with the USSR. In the turbulent information technology industry, it was hard to pick a single competitor as a target, so NEC's strategic intent, set in the early 1970s, was to acquire the technologies that would put it in the best position to exploit the convergence of computing and telecommunications. Other industry observers foresaw this convergence, but only NEC made convergence the guiding theme for subsequent strategic decisions by adopting "computing and communications" as its intent. For Coca-Cola, strategic intent has been to put a Coke within "arm's reach" of every consumer in the world.

Strategic intent is stable over time. In battles for global leadership, one of the most critical tasks is to lengthen the organization's attention span. Strategic intent provides consistency to short-term action, while leaving room for reinterpretation as new opportunities emerge. At Komatsu, encircling Caterpillar encompassed a succession of medium-term programs aimed at exploiting specific weaknesses in Caterpillar or building particular competitive advantages. When Caterpillar threatened Komatsu in Japan, for example, Komatsu responded by first improving quality, then driving down costs, then cultivating export markets, and then underwriting new product development.

Strategic intent sets a target that deserves personal effort and commitment. Ask the chairmen of many American corporations how they measure their contributions to their companies' success and you're likely to get an answer expressed in terms of shareholder wealth. In a company that possesses a strategic intent, top management is more likely to talk in terms of global market leadership. Market share leadership typically yields shareholder wealth, to be sure. But the two goals do not have the same motivational impact. It is hard to imagine middle managers, let alone blue-collar employees, waking up each day with the sole thought of creating more shareholder wealth. But mightn't they feel different given the challenge to "Beat Benz"—the rallying cry at one Japanese auto producer? Strategic intent gives employees the only goal that is worthy of commitment: to unseat the best or remain the best, worldwide.

Many companies are more familiar with strategic planning than they are with strategic intent. The planning process typically acts as a "feasibility sieve." Strategies are accepted or rejected on the basis of whether managers can be precise about the how as well as the what of their plans. Are the milestones clear? Do we have the necessary skills and resources? How will competitors react? Has the market been thoroughly researched? In one form or another, the admonition "Be realistic!" is given to line managers at almost every turn.

But can you *plan* for global leadership? Did Komatsu, Canon, and Honda have detailed, 20-year "strategies" for attacking Western markets? Are Japanese and Korean managers better planners than their Western counterparts? No. As valuable as strategic planning is, global leadership is an objective that lies outside the range of planning. We know of few companies with highly developed planning systems that have managed to set a strategic intent. As tests of strategic fit become more stringent, goals that cannot be planned for fall by the wayside. Yet companies that are afraid to commit to goals that lie outside the range of planning are unlikely to become global leaders.

Although strategic planning is billed as a way of becoming more future oriented, most managers, when pressed, will admit that their strategic plans reveal more about today's problems than tomorrow's opportunities. With a fresh set of problems confronting managers at the beginning of every planning cycle, focus often shifts dramatically from year to year. And with the pace of change accelerating in most industries, the predictive horizon is becoming shorter and shorter. So plans do little more than project the present forward incrementally. The goal of strategic intent is to fold the future back into the present. The important question is not, "How will next year be different from this year?" but, "What must we do differently next year to get closer to our strategic intent?" Only with a carefully articulated and adhered to strategic intent will a succession of year-on-year plans sum up to global leadership.

Just as you cannot plan a 10- to 20-year quest for global leadership, the chance of falling into a leadership position by accident is also remote. We don't believe that global leadership comes from an undirected process of intrapreneurship. Nor is it the product of a skunkworks or other techniques for internal venturing. Behind such programs lies a nihilistic assumption: the organization is so hidebound, so orthodox ridden that the only way to innovate is to put a few bright people in a dark room, pour in some money, and hope that something wonderful will happen. In this "Silicon Valley" approach to innovation, the only role for top managers is to retrofit their corporate strategy to the entrepreneurial successes that emerge from below. Here the value added of top management is low indeed.

Sadly, this view of innovation may be consistent with the reality in many large companies.[2] On the one hand, top management lacks any particular point of view about desirable ends beyond satisfying shareholders and keeping raiders at bay. On the other, the planning format, reward criteria, definition of served market, and belief in accepted industry practice all work together to tightly constrain the range of available means. As a result, innovation is necessarily an isolated activity. Growth depends more on the inventive capacity of individuals and small teams than on the ability of top management to aggregate the efforts of multiple teams towards an ambitious strategic intent.

In companies that overcame resource constraints to build leadership positions, we see a different relationship between means and ends. While strategic intent is clear about ends, it is flexible as to means—it leaves room for improvisation. Achieving strategic intent requires enormous creativity with respect to means: witness Fujitsu's use of strategic alliances in Europe to attack IBM. But this creativity comes in the service of a clearly prescribed end. Creativity is unbridled, but not uncorralled, because top management establishes the criterion against which employees can pretest the logic of their initiatives. Middle managers must do more than deliver on promised financial targets; they must also deliver on the broad direction implicit in their organization's strategic intent.

Strategic intent implies a sizable stretch for an organization. Current capabilities and resources will not suffice. This forces the organization to be more inventive, to make the most of limited resources. Whereas the traditional view of strategy focuses on the degree of fit between existing resources and current opportunities, strategic intent creates an extreme misfit between resources and ambitions. Top management then challenges the organization to close the gap by systematically building new advantages. For Canon this meant first understanding Xerox's patents, then licensing technology to create a product that would yield early market experience, then gearing up internal R&D efforts, then licensing its own technology to other manufacturers to fund further R&D, then entering market segments in Japan and Europe where Xerox was weak, and so on.

In this respect, strategic intent is like a marathon run in 400-meter sprints. No one knows what the terrain will look like at mile 26, so the role of top management is to focus the organization's attention on the ground to be covered in the next 400 meters. In several companies, management did this by presenting the organization with a series of corporate challenges, each specifying the next hill in the race to achieve strategic intent. One year the challenge might be quality; the next, total customer care; the next, entry into new markets; the next, a rejuvenated product line. As this example indicates, corporate challenges are a way to stage the acquisition of new competitive advantages, a way to identify the focal point for employees' efforts in the near to medium term. As with strategic intent, top management is specific about the ends—reducing product development times by 75 percent, for example—but less prescriptive about the means.

Like strategic intent, challenges stretch the organization. To preempt Xerox in the personal copier business, Canon set its engineers a target price of $1,000 for a home copier. At the time, Canon's least expensive copier sold for several thousand dollars.

---

[2]Robert A. Burgelman, "A Process Model of Internal Corporate Venturing in the Diversified Major Firm," *Administrative Science Quarterly,* June 1983.

Trying to reduce the cost of existing models would not have given Canon the radical price performance improvement it needed to delay or deter Xerox's entry into personal copiers. Instead, Canon engineers were challenged to reinvent the copier—a challenge they met by substituting a disposable cartridge for the complex image-transfer mechanism used in other copiers.

Corporate challenges come from analyzing competitors as well as from the foreseeable pattern of industry evolution. Together these reveal potential competitive openings and identify the new skills the organization will need to take the initiative away from better positioned players. Exhibit 1, "Building Competitive Advantage at Komatsu," illustrates the way challenges helped that company achieve its intent.

For a challenge to be effective, individuals and teams throughout the organization must understand it and see its implications for their own jobs. Companies that set corporate challenges to create new competitive advantages (as Ford and IBM did with quality improvement) quickly discover that engaging the entire organization requires top management to:

- *Create a sense of urgency,* or quasi crisis, by amplifying weak signals in the environment that point up the need to improve, instead of allowing inaction to precipitate a real crisis. Komatsu, for example, budgeted on the basis of worst case exchange rates that overvalued the yen.
- *Develop a competitor focus at every level through widespread use of competitive intelligence.* Every employee should be able to benchmark his or her efforts against best-in-class competitors so that the challenge becomes personal. For example, Ford showed production-line workers videotapes of operations at Mazda's most efficient plant.

EXHIBIT 1 Building Competitive Advantage at Komatsu

Protect Komatsu's Home Market against Caterpillar	Reduce Costs While Maintaining Quality	Make Komatsu an International Enterprise and Build Export Markets	Respond to External Shocks That Threaten Markets	Create New Products and Markets
Early 1960s: Licensing deals with Cummins Engine, International Harvester, and Bucyrus-Erie to acquire technology and establish benchmarks **1961:** Project A (for Ace) to advance the product quality of Komatsu's small- and medium-sized bulldozers above Caterpillar's **1962:** Quality Circles companywide to provide training for all employees	**1965:** C D (Cost Down) Program **1966:** Total C D program	**Early 1960s:** Develop Eastern bloc countries **1967:** Komatsu Europe marketing subsidiary established **1970:** Komatsu America established **1972:** Project B to improve the durability and reliability and to reduce costs of large bulldozers **1972:** Project C to improve payloaders **1972:** Project D to improve hydraulic excavators **1974:** Established presales and service department to assist newly industrializing countries in construction projects	**1976:** V-10 program to reduce costs by 10% while maintaining quality; reduce parts by 20%; rationalize manufacturing system **1977:** ¥ 180 program to budget companywide for 180 yen to the dollar when exchange rate was 240 **1979:** Project E to establish teams to redouble cost and quality efforts in response to oil crisis	**Late 1970s:** Accelerate product development to expand line **1979:** Future and Frontiers program to identify new businesses based on society's needs and company's know-how **1981:** EPOCHS program to reconcile greater product variety with improved production efficiencies

- *Provide employees with the skills they need to work effectively*—training in statistical tools, problem solving, value engineering, and team building, for example.
- *Give the organization time to digest one challenge before launching another.* When competing initiatives overload the organization, middle managers often try to protect their people from the whipsaw of shifting priorities. But this "wait and see if they're serious this time" attitude ultimately destroys the credibility of corporate challenges.
- *Establish clear milestones and review mechanisms* to track progress and ensure that internal recognition and rewards reinforce desired behavior. The goal is to make the challenge inescapable for everyone in the company.

It is important to distinguish between the process of managing corporate challenges and the advantages that the process creates. Whatever the actual challenge may be—quality, cost, value engineering, or something else—there is the same need to engage employees intellectually and emotionally in the development of new skills. In each case, the challenge will take root only if senior executives and lower level employees feel a reciprocal responsibility for competitiveness.

We believe workers in many companies have been asked to take a disproportionate share of the blame for competitive failure. In one U.S. company, for example, management had sought a 40 percent wage-package concession from hourly employees to bring labor costs into line with Far Eastern competitors. The result was a long strike and, ultimately, a 10 percent wage concession from employees on the line. However, direct labor costs in manufacturing accounted for less than 15 percent of total value added. The company thus succeeded in demoralizing its entire blue-collar work force for the sake of a 1.5 percent reduction in total costs. Ironically, further analysis showed that their competitors' most significant cost savings came not from lower hourly wages but from better work methods invented by employees. You can imagine how eager the U.S. workers were to make similar contributions after the strike and concessions. Contrast this situation with what happened at Nissan when the yen strengthened: top management took a big pay cut and then asked middle managers and line employees to sacrifice relatively less.

Reciprocal responsibility means shared gain and shared pain. In too many companies, the pain of revitalization falls almost exclusively on the employees least responsible for the enterprise's decline. Too often, workers are asked to commit to corporate goals without any matching commitment from top management—be it employment security, gain sharing, or an ability to influence the direction of the business. This one-sided approach to regaining competitiveness keeps many companies from harnessing the intellectual horsepower of their employees.

Creating a sense of reciprocal responsibility is crucial because competitiveness ultimately depends on the pace at which a company embeds new advantages deep within its organization, not on its stock of advantages at any given time. Thus, we need to expand the concept of competitive advantage beyond the scorecard many managers now use: Are my costs lower? Will my product command a price premium?

Few competitive advantages are long lasting. Uncovering a new competitive advantage is a bit like getting a hot tip on a stock: the first person to act on the insight makes more money than the last. When the experience curve was young, a company that built capacity ahead of competitors, dropped prices to fill plants, and reduced costs as volume rose went to the bank. The first mover traded on the fact that competitors undervalued market share—they didn't price to capture additional share because they didn't understand how market share leadership could be translated into lower costs and better margins. But there is no more undervalued market share when each of 20 semiconductor companies builds enough capacity to serve 10 percent of the world market.

Keeping score of existing advantages is not the same as building new advantages. The essence of strategy lies in creating tomorrow's competitive advantages faster than competitors mimic the ones you possess today. In the 1960s, Japanese producers relied on labor and capital cost advantages. As Western manufacturers began to move production offshore, Japanese companies accelerated their investment in process technology and created scale and quality advantages. Then as their U.S. and European competitors rationalized manufacturing, they added another string to their bow by accelerating the rate of product development. Then they built global brands. Then they deskilled competitors through alliances and outsourcing deals. The moral? An organization's capacity to improve existing skills and learn new ones is the most defensible competitive advantage of all.

To achieve a strategic intent, a company must usually take on larger, better financed competitors. That means carefully managing competitive engagements so that scarce resources are conserved. Managers cannot do that simply by playing the same game better—making marginal improvements to competitors' technology and business practices. Instead, they must fundamentally change the game in ways that disadvantage incumbents—devising novel approaches to market entry, advantage building, and competitive warfare. For smart competitors, the goal is not competitive imitation but competitive innovation, the art of containing competitive risks within manageable proportions.

Four approaches to competitive innovation are evident in the global expansion of Japanese companies. These are: building layers of advantage, searching for loose bricks, changing the terms of engagement, and competing through collaboration.

The wider a company's portfolio of advantages, the less risk it faces in competitive battles. New global competitors have built such portfolios by steadily expanding their arsenals of competitive weapons. They have moved inexorably from less defensible advantages such as low wage costs to more defensible advantages like global brands. The Japanese color television industry illustrates this layering process.

By 1967, Japan had become the largest producer of black-and-white television sets. By 1970, it was closing the gap in color televisions. Japanese manufacturers used their competitive advantage—at that time, primarily, low labor costs—to build a base in the private-label business, then moved quickly to establish world-scale plants. This investment gave them additional layers of advantage—quality and reliability—as well as further cost reductions from process improvements. At the same time, they recognized that these cost-based advantages were vulnerable to changes in labor costs, process and product technology, exchange rates, and trade policy. So throughout the 1970s, they also invested heavily in building channels and brands, thus creating another layer of advantage, a global franchise. In the late 1970s, they enlarged the scope of their products and businesses to amortize these grand investments, and by 1980 all the major players—Matsushita, Sharp, Toshiba, Hitachi, Sanyo—had established related sets of businesses that could support global marketing investments. More recently, they have been investing in regional manufacturing and design centers to tailor their products more closely to national markets.

These manufacturers thought of the various sources of competitive advantage as mutually desirable layers, not mutually exclusive choices. What some call competitive suicide—pursuing both cost and differentiation—is exactly what many competitors strive for.[3] Using flexible manufacturing technologies and better marketing intelligence, they are moving away from standardized "world products" to products like Mazda's mini-van, developed in California expressly for the U.S. market.

Another approach to competitive innovation—searching for loose bricks—exploits the benefits of surprise, which is just as useful in business battles as it is in war. Particularly in the early stages of a war for global markets, successful new competitors work to stay below the response threshold of their larger, more powerful rivals. Staking out underdefended territory is one way to do this.

To find loose bricks, managers must have few orthodoxies about how to break into a market or challenge a competitor. For example, in one large U.S. multinational, we asked several country managers to describe what a Japanese competitor was doing in the local market. The first executive said: "They're coming at us in the low end. Japanese companies always come in at the bottom." The second speaker found the comment interesting but disagreed: "They don't offer any low-end products in my market, but they have some exciting stuff at the top end. We really should reverse engineer that thing." Another colleague told still another story. "They haven't taken any business away from me," he said, "but they've just made me a great offer to supply components." In each country, their Japanese competitor had found a different loose brick.

The search for loose bricks begins with a careful analysis of the competitor's conventional wisdom: How does the company define its "served market"? What activities are most profitable? Which geographic markets are too troublesome to enter? The objective is not to find a corner of the industry (or niche) where larger competitors seldom tread but to build a base of attack just outside the market territory that industry leaders currently occupy. The goal is an uncontested profit sanctuary, which could be a particular product segment (the "low end" in

---

[3]For example, see M. E. Porter, *Competitive Strategy* (New York: Free Press, 1980).

motorcycles), a slice of the value chain (components in the computer industry), or a particular geographic market (Eastern Europe).

When Honda took on leaders in the motorcycle industry, for example, it began with products that were just outside the conventional definition of the leaders' product-market domains. As a result, it could build a base of operations in underdefended territory and then use that base to launch an expanded attack. What many competitors failed to see was Honda's strategic intent and its growing competence in engines and power trains. Yet even as Honda was selling 50cc motorcycles in the United States, it was already racing larger bikes in Europe—assembling the design skills and technology it would need for a systematic expansion across the entire spectrum of motor-related businesses.

Honda's progress in creating a core competence in engines should have warned competitors that it might enter a series of seemingly unrelated industries—automobiles, lawn mowers, marine engines, generators. But with each company fixated on its own market, the threat of Honda's horizontal diversification went unnoticed. Today companies like Matsushita and Toshiba are similarly poised to move in unexpected ways across industry boundaries. In protecting loose bricks, companies must extend their peripheral vision by tracking and anticipating the migration of global competitors across product segments, businesses, national markets, value-added stages, and distribution channels.

Changing the terms of engagement—refusing to accept the front runner's definition of industry and segment boundaries—represents still another form of competitive innovation. Canon's entry into the copier business illustrates this approach.

During the 1970s, both Kodak and IBM tried to match Xerox's business system in terms of segmentation, products, distribution, service, and pricing. As a result, Xerox had no trouble decoding the new entrants' intentions and developing countermoves. IBM eventually withdrew from the copier business, while Kodak remains a distant second in the large copier market that Xerox still dominates.

Canon, on the other hand, changed the terms of competitive engagement. While Xerox built a wide range of copiers, Canon standardized machines and components to reduce costs. Canon chose to distribute through office-product dealers rather than try to match Xerox's huge direct sales force. It also avoided the need to create a national service network by designing reliability and serviceability into its product and then delegating service responsibility to the dealers. Canon copiers were sold rather than leased, freeing Canon from the burden of financing the lease base. Finally, instead of selling to the heads of corporate duplicating departments, Canon appealed to secretaries and department managers who wanted distributed copying. At each stage, Canon neatly sidestepped a potential barrier to entry.

Canon's experience suggests that there is an important distinction between barriers to entry and barriers to imitation. Competitors that tried to match Xerox's business system had to pay the same entry costs—the barriers to imitation were high. But Canon dramatically reduced the barriers to entry by changing the rules of the game.

Changing the rules also short-circuited Xerox's ability to retaliate quickly against its new rival. Confronted with the need to rethink its business strategy and organization, Xerox was paralyzed for a time. Xerox managers realized that the faster they downsized the product line, developed new channels, and improved reliability, the faster they would erode the company's traditional profit base. What might have been seen as critical success factors—Xerox's national sales force and service network, its large installed base of leased machines, and its reliance on service revenues—instead became barriers to retaliation. In this sense, competitive innovation is like judo: the goal is to use a larger competitor's weight against it. And that happens not by matching the leader's capabilities but by developing contrasting capabilities of one's own.

Competitive innovation works on the premise that a successful competitor is likely to be wedded to a "recipe" for success. That's why the most effective weapon new competitors possess is probably a clean sheet of paper. And why an incumbents' greatest vulnerability is its belief in accepted practice.

Through licensing, outsourcing agreements, and joint ventures, it is sometimes possible to win without fighting. For example, Fujitsu's alliances in Europe with Siemens and STC (Britain's largest computer maker) and in the United States with Amdahl yield manufacturing volume and access to Western markets. In the early 1980s, Matsushita established a joint venture with Thorn (in the United Kingdom), Telefunken (in Germany), and Thomson (in France), which allowed it to quickly multiply the forces arrayed against Philips in the battle for leadership in the European VCR business. In fighting larger global rivals by proxy, Japanese companies have adopted a maxim as old as human conflict itself: my enemy's enemy is my friend.

Hijacking the development efforts of potential rivals is another goal of competitive collaboration. In the consumer electronics war, Japanese competitors attacked traditional businesses like TVs and hi-fis while volunteering to manufacture "next generation" products like VCRs, camcorders, and compact disc players for Western rivals. They hoped their rivals would ratchet down development spending, and in most cases that is precisely what happened. But companies that abandoned their own development efforts seldom reemerged as serious competitors in subsequent new product battles.

Collaboration can also be used to calibrate competitors' strengths and weaknesses. Toyota's joint venture with GM, and Mazda's with Ford, give these automakers an invaluable vantage point for assessing the progress their U.S. rivals have made in cost reduction, quality, and technology. They can also learn how GM and Ford compete—when they will fight and when they won't. Of course, the reverse is also true: Ford and GM have an equal opportunity to learn from their partner-competitors.

The route to competitive revitalization we have been mapping implies a new view of strategy. Strategic intent assures consistency in resource allocation over the long term. Clearly articulated corporate challenges focus the efforts of individuals in the medium term. Finally, competitive innovation helps reduce competitive risk in the short term. This consistency in the long term, focus in the medium term, and inventiveness and involvement in the short term provide the key to leveraging limited resources in pursuit of ambitious goals. But just as there is a process of winning, so there is a process of surrender. Revitalization requires understanding that process too.

Given their technological leadership and access to large regional markets, how did U.S. and European companies lose their apparent birthright to dominate global industries? There is no simple answer. Few companies recognize the value of documenting failure. Fewer still search their own managerial orthodoxies for the seeds for competitive surrender. But we believe there is a pathology of surrender (summarized in "The Process of Surrender") that gives some important clues.

It is not very comforting to think that the essence of Western strategic thought can be reduced to eight rules for excellence, seven S's, five competitive forces, four product life cycle stages, three generic strategies, and innumerable two-by-two matrices.[4] Yet for the past 20 years, "advances" in strategy have taken the form of ever more typologies, heuristics, and laundry lists, often with dubious empirical bases. Moreover, even reasonable concepts like the product life cycle, experience curve, product portfolios, and generic strategies often have toxic side effects: They reduce the number of strategic options management is willing to consider. They create a preference for selling businesses rather than defending them. They yield predictable strategies that rivals easily decode.

Strategy "recipes" limit opportunities for competitive innovation. A company may have 40 businesses and only four strategies—invest, hold, harvest, or divest. Too often strategy is seen as a positioning exercise in which options are tested by how they fit the existing industry structure. But current industry structure reflects the strengths of the industry leader; and playing by the leader's rules is usually competitive suicide.

Armed with concepts like segmentation, the value chain, competitor benchmarking, strategic groups, and mobility barriers, many managers have become better and better at drawing industry maps. But while they have been busy map making, their competitors have been moving entire continents. The strategist's goal is not to find a niche within the existing industry space but to create new space that is uniquely suited to the company's own strengths, space that is off the map.

This is particularly true now that industry boundaries are becoming more and more unstable. In industries such as financial services and communications, rapidly changing technology, deregulation, and globalization have undermined the value of traditional industry analysis. Map-making skills are worth little in the epicenter of an earthquake. But an industry in upheaval presents opportunities for ambitious companies to redraw the map in their favor, so long as they can think outside traditional industry boundaries.

Concepts like "mature" and "declining" are largely definitional. What most executives mean when they label a business mature is that sales growth has stagnated in their current geographic markets for existing products sold through existing

---

[4]Strategic frameworks for resource allocation in diversified companies are summarized in Charles W. Hofer and Dan E. Schendel, *Strategy Formulation: Analytical Concepts* (St. Paul, MN: West Publishing, 1978).

The Process of Surrender

In the battles for global leadership that have taken place during the last two decades, we have seen a pattern of competitive attack and retrenchment that was remarkably similar across industries. We call this the process of surrender.

The process started with unseen intent. Not possessing long-term, competitor-focused goals themselves, Western companies did not ascribe such intentions to their rivals. They also calculated the threat posed by potential competitors in terms of their existing resources rather than their resourcefulness. This led to systematic underestimation of smaller rivals who were fast gaining technology through licensing arrangements, acquiring market understanding from downstream OEM partners, and improving product quality and manufacturing productivity through companywide employee involvement programs. Oblivious of the strategic intent and intangible advantages of their rivals, American and European businesses were caught off guard.

Adding to the competitive surprise was the fact that the new entrants typically attacked the periphery of a market (Honda in small motorcycles, Yamaha in grand pianos, Toshiba in small black-and-white televisions) before going head-to-head with incumbents. Incumbents often misread these attacks, seeing them as part of a niche strategy and not as a search for "loose bricks." Unconventional market entry strategies (minority holdings in less-developed countries, use of nontraditional channels, extensive corporate advertising) were ignored or dismissed as quirky. For example, managers we spoke with said Japanese companies' position in the European computer industry was nonexistent. In terms of brand share that's nearly true, but the Japanese control as much as one-third of the manufacturing value added in the hardware sales of European-based computer businesses. Similarly, German auto producers claimed to feel unconcerned over the proclivity of Japanese producers to move upmarket. But with its low-end models under tremendous pressure from Japanese producers, Porsche has now announced that it will no longer make "entry level" cars.

Western managers often misinterpreted their rivals' tactics. They believed that Japanese and Korean companies were competing solely on the basis of cost and quality. This typically produced a partial response to those competitors' initiatives: moving manufacturing offshore, outsourcing, or instituting a quality program. Seldom was the full extent of the competitive threat appreciated—the multiple layers of advantage, the expansion across related product segments, the development of global brand positions. Imitating the currently visible tactics of rivals put Western businesses into a perpetual catch-up trap. One by one, companies lost battles and came to see surrender as inevitable. Surrender was not inevitable, of course, but the attack was staged in a way that disguised ultimate intentions and sidestepped direct confrontation.

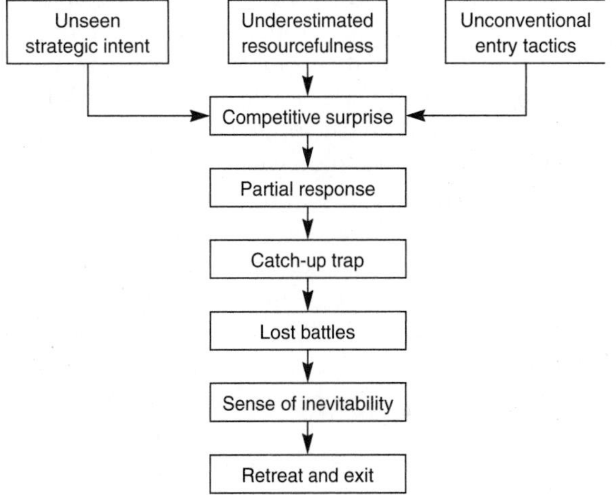

channels. In such cases, it's not the industry that is mature, but the executives' conception of the industry. Asked if the piano business was mature, a senior executive in Yamaha replied, "Only if we can't take any market share from anybody anywhere in the world and still make money. And anyway, we're not in the 'piano' business, we're in the 'keyboard' business." Year after year, Sony has revitalized its radio and tape recorder businesses, despite the fact that other manufacturers long ago abandoned these businesses as mature.

A narrow concept of maturity can foreclose a company from a broad stream of future opportunities. In the 1970s, several U.S. companies thought that consumer electronics had become a mature industry. What could possibly top the color TV? they asked themselves. RCA and GE, distracted by opportunities in more "attractive" industries like mainframe computers, left Japanese producers with a virtual monopoly in VCRs, camcorders, and compact disc players. Ironically, the TV business, once thought mature, is on the verge of a dramatic renaissance. A $20 billion-a-year business will be created when high-definition television is launched in the United States. But the pioneers of television may capture only a small part of this bonanza.

Most of the tools of strategic analysis are focused domestically. Few force managers to consider global opportunities and threats. For example, portfolio planning portrays top management's investment options as an array of businesses rather than as an array of geographic markets. The result is predictable: as businesses come under attack from foreign competitors, the company attempts to abandon them and enter others in which the forces of global competition are not yet so strong. In the short term, this may be an appropriate response to waning competitiveness, but there are fewer and fewer businesses in which a domestic-oriented company can find refuge. We seldom hear such companies asking: Can we move into emerging markets overseas ahead of our global rivals and prolong the profitability of this business? Can we counterattack in our global competitors' home markets and slow the pace of their expansion? A senior executive in one successful global company made a telling comment: "We're glad to find a competitor managing by the portfolio concept—we can almost predict how much share we'll have to take away to put the business on the CEO's 'sell list.' "

Companies can also be overcommitted to organizational recipes, such as strategic business units and the decentralization an SBU structure implies. Decentralization is seductive because it places the responsibility for success or failure squarely on the shoulders of line managers. Each business is assumed to have all the resources it needs to execute its strategies successfully, and in this no-excuses environment, it is hard for top management to fail. But desirable as clear lines of responsibility and accountability are, competitive revitalization requires positive value added from top management.

Few companies with a strong SBU orientation have built successful global distribution and brand positions. Investments in a global brand franchise typically transcend the resources and risk propensity of a single business. While some Western companies have had global brand positions for 30 or 40 years or more—Heinz, Siemens, IBM, Ford, and Kodak, for example—it is hard to identify any American or European company that has created a new global brand franchise in the last 10 to 15 years. Yet Japanese companies have created a score or more—NEC, Fujitsu, Panasonic (Matsushita), Toshiba, Sony, Seiko, Epson, Canon, Minolta, and Honda, among them.

General Electric's situation is typical. In many of its businesses, this American giant has been almost unknown in Europe and Asia. GE made no coordinated effort to build a global corporate franchise. Any GE business with international ambitions had to bear the burden of establishing its credibility and credentials in the new market alone. Not surprisingly, some once-strong GE businesses opted out of the difficult task of building a global brand position. In contrast, smaller Korean companies like Samsung, Daewoo, and Lucky Gold Star are busy building global-brand umbrellas that will ease market entry for a whole range of businesses. The underlying principle is simple: economies of scope may be as important as economies of scale in entering global markets. But capturing economies of scope demands inter-business coordination that only top management can provide.

We believe that inflexible SBU-type organizations have also contributed to the deskilling of some companies. For a single SBU, incapable of sustaining investment in a core competence such as semiconductors, optical media, or combustion engines, the only way to remain competitive is to purchase key components from potential (often Japanese or Korean) competitors. For an SBU defined in product-market terms, competitiveness means offering an end product that is competitive in price and performance. But that gives an SBU manager little incentive to distinguish between external sourcing that achieves "product embodied" competitiveness and internal development that yields deeply embedded organizational competences that can be exploited across multiple businesses. Where upstream component manufacturing activities are seen as cost centers with cost-plus transfer pricing, additional investment in the core activity may seem a less profitable use of capital than investment in downstream activities. To make matters worse, internal accounting data may not reflect the competitive value of retaining control over core competence.

Together a shared global corporate brand franchise and shared core competence act as mortar in many Japanese companies. Lacking this mortar, a company's businesses are truly loose bricks—easily knocked out by global competitors that steadily invest in core competences. Such competitors can co-opt domestically oriented companies into long-term sourcing dependence and capture the economies of scope of global brand investment through interbusiness coordination.

Last in decentralization's list of dangers is the standard of managerial performance typically used in SBU organizations. In many companies, business unit managers are rewarded solely on the basis of their performance against return on investment targets. Unfortunately, that often leads to denominator management because executives soon discover that reductions in investment and head count—the denominator—"improve" the financial ratios by which they are measured more easily than growth in the numerator—revenues. It also fosters a hair-trigger sensitivity to industry downturns that can be very costly. Managers who are quick to reduce investment and dismiss workers find it takes much longer to regain lost skills and catch up on investment when the industry turns upward again. As a result, they lose market share in every business cycle. Particularly in industries where there is fierce competition for the best people and where competitors invest relentlessly, denominator management creates a retrenchment ratchet.

The concept of the general manager as a movable peg reinforces the problem of denominator management. Business schools are guilty here because they have perpetuated the notion that a manager with net present value calculations in one hand and portfolio planning in the other can manage any business anywhere.

In many diversified companies, top management evaluates line managers on numbers alone because no other basis for dialogue exists. Managers move so many times as part of their "career development" that they often do not understand the nuances of the businesses they are managing. At GE, for example, one fast-track manager heading an important new venture had moved across five businesses in five years. His series of quick successes finally came to an end when he confronted a Japanese competitor whose managers had been plodding along in the same business for more than a decade.

Regardless of ability and effort, fast-track managers are unlikely to develop the deep business knowledge they need to discuss technology options, competitors' strategies, and global opportunities substantively. Invariably, therefore, discussions gravitate to "the numbers," while the value added of managers is limited to the financial and planning savvy they carry from job to job. Knowledge of the company's internal planning and accounting systems substitutes for substantive knowledge of the business, making competitive innovation unlikely.

When managers know that their assignments have a two- to three-year time frame, they feel great pressure to create a good track record fast. This pressure often takes one of two forms. Either the manager does not commit to goals whose time line extends beyond his or her expected tenure. Or ambitious goals are adopted and squeezed into an unrealistically short time frame. Aiming to be Number 1 in a business is the essence of strategic intent, but imposing a three- to four-year horizon on the effort simply invites disaster. Acquisitions are made with little attention to the problems of integration. The organization becomes overloaded with initiatives. Collaborative ventures are formed without adequate attention to competitive consequences.

Almost every strategic management theory and nearly every corporate planning system is premised on a strategy hierarchy in which corporate goals guide business unit strategies and business unit strategies guide functional tactics.[5] In this hierarchy, senior management makes strategy and lower levels execute it. The dichotomy between formulation and implementation is familiar and widely accepted. But the strategy hierarchy undermines competitiveness by fostering an elitist view of management that tends to disenfranchise most of the organization. Employees fail to identify with corporate goals or involve themselves deeply in the work of becoming more competitive.

The strategy hierarchy isn't the only explanation for an elitist view of management, of course. The myths that grow up around successful top managers—"Lee Iacocca saved Chrysler," "De Benedetti rescued Olivetti," "John Sculley turned Apple around"—perpetuate it. So does the turbulent business environment. Middle managers buffeted by circumstances that seem to be beyond their control desperately want to believe that top management has all the answers. And top management, in turn, hesitates to admit it does not for fear of demoralizing lower level employees.

The result of all this is often a code of silence in which the full extent of a company's competitiveness problem is not widely shared. We interviewed business unit managers in one company, for exam-

[5]For example, see P. Lorange and R. F. Vancil, *Strategic Planning Systems* (Englewood Cliffs, NJ: Prentice Hall, 1977).

ple, who were extremely anxious because top management wasn't talking openly about the competitive challenges the company faced. They assumed the lack of communication indicated a lack of awareness on their senior managers' part. But when asked whether they were open with their own employees, these same managers replied that while they could face up to the problems, the people below them could not. Indeed, the only time the workforce heard about the company's competitiveness problems was during wage negotiations when problems were used to extract concessions.

Unfortunately, a threat that everyone perceives but no one talks about creates more anxiety than a threat that has been clearly identified and made the focal point for the problem-solving efforts of the entire company. That is one reason honesty and humility on the part of top management may be the first prerequisite of revitalization. Another reason is the need to make participation more than a buzzword.

Programs such as quality circles and total customer service often fall short of expectations because management does not recognize that successful implementation requires more than administrative structures. Difficulties in embedding new capabilities are typically put down to "communication" problems, with the unstated assumption that if only downward communication were more effective—"if only middle management would get the message straight"—the new program would quickly take root. The need for upward communication is often ignored, or assumed to mean nothing more than feedback. In contrast, Japanese companies win, not because they have smarter managers, but because they have developed ways to harness the "wisdom of the anthill." They realize that top managers are a bit like the astronauts who circle the earth in the space shuttle. It may be the astronauts who get all the glory, but everyone knows that the real intelligence behind the mission is located firmly on the ground.

Where strategy formulation is an elitist activity it is also difficult to produce truly creative strategies. For one thing, there are not enough heads and points of view in divisional or corporate planning departments to challenge conventional wisdom. For another, creative strategies seldom emerge from the annual planning ritual. The starting point for next year's strategy is almost always this year's strategy. Improvements are incremental. The company sticks to the segments and territories it knows, even though the real opportunities may be elsewhere. The impetus for Canon's pioneering entry into the personal copier business came from an overseas sales subsidiary—not from planners in Japan.

The goal of the strategy hierarchy remains valid—to ensure consistency up and down the organization. But this consistency is better derived from a clearly articulated strategic intent than from inflexibly applied top-down plans. In the 1990s, the challenge will be to enfranchise employees to invent the means to accomplish ambitious ends.

We seldom found cautious administrators among the top managements of companies that came from behind to challenge incumbents for global leadership. But in studying organizations that had surrendered, we invariably found senior managers who, for whatever reason, lacked the courage to commit their companies to heroic goals—goals that lay beyond the reach of planning and existing resources. The conservative goals they set failed to generate pressure and enthusiasm for competitive innovation or give the organization much useful guidance. Financial targets and vague mission statements just cannot provide the consistent direction that is a prerequisite for winning a global competitive war.

This kind of conservatism is usually blamed on the financial markets. But we believe that in most cases investors' so-called short-term orientation simply reflects their lack of confidence in the ability of senior managers to conceive and deliver stretch goals. The chairman of one company complained bitterly that even after improving return on capital employed to over 40 percent (by ruthlessly divesting lackluster businesses and downsizing others), the stock market held the company to an 8:1 price/earnings ratio. Of course the market's message was clear: "We don't trust you. You've shown no ability to achieve profitable growth. Just cut out the slack, manage the denominators, and perhaps you'll be taken over by a company that can use your resources more creatively." Very little in the track record of most large Western companies warrants the confidence of the stock market. Investors aren't hopelessly short-term, they're justifiably skeptical.

We believe that top management's caution reflects a lack of confidence in its own ability to involve the entire organization in revitalization—as opposed to simply raising financial targets. Developing faith in the organization's ability to deliver on tough goals, motivating it to do so, focusing its attention long enough to internalize new capabilities—this is the real challenge for top management. Only by rising to this challenge will senior managers gain the courage they need to commit themselves and their companies to global leadership.

Case II–14
Intel Corporation (C): Strategy for the 1990s

George W. Cogan and Robert A. Burgelman

Introduction

The two years following Intel's decision to exit the DRAM business were difficult ones. Company revenues fell during 1985 and 1986 as Intel's top management discontinued several low-margin product lines and reduced the workforce of 25,400 by 7,200. Intel losses for 1986 exceeded $200 million. The entire industry suffered as it adjusted to the new Japanese capacity and slackening demand.

In 1987, Intel began to emerge from the recession. While the company adopted a sole sourcing strategy for its microprocessor products, demand grew dramatically for its 386™ microprocessor[1] product line. In the middle of 1989, the company's expected sales had nearly tripled to $3.1 billion. In 1989, it had the highest return on sales of any major semiconductor company in the world. (See Exhibits 1 and 2.)

As Andy Grove, Intel's CEO since 1987, described the emergence of the "new" Intel late in 1990, he wondered about the implications of the changing structure of the semiconductor industry on his company. He wondered what Intel's technology strategy should be and whether the Intel of the 1990s should plan to be a dominant player in the EPROM business. He also wondered about the emergence of RISC architecture and the implications that held for Intel's core microprocessor business. Finally, the growing importance of Intel's systems business raised some touchy issues about the company's relations with its customers.

[1]386 is a trademark of Intel Corporation.

DRAMS in 1990

After the decision to stop developing the 1 meg DRAM in late 1984, Andy Grove had traveled to Portland several months later to address the DRAM Technology Development Group. He had started his announcement to the group by saying: "Welcome to the mainstream of Intel."

While there had been significant resistance to the decision to exit DRAMs on the part of some high-level managers, the DRAM technology development group accepted the decision. Sun Lin Chou, then leader of the group, said:

> I guess one of the reasons that we didn't feel so bad about the DRAM decision is that we felt we had done our part by regaining a leading technical position with the 1 meg DRAM. We were allowed to continue development for several months, so that by the time we stopped, we had functioning 1 meg DRAM parts.
>
> The company was really caught in a no-win situation. We were trying harder and harder, but it seemed that our efforts would not lead to a big success.

Intel's experience in the DRAM marketplace mirrored that of several other U.S. competitors who also exited during the 1985–86 recession. In 1985, the entire DRAM market shrunk by over 50 percent to $1.4 billion. However, by late 1987, demand once again began to outpace supply, and DRAM suppliers enjoyed market growth and renewed profitability. By 1987, Japanese companies controlled the overwhelming majority of the DRAM market since only two U.S. manufacturers, Texas Instruments and Micron Technology, remained.[2]

By 1990, Japanese companies commanded 87 percent of the $8 billion DRAM market, U.S. companies held about 8 percent, and Korean companies held the remaining 5 percent.[3] Korean market share was likely to increase as Korean firms announced investment plans of over $4 billion by the early 1990s. In order to address marketing concerns that the company have a full product line, Intel, in 1987, had signed a long-term sourcing agreement with Samsung Semiconductor for DRAM chips under which Intel would market the Korean chips under its own name. *Electronic Buyer News* reported that

[2]Although IBM does not sell DRAMs, it is one of the world's largest producers for its own internal uses.

[3]These figures do not include U.S. captive suppliers (IBM and AT&T). If captive suppliers are included, Japan's share of the U.S. market falls to 65 percent. Captive estimate from G. Gilder, *Microcosm* (New York: Simon and Schuster, 1989), p. 152.

EXHIBIT 1 Selected Intel Corporation Financial Data (dollars in millions)

	Year ended December 31											
	1979	1980	1981	1982	1983	1984	1985	1986	1987	1988	1989	1990
Sales	663	854	788	900	1,122	1,629	1,364	1,265	1,907	2,875	3,127	3,921
COGS	313	399	458	542	624	883	943	861	1,043	1,506	1,721	1,930
Gross margin	350	455	330	358	498	746	421	404	864	1,369	1,406	1,991
R&D	67	96	116	131	142	180	195	228	260	318	365	517
SG&A	131	175	184	198	217	315	287	311	358	456	483	666
Operating profit	152	184	30	29	139	251	(61)	(135)	246	595	557	858
Interest and other	(3)	2	10	2	40	47	55	(76)	42	34	−96	336
Profit before tax	149	186	40	31	179	298	(6)	(211)	288	629	583	486
Income tax	71	89	13		63	100	(7)	8	40	176	192	336
Net income	78	97	27	31	116	198	1	(203)	248	453	391	650
Depreciation	40	49	66	83	103	114	166	173	171	210	190	292
Capital investment	97	152	157	138	145	388	236	154	301	477	351	680

	December 31											
	1979	1980	1981	1982	1983	1984	1985	1986	1987	1988	1989	1990
Cash and ST investment	34	127	115	85	389	230	188	74	630	970	1,064	1,785
Working capital	115	299	287	306	608	568	717	649	506	1,036	1,242	1,806
Fixed assets	217	321	412	462	504	778	848	779	891	1,122	1,284	1,658
Total assets	500	767	871	1,056	1,680	2,029	2,152	1,977	2,498	3,549	3,994	5,377
LT debt	0	150	150	197	127	146	270	287	298	479	412	345
Equity	303	432	488	552	1,122	1,360	1,421	1,245	1,276	2,080	2,549	3,592
Employees	14,300	15,900	16,800	19,400	21,500	25,400	21,300	18,200	19,200	20,800	22,000	24,600
ROS	11.8%	11.4%	3.4%	3.4%	10.3%	12.2%	0.1%	(16.0%)	13.0%	15.8%	12.5%	16.6%
ROA	21.9%	19.4%	3.5%	3.6%	11.0%	11.8%	.05%	(9.4%)	9.9%	12.8%	9.8%	12.1%
ROE	38.0%	32.0%	6.3%	6.4%	21.0%	17.6%	0.1%	(14.3%)	19.5%	21.8%	15.3%	18.1%

SOURCE: Intel annual reports.

Intel had sold more than 10 million 256K and 1-megabit DRAMs during 1988 through its commodity operation. Prevailing prices suggest that the DRAM reseller business generated well over $100 million in revenue by 1990.

The dramatic decline in U.S. position led some industry observers to predict the eventual downfall of the entire U.S. semiconductor industry. The concern over U.S. competitiveness and dependence on foreign suppliers led several companies to announce plans to form a joint DRAM venture. A group of semiconductor and computer companies[4] agreed in June 1989 to form U.S. Memories, Inc., investing an initial $50,000 each. The venture required $1 billion in capitalization over several years and intended to use IBM's design for a 4-

[4]The group included Hewlett Packard, Intel, IBM Corp., Digital Equipment Corp., LSI Logic Corp., National Semiconductor, and Advanced Micro Devices.

EXHIBIT 2 Selected Competitor Data for 1988

FY 1988 (in millions)	Intel	National Semiconductor	Texas Instruments	Advanced Micro Devices	Motorola	Hitachi	Toshiba	NEC	Fujitsu
Total sales	2,874	1,648	6,294	1,125	8,250	39,800	28,579	21,893	16,374
COGS	1,505	1,280	5,778	661	5,040	29,535	20,583	15,120	10,713
R&D	318	264		208	incl.				
SG&A	456	236		224	1,957	8,259	7,115	5,863	4,704
Other	(36)	55		18	642	(643)	(122)	344	108
Profit	631	(187)	516	14	611	2,649	1,003	566	849
Profit after tax	453	(23)	366	19	445	1,094	485	204	337
Depreciation	211	184	389	153	543	2,351	1,412	1,310	1,094
Capital expenditure	477	277	628	131	873	2,333	1,469	2,016	1,527
Total assets	3,550	1,416	4,427	1,081	6,710	44,969	27,673	23,426	18,532
LT debt	479	52	623	130	343	3,462	4,423	3,576	2,413
Total equity 1987	1,276	1,013	1,885	623	3,008	14,607	4,061	3,523	4,660
Total equity 1988	2,080	848	2,243	645	3,375	16,148	5,743	4,784	6,616

SOURCE: Annual reports.

megabit DRAM as its introductory product offering early in 1991. The unusual arrangement between competitors was likely to require federal antitrust clearance[5] and faced opposition from vocal critics.

New Technology Drivers

Until 1985, Intel managers thought of DRAMs as the company's technology driver. Historically, DRAMs had always been the first products to employ new technology. Even though it never went into production, the 1-megabit DRAM was Intel's first attempt at a 1-micron geometry. Sun Lin Chou said it was typical for DRAMs to precede logic products in linewidth reduction by at least one year.

In 1990, Sun Lin Chou expressed some skepticism in discussing the cumulative volume model for learning in the semiconductor industry:

> The traditional model of a technology driver says that the more you do, the more high-volume products you run, the more productive you get. That means in order to stay on the leading edge, you need a product you can ramp into high-volume production rapidly. There is some truth to the model, but it can be carried to an extreme.
>
> There are certainly ways of learning that can be carried out at much lower volumes. Our recent experience suggests that you can learn without massive volumes. If so, that takes away the requirement or urgency to have a traditional technology driver. We think it is possible to achieve mature yields by processing only about 10,000 wafers versus the old model's predicted requirement of 1,000,000 wafers. But you have to use intelligence.
>
> You don't learn quickly when you increase volume by brute force. You have to learn by examining wafers. Learning is based on the number of wafers looked at, analyzed, and the number of effective corrective actions taken. Even if you have processed 1,000 wafers, the technical learning probably only came from the 10 wafers you analyzed. Technical learning is time- and engineering-constrained, not number-of-wafers-constrained.
>
> There are also a great number of things you can do in an open loop system. For example, you can see or guess where particles are coming from and remove them without really knowing for sure whether they are a yield limiter. You don't take the time to get the data to justify the fix; you don't do a detailed study; you just fix what seems broken. You have an intuition about what to do. The Japanese have really led the way on this. You don't undertake an ROI analysis to figure out the cost/benefit for every little improve-

[5] *The Wall Street Journal,* June 21, 1989, p. B5, and *San Francisco Chronicle,* June 22, 1989, p. C1. Some companies (notably Apple and Sun Microsystems) were reluctant to invest in U.S. Memories, due to relationships with existing DRAM manufacturers. *San Francisco Chronicle,* September 26, 1989, p. C1.

ment. You just fix everything you can think of. Everyone can participate.

Craig Barrett, executive vice president and general manager of the Microcomputer Components Group, believed the importance of DRAMs to technology leadership had been overestimated by most industry observers:

> At one time DRAMs really were a technology driver for Intel. DRAMs are still the single biggest product in the industry as a whole. They are about $8 billion to $10 billion of a $50 billion market. And they are certainly a learning vehicle for some.
>
> When we got out of DRAMs we were concerned that we might suffer from the lack of volume. We tried to address that concern by selectively staying in the EPROM business. Even though the EPROM volume is not as big, it is a volume product. But, I would have to conclude that after two generations post DRAM we do not miss it as a technology driver.
>
> I think that the industry used the notion of technology driver as a crutch. We were late waking up to the fact that we did not need to run volume in order to learn. There are other ways to be intelligent. You don't have to depend on volume if you depend on good engineering.
>
> We have data to show that our learning as represented by lowering defect density has actually accelerated in the past two generations when plotted either as a function of time or as a function of cumulative wafers put through the fab. For each generation since 1985—1.5 micron, 1 micron, and most recently 0.8 microns—each defect density trend line is downward sloping with the most recent generations having the steepest slopes.
>
> While we have some volume from our EPROM line and we make lots of efforts to transfer learning from one facility to another, we focus on basic techniques to accelerate learning: design of experiments, statistical process control, and just plain good engineering.
>
> While we do have a lot of high-margin wafer starts, we still have a significant mixture of products. We have 256K EPROMs, 1 meg, 2 meg, and just recently 4 meg in addition to our microcontrollers, which are all very cost sensitive. We chose to stay in those commodity businesses partly because it does "keep us honest." Of course, it also represents a significant part of our revenue and it helps to amortize R&D expenditure.

Gerry Parker, vice president of Technology Development, had a slightly different perspective on the issue of technology drivers:

> There is no single technology driver at Intel. We focus our technology development on logic and nonvolatile memory products. More than ever before, we watch what the rest of the industry is doing and try to follow trends. The DRAM is the industry's driver, because it is the highest volume product, and DRAM suppliers are the biggest equipment purchasers. There have been some really fascinating developments in the industry. I think that the entire industry paradigm has shifted in the past several years.
>
> I spend a lot of time now following what the DRAM people are doing and talking with equipment manufacturers. A great deal of the know-how is now generated at the equipment suppliers. We try to stay in the mainstream by purchasing the most advanced equipment, but then we optimize it to maximum advantage for our products.
>
> For example, I know that a certain stepper vendor is developing a new tool that will accommodate a certain maximum chip size. It will not be able to process larger chips. The size is driven by the needs of Toshiba's next-generation DRAM. They are building the equipment to satisfy the demands of their largest customer.
>
> You can bet that all of Intel's next generation parts will be designed to capitalize on the DRAM tool. We will put that constraint on our designers. The equipment vendor will be tooled up to produce those steppers in volume and will be happy to supply us with a few machines. We could ask them to design a special tool for us, but it would be inferior because we wouldn't command the same level of attention that Toshiba gets.
>
> Attitude is important and has led to the changes. The Japanese really have taught us something. They expect excellence from equipment vendors and make *them* develop the expertise to provide the best possible equipment. If a piece of equipment has a problem, the vendor is right there in the fab area fixing it and he can make appropriate changes on the next generation.
>
> Our approach has traditionally been different. We would modify the equipment ourselves and not even tell the vendor. We sometimes didn't even let the vendors into our fabs. We have changed a lot in our openness, and we are beginning to use sole-source suppliers for each category of equipment, but we could still do more.
>
> I was talking to a guy at Applied Materials, one of our equipment suppliers, about the differences between our approach and that of the Japanese. In Japan, all the technicians set the machines to the exact settings that are specified by Applied Materials. If the process doesn't work, Applied Materials gets blamed. In the United States, we tend to be more inventive: each technician sets the machine to an optimum that he has determined. When you operate like that, it becomes more difficult to blame the vendor when the yields are down.
>
> As a result of this fundamental change in the equipment suppliers' role, learning now resides in the indus-

try, not just in the company. That is a complete shift. Just to prove it, look at this example. A Japanese ball bearing company, NMB,[6] with no expertise in the semiconductor industry, had $500 million in excess cash and decided to get into the DRAM business. They got vendors to sell them equipment and set it up, and they contracted with consultants to sell them a process and get it running. In a short time they are the most automated semiconductor factory in the world. That would never have happened even five years ago.

I certainly don't want to minimize the importance of process development. NMB now has to go out and buy a new process for the next generation. There is plenty of process development that distinguishes companies from each other. But, the latest equipment is essential to getting the highest yields. Equipment vendors allow Intel and even new start-ups to keep up with the latest industry advances.

EPROM and Flash

By the end of 1986, Intel had exited the DRAM and SRAM businesses, stopped the development of E²PROMs, sold its memory systems division, and sold its bubble memory subsidiary. Intel's only remaining position in memory businesses was in EPROMs. In 1986, Intel commanded a 21 percent share of the $910 million market versus 17 percent of an $860 million market two years earlier. In 1989, EPROMs were manufactured in five of Intel's fab sites.

Intel's continued dominance in the EPROM business arose partly from a successful legal battle against Hitachi and other Japanese companies accused of selling EPROMs below cost in the United States. Intel successfully fended off the attack through actions taken by the U.S. government.

In September 1986, Intel top management requested a middle-level manager to prepare a study of each memory business and make recommendations for Intel's long-term strategy. The manager recommended that Intel maintain its position in the EPROM business.

Intel top management decided to keep the EPROM operation as a relatively high volume product to drive learning, but primarily as an enabling technology for the microcontroller business. Intel's microcontrollers integrate EPROM functionality and use an EPROM process technology. In 1989, Intel remained the EPROM market leader with 21 percent market share of a $1 billion market.

Flash

The middle manager also recommended that the company devote resources to a new memory technology called *Flash*. He said:

> People say necessity is the mother of invention, and it sounds trite, but it's true. Those two years [1985–86] at Intel were incredibly stressful for the entire company. But, out of that time emerged several paradigm changes.
>
> One very important one was Flash memory. Flash is very similar to E²PROM in functionality, but it is much cheaper to make. Basically, it costs less than EPROM, but you can erase it electrically instead of with light. This is a major cost/functionality discontinuity in EPROM semiconductor technology and has significant implications. One can envision low end solid state reprogrammable systems, for instance, as well as simpler field service for ROM/EPROM based systems.
>
> Contrasting Flash to DRAM reveals some interesting perspectives. Flash does not have the flexible write functionality of DRAM, but it is nonvolatile. Additionally, Flash is actually a simpler-to-manufacture read/write technology because it is not constrained by the need for a large capacitor in each memory cell. About 80 percent of the current DRAM cell is active whereas only 5 percent of the Flash cell is. That means that Flash can shrink like mad. The best way to compete with the Japanese is to change the game.
>
> Another paradigm change has resulted in our working on a truly parallel processor, or neural network, that uses a version of Flash technology. By making an analog instead of a digital device, we can develop a low-precision but very-high-performance "trainable analog/memory processor." It remains to be seen what applications will evolve from this capability but it has exciting possibilities.
>
> If Flash leads to miniaturization of computers from portable to hand-held units, neural nets may solve handwriting recognition. This, combined with a notebook computer, would result in a very user-friendly tool for a large market.
>
> As you think about it, Flash may ultimately have implications for the microprocessor business. If you look out far enough, you can see a whole new era for semiconductor technology.

By 1990, some industry observers began to recognize the potential for Flash as a replacement for

[6]For more on NMB, see Gilder, *Microcosm,* p. 154–59. Takami Takahashi, NMB president, views DRAMs as the ultimate commodity: "A chip is merely a miniature ball bearing—flattened out, with a picture on it." In 1989, NMB was on a yearly sales run rate of $350 million, having reached sales of $200 million in 1988 on an estimated investment of $200 million in plant and equipment. The plant had a total of 160 employees working four shifts.

EXHIBIT 3 Cost/Drive Over Time, 2.5" 20-200 MB, Midyear OEM Quantities

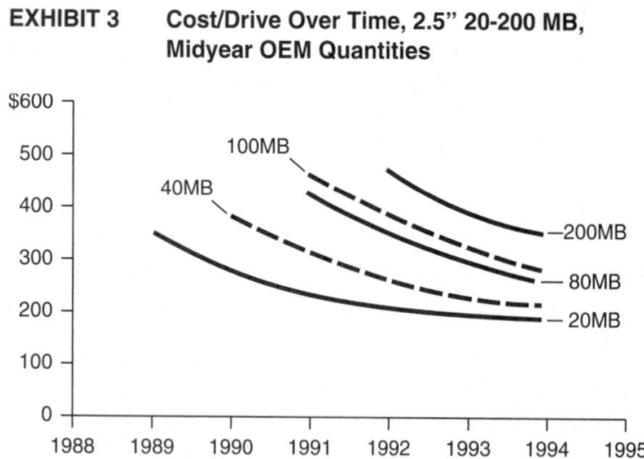

SOURCE: IDC.

EXHIBIT 4 PC Card Cost Projection

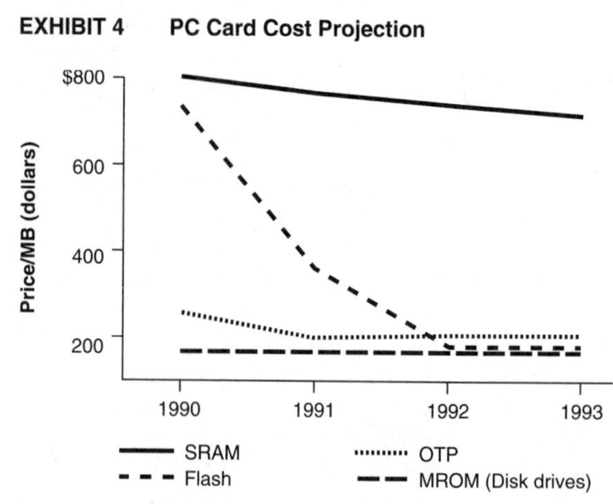

conventional magnetic disc drives in laptop computers.[7] Some industry specialists noted that solid state disks, when compared to traditional Winchester drives, can consume up to 300 times less power, are 15 times more durable, can withstand much more heat, and are up to 100 times faster. Other industry specialists, however, noted that there has been a 100-fold "shrink" in the size of 20–40-megabit drives since the late 1970s (from 2,300 cubic inches for the 14-inch drive to 23 cubic inches for the current 1-inch drive), and that during that time price has decreased by a factor of 10, and access time improved by a factor of 2.[8] Exhibit 3 shows projections of prices for various 2.5-inch disk drive capacities.

In the portable PC market, the London-based company Psion PLC already had plans to introduce two notebook computers in 1990 which would use Flash instead of magnetic storage. While the current installed base of portables is estimated at less than 5 million units, the future potential is estimated at more than 20 million.[9]

The market for ultraportables (falling between today's 6-pound notebook and the 1-pound pocket-type) was estimated to grow from less than 1 million in 1990 to 12 million in 1994.[10]

[7]Microsoft has decided to support the technology by releasing file-management software that lets MS-DOS treat Flash like disk drives.

[8]"You Can Take It With You," Forum on Portable Computers and Communications, Bear Stearns & Co., New York, October 2–3, 1990.

[9]Ibid.

[10]Ibid.

Although Flash was still more expensive than traditional magnetics, its learning curve was much steeper. Exhibit 4 shows price projections for different storage technologies.

In October 1990, Intel announced a credit-card size "Flash memory card" which will be available in 1- and 4-megabyte storage disk, and priced at $298 and $1,198, respectively. Intel said that the new storage drive will offer an important alternative to floppy and hard disk drives in portable computers, because it uses less power and offers improved performance. The reduced power demands, for instance, will ex-tend battery life between 10 and 100 times for portable computers. The company expected to begin mass production of the Flash memory card in December.

By 1994, Intel predicted it would have a 16-megabit Flash chip. The chip would enable a cost-competitive alternative to the industry standard 40-megabyte hard drive on a credit-card size format.

Western Digital was reportedly developing Flash subsystems that can be managed like magnetic media, and can be interfaced into a system like a disk drive.[11] Texas Instruments was also developing its own Flash technology which reportedly used less power than Intel's during data writing.

New Microprocessor Strategy

During the same week in October 1985 when Intel made the decision to close Fab 5 in Oregon for DRAM production, it announced shipment of the

[11]Ibid.

32-bit 80386. The electronics industry received the 386™ microprocessor with great enthusiasm. Just one year later, in the third quarter of 1986, customers had completed development of new products, and the first products to contain the 386™ were shipped. By then, the new microprocessor had garnered over 200 design wins by virtue of its upward compatibility with existing personal computer software and its broad applications in other markets.

The power of the 386's ability to leverage previous software led to the most rapid ramp up of production for any microprocessor in Intel's history. By the end of 1987, just two years after introduction, Intel had shipped an estimated 800,000 units as compared to 50,000 for the earlier 8086 at two years after its introduction. By 1989, some analysts believed that Intel was too dependent on the *i*386™ and its support chips, estimating that they generated nearly $1 billion, or between 30 and 40 percent of revenue for the company during FY 1988.

A new corporate strategy added to Intel's early success with the 80386. During previous generations, Intel supported a cross-licensing agreement with AMD in which AMD acted as a second source and provided development of support chips. Intel's top management made the decision to make AMD perform under the existing agreement or be prepared to act as a sole source for the 386™.[12]

Craig Barrett described some of the factors which figured in the decision:

> Basically, Intel got to the point where it could generate enough customer confidence to pull it off. There were at least several forces at work.
>
> Our quality thrust of the early 1980s began to pay off in improved consistency on the manufacturing line and overall better product quality. In addition, customer–vendor partnerships became more prevalent throughout our business. For example, we had recently started selling Ford a microcontroller product, the 8061. They proclaimed that total cost was more important than purchase price alone and decided to work with us closely and exclusively—sort of on the Japanese model. We learned a great deal from that which carried into our other customers and to our vendors.
>
> We had also decided to pursue a "vendor of choice" strategy in 1984 which led to improved customer satisfaction. Finally, the experience with earlier x86 generations led us to believe that we could accurately forecast demand for the 386™ and put sufficient manufacturing capacity in place.
>
> With improved manufacturing consistency and better forecast accuracy, we realized that it wasn't always necessary to have a second source to keep the customer satisfied. And, as our second-source deal with AMD came unraveled, we put in the capability to never miss a shipment by adding strategic inventory and redundant capacity. And, since then we have never missed an 80386 customer commitment.
>
> The pitfalls of our strategy are obvious. You can fall on your own sword. And it only takes once to lose the confidence of your customers. Also, the business is sufficiently profitable that everyone is gunning for you. They try to make clones of your products or substitutes.

Bob Reed, chief financial officer, underlined the importance of intellectual property to Intel and to the semiconductor industry:

> Intel has looked around for an edge against competitors. When we look back 10 years from now we may see that intellectual property protection[13] saved the U.S. semiconductor market. The protection will essentially lead to a segmentation of the semiconductor industry into maybe 10 industries, all with leaders. Intel's sole source strategy for the *i*386™ is a good example of a winning strategy. Now Motorola is also a sole source.
>
> This does not imply a much more complicated contractual relationship with customers. For example, Intel has no penalty clauses for nondelivery of parts; however, we never miss a delivery. The stakes have been raised on both sides of the table.
>
> At Intel, the legal department has grown from 5 to 20 internal people in the past five years. In addition, we retain outside counsel. We vigorously pursue anyone who infringes on our intellectual property rights.

In order to support the sole-sourcing strategy, Intel converted their new Israel facility, originally designed for EPROMs, to make microprocessor products. In addition, the Portland technology development group began developing a 1-micron version of the 386™, a significant reduction in chip size from the original 1.5-micron geometry.

While increased performance and the need for ever increasing price/performance advancements were the key force driving microprocessor development, high integration and increased functionality

[12]Intel believed that AMD did not earn rights to the 386™ design under the existing licensing agreements. Intel's decision led to a widely publicized dispute with AMD which was still in the final stages of binding arbitration at the time of this case development. IBM, however, continued to be allowed to manufacture Intel microprocessors for its own products.

[13]In a landmark decision in 1986, the U.S. Courts agreed with Intel that computer code embedded in silicon is covered by U.S. copyright laws, thus affording protection for Intel's chip designs.

EXHIBIT 5

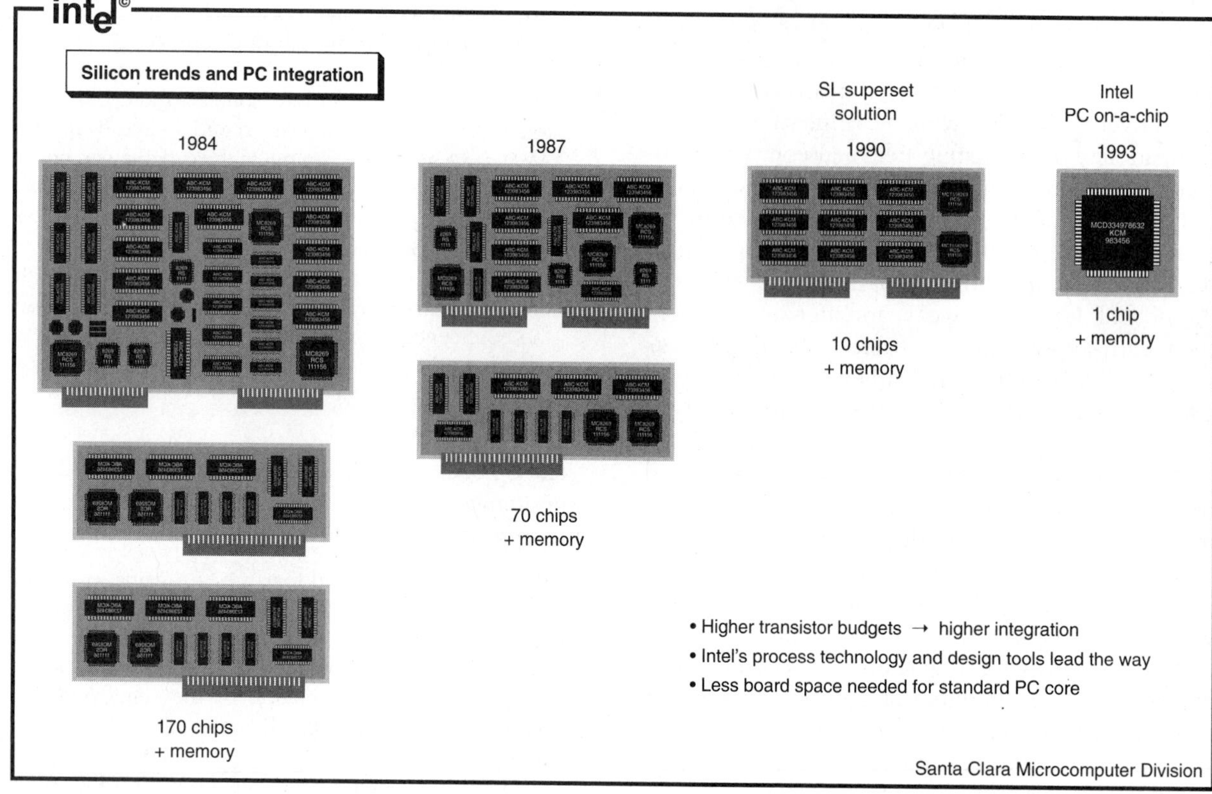

were also important. Increased functionality and integration depend on the ability to "shrink" the microprocessor, allowing more space to integrate new features. Jack Carsten, formerly an Intel senior vice president and currently a venture capitalist in Silicon Valley, said:

> Lots of people talk about the design team that developed Intel's 386™ chip. It's a great product. But, the great unsung heroes at Intel are the people who successfully developed the "shrink" technology for the 386™. That reduction in geometry led to higher performance parts as well as greatly increased yields.

Exhibit 5 shows the evolution of the result of the shrinking CPU technology.

Sun Lin Chou discussed the role of the Portland Technology Development group:

> In the past two years the situation has changed significantly. We don't just do process development in Portland. We have designers in Portland who leverage our ability to make use of leading-edge technology sooner. Some of those designers are old DRAM designers who have retrained.
>
> In the old days, memory was always the first product to use a new process. First we would get the yields up on memory, then a couple of years later the logic product would use the process. Stabilize the process on memory, then do logic. Since logic takes longer to design, it is easier to do it that way. Now we are faced with no DRAM. The concept of technology driver has changed.
>
> Our challenge is to get logic products up on new processes sooner than we ever have before. To do that, we accelerate and integrate the design process. We use the Portland designers to design standard cells which can then be used by the chip designer groups. We also take existing logic parts that have proven designs and use the new standard cells to generate "shrink" designs.
>
> Instead of using memory to ramp production, we are now using logic products redesigned with smaller geometries. That is a fundamental change, because demand is not infinite for logic products. We may only have to use a small fraction of one fab's capacity to satisfy the world demand for a particular logic product.

We also have a group of designers that actually work on new chip designs with the design group in Santa Clara. There was a lot of skepticism about having split design teams, but this arrangement allows us to have a set of designers who are much closer to the process. For example, the Portland design group designed the entire Cache RAM block that goes into the 80486™ chip.

The 80486™[14] was introduced in April 1989. With over 1 million transistors, the *i486*™ microprocessor contains nearly four times the circuit elements in the 386™. The *i*486 had taken a total of 130 person-/years in design effort, compared to 80 for the 386. It had benefited from a four-fold increase in proprietary specialized design tools created by Intel. The overall investment in the *i*486 development had been more than $200 million. In keeping with its strategy of upward compatibility, Intel has designed the new offering to run software developed for its predecessors. The 486™ was expected to be especially important in the growing market for a new class of "servers," which can store information for an entire corporation and send it out as needed to PCs in response to queries from different types of users (engineers, accountants, marketing specialists, senior executives). In 1990, the market for servers was projected go grow from $4 billion to $12 billion by 1994.[15]

RISC versus CISC

By 1990, Intel had established a dominant position in the personal computer microprocessor business based on CISC (complex instruction set computing) design. Every manufacturer of advanced IBM-compatible personal computers had to purchase the 386 or 486 microprocessor from Intel. Similarly, those manufacturers or their customers had to purchase operating system software from Microsoft Corporation[16] in order to maintain backward compatibility with the thousands of programs already developed for the PC market. During 1990, NCR was the first Intel customer to decide to use Intel microprocessors throughout its entire product line. Some analysts believed that Intel's penetration in the CISC-microprocessor market would continue throughout the 1990s (see Exhibit 6).

In the meantime, a new market for microprocessors led to the proliferation of microprocessor designs. The engineering workstation market characterized by high-performance graphics and computation ability was pioneered by Sun Microsystems. In some of its earlier systems, Sun used the Intel 386 chip, but instead of MS-DOS chose the UNIX operating system.[17]

Scott McNealy, president of Sun Microsystems, believed that Intel was charging too much for its processors, so he initiated the development[18] of a new processor using a computing architecture called RISC (reduced instruction set computing).[19] Following a strategy of "open" standards, McNealy made the Sun RISC chip design (SPARC) available to his competitors.

In addition to the SPARC chip, several other RISC chips had reached the market place by 1990, including offerings from MIPS and Motorola. Each of the new RISC chips was capable of supporting some version of the UNIX operating system environment.

In 1990, various analysts were debating the future of RISC versus CISC. One analyst observed that while RISC microprocessors were simpler than CISC ones, the system logic that surrounds the RISC microprocessor is more complex, and that all the RISC does is to transfer system complexity from the microprocessor to the system logic. This analyst also noted that RISC is far behind CISC on the learning curve, and that, for instance, in 1990, Intel alone shipped over 8 million 32-bit CISC microprocessors,

[14]486 is a trademark of the Intel Corporation.

[15]*Business Week,* November 26, 1990, p. 122.

[16]Microsoft was the sole source for the IBM-PC operating system, MS-DOS. In conjunction with IBM, Microsoft also developed a new operating system, OS2, which took advantage of the 286 and 386's multitasking features, while maintaining backward compatibility.

[17]Unlike MS-DOS, the UNIX operating system is capable of taking advantage of the multiprocessing feature of the 386. In addition, UNIX is an "open" program and available from multiple sources (although many of the versions are not compatible).

[18]While Sun designed the RISC chip, it did not have chip-making expertise and farmed out the actual manufacturing of the chip to several silicon foundries.

[19]The RISC (reduced instruction set computing) actually preceded the CISC (complex instruction set computing) architecture. Instructions are in the lowest level commands a microprocessor responds to (such as "retrieve from memory" or "compare two numbers"). CISC microprocessors support between 100 and 150 instructions while RISC chips support 70 to 80. As a result of supporting fewer instructions, RISC chips have superior performance over a narrow range of tasks and can be optimized for a specific purpose. Through combinations of the reduced instruction set, the RISC architecture can be made to duplicate the more complex instructions of a CISC chip, but at a performance penalty.

EXHIBIT 6 Intel X86 Compatible Computers Will Dominate PCs, Workstations, Midrange and Eventually All Computing

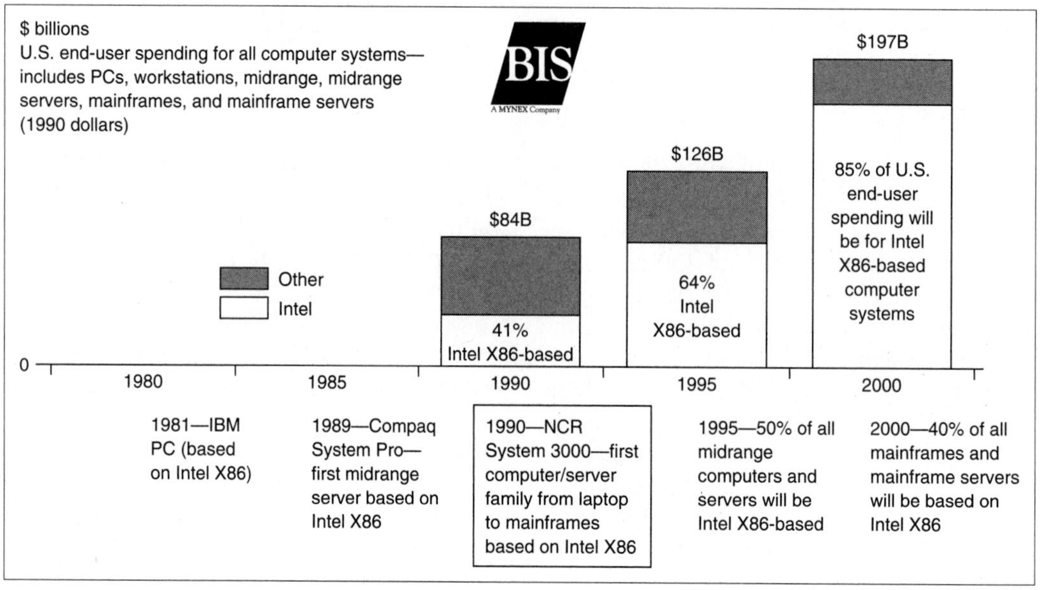

$ billions
U.S. end-user spending for all computer systems—includes PCs, workstations, midrange, midrange servers, mainframes, and mainframe servers (1990 dollars)

BIS
A MYNEX Company

Year	Total	Intel X86-based share
1990	$84B	41% Intel X86-based
1995	$126B	64% Intel X86-based
2000	$197B	85% of U.S. end-user spending will be for Intel X86-based computer systems

Legend: Other; Intel

Axis: 0; 1980; 1985; 1990; 1995; 2000

1981—IBM PC (based on Intel X86)

1989—Compaq System Pro—first midrange server based on Intel X86

1990—NCR System 3000—first computer/server family from laptop to mainframes based on Intel X86

1995—50% of all midrange computers and servers will be Intel X86-based

2000—40% of all mainframes and mainframe servers will be based on Intel X86

SOURCE: BIS CAP International

while the 10 RISC suppliers combined shipped no more than 200,000 units.[20]

Another analyst observed that the success of RISC versus CISC is likely to depend on whether a totally seamless software bridge can be created enabling all IBM-PC compatible application software to be run fast enough on UNIX-based machines. The question is who could do that, and what their incentive would be to do so.[21]

The *i*860™ Story

In 1988, Intel's official response to RISC architecture was to call it "the technology of the have nots." As several companies announced new RISC chips, Intel developed an internal jargon referring to the competitor chips as YARPs, for "yet another RISC processor."

Yet, within the Intel design organization, a designer named Les Kohn had been trying for several years to initiate a RISC program:

> I joined the company in 1982 after working for National on their 32000 processor. At that time, I realized that RISC architecture had some definite technical advantages. That was very difficult to see from Intel's perspective of the x86 architecture. So even at a technical level, there was no clear consensus that RISC is the right approach.
>
> Between 1982 and 1986, I made several proposals for RISC projects through the Intel product-planning system, but I wasn't successful. RISC was not an existing business and people were not convinced that the market was there. Also, the company had had a bad experience with a new architecture, the 432, which was not commercially successful. Experience makes skeptics. The design would have been way too big to do in a skunkworks.
>
> In 1986, I saw that our next generation processors would have 1 million transistor chips, and I started working on the idea of a RISC-based processor that would take full advantage of that technology. This proposal had more aggressive goals and was more convincing than previous ones. Several people, including

[20]Goldman Sacks, "The Future of Microprocessors," research report, April 23, 1990.

[21]Hambrecht & Quist, Inc., "Institutional Research: Intel Corporation," September 12, 1990.

Sai Wai Fu and Kanwar Chadha, got interested in the idea, and we drafted a product requirement document that outlined market size, pricing, and rough development cost. Then we had several breaks that made the project go.

First of all, we positioned it as a coprocessor to the 80486 and made sure that it could be justified on that basis. We designed it as a stand-alone processor, but made it very useful as an accessory to the 486™.

We made sure it was very different from the x86 family so that there would be no question in the customer's mind of which product to use. The real fortuitous part came when presentations to several large customers generated a lot of positive feedback to senior management. Feedback helps because at a technical level, senior managers are not experts.

There was also a whole group of customers who did not previously talk to Intel, because they were more interested in performance than compatibility. 3D graphics, workstation, and minicomputer accounts all got very interested. In the end, it looks like the *i*860[22] will generate a whole new business for Intel.

During the development of the RISC chip, it was code named the N10, and perceived by top management as a coprocessor for the *i*486™. The N10 had a 64-bit architecture with floating point and integer processing as well as enhanced graphics capability. According to Kohn, the chip utilized design concepts found in supercomputers. The design team of 50 wore tee shirts with a miniaturized CRAY supercomputer icon resting on a chip.

Kohn commented on Intel's unique position to produce a 1-million transistor RISC chip:

Intel has historically led the industry in having the most transistors—at least in terms of widely used, commercial microprocessors. To do it on the schedule we did it on requires a very close working relationship between technology development and the design teams.

In a lot of cases, RISC companies are working with external vendors for the fabrication of parts so they either have to design for the lowest common denominator of those technologies or they don't necessarily get access to the most advanced technology.

Another factor is the design tools. Intel made a strategic decision to invest in advanced CAD tools. Our new database manager allows us to manage the several thousand files that go into this chip. It made sure that people didn't make changes that got lost or that two different people weren't making changes to the same file at the same time. We also used a new generation of workstation-based circuit design that was very graphic, allowing the engineers to work directly with schematics and display results graphically.

In February 1989, Intel announced the *i*860 not as a coprocessor, but rather as a stand alone RISC processor. Top management decided to join the RISC processor race. Grove said:

We had our own marketing story for the chip, but our customers changed it. They said, "Listen, this isn't just a coprocessor chip. This could be the central processor of a super technical workstation." Occasional sarcastic jibes aside, we're in no position now to dump on RISC as a technology. Our chip shows what the real potential of RISC is.[23]

Craig Barrett viewed the *i*860 as part of a rational strategy having emerged through the championing of a top flight engineer:

There has been competition between the RISC and CISC architectures for some time. If we assume that the market will split, this gives us a position in both markets.

Intel's bread and butter clearly is still in the x86 family. There is a 586 on the drawing board and a 686 planned to follow that. If there was ever any question of which comes first, it could be answered very quickly. But if there are enough people out there who want to buy YARPs, then we call the *i*860 a YARP killer. It is the highest-performance RISC processor on the market.

Systems Business

Les Vadasz became senior vice president and general manager of the Intel Systems Business in 1985. In 1988, the business had nearly kept pace with the dramatic microprocessor growth so that it accounted for about $750 million of Intel's $2.8 billion in sales. In 1990, it was expected to contribute over $1 billion.

Originally, the Systems Business provided technology to enable the growth of Intel's semiconductor business. For example, development systems, which allowed customers to design systems and write software for microprocessor applications, provided a significant portion of the revenue.

---

[22]860 is a trademark of the Intel Corporation.

[23]*The Wall Street Journal,* February 28, 1989, pp. A1 and A8.

In 1985, top management had made the strategic decision to increase the systems business share of total revenue. Vadasz said:

> In 1985, the systems business was still devoted to accelerating the deployment of our silicon technology. We were providing our customers multiple choices at different levels of integration. If they wanted microprocessors or board level products, we could provide either.
>
> Now we are more like an independent business. We make a range of products: PC-compatibles for OEMs; mainframes through a joint venture;[24] and even parallel supercomputers based on the *i*386™ and *i*860™ processors. We also make PC enhancement boards and sell them through retail channels. Microprocessor-based computer technology is the future, even in supercomputers.
>
> We organize by having segmented strategies for each market. We must recognize that each of our segments requires a different business structure. For example, supercomputers and PCs require entirely different manufacturing disciplines. The PC enhancement business requires a retail understanding, its own sales force, a different kind of documentation, and, of course, its own product engineering.
>
> As you grow, and stake out new territory, you test and develop new capabilities for the company. Each new capability can then be deployed into other areas. But, you must exercise discipline in how you use your capabilities.

Several of the businesses started as ventures in the Intel Development Organization (IDO), which Vadasz also heads. Vadasz continued:

> IDO looks a bit like an internal venture capital fund. It is funded by the corporation and has its own mini board of Gordon Moore, Bob Reed, and me. It serves to isolate a new idea from the quarterly cycle of Intel's business. We create an isolated investment unit and see how it does. These units are managed with an iron hand, but on their own merits.
>
> The guiding question at Intel is: Where can we add intellectual value? Some semiconductor people used to grow crystal ingots [raw material for semiconductors], but they found they could not add value there. Others, specializing in crystal growth, became more effective suppliers. DRAMs have become like that. Manufacturing DRAMs does not tell you how to make computers. The lowest-value-added component in the chain always tends to spread, so you get perfect competition in that area.

Some industry observers believed Intel's Systems Business represented a bold strategy which could alienate its customers. Not only did Intel have a sole-source position, but it could even be considered a potential competitor to some of its customers, companies such as Compaq, Tandy, and Olivetti.

Questions in 1990

In reviewing the recent history of the company, Grove wondered how to top the "awesome $3 billion Intel." Among the U.S. semiconductor companies, Intel was clearly the leading performer in 1990, but what steps would be necessary to continue that performance?

During the strategic reorientation of 1985, Intel's top management had completely revised the company's strategic long-range planning (SLRP) system, and had resolved to emphasize a set of overriding corporate strategies which would guide lower levels in developing specific objectives. The three-point corporate strategy was:

1. Increase architectural and technological leadership.
2. Be our customers' preferred supplier.
3. Be a world-class manufacturer.

Five years later, this strategy still seemed right. The company continued to invest large amounts of resources in R&D (some $400 million in 1990) and its track record of innovation continued unabated.

However, some adjustments might be necessary. In particular, Grove wondered about the future role of the relatively low margin EPROMs in what was now "the microprocessor company." Should Intel get out of EPROMs to free resources for microprocessors, or should they continue, particularly in light of the potential future of Flash? He also questioned the role of RISC and the implications of Intel's endorsement of that technology. Was RISC a distortion of Intel's microprocessor strategy or part of it? What options could they pursue? Finally, he wanted to consider the larger environmental forces that could help or prevent Intel from sustaining its current growth and profitability throughout the 1990s.

---

[24]BIIN Computer, a joint venture with Siemens, was founded in the summer of 1988 to develop a fault-tolerant computer. The joint venture was dissolved in October 1989.

Case II–15 Intel Corporation (D): Microprocessors at the Crossroads

Dan Steere and Robert A. Burgelman

Intel's Good Fortune Is Surprisingly Good

Intel surprises its investors with its 4th qtr 1992 earnings. The semiconductor giant's stock rose $8.125 on Jan. 13, 1993, the day it reported its profits. Intel's rosy performance is attributed to its leadership in the microcomputer chip design market. Its financial performance record has made the company the new leader in Wall Street, taking the place of consumer companies, such as Coke, on which investment portfolios were previously based.

The New York Times, January 14, 1993

1993 was a very good year at Intel. Personal computers (PCs) based on the Intel Architecture represented over 85 percent of the nearly 30 million PCs sold worldwide in 1992.[1] Fierce competition among PC makers had rapidly lowered the cost of systems powered by Intel's flagship family of Intel486[2] microprocessors. PC unit sales skyrocketed, increasing by 17.7 percent in 1992. They were expected to continue double-digit annual growth into the foreseeable future. With the surge of demand for Intel's most advanced processors, for which Intel was the sole source, revenues and profits continued to set records with each quarterly earnings statement. On March 22, the next-generation Pentium processor was announced, delivering a two-fold performance increase over the fastest member of the previous generation.

However, Intel was being pressured from many directions. Industry observers and financial analysts questioned Intel's ability to maintain its recent growth and profitability. Intel's mainstay microprocessor business was facing a series of powerful competitive challenges and technology trends. In addition, Intel was pursuing opportunities in significant new markets. Each new push, while providing the prospect of new profits and rapid growth, would require large investments of both capital and management attention. As they left the annual strategic long-range planning (SLRP) sessions in October 1993, Intel senior managers weren't in a mood to rest on the company's recent success.

This case describes Intel's position and key developments in the worldwide microprocessor industry in 1993.

Company Background

On August 2, 1968, the *Palo Alto Times* announced that Robert Noyce and Gordon Moore had left Fairchild Camera and Instrument, a leader in the emerging field of semiconductors, to form a new company. Andy Grove, who had been Gordon Moore's assistant director of research at Fairchild, joined soon after to become Intel's director of research, rounding out the top management team. From the beginning, Intel was poised to attract the most talented research and development engineers this emerging field had to offer. Nearly a decade earlier, Noyce had shared credit for inventing the integrated circuit.[3] Gordon Moore, after working on the technical staff of Shockley Semiconductor, one of Silicon Valley's pioneers, had helped found Fairchild. Intel became the first company to specialize in producing large-scale integrated circuits (LSI). In 1969, Intel established its position as an industry leader by pioneering new semiconductor fabrication processes that simultaneously increased the number of circuits on a chip while also greatly reducing its production cost. In 1970, Intel introduced the world's first DRAM (dynamic random access memory). Over the next three years DRAMs replaced magnetic cores as the standard technology used by computers to store instructions and data as they executed programs.

By 1972, the 1103, Intel's original DRAM, was the world's largest selling semiconductor, accounting for over 90 percent of Intel's $23.4 million in revenue. DRAMs remained the core product line for Intel throughout the 1970s and early 80s. Initially,

[1]Source: International Data Corporation, 1993.

[2]Intel486, Intel386, *i*486, *i*386, OverDrive, Indeo Video, and Pentium are trademarks of Intel Corp.

[3]Noyce shared this distinction with Jack Kilby of Texas Instruments.

DRAMs were a very attractive business. Demand grew rapidly as innovations in production processes and memory design led to steadily increasing product performance and decreasing cost. Intel's leadership in design and fabrication yielded strong profits and healthy market share throughout the 1970s. However, by 1984, DRAMs had become a mature technology. Product features were standardized and performance was progressing along a steady, predictable path. Both design and fabrication technology were well understood by all major players in the industry. With many new firms investing heavily in production capacity in the late 1970s and early 80s, prices plummeted. Anticipating a large loss in the near future, and seeing the need to invest heavily in state-of-the-art production capacity to keep up, Intel decided to exit the DRAM industry in 1984.

In addition to DRAMs, Intel had pioneered a number of other breakthrough products. After inventing the EPROM (electrically programmable read-only memory), Intel lead the EPROM market until the late 1980s. But Intel's most notable invention was the microprocessor. Originally invented as a clever design for a hand-held calculator, the microprocessor became the central piece of hardware that enabled the explosion of the personal computer industry. Largely on the strength of its microprocessor technology, development tools, marketing support, and cross-licensing agreements allowing several vendors to function as alternative sources, Intel's 8088 microprocessor was selected by IBM for its first personal computer in 1981. As sales of IBM and IBM-compatible personal computers skyrocketed throughout the 1980s, Intel prospered. By 1993, the *New York Times* estimated that sales of Intel486 microprocessors accounted for 75 percent of revenues and 85 percent of earnings.[4] See Exhibit 1 for financial data on Intel Corporation.

Intel's Corporate Structure

In 1993, Intel was organized as a large matrix. (See Exhibit 2 for an Intel organization chart.) On one side of the matrix sat four products groups, Microprocessor Products Group (MPG), Mobile Computing Group (MCG), Semiconductor Products Group (SPG), and Intel Products Group (IPG). Each group carried profit and loss responsibility for its respective market (more on each group later). Matrixed through the products groups were a series of functional organizations. These included, among others: Technology and Manufacturing Group (TMG), Sales, Intel Architecture Labs (IAL), Finance, and Legal. These groups contained their own staff, facilities, and the like, and also supervised a series of "dotted line" reporting relationships with members of each product group. The functional organizations were responsible for supporting the product groups and for cultivating necessary expertise across the organization. A common structure at Intel was "two in a box." Each of the product groups and many of the divisions below were run by two people. Typically, one person would bring a technical background while the other's experience would be based in sales or finance. Even at the top, Andy Grove, Craig Barrett, and Gordon Moore, Intel's CEO, COO, and chairman, were shown as three in a box.

Intel's organization was in the process of continued evolution. MPG and MCG[5] led in the worldwide microprocessor industry and continued to grow rapidly. IPG had established a strong presence in PC enhancement products (such as fax modems and LAN[6] cards), manufactured leading edge supercomputers, and operated a significant OEM systems business. SPG continued as a leading supplier in several of the lower-margin markets for semiconductors, including microcontrollers, and the emerging market for Flash Memories. Divisional reorganizations were common as the product groups regularly realigned their organizations as they sought continued growth in their markets.

Microprocessor Products Group

Headed by Paul Otellini and Dr. Albert Yu, MPG was directly responsible for overseeing development of all Intel Architecture microprocessors[7] (see Exhibit 3 for an MPG organization chart and Exhibit 4 for an explanation of Intel processor names). Having just released the Pentium processor, MPG faced a fast-moving market filling with new challenges from large rivals. Vin Dham, vice president and general

[4]Source: *New York Times,* January 14, 1993.

[5]MCG, as it its name suggested, concentrated on microprocessors and supporting chip sets for the mobile computing market, while MPG focused on the desktop microprocessor market.

[6]Local area network adapter. This was a card that could be installed into a PC, allowing it to communicate with other PCs over a network.

[7]This does not include *i*860 or *i*960 RISC processors, which were used primarily for embedded-control applications (such as controlling the operations of a laser printer).

EXHIBIT 1 Intel Corporation Financial Data

	1992	1991	1990	1989
Net revenues	$5,843,984	$4,778,616	$3,921,274	$3,126,833
Cost of sales	2,557,407	2,315,559	1,930,288	1,720,979
Research and development	779,914	618,048	516,747	365,104
Marketing, general, and administrative	1,016,617	765,069	615,904	483,436
Operating costs and expenses	4,353,938	3,698,676	3,062,939	2,569,519
Operating income	1,409,046	1,079,940	858,335	557,314
Interest expense	(54,659)	(81,786)	(99,363)	(96,127)
Interest income and other, net	133,162	196,475	227,289	121,834
Income before taxes	1,568,549	1,194,629	966,261	583,021
Provision for taxes	502,000	376,000	336,000	192,000
Net income	$1,066,549	$ 818,629	$ 650,261	$ 391,021
Depreciation and amortization	$ 517,640	$ 418,250	$ 292,430	$ 237,160
Capital expenditure	1,745,000	1,366,540	971,980	659,260
Total assets	8,088,590	6,292,100	5,376,310	3,993,980
Long-term debt	358,810	362,530	419,970	412,480
Total equity	$5,817,380	$4,557,850	$3,591,510	$2,548,800

SOURCE: Intel Corp. annual reports.

manager of Microprocessor Division 5, 7 (MD5,7), the group which developed Pentium, explained: "When we started the development project in 1989, the competition was SPARC.[8] 'Beat SPARC' was our motto. Now for all intents and purposes, SPARC is not a threat. PowerPC[9] and Alpha[10] didn't exist. Suddenly they are the threats."

MPG faced competition from two directions. First was the continued battle within the Intel (or x86) architecture. The first processors claiming full compatibility with its flagship Intel 486 processors were entering the market. In addition, several new architectures based on RISC (reduced instruction set computing) technology were challenging Intel's ability to maintain state-of-the-art performance within the framework of its current architecture.

Microprocessor Industry Background

Intel's involvement in the microprocessor industry dates back to the world's first microprocessor, the 4004. Invented in 1971 to power an electronic calculator, this product was the predecessor of Intel's 8086 and 8088, which IBM adopted as its PC microprocessor architecture. Intel's product line progressed from the 8086 to the 80286 in 1982. During the early years of the PC industry, IBM and IBM-compatible PCs became the leading architecture. The Intel architecture became the highest volume microprocessor architecture by an overwhelming margin. However, at that time, a number of other vendors were licensed by Intel to produce Intel processor designs. Indeed in 1984, when the Intel architecture accounted for 59 percent of all 16-bit microprocessors, Intel's share of the microprocessor market was only 14.5 percent.

In 1985, with the introduction of the Intel386, Intel adopted a sole-sourcing strategy. The company no longer licensed the intellectual property necessary to copy the 386 or future generations. Competitors could still create products that functioned like an Intel processor; however, they had to use careful reverse engineering, a time-consuming and difficult process. Under this policy, Intel served as the only source for the 386 for four years. After introducing the first Intel486 in 1989, Intel was the sole source until mid-1993. As had been the case with earlier generations, the *i*486 family provided marked improvement in the response time of most PC software when compared with a 386 (see Exhibit 5 for a comparison of Intel processor generations). As the sole source, Intel reaped large margins on 486 sales as prices in the 386 market plummeted. 1993 found

[8]SPARC is a trademark of Sun Microsystems, Inc.

[9]PowerPC is a trademark of IBM, Motorola, and Apple Computer.

[10]Alpha is a trademark of Digital Equipment Corp.

EXHIBIT 2 Intel Corporation Organization Chart

Executive Office
G. Moore, A. Grove, C. Barrett

- Microprocessor Products Group
- Mobile Computing Group
- Semiconductor Products Group
- Intel Products Group

Strategic:
- Corporate Strategy
- Corporate Marketing Group
- Intel Architecture Laboratories
- Corporate Business Development

Operations:
- Technology and Manufacturing Group
- Sales
- Finance

Administration:
- Information Technology
- Legal
- Human Resources

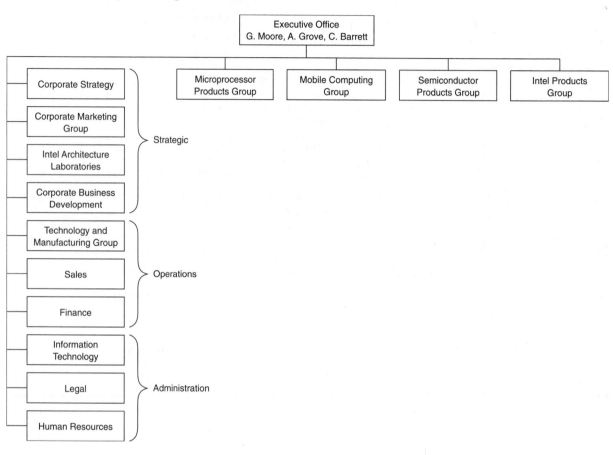

competitors entering the 486 market for the first time. See Exhibits 6 and 7 for market share and price trends in the 386 and 486 markets.

Because initial shipments were limited as production was ramped up, Pentium processors were rationed to leading systems designers throughout 1993. Industry analyst Infocorp, in a report released in July, expected Intel's customers to ship 1.5 million Pentium systems in 1993, over 9 million in 1995, and more than 28 million in 1996.[11] In the report Infocorp also said that it expected the P6 (the next generation processor) to be in production in 1996. In its third quarter earnings announcement, Intel reiterated its commitment to ship "hundreds of thousands of Pentium processors in 1993, and millions in 1994."

[11]*EDGE: Work-Group Computing Report,* July 26, 1993, p. 2.

Intel was also facing renewed competition from several RISC processor vendors. *Reduced instruction set computing* was a term used to describe a microprocessor design philosophy that emerged in the early 1980s. Microprocessor instructions are the lowest level commands a processor responds to (such as "retrieve from memory" or "compare two numbers"). RISC processors support fewer instructions (70–80) than CISC (complex instruction set computing) processors (100–150). As a result of supporting fewer instructions, RISC chips offer superior performance over a narrow range, and can be optimized for a specific purpose. The theory behind RISC was that as instructions were simplified, the processor could more efficiently execute the instructions used most often, leading to faster overall performance. Intel countered claims of superior RISC performance in general use by pointing out that the *i*486 and Pentium incorporated many RISC features and offered competitive performance in important benchmarks.

EXHIBIT 3 MPG Organization Chart

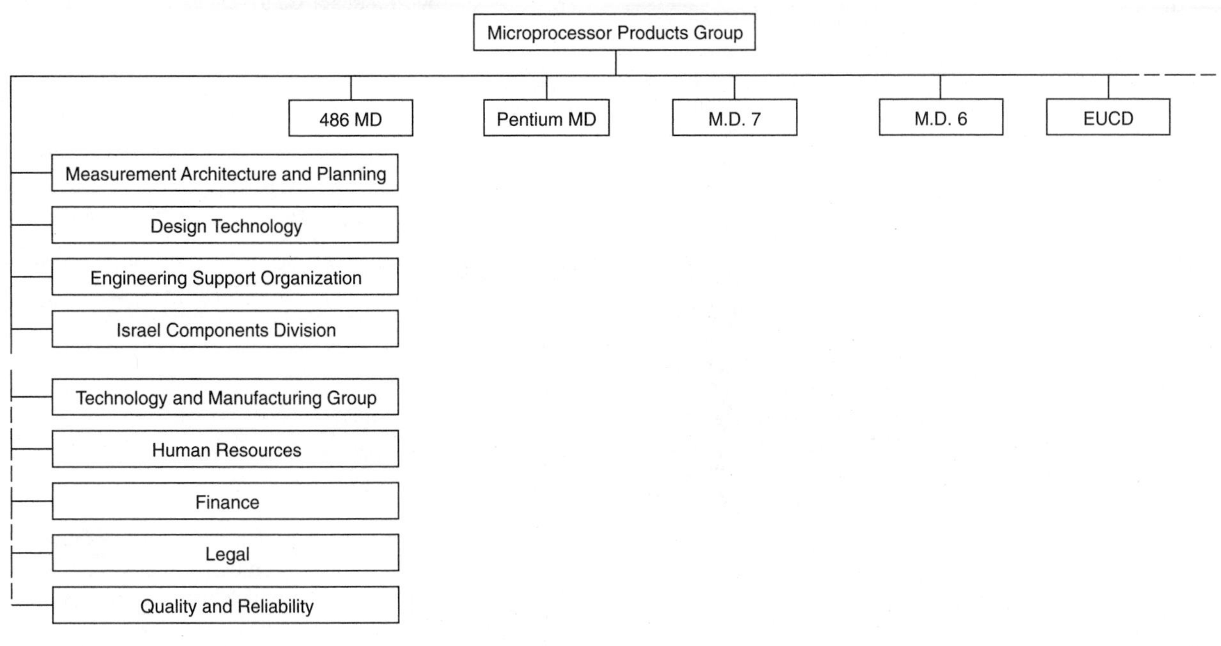

In the late 1980s RISC architecture had come to dominate the market for technical workstations. Market leaders Sun Microsystems, Hewlett-Packard, IBM, DEC (Digital Equipment Corp.), and Silicon Graphics each supported a proprietary RISC architecture which usually ran an operating system also provided by the workstation vendor (typically a proprietary version of UNIX). Because they were not compatible with the thousands of software programs written for Intel processors running Microsoft DOS and Windows operating systems, RISC processors had not been able to gain a presence in the much larger market for desktop PCs. See Exhibits 8 and 9 for unit sales of different processor types and different computer systems segments.

MPG's Organization

MPG was organized into product groups which carried responsibility for all aspects of a given product line. Intel's microprocessor lines were divided into MD3,4 (Microprocessor Division 3,4), which was responsible for Intel386 and Intel486 product lines; MD5,7, which encompassed the Pentium and the P7[12] product groups; and MD6, which was readying the P6, the sixth-generation Intel processor. EUCD (End User Components Division) marketed Intel's OverDrive[13] upgrade processors. IMD (Integrated Microcomputer Division) developed supporting chipsets which accompanied the microprocessors. Each of these groups contained its own design engineers and marketing resources, and maintained matrix relationships with other groups such as the sales organization, Technology and Manufacturing Group (TMG—which was responsible for developing process technology and managing production facilities), finance, and others. As with the rest of Intel, MPG's general managers maintained full profit-and-loss responsibility for their product lines.

Microprocessor Design

Dr. Albert Yu explained some of the background of microprocessor design:

[12]P7 was Intel's seventh generation processor. In 1993, Intel had development efforts underway for both P6 and P7.

[13]OverDrive was one of a family of processors designed to plug into a special socket in many PC systems to improve performance by replacing a less powerful microprocessor which was shipped with the system initially. Customers could buy these processors at a computer retailer and install the upgrade themselves.

EXHIBIT 4 Explanation of Intel Processor Names

Intel processors carry two basic designations, SX and DX. These refer to the feature set included on the processor chip. DX indicates that a math coprocessor (or floating-point unit) is included on-chip. SX is the same basic processor design without the math coprocessor. Because of the additional computational support, DX processors are more powerful (i.e., execute software more quickly) than SXs under normal conditions.

Every microprocessor operates with a clock set at a specific speed measured in megahertz (MHz). The clock speed is one determinant of performance. Given two processors with the same design, the one with the faster clock will execute software instructions more quickly. However, because there are many other aspects of a microprocessor architecture that determine performance, clock speed is not a reliable indicator of performance when comparing processors from different architectures. Clock doubling refers to a technique that allows a microprocessor to operate at two clock speeds—a high speed internally, and a lower speed for the processor's interaction with the rest of the system. This is done because many standard systems operate at one of several standard clock rates (33MHz is common in 486 systems). Because much of a processor's work does not involve the rest of the system, speeding up the internal clock offers a substantial performance improvement without changing the complexity of the surrounding system design. Intel's clock-doubled 486s are denoted with a 2 followed by the internal frequency (486DX2/66, 486DX2/50).

Therefore, an *i*486DX50 is a 50MHz 486 processor with an on-chip math coprocessor. An *i*386SX33 is a 33MHz 386 processor without an on-chip math coprocessor.

Versions of each generation of the microprocessor architecture follow a road map which usually contains three dimensions: performance, packaging, and features. Performance and packaging are rather obvious. For example, we offer a range of clock frequencies (*i*486: 25 MHz, 33 MHz, 50 MHz). The faster the clock, with all else equal, the faster the processor. There are also a well-known set of packaging[14] options that customers demand. Features are much less obvious. These refer to specific functions which may be included on the microprocessor chip which aren't necessarily part of the core processor. Our products serve three markets: servers, desktop PCs, and mobile computers. These markets look similar, with many of the same players (OEMs). However, the details [i.e., feature set required] are very different.

Another problem is the timing of certain features—if you include certain uses of your processor before the market is ready to implement it, you wind up going through a lot of engineering effort, and adding complexity and size (which translates into higher cost) to

EXHIBIT 6 Average Desktop/Tower PC Street Prices by Processor Q2 91–Q4 92

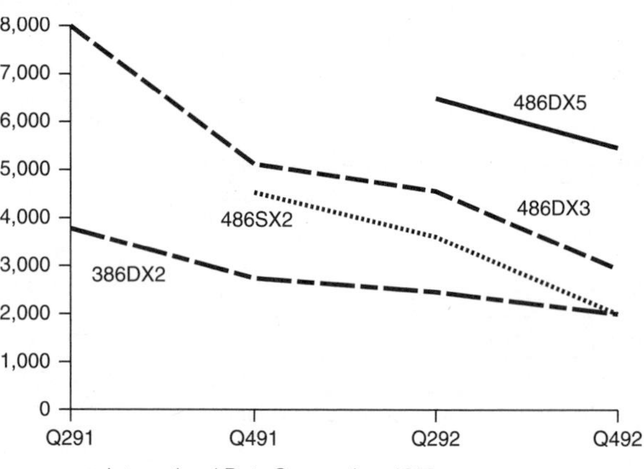

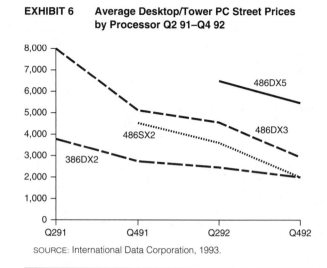

SOURCE: International Data Corporation, 1993.

[14]*Package* refers to the plastic or ceramic and metal case that encapsulates a microchip and connects it to leads on a circuit board. Packages will vary according to the type of system being designed. For example, Thin Quad Flat Pack is a special package for mobile computers that is more expensive but offers a very low profile to conserve space.

EXHIBIT 5 Comparison of Intel Processor Generations

Processor Generation	Date of Release	Price at Launch	1993 Price	MIPS at Launch	Highest MIPS	Transistor Count
8086	June 1978	$360	Discontinued	.33	.75	29,000
80286	February 1982	$360	$8	1.2	2.66	134,000
80386	October 1985	$299	$91	5	11.4	275,000
80486	August 1989	$950	$317	20	54	1,200,000
Pentium	March 1993	$995	N/A	112	N/A	3,100,000

SOURCE: *BYTE*, May 1993.

EXHIBIT 7 Trends in X86 Market Share, 1989–1992

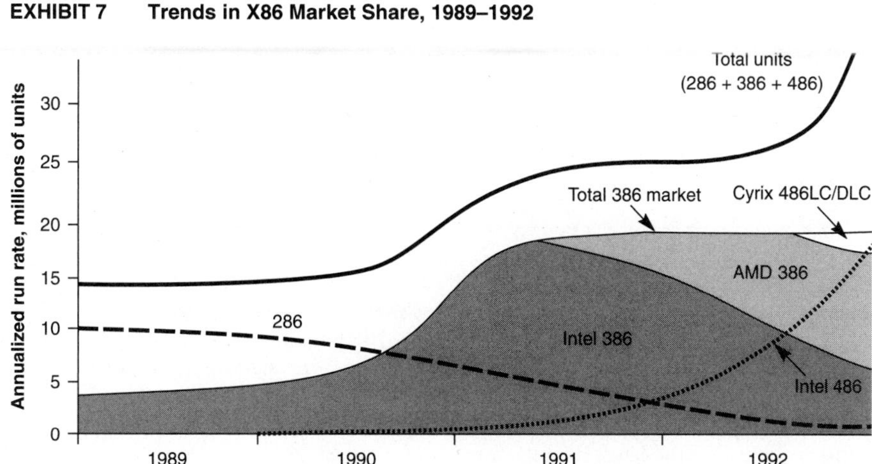

SOURCE: Microprocessor report estimates.

EXHIBIT 8 Worldwide PC Unit Shipments by Processor Type, 1981–1992

Vendor and Processor	1981	1982	1983	1984	1985	1986	1987	1988	1989	1990	1991	1992
8088/86	72	324	1,135	2,894	3,626	4,289	5,139	5,633	4,221	2,633	1,174	526
80286				61	610	1,875	4,387	6,652	8,284	7,968	5,318	2,847
80386SX								122	1,018	4,415	8,610	10,607
80386DX						42	449	1,323	2,373	3,276	3,832	3,258
80486SX											193	2,245
80486DX									5	162	969	2,278
Total Intel Architecture*	72	324	1,135	2,995	4,236	6,206	9,975	13,729	15,901	18,455	20,096	21,760
680X0**	5	18	66	665	626	919	1,564	2,048	2,443	2,883	3,363	3,865
RISC***						1	5	21	80	195	323	448
Other	1,209	4,675	8,066	8,369	5,793	5,890	5,823	3,319	2,751	1,922	1,535	1,063
Total PCs	1,286	5,016	9,267	11,989	10,655	13,016	17,366	19,477	21,176	23,456	25,317	27,136

*Total Intel is for all Intel and Intel compatible processors.
**680X0 indicates Motorola 68K architecture processors.
***RISC is all RISC processors combined—SPARC, MIPS, RS/6000, and the like.

SOURCE: International Data Corporation, 1993.

your design for something people don't care about and won't pay for. If you're late in providing a desired feature, you open the door for a competitor. Because of this, microprocessor feature sets are much more complicated than features for other semiconductors, such as DRAMs. There are many more variables which can be altered.

Having in-house manufacturing is very important. Design engineers in MPG work very closely with Gerry Parker's [Technology and Manufacturing] group to incorporate the design and manufacturing process. We are already defining process technology for 1997. This is a key element to success—the heart of the business. This is important to our ability to get the most into the smallest chip. If you look at our competition, the ones with their own manufacturing have chips that are compact and well designed. Competitors who don't [have their own manufacturing] have bigger chips.

EXHIBIT 9 Worldwide Unit Shipments of Computer Systems by Segment

	1990	1991	1992	CAGR (%)
Supercomputer	1,000	1.013	1.074	3.6
Mainframe	15,130	13,587	9,434	−21.0
Midrange	718,683	695,641	545,567	−12.9
Workstation	407,624	527,549	584,544	19.8

Volume is key to everything. A leading-edge design will take 50 to 100 top engineers two or three years to develop. Total development costs will probably range from $50 million to $100 million. In addition to that, the processor must make use of the latest manufacturing technology to be cost-effective. A leading-edge fab can require $700 million to $800 million in capital investment. You have to sell a lot of processors to recoup those costs.

Pentium processor design program. The following are excerpts from conversations with Vin Dham and Albert Yu on the Pentium program:

Vin Dham

The team goal has always been to minimize the performance difference between our architecture and the best RISC guys. If we're close, our customers won't switch. It isn't worth their while. Switching takes a lot of effort. Some of our largest OEMs recently told me not to worry about the RISC guys. I told them that if I don't do my job right, they'll be telling me to worry a couple of years from now. . . . In the early Pentium processor development we did extensive investigations and asked our customers, "What would it take to get you to switch?" They said it would take more than a 2X difference in performance. . . . Our biggest advantage is compatibility. As long as we can offer world-class performance, our customers will continue to choose our architecture to maintain compatibility with the huge software base written to the Intel architecture.

Compatibility costs us 10 percent to 30 percent in terms of performance because we have to have a more complex design. Complexity costs in two ways: (1) more transistors lead to a larger chip, which is more expensive to make; (2) it hurts on performance because a more complex design is often slower or harder to optimize. However, the difference in size isn't as great as the competition is advertising; we are currently compacting the Pentium processor to decrease the number of transistors and move it to a smaller (linewidth) process. This will reduce the size of the chip and the amount of heat it generates. When we finish this, about the time our competitors will have their chips available, we'll be on par. But sure, because they are starting from scratch, they don't have this added burden of complexity.

Albert Yu

Over a couple of generations, any architecture accumulates a compatibility burden. We have seen this with a couple of the original RISC architectures. This burden is not unique to Intel, but affects everyone over time. You always have opportunities to do something new with a new architecture [to improve performance]. But you have to [keep older structures in place along with the new features to] maintain software compatibility from one generation to the next. There is a lot of marketing hype from our competitors about RISC processors being superior to our architecture. RISC versus CISC is not a technical discussion. RISC means simplifying as much as possible. This is good in any setting. RISC is a set of techniques that can be applied to microprocessor design to increase overall throughput. We continue to apply these techniques to the Intel architecture. The 486 and Pentium architectures incorporate many of these design concepts.

Another trend we're facing at MPG is the increasing number of engineers required for each new generation of the architecture. There was as much innovation in the administration of the Pentium architecture development project as there was in the technology. The 386 team consisted of about 30 engineers, the 486 was roughly 80 engineers, and the Pentium processor design team was over 100 engineers. Right now we have even more engineers working on the P6. That's about as large as we can go. We have to find a way to handle the increased complexity of future generations through automating the design process rather than by simply adding more people.

We have made a big investment in proprietary design tools. For the last decade we have led the industry in the complexity of logic design. When we were putting 1 million transistors on a logic chip, the industry was at 500k. We have no choice but to do our own tools. This is also an advantage over our competition—they have to either build their own or work with less advanced, generally available tools.

Vin Dham

There are several tools that we develop in house that are important to our design capability and lead the industry—these are critical. You have to understand that some parts of a microprocessor are very complex and innovative, while others are composed of standard elements (such as SRAM cells). We can buy off the shelf tools for the standard elements but not for everything. Also, don't forget about the challenge of moving a new design into production. This is a big deal. We are constantly co-developing new design tools along with our leading-edge process technology. One of our key tools helps us move a design from the drawing board to our most advanced process technology faster than anyone else in the industry. However, the best tool is still by hand. We still lay out the critical elements of the processor by hand (less than 10% of the total transistors). No tool can absolutely optimize as well as the right person.

Product Quality

Along with continued emphasis on technical prowess, managers in MPG also sought to improve the reliability of new products. Vin Dham explained:

This was a big shift in focus from the 486 to the Pentium processor development efforts. We were lousy in quality and support to our customers. When the 486 came out, there were many bugs—bad bugs—which we didn't catch. One bug that was found by a customer surfaced after we had begun production—50,000 486s became key chains instantly. That's a lot of very expensive key chains! We were at our customers' mercy—they were finding the errors in our products. We were depending on them for our quality assurance. One customer found a bug in the 486, but didn't tell us about it. They worked around it in their system and then didn't want to tell us because it would be an advantage to their products over our other customers. We found out almost by accident from one of their people. This is a scary position to be in.

In terms of quality we learned many things from the 486 introduction that we have improved. For example, design work proceeds according to functional blocks owned by small teams of designers. A root-cause analysis of each bug reported for the 486 [an extensive analysis conducted after the release of the 486] identified that most of the bugs were coming from the interfaces between the functional blocks rather than from within a block. For the Pentium architecture we assigned a team to be responsible for the interfaces only, to be sure they were being handled properly. As the project was nearing completion, after each of my teams assured me there were no bugs, I offered to pay anyone $100 on the spot if they found a bug—I paid out a few hundred dollars. This was a lot cheaper than finding the bug later or having a customer find the bug for us. With Pentium processors, no bugs have gone to customers.

Another area we needed to build up was compatibility testing. In 1989, we had very little compatibility testing capability. Yet compatibility is our most important feature. We recognized that we needed to have a world-class compatibility testing capability. I went to Albert [Yu] and convinced him of this. Now, we are ahead of most of the world in this area. At first people said, "You're going to have to duplicate all the compatibility labs at IBM, Compaq, Dell, and the rest." It turned out that we only needed resources of the best one, not all of them. For the 386 there were two engineers verifying that it was compatible with the overall architecture. There were a few more on the 486, but it was too little too late. For the Pentium processor, the team was there from the start.

Customer Support

Vin Dham

In the past, we have, at times, provided lousy customer support. We designed the CPU and gave it to our customers to design their systems. We began to change this for the first time with the *i*486DX2/50.[15] We got much more involved in their design programs, as they transitioned to higher-end systems. We are also focusing on providing a more complete solution to our customers. For the Pentium architecture we provided a very comprehensive solution. We even designed and built some of the first Pentium systems. This allowed us to benchmark our customers and say, "Hey, guys, we can build a system that performs better than yours—here's how you can improve."

A good example of improved support is the bus function model. This is a software model of how key parts of our processor function. Our customers use this to design their systems to work with the new microprocessor. For the 486, we had a small independent software company do our bus function model. It was a disaster; they were late and had many problems with the model. This function is now in-house and worked well with our Pentium customers.

Corporate Marketing Group

The Corporate Marketing Group (CMG) got its start in the early 80s as a division of MPG. The End User Marketing Group was composed of a small team of five guerrilla marketers. Several smaller scale adver-

[15]For an explanation of Intel product names see Exhibit 3.

tising programs had been used to encourage end users to adopt the latest Intel technology. This included programs to help speed the transition from the 286 to 386 (which was known as Red X because it featured print ads with a large red X crossing out a 286 logo), and from the 386 to 486. However, "Intel Inside" was the first time Intel put together a large, comprehensive program geared toward turning the Intel name into a consumer brand. CMG managers pointed to Intel's microprocessor branding strategy as further evidence of the company's transition toward a branded-products company.

Intel Inside

In April 1990, Intel launched its first "Intel Inside" advertising campaign. Aimed directly at end users, rather than Intel's OEM customers, the Intel Inside program sought to influence customers to specify Intel microprocessors when they purchased a PC. This effort, which has been hotly debated in the industry, was the most noticeable effect of the changes being brought about by the CMG. 1993 found CMG managers committed to transforming Intel from a microcomputer company that marketed primarily to a small number of engineers, to a branded products company that marketed to both the traditional technical customers (its OEMs) as well as a mass, nontechnical, audience. CMG oversaw all Intel communications programs aimed at end users except those related to Intel's retail products marketed by IPG.

From 1990 to 1993, CMG invested over $500 million in programs designed to increase Intel's brand equity with end users. Intel Inside was the largest and most visible of these investments. It was composed of two broad thrusts. The first involved advertising and merchandising activities with OEMs. This included cooperative advertising with OEMs that displayed the Intel Inside logo in their print ads[16] and product catalogues. In addition there were promotions for OEMs that displayed the Intel Inside logo (usually a sticker) on their point of sale displays and packaging materials. The second thrust was a series of print and TV ad campaigns focused on Intel Inside and the associated brand promise which were placed directly by Intel. These print and television ad programs stressed Intel's guarantee of safety and advanced technology. Safety was seen both in terms of software compatibility and upgradeability.[17] Ads also emphasized Intel's latest technology, ranging from the clock-doubled *i*486DX/2 66 to Pentium.

While there was considerable debate in the computer and advertising industries as to the effectiveness of these programs, Intel managers maintained that the investment was well spent and was already showing significant signs of creating a strong brand. Company-sponsored research showed that end user awareness of the Intel brand name had increased significantly as had users' image of Intel as a technology leader versus competitors such as AMD and Cyrix.

By the end of 1991, over 300 OEMs participated in the program. However, not every OEM welcomed Intel Inside with open arms. Major OEMs such as Compaq and IBM were less enthusiastic about the program and refused to participate in some elements. These OEMs felt that Intel Inside decreased their ability to differentiate products from their competitors. "It was leveling the playing field," said Kevin Bohren, a Compaq vice president.[18] "We have to be careful to develop the program to both build the Intel brand and serve the needs of our customer base," agreed Sally Fundakowski, a CMG manager.

As 1993 continued, several questions revolved around Intel Inside. Much of the advertising sponsored by Intel had focused on two areas, Intel's promise of the most advanced technology and the safety of the huge software base written for Intel-based PCs. While these two attributes were considered to be pillars of Intel Inside's brand equity, there were questions about where Intel Inside should go next. Explains an Intel manager:

> There's been a strong debate about whether Intel Inside should include 386 processors. We have consistently touted the 486 as today's best technology and encouraged people to upgrade to a 486 system. So some people think we should focus Intel Inside only on the 486 and Pentium processor. Also, does the promise of unparalleled software compatibility hold true for a system with an Intel processor running NextStep, or Penpoint?[19] Some say that extending the brand weakens the promise, while others say, "What

[16]The OEM initiated the ad and was reimbursed a predefined amount by Intel.

[17]This refers to the OverDrive upgrade socket included in most *i*486 systems that allowed users to buy a more powerful Intel processor in the future to upgrade their system with the latest technology.

[18]*Business Week,* September 30, 1993, p. 32.

[19]Operating systems which were not compatible with Microsoft DOS or Windows.

good is all this money we've invested in the brand if you can't take advantage of it?"

Microprocessor Branding

In 1980, IBM chose the Intel 8088 microprocessor to power its first PC. The next generation, a 16-bit enhancement of the 8-bit 8088, was labeled the 8086. Successive Intel microprocessors followed the 80X86 naming convention (i.e., 80286, 80386, 80486). Advertisements often omitted the 80 from the beginning of the name. As competitors introduced Intel-compatible processors they followed the same convention. Intel managers felt that competitors were benefiting from brand equity being built up by Intel's promotions of its 386 and 486 processors.

After trying unsuccessfully to stop other suppliers from using the X86 branding convention, Intel decided that it should develop a name for its fifth generation processor that could not be copied by others. This led to the selection of the Pentium trademark. No Intel marketing or promotional materials mentioned 586. Tracking press accounts appearing before and just after the Pentium processor's introduction, Intel marketers reported that while initially there were more references to Intel's 586 than to the Pentium processor, one month after its release over 90 percent of the mentions used Pentium instead of 586.

Technology and Manufacturing Group

Intel's Technology and Manufacturing Group (TMG) was a functional organization which managed Intel's manufacturing sites (or fabs). TMG also developed and deployed Intel's latest semiconductor process technology. TMG engineers matrixed closely with product groups in MPG and SPG because of the close link between product and process design. Having publicly committed to building another $1 billion fab near Albuquerque, New Mexico, in early 1993, Intel continued to invest heavily in state-of-the-art fab capacity. "It's interesting," noted Gerry Parker, senior vice president and general manager of TMG. "This industry moves in cycles. A couple of years ago we [the industry] had too much advanced capacity. Now, everybody's fabs are full, you can't find excess capacity anywhere in the industry. . . . Fabless companies look great in times of overcapacity, but struggle when it goes the other way."

During the mid-1980s, as Intel considered exiting the DRAM business, there was great concern over Intel's loss of the DRAM as a technology driver. The generally accepted theory was that it took cumulative production of approximately a million units to obtain mature semiconductor yields. However, since halting DRAM production, Intel managers found that they could continue to drive high yields with lower volumes. Gerry Parker discussed his perspective on technology drivers:[20]

> There is no single technology driver at Intel. We focus our technology development on logic and nonvolatile memory products. More than ever before, we watch what the rest of the industry is doing and try to follow the trends. The DRAM is the industry's driver, because it's the highest volume product and because DRAM suppliers are the biggest purchasers [of fab equipment]. There have been some really fascinating developments in the industry. I think that the entire industry paradigm has shifted in the past several years.
>
> I spend a lot of time now following what the DRAM people are doing and talking with equipment manufacturers. A great deal of the know-how is now generated at the equipment suppliers. We try to stay in the mainstream by purchasing the most advanced equipment, but then optimize it to maximum advantage for our products."

While once very similar, DRAM and logic (including microprocessors) fabrication technologies had grown apart over the last decade. This is largely because leading logic products such as microprocessors have grown immensely more complex. The need to interconnect so many parts of a microprocessor has led designers to chips which differ significantly in their composition from memory chips. In recent estimates, a leading-edge factory built for logic production shared only about 40 percent of its equipment with a comparable DRAM factory. The minimum efficient scale is estimated to be between 3000 and 4000 wafer starts per week. Such a factory is estimated to cost roughly $400 million. One industry analyst estimated that a single wafer would yield approximately 60 486 CPUs at the current 0.8 micron process.

With each product generation, Intel followed a consistent pattern of introducing the most advanced CPU design on existing fab technology, and then moving it to the next process generation

[20]Excerpt taken from "Intel Corporation (C);" see Case II–14.

to improve profitability and product performance.[21] The 386 was introduced on 1.5-micron technology and then transferred to a leading edge 1.0-micron process. On the 1.0-micron process, the 386 measured 250 sq. mils versus 400 at 1.5 microns. This size reduction greatly increased the number of parts that could be produced with each silicon wafer. The 486 had been introduced on a 1.0-micron process and then moved to 0.8 microns. A similar progression was planned for the Pentium processor, which was introduced on Intel's current 0.8-micron technology. Industry analysts at Infocorp expected to see Pentium transition to a 0.65-micron process and run at approximately 100MHz by mid-1994.

RISC at Intel

In 1993, as its name implied, the Intel architecture was the singular focus of the company's microprocessor franchise. However, just three years earlier, the Intel architecture had been challenged internally by a new RISC architecture developed by a small team within the microprocessor design organization. Led by Les Kohn, the project was justified as a coprocessor for the 486. Several earlier attempts to create a new RISC-based architecture had been rejected. Code named N10, the new chip utilized design concepts found in supercomputers, according to Kohn. Dubbed the *i*860, the new processor was positioned by Intel as an ideal processor for advanced workstations.

With the *i*860, Kohn had finally been able to get support from many Intel managers for his new architecture. However, that very success had forced top management to consider the role RISC technology should play at Intel. Should future architectural bets be placed on the current CISC Intel architecture, on a new RISC architecture, or both? After a protracted debate, the Intel architecture won. This was partially due to the fact that Intel designers believed that they could continue to offer significant performance improvements by enhancing the existing architecture with RISC-like features. Kohn and most of his team had left Intel by 1993. However, RISC had become firmly established. Another RISC design, dubbed the *i*960, became a very popular microcontroller, specializing in computing-intensive tasks such as managing the operations of a laser printer. Dataquest estimated that the *i*960 was the world's highest volume RISC chip in 1992.[22]

Microprocessor Competition

Intel-Compatible Competitors

During the late 1980s, after Intel's decision to be the sole source for the microprocessors it created, several competitors emerged within the Intel or "x86" architecture. The two largest competitors, Advanced Micro Devices (AMD) and Cyrix, both offered popular 386 clones and were ramping up production of their versions of the leading 486 processors. In addition, both IBM and Texas Instruments, two of the world's largest semiconductor manufacturers, seemed poised to enter the market with 486 compatibles of their own. See Exhibit 10 for selected financial data on competitors.

AMD. AMD, the fifth-largest U.S. semiconductor company, is the highest volume Intel-compatible competitor. Through a series of cross-licensing agreements with Intel which date back to the late 1970s, AMD obtained the rights to many of Intel's basic patents on the x86 architecture. Having introduced its first Intel-compatible 386 processor in 1990, by 1992, AMD was the 386 market leader. AM386[23] processors accounted for over 50 percent of the 386 market in 1992.

Over the summer of 1993, AMD launched its first 486 compatibles. The new chips were delayed over six months by a legal dispute over AMD's rights to use key Intel intellectual property.[24] AMD initially lost a court decision on the matter. However, the decision was overturned in May. Immediately following the reversal, which was appealed by Intel, AMD announced that two 486-compatible processors were entering production. In July, AMD announced a new set of 486 compatibles which didn't rely on the Intel property in question.[25] AMD expected to achieve a 5 percent share of the 486 market by 1993, and a 20 percent share by the end of 1994. Industry analysts expected AMD's short-term market share to depend partially on its ability to add new manufacturing capacity. AMD's lineup included

[21]Microprocessors could be made to run faster on a smaller process because electrical signals don't have as far to travel.

[22]In terms of units sold.

[23]AM386 and AM486 are trademarks of AMD corporation.

[24]The intellectual property in question was microcode associated with the 486.

[25]They utilized internally developed microcode.

EXHIBIT 10 Selected Competitor Financial Data, Fiscal 1992

	IBM	Texas Instruments	AMD	Cyrix	Motorola
Net revenues	64,523,000	7,440,000	1,514,490	72,898	13,303,000
Cost of sales	35,069,000	5,250,000	746,490	28,003	8,508,000
Research and development	6,522,000	470,000	227,860	8,322	Not reported
Marketing, general, and administrative	19,526,000	1,300,000	270,200	23,383	3,838,000
Operating costs and expenses	61,117,000	7,020,000	1,244,550	31,705	12,346,000
Operating income	3,406,000	420,000	269,940	13,190	957,000
Interest expense	(12,432,000)	(51,000)	(17,230)		(157,000)
Interest income and other, net			18,910	375	
Income before taxes	(9,026,000)	369,000	271,620	13,565	800,000
Provision for taxes	(2,161,000)	122,000	26,620	5,152	224,000
Net income	(6,865,000)	247,000	245,000	8,413	576,000
Depreciation and amortization	4,793,000	610,000	152,310	2,490	1,000,000
Capital expenditure	8,911,000	1,039,000	373,110	9,120	2,383,000
Total assets	86,705,000	5,185,000	1,448,090	50,270	10,629,000
Long-term debt	7,108,000	909,000	25,760	150	1,258,000
Total equity	27,624,000	1,947,000	1,046,740	31,460	5,144,000

SOURCE: 1992 annual reports; for Cyrix, 1992 Prospectus.

low-power 3.3-volt versions of the AM486SX and the powerful clock doubled AM486DX2/66, comparable in performance with Intel's highest performing 486 processor. In each case, AMD's prices matched corresponding Intel parts. This was not surprising because Intel had been unable to fully meet 486 demand throughout the first half of 1993. In early October, Intel announced plans to drop fourth-quarter prices for some *i*486SX CPUs by 20 to 30 percent. AMD also announced that it was working on a Pentium-class processor, dubbed K-5, which would be available sometime in 1994.

CYRIX. Founded in 1987 by a group of engineers from Texas Instruments, Cyrix rallied around the slogan, "Become the Compaq[26] of the microprocessor industry." Having grown rapidly on the strength of its first product, a math coprocessor which worked with Intel microprocessors to speed numerical calculations, Cyrix entered the microprocessor market in 1991 with the Cy486SLC.[27] Fitting into a 386 socket and incorporating many features found in the *i*486 family, the Cy486SLC was more powerful than any member of the Intel 386 family, but was not as powerful as the *i*486SC25, Intel's entry-level 486. "That product was particularly appealing to OEMs who were caught during the transition from 386s to 486s with excess inventories of 386 motherboards. The motherboards couldn't accommodate a 486. The Cyrix part gave them a way to upgrade those boards," explained one Intel manager.

Late in May 1993, at Spring Comdex, Cyrix introduced a line of 6 Intel 486SX-compatible processors. The processors incorporated advanced power management features expected in Intel's pending S-series line of 486 processors slated for release in June 1993. The Cyrix parts were priced comparably with Intel's 486SX products. Two of the processors also incorporated clock-doubling technology which was invented and first introduced by Intel in early 1992. In addition, Cyrix announced the availability of two processors which allowed users to upgrade their 386 PCs by replacing the existing 386 CPU with a Cyrix 486. The two processors carried a retail price roughly half that of a comparable Intel upgrade kit. Cyrix also announced plans to enter production with its more powerful Cy486DLC line of processors during the summer of 1993. DLC processors were projected to offer performance comparable to Intel's leading *i*486DX processors. Cyrix was also develop-

[26]After Compaq Computer Corp., which became a leading PC systems manufacturer by selling IBM-compatible PCs.

[27]Cy386 and Cy486 are trademarks of Cyrix Inc.

ing a next-generation processor which would be compatible with the Pentium architecture. Dubbed M1, Cyrix claimed it would offer higher performance than the Pentium by optimizing the Pentium architecture's internal design. Cyrix claimed the part would be available in 1994 and would significantly undercut Intel's pricing.

Cyrix CEO Jerry Rogers, quoted in *PC Week* (December 28, 1992), noted:

> "The myth is that it takes hundreds and hundreds of engineers and four to five years to design a microprocessor." However, armed with a "get it right the first time" motto, a six-person engineering design team and an advanced CAD system, Cyrix was able to turn out its first 486-compatible chip in 18 months.

Cyrix depends on two large semiconductor partners for production capacity and access to crucial intellectual property. Cyrix did not have the rights to manufacture and sell Intel-compatible microprocessors. However, rights to key technologies necessary to duplicate the Intel architecture were widely cross-licensed during the late 1970s and early 80s. Texas Instruments and SGS Thompson Microelectronics, each of whom had rights to the necessary Intel technology, served as Cyrix's manufacturing and marketing partners. While these rights were initially challenged by Intel, U.S. courts upheld Cyrix's ability to design and market processors manufactured by its partners. In early 1993, the semiconductor trade press reported that Cyrix was searching for additional fab capacity, likely to be located in East Asia. Cyrix's capacity agreements with Texas Instruments reportedly were constraining shipments of *i*486-compatible processors. Cyrix managers publicly complained that they were not able to fill orders for their 486s because TI was not making enough production capacity available for Cyrix products. In August, Cyrix managers confirmed that Texas Instruments was preparing to use most of its microprocessor production capacity for its own line of 486-compatible CPUs. Cyrix successfully executed its first public stock offering during the summer of 1993.

Texas Instruments. Separately, Texas Instruments announced in early 1993 that it was sampling its own versions of Cyrix processors. TI was reported to have rights to produce and sell versions of Cyrix designs and to enhance Cyrix's base design with its own technology. TI's initial announcements indicated that its version of Cyrix processors was able to operate at higher frequencies due to a manufacturing process enhancement.

On October 7th, TI announced its plans to offer *i*486-compatible processors that incorporated a Cyrix core with additional TI technology. TI announced that its first product would be targeted at the rapidly growing niche of subnotebook PCs. The processor, named Potomac, would be demonstrated in November and was slated for full-scale production by January 1994. TI was reportedly planning to follow up with a full line of 486 compatibles and a Pentium competitor. As the second-largest U.S. semiconductor company, TI's entry was taken very seriously by industry analysts. TI's other recent microprocessor activity centered around its work with Sun Microsystems' SPARC RISC architecture. TI was the leading producer of advanced SPARC processors used in SUN workstations.

IBM. IBM, the world's largest PC maker and Intel's largest customer, fabricated versions of Intel's microprocessors under license from Intel. IBM's license allowed it to alter Intel's designs to increase performance or add additional features. Historically, IBM used this license to differentiate its PC product line from other OEMs through features like proprietary power management functions built into its SLC line of Intel-compatible processors. However, recently IBM's microelectronics division began selling components outside of IBM for the first time, and was actively seeking to supply other PC makers with its enhanced Intel-compatible microprocessors. IBM was reported to be readying a clock-tripled version of the 486 which could be sold to other PC OEMs. The processor, which was rumored to run at 99MHz internally and 33MHz externally, was being positioned directly against Intel's popular clock-doubled *i*486DX2-66, which ran at 66MHz internally and 33MHz externally.

MPG's 486 Strategy

In late 1992, Intel announced plans to introduce more than 25 versions of the Intel 486 processor during 1993. Microprocessor Product Group general manager Albert Yu noted, "Our competitors seek niches initially and then expand out of them." "AMD and Cyrix got into the 386 market because we left gaps," echoed another senior manager. "There were several holes in the 386 product line. Their 40MHz 386DX and 3.3-volt processors filled niches that Intel products didn't cover. We've worked to minimize holes in the Intel 486 processor family." Tom Macdonald, director of marketing for MD3-4 (the 386 and 486 product families), described the 486 strategy:

> We knew there were holes in the 386 but we focused more on 486. Once the 386 was designed, it was finished. We didn't add additional features. Our strategy for the 486 is to cover all the holes. We have a number of design teams working on a wide range of proliferations of the basic 486 design. The versions differ based on the speed of the processor clock (MHz), the package type, and other features (e.g., lower operating voltage, and the inclusion of power management features). Our design goal is to be the fastest processor at a given MHz (clock speed) and to offer the most MHz.

"When we were doing the 386 we weren't a $6 billion company; now we can make sure we don't leave holes," added an Intel designer who had been involved in several microprocessor generations. "In terms of pricing, AMD and Cyrix tend to charge slightly less than Intel with slightly more MHz (for example, AMD initially offered a 40MHz AM386DX for slightly less than an Intel 33MHz *i*386DX)," Macdonald concluded

PC Systems Manufacturers

A key part of Intel's success was the vibrant market for PC systems. PC systems manufacturers (or OEMs) faced one of the most intensely competitive markets in the world. Major systems manufacturers had seen gross margins decline from 35 to 45 percent[28] in 1990 to the mid-20% range in 1993 (see Exhibit 11 for a breakdown of market share and gross and operating margins for leading PC vendors). Major vendors such as IBM and Compaq spent most of 1992 and 93 in a price war with several rapidly growing, low-cost manufacturers such as Dell Systems, Gateway 2000, and Packard Bell. Several medium-sized OEMs and several more smaller players either entered bankruptcy, sold out, or merged with a competitor. In one such transaction, Tandy, a pioneer in the PC industry and eighth largest vendor, sold its PC operations to AST Corp., the Number 7 player. Noted one Intel manager, "All the major OEMs are struggling to survive on very thin margins. There's no money left in most of these guys to do advanced development. Instead of thinking about where next generation systems are going, they're trying to figure out how to survive next quarter." According to *Infoworld* (March 29, 1993):

> Most manufacturers, Compaq and AST included, angrily reject that term [commodity] and point to the ways their systems differ from others. But Dell president Joel Korcher said the term is entirely correct for systems that can be sold over the phone and shipped out by mail. . . ."We're about two steps up the food chain from rice. This is a commodity business and we like it just fine. Only a moron would say PCs aren't commodities."

New Challenges From RISC

Windows NT. A key element of Intel's rise in the microprocessor industry lay in its relationship with Microsoft. Brought together by IBM in 1980 to provide the two key components of the original IBM personal computer, Microsoft and Intel were the clear leaders in the world PC industry. In 1993 Microsoft's MS-DOS[29] operating system was running on 119 million PCs throughout the world.[30] Microsoft's Windows 3.1 operating environment (which ran in conjunction with DOS) was being run on over 30 million PCs, and Microsoft claimed to be selling over a million copies of Windows 3.1 per month. MS-DOS and Windows 3.1 accounted for over 86 percent of the world's installed base. MS-DOS was written to run only on Intel architecture microprocessors. Personal computers based on other microprocessor architectures, such as the RISC processors used in most workstations, couldn't run Microsoft's operating system, and therefore couldn't use any of the applications written for MS-DOS or Windows.

The success of Windows 3.1 had been a key factor in Intel's recent growth and profitability. Computer graphics require a great deal of processing. A graphical environment, such as Windows, requires more processing power than a character-based interface such as MS-DOS because the computer must process much more information to represent the environment. While Windows 3.1 can be run on a 286 PC, a 386 was generally considered the minimum processor for acceptable performance. In addition, 486 systems offered noticeable improvements in software responsiveness. This improvement in usability for the broad base of PC users (even those who did not change the tasks they used PCs to accomplish) helped attract new PC users and drove demand for Intel 486 processors as existing users

---

[28]For example, Compaq, a leading OEM, saw gross margins fall from 43 percent in 1990 to 24.1 percent in 1993.

[29]Windows 3.1, MS-DOS, and Windows NT are trademarks of Microsoft Corp.

[30]According to industry analyst IDC.

EXHIBIT 11 Top U.S. PC Vendors

Rank 1993/1992	Vendor	Projected 1993 U.S. Unit Shipments	Market Share (%) 1993	Market Share (%) 1992	Unit Growth (%) 1993	Gross Margin (%) Q2 '93	Gross Margin (%) Q2 '92	Operating Margin (%) Q2 '93	Operating Margin (%) Q2 '92
1/2	IBM*	1,924,000	13.9	11.7	40	30.6	46.9	(56.9)	8.6
2/1	Apple	1,870,000	13.5	13.0	22	32.5	44.3	(16.5)	11.6
3/3	Compaq	1,316,000	9.5	5.7	95	24.1	30.2	9.3	5.0
4/5	Dell	791,000	5.7	3.8	75	6.5	22.7	(14.0)	6.5
5/4	Packard Bell	777,000	5.6	5.1	30	N/A	N/A	N/A	N/A
6/6	Gateway 2000	621,000	4.5	3.6	45	16.4	16.8	8.1	9.5
7/8	AST	592,000	4.3	2.7	85	17.8	29.2	(27.5)	9.6
	All vendors	13,818,000	N/A	N/A	17.5	N/A	N/A	N/A	N/A

*IBM gross margin is for all hardware sales; operating margin is for all of IBM.

SOURCE: International Data Corporation 1993

upgraded to more powerful systems needed to run Windows effectively. Some analysts questioned the incremental improvement most users would notice when moving from a 486 to a Pentium system.

At Spring Comdex, in May 1993, Microsoft announced the release of its much anticipated Windows NT operating system. NT, which had been in development for four years, contained powerful features formerly found only in workstations, minicomputers, and mainframes. Initially, Microsoft positioned Windows NT for use in the highest powered desktop PCs, workstations, and for "servers," powerful PCs or minicomputers which contain large databases or applications (such as a corporate electronic mail system). Microsoft promoted NT as the ideal choice for servers used in client-server computing. In the client-server model, multiple "clients," usually desktop personal computers, used by groups of employees, customers, and so on, access the information stored on one or more servers through a network, and then process it on their PCs locally. This differs from the traditional mainframe and minicomputer model, where all of the processing is done at the server. Client-server computing was increasingly projected to replace more traditional arrangements (of mainframes and minicomputers accessed via terminals) as the dominant method of organizing corporate computing resources over the next decade. In keeping with the sophisticated features of Windows NT, the operating system required significantly more system resources than its desktop counterpart Windows 3.1. Where Windows 3.1 required a minimum system configuration of 1 megabyte of RAM (random-access memory—usually implemented with DRAM) and 10 megabytes of disk space (to store the operating system code), NT required a minimum configuration of 8 megabytes RAM and 70 megabytes of disk space.

While Pentium was considered capable of providing the necessary processing power and feature set for these larger, more complex applications, it was not the only microprocessor that NT embraced. Unlike earlier Microsoft operating systems, Windows NT was designed to be easily ported to run on multiple microprocessor architectures. Only a small percentage of the total operating system code was specific to the microprocessor architecture. This made it a relatively easy task to port the operating system to multiple architectures. At Comdex, versions of NT were announced for both the Intel and MIPS RISC architecture. In addition, Microsoft was working with both DEC and IBM to help them port NT to DEC's new Alpha RISC architecture and IBM's PowerPC architecture. Both Hewlett-Packard and Sun were believed to be actively considering a port of NT to their respective RISC architectures (PA-RISC and SPARC) as well. At NT's release, Microsoft officials announced that they expected to sell 1 million copies of NT during its first 12 months.

Chicago. In addition to the announcement of Windows NT, Microsoft was also working on the next version of its popular Windows 3.1 operating environment for mainstream desktop PCs. Code-named Chicago, Windows 4.0 was expected to be the first desktop version of Windows (i.e., one designed for a typical desktop PC) not to require MS-DOS. Industry analysts expected Chicago to sell at levels consistent with the 1.5 million copies per month currently estimated for Windows 3.1 when it began shipping in the second half of 1994. Initially, Chicago was expected to support only the Intel architecture.

Other operating system developments. NT's main competition was expected to come from the leading UNIX operating systems that dominated the workstation market and IBM's OS/2. Having similar advanced features as NT, including the ability to run both DOS and Windows 3.1 applications, OS/2 was being positioned by IBM as both an advanced desktop and server operating system. IBM expected to sell about 3 million copies of OS/2 in 1994.

With the heritage in mainframes, minicomputers, and workstations, leading UNIX operating system vendors such as Sun Microsystems, Hewlett-Packard, Santa Cruz Operation (SCO), IBM, Novell, and Digital Equipment Corp. were positioning UNIX as the operating system of choice for powerful desktops and servers. UNIX, which had been widely licensed by its creators at AT&T and several U.S. universities (primarily Berkeley and Carnegie Mellon), existed in many forms. In most cases a hardware vendor, such as Sun Microsystems, the market leader in workstations, supported an operating system that enhanced common characteristics of UNIX with proprietary modifications or extensions. These proprietary aspects usually required that software written for one version of UNIX be partially rewritten to run on another version.

Windows NT was not the only operating system being developed for multiple architectures. Over the summer, SunSoft, the software arm of Sun Microsystems, introduced SOLARIS 486.[31] SOLARIS was a version of UNIX which ran on all Sun workstations. Applications which had been written for SOLARIS on a SPARC processor (Sun's RISC architecture) could now be recompiled to run on an Intel 486 or Pentium system. SunSoft also announced a SOLARIS port to PowerPC.

In addition to its own operating system ports, SunSoft announced that it would help bring applications written for Microsoft Windows to the UNIX world, through a technology it called WABI. Short for Windows application binary interface, WABI would allow UNIX operating systems to run Windows applications by emulating the Windows-on-Intel environment. While WABI would be folded into SOLARIS, SunSoft publicly sought to license WABI to other operating system vendors. By the end of the summer, SunSoft announced that WABI had been licensed to IBM, Hewlett-Packard, SCO, and other leading UNIX providers.

On March 17, 1993, over 70 of the leading UNIX systems and software vendors announced plans to create a unified version of the UNIX operating system. Called COSE for common open software environment, the new set of specifications would create a common interface to which all UNIX applications developers could write. This would allow an ISV (independent software vendor) to write one version of an application which could then run, unaltered, on the various UNIX platforms. The interface would be implemented by each major UNIX vendor as a subset of its operating system. Six major UNIX operating system vendors (SunSoft, IBM, Hewlett-Packard, SCO, Univel, and Novell) announced their intention to develop a common set of standards by the end of 1993. Each expected to release upgrades to their current UNIX implementations by mid 1994. Each was also expected to continue to support the previous proprietary elements of their operating systems and to augment the new specification with proprietary extensions for certain leading-edge features not covered in the standard.

Silicon Graphics (MIPS). In the late 1980s MIPS, then an independent company, helped to found the ACE consortium. ACE, which stood for advanced computing environment, was led by MIPS, Compaq, and Microsoft. The purpose of the alliance was to advance desktop computers by moving from Intel's CISC processor architecture to the MIPS higher performance RISC architecture. Microsoft began development on Windows NT with the commitment to support both the Intel and MIPS architectures. In 1992, Compaq withdrew support for ACE, announcing that it would remain committed to the Intel architecture because it believed that Pentium and future generations of the Intel architecture would offer comparable performance to RISC architectures. ACE fell apart shortly after Compaq's announcement, and MIPS, nearing bankruptcy, was bought by Silicon Graphics, a leading consumer of its microprocessor technology.

However, Microsoft did not withdraw support for the MIPS architecture from Windows NT. In fact, the first version of NT was shipped on disks containing versions for both Intel- and MIPS-based systems in

---

[31]SOLARIS and SOLARIS 486 are trademarks of Sun Microsystems.

the same package. Coinciding with the NT release, several systems vendors, led by Acer, an established PC producer, announced powerful desktop systems based on MIPS processors and Windows NT. Other MIPS vendors to announce products slated to ship in 1993 were NetPower (a recent start-up founded by former MIPS CEO, Robert Miller), Carrera Computers Inc., DeskStation, NEC Technologies Inc., and Tangent Computer Corp. Several desktop PCs based on the MIPS microprocessors, which would run Windows NT, were announced for shipment in the fall of 1993 with prices ranging from $3,500 to $5,000 (comparable with announced prices and performance of the first Pentium systems).

MIPS remained an independent division of Silicon Graphics after its purchase in 1992. MIPS was a design center which relied on partners to manufacture and sell its products. In late 1993, MIPS's semiconductor partners were Toshiba Electronics, NEC Technologies, Siemens AG, Integrated Device Technologies (IDT), LSI Logic, and Performance Semiconductor. "We want to penetrate the PC market by providing double the performance of the Intel product line at the same price," said Jean-Claude Toma, RISC systems product marketing manager for Toshiba America Electronics Inc. (*PC Week,* June 28, 1993).

MIPS's product line was led by the powerful R4400[32] microprocessor, which provided integer performance, the usual benchmark for desktop PCs, that was approximately equal to the Pentium. However, the R4400 nearly doubled the floating point performance (an important performance metric for computing intensive applications like those run on workstations) of a Pentium processor. MIPS also announced plans to bring out a low-power version of its R4000 series, the R4200. Drawing just 1.5 watts of power (as compared with Pentium's 15 watts), the R4200 was projected to be the first processor capable of running Windows NT on a portable computer.

MIPS was also sharing design work with its manufacturing partners. Two of MIPS's partners, NEC and IDT, were working on in-house lines of low-cost, high-performance processors based on MIPS technology. Additionally, in June 1993, MIPS announced a joint development project for its next-generation design dubbed the T5. MIPS and its six partners would be contributing $150 million to develop the chip, which was expected to be completed in late 1994 or early 1995. MIPS claimed that T4 would offer roughly three times the performance of Pentium.

Alpha. Digital Equipment Corp. (DEC) also sponsored a strong Pentium competitor. Its Alpha 21064 processor, introduced in late 1992 as the first example of Alpha architecture, was currently the most powerful processor in existence. Having initially introduced Alpha in its workstation product line, DEC eventually planned to base its entire product line (mainframes, minicomputers, workstations, and desktop PCs) on the Alpha architecture. Of particular importance to DEC was the transition of its VAX product line, the world's leading minicomputers (and DEC's traditional core product), to Alpha processors.

DEC's Personal Computer Business Unit, which was in the process of mounting a large thrust to make DEC a major player in the PC business, announced that it planned to continue to offer Intel-based PCs as its primary product line.[33] Desktops and servers based on Alpha and Pentium processors and running Windows NT would be added at the top of the line in early 1994. Systems based on Alpha processors were expected to start around $7,000.

DEC also sought to position Alpha for use by other systems manufacturers. In early 1993, it announced that it had licensed Mitsubishi as a second source for its Alpha processors. DEC would be the sole producer of Alpha until late 1994, when Mitsubishi would begin production on its next-generation manufacturing process.

PowerPC. In the early summer of 1993 IBM, Motorola, and Apple announced the PowerPC 601, the first microprocessor to emerge from their joint venture, formed three years earlier. The 601 was advertised to provide comparable or superior performance to Pentium for less than half of the price.[34] On the day after the 601's announcement, Intel stock fell $5.25 to $87.38 per share. See Exhibits 12 and 13 for a comparison of the R4400, Pentium, and other leading microprocessors.

Having cost the partners nearly $1 billion, the PowerPC development program was lauded by many industry analysts as a very well managed joint venture. The PowerPC 601 remained on schedule

[32]R4400, R4000, and R4200 are trademarks of Silicon Graphics, Inc.

[33]DEC ranked ninth in microcomputer sales in 1992.

[34]It was rated by several industry publications as having comparable integer performance and approximately 50 percent better floating-point performance.

EXHIBIT 12 Comparison of Leading Microprocessors

	PowerPC 601 (IBM)	486DX2 (Intel)	Pentium (Intel)	R4000SC (MIPS)	R4400SC (MIPS)	SuperSPARC (SUN)	Alpha 21064 (DEC)	PA7100 (H-P)
Clock rate	66MHz	66MHz	66MHz	100MHz	150MHz	50MHz	150MHz	99MHz
SPECint92*	>60	32.2	64.5	61.7	88 (est.)	65.2	84.4	80.0
SPECfp92	>80	16.1	56.9	63.4	97 (est.)	83.0	127.7	150.6
Die area** (square mm)	121	81	294	184	184	256	234	196
Transistors (millions)	2.8	1.2	3.1	1.35	2.2	3.1	1.7	0.85
Process size***	0.65 micron	0.8 micron	0.8 micron	0.8 micron	0.6 micron	0.7 micron	0.75 micron	0.75 micron
Price	<$470	$542	$995	$640	$1120	$1199	$1096	N/A
Production	3Q93	Now	2Q93	Now	3Q93	Now	Now	Now

*SPECint92 and SPECfp92 are performance comparisons obtained by measuring the time required to complete a set of software routines, called benchmarks. These benchmarks are created and maintained by an independent testing organization. SPECint measures processor performance when executing integer calculations (the most common basic instructions in most desktop PC applications programs). SPECfp measures processor performance in executing floating point calculations which are necessary for many advanced applications found in workstations (such as 3D graphics and modeling).

**Die area is an important determinant of manufacturing cost. A larger die leads to fewer working parts from each silicon wafer processed, and therefore higher manufacturing cost per yielded processor.

***Process size refers to the smallest width of a feature that a semiconductor fabrication process is capable of producing. In 1993, 0.6-micron processes were considered to be state of the art.

SOURCE: *Microprocessor Report,* May 10, 1993.

and delivered impressive performance. The Somerset design center, which housed over 300 engineers from the three companies, was recognized as a world-class R&D center. PowerPC's manufacturing capabilities were also considered to be world-class, with both IBM and Motorola serving as foundries for various parts of the PowerPC product line. Initially, IBM would be the only producer of the 601 because it was designed in conjunction with a proprietary IBM manufacturing process. Motorola announced that it would come online with several follow-on products in 1994. Motorola planned a full line of PowerPC processors for applications ranging from microcontrollers to workstations to powerful servers.

Both Apple Computer and IBM committed to bring out systems based on PowerPC. From the beginning, Apple announced that it would transition its entire Macintosh product line from Motorola's 68K[35] microprocessor architecture to PowerPC. Apple expected to finish porting its Macintosh System 7[36] operating system to PowerPC by early 1994. The first PowerPC based Macintoshes would be released at that time. Initially, only Apple's highest performance Macs would be based on PowerPC. However, by 1996, PowerPC was expected to support the majority of the Macintosh product line. PowerPC Macs would be able to run any existing Macintosh application via emulation software (to convert from Motorola 68K instructions to PowerPC instructions). However, to truly take advantage of the superior performance of PowerPC, ISVs could recompile their applications to execute PowerPC instructions directly.[37] Over the summer, several of the largest Macintosh ISVs, including Microsoft, had publicly committed to port their Mac applications to Macintoshes running on PowerPC. PowerPC Macs were also slated to include DOS and Windows 3.1 emulation software. Developed from technology licensed directly from Microsoft by Insignia Solutions, Inc., the emulation software was claimed to allow PowerPC Macs to run any DOS or Windows 3.1 application as fast as an average Intel 486-based PC running Windows 3.1.

While IBM did not commit to move its PC product line away from the Intel architecture, it had big plans for PowerPC as well. IBM's first PowerPC systems were released in September. These first systems were high-performance technical workstations running IBM's AIX operating system (a version of UNIX). Because IBM's workstation products, and AIX, were based on the RS/6000 architecture, from

[35]This architecture originated with the Motorola 68000.

[36]Macintosh and System 7 are trademarks of Apple Computer.

[37]This is called native code.

EXHIBIT 13 Comparing Power PC with Pentium (from *MacWeek*, 9/20/93)

Microprocessor	Die Area (square inches)	Power Supply (volts)	Power Dissipation (watts)	Available Dies per Wafer* (8 in. wafer)
Pentium 1 (1993)	.416	5.0	14.0	114
Pentium 2 (1994)	.235	3.3	6.5	203
PPC 601 (1993)	.185	3.6	8.5	258
PPC 604 (1994)	.128	3.3	6.0	373

*Available dies per wafer indicates the number of dies of each processor which will fit on an 8" wafer. Fewer working processors will actually be obtained. Typical yields for a microprocessor are estimated by industry analysts to be as low as 20% for a new processor and as high as 95% for a mature semiconductor product.

SOURCE: Hambrecht and Quist.

which the PowerPC had been derived, few changes were needed to integrate PowerPC systems into this product line. IBM also announced its intention to use PowerPC as the basis for systems ranging from powerful, massively parallel supercomputers, to minicomputers, to workstations, to desktop PCs, to hand-held computers and consumer devices. At the time of the PowerPC launch, the IBM PC Company announced its intention to continue to manufacture systems based on the Intel architecture.

In addition to their individual efforts to develop software for PowerPC, IBM, Apple, and Motorola were also working together on the next-generation operating systems slated for PowerPC. PowerOpen was the name of a joint development effort by the three companies to unite UNIX and the Macintosh into a single operating system. Applications written for either AIX or System 7 would run without emulation on a PowerPC-based machine running PowerOpen. By the beginning of 1994, Apple was scheduled to deliver the Macintosh Applications Services tool kit. This kit would allow Macintosh applications to run on top of AIX via emulation. The schedule for the next step, which was to fully integrate the two operating systems into PowerOpen, was not clear.

The PowerOpen foundation, founded in 1991, was located in Burlington, Massachusetts. The mission for the foundation's staff of 12 was to establish a series of operating system standards and support operating system compliance for the PowerPC architecture. Any operating system vendor that implemented the PowerOpen standard would be able to run any PowerOpen application. The organization consisted of five founding sponsors (IBM, Apple, Motorola, Harris, and Groupe Bull) and two companies listed as principals (Thompson CSF and Tadpole Technologies). PowerOpen also listed 125 system vendors, applications developers, and academics as associate members. Both Harris and Groupe Bull planned to offer PowerOpen-compliant operating systems geared for servers and workstations.

Macintosh. In addition to Apple's involvement with the PowerPC and PowerOpen, Apple was taking additional steps toward redefining its business model. In June, Apple's Macintosh System Software Division, the group responsible for the Macintosh operating system, changed its name to AppleSoft and announced plans to license Macintosh System 7 (the current version) openly to systems vendors using either the PowerPC or Intel architecture. The PowerPC native version of System 7 was expected to be ready in early 1994. AppleSoft did not specify when System 7 for the Intel architecture would be available. In addition, AppleSoft confirmed that it would deliver the same Macintosh Applications Services tool kit it was preparing for PowerOpen to other UNIX operating system vendors. By the first quarter of 1994, Sun Microsystems' SOLARIS,

Hewlett-Packard's HP/UX,[38] and other popular versions of UNIX would be able to run applications written for the Macintosh.[39]

Intel Architecture Labs

While developing the 1990 strategic long-range plan, Intel managers saw a problem. While Intel's microprocessors had steadily increased in sophistication and performance, the system architecture Intel's customers were using had changed little in nearly a decade. "It was like we were putting a Ferrari engine in a Volkswagen," said one Intel manager. "We realized that we had to take more of a leadership position in the industry. Originally, IBM and other OEMs had set system design standards. With OEMs under extreme pressure to cut costs, most aren't thinking about this—they are focused on executing today to survive. Only a handful of OEMs have the ability to do research on next generation system architectures," he continued.

To address this problem, Intel Architecture Labs was formed by bringing together several small research departments from the product groups. IAL's first goal was to bring new technology into the systems around Intel microprocessors, ensuring Intel based PCs would remain competitive with other platforms such as Apple's Macintosh. The second goal was to chart the path of future technologies related to the PC and help eliminate roadblocks to the development of leading edge applications for the PC. IAL developed and maintained a series of industry roadmaps for microprocessors, supporting chip sets, operating system software, and application software. IAL was composed of both hardware and software researchers. "Most people don't realize Intel employs over 1,000 software engineers. That would make us the 10th largest PC software house if they were broken out," notes Richard Wirt, an IAL manager. "Increasingly our focus is on providing basic software technology that allows operating systems and applications to take advantage of leading edge microprocessor capabilities."

From 1990 to 1993, IAL proposed a series of basic hardware and software enhancements to the PC architecture. Three of these are described below as illustrations of IAL's activities.

PCI

By 1990, the use of popular graphics programs (including Windows) had increased the level of graphics performance needed for a desktop PC. The number of characters or pixels displayed on a screen had gone from 2,000 to 800,000 as computer graphics began to approach video quality. This meant that much more information needed to flow between the CPU and the display controller. This information flowed over the computer's bus, the electronic connection between the CPU and other system components. 386 and 486 CPUs had more than enough power for the graphics. However, the speed of the bus hadn't changed in 10 years. It was becoming a bottleneck because it was tied up with graphics and slowed down everything else. In response, IAL developed the PCI (peripheral components interconnect) bus which was being offered by Intel as a PC industry standard. "The PCI bus was developed to anticipate the needs of the next four to five generations of PCs because it allows the infrastructure of the PC platform to scale with future CPU generations," notes Gerry Holzhammer, a researcher in IAL who worked on PCI. "We developed PCI technology, and are giving it to the industry. While PCI as an architecture does not directly generate significant revenue for Intel, it is an important enabler for Intel's next-generation high-performance CPUs."

Some OEMs were reluctant to adopt PCI and other Intel system enhancements because it decreased their ability to differentiate their systems through proprietary graphics designs. "This was an initial reaction for some, but it hasn't been much of an issue as we've proven that this is the right technology for the future," notes one IAL manager.

Traditional Intel-based PC OEMs weren't the only ones interested in PCI. In July 1993, Apple Computer announced that it would adopt PCI for its second-generation PowerPC-based Macintoshes. In addition, DEC announced plans to offer a version of its Alpha RISC microprocessor with PCI functionality built into the microprocessor. Adopting PCI would

---

[38]HP/UX is a trademark of Hewlett-Packard Corp.

[39]Any Macintosh application written to run on a Motorola 68K processor would run on the UNIX machines via software emulation. Emulation usually leads to a significant decrease in application performance. However, the UNIX applications performed as well or better than when running on a Macintosh, because the UNIX machines were typically high-powered engineering workstations with much more processing power than an average Macintosh.

allow both Apple and DEC computers to use any peripheral cards built to the PCI specifications.[40]

INDEO™ Video

"Intel sees beauty in the PC like a cobbler sees beauty in shoes—it's the device that makes the company what it is. Our objective is always to increase the demand for PCs," explained Claude Leglise, marketing manager for Intel's Indeo video technology. "In the early 1980s the PC replaced two things—the Selectric (electric typewriter) and the HP35 (electronic calculator). Those two applications—word processing and spreadsheets—still overwhelmingly dwarf other uses of PCs. My group is helping evangelize the next addition to PC functionality, video. Our vision is to turn the PC into a communications device. Last year people bought 40 million PCs and 85 million TVs. We want to expand the market for PCs and we want to drive demand for more advanced Intel chips such as the Pentium processor and the P6. Several IAL technology thrusts are coming from this vision, including IAL's work on TAPI[41] and Indeo technology."

Digital Video requires a large amount of computing power. Traditionally, for a PC to run video, expensive add-in boards were needed with specialized hardware to decompress and display video. Indeo video software enabled PCs based on Intel486 or Pentium processors to decompress and display video without additional hardware. After being developed within IAL, Indeo video was incorporated into Microsoft's Video for Windows application and was offered to ISVs for incorporation into software for Intel-based PCs.

Intel actively evangelized Indeo video to the industry. It charged no licensing fee for the basic technology, in order to get new functions into the PC and to encourage new software to take advantage of it. "We are putting in place the building blocks to make the industry better," Leglise continues.

> Our model for application enhancement is to provide a product which works with some level of functionality on the existing installed base. That way people can get a taste of the new application without buying a new machine. However, more powerful machines provide better performance and people buy bigger machines (which incorporate more advanced Intel CPUs). For example, Indeo software works on any 486. However, you get a much larger video frame and more frames per second with a 486DX50 than you do with a 486SX25 (the lowest performance 486), and it gets even nicer with a Pentium processor.

Intel evangelized these technologies to the general software community in two ways. It was promoted jointly with partners such as Microsoft, by including it in industry standard software such as Microsoft's Video for Windows. SSTM (Strategic Software Technology Management), a group within Intel's sales organization which maintained ongoing relationships with the top 20 to 25 ISVs, also promoted the technology to key software developers.

"Providing this functionality straight off of the CPU is an ongoing technology trend," notes an IAL manager. "Usually, when new functions are introduced they require special hardware to assist the CPU. Five years ago optical character recognition required special parallel processing computers. Now, that can be done on a single processor. Also, don't forget about math coprocessors. Originally, they were extra components. Now they have been absorbed by the CPU. The same thing is happening with video. Cutting out that extra hardware makes the system less expensive and the applications easier to sell and use."

Pentium Compilers Project

In the early stages of the Pentium design process, MPG managers realized that few software applications were taking advantage of advanced features built into the 486 and planned for the Pentium, to speed up software performance. The 486 and Pentium maintained strict software compatibility with all previous Intel architecture microprocessors. However, new features were introduced which improved performance over the previous generations. Therefore, code written for the 286 worked perfectly well on a 486, but was slower than it could be. Part of the problem was caused by compilers which hadn't been updated to take advantage the new features (see the Appendix).

---

[40]A peripheral card, such as a modem or a LAN adapter card, must conform to the bus specification. The bus spec defines how the peripheral communicates with the system's microprocessor. In the past most competing system architectures used different bus specifications; therefore, peripheral cards for a Macintosh wouldn't work in a PC based on an Intel processor.

[41]Telephone API—a software interface between telephones and PBX systems to allow the PC to interact with the office phone system to take advantage of advanced features such as caller ID and conferencing.

Richard Wirt, leader of the compiler project, explains:

> One way the RISC architectures got performance improvements was by creating highly optimized compilers for their new architectures. In a performance-conscious applications environment a compiler can make a big difference. Using the compilers we have developed, we can improve the performance of an application by about 30 percent. That 30 percent improvement cost me $2 million to $3 million; it would cost the MPG guys a lot more to get that much of a boost.
>
> Beginning in 1990, we assembled an elite team of specialized software engineers to address this issue. Now we probably have one of the best compiler technology centers in the world. You have to remember that the compiler industry is fairly small and the people we have here represent some of the best minds in the world. After we developed the technology, we worked with all of the leading PC compiler companies to incorporate it into their products. The royalty for the license is nominal because the technology is key to our most advanced processors. We are already well underway with compiler development for the P6.

Conclusion

A man and a woman sat talking as the sun set outside the window of her 15th floor Manhattan office. "Listen," the woman, a seasoned financial analyst, said to her colleague, who had recently joined the firm (after graduating from a well-known West Coast business school).

> It's time to take another look at Intel. We have a strong buy recommendation on them, and our clients made a lot of money on those guys last year. Their stock doubled, they became the world's largest semiconductor company, and they're one of the most profitable companies in the information processing industry. But I'm wondering about what's in store for the next few years. With so much riding on their microprocessor franchise, and the increasing investments needed to stay ahead, what will these new competitors do to Intel's market position and profit prospects? There seem to be a lot of things going on in the industry right now, but nobody here has a good overall picture of what's going to shape the industry over the next 5 to 10 years. So, your first assignment is to prepare a recommendation evaluating Intel's strategies and prospects for the future. You took that class on corporate strategy in high-tech industries. Maybe it'll come in handy. What should Intel be doing right now, and what do you think of their growth prospects? Should we be buying their stock? Well, I've got to go. Everyone here will be looking forward to your evaluation and recommendations on Monday. Have a good weekend!

Her colleague sat back, looked at his cold cup of coffee . . .

APPENDIX: NOTE ON OPERATING SYSTEMS AND APPLICATIONS DEVELOPMENT

Independent Software Vendors (ISVs) such as Lotus Development, WordPerfect, Borland, and Microsoft write applications programs (word processors, spreadsheets, computer-aided design tools, etc.) which make PCs useful. In its most primitive form, an applications software program is a series of codes which signify specific operations that a microprocessor will carry out. A certain sequence of 1s and 0s specifies the operation or instruction desired. Each microprocessor architecture has a unique set of operations and a unique translation (different codes for each operation).

Most of a typical application is written in a high-level programming language such as C. A compiler then translates the program lines into binary code which runs with a specific operating system on a specific microprocessor architecture. Versions of popular programming languages exist for nearly every operating system. However, each microprocessor architecture has a unique structure. Commands can be structured in certain ways to take advantage of the microprocessor's design. An ISV can utilize these features to improve the performance of the program. The application then becomes tailored to the microprocessor and becomes difficult to transfer to a new processor. A program which is not written to take advantage of these features is called portable code. Portable code is usually somewhat slower. Therefore, a programmer can often trade off the ease of porting an application to multiple operating systems and microprocessors with the performance of a program. As one software manager explains: "A lot of times you see an ISV tailor one version of an application closely to its highest volume architecture and have a second, portable version, which is ported to other platforms."

The applications program must also be tested thoroughly before it can be sold. This is a complex process of feeding large combinations of inputs into the program to ensure that it works properly.

Testing can take up to 50 percent of the time involved in developing the application. Testing and post-release support often represent 30 to 50 percent of the ISV's product cost.

Emulation

Software which is written for a particular environment (microprocessor and operating system) can be made to run on a computer based on a different processor or OS. A software layer can be created to mimic the environment that the original program is written to run in. This software layer is called emulation software. Sun's WABI and Insignia's SoftPC are examples of emulation packages. Because of the extra processing required to mimic a different environment, an application runs slower in emulation than on its native architecture. The difference in performance of emulation environments varied widely. However, most emulators ran software 30 to 50 percent slower than on a native environment.

Case II–16
Allegheny Ludlum Steel (Abridged)

David A. Garvin

Richard (Dick) P. Simmons, CEO of Allegheny Ludlum Steel Corporation, summarized his business philosophy:

> Running a business is like life: it's a series of screw-ups. If you can identify them, prioritize them, and attack them quickly, you can then go on and be creative and innovative. That way, you are not devoting a massive portion of the company's efforts to just fixing things—generally, long after they should have been fixed.

Between 1980 and 1984, despite a prolonged recession, heavy increases in imports, and a very strong dollar, Allegheny averaged an annual return on investment of over 15 percent, making it the most consistently profitable domestic competitor in the specialty steel industry.

Even though Allegheny's stainless business had grown 4 to 5 percent annually while many competitors went bankrupt or ran large losses, it was rapidly losing share in its other business, silicon steel. Silicon imports had risen 400 percent during 1984; today they accounted for 30 percent of the market. Because silicon steels were less protected by tariffs and quotas than other steel products, foreign producers were expected to shift further attention to this area. Now, in June 1985, Allegheny had to make a choice. It could milk silicon as a cash cow, meet the Japanese threat head-on, or get out of the silicon business altogether. The context was dynamic: Allegheny might or might not achieve the needed breakthrough in its own silicon research; Armco, its major domestic competitor in silicon, was in serious financial trouble; and import quotas were under discussion. At the same time, Allegheny would soon need more stainless steel capacity. The least expensive option for stainless capacity was to convert some silicon capacity to stainless. Simmons recognized that the timing of the decision was as critical as the decision itself:

> What we're trying to do is keep our options open as long as possible. So you start with Simmons's management rule Number 1: don't make a decision before you have to make it, but then don't make it after you should have made it. There is an appropriate time at which a strategic decision has to be made, and that's what people like me get paid to do.

In the 1980s domestic producers of carbon steel, which accounted for 98 percent of U.S. steel tonnage and 90 percent of sales dollars, were besieged by imports and fighting for survival. Specialty steel producers were not in such dire straits, although they too were being hurt by imports. Specialty steels included stainless, grain-oriented silicon, and tool steels, as well as special alloys used in high-technology applications. Stainless steels, which accounted for 90 percent of the specialty market (exclusive of silicon), were growing at 4 percent per year. Total domestic production of stainless steel was around 1.2 million tons, and the average selling price per ton was approximately $2,500, compared with $350 to $400 for carbon steel. High-end silicon steels, which were used in electrical applications where minimizing energy loss was essential, competed in a market that had shrunk 40 percent—to 260,000 tons—in the last 10 years.

EXHIBIT 1 Organization Chart

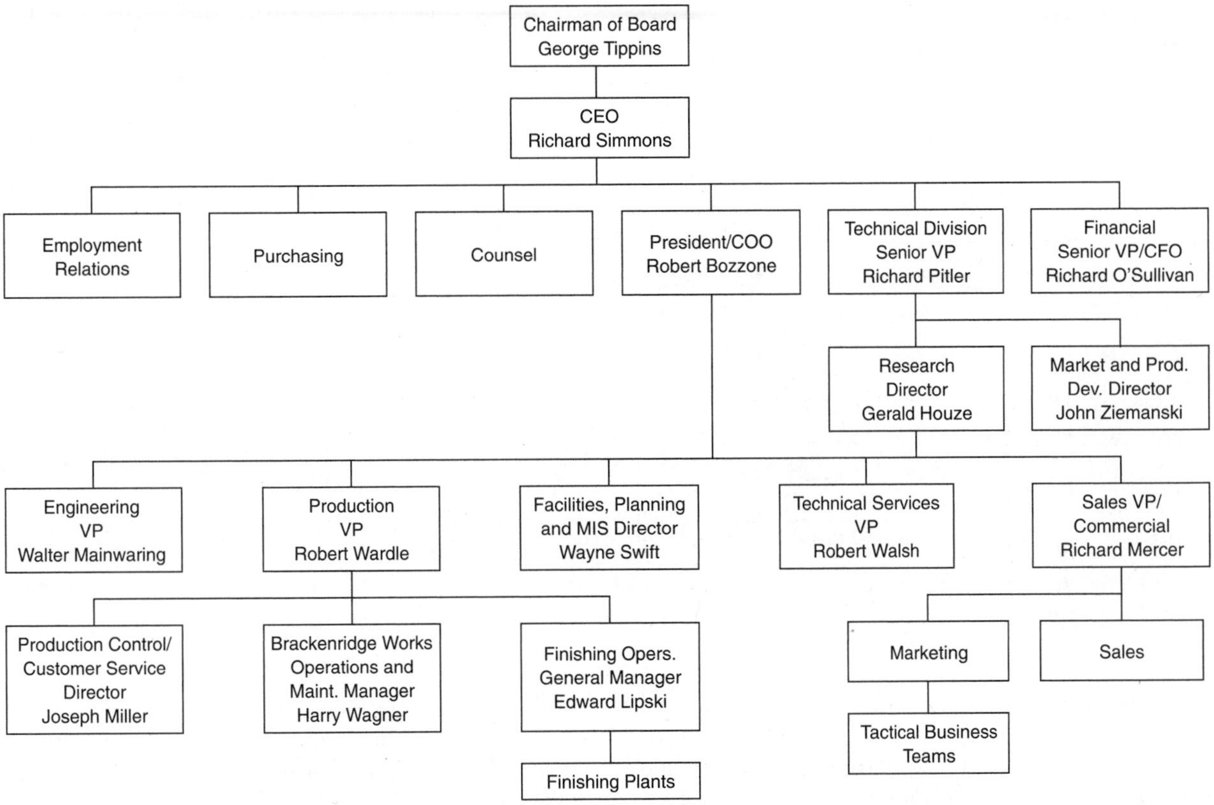

- Chairman of Board
George Tippins
  - CEO
Richard Simmons
    - Employment Relations
    - Purchasing
    - Counsel
    - President/COO
Robert Bozzone
      - Engineering VP
Walter Mainwaring
      - Production VP
Robert Wardle
        - Production Control/ Customer Service Director
Joseph Miller
        - Brackenridge Works Operations and Maint. Manager
Harry Wagner
        - Finishing Opers. General Manager
Edward Lipski
          - Finishing Plants
      - Facilities, Planning and MIS Director
Wayne Swift
      - Technical Services VP
Robert Walsh
      - Sales VP/ Commercial
Richard Mercer
        - Marketing
          - Tactical Business Teams
        - Sales
    - Technical Division Senior VP
Richard Pitler
      - Research Director
Gerald Houze
      - Market and Prod. Dev. Director
John Ziemanski
    - Financial Senior VP/CFO
Richard O'Sullivan

The Company

Background

In 1980 Dick Simmons and George Tippins, a Pittsburgh industrialist, headed a group of 17 managers that bought Allegheny Ludlum from Allegheny International for $195 million plus the assumption of $28 million in debt. Tippins, who bought 80 percent of the stock, became chairman, while Simmons remained as president and became CEO. In the spring of 1985, Robert (Bob) Bozzone, then executive vice president and chief operating officer, became president (see Exhibit 1).

Allegheny was the largest specialty steel producer in the country. Two-thirds of its 1984 sales of $764 million came from stainless and other high-tech alloys, the rest from silicon. All of its products were flat-rolled into coils. It considered two-thirds of its stainless tonnage to be commodity products: steels produced in standard grades, widths, and thicknesses, sold primarily on price to multiple customers.[1]

Customized versus Standard Products

Standard products lacked differentiation; many vendors had to meet identical specifications, or multiple customers bought the same product. Standard products were usually produced and sold in high volume, faced numerous competitors, and increasingly were sold through distribution centers at a price set by the market. Typical products included sheet used for milk trucks or strip used for consumer appliances.

[1]Allegheny Ludlum distinguished its two major product groups by the terms *commodity* and *specialty*. To avoid the confusion of discussing "specialty specialty steel" and "commodity specialty steel," the word *customized* is used here to indicate those specialty products tailored to customers' needs, and *standard* to indicate generic products bought by multiple customers and/or for multiple applications.

EXHIBIT 2 Flow Diagram of Primary End Processing Paths

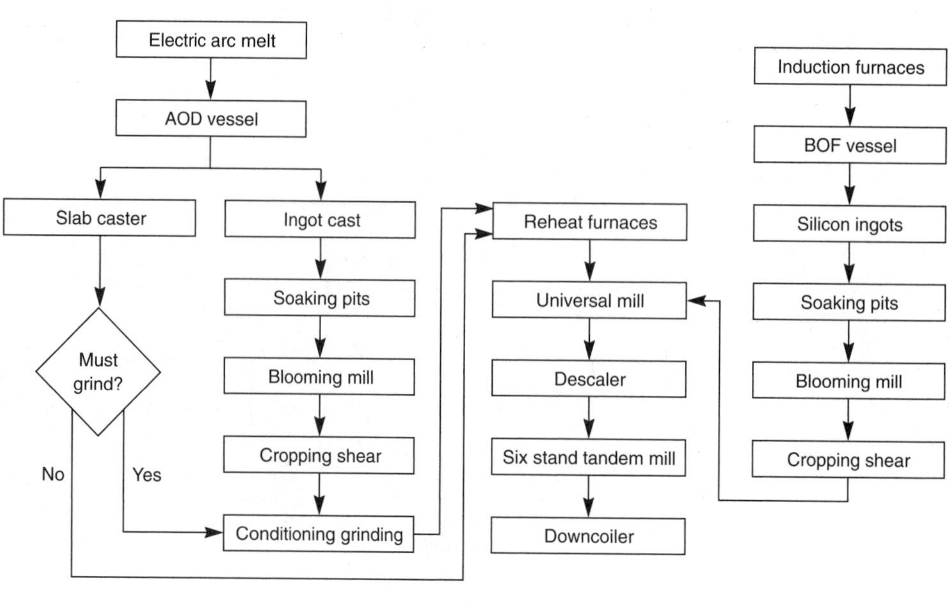

Customized products, by contrast, were tailored for direct customers by alloy, grade, size, finish, or other required property. Applications were specific and demanding, such as drawing 10″ deep to form a cooking pot or drawing to .002 inch to form a hypodermic needle. Customers often received extensive technical assistance from Allegheny on how to make the steel work well on their equipment. Profit margins on these products were higher than for standard products, either because the products were proprietary or because there were only one or two competitors.

Much of the time, customized and commodity products went through the melting, casting, and hot rolling processes no differently, and only took on their distinct identities later during the cold rolling and finishing operations (see Exhibit 2). The number and types of finishing steps—which rolling mills and annealing and pickling lines the steel passed through—took products down to a certain thickness or gauge, imparted certain properties critical to the application, or gave the products a certain edge or finish. Commodity grade 304, for example, required six steps after the hot strip mill; a more customized grade, 921, required 35 steps. In some cases, a product began to be customized as early as the Melt Shop. For example, grade 201 piston rings had a limit on the number of oxygen blows that could be used to correct temperatures during the melt. If the melter violated this limit, Technical Services downgraded the heat and it would be used for some other, less demanding application. Melters did more planning for such heats, making sure nothing would cause a delay and make the heat go cold.

Competition

Allegheny's domestic competitors were of three types: specialty steel divisions of larger carbon steel companies that made standard products, usually in a limited number of grades; smaller, free-standing companies that made either custom or standard products, but rarely both; and rerollers, who imparted finishing steps to semifinished steel. The larger, integrated producers were not well suited to making custom products; they did little R&D, and none was set up to offer extensive technical support. Unlike Allegheny, they were prone to initiating price cuts. The smaller, nonintegrated producers—whether of standard or custom products—had to buy their slabs or hot-roll bands (the semifinished coils of steel that came off the hot strip mill). That increased costs, as did finishing equipment that was less economically sized than Allegheny's. Small size was an advantage, however, in providing prompt delivery and reliable customer service.

The ability to react quickly to customers and/or to fill small orders was also a strength of rerollers; they inventoried certain grades and sizes that they could then finish, slit, and ship, sometimes converting commodity to custom products. The need for quick responsiveness and also for technical support had so far kept foreign producers out of most customized products (except for silicon steel). Imports were sold primarily to steel service centers which competed on price and delivery responsiveness.

Strategy

Allegheny's strategy was to be the low-cost producer of stainless steel commodities, and at the same time to pursue new niches for customized products. The links between the two were multiple and dynamic. Commodities carried part of the overhead of the company's high-volume facilities, allowing Allegheny to make custom steels in larger volume and at lower cost than its competitors. This meant that Allegheny's primary end delivered a low-cost, hot-roll band—whether then finished as a standard or custom product—at a cost no small competitor could match. The price premium commanded by Allegheny's custom products also supported the company's extensive research, market development, and technical services. These activities in turn developed new products and processes and reduced manufacturing costs through continued process improvements.

Support of low-cost production. Because raw materials accounted for up to 80 percent of variable costs for commodities, low-cost production required good contracts on alloys and other materials. Such savings benefited customized products as well. Low-cost production was also supported by an extremely rigorous standard cost accounting system, a low-cost routing system, and a system of objectives established annually by the managers themselves. Such efforts had increased net tons of steel per employee by almost 40 percent between 1979 and mid-1985.

Primary End

Melting and refining steel involved one of two routes at Allegheny. Most stainless was melted in an electric arc furnace (EAF) and then refined in an argon oxygen furnace (AOD); all silicon was melted in a coreless induction furnace and then refined in a basic oxygen furnace (BOF).

Stainless

From the AOD, over 90 percent of the melts went directly to the continuous caster, which cast slabs directly from the molten metal. Slabs were 8 inches thick, and weighed 10 to 15 tons. The concaster eliminated many of the steps associated with ingots, and had much lower yield losses. The surfaces of some directly cast slabs were so good they did not have to be conditioned on grinders.

Some stainless melts were teemed into ingot molds, cooled, stripped from the molds, heated in a soaking pit furnace, shaped by the blooming mill into large rectangular slabs, and their outer surface removed in slab conditioning. The ingot route was used for those melts that could not be concast, or when Brackenridge melting or casting was full.

Whether concast or ingot, a slab had to be reheated up to 2,300°F and prepared for the hot strip mill where powerful electronically controlled rollers reduced the thickness of the metal while improving its properties. The Universal Mill took the slab to a 1-inch thickness in five passes, while the Tandem Mill took it to a gauge of .080 to .300 inches. The slab had now become a hot-roll band, a flat coil of steel up to 50″ wide, weighing 25,000 pounds. It was rolled into a coil by the downcoiler.

Silicon

From the BOF, all silicon melts were teemed into ingots, and followed the same steps as stainless ingots except that the surface did not have to be conditioned, nor the slab reheated.

Stainless Finishing

Allegheny then finished its bands into sheet, strip, or plate. Sheets were flat-rolled into coils 24 inches or wider, strip less than 24 inches, while plate was at least 3/16″ thick. To make better use of equipment and reduce yield losses, coils could be built-up or welded together to form a 50,000 pound coil.

Before being finished, coils had to be softened and prepared. Annealing, shot blast, and pickling processes were used, the choice depending on the product's chemistry and intended use. The various cold-rolling mills reduced the thickness of the coils through a series of rolling operations to thicknesses as thin as .005 inch thick.

Finishing operations might also include bright anneal lines that protected the steel from oxidation, and other annealing and pickling steps. Slitters cut the steel into narrower widths; much strip, for example, was sold in 1.5- to 2-inch widths. Finished tonnage yield was about 83 percent of the melt tonnage.

Silicon Finishing

Silicon finishing included many steps similar to those for stainless, and special steps to improve its magnetic properties. These included magnesium oxide coating, a tunnel furnace in which grain growth was controlled, and several normalizing processes. Finished tonnage yield was about 50 percent of the melt tonnage.

Support of customized production. Customized production was supported by extensive customer interchange and the broadest technical development effort in the industry. Allegheny spent 2 percent of its sales dollars on research (about 10 times what its stainless competitors spent), and another 2 percent on technology, including equipment computerization, software programs, and process control. Its market development group obtained market intelligence; competitors either did not do this at all, or did it much less deliberately. And its technical services group worked closely with customers to create a match between their manufacturing processes and Allegheny's steels, while also providing metallurgical assistance to Allegheny's own line operators.

Organization

The Plant System

Most stainless was melted at the Brackenridge plant, and all silicon at nearby Natrona (see Exhibit 3). Brackenridge housed the continuous caster and the hot strip mill, which meant that silicon went to Brackenridge for hot rolling before being finished at Bagdad. Brackenridge produced hot-roll stainless bands for the four stainless finishing plants. Products were normally assigned to particular plants, although there was frequent overlap. Because the routing system aimed to maximize margins by minimizing costs, different capacity and product mix conditions led to different assignments.

Functions

Direct reporting to Simmons and Bozzone was divided by function (see Exhibit 1). In addition to the usual functions and activities, such as sales, engineering, and operations, the Technical Division, Technical Services, and the tactical business teams were of particular note.

The Technical Division

Headed by Richard (Dick) Pitler, the Technical Division encompassed both Research and Market and Product Development.

Research. About 20 percent of Research's work supported sales or manufacturing, 60 percent went toward new products or process improvements, and 20 percent was high-risk experiments. The division had its own melt shop where it could make small melts of new alloys; it also took steel off the plant floor to cut apart and examine. Multiple laboratories carried out work in heat treating, magnetic testing, electron optics, x-ray diffraction, corrosion testing, mechanical testing, and other areas.

Process improvements were often sought through physical and/or mathematical models. A model of the continuous caster, for example, used water, whose viscosity was similar to that of molten steel, to understand flow rates, eddies, traps and patterns in the caster's internal currents created by the submerged entry nozzle. As a result, several new nozzle designs were developed, each tailored to a particular grade of specialty steel, to get the right temperature distribution and flow.

Market and Product Development. This group of five had spent their working lives in the company; each combined a background in engineering, research, and some other functional field. Organized along major customer-industry lines, members spent 60 percent of their time on the road, introducing new Allegheny materials and making sure they were used properly. The group's director, John Ziemanski, noted: "Our ability to get in and talk to engineers early on gives us a leg up in anticipating market needs."

EXHIBIT 3 Allegheny's Plant System

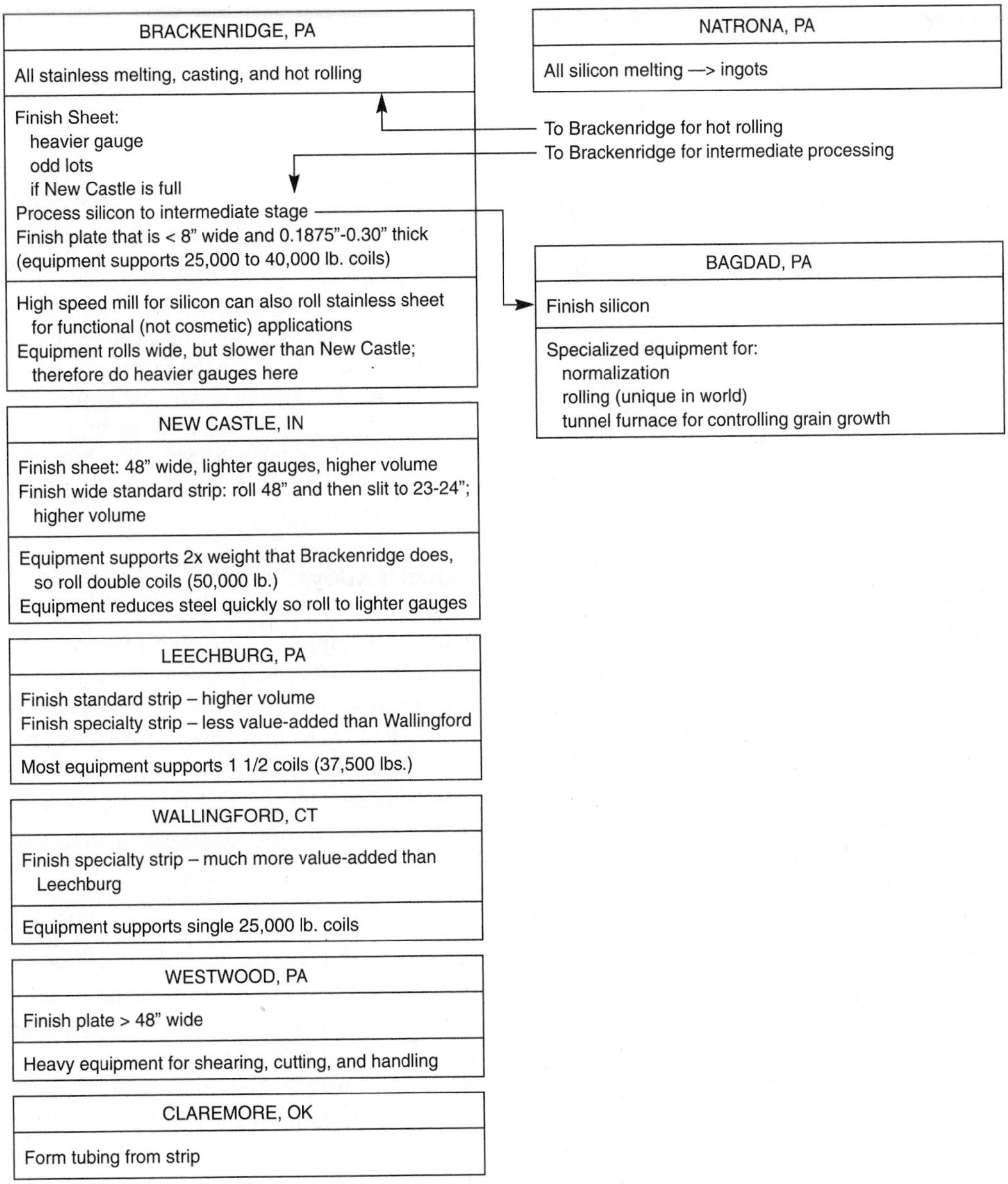

BRACKENRIDGE, PA
All stainless melting, casting, and hot rolling
Finish Sheet: heavier gauge odd lots if New Castle is full Process silicon to intermediate stage → (to Bagdad, PA: Finish silicon) Finish plate that is < 8" wide and 0.1875"-0.30" thick (equipment supports 25,000 to 40,000 lb. coils)
High speed mill for silicon can also roll stainless sheet for functional (not cosmetic) applications Equipment rolls wide, but slower than New Castle; therefore do heavier gauges here

NATRONA, PA
All silicon melting —> ingots

(From Natrona: To Brackenridge for hot rolling; To Brackenridge for intermediate processing)

BAGDAD, PA
Finish silicon
Specialized equipment for: normalization rolling (unique in world) tunnel furnace for controlling grain growth

NEW CASTLE, IN
Finish sheet: 48" wide, lighter gauges, higher volume Finish wide standard strip: roll 48" and then slit to 23-24"; higher volume
Equipment supports 2x weight that Brackenridge does, so roll double coils (50,000 lb.) Equipment reduces steel quickly so roll to lighter gauges

LEECHBURG, PA
Finish standard strip – higher volume Finish specialty strip – less value-added than Wallingford
Most equipment supports 1 1/2 coils (37,500 lbs.)

WALLINGFORD, CT
Finish specialty strip – much more value-added than Leechburg
Equipment supports single 25,000 lb. coils

WESTWOOD, PA
Finish plate > 48" wide
Heavy equipment for shearing, cutting, and handling

CLAREMORE, OK
Form tubing from strip

Technical Services

Headed by Robert (Bob) Walsh, and with a dotted line relationship to Pitler, Technical Services defined and coordinated the steelmaking process, decided whether a product met customer specifications and whether it would be shipped, and helped customers use existing products. It consisted of three subgroups: product services, metallurgical engineering, and quality assurance.

Product Services. Trained as metallurgists or as tool and die makers, members of this group tried to insure that Allegheny understood exactly what the customer needed, helped customers' operating personnel work with Allegheny materials, and suggested changes either in the customers' equipment and fabrication processes and/or in Allegheny's materials. Charles (Charlie) Rietdyke, a section manager for Technical Services, described the group's role:

> Everything starts with the customer: we must meet its requirements. Our metallurgists can determine if the material is within specifications, but that in itself says nothing about whether the customer can make the part with it. Our tool and die people help close that gap.

Metallurgical Engineering. These plant metallurgists defined the production process that orders would follow, monitored the process in operation, and provided technical assistance to operators on the floor. The parameters established by this group included the chemistry of the process, the number and types of annealing and rolling cycles the steel would go through, the temperatures and pressures at which operations would be run, and sometimes the specific pieces of equipment that could be used, or had to be used, for certain steps. Process definition was dynamic; as Leonard (Len) Greco, formerly of Tech Services and recently named operations manager at Wallingford, put it, "First we make it right, then we learn how to make it cheaply." The customer's intended use of the product was the starting point for defining the alloy and the kind of reductions that would be needed—without restrictions on cost. But because the number of passes in cold rolling affected the properties of the final product, subsequent experimentation included efforts to change the alloy to allow reductions in the number of passes needed, or to reach the same end point with the same alloy with fewer passes. Each was aimed at getting costs out of the product.

The assistance offered by plant metallurgists to line operators took many forms. Victor (Vic) Ardito, general manager of the Melt Shop, described their role:

> If you put somebody in a job where they have to make a decision that can't wait—like our melters, who always have another heat behind them—then they have to do something. If you leave them alone, they will play it safe, and you are always going to lose when they do that. But when our melters have a problem, they not only have round-the-clock telephone numbers to call, they also have the metallurgist there. So our melters end up making intelligent decisions—yes, with a certain amount of risk in them.

Quality Assurance. The third group in Tech Services had ultimate responsibility for deciding what did or did not meet customer requirements, and final say over whether or not a product would be shipped. It also decided which operating unit would be charged for defects. In making such decisions, Reno Giapponi, general supervisor of inspection and physical test at Wallingford (but better known to his colleagues as "God"), noted that: "The key thing is end use: will it make the product?" Deciding what to do in gray areas was often handled by direct customer contact: "This is what we have—can you use it?" QA also coordinated the company's response to customers' orders—within 48 hours for repeat orders, and from three days to three weeks for new orders. When asked whether the competition could respond as quickly, Pitler replied:

> They could be as fast, but they won't be as accurate. Or they'll say they can make anything. Although it sometimes feels as though customers have a memory span of five minutes, we think they come to us because we can do more for them. And, we think it helps our credibility to say, "We cannot give you a reasonable answer within too short a time," or, "No, we can't make this."

Exhaust Alloys

A recent example of the role played by the technical staff was their response to information that Market Development and Technical Services engineers had picked up from their engineering contacts in the auto industry. Domestic automakers wanted to switch to stainless steel for exhaust manifolds, but 30 to 50 percent of conventional 409 grade stainless (used successfully for catalytic converters for a decade) cracked when bent into these pretzel-like forms. Allegheny's engineers sensed a large potential market if a more malleable alloy could be developed. Their informal conversations spurred Bob Walsh to call a meeting of all the key players; in one day, the group pounded out the chemical, metallurgical, and process steps they would use for a high-performance exhaust alloy, called 409HP. Walsh and Pitler skipped the laboratory stage, and went directly to mill experiments on the shop floor, melting five full-scale (100-ton) heats in a week. Walsh recalled, "We got some out to customers for evaluation, and they confirmed our expectations. Now that we knew what 409HP could do, the question was cost and repeatability." By substituting 409HP for a whole week's 409 production, Allegheny got larger volumes out to customers. Thus, within six weeks, the company developed the new alloy, made 2,000 tons, got it out to customers where reject rates dropped to 1 to 3 percent, learned its costs, and defined a repeatable manufacturing process. These efforts were facilitated by Bozzone's and Simmons' familiarity with market and metallurgical issues. Gerald (Gerry) Houze, director of research, noted:

> Simmons and Bozzone had already seen Market Development's presentation, engine by engine, on the potential of this market. They also knew what we were trying to do technically and could make their own assessments. Technical literacy runs throughout the company, and makes it easy to sell a project like this.

Tactical Business Teams (TBTs)

Allegheny divided its products into six groups and delegated operating responsibility for managing these businesses to six tactical business teams. From most commoditylike to most customized, the six were stainless plate, stainless sheet, stainless standard strip, stainless customized strip, silicon, and high-tech alloys. The teams were headed by Marketing, and included the appropriate plant manager and representatives from Technical Services and Production Control. The TBT was held accountable for sales, conversion costs, variances, and the use of working capital and equipment—all measures under its direct control. Objectives were to meet the targeted variable margin dollars (revenues minus variable standard costs plus or minus variances) for the business, gain a good return on controllable assets, and achieve the "critical issues" for the year.

These teams worked on the middle ground between daily operating decisions and larger decisions with strategic impact. Although TBTs were, in Simmons's view, expected "to be the point dog on strategic issues affecting their businesses," members had to go to their functional bosses (or higher, if necessary) on such questions. The same recourse was available if a team member disagreed with the direction his or her team was taking. But this route was rarely taken, for as Reitdyke put it, "We would have to go up one level to resolve it, and that's ridiculous. If we can't settle it when we are so close to it, who else can?" Len Greco concurred:

> Having the team prevents someone from making a decision that doesn't take everything into account. Say Marketing wants to change the coil size for a customer, but that affects our equipment; as a team, we talk about it and see how our choices affect other people, and whether or not we can do it. Or maybe we are running into bottlenecks, so then Production Control can give us another route.

The system of plural management at Allegheny went beyond the TBT structure, however. Bob Walsh described how he viewed his job and that of his colleagues:

> Bob Wardle's [vice president for operations] job is to make a product at the lowest cost that meets customer standards and our objectives in the market. My job is to meet customer standards and our objectives in the market at the lowest cost. I cannot escape responsibility for costs; he cannot escape responsibility for quality and reliability. That's what Dick Simmons wants, and that's what trickles down. In this company's culture, there's no such thing as "*you* failed." Either *we* survive or *we* fail.

Control Systems

Evolution of the Systems

Allegheny's control system and plural management were Dick Simmons's response to the parochialism he had experienced in his first 15 years in the steel industry. Simmons believed functionally organized companies created department- and plant-focused thinking, as well as adversarial relationships so tangible "you could see them, you could taste them, you could smell them—almost like a religious war." When he returned to Allegheny in 1969 as vice president of manufacturing, he found each plant to be "an empire," and a profit center with its own cost system, making it impossible even to directly compare the costs of making the same product in different plants.

Simmons's first step was to turn plants into cost centers, a move that was perceived as being a staff reduction. He recalled: "We didn't just eliminate managers; we designed them out of the system." Next, Simmons instructed the controller to develop a standard direct cost system that allowed the costing of each coil. Some 100,000 standards were built into the database. (A standard was the variable conversion cost of performing an operation on a particular grade, size, and thickness of steel using a particular piece of equipment.) With this information, one could identify and compare the cost of producing the same grade, size, and thickness of steel on different equipment, or the cost of producing different grades, sizes, or thicknesses on the same equipment. This system became the foundation for choosing alternative routes in production scheduling, and for generating weekly (and now daily) variance reports in which variances were converted to dollars. The system reflected Simmons's philosophy:

> If you can measure it, you can manage it. But traditionally, the steel industry has thought in terms of tons. We converted everything to dollars because people bank dollars, live on dollars, and buy food with dollars; I wanted them to run their businesses on dollars too.

Simmons's third major step was to create the tactical business teams to push responsibility for profits below the level of president.

The Cost Accounting System

Standards were developed, and actual costs tracked, for every department, machine, process, grade, width, and gauge of steel. Work was actually tracked to the individual-coil level. By dividing the number of coils produced from a given batch of work, the variance per coil could be obtained and applied to the standard cost to give the actual cost of the coil. This database could be exploded in any way: by grade, by product, by customer, by thickness—in any fashion the TBT believed had value. To Allegheny's knowledge, no other competitor could track its coil costs so precisely.

Standard costs for purchased materials were based on historical experience and expectations of price changes. Standards for productivity and efficiency, by contrast, were based on best past performance, generally referred to as the "Olympic standard." These standards were renegotiated annually between Operations and Accounting. Each year, the company strove to take away most of the favorability by tightening standards; for example, in 1984, $11 million was taken out of the standards. Wardle commented, "If the variance is unfavorable, we ask, 'What are we doing wrong?' If it's favorable, we ask, 'What's wrong with the standard?' " As Allegheny's controller Charles (Chuck) May noted, "To loosen a standard, there has to be a very good reason."

Managing Day-to-Day Production

Managers used reports issued daily, weekly, or monthly to keep close tabs on production, costs, and profit margins. These reports, in turn, provided a barometer of the managers' effectiveness, and were the foundation of the incentive pay system.

Production reports, or "What happened yesterday?" Production managers received daily reports on yesterday's orders, production, and shipments (both planned and actual). Bob Wardle, who had grown up in maintenance and then engineering and who knew every piece of equipment by heart, commented on his use of these reports:

> Because of experience, I can usually go through this 17-page report on seven plants in 15 minutes, and know where to ask questions. When I see something unusual, I ask why and I'm on the phone. By 9:15, no matter what plant I'm at, I've talked to Joe Miller, to Harry Wagner, and to Eddie Lipski. By 9:30, I've talked to Bob Bozzone about what my problems are. Then he talks to Dick [Simmons] who demands to know every morning what happened yesterday. What makes this system work is the accuracy of the data and the speed with which we get it. That allows us to make decisions on the basis of facts—immediately.

Ardito also described how his morning began:

> We start with what happened yesterday. I review the morning report and talk to my supervisors. We put together a story and I talk to Harry by 9 o'clock. Every day he wants to know, "Were there any delays? Why? What are the costs?" It takes time, and sometimes the fellows grumble about having to spend the first hour of their day like this. But the key to keeping variances low is real-time responsiveness.

Efficiency reports. The cost system was also the basis for weekly efficiency reports that converted the four key variances of productivity, utilization, yield, and rejects to dollar values (see Exhibit 4A). These variances were calculated in the following way:

- *Productivity*—net tons per hour compared with standard tons per hour.
- *Utilization*—contact time (amount of time equipment was in contact with the work) divided by turn time (an eight-hour shift).
- *Yield*—tons of material coming off equipment divided by tons going on.
- *Rejects*—coils scrapped and heats aborted compared with total coils and total heats.

Every department head had to comment each week in writing on the variance report for his or her area. These comments were circulated to all other managers, including Simmons, and were one of the topics at Simmons's weekly meeting with officers. Once a month, TBT leaders joined the group to discuss their products, problems, and opportunities.

Sales and net margin reports. Issued monthly, these reports showed the net contribution margin for each major product category (e.g., chrome

EXHIBIT 4A An Efficiency Report—Weekly Summary

	Productivity				Total Productivity and Yield Variance $		Quality Cost Variance
Location & Department	Tons Produced	Productivity Variance $	Utilization Variance $	Yield Variance $	Week	MTD	MTD
Brackenridge							
#8-3 Melting and slab casting	8,764	$17,000	0	$79,000	$96,000	$87,000	0
#8-7 Natrona							
Induction furnace	5,647	3,000	5,000	(25,000)			
BOF	6,988	0	8,000	0	(9,000)	(9,000)	0
#8-2 Blooming and hot strip mill	16,515	6,000	36,000	42,000	84,000	117,000	11,000
#8-2 Coil buildup	5,454	3,451	(140)	(1,605)	1,706	1,706	0
#10 Conditioning	4,491	6,000	0	12,000	18,000	61,000	0
#3 Alloy finishing	16,126	2,584	(4,679)	24,906	22,811	59,775	15,000
#7-3 Silicon finishing	13,110	(16,635)	(28,826)	(42,360)	(87,821)	(104,115)	0
Primary operations	0	0	0	0	0	0	63,000
Quality costs in hot roll band variance	0	0	0	0	0	0	62,000
Total Brackenridge	77,095	21,400	15,355	88,941	125,696	213,366	151,000
#7 New Castle	14,852	43,279	(5,378)	(9,609)	28,292	58,049	10,000

EXHIBIT 4B A Sales and Net Margin Report (monthly)

				Net Margin			
Product and Grade	Pounds	Sales Dollars	Per Pound	Dollars	Per Pound	(%)	Plan N.M. Per Pound
Sheets: C.R.-CR NI	197,306	$202,265	$1.025	$ 85,418	$0.433	42	0.304
CR NI+	10,002	14,272	1.427	5,749	0.575	40	0.408
CR MN	1,882	1,990	1.057	1,099	0.584	55	0.460
ST CR	7,172	7,118	0.992	1,974	0.275	28	0.292
Low CR	12,544	8,778	0.700	3,410	0.272	39	0.190
Emission control	55,078	34,819	0.632	16,710	0.303	48	0.234
Hot rolled	14,702	9,658	0.657	3,001	0.204	31	0.131
Excess primes	6	4	0.714	0			
Commodity	17,698	16,131	0.911	6,490	0.367	40	0.196
Total stainless sheets	316,390	295,033	0.932	123,850	0.391	42	0.279

Note: These two reports are abbreviated, and are included only to show the kind of information Allegheny collects; they are not intended as the basis of any analysis.

CR = chrome, MN = manganese, NI = nickel, ST CR = straight chrome.

nickel) within major product lines (e.g., sheet) (see Exhibit 4B). They quickly revealed how each product line, and thus each TBT, was doing financially, and identified problems and opportunities. Marketing people took these slender reports on the road and were able to quote prices on the spot.

Margins, ROCI, and incentive pay. These net margin reports, together with a monthly report showing return on capital invested (ROCI), made up the report card for each TBT. ROCI indicated how well managers were using the company's working capital and equipment. (A typical ROCI calculation is shown in Exhibit 5.) Robert (Bob) Rutherford,

EXHIBIT 5 Return on Controllable Capital Invested, 1984 (units in thousands; sheet only)

	Plan		Actual	
	$	Non $	$	Non $
Sales:				
Tons		152,988T.		158,195T.
Dollars	$258,744		$295,033	
Net margin:				
Dollars	79,592		123,850	
As percent of sales		30.8%		42.0%
Operating profit (= net margin − period costs):				
Dollars			71,154	
As percent of sales				24.1%
Asset use:				
Inventory dollars (= raw materials + WIP) (Raw materials allocated by forecasted sales for three mos.) (WIP: each order @ standard cost)		45,800		
Inventory tons (= raw materials + WIP)				60,782T.
Total inventory weeks				14 weeks
Required weeks (# weeks required to produce projected sales volume)				7 weeks
Authorized weeks (# weeks of inventory above required weeks to increase sales via quick delivery)				7 weeks
Excess inventory (# weeks of inventory above authorized weeks)				0 weeks
Accounts receivable:				
Dollars (actual amount outstanding)			31,329	
Number of days outstanding				46.1 days
Net plant and equipment (percent of net book value of each piece of equipment on which products were processed; percent based on projected volume sheet will generate)			42,174	
Total controllable investment			$119,303	
Asset turnover (sales ÷ controllable investment)				2.47
Operating profit (asset turnover × percent operating profit; or, operating profit ÷ controllable investment)				59.6%

head of the TBTs for both standard and specialty strip, commented on his use of the ROCI report: "I'm looking for trends. The key measures for being out of control are days out for receivables and excess inventory weeks."

Margin dollars also counted heavily in calculating incentive pay for the 105 eligible managers. Seventy-five percent of their bonus was based on the company's operating profits and cash flow, the other 25 percent on individual and TBT achievements. This 25 percent was, in turn, divided between meeting margin dollar targets for the product line and achieving critical issues.

Planning and Critical Issues Program

Whereas the cost system reacted to problems, the critical issues program was designed to find opportunities and set priorities for the following year. The program had three levels—goals, critical success factors (CSFs), and critical issues (CIs)—that were redeveloped annually through a process coordinated by Wayne Swift, director of Facilities, Planning, and MIS. Input was also provided by a strategic planning process that identified major threats and opportunities that had to be addressed. Simmons commented:

"This process does not spit out financials. We only want to know from our CFO: Can we finance it? We look only at the best, the worst, and the most probable scenarios."

Simmons, Bozzone, Pitler, and Richard O'Sullivan, the chief financial officer, developed broad annual goals that meshed with the business plan and budget. Within this framework, a broader tier of management, including directors and plant managers, developed critical success factors. These were top priorities for the coming year, specific enough to assign to functions, but leaving open how particular people and departments would work toward realizing an objective; that was the role of critical issues.

Critical issues were task-oriented programs that supported CSFs. They were committed to individually by each of Allegheny's top 105 managers but included hundreds more below them. Because they included quantified objectives and timetables, critical issues were targets against which managers could be measured. Three times a year, at a meeting with the other participants in the program, managers spoke for about two minutes on what they had accomplished. As Swift pointed out, "In front of 104 peers, you don't get up and say you haven't done anything. You don't want to flop or be embarrassed."

Critical issues were developed by the people who would be held responsible for meeting them. Simmons described the process:

> We all get our chance. We argue and haggle, for an issue is not just accepted—unless someone says, "I want to do this." When we finally disseminate the plan at the end of the year, we will have agreed on a rather detailed list of problems and opportunities that everybody has signed onto.

An Example: Increasing Melt Capacity

Increasing melt shop capacity had been Vic Ardito's major critical issue for several years. Improvement had been steady: since 1977 capacity had doubled, but without any physical capacity being added (see Exhibit 6). Ardito described the improvement process: "We began working with the melters and general foremen, the people that run the show on each turn. They began to understand what was needed and they applied their creativity and began to make it happen. Many of the great ideas have come off the floor from the foremen."

The melt shop spent up to $650,000 a day on materials, so it began by asking, "What can we do to make the furnace accept cruddy materials?" Although it meant putting up with broken electrodes, strong fumes, and surging flames, the additional 1/4¢ per pound conversion cost was more than offset by the 4¢ picked up on materials bought.

To make better use of the 120-ton AOD—a $100 a minute operation—and the continuous caster, and

EXHIBIT 6 AOD and Caster Productivities

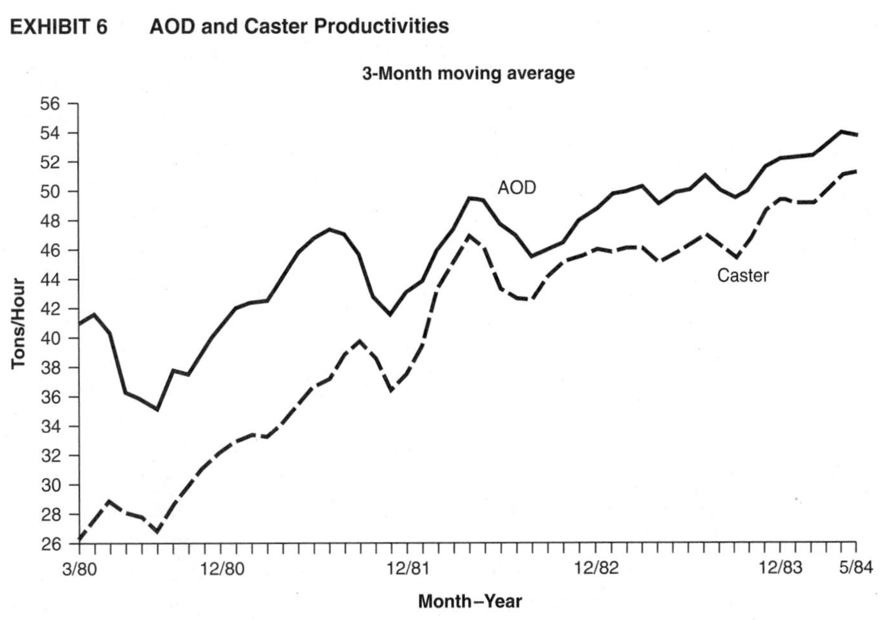

to solve shifting bottlenecks, the melters developed new methods. These included combining heats from two EAFs (which had smaller capacity than the AOD) in the AOD, losing less time between emptying one AOD heat and refilling it with another, and having a chemically identical heat ready to be cast at the moment the first heat was all the way through the caster.

To help the melt shop reach its tonnage goals, other departments had related critical issues. Research, for example, had to develop computer programs that would increase control over melt parameters while decreasing total melt time. Heretofore, bringing a heat to a desired end point meant testing it at several points and making ad hoc adjustments. This process was not only time-consuming but often compounded the original problem (much as a cook might compensate for too much thyme by adding too much basil). By contrast, research's computer program, which operated in real time, told melters how much oxygen to blow right now, or what materials to add in what quantities.

Tools and Techniques

Allegheny had developed other mechanisms to support the basic building blocks of the standard cost system, the critical issues program, and plural management. Among the most important were laboratory and production experiments and the low-cost routing system.

Experiments

Most of research's work was written up as experiments, which were of three types: laboratory experiments, mill experiments, and 710s. Laboratory experiments were forerunners of full-scale trials in the mill. Mill experiments and 710s, on the other hand, had to be scheduled around regular production. The difference between mill experiments and 710s lay in the degree of risk, and in how costs were accounted for.

The 710s were high-risk experiments. To encourage this kind of experimentation, 710s did not show up in production costs; they therefore did not detract from variable margins. They required signoffs from four vice presidents (Pitler, Walsh, Wardle, and Richard Mercer, vice president of Commercial) who had to agree that the process was reasonable, that it would not damage the equipment, and that it was worthwhile commercially.

While the dividing line between 710s and other mill experiments was not always clear, the latter typically aimed at modifying and improving something that was already known. This might be the simplification of an existing operation, a change in equipment use, or a metallurgical change. At least 100 mill experiments were performed yearly, compared with the usual one 710 per month. Costs of mill experiments were included in operating departments' budgets. When asked why he agreed to mill experiments, since they made his costs go up, Harry Wagner, works manager at Brackenridge and Natrona, replied:

> I'll do it if it sounds like a smart thing to do; we're not after mosquitoes with cannons here, so we don't want to spend a dollar to save a dime. Yes, it may mess up my operation temporarily, and give me a negative variance or at least raise costs. But it may also lower my long-run costs or improve my quality. If an experiment messes you up, they change the yardsticks. It's the bottom line that drives us.

Bob Walsh added: "You have to put your money where your mouth is. If you encourage people to innovate, then you don't penalize them when it results in a negative variance."

Experiments got started for several reasons. Research had developed something in its own labs that it wanted to test in the mill, a customer had a new material that it wanted to try in full production, or the company wanted to experiment with variations of current production practices, such as new chemistry or new process techniques, to improve quality or reduce costs. An additional important use of experiments was to open the door to new business, but on a small enough scale that the risks were minimized.

Low-Cost Routing

Allegheny's routing system provided options for routing products over different pieces of equipment. Most of the routing choices involved cold rolling and stainless finishing operations. In general, the greatest latitude was in breaking down coils to intermediate gauges; the least, in the final rolling of thin gauges and other finishing steps.

Routing options that were ultimately chosen on an economic basis were first screened and constrained by certain equipment, metallurgical limitations, and customer needs. These considerations included coil size (every piece of equipment had a maximum coil size, measured in weight, that it could support); the 24-hour rolling requirement (all silicon and 40 percent of stainless had to be rolled within 24 hours of being cast); and necessary end-product qualities that could be obtained only by using a particular piece of equipment. Within such constraints, Production Control identified all alternative equipment over which a product could, from a technical standpoint, be routed; it then tallied the costs associated with each step and ranked the routes by cost.

An invaluable tool for making these choices was Allegheny's proprietary computer program, Route Cost, developed by Wayne Swift to follow certain decision rules. Production Control used the program to schedule production, and Accounting used it to develop expected conversion costs for new products. No competitor had a similar program because none had the detailed standard cost accounting system needed to support it.

Route Cost was essential in helping Allegheny meet its overall objective of maximizing margins. Once equipment capacity limits were reached, however, its decision rules were overridden to avoid temporary bottlenecks that could lengthen delivery times. Then, critical units were scheduled first for high margin, specialty products, and less efficient equipment was brought onstream as necessary. The potential conflict between Production Control's need to look at capacity, equipment use, and scheduling for all product lines and the TBTs' desire to maximize their own margins was resolved by Marketing or, if necessary, by Bozzone and Simmons. In making such a decision, they relied heavily on margin reports.

Low-cost routing could also be overridden by customer service. Marketing put five or six items out of 4,000 monthly invoices on a hot list; Production Control then did whatever it had to to get the order out.

Capacity and Facility Decisions

In the near future, Allegheny faced decisions about both its stainless and silicon steel facilities. The market for stainless, as well as Allegheny's share, was expected to continue to increase. The company's melting and casting capacities, however, were approaching their limits. At the same time, there was no longer enough silicon volume to keep the Natrona melt shop running at anything close to capacity. Because Natrona could be adapted to melt stainless, the two capacity decisions were interlinked.

Silicon Markets and Products

Although Allegheny participated in the full range of silicon markets, its concerns focused on the high end. Competition for high-end power and distribution transformer markets centered on energy efficiency; the more energy efficient the steel, the lower the utility's operating costs. A competitor with a less efficient product could offer a more attractive initial price, or responsiveness to the unique design needs of each utility. A maturing utility infrastructure and more efficient steels had greatly shrunk tonnage demands.

Improving the magnetic quality of silicon was difficult to do; even more difficult was getting a process with 80 to 90 percent repeatability. Orienting the grains increased magnetic quality; getting the grains lined up and controlling their growth was at the heart of this difficult process. Indeed, only four companies in the world could make high-quality, grain-oriented silicon. Historically, Allegheny and Armco had shared the domestic market. But in 1984, Kawasaki Steel and Nippon Steel grabbed 30 percent of the U.S. market with their "high B" product that was 10 percent more efficient than the steel the Americans were making. At the low end, the Europeans, Brazilians, and Canadians were aggressively gaining share on the basis of price.

Allegheny had designated the achievement of a silicon product competitive with high B as a CSF, and was spending half its research dollars on this effort. Simmons also lobbied actively for silicon quotas—not tariffs, because, as he was quick to point out, foreign subsidies could be used to offset American tariffs. Yet even if quotas were achieved, the company would face competitive threats. Bozzone pointed out:

> The transformer people could go to Mexico or somewhere else and have their cores wound there, using Japanese steel. The product would then come into the country as a transformer rather than as steel. Or the Japanese could sell to the Swedes, without profit, to get around our quotas. I was meeting with some of the transformer people just a few weeks ago, and they are already looking at the Swedish option.

Silicon Options

Allegheny had several options for its silicon business.

1. *Meet the Japanese head on.* Under this option, the company would intensify its efforts to develop a product capable of competing with the Japanese in the high end of the market. Research and experimentation had raised magnetic quality 2–4 percent, bringing Allegheny's product to parity with Armco's; another 10 percent was a tall order. Bozzone acknowledged the company had a long way to go in achieving a repeatable process: "We try to understand the reaction of the metal, while the Japanese understand *why* things happen. We could accelerate the pace of R&D, but can we get close enough?" Even if Allegheny could improve the product's quality and process repeatability, pricing it to recoup the investment might be difficult. The Japanese had a history of accepting low returns or even selling below costs for long periods in markets they had targeted.

2. *Joint venture with the Japanese.* Allegheny could possibly get a license with Kawasaki Steel to produce some of its recipes. This would give Allegheny the opportunity to regain its competitiveness in the high end, and perhaps enhance low-end sales. Allegheny would still require a major silicon research effort, but it would be focused on finishing operations.

3. *Adapt some silicon facilities for making stainless.* Allegheny had over $100 million invested in silicon equipment, most of it depreciated. Some of the excellent finishing equipment was dedicated and could not be adapted for stainless use. Some equipment, such as a highly computerized, high-speed rolling mill and seven slitting lines, could be changed over permanently, at modest cost, or used alternately for silicon and stainless, with minor modifications such as in the lubrication system.

4. *Run silicon as a cash cow, and get out of the business.* This option would stretch out the time horizon for getting out of the business, while continuing to support 20–35 percent of the company's overhead. Allegheny would sharply reduce its research and technical support, and continue to cut prices. Bozzone, however, noted:

> Most businesses in which you could pull back on management attention and technical support are commodity businesses. But if you took away the support in this highly technical business, you might lose share even in the conventional end of the business. So we are not sure the cash cow approach would work.

Given the uncertainties of running silicon as a cash cow, Allegheny could instead take an immediate write-off of nonadaptable equipment, and get out of silicon quickly.

Stainless Markets and Capacity

Allegheny had increased its stainless sales 4–5 percent per year (in tons) for the last several years, and had incrementally raised its Brackenridge melt capacity to over 400,000 tons per year. While the hot end was in balance, it was reaching its limits for squeezing out more tonnage. Management estimated that it would need 150,000 tons by 1990. They anticipated two major sources of that increase: exhaust alloys, and supplying competitors that had closed their melt shops with hot-roll bands.

Natrona, by contrast, had melt capacity of 600,000 tons for silicon steel, but was currently producing no more than 40 percent of that. Allegheny had experimented with modifying one of the two BOFs at Natrona so it could refine some grades of stainless there. The potential capacity of the modified BOF would be a little more than half its silicon capacity, because a silicon heat was almost twice as fast as a stainless heat. While the quality of these heats was comparable to those from Brackenridge, the modified BOF could accommodate only some grades of stainless and entailed a cost penalty. Currently, that penalty came in two parts: a 3¢ premium for refining in the BOF rather than in the AOD, and a 5¢ premium for using ingots rather than the caster. Several steps could be taken, either singly or in combination, to deal with the stainless situation. But silicon needed strategic attention immediately.

PART III Enactment of Technology Strategy—Developing the Firm's Innovative Capabilities

Designing and Managing Systems for Corporate Innovation

In Part II, we discussed the design and evolution of a firm's technology strategy. Technological competencies and capabilities were viewed as the foundation of technology strategy. The evolution of technology strategy was examined in the context of a matrix of generative selective forces that shape innovation processes within the firm, within an industry, and in the broader system encompassing multiple industries or major segments within an industry. In Part III we take a somewhat different perspective, examining how a firm's innovative activities reflect its technology strategy and how the enactment of technology strategy serves to further develop its innovative capabilities.

Technology strategy is enacted through the performance of a sequence of key tasks (see "Creating and Implementing a Development Strategy" in Part IV), which serves to augment the firm's existing technological competences and to build new ones. At the start of this sequence is technology sourcing. In order to stay ahead of competitors, high-technology firms must source technology on a continuous basis. While many firms source some of their technology through licensing arrangements, R&D with other firms, consortia, strategic alliances, joint ventures, and acquisitions, high-technology firms must source the bulk of their new technology internally through investments in R&D. At the end of the sequence of key tasks is technical support and field service—companies selling technical equipment, for instance, need a capability to service the equipment and to train and keep their users up-to-date. Between technology sourcing and technical support are key tasks associated with the major corporate innovation challenges: the development of new products and new businesses.

Innovation Challenges in Established Firms

New Product and New Business Development

The major innovation challenges facing established firms derive from the evolutionary process model of strategy making, presented in Reading II-13 of this book. This model, reproduced in Exhibit 1, distinguishes be-tween *induced* and *autonomous* strategic processes.

Induced strategic action takes place in light of the firm's corporate strategy and in relation to its familiar external environments. Corporate strategy reflects top management's beliefs about the basis of the firm's past and current success.[1] These beliefs determine

[1]R. A. Burgelman, "A Model of the Interaction of Strategic Behavior, Corporate Context, and the Concept of Strategy," *Academy of Management Review* 8 (1983), pp. 61–70; "Intraorganizational Ecology of Strategy Making and Organizational Adaptation: Theory and Field Research," *Organization Science* 2 (1991); "Fading Memories: A Process Theory of Strategic Business Exit in Dynamic Environments," *Administrative Science Quarterly* 39 (1994), pp. 24–56; G. Donaldson and J. Lorsch, *Decision Making at the Top* (New York: Basic Books, 1983); K. Weick, "Substitutes for Corporate Strategy," in *The Competitive Challenge,* ed. D.J. Teece (Cambridge, MA: Ballinger, 1987), pp. 221–34.

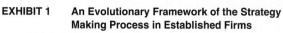

EXHIBIT 1 An Evolutionary Framework of the Strategy Making Process in Established Firms

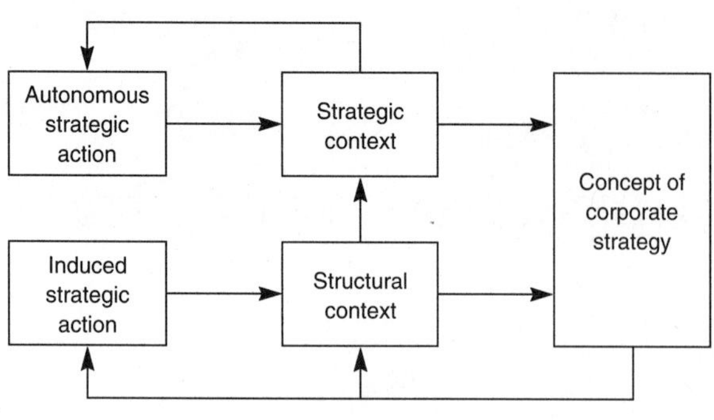

what the firm views as its distinctive (or core) competences and what the product-market domain is in which it can successfully compete. While in small firms corporate strategy and strategic action are usually closely linked, larger firms typically require the creation of a structural context to secure the link between strategy and action. The structural context serves to select strategic initiatives that fit with the corporate strategy and leverage the organizational learning on which the corporate strategy is based. The structural context encompasses administrative (e.g., resource allocation rules) and cultural (e.g., rules of expected behavior) mechanisms.

Autonomous strategic action is outside the scope of the current corporate strategy and opens up new environmental niches. Successful, autonomous initiatives lead to an amendment of the firm's concept of strategy through the process of strategic context determination. This involves middle-level managers in formulating a broader strategy for the initiatives of internal entrepreneurs and acting as organizational champions to convince top management to support these initiatives. The autonomous strategic process is guided by the strategic recognition capacity of senior and top managers, rather than by strategic planning.[2]

Exploiting innovation opportunities in the induced process. Typically, technological innovations associated with the induced process are incremental or architectural.[3] They emerge, in part, from the firm's R&D investments. Incremental or architectural innovations are not necessarily small innovations; for instance, developing a new air frame for the next-generation aircraft is an incremental (and perhaps, in part, architectural) innovation project for Boeing because it is well understood in the context of that firm's corporate strategy. But such a project involves a commitment of billions of dollars. Innovation in the induced process is also likely to shift from the "fluid" to the "specific" state (increased importance of process innovation relative to product innovation)[4] as products reach the mature stage in the life cycle of their underlying technologies. Adjusting to the changing basis of competition entailed by this shift often poses difficult managerial problems.[5] In the short to medium term, managing incremental and architectural innovations is the most significant innovation challenge facing established firms. To meet this challenge, firms must develop strong product and process development capabilities.

Exploiting innovation opportunities in the autonomous process. Typically, technological innovations associated with the autonomous process are radical.[6] Such opportunities emerge somewhat unexpectedly or serendipitously from the firm's R&D investments, especially corporate research. Radical innovations are not necessarily large, at least not initially. For instance, electronic fuel injection (EFI) was invented at Bendix Corporation by an individual engineer; now, however, EFI is a $100 million-plus segment in the automotive supply industry. Similarly, Steve Jobs and Steve Wozniak developed the personal computer in a garage, and total sales in the personal computer industry exceed $100 billion in 1995.

The innovation challenge posed by the autonomous strategic process is important for a firm's long-term survival and development, particularly because as firms grow large their capacity to maintain a growth rate based on pursuing opportunities in their

[2]R. A. Burgelman, "Corporate Entrepreneurship and Strategic Management: Insights from a Process Study," *Management Science* 29 (1983), pp. 1649–64; "Intraorganizational Ecology"; and "Fading Memories."

[3]R. M. Henderson and K. B. Clark, "Architectural Innovation: The Reconfiguration of Existing Product Technologies and the Failure of Established Firms," *Administrative Science Quarterly* 35 (1990), pp. 9–30.

[4]W. Abernathy, *The Productivity Dilemma* (Baltimore: The Johns Hopkins University Press, 1978).

[5]Burgelman, "Fading Memories."

[6]A. Cooper and D. Schendel, "Strategic Responses to Technological Threats," *Business Horizons,* 1976, pp. 61–69; R. A. Burgelman, "A Process Model of Internal Corporate Venturing in the Diversified Major Firm," *Administrative Science Quarterly* 28 (1983), pp. 223–44; Henderson and Clark, "Architectural Innovation."

mainstream areas of business eventually diminishes. Sooner or later, firms—Apple and IBM alike—must find and exploit growth opportunities in marginally related (or even unrelated) areas of business. Systematic research shows that such diversification is difficult and risky. Not surprisingly, various authors have argued that firms should maintain the "common thread"[7] and "stick to the knitting."[8] This may be good advice for firms that have not sufficiently exploited additional opportunities in their mainstream businesses through the induced strategic process; however, it overlooks the fundamental growth problem. To meet the innovation challenge associated with the autonomous process, firms must develop a capability to manage internal entrepreneurship.

A balancing act. Firms must also balance the relative emphasis on these two key challenges throughout their development. This is difficult, in part because the two innovation challenges require different management approaches, and there is a strong tendency for firms to address the challenges sequentially rather than simultaneously.[9]

The remainder of this chapter focuses on the management of corporate research and corporate entrepreneurship. This discussion highlights the innovation challenge associated with the autonomous process; the challenge associated with the induced process–new product development—is discussed in Part IV, "Creating and Implementing a Development Strategy."

Strategic Management of Corporate Research

Because of its long-range time horizon, high risk, and exploratory orientation, corporate research poses especially subtle and complex strategic management issues. Established high-technology firms typically spend a significant fraction of their resources—at least 5 to 10 percent of sales—on R&D activities. Most of these resources are allocated to R&D projects for mainstream businesses, but a sizable fraction—10 to 15 percent of the total R&D budget—is often spent on corporate research.[10] Corporate research is truly long-range, high-risk, and exploratory. The effort of Monsanto in the biotechnology area, described earlier, is an example, as is the establishment of the Palo Alto Research Center (PARC) by Xerox in 1970.[11] There are important issues associated with the strategic management of R&D activities in general, such as (1) whether the firm is putting its R&D dollars into those areas of technology that will provide the highest economic returns, and (2) how tightly R&D projects are linked to business objectives in those promising areas of technology.[12]

The Functions of Corporate Research

Rosenbloom and Kantrow[13] have provided a useful overview of the functions of corporate research; it indicates that corporate research helps meet the innovation challenges associated with the induced and autonomous strategic processes (see Exhibit 2).

Support of existing businesses (induced process). As Exhibit 2 suggests, activities in support of the firm's existing business comprise improvements in existing products and processes. Often, the corporate research group will have high-level experts in certain areas of science that divisional R&D groups or product developers cannot afford for themselves exclusively. Corporate research also can provide several services to the rest of the corporation: (1) help divisional R&D groups assess technological threats and opportunities through high quality intelligence work, (2) assist divisional R&D with their human resource management by helping recruit talented technical personnel, and (3) facilitate transfers of technology from corporate research to divisional R&D or product development groups.

New strategic directions (autonomous process). The key contribution of a corporate research capability, however, is to discover new areas of technology that may form the basis of entirely new businesses. For example, DuPont's invention of nylon, Corning's invention of optical fiber, and EMI's invention of the CT scanner created entirely new

---

[7]H. I. Ansoff, *Corporate Strategy* (New York: McGraw-Hill, 1965).

[8]T. J. Peters and R. H. Waterman, *In Search of Excellence* (New York: Harper & Row, 1983).

[9]R. A. Burgelman, "Managing the Internal Corporate Venturing Process," *Sloan Management Review,* Winter 1984 pp. 33–48.

[10]R. S. Rosenbloom and A. Kantrow, "The Nurturing of Corporate Research," *Harvard Business Review,* January–February 1982.

[11]B. Uttal, "The Lab that Ran Away from Xerox," *Fortune,* September 5, 1983.

[12]R. N. Foster, "Linking R&D to Strategy," *The McKinsey Quarterly,* Winter 1981.

[13]"The Nurturing of Corporate Research."

EXHIBIT 2

- Specify research charter.
- Research charter represents the shared understanding of the mission that research is expected to fulfill.

		Functions of Corporate Research	
		New Strategic Directions	Support of Existing Businesses
Innovations by:	Improving and strengthening understanding of technologies in use	Corporate diversification to new applications and markets	Product and process improvements
	Discoveries and developing new technologies	Corporate diversification to entirely new businesses	New processes for established products
Corporate service by:	Intelligence	Windows on new science and technology	Assessing threats and opportunities
	Human resources	Recruiting new kinds of skills	Recruiting talented people with high potential
	Technology transfer	Identifying acquisition candidates with needed technological expertise	From corporate research to operations

SOURCE: R. S. Rosenbloom and A. M. Kantrow, "The Nurturing of Corporate Research," *Harvard Business Review*, January–February 1982, pp. 115–23.

businesses for these firms. IBM's contributions to high-temperature superconductivity may one day pay off in new but as yet unimagined business opportunities. Rosenbloom and Kantrow[14] point out that corporate research may help a firm keep a window open on new science and technology, and Cohen and Levinthal[15] found that corporate research increases the firm's "absorptive capacity" of new technology. Furthermore, having top-level scientists at corporate R&D may help in the recruitment of other top technical personnel. Finally, corporate research may help in identifying acquisition candidates with the necessary technical expertise.

Effectively using the output of corporate research. Corporate research's role is to generate new technologies, some of which can be used effectively in the various parts of the organization responsible for new product development for existing businesses (induced strategic process). The transfer of technology from research to development, however, is a nontrivial problem for most firms. (See Reading III-3).

[14]Ibid.

[15]W. M. Cohen and D. A. Levinthal, "Absorptive Capacity: A New Perspective on Learning and Innovation," *Administrative Science Quarterly* 35 (1990), pp. 128–52.

Corporate research also generates technologies that cannot easily find a home in the firm's existing product development infrastructure. These require special arrangements to facilitate the technologies (autonomous strategic process). Later in this chapter a framework for designing such arrangements is presented.

Managing Key Interfaces

Corporate research–divisional R&D interface (induced process). Managing the interface between corporate research and divisional R&D is difficult because of the differing orientations and expectations of the groups involved.[16] Scientists in divisional labs or people in product development usually want to commission experimental studies or obtain expert help from corporate research. They tend to see corporate research as providing a service and expect corporate research to be responsive to their initiations and requests. Corporate research, on the other hand, tends to see itself as carrying out work at the frontier of areas of science that promise to be of great importance to the firm's long-term suc-

[16]R. A. Burgelman and L. R. Sayles, *Inside Corporate Innovation* (New York: Free Press, 1986).

EXHIBIT 3 Linkages between R&D Units

		Geographical			
		Closed		Open	
		Personal		Personal	
		Closed	Open	Closed	Open
Administrative	Closed	Tight Coupling			
	Open				No Coupling

cess and resists being asked to perform low-level technical problem solving. Members of corporate research want to be considered "advisers" who initiate improvements in the research programs of divisional R&D. Given these different expectations, careful use of administrative, geographical, and personal linkages is important to manage the interfaces effectively. These linkages are illustrated in Exhibit 3.

Geographical linkages are the physical proximity between R&D groups. Research conducted by Allen,[17] for instance, has shown the importance of proximity for communication between R&D personnel. Administrative linkages comprise the authority relationships of different groups (i.e., whether they report to the same superior). To the extent they do, it is of course easier to impose formal collaboration. Personal linkages refer to the informal network of contacts researchers develop in the firm. While the most elusive, these ties probably have the greatest impact on the quality of collaboration between research personnel.

Corporate research–business research interface (autonomous process). Developing new areas of business based on corporate research is an entrepreneurial task. It necessitates linking new technological solutions to market needs and obtaining additional resources to create a commercially viable new business, and thus requires inputs from corporate research and business research specialists. Managing the interface between corporate research and business research specialists, such as the interface between corporate research and divisional R&D, is difficult. Burgelman and Sayles[18] have identified several factors that affect the interface between corporate research and business research professionals (see Exhibit 4).

The work environments of corporate research and business research professionals are quite different. Corporate researchers operate in the well-established tradition of scientific research and have clearly described positions in the research management hierarchy (bench scientist, group leader, R&D manager, etc.). The scientific method guiding their work is well codified, and the databases they use are to a great extent systematic and objective. Moreover, the time pressures encountered are mostly self-generated because it is difficult for management to significantly compress the time needed to carry out critical experiments and virtually impossible to order scientific breakthroughs. The time to complete a scientific study is to a large extent determined by the logic of the scientific method. Business research professionals, on the other hand, operate in a less well defined research tradition and their work hierarchy is often less clearly defined. Their methods tend to be more ad hoc and less codified, and their databases tend to be less systematic and more subjective. Business research professionals are more likely to encounter externally generated time pressures (e.g., from customers with technical problems) that determine the time period within which a solution must be found.

The professional orientations of the two groups are also somewhat different. Corporate scientists consider serendipity (and the concomitant unpredictability) a way of life, and are mostly interested in pursuing new ideas and finding ways to improve technical performance in major ways. Corporate scientists expect their work to be evaluated primarily on the quality of the investigation rather than the commercial usefulness of its results. Business research professionals, on the other hand, usually operate in a planning framework requiring predictable commercial results. They are interested in the commercial impact of a technical idea rather than its novelty, and in whether it will solve a technical customer need within acceptable cost parameters.

Finally, differences in background and personal interests may impede effective interaction among the groups. Corporate scientists typically have PhDs and have built experience through deep and focused research. Conversely, business research professionals often do not have PhDs and have had broader and more diverse experiences.

---

[17] T. J. Allen, *Managing the Flow of Technology* (Cambridge, MA: MIT Press, 1977).

[18] *Inside Corporate Innovation.*

EXHIBIT 4 Systematic Differences between Business and R&D People

	R&D People	Business Research People
Work Environment		
1. Structure.	Well defined: existence of research tradition; clearly described positions	Ill defined: no real research tradition; positions less clearly defined
2. Methods.	Scientific and codified	Ad hoc and uncodified
3. Database.	Systematic and objective	Unsystematic and largely subjective
4. Work and time pressures.	Mostly internal; how long does it take?	Mostly external; how long do we have?
Professional Orientations		
5. Operating assumptions.	Serendipity	Planning
6. Goals.	"New" ideas/can it be improved?	"Big" ideas/does it work?
7. Performance criteria.	Quality of investigation	Quantity of results
Quality of Personnel		
8. Educational background.	PhD	Masters
9. Experience.	Deep and focused	Broad and diverse
Personal Interests		
10. Career objectives.	Become venture manager?	Become venture manager?

SOURCE: Burgelman and Sayles, *Inside Corporate Innovation.*

Linking Corporate Research to Corporate Development Strategy

Providing a clear charter for corporate research (see Exhibit 2) is important to facilitate its strategic management. In addition, top management must ensure that corporate research supports the firm's corporate development strategy. This requires that top management establish an effective process for deciding which new businesses and competences the firm wants to develop. Having a clear corporate development strategy makes it easier for top management to assess the strategic importance of different research areas with the help of the firm's chief scientist, corporate vice president of technology, or other senior representative of R&D.

Assessing technological opportunity. Rosenberg[19] outlines how the high uncertainty involved in technological changes makes it extremely difficult to assess associated business opportunities even after their technological feasibility has been established. For instance, one of the most important applications of the laser has been telecommunications. However, "patent lawyers at Bell Labs were initially unwilling even to apply for a patent on the laser, on the grounds that such invention had no possible relevance to the telephone industry."[20] Rosenberg goes on to discuss five dimensions of the fundamental uncertainty that constrain the ability to predict the value of radically new technologies:

1. Technological innovations come into the world in primitive conditions and with properties and characteristics whose usefulness cannot be immediately appreciated (e.g., the laser was not an obvious substitute for something that already existed).
2. The impact of technological innovations often depends on improvements in complementary inventions (e.g., the usefulness of the laser in telecommunications depended on the availability of fiber optics).
3. Major technological innovations often constitute entirely new technological systems, but it is difficult to conceptualize such systems (e.g., the telephone was originally conceptualized as primarily a business instrument).
4. Major technological innovations often had their origins in attempts to solve very specific prob-

[19]N. Rosenberg, "Uncertainty and Technological Change," paper prepared for the Conference on Growth and Development: The Economics of the 21st Century, organized by the Center for Economic Policy Research of Stanford University, June 3–4, 1994.

[20]Ibid., p. 5.

lems and lead to unanticipated uses (e.g., the steam engine was invented specifically as a device for pumping water out of flooded mines).

5. The ultimate impact of technological innovations depends on the ability to effectively link them to specific categories of human needs (e.g., it was David Sarnoff, not Marconi, who linked the possibility of wireless communication to extended human needs).

Assessing technological opportunities is an integral task of top corporate research management. Rosenbloom and Kantrow[21] report criteria used by George Pake, former vice president of corporate research at Xerox, to assess technological opportunities. Pake asked the following questions:

- Are first-class researchers available to pursue them?
- Is major investment likely to yield major advances?
- How many years will it take before we see useful results?
- How many failures and successes have others had in this area?

If a proposal survived this initial screening, and before committing resources, Pake and others at Xerox then asked:

- Can the expert technology be obtained from vendors or through acquisition?
- What costs would be incurred by displacing an existing research program to implement the new proposal?
- Is there enough hope that a successful result can be transferred downstream?
- Will the necessary capital be available?

Clearly, answering these kinds of questions involves qualitative judgment as well as quantitative analysis. The capacity of top management to evaluate the quality of the thinking of R&D managers, group leaders, and bench scientists in corporate research is crucial here.

The role of different levels of corporate research management. The key operational levels in corporate research are:

- Technicians (usually having a bachelors or masters degree in science or engineering and responsible for helping scientists with the implementation of experiments, data analysis, etc.).
- Bench scientists (usually having a fairly recent PhD in science or engineering and responsible for specific research projects).
- Group leaders (usually having a PhD in science or engineering and a strong track record as a "respected peer" in their specialty, and responsible for a number of bench scientists and their projects).
- R&D managers (senior managers to whom a number of group leaders report).
- Director of corporate R&D (responsible for the overall corporate research effort).[22]

The director of corporate research will usually report to a vice president in charge of all the firm's R&D and technology efforts. Sometimes, the firm will have a chief scientist and/or a scientist advisory board to help the CEO and top management with decisions concerning R&D and technology. Also, sometimes the firm will have a parallel ladder of scientific positions to recognize the levels of achievement of scientists who do not wish to become "managers" (see "Duval Research Center," Case III-2).

While the ultimate responsibility for corporate research rests with top management, Burgelman and Sayles[23] found that many critical decisions are actually made by senior (but not top) managers. R&D managers established general directions and broad research programs for their group leaders and the bench scientists that report to them, but for the most part tried to keep their staff honest by asking questions and demanding reviews. A critical factor seemed to be the intellectual respect the R&D manager commanded from not being easily snowed by the researchers. Also, the group leader played a very important role in making substantive judgments. Group leaders experienced most intensely the tension between relevance of a scientific area to the corporation and the need to do good science. At the same time, group leaders were often involved in starting a new venture based on corporate research. They usually were sufficiently close to the actual research work to fully understand how a particular technical solution might satisfy a market need, and were sufficiently familiar with, and networked in, the corporate environment to be able to act as product champion.

Allocating resources to corporate research. Once areas of corporate research receive top management support based on their relevance to

[21] "The Nurturing of Corporate Research," p. 121.

[22] Burgelman and Sayles, *Inside Corporate Innovation*.

[23] Ibid.

corporate strategy and the abundance of their technological opportunities, resources can be allocated to them. Corporate research, however, is inherently inertial: to overcome the conceptual and empirical hurdles associated with discovery and invention, scientists need to be tenacious and persistent. Not surprisingly, the trajectories of corporate strategy and corporate research are likely to diverge. Also, technological opportunities may not materialize at the rate or the magnitude originally anticipated. While it would be dysfunctional to disrupt the long-term horizon of corporate research projects, it is necessary to monitor the pattern of resource allocation. The strategic management of corporate research requires both rigorous scientific scrutiny by research management and close financial scrutiny by business management. Some companies, notably Merck, have found it useful to apply an options valuation framework to investments in corporate research.[24]

Managing Corporate Entrepreneurship

The Managerial Challenge Posed by Autonomous Strategic Action

Technology-based internal entrepreneurial activity often emerges spontaneously.[25] This is not surprising because firms almost continuously bring in new talent that interacts with the firm's existing resources, competencies, and capabilities in ways that cannot be fully anticipated.[26] Here are some examples:

- In 1966, calculators were largely mechanized. A young man working for one of the calculator companies brought a model for an electronic calculator to Hewlett-Packard. His own firm was not interested in it because they didn't have the electronic capability. In spite of unfavorable market research forecasts, William Hewlett personally championed the project.[27]
- In 1980, Sam H. Eletr, a manager in Hewlett-Packard's labs, tried to persuade the company's new product people to get into biotechnology. "I was laughed out of the room," he said. But venture capitalists didn't laugh. They persuaded Mr. Eletr to quit Hewlett-Packard and staked him $5.2 million to start a new company. Its product: gene machines, which make DNA, the basic material of the genetic code—and the essential raw material in the burgeoning business of genetic engineering. Now, three years later, Hewlett-Packard has formed a joint venture with Genentech Inc. to develop tools for biotechnology. One product it is considering: gene machines.[28]

How should corporate management deal with autonomous strategic initiatives? Clearly, not every new initiative can or should be supported. Yet it seems reasonable to ask whether the top management of the firms in these examples made a strategic decision not to pursue the initiatives of their internal entrepreneurs. From a strategic management perspective, it is insufficient to reject the electronic calculator because "we don't have an electronics capability" or the gene-making machine because "we are not in biotechnology." There must have been important competencies in the firm that allowed the internal entrepreneurs to come up with their idea and perhaps even develop a prototype. Even if there was no apparent relationship with current capabilities and skills, it was important for top management to consider the potential implications of the initiative for the firm's strategic position. In the case of calculators, for instance, top management of the mechanical calculator firm might be expected to have considered the strategic implications of someone else bringing an electronic calculator to market successfully. Because autonomous action explores the boundaries of the firm's set of core and distinctive competencies and the corresponding product-market opportunities, it is a vital part of the strategic process in established firms.

The Use of New Venture Divisions

One way top management has tried to take advantage of the autonomous strategic initiatives that often emerged based on technologies developed in corporate research was to create a separate new venture division, or NVD. The premise was that internal entrepreneurs should be allowed to pursue ventures unencumbered by the constraints of the firm's mainstream business management. Having reached criti-

---

[24]N. A. Nichols, "Scientific Management at Merck: An Interview with CFO Judy Lewent," *Harvard Business Review*, January–February 1994.

[25]Burgelman, "A Process Model."

[26]E. T. Penrose, *The Theory of the Growth of the Firm* (Oxford: Blackwell, 1968).

[27]R. M. Atherton and D. M. Crites, "Hewlett-Packard: A 1975–1978 Review," Harvard Case Services, Boston, MA, 1980.

[28]"After Slow Start, Gene Machines Approach a Period of Fast Growth and Steady Profits," *The Wall Street Journal*, December 13, 1983.

EXHIBIT 5 Interface Problems Involving the NVD

	NVD–Operating Divisions Interfaces	NVD–Corporate Management Interfaces
Strategic interferences	■ Domain protection issues ■ Synergy considerations	■ Lack of diversification strategy ■ Limits to rate of strategic change that can be absorbed ■ Effects on corporate image
Administrative/cultural frictions	■ Rigidities resulting from management system ■ Personnel transfer issues	■ Circumvention of corporate rules and regulations ■ Inadequate measurement and reward systems ■ Resistance to institutionalization

SOURCE: Adapted from R. A. Burgelman, "Managing the New Venture Division: Research Findings and Implications for Strategic Management," *Strategic Management Journal,* January–March 1985.

cal mass, a new venture could then be transferred to an operating division as a new business unit or department or, if sufficiently large, the venture could become a freestanding division in its own right. The prospect of becoming the general manager of a major new business in the corporate context was a strong incentive for would-be corporate entrepreneurs. Fast[29] and Burgelman and Sayles,[30] however, have documented serious problems associated with the NVD design. (Note: "Medical Equipment (A)," Case III-7, offers the opportunity to discuss this design option in depth.) The problems as documented by Burgelman[31] are summarized in Exhibit 5.

NVD–operating division interface problems. In the NVD's interface with the operating divisions, potential strategic interferences revolve around product-market domain and synergy issues. The product-market domain of new ventures is meant to involve business areas outside the strategies of the operating divisions, but down the road there are often conflicts of strategic interests. For instance, an operating division may want to absorb a new venture while its manager is still trying to demonstrate that it will be sufficiently large to warrant creating a separate division. Also, an operating division may be concerned if the sales force of a new venture begins to contact its existing customers.

Besides potential strategic interferences, administrative frictions may emerge. A uniform corporate management system may make it difficult for a new venture to get resources from an operating division because divisional managers feel they have to stick to their action plans (which do not include helping fledgling ventures). Personnel transfers between divisions and new ventures are difficult when capable divisional personnel are concerned about being reintegrated in the corporate mainstream if a new venture folds.

NVD–corporate management interface problems. A key problem facing the NVD is that the firm lacks a clear corporate diversification strategy. In addition, corporate management often has no clear idea about the rate of strategic change the firm can sustain. Finally, top management may belatedly become concerned about the effects of a venture's activities on the corporate image. For instance, if a venture sold a deficient piece of equipment, the ramifications for the corporation would extend far beyond the effects on the venture itself. Not being sure what to expect, top management often adopts a vacillating stance toward new ventures. Venture managers are aware of this and realize they have only limited time to make a mark. This puts enormous pressure on venture managers to show fast growth within a narrow time window.

Administrative frictions in the NVD–corporate management interface sometimes result from the venture's occasional circumvention of corporate rules and regulations: sometimes the venture manager will feel compelled to cut corners in corporate standard operating procedures in order to survive.

---

[29]N. D. Fast, *The Rise and Fall of Corporate New Venture Divisions* (Ann Arbor, MI: U.M.I. Research Press, 1979).

[30]Burgelman and Sayles, *Inside Corporate Innovation.*

[31]R. A. Burgelman, "Managing the New Venture Division: Research Findings and Implications for Strategic Management," *Strategic Management Journal,* 1985.

Also, the lack of measurement and reward systems tailored to the tasks of developing a new venture may motivate dysfunctional actions. For example, if the size of a business (sales volume or number of personnel) is the major criterion for managerial compensation, it should come as no surprise that venture managers will try to grow their venture quickly, sometimes at the expense of other considerations. Furthermore, venture managers are likely to resist attempts on the part of corporate management to institutionalize their venture—to act more like the rest of the corporation—as long as they feel that the corporate ways and means are impeding their struggle for success in the market as well as in the internal corporate context.

A Framework for Assessing Internal Entrepreneurial Initiatives

How can corporate management improve its capacity to deal with autonomous strategic action if simply putting such an initiative in a separate new venture division often does not work? A first step in addressing this question is recognizing that different ventures have different needs and not all ventures can be effectively treated in the same way. The next step is to develop an analytical framework that can be used to assess entrepreneurial initiatives and that leads to tentative conclusions about the use of a variety of organization design alternatives to effectively structure the relationship between entrepreneurial initiatives and the corporation. The proposed conceptual framework focuses on two key dimensions of strategic decision making concerning internal entrepreneurial proposals: the expected strategic importance for corporate development, and the degree to which proposals are related to the core capabilities of the corporation, i.e., their operational relatedness. (See Exhibit 6.)

Assessing strategic importance. Assessing strategic importance involves considering the implications of an entrepreneurial initiative for the firm's product market position. In the example of gene machines at Hewlett-Packard, the assessment of strategic importance would address the question of whether failing to pursue the initiative would prevent the corporation from moving into bioelectronics, a potentially important new area of electronic instrumentation.

How can management assess the strategic importance of an entrepreneurial initiative? While this is an important responsibility, it often is one for which top management is not well equipped. Corporate-level managers in established firms tend to rise through the ranks, having earned their reputation as head of one or more of the firm's operating divisions. By the time they reach the top management level, they have developed a highly reliable frame of reference to evaluate business strategies and resource allocation proposals pertaining to the corporation's main lines of business. By the same token, their substantive knowledge of new technologies and markets is limited. Top management tends to rely on corporate staff, consultants, and informal interactions with colleagues from other companies to assess new business fields. Such information sources have merit, but they are no substitute for efforts to understand the substantive issues associated with an autonomous initiative. Top managers depend on middle-level managers, who are closer to new technologies and markets, and who champion autonomous initiatives based on their own substantive assessments. Such interactions improve top management's capacity to make strategically sound assessments. Examples of critical issues to be addressed in these substantive interactions are:

- How does this initiative maintain the firm's capacity to move in areas where major current or potential competitors might move?
- How does this help the firm determine where *not* to go?
- How does it help the firm create new defensible niches?
- How does it help mobilize the organization?
- To what extent could it put the firm at risk?
- When should the firm get out of it if it does not seem to work?
- What is missing in the analysis?

Strategic assessment may result in characterizing a proposal as *very* or *not at all* important. In other cases, the situation will be more ambiguous and lead to assessments such as "important for the time being" or "may be important in the future." Key to the usefulness of the analysis is that such assessments are based on specific, substantive factors.

Assessing operational relatedness. Operational relatedness concerns the degree to which an entrepreneurial initiative requires competencies and capabilities that differ from the corporation's core competencies. Entrepreneurial initiatives typically are based on new competencies and may have the

EXHIBIT 6 Toward an Assessment Framework

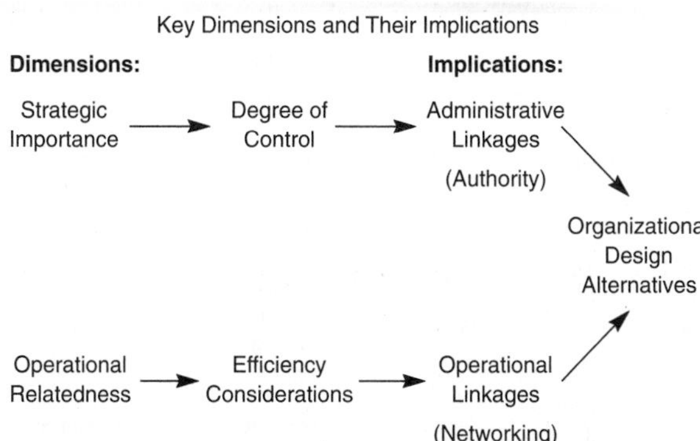

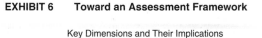

SOURCE: R. A. Burgelman, Managing Corporate Entrepreneurship: New Structures for Implementing Technological Innovation, *Technology in Society* (December 1985), pp. 91–103.

potential for positive or negative synergies with existing competencies/capabilities. Also, internal entrepreneurs often weave together pieces of technology and knowledge from separate parts of the organization that would otherwise remain unused.

In order to be able to make the required assessment of operational relatedness, corporate management again needs to rely on substantive interactions with middle-level managers who champion entrepreneurial projects. Critical issues and questions to be addressed include:

- What key capabilities are required to make this project successful?
- Where, how, and when will the firm get them if it doesn't have them yet, and at what cost?
- Who else might be able to do this, perhaps better?
- How will these new capabilities affect the capacities currently employed in the firm's mainstream business?
- What other areas may possibly require successful innovative efforts if the firm moves forward with this project?
- What is missing in the analysis?

To help top management with this assessment it is useful to develop a competencies/capabilities inventory that indicates how they are deployed in the firm's current businesses. In light of this, new initiatives will sometimes be classified as *very* or *not at all* related. In other cases, the situation will lead to a *partly related* assessment. These assessments should again be made in specific, substantive terms for each initiative.

Design Alternatives for Corporate Entrepreneurship

Having assessed an entrepreneurial initiative in terms of its strategic importance and operational relatedness, corporate management must choose an organization design for structuring the relationship between the new business opportunity and the corporation that is commensurate with its position in the assessment framework. This involves various combinations of administrative and operational linkages.

Determining administrative linkages. The assessment of strategic importance has implications for the degree of control corporate management must maintain over the new business development. The premise is that firms, like individuals, want to exert control over the factors likely to affect their strategic position and thus their freedom to act and pursue their objectives. This, in turn, has implications for the administrative linkages to be established. If strategic importance is high, strong administrative linkages are in order. This means, basically, that the new business must be folded into the existing structural context of the firm. Corporate management will want a say in the strategic management of the new business through direct reporting relationships as well as involvement in planning and budgeting processes, and in trade-offs between the strategic concerns of the new and existing businesses. Measurement and reward systems must reflect clearly articulated strategic objectives for the new business development.

Low strategic importance, on the other hand, should lead corporate management to examine how the new business can best be spun off. In more ambiguous situations where strategic importance is judged to be somewhat unclear, corporate management should relax the structural context and allow the new business some leeway in its strategic management. In such situations, the strategic context of the new business remains to be determined. This requires mechanisms facilitating substantive interaction between middle and corporate levels of management, and measurement and reward systems capable of dealing with as yet unclear performance dimensions and strategic objectives.

Determining operational linkages. The degree of operational relatedness has implications for the efficiency with which both the new and the existing businesses can be managed. The premise here is that firms seek to organize their operations in such a way that synergies are maximized while the cost of transactions across internal organizational boundaries is minimized. This, in turn, has implications for the required operational linkages. If operational relatedness is judged to be high, tight coupling of the operations of the new and existing businesses is in order. Corporate management should ensure that both new and existing capabilities and skills are employed well through integration of work flows, adequate mutual adjustment between resource users through lateral relations at the operational level, and free flows of information and know-how through regular contacts between professionals in the new and existing businesses.

In contrast, low operational relatedness may require complete decoupling of the operations of new and existing businesses to avoid interferences. In situations where operational relatedness is partial and not completely clear, loose coupling seems most adequate. In such situations, the work flows of new and existing businesses should remain basically separate, and mutual adjustment is achieved through individual integrator roles or task force types of mechanisms, rather than directly through the operational level managers. Information and know-how flows, however, remain uninhibited. Exhibit 6 summarizes the key dimensions and their implications of the assessment framework.

EXHIBIT 7 Organization Designs for Corporate Entrepreneurship

Design Alternatives

Operational Relatedness	Very Important	Uncertain	Not Important
Unrelated	3 Special Business Units	6 Independent Business Units	9 Complete Spin-Off
Partly Related	2 New Product Department	5 New Venture Division	8 Contracting
Strongly Related	1 Direct Integration	4 Micro New Venture Department	7 Nurturing and Contracting

Strategic Importance

SOURCE: R. A. Burgelman, "Designs for Corporate Entrepreneurship in Established Firms," *California Management Review* (Spring 1984), pp. 154–166.

Choosing Design Alternatives

Various combinations of administrative and operational linkages produce different design alternatives. Exhibit 7 shows nine such design alternatives.

The design alternatives discussed here are not exhaustive, and the scales for the different dimensions used in the assessment framework remain rudimentary. Much room is left for refinement through further research. By the same token, the framework represented in Exhibit 7 provides a conceptual underpinning for a number of practices adopted by established firms.

Direct integration. High strategic importance and operational relatedness require strong administrative and operational linkages. This means there is a need to integrate the new business directly into the mainstream of the corporation. Such integration must anticipate internal resistance for reasons well documented in the organizational change literature. The role of "champions"—those who know the workings of the current system very well—is likely to be important in such situations. The need for direct integration is perhaps strongest in highly integrated firms, where radical changes in product concept and/or in process technologies could threaten the overall strategic position of the firm. For instance, the development of "float glass" by Pilkington Glass, Ltd., had immediate and far-ranging implications for all glass makers, including Pilkington.[32]

New product department. High strategic importance and partial operational relatedness require a combination of strong administrative and medium-strong operational linkages. This may be achieved by creating a separate department around an entrepreneurial project in that part (division or group) of the operating system where the potential for sharing capabilities and skills is signifi-cant. Corporate management should monitor the project's strategic development in substantive terms and not allow it to be folded ("buried") into the overall strategic planning of that division or group. For instance, there was strong resistance to developing electronic fuel injection (EFI) in the Automotive Group at Bendix Corporation. Only when a new group-level manager took charge and brought in new technical competences was EFI serious pursued by Bendix.

[32]B. Twiss, *Managing Technological Innovation* (London: Longman, 1980).

By that time, however, Bosch, which had licensed the technology from Bendix, was far ahead in EFI.

Special business units. High strategic importance and low operational relatedness may require the creation of specially dedicated new business units. Strong administrative linkages are necessary to ensure the attainment of explicit strategic objectives within specified time horizons throughout the development process. It will often be necessary to integrate some of these business units into a new operating division in the corporate structure. IBM's use of the Special Business Unit design to enter the personal computer (PC) business is an example. In the mid-1980s, the Special Business Unit was disbanded and the PC activities were folded into IBM's mainstream organization. Corning Inc. has been able to use wholly owned subsidiaries to capitalize on new opportunities that emerge, at least in part, from its considerable corporate R&D efforts.

Micro new ventures department. Uncertain strategic importance and high operational relatedness seem typical for the "peripheral" projects that are likely to emerge in the operating divisions on a rather continuous basis. For such projects, administrative linkages should be loose. The venture manager should be allowed to develop a strategy within budget and time constraints but should otherwise not be limited by current or divisional or even corporate level strategies. Operational linkages should be strong, to take advantage of the existing capabilities and skills and to facilitate transferring back newly developed ones. Norman Fast[33] has discussed a "micro" new ventures division design, which would seem to fit the conditions specified here. Fast describes how the DuPont company, during the 1970s, moved away from a corporate new venture division to scale down the type of new ventures pursued and to tie these more strongly to the firm's operating divisions.

New venture division (NVD). This design is proposed for situations of maximum ambiguity in the assessment framework. The NVD may serve best as a "nucleation" function. It provides a fluid internal environment for projects with the potential to create major new business thrusts for the corporation, but of which the strategic importance remains to be determined as the development process unfolds. Administrative linkages should be fairly loose. Middle-level managers supervising a few ventures are expected to develop "middle range" strategies for new fields of business: bringing together projects which may exist in various parts of the corporation and/or can be acquired externally, and integrating these with some of the venture projects they supervise to build sizable new businesses. Operational linkages should also be fairly loose, yet sufficiently developed to facilitate the transfer of relevant know-how and information concerning capabilities and skills. Long time horizons—8 to 12 years—are necessary, but ventures should not be allowed to languish. High-quality middle-level managers are crucial to make this design work.

Independent business units. Uncertain strategic importance and negligible operational relatedness may make this arrangement appropriate. The firm may want to maintain controlling ownership with correspondingly strong board representation, but also offer part of the ownership to partners and to the venture's management. This provides corporate management with the option either to bring the venture into the corporation as a wholly owned subsidiary at a later date, or to spin it off completely. IBM, during the early 1980s, had several independent business units,[34] most of which were later spun off. An example of joint ownership is provided by the way Bank of America organized its venture capital business.[35] ("PC&D," Case III-8, offers the opportunity to discuss this design option in depth.)

Nurturing plus contracting. In some cases, an entrepreneurial proposal may be considered unimportant for the firm's corporate development strategy, yet be strongly related to its operational capabilities and skills. Such ventures typically will address market niches that are too small for the company to serve profitably but that offer opportunities for a small business. Top management may want to help such entrepreneurs spin off from the corporation and may, in fact, help the entrepreneur set up his or her business. This provides a known and, in all likelihood, friendly competitor in those niches, keeping out other ones. Instead of administrative or ownership linkages, there may be a basis for long-term contracting relationships in which the corpora-

[33] *The Rise and Fall of Corporate New Venture Divisions.*

[34] "Meet the New Lean, Mean IBM," *Fortune,* June 13, 1983, p. 78.

[35] "Despite Greater Risks, More Banks Turn to Venture-Capital Business," *The Wall Street Journal,* November 28, 1983.

tion can profitably supply the entrepreneur with some of its excess capabilities and skills. Strong operational linkages related to these contracts may facilitate transfer of new or improved skills developed by the entrepreneur.

Contracting. The possibilities for nurturing would seem to diminish as the required capabilities and skills of the new business are less related. Yet there may still be opportunities for profitable technology licensing arrangements and for learning about new or improved capabilities and skills through some form of operational linkages.

Complete spin-off. If strategic importance and operational relatedness are both low, complete spin-off may be most appropriate. A decision based on a careful assessment of both dimensions is likely to lead to a well-founded decision from the perception of both the corporation and the internal entrepreneur.

Implementing Design Alternatives

In order to implement designs for corporate entrepreneurship effectively, three major issues and potential problems must be considered. First, corporate management and the internal entrepreneur should view the assessment framework as a tool to clarify—at a particular moment—their community of interests and interdependencies and to structure a non-zero sum game. Second, corporate management must establish measurement and reward systems capable of accommodating the incentive requirements of different designs.[36] Third, as the development process unfolds, new information may modify the perceived strategic importance and operational relatedness, which may require a renegotiation of the organization design. The organization design framework must thus be used dynamically, with ventures potentially moving from one type of arrangement to another.

To deal effectively with implementation issues and potential problems, corporate management must recognize internal entrepreneurs as "strategists" and perhaps even encourage them to think as such. This is necessary because the stability of the relationship will depend on both parties' feeling that they have achieved their individual interests to the greatest extent, given the structure of the situation. On the part of corporate management, this implies attempts to appropriate benefits from the entrepreneurial endeavor, but only to the extent that they can provide the entrepreneur with the opportunity to be more successful than if he or she were to go it alone. This, in turn, requires simultaneously generous policies to help internal entrepreneurs based on a sound assessment of their proposals and unequivocal determination to protect proprietary corporate capabilities and skills vigorously. During the early 1980s, companies in Silicon Valley, for instance, increased their legal staffs in part to defend themselves from intellectual property being siphoned off by unwanted spin-offs.[37]

Conclusion

In his early work, Schumpeter[38] distinguished between entrepreneurial and managerial types of economic activity. The role of the Schumpeterian entrepreneur was to change the pattern of resource allocation in the economy. In the process of innovation, entrepreneurs created a gale of "creative destruction." In his later work, Schumpeter[39] viewed large organizations as the main engine of the innovation process. While there have been doubts about the innovative capability of large established corporations, there is little doubt that they continue to play a key role in innovation. Through their ability to fund corporate research, large established corporations provide a substratum of discovery and invention that feeds the innovation process. Many start-ups have been built on ideas that originated within large established corporations. The spin-offs from Hewlett-Packard, Intel, and Apple, for instance, testify to this. Large established corporations thus fulfill an important function that could not easily be performed by small firms or by the government. Also, it is sometimes argued that the innovation process in large established corporations is more costly than in start-ups. But this ignores the fact that many start-ups are usually competing to bring a new product to market and that most of these fail. If the costs incurred by all the failing start-ups were considered together with the cost of the winning start-up to

[36] B. Holmstrom, "Agency Cost and Innovation," *Journal of Economic Behavior and Organization* 12 (1989), pp. 305–27.

[37] "Spin Offs Mount in Silicon Valley," *The New York Times,* January 3, 1984.

[38] J. A. Schumpeter, *The Theory of Economic Development* (Cambridge, MA: Harvard University Press, 1934).

[39] J. A. Schumpeter, *Capitalism, Socialism, and Democracy* (NY; Harper and Brothers, 1942).

calculate the total cost of the innovation, it is not clear that the innovation process involving start-ups would always be more efficient than that involving large established firms.

Here we argue that the early Schumpeterian process is, to some extent, reenacted in established corporations. Established corporations maintain their growth and their long-term viability by taking advantage of internal entrepreneurs' exploration of the potential of the dynamic resource combinations that they have assembled. Internal entrepreneurs, like external ones, enact new opportunities and change the resource allocation pattern within the firm. To facilitate and manage this process better, new organization designs are necessary. This, in turn, requires a richer theory of the firm and a more nuanced view of the role of hierarchies, contracts, and markets. The conceptual foundations of these developments are currently being laid in such fields as the economics of internal organization, agency theory, the theory of legal contracts, and evolutionary theories of strategy and organization. As usual, practitioners are already experimenting with new organizational forms and arrangements. In the process, they generate new data and lay the basis for new research questions. A better understanding of the process of corporate entrepreneurship will facilitate the collaboration between firms and their internal entrepreneurs.

Technology Sourcing

Case III–1 *Aerospace Systems (A) and (B) (condensed)*

A. Ruedi and P. Lawrence

Dr. Roger Simon had just passed up an opportunity to teach at Yale, preferring instead to stay on at Aerospace and set up a new corporate research lab. Looking forward to his new role as director, he knew it would be a big job; one which would be not only profitable but challenging as well. In his short time at the Atomic Energy Division, Simon had convinced both his division president and the president of the corporation, Al Douglas, of the need for a central research facility staffed by top-notch scientists working at the frontiers of their disciplines. He now had to draw upon all his previous experience working at the Manhattan Project and in the Zeta Labs to build a research organization which would enable Aerospace to remain competitive in the future.

Aerospace had adapted successfully to previous changes in business strategy, but over the past 20 years most of the technical accomplishments were in the area of classical physics applied to large aircraft moving at high velocities. With the recent advances in quantum mechanics and relativity, the nature of the industry was changing dramatically, and, to keep abreast of these changes, Simon felt that Aerospace had little choice but to embark on this expensive undertaking. Only within a central research facility could a company as large and diverse as Aerospace attract and maintain a critical mass of fundamental scientists working at the forefront of their fields.

Simon had been recruited initially as a research scientist, but in less than a year he found himself planning for a \$3.5 million technical center with a projected annual budget at \$5 million. This represented a major commitment by the board to the role of basic research in its future business strategies, but money alone would not guarantee success. Simon had to confront the generic difficulty of establishing a research group working in areas of high uncertainty within a business environment where investments must be justified by performance.

Harvard Business School case 9-474-164.

Aerospace Systems: A Company in Transition

In 1959, Aerospace was one of the largest companies in the industry, with contract sales to the U.S. government of well over a billion dollars per year. From its founding in 1933, Aerospace grew rapidly to become one of the largest producers of aircraft in the world until the close of World War II, when—

almost overnight—90 percent of its contracts with the Defense Department were canceled. In adjusting to this, Aerospace adopted a policy of diversification with less emphasis upon production and more upon contracts for complex systems requiring greater technical competence. By the 1950s, Aerospace was again one of the largest competitors in the field. With the change in business strategy, the older production-oriented structure, in which the heads of the major functions all reported to the chief executive, soon became unwieldy. To provide better support for its diversified activities, Aerospace decentralized its operations into eight separate divisions.[1] Each was given greater autonomy, being responsible to corporate headquarters solely on a profit basis, and during the decade of the 1950s many became the largest, or second largest, producer of their product or system in the world.

For a time, decentralization proved to be an effective organizational solution to the problems of diversification and growth, but by the late 1950s there was a growing tendency within the divisions toward parochialism and interdivisional competition leading to redundance and a concentration on short-run problems. Each division had its own research staff, but they tended to work on rather short-range projects. The one exception was in the Atomic Energy (AE) Division, which employed the largest number of PhD scientists, but the work here was done primarily for the Atomic Energy Commission, and this tended to limit both the scope of research activities and opportunities to draw upon this classified work in the other divisions. Several previous attempts had been made to establish a corporate research lab using AE scientists, but the resistance by other divisions stymied these efforts until the arrival of Dr. Roger Simon in July 1960.

Simon was well-known in scientific circles as a theoretical chemist with numerous publications to his credit. An eminent scientist, he had nonetheless become increasingly interested in management. It was this which caused Simon to leave Zeta Labs on two occasions for research positions elsewhere. Speaking of his desire to become a manager, Dr. Simon said:

> I had been doing science for a good many years, and although I still had a certain amount of ambivalence, I felt that I ought to try my hand at a little bit of organization, to organize the world about me. The opportunity at Alfa Steel seemed interesting, something called an assistant director of research. But it turned out that except for a small amount of fundamental work, they did not even do applied research; they put food in cans to see how long it would take for the cans to erode. I decided that this was simply not the place for me. I had the option of returning to Zeta with continuity of service, and I did.
>
> At Zeta, I spent my time totally involved with scientific matters, and I suppose nobody ever thought of me as a manager, although I did begin to express some of these views before I left. I thought—well, maybe I could knit together a chemical physics group for them. I was in fact the leader of that group without the title, simply because I was able to generate sufficient excitement of ideas—and most theoretical chemists are motivated by such ideas. To this day, the theoretical chemists at Zeta do not interact much with the rest of the lab, which is primarily physics oriented. They are a resource which is not fully utilized, and they can be tolerated because the laboratory is so successful anyway. My proposal was to make use of this resource for the company without destroying its scientific competence. They were willing to think about it, but they were not willing to do anything about it. I decided to leave again, since there was this interesting opportunity at AS.
>
> While I was at the Gordon conference,[2] a fellow from AE invited me to stop by and present a paper there. While I was there I was offered a job. I spoke to Howard Elliott, the director of research, and to the vice president of AE. What I noticed at AE was what I thought was a remarkable group of scientists. There were a lot of poor ones too—but nevertheless a remarkably high density of good scientists. But they were unconnected, they weren't interacting even among themselves, and they were unrecognized. I thought they were, as a group, as high quality as you could find at Zeta. Now there are a very few industries that have an opportunity like that. Some of these fellows were actually world authorities in their fields, like Bruce Nelson and Carl Nadel.
>
> I told Howard Elliott, the director of research, that I would only be interested in coming if I had the chance to do some organization, particularly with these resources—it seemed like an exciting idea to bring them together somehow. I really had no firm idea how to do it. I had never thought of that sort of thing. I guess it was sort of rash to think I could do it. I finally joined AE as a research advisor, with the promise that I would become associate director of research after about six months. Howard Elliott was not interested in me as a manager, he was interested in hiring me as a

---

[1]These were the Radar, Aircraft, Space Systems, Rocket Engines, Electronic Systems, Atomic Energy, Information Systems, and Submarine Systems Divisions.

[2]A series of yearly scientific conferences devoted to solid-state physics and solid-state chemistry.

scientist—but he could only get me as a scientist by permitting me to do some organization.

At that time, the research department was divided into four subdivisions: physics, chemistry, electron physics, and metallurgy. Each one was headed by a department head—all were competing for Howard Elliott's job. There was no coherence; they were all busy building up their empires by acquiring more contracts.

Supervisors and group leaders also spent much of their time doing paperwork and had little time to do science. That is the main reason why some of the better scientists didn't want to be bothered with becoming group supervisors.

Average scientists behaved as if they were working for one of the national laboratories; they did research essentially for the AEC and were responsible for getting out the data—that was all. Some of the research was good, some of it wasn't so good. Nobody thought they were working for AE, to say nothing of AS. Everyone had a special relationship with some sponsor at the AEC. There was a great deal of brochuremanship, of time being wasted in getting contracts. Scientists were entrepreneurs in their own right; they had control over consultants, travel, recruiting, and equipment. They were not called upon to think about the relation of their scientific problem to anything else. It was a more pure researchy attitude than you would find at a university.

An executive no longer with AE described the situation as follows:

Howard Elliott was a great guy, but he had to evaluate everything from three angles before he could make a decision. He was very soft spoken and technically very good. At meetings he would criticize things technically and everybody loved him and respected him. Roger Simon with his extremely dynamic approach to life was getting in there, muddying up the waters like crazy, and stirring things around to find out where the mud was going to travel.

When Howard Elliott had a skiing accident and was sent to the hospital, Roger Simon became acting director of research. In the meantime, Howard Elliott had received several offers from various universities and he confided to Roger Simon that he was thinking of leaving. Roger Simon recalls:

That was a bit disconcerting to me because I thought it was unfair of him to have recruited me a few months before and then to run out before my feet were wet. I told him that I would have preferred him to stay on, while I myself was thinking of going because this was such a mess. At that time, I had a nice offer from Yale University at $24,000 a year.

At this time, Sinclair Reed (the division president) was attempting to get a million dollars of internal funds to replace a like amount withdrawn by the AEC. Howard Elliott was still director of research, and I told Sinclair that my decision as to whether or not I would go to Yale hinged upon whether or not they got that million dollars. Without it, I was not interested in staying because there was too much instability.

To me, Sinclair was the ultimate; if I put enough pressure on him, then he could settle the problem. What I did not realize then was that he was not the ultimate, that putting pressure on him just squeezed him. Howard Elliott felt crushed more than anyone else, and after some discussion with Sinclair Reed he finally quit and I became acting director of research without any obligation to stay on.

With the issue of the million dollars still pending, Roger Simon proceeded to tackle what he considered his two main problems. The first was to "weed out the deadwood."

The lab was in considerable turmoil as a result of Roger Simon's promotion. The section heads were disgruntled because their chance for promotion seemed to have vanished, and the bench scientists were apprehensive about the future of their jobs. These anxieties were not relieved when Simon promoted Bruce Nelson and Carl Nadel to associate directorships. Nelson had never held an administrative position, although he had a worldwide reputation as a scientist; Nadel, who had been in and out of management positions at the group leader level, was also well known as a scientist.

The unrest and anxiety produced by these rapid changes were utilized by Simon to get rid of many people he thought incompetent or useless. Those people who, in concert with Nelson and Nadel, Simon thought were valuable, were privately reassured of their positions and future with the company. In several instances, Simon promoted people to positions of group leader based primarily on the criterion of scientific accomplishment. In like fashion, Bod Nordson, an ex-physicist turned administrator who had been with the research department for only a few months as administrative liaison, was promoted to research administrator. Nelson, Nadel, and Nordson became, with Roger Simon, the management team for AE's research department.

The second problem facing Roger Simon was to get the better scientists to relate their activities to the corporation and interact with others:

I had already begun to motivate some scientists to relate to the overall mainstream of effort at AE. For example, Bill Tresbon and his group were working quietly on the electronic properties of metals and conductivity. Tresbon told me that he discovered a very interesting high-field superconductor. I woke up one morning a few days after this and said to myself, "Why the devil don't they make a magnet?"

Of course, this was unheard of as far as they were concerned. They were not interested in this. They were going on to something else. So I went down to see one of the men in Tresbon's group, as Tresbon was away, and said, "Look, why don't you try to make a magnet? But first we'll have to draw a wire," and he said, "Tresbon won't like that . . . it's such an applied thing," and I said, "Well, you know you might learn something from this."

"Besides," he said, "you haven't got any money."

"How much will it take?"

"About $50,000."

"You start making that magnet and I'll get you the $50,000."

Very reluctantly he began, and we had the first superconductive wire of this type in the country. I said to Sinclair, "I'm going to make you very happy," and I told him about the discovery. "You do make me happy," he said; and I said, "Well, if you're so happy, get me $50,000 so that these fellows can go ahead," and he did.

When Tresbon came back, he was ready to go through the ceiling, but the day after the first sample of wire came in, it was interesting to see the reaction. It carried 10 to 15 times as much current as the original slab, and it went to much higher fields. The point is—by having taken the first technological step, they added to their store of scientific knowledge. Then they became very interested and they got into the magnet race. And these two guys, all by themselves, successfully competed with much larger efforts at Ipsylon, Zeta, and Gamma Labs.

There were several instances like this and apparently Sinclair Reed came to the conclusion that this was the time to ask Douglas not only for the million dollars, but to establish some sort of central research effort, and he asked me to write a report telling Douglas what he would have to do to establish a research facility of this kind.

Roger Simon had two weeks to prepare his proposal. He achieved this by working together with Nelson, Nadel, and Nordson. The four men would discuss the issues, then Simon dictated his ideas, which were subsequently edited by Nadel and Nordson. The brochure (Appendix) suggested a research laboratory geographically separate from AE, although organizationally part of AE, reporting to Reed.

Though the line of argument and the tone that the brochure would take had been discussed by Simon with Reed before publication, Reed did not read the final document until the day before it was to be presented to Mr. Douglas. Reed was in agreement with the general content and took the lead in presenting the idea of a geographically separate, corporate-oriented research center.

During the course of the meeting, Mr. Douglas's primary concern appeared to be how one might obtain the necessary interdivisional acceptance and utilization of the research effort if this corporate-oriented effort was to be part of a single division. Reed responded with the key suggestion that the central research function be removed from his jurisdiction and placed under that of the general office. Although Reed's extemporaneous offer was well received by Douglas, no conclusions were reached at the meeting. In recalling the next few days, Mr. Simon said:

Things went on for a couple of weeks; there was no comment from Douglas and no report as to what his decision was. I asked Sinclair how things were going and he said, "I haven't heard anything so it looks pretty grim," so I said, "Well, Sinclair, summer is coming along and I think I'm going to accept the job at Yale University." Sinclair said, "Let's go down and see Douglas before you make up your mind." So we went down to see Douglas and talked with him. This is the longest talk I ever had with Douglas. And then I detected after some minutes that there was a rapport between Douglas and me and right then and there I decided, "Well, this is a big company and they are good scientists. It will not only be challenging, but profitable, to establish a lab in an organization like this."

Alan Douglas recalled the meeting with Dr. Simon and events that led up to it:

There were two thoughts in my mind. The first and foremost was the need to upgrade the technical excellence of the corporation and the fact that I, myself, did not possess the requisite technical background to accomplish this without a staff. Secondly, the intrinsic value of a science effort in the corporation during this period.

Then I started hearing about Roger Simon. Sinclair Reed talked to me about Roger Simon quite often, mentioning his intellectual capabilities and his abilities to form a lab, and I began to get interested. I began to talk to Roger Simon because his background was so different from mine that we had to go through an adjustment period before we could understand each other. In fact, he gave me a series of lectures which gave me some feeling about what the science that he had in mind was about. It developed at this point that he was also a good administrator since he was running that lab at AE.

The mental cycle that I went through was something like this: Here was this group working under contract for the AEC, working on their own problems because you can't get a first-rate scientist to work on anything unless it is a problem he is interested in. But the restraining interest of government was considerable and I started to give some thought about funding this research out of internal funds. The question was how to set up the lab. The idea of taking any of our research and development funds and putting them into that kind of an organization was not very popular with the divisional people who are product and development oriented.

Dr. Simon recalled his relationship with Mr. Douglas in this period as follows:

In view of the urgency connected with the upgrading of science in the corporation and because of the variety of unbalanced pressures to which I thought Douglas would be subjected, what I had to do was to learn to motivate him. I thought, "How can I motivate Douglas? I can't really motivate him because of my management experience, because I have none. I may have some brash ideas, but I can't really represent myself as a distinguished manager." The only thing I had to go on was my hopefully distinguished reputation as a scientist—a reputation which very few people at AS had the equivalent of; the only other people might be a few in the research department at AE—Nelson, Nadel, and Tresbon. So I made no effort; in fact, I told him point blank I was no manager but that I was a good scientist. I told him I was fed up with the way science was being managed at AS and for that reason I was going to Yale University. At this point he said, "Well, I want you to think about it a little longer."

I thought about it a little longer and went back a couple of days later, and he said, "We have been trying to establish a central research activity for a long time, but we have not had the man whom we could count on to do it. We now think we have." I sat there very quietly. Then I warned him again that I had no experience as a manager, that he was gambling, that he would have to give me the authority to do this thing the way I wanted to do it, not to make me a shunt to him or anybody else. And he agreed! It was a startling thing, he agreed!

By July, the Aerospace System's board of directors had approved the establishment of a corporate research center as outlined in Dr. Simon's proposal and recommended by Al Douglas. The research center was to become a separate division in October 1962 and in the interim period remain dependent on the Atomic Energy Division for facilities and administrative support. Prior to the board meeting, Simon was spending most of his time in the day-to-day operations of the AE lab, but with this go-ahead decision things began to move fast.

In preparation for the early discussions with architects, Simon and his associate directors had to spend many late nights discussing what the laboratory would look like in terms of size and disciplines so they could pin down an appropriate physical layout. Building upon his initial proposal, Simon wanted to construct a lab based upon key scientific disciplines, for only in this way did he feel he could combine both specialization and flexibility in a single research unit. Each researcher would be eminent in the field, but the fields, being basic, could combine in numerous ways, depending upon the interests generated. To support this, senior staff members would have their own lab, but in a facility which was compact to facilitate interaction. As the lab evolved in these meetings, other factors such as the size and location of offices, the library, and even the cafeteria were all designed to maintain a stimulating collegial atmosphere.

Beyond these architectural considerations there were a great many other issues raised but not yet fully resolved. The whole problem of financial support was only one of these. Based on their experience in AE, they knew of the dangers associated with government contracts, but they were still not certain what the actual mix of outside to inside support should be. Related to this was the issue of whether divisions should be encouraged to pay for work in the laboratory on a "contract" basis, or whether all research should be corporately funded. This in turn raised the question of how the interface between the lab and the divisions could be arranged to promote autonomy of the lab while still having it in touch with the divisions.

Another problem they talked about dealt with the administrative components of the lab. To what extent should the day-to-day operation and liaison responsibilities be centralized and kept from the scientists? Since they were planning to spend in the order of $100,000 per person in each of 15 key scientific areas and they hoped to recruit top people in each field, they wanted to avoid bureaucratic red tape and too many levels of management, which would constrain this talent. One possibility was for Simon, Nelson, and Nordson to have the key scientists report directly to them as a group. However, they felt that key personnel might end up spending too much of their time in meetings rather than in their labs. Simon and his group talked often about this problem in an effort to get a balance between autonomy for the individual scientists and some unity of purpose in the lab.

In addition to these questions on financing and direction, Simon and his team also were beginning to grapple with several related issues. Where would they recruit these scientists? Would they try to attract researchers from the other divisions as well as go outside? What type of compensation scheme would they offer to attract and motivate these people? And how would this be tied into performance evaluations?

APPENDIX: A MASTER RESEARCH PLAN FOR AEROSPACE SYSTEMS

Definition

It is best to begin with the definition of terms. By *research* I shall mean something distinct from *development,* though the separation can never be complete. With this in mind, I classify under the heading of *research* those activities which are devoted to the creation of new understanding of both phenomena and materials.

Need for a Research Program

Aerospace Systems, in consort with the rest of the industry, has as yet not demonstrated outstanding capacity in research in the sense in which I have defined it. It is important to note that research is a different activity in the sense that it is involved with the creation of new knowledge, and very often this is offered in terms of the molecular and submolecular mechanisms which underlie materials and phenomena. The developments at AS cited above have, with minor exception, all been based on the sound application of scientific principles which were thoroughly established at the time the developments were initiated. One might say that the science of yesterday is the engineering development of today. The converse is obvious. The engineering which we will do tomorrow will be the direct descendent of the research we do today.

Why is it that we can no longer rely solely on engineering applications? Even more important, the need for research stems from the fact that today's accelerated pace has drastically reduced the delay time between the moment when new science is created and the instant when it is utilized as a tool of development. It has become customary for the same organization to create the science and to exploit the development.

Functions of a Profitable Research Laboratory

If it is granted that the corporation must literally pursue research, there must next follow an understanding as to how a group of individuals, synthesized into a laboratory, can come up with the necessary knowledge that the corporation seeks to exploit.

Maintaining lines of communication with the external scientific community. It is vital to become aware of new and exciting developments in the world of science as soon as they happen. In today's highly competitive atmosphere, time—even a little time—is a valuable commodity, and only early cognizance of important developments can provide the necessary time. There is no better way to establish broad lines of communication with the world of science than through the natural personal relationships which occur among scientists who are peers. If the laboratory has gained the respect of the scientific community and its scientists are similarly respected, then they will be welcomed within the most elite professional circles. The normal give-and-take of information which occurs within these groups will provide for the early transmission of news.

Many modern developments are so specialized that they can only be interpreted by someone who has a working familiarity in a new field. Thus, it may sometimes be of value to support a small research effort in order to keep an eye on the new field.

Stimulating other laboratories. An important function of a research laboratory is that of stimulating the community of science to work on problems which are of interest to the parent firm. This can, perhaps, best be indicated by the example of Bell Telephone Laboratories and the transistor. When the transistor effect was first discovered by Brattain and Bardeen, it was realized immediately that the effect could be converted into a useful device which Bell could use to replace costly, short-lived, and less reliable vacuum tubes which were found by the millions in the Bell System. On the other hand, there were grave materials problems of a fundamental nature, and even Bell's large staff could not be expected to solve them within a reasonable period of time. By inducing some of their most outstanding people to work and publish in this area, they succeeded in stimulating the entire world to concentrate on the field of solid-state physics. So popular did the subject become that the solid-state sessions at the Physical Society meetings permitted standing room only. The scientific community published the results of its work and the literature was available to

Bell. In a sense, Bell achieved immense amplification of its own effort, and in fact they were able to actually use transistors in the Bell systems within a very few years. That other firms manufactured and sold transistors was of secondary importance. Bell only wanted to use them.

It is clear that this sort of strategy cannot be pursued with a second-rate staff. To nucleate interest, it is not enough to publish work in the field. The work must be imaginative, exciting, and clearly indicative of the possibilities for further inquiry.

Advising and consulting with development groups. This is a fairly obvious function of a research laboratory. Sometimes a development individual's problem can be solved as soon as he or she contacts the appropriate researcher. The latter may have sufficient knowledge concerning the recent literature in the field so that the solution involves little more than the location of a specific reference. Alternatively, the knowledge may be available but not published and yet the researcher may know of it. Sometimes the development person may be able to enlist the collaborative effort of the researcher in the development problem itself.

The Research Scientist

When the need for research is accepted, there must be a simultaneous acceptance of the fact that the research scientist is a different species from the engineer. Because of this, a whole new host of problems arises for which the solutions developed to fit the engineer are inappropriate. These problems are discussed here, but first a few words are in order concerning the motivation and attitudes of the truly outstanding and creative research scientist. Analyses of the scientist have appeared in many reports and are well documented. These remarks combine our own experiences with those of other well-known and well-established research organizations. *AS has been attempting to deal with the research scientist with methods applied previously to engineers.* An immediate result is that AS is not regarded by scientists as an especially desirable place to work.

It must be accepted from the very beginning that most scientists are profession oriented and not company oriented. It is not very far from the truth to say that scientists regard the company partly as a means to an end, that is, a means to advance scientific research. But the company wishes to use science as a means to its end, that is, to earn profits. Therefore, it is necessary that a compromise be made. The company must make peace with the world of science in order to extract information from it and to secure maximum allegiance from its workers.

To attract these top-notch research scientists, the company must display an enthusiasm for good science as an end in itself. It is generally true that the degree of company-oriented enthusiasm shown by the scientist is directly proportional to the degree of science-oriented enthusiasm displayed by the company. The surest way to alienate a talented research worker is to tolerate good science passively while exhibiting enthusiasm actively for the technical activities which are clearly directed toward a commercial goal. The enthusiasm must be felt; it cannot be produced by edict. But if senior management cannot honestly display enthusiasm for science, then it is probably fair to say that only among a few members of senior management does enthusiasm for science per se exist.

The research scientist considers himself or herself a professional person. There is a large complex of small indignities at AS which militate against providing the scientist with the necessary dignity and atmosphere. Each one of these items considered by itself seems so trivial as to be of no consequence, but the entire complex of annoyances makes for a complaint of some significance. It is also true that some of the individual annoyances are not annoyances at all, but are merely regarded so by the research workers.

In this instance, we have an example of the importance of recognizing the personal characteristics of research workers as distinct from those of engineers.

In personal nonscientific behavior, the scientific worker is no more a logical individual than is any other person. For example, capable scientists are often completely unimpressed by an appeal for economy from management. This, in spite of the irrefutable argument that all funding, no matter how generous, is limited. One might say that this is an aspect of the real world which is not real to scientists.

If a company means to establish a research laboratory, it must be prepared to put up with all the seemingly illogical intangibles that go along with it.

Managerial Authority Required by a Research Laboratory

An atmosphere in which creative ideas will flourish can only be attained with certain managerial authorities granted to the laboratory by the corporation's senior management. Two such areas are the control and direction of the research program. One cannot employ creative individuals with national reputations and then tell them what to do; creative talent is often intimately bound to an independent nature. The principal elements of control available to the research director are: (1) the careful selection of personnel at the time of employment, and (2) those influence methods associated with the personal rather than business relationship with the scientist. For example, it is only reasonable to select as employees workers whose natural interests are in those fields upon which it is felt that the company should concentrate. One also attempts to employ responsible individuals who will understand the nature of their obligation to the company. But once employed, scientists must be allowed to work on tasks to which enthusiasm drives them. That extra spark that is needed to inspire a new idea will only come from the drive for understanding that the scientist finds within.

Another attribute of the better scientist helps channel the laboratory's energies into the desired fields. This is the fact that very few scientists enjoy working in isolation. Ordinarily they like to discuss their problems with colleagues whose interests are similar. Thus, if some central theme of scientific interest pervades the laboratory, the new employee will tend to gravitate towards it.

The important thing is to make everyone desirous of being a member of the team. The personality of the director may be used as a control element by appropriate use of enthusiasm or by development of interest through the active collaboration of the director in a new field.

If under this system workers occasionally pursue lines of inquiry which are not of immediate use to the company, then this is the price which must be paid in order to establish an atmosphere in which creative thinking will flourish, and to which outstanding personnel will be attracted.

The company must also make it clear that they will not be perpetually anxious about how their funds are being applied to research. They must be confident in the judgments of the research management. Constant detailed accounting of the manner in which funds are utilized should not be necessary.

Those limitations which the corporate management wishes placed on its research effort should be clearly and publicly delineated. Outside of these, research management should be given a free hand to create the most fertile environment that its ingenuity can provide.

It is clear that the principal emphasis must be placed on the acquisition of outstanding personnel. The success of the entire venture will stand or fall on the company's ability to recruit talented people. The more creative scientist (measured by some suitable standard) may be 100 times as creative as the average. On this basis, it is well worthwhile for the company to spend two or three times the average in support of such a person; the return per dollar is 30 to 50 times greater.

Management's Attitude toward the Research Program

I have noted previously that one of the essential requirements for a productive research laboratory is a display of enthusiasm for good science on the part of the senior corporate and divisional managements. Displaying enthusiasm for science is an expensive thing, in connection with which more often than not direct financial return cannot be visualized. For example, it may be necessary at times to sponsor research projects having no direct bearing on current company interests. It will be necessary to have scholarly academic visitors whose consultant fees are high and who do little more than raise the morale of the organization. It may be necessary to provide scientists with paid sabbaticals during which they can visit other research institutes or universities. At times it will be necessary to sponsor topical scientific conferences, even to the extent of publishing the proceedings. It may even be necessary to employ scientists on a full-time basis who spend only a part of their time in the company laboratory; for example, some of their time may be devoted to teaching.

The Returns of Research

Nobody can guarantee in advance just what return, if any, will be realized on the very appreciable sum of money which must be invested to establish an adequate research program. It therefore requires faith on the part of the investor that given first-class personnel surrounded by an atmosphere within which creative activity can flourish, the chances for profit are excellent. Faith is in a large measure familiarity. That the value of such a very unconventional mode of business function as has been described should be real can only become clear with sufficient familiarity.

Many businesspeople, although highly intelligent and extremely sensitive to reasonable arguments, find it difficult to bring themselves to risk funds in a research effort because they have not acquired the necessary intimate familiarity with the details of the research process.

Another bitter pill must be swallowed. This is the fact that once having mounted the best possible kind of effort, no major advantage over competitors who have mounted similar efforts can be assured. The best that can be hoped for is the ability to remain abreast of the leaders, not to outdistance them. The aspects here are negative rather than positive in the sense that the firm without a first-class research effort will almost surely fall far behind.

Probably the best that can be done in the way of assuring a profitable research effort is to employ an outstanding research director and to place one's faith in him or her. The chances are, if the director is competent and it is possible to provide an atmosphere in which to recruit outstanding scientists, the effort will be profitable given enough time. This is at once the very most and very least that one can do.

I have deliberately emphasized the scientific rather than the applications aspects of some activities at AE. This is not to belittle the importance of an effective applied research effort. The scientific advances which AE scientists are apparently capable of making would have little significance for the company if there did not exist an effective product development department to which the research effort could be eventually coupled. I emphasize these specific activities in the realm of pure science because this is an exceedingly valuable effort currently owned by the company which has attracted too little attention.

The research discussed is of a caliber and significance equal to that found at the best universities or at an outstanding research institute. The fact that such work can be done indicates that AS has a nucleus of talent in these fields. In spite of the outstanding work which I have just described, however, this nucleus has not fulfilled its potential and in fact is in danger of dissolution. If we lose this group of scientists, it is questionable whether the company will ever mount a similar research effort in the future. In today's competitive market, it will be almost impossible to recruit such talent again.

The Need for Centralization

What is the trouble? Why has not the group fulfilled its potential? The answer is many-faceted. In the first place, the whole of a laboratory should be greater than the sum of its parts. There should be an integration of effort. Scientists should interact spontaneously with one another. There should be a feeling of teamness. The laboratory should reach a kindling temperature. Interaction is instrumental in achieving this kindling temperature, and it is also necessary for the research effort to attain a critical mass.

At AE, there has not been much spontaneous interaction and I suspect the same is true of the other divisions of AS. Certain things catalyze interaction. Instead of the things necessary for such catalysis, it seems as if just those which act to quench interaction have been present. For example, most of AE's research is supported by external sponsors. The resulting project system has compartmentalized the scientist's time and equipment. If scientists are stimulated by colleagues to investigate a problem outside the scope of their immediate project, how will they charge the time? More important, where will they find the equipment to pursue their interest? In the end, one's mind also becomes compartmentalized and one is no longer susceptible to stimulation. There are several individuals who exemplify this effect at AE.

To achieve an integrated effort, there must be a centralized research effort within AS. This will have to come to pass before the kind of research I have been discussing can be realized. As it stands, there are not only costly redundancies within the company, but there is obvious interference between divisions. It seems unreasonable in the light of the scarcity of topflight research personnel that AS should further scatter its talents among its own several parts. Unfortunately, there is an unsymmetrical distribution of both profitability and research talent among the various subdivisions of AS. For example, Rocket Engines and Electronic Systems are capable of large earnings, but there is little question that the largest concentration of research talent, as opposed to development talent, is lodged at AE. Therefore, AE would have to play a major role in the process of centralization. Of course, opposition to this concept may arise, but this has little bearing on the fact that it is required on the grounds of logic.

Consider the case of the high-field superconducting program. It was a real stroke of luck that we, with our very small effort (supported entirely by AEC funds), were able to effect a breakthrough which our large and capable competition had not achieved. Because AS had not supported this research, our proprietary position was somewhat compromised, but worse yet we had neither equipment, nor funds, nor personnel to capitalize on this breakthrough and to fully exploit the time advantage which had been given us.

Any research laboratory, in order to be successful, ought to have one or at the most only a few themes at a time. The development of high-field superconductors seemed to provide excellent opportunity to bring the integration of purpose which can be initiated by so powerful a central theme, but very little of this plan could be effected as there are no uncommitted funds for the support of a diversified program of this sort. In this instance, time is a critical element since there are very large research efforts functioning in the hands of our competitors. Worse yet, the capital equipment is not available.

I have quoted at length the high-field superconductor story to emphasize how ineffective our system is from the point of view of sponsoring a mobile and highly competitive research program. There is so much inertia associated with the ponderous mechanism for making up our collective mind that whatever advantage in time our research effort may have given us erodes until no advantage remains. I would say that all of this stems from the lack of a master plan for research, a commitment in advance to do certain things, and a placing of confidence in the person of some trusted and highly competent research director. The establishment of a corporate research center would undoubtedly provide some of the basis for the elimination of such difficulties. It would at least give us a master plan to which we could refer all decisions which have to be made in a hurry.

A master plan would have some further advantages. Where AEC or DOD sponsorship ceases for a project of scientific excellence before such work can be completed and published, the company should see to it that such work is completed. This is a part of the principle that the company should make peace with the world of science to establish an atmosphere and reputation which will attract the more outstanding personnel.

The Opportunity Exists

In spite of the above criticisms, AS is situated at a point in time and space (circumstance and geography) which is especially opportune for the establishment of the best industrial research laboratory on the West Coast.

West Coast industrial laboratories are all of the same type, heavily involved with government contracts and committed to cost-plus research. There is little project security—even job security is uncertain—and in fact, a large class of what might be called migrant scientific workers exists who follow the contracts from company to company. Each laboratory has a few competent people, but no one is able to acquire the critical mass necessary to mount a really outstanding research effort.

Most of the personnel engaged by these laboratories continue on their jobs because, among other reasons, they prefer to live on the West Coast. If any one company would give the clear sign that it meant to conduct its affairs in a manner similar to the outstanding East Coast laboratories (Bell, GE, IBM), it would very rapidly accumulate the best personnel now scattered among the many similar mediocre firms. For AS to give this sign, it will have to give public demonstration to the acceptance of those precepts mentioned above. The establishment of this laboratory will require considerable initial expense. AS will have to let it be known publicly that such expense has not been spared and that the research is being heavily financed by company funds. Furthermore, it would have to be made clear that it was research, not development, which would be sponsored, and that the company was willing to be quite patient in connection with the time schedule for results, perhaps looking 5 to 10 years into the future.

A Master Research Plan

Development of a research theme. A master plan for research at AS requires, first, the statement of a theme or themes. An industrial research laboratory ought to be concerned with but a few all-consuming central research themes at any time.

To be appropriate to AS, a research theme should fulfill two criteria. First, it should be the frontier of science. Second, it should evolve naturally from the corporation's fields of interest.

By tradition, AS has been a physics-based organization. It is, therefore, doubly appropriate that AS should concentrate primarily on physical research.

Fields of research. It is appropriate that the phase of the master plan which indicates the areas of research of interest to the corporation be indicated in terms of those scientific disciplines for which we desire coverage. It will be the job of research management to integrate these diverse interests into a unified effort, now supporting one theme, and later, perhaps, another. In examining the list of disciplines, it must not be assumed that the people assigned to one discipline will be limited to that particular field. People of the proper caliber will be able to work in a number of the areas contained within the list. One attribute of a good scientist is interest in allied disciplines. Through such cross-fertilization, progress is made.

Many of the subjects can overlap; many of the people who are working at one time in one area might very easily work at another time in another area. It is only through juxtaposing people with such overlapping interests that it is possible to achieve the interaction and integration of purpose which is required to advance a currently important research theme. What is important is to have all of these people on board all of the time. It may seem expensive if at times we are not using all of them in connection with fields which are of primary interest to the company, but we cannot tolerate the lag which is involved in acquiring them only when we need them.

Personnel for the central research laboratory. Since the research center is to be representative of the entire corporation, it ought to draw upon personnel from all divisions as required. The staff, however, should not come exclusively from the present divisions and a large fraction of the required staff will have to be recruited from universities and other laboratories. The contribution of manpower from each of the divisions of AS to the initial staffing of the research center should depend on the qualifications of the scientists themselves, and no requirements should be imposed regarding proportionality to a division's size, solvency, or seniority. Any conflict based on this issue is liable to immobilize the plan at the outset. Any compromise to questions of personality is liable to do the same. If a large sum of money is to be invested, we ought to be sure that it is put to the best possible use. The corporate director of research should report directly to the general offices and be charged with the responsibility of showing no special bias towards any of the operating divisions.

We will need to recruit for the several disciplines not now adequately covered. Such recruiting must place very strong emphasis on the acquisition of creative people. Recruiting will be slow because of the lack of availability of adequate personnel. It should be reiterated that such personnel will be attracted to the corporate research center only if the proper image can be created. Everything must be done to produce and maintain this image. Once we acquire outstanding personnel and are provided with proper funding and adequate working conditions, the rest will almost take care of itself.

Size of the central research laboratory. The corporate research center should have a minimum size in order to achieve the critical mass necessary for effective functioning. It has to be large enough to cover the wide variety of disciplines listed. It must have breadth in order to be cognizant of the latest developments in these fields. It must have depth in order to make it possible for AS to deploy its forces in the most efficient manner to meet the demands of the moment. It must be large enough to provide the community of science with a purposeful and respected image. It must provide a sufficient variety of fields to attract and interest people of stature. It must promise a top-notch potential staff member an association with colleagues sufficiently learned and versatile to supply the investigator with all desired support information.

How large is large enough? My best estimate gleaned from actual working experience is about 100 scientists of PhD caliber. Each of these must have support to the extent of about one technician per scientist so that the entire research organization should involve about 200 direct people.

The number of people enumerated in the list below represents senior people, all of whom have the PhD degree or equivalent. The total of the list is 93. To allow for imperfect estimates, we propose to round the figure off at 100. In addition to these, and the 100 supporting technicians, there will be need for a staff of service and clerical personnel concerned with administrative service duties, a library, and a shop.

Facility needs. In the previous section of this discussion, examples of impendences have been given, and it has been argued that a certain degree of managerial autonomy and stability of funding is necessary. For these reasons, and others previously noted, a research center separate from the present AS divi-

Physics	
Theoretical physics	8
Metal physics	5
Nonmetallic solids	7
Plasma physics	5
Geophysics	2
Nuclear physics	5
Field physics	5
Space physics	4
Surface physics	1
Biophysics	1
High-temperature materials	6
Device physics	4
	53

Physical Metallurgy	
Mechanical properties	6
Structure	4
	10

Chemistry	
Electrochemistry	4
Chemical kinetics	3
Radiation	2
Chemical thermodynamics	1
Theoretical chemistry	2
Combustion chemistry	2
Polymer chemistry	2
Surface chemistry	2
Biochemistry	1
Analytical chemistry	2
	21

Mathematics	
Statistics	1
Information theory	2
Operational analysis	3
Logic	1
Numerical analysis	2
	9

sions appears desirable and necessary. It would require approximately 120,000 square feet of laboratory and office space to house the number of people noted. This figure is, of course, only approximate and is presented here merely as a guide for further study.

Reading III–1 *The Lab that Ran Away from Xerox*

Bro Uttal

On a golden hillside in sight of Stanford University nestles Xerox's Palo Alto Research Center, a mecca for talented researchers—and an embarrassment. For the $150 million it has lavished on PARC in 14 years, Xerox has reaped far less than it expected. Yet upstart companies have turned the ideas born there into a crop of promising products. Confides George Pake, Xerox's scholarly research vice president: "My friends tease me by calling PARC a national resource."

Not that the center has been utterly barren of benefits for Xerox. The company's prowess in designing custom chips, to be used in future copiers, comes largely from PARC. So do its promising capabilities in computer-aided design and artificial intelligence. PARC did most of the research for Xerox's laser printers, now a $250-million-a-year business growing at 45 percent annually and expected to turn a profit in 1984.

But Xerox hasn't cashed in on PARC's exciting research on computerized office systems, which was the center's original reason for being. According to Stanford J. Garrett, a security analyst who follows Xerox for Paine Webber, the company's office systems business lost a horrific $120 million last year and will probably drop $80 million in 1983. "Xerox has got a lot out of PARC," says Garrett, "but not nearly as much as it could have or should have."

Why has Xerox had trouble translating first-rate research into money-making products? Partly because the process takes time at any large company—often close to a decade. Sheer size slows decision making, and the need to concentrate on existing businesses impairs management's ability to move deftly into small, fast-changing markets. This is a special problem for Xerox, still overwhelmingly a one-product company whose copiers accounted for three-quarters of last year's $8.5 billion in revenues and almost all the $1.2 billion in operating profits.

Serious organizational flaws, acknowledged by high Xerox executives, have also proved a handicap. PARC had weak ties to the rest of Xerox, and the rest of Xerox had no channel for marketing products based on the researchers' efforts. The company has revamped office equipment marketing five times in the last six years. "Xerox has creaked, twisted, and groaned trying to find out how to use PARC's work," says an insider. While Xerox has groaned, disgruntled researchers have left in frustration. These Xeroids, as they call themselves, have showered PARC's concepts—for designing personal computers, office equipment, and other products—on competing companies.

PARC's influence outside the walls of Xerox is an ironic tribute to the ambitious vision of the man who founded the center in 1969. C. Peter McColough, then Xerox's president, charged PARC with providing the technology Xerox needed to become "an architect of information" in the office. The new center, in a mutedly elegant three-story building whose rock-garden atria foster meditation, quickly lured many of the nation's leading computer scientists, offering what an alumnus calls "a blank check and 10 years without corporate interference."

Roughly half of PARC's money went for research in computer science and half for research in the physical sciences. Most of the glamour radiated from the computer crew. Members were notorious for long hair and beards and for working at all hours—sometimes shoeless and shirtless. They held raucous weekly meetings in the "bean-bag room," where people tossed around blue-sky concepts while reclining on huge pellet-filled hassocks. PARC's hotshots were not just playing at being geniuses. Before long, computer scientists recognized PARC as the leading source of research on how people interact with computers.

The hands-off policy at Xerox's headquarters in Stamford, Connecticut, proved a double-edged sword. PARC researchers used their freedom to explore concepts for personal computing that have since swept the industry. All sorts of computers, including some from Apple and IBM, now offer "bit mapped" displays, which PARC championed 10 years ago. Such displays link each of the thousands of dots on a video screen to a bit of information stored in computer memory, thus allowing the computer to change each dot and create very fine-grained images. Apple's new, easy-to-use Lisa flaunts a display that can be divided into "windows" for viewing several pieces of work at once, as well as a pointing device, or "mouse," for giving commands. PARC did the lion's share of work on both ideas.

But Xerox's loose management also encouraged PARC to overstep its charter, which was to do research, not nuts-and-bolts product development. By the mid-1970s, the center was hard at work on the Alto, an expensive machine with some of the attributes of a personal computer, which was supposed to serve as a research prototype. Alto and its software became so popular inside Xerox, where PARC installed a couple of thousand of the systems, that some renegade researchers began to see them as commercial products. Out of top management's sight, they slaved like distillers of moonshine whiskey to develop the Alto for the market.

Product development, however, was the turf of another Xerox group, which was championing a rival machine called the Star, later to reach the market as Xerox's 8010 workstation. Unlike a personal computer, which generally relies on its own processing power and memory, the Star worked well only when linked with other Xerox equipment. (See "Xerox Xooms toward the Office of the Future," *Fortune,* May 18, 1981.)

PARC rebels not only took on the development group, but also dominated a Xerox unit set up to test-market research prototypes. This group got over 100 Altos installed in the White House, both houses of Congress, and a few companies and universities. Unwilling to support rival machines, Xerox guillotined the Alto and in 1980 liquidated the whole test-marketing group.

Veterans of that group have been the chief evangelists of PARC technology. John Ellenby, one of the unit's managers, later founded Grid Systems. His Compass computer approximates some prescient PARC concepts first used in the Alto. It's portable, uses a bit-mapped display, and easily hooks up with remote computers. At $8,000 to $12,000, the Compass sounds too costly to be popular, but Grid expects revenues of more than $28 million in 1983, its first full year of operations; in August, Grid said it was on the verge of profitability.

Another manager of the test-marketing unit, Ben Wegbreit, had previously been one of PARC's brightest technical talents. Convergent Technologies of Santa Clara, California, founded in 1979 to make workstations, picked off Wegbreit and two colleagues to design software. Convergent's word processing program shows some of its origins in the form of a "piece table," a type of software developed at PARC. It allows computers with fairly small memories to process long documents. It does this by storing only the changes made when editing, along with the original version, instead of the original plus a full-length edited version, as other programs do.

Conveniences like that have helped Convergent land contracts that could produce some $450 million in sales to big computer companies that haven't developed their own desktop systems.

Charles Simonyi, who defected from Hungary at 17, styles himself "the messenger RNA of the PARC virus." He worked at the center for seven years, mostly on Bravo, a text-editing software program for the Alto that never reached the market. "We weren't supposed to do programs like that," he confesses, "so Bravo started out as a subterfuge. But when people at Xerox saw it, they wanted to use it inside the company. Bravo was why people used Altos, just as VisiCalc was the reason people bought the Apple II." Simonyi expected some brilliant executive to see his product's market potential. "That wasn't dumb," he says, "but it was naive to assume such a person would come from Xerox." Simonyi found a warmer welcome at Microsoft Corporation, based in Bellevue, Washington, which rang up $50 million in sales of personal-computer software in the year ended last June. A big chunk of this year's sales, which should approach $100 million, will come from Microsoft Word, a streamlined version of Bravo.

Lisa is the unkindest cut of all. In December 1979, Steve Jobs, then Apple's vice chairman, visited PARC with some colleagues to poke around. They saw Smalltalk, a set of programming tools. "Their eyes bugged out," recalls Lawrence Tesler, who helped develop Smalltalk. "They understood its significance better than anyone else who had visited." Seven months later, Jobs hired Tesler, having decided to use many Smalltalk features in the Lisa.

The Lisa had to be priced at $10,000, two to four times Jobs' earlier estimates. But it seems to be taking off. Apple claims to have shipped as many Lisas in July, the first month they were available, as Xerox has shipped Stars, or 8010s, in 19 months of availability. The Star, which embodies many concepts used in the Lisa, has been ill-starred. The influential *Seybold Report on Professional Computing* calls it "a jack-of-all-trades which does none really well." Sales suffered initially because some of the Star's software was late in coming to market.

Office equipment analysts have started referring to PARC-style systems as "Lisalike," not "Starlike." Apple's next computer, Macintosh, scheduled to ripen into a commercial product by the end of this year, could further identify Apple with PARC's ideas. The engineering manager for Macintosh came from PARC, where his last big project was a personal computer.

From this, Xerox might appear to have muffed the chance to make it big in personal computers with PARC's creations. Some Xeroids are sure the company could have been an early winner if only it had launched a less expensive Alto in the late 1970s. Unlike the Star, the Alto was an "open" computer, easy for outsiders to program. Independently written software has helped touch off the personal computer explosion, so the dissidents have a point. Because the Star is "closed," outsiders can't write programs for it.

To mourn the Alto, though, is to blame unfairly those who killed it. Xerox was out to produce office equipment, and no office equipment supplier, including IBM, foresaw that personal computers would compete with their wares. It was inconceivable that the cost of computer memory would decline 31 percent a year, as it has for the last five years, or that today's microcomputers would be as powerful as yesterday's mainframe computers. Xerox and its ilk concentrated not on freestanding personal computers but on clusters of workstations that share the use of computer hardware. That way, customers could spread high hardware costs across many workers. And suppliers could defray the costs of their prized sales forces with big-ticket orders.

Besides, Xerox had, and still has, ulterior motives in the office. Competition in the copier market keeps growing, and the company's chief aim has been to protect copier installations by strengthening its control of large, lucrative accounts. Companies that can sell complete office systems—workstations with reliable software, printers, and data-storage devices, all linked into a network—have a stronger lock on their customers than do suppliers of standalone equipment. Thus, the Star, which works well only when hooked up with other Xerox gear, seemed to fit the company's strategy better than free-standing little computers would.

The complete-system approach, moreover, was more compatible with Xerox's expansive ways of thinking than the alternative of making piecemeal improvements on an individual machine like the Alto. Big companies often can't make the modest efforts needed to probe emerging markets. "It's a problem when you're getting your feet wet in a new business," says Jack Goldman, formerly Xerox's research chief. "In a large company, every product must be a home run to justify the costs of marketing and development."

That has been especially true at Xerox, which owes its existence to xerography, one of the longest homers on record. Top management "followed the big-bank strategy," says one veteran. "They wanted to build absolutely the best office system instead of taking things bit by bit." At PARC, the company's urge to build the best at the expense of the merely better, like an Alto, had its own name: biggerism.

Biggerism could pay off in some ways, to be sure. Xerox has big hopes for Ethernet, a PARC-invented network that uses a cable and translating devices to connect different types of office equipment. By souping up the performance of PARC's original version of Ethernet, Xerox drastically raised the cost of hooking up, to as much as $5,000 per connection. That move discouraged sales and deterred other equipment makers from adapting their machines to talk through Ethernet. But now, improved chip technology has sliced the cost of connecting by about two-thirds. Over 70 office equipment makers are using Ethernet or plan to, including Apple. The temporary setback helped keep Ethernet from becoming *the* industry standard, but it is *a* standard. (The only other company likely to set a standard is IBM.)

Xerox still thinks PARC's work can produce some big hits. No one is more convinced than John Shoch, a remarkably hard-boiled former PARC researcher who became the company's office systems chief last October. His first priority is to expand the number of Xerox products that will communicate over Ethernet (20 do now, including laser printers and facsimile machines). Making a winner out of the Star will take more effort. Because the technology is old and the system tries to do so many things, the workstation seems expensive and inept in many functions, especially compared to Lisa.

Shoch wants to bring out a less costly version of the $15,000 Star, which he sees as one claw of a pincer's movement to narrow the Lisa's potential market share. The other claw, in his view, will be IBM's personal computer armed with a Lisa-like set of programs written by VisiCorp. Priced at some $7,000, that system won't compete directly with the Star but will be far cheaper than the Lisa. It will also tap into Ethernet—thanks to a helping hand from Xerox. Says Shoch: "There's going to be a squeeze between the lower priced Star and commodity-type computers that run better software. It'll be a tough place to compete."

The company's support of PARC has never wavered. This year's budget of $35 million or so will set a record. But changes have taken place. Last March, Xerox appointed a new director of PARC, William Spencer. A veteran of two decades at Bell Labs, Spencer admires AT&T's ability to transfer technology out of the lab by attaching satellite labs to major manufacturing plants. "PARC's main shortcoming," he feels, "has been a lack of management attention. We started things that didn't match what was going on in other parts of Xerox."

Spencer is trying to produce a better fit by meeting a couple of times a year at PARC with Xerox's division managers, some of whom haven't visited for years. Every three weeks or so he breakfasts with Shoch, and they've started a joint hiring program: some new researchers will spend their first year or so at PARC, then join the office systems group.

Time is on Spencer's side. Having taken its lumps in the office systems business, Xerox has a better fix on what kinds of products make sense. While Shoch's division still struggles to discover a successful way of selling office systems, PARC, having created much of the technology McColough sought, is stepping up its work on a new frontier: very-large-scale integrated circuits used for everything from diagnosing copier breakdowns to connecting personal computers with mainframes. "The foundation for our future will be the next generation of chips," says Spencer, who originally came to PARC to set up a line for making them. "Office systems is a smaller part of our work now."

When a company wants to make it big in a new business, a solid base of technology is necessary. But it's hardly sufficient. Without a clear understanding of corporate strategy and pressure from a hungry marketing group, even the best technologists can get out of hand. The tricky part is to strike a balance between encouraging creativity and getting your money's worth.

Case III–2
Duval Research Center

M. A. Maidique

"Duval has a dual ladder system," explained Jim Breitmaier, vice president of R&D, Duval Plastics Corporation. "However, it's not working well."

Two years ago, we created the Fellow position because there was a feeling, particularly among the younger scientists, that our dual ladder didn't go far enough. But the technical people continue to complain that the managers have more status in the hierarchy than they do.

Recently, I've begun to question the effectiveness of the dual ladder, at least our version of it. Can the dual ladder upgrade the status of the technical people? And, more importantly, is it a practical way to get scientists more involved in decision making? I have a hunch that our system can be significantly improved but I don't yet know what changes to make.

EXHIBIT 1 Sales and Net Income 1968–1977 (in millions)

	Sales	Net Income	R&D
1977	560	46	27
1976	512	42	24
1975	470	15	21
1974	525	24	19
1973	472	35	17
1972	357	27	NA
1971	302	17	
1970	304	22	
1969	270	27	
1968	240	24	

SOURCE: Duval Plastics Corporation, Annual Report, 1977.

Duval Plastics Corporation

Duval traced its origins to a chemical business established in 1900 by Alphonse Duval in Wilmington, Delaware. From the original chemical business, the company had branched out to plastics after World War II. Although by now Duval manufactured a wide variety of other products, the Duval Plastics Corporation is principally a specialty plastics manufacturer. Duval leadership in the specialty plastics industry is seen by management as strongly influenced by the firm's early commitment to search for better materials and more efficient ways of forming them into useful products. Jacques Duval, the company chairman, described the Duval team as committed to "making our science useful."

Research and development was a deeply rooted tradition at the Duval Plastics Corporation. The origin of Duval's R&D center was one of the first plastics research labs in the nation, established in 1918 by Thomas Murphy.

The commitment to research evidenced by Dr. Murphy's pioneering labor paid off. Over the decades following the First World War, the company had introduced a wide variety of new plastic materials. The company also pioneered in plastics manufacturing. The first automated plastics processes had been developed at Duval.

Research concepts had been successfully turned into sales and profits at the Duval Plastics Corporation. Net profits in 1977 reached $46 million on sales of $560 million while R&D expenditures increased to $27 million, a new record (see Exhibit 1). Less than 5 percent of these R&D expenditures were financed by the government.

The company's 30,000 products fall into three broad categories: *Consumer products* that include a wide variety of plastic tablewares and housewares for preparing, serving, and storing food and plastic components for other kitchen utensils; *electrical and electronic products* used widely in consumer, industrial, aerospace, military, and telecommunications equipment; *technical and other* products that include such wide applications as laboratory plastic equipment, clinical chemistry instruments, and spe-

EXHIBIT 2 Product Breakdown by Industry Segment* (in millions)

	Consumer Products	Consumer Durable Components	Capital Goods Components	Health and Science	General Corporate
Net sales	149	168	132	110	—
Income from operations	28	37	22	13	43*
Total assets	74	86	64	75	240†

*Corporate research and development projects which are designed to benefit a wide range of products and processes.
†Includes cash, short-term investments, and investments in associated companies.

cialized diagnostic testing systems. (See Exhibit 2 for a product breakdown by industry segment.)

The Plastics Research Center

From its modest beginning 60 years earlier, Duval's Research Center had grown to a complex of several buildings located in Wilmington, Delaware, and surrounded by over 500 acres of meadowlands and hills. In late 1975, the center extended its activities to include a laboratory on the outskirts of Munich, Germany.

The Research Center's organization included 150 scientists and engineers with bachelor's and advanced degrees in 30 disciplines, including 62 PhDs. Two hundred fifty technicians, secretaries, and other supporting personnel made up the remainder of the center's organization.

Several of the Plastics Research Center's PhDs had gone on to senior management positions at Duval. The president of Duval, Dr. Jonathan Glasgow, had started out as a chemist in one of the Plastics Research Center's laboratories in 1960. Dr. Selden Loring, vice chairman of the board and director of the Research Division, had begun his career as a researcher in 1945. Dr. James Breitmaier, vice president R&D, had likewise begun his career as a research scientist in 1965.

Research, development, and engineering activities at the Plastics Research Center cover a very wide range. Five broad areas, however, account for most of Duval's R&D activities:

1. Materials sciences.
2. Physical sciences.
3. Life sciences.
4. Product development.
5. Process research and development.

To accomplish its broad range of R&D goals, Duval had over the years assembled a cadre of scientists with impressive credentials and diverse backgrounds. The Plastics Research Center includes scientists with degrees in analytical, physical, and organic chemistry; ceramics; metallurgy; and crystallography. There are also electrical and mechanical engineers, computer scientists and product designers, optical physicists, and mathematicians. During the last decade, Duval has also recruited a team of biochemists, biomedical engineers, immunologists, and microbiologists.

Duval's management could point to several examples to demonstrate the wide freedom that Duval scientists enjoyed in their research pursuits. The curiosity and enterprising abilities of Duval's scientists had led the company far afield, from plastics materials research to fields such as biochemistry, immunology, and blood analysis.

Organization

The Plastics Research Center is one of the three main organizational blocks of the Duval Plastics Corporation that report directly to the chairman, Jacques Duval. President Jonathan Glasgow is primarily responsible for domestic operations and has responsibility for most of the company's 45 manufacturing plants and its 15,000 employees. Vice Chairman Charles Duval, the chairman of the board's cousin, has responsibility for international operations. About one-third of Duval's sales were made to customers outside the United States. Vice Chairman Selden Loring is responsible for the Research Division. (See organization chart in Exhibit 3.)

Neither of the Duvals was a technical person. They had both, however, graduated in business from Stanford University. Thus, President Glasgow, a PhD physical chemist, in conjunction with Selden Loring, exerted a great deal of influence over technical decisions.

Jon Glasgow explained his role:

> It would be difficult for me to play a key role in the company's technological decisions if I had not had

EXHIBIT 3 Duval Plastics Corporation Organization

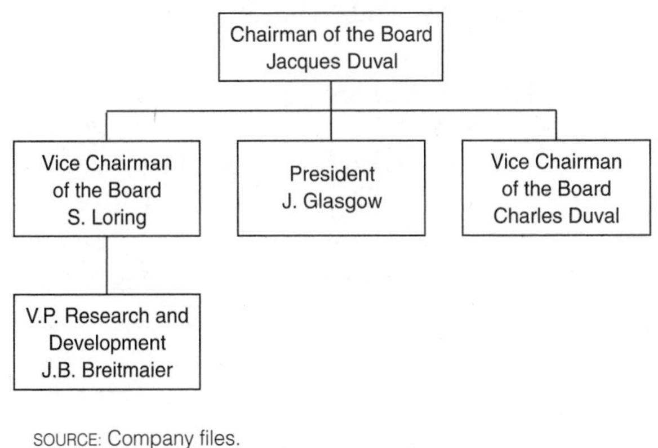

SOURCE: Company files.

> the technical training that I have. At Duval, I headed up the physics and electronics lab before assuming general management responsibilities. My technical background is not absolutely essential but it does give me credibility with the technical people. But my real role is that of a "creative intermediary", who brings together the technology and the market opportunity.
>
> As a minimum, the manager of a technology firm must have enough highly qualified technical people around him so that he can have access to sound judgments regarding technology. The key to this access is a management style that allows the right communications to come up through the organization to the president's office.

Some of these technical inputs had been provided by many years at Duval by Dr. Selden Loring, who had distinguished himself in the company by his technical work as well as by building an outstanding research team. While Selden Loring directed Duval's technical efforts, he also took care to groom a successor. Loring had decided many years before that Jim Breitmaier would succeed him.

Dr. James Breitmaier was now responsible for all of the line operations of the Plastics Research Corporation, including the European lab. Reporting to Dr. Breitmaier were four line, director-level departments:

1. Research.
2. Development (process and product).
3. Bubble memories.
4. European R&D.

Also reporting were two staff departments:

1. Planning.
2. Administrative and technical services.

The Dual Career Ladder

The first rung of a parallel career ladder for scientists and engineers, the Senior Associate, had existed for 20 years at Duval (Exhibit 4).[1] However, over the last few years a feeling had developed, particularly among the younger scientists, that the ladder didn't go far enough.

EXHIBIT 4 Parallel Ladder Structure

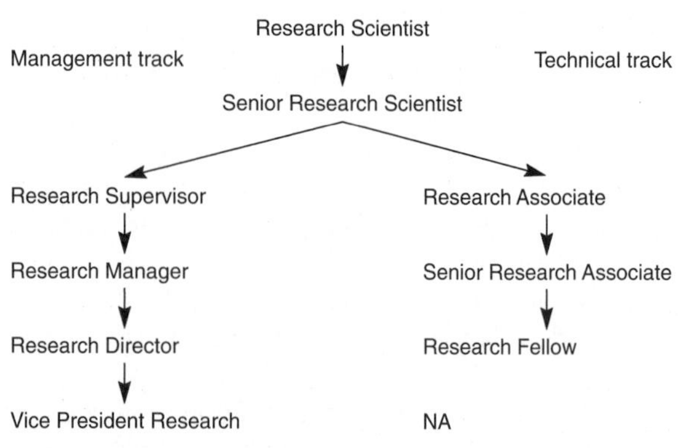

Partially in response to this sentiment Dr. Breitmaier had established the Fellow position in 1977. "I guess you could call me the 'champion' of the Fellow concept," said Breitmaier.

"The first two Fellows, Dave Marein and Bernie Dante, were chosen without formal guidelines," Breitmaier explained.

> They are outstanding scientists, however, and certainly no one would question their appointments. But in the future we must be more careful, more systematic about the appointments. That's why we have prepared a document to establish ground rules for future appointments to the Research Associate and Fellow positions (Exhibit 5).
>
> I think that the creation of the Research Fellow position has been a positive step. However, there remain a lot of unanswered questions about the parallel ladder concept and how it should be implemented. I've still to resolve a number of difficult issues.
>
> Two years ago, for example, research, development, and engineering were one organization.[2] Thus the issue of whether there should be an Engineering Fellow, or a Development Fellow, wouldn't have come up. We are now discussing whether we shouldn't create such positions [see Exhibit 6 for proposal]. There are clearly pros and cons. We want to stimulate first-class technical work throughout the company. But will this dilute the significance of appointment to a Fellow position?

[1]The parallel ladder is a dual hierarchy system, widely employed by U.S. technology-based systems since the early 1960s, which aimed at improving the status and the compensation levels of distinguished scientists and engineers.

[2]Now most of the company's engineering and development is done at the operating divisions.

EXHIBIT 5 Research Associate/Research Fellow Position Definition

Objective

To provide for the professional career advancement of those members of the Plastics Research Center who have made significant research contributions and whose talents and skills lie particularly in the scientific and technological fields.

Background

Duval has established a series of research positions and titles for senior members of the technical staff, ranging from the Associate level to the post of Fellow. This memorandum outlines the procedures, qualifications, and guidelines to be used in considering candidates for promotion to the Associate position or higher in this series.

Procedures

Proposals for promotion of a candidate will be prepared by the immediate supervisor and presented to the Research Center Staff, who will make a recommendation to J. B. Breitmaier for final decision. The supervisor should present a written proposal two weeks in advance of meeting with the staff and should expect to present and discuss the proposal personally.

Qualifications

Advancement to Associate and to higher posts will depend on identification and recognition of scientific and technical stature of the candidate and contributions made. These qualities should be considered from the viewpoint of the company as well as from the viewpoint of the scientific community worldwide.

Strict quantitative measures are not adequate and can only serve as guidelines together with qualitative factors in considering the merits of a proposal. Some suggested guidelines and factors are included below. A candidate will seldom meet all of the qualifications fully, but should meet most.

Business Contribution

- Should be identified as key contributor to inventions and/or developments which are important to the company business.
  - At the *Associate* level, these contributions may not yet be reflected in significant new sales volume.
  - At the *Senior Associate* level, the candidate will usually be associated with significant sales volume contribution and with several invention/development areas.
  - At the *Fellow* level, the candidate will usually be identified as introducing an important discontinuity in the flow of corporate technology, resulting in the opening of new business(es).
- In considering business contribution qualifications, it will be useful to judge:
  - How far away from traditional Duval technology has the candidate taken us successfully?
  - What degree of professional risk was assumed?
  - How consistently has the candidate demonstrated ability to originate ideas and solutions over time?
  - What degree of autonomy has been accorded the candidate in the choice of program?

Technical Stature

The *Associate* candidate will usually have several patent disclosures, may have one or more issued patents and a few published technical papers of recognized quality.

A *Senior Associate* is usually recognized by the organization as an expert in a limited field and is consulted by peers and by marketing specialists on occasion.

The *Fellow* candidate will normally be widely known in the scientific community, with more than 20 issued patents, of which several are in commercial use.

Fellows are recognized as corporate experts in their field, and are consulted by peers, by marketing, and by management. They are looked to as setting a standard of technical excellence for the corporation.

In considering the technical stature qualifications, it may be useful to list:

- Publications and their significance.
- Patents and their impact.
- Professional society prizes/awards.
- Editorial activities—professional journals/books.
- Invited-speaker role at professional meetings.
- NSF reviewer role.

3-10-79

SOURCE: Company files.

EXHIBIT 6 Engineering Fellow/Associate Proposal

TO: Research Center department heads
FROM: J. B. Breitmaier and A. B. Johnson*
DATE: December 15, 1978
SUBJ: Engineering Fellow/Associate Advisory Committee

Attached is the proposal for the procedure and qualifications for the positions of Engineering Fellow, Senior Engineering Associate, and Engineering Associate. This proposal has been approved by us and the appropriate people in the Personnel organization and now needs to be made ongoing.

We would like each of you to be a member of the first Advisory Committee for Engineering Fellow/Associate. We have asked Mike Cassandino† to be the chairman and he will be contacting you regarding your first meeting.

We feel this is a definite step forward in recognizing and rewarding exceptional engineering talents as well as more closely tying together the Research Center to the operating divisions.

Proposal

To formalize between the Plastics Research Center and the Operating Divisions the process for selection of Engineering Associate and Senior Engineering Associate, and to recognize a new level of corporate engineering contributions through the new position of Engineering Fellow.

System's Objective

To recognize and reward those individuals employed by Duval who have made significant-measurable-outstanding engineering contributions to the company.

Qualifications

These positions are considered a reward for past accomplishments rather than anticipated future behavior. The guidelines are as follows:

	Associate		Fellow			
Qualification	A1	A2	F1	F2	F3	F4
Contribution to D.P.C. profitability (in millions of dollars)	1–2	2–10	10–30	30–60	60–100	>100
Contributions (multiple) recognized outstanding in the field by:						
Division	Yes	Yes	Yes	Yes	Yes	Yes
Corporation (WW)	No	Yes	Yes	Yes	Yes	Yes
USA	No	No	Yes	Yes	Yes	Yes
World	No	No	No	No	Yes	Yes
Recognized as a consultant by:						
Peers	Yes	Yes	Yes	Yes	Yes	Yes
Division	Yes	Yes	Yes	Yes	Yes	Yes
Corporation (WW)	No	Yes	Yes	Yes	Yes	Yes
Recipient of individual outstanding contributor award or equivalent	0	1	2	3	4	5
Number of patents/awards	0–5	5–10	10–15	15–20	20–25	>25
Performance rating last three years	EX/OS	EX/OS	EX/OS	EX/OS	EX/OS	EX/OS

Qualifier

1. Should not be in the "mainstream" of management, but instead have a specific technical orientation.
2. Individual can have people reporting to him or to her.
3. Contributions can be accumulative and it would be possible to move progressively higher in group number as additional contributions are made.
4. The first three guideline factors will represent 80 percent of the qualifying needs.
5. Since all of these individuals contribute more towards future growth than short-term profitability, we did not feel additional compensation on a regular basis would be desirable. However, they should be considered for such rewards as stock options.

Approval Process

1. All recommendations for these positions should be screened first by the Advisory Committee consisting of three Engineering Division Directors, two Plastic Research Center Directors, and one Fellow.
2. At least 50% of the Advisory Committee should be rotated every three years.

EXHIBIT 6 ***(concluded)***

3. The Advisory Committee should meet formally three times a year with candidates for all levels proposed by the appropriate director (sponsor).
4. All recommendations from the Advisory Committee must be unanimous and will need the final approval of Dr. Breitmaier and Mr. Johnson.

*Vice president, Engineering Division.
†Director, Personnel Department.

SOURCE: Company files.

Then there is the question of how many Fellows and Associates to appoint. Right now we have 2 Fellows, 8 Senior Associates, and 15 Associates out of a pool of 300 technicians and scientists. But technical people point out that there are over twice as many managers, 20, as there are Senior Associates, the equivalent ladder position. With more opportunities available, this signals to some that we are still emphasizing managers.

But the crux of the problem is improving the quality of our technological decisions, finding better ways to integrate decision making and technology.

Although I enjoy technical work, I generally don't make technical decisions myself. I don't get involved in, accept, or reject decisions on projects that have less than a $5,000 sales potential, and 20 percent of the programs we're involved in are below this level.

The burden of decision making falls on the six department directors and their supporting managers. But I try to stay abreast of what is going on technically. I have often said to Fellows and Associates, "Drop in and talk whenever you want." And quite a few do come in.

It's very important for us to maintain the highest quality technical communications. In the early stages of a project development, using traditional business tools such as IRR and ROA are not very useful. It's really technical judgment that counts. You can't analyze the project in numerical terms until it gets into the very latest stages of development. (Duval had defined five new project development stages.)

Stage	Objective
1. Basic research	Basic knowledge
2. Applied research	Technical feasibility
3. Exploratory development	Commercial feasibility
4. Scheduled development	Production and initial sales
5. Commercial development	Profit

At present, technical requests are evaluated by our technical directors in conjunction with managers from the line divisions. Perhaps some of the dual ladder people should be automatically included in these committees.

Interviews with Technical Staff's Division Scientists

Several scientists on the technical ladder and younger aspirants were questioned by the casewriter regarding their attitudes towards the Duval ladder system.

Bernie Dante, Research Fellow, PhD physical chemistry, MIT, 25 years at Duval, 18 patents, 27 publications.

I've been a Research Fellow since the program began in 1977, along with Dave Marein. Earlier I had been the manager of a small chemistry department. Now I have less administrative responsibility; otherwise, I do the same kind of work.

The Fellow position was created in part as a response to the criticisms by younger scientists. They argued that the dual ladder didn't go far enough. The ladder now, for the Fellow position, has no salary limit.

But people still complain that it is tough to get ahead in the technical ladder. There are eight Senior Research Associates, and this may be too few compared to the over 20 managers.

However, when you get there the dual ladder positions are fully equivalent. And I haven't heard anyone else say otherwise. Of course this doesn't mean that the technical people control the management decisions.

In principle, the dual ladder system is modeled on the achievements of Dr. W. George. Dr. W. George, who started out as a research scientist, became the "Dean of the Fellows" at Duval. He has one of the most impressive technical records in the history of the company. Altogether he has about 40 patents. He was a research director until he retired a couple of years ago.

Patents, in part for historical reasons, are an important part of the Duval corporate strategy. For many decades, Duval has thrived on a number of unusual material and process innovations.

Recently David Marein, the only other person thus far appointed to the Fellow position, coinvented bubble memories. (Marein and a Bell Labs scientist are considered the coinventors of bubble memories.) This was a major development, though quite a bit outside of our main plastics business, where I have done most of my own work.

Every year, Duval is granted about 50 patents. We generally follow a policy of patenting first, to assure protection, and then publishing. Sometimes, however, to get the benefit of outside reaction, we will publish before a patent issues.

It's tough, however, to evaluate the value of patents. Material patents, for instance, are easier to defend. In general, it's very difficult to evaluate the potential of an R&D idea. It's far easier to reward product development and sales.

I'm delighted to have been selected a Research Fellow, but in a sense I am not absolutely clear about the need for the position. To me the achievements that lead to the position are a great reward in themselves.

On the other hand, maybe I'm too influenced by the old times when any of us could drop in and talk to Glasgow and Loring. Then the labs used to be next to the administrative building. Now we're at the Center, 15 miles away. I don't know how the younger guys feel about this, that is, the ones that don't know the top management people personally.

Charlie Lucas, Senior Research Associate, PhD, Cornell, physics, 17 years at Duval, 40 papers, 9 patents.

The second ladder is a bunch of nonsense. I don't care what they call me even if it's "Lord King of Research." Let me point out at the outset that at least half of my peers would disagree with my views on this.

The key issue to me is who tells you what to do. I have no more say in what goes on now than before. I'm likely to report to someone 10 or 12 years my junior. I control no funds, no people. I can only sign for $100. But, on the other hand, I see no way that this could be changed. That is, no way short of anarchy.

There is a lot of pressure around here to be a manager. It's a very prestigious and powerful position. It's the goal of many of our research people. Some of them don't really belong in research. They are interested in management, not science. They'd just as soon manage an underwear factory.

Yet often they make technical decisions. But when a project fails, doesn't make a buck, the failure trickles back to us and we bench scientists shoulder the criticism.

But don't get me wrong. Being a manager is difficult. For me it would be almost impossible. I don't like to tell others what to do. I have an inferiority complex about ordering others around.

Becoming a Research Fellow is to a certain extent a matter of luck. You can't judge people's technical ability, so what do you do? You make the appointment depend on the commercial success their developments have had.

In the physics group, for instance, there is a small chance of a big commercialization success so there is a small chance of becoming a Fellow. It helps, however, if you're working on one of the big projects (projected ultimate market of $5 million or more). Then you have the best access to funds, space, people, and any other resources you might need. But a lot of exploratory research still winds up being aborted.

It's the old, paradoxical tension between basic research and commercialization. If you're Bell Labs—and everyone aspires to be Bell Labs—you presumably can ignore it. Duval can't. We are not Bell Labs.

Yet no one would disagree with the appointments to the Fellow level that have thus far been made. Most people believe that more should be made.

There should be a Senior Fellow position but there is no one at this point to appoint at that level. Only Dr. George, who is now retired, would have qualified. He was responsible for more important inventions than anyone else in the company. He has over 40 patents.

But why worry so much about the dual ladder? All that people should be told is, "Look, there are two ways to go, management or individual contributor. And you should think very hard about this."

Bill Osell, Research Scientist, PhD immunogenetics, Columbia, 30 years old, three years at Duval.

I've had a unique opportunity here at Duval to set up a new program in immunology. The funding has been fantastic. Basically they allowed me to do my own thing. The support for my program, in general, has been excellent. This is very important to all scientists.

In the long term, I have a choice between climbing the technical or management ladder. The question is how long will I be able to retain my present productivity, that is, my output in terms of publications and patents. To advance in the Duval parallel ladder, you need to develop an international reputation. Several of our scientists, for instance, are members of the National Academy of Sciences. But getting to the top of the ladder has its rewards. Bernie Dante, for instance, might make more than the president of Duval. His job is also very, very secure.

On the other hand, promotions in the scientific end are basically conservative, that is, progress up the ladder is slow. We are top heavy in managers.

But nonetheless, management is a real alternative for me. I like working with people and organizing. If I run out of technical ideas, I'll give it a try.

Robert Richards, Senior Research Associate, chemist, MS protein chemistry, RPI, PhD work (complete except for thesis), Stanford University, 28 patents, 32 published papers, 14 years at Duval, Fundamental Life Sciences Department. Present projects: waste conversion, tissue culture fermentation.

The parallel ladder is a great concept, that is, it has the potential to be a great system. But to work, it has to be an equal partnership between scientists and management.

We are still far from this ideal at Duval. But things are better than they were a few years ago. At one time, the parallel ladder was simply a dumping ground for scientists that had failed as managers. This is no longer the case. But management and economics still dominate the technical people.

Ideally, the managers should make the budget, planning, and personnel decisions while the scientists make the decisions on the technical programs. In short, there should be an equal partnership. This is the only way the positions on the ladder could be fully equivalent.

Right now they aren't. Take compensation, for instance. Equivalent positions on the ladder have equivalent salary ranges. But it takes much longer in elapsed time for a technical person to get to the equivalent managerial level. You're penalized for being on the technical side.

The differences manifest themselves in other ways, too. The managers have larger, better furnished and located offices, and easier access to clerical and secretarial assistance.[3] What all this adds up to is that the "equivalent" management positions have more status and recognition in the Duval community.

Managers can also rise higher in the hierarchy than technical people. The highest position I can aspire to on the technical track is a Research Fellow, which is rated on the ladder as a director-level equivalent. However, there is no equivalent Senior Research Fellow that could be, at least theoretically, equivalent to a corporate vice president. But I recognize that it has to stop there. There can be only one president. But why shouldn't the president have one or more VP-level technical advisors?

Duval has actually gone backwards in this regard. The Fellows used to report to our vice president, Jim Breitmaier, but now they report to the director of research. It's been like that, one step forward, a half-step backward.

But maybe the most significant problem is that the judgment of technical people is not yet weighed sufficiently. If you're in a meeting, it's always the management people that have the final say, even on technical issues. It's simply not an equal partnership.

But the problems, I believe, are solvable. Our present system can be improved. One thing that we have going for us is that Jim [Breitmaier] listens and people are willing to speak their mind to him. I am basically optimistic that future changes will be for the better.

[3]Parking for the R&D Center was on a first-come, first-served basis from technicians to James Breitmaier.

Conclusion

Jim Breitmaier had recently done a good deal of thinking about the Duval dual career structure. He was intimately familiar with the prevailing attitudes and reservations regarding the Duval dual ladder system at the Plastics Research Center. He thought some changes could be constructive but he hadn't yet decided what these might be and when they should be implemented. Jim had recently obtained access to an excerpt from a consultant's report that discussed the recent literature on dual career ladders (Appendix). He wondered how relevant these academic findings might be to his own operation.

APPENDIX: DUVAL RESEARCH CENTER

Parallel Ladders: The Modern View

To the modern researcher the parallel ladder, in MIT's Ed Roberts's words, "is an oversimplified solution to a complex problem." Thus, the focus of management research has in the last decade shifted to the study of the overall problem of the organizational implications of technical careers.

The groundwork for understanding the dual ladder dilemma is laid out in Schoner and Harrell's study.[1] Schoner and Harrell surveyed the attitudes of 100 engineers and managers in an electronics company that had implemented the dual ladder concept. They designed nine questions that measured morale, attitudes towards the dual ladder, and attitudes towards recognition. Only in two questions are the differences in response between the technical and management groups statistically significant:

1. The technical personnel—much more so than the management group—felt that they were underpaid.

2. A significant minority of technical personnel were dissatisfied with being on the technical ladder.

However, surprisingly, morale was high *throughout the firm*. There were no significant morale differences between the managerial and the technical groups. This data led the authors to conclude that

> high morale among technical personnel does not *necessarily* depend on their having equal prestige in the company, or on being paid on the same scale [author emphasis].

[1]B. Schoner and T. W. Harrell, "The Questionable Dual Ladder," *Personnel,* January/February 1973.

EXHIBIT A Organizational Roles for Technically Trained Personnel at Mid-Career

Orientation at Mid-Career		Organizational Evaluation of Potential: High	Organizational Evaluation of Potential: Low ("ordinary")
	Technical	Independent contributor Policy specialist "Idea innovator" "Internal entrepreneur" (1)	Technical support Expert on "formatted" tasks (2)
	People	Top management Sponsor Development as policy (3)	Mentor Individual development functions (4)
	Nonwork	Specialist Internal consultant (5)	(6)

The reason is that technical people "tend to look to their professional colleagues (which may be outside the firm) for recognition."

Thus, to Schoner and Harrell the paradoxical finding of universally high morale in a situation in which the dual ladder had failed to confer equal prestige on the managerial and technological groups "suggests that the dual ladder policy is based on a misconception of what engineers and scientists really want from their jobs."

However, despite these caveats, the dual ladder has proliferated. One survey of 22 technology-based companies found that 75 percent had "some kind of parallel ladder system,"[2] while another study of 10 similar firms found that 70 percent had "certain dual hierarchies."[3] The widespread character of the dual ladder combined with the contradictions pointed out by the Schoner and Harrell study highlight the need for a more sophisticated examination of the dual ladder dilemma.

Lotte Baylyn, in a continuing study of MIT graduates, attempts such an analysis by segmenting the mid-career technically trained professional into three groups:[4]

1. Technically oriented.
2. People oriented.
3. Nonwork oriented.

These groups are then further subdivided into "high" and "low" (or ordinary) organization potential. This results in the six cells given in Exhibit A. According to Professor Baylyn, each of these cells has its own characteristics and must be considered individually. Baylyn notes that "most organizations are geared to cell 3, to people-oriented employees who will rise to top positions in the company." The difficulties that dual ladder systems face are clarified by the Baylyn model:

> The trouble with the technical ladder is that it has so often been used for cell 4 employees that it has lost its value for those in cell 1 for whom it is really intended. In other words, the technical ladder has been implemented in most companies in such a way that it has not differentiated between high- and low-potential employees. Companies must find a place for the "plateaued" manager—the people-oriented employees who will not make it at the top; they must also find ways of allowing their potential technical people to expand in influence and express their particular competences. But the same mechanism cannot easily serve both these needs, and the technical ladder has too often been asked to do just that.[5]

[2]Stanford University, *Motivation of Scientists and Engineers,* Stanford Graduate School of Business, Stanford University, 1959, pp. 14–16.

[3]John W. Riegel, *Administration of Salaries and Intangible Rewards for Engineers and Scientists* (Ann Arbor: Bureau of Industrial Relations, University of Michigan, 1958), p. 23.

[4]Lotte Baylyn, "An Analysis of Mid-Career Issues and Their Organization Implications," to appear in J. E. Paap (ed.), *New Dimensions in Management of Human Resources* (London: Prentice Hall International).

[5]Ibid.

The dual ladder decision is an important one for a technically based company. But it is subtle enough to demand a careful analysis of precisely what group it is that is to be rewarded. And it must not be allowed to become "a 'booby prize' for those that fail to make the more prestigious administrative ladder," since for most engineers "success seems to consist in winning a place in management."[6]

But perhaps most important for high-level technical contributors—dual ladder or not—is that they, in Baylyn's words, "must not be isolated from the decision-making top management group." A corollary to this idea is that top managements that pursue this policy—quite apart from the motivational benefit—will doubtlessly be better able to make sound, well-informed technological decisions.

Reading III–2
Financial Engineering at Merck

Thomas Luehrman

Last year Merck & Co., Inc., invested well over $2 billion in R&D and capital expenditures combined. The company spent much of the money on risky, long-term projects that are notoriously difficult to evaluate. Indeed, the critics of modern finance would argue that such projects should not be subjected to rigorous financial analysis, because such analysis fails to reflect the strategic value of long-term investments. Yet at Merck, it is the longest horizon, most strategic projects that receive the most intense and financially sophisticated analyses. In fact, Merck's finance function is active and influential with a highly quantitative, analytical orientation. The company is seldom, if ever, criticized for being shortsighted.

[6]Leonard Sayles and G. Strauss, *Managing Human Resources,* p. 386.

Reprinted by permission of *Harvard Business Review,* January–February 1994, pp. 94–96.

Why doesn't all this analysis choke off long-term investing, as critics of modern finance theory say it should? In part because Merck is a leader in building financial models of scientific and commercial processes and in using those models to improve business decisions. Rather than relying on static, single-point forecasts, Merck's models use probability distributions for numerous variables and come up with a range of possible outcomes that both stimulate discussion and facilitate decision making.

For example, Merck's Research Planning Model, now 10 years old, integrates economics, finance, statistics, and computer science to produce disciplined, quantitative analyses of specific elements of Merck's business. This model does not make decisions. Instead, it provides Merck executives with cogent information both about risks and returns and about financial performance for specific projects and activities.

The Research Planning Model

In 1983, major drug development projects at Merck were not formally, prospectively evaluated as capital investments. They faced rigorous *scientific* scrutiny, to be sure, but comparatively little economic or financial scrutiny. Judy Lewent, then chief financial advisor to Merck's Research Division, sought to create two specific capabilities in a comprehensive Research Planning Model: the ability to assess risk and return, project by project, prior to the commitment of significant funds; and the ability to assess the contribution of the research laboratories to the health and performance of the entire corporation.

To build the Research Planning Model, Lewent and her staff used a technique known as *Monte Carlo simulation.* Computers a decade ago were primitive, and no usable commercial software packages existed. So Merck had to create its own simulation "engine," encode the necessary probability distributions, and write computer programs to handle variables associated with pharmaceutical R&D. The model's inputs include scientific and therapeutic variables, capital expenditures, production and selling costs, product prices and quantities, and macroeconomic variables like interest, inflation, and exchange rates. For all these variables, the model

EXHIBIT 1 Merck's Research Planning Model

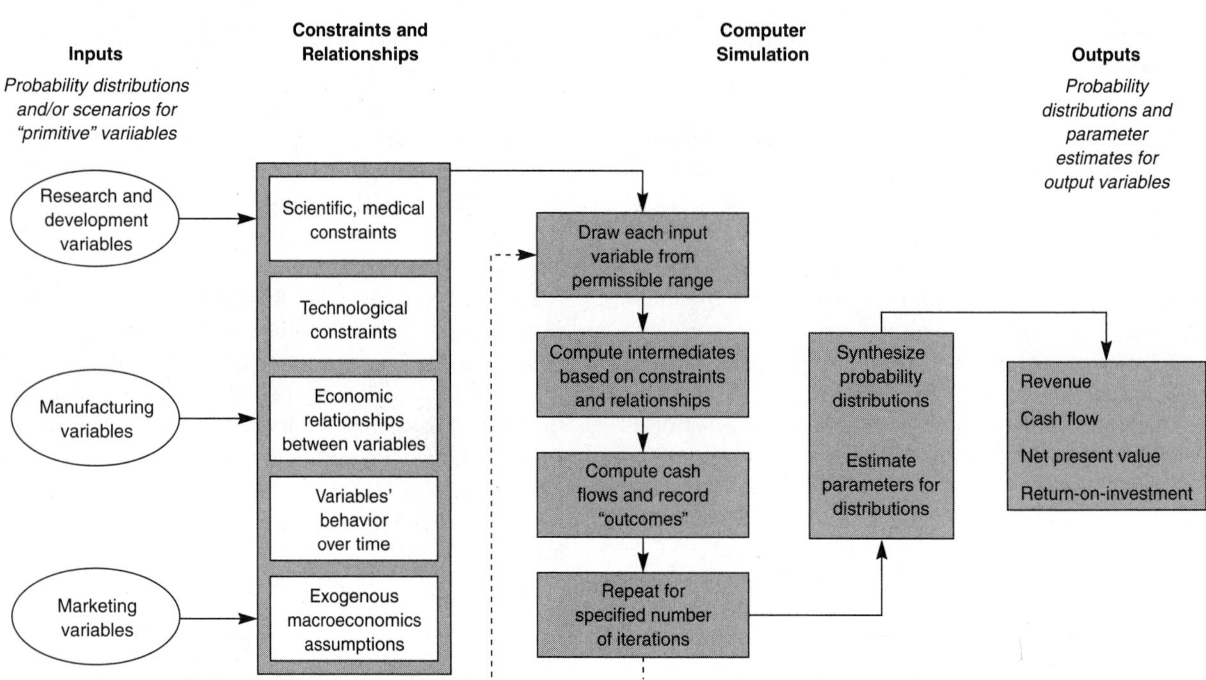

uses ranges rather than point estimates, for example, "optimistic," "expected," and "pessimistic" values for a variable or actual probability distributions.

The computer repeatedly draws values from permissible ranges and computes outcomes based on specified relationships between the variables and other parameters. In this way, the model synthesizes probability distributions for key output variables, such as annual nominal- and constant-dollar forecasts of revenues, cash flow, return-on-investment, and net present value (NPV). Hence, the output from the model is not merely a point forecast for, say, NPV, but a frequency distribution showing the probability that a project's NPV will exceed a certain level. Summary statistics, such as standard deviation per unit of time, can be computed from the synthesized distribution and then used in other analyses, such as an option analysis.

What are the payoffs of all this sophistication? In short, better decisions. With this model, Merck neither disregards the uncertainty associated with drug development as unquantifiable nor grossly oversimplifies that uncertainty with point estimates. Instead, the realities of the pharmaceutical industry are explicitly acknowledged and quantified in a disciplined fashion by probability distributions. And rather than looking at R&D as a collection of scientific problems, the model allows management to view it in the context of the whole business. In this light, the very different commercial implications of seemingly similar scientific problems emerge, and executives can tailor investment decisions accordingly. Finally, the model's broad financial perspective and its formal treatment of uncertainty are boiled down into cash flows and present values: the "coin of the realm" in finance.

In all these respects, Merck's financial analysis of the R&D process is not only compatible with modern finance theory but can even be said to exemplify best current practice. For example, in the model's first year, 1984, its output helped shape an important internal debate about whether or not R&D could produce enough new products to turn Merck into a growth company without diversifying out of pharmaceuticals. The model confirmed this possibility, and, indeed, over the next five years, Merck's market capitalization grew at an average rate of more than 45 percent per year. By 1989, the Research Planning Model was used to evaluate every significant research-and-development program in the company over a 20-year horizon. (See Exhibit 1.)

Reading III–3
The Transfer of Technology from Research to Development

H. Cohen, S. Keller, and D. Streeter

In this paper, we will discuss some observations we have made in our own laboratories on the transfer of technology from research to development. We have tried to assemble "data" on transfers or attempted transfers that have occurred over the past 15 years. We have inspected these findings to see whether some common features could be recognized.

IBM's Research Division is a separate division of the company, independent of product groups, and reporting directly to the chief operating executives in the corporate office. The division is not, however, a staff advisory group but is charged with two major functions: to contribute to the technologies required for the product line by supporting current technologies and by finding new alternatives, and to contribute to those fields of science which underlie present product technologies and which may provide future ones. Product development is carried out in the laboratories of the groups' development divisions. There are 27 of these throughout the world. Thus, our Research Division, with its three laboratories in Yorktown Heights, San Jose, and Zurich, faces a development community about 10 times our size, well spread geographically, and covering a very large range of technical areas. In only one case, at San Jose, are research and development laboratories located at the same site.

Since completing the data taking and analysis reported here, we have used some of the notions to help guide research managers and project leaders with new transfers as they have come about. In doing this, we have begun to perceive other aspects that we hope will bear further generalizations, perhaps in later reports. In addition, we have added to our divisional staff a full-time marketing representative as program manager for technology transfer, and a full-time cost estimator. The former serves to make the corporate and divisional marketing representatives knowledgeable about our work and to bring their requirements to us. The latter helps us prepare our case with our development colleagues.

Research Management 22, no. 3 (May 1979), pp. 11–17. Reprinted with permission.

Methodology

First, let us set out some terminology. Transfers will be called successful if the technology has moved from research to a development laboratory and then has become a product or a part of a product or an important enhancement of a production process. A nonsuccessful transfer will be one in which the technology has left research but has not appeared as a product. A nontransfer refers to research projects that were intended for transfer but were never accepted in development.

We began our study with two parallel steps: first, we wrote down the "well-known" lore in the company having to do with the transfer problem; and second, we examined a long list of all the projects in the laboratories over a 15-year period that we felt were intended to be transferred (remember that part of our mission has always been to work in science as well as in applied projects).

The prejudices about what was required for a good transfer were collected from research and development managers and staff members who had been involved in transfers. Here are some of them:

1. There must be an advanced technology group in the receiving organization to enable transfer to take place. (*Advanced technology* is the term used in the company for an advanced effort in the development laboratory not directly supporting a currently planned product but aimed at follow-on or replacement products.)
2. Advanced technology competes with research, often blocking transfer.
3. Transfer occurs when "outsiders" recognize the value of the technology. These outsiders may be external to the company, or they may be internal users of the technology but not prospective developers.
4. The external marketplace can play an effective role in pressuring a transfer to take place.
5. Once a project has transferred, it is useful to maintain some level of work in research, overlapping and complementing the newly initiated work in the division.
6. There should be joint participation, by research and development, when the project is still in research. The transfer can be most easily facilitated with the transfer of people from the joint program to the receiving organization.
7. Physical proximity of research to the receiving organization is important.

We examined the long list of projects and divided it into new lists of successful, nonsuccessful, and nontransfers. From these, we chose projects that represented the functional areas of our research programs: logic and memory, storage, input/output and communications, systems and programming, and computer applications. We actually reviewed only 18 projects so that we can certainly make no claims to completeness even within our own laboratories. A description of each of the case histories is given in the Appendix. Furthermore, we conducted our examination in an "anthropological" mode of observation and discussion through interviews without trying to quantify results. We have, therefore, arrived at some views and suggestions and not at hard-and-fast conclusions or rules of conduct.

From the original prejudices or "lore" noted above, we produced an interviewing guide and then interviewed more than 50 people who were involved in the transfers. Most, but not all, of these are or were in the research division so that we have more a research view than a general one. Case histories were prepared for each of the projects. The case histories and key factor suggestions were reviewed, testing the original prejudices, sometimes replacing or confirming them, sometimes adding new factors of interest. We finally replaced the original list with a new set of factors or ingredients of a transfer to which we gave an ordering of importance. In the following two sections, we will discuss these technology transfer factors in order of relative importance. In the discussion, we will point out examples from specific projects to help explain the factors.

Primary Factors

Technical understanding

It is essential that research understand the main technical issues of the technology before passing it on. This may seem obvious. However, in some cases we studied this did not seem to be true, and this is why we believe the technical base for each project must be considered carefully. In the germanium project, while the materials and processing problems were understood, the limitations in the advantages of germanium over silicon only became apparent after several years of research activity. These had less to do with devices that were created and more to do with device implementation in packaging and circuitry.

In addition, the target of achieving a very-high-speed device, a rather restricted goal, could also be achieved with silicon, whose development was continuing to make progress. Another example can be drawn from the beam addressable file project. There were problems in obtaining the laser arrays for addressing and problems in obtaining a material with the desired properties. At the same time, research tried very early in the game to obtain development assistance in the program. It turned out that this was premature. In addition, we had not successfully evaluated the benefits of this technology over what was available in the conventional magnetic recording. Since we didn't have the technology in hand (lack of addressing arrays or appropriate materials) and since we had not fully assessed the advantages over existing technology and the latter's limitations or lack of them, the project was destined to be unsuccessful insofar as the transfer process was concerned.

When a research project is aimed at transferring to development toward product status, it is important to understand where it will fit in the product line and what requirements must be met to reach that fit. While research cannot do its own marketing, it cannot waste time solving problems that don't exist or producing technology that cannot be sold by IBM. A basic ingredient of a technology is its cost. This can be considered at least in a preliminary estimate fashion for hardware but is, obviously, very difficult for programming. Both of the large systems projects we referred to failed in this respect.

Fortunately, for devices, circuits, and other hardware, the research work itself requires that at least one possible means of manufacturing be exhibited. Alternatives and improvements can be left for development and manufacturing engineering. For software, especially systems programming, "manufacture" or implementation in development is not well understood. Research results in software have not seemed to have directly affected eventual implementation methods.

Feasibility

Several projects never demonstrated the feasibility of research concepts because the time pressures forced transfer before demonstration could be accomplished. One thing that we learned was that we have to sometimes bridle our enthusiasm to keep from pushing an idea before we understand it well enough and can demonstrate its feasibility. Research and the receiving division must reach an agreement on what constitutes feasibility. Clearly, this will depend on the topic. For an algorithm such as the Fast Fourier Transform, the requirement is a running program that does better than existing methods. For hardware it will be a working device or even a system of components, performing a function, together with a demonstrated fabrication methodology. The program in magnetic films for memories is one in which feasibility was shown. However, magnetic films never became a product due to advances made in core memories and the quick growth in semiconductor memory technology.

In some cases, there are entire application systems or languages where the feasibility implies acceptability to the end user. This might be an end user in, say, medical diagnosis or the airline business, and must involve some kind of joint study with real users before feasibility can be demonstrated.

Advanced development overlap

For those projects that are transferred out, research must determine whether to maintain activity, either to support development or to defend its concepts, or to explore advanced or related technologies. The successful research development of FETs was followed by an abrupt discontinuation of almost all research in semiconductors for a short period. This was a mistake. The difficulty experienced in getting the development division to pick up the one-device memory cell in 1967 may have been partly due to a relative disinterest by research management in semiconductors just at that time as it turned its attention to other areas.

In planning applied projects, and especially as they near transfer, careful preparations have to be made for the proper kind of overlap program. For certain research projects, in particular, systems work, the creation of a special, advanced development effort is often the answer to problems of scaling-up, or to answer questions of marketability or economic feasibility before making a full product commitment. This may require bringing to the research laboratories new kinds of people. For example, with APL, a complete working system with customers was running before transfer.

Growth potential

There have been several research programs that suffered from being too narrowly aimed at a specific need and not having clear paths to technical growth and to growth in product applicability. Examples of this are the germanium and the beam addressable file programs.

Unless there is a prospect of technical advancement, the transfer may not be successful due to the fact that existing technologies "stretch" themselves. The challenge of a new technology forces an existing one to extend itself, to advance its goals, to expand its potential in the face of competition. Frequently, this stretching removes the advantages of this challenge, resulting in its demise. This was exactly the case with the beam addressable file. The germanium project and the magnetic thin film program afford other examples. The cryogenic computer work of the early 1960s is another example. The thin superconducting film memories developed at that time lost out to the advances being made by magnetic films and the cryotron logic lost out to the constant advances made by silicon circuitry. In all of these cases, not enough attention was paid to the growth potential in the new technology.

While research could perhaps take credit for stimulating or forcing advances in the existing technologies by offering competing alternatives, it certainly can't be the organization's major ambition or goal. To avoid being caught itself, Research has to constantly and carefully look over its shoulder at what is coming along.

Existence of an advocate

No matter how elegant the research results are or how much benefit they appear to have for the company, someone in research must take the responsibility to see that the results reach the right place. Our study indicates that a strong proponent actively selling the research results is necessary for transfer. It is obviously not sufficient; the several projects that failed to transfer or failed to become products also had research champions. Properly timed seminars for publicizing and explaining transferable research concepts have been helpful when used. The effectiveness of the research champion has been enhanced in several cases via a push-pull provided by an external champion.

Advanced technology activities in a development laboratory

The major conclusion is that advanced technology programs in the development laboratories are helpful and often necessary for transfer from research. In a very clear-cut fashion, the presence of "ad tech" groups aided in our moving electron beam technology and magnetic bubbles work from research to development. Both of these transfers have and are taking place continuously. Materials and knowledge of materials processing, device and circuit invention, and application techniques have all moved out. Interest in electron beam fabrication methods was high enough amongst individuals in ad tech, and their connection to research was useful in smoothing the way. With respect to bubbles, the ad tech lab in development had the talents and experience to pick up its technology. Thus, without formal contracting or negotiating, the presence of skilled and research-minded people in the development labs, and their relative freedom from close-in product demands, made it easier to effect the transfer.

In other hardware projects, divisional ad tech has served a critical function and has often looked to be competitive or even obstructional to research. Our case studies show that most of the time, the higher hurdles created by ad tech skepticism or resistance were, in the end, beneficial. For LSI-FET, research had to do the work and carry materials processing, device and circuit design, and design automation very far along, further than the research image of itself was comfortable with. However, the results were convincing, the corporation took on FETs in a confirmed fashion, and research benefited by having seasoned people in silicon technology, ready for subsequent efforts.

There is a similar record for magnetic films. The initial hurdles put up by the relevant development organization required very solid results and a thorough involvement of research people, not only in technology but also in systems usage and its economy. In the cases of the already mentioned beam addressable file and germanium programs, ad tech groups were correctly negative. By and large, having an ad tech activity in a divisional development laboratory is a positive asset to technology transfers.

All of the above is relevant to hardware technology. In the case of software activities, the picture is not as clear. In one case, that of APL, it was protected and developed slowly inside research. While it created its technology, it also created a user audience and usage patterns. Keeping it in research longer than might have been thought desirable had the benefit of producing a new language and tools for its operation, not seriously reduced in effectiveness by having to comply with then-current marketing philosophy. Thus, research, willing or not, provided the advanced technology phase for APL.

There is a class of programming results that really does not require very much further development. The FFT, VM Monitor, and ASTAP contributions were passed on fairly directly, but in each case the successful transfer came about by negotiating what level of programming would be acceptable.

In general, in the software area it is a little more difficult to define the role of ad tech groups in the development sector.

External pressures

For many of the hardware projects that were transferred and for some of the software ones, the presence of some form of the same technology in a competitor's laboratory or a product announcement has helped transfer. For our work in LSI-FETs, most of the industry was beginning preparation for FET componentry while our components development groups were still concentrating on bipolars. Research was able to draw attention to the competition when it was needed. For magnetic thin films, a competitor had announced a memory product before our product was close to announcement, but it was clear from the published work of research activities in several laboratories that a number of companies were working on magnetic films. At the time we were urging a development lab to become interested in electron beam technology, some manufacturers were publicly talking about methods and preliminary results. Reports of work on bubbles at other laboratories have kept product development people interested enough to make the continuous transfer that is occurring easier.

In other projects, however, there was no competitive pressure. In the applications area, cryptography and Fast Fourier Transforms were unique to research and IBM. The beam addressable file was not specifically pushed by competitors, although their people had similar projects underway. In the S.S.A., there was an immediate development following the research work in order to fulfill a government contract.

In general, for hardware, parallel activity elsewhere has helped research to transfer to development. It has also created an external standard against which to judge the research progress and achievement. When there is no outside activity we can expect greater difficulty in making judgments ourselves and in transferring.

For the applications results, external pressure has not played an important role. For the systems and programming transfers, competition has played a part in the past and may again in the future.

Joint programs

Joint programs can have several forms. They can involve support by money or by people. They may involve research people in development laboratories or development people in our laboratories. The most interesting observation from our case studies is that there was no joint activity in any of the systems and programming projects. There may have been a number of reasons, but for the most part this seemed to have been because of an inability by research to convince development managers that our ideas were any better or might be more productive than their own.

There were (or are) activities involving jointly planned programs or lending of people in LSI-FET, magnetic bubbles, and in magnetic thin films. In the germanium and electron beam projects, research took on development people in training or as a mode of entry hiring into the company. In general, we conclude that joint programs are good to have but do not ensure success.

Secondary Factors

Timeliness

Timeliness may enter in several ways. For one, research may try to provide a new or unique technology early because there are other candidates for a new product. More often research will have to be concerned about product cycles and when entry of improvements or even a new technology in a conventional product area is feasible. Good timing is important but it is not sufficient for successful transfer. If what we have is good enough, timeliness may not even be necessary.

Internal users

In addition to the useful pressure that external competition may create in helping to move a technology to the development laboratories, in some cases internal IBM users can play a similar role. A demand from hardware systems people, in one of the development labs, for low-cost, high-density FET circuitry helped in getting our divisional components people to pick up the research results. Internal use of APL helped create pressure on the sales side of the business. Hopefully, internal users of magnetic bubbles will grow and augment the market for device and circuit manufacture. If such internal-user demands do not naturally arise, perhaps research labs should stimulate them.

Government contracts

In one of the cases studied, magnetic bubbles, the presence of a government contract was useful in furthering the research work itself and in providing a good stimulus for transfer. In the early days of magnetic thin film research, contracts were helpful in getting started in the technology. Another contract supported some early work in sparse matrices. The difficulty of the government's requirements for the Social Security Page Reader forced a collaboration between research and development that probably would not have taken place otherwise. The collaboration produced technical advances that were useful in subsequent products. In effect, the stiff external requirements forced the development groups to look to research for advanced work.

High-level involvement

Occasionally, research has turned to corporate management for help in transfer. This was true in the case of LSI-FETs. At other times, staff committees were involved. In general, however, this has not been an important or even an effective mechanism for research to use.

Individual corporate responsibility

In one case, cryptography, an individual with a corporate watchdog role was useful. In general, this is rare and this may be important only when there is a totally new area of technical endeavor, such as cryptography, for us to deal with.

Proximity

In practically no case was the proximity of a development laboratory to a research laboratory an important factor. At times, being close was convenient and saved money, but no transfer failed because of distance.

APPENDIX: THE 18 CASE STUDY PROJECTS

Large-Scale Integration—N-Channel Field Effect Transistors (Successful)

In 1963, the Yorktown Heights laboratory began work on integrated silicon circuitry. This included silicon processing techniques, involving considerable physics and chemistry, device and circuit design, light table development for mask making and other optical lithographic requirements, and a design automation program. The devices were primarily FETs—field effect transistors—but the methodology evolved proved to be useful for bipolar devices and circuits as well. The general idea of large-scale integration was transferred to the component development laboratories in 1966, but it was not until 1968 that the specific technology for FET was finally adopted. This transfer provided the basis for IBM's main memories of the early 1970s and for the logic in most of the company's terminals and small machines in the same period.

Electron Beam Fabrication Methods (Successful)

In the early 1960s, the Yorktown Heights laboratory used electron beams to produce an optically read storage disk. Its original use was as the dictionary in a Russian translation system. Some of this early "photostore" technology was transferred as early as 1963 into special-purpose storage products. From that time on, there were a number of parallel research activities: the beam column itself including an improved filament, the software to automatically run circuit patterns and, importantly, efficient sensitive resists for the lithographic processing. These were transferred continuously into the component development laboratories beginning about 1966. Electron beam fabrication methods are now in use in the lithographic processes of circuit chips.

The Germanium Program (Nontransfer)

Germanium has a higher mobility than silicon and, in the early days of transistors, was widely used for point contact and junction transistors. With the coming of integration in the early 1960s, there was a brief period of competition between germanium and silicon for use in integrated circuits. The Yorktown laboratory started a program in 1964 which was supported by funds from the Components Development Division. With this support, the program grew to a rather large size. As the silicon technology advanced, the germanium studies experimented with low-temperature environments (liquid nitrogen) to gain further speed and other advantages. Both were aimed at a high-speed circuit requirement for a large computing system which was in design at the time. By 1968, however, it had become apparent that although germanium might meet the requirements of speed for this particular computer project, the power required to attain these speeds was very high. Although this was also true of silicon, silicon had much more attractive characteristics at medium and low speeds and appeared to have greater growth and extendibility prospects. The project was terminated in 1968, and the use of germanium in computer circuitry has disappeared.

One Device Memory Cell (Unsuccessful)

Until 1966, integrated circuits for memory in the research laboratory and in development in IBM had used a number of transistors for each memory cell. A cell is the physical location of memory bit storage. At this time, a research staff member invented a memory circuit, which required only one device, and a patent was issued in 1968. Attempts were made to interest the development laboratories in this circuit which gave a very large decrease in cell area and therefore represented a primary means of increasing memory density on a chip and increasing speed. Unfortunately, other designs had already been adopted for current development in 1967 and little headway was made. Eventually, cell designs of this kind did appear in IBM memory technology but an early lead was lost.

Magnetic Thin Film Memory (Unsuccessful)

Early work on using thin magnetic films to form memories was carried on in IBM, Lincoln Laboratories, Univac, and other laboratories. In 1960, joint preliminary studies by IBM research and a development group resulted in a research project in the Zurich laboratory. This was successful to the extent that the technology was brought from Zurich to Yorktown Heights and with further work was transferred to a components development laboratory. By 1964, a product design for a very fast memory was completed. Plans were made to use the memories in a large computer. In research, further activity produced new technical ideas for other versions of thin film memories. While all of this was happening in magnetic thin films, the major memory product was ferrite cores which were being continuously improved as to size and speed. Also, the first transistor memories were being considered. In the end, only one computer system with a fast magnetic thin film memory was shipped. It had made its goals but the technology, by 1968, had been overtaken by transistor memories. In 1969, efforts were terminated by both research and development.

Beam Addressable Storage (Nontransfer)

In the mid-1960s, before the serious advent of magnetic bubbles as a storage candidate, much thought was given to replacing magnetic induction recording with a beam addressable storage system. To gain high bit-density, magnetic domain sizes on disks and tapes have been continuously reduced, hence requiring the magnetic head to move closer to the disk surface. As the head-to-surface gap becomes smaller, design and operational control become more difficult and more costly. Beam addressed disk storage did not have this limitation and therefore looked interesting. A research project was underway in the San Jose laboratory by 1968. It used a magneto-optic effect: originally a europium oxide–coated disk was written on by a light beam produced by low-temperature injection lasers. At first, the disk surface materials also had to be operated at liquid nitrogen temperatures. New disk coatings were found and plans were made to do the work necessary to bring continuously operating room temperature semiconductor lasers into the system. A deeper understanding of the physical mechanisms involved in the transduction of light energy through a thermal phase to a change in magnetic phase was studied. As all of this was being done, the magnetic induction recording technology in the neighboring development laboratory was spurred to significant improvements. Higher densities of magnetic bits and dramatically smaller head-to-disk gaps were found feasible. The projected densities and costs of magnetic induction recording became equal to or better than those set out as goals for the beam addressable project, and it was terminated.

Magnetic Bubbles (Successful)

Although IBM researchers had worked with the interesting garnet crystal materials and were aware of magnetic effects themselves and those observed at the Bell Laboratories and Philips Eindhoven laboratory, it was not until the announcement by the Bell Labs of its bubble technology and its patent in the area that interest was really spurred. Research groups were formed in 1969, and a small NASA contract was accepted in 1971 calling for a simple operating chip with bubbles of rather large diameter. The contract was completed in 1972. New materials, including an amorphous substitute for the garnet crystals, began to come out of the research activities. Inventions of new bubble devices and of a new system concept, the bubble lattice file, appeared. However, efforts to interest the component development laboratories and computer system development groups in the company were not successful. Research then undertook a campaign to interest not only the technology developers in the company but also future systems users. Finally, the storage development laboratory became interested and early research work was transferred. Research continues to work on advanced concepts in bubble storage.

Copier Technology (Successful)

In the early 1960s, relatively basic work was started in the San Jose Research laboratory on organic photoconductors. Although there was not a specific product goal in mind, it was thought that microfilms or perhaps copiers might require such photosensitive materials. The early studies led to the discovery of a very-high-sensitivity photoconductor just at the time when technology for an office copier was required. A robot model was built to show that the new material would work. Since this was a new product area, there was no development group to accept the work. Eventually some of the research people carried the technology into development while others created an advanced technology group for the development division.

Social Security Page Readers (Successful)

Character and pattern recognition had been a research field in the computer sciences all throughout the 1950s. In the early 1960s, the Yorktown Heights group developed a system for character recognition with multiple scanners and software and hardware for processing recognition logic flexible enough to operate on a wide variety of fonts. In product development, however, character recognition concentrated on special single fonts such as might be employed in a bank check reader. When the Social Security Administration requested a multifont page reader in 1963, the research facility and its processing experience was used to show feasibility. A joint effort was carried on by research and the development laboratory for two years involving transfers of people both ways. When the page reader product was delivered to the Social Security Administration, a large number of the research concepts were included.

System Y (Unsuccessful) System A (Unsuccessful)

These were two large projects—one in the mid-1960s, the other in the early 1970s. One dealt with an ad-vanced hardware design for a computer and the other a software architecture. We cannot discuss these projects in any detail because some of the results are still sensitive. However, they were similar in the following respect: in each there were some extremely interesting and potentially powerful concepts developed while they were in research (Yorktown Heights). In both cases, this was only a short period of time, one year, and before these concepts could be worked to any degree of feasibility, the projects were moved almost intact into a development program. In hindsight, it appears now that not enough understanding was provided during the research period.

APL (Successful)

The concepts of the APL language were brought to IBM by the research staff member who conceived of them at Harvard. The language was unique in that it developed a new notation and syntax and among other attractive features allowed for the powerful operators on vectors and matrices that are desired by people in many kinds of mathematical applications in science. After a trial as a batch system, a time-sharing implementation was created, nominally for use in the Yorktown Heights laboratory. Classes were taught and very quickly a large number of researchers began to use the system. Other users came on to the system from other parts of IBM. All of this was carried on relatively informally, and as the user set grew and the language became well known it served as a proof to the development and marketing groups in the company that APL deserved to become a product. This finally happened in 1970.

M-44 (Successful)

This was the local name at the Yorktown Heights laboratory for a project in the early 1960s that tested concepts for virtual memory and virtual machines. An older computer was physically modified and a new operating system created to try out the ideas. For example, the notion of paging, bringing blocks of data from disk or drum to main memory in an ordered fashion so as to give the user the impression of an enhanced or virtual memory, was tested by literally coding algorithms and trying them out. The virtual machine concept was first used in this experimental system. The research results were positive and were quickly transferred to development groups for use in time-sharing systems in the late 1960s and virtual memory and machine systems in the 1970s.

VM Monitor/Statistics-Generating Package (Successful)

These are two related software programs that enable users of VM, one of IBM's main operating systems, to measure the performance of their workload on the systems. The programs were developed in Yorktown Heights for use on the local computing systems to help understand computing efficiency and improvements. They were transferred relatively smoothly to a development division and have become part of the VM system provided for customers.

Cryptography (Successful)

Data security became an issue in IBM in the late 1960s. Corporate responsibility was assigned to an individual who stimulated interest and activities amongst the mathematicians at Yorktown Heights. Simultaneously, others in the laboratory were coding and designing hardware for some new encryption methods. Attempts were made in 1970 to interest advanced technology groups in the terminal development laboratories, but there were no takers. However, in 1971, a special product was produced by the same development laboratory for a banking customer. The cryptographic code developed by that laboratory was sent to Yorktown Heights for testing and it was easily broken. The new technology, ideas, hardware, and software that had been underway at research were quickly put into use instead, and the transfer was effected. An enhanced version of these codes has now become the federal cryptographic standard.

Fast Fourier Transform (Successful)

This now well-known algorithm came into being in its present easily computed form through the joint efforts of two IBMers in research and a staff member of the Bell Labs in 1963. The algorithm was suggested to solve a particular problem in low-temperature physics and programmed at Yorktown Heights. Its amazing usefulness was publicized and propagated to IBM customers and scientists by reports, papers, newsletters, and a large number of personal contacts. Within four years' time, programs were available, special hardware was under development, and the algorithm was on its way to becoming one of the most widely used in all of scientific computing. Important extensions are still being made.

ASTAP (Successful)

This is an acronym for an internal IBM circuit analysis program. Between 1963 and 1975, mathematicians in the Yorktown Heights laboratory made a number of contributions. Two of these, methods for handling "stiff" differential equations and for dealing efficiently with sparse matrices, have made huge improvements in circuit analysis running times. They have also led to a large number of independent mathematical investigations by workers in the field in a number of other institutions.

Graphic Document System (Unsuccessful)

This project began as a possible solution to the problem of mapping electric utility holdings. It was stimulated by a known customer need and it allowed field maps, roughly sketched on the job, to be easily and swiftly transformed into properly dimensioned, annotated, and rectified maps. The system used special hardware and required new software. It was used in a test with one of the major regional utility companies and proved effective in this trial. Using the mapping system as a base, a drafting system was also evolved and tested in one of IBM's development laboratories. Both projects have since wandered through a number of development projects in both domestic and European development laboratories, but no products have resulted.

Reading III–4
Absorptive Capacity: A New Perspective on Learning and Innovation

Wesley M. Cohen and Daniel A. Levinthal

Introduction

Outside sources of knowledge are often critical to the innovation process, whatever the organizational level at which the innovating unit is defined. While the example of Japan illustrates the point saliently at the national level,[1] it is also true of entire industries, as pointed out by Brock[2] in the case of computers and by Peck[3] in the case of aluminum. At the organizational level, March and Simon[4] suggested most innovations result from borrowing rather than invention. This observation is supported by extensive research on the sources of innovation.[5] Finally, the importance to innovative performance of information originating from other internal units in the firm, outside the formal innovating unit (i.e., the

---

Administrative Science Quarterly 35 (1990), pp. 128–52.

[1]D. E. Westney and K. Sakakibara, "The Role of Japan-Based R&D in Global Technology Strategy," in *Technology in the Modern Corporation,* ed. M. Hurowitch (London: Pergamon, 1986), pp. 217–32; E. Mansfield, "The Speed and Cost of Industrial Innovation in Japan and the United States: External vs. Internal Technology," *Management Science* 34, no. 10 (1988), pp. 1157–68; N. Rosenberg and W. E. Steinmueller, "Why Are Americans Such Poor Imitators?" *American Economic Review* 78, no. 2 (1988), pp. 229–34.

[2]G. W. Brock, *The U.S. Computer Industry* (Cambridge, MA: Ballinger, 1975).

[3]M. J. Peck, "Inventions in the Postwar American Aluminum Industry," in *The Rate and Direction of Inventive Activity,* ed. R. R. Nelson (Princeton: Princeton University Press, 1962), pp. 279–98.

[4]J. G. March and H. A. Simon, *Organizations* (New York: Wiley, 1958).

[5]For example: W. F. Mueller, "The Origins of the Basic Inventions Underlying DuPont's Major Product and Process Innovations, 1920 to 1950," in *The Rate and Direction of Inventive Activity,* ed. R. R. Nelson (Princeton: Princeton University Press, 1962), pp. 323–58; D. Hamberg, "Invention in the Industrial Research Laboratory," *Journal of Political Economy* 71 (1963), pp. 95–115; S. Myers and D. C. Marquis, "Successful Industrial Innovations," Washington, DC: National Science Foundation, NSF 69–17, 1969; R. Johnston and M. Gibbons, "Characteristics of Information Usage in Technological Innovation," *IEEE Transactions on Engineering Management* 22 (1975), pp. 27–34; E. von Hippel, *The Sources of Innovation* (New York: Oxford University Press, 1988).

R&D lab), such as marketing and manufacturing, is well understood.[6].

The ability to exploit external knowledge is thus a critical component of innovative capabilities. We argue that the ability to evaluate and utilize outside knowledge is largely a function of the level of prior related knowledge. At the most elemental level, this prior knowledge includes basic skills or even a shared language but may also include knowledge of the most recent scientific or technological developments in a given field. Thus, prior related knowledge confers an ability to recognize the value of new information, assimilate it, and apply it to commercial ends. These abilities collectively constitute what we call a firm's absorptive capacity.

At the level of the firm—the innovating unit that is the focus here—absorptive capacity is generated in a variety of ways. Research shows that firms that conduct their own R&D are better able to use externally available information.[7] This implies that absorptive capacity may be created as a byproduct of a firm's R&D investment. Other work suggests that absorptive capacity may also be developed as a byproduct of a firm's manufacturing operations. Abernathy[8] and Rosenberg[9] have noted that through direct involvement in manufacturing, a firm is better able to recognize and exploit new information relevant to a particular product market. Production experience provides the firm with the background necessary both to recognize the value of and implement methods to reorganize or automate particular manufacturing processes. Firms also invest in absorptive capacity directly, as when they send personnel for advanced technical training. The concept of absorptive capacity can best be developed through an examination of the cognitive structures that underlie learning.

[6]E. Mansfield, *Economics of Technological Change* (New York: Norton, 1968).

[7]J. E. Tilton, *International Diffusion of Technology: The Case of Semiconductors* (Washington, DC: Brookings Institution, 1971); T. J. Allen, *Managing the Flow of Technology* (Cambridge, MA: MIT Press, 1977); D. C. Mowery, "The Relationship between Intrafirm and Contractual Forms of Industrial Research in American Manufacturing, 1900–1940," *Explorations in Economic History* 20 (1983), pp. 351–74.

[8]W. J. Abernathy, *The Productivity Dilemma* (Baltimore: Johns Hopkins University Press, 1978).

[9]N. Rosenberg, *Inside the Black Box: Technology and Economics* (New York: Cambridge University Press, 1982).

Cognitive Structures

The premise of the notion of absorptive capacity is that the organization needs prior related knowledge to assimilate and use new knowledge. Studies in the area of cognitive and behavioral sciences at the individual level both justify and enrich this observation. Research on memory development suggests that accumulated prior knowledge increases both the ability to put new knowledge into memory, what we would refer to as the acquisition of knowledge, and the ability to recall and use it. With respect to the acquisition of knowledge, Bower and Hilgard[10] suggested that memory development is self-reinforcing in that the more objects, patterns, and concepts that are stored in memory, the more readily is new information about these constructs acquired and the more facile is the individual in using them in new settings.

Some psychologists suggest that prior knowledge enhances learning because memory—or the storage of knowledge—is developed by associative learning in which events are recorded into memory by establishing linkages with preexisting concepts. Thus, Bower and Hilgard[11] suggested that the breadth of categories into which prior knowledge is organized, the differentiation of those categories, and the linkages across them permit individuals to make sense of and, in turn, acquire new knowledge. In the context of learning a language, Lindsay and Norman[12] suggested the problem in learning words is not a result of lack of exposure to them but that "to understand complex phrases, much more is needed than exposure to the words: a large body of knowledge must first be accumulated. After all, a word is simply a label for a set of structures within the memory system, so the structures must exist before the word can be considered learned." Lindsay and Norman further suggested that knowledge may be nominally acquired but not well utilized subsequently because the individual did not already possess the appropriate contextual knowledge necessary to make the new knowledge fully intelligible.

The notion that prior knowledge facilitates the learning of new related knowledge can be extended

[10]G. H. Bower and E. R. Hilgard, *Theories of Learning* (Englewood Cliffs, NJ: Prentice Hall, 1981).

[11]Ibid.

[12]P. H. Lindsay and D. A. Norman, *Human Information Processing* (Orlando, FL: Academic Press, 1977).

to include the case in which the knowledge in question may itself be a set of learning skills. There may be a transfer of learning skills across bodies of knowledge that are organized and expressed in similar ways. As a consequence, experience or performance on one learning task may influence and improve performance on some subsequent learning task.[13] This progressive improvement in the performance of learning tasks is a form of knowledge transfer that has been referred to as "learning to learn."[14] Estes,[15] however, suggested that the term "learning to learn" is a misnomer in that prior experience with a learning task does not necessarily improve performance because an individual knows how to learn (i.e., form new associations) better, but that an individual may simply have accumulated more prior knowledge so that he or she needs to learn less to attain a given level of performance. Notwithstanding what it is about prior learning experience that may affect subsequent performance, both explanations of the relationship between early learning and subsequent performance emphasize the importance of prior knowledge for learning.

The effect of prior learning experience on subsequent learning tasks can be observed in a variety of tasks. For instance, Ellis suggested that "students who have thoroughly mastered the principles of algebra find it easier to grasp advanced work in mathematics such as calculus."[16] Further illustration is provided by Anderson, Farrell, and Sauers,[17] who compared students learning LISP as a first programming language with students learning LISP after having learned Pascal. The Pascal students learned LISP much more effectively, in part because they better appreciated the semantics of various programming concepts.

The literature also suggests that problem-solving skills develop similarly. In this case, problem-solving methods and heuristics typically constitute the prior knowledge that permits individuals to acquire related problem-solving capabilities. In their work on the development of computer programming skills, Pirolli and Anderson[18] found that almost all students developed new programs by analogy-to-example programs and that their success was determined by how well they understood why these examples worked.

We argue that problem solving and learning capabilities are so similar that there is little reason to differentiate their modes of development, although exactly what is learned may differ: learning capabilities involve the development of the capacity to assimilate existing knowledge, while problem-solving skills represent a capacity to create new knowledge. Supporting the point that there is little difference between the two, Bradshaw, Langley, and Simon[19] and Simon[20] suggested that the sort of necessary preconditions for successful learning that we have identified do not differ from the preconditions required for problem solving and, in turn, for the creative process. Moreover, they argued that the processes themselves do not differ much. The prior possession of relevant knowledge and skill is what gives rise to creativity, permitting the sorts of associations and linkages that may have never been considered before. Likewise, Ellis[21] suggested that Harlow's[22] findings on the development of learning sets provide a possible explanation for the behavioral phenomenon of "insight" that typically refers to the rapid solution of a problem. Thus, the psychology literature suggests that creative capacity and what we call absorptive capacity are quite similar.

To develop an effective absorptive capacity, whether it be for general knowledge or problem solving or learning skills, it is insufficient merely to expose an individual briefly to the relevant prior knowledge. Intensity of effort is critical. With regard to storing knowledge in memory, Lindsay and Nor-

---

[13]H. C. Ellis, *The Transfer of Learning* (New York: Macmillan, 1965).

[14]Ibid.; W. K. Estes, *Learning Theory and Mental Development* (New York: Academic Press, 1970).

[15]Estes, *Learning Theory and Mental Development.*

[16]Ellis, *The Transfer of Learning.*

[17]J. R. Anderson, R. Farrell, and R. Sauers, "Learning to Program in LISP," *Cognitive Science* 8 (1984), pp. 87–129.

[18]P. L. Pirolli and J. R. Anderson, "The Role of Learning from Example in the Acquisition of Recursive Programming Skill," *Canadian Journal of Psychology* 39 (1985), pp. 240–72.

[19]G. F. Bradshaw, P. W. Langley, and H. A. Simon, "Studying Scientific Discovery by Computer Simulation," *Science* 222 (1983), pp. 971–75.

[20]H. A. Simon, "What We Know about the Creative Process," in *Frontiers in Creative and Innovative Management,* ed. R. L. Kuhn (Cambridge, MA: Ballinger, 1985), pp. 3–20.

[21]Ellis, *The Transfer of Learning.*

[22]H. F. Harlow, "The Formation of Learning Sets," *Psychological Review* 56 (1949), pp. 51–65; "Learning Set and Error Factor Theory," in *Psychology: A Study of Science,* vol. 2, ed. S. Koch (New York: McGraw-Hill, 1959), pp. 492–537.

man[23] noted that the more deeply the material is processed—the more effort used, the more processing makes use of associations between the items to be learned and knowledge already in the memory—the better will be the later retrieval of the item. Similarly, learning-set theory[24] implies that important aspects of learning how to solve problems are built up over many practice trials on related problems. Indeed, Harlow[25] suggested that if practice with a particular type of problem is discontinued before it is reliably learned, then little transfer will occur to the next series of problems. Therefore, he concluded that considerable time and effort should be spent on early problems before moving on to more complex problems.

Two related ideas are implicit in the notion that the ability to assimilate information is a function of the richness of the preexisting knowledge structure: learning is cumulative, and learning performance is greatest when the object of learning is related to what is already known. As a result, learning is more difficult in novel domains, and, more generally, an individual's expertise—what he or she knows well—will change only incrementally. The above discussion also suggests that diversity of knowledge plays an important role. In a setting in which there is uncertainty about the knowledge domains from which potentially useful information may emerge, a diverse background provides a more robust basis for learning because it increases the prospect that incoming information will relate to what is already known. In addition to strengthening assimilative powers, knowledge diversity also facilitates the innovative process by enabling the individual to make novel associations and linkages.

From Individual to Organizational Absorptive Capacity

An organization's absorptive capacity will depend on the absorptive capacities of its individual members. To this extent, the development of an organization's absorptive capacity will build on prior investment in the development of its constituent, individual absorptive capacities, and, like individuals' absorptive capacities, organizational absorptive capacity will tend to develop cumulatively. A firm's absorptive capacity is not, however, simply the sum of the absorptive capacities of its employees, and it is therefore useful to consider what aspects of absorptive capacity are distinctly organizational. Absorptive capacity refers not only to the acquisition or assimilation of information by an organization but also to the organization's ability to exploit it. Therefore, an organization's absorptive capacity does not simply depend on the organization's direct interface with the external environment. It also depends on transfers of knowledge across and within subunits that may be quite removed from the original point of entry. Thus, to understand the sources of a firm's absorptive capacity, we focus on the structure of communication between the external environment and the organization, as well as among the subunits of the organization, and also on the character and distribution of expertise within the organization.

Communication systems may rely on specialized actors to transfer information from the environment or may involve less structured patterns. The problem of designing communication structures cannot be disentangled from the distribution of expertise in the organization. The firm's absorptive capacity depends on the individuals who stand at the interface of either the firm and the external environment or at the interface between subunits within the firm. That interface function may be diffused across individuals or be quite centralized. When the expertise of most individuals within the organization differs considerably from that of external actors who can provide useful information, some members of the group are likely to assume relatively centralized "gatekeeping" or "boundary-spanning" roles.[26] For technical information that is difficult for internal staff to assimilate, a gatekeeper both monitors the environment and translates the technical information into a form understandable to the research group. In contrast, if external information is closely related to ongoing activity, then external information is readily assimilated and gatekeepers or boundary-spanners are not so necessary for translating information. Even in this setting, however, gatekeepers may emerge to the extent that such role specialization relieves others from having to monitor the environment.

A difficulty may emerge under conditions of rapid and uncertain technical change, however, when this interface function is centralized. When information

[23] *Human Information Processing.*

[24] Harlow, "The Formation of Learning Sets" and "Learning Set and Error Factor Theory."

[25] "Learning Set and Error Factor Theory."

[26] Allen, *Managing the Flow of Technology;* M. L. Tushman, "Special Boundary Roles in the Innovation Process," *Administrative Science Quarterly* 22 (1977), pp. 587–605.

flows are somewhat random and it is not clear where in the firm or subunit a piece of outside knowledge is best applied, a centralized gatekeeper may not provide an effective link to the environment. Under such circumstances, it is best for the organization to expose a fairly broad range of prospective "receptors" to the environment. Such an organization would exhibit the organic structure of Burns and Stalker,[27] which is more adaptable "when problems and requirements for action arise which cannot be broken down and distributed among specialist roles within a clearly defined hierarchy."

Even when a gatekeeper is important, his or her individual absorptive capacity does not constitute the absorptive capacity of his or her unit within the firm. The ease or difficulty of the internal communication process and, in turn, the level of organizational absorptive capacity are not only a function of the gatekeeper's capabilities but also of the expertise of those individuals to whom the gatekeeper is transmitting the information. Therefore, relying on a small set of technological gatekeepers may not be sufficient; the group as a whole must have some level of relevant background knowledge, and when knowledge structures are highly differentiated, the requisite level of background may be rather high.

The background knowledge required by the group as a whole for effective communication with the gatekeeper highlights the more general point that shared knowledge and expertise are essential for communication. At the most basic level, the relevant knowledge that permits effective communication both within and across subunits consists of shared language and symbols.[28] With regard to the absorptive capacity of the firm as a whole, there may, however, be a trade-off in the efficiency of internal communication against the ability of the subunit to assimilate and exploit information originating from other subunits or the environment. This can be seen as a trade-off between inward-looking versus outward-looking absorptive capacities. While both of these components are necessary for effective organizational learning, excessive dominance by one or the other will be dysfunctional. If all actors in the organization share the same specialized language, they will be effective in communicating with one another, but they may not be able to tap into diverse external knowledge sources. In the limit, an internal language, coding scheme, or, more generally, any particular body of expertise could become sufficiently overlapping and specialized that it impedes the incorporation of outside knowledge and results in the pathology of the not-invented-here (NIH) syndrome. This may explain Katz and Allen's[29] findings that the level of external communication and communication with other project groups declines with project-group tenure.

This trade-off between outward- and inward-looking components of absorptive capacity focuses our attention on how the relationship between knowledge sharing and knowledge diversity across individuals affects the development of organizational absorptive capacity. While some overlap of knowledge across individuals is necessary for internal communication, there are benefits to diversity of knowledge structures across individuals that parallel the benefits to diversity of knowledge within individuals. As Simon[30] pointed out, diverse knowledge structures coexisting in the same mind elicit the sort of learning and problem solving that yields innovation. If there exists a sufficient level of knowledge overlap to ensure effective communication, interactions across individuals who each possess diverse and different knowledge structures will augment the organization's capacity for making novel linkages and associations—innovating—beyond what any one individual can achieve. Utterback,[31] summarizing research on task performance and innovation, noted that diversity in the work setting "stimulates the generation of new ideas." Thus, as with Nelson and Winter's[32] view of organizational capabilities, an organization's absorptive capacity is

[27]T. Burns and G. M. Stalker, *The Management of Innovation* (London: Tavistock, 1961), p. 6.

[28]R. Dearborn and H. A. Simon, "Selective Perception in Executives," *Sociometry* 21 (1958), pp. 140–44; D. Katz and R. L. Kahn, *The Social Psychology of Organizations* (New York: Wiley, 1966); T. J. Allen and S. D. Cohen, "Information Flows in R&D Labs," *Administrative Science Quarterly* 20 (1969), pp. 12–19; M. L. Tushman, "Technical Communication in R&D Laboratories: The Impact of Project Work Characteristics," *Administrative Science Quarterly* 21 (1978), pp. 624–44; T. R. Zenger and B. S. Lawrence, "Organizational Demography: The Differential Effects of Age and Tenure Distributions on Technical Communication," *Academy of Management Journal* 32 (1989), pp. 353–76.

[29]R. Katz and T. J. Allen, "Investigating the Not Invented Here (NIH) Syndrome: A Look at the Performance, Tenure, and Communication Patterns of 50 R&D Project Groups," *R&D Management* 12 (1982), pp. 7–12.

[30]"What We Know about the Creative Process."

[31]J. M. Utterback, "The Process of Technological Innovation within the Firm," *Academy of Management Journal* 12 (1971), pp. 75–88.

[32]R. R. Nelson and S. Winter, *An Evolutionary Theory of Economic Change* (Cambridge, MA: Harvard University Press, 1982).

not resident in any single individual but depends on the links across a mosaic of individual capabilities.

Beyond diverse knowledge structures, the sort of knowledge that individuals should possess to enhance organizational absorptive capacity is also important. Critical knowledge does not simply include substantive, technical knowledge; it also includes awareness of where useful complementary expertise resides within and outside the organization. This sort of knowledge can be knowledge of who knows what, who can help with what problem, or who can exploit new information. With regard to external relationships, von Hippel[33] (1988) has shown the importance for innovation of close relationships with both buyers and suppliers. To the extent that an organization develops a broad and active network of internal and external relationships, individuals' awareness of others' capabilities and knowledge will be strengthened. As a result, individual absorptive capacities are leveraged all the more, and the organization's absorptive capacity is strengthened.

The observation that the ideal knowledge structure for an organizational subunit should reflect only partially overlapping knowledge complemented by nonoverlapping diverse knowledge suggests an organizational trade-off between diversity and commonality of knowledge across individuals. While common knowledge improves communication, commonality should not be carried so far that diversity across individuals is substantially diminished. Likewise, division of labor promoting gains from specialization should not be pushed so far that communication is undermined. The difficulties posed by excessive specialization suggest some liabilities of pursuing production efficiencies via learning by doing under conditions of rapid technical change in which absorptive capacity is important. In learning by doing, the firm becomes more practiced and hence more capable at activities in which it is already engaged. Learning by doing does not contribute to the diversity that is critical to learning about or creating something that is relatively new. Moreover, the notion of "remembering by doing"[34] suggests that the focus on one class of activity entailed by learning by doing may effectively diminish the diversity of background that an individual or organization may have at one time possessed and, consequently, undercut organizational absorptive capacity and innovative performance.

It has become generally accepted that complementary functions within the organization ought to be tightly intermeshed, recognizing that some amount of redundancy in expertise may be desirable to create what can be called cross-function absorptive capacities. Cross-function interfaces that affect organizational absorptive capacity and innovative performance include, for example, the relationships between corporate and divisional R&D labs or, more generally, the relationships among the R&D, design, manufacturing, and marketing functions.[35] Close linkages between design and manufacturing are often credited for the relative success of Japanese firms in moving products rapidly from the design stage through development and manufacturing.[36] Clark and Fujimoto[37] argued that overlapping product development cycles facilitate communication and coordination across organizational subunits. They found that the speed of product development is strongly influenced by the links between problem-solving cycles and that successful linking requires "direct personal contacts across functions, liaison roles at each unit, cross-functional task forces, cross-functional project teams, and a system of 'product manager as integrator.'"[38] In contrast, a process in which one unit simply hands off the design to another unit is likely to suffer greater difficulties.

Some management practices also appear to reflect the belief that an excessive degree of overlap in functions may reduce the firm's absorptive capacity and that diversity of backgrounds is useful. The Japanese practice of rotating their R&D personnel through marketing and manufacturing operations, for example, while creating knowledge overlap, also enhances the diversity of background of their personnel. Often involving the assignment of technical personnel to other functions for several years, this practice also suggests that some intensity of experience in each of the complementary knowledge domains is necessary to put an effective absorptive capacity in place; breadth of knowledge cannot be superficial to be effective.

---

[33] *The Sources of Innovation.*

[34] Nelson and Winter, *An Evolutionary Theory of Economic Change.*

[35] Mansfield, *Economics of Technological Change,* pp. 86–88.

[36] Westney and Sakakibara, "The Role of Japan-Based R&D in Global Technology Strategy."

[37] K. B. Clark and T. Fujimoto, "Overlapping Problem-Solving in Product Development," Technical Report, Harvard Business School, 1987.

[38] Ibid., p. 24.

The discussion thus far has focused on internal mechanisms that influence the organization's absorptive capacity. A question remains as to whether absorptive capacity needs to be internally developed or to what extent a firm may simply buy it via, for example, hiring new personnel, contracting for consulting services, or even through corporate acquisitions. We suggest that the effectiveness of such options is somewhat limited when the absorptive capacity in question is to be integrated with the firm's other activities. A critical component of the requisite ab-sorptive capacity for certain types of information, such as those associated with product and process innovation, is often firm-specific and therefore cannot be bought and quickly integrated into the firm. This is reflected in Lee and Allen's[39] findings that considerable time lags are associated with the integration of new technical staff, particularly those concerned with process and product development. To integrate certain classes of complex and sophisticated technological knowledge successfully into the firm's activities, the firm requires an existing internal staff of technologists and scientists who are both competent in their fields and are familiar with the firm's idiosyncratic needs, organizational procedures, routines, complementary capabilities, and extramural relationships. As implied by the discussion above, such diversity of knowledge structures must coexist to some degree in the same minds. Moreover, as Nelson and Winter's[40] (1982) analysis suggests, much of the detailed knowledge of organizational routines and objectives that permit a firm and its R&D labs to function is tacit. As a consequence, such critical complementary knowledge is acquired only through experience within the firm. Illustrating our general argument, Vyssotsky,[41] justifying the placement of Bell Labs within AT&T, argued:

> For research and development to yield effective results for Bell System, it has to be done by . . . creative people who understand as much as they possibly can about the technical state of the art, and about Bell System and what System's problems are. The R&D people must be free to think up new approaches, and they must also be closely coupled to the problems and challenges where innovation is needed. This combination, if one is lucky, will result in insights which help the Bell System. That's why we have Bell Labs in Bell System, instead of having all our R&D done by outside organizations.

[39]D. M. S. Lee and T. J. Allen, "Integrating New Technical Staff: Implications for Acquiring New Technology," *Management Science* 28 (1982), pp. 1405–20.

[40]*An Evolutionary Theory of Economic Change.*

[41]V. A. Vyssotsky, "The Innovation Process at Bell Labs," Technical Report, Bell Laboratories, 1977.

Path Dependence and Absorptive Capacity

Our discussion of the character of absorptive capacity and its role in assimilating and exploiting knowledge suggests a simple generalization that applies at both the individual and organizational levels: prior knowledge permits the assimilation and exploitation of new knowledge. Some portion of that prior knowledge should be very closely related to the new knowledge to facilitate assimilation, and some fraction of that knowledge must be fairly diverse, although still related, to permit effective, creative utilization of the new knowledge. This simple notion that prior knowledge underlies absorptive capacity has important implications for the development of absorptive capacity over time and, in turn, for the innovative performance of organizations. The basic role of prior knowledge suggests two features of absorptive capacity that will affect innovative performance in an evolving, uncertain environment.[42] Accumulating absorptive capacity in one period will permit its more efficient accumulation in the next. By having already developed some absorptive capacity in a particular area, a firm may more readily accumulate what additional knowledge it needs in the subsequent periods in order to exploit any critical external knowledge that may become available. Second, the possession of related expertise will permit the firm to better understand and therefore evaluate the import of intermediate technological advances that provide signals as to the eventual merit of a new technological development. Thus, in an uncertain environment, absorptive capacity affects expectation formation, permitting the firm to predict more accurately the nature and commercial potential of technological advances. These revised expectations, in turn, condition the incentive to invest in absorptive capacity subsequently. These two features of absorptive capacity—cumulativeness and its effect on expectation formation—imply that its development is domain specific and is path or history dependent.

The cumulativeness of absorptive capacity and its effect on expectation formation suggest an extreme case of path dependence in which once a firm ceases investing in its absorptive capacity in a quickly

[42]W. M. Cohen and D. A. Levinthal, "Fortune Favors the Prepared Firm," Technical Report, Dept. of Social and Decision Sciences, Carnegie Mellon University, 1989.

moving field, it may never assimilate and exploit new information in that field, regardless of the value of that information. There are two reasons for the emergence of this condition, which we term *lockout.*[43] First, if the firm does not develop its absorptive capacity in some initial period, then its beliefs about the technological opportunities present in a given field will tend not to change over time because the firm may not be aware of the significance of signals that would otherwise revise its expectations. As a result, the firm does not invest in absorptive capacity and, when new opportunities subsequently emerge, the firm may not appreciate them. Compounding this effect, to the extent that prior knowledge facilitates the subsequent development of absorptive capacity, the lack of early investment in absorptive capacity makes it more costly to develop a given level of it in a subsequent period. Consequently, a low initial investment in absorptive capacity diminishes the attractiveness of investing in subsequent periods even if the firm becomes aware of technological opportunities.[44] This possibility of firms being locked out of subsequent technological developments has recently become a matter of concern with respect to industrial policy. For instance, Reich[45] declaims Monsanto's exit from "float-zone" silicon manufacturing because he believes that the decision may be an irreversible exit from a technology, in that "each new generation of technology builds on that which came before, once off the technological escalator it's difficult to get back on" (p. 64).

Thus, the cumulative quality of absorptive capacity and its role in conditioning the updating of expectations are forces that tend to confine firms to operating in a particular technological domain. If firms do not invest in developing absorptive capacity in a particular area of expertise early on, it may not be in their interest to develop that capacity subsequently, even after major advances in the field. Thus, the pattern of inertia that Nelson and Winter[46] highlighted as a central feature of firm behavior may emerge as an implication of rational behavior in a model in which absorptive capacity is cumulative and contributes to expectation formation. The not-invented-here syndrome, in which firms resist accepting innovative ideas from the environment, may also at times reflect what we call lockout. Such ideas may be too distant from the firm's existing knowledge base—its absorptive capacity—to be either appreciated or accessed. In this particular setting, NIH may be pathological behavior only in retrospect. The firm need not have acted irrationally in the development of the capabilities that yields the NIH syndrome as its apparent outcome.

A form of self-reinforcing behavior similar to lockout may also result from the influence of absorptive capacity on organizations' goals or aspiration levels. This argument builds on the behavioral view of organizational innovation that has been molded in large part by the work of March and Simon.[47] In March and Simon's framework, innovative activity is instigated due to a failure to reach some aspiration level. Departing from their model, we suggest that a firm's aspiration level in a technologically progressive environment is not simply de-termined by past performance or the performance of reference organizations. It also depends on the firm's absorptive capacity. The greater the organization's expertise and associated absorptive capacity, the more sensitive it is likely to be to emerging technological opportunities and the more likely its aspiration level will be defined in terms of the opportunities present in the technical environment rather than strictly in terms of performance measures. Thus, organizations with higher levels of absorptive capacity will tend to be more proactive, exploiting opportunities present in the environment, independent of current performance. Alternatively, organizations that have a modest absorptive capacity will tend to be reactive, searching for new alternatives in response to failure on some performance criterion that is not defined in terms of technical change per se (profitability, market share, etc.).

A systematic and enduring neglect of technical opportunities may result from the effect of absorptive capacity on the organization's aspiration level when innovative activity (e.g., R&D) contributes to absorptive capacity, which is often the case in technologically progressive environments. The reason is that the firm's aspiration level then depends on the very innovative activity that is triggered by a failure to meet the aspiration level itself. If the firm engages

[43]Ibid.

[44]A similar result emerges from models of adaptive learning. B. Levitt and J. G. March, "Organizational Learning," *Annual Review of Sociology* 14 (1988), pp. 319–40, noted that "a competency trap can occur when favorable performance with an inferior procedure leads an organization to accumulate more experience with it, thus keeping experience with a superior procedure inadequate to make it rewarding to use" (p. 322).

[45]R. B. Reich, "The Rise of Techno-Nationalism," *Atlantic,* May 1987, pp. 63–69.

[46]*An Evolutionary Theory of Economic Change.*

[47]*Organizations.*

in little innovative activity, and is therefore relatively insensitive to the opportunities in the external environment, it will have a low aspiration level with regard to the exploitation of new technology, which in turn implies that it will continue to devote little effort to innovation. This creates a self-reinforcing cycle. Likewise, if an organization has a high aspiration level, influenced by externally generated technical opportunities, it will conduct more innovative activity and thereby increase its awareness of outside opportunities. Consequently, its aspiration level will remain high. This argument implies that reactive and proactive modes of firm behavior should remain rather stable over time. Thus, some organizations (like Hewlett-Packard and Sony) have the requisite technical knowledge to respond proactively to the opportunities present in the environment. These firms do not wait for failure on some performance dimension but aggressively seek out new opportunities to exploit and develop their technological capabilities.[48]

The concept of dynamically self-reinforcing behavior that may lead to the neglect of new technological developments provides some insight into the difficulties firms face when the technological basis of an industry changes—what Schumpeter[49] called "the process of creative destruction." For instance, the change from electromechanical devices to electronic ones in the calculator industry resulted in the exit of a number of firms and a radical change in the market structure.[50] This is an example of what Tushman and Anderson[51] termed competence-destroying technical change. A firm without a prior technological base in a particular field may not be able to acquire one readily if absorptive capacity is cumulative. In addition, a firm may be blind to new developments in fields in which it is not investing if its updating capability is low. Accordingly, our argument implies that firms may not realize that they should be developing their absorptive capacity due to an irony associated with its valuation: the firm needs to have some absorptive capacity already to value it appropriately.

Absorptive Capacity and R&D Investment

The prior discussion does not address the question of whether we can empirically evaluate the importance of absorptive capacity for innovation. There is a key insight that permits empirical tests of the implications of absorptive capacity for innovative activity. Since technical change within an industry—typically incremental in character[52]—is often closely related to a firm's ongoing R&D activity, a firm's ability to exploit external knowledge is often generated as a byproduct of its R&D. We may therefore consider a firm's R&D as satisfying two functions: we assume that R&D not only generates new knowledge but also contributes to the firm's absorptive capacity.[53] If absorptive capacity is important, and R&D contributes to it, then whatever conditions the firm's incentives to learn (i.e., to build absorptive capacity) should also influence R&D spending. We may therefore consider the responsiveness of R&D activity to learning incentives as an indication of the empirical importance of absorptive capacity. The empirical challenge then is to understand the impact of the characteristics of the learning environment on R&D spending.

We construct a simple static model of firm R&D intensity, which is defined as R&D divided by sales. Normalization of R&D by firm sales controls for the effect of firm size, which affects the return per unit of R&D effort. This model is developed in the broader context of what applied economists have come to believe to be the three classes of industry-level determinants of R&D intensity: demand, appropriability, and technological opportunity conditions.[54] Demand

---

[48]This argument that such reactive and proactive behavior may coexist in an industry over the long run assumes that there is slack in the selection environment and that technologically progressive behavior is not essential to survival. One can, alternatively, identify a number of industries, such as semiconductors, in which it appears that only firms that aggressively exploit technical opportunities survive.

[49]J. A. Schumpeter, *Capitalism, Socialism and Democracy* (New York: Harper and Row, 1942).

[50]B. A. Majumdar, *Innovations, Product Developments and Technology Transfers: An Empirical Study of Dynamic Competitive Advantage. The Case of Electronic Calculators* (Lanham, MD: University Press of America, 1982).

[51]M. L. Tushman and P. Anderson, "Technological Discontinuities and Organizational Environments," *Administrative Science Quarterly* 31 (1986), pp. 439–65.

[52]Rosenberg and Steinmueller, "Why are Americans Such Poor Imitators?"

[53]We refer readers interested in the details of the theoretical and subsequent empirical analysis and results to W. M. Cohen and D. A. Levinthal, "Innovation and Learning: The Two Faces of R&D," *Economic Journal* 99 (1989), pp. 569–96, from which the following discussion is drawn.

[54]W. M. Cohen and R. C. Levin, "Empirical Studies of Innovation and Market Structure," in *Handbook of Industrial Organization,* ed. R. C. Schmalensee and R. Willig (Amsterdam: Elsevier, 1989), pp. 1059–1107.

EXHIBIT 1 Model of Absorptive Capacity and R&D Incentives

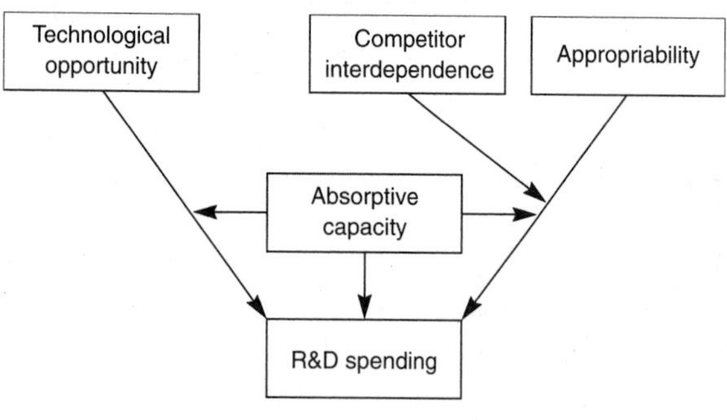

is often characterized by the level of sales and the price elasticity of demand. The latter indicates the degree to which a firm's revenue will increase due to a reduction in price. For example, in the case of a process innovation that reduces the cost of production and, in turn, the product price, the price elasticity of demand reflects the associated change in total revenue that influences the economic return to innovative effort. Appropriability conditions refer to the degree to which firms capture the profits associated with their innovative activity and are often considered to reflect the degree to which valuable knowledge spills out into the public domain. The emphasis here is on valuable knowledge, because if a competitor's knowledge spills out but the competitor has already exploited a first-mover advantage in the marketplace, this knowledge is no longer valuable to the firm and does not constitute a spillover by our definition. The level of spillovers, in turn, depends on the strength of patents within an industry, the efficacy of secrecy, and/or first-mover advantages. Technological opportunity represents how costly it is for the firm to achieve some normalized unit of technical advance in a given industry. As typically conceived, there are two dimensions of technological opportunity.[55] The first, incorporated in our model, refers simply to the quantity of extraindustry technological knowledge, such as that originating from government or university labs, that effectively complements and therefore leverages the firm's own knowledge output. The second dimension of technological opportunity is the degree to which a unit of new knowledge improves the technological performance of the firm's manufacturing processes or products and, in turn, the firm's profits. For example, given the vitality of the underlying science and technology, an advance in knowledge promises to yield much larger product-performance payoffs in the semiconductor industry than in steel.[56]

The basic model of how absorptive capacity affects the determination of R&D expenditures is represented diagrammatically in Exhibit 1. We postulate that learning incentives will have a direct effect on R&D spending. We also suggest that where the effect of other determinants, such as technological opportunity and appropriability, depend on the firm's or rivals' assimilation of knowledge, absorptive capacity—and therefore learning incentives—will mediate those effects. Finally, we suggest that the effect of appropriability conditions (i.e., spillovers) will be conditioned by competitor interdependence. In this context, we define interdependence as the extent to which a rival's technical advances diminish the firm's profits.

Two factors will affect a firm's incentives to learn, and, therefore, its incentives to invest in absorptive capacity via its R&D expenditures. First is the quantity of knowledge to be assimilated and exploited: the more there is, the greater the incentive. Second is the difficulty (or, conversely, the ease) of learning. Some types of information are more difficult to assimilate and use than others. We interpret this to mean that per unit of knowledge, the cost of its absorption may vary depending on the characteristics of that knowledge. As learning is more difficult, more prior knowledge has to have been accumulated via R&D for effective learning to occur. As a result, this is a more costly learning environment. In such a setting, R&D is more important to building absorptive capacity and the more R&D effort the firm will need to have expended to achieve some level of absorptive capacity. Thus, for a given level of a firm's own R&D, the level of absorptive capacity is diminished in environments in which it is more difficult to learn. In addition, we are suggesting that a more difficult learning environment increases the marginal effect of R&D on absorptive capacity. In contrast, in environments in which learning is less demanding, a firm's own R&D has little impact on

[55]Ibid.

[56]This second dimension is incorporated in the model developed in Cohen and Levinthal, "Innovation and Learning." We do not incorporate this second dimension in the present model because all the qualitative theoretical and empirical results associated with this second dimension of technology opportunity are the same as those associated with the first considered here.

EXHIBIT 2 Model of Sources of a Firm's Technical Knowledge

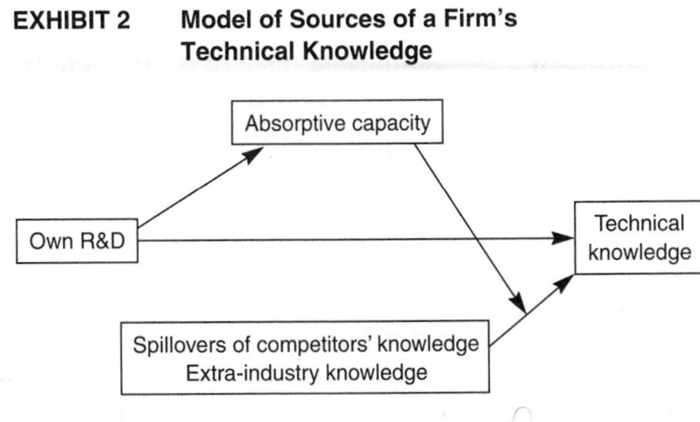

its absorptive capacity. In the extreme case in which external knowledge can be assimilated without any specialized expertise, a firm's own R&D would have no effect on its absorptive capacity.

We have argued that the ease of learning is in turn determined by the characteristics of the underlying scientific and technological knowledge. Although it is difficult to specify a priori all the relevant characteristics of knowledge affecting the ease of learning, they would include the complexity of the knowledge to be assimilated and the degree to which the outside knowledge is targeted to the needs and concerns of the firm. When outside knowledge is less targeted to the firm's particular needs and concerns, a firm's own R&D becomes more important in permitting it to recognize the value of the knowledge, assimilate, and exploit it. Sources that produce less targeted knowledge would include university labs involved in basic research, while more targeted knowledge may be generated by contract research labs, or input suppliers. In addition, the degree to which a field is cumulative, or the field's pace of advance, should also affect how critical R&D is to the development of absorptive capacity. The more that findings in a field build on prior findings, the more necessary is an understanding of prior research to the assimilation of subsequent findings. The pace of advance of a field affects the importance of R&D to developing absorptive capacity because the faster the pace of knowledge generation, the larger the staff required to keep abreast of new developments. Finally, following Nelson and Winter,[57] the less explicit and codified the relevant knowledge the more difficult it is to assimilate.

To structure the analysis, we assumed that firms purposefully invest in R&D to generate profit and take into account R&D's dual role in both directly generating new knowledge and contributing to absorptive capacity. Knowledge is assumed to be useful to the firm in that increments to a firm's own knowledge increase the firm's profits while increments to rivals' knowledge diminish them. We posit a simple model of the generation of a firm's technological knowledge that takes into account the major sources of technological knowledge utilized by a firm: the firm's own R&D knowledge that originates with its competitors' R&D, spillovers, and that which originates outside the industry. Exhibit 2 provides a stylized representation of this model in which, first, the firm generates new knowledge directly through its own R&D, and second, extramural knowledge, drawn from competitors as well as extraindustry sources such as government and university labs, also contributes to the firm's knowledge. A central feature of the model is that the firm's absorptive capacity determines the extent to which this extramural knowledge is utilized, and this absorptive capacity itself depends on the firm's own R&D. Because of this mediating function, absorptive capacity influences the effects of appropriability and technological opportunity conditions on R&D spending. Thus, the effects of appropriability and technological opportunity are not independent of R&D itself.

A key assumption in the model is that exploitation of competitors' research findings is realized through the interaction of the firm's absorptive capacity with competitors' spillovers. This interaction signifies that a firm is unable to assimilate externally available knowledge passively. Rather, to utilize the accessible R&D output of its competitors, the firm invests in its absorptive capacity by conducting R&D. Exhibit 2 also illustrates that, like its assimilation of competitors' R&D output, a firm's assimilation of extraindustry knowledge—the dimension of technological opportunity considered here—is constrained by its absorptive capacity. According to our model, therefore, the factors that affect learning incentives (i.e., the ease of learning and the quantity of available knowledge) influence the effects of appropriability and technological opportunity conditions on R&D.

Direct effect of ease of learning. As shown formally in Cohen and Levinthal,[58] this model implies that as the ease of learning diminishes, learning becomes more dependent on a firm's own R&D, and R&D spending increases because of two effects.

[57] *An Evolutionary Theory of Economic Change.*

[58] "Innovation and Learning."

First, the marginal impact of R&D on absorptive capacity is greater in more difficult learning environments. As the learning environment becomes more difficult, however, there is a second, more subtle effect. Since, ceteris paribus, a more difficult learning environment lowers firms' absorptive capacities, R&D activity becomes more of a private good in the sense that competitors are now less able to tap into the firm's R&D findings that spill out.

Technological opportunity. We predict that an increase in technological opportunity—the amount of available relevant external technical knowledge—will elicit more R&D in more difficult learning environments. Greater technological opportunity signifies greater amounts of external information, which increase the firm's incentive to build absorptive capacity, and a more challenging learning environment increases the level of R&D necessary to build absorptive capacity.

Appropriability. We predict that spillovers will provide, in part, a positive incentive to conduct R&D due to the interaction of spillovers with an endogenous absorptive capacity. Traditionally, spillovers have been considered only a deterrent to R&D activity.[59] In the standard view, a firm's incentive to invest in R&D is diminished to the extent that any findings from such activities are exploited by competitors and thereby diminish the innovator's own profits. In our framework, however, this negative appropriability incentive associated with spillovers is counterbalanced by a positive absorptive-capacity-building incentive. The more of its competitors' spillovers there are out there, the more incentive the firm has to invest in its own R&D, which permits it to exploit those spillovers.

We have shown elsewhere[60] that when this absorption incentive is large, as when learning is difficult, spillovers may actually encourage R&D. The relative magnitude of the absorption incentive is greater when firms within an industry are less interdependent in the sense that rivals' technical advances have less of an effect on the firm's own profits. With less interdependence, the degree to which rivals gain from the firm's R&D spillovers at the firm's expense diminishes relative to the benefit of being able to exploit the rivals' spillovers. Either a more competitive market structure or a higher price elasticity of demand for the firm's product can diminish interdependence in an industry.

Methods

Data and Measures

To test the predictions of our framework for R&D activity, we used cross-sectional survey data on technological opportunity and appropriability conditions in the American manufacturing sector collected from R&D lab managers by Levin et al.,[61] and the Federal Trade Commission's Line of Business Program data on business unit sales, transfers, and R&D expenditures. The dependent variable, R&D intensity, was defined as company-financed business-unit research and development expenditures, expressed as a percentage of business unit sales and transfers over the period 1975 through 1977. The data on interindustry differences in technological opportunity and appropriability are industry (line of business) mean scores computed as an average over all respondents within a given industry. The sample consists of 1,719 business units representing 318 firms in 151 lines of business.

The data pose two estimation issues. First, some 24 percent of the firms performed no R&D in at least one year. If the independent variables reflect both the probability of conducting R&D, as well as the amount of R&D spending, then a Tobit analysis would be appropriate. Alternatively, a firm may require some initial level of absorptive capacity before it is influenced by the characteristics of the learning environment. In this case, the variables reflecting the ease of learning only affect the amount of R&D conducted by firms engaging in R&D activity and not the probability of engaging in R&D activity. In light of the uncertainty over the appropriate estimation technique, we explored the robustness of the results by analyzing a Tobit and an OLS (or GLS)

---

[59]For example: R. R. Nelson, "The Simple Economics of Basic Research," *Journal of Political Economy* 67 (1959), pp. 297–306; K. J. Arrow, "Economic Welfare and the Allocation of Resources for Invention," in *The Rate and Direction of Inventive Activity,* ed. R. R. Nelson (Princeton, NJ: Princeton University Press, 1962), pp. 609–25; M. A. Spence, "Cost Reduction, Competition, and Industry Performance," *Econometrica* 52 (1984), pp. 101–22.

[60]Cohen and Levinthal, "Innovation and Learning."

[61]R. C. Levin, A. K. Klevorick, R. R. Nelson, and S. G. Winter, "Questionnaire on Industrial Research and Development," Dept. of Economics, Yale University, 1983; "Appropriating the Returns from Industrial R&D," *Brookings Papers on Economic Activity,* 1987, pp. 783–820.

specification. The second estimation issue is the presence of heteroscedasticity. We found the assumption of homoscedasticity to be violated, with the logarithm of the error variance being a linear function of the exogenous variables and the number of respondents to Levin et al.'s survey.[62] Unless otherwise noted, the results we report in this section reflect robust effects that hold across three different estimation methods, including ordinary least squares (OLS), generalized least squares (GLS) in which we adjust for heteroscedasticity, and Tobit, which was used when we included the observations for which R&D expenditures were zero.

We tested our predictions in the context of an empirical model of business unit R&D intensity in which technological opportunity, appropriability, and demand conditions are considered as the principal industry-level determinants of firms' R&D spending. While data constraints do not permit observation of the direct effect of the ease of learning or its determinants on firms' R&D spending, we were able to examine how these variables condition the influence on R&D of technological opportunity and appropriability conditions.

Technological opportunity was assessed with variables measuring the "relevance" or "importance" for technological progress in each line of business of what are considered to be two critical sources of technological opportunity—the science base of the industry and extraindustry sources of knowledge.[63] These measures are drawn from Levin et al.'s survey, in which R&D managers indicated on a 7-point Likert scale the relevance of 11 basic and applied fields of science and the importance of external sources of knowledge to technological progress in a line of business. The basic fields of science include biology, chemistry, mathematics, and physics, and the applied fields of science include agricultural science, applied math/operations research, computer science, geology, materials science, medical science, and metallurgy.[64] The five extraindustry sources of knowledge considered here included equipment suppliers (EQUIPTECH), materials suppliers (MATERIALTECH), downstream users of the industry's products (USERTECH), government laboratories and agencies (GOVTECH), and universities (UNIVTECH). We interpreted the measures of the relevance or importance of each field or knowledge source to index the relative quantity of knowledge generated by that field or source that is potentially useful. We then distinguished across the eleven scientific fields and the five extraindustry knowledge source variables on the basis of the ease of learning associated with each. We suggested above that one important determinant of the ease of learning is the degree to which outside knowledge is targeted to a firm's needs and concerns. One can readily distinguish among both the eleven fields and the five extraindustry knowledge sources on that basis. The knowledge associated with the basic sciences is typically less targeted than that associated with the applied sciences. We also distinguished among the extraindustry knowledge sources on the same basis. A priori, we ranked university labs, government labs, materials suppliers, and equipment suppliers as providing increasingly more targeted knowledge to firms. We did not rank the relative effect of knowledge originating from users because, as suggested by von Hippel,[65] users will often provide a product idea to potential suppliers, but the informativeness of the "solution concept" is quite variable. Therefore, the targeted quality of the information is variable as well.

To represent intraindustry spillovers of R&D, we employed measures from Levin et al.'s survey of the effectiveness of six mechanisms used by firms to capture and protect the competitive advantages of new processes and new products: patents to prevent duplication, patents to secure royalty income, secrecy, lead time, moving quickly down the learning curve, and complementary sales and service efforts. We employed the maximum value of the effectiveness scores attained by these mechanisms as our measure of appropriability or spillovers, and label this variable APPROPRIABILITY; a high level of APPROPRIABILITY reflects a low level of spillovers.

In our theory, we predicted an interaction effect by which, as the ease of learning diminishes, or firms become less interdependent, the effect of spillovers on R&D spending should become more positive (or less negative). In the absence of any direct measure of the ease of learning, we distinguished categorically between those industries in which basic science was more relevant to technical progress than the rel-

[62]Ibid.

[63]Cohen and Levin, "Empirical Studies of Innovation and Market Structure."

[64]Although geology was classed as a basic science by Levin et al. (see note 61), we classed it as an applied science because of its inductive methodology and intensive use by firms in the extractive sector.

[65]E. von Hippel, "Successful Industrial Products from Customer Ideas," *Journal of Marketing* 42 (1978), pp. 39–49.

EXHIBIT 3 Analysis of R&D Intensity

	Regression Coefficient		
Variable	OLS (N = 1302)	GLS (N = 1302)	Tobit (N = 1719)
Intercept	−5.184**	−2.355*	−4.086**
	(1.522)	(1.037)	(1.461)
APPROPRIABILITY × C4	.213	.342**	.368**
	(.128)	(.103)	(.130)
APPROPRIABILITY × PELAS	−.192	−.200*	−.176
	(.106)	(.091)	(.103)
APPROPRIABILITY × DUMAPP	.448*	.248	.211
	(.202)	(.143)	(.194)
APPROPRIABILITY × DUMBAS	.302	.174	.094
	(.208)	(.144)	(.206)
USERTECH	.470**	.397**	.612**
	(.104)	(.069)	(.107)
UNIVTECH	.374**	.318**	.395**
	(.131)	(.091)	(.147)
GOVTECH	.221*	.069	.137
	(.106)	(.079)	(.107)
MATERIALTECH	−.258**	−.074	−.303**
	(.098)	(.070)	(.100)
EQUIPTECH	−.401**	−.484**	−.574**
	(.111)	(.077)	(.117)
Biology	.314**	.185**	.276*
	(.102)	(.071)	(.114)
Chemistry	.289**	.081	.191*
	(.084)	(.062)	(.088)
Math	.184	.151	.123
	(.131)	(.097)	(.143)
Physics	.373**	.323**	.310*
	(.117)	(.091)	(.128)
Agricultural Science	−.441**	−.273**	−.308**
	(.088)	(.064)	(.099)
Applied Math/Operations Research	−.237	−.117	−.366*
	(.148)	(.102)	(.152)
Computer Science	.294*	.116	.433**
	(.124)	(.090)	(.122)
Geology	−.363**	−.240**	−.365**
	(.084)	(.061)	(.097)
Materials Science	−.110	−.150	.116
	(.125)	(.095)	(.118)
Medical Science	−.179	−.133	−.133
	(.093)	(.070)	(.103)
Metallurgy	−.315**	−.195**	−.393**
	(.077)	(.053)	(.089)
NEWPLANT	.057**	.049**	.045**
	(.008)	(.006)	(.007)
PELAS	.936	1.082*	.892
	(.611)	(.527)	(.573)
INCELAS	1.077**	.587**	1.112**
	(.170)	(.131)	(.188)
DGROWTH	.068	−.074	.004
	(.090)	(.053)	(.105)
	.287		

*$p < .05$; **$p < .01$.
SOURCE: W. M. Cohen and D. A. Levinthal, "Innovation and Learning: The Two Faces of R&D," *Economic Journal* 99 (1989), pp. 590–591, 569–596). Standard errors are in parentheses.

atively more targeted applied sciences and assumed that learning was generally less difficult in industries that fell into the latter category. Thus, we created a dummy variable, DUMBAS, that equals 1 when the average value of the relevance scores associated with the basic fields exceeds that associated with the applied fields and that equals 0 otherwise. We specified the dummy variable, DUMAPP, analogously. To capture the interdependence of firms, we employed measures of industries' competitiveness as represented by each industry's four-firm concentration ratio (C4) and industry-level estimates of the price elasticity of demand (PELAS).

To further control for industry demand conditions, we used industry estimates developed by Levin[66] of price elasticity (PELAS) and income elasticity (INCELAS) and a demand time-shift parameter (DGROWTH). Finally, we included another control variable that may also reflect technological opportunity, industry maturity. We used a somewhat crude measure of industry maturity, NEWPLANT, that measures the percentage of an industry's property, plant, and equipment installed within the preceding five years.

Results

Technological opportunity. Our theory suggests that when the targeted quality of knowledge is less (i.e., learning is more difficult), an increase in the relevance (i.e., quantity) of knowledge should have a more positive effect on R&D intensity. Therefore, the coefficient estimates of the variables measuring the relevance of the four basic scientific fields should exceed those of the variables measuring the relevance of the seven applied scientific fields. Confirming the prediction, Exhibit 3 indicates that the estimated coefficients for the applied sciences are, with the exception of computer science, lower than that for the basic sciences. The similarity of the estimate of the effect of the relevance of computer science, an applied science, to those of some of the basic sciences suggests that the assumption may not be correct that only one determinant of the ease of learning, the targeted quality of the field, varies systematically across the fields of applied and basic science. Another determinant of the ease of learning postulated above is a field's pace of advance, where faster pace should require more R&D to permit assimilation, and the pace of advance in computer science has been relatively rapid over the past two decades.

To further test the prediction that the coefficient values of the less targeted, basic-science field variables would exceed those of the applied fields, we estimated a specification, otherwise identical to the first, in which we constrained the coefficients of the basic sciences to be the same and the coefficients of the applied sciences to be the same. This shows the effect on R&D spending when the overall technological opportunity associated with basic science and applied science, respectively, changes. The constrained coefficient estimates of the effect of the technological opportunity associated with the basic and applied sciences are significantly different (at the $p < .01$ level) across all estimation methods, with the former equal to .189 and the latter equal to $-.080$ in the GLS estimation. Therefore, relative to the effect of an increase in the technological opportunity associated with applied science, an increase in that associated with basic science elicits more R&D.

Our predicted ranking of the coefficient magnitudes associated with the extraindustry sources of knowledge, reflecting increasingly targeted knowledge from these sources, is largely confirmed. The coefficient estimate for the importance of knowledge originating from universities exceeds that for government labs, which, in turn, is greater than that for materials suppliers, which exceeds that for equipment suppliers. The difference between coefficient values is statistically significant in the case of government sources versus materials suppliers for both the OLS and Tobit results ($p < .01$) and in the case of materials suppliers versus equipment suppliers in the GLS results ($p < .01$). While we had no prediction regarding the coefficient value for USERTECH, the consistently high value of the coefficient estimate may reflect some element of demand conditions. Consistent with this, we have observed the variable USERTECH to be significantly correlated with measures of the importance of product differentiation.[67]

Appropriability. The results largely support the prediction that the ease of learning conditions the effect of knowledge spillovers. The effect on R&D intensity of increasing appropriability (i.e., diminishing spillovers) was significantly greater ($p < .05$) in

[66]R. C. Levin, "Toward an Empirical Model of Schumpeterian Competition," Technical Report, Dept. of Economics, Yale University, 1981.

[67]Compare Cohen and Levinthal, "Innovation and Learning."

those industries in which the applied sciences are more relevant to innovation than the basic sciences. This result suggests that the positive absorption incentive associated with spillovers is greater in industries in which the difficulty of learning is greater. Second, there is a significant positive effect ($p < .01$) of the interaction between market concentration and the appropriability level. As market concentration increases (indexing a diminution in competitiveness), the positive effect of a given appropriability level on R&D intensity increases, as predicted. Likewise, the effect of the interaction of the price elasticity of demand and the level of appropriability is negative (but only significant at $p < .05$ in the GLS estimate), providing additional support for the proposition that the positive effect of spillovers will increase in industries in which firms are less interdependent. The results suggest that the learning environment affects the impact of spillovers on R&D spending and that the importance of the positive absorptive-capacity-building incentive relative to that of the negative appropriability incentive is conditioned by the degree of competitor interdependence.

While we have shown that the learning environment modifies the effect of appropriability conditions, the question remains whether spillovers may, on balance, actually encourage R&D in some industries. To explore this possibility, we examined the effect of spillovers in the four two-digit SIC code level industries for which our sample contains enough lines of business to permit separate industry regressions. These include SICs 20 (food processing), 28 (chemicals), 35 (machinery), and 36 (electrical equipment). Due to the reduction in the degrees of freedom for industry-level variables, we simplified the estimating equation to consider only the direct effect of APPROPRIABILITY, and the science field variables were summarized as the maximum relevance scores attained by the basic and applied fields, respectively. In SICs 28 and 36, the effect of the APPROPRIABILITY variable was negative and significant at conventional levels, implying that R&D intensity rises with spillovers. In the Tobit results, the sign was also positive for SICs 28 and 36, but the coefficient estimates were not quite significant at the .05 confidence level. Thus, in SICs 28 (chemicals) and 36 (electrical equipment), R&D intensity rose with spillovers when we controlled for other industry-level variables conventionally thought to drive R&D spending, including technological opportunity and demand conditions. Although the analyses showing a positive effect of spillovers in these two industry groups do not represent a direct test of our model, the results suggest, particularly when considered with the interaction results, that the positive absorption incentive associated with spillovers may be sufficiently strong in some cases to more than offset the negative appropriability incentive.

Implications for Innovative Activity

Drawing on our prior work,[68] we offer some implications of absorptive capacity for the analysis of other innovative activities, including basic research, the adoption and diffusion of innovations, and decisions to participate in cooperative R&D ventures, that follow from the preceding analyses.

The observation that R&D creates a capacity to assimilate and exploit new knowledge provides a ready explanation of why some firms may invest in basic research even when the preponderance of findings spill out into the public domain. Specifically, firms may conduct basic research less for particular results than to be able to provide themselves with the general background knowledge that would permit them to exploit rapidly useful scientific and technological knowledge through their own innovations or to be able to respond quickly—become a fast second—when competitors come up with a major advance.[69] In terms of our discussion of the cognitive and organizational aspects of absorptive capacity, we may think of basic research as broadening the firm's knowledge base to create critical overlap with new knowledge and providing it with the deeper understanding that is useful for exploiting new technical developments that build on rapidly advancing science and technology.

This perspective on the role of basic research offers a rather different view of the determinants of basic research than that which has dominated thinking in this area for the 30 years since Nelson's[70] seminal article. Nelson hypothesized that more diversified firms will invest more heavily in basic research because, assuming imperfect markets for information, they will be better able to exploit its wide-ranging and unpredictable results. Nelson thus

---

[68]Ibid.; W. M. Cohen and D. A. Levinthal, "Participation in Cooperative Research Ventures and the Cost of Learning," Technical Report, Dept. of Social and Decision Sciences, Carnegie Mellon University, 1987.

[69]N. Rosenberg, "Why Do Firms Do Basic Research (with Their Own Money)?" *Research Policy* 1990.

[70]"The Simple Economics of Basic Research."

saw product-market diversification as one of the key determinants of basic research.[71] Emphasizing the role of basic research in firm learning, our perspective redirects attention from what happens to the knowledge outputs from the innovation process to the nature of the knowledge inputs themselves. Considering that absorptive capacity tends to be specific to a field or knowledge domain means that the type of knowledge that the firm believes it may have to exploit will affect the sort of research the firm conducts. From this vantage point, we would conjecture that as a firm's technological progress becomes more closely tied to advances in basic science (as has been the case in pharmaceuticals), a firm will increase its basic research, whatever its degree of product-market diversification. We also suggest, with reference to all firm research, not just basic research, that as the fields underlying technical advance within an industry become more diverse, we may expect firms to increase their R&D as they develop absorptive capacities in each of the relevant fields. For example, as automobile manufacturing comes to draw more heavily on newer fields such as microelectronics and ceramics, we expect that manufacturers will expand their basic and applied research efforts to better evaluate and exploit new findings in these areas.

The findings on the role of absorptive capacity and the ways in which it may be developed also have implications for the analysis of the adoption and diffusion of innovations. Our perspective implies that the ease of learning, and thus technology adoption, is affected by the degree to which an innovation is related to the preexisting knowledge base of prospective users. For example, personal computers diffused more rapidly at the outset among consumers and firms who had prior experience on mainframes or minicomputers. Likewise, software engineering practices seem to be adopted more readily by programmers with previous Pascal rather than Fortran experience because the structure of Pascal more closely reflects some of the underlying principles of software engineering.[72] Our argument also suggests that an innovation that is fully incorporated in capital equipment willdiffuse more rapidly than more disembodied innovations that require some complementary expertise on the part of potential users. This is one of the anticipated benefits of making computers more user-friendly.

The importance of absorptive capacity also helps explain some recent findings regarding firms' cooperative research ventures. First, Link[73] has observed that cooperative research ventures are actually found more typically in industries that employ more mature technologies rather than in industries in which technology is moving ahead quickly—as seems to be suggested by the popular press. Second, it has been observed that cooperative ventures that have been initiated to pursue basic research, as well as more applied research objectives, have been subject over the years to increasing pressure to focus on more short-term research objectives.[74] The simple notion that it is important to consider the costs of assimilating and exploiting knowledge from such ventures provides at least a partial explanation for these phenomena. Many cooperative ventures are initiated in areas in which the cost to access the output of the venture is low, or they often gravitate toward such areas over time. Conversely, those who are attempting to encourage cooperative research ventures in quickly advancing fields should recognize that the direct participation in the venture should represent only a portion of the resources that it will take to benefit from the venture. Participating firms also must be prepared to invest internally in the absorptive capacity that will permit effective exploitation of the venture's knowledge output.

Conclusion

Our empirical analysis of R&D investment suggested that firms are in fact sensitive to the characteristics of the learning environment in which they operate. Thus, absorptive capacity appears to be part of a firm's decision calculus in allocating resources for innovative activity. Despite these findings, because absorptive capacity is intangible and its benefits are indirect, one can have little confidence that the appropriate level, to say nothing of the optimal

[71]Markets for information often fail because they inherently represent a situation of information asymmetry in which the less informed party cannot properly value the information he or she wishes to purchase, and the more informed party, acting self-interestedly, attempts to exploit that inability. See O. E. Williamson, *Markets and Hierarchies: Analysis and Antitrust Implications* (New York: Free Press, 1975).

[72]G. Smith, W. M. Cohen, W. Hefley, and D. A. Levinthal, "Understanding the Adoption of Ada: A Field Study Report," Technical Report, Software Engineering Institute, Carnegie Mellon University, 1989.

[73]A. N. Link, "Cooperative Research Activity in U.S. Manufacturing," Technical Report, University of North Carolina, Greensboro, 1987.

[74]D. C. Mowery and N. Rosenberg, *Technology and the Pursuit of Economic Growth* (New York: Cambridge University Press, 1989).

level, of investment in absorptive capacity is reached. Thus, while we have proposed a model to explain R&D investment, in which R&D both generates innovation and facilitates learning, the development of this model may ultimately be as valuable for the prescriptive analysis of organizational policies as its application may be as a positive model of firm behavior.

An important question from a prescriptive perspective is, When is a firm most likely to underinvest in absorptive capacity to its own long-run detriment? Absorptive capacity is more likely to be developed and maintained as a byproduct of routine activity when the knowledge domain that the firm wishes to exploit is closely related to its current knowledge base. When, however, a firm wishes to acquire and use knowledge that is unrelated to its ongoing activity, then the firm must dedicate effort exclusively to creating absorptive capacity (i.e., absorptive capacity is not a byproduct). In this case, absorptive capacity may not even occur to the firm as an investment alternative. Even if it does, due to the intangible nature of absorptive capacity, a firm may be reluctant to sacrifice current output as well as gains from specialization to permit its technical personnel to acquire the requisite breadth of knowledge that would permit absorption of knowledge from new domains. Thus, while the current discussion addresses key features of organizational structure that determine a firm's absorptive capacity and provides evidence that investment is responsive to the need to develop this capability, more research is necessary to understand the decision processes that determine organizations' investments in absorptive capacity.

Case III–3
Advanced Drug Delivery Systems: ALZA and Ciba-Geigy (A)

Mark W. Cunningham, Reinhard Angelmar, and Yves Doz

In midsummer 1977, the management teams of Ciba-Geigy's Pharma Division in Basle, of its U.S. division in Summit, New Jersey, and of ALZA Corp., of Palo Alto, California, had to decide whether to cooperate in the development and commercialization of pharmaceutical products using Advanced Drug Delivery Systems (ADDS) and, in the event of a positive decision, what form such cooperation should take.

In order to allow an understanding of the context of this decision, this case reviews key aspects of the pharmaceutical industry in 1977, presents the ADDS field, and profiles briefly the two companies: ALZA and Ciba-Geigy.

The Pharmaceutical Industry: Recent Evolution

The worldwide pharmaceutical market in 1977 was worth around $48 billion, the largest geographical market being the United States with some 16 percent, followed by Japan with 11 percent (see Exhibit 1). Worldwide sales of pharmaceutical companies in current terms had been growing at an average rate of 12 percent since 1960, and 15 percent since 1970. The average rate of return on net worth over the last 15 years had been 18 percent, which was considerably above the average for other major industries (11 percent). The financial performance of several of the leading companies was well above this figure.

However, there were indications that the future might not be quite as rosy. Valuable new drug discoveries, which had been the main motor for

EXHIBIT 1 Worldwide Pharmaceutical Market

	1977 ($ millions)	Percent of World Total	Sales per capita (dollars)
United States of America	$ 7,800	16.3%	$36
Japan	5,400	11.3	48
Federal Republic of Germany	4,100	8.5	67
France	2,900	6.0	55
Italy	1,800	3.8	32
Brazil	1,500	3.1	14
Spain	1,200	2.5	33
United Kingdom	1,200	2.5	21
Argentina	900	1.9	35
Mexico	800	1.7	13
Others	20,400	42.5	
Total	$48,000	100.0%	

EXHIBIT 2 U.S. Pharmaceutical Industry Performance

A. Patent Life and R&D Expenditure

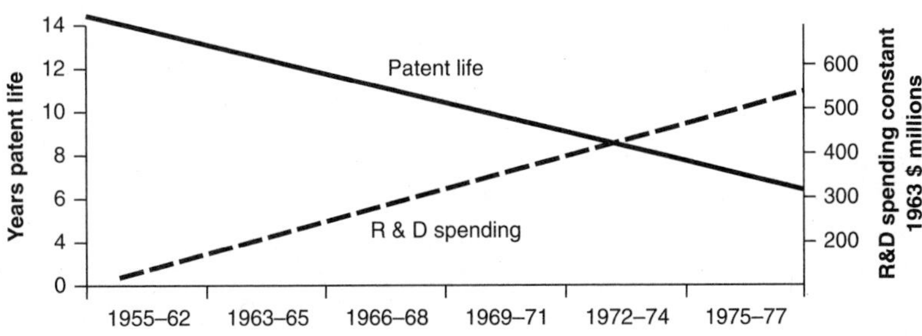

SOURCE: *The Economist.*

B. Registration of New Chemical Entities

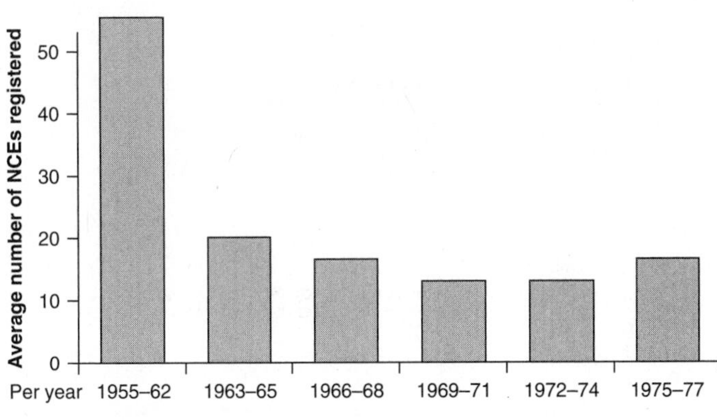

SOURCE: *The Economist.*

growth, had become rarer, the development process much longer and more expensive, and the lucrative period of patent protection correspondingly shorter (see Exhibit 2).

Though there were nearly 10,000 companies in the ethical drug business worldwide, 90 percent of sales were made by the hundred largest. The top 25 companies shared less than 50 percent of sales and the largest individual market share was 3.5 percent. Exhibit 3 shows the top 15, their country of origin, and the importance of pharmaceuticals in group sales. Exhibit 4 shows the areas of activity of leading pharmaceutical companies and their R&D profile.

Product innovation was the main key both to profitability and to growth, but new drug discoveries remained partly serendipitous. Companies' labs screen for activity and toxicity large numbers of natural and synthetic substances which, because of their molecular characteristics, are thought to have a potential use in one or another therapeutic area. This primary screening is usually done on animals. Only about 1 in 1,000 of the chemicals so tested proves sufficiently active and nontoxic to deserve trials on human beings.

The product development process was very slow, with anywhere between 1 to 10 years of research (developing and screening chemical substances), and around 9 years for preclinical and clinical trials leading up to the application for registration. Then three more years of trials were likely to be needed for registration (see Exhibit 5). By the mid-1970s, estimates of the average R&D expenditures per new drug actually introduced by a major pharmaceutical company, taking into account the very high dropout rate during clinical tests, ranged between $25 million and $80 million.

The serendipitous nature of discovery and the need to spread risks and to smooth out the activity

EXHIBIT 3 Leading Pharmaceutical Companies, 1977

	Country	1977 Pharmaceutical Sales ($billions)	Pharmaceutical as a Percent of Group Sales	World Market Share	Percent of Sales in Home Country	Percent of Sales from Top Four Products
1. Hoechst-Roussel	Federal Republic of Germany	$1.6	16%	3.3%	67%	—
2. Merck & Co.	United States of America	1.4	84	2.9	45	49
3. Bayer	Federal Republic of Germany	1.3	13	2.7	69	—
4. Ciba-Geigy	Switzerland	1.2	28	2.5	2	22
5. Hoffman La Roche	Switzerland	1.2	51	2.5	10	—
6. American Home Products	United States of America	1.1	39	2.3	31	37
7. Warner Lambert	United States of America	1.0	40	2.1	43	36
8. Pfizer	United States of America	1.0	50	2.1	51	50
9. Sandoz	Switzerland	0.9	48	1.9	5	—
10. Eli Lilly	United States of America	0.9	53	1.9	37	60
11. Upjohn	United States of America	0.7	66	1.5	37	53
12. Boehringer	Federal Republic of Germany	0.7	77	1.5	69	—
13. Squibb	United States of America	0.7	50	1.5	33	38
14. Bristol Myers	United States of America	0.7	30	1.5	31	—
15. Takeda	Japan	0.6	65	1.3	6	—

SOURCE: U.N. 1979 report and ADL Insight.

EXHIBIT 4 Drug Companies

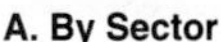

A. By Sector

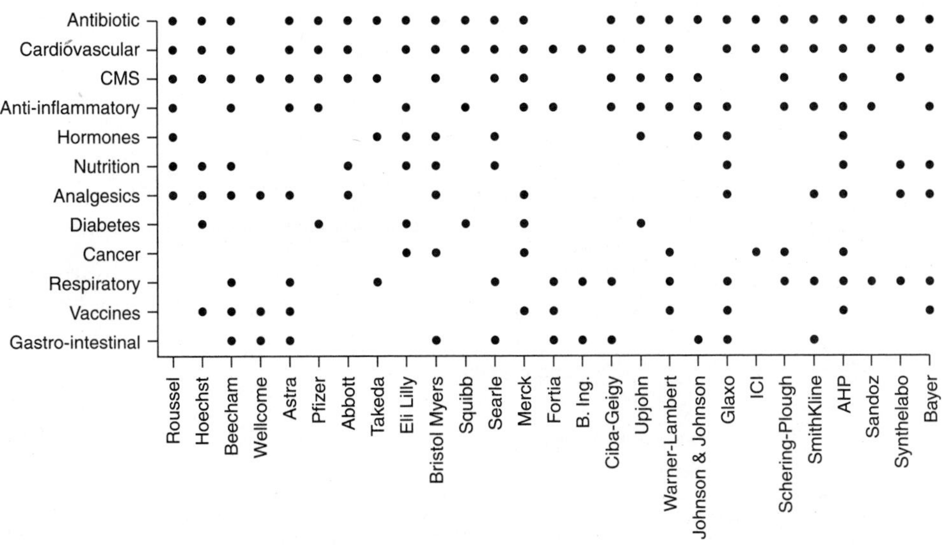

SOURCE: Annual reports.

B. Selected R&D Characteristics of Leading Pharmaceutical Companies

	Basic research emphasis	Development emphasis	Historic productivity	Recent productivity	Licensing relationships
Maximum:			2	3	1
Abbott	•	•	+	+	+
American Home		•			+
Ciba-Geigy	•	•	+		+
Johnson & Johnson	•	•	+	++	+
Lilly	•	•	+	+	+
Merck	•	•	++	+++	
Pfizer	•	•		+	+
Roche	•		+		+
Schering-Plough	•	•	+		+
SmithKline	•	•		++	
Squibb		•		+	+
Upjohn	•			+	+
Warner-Lambert		•	+		+

SOURCE: ADL Impact.

of development groups created economies of scale in pharmaceutical R&D. R&D spending amongst leading companies varied from 5 percent of turnover to over 12 percent, with an industry average of 8 percent (up from 7 percent in the 1960s). Companies could be divided into two main groups: those which depended heavily for growth and profits on product innovation; and those which relied on process skills to produce me-too products rapidly and cheaply, and on marketing skills to sell them. Ciba-Geigy, Merck, Eli Lilly, and most of the other top companies belonged to the first group.

Despite the slowdown in successful introductions, the industry still judged that the prerequisite for success was a large and well-focused R&D program and was increasing spending in this area. Companies were concentrating their efforts on a smaller number of indications with proven market potential and trying, where possible, to build on their existing expertise. It seemed likely that the smaller compa-

EXHIBIT 5 Development Process for Typical Pharmaceutical Product

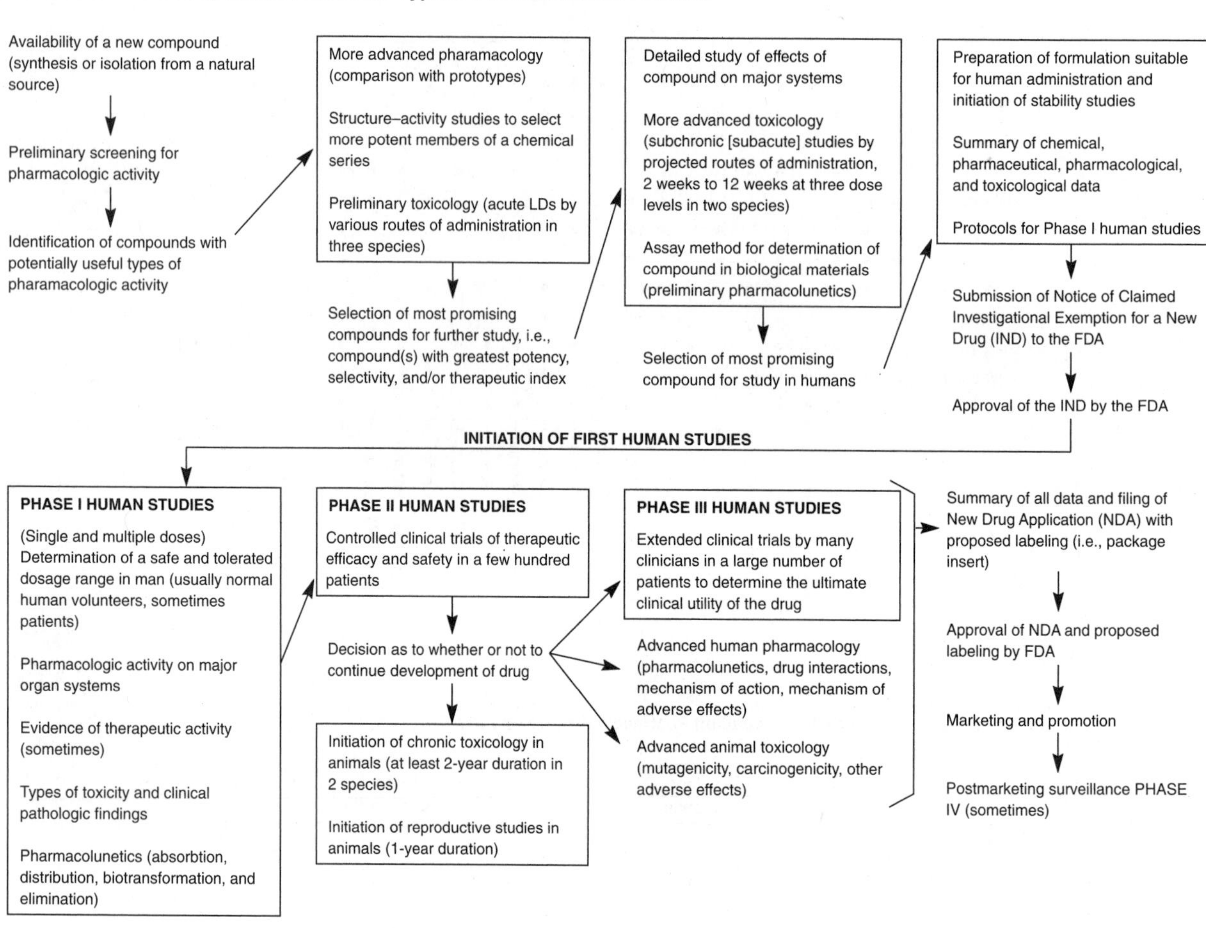

SOURCE: Frank G. Standaert, Department of Pharmacology, Georgetown University Schools of Medicine and Dentistry, Washington, D.C.
FROM: Bezold, "The Future of Pharmaceuticals"

nies would continue to have a high success rate in discovery, but that they would be forced by the costs of development to seek partners and licensees to exploit their discoveries.

Marketing costs were estimated to average 12 percent of turnover. Doctors were the key in ensuring the success of new drugs since neither the patients nor the actual buyers or payers (hospital administrators, health plan officials) knew much about them. Many drug companies ran separate sales forces (detailers) for different therapeutic areas or target groups. It was felt that detailers could not be expected to promote a full range of several hundred products. Thus, drugs suitable for hospital use might be promoted by one sales force, those for general practitioners' prescription by a second, and those for self-medication by yet another. The sales forces of Ciba and Geigy had not been combined when the two companies merged, and it was usual also for sales forces to remain separate when a large company acquired a smaller, specialized one.

Marketing and the establishment of a differentiated position for brands became increasingly important. While patents could prevent direct reproduction of a drug, they did not stop the competition issuing a slight chemical modification with similar action. Generally speaking, the first product into a new area, or the first to achieve a significant improvement (such as better efficacy, lesser side effects, easier formulation into oral form, etc.) over existing products in an established one became the physicians' drug of choice. This pattern increased both the risks and potential rewards of the R&D process. A good product reaching the market too

EXHIBIT 5 *(continued)*

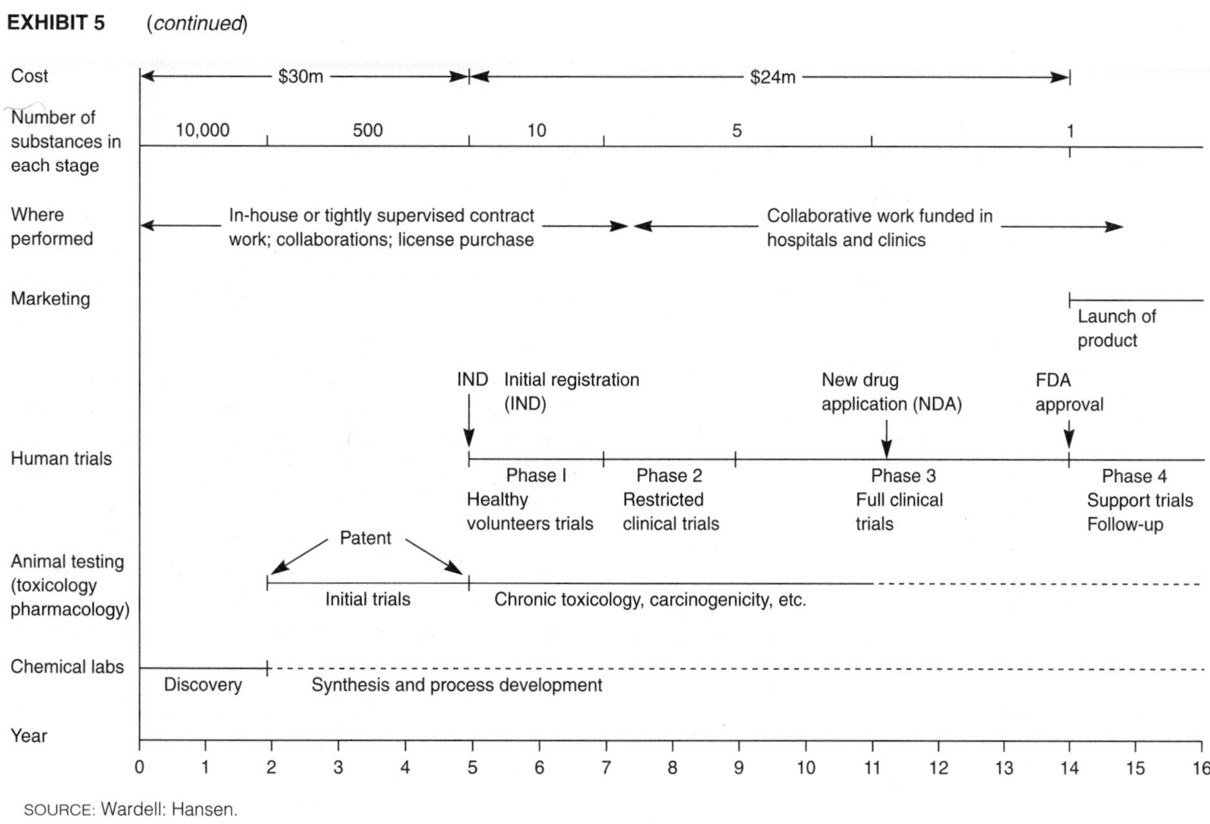

SOURCE: Wardell: Hansen.

late might not even cover its development costs. The potential of a product was thus intimately tied to the progress being made by competitors working on the same problem. Late entrants could try for a coattails effect identifying themselves with the leader and relying on marketing muscle for sales. However, generally, an attempt was made to differentiate with a different dosage form, or by claiming a wider range of applications.

The importance of first entry and the need to spread costs of development over a wide sales base led all the major ethical drug companies to establish overseas subsidiaries. These had their own marketing and sales organizations and many formulated and packaged products, though the production of active ingredients was usually centralized to achieve economies of scale. The subsidiaries generally operated with a considerable degree of autonomy.

The three Basle-based Swiss companies (Ciba-Geigy, Hoffmann-La Roche, and Sandoz) sold 95 percent of their product abroad, exporting the majority of their active ingredients from headquarters. U.S. companies still served mainly their domestic markets but were internationalizing rapidly. Japanese suppliers remained so far almost entirely domestic.

Advanced Drug Delivery Systems (ADDS)

The active ingredient of a pharmaceutical product cannot usually be administered in its natural state. It has to be combined with a delivery vehicle or dosage form such as a pill, syrup, and the like (Exhibit 6). Most conventional drug delivery methods have the same limitation: they do not permit the physician consistently to reach and maintain the optimum level of active ingredient (AI) in the pa-tient's blood and tissues (Exhibit 7). Until the 1930s the dosage form was largely the province of the pharmacist who formulated active ingredients and inert materials into pills, liquids, and ointments, whereas the pharmaceutical companies concerned themselves with the discovery and production of active ingredients.

With the therapeutic explosion of the next two decades and the downstream integration of the

EXHIBIT 6 Conventional Delivery and Dosage Forms

1. *Oral forms* (pills, capsules, syrups, powders, etc.) are easy to apply and are generally well accepted by patients. Their main disadvantages are that they affect and are affected by the properties of the individual's gastrointestinal (GI) tract and that their active ingredients are often rapidly metabolized by the liver. They are generally only suitable for drugs with long half-lives (resistance to metabolism), and because of their rapid metabolism in the liver they often have to be applied in much larger doses than the intended treatment area really requires.

2. *Parenteral forms* (injections, infusions) are largely used for drugs which have too short a half-life for oral dosage or are not absorbed by the GI tract. Many antibiotics fit into this category. This form has the great disadvantage that it is not generally suitable for self-medication and is restricted to hospitals and clinics in the main.

3. *Topical forms* (ointments, creams, liquids) are for external application generally, treating such surface conditions as wounds, burns, and eczema. However, where a drug permeates the skin easily, it can be used to treat internal conditions (nitroglycerine ointments for angina and various bronchial treatments).

4. *Rectal forms* (suppositories) have a more uniform absorption than oral products without their effect on the stomach, but they are not well accepted by patients in a large part of the world.

5. *Inhaled forms* (atomizers) are generally used for respiratory complaints; although the lungs provide easy access to the blood stream, they are also fragile.

pharmaceutical companies, the delivery vehicle began to get more attention. Companies were looking for ways to differentiate their products, and it was felt that an increase in convenience to the user would not only do this but also improve compliance and therefore efficacy of treatment.

Marketing departments were asking for once-a-day treatments and while most of research's efforts in this area went into searching for drugs with longer active lives (resistance to metabolism), many of the large pharmaceutical companies also worked on slow-release delivery systems. They established pharmacokinetics departments to study the absorption, distribution, metabolism, and excretion of drugs. These functions were still very imperfectly understood. Most prior research had concentrated solely on the empirical observation of the effects of drugs.

Several slow-release systems were developed. Such systems were generally expensive to produce and their success in the marketplace had been very mixed. Ciba-Geigy had one in-house–developed slow-release product, Slow-K, which had been a major success, turning a commodity chemical into a high-margin product.

Many of the slow-release formulations marketed since the mid-1960s had not been commercial successes because there was no very strongly perceived need for them. Patients often did not mind taking medication several times a day; indeed, for many short treatments, they found this more reassuring. Doctors saw no reason to change their prescribing habits, and the detailers saw no particular reason to push slow-release at the expense of a well-known traditional form of the same drug.

While many pharmacologists and physicians felt that slow-release was a marketing gimmick and that conventional delivery systems were adequate for therapeutic needs, others agreed with Dr. Alex Zaffaroni, the founder and president of ALZA Corporation, who said that one should be aiming to achieve complete control of the release and movement of the drug within the body in order to satisfy the "Laws of Minima" which he defined as follows:

> The physician's objective should be to achieve the desired results with the "minimum of interaction of therapeutic agents with body tissues." The drug with the shortest practical half-life should be chosen; the formulation should contain as few other substances as possible; the application site should be chosen to reduce the number of tissue compartments traversed on the way to the treatment site; dosage should be as low and as infrequent as possible.

Dr. Zaffaroni said that "therapeutic systems" should be developed to allow control of the rate of release of a drug as well as its quantity. The release profile for such products would be similar to that shown in Exhibit 8.

Though in its broadest sense an advanced drug delivery system (ADDS) could be said to be any new delivery vehicle offering improvements over existing methods, the term will be applied here only to those which could be used in "therapeutic systems" as defined by Dr. Zaffaroni. Though ALZA seemed to have the largest number of systems at an advanced stage of development (Exhibit 9), a number of other companies were known to be working along similar lines. Dr. Zaffaroni felt that the commercial potential of optimized delivery systems, or ADDS, was enormous:

1. They would permit the use of some substances which were currently too toxic or short-lived for commercialization.

EXHIBIT 7 Drug Concentration in Blood and Tissues

The concentration of the drug in blood and tissues varies greatly over time and depends on several factors:

1. The quantity of active ingredient (AI) administered and frequency of dosage.
2. The rate of breakdown of the carrier material, which varies from patient to patient.
3. The rate of absorption of the AI (also variable).
4. The half-life of the AI (the time it takes the body to metabolize and deactivate the drug): the shorter the half-life, the larger the dose or more frequent its application.

The graph below shows the typical concentration in the blood of a drug administered four times daily in conventional form.

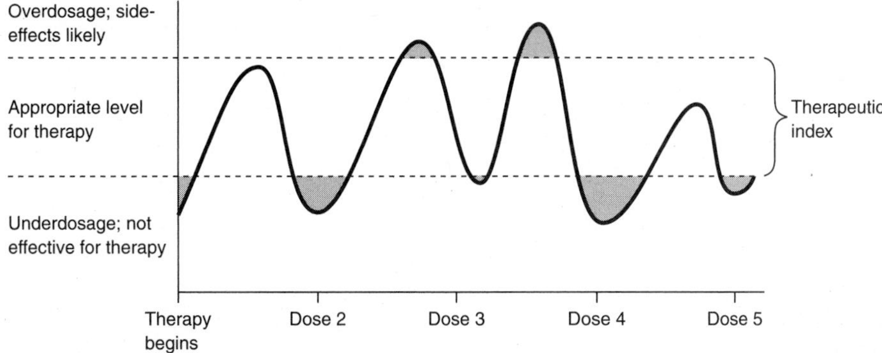

Drugs can be positioned on a therapeutic index which is defined as the relationship between the minimal curative dose and the maximal tolerated one. Where the index is wide, as in the figure above, such variations may be acceptable, if not optimal. Where it is narrow, as in the graph below, large fluctuations cannot be permitted; toxic side effects occur when the concentration is too high, and the drug is ineffective when it is too low. The usual solution to this problem is to increase the frequency of dosage, but this often causes patient compliance problems, particularly in long-term treatments.

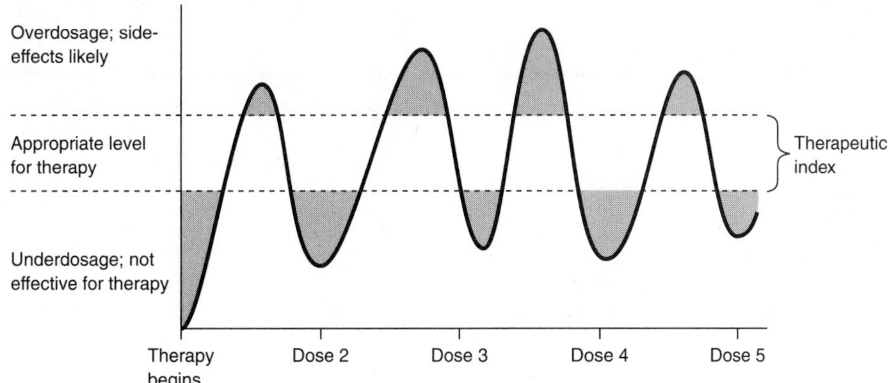

Many drugs of proven activity have been rejected in preclinical and clinical tests because their narrow therapeutic index caused toxic side effects when they were applied in conventional oral or parenteral form.

2. They could be used to repackage or improve existing products, extending their effective life and diminishing the ill-effects of loss of patent protection.

3. They could add value to generics through differentiation.

4. They could open up for commercialization markets in which patient compliance was a serious problem (e.g., contraception in the Third World).

However, there were still a number of medical, commercial, and technical question marks hanging over ADDS.

The validity of the "Rules of Minima" was by no means accepted by the pharmacological establishment, though to the layman they seemed to make sense. There were worries that a steady release rate for a drug might more easily lead to tolerance in the

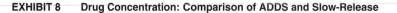

EXHIBIT 8 Drug Concentration: Comparison of ADDS and Slow-Release

Overdosage; side-effects likely
ADDS
Slow-release
Appropriate level for therapy
Underdosage; not effective for therapy
24 hours
Therapy begins
Dose 2

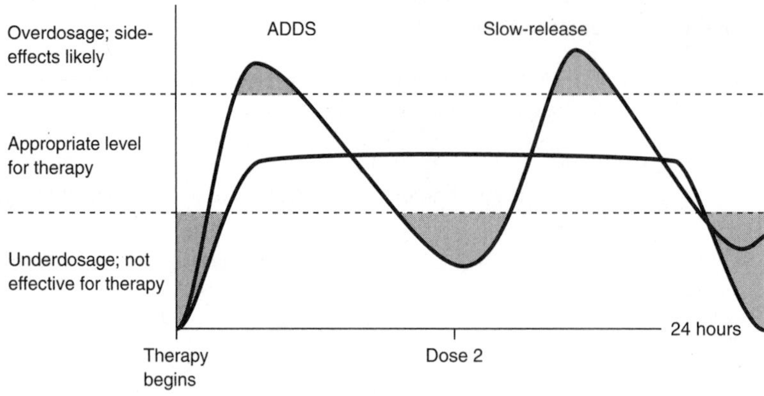

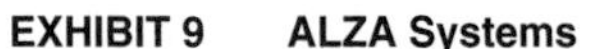

EXHIBIT 9 ALZA Systems

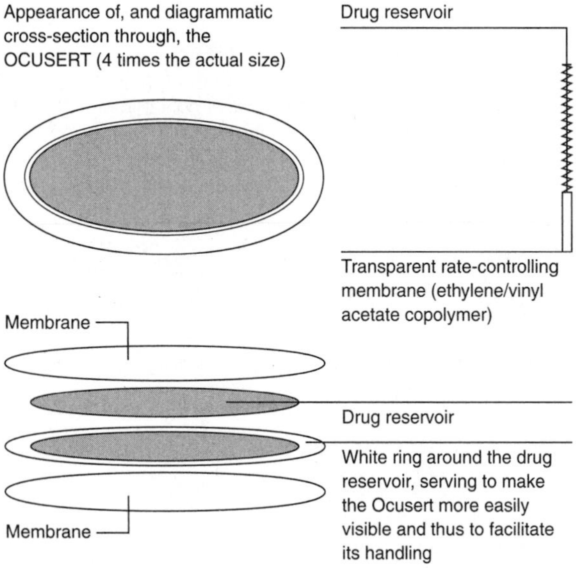

Appearance of, and diagrammatic cross-section through, the OCUSERT (4 times the actual size)
Drug reservoir
Transparent rate-controlling membrane (ethylene/vinyl acetate copolymer)
Membrane
Drug reservoir
White ring around the drug reservoir, serving to make the Ocusert more easily visible and thus to facilitate its handling
Membrane

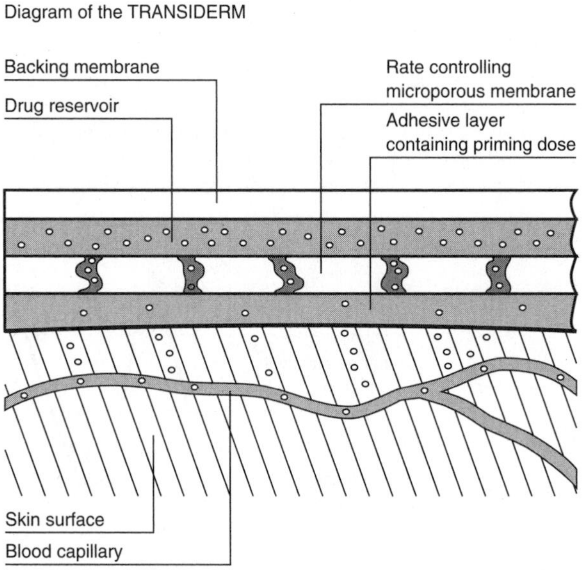

Diagram of the TRANSIDERM
Backing membrane
Drug reservoir
Rate controlling microporous membrane
Adhesive layer containing priming dose
Skin surface
Blood capillary

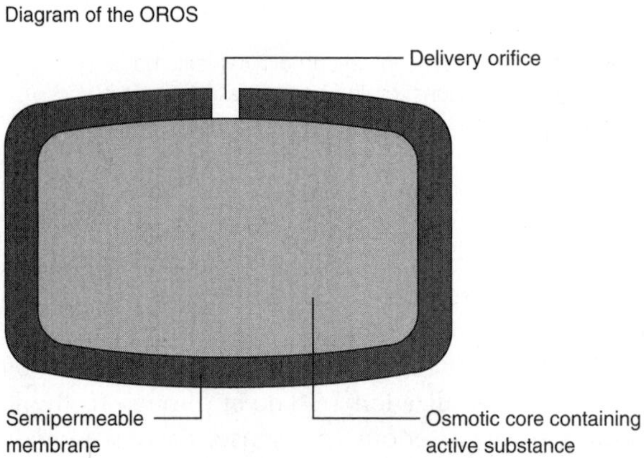

Diagram of the OROS
Delivery orifice
Semipermeable membrane
Osmotic core containing active substance

EXHIBIT 9 *(concluded)*

Diagram illustrating details of the AR, MED infusor

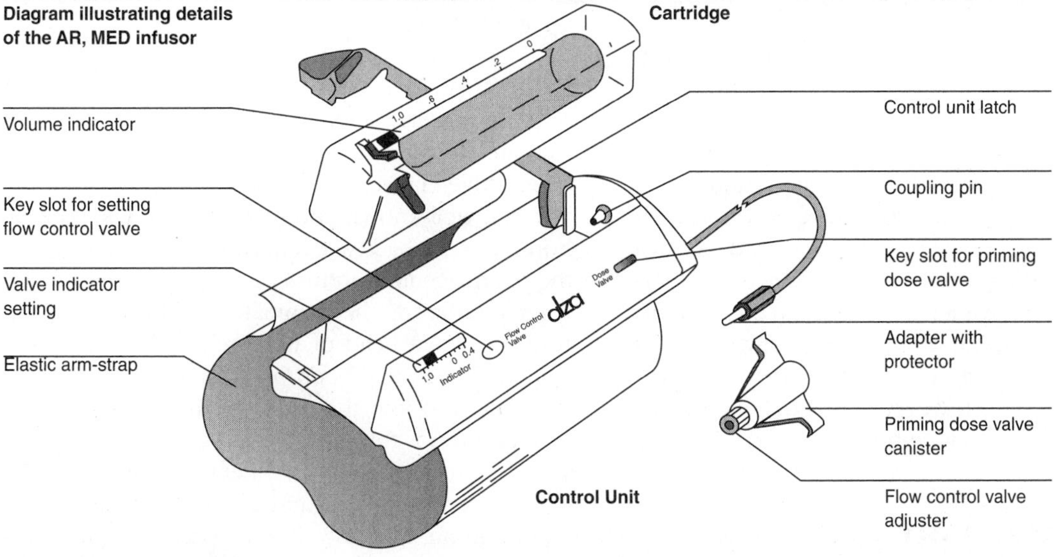

Cartridge
Volume indicator
Key slot for setting flow control valve
Valve indicator setting
Elastic arm-strap
Control unit latch
Coupling pin
Key slot for priming dose valve
Adapter with protector
Priming dose valve canister
Flow control valve adjuster
Control Unit

Diagrammatic cross-section through the PROGESTASERT

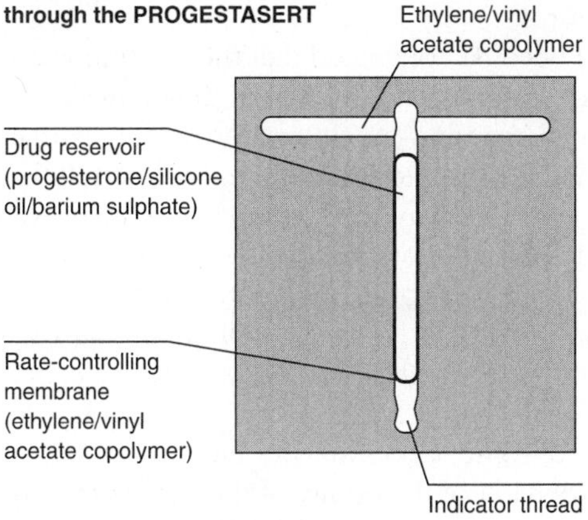

Ethylene/vinyl acetate copolymer
Drug reservoir (progesterone/silicone oil/barium sulphate)
Rate-controlling membrane (ethylene/vinyl acetate copolymer)
Indicator thread

Diagram illustrating how the PROGESTASERT operates

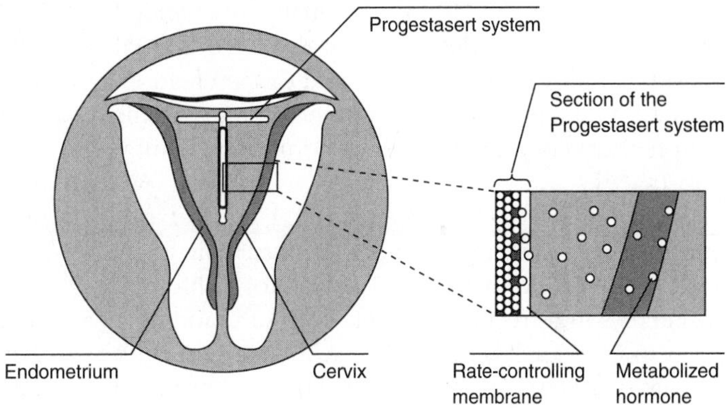

Progestasert system
Section of the Progestasert system
Endometrium
Cervix
Rate-controlling membrane
Metabolized hormone

body and therefore to larger and larger doses, or to ineffectiveness. Many felt that the therapeutic index of the vast majority of drugs was sufficiently wide for conventional delivery vehicles to be acceptable, and that the potential for ADDS was therefore limited.

There were also doubts about the practicality of designing sophisticated delivery vehicles and then trying to squeeze drugs into them. The absorption characteristics and modes of action of most drugs were imperfectly understood. Achieving true control of their release might well require custom designing of the system for each individual case.

ADDS were very much more expensive to produce than conventional forms; the production and packaging of pills, ointments, syrups, and injectables formed a very low proportion of overall cost. Techniques were generally well known, and techniques were standard throughout the industry. In the case of ADDS, the delivery vehicle generally cost more than its contents.

Registration was likely to be relatively easy to obtain for systems including established drugs since the efficacy of the latter would already have been proven. The main problem would be proving efficacy superior to that of the industry standard in order to justify a higher price.

The pharmaceutical industry's main areas of expertise were the synthesis and efficient production of active chemicals. The compounding of the final product was a relatively simple process. ADDS would require a new type of development and production know-how: familiarity with polymers, plastics, adhesives, molding systems, and so on. Engineers would find themselves in the front line for the first time and the expertise required was not easy to acquire.

Commercial potential was equally uncertain. Many of the ADDS devices would require the patient and physician to learn new application methods (the main exception to this was ALZA's OROS), though they offered greater convenience thereafter. The medical establishment was generally thought to be conservative and slow to accept new forms of treatment. The very low acceptance rate for ALZA's Progestasert and OCUSERT, both of which had therapeutic and user advantages, seemed to confirm this view. The introduction of a radically new system is best achieved through a well-trained and product-specific sales force. However, this is only economic for extremely high-volume products.

ALZA Corporation

ALZA was founded in 1968 by Dr. Alejandro (Alex) Zaffaroni. ALZA's mission, essentially unchanged from the start, was described by the 1976 annual report as follows: "ALZA is devoted to the creation, development, and marketing of therapeutic systems for precisely controlled delivery of drugs and natural substances."

ALZA occupied nine well-appointed, even luxurious, modern buildings in the Stanford University Industrial Development Park, Palo Alto, California, just across the street from Hewlett-Packard and next door to IBM. Each building was self-contained, with its own cafeteria and social facilities, to promote close personal contacts among subgroups. The whole was surrounded by landscaped grounds complete with sculptures which often served as an outside meeting room and canteen.

While the company had, until now, functioned mainly as a research organization financed by capital, it had recently launched three products, and its declared intention was to become an integrated pharmaceutical company handling its own production and marketing. The emphasis had thus far been on the development of systems, on the assumption that once these were perfected, generic or proprietary compounds would be found to fill them.

ALZA's technology was largely unique in 1977, and there was no other company or research center with a similar mix of materials, engineering, and pharmaceutical expertise. The company's projects and products and their principal features are summarized in Exhibit 10.

Origins of ALZA

Dr. Zaffaroni was a biochemist of Urugayan origin who had joined Syntex in 1951 and contributed considerably to its meteoric growth. Though he had not been active in research for many years, Dr. Zaffaroni was still well-known and respected for his work on hormones. He had excellent connections throughout the pharmaceutical industry and in academic circles.

Dr. Zaffaroni had initiated delivery systems research while head of Research and Marketing at Syntex. Syntex had been one of the very few small companies to join the ranks of the major pharmaceutical groups through internal growth in the post-war period. Its success had been equally the result of a highly innovative and succesful research program and an aggressively entrepreneurial business policy, in both of which Dr. Zaffaroni had played a significant role.

He had become convinced that the enormous scientific and commercial potential of the delivery systems field demanded much greater resources than Syntex was prepared to underwrite. He also felt that the most effective way to develop a new idea was from scratch and as an independent new venture, rather than in large company laboratories.

He left Syntex and put $2 million of his own money into the start-up company ALZA. He persuaded Syntex to release patents, research programs, and some personnel to him in return for about 25 percent of the equity of the new company. These shares were later distributed to Syntex shareholders as supplementary dividends.

Using contacts developed while at Syntex, Alex Zaffaroni had assembled a first-rate team of 90 researchers and technicians by 1970. Among them were such ADDS pioneers as Dr. Higuchi, for whom ALZA financed a Development Institute at the University of Kansas. He had also recruited a team of well-known scientists from leading universities to form a Board of Scientific Advisors and to act as consultants to ALZA.[1]

Dr. Zaffaroni was a charismatic and paternalistic leader who managed to inspire not only loyalty and enthusiasm in his employees, but also a sense of mis-

[1]One of these was Dr. Robert Woodward, professor of science at Harvard. He was also a member of the Ciba-Geigy board of directors and head of a research institute funded by Ciba-Geigy.

EXHIBIT 10 Principal Features of ALZA Drug Delivery Systems

SYSTEM	POTENTIAL USE LENGTH OF ACTION	COMPETING METHODS LENGTH OF ACTION	ALZA PRODUCT & THERAPY	CORE TECHNOLOGY	DATE OF INTRODUCTION	COMMERCIAL POTENTIAL	PRINCIPAL ADVANTAGES	PRINCIPAL DRAWBACKS
Ocusert Eye-insert with reservoir and rate-controlling membrane	Glaucoma, Trachoma, Conjunctivitis, other infections 1 week +	Eye drops, ointments, systemic medicines. Surgery 3 hrs. to perm.	Ocusert Pilocarpine Glaucoma	Polymer membranes	1975	Glaucoma $20 m market. Others big but not known	Controlled delivery. Smaller dose, fewer side effects. Patient compliance	Expensive. Doctor and patient need special training
Intra-uterine device Drug or hormone release through membrane	Contraception Menstrual control 1 year	The "pill", other IUDs, surgery, diaphragms, etc. 1 day to perm.	Progestasert Contraception	Polymer membrane	1976	Contraception $500m + worldwide	Reduced menstrual problems. Reduced hormone intake. Patient compliance	Expensive. Doctor must be trained. Ectopic pregnancies. Strong competition
OROS Oral steady release drug in semi-permeable membrane	Almost all systemic drugs suitable for oral use. 1 day	Microcapsules, matrix slow-release. Regular pills 4 hrs to 1 day	None as yet. Prototype	Polymer membrane. Osmosis	1980? If suitable drug found	Impossible to quantify. Thought to have biggest potential	Steady release unaffected by acidity changes. Less irritation. Patient compliance	Expensive. Need for 24 hr. dose unclear. Many competitors
Transiderm Patch stuck to skin containing reservoir and rate-controlling membrane	Anti-nausea; angina, hormonal imbalance, many others. 3 days–2 weeks	Ointments, creams, adhesive patches. Without rate control 4 hrs. +	None as yet. Prototype	Polymer membrane. Adhesives	1979? If trials scopolamine successful	Very large	Steady release drug. By-passes liver. Treatment easily stopped. Patient compliance	Not suitable for all drugs. Relatively expensive
Chronomer Injectable bio-erodible polymer containing drug	Diabetes, hormonal imbalance, narcotic antagonists contraception Up to 1 year	Implants. Depot injections. Erodible polymers. Up to 1 year	None as yet. Still basic research	Biodegradable polymers. Drug inclusion	1983?	Very large	Long-term steady release. Can be removed. Patient compliance	Not yet known
Portable intra-venous infusor	All treatments that need infusion. Cancer chemotherapy, anaesthetics Up to 12 hrs	Static drip on pole. Mechanical pumps (heavy) Several hrs.	AR/MED. Infusor Purchaser decides use	Elastomers	1976 in prototype form	Limited	Portability, ease of use	Expensive. Small-scale production
Osmotic Minipump Implantable drug reservoir and release mechanism	Basic biomedical research in animals. Toxicology studies Up to 7 days	Injections, medicated food, external infusion implanted polymers 4 hrs, to 1 yr.	ALZET. Potential for all medical & veterinary research	Osmosis	1976	Small	No true alternative for steady release research. Ease of use.	

EXHIBIT 11 Partial Organization Chart for ALZA Corporation—1977

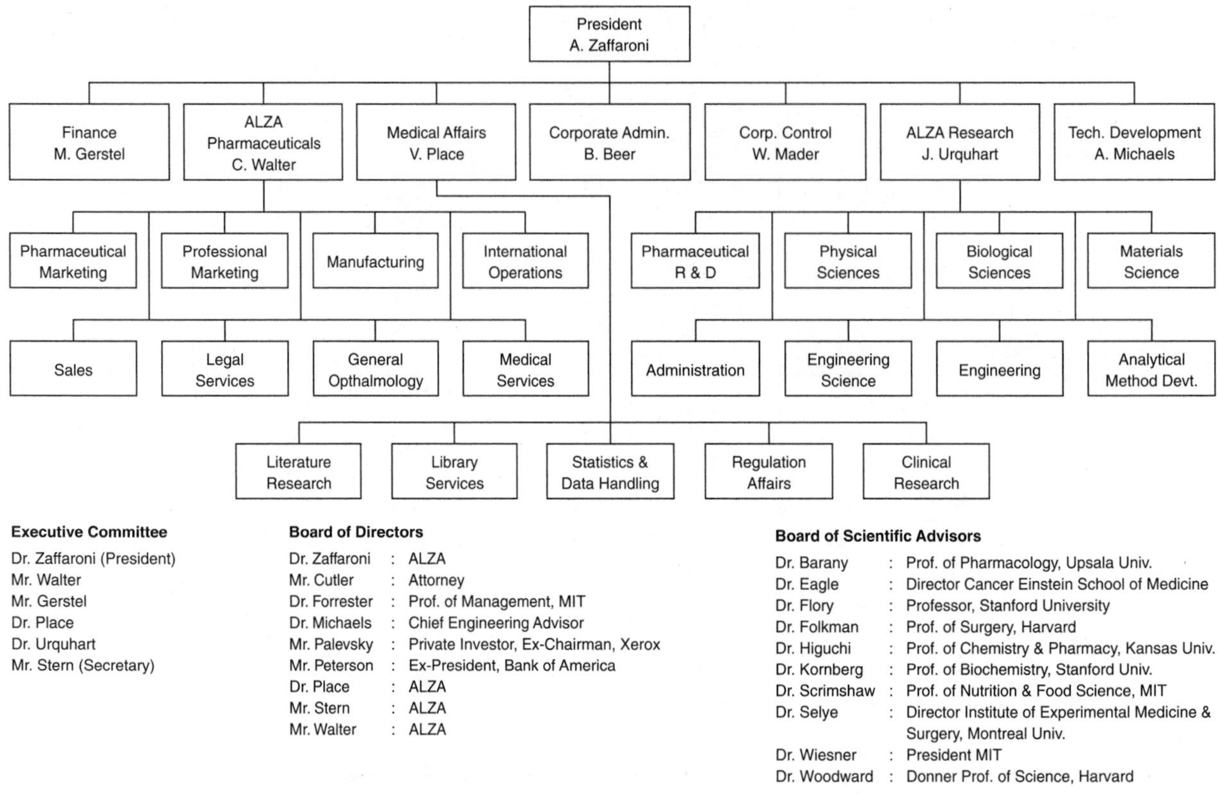

SOURCE: ALZA documentation.

sion as great as his own. He believed in hiring the best people and giving them the best possible conditions to work in. He was particularly concerned to foster an entrepreneurial spirit in ALZA and he encouraged initiative on the part of his employees. Strong emphasis was placed on the generation of ideas and on creative development of them, and budgetary control was not tight. Cost considerations came very far down on Dr. Zaffaroni's list of priorities. Though he now concentrated chiefly on strategic issues, Dr. Zaffaroni continued to be involved in the decision-making process at almost all levels.

ALZA Organization

Dr. Zaffaroni was both chairman of the board and president (CEO) of the company; five of the nine directors were nonexecutive appointees. The management committee which ran the company consisted of the heads of research, medicine, production, and finance, and Dr. Zaffaroni and the company secretary. A partial organization chart for ALZA can be found in Exhibit 11.

Almost all the key scientists and managers had held their positions since the founding of the company. Many of those in positions of responsibility were still in their 20s or 30s. The atmosphere was informal with an open-door policy running right to the top, and the hierarchical structure was very ill defined. Wages were not exceptionally high and there were few performance-linked bonuses, but many employees benefited from stock options.

Research was generally carried on by multidisciplinary teams whose members also belonged to departments organized along functional lines. Research was considered the core of the company, and in 1977 it accounted for 220 of the 550 ALZA employees. These included a large number of materials engineers and polymer chemists. The medical department, concerned mostly with the clinical trials necessary for registration of products, employed another 30 people.

ALZA Pharmaceuticals had been formed in 1973 as a subsidiary which would combine the manufacturing, marketing, and sales functions.

Manufacturing acquired a new 67,000-square-foot facility in the industrial park and with the pilot plant had acquired 150 process workers and technicians by 1975. The capacity acquired was expected to be sufficient to meet demand into the 1980s. This function was run very much as a separate unit with little contact between research and manufacturing below executive level.

The marketing department concentrated at first on raising awareness of the eye-insert OCUSERT, publishing scientific papers, sponsoring symposia on glaucoma, and producing training films and literature. A field force was trained not only in opthalmic applications of ADDS but also in other potential fields and in membrane technology. Between 1974 and 1976 a similar program was followed for Progestasert, a contraceptive device launched in 1976. By 1976 ALZA had a direct field sales force of 70 representatives and regional managers. The majority specialized in contraception, which was the larger market and which was prescribed by a greater number of doctors.

ALZA Operations 1968–1977

Between 1969 and 1976 ALZA raised $73 million in capital. Of this, $12 million came from companies interested in distribution of ALZA products or in ALZA research contracts (e.g., Merck). Of the rest, $37 million came from private placements and warrants, and $26 million from publicly offered stock. The only major stockholder was Dr. Zaffaroni, who in 1977 held roughly 13 percent of the 7.8 million shares.

In 1970, ALZA was predicting the launch of the first product (unspecified) by 1972. It could be OCUSERT, Progestasert, or an unnamed product for cattle. By 1972, ALZA was still far from a launch, development times having been underestimated. No new launch date was given.

In 1973 the first new drug applications, for OCUSERT and Progestasert, were presented to the U.S. Food and Drug Administration (FDA) and by the end of 1974 the production facilities for these were largely in place. The establishment of the latter before approvals had been obtained was a calculated risk. ALZA needed to get products into the marketplace as quickly as possible not only to provide revenue but also to maintain the company's credibility in the stock market.

Approval for OCUSERT came in 1974 and it was launched in 1975. Progestasert was approved in 1975 and launched in 1976. Both products enjoyed a high degree of interest in the medical press and both appeared to perform up to expectations in all respects except sales volume. ALZA had no doubt that the products were significant technical advances over existing systems and felt that the warm reception given to them by those asked to test them would translate into industrywide acceptance.

In any event, the sales which had been expected to put the company into profit in 1977–78 were well below estimates. Sales of $2.8 million were registered in 1976, and around $6 million in the year ending June 1977. However, there were indications that a high proportion of the latter sum consisted of sale-or-return consignments filling the distribution pipeline. Far from rising, it seemed that the real sales trend was downwards.

The initial resistance to new concepts had turned out to be much stronger than expected. The Progestasert device had to be inserted by physicians, and though the action was said to be easy it had to be learned. Physicians were somewhat reluctant to recommend a new device, taking a conservative wait-and-see attitude. The ALZA sales force might have been able to overcome these problems if there had not also been price resistance to the product. It was more expensive than competing IUDs and represented a much higher one-time outlay than the pill. To add to Progestasert's difficulties, there were indications that it did nothing to prevent ectopic pregnancies, those occurring outside the womb.

OCUSERT had to be inserted by the patients; since many of these were elderly and already very sensitive about their eyes, the product met with user resistance. This patient group was not only inherently conservative, but also very price sensitive, and OCUSERT was considerably more expensive per treatment day than eyedrops. The clear advantages of the product (once-a-week application and few side effects) were insufficient in themselves to sell it.

ALZA's Situation in 1977

The separate sales forces, unable to spread their costs across a range of products, became a serious drain on the company's stretched resources. Marketing expenditure for 1974–1977 exceeded $20 million and was running at an annual rate of $6.5 million.

Annual operating losses for 1975 to 1977 exceeded $15 million, and with sales in 1977 barely

EXHIBIT 12 Statement of Operations

	Years Ended June 30				
	1973	1974	1975	1976	1977
Net sales	$ —	$ —	$ —	$ 2,401,000	$ 6,102,000
Research revenue	—	—	250,000	399,000	1,108,000
Total revenue	—	—	250,000	2,800,000	7,210,000
Costs and expenses:					
Costs of products shipped	—	—	—	1,136,000	3,720,000
Start-up manufacturing costs	—	762,000	710,000	1,099,000	—
Research and product development expenses	6,073,000	6,751,000	7,515,000	8,434,000	8,087,000
General, administrative, and marketing expenses	1,470,000	2,937,000	6,125,000	7,223,000	9,077,000
Interest, net	(961,000)	(1,400,000)	(698,000)	462,000	1,296,000
Total costs and expenses	6,582,000	9,050,000	13,652,000	18,354,000	22,180,000
Loss before items below	(6,582,000)	(9,050,000)	(13,402,000)	(15,554,000)	(14,970,000)
Excess of sales value over cost of products previously shipped	—	—	—	420,000	—
Equity in net loss of Dynapol	(407,000)	(1,251,000)	(1,624,000)	(1,153,000)	(1,261,000)
Net loss	$(6,989,000)	$(10,301,000)	$(15,026,000)	$(16,287,000)	$(16,231,000)
Net loss per share	$(1.37)	$(1.83)	$(2.47)	$(2.30)	$(2.12)
Weighted average number of shares outstanding	$ 5,086,000	$ 5,642,000	$ 6,080,000	$ 7,086,000	$ 7,667,000

SOURCE: ALZA annual reports.

covering manufacturing costs, it was clear that the company's cash flow crisis was not a short-term phenomenon. ALZA's capital reserves had been exhausted. By June 1977, $14 million of a $20 million line of credit had already been taken up and the company was in default of loan conditions. The company's stock was selling at half of 1976 prices (Exhibits 12, 13, 14).

Faced with an increasingly precarious financial situation, Alex Zaffaroni devoted most of 1977 to the search for a long-term solution.

He approached almost all the major pharmaceutical and chemical companies with proposals for a comprehensive partnership which would secure the future of ALZA. In April 1977, Dr. Zaffaroni contacted a member of Ciba-Geigy's board of directors who introduced him to Dr. Gaudenz Staehelin, head of Ciba-Geigy's Pharma Division. Dr. Zaffaroni proposed that Ciba-Geigy take a major equity position in ALZA in return for licenses to existing and future technologies.

Ciba-Geigy AG

The Group

Formed by a merger between two major chemical companies in 1970, Ciba-Geigy AG was a diversified multinational with headquarters in Basle, Switzerland, subsidiaries in 60 countries, and sales representation in many more. 1976 group sales were 9.5 billion Swiss francs; 98 percent of end-product sales were made abroad but much of the manufacturing, particularly of active ingredients (AIs), was done in Switzerland. The group employed 75,000 people worldwide, of whom 21,000 were in Switzerland.

EXHIBIT 13 Balance Sheet June 30, 1976, and 1977

Assets	1976	1977
Current assets:		
Cash	$ 1,129,000	$ 1,626,000
Certificates of deposit and bankers' acceptances	3,352,000	—
Receivables	722,000	1,544,000
Inventories, at cost	1,860,000	2,979,000
Prepaid expenses and other	544,000	756,000
Total current assets	7,607,000	6,905,000
Property, plant, and equipment:		
Prepaid land leases	1,062,000	1,062,000
Buildings	9,747,000	9,933,000
Equipment	5,198,000	6,253,000
Leasehold improvements	934,000	1,097,000
Construction in progress	507,000	597,000
	17,448,000	18,942,000
Less accumulated depreciation and amortization	(2,654,000)	(3,612,000)
Net property, plant, and equipment	14,794,000	15,330,000
Other, net	1,076,000	1,108,000
	$23,477,000	$23,343,000
Liabilities and Shareholders' Equity		
Current liabilities:		
Accounts payable	$ 773,000	$ 357,000
Accrued liabilities	554,000	333,000
Bank loan	—	14,200,000
Current portion of long-term debt	17,000	19,000
Total current liabilities	1,344,000	14,909,000
Long-term debt, noncurrent portion	2,766,000	1,747,000
Commitments		
Shareholders' equity:		
Common stock, $1 par value: 10,000,000 shares authorized, 7,796,391 shares outstanding, 7,609,071 in 1976	7,609,000	7,796,000
Paid-in capital	71,786,000	73,911,000
ALZA's ownership interest in Dynapol, subject to restriction	(1,471,000)	(232,000)
Deficit	(58,557,000)	(74,788,000)
Total shareholders' equity	19,367,000	6,687,000
	$23,477,000	$23,343,000

SOURCE: ALZA financial statement.

Ciba-Geigy's facilities in and around Basle constituted practically a town by themselves, consisting of many office buildings, laboratories, and production plants, some of them dating from the 19th century. The company had its own social clubs, shops, and sporting facilities.

Company top management was largely drawn from a relatively small circle of old Basle families, and business and civic responsibilities were often intertwined. Many managers held high rank in the Swiss army. Most managers at Basle were Swiss and though the official language of Ciba-Geigy was English, many foreigners found that a mastery of Swiss German was essential to integration.

Basle was also the home of two other major chemical and pharmaceuticals companies, Hoffmann-La

EXHIBIT 14 Statement of Changes in Financial Position Five Years Ended June 30, 1977

	Year ended June 30				
	1973	1974	1975	1976	1977
Sources of working capital:					
Net proceeds from rights offering	$	$	$	$14,435,000	$
Exercise of stock options and warrants and issuance of stock under employee stock purchase plan	1,728,000	9,399,000	478,000	337,000	94,000
Sale of common stock		5,000,000	2,500,000	2,000,000	1,500,000
Issuance of common stock for patents and licenses	44,000		91,000	79,000	13,000
Warrants issued in connection with bank credit agreement				750,000	660,000
Bank loan under revolving credit agreement			4,000,000	1,000,000	13,200,000
Additions to long-term debt			1,800,000		
Exchange of common stock with Dynapol					23,000
	1,772,000	14,399,000	8,869,000	18,601,000	15,490,000
Applications of working capital:					
Net loss	6,989,000	10,301,000	15,026,000	16,287,000	16,231,000
Reduced by items not requiring working capital during the period:					
Depreciation and amortization	(385,000)	(538,000)	(685,000)	(915,000)	(1,000,000)
Sale of property, plant and equipment for note receivable	(597,000)				
Amortization of deferred interest				(333,000)	(447,000)
Write-off of advance royalties			(173,000)	(81,000)	
Write-off of advances to ALZA Mexicana, S.A.			(321,000)	(490,000)	(315,000)
Equity in net loss of subsidiaries	(406,000)	(1,350,000)	(1,695,000)	(1,153,000)	(1,261,000)
Total used in operations	5,601,000	8,413,000	12,152,000	13,315,000	13,208,000
Bank loan reclassified as current liability					14,200,000
Payment of bank loan				4,000,000	
Additions to property, plant, and equipment, net	1,291,000	3,738,000	5,331,000	1,857,000	1,494,000
Patents, patent applications, and licenses	44,000		87,000	127,000	27,000
Long-term note receivable	597,000			490,000	315,000
Advances to ALZA Mexicana, S.A.		305,000	253,000		
Deferred interest expense resulting from valuation of bank credit agreement warrants				417,000	462,000
Other, net	31,000	72,000	68,000	89,000	51,000
	7,564,000	12,528,000	17,891,000	20,295,000	29,757,000
Increase (decrease) in working capital	$(5,792,000)	$ 1,871,000	$(9,022,000)	$ (1,694,000)	$(14,267,000)

SOURCE: ALZA financial statement.

Roche and Sandoz. The two had one of the highest per capita incomes in the world (it was also a banking center), but the overall impressions given at all times, except Carnival, were of conservatism, sobriety, and order.

Ciba-Geigy's headquarters organization in Basle consisted of the Corporate Executive Committee (*Konzernleitung*, or KL), a number of corporate staff functions, and the divisional managements of four of the six Ciba-Geigy divisions: Pharmaceuticals, Agrochemicals, Dyestuffs and Chemicals, and Plastics and Additives. Divisional management for the Ilford Division was located in the United Kingdom, and Airwick was based in the United States and France.

Ciba-Geigy's operations in the countries were carried out by group companies which were also organized along divisional lines. While division managements at headquarters were responsible for worldwide strategies, direct authority over local divisional operations rested with group companies. The latter's plans were reviewed by regional corporate staff units.

EXHIBIT 15 Ciba-Geigy A.C. 1977: Partial Organization Chart

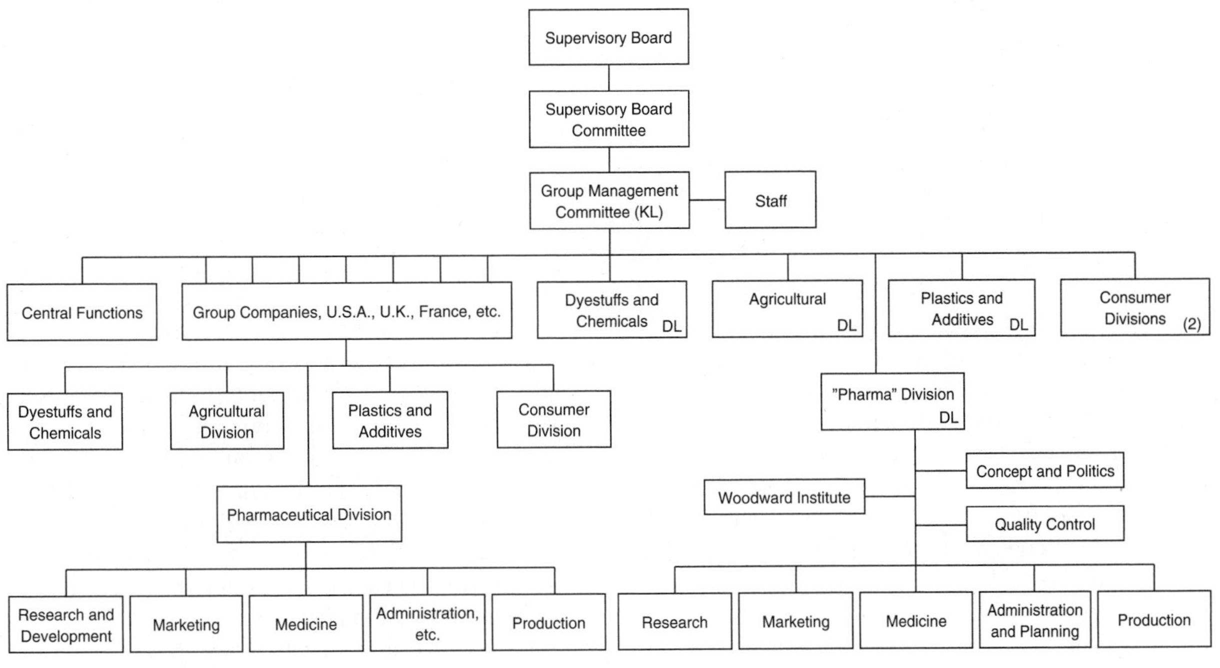

Integration of regional and divisional perspectives took place mainly in the KL. Each KL member was responsible for one or several divisions and regions (a partial organization chart can be found in Exhibit 15).

Ciba-Geigy Pharmaceuticals Division

The Pharmaceutical Division (usually referred to as Pharma) was the largest of Ciba-Geigy's divisions with 28 percent of group sales in 1976, and an even larger share of profits. Its 2.5 percent worldwide market share placed it among the leading companies in the industry. Although it was represented in more than 60 countries, its top four markets (United States, West Germany, Japan, and United Kingdom) accounted for about 42 percent of divisional sales.

The division concentrated almost exclusively on prescription drugs in five areas: cardiovascular preparations, antirheumatics and other anti-inflammatory preparations, psychotropic and neurotropic drugs, medicines for the treatment of various infectious diseases, and a more heterogeneous range of preparations including dermatologicals and drugs for coughs and colds.

Many of Ciba-Geigy's products in the first three areas were for long-term (chronic) treatment. These products had the advantage of yielding steady sales once a new patient was acquired but involved risks of unpredictable side-effects.

In the past, Ciba-Geigy had shown somewhat more concern for drug delivery forms than many of its competitors. It had launched a number of products of a nontraditional nature. Slow-K, a slow-release product introduced not long ago, had demonstrated both Ciba-Geigy know-how in this area and the commercial value of new delivery forms. There were also slow-release forms of injectable corticoids and Slow Trasicor.

Although the division had been regularly spending a high proportion (about 11 percent) of revenue on R&D, industry analysts rated its recent R&D productivity lower than that of other leading companies (Exhibit 4).

About two-thirds of the R&D effort was spent in Basle. Among the other three research centers, only the one in the United States (Summit) had all the functions necessary for complete product development. There was some funding of university projects, and the company backed two semi-independent research institutes. Few of the important products had been obtained through licenses or joint research projects, and cooperation with other pharmaceutical companies had been both rare and, save one ex-ception, unsuccessful.

Ciba-Geigy's R&D organization comprised many highly specialized experts. Most researchers in Basle were Swiss or German, and many of them had been with Ciba-Geigy for a number of years, whereas staff in the United States was mostly American and turnover was fairly high. Researchers and other staff were classified into a highly differentiated system of hierarchical ranks. The structure of the research department was both broad and deep. It was organized along functional lines, and there were four levels below the head of research.

The product development process was organized in such a way that a product passed sequentially through a number of different departments, first within R&D, then in Medicine, Technical Operations and, finally, Marketing.

Group companies had considerable freedom in developing their own strategies and programs, including the possibility to refuse introduction of products developed by Basle. Group company autonomy tended to increase in proportion to the importance of the subsidiary. In this regard, observers noted that some of Ciba-Geigy's most important products worldwide had not been introduced by its U.S. subsidiary.

Case III–4
ALZA Corporation (A)

Mark W. Cunningham, Reinhard Angelmar, and Yves Doz

The possibility of a partnership with or takeover by Ciba-Geigy was viewed with great concern by ALZA. For Alex Zaffaroni, as well as for almost all the scientists and managers on his team, the development of ADDS (advanced drug delivery systems) had become a life's dream; success would be the fulfillment of a vision. To abandon the crusade or reduce their commitment was out of the question. Yet recent results had been very disappointing. The first major products, OCUSERT and Progestasert, had been slow to develop and, when finally introduced, had not met with the expected success in the market. Further product introductions were a few years down the road. ALZA would not be able to hang on that long without outside help even if it shed its production and marketing operations and became a pure research organization once again.

Dr. Zaffaroni was desperate to maintain his research team intact for several reasons.

First, most ALZA employees trusted him blindly to find a solution to the financial crisis. They were fully aware of the gravity of the situation, but as the crisis deepened, very few of them started to explore other job opportunities and only a handful actually left.

Second, the effective development of ADDS demanded tight interaction between a variety of different technologies. Unless a viable research team in each technology could be maintained, ALZA's ability to conceive and develop new products would soon be jeopardized.

Third, he was ethically committed to maintaining a positive and creative climate in his company and could hardly imagine an ALZA run on a shoestring.

Dr. Zaffaroni's experience at Syntex had made him wary of large corporations and large-scale R&D efforts, though Syntex had been one of the most successful companies and he had been one of its leaders. Very few of the key staff of ALZA had large-company experience. They therefore viewed any link with a big organization with some degree of uneasiness and suspicion. Yet all were aware that this might be the only way to save ALZA.

This case provides additional information on ALZA's management organization and predicament in 1977, which will help the reader better understand its approach to a possible partnership with Ciba-Geigy.

ALZA's Strategy

While ALZA's devotion to its scientific mission—the development and commercialization of ADDS—remained constant throughout its history, the concept of how to achieve that mission evolved somewhat over time, at least partly under the pressure of events.

Alex Zaffaroni first envisaged a company that would evolve from R&D towards manufacturing and marketing as its products were developed and received FDA approval. OCUSERT and Progestasert had been seen as the first steps in ALZA's evolution into an integrated pharmaceutical company. Yet it was clear from the start that ALZA had neither the resources nor the competence to compete with major companies in the discovery and synthesis of new active ingredients and the manufacture of existing ones.

Research was therefore concentrated on the delivery systems and the screening of existing generic or proprietary active ingredients for suitability. Progestasert and OCUSERT both used drugs in the public domain, as would the first transdermal system (expected to use scopolamine against motion sickness).

Cooperation with outsiders was inevitable to a greater or lesser degree. From the very beginning, discussions with pharmaceutical companies centered on the licensing of active ingredients by ALZA, and/or of delivery systems by the partner. The first contact with Ciba-Geigy USA, which was of this kind, occurred in 1971, but produced no concrete results.

Dr. Zaffaroni was concerned to avoid excessive contact with the majors. There was, at first, no question of undertaking contract research; ALZA had as much money as it needed and wished to avoid the transfer of its technology to potential competitors. However, in 1976 long-term research agreements were signed with Merck (cardiovascular and anti-inflammatory applications of OROS) and Boehringer Ingelheim of West Germany (antihypertensives in transdermal systems). Both agreements were for contract research giving ALZA clear objectives and budgets. Intercompany project teams were not set up, and the emphasis was on the provision of a service rather than collaboration. Neither project had progressed very far by 1977, though they yielded revenues of $1.7 million in that year.

This change in policy partly reflected ALZA's need for new sources of revenue, but also the feeling that it was now strong enough to stand the contact with outside cultures. It was also felt that the launch by leading pharmaceutical companies of major products based on ALZA's systems would enhance ALZA's credibility and bring in royalties. There were no exclusivity provisions that would prevent ALZA from using what they learned in these projects for other products.

Overseas marketing agreements were sought for the ALZA products because a dedicated international sales force would be impossibly expensive. However, they were deliberately restricted to small, geographically limited concerns. Marketing in the United States was kept in-house to retain control and added value. The United States was the largest market for ALZA's products and thought likely to be the most receptive to new and better methods of treatment.

Manufacturing was retained at Palo Alto because it was central to the strategy of integration and because ALZA did not feel that anyone else had the necessary skills to handle it.

Dr. Zaffaroni was concerned that ALZA should not be allowed to grow too large for its entrepreneurial spirit and that its concern for the individual be maintained. Growth would therefore be achieved not through internal diversification but through the formation of spin-off companies exploiting research groups' expertise in new areas. These would operate independently and would be funded at least partly by outside capital. They would provide new opportunities for scientists and managers from the mother company. The first of these affiliates, Dynapol, was formed in 1972 to exploit ALZA expertise in polymer and other technologies in the nutritional field.

ALZA Organization

Authority in ALZA stemmed from Dr. Zaffaroni, the founder, chairman of the board, and president. Though the board of directors included the vice presidents in charge of medical affairs and ALZA Pharmaceuticals (the commercial and production organization), and the part-time company secretary, the remaining members were essentially outside advisors. Several had investments in ALZA and all were now close friends of Dr. Zaffaroni.

The Board of Advisors consisted of 10 very distinguished scientific academics who served to keep ALZA in touch with the latest developments in their fields and exercised their influence on its behalf. They also added to its prestige and credibility. They played no active role in the running of the company.

Reporting to Dr. Zaffaroni were the heads of finance, pharmaceuticals, research, medical affairs, control, technical development, and administration. The first four formed the management committee with Dr. Zaffaroni.

Finance Division. Mr. Martin Gerstel, head of the Finance Division, had joined the company direct from the Stanford MBA program in which he had distinguished himself. He had previously been a financial analyst at Cummins following a BS in industrial engineering.

Pharmaceuticals Division. The Pharmaceuticals Division had been formed in 1973 to handle the production and marketing of the company's systems. It provided the infrastructure and services of an integrated pharmaceutical company, which had not until then been required. It was set up as a separate unit operating from dedicated facilities on a 10-acre site not far from the main ALZA buildings. The original production facilities had become the pilot plant. A factory intended to manufacture Progestasert on a large scale had just been completed in Mexico and was owned only 49 percent by ALZA for legal reasons.

The Pharmaceuticals Division was headed by Dr. Carroll Walter, formerly VP of Syntex Laboratories, who was supported by sales, marketing, and production executives recruited mainly from the pharmaceutical industry. Nearly half of ALZA's employees (250) were still in pharmaceuticals, but the division's rapid buildup of staff in 1975–76 had been followed by dismissals in both production and sales departments in the financial crisis of 1977.

Research Division. Dr. Urquhart, the head of research, had been a professor of physiology at Pittsburg University and of biomedical engineering at USC before joining ALZA in 1969. Until 1975 the division had devoted itself exclusively to ALZA's internal projects, but in 1976 contracts for long-term joint-development projects had been signed with Merck (OROS) and Boehringer Ingelheim (Transderm). Dr. Urquhart was supported by directors for Pharmaceutical R&D; Physical Biological, Materials and Engineering Science Administration; Engineering; and Analytical Methods.

Though it was possible to be involved exclusively in basic research in a narrow field, most of the members of these departments worked on multidisciplinary project teams. Thus, a polymer chemist might report for most day-to-day purposes to a project leader who was a biologist or engineer. The division still employed 220 people in mid-1977, having undergone very little pruning. It was acknowledged to be the company's essential core.

Dr. Felix Theeuwes (OROS), a Belgian chemist with an academic background, and Dr. Janet Shaw (OCUSERT), a British physiologist and biologist who joined from Institutional Research, were typical of ALZA's project leaders. Most had distinguished backgrounds in research and had either invented the systems they were developing or had been associated with them from the start. Mr. Peter Carpenter, a Chicago MBA with a chemistry degree and considerable consulting experience, had been hired as a project leader in 1977 but rapidly took over responsibility for planning.

Medical Affairs. Dr. Virgil Place, head of the Medical Affairs Division, had been director of clinical pharmacology at Syntex. The department was responsible for literature research and library services, data processing, and regulatory affairs. The department also set up the clinical research required for the registration of new products and for the marketing information package. Pharmaceutical companies generally consider the latter role crucial to the successful launch of any new product, particularly if it uses unfamiliar concepts. The Clinical Research Department had to cover such diverse fields as opthalmology, gynecology, and cardiology with a very limited staff (seven nurses, two trials managers and two research assistants).

A series of highly detailed organization charts had been drawn up in 1974, but their release had never been authorized by Dr. Zaffaroni; he felt that the company's interests were best served by playing down the formal structure. His objective was to keep relationships within the company as fluid as possible since he believed that flexibility and multichannel communications were essential to the maintenance of the entrepreneurial spirit of ALZA. This was considered particularly important in the R&D and medical areas.

Consequently, though their immediate responsibilities and reporting lines were clear to ALZA employees, they had little sense of the company's overall structure. Individuals were given the titles traditional in the industry (principal, senior, and junior scientist) but the exact status of each individual was not clear in all situations; a senior scientist in charge of a project might even have a vice president reporting to him or her if the latter had special skills essential to the project.

The lack of role definition could cause problems. A high proportion of scientists joining ALZA left again very rapidly because they found it hard to fit in. They were given few clear orders and were expected to propose their own work program or sign on for those of others. The organization demanded and received a very high degree of commitment from its members. Very few left after the first few months, and all seemed not only prepared but also happy to work long hours.

In some senses the atmosphere was similar to that in university research departments with their emphasis on creativity and the free flow of ideas. This was not surprising since most employees came from that background. It was a challenging environment but also, for those who were fully committed, a very supportive one. People believed that what they were doing was not only worthwhile but also unique. They were an elite band.

There was no restriction on contacts between departments and Dr. Zaffaroni and his vice presidents were well known to all the research staff. Intellectual standards were said to be extremely high; most lab technicians/assistants had graduate degrees and were genuine actors in the research process rather than order-followers. However, it was clear to all concerned that "when the chips are down, there's one person to say this is the way we'll do things": that person was Dr. Zaffaroni.

The Role of Dr. Zaffaroni

Dr. Zaffaroni had very strong personal beliefs which were central to the way ALZA had been set up and continued to be run. He believed that one of a company's or chief executive's main tasks was to enhance the job satisfaction and promote the personal growth of his employees. He provided the appropriate framework in the form of an attractive, almost luxurious working environment, and tried to ensure that his researchers were not disturbed by administrative or budgetary controls.

He promoted the intellectual content of work, the scientifically elegant solution to a problem, and though he was aware that this might lead to operational inefficiencies, he felt that this attitude was the only one possible in a high-technology research-dependent organization. Employees were encouraged to take an interest in areas in which they had neither experience nor qualifications, and several scientists ended up in marketing or general management.

Dr. Zaffaroni believed in recruiting the best available brains and was prepared to go to great lengths to get the people he wanted. ALZA bought Virgil Place's consulting company, and set up a shell company for Alan Michaels, the first head of research and an expert in core membrane technology, which was eventually bought out on advantageous terms. Dr. Higuchi, the originator of much of the ADDS theory, wanted to continue to teach in Kansas, so an institute was set up around him, which was later sold to Merck when he wanted to move on.

Alex Zaffaroni believed that one major objective of the company must be to foster the personal growth of its employees. To this end, the organization must be adapted to the individual rather than the other way around. One way of encouraging personal and organizational growth was to allow research groups or individuals to form spin-off companies that would exploit ALZA technologies in new fields. The first of these was Dynapol, set up to work in nutrition.

Perhaps the most important element of Dr. Zaffaroni's leadership was his ability to inspire those around him with his own enthusiasm and sense of mission. It was a major factor in the very low turnover of scientists which was maintained even when the going got tough. He was respected for his past scientific achievements, for his obvious concern for his colleagues, and for his refusal to compromise quality for commercial convenience. He was somebody of whom his employees and colleagues could be proud.

Dr. Zaffaroni's ability to attract and retain the faith of investors was also of a high order; though the first $2 million came from his own pocket, by 1976 he had raised more than $70 million from private placements and public issues. A great deal of this money came from friends and acquaintances both within and outside the industry. The list of highly distinguished scientific advisors and consultants also helped maintain the confidence of investors. The technique was later adopted by the biotechnology start-ups of the late 1970s.

The Financial Crisis

Since the start of operations in 1968, ALZA had accumulated a deficit of around $75 million. Cumulative operating revenues (at various points investment income and interest were sizable) had reached $10 million by mid 1977. Annual operating losses had jumped from $9 million to $13.5 million in 1975 with the buildup of overheads, and had been running at around $15 million for the last two years. (A statement of operations for 1973–1977 can be found in Exhibit 12 of Case III–3.)

The balance sheet (see Exhibit 13 of Case III–3) shows the extreme gravity of the company's liquidity crisis. Current assets were very largely inventory and amounted to $5.6 million, while current liabilities were over $17 million because the bank loan had become due as soon as ALZA failed to meet working capital and net worth conditions. The banks were pressing either for repayment or for proof of a new source of funds which would guarantee survival. They had agreed not to force ALZA into liquidation so long as negotiations with a real chance of succeeding were in progress with potential partners.

ALZA calculated that the company's cash shortfall over the next five years would be somewhere between $30 million and $50 million, depending on the speed with which successful new products could be brought to the market and on the readiness of the banks to extend payment terms.

The Search for Partners

The search for financing occupied Martin Gerstel and Dr. Zaffaroni to the exclusion of almost all other activities from late 1976 onwards. The company's Scientific Advisors and non-executive board members were also mobilized.

It was clear from early 1976 that some additional financing would probably be necessary, but the real extent of this only became clear with the early sales figures for Progestasert. The company's financial position (see above) and operational difficulties led its investment bankers to advise that a public issue of stock would not be taken up by the market. Private placements would yield little or nothing for the same reasons. ALZA was already in default of the terms of its bank loans by 1977 and had no surplus from which to pay interest charges. There was therefore no possibility of further bank financing.

Since ALZA could not raise money in expectation of pure financial return, it was obliged to look for a partner interested in its research expertise, existing technology, or both. In the first half of 1976 ALZA had signed agreements with Merck and Co., one of the biggest U.S. pharmaceutical companies, and with Boehringer Sohn, Ingleheim am Rhein from West Germany.

Merck had agreed to finance a three-to-five-year joint-development program for cardiovascular and anti-inflammatory systems using the OROS technology. It also bought $3.5 million of ALZA stock at over $20 a share with an option for $1.5 million more. Boehringer Ingleheim had signed up for a long-term joint development of transdermal systems but bought no equity.

There was no immediate prospect of an increase in the financial commitment of either of these companies, and it was now clear that similar agreements with other companies would be insufficient to save ALZA. At least half of any research payment represented real costs to ALZA, so the contribution to overheads and loan repayments would always be fairly small.

Approaches made to almost all the remaining major pharmaceutical companies failed to produce a positive response. Dr. Zaffaroni also approached a large number of companies in the chemical and petrochemical industries, though he felt that purchase by a company outside pharmaceuticals was not in ALZA's best interests. Arco expressed interest, but in detailed discussions had failed to come up with a real offer.

ALZA and Ciba-Geigy

The first contact with Ciba-Geigy USA in 1971 had not led to any further discussions, though it had revealed that company's interest in this area. Dr. Zaffaroni met the Ciba-Geigy main board (KL) member responsible for their Pharma Division at a scientific conference in March 1977 and suggested cooperation. He was put in touch with the head of Pharma Division, Dr. Staehelin, and flew to Basle to meet him in April. The meeting was very successful on a personal level and it was followed in May by a Ciba-Geigy visit to Palo Alto.

The Ciba-Geigy team consisted of the Swiss heads of research (Dr. Heusler) and production (Dr. Goetz) and the head of Pharma US (Mr. Mackinnon). They were not authorized to negotiate in any way, but looked at the ALZA operation and took a great deal of financial and technical data away with them. Nothing of importance was heard from them for some time despite the obvious need for a quick decision, but in late July Dr. Zaffaroni heard that Ciba-Geigy was ready to discuss the terms of a possible collaboration or purchase.

He did not know what these terms might be. Possibilities ranged from outright purchase of all shares and integration into Ciba-Geigy to a large-scale research contract with little or no infusion of capital. As far as Ciba-Geigy knew, negotiations with another potential buyer, possibly Arco, were still in progress.

ALZA Assessment of Ciba-Geigy

Ciba-Geigy's financial soundness and commercial power were not in doubt, and it could afford to offer ALZA generous financial terms. It seemed likely that organizationally ALZA would be associated with the U.S. subsidiary, though the bulk of research was done in Basle.

Ciba-Geigy had one major sustained-released preparation on the market (Slow-K, which used a wax-matrix system) and a number of slow-release variants of major products. It seemed to have a fair amount of pharmacokinetic and systems development experience. The system which seemed to interest them the most was OROS.

The Swiss company produced a wide range of patented and generic compounds, many of which might be suitable for inclusion in ALZA systems. It also had considerable marketing and distribution strength worldwide. There was a visioncare section and though research in endocrinology was being carried out, Ciba-Geigy had only little presence in contraception.

Dr. Zaffaroni's impression was that Dr. Staehelin would wish to preserve ALZA's unique character, but he had no clear indication of the thinking of the Research Department and American subsidiary. Professor Woodward, an ALZA scientific advisor and CIBA-Geigy main board member, was very much in favor of linking the two companies.

Objectives of ALZA and Ciba-Geigy

ALZA's negotiating strategy would depend on the relative importance of different objectives, some of them perhaps conflicting, and upon its perception of the objectives of Ciba-Geigy.

The primary objective of ALZA was survival. The banks were ready to foreclose on their loans and effectively bankrupt the company. This would not necessarily mean the end of ALZA because a restructuring might be possible, but it would undergo a radical change. It might, for example, become a research and development laboratory relinquishing the ambition to become an integrated concern and living off research contracts and royalties.

However, Dr. Zaffaroni wished to see his company changed as little as possible. He wanted to preserve its unique character: the excellent working conditions, the freewheeling creativity, the employees' sense of commitment. Therefore, the second main objective was to retain ALZA's autonomy, or at least a degree of freedom of action; Ciba-Geigy might be prepared to save ALZA but only under terms which would be less acceptable than a restructuring—integration as an in-house research unit of Ciba-Geigy, for example.

Dr. Zaffaroni believed that if the company could hang on for another three to five years, the next generation of ADDS, principally OROS and transdermal systems, would make it financially viable. They had applications for a much wider range of treatments than the first generation. He therefore wanted to keep ALZA's options for the future as open as possible.

A third objective was to retain as much as possible of the technology already developed under ALZA's control, and to maintain a real interest in future developments. The granting of exclusive rights to all or part of the technology would jeopardize ALZA's long-term development.

The position of Ciba-Geigy with regard to these issues was by no means clear. ALZA could be regarded primarily as an almost risk-free investment if majority control was obtained because of the tax advantages available. ALZA had several years of losses and R&D and capital depreciation that could be written off against the profits of Ciba-Geigy's American subsidiary.

A deal could be seen as a means of getting Ciba-Geigy up to speed in a promising new area through technology transfer, or as a quick way of getting new or revitalized products onto the market. However, the interests and positions of Basle and Summit management within Ciba-Geigy might not necessarily be identical.

Case III–5
Ciba-Geigy Limited: Pharmaceutical Division (A)

Mark W. Cunningham, Reinhard Angelmar, and Yves Doz

When Dr. Gaudenz Staehelin was appointed chairman of the Pharma Divisional Committee (*Division sleitung,* or DL) in 1975, he as the first nonscientist to hold this position. A lawyer by training, the soft-spoken, 39-year old scion of an old Basle family had entered the company in 1964. Before his nomination to Pharma, Dr. Staehelin had worked in the company's corporate legal department. He had been deeply involved in the complex legal and organizational aspects of the 1970 merger between Ciba and Geigy.

The appointment of a nonscientist as DL chairman was interpreted by Pharma staff as a signal of possible change in the division's way of operating. The division's evolution since the 1970 merger provided further grounds for this expectation: internal estimates suggested that the division had dropped from second to fourth place in world pharmaceutical sales since 1970; moreover, there were few promising new compounds in the pipeline. At the same time, the total group was becoming more dependent on the Pharma Division for growth and profits, as the industrial divisions (dyestuffs and chemicals and plastics and additives), the traditional backbone of the company, were being hit by the recession.

One of Dr. Staehelin's first moves was to develop an explicit statement of the division's mission, objectives, and strategies in the form of a divisional *Leitbild* (charter). It stated the intention

> to maintain and improve . . . our leading position in the health care industry . . . We intend to concentrate on the pharmaceutical business . . . [but] to extend the scope of our activities and to develop from a Pharmaceutical Division to a Health Care Division.

The growth and profitability targets set by the Leitbild were significantly above the industry average.

Organization Structure

Ciba-Geigy's worldwide Pharma Division comprised the divisional management in Basle, with the staff functional units directly subordinated to the divisional management (research, medical, technical operations, marketing, administration, and planning), and the Pharma divisions of group companies (Exhibit 1).

Divisional Management

The chairman of the division was chiefly responsible for worldwide strategies and their implementation through local divisions, for the management of the worldwide functional groups in Basle and, in regard to the R&D process, for decisions concerning the research program, the inclusion of new preparations (including licensed products) in the development process, their inclusion in the product line, and product withdrawal.

Dr. Staehelin was highly sensitive to Ciba-Geigy's tradition of decision making by consensus. This meant that major decisions were in fact taken by the divisional management committee which, in addition to the chairman, included the heads of the functions (see Exhibit 2). The arrival of Dr. Staehelin in the Pharma Division had coincided with or preceded other changes in DL and other key positions:

- Dr. Karl Heusler, 54 years old, was appointed head of Pharma research in 1974. Dr. Heusler, a chemist, had entered Ciba in 1951. After a distinguished scientific career in the area of stereoid synthesis, Dr. Heusler had successively occupied the positions of head of the Woodward Research Institute, head of chemistry with Ciba and, after the merger, head of chemistry of Ciba-Geigy.
- While Prof. Oberholzer remained in place as head of the Medicine Division, immediately below him Dr. P. Loustalot (54 years old and with 25 years' service in Ciba-Geigy) had recently taken over the responsibility for all Phase 3 and 4 clinical trials.
- Dr. Götz, 41 years old, had moved from pharmacy research to production and had taken over the production function in 1975 after many years spent abroad establishing new units.
- Mr. Orsinger, 48 years old, and in marketing since he returned to headquarters in 1967, had taken over the function in 1975.

The Worldwide Functional Groups in Basle

Research Basle. Research Basle had the following four missions:

1. Provide new candidate-compounds and preparations for development.
2. Contribute to the development of selected compounds by performing human/clinical pharmacology (Phase I) studies.
3. Provide scientific support to Pharma divisions in group companies (e.g., for marketed products).
4. Provide evaluation and expert opinion on third-party products.

Basle research accounted for about two-thirds of the division's annual research effort. All of Ciba-Geigy's

EXHIBIT 1 Ciba Geigy Pharma Division, 1978

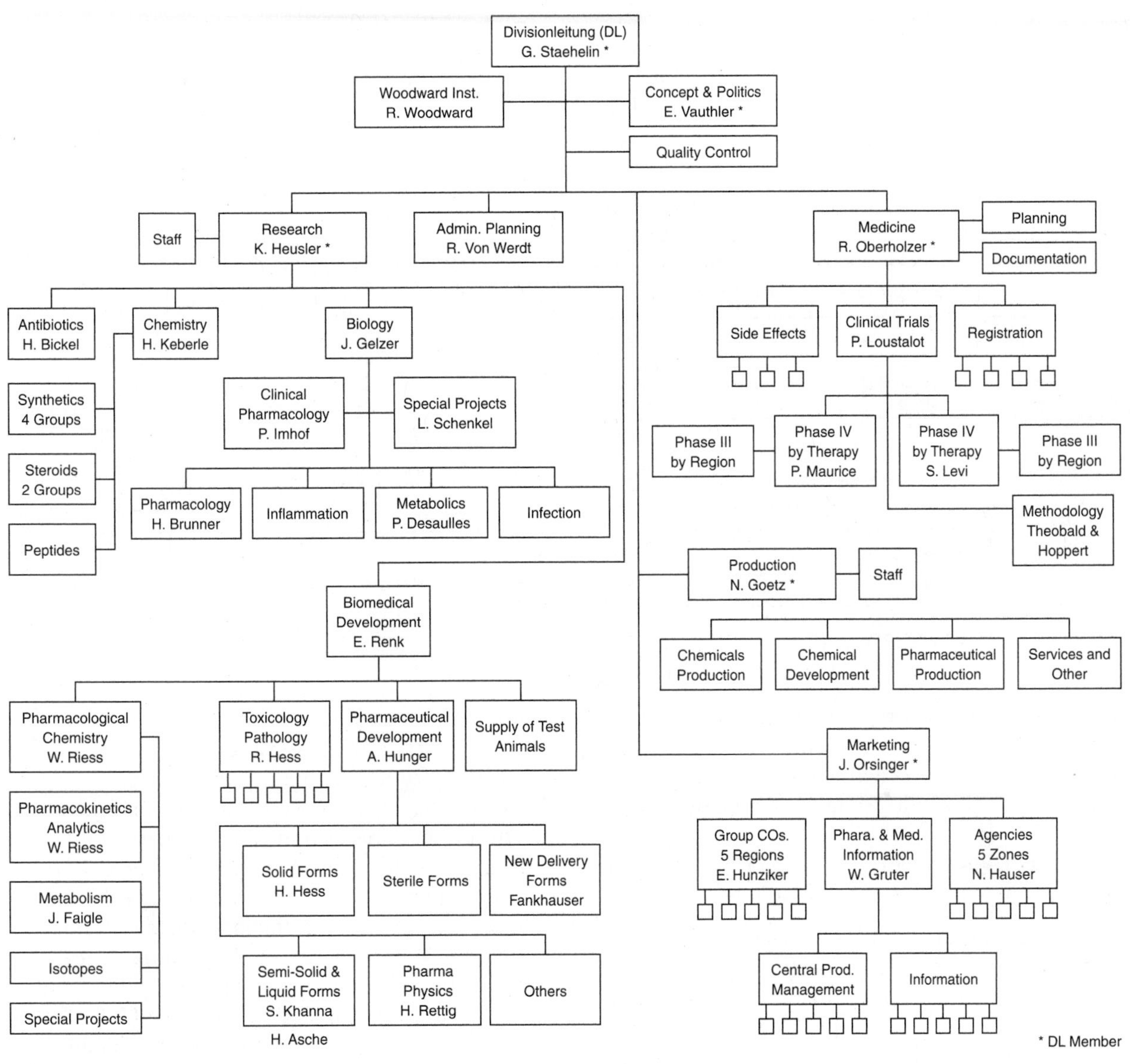

internally developed products had their origin in Basle.

Except for India, which had a research unit specializing in tropical diseases, only the U.S. division had a research unit capable of drug discovery and preclinical development. Its size was about one-third that of the Basle unit.

Basle research had no direct authority over research carried out in group companies. Divisional management, which in principle had the power to coordinate worldwide research, had not taken an active role in research strategy formulation. In particular, there was no clear policy concerning the assignment of specific research programs to research units. This had led to some duplication of effort and communication and cooperation problems, especially between Basle and the United States.

The U.S. division felt that its size, the highly competitive nature of the U.S. market, and the scientific resources available in the United States all argued for a greatly expanded role for the U.S. research

EXHIBIT 2 Ciba-Geigy A.G. 1977

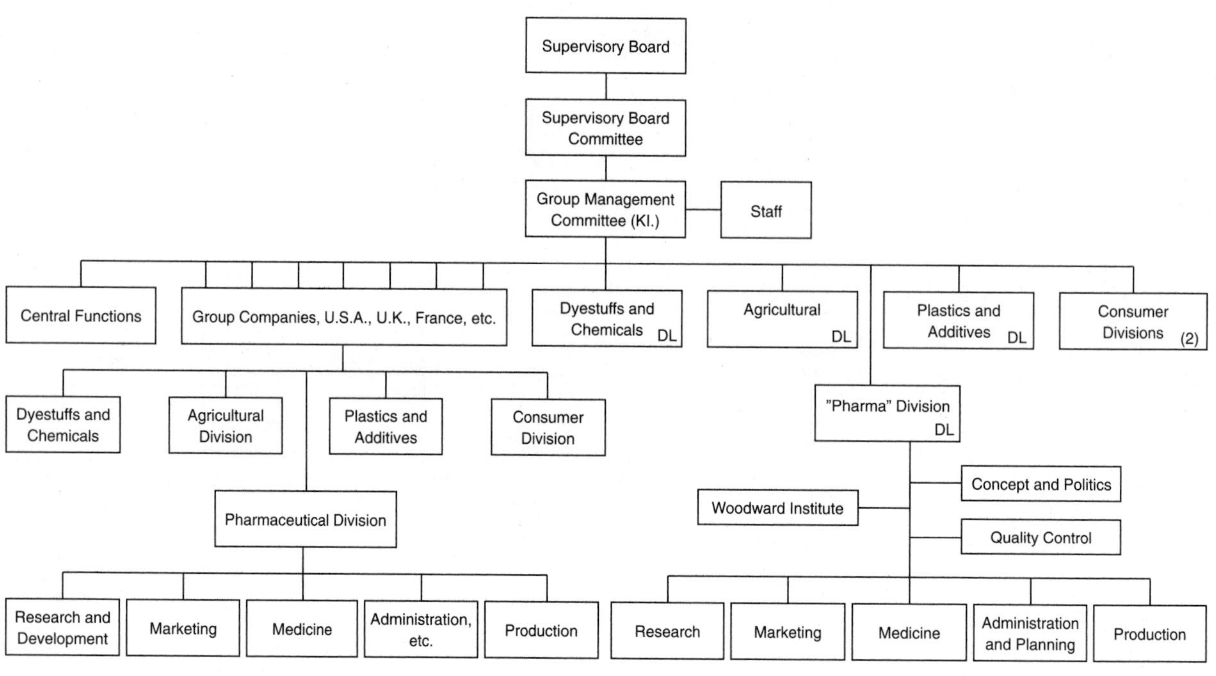

unit. Basle managers typically responded that U.S. research was too narrowly focused on the U.S. market, and that this parochial orientation was inappropriate for a worldwide operating company.

Medical Department. Its major missions in regard to new product development were:

1. Plan, initiate, and oversee the conduct of clinical studies at headquarters and by medical departments of group companies (Phases II, III and IV).
2. Design and develop new methodology for clinical research.
3. Ensure the coordination of the clinical activities of group company Pharma divisions worldwide.
4. Ensure timely registration and revalidation of products with appropriate authorities worldwide.

Only about 20 percent of the division's total medical expenditures were spent by the Basle Medical Department. This reflected the fact that the bulk of the clinical studies were performed outside Switzerland and paid for by group companies.

Like the Research Department, the Medical Department in Basle had no direct authority over the medical departments of group companies (MEGROCs). Group companies were free to decide whether or not to conduct clinical trials on a compound proposed by Basle, and with what priority and speed.

Typically, there were many intermediaries between the physician in Basle in charge of a compound and the clinical investigators actually conducting clinical trials in the countries. Persons involved in Basle were: the immediate superior (the *Bereichsleiter* in charge of the indication area for which the compound was targeted), the medical coordinator for the region, the head of Clinical Research, and the head of the Medical Department. The main intermediaries in each country were: the head of the Medical Department and the physician responsible for the indication area. The difficulties of managing international clinical trials created personnel problems for the Basle medical departments: recruitment of highly qualified specialists was difficult and physician turnover was high.

Technical Operations. The major contributions of this unit during the new product development process were:

1. The production of sufficient amounts of active ingredient to enable preclinical and clinical testing.

2. The development of delivery (dosage) forms.
3. The scaling-up of production processes in preparation for market introduction.

With production of active substances concentrated in Switzerland, most of the technical development of new products was carried out in Basle. Only the U.S. unit had complete technical development facilities which were managed independently of Basle.

Marketing. Marketing's role in regard to new product development was as follows:

1. Define and help build the division's product range . . . in such a way that it meets the needs of the market and is consistent with divisional goals.
2. Elaborate marketing strategies for products or groups of products to ensure best possible local and worldwide market penetration and profitability.

Group companies were free to decide which products to introduce and with what strategy.

The Pharma Divisions of Group Companies

Divisional management at Basle had no direct control over the actions of local divisions, though it often had considerable influence. Financial and operational targets were set by the KL (*Konzernleitung*) after discussions with the DL. Contributions to parent company expenses and profits were the main target variables. The annual budget and the long-term plans for the divisions were agreed to between the countries and Basle, and performance was then monitored by the latter. Group companies considered generally that their primary task was to meet the stated objectives and that the means by which they did so were their affair. This attitude was actively encouraged by Dr. Staehelin, who felt that country organizations were in the best position to judge their own market and should be free to act as "independent, entrepreneurial units."

In regard to new products, this meant that countries made their own evaluations of the probability of the commercial success of a compound under development in Basle and, on this basis, decided whether to conduct clinical trials or introduce the product. In fact, Basle frequently had to sell its potential products to the countries. Countries could also license in products in order to round out their product range.

The U.S. group company, in particular, has a reputation for going its own way, in Pharma as well as in the other divisions. It had not launched VOLTAREN, an antirheumatic product which by 1976 had become the company's second most important seller, or TRASICOR, a cardiovascular product (number 4 in 1977). Both of these products were developed internally and both were rejected by the United States. On the other hand, several products had been licensed from the outside to fill gaps in the range.

R&D in the Ciba-Geigy Pharma Division

R&D in the Pharma division, Basle, mainly comprised the following activities:

- Drug discovery (chemistry, biology-nonclinical development, toxicology, pharmacokinetics, pharmaceutical development, analytics, chemical development, biotechnological development).
- Medicine (human pharmacology/clinical pharmacology, clinical research, drug monitoring).
- Licensing in and out of products.
- R&D activities of affiliated firms and institutions.
- Various R&D management and support functions (e.g., patents and documentation).

Exhibit 3 shows the main R&D functions, their relationship over time, and the departments responsible for each.

Financial Resources for R&D

The overall level of R&D effort amounted to about 11 percent of sales. Because of the increasingly stringent regulatory requirements, the amount of resources devoted to developmental activities had been increasing. At present, drug discovery absorbed about 27 percent, nonclinical development 24 percent, and medical activities 27 percent of the total R&D budget.

One of the motives for the 1970 merger had been to benefit from economies of scale in R&D. Consequently, division management had attempted to contain the rise of R&D costs after the merger. The ambitious profitability targets set by the 1976 *Leitbild* and the recent economic recession had led to a virtual freeze on R&D expenditures.

Shifting of resources between research projects and programs was difficult. The major reasons for this were: the fragmentation of the R&D activities across many different departments, the lack of an organizational process for setting clear and opera-

EXHIBIT 3 Main Tasks and Departments in Ciba-Geigy R&D Process

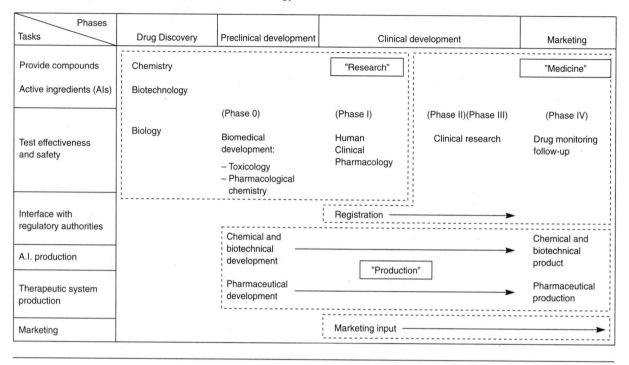

Tasks \ Phases	Drug Discovery	Preclinical development	Clinical development	Marketing
Provide compounds Active ingredients (AIs)	Chemistry Biotechnology		"Research"	"Medicine"
Test effectiveness and safety	Biology	(Phase 0) Biomedical development: – Toxicology – Pharmacological chemistry	(Phase I) Human Clinical Pharmacology (Phase II)(Phase III) Clinical research	(Phase IV) Drug monitoring follow-up
Interface with regulatory authorities			Registration →	
A.I. production		Chemical and biotechnical development →	"Production"	Chemical and biotechnical product
Therapeutic system production		Pharmaceutical development →		Pharmaceutical production
Marketing			Marketing input →	→

tional R&D priorities, the absence of objective data that could justify the shift vis-à-vis the staff concerned, an R&D culture that discouraged competition for resources, and a tradition of letting researchers work on their own projects (officially up to 30 percent of their time).

Human R&D Resources

One consequence of the containment and the recent freeze of R&D expenditures was a virtual ban on outside hiring except at the most junior levels. This meant that a department that wished to change its know-how basis could do so only by attracting staff with the requisite know-how from central R&D or by retraining its staff. Yet most Ciba-Geigy scientists were very reluctant to change discipline, or even project, and only with difficulty could they be reassigned against their will. Since the company had a tradition of long-term employment, they could hardly be dismissed either. Every department contained some scientists, often senior and highly paid, who were not optimally productive.

Ciba-Geigy AG had three official hierarchies existing side by side; two of them indicated the level of managerial or scientific responsibility, and the third the legal status of the individual. Prestige was generally measured by position in the legal hierarchy, which had six levels. No criteria for promotion were made explicit, though length of service requirements generally had to be met; each promotion was proposed by section heads, cleared by division heads, checked by personnel and finally authorized by the KL. There were strict quotas on the numbers of managers at each grade.

The management grades were fairly straightforward and linked to the size of importance of responsibilities. Scientists were assessed on knowledge, creativity, communication, initiative, and contribution (the first two having the heaviest weighting) and promoted after well-established intervals. Those wishing to remain pure researchers could acquire special status, but those wishing to enter research administration had to switch to the business hierarchy after a certain point. Remuneration was tightly linked to grade, and there were very few incentives directly linked to performance in the short term.

In-House versus Contract Research

Almost all research work was done in-house. Though there were well-established links with professors and researchers at many universities, and some funding was made available to them, their work was usually of little immediate relevance to current Ciba-Geigy projects. Such relationships were intended mainly to keep the company up-to-date with the latest theoretical work. The Friedrich Miescher Institute at Basle, funded largely by Ciba-Geigy, did basic research work. True coordination with programs within the company was not attempted. The institute was perhaps valued most as a recruiting ground. The relationship with the Woodward Institute in the U.S. was somewhat closer, however.

Joint research projects had been undertaken with several large companies. Though there had been several successes, many had broken down because of divergent objectives. There was generally a feeling in research circles that Ciba-Geigy research was second to none and that the money was better kept in the family.

The New Product Development Process

Individual compounds moved from the chemistry lab to the marketplace by the successive efforts of individuals in the research and medical departments. Within research, primary responsibility rested with the *Sachbearbeiter* (in chemistry) and the project leader (in biology). Upon completion of Phase I preclinical development, the compound was turned over to the clinical trial sponsor in the medical department. The marketing aspects were handled by the product management group with responsibility for the product's indication area.

The decision on whether to promote a compound to the next phase of development had important financial consequences and therefore was made at higher levels of management, including the DL during the later phases. The decision-making bodies, typically, comprised representatives of the various functions involved in the development process. In general, no decisions would be made unless a consensus among the different parties existed.

There was a general feeling that the development process was too slow. A variety of reasons were given. Some managers felt that the *Sachbearbeiters* and project leaders, who generally were work-bench scientists, lacked a sense of urgency and tended to prolong work on a compound out of a sense of scientific curiosity. The researchers complained that management took too long for deciding which compounds to promote to the next phase. They also perceived the physicians in the medical department as having a negative attitude toward "their" compounds, tending to reject or repeat studies done in human pharmacology (Phase I) and generally searching for data that would justify killing the compound. They also felt that there was a strong resistance to products that went outside Ciba-Geigy's traditional areas of expertise.

The fractionation of the technical development activities was also cited as an obstacle to speedy development:

- Toxicology and pharmacological chemistry reported to the head of biomedical development, one of three areas in the research department.
- Pharmaceutical development (this involved delivery forms) reported to the head of technical operations (production).
- Chemical and biotechnical development reported to the head of technical operations.

The ADDS Task Force

Dr. Staehelin's objective was to achieve above-average growth in pharmaceuticals and at least to regain the Number 2 position worldwide. Because of the decline in new chemical entities, this would require more effective exploitation of the existing product range and of the products already under development.

When Dr. Abt, head of the market research unit in the marketing department, suggested early in 1977 that ADDS might be a vehicle for superior growth, Dr. Staehelin responded by setting up a task force with the brief to investigate the attractiveness and practical feasibility of ADDS for the Pharma Division.

Task Force Composition and Views

Dr. Abt chaired the task force. Pharmaceutical development was represented by two members, notably Dr. Hunger, the head of the group. Basle research was represented by Dr. Riess, the head of pharmacological chemistry, and Dr. Fuchs from human pharmacology. Dr. Doebel was Summit's delegate to the task force, and two more members with different backgrounds rounded out the group. The heterogeneous nature of the group guaranteed that different perspectives on ADDS were aired.

Marketing saw some possibilities for enhancing the existing product line via ADDS and insisted on the importance of having oral one-a-day formulations for new products whenever possible. It saw also a few possibilities for using ADDS to turn generics into commercially viable products.

The majority of those working in pharmaceutical development felt that there was nothing particularly new or startling in the ADDS concept; they had been working on new delivery forms for many years.

Research suggested that it would be nice to do some basic research on "experimental pharmaceutical development" with substances requiring special delivery forms (e.g., immunostimulators, peptides).

Speaking for the U.S. group, Dr. Doebel emphasized its commitment to ADDS via the HEMAC project, a polymer-based oral slow-release system, on which 12 persons were working (mostly in U.S. central research). He argued that HEMAC should be adopted throughout the division, and that future ADDS research should build on U.S. experience.

The group also attempted to assess Pharma's total existing resources in the area of delivery systems:

- Of a total staff of 247 devoted to pharmaceutical development (110 in Basle, 62 in the United States), about 28 were involved in developing slow-release formulations, and only 14 (including the 12-person HEMAC group) were carrying out exploratory research on new delivery systems. The bulk of the staff was totally absorbed by normal product development tasks and had no free capacity to work on special projects.
- Pharmacological chemistry contributed to delivery systems research mainly through pharmacokinetics (the study of how drugs are distributed in the body) and drug metabolism (the study of how the body breaks down the drugs). Existing capacities were barely sufficient to handle ongoing projects.
- Capacities in biology and medicine (clinical research) were insufficient for systematic testing of delivery systems

Recommendations of the ADDS Task Force

The general conclusion of the task force was that delivery systems would become increasingly important in the future. It made four specific recommendations:

1. Additional capacity for basic ADDS research should be created within the division. The mission of the new unit should be to cooperate during preclinical development with biology to develop new delivery systems for specific, interesting substances. The unit could be created in Basle by adding one or two researchers to the three already working on such problems (one in central research and two in pharmaceutical development).

2. Whenever possible, oral once-a-day formulations should be available for all new product introductions. The consequent change in the division's development policies would require about 20 additional persons, mostly in pharmaceutical development.

3. In cases where specific needed technologies were not available in-house, outside development contracts should be pursued. ALZA was cited as one among several possible sources. The task force pointed out that third-party contracts would not solve the present development capacity constraint, as any new system would require extensive in-house testing. Outside contracting would also involve additional coordination costs.

4. HEMAC should be adopted outside the United States in those situations where its superiority to other systems could be shown.

Ciba-Geigy Views on ALZA: Early 1977

ALZA was one of the companies the task force members had in mind for carrying out ADDS contract research. Various individuals at Ciba-Geigy had had personal contacts with Dr. Zaffaroni over the years; others had formed their opinions through reading articles by him and his associates.

People in pharmaceutical development in Basle were generally skeptical regarding the ALZA systems, which they saw as being either unfeasible or mere gimmicks. Incompatibilities of personal styles had turned some U.S. research managers strongly against Dr. Zaffaroni. Marketing interpreted the lack of success of Progestasert and OCUSERT partly as a demonstration of strong market resistance to ALZA's unconventional delivery systems.

Others, particularly researchers not specialized in delivery systems, tended to have more positive attitudes. For example, Dr. Heusler, who was familiar with Dr. Zaffaroni's work on steroid synthesis, considered him to be a first-rate scientist. Dr. Schenkel, who headed the endocrinology lab in the biology group, had come away from a recent presentation by Dr. Zaffaroni convinced that some of his systems provided a solution to problems that had escaped solution until then.

In 1971, a high-level U.S. research manager had visited ALZA and explored possibilities for cooperation. He was told that as a matter of principle ALZA was not interested in cooperating with large pharmaceutical companies, except as a potential source of compounds for ALZA systems. Since then, no official contact between ALZA and Ciba-Geigy had taken place.

Ciba-Geigy Assesses the ALZA Opportunity

In April 1977, Dr. Vischer, member of the KL and former chairman of the Pharma division, informed Dr. Staehelin that he had been contacted by Dr. Zaffaroni, who wanted to find a buyer for ALZA, which was in financial difficulties. According to Dr. Vischer, Dr. Zaffaroni was very pressed by time and needed a really fast decision.

Dr. Staehelin, who had just learned about the recommendations of the ADDS Task Force, decided immediately to send a party consisting of Dr. Götz, Dr. Heusler, and Mr. MacKinnon, head of the U.S. Pharma Division, to ALZA in order to make a first assessment of the situation. On the basis of their report, he invited Dr. Zaffaroni to Basle. During their first meeting, he and Dr. Zaffaroni immediately established a strong personal rapport and decided to start negotiations between the two companies.

In May, the DL set up a project team with the task of studying in depth the possibility of gaining access to ALZA's technology. The project group in turn appointed three subgroups to carry out a thorough investigation of the scientific/technical, financial, and marketing aspects. All groups potentially involved in a collaboration were represented.

Assessment of ALZA's Technology

The full range of ALZA technologies is included in Exhibit 10 of Case III–3. The intrauterine and ocular devices and the osmotic minipump were already on sale and seemed to work well.

The transdermal delivery system (TTS) was available in prototype and thought to be two to four years from launch with scopolamine. The TTS-system would deliver regular quantities of a drug for periods from one day to one week. Boehringer-Ingelheim had a non-exclusive license for one of their substances.

The OROS system (oral sustained release) seemed to be technically very advanced and only waiting for test programs with suitable ingredients. Merck was already testing this product which was the one of most immediate interest to Ciba-Geigy.

ALZA was thought to possess advanced polymer technology and to be highly innovative but somewhat weak in development and production. It was estimated that without outside help, it would take Ciba-Geigy several years and considerable additional resources to acquire a similar level of expertise. Patent coverage of ALZA's inventions was extremely tight.

Exhibit 4 indicates potential Ciba-Geigy–ALZA projects, by indication area and by type of ALZA system to be used.

EXHIBIT 4 New Drug Delivery Systems (Potential ALZA Projects)

System \ Indication	Cardio-vascular, Diuresis	Anti-inflammation	CNS	Others	Total
OROS	12	2	2	4	20
Transdermal	3	—	1	3	7
CHRONOMER (Inject./Implant.)	—	—	—	5	5
OCUSERT	—	1	—	2	3
New systems	1	—	—	4	5
	16	3	3	18	40

SOURCE: Ciba-Geigy internal report.

EXHIBIT 5 Ciba-Geigy Estimate of 1981–1987 Sales of ALZA-Related Products

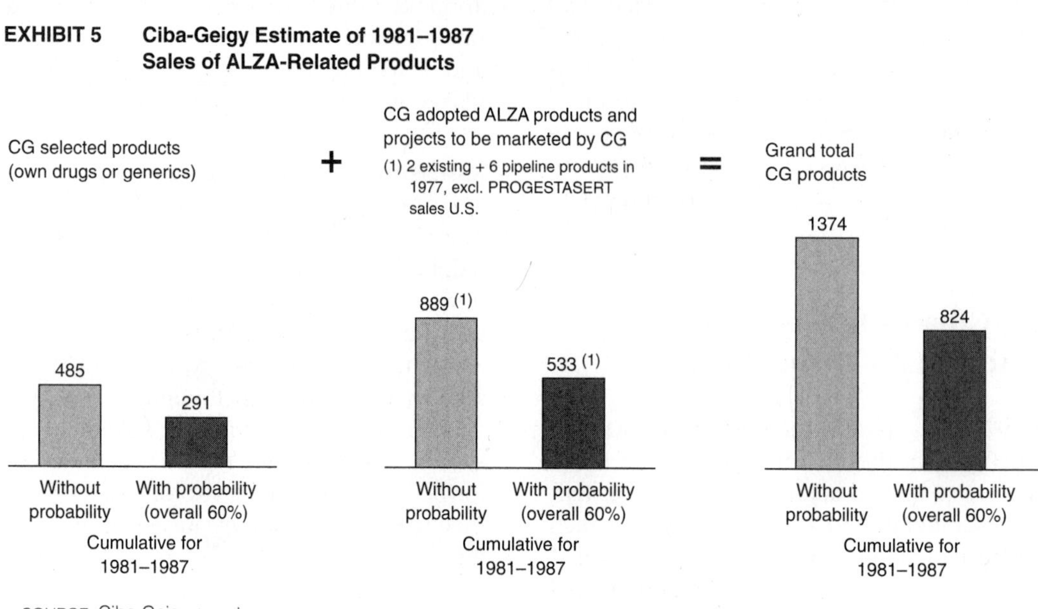

SOURCE: Ciba-Geigy report.

Marketing Assessment

Neither of the two major products, Progestasert and OCUSERT, had performed up to expectations in the marketplace. The former was affected by general doubts about IUDs after the Dalcon Shield scare, was expensive, and demanded new application techniques. OCUSERT was also much more expensive than the eye-drop alternative for glaucoma and demanded application skill of a largely elderly customer group.

Sales of these products had been expected to put ALZA into profit by 1977–78 but with sales of $2.8 million in 1976, and indications of less than twice that in 1977, they were hardly meeting direct costs, let alone contributing to marketing expenses. No other major product was within three years of introduction.

The project team estimated cumulative 1981–1987 sales of Ciba-Geigy–ALZA products at $824 million (Exhibit 5).

Financial Assessment

Sizeable manufacturing and marketing organizations had been built up by ALZA for the new products, and general, administrative, and marketing expenses had risen from $1.3 million (22 percent of costs) in 1974 to $8.1 million (46 percent) in 1976.

By the middle of 1977, the company had an accumulated deficit of $69 million and an annual operating loss of $15 million. Bank debt stood at $14 million and a $20 million line of credit arranged with a number of banks in 1973 was expected to be exhausted by the end of the year.

Merck had invested $3.5 million since 1975 as part of its research agreement and was under no obligation to increase its holding. Share prices, which had stood at a high of $36 in January 1970, had been dropping steadily since January 1976, and in June 1977 stood at $7.50. There were 7.8 million shares outstanding, of which 13 percent were held by Dr. Zaffaroni. There were no other major shareholders. ALZA's financial position is summarized in Exhibit 6.

Ciba-Geigy's financial experts ruled out acquisition of 100 percent of ALZA's stock because its price, calculated at present stock values, would have amounted to about $70 million. In addition, an after-tax cash infusion of $20 million to $25 million would still have been necessary.

Other arrangements considered were:

1. A license agreement covering ALZA's patents and know-how.
2. R&D contracts for specific projects.
3. A loan which would entitle Ciba-Geigy to the rights under 1 above.
4. Acquisition of 80 percent of ALZA's stock, which would cost about $35 million. This would give

EXHIBIT 6 Ciba-Geigy Summary of ALZA Financial Position, 1977

Balance Sheet (in millions)

	June 30, 1977	June 30, 1976
Current assets	$ 6.9	$ 7.6
Fixed assets	16.4	15.9
Total assets	23.3	23.5
Bank debt	14.2	1.0
Total liabilities	16.6	4.1
Common stock	7.8	7.6
Paid-in capital	68.0	65.9
Deficit	(69.1)	(54.1)
Stockholders' equity	6.7	19.4

ALZA management has estimated that their bank debt will be $20 million by the end of 1977; stockholders' equity will be approximately zero.

Operating Statement (in millions)

	1977	1976	1975	1974	1973
Income	$ 7.2	$ 2.8			
Total cost and expenses	22.2	18.4	15.9	11.0	7.2
R&D cost and expenses	8.1	8.4	9.0	8.1	6.9
Operating loss	(15.0)	(15.6)	(15.9)	(11.0)	(7.2)

SOURCE: Ciba-Geigy internal report.

Ciba-Geigy control of ALZA and allow it to consolidate ALZA with the U.S. group company and lead to tax savings estimated at $27 million.

Ciba-Geigy's Options

The opportunity to collaborate with ALZA had to be compared with other ways of building up ADDS expertise.

One alternative consisted in collaborating with other firms on specific ADDS projects. Other small firms with specialized ADDS expertise existed, but none seemed to offer the same breadth and quality of ADDS expertise as ALZA.

A second alternative consisted in building up ADDS expertise in-house. This alternative, which fit with the division's traditional behavior, was favored by the pharmaceutical development group. Although their tests showed that the ALZA systems seemed to work, they remained skeptical. Their most favorable comment was, "It's an interesting idea." They were convinced that they could do whatever was necessary by themselves if given the appropriate resources.

Support for collaboration with ALZA was based on a variety of reasons. Mr. MacKinnon and other managers of the U.S. division felt that ALZA provided a unique opportunity for increasing Summit's role as an R&D center and could yield real benefits to the division. Internal build-up of ADDS capacity would most likely benefit Basle research. But it would be difficult for Basle to ignore Summit when collaborating with another U.S. company. The fact that the U.S. unit had been involved since the first approach to ALZA was in itself already highly significant. The few Summit researchers who felt that ALZA was based more on superb salesmanship than on valid scientific concepts were clearly a minority.

Most researchers in Basle outside the pharmaceutical development group thought that ALZA's systems were sound. Dr. Keberle, head of chemistry, who had started work on pharmacokinetics and metabolism at Ciba in the 1960s, was confident that the systems would work. Researchers in biology (e.g., Dr. Schenkel) thought that the ALZA systems would allow the rapid development of interesting compounds with a short half-life, for which no satisfactory delivery systems existed yet.

Dr. Heusler, as head of research, saw speed as the major advantage of a collaboration with ALZA. Building up internal resources comparable in competence to ALZA, in his estimate, would take at least five to eight years, provided the necessary qualified personnel could be attracted to Basle. This would be too late to fill the gap he foresaw on the basis of the products presently in the R&D pipeline. From the point of view of technical operations, Dr. Götz saw the potential for a broadening of Basle's expertise with polymer-treatment and laser-drilling (for the OROS system).

In thinking about the various arguments concerning the collaboration with ALZA, Dr. Staehelin felt strongly that ALZA could give more to Ciba-Geigy than just its technology. His own company was well-organized but somewhat rigid. ALZA seemed to be run on a completely different basis. A collaboration with ALZA would expose his organization to valuable new forms of thinking and acting. But how should the relationship be structured in order to get the full benefit of ALZA's scientific and organizational know-how?

In mid-July 1977, time was running out for ALZA. Dr. Zaffaroni made it very clear to Dr. Staehelin that ALZA would go under unless a potential partner came up with a firm proposal within the next few weeks.

About Our Research

We spent more than five years studying the internal workings of 15 strategic alliances around the world. We sought answers to a series of interrelated questions. What role have strategic alliances and outsourcing agreements played in the global success of Japanese and Korean companies? How do alliances change the competitive balance between partners? Does winning at collaboration mean different things to different companies? What factors determine who gains most from collaboration?

To understand who won and who lost and why, we observed the interactions of the partners first-hand and at multiple levels in each organization. Our sample included four European-U.S. alliances, two intra-European alliances, two European-Japanese alliances, and seven U.S.-Japanese alliances. We gained access to both sides of the partnerships in about half the cases and studied each alliance for an average of three years.

Confidentiality was a paramount concern. Where we did have access to both sides, we often wound up knowing more about who was doing what to whom than either of the partners. To preserve confidentiality, our article disguises many of the alliances that were part of the study.

Reading III–5
Collaborate with Your Competitors—and Win

Gary Hamel, Yves L. Doz, and C. K. Prahalad

Collaboration between competitors is in fashion. General Motors and Toyota assemble automobiles, Siemens and Philips develop semiconductors, Canon supplies photocopiers to Kodak, France's Thomson and Japan's JVC manufacture videocassette recorders. But the spread of what we call *competitive collaboration*—joint ventures, outsourcing agreements, product licensings, cooperative research—has triggered unease about the long-term consequences. A strategic alliance can strengthen both companies against outsiders even as it weakens one partner vis-à-vis the other. In particular, alliances between Asian companies and Western rivals seem to work against the Western partner. Cooperation becomes a low-cost route for new competitors to gain technology and market access.[1]

Yet the case for collaboration is stronger than ever. It takes so much money to develop new products and to penetrate new markets that few companies can go it alone in every situation. ICL, the British computer company, could not have developed its current generation of mainframes without Fujitsu. Motorola needs Toshiba's distribution capacity to break into the Japanese semiconductor market. Time is another critical factor. Alliances can provide short-

Reprinted by permission of *Harvard Business Review,* January–February 1989, pp. 133–139.

[1]For a vigorous warning about the perils of collaboration, see R. B. Reich and E. D. Mankin, "Joint Ventures with Japan Give Away Our Future," *Harvard Business Review,* March–April 1986, p. 78.

cuts for Western companies racing to improve their production efficiency and quality control.

We have spent more than five years studying the inner workings of 15 strategic alliances and monitoring scores of others. Our research (see the insert "About Our Research") involves cooperative ventures between competitors from the United States and Japan, Europe and Japan, and the United States and Europe. We did not judge the success or failure of each partnership by its longevity—a common mistake when evaluating strategic alliances—but by the shifts in competitive strength on each side. We focused on how companies use competitive collaboration to enhance their internal skills and technologies while they guard against transferring competitive advantages to ambitious partners.

There is no immutable law that strategic alliances *must* be a windfall for Japanese or Korean partners. Many Western companies do give away more than they gain—but that's because they enter partnerships without knowing what it takes to win. Companies that benefit most from competitive collaboration adhere to a set of simple but powerful principles.

Collaboration is competition in a different form. Successful companies never forget that their new partners may be out to disarm them. They enter alliances with clear strategic objectives, and they also understand how their partners' objectives will affect their success.

Harmony is not the most important measure of success. Indeed, occasional conflict may be the best evidence of mutually beneficial collaboration. Few alliances remain win-win undertakings forever. A partner may be content even as it unknowingly surrenders core skills.

Cooperation has limits. Companies must defend against competitive compromise. A strategic alliance is a constantly evolving bargain whose real terms go beyond the legal agreement or the aims of top management. What information gets traded is determined day to day, often by engineers and operating managers. Successful companies inform employees at all levels about what skills and technologies are off-limits to the partner and monitor what the partner requests and receives.

Learning from partners is paramount. Successful companies view each alliance as a window on their partners' broad capabilities. They use the alliance to build skills in areas outside the formal agreement and systematically diffuse new knowledge throughout their organizations.

Why Collaborate?

Using an alliance with a competitor to acquire new technologies or skills is not devious. It reflects the commitment and capacity of each partner to absorb the skills of the other. We found that in every case in which a Japanese company emerged from an alliance stronger than its Western partner, the Japanese company had made a greater effort to learn.

Strategic intent is an essential ingredient in the commitment to learning. The willingness of Asian companies to enter alliances represents a change in competitive tactics, not competitive goals. NEC, for example, has used a series of collaborative ventures to enhance its technology and product competences. NEC is the only company in the world with a leading position in telecommunications, computers, and semiconductors—despite its investing less in R&D (as a percentage of revenues) than competitors like Texas Instruments, Northern Telecom, and L.M. Ericsson. Its string of partnerships, most notably with Honeywell, allowed NEC to leverage its in-house R&D over the last two decades. Western companies, on the other hand, often enter alliances to avoid investments. They are more interested in reducing the costs and risks of entering new businesses or markets than in acquiring new skills. A senior U.S. manager offered this analysis of his company's venture with a Japanese rival: "We complement each other well—our distribution capability and their manufacturing skill. I see no reason to invest upstream if we can find a secure source of product. This is a comfortable relationship for us."

An executive from this company's Japanese partner offered a different perspective:

> When it is necessary to collaborate, I go to my employees and say, "This is bad, I wish we had these skills ourselves. Collaboration is second best. But I will feel worse if after four years we do not know how to do what our partner knows how to do." We must digest their skills.

The problem here is not that the U.S. company wants to share investment risk (its Japanese partner does too) but that the U.S. company has no ambition *beyond* avoidance. When the commitment to learning is so one-sided, collaboration invariably leads to competitive compromise.

Many so-called alliances between Western companies and their Asian rivals are little more than sophisticated outsourcing arrangements (see the insert "Competition for Competence"). General

Competition for Competence

In the article "Do You Really Have a Global Strategy?" (*Harvard Business Review,* July–August 1985), Gary Hamel and C. K. Prahalad examined one dimension of the global competitive battle: the race for brand dominance. This is the battle for control of distribution channels and global "share of mind." Another global battle has been much less visible and has received much less management attention. This is the battle for control over key technology-based competences that fuel new business development.

Honda has built a number of businesses, including marine engines, lawn mowers, generators, motorcycles, and cars, around its engine and power train competence. Casio draws on its expertise in semiconductors and digital display in producing calculators, small-screen televisions, musical instruments, and watches. Canon relies on its imaging and microprocessor competences in its camera, copier, and laser printer businesses.

In the short run, the quality and performance of a company's products determine its competitiveness. Over the longer term, however, what counts is the ability to build and enhance core competences—distinctive skills that spawn new generations of products. This is where many managers and commentators fear Western companies are losing. Our research helps explain why some companies may be more likely than others to surrender core skills.

Alliance or Outsourcing?

Enticing Western companies into outsourcing agreements provides several benefits to ambitious OEM partners. Serving as a manufacturing base for a Western partner is a quick route to increased manufacturing share without the risk or expense of building brand share. The Western partners' distribution capability allows Asian suppliers to focus all their resources on building absolute product advantage. Then OEMs can enter markets on their own and convert manufacturing share into brand share.

Serving as a sourcing platform yields more than just volume and process improvements. It also generates low-cost, low-risk market learning. The downstream (usually Western) partner typically provides information on how to tailor products to local markets. So every product design transferred to an OEM partner is also a research report on customer preferences and market needs. The OEM partner can use these insights to read the market accurately when it enters on its own.

A Ratchet Effect

Our research suggests that once a significant sourcing relationship has been established, the buyer becomes less willing and able to reemerge as a manufacturing competitor. Japanese and Korean companies are, with few exceptions, exemplary suppliers. If anything, the "soft option" of outsourcing becomes even softer as OEM suppliers routinely exceed delivery and quality expectations.

Outsourcing often begins a ratchetlike process. Relinquishing manufacturing control and paring back plant investment leads to sacrifices in product design, process technology, and, eventually, R&D budgets. Consequently, the OEM partner captures product-development as well as manufacturing initiative. Ambitious OEM partners are not content with the old formula of "You design it and we'll make it." The new reality is, "You design it, we'll learn from your designs, make them more manufacturable, and launch our products alongside yours."

Reversing the Verdict

This outcome is not inevitable. Western companies can retain control over their core competences by keeping a few simple principles in mind.

A competitive product is not the same thing as a competitive organization. While an Asian OEM partner may provide the former, it seldom provides the latter. In essence, outsourcing is a way of renting someone else's competitiveness rather than developing a long-term solution to competitive decline.

Rethink the make-or-buy decision. Companies often treat component manufacturing operations as cost centers and transfer their output to assembly units at an arbitrarily set price. This transfer price is an accounting fiction, and it is unlikely to yield as high a return as marketing or distribution investments, which require less research money and capital. But companies seldom consider the competitive consequences of surrendering control over a key value-creating activity.

Watch out for deepening dependence. Surrender results from a series of outsourcing decisions that individually make economic sense but collectively amount to a phased exit from the business. Different managers make outsourcing decisions at different times, unaware of the cumulative impact.

Replenish core competences. Western companies must outsource some activities; the economics are just too compelling. The real issue is whether a company is adding to its stock of technologies and competences as rapidly as it is surrendering them. The question of whether to outsource should always provoke a second question: Where can we outpace our partner and other rivals in building new sources of competitive advantage?

Motors buys cars and components from Korea's Daewoo. Siemens buys computers from Fujitsu. Apple buys laser printer engines from Canon. The traffic is almost entirely one way. These OEM deals offer Asian partners a way to capture investment initiative from Western competitors and displace customer-competitors from value-creating activities. In many cases this goal meshes with that of the Western partner: to regain competitiveness quickly and with minimum effort.

Consider the joint venture between Rover, the British automaker, and Honda. Some 25 years ago, Rover's forerunners were world leaders in small car design. Honda had not even entered the automobile business. But in the mid-1970s, after failing to penetrate foreign markets, Rover turned to Honda for technology and product-development support. Rover has used the alliance to avoid investments to design and build new cars. Honda has cultivated skills in European styling and marketing as well as multinational manufacturing. There is little doubt which company will emerge stronger over the long term.

Troubled laggards like Rover often strike alliances with surging latecomers like Honda. Having fallen behind in a key skills area (in this case, manufacturing small cars), the laggard attempts to compensate for past failures. The latecomer uses the alliance to close a specific skills gap (in this case, learning to build cars for a regional market). But a laggard that forges a partnership for short-term gain may find itself in a dependency spiral: as it contributes fewer and fewer distinctive skills, it must reveal more and more of its internal operations to keep the partner interested. For the weaker company, the issue shifts from "Should we collaborate?" to "With whom should we collaborate?" to "How do we keep our partner interested as we lose the advantages that made us attractive to them in the first place?"

There's a certain paradox here. When both partners are equally intent on internalizing the other's skills, distrust and conflict may spoil the alliance and threaten its very survival. That's one reason joint ventures between Korean and Japanese companies have been few and tempestuous. Neither side wants to "open the kimono." Alliances seem to run most smoothly when one partner is intent on learning and the other is intent on avoidance—in essence, when one partner is willing to grow dependent on the other. But running smoothly is not the point; the point is for a company to emerge from an alliance more competitive than when it entered it.

One partner does not always have to give up more than it gains to ensure the survival of an alliance. There are certain conditions under which mutual gain is possible, at least for a time:

The partners' strategic goals converge while their competitive goals diverge. That is, each partner allows for the other's continued prosperity in the shared business. Philips and Du Pont collaborate to develop and manufacture compact discs, but neither side invades the other's market. There is a clear upstream/downstream division of effort.

The size and market power of both partners are modest compared with industry leaders. This forces each side to accept that mutual dependence may have to continue for many years. Long-term collaboration may be so critical to both partners that neither will risk antagonizing the other by an overtly competitive bid to appropriate skills or competences. Fujitsu's one to five size disadvantage with IBM means it will be a long time, if ever, before Fujitsu can break away from its foreign partners and go it alone.

Each partner believes it can learn from the other and at the same time limit access to proprietary skills. JVC and Thomson, both of whom make VCRs, know that they are trading skills. But the two companies are looking for very different things. Thomson needs product technology and manufacturing prowess; JVC needs to learn how to succeed in the fragmented European market. Both sides believe there is an equitable chance for gain.

How to Build Secure Defenses

For collaboration to succeed, each partner must contribute something distinctive: basic research, product development skills, manufacturing capacity, access to distribution. The challenge is to share enough skills to create advantage vis-à-vis companies outside the alliance while preventing a wholesale transfer of core skills to the partner. This is a very thin line to walk. Companies must carefully select what skills and technologies they pass to their partners. They must develop safeguards against unintended, informal transfers of information. The goal is to limit the transparency of their operations.

The type of skill a company contributes is an important factor in how easily its partner can internalize the skills. The potential for transfer is greatest when a partner's contribution is easily transported (in engineering drawings, on computer tapes, or in the heads of a few technical experts); easily interpreted (it can be reduced to commonly understood equations or symbols); and easily absorbed (the skill or competence is independent of any particular cultural context).

Western companies face an inherent disadvantage because their skills are generally more vulnerable to transfer. The magnet that attracts so many companies to alliances with Asian competitors is their manufacturing excellence—a competence that is less transferable than most. Just-in-time inventory systems and quality circles can be imitated, but this is like pulling a few threads out of an oriental carpet. Manufacturing excellence is a complex web of employee training, integration with suppliers, statistical process controls, employee involvement, value engineering, and design for manufacture. It is difficult to extract such a subtle competence in any way but a piecemeal fashion.

There is an important distinction between technology and competence. A discrete, stand-alone technology (e.g., the design of a semiconductor chip) is more easily transferred than a process competence, which is entwined in the social fabric of a company. Asian companies often learn more from their Western partners than vice versa because they contribute difficult-to-unravel strengths, while Western partners contribute easy-to-imitate technology.

So companies must take steps to limit transparency. One approach is to limit the scope of the formal agreement. It might cover a single technology rather than an entire range of technologies; part of a product line rather than the entire line; distribution in a limited number of markets or for a limited period of time. The objective is to circumscribe a partner's opportunities to learn.

Moreover, agreements should establish specific performance requirements. Motorola, for example, takes an incremental, incentive-based approach to technology transfer in its venture with Toshiba. The agreement calls for Motorola to release its microprocessor technology incrementally as Toshiba delivers on its promise to increase Motorola's penetration in the Japanese semiconductor market. The greater Motorola's market share, the greater Toshiba's access to Motorola's technology.

Many of the skills that migrate between companies are not covered in the formal terms of collaboration. Top management puts together strategic alliances and sets the legal parameters for exchange. But what actually gets traded is determined by day-to-day interactions of engineers, marketers, and product developers: who says what to whom, who gets access to what facilities, who sits on what joint committees. The most important deals ("I'll share this with you if you share that with me") may be struck four or five organizational levels below where the deal was signed. Here lurks the greatest risk of unintended transfers of important skills.

Consider one technology-sharing alliance between European and Japanese competitors. The European company valued the partnership as a way to acquire a specific technology. The Japanese company considered it a window on its partner's entire range of competences and interacted with a broad spectrum of its partner's marketing and product-development staff. The company mined each contact for as much information as possible.

For example, every time the European company requested a new feature on a product being sourced from its partner, the Japanese company asked for detailed customer and competitor analyses to justify the request. Over time, it developed a sophisticated picture of the European market that would assist its own entry strategy. The technology acquired by the European partner through the formal agreement had a useful life of three to five years. The competitive insights acquired informally by the Japanese company will probably endure longer.

Limiting unintended transfers at the operating level requires careful attention to the role of gatekeepers, the people who control what information flows to a partner. A gatekeeper can be effective only if there are a limited number of gateways through which a partner can access people and facilities. Fujitsu's many partners all go through a single office, the "collaboration section," to request information and assistance from different divisions. This way the company can monitor and control access to critical skills and technologies.

We studied one partnership between European and U.S. competitors that involved several divisions of each company. While the U.S. company could only access its partner through a single gateway, its partner had unfettered access to all participating divisions. The European company took advantage of its free rein. If one division refused to provide certain information, the European partner made the same request of another division. No single manager in the U.S. company could tell how much information had been transferred or was in a position to piece together patterns in the requests.

Collegiality is a prerequisite for collaborative success. But *too much* collegiality should set off warning bells to senior managers. CEOs or division presidents should expect occasional complaints from their counterparts about the reluctance of lower level employees to share information. That's a sign that the gatekeepers are doing their jobs. And senior management should regularly debrief operating personnel to find out what information the partner is requesting and what requests are being granted.

Limiting unintended transfers ultimately depends on employee loyalty and self-discipline. This was a real issue for many of the Western companies we studied. In their excitement and pride over technical achievements, engineering staffs sometimes shared information that top management considered sensitive. Japanese engineers were less likely to share proprietary information.

There are a host of cultural and professional reasons for the relative openness of Western technicians. Japanese engineers and scientists are more loyal to their company than to their profession. They are less steeped in the open give-and-take of university research since they receive much of their training from employers. They consider themselves team members more than individual scientific contributors. As one Japanese manager noted: "We don't feel any need to reveal what we know. It is not an issue of pride for us. We're glad to sit and listen. If we're patient we usually learn what we want to know."

Controlling unintended transfers may require restricting access to facilities as well as to people. Companies should declare sensitive laboratories and factories off-limits to their partners. Better yet, they might house the collaborative venture in an entirely new facility. IBM is building a special site in Japan where Fujitsu can review its forthcoming mainframe software before deciding whether to license it. IBM will be able to control exactly what Fujitsu sees and what information leaves the facility.

Finally, which country serves as "home" to the alliance affects transparency. If the collaborative team is located near one partner's major facilities, the other partner will have more opportunities to learn—but less control over what information gets traded. When the partner houses, feeds, and looks after engineers and operating managers, there is a danger they will "go native." Expatriate personnel need frequent visits from headquarters as well as regular furloughs home.

Enhance the Capacity to Learn

Whether collaboration leads to competitive surrender or revitalization depends foremost on what employees believe the purpose of the alliance to be. It is self-evident: to learn, one must *want* to learn. Western companies won't realize the full benefits of competitive collaboration until they overcome an arrogance borne of decades of leadership. In short, Western companies must be more receptive.

We asked a senior executive in a Japanese electronics company about the perception that Japanese companies learn more from their foreign partners than vice versa. "Our Western partners approach us with the attitude of teachers," he told us. "We are quite happy with this, because we have the attitude of students."

Learning begins at the top. Senior management must be committed to enhancing their companies' skills as well as to avoiding financial risk. But most learning takes place at the lower levels of an alliance. Operating employees not only represent the front lines in an effective defense but also play a vital role in acquiring knowledge. They must be well briefed on the partner's strengths and weaknesses and understand how acquiring particular skills will bolster their company's competitive position.

This is already standard practice among Asian companies. We accompanied a Japanese development engineer on a tour through a partner's factory. This engineer dutifully took notes on plant layout, the number of production stages, the rate at which the line was running, and the number of employees. He recorded all this despite the fact that he had no manufacturing responsibility in his own company, and that the alliance didn't encompass joint manufacturing. Such dedication greatly enhances learning.

Collaboration doesn't always provide an opportunity to fully internalize a partner's skills. Yet just acquiring new and more precise benchmarks of a partner's performance can be of great value. A new benchmark can provoke a thorough review of internal performance levels and may spur a round of competitive innovation. Asking questions like, "Why do their semiconductor logic designs have fewer errors than ours?" and "Why are they investing in this technology and we're not?" may provide the incentive for a vigorous catch-up program.

Competitive benchmarking is a tradition in most of the Japanese companies we studied. It requires many of the same skills associated with competitor analysis: systematically calibrating performance against external targets; learning to use rough estimates to determine where a competitor (or partner) is better, faster, or cheaper; translating those estimates into new internal targets; and recalibrating to establish the rate of improvement in a competitor's performance. The great advantage of competitive collaboration is that proximity makes benchmarking easier.

Indeed, some analysts argue that one of Toyota's motivations in collaborating with GM in the much-publicized NUMMI venture is to gauge the quality of GM's manufacturing technology. GM's top manufacturing people get a close look at Toyota, but the reverse is true as well. Toyota may be learning whether its giant U.S. competitor is capable of closing the productivity gap with Japan.

Competitive collaboration also provides a way of getting enough to rivals to predict how they will behave when the alliance unravels or runs its course. How does the partner respond to price changes? How does it measure and reward executives? How does it prepare to launch a new product? By revealing a competitor's management orthodoxies, collaboration can increase the chances of success in future head-to-head battles.

Knowledge acquired from a competitor-partner is only valuable after it is diffused through the organization. Several companies we studied had established internal clearinghouses to collect an disseminate information. The collaborations manager at one Japanese company regularly made the rounds of all employees involved in alliances. He identified what information had been collected by whom and then passed it on to appropriate departments. Another company held regular meetings where employees shared new knowledge and determined who was best positioned to acquire additional information.

Proceed with Care—But Proceed

After World War II, Japanese and Korean companies entered alliances with Western rivals from weak positions. But they worked steadfastly toward independence. In the early 1960s, NEC's computer business was one-quarter the size of Honeywell's, its primary foreign partner. It took only two decades for NEC to grow larger than Honeywell, which eventually sold its computer operations to an alliance between NEC and Group Bull of France. The NEC experience demonstrates that dependence on a foreign partner doesn't automatically condemn a company to also-ran status. Collaboration may sometimes be unavoidable; surrender is not.

Managers are too often obsessed with the ownership structure of an alliance. Whether a company controls 51 percent or 49 percent of a joint venture may be much less important than the rate at which each partner learns from the other. Companies that are confident of their ability to learn may even prefer some ambiguity in the alliance's legal structure. Ambiguity creates more potential to acquire skills and technologies. The challenge for Western companies is not to write tighter legal agreements but to become better learners.

Running away from collaboration is no answer. Even the largest Western companies can no longer outspend their global rivals. With leadership in many industries shifting toward the East, companies in the United States and Europe must become good borrowers—much like Asian companies did in the 1960s and 1970s. Competitive renewal depends on building new process capabilities and winning new product and technology battles. Collaboration can be a low-cost strategy for doing both.

Corporate Innovation

Case III-6
Allstate Chemical Company: The Commercialization of Dynarim

Artemis March and David A. Garvin

In February 1986, Pete Kennedy, director of the Dynarim project, and his boss, Eric Reinhalter, sat down with Jack Cousins, president of Allstate Chemical Company, to discuss the future of the new Dynarim product. Dynarim, a liquid resin fabricated into structural parts by a new molding technology, now had repeat orders approaching $1 million. The project had been housed in an incubator group called Commercial Development for the past two years, but it could not remain there indefinitely. Cousins therefore wanted to review its status and future location, even though a move was not yet imminent.

The Company

Allstate Chemical in the 1970s

Allstate Chemical Company (ACC) produced commodity and specialty chemicals and distributed commodity chemicals for virtually every major chemical producer in the United States. Its distribution philosophy, supported by the largest distribution network in the country, was "Tell us what you want, and we will get it to you." ACC itself supplied about 15 to 20 percent of the product sold through its network. Distribution accounted for about half of total revenues. Another 15 percent of sales came from the production of diverse specialty chemicals such as adhesives, foundry products, and electronics chemicals, most of which ACC had acquired during the last decade. Like Allstate's existing divisions, these additions operated with considerable autonomy and possessed the full range of functions needed for P&L accountability. (See Exhibit 1.)

Relationship with the corporation. Allstate Chemical was a wholly owned subsidiary of the $8 billion Allstate Oil Corp. (AOC). During most of the 1970s, according to Jack Cousins, who became president of ACC in mid-1983,

> chemicals were not perceived as a significant growth or investment area. It was tacitly understood that our mission was to provide a positive cash flow to the corporation for use in other areas.

Refinery closings and divestment of some oil-producing properties in the late 1970s reduced the pressure on ACC to be a cash provider and generated funds for reinvestment in businesses other than oil. For the first time, chemical distribution and specialty chemicals were targeted for reinvestment and growth. Corporate expected a high return from the chemical business—12 to 13 percent ROI—as well as long-term growth. This sometimes produced conflicts: $4 million per year for a development project, for example, translated into 1/2 percent less ROI.

Strategic shift toward specialty chemicals in the 1980s. Such pressures from AOC were one of several factors leading ACC management to decide that its future lay in specialty chemicals (coupled with a continued focus on distribution) rather than commodities. Because of differences between the two types of chemicals, major organizational and policy changes were required to support the shift.

Customers bought commodity chemicals to meet a specification and because the price was right. Products were generic, and the market determined their price. Purchasing departments made the buying decisions, largely on the basis of price, quality, and delivery. Commodities were sold to end users and fabricators. Because the cost of the chemical was a key part of these customers' costs, a supplier that was 1–2¢ high usually lost the business. This emphasis on cost led to in-house manufacturing, in which, one manager noted, "life revolves around the plant because low cost wins the game." Although high volume had brought ACC healthy profits, margins were less than for specialties, where performance set the price.

In specialties, the approach was usually to start from the customer's use and work backward. Applications were critical. Specialty chemicals were usually a small part of the price of the customer's product; as long as products performed as needed, business was not lost over pennies. Purchasing played a largely administrative role because deci-

EXHIBIT 1 Selected Financial Data (in millions)

	1985	1984	1983	1982	1981
Sales and operating revenues	$1,500	$1,500	$1,200	$1,200	$1,300
Operating income	70	55	0	30	40
Identifiable assets	500	500	420	400	460
Funds provided from operations	60	50	20	45	50
Additions to plant, property, and equipment	40	20	20	30	35
Depreciation, depletion, and amortization	25	25	20	20	15

Note: All figures have been rounded.

SOURCE: 1985 Annual Report.

sions to buy or specify critical ingredients were made by design engineers and plant people. These demands increased the need for marketing and technical staff. Because specialties were sold in the tens of millions of pounds per year rather than in billions, they were more likely to be made in batches than by continuous processes. This enormously reduced the scope and cost of capital investment—from hundreds of millions of dollars to tens of millions. But commodity plants could not be converted to specialty production. Specialties, however, allowed a company to forgo in-house manufacturing, particularly in the early, risky stages of a product's life. Cousins explained:

> With an uncertain new product, why own a plant when you can rent a reactor? You would only want to bring manufacturing in-house if you had a well-established, high-volume product, or if you couldn't protect the technology, or if the manufacturing sequence was very complex and an outside company couldn't do it right or very consistently.

In specialties, ACC management felt it was important to be a leader rather than a follower. An early entrant could not only gain market share, set the price and ground rules, and gain lead time; it could also dictate the performance parameters a competitor would need to exceed to displace it. Later entrants had to provide significantly better performance, because their products were seldom "drop-ins" for the customer's equipment and process. Switching costs might include new molds or repiping and, most significantly, requalification testing, which could take years and cost millions of dollars. Second entrants also had to overcome reluctance to change from the known to the unknown.

Between 1980 and 1985, Allstate closed and sold several commodity businesses, including plants, and added specialties by acquiring and building facilities and using outside processors. Specialties doubled from 15 percent of Allstate's business to 30 percent, while distribution of commodities continued to account for about half of the company's sales. George Prince, general manager of the Polyesters Division, which now derived most of its profits from specialties, commented on what the changes had meant for his division.

> You have much more exposure in the corporation when you're identified as a division that needs to be grown. We have made timely acquisitions that fit our technological and customer base, and we intend to make more since the corporation is now willing to fund them. Our staff has increased dramatically. Two years ago, we did no market development. But now, for example, we are trying to get engineers to design in our resins for the Pontiac Firebird, and that requires marketing.
>
> Specialties are also more quality oriented, and there's been more emphasis on how we control processes and how we report data to customers. For that reason, we do all of our own specialty manufacturing, and are investing in things like computer control of reactors. Our productivity has gone up because we're not making off-spec product.

Research, 1977–1986

Formation of Venture Research

Until 1977, Allstate Chemical had no significant central research organization. Small research groups in each division focused on short-term technical service to customers. Under the impetus of Cousins, who was then administrative vice-president for research, engineering, and finance, 25 percent of the company's research budget and people were pulled from the divisions to form Venture Research (VR).

VR's charter was to develop projects that would lead to major new businesses, with *major* defined as at least several hundred million dollars in annual sales. The group was to look for home runs outside existing division interests. Initially, Cousins and other senior managers wanted VR to focus on breakthrough process changes for producing high-volume, commodity chemicals. To head VR, Allstate recruited Dick Winthrop, whose process work at a competitor had won several industry awards.

Research strategy: From process/commodity focus to product/specialty. Process research required a broad range of chemical and engineering skills, a large commitment of people for long periods, and heavy investments in capital equipment. During the research stage, for example, this might mean building a series of reactors of increasing size, each of which could study a larger number of process variables. If the researchers succeeded in creating a commercially viable reaction, engineers would then have to create the equipment to make it. Process research typically started with petrochemicals that could be refined from crude oil (such as benzene), and sought cheaper ways to produce derivative monomers (such as styrene) or polymers (such as polystyrene), by significantly reducing the costs of raw materials, of capital, or both.[1]

VR's initial strategy aimed to replicate what Winthrop had accomplished at Sohio. Process changes had so dramatically lowered Sohio's price for a high-volume monomer that they had "knocked the bottom out of the market," as one manager put it. Although Allstate did develop two new processes, neither achieved commercial success. In one case, the cost advantage was not large enough; in the other, ACC had to compete with potential customers' captive monomer production. The 1981–83 industry recession and the domestic industry's shift to offshore production dealt the final blows to ACC's process/commodity research strategy. Cousins ruefully acknowledged: "It took five years and $50 million to see that this was the wrong way to go."

As process research was cut back, VR slowly gravitated toward product/specialty research. By 1984, its charter had shifted to supporting and strengthening the divisions. Prince described Polyesters' changing relationship to VR:

> We used to do almost no new product development; what we did was hand-holding, fire-fighting, and low-level product improvement to satisfy specific customer needs. Now we are identifying market opportunities and developing new chemistries for which we want VR's expertise. We want them to do original chemistry, to invent new polymers that we develop for the market. Therefore, we need close contact to see that they are on track—we don't want them doing any blue-sky stuff. So when we see an opportunity for expanding our product line, I lobby Jack and the others, and they go to Dr. Winthrop and tell him to work on it.

Less capital intensive than process research, polymer research normally involved working with a certain type of chemistry (such as esters, urethanes, or alcohols) to produce either an entirely new molecule or improvements in the performance of existing molecules. Results were typically the product of years of studying such basic phenomena as what made adhesives work. According to Cousins, the shift in research strategy was brought about by a combination of "SEP oversight, reviews of projects, yelling, and handholding."

Strategic Expansion Project (SEP) Board

Shortly after becoming president, Cousins established the Strategic Expansion Project Board to oversee research. Its members were Cousins and five group vice presidents, and its charter was to identify and fund those research projects that had significant strategic and commercial potential. The board looked for projects that fit Allstate's strength in technology or markets, and could open up new businesses. Such projects had to be more than mere line extensions, which remained the responsibility of divisions. VR could still fund projects at a relatively low level from its own budget, but continued funding, or significant expansions of the work, required board approval. SEP-approved projects were funded from "Jack's budget" until they broke even.

With this mechanism, the company's chief operating officers supported the start-up costs of new businesses from company rather than division profits, and exercised control over funding. If necessary, the board could kill a project that was not showing significant progress or whose commercial potential had waned. Cousins was satisfied that commercial considerations now guided Allstate's research in new areas. He noted, however, that "Dick Winthrop doesn't totally approve of this approach. There are areas he would like to expand that don't have a chance of succeeding commercially. But he knows that I will not approve a test-tube project." Winthrop conceded that "they have shelved a few projects I would like to have continued," but pointed out the board's usefulness in giving VR direction:

> They advise us of areas to keep away from and give me guidance on time frames and capital expenditures so that I, in turn, can provide better guidance to the projects. The cross-play between divisions is valuable, and they may see areas we don't know about. But I would like them to do more in the way of suggesting areas of R&D that would be good for Venture Research.

One of VR's earliest polymer projects—and one that did gain SEP approval—was eventually commercialized as Dynarim. In the beginning, however, Dynarim was a molecule without a purpose or a home.

---

[1]Monomers are small molecules (i.e., molecules having low molecular weight), usually in liquid form. Also called resins or prepolymers, they are an intermediate product that needs further processing (polymerization plus molding into a part) to make a final product. Monomers are the bricks and mortar for constructing the polymer "house." Polymers are large molecules that have been put together to create a solid material that, when molded, has desired properties such as stiffness or strength.

The RIM Polymer Project

V110: A neat molecule with no use, 1976–1980. Originally, the project had sought to plug a hole in the high end of Allstate's ester product line. In 1976, Hank Benoit and Joe Finnigan, both research chemists, were asked to create a molecule that would outperform competitors' vinyl esters. Benoit and Finnigan invented a family of low-molecular-weight, liquid resins. During the next few years, they explored innumerable variations in the family's chemistry and spatial configuration; eventually, they narrowed the field to four molecules. By 1980, Winthrop had selected one of the four, V110, as clearly superior. Yet despite agreement among the coinventors, their section head, Ron Church, and Winthrop that they had a "neat molecule," and despite efforts to involve the divisions, no one was interested in or could find applications for V110.

The polymer had excellent properties when molded: strength, stiffness, and resistance to high temperatures. But it was too brittle for commercial use without the addition of other materials. Fiberglass reinforcement eliminated the brittleness, but processing difficulties with the fiberglass resin sometimes created consistency problems with the product. These problems disappeared if a new molding technique, reaction injection molding (RIM), was used instead of conventional compression molding. But fabricators were resistant to the different type of fiberglass handling required to make large RIM parts.

Adding RIM technology. RIM technology and equipment were first developed in Europe. By 1980, approximately 500 machines had been installed in the United States, with ownership distributed about equally between multiple independent molders and a few captive producers, mostly in the auto industry. By contrast, compression (or press) molding equipment was owned primarily by 20 major end users, 6 of whom dominated the business. The differences in equipment distribution reflected the technologies' cost differences. Press molding required enormous heat and pressure, and thus enormous equipment and energy, to make parts. RIM, on the other hand, could fabricate large parts using smaller, cheaper equipment. For a part 8 inches by 5 feet (such as an automobile bumper), the contrast was between a 750-ton, $400,000 machine and a 25-ton, $200,000 machine. RIM's energy costs, molding costs, and tooling costs were much lower as well.[2] The major reason for these differences was that RIM polymerized the liquid monomers (the reaction) and formed them into a solid part (injection molding) in one step, rather than the two required by compression molding.

Not all monomers, however, were suitable for use in this process. Because the reaction occurred very quickly, RIM required liquid materials, such as urethane, that flowed easily at room temperature and reacted quickly with an isocyanate. The Allstate V110 team realized that its molecules so reacted, and thus made the link to RIM. Moreover, the result was a rigid product that could be used for structural parts, unlike the usually floppy, urethane-based products. Winthrop commented:

> Once we recognized the technological opportunity, it took six months to get the project redirected and the chemists working on tailoring a molecule for RIM use. We also needed someone who knew plastics markets to head the commercial development of the RIM project [the new name of the V110 project].

Market and applications development, 1980–1983. Pete Kennedy was recruited from Du Pont in August 1980 to identify market opportunities for V110, to reorient Allstate's chemists to those markets, and to develop a business strategy. Cousins commented:

> We knew we had a neat molecule in one of our VR projects, but we didn't know how to talk to the market. We had always made interesting molecules and then tried to figure out how to use them. Now, instead of working in a vacuum, we needed to bring information from the market into the lab. But we weren't set up to do that. So we hired Pete Kennedy, a hybrid, a PhD chemist with street experience, who understood pricing and marketing, and who knew the auto market.

Initially, there was some uncertainty about whom Kennedy should work for. As a first step, Cousins decided to place him within the VR organization, reporting to Winthrop.

Kennedy began visiting design engineers and materials people in the automotive and aerospace industries to identify their needs for V110-based

---

[2]RIM had even greater cost advantages over injection molding, the third major molding technique. Huge clamping forces were required for injection molding, making it inappropriate for large parts. For most purposes, the primary comparison was therefore between RIM and compression molding.

materials, to generate and validate industry interest, and to develop market pull. He encouraged customers to test Allstate's materials and worked with molders to make prototypes. He also began to create an applications laboratory, noting that it "is one of the first things you add when you want to commercialize a product." Such a laboratory duplicated customers' facilities, running parts on the same kinds of equipment and then testing them. For this reason, within a few months of his arrival Kennedy got approval to buy a RIM machine for $80,000. A VR project manager pointed out the importance of an applications laboratory, which was a new concept for Allstate:

> You need both a pilot plant and an applications laboratory for product development. The applications or field support staff provide know-how to the customers and to the molders. They show them how to make the part, and demonstrate that it won't tear up their equipment. They give customers the comfort of knowing their parts can in fact be made.

Kennedy identified a wide range of materials that could be of use to customers. The project broadened from V110 to a larger category of potential products: high-performance engineering materials that could be RIMed.[3] A few of these would displace existing urethane and thermoplastic materials, but most would try to displace metal. Kennedy commented:

> I am not committed to V110, but to a market with opportunities for new chemistries. I have an open strategy on materials. I want to create engineering-type RIM polymers that customers want. If my product becomes obsolete, I want to be the one to obsolete it.

Despite his charter to tailor V110 to the market, Kennedy initially lacked both staff and authority. The four research chemists still reported to Ron Church. Friction between the two slowed the project. Benoit recalled:

> When Kennedy joined us, there was a period of severe adjustment. I resisted him for six months before I saw the light. Then I began to see that we needed to work toward performance requirements to commercialize a product. Before, we had just varied things willy-nilly: "Gee, what happens if we do this?" But when Kennedy talked to customers, they would say, "We need X, can you formulate it to do that?" Of course, they don't give you clear specifications. They are more likely to say, "If I can bang it against the side of my desk and it doesn't crack, it's good," rather than tell you what tensile strength they want. So you need to translate such comments into something concrete. Pete Kennedy can do that.

By stimulating market interest, Kennedy built internal credibility for the project. And by building relationships with individual chemists and helping them solve technical problems, he began reorienting RIM research toward market needs.

Product and process development, 1980–1983. Because molders resisted using fiberglass reinforcement, Kennedy wanted to begin work on a new resin that did not require it. Top management soon wanted the RIM team to cut back pilot runs for V110 process specification so it could devote most of its energy to creating such a molecule. But, because Kennedy also felt Allstate had "to have a product we could make and a way we could make it," he thought it was just as imperative to do extensive applications development on V110 materials and define a manufacturing process for that molecule as it was to start work on a new molecule. He therefore went down two tracks: initiating work on a molecule that did not require fiberglass reinforcement while doing as much applications work and as many pilot runs as he could get through. He summarized his approach: "No one said no, and I didn't ask." In the words of his eventual boss, Eric Reinhalter, Kennedy

> went from using "springs and mirrors" to "officially condoned bootlegging." He began operating, perhaps subconsciously, as the general manager of a business that did not yet exist, talking to customers, making prototypes, and looking into manufacturing possibilities.

Process development entailed two major tasks: specifying the process variables, and getting a manufacturing organization in place. Allstate's pilot plant, which was run by VR, could make virtually any chemical Allstate made or was likely to. Batches of V110 made in the pilot plant were studied to identify key variables and their interactions, or used for prototypes and customer evaluations. By the end of 1983, Kennedy felt that Allstate still needed to

---

[3]Polymers could be divided into three groups on the basis of broad performance capabilities. At the low end were plastics used in applications such as packaging, toys, and housewares. Engineering materials were higher-performance polymers that stood up to certain temperatures, were chemically resistant, and had desirable characteristics for particular work applications. Structural polymers were a subset of engineering materials. Usually reinforced, they could substitute for metal and be designed into structures where they performed load-bearing functions. V110 was a structural engineering polymer.

understand much more about these interactions to define "the window within which we could safely operate" the V110 process, which included a very flammable reactant.

Eventually, commercial-scale manufacturing of V110 would be necessary. Since Allstate had no reactor available with the right capabilities, Kennedy opted for toll processing—manufacture of the chemical by an outside processor under contract. Allstate management often used toll processors, and Kennedy found it appropriate at this stage of V110 development: "Before we make any dedicated capital investment that could become obsolete, I want to be sure that the product has a stable position and its chemistry is the final one."

A Market-Driven Technology Strategy

Guiding product development toward market-based performance targets was a new approach to research at Allstate. Through presentations and one-to-one meetings with chemists, Kennedy advocated this approach in the 1980–1983 period. He recalled:

> I was saying, "Make me a molecule that does these things." This was scary to chemists because they didn't have a basic molecule to work from. Instead, they had all of nature to deal with, so they didn't even know where to begin. Most were impressed with the elegance of the analysis, but found it hard to use. Even today, it hasn't become part of our working environment; when Venture Research designs a new molecule, it still does it the old way.

The method articulated by Kennedy provided a starting point for structuring the approach to polymer design. It established product performance targets and then identified process parameters that immediately eliminated much chemistry from consideration. The researchers then concentrated their search within those classes of polymers whose spatial relationships made them likely to meet the desired performance and process parameters. (See Exhibit 2.)

One of Kennedy's tools for communicating this approach was a positioning chart for RIM resins. (See Exhibit 3.) For each of seven key attributes, such as stiffness, he compared the performance ranges covered by existing thermoplastics and RIM materials with those that were currently unserved. For example, thermoplastics covered almost the entire range of stiffness, but existing RIM materials showed major gaps in this area. Such gaps, which could be met by engineering-type RIM resins, would become the focus of Allstate's research, and the basis for refining and varying the V110 family of molecules.

The Formation of Commercial Development

After setting up the SEP board and clarifying Venture Research's role, Cousins considered other ways to link research more closely with marketing. One was to push the specialty divisions to become more market-sensitive. A second was to let Venture Research develop its own marketing efforts, an option he rejected because "they tend to be naive about marketing, and research management might not listen." The third option, which was eventually adopted, was to create a high-level group with the commercialization of new businesses as its main charter, and the spread of marketing as a secondary goal.

CD leadership and organization. To head this new group, called Commercial Development (CD), Cousins wanted

> a marketing animal with on-the-ground success in markets and technologies similar to ours. He had to know enough technology to talk with research. His personal makeup had to be consistent with our culture—laid back and informal.

In Eric Reinhalter, he found someone who had developed, marketed, and sold applications for polymer materials to large end users for over 20 years. Originally, he was slated to report to the SEP Board, but after insisting that he have one formal boss, Reinhalter was assigned to report directly to Cousins, and joined the company in January 1984. He commented:

> I felt that a clear reporting relationship to one senior manager was essential. Jack's choice that it be him sent a signal that CD would be an important new effort, and it has worked well for both of us. I keep Jack informed, but he manages me by exception rather than on a day-to-day basis. I also defer to the SEP board—of which I am a member—and it treats me as an unequal equal.

Transfer of RIM to CD

Reinhalter was offered three projects; he accepted them all. Of these, RIM was the most mature and the only one with a product. The CD group began quite

EXHIBIT 2 Key Steps in Market-Driven Technology Strategy for Engineering RIM Resins

1. *Product Performance Targets:* Establish performance characteristics the product must meet.

   For engineering RIM polymers, seven such characteristics and their ranges were established, including:

flexural modulus (stiffness)	250,000–500,000 psi
tensile strength	8,000 psi (minimum)
(etc.)	

A resin had to meet all seven characteristics within the target range, giving considerable latitude for trade-offs, experimentation, and judgment, resulting in multiple resins with a different balance of properties.

2. *Process Parameters:* Establish boundaries within which the resins must fall in order to be processed on equipment chosen.

   RIM processing equipment required:

   a. Materials must be liquid (low viscosity) at operating temperatures in order to flow properly.
   b. Individual components must be transportable as liquids at temperatures less than 300°F.
   c. There must be no by-products because all reactions will take place very quickly in the mold.

   This eliminated many materials from consideration.

3. *Polymer Architecture:* Because broad classes of spatial relationships are associated with certain performance features, it is possible to eliminate whole classes of polymers from consideration and concentrate on those most likely to meet targets.

   With regard to RIM materials:

   a. Linear polymers tended to be stiff, have high viscosity, and high melting points, features that made them prime candidates for RIM resins. Branched linear polymers, being less stiff, lower in viscosity, and having lower melting points than unbranched, were easily eliminated from consideration, whatever their chemistry.

   b. Higher molecular weight polymers were always tougher, and longer molecules had higher molecular weight. However, getting the molecular weight up required more cycle time, thereby increasing manufacturing costs. Was it possible to design a molecule that acted like longer/higher-weight molecules but in fact required less molecular weight? Yes, if one constructed it to take advantage of certain kinds of bonding between molecules whose effect took the place of single, large molecules.

4. *Conclusion:* It is possible and efficient to design polymers to fit market-determined performance features and hardware requirements by concentrating one's research in areas most likely to pay off according to a structural analysis linking polymer morphology with performance tendencies.

small; it consisted of the technical people Reinhalter inherited from the three projects, plus three business analysts. Kennedy was immediately appointed sole project manager for RIM. He observed:

> I now had a boss who understood business and marketing. Eric validated my feelings about what I had been doing—that markets were key. The project now had a place in the organization and it fit the new strategic direction.

One of Reinhalter's early initiatives was a contest to name V110 to give it a new, commercial identity and team mentality. The winner was *Dynarim*. Dynarim referred to the entire family of RIM resins, and Dynarim 1100 referred to V110 specifically.

If RIM had not been housed within Commercial Development, it would have been sent to a division. That option, however, had little support. There was no obvious fit with any existing division; and RIM would have had to compete with more established profitable products for funds and attention.

The Role of CD

Cousins had given CD a deliberately broad charter. He wanted it to manage two or three projects at a time ($2 million to $4 million per year per project meant more were too expensive), to guide research, and to bring more of a marketing perspective to the company. But he had only rough guidelines for deciding when projects should be transferred into and out of CD. He did not want to saddle a division with foreign technologies, products, or markets. He was also inclined to put a project in CD if a division lacked critical skills to make the project successful; he commented, "With RIM, for example, we put it in CD because we didn't have market development

EXHIBIT 3 RIM Resin Positioning

A shows that IM materials cover the whole performance spectrum for this feature.
B shows major holes in the performance spectrum being met by existing RIM materials, c. 1980–1981.
C shows how Allstate proposes to fill those gaps in areas most important to market (300–1,500 range).

Performance targeted for Allstate reactive resins

A Thermoplastics (injection molding)

Polyethylene, polypropyline, ABS polystyrene, etc.	Nylon, acetal, etc.	Mineral and glass reinforced thermoplastics			
		Mineral reinforced plastics	Glass reinforced nylon and polycarb	Glass reinforced PET polyester	

B Reactive molding resins

C Target performance for Dynarim resins

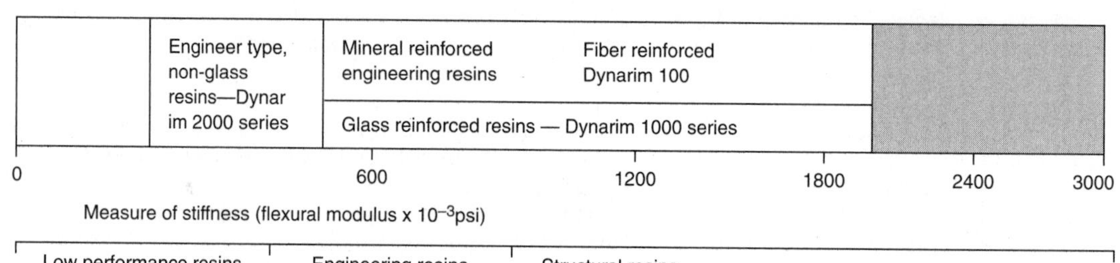

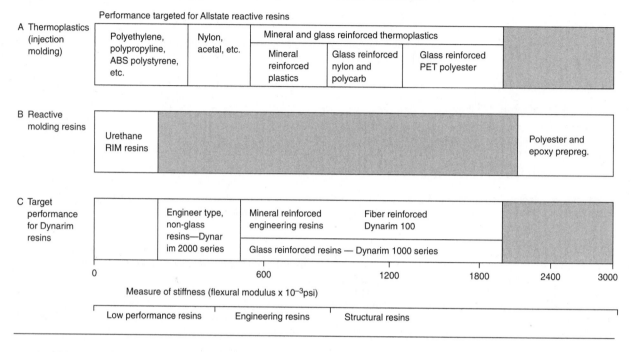

skills in the divisions." Once projects were assigned to CD, Cousins wanted it to be a portfolio manager, providing research and marketing direction, functioning as an intermediary between VR and the divisions. Most of all, Cousins wanted to avoid redundancy:

> If a division already has a certain capability, we shouldn't set up anything in CD that duplicates it. I don't want CD to worry about process development or manufacturing—that's a distraction. I don't want a self-contained business unit; I want them to develop a product that can be handed off to a division. For example, why should we recreate a custom manufacturing facility for Dynarim when we already have six or eight divisions set up to manufacture?

George Prince summarized his view of CD's role:

> CD should work with chemistries we in the divisions don't practice but which are akin to our markets. Process development should take place before a project goes too far: is there a known process? Do we have the equipment? The expertise? This should be coordinated—the marketing by CD, the chemistry by VR, and the engineering and manufacturing by a division. CD should do very little manufacturing, but they need to be able to scope out what's required.

Before a product was handed off to a division, Prince thought that its commercial feasibility needed to have been demonstrated:

> First you need a commercial process, and the demonstration that it is economically feasible. Then a division can take it and commercialize it. But if it's still hard to meet specifications consistently on scaled-up production, then we shouldn't take it.

While he thought it was possible in some cases for a product to be handed off directly from Venture Research to a division, Prince felt that CD, with greater resources for product and market development, could generally take a project earlier than a division. He commented: "If Venture Research can take a product from A to H, then CD might need to get it to L or M before a division takes it."

According to CD's own mission statement, its goal was to identify, develop, and commercialize profitable new business opportunities. In Reinhalter's view, this meant CD had to be active in four areas:

> We have to develop the product, get it made, develop the market, and have applications people who go to the customer. Applications development is the norm in

> specialties; you have to work with the customer to make the part. Marketing includes everything needed to sell the product: creating demand from the end user, calling on molders who fabricate it—whatever it takes. We must also demonstrate the ability to sell the product and to make it. But it can actually be made anywhere; we just need someone on the team who is responsible for getting it made right and who can deal with any problems.

The growth in staff for the RIM project reflected these priorities. Between 1984 and 1986, applications development expanded to nine people, research (renamed product development) to eight, and marketing to five. The marketing and sales people both developed markets and handled accounts. One manufacturing engineer served as liaison with the toll processor.

Reinhalter distinguished between three key manufacturing activities: demonstrating manufacturability, process development, and production responsibility. Demonstrating the manufacturability of a new product was, in his view, the responsibility of the seller. Thus, Winthrop had to convince Reinhalter a product could be made, and he in turn had to convince the SEP board and Cousins. Both paper exercises and physical demonstrations were usually required. Process development then followed. Reinhalter believed it should be done by whoever had the most expertise, but in practice, it usually fell to the group with the greatest interest. Reinhalter commented:

> CD should not be manufacturing intensive; it needs only enough process development expertise to get a particular job done. With Dynarim, I would have been happy to have an existing division handle it, but none stepped forward—they all had jobs already. So we developed the process and transferred it to production.

Kennedy supported this approach, with qualifications. He too wanted to minimize CD's work-in-process development, but at the same time wanted to be certain the product fit tight parameters. He commented:

> I have no product until I can make it. You must tie down the interface between manufacturing and product performance, so you can't turn it over to someone who doesn't know that a 700 viscosity gives you a different product from 600. But I will do the minimum necessary to assure myself that I have the product I want. If I can get this from a division, fine; if I have to go outside, I will; and if I have to do it myself, I will.

Finally, once it became clear that a potential new business had emerged, full-scale manufacturing was necessary. Reinhalter wanted clear responsibility for manufacturing lodged somewhere in the company. But he cared less about where it was lodged than that there was someone who could be held accountable.

Although Reinhalter agreed with CD's original charter, he felt the mission had become less clear over time. "We have to decide if the plate is full enough already. Should we keep adding more? Do we really want to move things in and out?" He also pointed to a possible conflict between CD's original charter and the recruitment and motivation of staff. Reinhalter argued that operating people who had a personal stake (which he called psychological ownership) in a program would do a better job than "pass-through people," but recognized they would probably have trouble letting go of projects.

The Dynarim Project, 1984–1986

Kennedy developed a strategic plan in 1984 with the goal of becoming the worldwide leader in engineering-type RIM materials. He argued that RIM hardware had opened up new opportunities for high-performance materials, that a large, unserved market for such materials already existed, and that Allstate was far ahead in grasping this opportunity and developing the required products. Accordingly, applications development on the Dynarim 1100 series expanded; by 1985, heavy product development was underway on the Dynarim 2000 series as well. Molecules in the 1100 series were iterations based on the original V110 chemistry, and were targeted for large, structural, nonappearance parts used in transportation equipment. Dynarim 2000 was based on a new chemistry that could be used with or without reinforcement; it would eventually take RIM resins into such markets as cabinetry for business and medical equipment.

During 1984–1985, interest in Dynarim picked up at General Motors for use as tire covers (the platform covering the well in which spare tires were placed, which became the floor of the trunk). Covers for several models were tested, and the first order, for use in selected Cadillacs, Oldsmobiles, and Buicks, came in April 1985. A year later repeat orders had generated $1.4 million in sales. Kennedy was confident that business would soon expand, both to other auto models and to additional parts. In both areas, testing and evaluation were well under way.

Toll processing continued to be the manufacturing method of choice, despite the cost premium of

10 cents per pound and the need to share proprietary information. Patents on Dynarim reduced anxiety about sharing such information. Toll processing was also consistent with Cousins' desire to reduce capital intensity, and his view that manufacturing was not a competitive key, at least at that time.

Managing a toll processor required skills similar to those needed to manage an in-house manufacturing operation; these included getting raw materials to the processor, paying bills, and handling off-spec production. It also required the ability to identify appropriate processors in the first place, and then to negotiate and administer contracts. Because the manufacturing engineer assigned to the RIM project was only 24 years old and had little experience in these areas, an engineer from polyesters acted as a consultant.

Allstate managers thought they might want to bring Dynarim manufacturing in-house within three to five years. Some of the factors that would shape the decision would be the size of the required investment (about $2.5 million to convert an existing plant, $5 million to build a new one), the company's willingness and ability to make the investment, whether Allstate had a plant with the right equipment that was underused at the time, EPA regulations, and projected volume.

Future Dynarim Decisions

Eventually, decisions would have to be made about moving Dynarim out of Commercial Development. Issues involved timing, location, and the size of the group to be moved. But no one felt decisions were needed soon. Reinhalter, for example, observed:

> It's not important to me to define the future if the trend is right. I am not preoccupied with whether or not Dynarim goes to a division, although I would prefer to leave it where it is until it's obvious that it's time to change. When there's a compelling reason to move, it should be obvious—for example, if we need a sales force. But if you change, don't screw up what made it work before.

Cousins also felt no urgent need to move Dynarim to a division. But he cautioned:

> Leaving it forever in CD is not an option, although I'm perfectly comfortable with it in CD this year and next. Polyesters probably wouldn't even want it right now because they are profit oriented and Dynarim is still losing money. But I don't want CD to spend all its time on RIM, either.

Reinhalter's primary concern was keeping the project team intact, or at least allowing whoever wanted to move with the product to be able to do so. Reinhalter explained:

> I don't want to lose the momentum that's been built by having critical mass. I worry about culture change. Pete Kennedy built an environment here—I just added to it—where we do more than we think we can. The can-do attitude has generated extremely rapid progress, and that could get lost if the team were broken up.

Although Polyesters remained the division most likely to receive Dynarim, an alternative was for it to go to a new division. The choice was complicated because Dynarim had already spun off a new product, Dynatech, that was being developed in Polyesters. In the long run, there were three possibilities: Dynarim could join its sister product in the Polyesters Division, the two products could form the basis of a new division, or Dynatech could remain in Polyesters while Dynarim became the core of a new business unit.

Dynatech's chemistry was identical to Dynarim 1100's, for the V110 molecule was the foundation of both products. Dynarim, however, was then RIMed, forming a polymer and a part in a single operation, while Dynatech was to be used in compression molding. Once the Dynatech project had a marketable product, press-molding fabricators would buy V110 resin, combine it with a fiberglass resin to form a sheet-molding compound (SMC), and then mold a part. The resulting parts would be similar in performance to Dynarim,[4] and thus superior to vinyl ester's performance. Compared with other SMCs, Dynatech's fumes would be much less noxious, an advantage in dealing with environmental regulations. Finnigan thought the use of compression molding gave Dynatech a financial advantage as well:

> If a fabricator were starting from scratch, it would make sense to buy RIM equipment for large parts. But few of them have RIM equipment yet, while lots of them have heavily depreciated press-molding equipment. With both products, we can cover all the bases.

---

[4]Kennedy disputed this in part, pointing out that the vertical walls of large press-molded parts were weaker than the walls of similar parts that had been RIMed. These differences resulted from the rates at which resins flowed in the two processes. In Kennedy's view, the consequence was that Dynarim could cross over more easily into Dynatech markets than the reverse. Prince disagreed; he believed that RIM products were restricted to non-appearance applications, while Dynatech could be used in appearance applications such as car fenders.

Dynatech had emerged from an SEP-funded project in 1984 that focused on polyester fabrication processes. The project had been instigated by Finnigan, who saw an opportunity for Polyesters to do something with the V110 chemistry. The year's work convinced Prince that Dynatech was a commercially feasible product, and Polyesters then picked up its funding. Prince described the difference between his division's acceptance of Dynatech in 1985 and its resistance to Dynarim in 1984:

> Both Dynatech and Dynarim will concentrate on the transportation industry, with automotive being our initial target. We already market our specialty polyesters to domestic auto producers, and work with the press molders that fabricate auto parts. While we have lots of expertise in compression molding, we know little about RIM and have no relationships with RIM molders. So Dynatech fit our customers' business and equipment without our having to fiddle, while Dynarim would have required our hiring several people we couldn't afford.

Markets for Dynatech and Dynarim 1100 overlapped—although just how, and to what extent, was still unclear. Currently, both products were expected to replace metal in nonappearance structural applications in transportation and other equipment. Estimates of potential crossover in each direction varied. Most Allstate managers viewed the overlap as broadening Allstate's market coverage, rather than as a source of competitive problems. In fact, both Dynatech and Dynarim had based applications engineers in the same Detroit office. These people talked to one another constantly, exchanged leads, and, according to Reinhalter, seldom fought over applications. In most cases, the line dividing the two products was obvious: the size, shape, and volume of a part usually dictated whether RIM or compression molding should be used. If product choice was not resolved at this level, customers were likely to make the decision. Reinhalter pointed out: "Our customers are very sophisticated, so they know which method is better for their application. They also have preferred molders or fabricators that they want to use."

While end user applications were similar for the two products, there were subtle but (in Kennedy's view) critical distinctions between the required marketing processes. RIM was strongly end user driven, while Polyesters' SMCs were more processor driven. Kennedy observed:

> The SMC community is relatively small and composed of big, influential processors who create a creditable supply for, say, a General Motors. GM determines only the performance specs and leaves it to the processor to choose particular materials from particular vendors. Quality is controlled by the processors' skill. We, on the other hand, want the end user to specify a particular material; the specifications are for a particular formulation, not just for performance. Quality would then be controlled by the materials.

While Prince acknowledged that, in the past, Polyesters had tried to sell against performance specifications, Allstate's new emphasis on specialties was affecting the division's marketing approach:

> We now spend time with end users, talking with their engineers to try and get our resins designed into products. We want them to tell fabricators to make the parts from our resins; then we work with molders to make it easy for them to do so.

These considerations affected the eventual location of the two new products. Cousins, for example, thought the organizational separation of the two was "fine for now," but he noted that eventually they were "likely to become the same business." Because of the similarity of product and end user markets, Cousins indicated he "would have no hesitation putting the two products together."

Prince, on the other hand, believed that the size of the eventual Dynarim market was a key consideration in deciding where it should go. If it appeared that that market would be $50 million to $100 million, then Dynarim had grounds for becoming a new division. But if it looked more like a market of $5 million to $15 million, Prince believed it made more sense to "graft Dynarim onto an existing division," most likely Polyesters because "our ultimate customers are similar."

Reinhalter and Kennedy both favored continued separation of the two products. Surface similarities, they argued, were less important than differences in how the two were marketed, sold, distributed, and used. Therefore, Dynatech was best handled by Polyesters, while Dynarim would be better off as the core of a new division. RIM technology, they added, did not fit within the existing corporate structure, and was properly the basis of a new business unit. If a division like Polyesters were to absorb Dynarim, it would then have to add a significant number of RIM specialists—possibly absorbing most of Kennedy's group in the process.

Although Kennedy and Reinhalter felt the immediate issue was achieving commercial success with Dynarim, they knew such success would reopen the location issue. To create a new division, they would have to develop strong arguments favoring the separation of the two products.

Reading III–6
Managing the Internal Corporate Venturing Process: Some Recommendations for Practice

R. A. Burgelman

Internal corporate venturing (ICV) is an important avenue for corporate growth and diversification.[1] Systematic research, however, suggests that developing entirely new businesses in the context of established firms is very difficult even when a separate new venture division is created for this purpose.[2]

Stage Models of ICV

Typical conceptualizations of ICV use a "stage model" approach.[3] Stage models provide a framework for discussing many important problems concerning the sequential development of new ventures. They focus on within-stage problems as well as on issues pertaining to the transition between stages. They emphasize the different requirements of different stages in terms of key tasks, people, structural arrangements, leadership styles, and the like. The problems most naturally addressed in a stage model are the ones that are important in growing any new business. But, many of the more difficult problems generated and encountered by ICV result from growing a new business in the context of an established organization. They result from the fact that strategic activities related to ICV take place at different levels of management simultaneously. Such problems are not easily incorporated in a stage model and tend to be discussed only in somewhat cursory fashion.

A Process Model of ICV

Recently, I have proposed a new model based on the findings of an exploratory study of the complete process through which new ventures take shape in the context of the new venture division (NVD) in large, diversified firms.[4] Exhibit 1 shows the "process model" of ICV. The methodology of the study is briefly described in the Appendix.

Exhibit 1 shows the *core* processes of ICV as well as the *overlaying* processes (the corporate context) in which the core processes take shape. The core processes of ICV comprise the activities through which a new business becomes defined and its development gains impetus in the corporation. The core processes subsume the managerial problems and issues that are typically addressed in stage models of ICV. The overlaying processes comprise the activities through which the strategic and structural contexts are determined. Structural context refers to the various organizational and administrative mechanisms put in place by corporate management to implement the current corporate strategy. Strategic context refers to the process through which the current corporate strategy is extended to accommodate the new business resulting from ICV efforts. Both the core and overlaying processes involve key activities (the shaded area) and more peripheral activities (the nonshaded area), situated at different levels of the organization.

Major Problems in the ICV Process

The process model indicates that ICV involves the interlocking strategic activities of managers at differ-

Reprinted from *Sloan Management Review*, Winter 1984, vol. 25, no. 2, pp. 33–48, by permission of the publisher.

[1]An overview of different forms of corporate venturing is provided in E. B. Roberts, "New Ventures for Corporate Growth," *Harvard Business Review* 58 (July–August 1980), pp. 132–42.

[2]An overview of early studies on new ventures is provided in E. von Hippel, "Successful and Failing Internal Corporate Ventures: An Empirical Analysis," *Industrial Marketing Management* 6, pp. 163–74. Von Hippel has noted the great diversity of new venture practices. Some of this diversity, however, may be due to a somewhat unclear distinction between new product development and new business development. Von Hippel also identifies some key factors associated with success and failure of new ventures but does not document how the *process* takes shape.

Concerning the use of the new venture division (NVD) design, see N. D. Fast, "The Future of Industrial New Venture Departments," *Industrial Marketing Management* 8, pp. 264–79. Fast has observed the precarious, unstable function of NVD in many firms. He explains the evolution in terms of shifts in corporate strategy and/or in the political position of the NVD.

[3]For a recent example of a stage model, see J. R. Galbraith, "The Stages of Growth," *Journal of Business Strategy*, 1983.

[4]R. A. Burgelman, "A Process Model of Internal Corporate Venturing in the Diversified Major Firm," *Administrative Science Quarterly* 28 (1983), pp. 223–44.

EXHIBIT 1 Key and Peripheral Activities in a Process Model of ICV

(Shaded = Key activities)

Levels	Definition (Core processes)	Impetus (Core processes)	Strategic Context (Overlaying processes)	Structural Context (Overlaying processes)
Corporate management	Monitoring	Authorizing	Rationalizing (key)	Structuring (key)
New venture division management	Coaching Stewardship	Strategic building (key)	Organizational championing; Delineating (key)	Negotiating
Group leader/Venture manager	Technical and need linking (key)	Product championing; Strategic forcing (key)	Gatekeeping Idea generating Bootlegging	Questioning

(Selecting: spans Strategic Context and Structural Context between corporate management and new venture division management; Product championing and Organizational championing link across cells.)

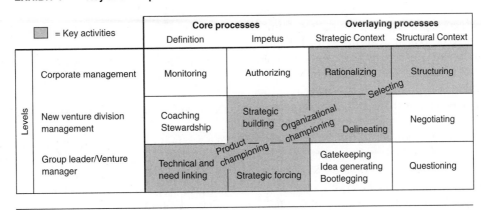

ent levels in the organization. These strategic activities are enacted without an existing master plan in which they all neatly fit together. Exhibit 2 provides an overview of some of the problematic aspects of the strategic situation at each level in each of the processes that constitute ICV.

Vicious Circles in the Definition Process

At the corporate level, managers tend to have a highly reliable frame of reference to evaluate business strategies and resource allocation proposals pertaining to the main lines of business of the cor-

EXHIBIT 2 Major Problems in the ICV Process

Levels	Definition (Core Processes)	Impetus (Core Processes)	Strategic Context (Overlaying Processes)	Structural Context (Overlaying Processes)
Corporate management	Top management lacks the capacity to assess the merits of specific new venture proposals for corporate development.	Top management relies on purely quantitative growth results to continue support for a new venture.	Top management considers ICV as insurance against mainstream business going bad. ICV objectives are ambiguous and shifting erratically.	Top management relies on reactive structural changes to deal with problems related to ICV.
NVD management	Middle-level managers in corporate R&D are not capable of coaching ICV project initiators.	Middle-level managers in new business development find it difficult to balance strategic building efforts with efforts to coach the venture managers.	Middle-level managers struggle to delineate the boundaries of a new business field. They spend significant amounts of time on political activities to maintain corporate support.	Middle-level managers struggle with unanticipated structural impediments to new venture activities. No incentive for star performers to engage in ICV activities.
Group leader Venture leader	Project initiators cannot convincingly demonstrate in advance that resources will be used effectively. They need to engage in scavenging to get resources.	Venture managers find it difficult to balance strategic forcing efforts with efforts to develop the administrative framework of the emerging ventures.	Project initiators do not have a clear idea which kind of ICV projects will be viable in the corporate context. Bootlegging is necessary to get a new idea tested.	Venture managers do not have a clear idea what type of performance will be rewarded except fast growth.

poration. By the same token, their capacity to deal with substantive issues of new business opportunities is limited, and their expectations concerning what can be accomplished in a short time framework is often somewhat unrealistic. Also, ICV proposals compete for scarce top management time. Their relatively small size combined with the relative difficulty in assessing their merit make it at the outset seem uneconomical for top management to allocate much of their time to them. Not surprisingly, top managers tend to *monitor* ICV activities from a distance.

Middle-level managers in corporate R&D (where new ventures usually originate) experience a tension between their resource *stewardship* and *coaching* responsibilities. Such managers tend to be most concerned about maintaining the integrity of the R&D work environment, which is quite different from a business-oriented work environment.[5] They are comfortable with managing relatively slow moving exploratory research projects and well-defined development projects. But they are reluctant to commit significant amounts of resources (especially people) to suddenly fast moving areas of new development activity which fall outside of the scope of their current plans and which have not yet demonstrated technical and commercial feasibility.

Operational-level managers typically struggle to conceptualize their still somewhat nebulous (at least to outsiders) business ideas, which makes communication with management difficult. The results of their *technical* and *need-linking* efforts often go against conventional corporate wisdom. They cannot clearly specify the development path of their projects, and cannot demonstrate in advance that the resources they need will be used effectively in uncharted domains.

Demonstrating technical feasibility

The lack of articulation between different levels of management results in a vicious circle in resource procurement. Resources can be obtained if technical feasibility is demonstrated, but demonstration itself requires resources. *Product championing* activities serve to break through this vicious circle. Using bootlegging and scavenging tactics, the successful project champion is able to provide positive information reassuring middle-level management and providing them with a basis for claiming support for ICV projects in their formal plans. This dynamic explains the somewhat surprising finding that middle-level managers often encourage and do not just tolerate such sub-rosa activities.

Demonstrating commercial feasibility

Even when a technically demonstrated product, process, or system exists, corporate management is often reluctant to start commercialization efforts because they are unsure about the firm's capabilities to effectively do so. To overcome such hesitancies, product champions engage in corner cutting: activities which deviate from the official corporate ways and means (e.g., contacting customers from other divisions for tryouts, hiring sales people in disguise). Or they may choose an approach that is more acceptable in the light of corporate management's concerns but which may not be optimal from the long-term strategic point of view (e.g., propose a joint venture with another firm).

Managerial Dilemmas in the Impetus Process

Product championing resulting in preliminary demonstration of technical and commercial viability of a new product, process, or system sets the stage for the impetus process. In the course of the impetus process, an ICV project receives "venture status," that is, it becomes a quasi-independent new business with its own budget and general manager. Often the product champion becomes the venture manager. Even though there are misgivings expressed about it, this happens naturally. First, for the product champion this constitutes the big, but also the only, reward. Second, there is usually just nobody else around who could take over and continue the momentum of the development process.

Continued impetus depends on the *strategic forcing* efforts of the venture manager level: attaining a significant sales volume and market share position within a limited time horizon.[6] Strategic forcing efforts center around the original product, process,

[5]These differences are discussed in greater depth in R. A. Burgelman, "Managing Innovating Systems: A Study of the Process of Internal Corporate Venturing," unpublished doctoral dissertation, Columbia University, 1980.

[6]The need for strategic forcing is also consistent with the findings that suggest that attaining large market share fast at the cost of early profitability is critical for venture survival. R. Biggadike, "The Risky Business of Diversification," *Harvard Business Review* 57 (May–June 1979), pp. 103–11.

or system. To implement a strategy of fast growth, the venture manager attracts generalist helpers who can cover a number of different functional areas reasonably well. With the growth of the venture organization and under competitive pressures due to product maturation, efficiency considerations become increasingly important. New functional managers are brought in to replace the generalists. They tend to emphasize the development of routines, standard operating procedures, and the establishment of an administrative framework for the venture. This, however, is time-consuming and detracts from the all-out efforts to grow fast. Thus, the venture manager is increasingly faced with a dilemmatic situation: continuing to force growth versus building the organization of the venture. Growth concerns tend to win out, and organization building is more or less purposefully neglected.

Whilst the venture manager creates a "beachhead" for the new business, the middle level engages in *strategic building* efforts to sustain the impetus process. Such efforts involve the conceptualization of a master strategy for the broader new field within which the venture can fit. They also involve the integration of projects existing elsewhere in the corporation and/or of small firms that can be acquired with the burgeoning venture. These efforts become increasingly important as the strategic forcing activities of the venture manager reach their limit. At the same time, the administrative problems created by the strategic forcing efforts require increasingly the attention of the venture manager's manager. Hence, like the venture manager, the middle-level manager is also confronted with a serious dilemma: focusing on expanding the scope of the new business versus spending time coaching the (often recalcitrant) venture manager and building the organization. Given the overwhelming importance of growth, the coaching activities and organization building tend to be more or less purposefully neglected.

Corporate-level management's decision to *authorize* further resource allocations to a new venture are to a large extent dependent on the credibility of the managers involved. Credibility, in turn, depends primarily on the quantitative results produced. Corporate management tends to develop somewhat unrealistic expectations about new ventures. They send strong signals concerning the importance of making an impact on the overall corporate position soon. This, not surprisingly, reinforces the emphasis of the middle and operational levels of management on achieving growth.

New product development lags behind

The lack of attention to building the administrative framework of the new venture prevents it from developing a continuous flow of new products. Lacking carefully designed relationships between R&D, engineering, marketing, and manufacturing, new product schedules are delayed and completed new products often show serious flaws.

The demise of the venture manager

Major discontinuities in new product development put more stress on the middle-level manager to find supplementary products elsewhere to help maintain the growth rate. This, in turn, leads to even less emphasis on coaching the venture manager. The new product development problems also tend to exacerbate the tensions between the venture manager and the functional managers. Eventually, the need to stabilize the venture organization is likely to lead to the demise of the venture manager.

The Indeterminate Strategic Context of ICV

The problems encountered in the core processes of ICV are more readily understood when examining the overlaying processes within which ICV development takes shape. Corporate management's objectives concerning ICV tend to be ambiguous. Top management does not really know which specific new businesses they want until the latter have taken some concrete form and size, and decisions must be made whether to integrate them or not in the corporate portfolio through a process of *retroactive rationalizing*.

Middle-level managers struggle with *delineating* the boundaries of a new business. They are aware that corporate management is interested in broadly defined areas like the "health field" or "energy." But it is only through the middle-level manager's strategic building and the concomitant articulation of a master strategy for the ongoing venture initiatives that the new business fields become concretely delineated and the possible new strategic directions determined.

At the operational level, managers engage in *gatekeeping, idea generating,* and preliminary *bootlegging* activities which may lead to the definition of ICV projects in new areas and/or in new business fields which are already emerging as a result of the ongoing ICV activities. These activities are autonomous because they are basically independent of the current strategy of the firm. Managers at this level have no clear idea at the outset which kinds of ICV projects will be viable in the corporation, but they seem to have a sense for avoiding those that have no chance of receiving support (e.g., because there have been some earlier failures in the area, or there are some potential legal liabilities associated with it).

Determining the strategic context

The indeterminateness of the strategic context of ICV requires middle-level managers to engage in *organizational championing* activities.[7] Such activities are of a political nature, and time-consuming. They require an upward orientation (as one venture manager put it) which is very different from the venture manager level's substantive and downward (hands-on) orientation. The middle-level manager must also spend time to work out the frictions with the operating system that may exist when the strategies of the venture and of mainstream businesses interfere with each other. The need for these activities tends to reduce further the amount of time and effort spent by the middle level on coaching the venture manager.

Oscillations of corporate strategy

New ventures take between 8 and 12 years on the average to become mature, profitable new businesses.[8] Top management's time horizon, however, is usually limited to three to five years. Corporate management's objectives tend to be shifting: new ventures are viewed by top management as insurance against mainstream business going bad rather than as a corporate objective per se.[9] Middle managers are aware that there are short-term windows for corporate acceptance which must be taken advantage of. This also puts pressure on them to grow new ventures as fast as possible.

The Selective Pressures of the Structural Context

Top management establishes a structural context to support the corporate strategy. The structural context provides strategic actors at operational and middle levels of management with signals concerning the types of projects that are likely to be supported and rewarded. It operates as a selection mechanism on the strategic behavior in the organization. ICV projects, by definition, fall outside the scope of the current corporate strategy and must overcome the selective pressures of the structural context.

The incompleteness of the structural context

Establishing a separate new venture division facilitates the definition and early impetus processes of ICV projects. But, by itself, the new venture division constitutes an incomplete structural context. In the absence of measurement and reward systems tailored specifically to the requirements of new venture activities, venture managers do not have a clear idea what performance is expected from them except in terms of reaching a large size for their new business fast. Middle-level managers of the new venture division experience resistance from managers in the operating divisions when activities overlap. Ad hoc negotiations and reliance on political savvy substitute for long-term based, joint optimization arrangements. This leads, eventually, to severe friction between ICV and mainstream business activities.[10]

Reactive changes in the structural context

When ICV activities expand beyond a level that corporate management finds opportune to support in light of their assessment of the prospects of mainstream business activities, or when some highly visible failures occur, changes are effected in the structural context to consolidate ICV activities. These changes seem reactive and indicative of the lack of a clear strategy for diversification in the firm.[11]

---

[7]The importance of the middle-level manager in ICV was already recognized by Von Hippel, "Successful and Failing Internal Corporate Ventures." I. Kusiatin, "The Process and Capacity for Diversification through Internal Development," unpublished doctoral dissertation, Harvard University, 1976; and M. A. Maidique, "Entrepreneurs, Champions, and Technological Innovations," *Sloan Management Review* 21, pp. 59–76, also have discussed the role of a "manager champion" or "executive champion."

[8]Biggadike, "The Risky Business."

[9]R. A. Peterson and D. G. Berger, "Entrepreneurship in Organizations: Evidence from the Popular Music Industry," *Administrative Science Quarterly* 16 (1971), pp. 97–106.

[10]These frictions are discussed in more detail in R. A. Burgelman, "Managing the New Venture Division: Research Findings and Implications for Strategic Management," *Strategic Management Journal* 6 (1985), pp. 39–54.

[11]Ibid.

EXHIBIT 3 Recommendations for Making ICV Strategy Work Better

		Core Processes		Overlaying Processes	
		Definition	Impetus	Strategic Context	Structural Context
Levels	Corporate management	ICV proposals are evaluated in light of corporate development strategy. Conscious efforts are made to avoid subjection to conventional corporate wisdom.	New venture progress is evaluated in substantive terms by top managers who have experience in organizational championing.	A process is in place for developing a long-term corporate development strategy. This strategy takes shape as a result of an ongoing interactive learning process involving top and middle levels of management.	Managers with successful ICV experience are appointed to top management. Top management is rewarded financially and symbolically for long-term corporate development success.
	NVD management	Middle-level managers in corporate R&D are selected who have both technical depth and business knowledge necessary to determine minimum amount of resources for project, and who can coach star players.	Middle-level managers are responsible for the use and development of venture managers as scarce resources of the corporation, and facilitate intrafirm project transfers if the new business strategy warrants it.	Substantive interaction between corporate- and middle-level management leads to clarifying the merits of a new business field in light of the corporate development strategy.	Star performers at middle level are attracted to ICV activities. Collaboration of mainstream middle level with ICV activities is rewarded. Integrating mechanisms can easily be mobilized.
	Group leader Venture leader	Project initiators are encouraged to integrate technical and business perspectives. They are provided access to resources. Project initiators can be rewarded other than by becoming venture managers.	Venture managers are responsible for developing the functional capabilities of emerging venture organizations, and for codification of what has been learned in terms of required functional capabilities while pursuing the new business opportunity.	Slack resources determine the level of the emergence of mutant ideas. Existence of substantive corporate development strategy provides preliminary self-selection of mutant ideas.	A wide array of venture structures and supporting measurement and reward systems clarifies expected performance for ICV personnel.

Managing the Corporate Context of ICV

The process model suggests that, at the corporate level of analysis, ICV is based on *experimentation and selection,* not a strategic planning process.[12] It is characterized by ambiguity, discontinuity, even an element of anarchy. Having identified some of the major problems in the ICV process, recommendations for improving the strategic management of ICV can be proposed. These can serve to alleviate, if not eliminate, these problems by making the corporate context more hospitable to ICV. Improvement of the overlaying process will, presumably, allow management to focus more on the problems that are inherent in the core processes and less on those that result from having to "fight the system." Exhibit 3 summarizes the recommendations.

Elaborating the Strategic Context of ICV

Top management should recognize that ICV is an important source of strategic renewal for the firm, and not just insurance against poor mainstream

[12]This argument is further developed in R. A. Burgelman, "Corporate Entrepreneurship and Strategic Management: Insights from a Process Study," *Management Science* 29 (1983), pp. 1349–64.

business prospects. ICV should therefore be considered an integral and continuous part of the strategy-making process.

The need for a corporate development strategy

To dampen the oscillations in corporate support for ICV, top management should create a process for developing an explicit and substantive long-term (10 to 12 years) strategy for corporate development, supported by a resource generation and allocation strategy. Both should be based on ongoing efforts to determine the remaining growth opportunities in the current mainstream businesses and the resource levels necessary to exploit them. Given the corporate objectives for growth and profitability, a resource pool should be reserved for activities outside the mainstream business. This pool should not be affected by short-term fluctuations in current mainstream activities. ICV as well as other types of activities (e.g., acquisitions) should be funded out of this pool. The existence of this pool of slack resources would allow top management to affect the rate at which new venture initiatives will emerge, if not their particular content.[13] This approach reflects a broader concept of strategy making than maintaining corporate R&D at a certain percentage of sales.

Substantive assessment of venture strategies

To more effectively determine the strategic context of ICV, and to reduce the political emphasis in organizational championing activities, top management should increase its capacity to make substantive assessments of the merits of new ventures for corporate development. Top management should learn to assess better the strategic importance to corporate development and the degree of relatedness to core corporate capabilities of ICV projects.[14]

One way to achieve this capability is for top management to include members with significant experience in new business development in the top management team. In addition, top management should require middle-level organizational champions to explain how a new field of business would further the corporate development objectives in *substantive* rather than purely numerical terms. Middle-level managers should have to explain how they create value from the *corporate point of view* with the new ventures they sponsor. Operational-level managers would then have a better chance to find out early which of the possible directions their envisaged projects could take will be more likely to receive corporate support.

Such increased emphasis on the part of top management would not necessarily mean having greater input in the specific directions of exploratory corporate R&D. Rather, it would increase their influence on the *business directions* that grow out of the exploratory R&D substratum.

Refining the Structural Context

Top management also needs to fine-tune the structural context and make it more compatible with the requirements of ICV.

More deliberate use of the new venture division (NVD)

Often, the NVD becomes the recipient of "misfit" and "orphan" projects existing in the operating system, and serves as the trial ground for possibly ill-conceived business ideas of the corporate R&D department. In some instances, greater efforts would seem to be in order to assess the possibilities of accommodating new venture initiatives in the mainstream businesses rather than transferring them to the NVD. In other instances, projects should be developed using external venture arrangements or be spun off. Such decisions should be based on an examination of where a project fits in the strategic context. They should be easily implementable by having a wide range of structures for venture-corporation relationships available.

Also, the NVD is a mechanism for *decoupling* the activities of new ventures and those of mainstream businesses. But, this decoupling usually cannot be perfect. Hence, integrative mechanisms (e.g., "steering committees") should be established to deal constructively with conflicts that will unavoidably and unpredictably arise.

---

[13]Ibid.

[14]These two dimensions would seem to be important in deciding what type of arrangements to use. For instance, high strategic importance and high degree of relatedness might suggest the need to integrate the new project directly into the mainstream businesses (even if there is resistance). Very low strategic importance and very low degree of relatedness might suggest complete spin-off as the best approach. The NVD would seem to be most adequate for more ambiguous situations on both dimensions.

Finally, top management should facilitate greater acceptance of differences between the management processes of the NVD and the mainstream businesses. This may lead, for instance, to more careful personnel assignment policies and to greater flexibility in hiring and firing policies in the NVD to reflect the special needs of emerging businesses.

Such measures to use the NVD more deliberately (and selectively) will reduce the likelihood of reactive changes in the structural context.

Measurement and reward systems in support of ICV

Perhaps the most difficult aspect of the structural context concerns how to provide incentives for top management to seriously and continuously support ICV as part of corporate strategy making. Corporate history writing might be an effective mechanism to achieve this. This would involve the careful tracing and periodical publication (e.g., a special section in annual reports) of decisions whose positive or negative results may become clear only 10 or more years after the fact. Corporate leaders (like political ones) would, presumably, make efforts to preserve their position in corporate history.[15]

To reduce the destructive emphasis on fast growth at middle and operational levels of management, the measurement and reward system must be tailored to the special nature of the managerial work involved in ICV. This would mean, for instance, greater emphasis on accomplishments in the areas of problem finding, problem solving, and know-how development than on volume of dollars managed. Efforts to develop the venture organization and the venture manager should also be included. These measures will alleviate the problems resulting from the pressures to grow fast, and more emphasis will be given by middle managers to coaching their venture managers, and to the administrative development problems of new ventures which otherwise tend to be neglected. More flexible systems for measuring and rewarding performance should accompany the greater flexibility in structuring the venture-corporate relations mentioned earlier. In general, the higher the degree of relatedness (the more dependent the new venture is on the firm's resources) and the lower the expected strategic importance for corporate development, the lower the rewards the internal entrepreneurs will be able to negotiate. Milestone points could be agreed upon to revise the negotiations as the venture evolves. To make such processes symmetrical (and more acceptable to the nonentrepreneurial participants in the organization), the internal entrepreneurs should be required to substitute negotiated for regular membership awards and benefits.

Furthermore, to attract "top performers" in the mainstream businesses of the corporation to ICV activities, at least a few spots on the top management team should always be filled with managers who have had significant experience in new business development. This will facilitate the determination of the strategic context and will eliminate the perception that NVD participants are not part of the real world and thus have not much chance to advance in the corporation as a result of ICV experience.[16]

At the operational level, where some managerial failures are virtually unavoidable given the experimentation and selection nature of the ICV process, top management should create a reasonably foolproof safety net. Product champions at this level should not have to feel that running the business is the only possible reward for getting it started. Systematic search for and screening of potential venture managers should make it easier to provide a successor for the product champion *in time*. Avenues for recycling product champions/venture managers should be developed and/or their reentry into the mainstream businesses facilitated.

Managing the Core Processes of ICV

Increasing top management's capacity to manage the corporate context of ICV will, in turn, facilitate the management of the core processes of ICV development. To alleviate some of the specific problems mentioned earlier, some further recommendations can be proposed.

[15]Some firms seem to have developed the position of corporate historian. Without underestimating the difficulties such a position is likely to encounter, one can imagine the possibility of structuring it in such a way that the relevant data would be recorded. Another instance, possibly a board-appointed committee, could periodically interpret this data along the lines suggested.

[16]As some people in my study pointed out, there is no need to take the risks of new business development if you are identified as a star performer. Such performers are put in charge of the large, established businesses where their capabilities will presumably have maximum leverage.

Managing the Definition Process

The ICV projects in my study typically started with an initiative at the group leader level (first-level supervisor) in the corporate R&D department. Such initiatives were rooted in the periphery of the corporate technological capabilities, reflected the creative insight and entrepreneurial drive of the initiator, and were influenced by the latter's perception of the chances of getting the venture eventually accepted by top management as a major new area for the firm.

Of the many ICV projects that start the definition process, only a few reach "venture" status. Some of the ones that do not make it to that transition may find a home for further development as a new product line in one of the operating divisions; others may just be stopped, and result only in an extension of the corporation's knowledge base. Some of the ones that do not make it, however, could possibly have succeeded, and some of the ones that do obtain venture status should not have. Timely assessment of the true potential of an ICV project remains a difficult problem. This follows from the very nature of such projects: the many uncertainties around the technical and marketing aspects of the new business, and the fact that each case is significantly different from all others. These factors make it quite difficult to develop standardized evaluation procedures and development programs without screening to death truly innovative projects.

Managing the definition process effectively thus poses serious challenges for middle-level managers in the corporate R&D department. They must facilitate the integration of technical and business perspectives, and must maintain a lifeline to the technology developed in corporate R&D as the project takes off. As stated earlier, the need for product championing efforts, if excessive, may cut that lifeline early on and lead to severe discontinuities in new product development after the project has reached the venture stage. The middle-level manager's efforts must facilitate both the product championing efforts and the continued development of the technology base, by putting the former in perspective and by making sure that the interface between R&D and business people works smoothly.

Facilitating the integration of R&D—business perspectives

To facilitate the integration of technical and business perspectives, the middle manager must understand the operating logic of both groups and must avoid getting bogged down in technical details, yet have sufficient technical depth to be respected by the R&D people. Such managers must be able to motivate the R&D people to collaborate with the business people toward the formulation of business objectives against which progress can be measured. The articulation of business objectives is especially important for the venture's relations with corporate management if the latter become more actively involved in ICV and develop a greater capacity to evaluate the fit of new projects with the corporate development strategy.

Middle-level managers in R&D must be capable to make the two groups give and take in a process of mutual adjustment toward the common goal of advancing the progress of the new business project. One of the key things here is creating mutual respect between technical and business people. Example setting by the R&D manager of showing respect for the business people's contribution is likely to have a carryover effect on the attitudes of the other R&D people. Regular meetings between the two groups to evaluate, as peers, the contribution of the different members of the team is likely to lead to much better integrated efforts.

The middle manager as coach

Such meetings also provide a vehicle for better coaching the product champion. The latter is really the motor of the ICV project in this stage of development. There are some similarities between this role and that of the star player in a sports team. Often, the situation with respect to product champions as star players is viewed in either-or terms: either they can do their thing, and then chances are that we will succeed, but there will be discontinuities, not fully exploited ancillary opportunities, and so on; or, we harness them, and they won't play.

A more balanced approach is possible if the R&D manager uses a process in which the product champion is recognized as the star player, but is, at times, challenged to maintain breadth by having to respond to queries like:

- How is the team benefiting more from this particular action than from others that the team may think to be important?
- How will the continuity of the efforts of the team be preserved?
- What will be the next step?

To back up this approach, the middle manager should have a say in how to reward the members on the team differently. This, of course, refers back to the determination of the structural context, and reemphasizes the importance at the corporate level to recognize that different reward systems are necessary for different types of business activities.

Managing the Impetus Process

Pursuing fast growth and administrative development of the venture simultaneously is a major challenge during the impetus process. This challenge, which exists for any start-up business, is especially difficult for one in the context of an established firm. This is so because managers in ICV, typically, have less control over the selection of key venture personnel yet, at the same time, have more ready access to a wide array of corporate resources.[17] Thus, there is much less pressure on the venture manager and the middle-level manager to show progress in building the organization than there is to show growth.

The venture manager as organization builder

A more adequate measurement and reward system should force the venture manager to balance the two concerns better. The venture manager should have leeway in hiring and firing decisions but should also be held responsible for the development of new functional capabilities and the administrative framework of the venture. This would reduce the probability of major discontinuities in new product development mentioned earlier. In addition, it will provide the corporation with codified know-how and information which can be transferred to other parts of the firm, or to other new ventures even if the one from which it is derived ultimately fails as a business. Know-how and information thus become important outputs of the ICV process, in addition to sales and profit dollars.

Often, the product champion will not have the required capabilities to achieve these additional objectives. In such cases, the product champion should be warned that the business will probably have to be taken away from him or her at some later date unless the capability to handle the growing complexity of the new business organization is demonstrated. The availability of compensatory rewards and of avenues for recycling the venture manager would make it possible for management to tackle deteriorating managerial conditions in the new business organization with greater fortitude. Furthermore, the availability of a competent replacement (as a result of systematic corporate search) may induce the product champion to relinquish the venture rather than see it go under.

The middle-level manager as corporate strategist

Increasing the capacity of top management to assess new venture projects will reduce the need for organizational championing and free up time for the middle-level manager for more intensive coaching of the venture manager in his or her efforts to build the venture organization. This aspect of the middle-level manager's job should also be more explicitly considered in the measurement and reward system at this level.

The encouragement of star performers at the middle level to get involved in new business development will also enhance their key role in the development of corporate strategy. By getting deeply involved in new business development, such middle-level managers will not only learn to manage the ICV process, they will also get to know the new businesses which may be part of the mainstream by the time they reach top-level positions. Because new ventures often intersect with multiple parts of mainstream businesses, they will learn what the corporate capabilities and skills—and the shortcomings in them—are, and learn to articulate new strategies and build new businesses based on new combinations of corporate capabilities and skills. This, in turn, may also enhance the realization of the possibilities for new operational synergies existing in the firm. Middle-level managers thus become crucial linking and technology transfer mechanisms in the corporation.

Conclusion: No Panaceas

The recommendations presented in this paper may make the ICV development a better managed process, that is, one less completely governed by the process of "natural selection." Yet, the implication is not that this process can or should become a

---

[17]Often, new ventures seem to be used for assigning personnel who do not fit well in the mainstream businesses (or are out of a job there).

planned one; or, that the fundamentally discontinuous nature of entrepreneurial activity can be avoided. Ultimately, ICV remains an uncomfortable process for the large, complex organization as it upsets its carefully evolved routines and planning mechanisms, threatens its internal equilibrium of interests, and requires a revision of the very image it has of itself.

The motor of corporate innovation consists of the strategic behaviors of individuals at different levels, willing to put their reputation and their career on the line in the pursuit of the big opportunity. As individuals, they act against and/or in spite of the system; not because they value corner cutting and risk taking per se, but because they must respond to the logic of the situation. And for radical innovation to take place, that logic entails—as Schumpeter posited some 70 years ago—the escape from routine, that is, from the very stuff of which large, complex organizations traditionally are made. Yet, the success of such innovations is ultimately dependent on whether they can become institutionalized. This may pose the most important challenge for managers of large, established firms in the 1980s.

This paper has proposed that managers can make a strategy involving radical innovations work better if they increase their capacity to conceptualize the organization's innovation efforts in process model terms. The recommendations, based on this point of view, should result in a somewhat better use of the individual entrepreneurial resources of the corporation, and thereby in an improvement of the corporate entrepreneurial capability.

APPENDIX: A FIELD STUDY OF ICV

A qualitative method was chosen as the best way to arrive at an encompassing view of the ICV process.

Research Setting

The research was carried out in one large, U.S.-based, high-technology firm of the diversified major type which I shall refer to as GAMMA. GAMMA had traditionally produced and sold various commodities in large volume, but it had also tried to diversify through the internal development of new products, processes, and systems so as to get closer to the final user or consumer and to catch a greater portion of the total value added in the chain from raw materials to end products. During the 1960s, diversification efforts were carried out within existing operating divisions, but in the early 1970s, the company established a separate new venture division (NVD).

Data were obtained on the functioning of the NVD. The charters of its various departments, the job descriptions of the major positions in the division, the reporting relationships and mechanisms of coordination, and the reward system were studied. Data were also obtained on the relationships of the NVD with the rest of the corporation. In particular, the collaboration between the corporate R&D department and divisional R&D groups was studied. Finally, data were also obtained on the role of the NVD in the implementation of the corporate strategy of unrelated diversification. These data describe the historical evolution of the structural context of ICV development at GAMMA before and during the research period.

The bulk of the data was collected in studying the six major ICV projects in progress at GAMMA at the time of the research. These ranged from a case where the business objectives were still being defined to one where the venture had reached a sales volume of $35 million.

Data Collection

In addition to the participants in the six ICV projects, I interviewed NVD administrators, people from several operating divisions, and one person from corporate management. All in all, 61 people were interviewed. The interviews were unstructured and took from one and a half to four and a half hours. Tape recordings were not made, but the interviewer took notes in shorthand. The interviewer usually began with an open-ended invitation to tell about work-related activities, then directed the discussion toward three major aspects of the ICV development process: (1) the evolution over time of a project, (2) the involvement of different functional groups in the development process, and (3) the involvement of different hierarchical levels in the development process. Respondents were asked to link particular statements they made to statements of other respondents on the same issues or problems and to give examples, where appropriate. After completing an interview, the interviewer made a typewritten copy of the conversation. All in all, about 435 legal-size pages of typewritten field notes resulted from these interviews.

The research also involved the study of documents. As could be expected, the ICV project participants relied little on written procedures in their day-to-day working relationships with other participants. One key set of documents, however, was the set of written corporate long-range plans concerning the NVD and each of the ICV projects. These official descriptions of the evolution of each project between 1973 and 1977 were compared with the interview data.

Finally, occasional behavioral observations were made, for example, when other people would call or stop by during an interview or in informal discussions during lunch at the research site. These observations, though not systematic, led to the formulation of new questions for further interviews.

Case III–7
Medical Equipment (A)

R. A. Burgelman and T. J. Kosnik

Introduction

In January 1977, Daniel Burns was confronted with a thorny situation as he assumed his new responsibilities as director of Gamma Corporation's New Venture Division (NVD). Burns had been asked to review the performance of each of the projects underway in the NVD and to decide what actions, if any, were needed. One venture, the Medical Equipment Project, had experienced explosive growth in the early 1970s. However, the drastic increase in revenues had not been accomplished without problems. During the course of his evaluation, Burns discussed the history of Medical Equipment with Dr. Stephen Sherwood, the venture manager. He also consulted with Dr. Franz Korbin, who had managed Sherwood's efforts for several years before Burns had arrived. In the course of his discussions with other individuals within and outside Medical Equipment, Burns gained additional observations.

Burns was reviewing those conversations as he prepared for his meeting with Dr. Korbin. He had asked Korbin to come to the meeting with recommendations about what should be done with Medical Equipment and with Dr. Sherwood. Burns wondered what Korbin might recommend. He was also thinking through what his options were in response to Korbin's potential suggestions.

Gamma Corporation and the New Venture Division

Gamma Corporation is a multibillion dollar U.S.-based industrial company. It started out as a holding company and operated for many years as a group of relatively autonomous components with limited direction from top management. The change from a holding company to a more integrated diversified firm occurred gradually through the 1960s. This integration was formalized through the adoption in the early 1970s of a comprehensive long-term program to improve all elements of human resources and business management. In recent years, a formal, unified management system has been instituted throughout the corporation. In the context of this new system, the operating components of Gamma develop interlocking objectives that are consistent with overall corporate objectives and goals. Gamma's Management Committee, with the support of the executive staff, oversees this process. It is deeply involved in setting overall direction, and monitors the evolution of business strategies and the allocation of capital.

The implementation of a uniform corporate management system was paralleled by an effort to introduce a uniform, integrated strategic planning approach for the management of Gamma's businesses. Gamma's businesses are now organized into strategic business units (SBUs). More than 150 SBUs are divided into six categories according to the criteria of present and expected future performance in terms of profitability, growth rate, and competitive position. The first four categories represent ongoing businesses offering successively lower gradations of business strength and potential. The fifth category represents business areas where withdrawal is indicated. The sixth is made up of emerging new businesses.

This large agglomeration of widely diversified but partially related businesses is grouped into a dozen major operational divisions under the administrative umbrella of corporate management and its executive staff.

Gamma's Unrelated Diversification Efforts

In view of its strategy of relying on the development of a "sustainable technical advantage" to compete in a particular market, Gamma has consistently spent vast amounts of resources on R&D activities both at the divisional and corporate levels. As a result, the firm has one of the highest records of obtaining annual awards for significant technological developments. The bulk of Gamma's business, however, traditionally consists of selling "commodities" and "intermediates" to major firms in the steel, auto, construction, appliance, textile, pharmaceuticals, and food industries, among others. Gamma's direct contacts with final consumers or users, though substantial in an absolute sense, have constituted a relatively minor part of its business.

During the late 1960s, corporate management wished to dampen the effects of the business cycle on Gamma's activities, to protect itself from the long-range threats to its basic commodities and intermediate businesses, and to catch a greater part of the value added in the chain from raw materials to finished products. As a result, Gamma became interested in developing new business opportunities in unrelated areas, especially in the direction toward reaching the final consumer or user.

Before the creation of the New Venture Division (NVD) in 1970, such unrelated diversification efforts were carried out in the context of the operating divisions, with the help of the corporate R&D department. But, by the end of the 1960s, corporate management had become increasingly concerned about the relevance of the corporate R&D efforts for future growth and diversification in unrelated areas, and about its ability to turn new ideas into new businesses through the divisions.

The New Venture Division

By 1970, a separate group was formed for the corporate development efforts. At the outset, this group was loosely organized. It encompassed New Business Development (NBD) and New Business Research (NBR) departments. In 1971, the corporate R&D (CR) department was integrated into this group. The heads of all these departments reported directly to the corporate vice president for technology. Initially, the idea was to generate new technical projects in the corporate R&D department, manage them through a development phase, and then transfer them as new departments to existing divisions, or grow them into new free-standing divisions.

The new NBD department comprised the Gascoal, Firefit, Environmental Systems, Farming Systems, Sea Products, and Medical Equipment Projects. These six projects were managed as new ventures with their own organizations under the supervision of the NBD manager.

During 1973, the concept of a New Venture Division (NVD) took clearer shape. The appointment of a first NVD director, to whom the NBD, NBR, and CR departments now reported, resulted in a more integrated management structure for the NVD. Don Sharp, the newly appointed NVD director, had been the NBD department head before taking up his new responsibilities. He was replaced as NBD manager by Dr. Franz Korbin. Exhibit 1 illustrates this management structure as it existed in January of 1973.

Don Sharp and Franz Korbin were generally considered among the top-notch managers in the entire corporation. They were consistently referred to as brilliant conceptualizers and strategists, as the typical high-level entrepreneurial managers. One observer articulated their philosophy:

> Sharp's and Korbin's approach was for you to learn while you are doing. Once you have a strategic concept you should start something, push it on its feet, and let it run and grow fast and thereby secure continued support from top management.

EXHIBIT 1 **Gamma Corporation: New Venture Division Organization Chart**

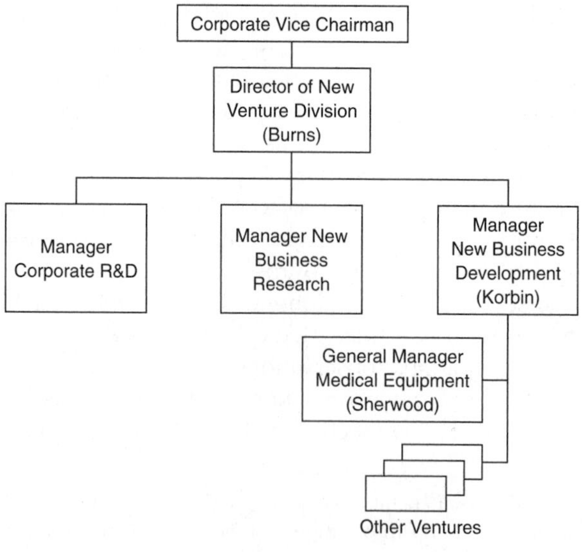

In this philosophy, the role of the entrepreneurial venture manager was very important. It encouraged strategic initiatives at lower levels, and allowed people to run hard within the as yet vaguely delineated boundaries of new business arenas.

However, by the end of 1976, the point had been reached where the number of projects and the total amount of required resources surpassed the corporation's readiness to absorb and fund. In view of a perceived need for consolidating the unrelated diversification efforts, corporate management promoted Don Sharp to the presidency of one of the operating divisions and brought Dan Burns in as the new NVD director in January of 1977. Burns was generally known in the corporation as the solid business type: realistic, cautious, and oriented towards "the numbers." He was expected to pull things together more, to establish a managerial rather than an entrepreneurial style throughout the NVD.

The Medical Equipment (ME) Venture

Burns was aware that Gamma Corporation had been interested in the health care field for many years. As early as the 1960s, the company had acquired a pharmaceuticals firm. Although that firm was subsequently divested in the 1968–69 recession, it provided part of the seeds from which the Medical Equipment Venture emerged. Other seeds included the company's experience in producing chemical reagents, nuclear medicine equipment, and electronic gear.

Evolution of the Project

From his conversation with Korbin, Sherwood, and others, and from a detailed study of the written long-range plans for the venture in the period 1973–76, Burns had obtained a fairly clear chronology of the venture's development. Exhibit 2 provides an overview of the evolution of the venture's sales volume and net income in the period 1970–77.

In 1968, Dr. Stephen Sherwood and several associates developed a business plan for a venture to take advantage of various technologies available within Gamma for measurement instruments. An instruments department was formed in the Electronics Division, and they began to explore potential high-growth areas, including the medical instrumentation business. At the same time, although the pharmaceutical company was divested, Gamma kept the medical instruments part of that firm.

The corporate R&D group of Gamma was interested in exploring the medical instruments area. When in 1969 the recession forced a reduction in the resource allocation to instruments in the Electronics Division, Sherwood was transferred to corporate R&D where he continued to explore potential applications in the medical technology area.

At a think tank session in R&D, another scientist mentioned a novel idea for a computerized blood analyzer. The idea was for a clinical centrifugal analyzer. In Sherwood's words,

> [It was] . . . an entirely new concept—not at all a me-too type of product. So I made some proposals that were accepted. The other scientist had very fixed ideas about how the product should look as a commercial product. But I had experience in commercial computers and knew the need to match a technology with a market configuration . . . that you must develop a "needs oriented" approach. As the project manager, I insisted on doing market research. . . . We ended with a radical departure from the original approach. We used only the nucleus of the physical concepts.

For the first three years, the Medical Equipment Project was essentially focused on the development of one product: the blood analyzer, which was named the ANABASE system. Later, other products and projects were added. However, the ANABASE system was still the mainstay of the business in 1976.

EXHIBIT 2 Evolution of Sales and Net Income, 1970–1977 (in thousands of dollars)

	1970	1971	1972	1973	1974	1975	1976	1977	1978
Sales	700	1,200	2,000	5,000	10,000	18,000	32,000	40,000*	60,000*
Net income	(470)†	(720)†	(760)†	(720)†	(1,000)†	(860)†	330†	350*	3,000*

*Estimated.
†Exclusive related corporate R&D expenditures.

In 1972, Sherwood proposed to sell the ANABASE system via a sales force specifically for the Medical Equipment Project. He met with organizational resistance, partly because management of Gamma was unsure of its ability to market to medical institutions.

Sherwood had told Burns:

> When we proposed to sell the ANABASE product by our own selling force, there was a lot of resistance out of ignorance. Management did numerous studies, had outside consultants on which they spent tens of thousands of dollars; they looked at XYZ Company for a possible partnership.
>
> Management was just very unsure about its marketing capability. I proposed to have a test marketing phase with 20 to 25 installations in the field. We built our own service group; we pulled ourselves up by the "bootstraps." I guess we had more guts than sense.

By 1973, corporate management began to realize the substantial potential of the ANABASE business, and a new competitive arena was defined by the management of the New Venture Division (NVD) and endorsed by corporate management. According to the corporate long-range plan of 1973, the corporation wanted to

> become a leading supplier of coordinated mechanical systems and related products in a market currently dependent on manpower, and limited annual operations for clinical testing in hospitals and private laboratories.

In 1974, the project obtained official venture status, and moved to the jurisdiction of the New Business Development department (NBD) in the NVD. Dr. Sherwood reported there to Dr. Korbin. During 1974, the ME venture continued to grow very rapidly because of the market success of the ANABASE system domestically and internationally, leading to a doubling of the 1973 $5 million sales volume. The newly formed ME venture encompassed, in addition to the ANABASE project and the selling of reagents, a radio-diagnostic product line and immunoassay technology. The backbone of the venture in terms of sales volume, however, was formed by the ANABASE system.

During 1975, the business strategy for the ME arena continued to be based primarily on market penetration with the ANABASE system, which had been further improved and expanded to include computerized data processing components. Sales volume reached over $15 million for the year. The venture's development efforts were primarily absorbed in the straightening out of product quality problems with the ANABASE product.

The further development of the biomedical technology (hardware and reagents) remained the responsibility of the corporate R&D department. Korbin and Sherwood recognized that these continued efforts would be very important for the venture to be able to reach the corporate objectives in terms of size for new ventures.

New product development for the ME arena, started in 1973, had resulted in the introduction of the ANALYZ automated immunoassay system for tests involving hormones, steroids, and therapeutic drugs, and in a radio-diagnostic product line for the detection of pathology of organs. These new products for the ME arena differed from the ANABASE product in that they attempted to conform more closely to an "integrated systems" approach, which had become the keystone of the ME arena strategy:

> Whereas ANABASE was designed to utilize reagents available from multiple sources in relatively low dollar volumes, subsequent products have been designed to utilize consumables primarily and in much higher dollar volumes, relative to those of the hardware. The use of sole-source consumables is traditionally repugnant to most customers, so it was necessary to demonstrate strong credibility in the marketplace before moving too far in that direction. Present indications suggest the achievement of that credibility.

By 1975, the ME venture had identified the key characteristics of the new business field in which it was operating: high technology; pull-through demand engendered by public desire for health care; cost and efficiency pressures; strong regulatory pressures; high competition from largely fragmented and specialized suppliers. These characteristics reinforced the importance of the "systems approach" articulated by venture management for the ME field:

> The development of automated methods with consumables, service, and education to maximize reliability, efficiency, and economy for the users.

Korbin and Sherwood showed a strong awareness of the continued importance of the marketing function, and the dangers of becoming technology and/or facilities oriented. They were explicit in stating what they perceived to be the key to success for the venture in the 1975 long-range plan:

> Success is dependent on the ability to identify needs sufficiently in advance of their realization to permit the long lead times associated with high technology and cumbersome regulations.

In response to concerns about too limited a product range for the ME venture, there had been efforts to look around in the company for other, health-related projects which might be agglomerated with the venture. A major new arena concerned "blood banking," for which applicable technology was being developed in two different divisions.

In 1975, it also became clear that the future growth of the ME arena would be accomplished through products acquired from outside the corporation rather than exclusively from internal development. The venture was expected to be able to make such acquisitions because of its capability to offer private inventors or small companies strong marketing organization and product engineering functions. Imaging instrumentation and microbiological applications were envisaged to offer good opportunities in this respect. The choice of the imaging arena highlights the growth in understanding the nature of the opportunities in the ME field. The long-range plan stated:

> The "imaging" arena breaks down the classical separation between radiology, nuclear medicine, and other disciplines, just as ANALYZ breaks down the dichotomy between nuclear medicine and pathology; and our planned activities in microbiology are likely to cross into the hematology segment. Such states of market flux, or discontinuities, are prime targets for rapid growth in the ME business strategy.

Still another new arena concerning support devices for patients—ranging from artificial hip joints to artificial organs—was identified in 1975 as one where a systems approach would be feasible. The exact content of this arena had not yet been defined, but it was already clear that the opportunities in the low end of the technology spectrum would be marginal. As with the ANABASE product and with a particular product in the blood banking arena, management envisioned that here, too, a first product based on entirely new technology would serve as the nucleus around which a variety of other products could evolve.

During 1976, the acquisition of a company with imaging technology was accomplished. Initial reaction to ANALYZ seemed favorable. A new radiodiagnostic product line had also been favorably received by customers, even though slower penetration than for ANALYZ was expected. For the patient support devices arena, the strategic design was more clearly articulated during 1976. The potential for value upgrading of traditional raw materials was perceived to be great.

The ME venture continued to grow very rapidly, with sales of over $30 million for the year. During 1976, the ANABASE product line was reaching a stage of maturity. Sales for this product alone were more than $20 million.

The outlook for the future was quite optimistic in 1976. It was expected that the new government administration would mark the advent of "national health insurance," which would lead to an expected increase in diagnostic testing expenditures of 150 percent in 1980 over the 1975 forecast, and would result in substantial changes in health care delivery patterns. This anticipated change led to a further refinement of the original arena's new product development strategy:

> Product development strategies are setting objectives for small, freestanding, fast, discretionary, low-skilled labor systems which can be combined to allow higher-capacity systems for the hospital setting with high reliability through redundancy.

For 1977, the new blood bank product line was expected to begin penetrating the market. Still another product, for rapid cardiac diagnosis, was scheduled to be introduced during 1977. The latter product was oriented toward a first penetration of the physician's office and the clinical, rather than therapeutic, segment of the market. Sales volume was expected to reach $40 million. Even if the venture would absorb all related corporate R&D expenditures, management expected to show a small profit for the year.

Roles of Key Players in the Development Process

Burns also had tried to develop a clear understanding of the specific contribution of Korbin and Sherwood in the development of the Medical Equipment Venture. In an earlier conversation, Sherwood had explained to Burns that there had been three phases in the development from a prototype product to commercially viable large-scale production of the ANABASE system. First was the technology development stage, in which the various new technologies were integrated, tested, and refined to produce a system that was reliable and easy to use. That phase took nearly three years. To some extent, technology development continued throughout the product life cycle as problems were discovered and enhancements were made. For example, the number of samples that the system was able to analyze simultaneously was increased in later models. In addition, the data processing capabilities of the system for the handling of patient records throughout the laboratory test process had been enhanced.

The second phase was market development. During that period, the contacts were made in the medical community which were necessary for the introduction and testing of the new product. Announcements about the product and its capabilities were made to the public. In the case of ANABASE, the first product announcements were made before Sherwood and his colleagues were certain about how the commercial product would actually function. As part of the market development phase, versions of the system were installed and tested in the field. These "beta test sites" provided the Medical Equipment Project with valuable information about how to improve the system that was to be offered during the subsequent phase.

The third phase of the process was commercialization. During that period, the manufacturing capability to produce the product in volume was established, and thoroughly tested systems were shipped to customer sites.

Dr. Sherwood had shared his views about that part of the process:

> Commercial development is a continuum, stretching over a three- to five-year period. That must be an integrated process, a continuous path. When you have different groups with different organizational barriers, you have problems. For instance, between production engineers and the people who look for a product adequate for the market. I want to generate an organization that would make that continuous process possible.

Daniel Burns realized that a large amount of the credit for the development of the Medical Products Venture to a $30 million business belonged to Dr. Sherwood. At the same time, the business was experiencing difficulties that seemed to be getting more acute as it grew larger.

Sherwood's role had been similar in some ways to that of an entrepreneur starting a new business. He had had to find the resources from within and outside Gamma Corporation to propel the ANABASE project through the technological development and market development phases to commercialization. He worked long hours throughout the process, driving the people who worked for him to do the same. He was, in the eyes of everyone with whom Burns met, the champion of the ANABASE product line. His single-minded commitment to the success of the project had forced the team over some difficult hurdles.

However, Sherwood was, like many entrepreneurs, not oriented toward long-term strategic thinking. In the words of one of his subordinates:

> Some of the problems probably relate to being a new venture and reaching a certain size. But another part is probably due to Dr. Sherwood's efforts to organize the venture in a way that is orienting us toward solving particular problems of an immediate nature, without taking into account some of the broader implications of the design.

There was also concern that Sherwood was unable or unwilling to delegate responsibility. One of his subordinates had intimated that

> Sherwood can't cut the rope. Once you pass the $15 million mark you must start delegating or you just get overwhelmed. He can't do that; he has to be in on all decisions. He even wants to decide the colors of the rooms. He'd run down the hall to have a say in that, too.

The people Sherwood had brought in under him on the Medical Equipment Venture were usually generalists rather than technical or functional specialists. Sherwood also had hired a number of people from outside Gamma Corporation to staff the new venture. Thus, both the organizational form and the people who filled the key roles contributed to the entrepreneurial atmosphere in which a manager was responsible for a variety of activities in different functional areas. For instance, Sherwood's right-hand man was an MBA from a well-known western business school. He had been in charge of both R&D and manufacturing of the reagents for ANABASE. He had interviewed and hired research engineers for the project, and his lack of technical background led to several serious mistakes. Individuals not competent to carry out the work on new products were brought on board, and the development timetable suffered.

Sherwood's practice of hiring for the Medical Equipment Venture from outside Gamma had created some resentment among longtime Gamma personnel. The Gamma old-timers thought that Sherwood did not trust their competence. He was alleged to have said that "you can't hire good people from within the Gamma Corporation."

Some people felt that many of the outside hires did not have the best interests of Gamma at heart. One longtime Gamma employee, now a manager in the venture, had told Burns:

> These tend to be opportunistic people who are often more interested in making a name for themselves, so that they can jump to a next, even better position. They will tend to push the things in their area, so that they can put on their resumes specific things that they have accomplished, but which in the overall framework of the new business may not be the best things. We have quite a bit of this hotshot type of routine.

As the Medical Equipment Venture grew, there was a need for strong financial managers to develop the systems and procedures to run the business more efficiently. In order to deal with the operating problems and create a more continuous flow for new product development, some of the generalists were replaced by functional specialists. These managers, in turn, put pressure on Sherwood to pay more attention to the development of internal systems. The manufacturing systems, in particular, had been neglected in the rush to build sales volume rapidly. The manufacturing function in the venture had been haphazard, confusing, and poorly planned. The new manufacturing manager had told Burns:

> Sherwood and Korbin made a very good strategic move by going from R&D directly to the marketplace. They minimized investment, bought time, and tried to maximize the cash flow. But coming from an R&D environment, they missed in the selection of key manufacturing people. That's still an ongoing problem. There is still some normalization to be done.

As a result of some of these pressures toward more professional management, conflicts had arisen between Sherwood and the new managers. In mid-1976, a recently hired, very capable marketing manager had left for the competition.

Sherwood had been preoccupied with rapid growth for the Medical Equipment Venture. He had felt that in order for the venture to reach maturity as a new business organization within the Gamma corporate structure, it was necessary to reach sales volumes of $50 million to $100 million within 5 to 10 years after the project began.

Sherwood had focused his efforts on the development and marketing of the ANABASE system. He became so caught up in that process that the new product development activities suffered. Relationships with corporate R&D were neglected. As a result, the flow of new product development was not yet brought under control. In the opinion of one of Sherwood's associates:

> Every ounce of effort with Dr. Sherwood is spent on the short run. There is no strategizing. New product development has been delayed, has been put to corporate R&D. . . . Every year we have doubled in size, but things never get any simpler.

There were serious communications problems within the Medical Equipment Venture and between the venture and the rest of Gamma Corporation. The product managers were often involved in disputes with the manufacturing and accounting functions. The venture had all but severed relations with corporate R&D, despite the fact that R&D was developing new medical products for them. One transferee from corporate R&D to the venture had told Burns:

> We were basically separated from the R&D group in the venture. The people in that group wanted to identify themselves. They did it to such an extent that they put a wall between themselves and us. In a way it was ironic. We were funded by the venture, and the technology that we developed was not accepted by them. Now, however, we are trying to reestablish the working relationship.

After the transfer of the ANABASE project as a new venture to the NBD department, Sherwood reported to Dr. Korbin. Burns knew that Dr. Korbin had also played a crucial role in the evolution of Medical Equipment. In the words of one of the people from Gamma's R&D group:

> You need a champion at the technical level to start it. But then you also need an "organizational champion" who, ideally, should come from outside R&D. . . . For Medical Equipment, Dr. Sherwood was the "product champion" here in the lab, and Dr. Korbin was the guy who was running around in the corporation and whispering in the right people's ears.

Korbin had earned the respect of peers and subordinates by the way he had handled his relationship with Medical Equipment as well as a number of other ventures before it. He was willing to take risks and to allow the venture manager a great deal of latitude in running the business. He sought out and worked with a wide range of product champions like Sherwood. He had an uncanny ability to cut deep into the heart of a problem, despite its complexity. One researcher said of Korbin:

> He doesn't need the in-depth familiarity with the technical aspects. He has the intellectual ability to transcend jargon, to thread through the logic in spite of the jargon.

Korbin had described his management approach to Burns as follows:

> First, I look for demonstrated performance on an arbitrarily—sometimes not even the right one—chosen tactic. For instance, doing "X" may not be the right move, but it can be done and one can gain credibility by doing it. So, what I am really looking for is the ability to predict and plan adequately. I want to verify the venture manager's claim that he or she knows how to predict and plan, so a "demonstration project" is needed, even if it is only an experiment. The second thing that I look for is the strategy of the business. That is most important. The strategy should be attractive and workable. It should answer the question where he or she wants to be in the future and how to get there. It is important for two reasons. First, once you have a strategy and can answer those questions, and I can verify a piece of it through a demonstration project, I can give strategic guidelines; I can let people make more independent decisions. That builds momentum, and I don't have to go to top management every day; so, it's also very important from an operational viewpoint. Second, it allows planning. And that, in turn, allows me to go to the corporation and stick my neck out.

Korbin had been the architect of the broader strategic design which guided the venture's development after 1973. This strategic design included:

1. Internal growth through new product development.
2. Agglomeration of medical-related projects from other parts of the company under the administrative umbrella of Medical Equipment.
3. External growth through the acquisition of related small companies.

As a consequence of this design, Dr. Korbin played an active role in attracting other projects from around the company to the Medical Equipment Venture. One manager described this approach:

> It was the genius of Dr. Korbin to attempt to get a better focus by bringing all of the capabilities relevant to the medical equipment field existing in the corporation under one management. That is to say, the refrigeration know-how of the Industrial Gases Division, the plastics know-how of Packaging Products, and the electronics know-how of Medical Equipment.

The product development and agglomeration process resulted in three lines of business within the Medical Equipment Venture: clinical chemistry (the original blood analyzer), nuclear medicine and imaging, and blood banking. The products for nuclear medicine were also used in laboratories to perform tests involving nuclear materials. While the technology was different, the marketing requirements meshed closely with the blood analyzer business.

The blood banking business was conceptually different from the original laboratory diagnostic products. It consisted of equipment which froze blood for subsequent use in transfusions to patients. Several managers speculated that it might be necessary to create separate organizations for the different product lines if they grew rapidly to a sufficient size. However, for the time being, they had agreed with Korbin that a critical mass was needed in order for a venture to succeed, and that combining the different products under one management was the best approach.

In 1976, only one outside company had been acquired and folded into the Medical Equipment Venture. However, there was no problem in taking that approach if an opportunity presented itself. Dr. Korbin was somewhat concerned that Dr. Sherwood might have overlooked such opportunities in the turmoil of fighting fires that sprang up in the day-to-day operations of the business.

Conclusion

As Burns reviewed the jumble of facts and opinions that had been uncovered in his discussions, he wondered what could have been done better in the case of the Medical Equipment Venture. What might the director of the NVD and senior management of Gamma have done to take advantage of Sherwood's entrepreneurial talents without letting things get out of hand? Were there things that Dr. Korbin might have done differently? He had championed the project to his superiors and brought related initiatives under one roof, but what might he have done for Sherwood? As for Sherwood himself, how might he have avoided some of the difficulties? The lessons learned from Medical Equipment were important, as other new ventures were likely to encounter similar situations in the future. Burns recalled that he had not been able to resist telling Sherwood at one point in his conversations with him that "you guys are so different. The corporation doesn't understand you. You must involve us more in the business."

Burns also wondered what should be done next. It was not clear what approach Dr. Korbin might propose when he arrived for the meeting. Burns wanted to have clear in his mind the advantages and the risks associated with each alternative. He wondered what potential solutions to the problem he might have overlooked. He felt he should have a tentative position about which action to take in case he was asked during the discussion. Finally, Burns was troubled that so much of his energies since he had taken over the NVD had been devoted to fire fighting, operating decisions like the one facing him with regard to Sherwood. He knew that some careful strategic thinking was necessary to determine what steps to take next with regard to the Medical Equipment Venture once the decision about the venture manager was made.

Reading III–7 *Agency Costs and Innovation*

Bengt Holmstrom

1. Introduction

For an increasing number of firms, innovation has become an urgent concern. With the lifetimes of products shortened due to an accelerating pace of technological change, the fight against obsolescence is raising new and unprecedented challenges everywhere. Business consultants, ever sensitive to the needs of the hands that feed them, have jumped into the act with a new gospel tailored to the management of innovation: bureaucratic procedures are to be replaced by a culture that encourages action, allows freedom to experiment, and exhibits substantial tolerance for errors; formal planning models, extensive information collection, and centralized decision making are all to be significantly curtailed.

Concerns about the innovativeness of U.S. firms have surfaced on the political front as well. The debate on a national industrial policy has touched on the need for a government agenda to encourage research and development. Such government intervention is based on a distrust for the ability of markets to steer capital to its best use, and understandably has met with skepticism. But whatever one's views, it is clear that the questions are important and topical. At stake is the preeminence of the United States as the industrial leader of the world.

My intention is not to join the debate on the need for increased innovation either on the national or the firm level, though in a larger historical perspective the attention seems appropriate; the West grew rich primarily because it was willing to experiment.[1] Rather I want to discuss the most efficient forms for organizing innovative activity in the private sector. If innovation is to be encouraged, which private institutions are best positioned to undertake it?

Stylized facts seem to indicate that small firms have been responsible for a disproportionate share of significant innovations in the past.[2] I'm aware that the validity of this claim can be debated and that the conclusions are sensitive to what one counts as innovation. Also, a higher success rate does not prove a comparative advantage; small firms could be innovating too much.[3] Yet, the casual evidence suggests the hypothesis that large firms are at a comparative disadvantage in managing truly innovative research. My specific purpose is to study whether current theories of organization, particularly those based on transaction cost and incentive considerations, can lend support for such a claim.

I will discuss two types of reasons why large firms might (rationally) innovate less. One has to do with the internal organization of the firm and the other with the firm's relationship to the capital market. On the internal side the main theme is that the large corporation has emerged primarily to serve production and marketing goals and that in pursuing those objectives effectively it has to organize in a way that compromises innovation incentives. Providing incentives for both types of activities within one organization is more costly than providing them through separate organizations. Ultimately the reasons for this can be traced back to the loss in reliable performance measures that attend integration. Weaker performance measures lead the firm to take other steps to ensure proper behavior. In general terms they involve affecting the opportunity costs of the employees. More rigid rules and less discretion are primary consequences. Such bureaucratization is hostile to innovation both directly by restricting experimentation and indirectly by screening out innovative personalities.

On the external side I will argue that a concern for reputation in the capital market will lead a large firm to act more cautiously in taking risks. Past per-

Journal of Economic Behavior and Organization 12 (1989), pp. 305–27.

[1]For a particularly compelling account, see N. Rosenberg and D. Birdzell, *How the West Grew Rich* (New York: Basic Books, 1985).

[2]See, for instance, Chapter 11 in F. Scherer, *Innovation and Growth,* 2nd ed. (Cambridge, MA: MIT Press, 1984).

[3]Small firms may be forced to innovate in order to distinguish themselves or be able to compete with large firms.

formance is an important signal for future potential and will determine the terms under which new capital will be made available. This has a tendency to make the firm myopic in its behavior. For a small firm which has less flexibility in choosing its activities, this problem is less severe. The extreme case is a start-up firm, singularly devoted to the development of a new product.

In presenting the details of these arguments I will draw unrestrainedly from the growing literature on transaction cost and incentive contracting; in particular, the recent efforts to identify the economic purpose of the firm. I will spend a fair amount of time interpreting this literature before applying the insights to the innovation issue at hand. I hope some of the discussion will be of independent interest to institutional economics in general.

The paper is organized as follows. Section 2 identifies some of the incentive dilemmas. Section 3 makes preliminary observations through the lens of a simple principal agent model. Sections 4 through 6, the body of the paper, develop the details of the internal organization problems that handicap innovation in large firms. Section 7 discusses the pressures from capital markets. A summary and conclusion are offered in Section 8.

2. The Incentive Dimensions of Innovation

In the simplest abstraction, innovation decisions are just investment decisions and as such part of the standard problem of how to allocate capital. One would expect modern finance theory to give good general advice on how to manage investments into research and development. But a quick look at finance textbooks reveals answers that are based on a very stylized conception of the problem and rather less illuminating than one would hope. Mainly, the student is told that the decision to invest should be based on a straightforward net present value calculation, in which the expected future return stream from the contemplated project is discounted using a cost of capital that reflects the appropriate social risk inherent in that stream. The most striking part of the advice is that projects should be evaluated this way without regard to individual portfolios or capital constraints.

Practitioners do not follow these simple rules. Firms do care about idiosyncratic risk and they are exceedingly conscious of capital constraints. In any given year there is a limited amount of money to be allocated among proposed projects and, typically, the demand for funding vastly exceeds the amount set aside for investment in that year. This imbalance is not resolved in a decentralized fashion by creating an internal-cost-of-capital schedule. Rather, the dilemma is dealt with by various idiosyncratic rules that all turn on more or less intense centralized scrutiny of the proposals put forward. For financial indicators firms rely on internal rates of return (with hurdle rates substantially above the cost of capital implied by market rates) as well as payback criteria more commonly than on net present values.

Likewise, capital markets do not allocate funds to firms in the stylized fashion prescribed by net present value theory. Rationing of capital is commonplace, and the cost of funds is very much perceived to depend on the source from which they are obtained.

By now it is well recognized where the discrepancies between standard theory and practice lie. Reallocating shares in the stock market is a very different type of activity than supplying fresh funds to a company. Marginal transfers of shares have little or no impact on the operation of a firm, while new funds change the firm's production set. The source of funds, the amount of capital, and the terms on which these funds are made available all influence the operation of the firm and the behavior and prospects of its members. Potential incentive problems are easy to envision, which suggests that the variety of institutions mediating capital from markets to firms (as well as capital within firms) is best understood in terms of their effectiveness in monitoring and managing the incentives of the people involved in using that capital.[4] As well, this is the appropriate perspective for discussing comparative advantage in innovation, since the process of innovation is mainly one of matching financial capital with the human capital behind the ideas.

The use of incentive contracts to reduce the costs of transacting under asymmetric information has been studied extensively. The standard framework considers a principal and, typically, one but sometimes many agents. Normally, the party with supe-

[4]Those who think the problem is in management practice rather than the theory should be reminded of the speed with which financial markets have adopted modern asset pricing theories. Understanding net present value analysis is trivial compared with learning option pricing and valuation of other derivative securities.

rior information is the agent, while the principal is the capital owner. In talking about investment incentives, the first question to ask is why there should be a problem. Why would the agent not want to act in the best interests of the principal? Suppose that the agent does nothing but give investment advice. Suppose the principal pays a flat fee for the advice. Then the agent would have no reason not to tell what is known. This is not as uncommon a case as one might think. Evaluators of projects, accountants who are to judge the veracity of financial statements, for instance, are paid on a noncontingent basis. Contingent fees would do little but create distorting incentives to report honestly what's observed.

More than evaluation expertise is needed to make a straight salary contract undesirable. Three ways of introducing preference incongruities are commonly considered. The first one recognizes that investments require efforts by the agent that cannot be compensated directly, because of problems with observability. To motivate private expenditures, contingent fees based on what's observable (e.g., the output of the project) will be necessary. Such incentive schemes introduce risk preferences for the agent, assuming that the agent is risk averse or does not have enough financial resources to buy out the principal.

A second possibility is that the agent owns part of the project, say the idea, and is shopping around for an equity partner. Since the agent knows the value of the project better than the potential partner, there is a problem in deciding on the right price. A contingent fee schedule is a means by which ex ante asymmetries in information can be reduced.

Finally, a third case recognizes that the agent may have a direct interest in the project, contingent fees notwithstanding. One plausible reason is that the agent's market value will depend on undertaking the project as well as on its outcome. Thus, investments commonly yield financial returns as well as human capital returns. Some kind of contract will be needed to align incentives more closely.

All three incentive dimensions seem relevant for managing innovation. Indeed, the agency costs associated with innovation are likely to be high, because innovation projects are: (*a*) risky—there is a high probability of failure, but also prospects for extraordinary returns; (*b*) unpredictable—many future contingencies are impossible to foresee; (*c*) long-term and multistage—the project has an invention, a development, and a completion stage, and can be terminated between those; (*d*) labor intensive—all stages require substantial human effort; (*e*) idiosyncratic—not easily comparable to other projects. It turns out that contracting under this set of circumstances is particularly demanding.

3. Some Insights from Agency Theory

As will become clearer in the next section, standard principal-agent models do not get to the core of the institutional choice question, because their results do not depend on the organizational location of the agency relationship. Yet, the models can shed light on a number of organizational issues. In this section I will work with a particularly simple principal–agent model to identify some trade-offs that I think are central to the innovation questions I have set to discuss. The model is described in full in Holmstrom and Milgrom;[5] my discussion relies in part on extensions contained in Holstrom and Milgrom.[6]

Basic Model

Consider a single innovation project, which yields an uncertain payoff x. As well, the payoff depends on what the agent does, but not so that it fully reveals the agent's role. Let the specific relationship be

$$x = e + \text{normal error term} \tag{1}$$

where e represents the agent's action (effort.)

Assume that the principal and the agent have an identical understanding of the stochastic project returns. Both believe the normal error term has mean μ and variance σ^2. Thus, the agent has no superior information about project returns before acting. This may be a reasonable assumption if we are at the initial stages of a research undertaking. Note that with this return specification, the agent is in effect choosing the mean of a normal distribution. If he acts e, the mean is $e + \mu$. The variance is not within the agent's control.

The principal is unable to observe directly what the agent does; that's what gives rise to the incentive problem. Let x be verifiable in the sense that

[5]B. Holstrom and P. Milgrom, "Aggregation and Linearity in the Provision of Intertemporal Incentives," *Econometrica* 55, no. 2 (1987), pp. 303–28.

[6]B. Holmstrom and P. Milgrom, "Assigning Tasks to Agents," mimeo, Yale University, 1989

enforceable contracts can be written on it. A contract specifies payments $s(x)$ to the agent when x occurs, leaving the principal with the residual $x - s(x)$.

The principal is risk neutral and the agent is risk averse with preferences described by the exponential utility function $-\exp\{-r(s(x) - c(e))\}$. Here r is the coefficient of absolute risk aversion and $c(e)$ the cost function. The natural interpretation of cost is in terms of opportunity loss. Working on the project limits the income that can be generated from other sources.

The problem is to choose s so that it encourages adequate effort, without overly burdening the agent with risk. Under suitable assumptions, the second-best contract (i.e., the best contract given the informational restrictions of the model) take the linear form: $s(x) = ax + b$.[7] The best choice of a is derived by maximizing the certain equivalent of joint surplus, which, given the linear rule, is $\mu + e - (1/2)r\alpha^2\sigma^2 - c(e)$, subject to the agent's first order condition $c'(e) = a$. To give an explicit example of a solution, suppose $c(e) = ke^2/2$. Then, the best piece rate is

$$\alpha = (1 + kr\sigma^2)^{-1} \qquad (2)$$

which also is the agent's choice of effort. The salary component β will be set so that the agent is willing to participate in the project; it is a mere transfer of wealth between the principal and the agent and of little interest here.

Formula (2) precisely accords with one's intuition: the agent's share is higher, the lower is his aversion to risk (lower r), the lower is the risk (the variance) and the lower is the cost of action. The solution reflects a trade-off between risk sharing and incentives to supply effort. For optimal effort one should choose $\alpha = 1$ and for optimal risk sharing $\alpha = 0$. Only if risk is absent or the agent is risk neutral can one avoid the agency costs associated with limited observability. The joint surplus (under the best contract) is in fact: $\mu + 1/2k^{-1}(1 + rk\sigma^2)^{-1}$, which is less than the first-best surplus: $\mu + (1/2)k^{-1}$. Note that welfare varies positively with α.

Monitoring

This basic model can be enriched in various ways. One is to introduce a monitoring variable y. By a monitor I mean any signal of the agent's action other than the outcome. It could be the principal looking over the agent's activities or information obtained from observing agents in related activities. If $y = e +$ a normal error term, as in (1), then the optimal schedule is linear in the two variables: $s(x,y) = \alpha x + \gamma y + \beta$. One finds that the higher is the risk of a project, the more intensive additional monitoring will be. Higher project risk forces a reduction in the coefficient α, that is, in the agent's outcome share. This reduces effort. Consequently, the incentive coefficient γ on the monitoring variable will be raised, since the marginal cost of effort has gone down (convex cost function). But an increase in the monitoring coefficient will increase the risk stemming from errors in monitoring and it becomes valuable to invest more in monitoring to reduce that error.

An executive, trying to encourage more innovation, recently observed: "I try to give people a feeling that it's okay to fail, that it's important to fail." Indeed, incentives for innovation must provide for more tolerance, since innovation is intrinsically risky and progress more erratic than with standard investments. But the consequence is equally important to recognize: direct, close-handed monitoring of the agent's activities must be introduced to compensate for the weaker output rewards. (However, as I will discuss later, monitoring information may often not be possible to use as effectively as envisioned here.)

Project Choice

How do agency costs affect the choice of projects? And how do projects get assigned across agents? These are the most interesting questions in the context of innovation. Using my earlier example, a project is identified with the characteristics (μ, σ^2, k). The best (single) project to choose maximizes the net welfare: $\mu + 1/2k^{-1}(1 + rk\sigma^2)^{-1}$. One notes that the best project is not determined by standard net present value rules. A concern for risk is present even though the principal is risk neutral.[8] The reason is that the worker is carrying (by design) some undiversified risk.

[7] I'm simplifying the description of the model considerably. The actual model views the agent as choosing the drift rate of a stochastic process over time. I'm describing the reduced form.

[8] Risk neutrality is a rather natural assumption here if one interprets risk as being idiosyncratic. Formally, the assumption can be rationalized in a model where both systematic and idiosyncratic risk are present. It is easy to show that the agent's contract would filter out the systematic risk and effectively be based only on the idiosyncratic component.

The implication is that, to a degree, advantages in technology (high μ) will be traded off against incentive considerations. A more uncertain technology is more costly from an incentive point of view and might be passed up in favor of more routine ones despite their lower returns. By the earlier monitoring logic, there would also be value in choosing projects that are correlated with each other. Overlapping or competing projects could make sense, since they would reduce the incentive costs even if duplication might otherwise be technologically wasteful. This would be an argument for carrying out many projects within the same firm. However, in the case of innovations, since their risks are rather idiosyncratic, one would not expect significant gains from such integration.

Considering the cost function $c(e)$, it is interesting to observe that a low-cost technology may be worse than a high one. Even if $c_1(e) < c_2(e)$ for *every e,* the latter cost function may be preferred. As an example, suppose $c_1(e) = e_2/2$ and the optimal incentive contract leads the agent to choose $e_2 = 1/2$ (this is optimal by appropriate choice of risk aversion and variance). Compare it to the following cost function: $c_2(e) = 1/8$ whenever $e < 1/2$ and infinity beyond that. Since $c_1(1/2) = 1/8$, the first cost function is uniformly lower than the second. Yet, the second cost function will be preferred, since with that one we can get the agent to choose 1/2 without imposing any risk.

An important general point hides behind this trivial example. Sometimes it is more effective to provide incentives by changing the agent's opportunity cost than by offering financial rewards; and quite generally this is a valuable additional incentive instrument. How does one change the opportunity cost? By controlling the agent's options to spend time and effort on alternative activities. The situation above could be interpreted in these terms. The first cost function applies when the agent can divide his or her time between working for the principal and working on a private project (e.g., watching TV at home). It corresponds to the opportunity cost of having less time to devote to the private project when more time is spent on the principal's. Under cost function c_2 the private option is removed. The agent's cost goes up uniformly, because the benefit from spending the balance of time at home is no longer available. However, with the option removed, no further incentives for effort need be provided. Forcing the agent to come into the office is an example in point; indeed, fixed salaries are more prevalent in office jobs than in jobs performed at home.

This discussion shows that the cost of providing incentives for a given task importantly depends on what other activities the agent is allowed to engage in, be that in private or within the firm. Loosely speaking, the more flexibility the agent has, the costlier it is to induce him or her to work on a given project. As a consequence, it may be optimal to reduce the agent's flexibility by eliminating marginal tasks, that is, tasks which do not contribute enough in net receipts to offset increased costs of providing incentives for more important tasks. (For more on this, see Holmstrom and Milgrom.)[9]

A significant factor in determining how much flexibility to allow the agent is how accurately one can measure the agent's performance in his or her major tasks. Let me illustrate this point by extending the earlier example a bit further. Suppose the agent could allocate some effort (e') to an outside activity with nonstochastic return $f(e')$. There is no cost to effort, but the total amount of effort, $e + e'$, cannot exceed 1; i.e., $c(e + e') = 0$ for $e + e' \leqq 1$ and infinity for $e + e' > 1$. Assume $f(e') = \lambda_1 e'$, for $e' \leqq n < 1$ and $\lambda_1 n + \lambda_2(e' - n)$ for $e' > n$, where $\lambda_1 > 1 > \lambda_2 > 0$; in other words, f is piecewise linear with a kink at $e' = n$. Note that ideally, the agent should devote time n to the outside and the rest to the principal's project. However, if the principal offers an incentive $\alpha < \lambda_2$ the agent will work only on the outside option. Thus, α must be at least λ_2 if the second option is around and it is desirable to have the agent work for the principal at all. The latter can be assured by choosing parameters so that $f(1) < 1$.

When there is little noise in output x (σ^2 small), the best alternative is to choose α just larger than λ_2. The cost of imposing risk on the agent is $(r/2)(\lambda_2)^2\sigma^2$, which is lower than the opportunity cost of forgoing the outside return: $(\lambda_1 - \lambda_2)n$. However, as σ^2 increases, it becomes increasingly costly to keep α above λ_2. When $\sigma^2 > (\lambda_1 - \lambda_2)n\{(r/2)(\lambda_2)^2\}^{-1}$, it is better to exclude the outside activity altogether, allowing the principal to set $\alpha = 0$.

The logic here can be generalized to several outside activities.[10] As risk increases, more outside activities will be eliminated. The upshot is that *the agent's flexibility will be more restricted the poorer*

[9]For more on this, see Holmstrom and Milgrom, "Assigning Tasks to Agents."

[10]In "Assigning Tasks to Agents," a model with a continuum of outside projects is used.

the performance measures for the main tasks. In more familiar terms: responsibility and authority must be in a balanced relationship. This control principle will play a central role both in the argument for corporate bureaucratization and the capital market discussion that follow. In passing I note that there is recent empirical evidence on the relevance of this prediction. Anderson and Schmittlein[11] found that in the electronics industry, the use of in-house salespeople (rather than independent agents) correlates significantly and positively with the uncertainty of the environment in which they operate.

Project Assignment

The second main principle I want to bring up is that of uniformity in tasks. Suppose several projects are to be allocated between two identical agents. Assume only total cost of effort matters to the agents. The projects differ in their risk characteristics, but are similar in their expected returns. Let $x_i = f(e_i) +$ normal error term, be the return of project i, where f is concave and error terms are independent. (The linearity result extends easily to this case.) Assume the principal only observes the aggregate output of each agent. Then the following holds: the best allocation of projects is such that the *projects assigned to one agent are uniformly more risky than the projects assigned to the other.*[12]

The proof is trivial. One can always switch around two projects between the agents without affecting output (since projects have identical return functions f). Thus, only risk considerations matter. Risk is minimized by assigning the agent with the lower incentive coefficient all projects with a variance above some cutoff level (determined endogenously by the cost function) and assigning all low risk projects to the agent with the higher incentive coefficient. (If it is optimal to give both agents the same incentive coefficient, then the assignment does not matter, but of course this is rarely the case.)

The intuition can be phrased as follows. If an agent is given both high-variance projects and low-variance projects (relative to the other agent), the presence of high-variance projects in the portfolio will force the incentive coefficient down, forgoing the opportunity to offer stronger incentives for the low-variance projects. On the other hand, if projects are split according to risk, one of the two agents can be offered strong incentives, while only the other one will have to operate under weak incentives because of risk. (Since projects are independent and utility exponential, diversification issues do not arise.)[13]

Thus, the agency costs are lower if the projects offered to the agents are uniform rather than diverse. The insight here can be looked at another way: when agents choose between homogeneous proj-ects, incentive problems associated with the allocation of effort are eliminated—only overall effort remains an issue. The implication is that innovation activities may mix poorly with relatively routine activities in an organization. (The point remains even if the organization is hierarchical; at some level attention must be allocated between both kinds of projects.)

The idea that incentives for different activities need to be in balance is of course relevant more generally. Thus, where cooperation between agents is desirable, individual incentives must be reduced.[14] For this reason it may again pay to separate tasks which require cooperation from tasks in which strong individual incentives are invaluable. Cooperation and competition do not coexist comfortably, at least within a narrow group.

Before I close this section, a qualification is in order. The model I have been using to guide my intuition is one in which effort incentives are paramount and no asymmetries in information are present, other than those regarding effort. The case in which the agent is better informed about project returns at the time of contracting may lead to somewhat different conclusions. (Information that arrives after a contract is signed and a project is selected does not change anything substantively.) Adverse selection, as this case is referred to, also raises a new issue: how to elicit information from the agent so that relatively efficient decisions (e.g., project choices) can be made. I will return to discuss this later. Let me just make one observation for future reference: in an effort to restrict the information rents of

[11] E. Anderson and D. Schmittlein, "Integration of the Sales Force: An Empirical Investigation," *Rand Journal of Economics* 13, no. 3 (1984), pp. 385–95.

[12] This same result has been independently arrived at by J. Minahan, "Managerial Incentive Schemes and the Divisional Structure of Firms," mimeo, University of Massachusetts at Boston, 1988.

[13] With appropriate modifications, the result extends to cases in which individual project returns are observed, so that each project has its own incentive coefficient α_i. Also, one can allow individual return functions f_i, and agents with different risk aversion and cost functions. See Holmstrom and Milgrom, "Assigning Tasks to Agents."

[14] E. Lazear, "Pay Equality and Industrial Politics," *Journal of Political Economy* 97, no. 3 (1989), pp. 561–80.

the informed, allocational distortions will arise. For instance, an entrepreneur shopping for an equity partner will receive too little funds and will end up bearing too much risk. More generally, when bargaining takes place under conditions of adverse selection, some of the surplus is dissipated, either because agreements will not be reached when they should or because there will be costly delays.

4. Incomplete Contracts and Institutional Choice

That incomplete contracting plays a central role in understanding institutional choice has been stressed by Williamson in his long line of research on organizations.[15] Were it the case that parties could sign comprehensive contracts, that is, contracts which fully specify each side's responsibilities in all future contingencies, the organizational context of the contract would not matter, really.[16] Grossman and Hart[17] have sharpened the argument by introducing the important distinction between residual decision rights, implied by institutional choice, and specific rights conferred by explicit contract. In this terminology, the ownership of a firm is identified with the residual rights to the firm's assets: its tangible assets (machines, buildings, cash, etc.) as well as its intangible ones (patents, brand names, reputation, etc.). This is a significant extension of the traditional view of ownership as an entitlement to the firm's residual income stream.

Residual rights become important when one encounters situations not covered by specific contracts. If a disagreement arises on how to resolve the matter, parties will have to negotiate a solution (with the courts offering final arbitration if necessary). What each side will get will depend on its bargaining position, which in turn is a function of its residual rights. Thus residual rights and institutional choice play a central role in imputing returns to each side.[18] Ownership of assets is an indirect way of choosing an incentive scheme for the transactors. The key point is that such variation in incentives could not be had by specific contract alone, since contracting is necessarily incomplete.

Relationship Specific Investments

The transactions cost literature has made asset specificity a key component in the analysis of integration. The central hypothesis is that integration—the purchase of the decision rights to all relevant physical assets by one party—will be an economically efficient arrangement in situations where asset specificity is high. A concentration of decision rights in one hand will provide the owner with all the rents and hence make initial ex ante investments worthwhile. By contrast, nonintegration prevents owners from fully appropriating the returns to their initial investments, causing inefficient decisions ex ante.

The simplest case is one in which there are two indispensable and entirely relationship-specific assets. Under separate ownership, each side will capture only half of the investment returns (assuming an even split of rents), while under integrated ownership the full returns are appropriated by the single owner. (With a single asset, the corresponding comparison would be between joint ownership and individual ownership.)

There are several qualifications to this conclusion. Two are particularly relevant. First, it is essential that the parties cannot contract on the initial investment itself.[19] If they could, the distribution of rents would not affect efficiency. Second, it is implicitly assumed above that the costs of investment get transferred under integration; it is the single owner who pays for all investments. Were it so that the other party remains responsible for the costs of investing in the asset he or she manages, he or she will lose all incentives to invest under integration and this may become a much worse alternative.

---

[15] O. Williamson, *Markets and Hierarchies: Analysis and Antitrust Implications* (New York: Free Press, 1975); *The Economic Institutions of Capitalism* (New York: Free Press, 1985).

[16] Traditional contract models are typically comprehensive. However, I note that the model in the previous section can be interpreted as a reduced form incomplete contract model if there are return streams that cannot be split between parties (e.g., $\alpha_i = 0$ or 1).

[17] S. Grossman and O. Hart, "The Costs and Benefits of Ownership: A Theory of Vertical and Lateral Integration," *Journal of Political Economy* 94 (1986), pp. 691–719.

[18] More often, of course, the knowledge of rights (and how they might affect potential bargaining) will control behavior without actual bargaining ever taking place. An implied governance structure comes to frame the relationship and affect the incentives of the transacting parties.

[19] Actually, the requirement is stronger. Even if investment decisions cannot be directly observed, it may be the case that short-term contracts (based on imperfect information) can provide adequate investment incentives. On this, see D. Fudenberg, B. Holmstrom, and P. Milgrom, "Short-term Contracts and Long-term Agency Relationships," forthcoming in *Journal of Economic Theory*.

Thus, whether ex ante investments will be more efficient under integration depends on what rights and responsibilities can be transferred. Certain assets are inalienable, most importantly those related to human capital. The right to decide to supply one's human services to an enterprise cannot be sold (because of involuntary servitude). Likewise, the decision on how much effort to expend remains a private matter, irrespective of organizational context (because effort cannot be observed).[20] Consequently, the incentives to invest effort into an enterprise can be expected to be diluted for an entrepreneur who sells his or her company but remains in his or her former managerial position. Benefits to integration rest on the assumption that ex ante investment decisions do not relate significantly to human efforts, but rather to decisions on expenditures of a monetary kind. I will return to this important point in the next section.

Coordination

In the example above, the distribution of decision rights matters, because it influences the division of ex post surplus. (Surplus is only a function of ex ante investments, not of the bargaining process, which costlessly is assumed to achieve an efficient outcome).[21] In general, of course, decision rights affect all aspects of bargaining, including, importantly, the costs of reaching an agreement.[22] If there is surplus to be divided, and both sides can threaten to dissipate it by withdrawing the use of critical assets, haggling over the division of the surplus can be expected. Such bargaining can be productive if it generates information about the best way to proceed. But if it is relatively clear what the right course of action is and haggling only occurs because parties try to enhance their own share at the expense of the other side's, then bargaining merely reduces surplus. Vesting decision rights with one party is a way of eliminating those costs.

Present modeling technology suggests that we introduce asymmetric information in order to capture such costs. So assume that one side has private information about the value of continuing the relationship in a contingency that lies outside an explicit contract. If both parties have ownership of an indispensible asset, we know from bargaining under asymmetric information that costly delays will result from haggling. The informed will try to extract rents from his or her private information and the uninformed will try to keep rents as low as possible. By contrast, if either party is given title to both assets, bargaining costs will go to zero. If the informed gets the assets, he or she will simply impose the best continuation given his or her information. And rather interestingly, the same is true if the uninformed is made the single owner. With nothing at stake, one can expect the informed to reveal his or her information quickly and in an unbiased fashion. Thus, for effective coordination of information, low-powered incentives may be necessary.

Note, however, that if one side has human or other nontransferrable assets that are instrumental to realizing the surplus, then that side should be given all assets. Simon's[23] suggestion that employers should be given the right to decide on the allocation of workers to tasks because of their better information implicitly assumes that the employers could otherwise hold up bargaining—or that bargaining among workers would be costly.

To sum up, the main arguments for integrating are two: incentives for investment in relationship-specific assets and improved coordination of decision making. How relevant are these for innovation? It seems to me that they do not provide strong reasons for placing innovation activities in a large firm. Relationship-specific investments are significant, but limited to relatively small groups. They do not require large-scale integration. Neither does there seem to be a great need to coordinate decisions among different research projects as the argument based on costly bargaining would demand. Indeed, it appears that large firms frequently make an effort to keep different innovation projects separate. By contrast, it is easy to understand that coordination gains can be significant in the production, marketing, and development of

[20]It is true that a change in ownership transfers the rights to design incentive mechanisms and that way gives indirect control over human capital decisions. This dimension has not been carefully studied.

[21]For more detailed models of this variety see Grossman and Hart, "The Costs and Benefits of Ownership," and also O. Hart and J. Moore, "Property Rights and the Nature of the Firm," mimeo, Massachusetts Institute of Technology. The latter presents a very accessible reduced form analysis, which covers cases with many assets and many interested parties.

[22]Bargaining costs are discussed at length in P. Milgrom and J. Roberts, "Bargaining and Influence Costs and the Organization of Economic Activity," RP 934, Graduate School of Business, Stanford University, 1987.

[23]H. Simon, "A Formal Theory of the Employment Relationship," *Econometrica* 19 (1951), pp. 293–305.

established products. In this view, firms grow large with the increased size of product markets.[24]

5. Appropriation and Measurement Problems

I stressed above that human capital is an asset that cannot be transferred and therefore incentives for effort may be significantly diluted by removing title to transferrable assets from those whose efforts are central to production. I believe innovation requires significant personal sacrifices particularly in acquiring information. The coordination benefits discussed above were conditional on fixed information. Coordination aids the elicitation of information, but makes the incentives to invest in information correspondingly worse. Appropriating the returns from such efforts is the major problem with integration.

Why can the firm not duplicate market incentives, for instance, by giving the innovator the rights to patents that might come with the innovation? There are several difficulties. First, the employee is using the firm's assets, human and physical, in the process of innovating. If he or she would receive all the benefits, without having to bear the costs, a serious misalignment would arise. He or she would undertake innovation with an eye on enhancing his or her human capital. Excess and wrong kinds of innovation would be likely: bad projects might be undertaken and cost-intensive projects would be disproportionately favored. The firm might try to charge fees for using its assets, but the allocation of costs poses a dilemma. Even the best intentioned firm does not know capital costs, as accountants would be the first to tell.[25] In addition, as an interested party, the firm has control of many levers to make accounting measures less reliable. The implication is that individual incentives based on innovation returns must be tempered to provide the agent with a properly balanced objective (as in the simple agency model of section 3). As Williamson[26] has emphasized, low-powered incentives come to replace high-powered incentives (based on net receipts) upon integration.

Another appropriation problem concerns the rights to decide on the continuation of projects. Innovations occur in several stages. It is easy to imagine situations in which the project leader would like to continue the project when the firm would not. He or she has much human capital at stake, which the firm cannot appropriate in turn. He or she is also likely at this stage to have private information on the success probability. Renegotiation of continuation rights would have to take place under conditions of asymmetric information. As mentioned earlier, bargaining under asymmetric information is difficult and will not allow the informed to receive all the rents. This feeds back on the incentives to invest human capital in the project at the initial stage. It is true that some of the same problems could be encountered in market arrangements as well. A lender could refuse additional capital. But if it is deemed desirable ex ante, long-term financing can be arranged at the outset. Long-term financing within the firm might not be as easily arranged, partly because the innovator is not bearing research costs as he or she would as an independent entrepreneur.

Indirectly, the arguments above make reference to the problems of measuring marginal product. Difficulties in identifying relevant costs and benefits, so as to make the innovator bear his marginal share, are central. Of course, even as an individual entrepreneur, measurement problems are substantial. The entrepreneur does not know all the relevant figures either—for instance, what future returns he or she will get. But the knowledge that the money will flow into his or her own pockets, that nothing will be taken away, still provides appropriate incentives. It is when financial accounts are integrated that the difficulties of measurement become consequential and severe.

To give an example of how integration destroys performance information, consider a scenario in which a smaller research-oriented firm is bought up by a corporation.[27] Assume both firms are publicly traded before the acquisition. After the acquisition, the small firm's stock would typically be withdrawn from the market. Evidently that would eliminate a critical information variable that could be used to evaluate managerial performance. The market would no longer monitor the purchased firm separately, and the value of that portion of activities

[24]To explain horizontal integration and conglomerates appears much more difficult. The incomplete contract paradigm has not cast much light on that important puzzle.

[25]Since a firm does not put its individual assets (or divisions) regularly on sale, important market information on asset value is missing. See discussion below.

[26]*The Economic Institutions of Capitalism.*

[27]This discussion is from B. Holmstrom and J. Tirole, "The Theory of the Firm," in *Handbook for Industrial Organization,* ed. R. Schmalensee and R. Willig (New York: Elsevier, 1989).

would be confused with contributions from the rest of the corporation.

The story is not complete, however, without asking why the corporation cannot continue to trade both stocks. In fact, it can, as evidenced by the recent merger of EDS with General Motors. GM, after purchasing EDS, started to trade GM-E stock, a stock without voting rights, but with a value based on EDS performance. Presumably, this was done to maintain an outside monitor of EDS. Indeed, EDS management got hefty shares in the new stock, as a continuation of their extensive stock incentive plans in EDS when it still was an independent company.

The experiment has not had a very successful history, at least to date. The alleged difficulties relate to disagreements in transfer pricing. Apparently the two managements are trying to resolve disputes arising from an incomplete contract. Since GM holds the main control rights, EDS management does not have their premerger bargaining power to extract surplus when unspecified contingencies are encountered. Also, the price of GM-E shares become to some extent manipulable by GM. This does not by itself render the stock valueless. It can be protected by covenants, and in the GM-EDS case it was. However, covenants change the nature of the stock; a GM-EDS share is no longer a pure piece of the economic value of EDS (even with the transfer problems factored in). One would also expect a reduced market interest in information acquisition (indeed, trading in GM-E shares has been lackluster). For all these reasons, it is clear that today's price of GM-E stock does not reflect the contributions of its management as effectively as the premerger price of EDS would have done.

To compensate for the dilution in incentives that attend appropriation and measurement problems, the integrated firm could intensify monitoring, and I think it does.[28] But as I will argue in the next section, there are serious impediments that compromise the effectiveness of internal monitoring. The information may be accurate, but the firm cannot act on it as strongly, because of potential collusion between the monitor and the ones he or she monitors. The key point is that verifiability is an endogenous variable, which depends on the incentives of those who collect the information. What makes market information so powerful is not its accuracy relative to information within the firm (one would expect it to be less accurate, in fact), but rather that market monitors express their conviction by "putting their money where their mouth is."

[28]In an influential article, Alchian and Demsetz have argued that firms emerge in response to problems of joint production. One needs a monitor to meter inputs. To give the monitor the right incentives to monitor, he should be made the owner (receive the residual returns). In the scenario I'm sketching, the argument goes reversely. When two firms are combined, a joint production problem is created (or made more serious), because cost and benefit streams will be confounded. Monitoring is a consequence of integration, not a reason for it. See A. Alchian and H. Demsetz, "Production, Information Costs, and Economic Organization," *American Economic Review* 62 (1972), pp. 777–95.

6. The Bureaucratization Dilemma

To say that increased size brings increased bureaucracy is a safe generalization. To note that bureaucracy is viewed as an organizational disease is equally accurate. The biggest patient is the government, whose bureaucratic manners are notorious, though some of the largest corporations appear almost as badly afflicted.

Undoubtedly, there are bureaucratic excesses in corporations. But the fact that bureaucracy is so universal and that it survives even in situations where choice of organizational form is free and subject to strong competitive forces should suggest some virtues. One is inclined to believe that if there were an easy way out of the dilemma, it would surely have been found by now.

Influence Costs

In fact, Milgrom[29] has argued that bureaucratic rules are a rational way of curbing detrimental influence activities in hierarchies. Concentrated authority will invite such activity. Subordinates will try hard to influence a superior's decisions to the extent such decisions impact on their welfare. Many decisions do. Plainly, some jobs are better than others and if the superior is in charge of allocating jobs, that's worth attention. Getting allocated more resources is also beneficial. It enhances one's value in the corporation as well as one's social status. Pleasing the superior may help in getting better wage raises. And so on. In general, the more discretion the superior has, the more intensive become the efforts to influence. As

[29]P. Milgrom, "Employment Contracts, Influence Activities, and Organization Design," *Journal of Political Economy* 96, no. 1 (1988), pp. 42–60.

we all know, authority tends to engender remarkable attention, some of it less desirable.

Why should the boss pay attention to the influence attempts of his or her subordinates? An important reason is that the boss may be in charge of evaluating performance in order to make the right job-skill matches. He or she will have to observe signals of ability and cannot close his or her ears and eyes to efforts by the subordinate to look good. The result is that subordinates may divert energies to prove their worth in ways that are less productive. The market is not immune to these afflictions either; career concerns give rise to distorted behavior in any situation where performance is being evaluated.[30] But within the firm, subordinates are being watched more closely and therefore receive more returns from signaling their value. Market authority, being more dispersed, offers less easily identified targets for influence activity. Thus, potential influence costs are higher in hierarchies.

Collusion

A less benign reason why the boss may care to be influenced is that bribes can be offered. In effect, the superior and the subordinate can collude.[31] Monetary transfers may be less common, because evidence of such transfers can leak out relatively easily. Also, people are not entirely unscrupulous. But transfers in kind tend to be viewed more innocently and are certainly prevalent. In exchange for personal services, flattery, and the like, more favorable decisions can be expected. Forgiveness will be a common response to mistakes. The strength of reciprocity can be assumed to grow with time and with the intensity of contact. Hierarchies are more fertile ground than markets in that regard.

Influence activities and collusion may severely compromise the integrity of subjective monitoring information. In its most extreme form collusion may render the monitoring information entirely useless. If the subordinate and superior form a team, they can always extract the maximal bonus from the firm. Consequently, monitoring information will have to be ignored. But even with more scrupulous behavior, monitoring information is not apt to be as useful as objective evaluation measures. In order to reduce potential or actual collusion, the firm will want to place constraints on the monitor's scope of discretion. For instance, bonuses may be permitted only so often or to so many in a given time period. But, of course, this will reduce the degree to which monitoring information bears on actual performance. One is caught in an unpleasant trade-off between allowing some collusion or ignoring part of the relevant information. Either way the effectiveness of monitoring is reduced.[32]

Another response to collusion is to ask for documentation. On what basis were bonuses awarded? This tends to eliminate purely subjective impressions. It shifts the monitoring focus towards more verifiable but less performance related measures. Wage and promotion policies based on seniority and other objective factors can be understood in this light.[33] Direct constraints may be imposed on subordinate conduct (e.g., time cards), to the point where checking for obvious errors and violations of the rules becomes the prime activity of the monitor. This is most common in government organizations, where comparison data and other performance measures are most lacking.

While explicit rules and policies are common, it is worth adding that the mere fear of being suspected of favoritism can lead a superior to discount performance in making wage and promotion decisions, even if he or she had the discretion to act freely on the information. Suspected favoritism would lower employee morale and invite attempts to purchase favors. Thus, one can expect organizations to be even more rule bound than the explicit evidence would suggest.

I want to stress that what gets this bureaucratic "misery" all started is the loss of performance measures higher up in the hierarchy. The integrity of subjective evaluations is a function of the monitor's

---

[30]B. Holmstrom, "Managerial Incentives—A Dynamic Perspective," in *Essays in Honor of Lars Wahlbeck* (Helsinki: Swedish School of Economics, 1982).

[31]J. Tirole, "Hierarchies and Bureaucracies," *Journal of Law, Economics and Organization* 2 (1986), pp. 181–214.

[32]It should be mentioned that collusion need not be bad. If two productive agents can monitor each other more effectively than the principal can, then it will often be desirable to allow them to collude, that is, allow them to make cooperative agreements about how hard to work. The principal induces collusion by making the agents responsible for each other's outcomes. The general issue is what kinds of trades one should allow between agents. Since markets are incomplete, the principal will want to regulate the agents' trade. See H. Itoh, "Essays on the Internal Organization of the Firm," unpublished doctoral dissertation, Graduate School of Business, Stanford University, 1988. Also see Holmstrom and Milgrom, "Assigning Tasks to Agents."

[33]Milgrom and Roberts, "Bargaining and Influence Costs and the Organization of Economic Activity."

incentives. An owner will not have to worry about bribes from an employee (this conclusion may change if there are many employees). If he or she accepts personal services in exchange for higher bonuses, this is merely an efficient trade. But when the monitor does not bear all the financial consequences of his or her actions, such trades will be excessive. The lesser his or her responsibility, the bigger the potential distortions. Stricter limitations on the use of information is implied.

In sum, the internal labor market in hierarchies will be pushed towards bureaucratic manners as a rational response to monitoring and influence problems.[34] The basic principle at work here is the principle of inflexibility featured in section 3. The more difficult it is to reward agents, because performance information becomes unreliable or diffuse, the more heavily the agent's opportunity costs will have to be controlled. This is precisely what the bureaucratic constraints are meant to accomplish. That these tendencies will be hostile to innovation seems plausible. Let me elaborate on a few of the main points.

By definition, rules and rigidities inhibit or discourage activities that are exceptional. Extensive capital budgeting procedures are a particularly severe impediment. Funding requests have to pass many layers of approval in order to bring the decision to a level that carries sufficient responsibility. The chances that unfamiliar and innovative projects get accepted are diminished.[35] In part this bias will reflect attempts by superiors to protect their specialized investments in human capital. New products and production methods may be a potential threat to their position of leadership.

The move towards verifiable but less relevant performance measures is equally troublesome. Subjective monitoring would be particularly valuable for innovation, since success is so uncertain. Exceptional tolerance for failure is essential. But such performance cannot be checked by conformance to organizational rules or by evaluation reports that can be readily substantiated.

Monitoring limitations suggest that the firm seeks out activities which are more easily and objectively evaluated. Assignments will be chosen in a fashion that are conducive to more effective control. Authority and command systems work better in environments which are more predictable and can be directed with less investment in information. Routine tasks are the comparative advantage of a bureaucracy, and its activities can be expected to reflect that.

Finally, in bureaucracies, promotions no longer serve the exclusive purpose of matching skills with tasks. The ability and responsibility of the firm to act as a human capital filter are being compromised as a consequence. Promotions based on measures weakly related to performance are one reason. A more important reason is that employees who have done well and deserve to be rewarded will have to be promoted rather than paid in cash. Promotion as a reward is less subject to misuse by a superior than cash rewards. By promoting the subordinate to a new, presumably more demanding task, the superior subjects himself or herself to outside judgments. Favoritism will become more visible. But then one must make sure that promotion to a new task does not result in a serious misassignment. This forces the firm to operate with employees whose characteristics are of more general use. Employees have to conform to the general culture and objectives of the firm. But innovators are not necessarily good managers as John Sculley must have realized at the Apple company when he wanted Steve Jobs out. Uniformity in the treatment of employees translates into uniformity in their characteristics, which may well screen out innovative personalities.

7. Capital Market Effects

One of the remarkable features of modern capital markets is that investors are willing to part with their money in such huge quantities with so limited explicit assurances of getting anything back. Behind this magic is a sophisticated network of institutional arrangements that controls management behavior. Much of the control is indirect through reputation. When firms go to borrow more money, which most have to do with some frequency, a good credit record and a healthy condition are invaluable. For the manager of the publicly held company, the pressures to perform and look good are greatest, because of the continuous assessment that stock prices provide. In this section, I want to mention two

---

[34]A rather different reason why a firm may find it valuable to promote internal uniformity can be provided along the lines of Kreps, who argues that a uniform corporate culture is an important vehicle for nurturing the firm's reputation. See D. Kreps, "Corporate Culture and Economic Theory," mimeo, Graduate School of Business, Stanford University, 1984.

[35]For an opposite discussion see R. Sah and J. Stiglitz, "The Architecture of Economic Systems: Hierarchies and Polyarchies," *American Economic Review* 76, no. 4 (1986), pp. 716–27.

reasons why reputation concerns may lead to conservatism and why the problem can be expected to be more severe for larger firms.

In large part, the market learns from a firm's past what to expect from it in the future. Extrapolation is rational since there are characteristics in the stochastic process of returns that have permanence. But the firm is not a passive player in this learning process. Management can make decisions that influence perceptions about the firm's potential. A simple scenario is the following. An investment decision has to be made today. The investment options vary in their return patterns. Some have returns far in the future and others in the nearer term. The market knows exactly the same as management: the investment options, the return distributions, and so on. However, the market cannot observe the management's decision directly; it can only infer what the management will do.

In this situation there may be a tendency for management to act myopically. By choosing projects with faster paybacks, early returns are enhanced on average. This raises market expectations about management and firm potential. Of course, later returns will be lower on average, offsetting some of the early gains. Exactly how the trade-off works out in the management's mind requires a specification of its preferences. What one can show is that if management is paid based on expected marginal product in each period, and management is less patient than capital markets (because of incomplete income smoothing), then there will be a bias towards the shorter term. Note well that this happens even though the market in the end is not fooled by management's choice. The market expects the bias, but this only reinforces management's need to show short-term results.[36]

Because market expectations will be correct, this story is perfectly consistent with informationally efficient markets as Stein[37] has observed. More strikingly, a management that tries to maximize the market value of the firm (i.e., current price) would be led to choose short-term projects. Thus, the common complaint about myopic and conservative American management may be well founded, but an inevitable consequence of our competitive system.

Since innovations tend to pay off in the distant rather than near future, this type of reputation story would suggest that innovations will not be undertaken sufficiently often. However, one has to explain why the problem is more severe in large firms. There are two reasons that fit the paradigm. One is that a disproportionate number of large firms are publicly traded. With the constant monitoring from markets, large firms are forced to be more myopic. The second reason is that large firms have more flexibility and independence. The argument for myopia turns on the fact that the market cannot observe the actual actions of management. If management could validate what it is doing, the problem would disappear. That some evidence can be presented is clear and explains why behavior is not entirely myopic. But the more activities there are, the more opportunity there is for unobserved allocations that inflate early performance.

These problems of risk taking are of course also present within the firm. In an organization that uses promotion as the main vehicle for rewarding performance, an aversion to risk can be expected among those who see their chances for promotion to be good.

A related reputation story has been presented by Diamond.[38] In his model projects are financed by debt. Projects can be risky or safe and firms can be either good or bad risks. What he shows is that over time, as the firm establishes a reputation for being a good business, interest rates charged on its borrowing will come down. Because of the option feature of debt contracts, firms will take risky projects when interest rates are high and safe projects when they are low. Putting the two together means that firms start off choosing risky projects but later revert to safe ones. The increased value of reputation makes it eventually not worth risking. Thus, established firms can be expected to guard their reputation by becoming conservative.[39]

---

[36]For explicit models that feature myopic behavior, see M. Narayanan, "Managerial Incentives for Short-term Results," *Journal of Finance* XL, no. 5 (1985), pp. 1469–84; T. Campbell and A. Marino, "On the Incentives for Managers to Make Myopic Investment Decisions," mimeo, University of Southern California, 1988; J. Stein, "Efficient Stock Prices, Inefficient Firms: A Signal-Jamming Model of Myopic Corporate Behavior," forthcoming in *Quarterly Journal of Economics*.

[37]"Efficient Stock Prices, Inefficient Firms."

[38]D. Diamond, "Reputation Acquisition in Debt Markets," mimeo, University of Chicago, 1987.

[39]Another implication from a concern for market reputation is that uniformity in activities and products is conducive to reputation maintenance. A retailer who sells both high- and low-quality items will confuse the quality of observations. For the same reason, it seems plausible that pressure for uniformity in project choice may manifest itself when dealing with capital markets. Mixing innovations and routine projects may raise the cost of capital above the average of undertaking the two separately.

I believe both reputation stories touch on relevant dimensions of the problems of channeling capital from markets to firms. Certainly, they are not the only ones that bear on innovation. Unfortunately, our present understanding of investment processes is so limited that it is hard to present a very comprehensive picture. As the discussion in section 2 indicated, finance theory is at a loss in explaining the rich variety of institutions set up to intermediate capital flows. Nor is the role of firms in this process clear. Why is centralized capital budgeting so universal a phenomenon? Is it so that capital budgeting reflects a comparative advantage in distributing funds or is it an inevitable consequence of the bureaucratization dilemma discussed before? These questions are very central in understanding how innovation is distributed across firms, but the answers are not yet available.

8. Conclusion

According to the theses above, integration is primarily motivated by coordination benefits and improved incentives for investment in nonhuman assets. Large-scale production and marketing activities are the main beneficiaries. Innovation, being a small-scale activity initially at least, will not gain much by this argument. On the cost side, integration suffers from weaker incentives to invest in human assets. These are the incentives most essential for successful innovation. Performance measures will be confounded and objective market assessments lost. Internal monitoring cannot compensate for this fully, because of potential collusion problems that attend weaker performance measures for the monitor. The firm will restrict freedom by bureaucratic rules in a rational effort to control incentives indirectly. More uniformity in activities and personnel will follow. Both are hostile to innovation.

Innovation activity requires exceptional tolerance for failure; lest tolerance translate into slack, monitoring has to be intensified. How can one improve the incentives for the monitor? By making him or her financially responsible for the consequences of his or her judgments. Venture capitalism is a solution of this kind. Venture capitalists are specialists in evaluating the quality of potential innovations. Also, they hold a substantial stake in the companies they oversee. The fact that venture capitalists eventually withdraw, once the firm is up and running suggests that their monitoring services are no longer as valuable. One reason is that the initial asymmetries in information have been reduced and the market can take over the role of monitoring; indeed, the venture capitalist often leaves when the firm goes public. Another reason may be that the firm is turning from innovation towards reaping the financial rewards from its successful discoveries, and the needs for monitoring are thereby reduced.

For an established corporation, turning up the rate of innovation will by this logic require decentralization. The innovative parts of the business have to be made more independent and financially more responsible. It appears that firms which are innovation oriented are also more decentralized. Not infrequently, departments or divisions of research and development are spun off.

The new organizational advice from business consultants to decentralize is supported by this analysis, but with important qualifications. The advice does not apply across the board, but only to firms that should intensify innovation because of obsolescence of products. Bureaucracy will continue to have a place as an efficient form of organizing large-scale production.

Case III–8
PC&D, Inc.

E. T. Christiansen, R. G. Hammermesh, and J. L. Bower

When we promoted you to the presidency five years ago, we expected that there would be changes, but we never expected you to diminish the importance of the old line businesses to the extent that you have. I think you have erred in doing so. . . .

The new entrepreneurial subs are certainly dynamic and have brought positive press to the company. But, by investing all new resources in them, you are jeopardizing the health of the company as a whole. . . .

My division's reputation has been built over the past 50 years on the superior quality of its products and sales force. But, as the leadership of our products begins to erode, my salesmen are beginning to leave.

Harvard Business School case 9-380-072.

> Without resources, I cannot stop this trend, and, as much as it saddens me to say so, I am losing my own motivation to stay with the company.

These were some excerpts from a letter that the senior vice president and head of the Machinery Division, George McElroy, 58, sent to John Martell, president of PC&D, Inc., in February 1976. McElroy was highly respected in both the company and the industry, a member of the board of directors, and a senior officer of the company for 20 years. Therefore, Martell knew that it was important to respond and resolve the issues with McElroy successfully. At the same time, Martell had no intention of giving up his own prerogatives to direct the company.

History of PC&D, Inc.

The Payson & Clark Company

Payson & Clark, the forerunner of PC&D, Inc., was founded during the merger movement around the turn of the century. Four regional machinery companies merged to form a national industrial machinery manufacturing corporation named after the two largest enterprises in the merger, Payson and Clark. With the growth of industry across the country at the time, the demand for heavy machinery took off. The new company benefited from economies of scale, in both production and distribution, and grew and prospered.

By 1965, Payson & Clark Company was an old, stable company, still producing machinery. With revenues of $300 million and net after-tax profits of $6 million, it was still the largest firm in the industry. (See Exhibits 1 and 2 for additional financial information.) The company offered the most complete line of heavy industrial equipment in the industry; the different available configurations of standard and custom models filled a large, encyclopedic sales manual. The consistently high quality and unusual breadth of the product line had made attracting high-caliber salesmen relatively easy. These people were highly knowledgeable in the applications of the product line and saw themselves as consultants to their industrial customers.

While Payson & Clark was the leader in quality and breadth of its product line, it was not the leader in innovations. It left expensive R&D to others, copying products after they were widely accepted. It could afford to follow others primarily because the industry itself was essentially the same as when the company was founded. Its growth depended on the general growth of industry in the United States, efficiencies in purchasing raw materials, and the scale and automation of production. Indeed, the company's major innovation came in the early 1950s with the introduction of plastics in some of the models.

The company was structured in 1965 as it had been in the 1920s, with a standard functional organization and highly centralized chain of command.

EXHIBIT 1 Payson & Clark Company Income Statement, 1956–1965 (in millions except per share data)

	1956	1957	1958	1959	1960	1961	1962	1963	1964	1965
Sales	$177.6	$190.7	$205.0	$220.5	$237.2	$247.9	$259.1	$273.3	$288.1	$302.7
Cost of goods sold	136.1	145.8	157.6	171.0	184.4	192.4	202.1	218.7	230.8	243.6
Gross profit	41.5	44.9	47.4	49.5	52.8	55.5	57.0	54.6	57.3	59.1
Depreciation	5.0	5.0	5.0	4.0	4.0	4.0	4.0	4.0	3.5	3.5
Marketing and general and administrative	18.2	19.7	20.5	22.2	25.6	27.5	28.4	28.0	30.0	33.3
Engineering and product development	8.1	8.6	9.9	10.1	10.6	11.0	11.4	8.8	9.2	7.1
Total expenses	31.3	33.3	35.4	36.3	40.2	42.5	43.8	40.8	42.7	43.9
NBIT	10.2	11.6	12.0	13.2	12.6	13.0	13.2	13.8	14.6	15.2
Interest	3.0	4.0	4.0	4.0	3.0	3.0	3.0	3.0	3.0	3.0
Profit before tax	7.2	7.6	8.0	9.2	9.6	10.0	10.2	10.8	11.6	12.2
Tax	3.6	3.8	4.0	4.6	4.8	5.0	5.1	5.4	5.8	6.1
Profit after tax	$ 3.6	$ 3.8	$ 4.0	$ 4.6	$ 4.8	$ 5.0	$ 5.1	$ 5.4	$ 5.8	$ 6.1
Earnings per share	$1.29	$1.36	$1.44	$1.65	$1.72	$1.80	$1.83	$1.94	$2.08	$2.19
Average stock price	$18	$22	$19	$30	$29	$29	$27	$31	$35	$33

EXHIBIT 2 PC&D, Inc. Payson & Clark Company Balance Sheet, 1956–1965 (in millions)

	1956	1957	1958	1959	1960	1961	1962	1963	1964	1965
Assets										
Cash and securities	$ 6	$ 7	$ 3	$ 1	$ 2	$ 2	$ 2	$ 1	$ 1	$ 1
Accounts receivable	33	36	38	39	41	43	45	47	51	55
Inventories	56	61	64	66	69	74	78	82	88	91
Total current assets	95	103	105	106	112	119	125	130	140	147
Plant and equipment	65	60	60	61	63	67	65	65	64	65
Investments in joint ventures							5	10	11	14
Total assets	$160	$163	$165	$167	$175	$186	$195	$205	$215	$226
Liabilities and Net Worth										
Accounts payable	$ 31	$ 33	$ 36	$ 38	$ 46	$ 54	$ 62	$ 65	$ 70	$ 75
Accrued liabilities	7	9	10	11	13	17	22	25	31	36
Long-term debt due	6	6	6	6	6	6	6	6	6	6
Total current liabilities	44	48	52	55	65	77	86	96	107	117
Long-term debt	52	47	41	35	29	23	18	12	6	—
Total liabilities	96	95	93	90	94	100	104	118	113	117
Common stock	27	27	27	27	27	27	27	27	27	27
Retained earnings	37	41	45	50	54	59	64	70	75	82
Total liabilities and net worth	$160	$163	$165	$167	$175	$186	$195	$205	$215	$226

Its top executives were old-time managers, the average age being 55. Many had spent their entire careers with the firm and could remember the days when old Mr. Payson had kept tight reins on the company in the 1930s and 1940s. Harold C. Payson IV, aged 53 in 1965, was president of the company from the late 1940s and president and chairman since 1955. Although the company was publicly held, the Payson family still owned a considerable amount of the stock.

In the early 1960s, Harold Payson began to consider succession. He wanted to leave the company in good condition not only for his own personal pride but for the betterment of his heirs. From discussions with his investment bankers and friends in the business world, Mr. Payson had recognized that an association with a high-technology, high-growth industry would strengthen Payson & Clark's image. One way in which Mr. Payson sought to implement this suggestion was to use some of the excess capital thrown off by the machinery business to enter into joint ventures with young, new companies developing high-technology, innovative products. Several such investments were made in the early 1960s, including one with the Datronics Company in 1962.

Datronics Company

In 1965, the Datronics Company was 10 years old with revenues of $50 million. (See Exhibits 3 and 4 for additional financial information.) The company had started as an engineering firm subsisting on government research grants and contracts. As a by-product of the governmental projects, the company also developed several types of sophisticated electronic equipment with wide applications to industry. The company concentrated its efforts on R&D, however, and subcontracted the production and bought marketing services for its commercial products. The lack of control over marketing and production and the lost profits passed to the marketers and subcontractors displeased the company's young president, John Martell. In his opinion, the growth of the company was limited until the right product emerged to justify going to a full manufacturing and marketing company.

Following Payson & Clark's investment in 1962, Datronics' engineers developed an exciting new product toward the end of 1964 which promised to sell extremely well due to its increased capacity and lower cost. John Martell saw the promise of the new product as the waited-for opportunity to

EXHIBIT 3 Datronics Company Income Statement, 1956–1965 (in millions except per share data)

	1956	1957	1958	1959	1960	1961	1962	1963	1964	1965
Contracts	$1.2	$6.4	$8.2	$7.5	$ 8.0	$7.9	$ 6.0	$ 4.3	$ 3.4	$ 2.4
Sales			.2	2.1	4.4	8.1	14.3	22.5	34.2	48.1
Revenues	1.2	6.4	8.4	9.6	12.4	16.0	20.3	26.8	37.6	50.5
Cost of goods sold	1.0	4.5	6.0	6.9	8.9	11.5	14.7	19.6	27.8	37.9
Gross profits	.2	1.9	2.4	2.7	3.5	4.5	5.6	7.2	9.8	12.6
Expenses	.5	.6	.7	.7	.7	.7	.9	.9	1.0	1.1
R&D		.7	.8	1.0	1.2	1.5	2.2	3.0	4.0	5.1
Profit before tax	(.3)	.6	.9	1.0	1.6	2.3	2.5	3.3	4.8	6.4
Tax	(.15)	.2	.4	.5	.8	1.1	1.2	1.6	2.4	3.2
Net profit	$ (.15)	$.4	$.5	$.5	$.8	$1.2	$ 1.3	$ 1.7	$ 2.4	$ 3.2
Earnings per share	($1.50)	$4	$5	$5	$8	$ 12	$10.40	$13.60	$19.20	$25.60

expand the company. It was clear, however, that a major influx of capital was needed to bring the product to the market, build a sales force, and begin volume production. Therefore, Martell began a search for external capital that included a presentation to the joint venture partner, Payson & Clark, which already owned 20 percent of Datronics' stock.

Meanwhile, Harold Payson had been following the activities at Datronics closely and was quite aware of the growth potential of the company before John Martell's visit. Further, he recognized that Datronics, once its manufacturing operations started, would have a continual need for new capital. If Payson & Clark invested once, it would not be long until another request for resources came from Datronics. With these factors in mind, Payson decided that the most beneficial arrangement for both parties would be for his company to acquire Datronics. Martell agreed to this offer and negotia-

EXHIBIT 4 Datronics Company Balance Sheet, 1956–1965 (in millions)

	1956	1957	1958	1959	1960	1961	1962	1963	1964	1965
Assets										
Cash	$.05	$ .10	$ .10	$ .40	$ .20	$ .60	$ .60	$ .65	$ 1.56	$ .70
Inventories	.20	2.60	2.70	3.70	5.20	6.20	6.80	10.15	15.22	20.10
Accounts receivable		.30	.50	1.00	2.00	2.20	3.00	4.00	5.12	6.00
Total current assets	.25	3.00	3.30	5.10	7.30	9.00	10.40	14.85	21.90	26.80
Plant and equipment	.50	1.00	1.20	1.40	2.00	3.10	5.10	7.50	8.5	9.0
Total assets	$.75	$4.00	$5.50	$6.50	$9.30	$12.10	$15.50	$22.35	$30.40	$35.8
Liabilities and Net Worth										
Accounts payable	.10	2.15	2.20	2.60	3.65	4.75	5.50	8.78	12.10	14.25
Accrued liabilities	.10	1.00	1.05	1.25	1.65	2.25	1.70	2.77	3.80	3.85
	.20	3.15	3.25	3.85	5.30	7.00	7.20	11.55	15.90	18.10
Notes payable	.60	.50	1.40	1.30	1.85	1.75	2.50	2.2	3.5	3.5
Total liabilities	.80	3.65	4.65	5.15	7.15	8.75	9.70	13.75	19.45	21.60
Additional paid-in capital	—	—	—	—	—	—	1.125	2.225	2.225	2.225
Common stock ($1 par)	.10	.10	.10	.10	.10	.10	.125	.125	.125	.125
Retained earnings	(.15)	.25	.75	1.25	2.05	3.25	4.55	6.25	8.65	11.85
Total liabilities and net worth	$.75	$4.00	$5.50	$6.50	$9.30	$12.10	$15.50	$22.35	$30.40	$35.80

tions for a friendly takeover were consummated. Payson & Clark acquired Datronics for $42 million in November 1965. John Martell himself received $8.4 million in cash, notes, and securities.

The acquisition provided an opportunity for the Payson & Clark Company to update its image. Patterning itself after other successful growth companies of the time, it changed its name to PC&D, Inc., to denote the beginning of a new era in the company.

PC&D, Inc., 1965–1970

After the acquisition, Harold Payson restructured the company with the help of consultants, setting up a divisional organization. The old Payson & Clark Company now became the Machinery Division, headed by George McElroy, formerly vice president, manufacturing. The Datronics Company became the Electronics Division, headed by John Martell.

The Electronics Division

At the time of the acquisition, the Datronics Company consisted of several scientific labs, some test equipment, 10 professional engineers, administrative staff, and John Martell.

Martell, an electrical engineer by training, was in his mid-30s. He was energetic and a risk taker by nature, and even as a child in Iowa could not imagine working for someone else all his life. After college at MIT, he worked for eight years at a large, scientific equipment company in the Boston area. Initially, he was hired for the research group, but he was more attracted to the management positions in the company. He transferred first to the Corporate Planning Office and then became plant manager for one of the divisions. With his technical competence and management experience, it was not surprising that he was approached by several of the more innovative of the company's research engineers to invest in and head up a new, independent R&D company. Martell bought in for 25 percent of the founding stock and, thus, began the Datronics Company.

During his term as president of Datronics, Martell was highly regarded by the small group of employees. While he had a respectable command of the technology, he left the research to the engineers, devoting his time to developing sources of challenging and lucrative contracts.

After the acquisition by the Payson & Clark Company, Martell retained full control of the operations of his old organization that was now the Electronics Division. He hired an experienced industrial marketer from a large technical firm to set up the marketing operations and a friend of his from his old employer to head up the production operations. As expected, the demand for the division's new product was very high. Five years later, by 1970, the division was a successful growing enterprise, having expanded into other electronics fields. It had 700 employees, marketing offices established or opening throughout the United States, Europe, and Japan, plants at three different sites, and revenues of over $160 million. The business press reported these activities very favorably, giving much credit to the leadership of Martell.

The Machinery Division

Meanwhile, the Machinery Division continued to be the stalwart of the industry it always had been, retaining its structure and activities of the earlier time. George McElroy, division manager and senior vice president, was considered the mainstay of the division. He had joined the company in the early 1950s and was primarily responsible for the plastics innovations of that time. Advisor and confidant of Payson, McElroy was thought by his subordinates to be the next in line for the presidency.

As for Harold Payson himself, he limited his involvement in the company's internal affairs to reviewing budgets and year-end results, and spent most of his time with community activities and lobbying in Washington. He felt justified in this hands-off policy because of the quality of both his division vice presidents, McElroy and Martell. PC&D's performance further supported Payson's approach. Revenues climbed to $530 million, and profits after tax to $14 million by 1970. The solid 26 multiple of its stock price reflected the confidence in PC&D's prospects. (See Exhibits 5 and 6.)

The compensation schemes reflected the extent to which Harold Payson allowed the division managers to be autonomous. McElroy's compensation was 90 percent salary, with a 10 percent bonus based on ROI. Martell received two thirds of his pay as a bonus based on growth in revenues. Compensation policies within each division were entirely at the discretion of either Martell or McElroy. In general,

Martell made much greater use of incentive compensation than McElroy.

1970 Change at PC&D

Toward the end of 1970, Harold Payson decided that it was time to limit his involvement to that of chairman of the board and to name a new president of PC&D. He, himself, supported the appointment of George McElroy as the next president. McElroy was the next senior officer in the company and, after years of working with Harold Payson, held many of the same views as to the traditional values of PC&D. However, Payson agreed with the school of thought that chief executives should not choose their own successors. He therefore established a search committee, consisting of three outside members of the board of directors. (See Exhibit 7 for a list of board members.) A thorough job was done. The committee interviewed several candidates within PC&D, including John Martell and George McElroy. Outside candidates were also considered. The committee utilized executive search firms and consultants to identify candidates and carefully compared external and internal prospects. The result was the nomination of John Martell. While his relative youth was a surprise to some, the search committee's report explained the thinking behind the choice that "during the past five years, PC&D has experienced an exciting and profitable period of growth and diversification. But it is essential that the company not become complacent. One of our major criteria in choosing a new president was to find a person with the energy and vision to continue PC&D's growth and expansion." The board unanimously approved the selection of John Martell as president and CEO.

Martell began his new position with the board's mandate in mind. He planned to continue the diversification of PC&D into high-growth industries. He expected to follow both an acquisition mode and a start-up mode, using the excess funds from the Machinery Division and PC&D's rising stock to finance the growth. For start-ups, Martell planned to use joint ventures supporting newer companies, much as the old Payson and Clark Company had supported his venture in its early days.

EXHIBIT 5 PC&D, Inc. Income Statement, 1966–1970 (in millions except per share data)

	1966	1967	1968	1969	1970
Sales					
Machinery	$315.1	$327.5	$340.2	$354.1	$368.2
Electronics	66.1	84.7	106.7	132.3	161.4
Total	381.2	412.2	446.9	486.4	529.6
Cost of goods sold:					
Machinery	251.7	264.3	271.8	284.7	297.9
Electronics	49.6	63.0	79.6	96.8	118.5
Total	301.3	327.3	351.4	381.5	416.4
Gross margin	79.9	84.9	95.5	104.9	113.2
Expenses:					
Marketing general and administrative expense	46.1	48.3	50.3	51.6	53.1
Product development—Machinery	6.9	4.6	4.7	4.1	4.5
R&D—Electronics	4.2	5.3	10.3	17.8	27.3
Total	52.2	58.2	65.3	73.5	84.9
NBIT	24.7	26.7	30.2	31.4	28.3
Interest	3.0	3.0	0.2	0.2	0.2
Profit before tax	21.7	23.7	30.0	31.2	28.1
Taxes	10.8	11.8	15.0	15.6	14.0
Net profit	$10.9	$11.9	$15.0	$15.6	$14.1
Earnings per share	$3.63	$3.97	$5.00	$5.20	$4.70
Average stock price	$94	$111	$145	$146	$103

EXHIBIT 6 PC&D, Inc. Balance Sheet, 1966–1970 (in millions)

	1966	1967	1968	1969	1970
Assets					
Cash and securities	$ 2	$ 5	$ 9	$ 7	$ 11
Accounts receivable	67	71	77	87	101
Inventories	118	128	145	166	180
Total current assets	187	214	231	260	292
Plant and equipment	83	95	97	108	120
Investments in joint ventures	10	11	12	12	10
Goodwill	6	6	5	5	5
Total assets	$286	$320	$345	$385	$427
Liabilities and Net Worth					
Accounts payable	$90	$96	$103	$111	$127
Accrued liabilities	31	33	31	32	35
Long-term debt due	1	1	1	2	3
Total current liabilities	122	130	135	145	165
Long-term debt	16	30	35	49	57
Total liabilities	138	160	170	194	222
Common stock and paid-in capital	55	55	55	55	55
Retained earnings	93	105	120	136	150
Total liabilities and net worth	$286	$320	$345	$385	$427

Martell brought to his position a very definite management style. He was a strong believer in the benefits accruing from an opportunistic, entrepreneurial spirit and he wanted to inject PC&D with this kind of energy. However, he was concerned that the kind of people with this kind of spirit would not be attracted to work with PC&D because of the stigma, real or imagined, of being attached to a large company.

As Martell commented:

> It was my experience that there are two worlds of people, some of whom are very secure and comfortable and satisfied in their career pursuits in large institutionalized companies, and others of whom are, I think, wild ducks, and who are interested in perhaps greater challenges that small companies present in terms of the necessity to succeed or die.
>
> In many work environments, the constraints placed upon the individual by the nature of the institution are such as to sometimes make people uncomfortable.
>
> The decision-making process is long and involved, sometimes not known, in the sense that the people who act upon decisions are not in close proximity to those who benefit or suffer from the effects of those decisions.
>
> The formalization of the decision-making process is frequently an irritant, and for people who are unusually energetic and demanding, in the sense of desiring themselves to take action and to have their actions complemented by the actions of other people upon whom

EXHIBIT 7 PC&D, Inc. Members, Board of Directors, 1970

Harold Payson IV, President—PC&D
George McElroy, Senior Vice President—Machinery Division, PC&D
John Martell, Vice President—Electronics Division, PC&D
Carl Northrup, Treasurer—PC&D
David S. Curtis, Partner—Barth & Gimbel, Wall Street brokerage firm
Elizabeth B. Payne, Partner—Payne, Bartley, & Springer, Washington law firm
Charles F. Sprague, President—Forrest Products, Inc. (a large manufacturing firm)
Gardner L. Stacy III, Dean—Business School, State University
James Hoffman, Vice President—Baltimore Analysts Association (an international firm)

they are dependent, I would characterize these people as perhaps being wild ducks rather than tame ducks. In that sense, I wanted more "wild ducks" in our company.

Martell himself credited the success of the Electronics Division to Payson's willingness to turn the reins completely over to him. The secret, Martell thought, was in spotting the right person with both ability and integrity. Corporate headquarters' role should be to provide resources in terms of both money and expertise as needed, to set timetables, to provide measurement points and incentive, and then to keep hands off.

While the board's directives were clear to Martell, the specifics for implementation were not. Not only were the larger questions of which way to diversify or how to encourage innovation unanswered, but how to plan and whom to involve were also unclear. Martell was not given the luxury of time to resolve these issues. Within the first week in his new position, three professionals from the Electronics Division called on Martell. Bert Rogers and Elaine Patterson were key engineers from the Research Department and Thomas Grennan was head of marketing, western region. They had been working on some ideas for a new product (not competing with any PC&D current lines) and were ready to leave the company to start their own business to develop and market it. Indeed, they had already had a prospectus prepared for their new venture. They were hoping either Martell personally or PC&D, Inc., might be able to provide some venture capital. The president particularly liked these three and admired their willingness to take such personal risks with a product as yet unresearched as to market or design. Indeed, with his energy and can-do aggressive style, Tom Grennan reminded Martell of himself just a few years ago when he left to start the Datronics Company.

Martell liked the product and saw the idea as a possible route for continuing the diversification and growth of PC&D. But there was a problem. It was clear from the presentation of the three that much of their motivation came from the desire to start their own company and, through their equity interest, to reap the high rewards of their efforts if successful. Martell did not fault this motivation, for it had been his as well. He could not expect PC&D's managers to take large personal risks if there was no potential for a large payoff. Further, a fair offer to the group, if in salary, required more than PC&D could afford or could justify to the older divisions. Martell told Rogers, Patterson, and Grennan that he was very interested and asked if he could review the prospectus overnight and get back to them the next day. That night, he devised a plan of which he was particularly proud. The major feature of the plan Martell called the Entrepreneurial Subsidiary. Martell presented this proposal to Grennan, Rogers, and Patterson the next day. They readily accepted and a pattern for most of PC&D's diversification over the next five years was begun.

The Entrepreneurial Subsidiary

Martell's plan was as follows:

When a proposal for a new product area was made to the PC&D corporate office, a new (entrepreneurial) subsidiary would be incorporated. The initiators of the idea would leave their old division or company and become officers and employees of the new subsidiary. In the current example, the new subsidiary was the Pro Instrument Corporation with Grennan as president and Rogers and Patterson as vice presidents.

The new subsidiary would issue stock in its name, $1 par value, 80 percent of which would be bought by PC&D, Inc., and 20 percent by the entrepreneurs involved—engineers and other key officers. This initial capitalization, plus sizable direct loans from PC&D, Inc., provided the funds for the research and development of the new product up to its commercialization. In the case of Pro Instruments, Patterson and Rogers hired 10 other researchers, while Grennan hired a market researcher and a finance/accounting person. These 15 people invested $50,000 together and PC&D invested another $200,000.

Two kinds of agreements were signed between the two parties. The first was a research contract between the parent company and the subsidiary, setting time schedules for the research, defining requirements for a commercializable product, outlining budgets, and otherwise stipulating obligations on both sides. In general, the sub was responsible for the R&D and production and testing of a set number of prototypes of a new product, while the parent company would market and produce the product on an international scale. Pro Instruments' agreement stipulated two phases, one lasting 18 months to produce a prototype, and another lasting 6 months to test the product in the field and produce a marketing plan. Detailed budget and personnel needs were outlined, providing for a $900,000 working capital loan from PC&D during the first phase and $425,000 during the second.

While PC&D, Inc., had proprietary rights on the product and all revenues received from marketing it, the agreement often included an incentive kicker for the key engineers in the form of additional stock to be issued if the finished product produced certain specified amounts of revenue by given dates. Indeed, this was the case for Pro Instruments: 5,000 shares in year 1, to be issued if net profits were over $250,000; 20,000 shares in year 2 if profits were over $1 million; and 10,000 in year 3 if profits were over $3 million.

The second agreement specified the financial obligations and terms for merger. Once the terms of the research contract were met, PC&D, with board approval, had the option for a stated period of time (usually four years) to merge the subsidiary through a one-for-one exchange of PC&D stock for the stock of the subsidiary. The sub was then dissolved. To protect the interests of entrepreneurs, PC&D was required to vote on merger of the sub within 60 days if the sub met certain criteria. For Pro Instruments, the criteria were (1) the product earned cumulative profits of $500,000 and (2) if the earnings of PC&D and the sub were consolidated, dilution of PC&D's EPS would not have occurred over three consecutive quarters. If PC&D did not choose to merge during the 60 days, then the sub had a right to buy out PC&D's interest.

Since PC&D's stock was selling for $103 in 1970 and subsidiary stock was bought for $1 per share, the exchange of stock represented a tremendous potential return. Depending on the value of PC&D's stock at the time of merger, the net worth of the "entrepreneurs" who originally invested in the sub multiplied overnight. Indeed, as subs were merged in ensuing years, typical gains ranged from 100 to 200 times the original investments in the entrepreneurial sub. For example, PC&D exercised its option to merge Pro Instruments when its product was brought to market in 1972. Thomas Grennan, who had bought 6,000 shares of Pro Instruments stock, found his 6,000 shares of PC&D valued at $936,000 (PC&D common selling for $156 on the New York Stock Exchange at the time). By the end of 1974, Pro Instruments' new product had earned $50 million in revenue and $4.8 million in profits, thus qualifying the original entrepreneurs for stock bonuses. Grennan received another 4,200 shares valued at $684,600. Thus, in four years, he had earned about $1.6 million on a $6,000 investment.

By setting up entrepreneurial subs like Pro Instruments, Mr. Martell had several expectations. In the process of setting up a subsidiary with the dynamics of a small, independent group, Martell hoped to create the loyalty, cohesion, and informal structure conducive to successful research and development efforts. The sub would have a separate location and its own officers who decided structure and operating policies. Further, it provided the opportunity to buy into and reap the benefits of ownership in the equity of a company. In Mr. Martell's words:

> I think the concept of the entrepreneurial subsidiaries was the outgrowth of the insight that in many industrial corporations the system of rewards is perhaps inverted from what many people think it should be; that the hierarchy of the institution commends itself to those people who are capable of managing other people's efforts, and those people at lower echelons who are unusually creative and who, as a result of their creativity and innovation and daring in the technical sense or perhaps in a marketing sense, are unusually responsible for the accomplishments of the business, are very frequently forgotten about in the larger rewards of the enterprise.
>
> I, on the other hand, recognized that such persons are frequently, perhaps by training, inclination, or otherwise, not capable of marshaling the financial resources or organizing the manufacturing and marketing efforts required to exploit their creativity. Without the kind of assistance that PC&D was capable of lending to them—an assured marketing capability was often a key concern—they are wary of undertaking new ventures.

Further, it was Mr. Martell's opinion that the organizational and incentive structure of the entrepreneurial sub would attract the best engineers from older, more secure firms to PC&D—the so-called wild ducks.

More important, Martell hoped to encourage the timely development of new products with minimal initial investment by PC&D. If Pro Instruments, for example, did not meet its timetable with the original money invested, its officers would have to approach PC&D for new money just as if they were an outside company. PC&D would then have multiple opportunities to review and consider the investment. If the entrepreneurial sub failed or could not get more money from the parent, PC&D was under no obligation to keep the company alive or to rehire its employees. If loans were involved, PC&D could act as any other creditor. As Martell observed,

> The benefit to PC&D shareholders was in the rapid expansion of PC&D's products, the size of the company, the ability of the company to compete in the marketplace in a way which PC&D, dependent upon

> only internal development projects, could never have achieved, or could have achieved only at much greater costs and over a longer period of years.

However, Martell felt the stock incentives would properly reward the genius of creative engineers for the service performed without having to pay high salaries over a long, potentially unproductive period after the initial product was developed. Employees did not have to be rehired, nor were they obligated to continue employment, even if the sub was merged. Those that were rehired would be paid at the normal salary levels of comparable people at PC&D. The reasoning here was that

> there were two criteria for establishing an entrepreneurial subsidiary. The first criterion was that the R&D objectives of the subsidiary could not be reached except under the aegis of the subsidiary, because it involved people who were not involved in PC&D's main lines of business.
>
> The other criterion was that considerable career risk must exist for the people who would leave their established positions within the management structure of PC&D to undertake the entrepreneurial venture of the new subsidiary. Also, the people, in some part, had to be new talent who came from outside PC&D. When I refer to career risk, I mean for example that if a director of engineering at PC&D left his or her post to join an entrepreneurial subsidiary, a new director of engineering would be appointed, and given the lack of success of the entrepreneurial subsidiary, there would in effect be no position of director of engineering to which the person could return. Moreover, it is probable that we would not want the individual to return.

The stock incentive also motivated the engineers to produce without having to commit any resources of the parent company for the future, since the corporation was not required to merge the sub or to produce and market the new product. The incentive kicker, moreover, would ensure quality. A product that was rushed through development would be more likely to have problems and not reach revenue goals.

Another advantage of the entrepreneurial sub was its effect on decision making. Without the need to go through the entire corporate hierarchy, decisions would be made closer to the operating level. This would enhance the quality of decisions because managers performed best, according to Martell, when given objectives and resources from top managers but with operating decisions left unfettered.

Finally, Martell expected that the entrepreneurial sub would be the training and proving ground of PC&D's future top managers. By providing the means for these executives to gain great personal wealth, Martell expected to gain their loyalty and continued efforts for both himself and PC&D.

PC&D: 1970–1975

During the first five years of Martell's presidency, PC&D's growth was quite impressive. With revenues topping the billion dollar mark in 1975, growth had averaged about 15 percent in revenues and 35 percent in profits after tax during the five years. (See Exhibits 8 and 9 for financials.) Such growth had been achieved, to a large extent, from new products developed in entrepreneurial subsidiaries. In 1975, sales of $179.2 million and profit before taxes and interest of $22.1 million came from these new products.[1] All together, 11 entrepreneurial subsidiaries had been organized during the 1970–75 time frame. Of these, four had successfully developed products and had been merged into PC&D—one in 1972, one in 1973, and two in 1974. The other seven were younger and work was still in process. None had failed so far.

Most subsidiaries grew out of needs of the Electronics Division or Pro Instruments. Competitors in the electronics equipment industry were beginning to integrate backward, lowering costs by producing their own semiconductors. The need to remain cost competitive caused PC&D to establish entrepreneurial subs to develop specialized components, including semiconductors, assuming that these could be both used by PC&D and sold in outside markets. In the process of selling semiconductors to outside customers, ideas for new products using PC&D components were stimulated, and new subs were formed to develop these equipment products. The cost of merging the two types of subs, components or equipment, differed, however. Equipment subs were cheaper in so far as they could share the already existing sales force of the Electronics Division; many parts could be standard ones already utilized in other products; and the processes were similar to other Electronics products. But with semiconductors, new plant, new sales channels, new manufacturing processes, and new skills at all levels had to be built. While to Martell the move into semiconductors promised a large cash flow in the future

---

[1]Of PC&D total assets in 1975, approximately 40 percent were devoted to the Machinery Division, 35 percent to the traditional Electronics Division, and 25 percent to the entrepreneurial subsidiaries.

EXHIBIT 8 PC&D, Inc. Income Statement, 1971–1975 (in millions)

	1971	1972	1973	1974	1975
Sales:					
Machinery	$382.9	$397.8	$412.5	$426.9	$ 440.6
Electronics*	193.6	235.6	300.1	397.4	561.4
Total	$576.5	$633.4	$712.6	$824.3	$1,002.0
Cost of goods sold:					
Machinery	311.3	322.6	338.2	350.9	359.1
Electronics	145.2	174.3	216.1	282.2	421.1
Total	456.5	496.9	554.3	633.1	780.2
Gross margin	120.0	136.5	158.3	191.2	221.8
Expenses:					
Marketing general and administrative expense	54.7	56.3	59.1	63.3	67.7
Development—Machinery	5.0	5.1	5.2	5.2	5.3
R&D—Electronics	28.4	29.5	30.7	31.9	33.5
Total	88.1	90.9	95.0	100.4	106.5
Profit before interest and taxes	31.9	45.6	63.3	90.8	115.3
Interest	0.2	3.0	3.0	7.0	11.0
Profit before tax	31.7	42.6	60.3	83.8	104.3
Taxes	15.8	21.3	30.1	41.9	52.1
Net profit	$ 15.9	$ 21.3	$ 30.2	$ 41.9	$ 52.2
Earnings per share	$5.30	$6.45†	$8.39	$10.47	$13.05
Average stock price	$106	$156	$158	$163	$238

*Sales figures for Electronics include both sales by the original division plus sales of new subsidiaries after they are merged. Thus in 1975, the $561.4 million in sales for Electronics includes $179.2 from products developed in subsidiaries. Profit before interest and taxes from new products was $22.1 million.

†Number of shares increased in 1972 by .3 million from the merger of Pro Instruments. They increased in 1973 by .3 million from merger of Sub #2, and again by .4 million in 1974 from the merger of Subs #3 and #4. Thus in 1974, there was a total of 4 million shares outstanding. In late 1973, there was a secondary offering of 1 million shares.

in a booming industry, some in the company were concerned that the current cash drain was not the best use of scarce cash resources.

When Martell first became president, he made few changes in PC&D's organization structure. McElroy continued as vice president, Machinery Division, and retained control over that division's structure and policies. Martell himself retained his responsibilities as manager of the Electronics Division. This he did reluctantly and with all intentions of finding a new executive for the job; however, the unexpected nature of his promotion left Martell without a ready candidate.

As the subs began to be merged, beginning with Pro Instruments in 1972, questions of organization began to arise. In typical fashion, Martell wanted to pass involvement in these decisions down to the appropriate managers. There was also no question that Pro Instruments' president, Tom Grennan, had proven himself with the new subsidiary. So in 1972, Martell appointed Grennan to division vice president, electronics, based on Grennan's superlative performance. Further, because the products were complementary, all of the subs that were merged in this period were placed in the Electronics Division. Moreover, in recognition of the increased number of products, Grennan did reorganize the Electronics Division. He appointed his Pro Instruments colleague, Bert Rogers, to director of research, which was organized by product area. Manufacturing, also organized by product, reflected the development by subsidiary as well. Marketing, on the other hand, was organized by region as it had been previously. Until they were merged, however, subsidiary presidents went directly to Mr. Martell for resolution of problems that arose. (See Exhibit 10 for an organization chart in 1975.)

By 1975, the Electronics Division's enlarged marketing and production departments employed 4,000 people with production plants in three different locations. Electronics now had sales of $561.4 million as compared to Machinery's $440.6 million.

EXHIBIT 9 PC&D, Inc. Balance Sheet, 1971–1975 (in millions)

	1971	1972	1973	1974	1975
Assets					
Cash and securities	$ 10	$ 5	$ 2	$ 2	$ 3
Accounts receivable	117	131	155	171	213
Inventories	200	223	270	327	401
Total current assets	327	359	427	500	617
Plant and equipment	122	124	125	178	232
Investments in joint ventures	10	8	10	9	6
Investments in subsidiaries	5	10	21	16	25
Goodwill	4	4	3	3	2
Total assets	$468	$505	$586	$706	$882
Liabilities and Net Worth					
Accounts payable	$151	$160	$179	$193	$243
Accrued liabilities	37	41	46	51	65
Long-term debt due	4	4	4	6	7
Total current liabilities	192	205	229	250	315
Long-term debt	55	58	84	138	193
Total liabilities	247	263	313	388	508
Common stock and paid-in capital	55	55	56	57	57
Retained earnings	166	187	217	261	317
Total liabilities and net worth	$468	$505	$586	$706	$882

While successful development projects from subsidiaries had been largely responsible for the sales growth at PC&D, this result had not come without costs. First, the subsidiaries required funds—$60 million by the end of 1975. Some of these funds came from retained earnings, but much was new money raised in the form of long-term debt. Further, stock issued to capitalize subs and pay bonuses to "entrepreneurs" had a diluting effect on PC&D's shares. If all subsidiaries were merged and successful, the number of new shares could be significant. While raising such a sizable amount of new funds was not particularly difficult for a company as large as PC&D, the needs arising from the subsidiaries left little new money for the core businesses of PC&D. The Machinery Division, for example, had not had their development budget increased at all during the five years ending 1975.

Current Concerns

Despite PC&D's recent successes, Mr. Martell was not without worries. Several problem areas had appeared in both the Electronics and Machinery Divisions.

In Electronics, personnel and products originating in subsidiaries now equaled or surpassed those from the original division. It had been part of the strategy of the entrepreneurial subsidiaries to use them as devices to attract talent from other firms. A key researcher hired from outside was encouraged to hire, in turn, the best of his or her former colleagues. Thus, the loyalty and friendships between key "entrepreneurs" and their staffs were often strong and long-standing. As the entrepreneurial subsidiaries were merged, their personnel tended to retain this loyalty to the president or key officers of the old sub rather than transferring it to PC&D. Thus, several warring spheres of influence were developing in the division, particularly in the research department and between research and other departments. Martell was concerned that such influences and warring would lead to poor decisions and much wasted energy in the division.

Turnover in Electronics was also increasing. This was of particular concern to Martell for it was just those talented engineers that the entrepreneurial subsidiaries were meant to attract that were beginning to leave. For example, Elaine Patterson, formerly of Pro Instruments, left during 1975 to start her own company, taking 20 research engineers with her. The source of the turnover was unclear but possible factors included distaste for the kind of warring atmosphere mentioned above and the inability to be a part of a large corporate R&D department with its demand for budgets and reports.

For many employees, the sudden absence of monetary incentives changed the climate drastically, however. This lack of incentive, coupled with the discovery that the most challenging projects were taken on by newly formed subsidiaries which favored hiring outside expertise, caused dissatisfaction. For Martell, such turnover was of greatest concern in the long run, for the inability to create a strong central R&D department in the Electronics Division created a continuing need for more entrepreneurial subs. These subsidiaries were still too new an idea for Martell to want to risk his entire future R&D program on their successes. Further, most of the new products were in highly competitive areas. Without continuing upgrades, these products would soon become obsolete. A strong central R&D department was needed for follow-up development of products started by subsidiaries.

Finally, Martell was concerned by recent indications of rather serious operating problems in the Electronics Division. This was particularly disturbing in that Martell had placed complete faith in Grennan's managerial ability. The most recent cost report, for example, indicated that marketing, G&A, and engineering expenses were way out of line in the division. Further, the marketing and production departments reported problems in several products originating in the subs. One product, with expected obsolescence of four years, now showed a six-year breakeven just to cover the engineering and production costs. Another product, completing its first year on the market, had been forecasted by the subsidiary to achieve $20 million in sales in its first two years. However, during the first six months, losses had been incurred because of customer returns. A report on the causes of the returns showed a predominance of product failures. The chances for breakeven on this product looked bleak. While

EXHIBIT 10 Organization Chart, 1975

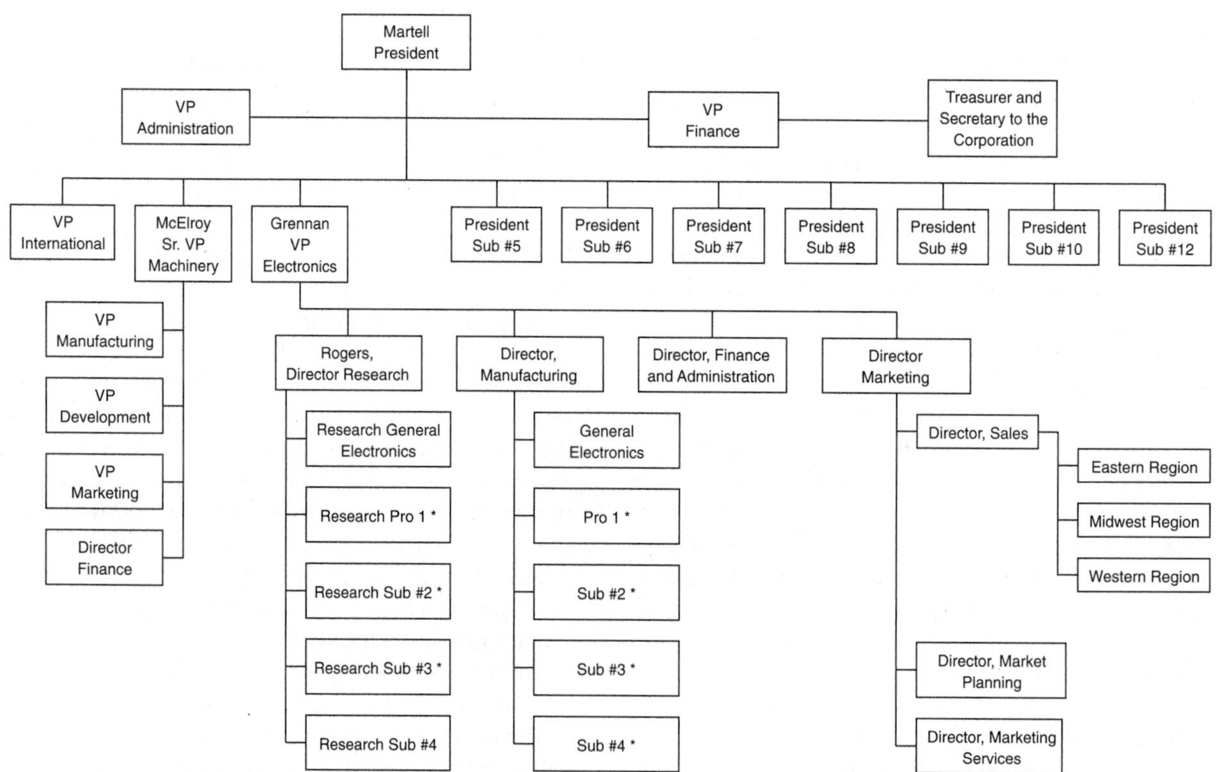

* Reference to subsidiaries indicates origin of personnel and product.

none of these problems had affected operating results yet, Martell was especially concerned that these operating problems would have a negative impact on first-quarter 1976 earnings.

Martell had not confronted Grennan with these operating problems as yet. He had wanted to see how the division itself was attacking these issues through its long-range plan. Martell had requested Grennan to prepare a long-range plan (five years) as well as the usual one-year operating plan. The product of this effort had only arrived recently (February 1976) and Martell had not had a chance to study it. (Table of Contents is reproduced in Exhibit 11.) Its 100-page bulk loomed on Martell's desk. Quick perusal had indicated maybe four pages of prose scattered through the plan, and dozens of charts, graphs, and tables of numbers, every one of which manifested an upward trend.

In an attempt to get employee feedback on all of these problems, Martell had contracted an outside consulting firm to carry out confidential interviews with personnel in the Electronics Division. The interviews found middle managers quite concerned over the "confusion in the division" which was causing a loss of morale there. The consultant's report cited concrete problems, including lost equipment, missed billings, and confusion in the plant. Typical comments from lower level personnel included:

EXHIBIT 11 PC&D, Inc.

Electronics Division
1976 Operating Plan
1977–1980 Long-Range Outlook

Table of Contents

Either upper management is not being informed of problems or they don't know how to solve them.

Morale is very poor, job security is nil.

There is little emphasis on production efficiencies.

Scrap is unaccounted for.

Market forecasts are grossly inaccurate.

Production schedules have a definite saw-tooth pattern. There is very little good planning.

There are no systematic controls.

These were not the sort of comments Martell expected from the division responsible for the major portion of PC&D's future growth. His concern, at this time, was not so much the problems themselves, but what was being done about them. His preferred policy was obviously to stay out of day-to-day operating problems. He wondered how long it was prudent to allow such problems to continue without some intervention on his part.

Meanwhile, the Machinery Division had its own problems. The last major construction of new plant had been in the early 1950s. Since that time, McElroy had upgraded production methods, which succeeded in checking rising costs. However, since 1965, resources for such improvements had not been increased, and, with inflation in the 1970s, less and less could be done on a marginal basis. McElroy was currently of the opinion that capacity was sufficient for the short term, but that it was impossible to remain state-of-the-art.[2] Indeed, the Machinery Division's products were beginning to fall behind the new developments of competitors. Further, the costs of Machinery's products were beginning to inch up. As the production line aged, quality control reported an increasing percentage of defective goods. In contrast to the situation in Machinery, the rather extensive investment in new plant for the production of semiconductors did not sit too well with McElroy, who was concerned with the lack of flexibility that could result from backward integrating and thought component needs should be farmed out to the cheapest bidder from the numerous small components firms. Martell was concerned how long he could keep McElroy satisfied without a major investment in Machinery and how long he could count on the cash flow from Machinery for other users.

Also, turnover, a problem never before experienced in the Machinery Division, had appeared. Here, however, it was the salespeople who were leaving. Martell worried over this trend, for the sales force was the strength of the division. According to the head of marketing, the salespeople considered themselves the best in the industry, and they did not wish to sell products which were not the best. They saw Machinery's products no longer as the best in quality or state-of-the-art. Further, they did not wish to work for a company where they felt unimportant. Whether true or not, the sales force certainly appeared less aggressive than in previous times.

Thus, Martell was not overly surprised to receive McElroy's letter nor was he certain that some of McElroy's anger concerning the Electronics Division was not justified. Martell knew he had to do something about McElroy, as well as Grennan and the Electronics Division. He also had to decide whether entrepreneurial subsidiaries should continue to be part of PC&D's research and development strategy. Finally, all of Martell's decisions concerning the divisions and subsidiaries needed to be consistent with a strategy that would continue PC&D's growth.

---

[2] McElroy suspected that the Machinery Division would require an investment of $100 million to $125 million over two to three years to revitalize the product line and plant and equipment. McElroy felt that in the long term the return on this investment would match the division's historic ROI.

PART

IV Creating and Implementing a Development Strategy

Creating and Implementing a Development Strategy

In technology-intensive environments, development projects are where the action is. They're where the "rubber meets the road." Through a combination of product and process enhancement activities such development projects can provide a host of benefits for an organization. First, they can lead to market success in a rapidly changing, intensely competitive setting. New products and their associated manufacturing processes and delivery systems can leapfrog the competition, create strong barriers that others must hurdle just to stay in the game, and establish a leadership position as a dominant design. Furthermore, they can be the vehicle for entering new distribution channels and garnering new customers, and they can complement existing offerings by rounding out the line and targeting untapped niches.

Nearly as important as the promise of market success is the impact that effectively executed development projects can have on resource utilization: they not only capitalize on prior research efforts, but leverage and enhance existing assets. What sales force or factory won't perform better with a new product that is hot in the market place than with an old, no longer distinctive product? Additionally, new products and new processes provide the means for an organization to overcome past weaknesses and establish an even stronger resource base for the future.

Still a third area of promise associated with the commercialization of new products and processes is that of organizational renewal and change. Organizations consist of people, and people become excited when they see growth opportunities being captured by new products and processes. Furthermore, the adoption and implementation of new technologies that transform aging assets can enable a business to recruit, train, and develop better people than its competitors. Being part of the team that succeeds in achieving its development goals is rewarding and fulfilling.

Unfortunately, far too often the reality surrounding many development projects is that although they begin with great expectations on the part of all involved, they fall far short in the end. Even projects with milestone dates, resource plans, and aggressive market goals often slip as they encounter unexpected problems and organizational miscues, arriving late and no longer on target for the market place (see Exhibit 1).

Why is it that so many development projects fail to deliver fully on their planned goals and anticipated benefits? Why do firms—even those that explicitly recognize the importance of product development—find it so challenging to focus resources and execute projects as intended? Additionally, why don't the increased dosages of management attention that inevitably result when major projects slip seem to have any impact on project effectiveness?

EXHIBIT 1 The Reality of Many Development Projects: Schedule Slippage in the A14 Stereo Project

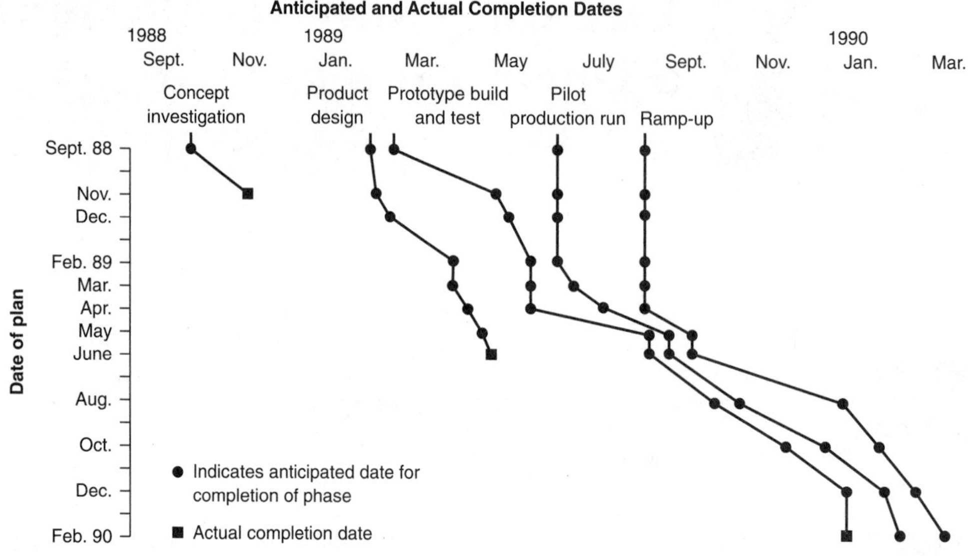

SOURCE: Adapted from S. C. Wheelwright and K. B. Clark, *Revolutionizing Product Development* (New York: Free Press, 1992), p. 11.

The perspective of this chapter is that an organization can achieve robust and predictable development capabilities that will achieve their intended goals in the marketplace, within the organization, and for the individuals involved. However, doing so requires a host of skills, tools, and concepts that in many instances differ significantly from the natural inclinations common in organizations. At the core of this need for change is management itself. In too many instances, management at all levels fails to provide the leadership required for success. The heart of the problem is management, but management is also the solution.

The magnitude of the change required on management's part is captured clearly by Exhibit 2. As illustrated, most senior managers play little, if any, role in the early stages (knowledge acquisition, concept investigation, and basic design) of a development effort. Once a project progresses to the point of building prototypes and trying to demonstrate the performance characteristics (or lack thereof) of those prototypes, management comes to life and remains attentive until prototyping problems have been resolved. When the product is introduced, all too often customers discover a number of remaining issues and problems, and management again focuses its attention on the effort.

The problem with such a pattern is that management is only reactive. As suggested by the shaded curves in Exhibit 2, the greatest amount of management's energy on the project is expended when the ability to influence its outcome is at a minimum. It would be far more effective to focus management attention and effort on development activity at the front end, or even the preproject phase, of development. To do so, however, management must have the appropriate skills, tools, and methods to provide the foundation for a different type of involvement in development. Once accomplished, management can then spend a far greater portion of its energies assessing the lessons learned from individual projects, using them to improve development capability on an ongoing basis, and laying the groundwork for subsequent projects.

The remainder of this chapter is organized around three areas of management activity: preproject or front-end planning, project execution, and postproject learning. This combined set of management activities is what constitutes the development strategy for a business. The concepts, frameworks, and tools that have been found particularly effective in each of these areas will be described, and the subsequent readings and case studies will elaborate on those and illustrate their use in practice. This chap-

EXHIBIT 2 Timing and Impact of Management Attention and Influence

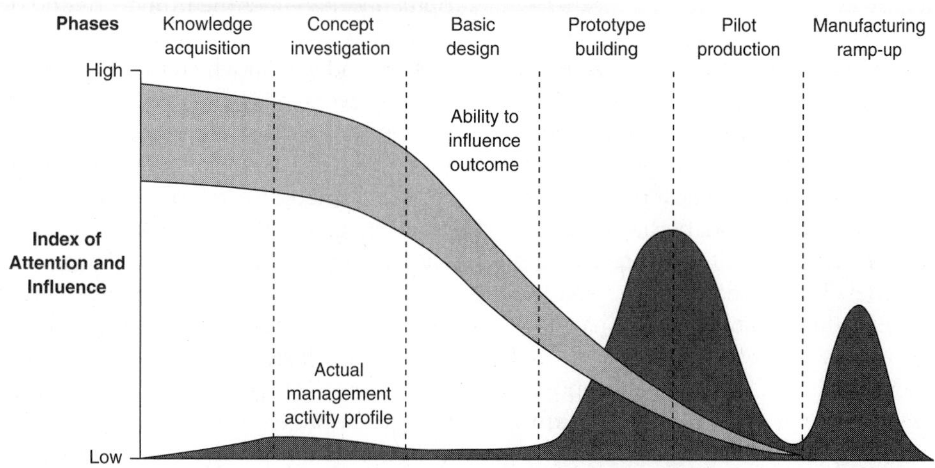

SOURCE: R. H. Hayes, S. C. Wheelwright, and K. B. Clark, *Dynamic Manufacturing* (New York: Free Press, 1988), p. 279. See also F. Gluck and R. Foster, "Managing Technological Change: A Box of Cigars for Brad," *Harvard Business Review,* September–October 1975, p. 141.

ter begins by providing an overview of development strategy and a detailed examination of the preproject stages, including a descriptive framework for categorizing individual development projects into different types. Next, four alternative team structures for organizing the resources used to carry out a development effort are outlined. These can be used effectively to match individual project needs and requirements with the organization's resources and business objectives. The final portion of this chapter focuses on specific ways an organization can learn across a series of development efforts and apply that learning to achieve continual improvement in development speed, productivity, and quality. In addition, an expanded role for management in achieving longer-term development goals is outlined.

Development Strategy and Preproject Management

While individual development projects are where much of the action is, senior management can have its greatest leverage in the preproject stages. There are two quite different views, however, as to the nature of senior management's role in these preproject activities. Both appear to be based on a similar overall concept of how development activity can be planned and managed, but the specific senior management activities under each approach are radically different, as are the results. We'll refer to the more frequently encountered approach as the *traditional senior management approach* and the alternative as the *development strategy leadership approach*.

The overall conceptual view of development activity for both approaches is that of the development funnel, shown in Exhibit 3. As suggested in this figure, organizations encounter a range of product ideas and concepts that can be investigated as potential new products and processes. From that range of possibilities, the organization must pick a handful of specific projects to which resources will be applied, with the goal of creating on-target, on-

EXHIBIT 3 The Development Funnel

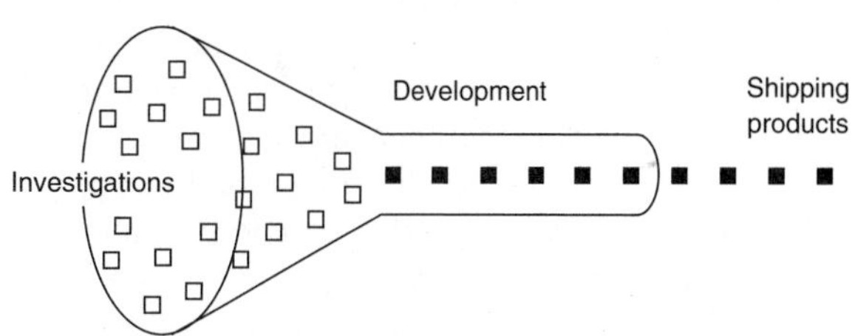

SOURCE: Adapted from R. H. Hayes, S. C. Wheelwright and K. B. Clark, *Dynamic Manufacturing* (New York: Free Press, 1988), p. 295.

time, on-budget products and processes that can be introduced to the market place in an effective and efficient manner.

The *traditional role* of senior management in the development funnel is to select, consider (screen), and evaluate a handful of project ideas from all of those available, and then make "go/no-go" decisions with regard to those projects. Senior management thus reacts to the possibilities raised from throughout the organization (and perhaps adds a few ideas of its own) and commits resources to get selected projects developed and into the market place. Unfortunately, this traditional view has several shortcomings and weaknesses.

First, it assumes that the set of concepts proposed by the organization adequately covers the firm's opportunities and needs for new products and processes. Second, it assumes that senior management will have the required information to properly decide which product ideas to develop, and in the context of ongoing business and product line strategies. Third, this view presumes that advanced development and technology work will have occurred before each development project receives its initial funding and approval. Finally, it assumes that senior management will adequately consider the capacity and resources requirements for prospective individual projects and for the mix of projects already approved. Unfortunately, few of these assumptions hold in practice, and the traditional approach ends up, again, being reactive, piecemeal, and tactical rather than proactive, comprehensive, and strategic.

A much more effective way to achieve the full potential of senior management involvement in development activity is the *development strategy leadership approach*. While based fundamentally on the idea of the development funnel, it creates a far more proactive role for senior management and incorporates a number of tools and techniques that facilitate senior management effectiveness. First, it seeks to put senior management in the position of motivating, guiding, and leading the organization to create the best set of projects. This includes articulating a set of criteria for what would constitute the "correct set" of development projects and connecting the process by which those criteria are applied with product, market, and technology strategies. Senior management thus helps to ensure that selected projects make the best use of existing resources, fit with ongoing business strategies, and are likely to achieve the firm's development objectives. Development projects are the means by which a firm enhances its capabilities; the aggregate set of approved projects is the basis for creating the development capabilities the firm needs and desires in the future.

A second way in which this approach creates substantial leverage is by placing senior management in the position of setting guidelines, general boundaries, and charters for individual projects so that those assigned to carry out such projects can focus their energies in the ways most likely to fulfill senior management's expectations. Thus, this approach avoids having senior management involved in too much of the detailed specification-setting refinements, and instead emphasizes broad boundaries that differentiate projects and set clear objectives for what each project is to accomplish.

Third, after creating an appropriate set of projects and defining the boundaries and charters for each project within that set, senior management is in a much better position to make resource allocation and timing decisions that recognize available development capacity and the need to avoid overcommitting scarce resources. It is easier to track a handful of on-target projects than to jump from one project to another as the organization gradually recognizes that its development resources are overcommitted by a factor of two or three. Having contracted with individual development teams as to the charter and bounds of each project, senior management can focus its attention on providing tools and support so that all approved projects move ahead on schedule, rather than constantly reallocating resources in response to current crises and delays.

The results of such a development strategy leadership approach have been described by Clark and Fujimoto in their study of the worldwide automotive industry.[1] These authors looked at major new car development programs in European, American, and Japanese auto companies and measured results in terms of project cycle time, resource requirements, and product quality. Their findings confirm that automotive companies that use the traditional approach take 20–25 percent longer, require almost twice as many engineering hours, and tend to have significantly lower product quality than do firms where senior management follows the development strategy leadership approach. Clark and Fujimoto also discovered that the benefits of the latter

[1]K. B. Clark and T. Fujimoto, *Product Development Performance* (Boston: Harvard Business School Press, 1991).

approach were becoming sufficiently clear that the major auto companies following the traditional approach were focusing significant energy and resources on developing the ability to pursue the development strategy leadership approach.

To understand what is required of senior management to effectively carry out this new approach, it is helpful to examine its three distinctive activities. The following subsections discuss how senior management can create the right set of projects, charter and bound individual projects within that aggregate set, and then balance the supply and demand of resources to best achieve the firm's development objectives.

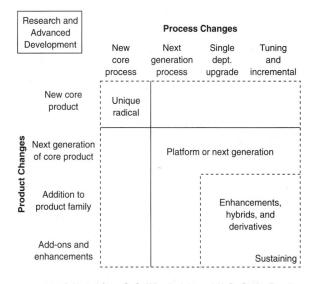

EXHIBIT 4 Creating the Mix of Product/Process Development Projects

Research and Advanced Development

Product Changes \ Process Changes	New core process	Next generation process	Single dept. upgrade	Tuning and incremental
New core product	Unique radical			
Next generation of core product		Platform or next generation		
Addition to product family			Enhancements, hybrids, and derivatives	
Add-ons and enhancements				Sustaining

SOURCE: Adapted from S. C. Wheelwright and K. B. Clark, *Revolutionizing Product Development* (New York: Free Press, 1992), p. 93.

Creating the Aggregate Set of Projects

For an organization to get the most out of its development resources, it is essential that the right mix of projects—those that use available resources to support existing market segments and to open up new market segments while appropriately utilizing new technologies—get created and proposed to the organization. In terms of the funnel in Exhibit 3, this process can be compared to widening the mouth of the funnel so that a complete range of alternatives is investigated before specific choices are made. This task, however, goes beyond simply encouraging the generation of more ideas; it involves combining and bundling ideas that will allow the organization to most effectively cover the needed areas of new product and process development. Thus, it is essentially a matter of creating and defining the alternatives that the firm can pursue, not simply investigating and screening those that naturally arise.

One way to characterize and organize this task is by using a two-dimensional diagram (see Exhibit 4) that defines individual projects according to the degree of change in the product and manufacturing process a specific project entails. The greater the degree of change along either dimension, the more resources are likely to be needed in completing that project.

The two-dimensional construct of Exhibit 4 (called the aggregate project matrix), classifies individual projects into five types. The three central types—derivative/enhancement/hybrid, platform/next generation, and unique/radical—are known as commercial development projects. They lead to new products and processes, providing the benefits typically sought through the application of development resources. The fourth category—sustaining—often uses similar development resources as commercial development projects, but does not create new products or processes. Rather, sustaining projects maintain or support existing products and processes or tailor those for a single customer. When new commercial development efforts are introduced to the marketplace before they are fully ready, the sustaining effort needed to make engineering change orders and other modifications so that products will perform up to customer expectations can be substantial. One reason for explicitly identifying such sustaining projects is to recognize the resource needs of those projects and the fact that they can often divert attention from the more traditional, visible, and higher leverage development efforts.

The fifth category—research and advanced development—is generally the technical precursor to a commercial development effort. These projects prove the feasibility of a given product or process concept and validate the existence of the technical knowledge and invention required to make the concept a commercial success. Because invention and technical exploration so often yield unpredictable outcomes, research and advanced development usually precede a commercial development project to ensure that development activities will have a very high probability of technical and market success.

For any ongoing business, a mix of all five types of projects is essential to long-term success. While the majority tend to be created, defined, and resourced within the organization, it is possible for some portion to be subcontracted or partnered with other organizations. For instance, it is not unusual for a business to develop relationships with an industry association group or a university, with the intent of having that group be the source of much of the research and advanced development effort needed by the business. Similarly, firms will often acquire another business to gain ownership of a unique/radical new product or process, or will subcontract to a service organization or field support group part of the sustaining effort needed for the existing product line. It is less common that firms will subcontract or partner platform/next-generation efforts unless these happen to be the first such effort or represent a diversification move. The key point is that one of senior management's roles is to recognize explicitly the needs of its business for an appropriate mix of these projects, and then to determine the most effective way to get those projects completed—whether in-house, through acquisitions, with a partner, or with a subcontractor.

The proportion of effort needed in each of these five areas depends in part on the firm's strategy, but also on the technical opportunities available and the maturity of the firm's product lines. For instance, a large firm that dominates many of its markets, tends to have a broad product line, and may contemplate only incremental changes in its basic technology (such as Kodak in its film business) is likely to support a few selected research and advanced development projects and an occasional platform or next-generation effort (such as developing a whole new line of film), but will focus most of its development resources on enhancement/derivative/hybrid projects or on sustaining and supporting its existing product lines. In the biotech industry, on the other hand, a firm might spend the vast majority of its development resources on research and advanced development, unique/radical projects, and an occasional wholly new platform. Such a firm would view itself as part of a young, emerging industry where the leverage is in establishing strong positions in whole new areas with radical new products.

There is no single best mix of projects for every company, or even for all the companies in a single industry. What is important is for senior management to understand where the opportunities exist, where the payback will be greatest, and what mix and proportion of different types of projects will best enable the firm to accomplish its business strategy.

Chartering and Bounding Individual Projects

After deciding on the mix and proportion of project types, senior management needs to help create expectations as to what individual projects are intended to accomplish, where they fit in the overall set of projects, and what resources will be made available to the team executing each project. Here again, using the five types of projects is one way for management to establish and bound individual project expectations and temper and balance project objectives and resources. For instance, *derivative projects* can range from cost-reduced versions of existing products to add-ons or enhancements for an existing production process. Development work on a derivative project typically will take less time and fewer resources and be constrained in its performance achievements by the existing platform product or process from which it is derived. Thus, these projects typically require less creativity and are more predictable in their outcomes.

Breakthrough projects, on the other hand, involve significant changes to existing products and processes and thus require much more creativity, greater degrees of freedom, and more time and resources. Like the initial efforts to develop the compact disc or fiber optics, they create whole new product and process categories that can define a new market. Their results and requirements are much less certain than those of derivative projects and typically require a more experienced and aggressive effort. They tend to be high risk and high return, both to the organization and to those who work on them.

Because breakthrough products often incorporate revolutionary new technologies or materials, they may require dramatic changes in manufacturing processes. This requires that the development team be given considerable latitude in designing both the product and the process. Often this includes providing access to a variety of advanced development projects and their results so that multiple new technologies can be called upon to achieve the dramatic results expected.

Platform projects, which fall in the middle of the commercial development spectrum, are considerably harder to define and bound because they need to be compatible with existing products and processes and yet be sufficiently new and bold that they can serve as a basis for subsequent derivatives, enhancements, and other variations of a basic product/process. For instance, Honda's 1990 Accord line is an example of a new platform that replaced its 1986 platform. Honda introduced a number of significant changes in both product and process, but no fundamentally new technologies. Similarly, in the early 1990s, Kodak's single-use camera—available in several different versions—was built off of a single platform, while the over 200 versions of Sony's Walkman were derived from one of three platforms, each of which was overhauled and redesigned (i.e., a new generation created) every two or three years.

How individual projects are chartered and bounded is important in giving focus and purpose to the development team charged with completing each project. The resulting product line, its basic architecture, its product families, and its range of variations will be the consequence of the set of breakthrough, platform, and derivative projects pursued in development. Organizations have discovered tremendous advantage in differentiating types of development projects such that they can leverage scarce development resources, address markets appropriately, and provide distinctive products offering competitive advantage. Chartering and bounding individual projects is a critical step contributing to the organization's success in achieving

EXHIBIT 5 Creating Product Families via Development Projects

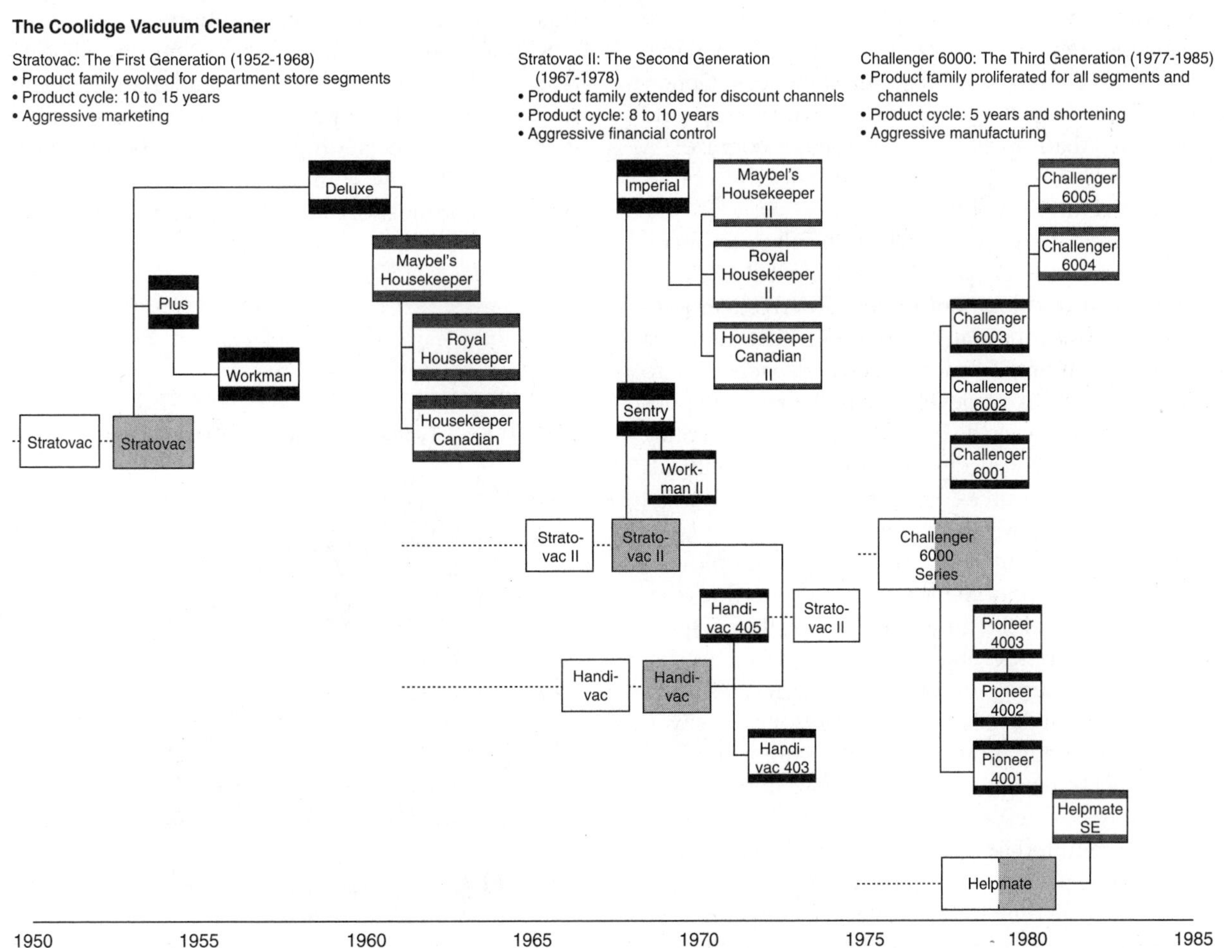

SOURCE: S. C. Wheelwright and W. E. Sasser, Jr., "The New Product Development Map," *Harvard Business Review*, May–June 1989, pp. 112–25.

these goals. An example of how this might play out over time is shown in Exhibit 5 for a fictitious vacuum cleaner company. The exhibit outlines three generations of product, each involving one or more new platforms and a number of carefully selected and positioned derivative projects aimed at different segments and distribution channels. Senior management can play a pivotal role in creating and guiding product and process generations and architectures.

Developing and Applying Resources to Selected Development Projects

It is perhaps easiest to understand senior management's role in providing and allocating resources by identifying the two most common problems firms have in this area: undertaking many more projects than can possibly be completed with the available resources, and assigning critical resources to work on several projects concurrently. Both problems reflect a lack of discipline and management's unwillingness to make hard choices. Generally, their impact is far more detrimental and pervasive than most organizations recognize. A simple example can help to illustrate the consequences of these problems.

Suppose a firm has a total of 80 full-time development and design people available to work on commercial development projects (derivative, platform, and breakthrough). This means that a total of 960 people-months can be allocated each year to these three types of development projects. Experience in industries as diverse as computers, scientific instruments, medical devices, and pharmaceuticals suggests that resources are typically overcommitted to the extent shown in Exhibit 6. As suggested, the representative firm with 80 full-time employees engaged in development activity might find that over one-third of the time actually available is spent on nondevelopment engineering tasks (such as sustaining engineering or other special requests the organization might place on these resources). Even more importantly, however, if one were to take all the projects currently considered active and estimate the amount of resources (in development people-months) required for completion and consider their desired completion dates, one would find that the firm had overcommitted its available development capacity by a factor of two or three. That is, the vast majority of firms have many more projects underway than they have resources to staff and complete by the desired introduction dates. This puts development activity in a catch-22 mode: priorities continually shift and people are moved from one project to another as the organization robs Peter to pay Paul in hopes of completing projects as scheduled. Of course, everybody knows that project commitments far exceed resources, making a game out of who will get priority and what projects will slip.

In addition, because there are not sufficient resources for all projects, the tendency is to commit particularly critical resources to as many as six or eight concurrent projects. Unfortunately, recent studies suggest that overcommitting individual resources actually reduces their effective capacity. That is, overcommitted individuals end up spending additional time going to meetings, getting back up to speed, correcting trivial errors, and so forth, thereby reducing their effective development capacity when it is most needed. This further exacerbates the overcommitment problem, leading inevitably to frustration, disappointment, and burnout.

Senior management must have the discipline to decide which projects are most important, to charter and bound those projects appropriately, and to commit to projects only up to the point where capacity will allow completion of all the resourced projects. For most organizations, this means cutting

EXHIBIT 6 Typical Development Capacity Predicament

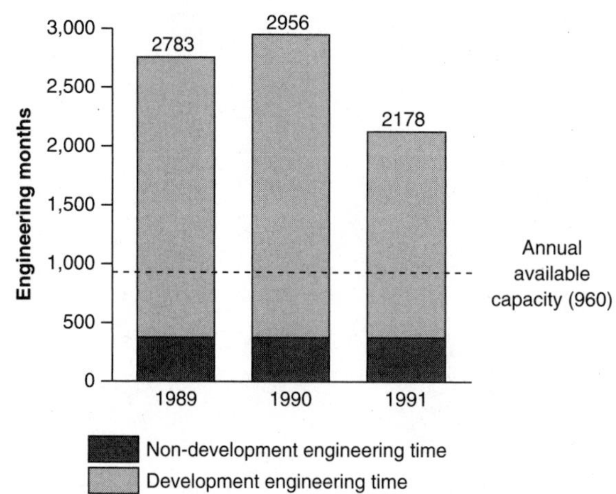

SOURCE: S. C. Wheelwright and K. B. Clark, "Creating Project Plans to Focus Product Development," *Harvard Business Review,* March–April 1992.

the current number of projects by one-half to two-thirds—a difficult pill to swallow. It always seems easier to pretend that all projects underway could be completed if everyone worked harder and longer. Experience suggests that this is a fiction, and that the best way to complete more projects on time, on budget, and on target is to do fewer projects and to assign scarce resources to, at most, one major and one minor project. However, when an organization has historically done the opposite, it requires senior management commitment and leadership to make this new set of principles a reality and to impose the discipline needed to avoid the all-too-common over-commitment. As chaos is reduced and focus on development resources increases, it is much easier for senior management to identify the additional resources and capabilities that are required and justified, and to make appropriate changes. This puts senior management in a proactive role, helping to build the organization's development capabilities, rather than leaving it in a reactive role that inevitably dissipates much of the development activities' potential effectiveness.

In summary, senior management can have its greatest impact, either positive or negative, during the preproject phase. By shifting to a proactive mode and adhering to a handful of principles and guidelines, senior management can help the entire organization leverage its existing capabilities and enhance its future capabilities. Much of this can be done around the aggregate project plan framework of Exhibit 4 and the repeated application of the following eight step procedure.

1. Define the primary types of commercial development, advanced development, and sustaining activity projects.
2. Determine the FTEs (full-time equivalents) and cycle time requirements for representative projects of each of those types.
3. Identify existing resources and compare those with the capacity required to complete existing projects on time.
4. Compute the implied capacity utilization from Step 3 and make the adjustments to bring supply and demand into balance.
5. Determine the mix of project types required in the future to achieve the firm's business objectives.
6. Estimate the number of projects of each type that can be undertaken to provide the desired mix and yet not overcommit existing development resources.
7. Create and define the set of specific projects that will be underway at various points of time in the future.
8. Work to increase the productivity of the development resources, thereby enhancing development capacity and capability in future time periods.

Project Organization and Management

Effective product and process development requires the integration of specialized capabilities. Such integration is difficult in most circumstances, but particularly challenging as organizations grow and mature and as functional groups become more specialized. Even the way these functions are organized creates complications for development activity: marketing typically is organized by product families and market segments; engineering is organized around functional disciplines and technical focus; manufacturing is often a mix between functions, process technologies, and product/market structures. The result is that, in firms of any substantial size, organizing and leading an effective development effort that integrates the tasks required on the part of all the functions is a major challenge.

If any one word has been used excessively in the past few years as a means to capture the opportunity available from more effective project management, it is *teams*. Unfortunately, much of the literature on product development teams does little to distinguish between different types of teams, the characteristics that make one team more appropriate in a given setting than another, and the ways in which different types of teams can be managed most effectively. A particularly useful perspective on the range of development teams that an organization might apply to a given development project is that provided by Clark and Fujimoto,[2] whose classification arrays teams along a spectrum: from those that are largely functionally oriented, with only loose connections across the functions, to those that are autonomous and integrated, with only loose connections to the individual functions. This spectrum is summarized in Exhibit 7. While such a classification scheme is not unique, it is a useful way to organize quite different structures associated with very different leadership roles, each of which has its own strengths and weaknesses.

[2]Ibid.

EXHIBIT 7 Types of Development Teams

1. Functional Structure

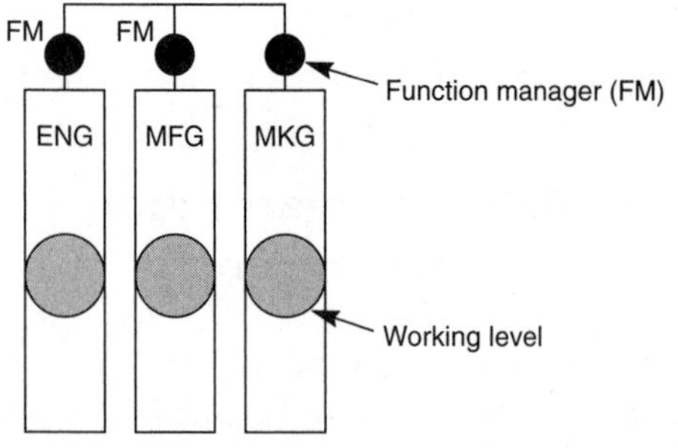

2. Lightweight Project Manager

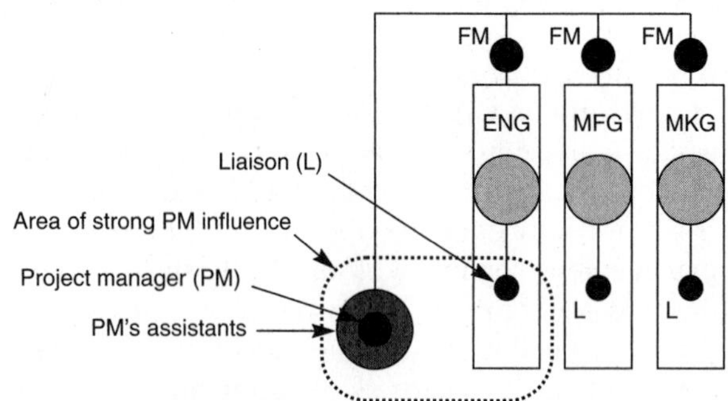

3. Heavyweight Project Manager

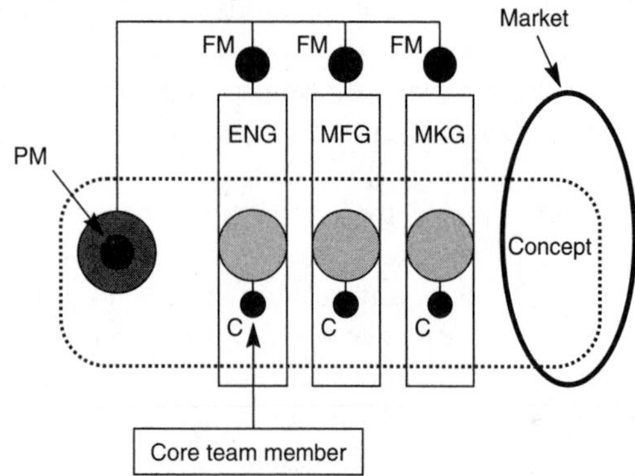

4. Autonomous Project Team

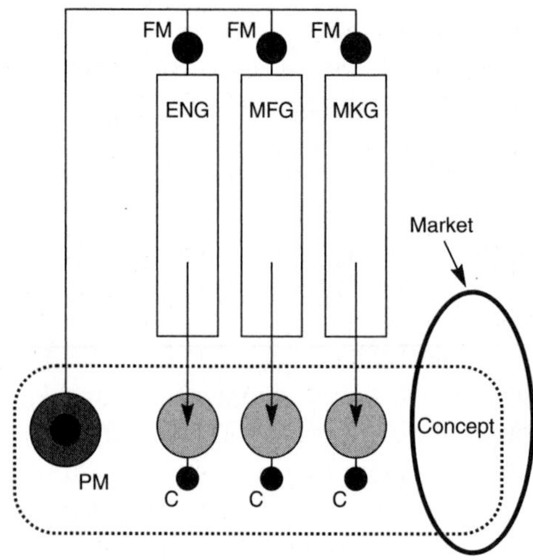

SOURCE: K. B. Clark and S. C. Wheelwright, "Organizing and Leading 'Heavyweight' Development Teams," *California Management Review* 34, no. 2 (1992), pp. 9–28.

Functional Team Structure

In the traditional functional organization typical of many large, mature firms, people are grouped primarily by discipline, each working under the direction of a specialized subfunction manager and a senior functional manager. The different subfunctions and functions coordinate ideas through detailed specifications that all parties agree to at the outset and through occasional meetings where issues that cut across groups are discussed. Over time, primary responsibility for a development effort passes sequentially—although often not smoothly—from one function to the next, a transfer often referred to as "throwing it over the wall."

The functional development team structure has several advantages and disadvantages. One strength is that managers who control a project's resources also control the performance of individual tasks in their functional area. Thus, responsibility and authority are usually aligned. However, tasks must be subdivided at the project's outset—the entire development process must be unpacked into separable, somewhat independent subactivities. But on most development efforts, not all required tasks are known at the outset, nor can they all be easily or realistically subdivided. Coordination and integration can suffer as a result.

Another major strength of this approach is that because most career paths are functional, at least until a general management level is reached, the work done on a project is judged, evaluated, and rewarded by the same subfunction and functional managers who make decisions about career paths. The associated disadvantage is that individual contributions to a development project tend to be judged largely independently of overall project success. The frequently cited tenet is that individuals cannot be evaluated fairly on outcomes over which they lack control. But as a practical matter, that often means that those directly involved in the details of the project are not responsible for the overall results finally achieved.

Finally, the functional project organization brings specialized expertise to bear on the key technical issues. The same person or small group of people may be responsible for the design of a particular component or subsystem over a long series of development efforts. Thus, the functions and subfunctions capture and apply the benefits of prior experience and become the keepers of the organization's depth of knowledge over time and across projects. The disadvantage is that every development project differs in its objectives and performance requirements, and it is unlikely that specialists developing a single component will do so very differently on one project compared to another. The best component or subsystem is defined by technical parameters in the areas of their expertise, rather than by overall system characteristics or specific customer requirements dictated by the unique market at which the development effort is aimed.

Lightweight Team Structure

Like the functional development structure, those assigned to the lightweight team reside physically in their functional areas, but each functional organization designates a liaison person to represent it on the project coordinating committee. These liaison representatives work with a lightweight project manager, usually a design engineer or product marketing manager, who coordinates different functions' activities. This approach usually occurs as an add-on to a traditional functional organization, with a functional liaison person having that role added to his or her duties. The overall coordination assignment of the lightweight project manager, however, tends not to be present in the traditional functional structure.

It is important to recognize that project managers are lightweight in two significant respects. First, they are generally middle- or junior-level people who, despite considerable expertise, have little status or influence in the organization. Such people have spent a handful of years in a function, and the present assignment is seen as a broadening experience—a chance for them to move out of the function. Second, although they are responsible for informing and coordinating the activities of the functional organizations, the key resources (including engineers on the project) remain under the control of their respective functional managers. The lightweight project manager does not have power to reassign people or reallocate resources, and instead concentrates on confirming schedules, updating timelines, and expediting across groups. Such project leaders typically spend no more than 25 percent of their time on a single project.

The primary strengths and weaknesses of the lightweight project team are those of the functional project structure, but now at least one person over the course of the project looks across functions and seeks to ensure that individual tasks—especially those on the critical path—get done in a timely function, and that everyone is kept aware of potential cross-functional issues and what is going on elsewhere in this particular project.

Thus, improved communication and coordination are what an organization expects when moving from a functional to a lightweight team structure. Because power still resides with the subfunction and functional managers, however, hopes for improved efficiency, speed, and project quality are seldom realized fully. Moreover, lightweight project leaders find themselves tolerated at best, and often ignored or even preempted. This can easily become a no-win situation for the individual thus assigned.

Heavyweight Team Structure

In contrast to the lightweight setup, the heavyweight project manager has direct access to, and responsibility for, the vast majority of those involved in the project. Such leaders are heavyweights in two respects. First, they are senior managers within the organization and may even outrank the functional managers. In addition to having expertise and experience, they also wield significant organizational clout. Second, heavyweight leaders have primary influence over the people working on the development effort and supervise their work directly through key functional people on the core teams. Often the core group of people is dedicated and physically colocated with the heavyweight project leader. However, the longer-term career development of individual contributors continues to rest not with the project leader—although that heavyweight leader makes significant input to individual performance evaluations—but with the functional manager, because members are not assigned to a project team permanently.

The heavyweight team structure has a number of advantages and strengths, along with associated weaknesses. In many instances, the advantages of the team approach bring with them potential disadvantages that may hurt development performance if not recognized and averted. Take, for example, the advantages of ownership and commitment, one of the most striking advantages of the heavyweight team. Identifying with the product and creating a sense of esprit d'corps motivate core team members to extend themselves and do what is needed to help the team succeed. But such teams sometimes expand the definition of their role and the scope of the project, and get carried away with themselves and their abilities. Even when the team does stay focused, the rest of the organization may see itself as second-class. Although the core team may not make the distinction explicit, it happens because the team has responsibilities and authority beyond those commonly given to functional team members. Thus, such projects inadvertently can become the "haves" and other, smaller projects the "have-nots" with regard to key resources and management attention.

Another potential concern is that the heavyweight team will want the same control over secondary activities (such as prototyping, analytical testing, and quality assurance) that it has over the primary tasks performed by dedicated team members. Thus, when waiting for these secondary tasks to be performed, the team's natural response is to demand top priority from the support organization, or to be allowed to go outside and subcontract to independent groups. While these may sometimes be the appropriate choices, senior management must establish make-buy guidelines and clear priorities applicable to all projects—perhaps changing service levels provided by support groups—or have support groups provide capacity and advisory technical services, but letting team members do more of the actual task work in these support areas. Whatever actions the organization takes, the challenge is to achieve a balance between the needs of the individual heavyweight project and of the broader organization.

Another advantage of the heavyweight team is the integration and integrity it provides through a system solution to a set of customer needs. Getting all of the components and subsystems to complement one another and to effectively address the fundamental requirements of the core customer segment can result in a winning platform product/process. The team achieves an effective system design by using generalist skills applied by broadly trained team members, with fewer specialists and, on occasion, less depth in individual component solutions and technical problem solving. The extent of these implications is aptly illustrated by the nature of the teams Clark and Fujimoto encountered in their study of the auto industry.[3] Clark and Fujimoto found that for U.S. auto firms in the mid 1980s, typical platform projects organized under a traditional functional or lightweight team structure entailed full-time work for several months by approximately 1,500 engineers. In contrast, a handful of Japanese platform projects carried out by heavyweight teams utilized only 250 engineers working full-time for several months. The implications of 250 versus 1,500 full-time equivalents (FTEs) with regard to breadth of tasks, degree of specialization, and need for coordination are significant and help explain major differences in project results as measured by product integrity, development cycle time, and engineering resource utilization.

But the lack of depth may also be a disadvantage of the heavyweight team. Some individual components or subassemblies may not attain the same level of technical excellence they would under a more traditional functional team structure. For instance, generalists may develop a windshield wiper system that is complementary with and integrated into the total car system and its core concept. But they also may embed in their design potential weaknesses or flaws that could have been caught by a functional team of specialists who had developed a long series of windshield wipers. To counter this potential disadvantage, many organizations order more testing of completed units to discover possible flaws, and have components and subassemblies reviewed by expert specialists. In some cases the quality assurance function has expanded its role to ensure that sufficient technical specialists review designs at appropriate points so that such weaknesses can be discovered early and their detrimental effects minimized.

[3]Ibid.

Autonomous Team Structure

With the autonomous team structure, or "tiger team," individuals from the different functional areas are formally assigned, dedicated, and colocated to the project team. The project leader, a heavyweight in the organization, is given full control over the resources contributed by the different functional groups. Furthermore, the project leader becomes the sole evaluator of the contribution made by individual team members. In essence, the autonomous team is given a clean sheet of paper; it is not required to follow existing organizational practices and procedures, but is instead allowed to create its own. This includes establishing incentives and rewards as well as norms for behavior. However, the team will be held fully accountable for the final results of the project: success or failure is its responsibility, and no one else's.

The fundamental strength of the autonomous team structure is focus. Everything the individual team members and team leader do is concentrated on making the project successful. Thus, tiger teams can excel at rapid, efficient new product and process development. They handle cross-functional integration in a particularly effective manner, possibly because they attract and select team participants much more freely than do the other project structures. Tiger teams, however, take little or nothing as given. They are likely to expand the bounds of their project definition and tackle redesigns of the entire product, its components, and subassemblies rather than looking for opportunities to utilize existing materials, designs, and organizational relationships. Their solution may be unique, making it more difficult to fold the resulting product and process—and in many cases, the team members themselves—back into the traditional organization upon project completion. As a consequence, tiger teams often become the birth place of new business units or they experience unusually high turnover following project completion.

Senior managers, because they are asked to delegate much more responsibility and control to the team and its project leader than under any other organization structure, often become nervous at the prospects of a tiger team. Unless clear guidelines have been established in advance, it is extremely difficult during the project for senior managers to make midcourse corrections or exercise substantial influence without destroying the team. More than one team has gotten away from senior management and created major problems.

One aspect of selecting an appropriate team structure that should be readily apparent is the need to match that team structure not only with the capabilities and resources of the organization, but also with the type of project that is to be assigned to the development team. While many different considerations are important in such a matching of the team structure to the type of project, it is generally the case that projects requiring deep technical excellence are best done under a functional structure. Projects requiring an outstanding system solution, such as is typical of a new platform or next-generation product concept, are often best done by a heavyweight project team. In most instances, younger, less experienced workers on a lightweight project team can handle derivative and enhancement projects, thus gaining valuable training. Because many of the choices are constrained by the platform from which the derivative or enhancement comes, such lightweight teams are able to deliver quite effectively. Finally, radical or breakthrough projects, as often associated with the very first generation of a whole new product or process, are often best carried out by a more autonomous tiger team.

Looking across different industries, it is also quite clear that the maturity of an industry and its technologies can have a direct bearing on the type of development team structure most likely to be found in the companies within that particular industry. For most start-up companies, the entire organization is often an autonomous tiger team simply because everyone is focused on a new product or process, and that is where the company's future lies. As second and third generations of the dominant product and process are developed, they too may continue to be carried out by a heavyweight project team consisting of virtually all the senior managers in the business. This is likely to be the case particularly where the company can grow substantially with a fairly narrow product line and simply by introducing succeeding generations of new products in that line. However, as companies mature and expand, adding multiple product lines, seeing some of those product lines require many more resources of a sustaining and operating nature, it is likely that they will shift their basic business organization to a functional structure. Thus, it is natural at that point to have product and process development also take on a more functional appearance, with the vast majority of resources being owned by the functions and the tasks being conducted under the direction of those individual functions.

That functional structure for the basic organization as well as its development efforts may then continue for years and even decades if a firm dominates its industry and if the rate of technical change is not too great. However, such a firm may become slow and less responsive over time. Like many of the industrial giants of the 1980s and early 1990s, it may find itself challenged as new technologies, competitors, and markets create a rapid onslaught of new product and process development opportunities. The functional structure is simply unable to keep up with all of those possibilities in a timely fashion. At that point such a large organization may start adding lightweight project coordinators in hopes of avoiding drastic organizational restructuring moves, while seeking diligently to improve its product development activities. Finally, it may become painfully obvious that on a few critical projects a totally new approach is needed. Some firms will choose to do that with a tiger team removed from the main organization; others might seek to develop a new capability for implementing heavyweight project teams. Industries such as automobiles, steel, and pharmaceuticals have followed patterns not unlike that just described.

The challenge for any single firm is to make sure that its dominant approach to organizing development teams matches its environment and its strategic imperatives, and that the firm develops capabilities and resources that allow it to apply alternative modes when they are deemed most appropriate for particular projects. Especially critical is making sure that the organization's human resource selection, training, and development policies as well as its organizational systems provide the mix of skills in the quantities needed by the overall development strategy. In theory, an organization might well choose to develop a portfolio of approaches that would cover all four types of development team structures in order to match them to a full range of development projects it seeks to undertake. However, experience suggests that most organizations have a tendency to adopt a dominant orientation or a standard approach to leading and organizing development projects. That dominant orientation in firms determines what is easy and likely to work, and what is hard and likely to be less effective. It thus determines the range of approaches and projects a firm can hope to apply and carry out.

Of the four development team structures outlined in Exhibit 7, two typically represent dominant orientations—the functional structure and the heavyweight team. Firms whose basic systems, skills, practices, and mechanisms are functional, for example, will find it relatively easy to implement lightweight teams. The lightweight setup is largely functional with an overlay of light coordination. Moving to a heavyweight team, however, is much more difficult and is unlikely to be fully successful if the functional structure remains the dominant orientation. Without basic changes in systems, practices, attitudes, and behaviors, attempts to add a heavyweight team capability in what is essentially a functional organization may create a "middleweight" approach, but is unlikely to build a heavyweight team.

In contrast, firms that have teams as their dominant orientation and have built their systems, training efforts, communication structures, and patterns of leadership around heavyweight teams will find it relatively easy to implement autonomous tiger teams. However, even though the heavyweight team has a functional organization carrying out some of its detailed work and support activities, conducting lightweight or even functional projects often involves adjustments in the standard approach and their lightweight teams are likely to be somewhat "heavier" than if their dominant orientation were functional.

The experience of Chaparral Steel illustrates the challenges and advantages of building capability for several approaches in development. Located in Midlothian, Texas, 30 miles south of Dallas, by the early 1990s Chaparral was producing well over 1 million tons per year of steel products used in forging (high alloy) and construction (structural) products. Using an electric furnace, a continuous caster, and a rolling mill to convert steel scrap into various milled products, Chaparral had continued to improve its performance through a variety of product and process development efforts. Chaparral defined three types of projects: major advanced development, platform, and incremental. Projects of the first type might require an expenditure of $3 million to $5 million over a period of three to five years, but would provide a breakthrough product or process. Platform projects might require $500,000 to $1 million in development expenses and take 12 to 24 months to execute. Incremental projects typically would incur development expenditures of $100,000 to $200,000, last a few months, and provide very quick payback. At any point in time the organization might have 40 or 50 development projects underway, of which no more than a couple would be major advanced development efforts, perhaps three to five would be platform efforts, and the remainder would be incremental efforts.

Because of the cost competitiveness of its industry and the operating demands required for profitable products and processes, Chaparral has chosen to conduct all of its development efforts on its factory floor and staff them primarily with line people. However, the team structure and project leadership used for each of the three types varies considerably. Incremental projects are almost all done by functional subgroups with a lightweight project manager. With so many projects going on and with projects so common, everyone understands the role of the lightweight project manager and wants to be supportive: they know, at some point, they will be one of those lightweight project managers and will desire the same kind of treatment. Thus, the support and cooperation provided to lightweight project managers tends to be substantially greater than in many traditional functional organizations. The platform projects are headed up by heavyweight project managers who have probably been department managers; following completion of the platform effort, they will go back to being a department manager. The advanced development projects are put under the direction of one of seven general foremen who report directly to the vice president of manufacturing (or one of the other vice presidents). These major projects start as advanced development efforts; once technical feasibility is proven, they quickly become breakthrough projects but with little or no change in team composition.

This mix of approaches has served Chaparral well in addressing the range of development opportunities and challenges faced in its business. Depending on the mix of technical depth, the coordination and integration of known tasks, the level of system integration, and the degree of breakthrough and new thinking required, Chaparral can pick a team structure, project manager, and overall management approach that makes sense for the situation. Expectations have been established over more than a decade, and thus procedures and approaches—as well as their governing principles—are well known throughout the organization.

Tools that Aid Development Project Completion

An area of substantial promise for improving the consistency and performance of development teams is that of new tools and techniques. Many of these are computer-based and range from computer-aided design/computer-aided manufacturing (CAD/CAM) systems used by mechanical engineers and others, to computer-aided engineering and drafting systems used by designers and architects, and on to finite-element analyses used by material scientists and others. In addition, new computer simulation and analytical tools are being developed to aid chemists and physicists in such diverse areas as consumer products and pharmaceuticals.

While numerous advances in the nature and application of such computer-based tools are likely to occur in the coming decade, other "low-tech" tools are also being developed and finding wide acceptance. A tool such as quality function deployment (QFD) developed first at Toyota and now applied throughout a number of industries is a systematic procedure for linking customer requirements to design parameters. Thus, it serves to apply rigor and completeness to cross-functional problem-solving activities that are common in most complex, system-based development efforts.[4] Even such organizational processes as just-in-time (JIT), value-added analysis, and fast cycle time techniques are proving useful when applied to the tasks of new product and new process development. This coming decade is likely to see a number of these tools applied much more broadly and systematically in building an organization's development capabilities.

Finally, a number of more traditional tools that long have been considered an important part of new product and process development methodologies are likely to be enhanced, extended, and even completely rethought to make them more effective in the competitive environment of the 1990s. One example of such a traditional tool is prototyping. Physical models and prototypes are used by various engineering disciplines to test product and process concepts and multiple iterations in the design and development process. Clearly, computers have extended and enhanced the way in which such pro-

---

[4]See Chapter 9 in S. C. Wheelwright and K. B. Clark, *Revolutionizing Product Development* (New York: Free Press, 1992). See also J. R. Hauser and D. Clausing, "The House of Quality," *Harvard Business Review*, May–June 1988, pp. 63–73.

totypes can be created and subsequently analyzed. As technologies continue to advance, the sophistication and range of prototyping activities will advance as well.

Learning across Development Projects

In a world of intense international competition where customers are sophisticated and demanding, and technologies are diverse and dramatic in their effects, organizations that stand still in product and process development will neither prosper nor survive. The ability to sustain significant improvements in development over long periods of time rests on the capability to learn from experience. What is crucial in improving development is insight and understanding about how the organization works in practice. Studies that benchmark the best practice among competitors or that generate new concepts and frameworks may prove valuable in establishing perspective, but solving the problems that limit performance requires a detailed understanding of the root causes of those problems as they play out in the specific circumstances of the organization's development process. Thus, learning from experience is crucial. In the context of product and process development, learning from experience means learning from development projects.

But organizational learning is not a natural outcome of development projects, even in successful development efforts. There seem to be two fundamental problems. The first is that the performance that matters is often a result of complex interactions within the overall development system. Moreover, the connection between cause and effect may be separated significantly in time and place. In some instances, for example, the outcomes of interest are only evident at the conclusion of the project. While symptoms and potential causes may be observed by individuals at various points along the development path, systematic investigation requires observation of the outcomes followed by an analysis that looks back to find the underlying causes. The second problem is that incentives in the organization favor pressing forward to the next project. Without concerted effort and focused attention on learning from the project that has just been completed, it is unlikely that engineers, marketers, or manufacturers will naturally devote time and energy to yesterday's problems. Most companies learn very little from their development experience. Those that do learn and understand the power in improvement do have developed tools and methods to help people—individually and collectively—gain insight and understanding and focus energy and attention on the problem of learning. While relatively little has been written and systematically studied with regard to how organizations learn about development activity and create capabilities to more effectively carry out such activities, a handful of observations can be made.

First, for an organization to learn across development projects, management must focus attention on the *need* for such learning. The way most organizations learn is within the functions along which they are organized, where those functions carry out repetitive tasks and gradually develop tools, systems, and procedures that incorporate their past experience and enable them to conduct those tasks more effectively. Since most development efforts are cross-functional or at least the leverage often occurs at the interfaces of the functions, learning about development requires a cross-functional perspective. Recent experience would suggest that project leaders are often in the best position to recognize the need for such learning and to capture the experiences of the development efforts they have been involved in, and turn those into systems, tools, and procedures that others in the organization can apply. However, that requires that project leadership become a significant step in multiple career paths, and an assignment that one might retain for an extended period of time. For example, an organization might well have younger project leaders start as lightweight coordinators and then gradually move to bigger projects, eventually becoming heavyweight project managers. A cadre of project leaders within the organization might then be developed who have a strong vested interest in capturing and applying the learning from individual development efforts.

A second observation is that learning from past development experience requires that lessons be identified, analyzed, captured, and then incorporated into the way the organization carries out its development activity. A particularly useful tool, but one not yet widely applied, is that of the *project audit.* This might well be undertaken by a cross-functional team (prior to their being assigned responsibility for a development project) that examines a recently completed project, compares it to other recently completed development efforts, and identifies high-leverage areas of opportunity where new tools, systems, or procedures might be of great benefit.

A third observation is that if improving development capability is important, senior management will need to provide leadership and guidance—with regard to goals and objectives, but also in terms of resources, organizational attention, and new skills. Thus, an essential aspect of a development strategy for a given business is not just identifying the set of projects to be undertaken, the development team structures for doing so, or the tools and techniques to be used by the team. These are all important, but in addition, forethought must be given to how the organization will learn, how that learning will be captured, the way in which it subsequently will be applied, and the results to be expected. Like so many issues, effective commercialization of products and processes depends on good management..

New Product Development

Case IV–1
Apple Computer (A)

J. S. Gable, S. Tylka, and M. A. Maidique

As Wil Houde, vice president and general manager of the Apple Computer Personal Computer Systems Division (PCSD), turned to look at the clock, his eyes fell upon a white teddy bear sitting on his shelf. For months that bear had been symbolically rotated between individuals responsible for solving the problems associated with Apple's newest product, the Apple III. The bear was his for now.

As part of his new responsibilities, Houde was about to present a major proposal at an Apple executive committee meeting in February 1981. He was not especially concerned that his proposal would be accepted. After all, it had been shaped in consultation with nearly everyone who would be there. However, he couldn't help wondering if this approach to the problem was correct. Probably, he reflected, it was.

Apple Computer History

In 1975, the Apple Computer Company was founded as a partnership. Microcomputers—computers based on the recently developed microprocessor chip—were new in 1975. The chips on which these small computers were based had an active area smaller than a fingernail and computing power greater than a room filled with vacuum tube computers.

The year the Apple partnership was founded, Steve Wozniak, 24, was working at Hewlett-Packard designing hand-held calculators, while Steve Jobs, 22, was designing video games at Atari. The two computer buffs were interested in having their own microcomputer, but they really couldn't afford their cheapest option, a $600 kit. Jobs recalls:

> We bought one microprocessor chip (between the two of us) and designed a microcomputer. Woz designed about 75 percent of it, and with some Hewlett-Packard and Atari parts, we built one. Our first computer, the Apple I, looked like a mess, but it worked.

Jobs and Wozniak belonged to the Home Computer Club in Palo Alto. As was the group custom, they showed off their Apple I. It wasn't much to look at, being little more than a single printed circuit board with wire streaming out from it, but all their friends wanted one. They were soon spending all their spare time building computers. Jobs explained:

> It took about 40 hours to get a working model: 20 hours to build one, and 20 hours to troubleshoot it. We decided that we could cut our time in half if we made a printed circuit board. So Woz sold his HP calculator and I sold my VW van for $1,325. This was the beginning of Apple Computer.

In 1976, a friend of Jobs laid out a printed circuit board (PCB) for the computer. The PCB made the computer production process much easier. Users could now insert the parts with a higher probability that the board would work. The PCB design cost $2,500. Jobs and Wozniak planned to make 100 boards and to sell them for $50 each, leaving them with $2,500 in profit. Maybe, they thought, they could recoup their initial investment of a calculator and a van.

Initially the partners sold the boards to hobbyists through trade magazines. But Jobs was interested in expanding business through other distribution channels. "I went to the original computer store in Mountain View (California) called the Byte Shop. The owner was really excited and said he'd take 50 of them. Dollar signs!"

But the owner added the condition that the boards be fully assembled. At that time all computers were kits, so Jobs and Wozniak went to local parts distributors and convinced them to sell $25,000 worth of parts on net-30-days terms. Jobs explained, "We bought the parts on sheer enthusiasm. We had no collateral—our VW and calculator were long gone. We didn't even know what net-30-days meant."

First, Jobs and Wozniak built 100 boards in their garage. They took 50 down to the Byte Shop and were paid cash. "We paid off the suppliers in 29 days, and we've run our business on cash flow ever since." They farmed out the assembly of the printed circuit boards and then plugged in the integrated circuits. About 200 Apple I computers were sold.

Apple II

By the fall of 1976, Jobs and Wozniak had designed a new home computer, the Apple II. The Apple II computer mainframe was similar to Apple I, but it had additional circuitry, a keyboard, and was packaged in a plastic housing. "We had learned a lot from the Apple I. We learned that 8K bytes of memory really weren't enough. We were using the new 4K RAMS (Read and Write Memories). At that time no one else was using RAMS. Going out with a product using only dynamic memories was a risky thing." On the other hand, the manufacturing process in the Apple II was essentially the same process originally worked out in the garage for the Apple I.

Wozniak designed most of the internal working of the new computer while Jobs was primarily responsible for its overall concept and appearance. Jobs wanted to strip the computer of its mysterious and sometimes threatening reputation. This led to a low profile, a plastic case, and no blinking lights or confusing knobs and dials. In many ways this design philosophy made the Apple II the first truly successful "personal computer." Apple also made available every piece of technical data relating to the machine, a highly unusual move in an industry where secrecy had always been tightly maintained. This open policy allowed sophisticated users to design circuit boards that could plug into the computer and expand its capabilities. In fact, several empty slots were built into the Apple II for just this purpose. Independent vendors began marketing hardware and software enhancements.

At this point, the two Steves were hesitant about going into business by themselves. They showed their prototype to others at the computer club. Commodore showed a special interest in the Apple II. (The Apple II almost became the Commodore I.) The partners also took their Apple II prototype to both Hewlett-Packard and Atari. Jobs stated:

> Atari rightfully said, "We have so much going on we have to stay focused on games," which was true. Hewlett-Packard's response was that Woz and I didn't have degrees and couldn't possibly know what we were doing. They decided to do it themselves and have since then. (Back in 1976, Hewlett-Packard was working on the HP-85.)

Each step along the way, the partners were virtually forced into the business, from design to manufacturing to marketing. But as Jobs explained, in time they found themselves more and more excited:

> You don't realize that there's a feeling developing, the feeling of being able to make something (especially an artifact) and see it get out in the world. It's up there with the "best" of feelings. It is an underlying passion that entrepreneurs feel that stems from the idea that you really can impact the world. You really can change how this world is being run.

During 1976, Jobs realized that the market was growing faster than they could internally finance.

> We needed some more money, so I called up a venture capitalist and he tooled over in his Mercedes. He said that he basically invested in companies right before they were about to take off, and we still had a few years. (He later ended up investing, at a substantially higher price.) But he gave me the name of a friend, Mike Markkula, who invested in riskier operations. So I called up Mike, and he tooled over in his Corvette.

Markkula was 32 when he went to discuss the business with Jobs. He had been in marketing at Fairchild Semiconductor and later became a marketing manager at Intel Corporation. Then he "retired." Markkula advised Jobs that he needed a business plan and together they worked on the project.

At this time the company developed its first business strategy. Their concept was to use microprocessor technology to create a personal computer for individuals to use in a wide variety of applications. They also needed a name for the company. Jobs explains how they arrived at that name:

> I had traveled some before I worked for Atari. In fact, I went to India and—like most tourists—ended up with dysentery. So when I returned to the States, I was interested in diet. I believe that man is architected as a fruitarian, and basically, that is the way we should eat. And the apple is the staple of the fruits. So we needed a name, and people were suggesting all of these funny, technical-sounding names like XXX or Matrix Manipulation. Just to spur creativity, I deemed that we would call it Apple Computer unless someone had a better idea by 5:00 P.M. Well, it stuck and it got us ahead of Atari in the phone book.

Most of the initial cash invested in Apple Computer came from Markkula, who invested $91,000 in January 1977. Jobs and Wozniak put up $2,654.48 each. Another $517,500 was raised from various venture capitalists in early 1978. This made Apple a rather inexpensive start-up. As Jobs commented, "It was clear that we didn't necessarily want Markkula's money—we wanted Markkula. I really admire Mike. He's a really good coordinator." They then hired Mike Scott, who had been an office mate of Markkula at Fairchild, to be the president. Markkula became chairman of the board and vice president of marketing, and Jobs, vice president of product development.

Meanwhile, other firms had also become interested in the personal computer market. In early 1977, Commodore announced the Pet, the first personal computer, priced at $495. Interest in the product was intense, but no one could get one. In hopes of purchasing a Pet, people mobbed the Commodore booth in April 1977, at the first West Coast Computer Fair in San Francisco. However, Commodore had problems. The price of Pet computers had been raised to $595, $100 over their advertised price. More importantly, they weren't actually available until August—or September—or October.

But Apple was right across the hall introducing the Apple II. Moreover, the Apple II could do some things that the Pet could not, such as color graphics and sound effects. Although the Apple II was somewhat more expensive than the Pet, priced between $1,195 and $1,395, it *was* available.

The Apple II was a product for which the customer had very low expectations, in part because it had little competition. The early personal computers were purchased by hobbyists. Customers were 98 percent male, typically 25 to 45 years old, earned a salary over $20,000 a year, and had the knowledge to program their own routines. (There was little standard software available.) Customers, for instance, commonly programmed games such as Star Trek and Adventure.

The Apple Computer Company

Apple's first full fiscal year of operations was 1978. (For financial data, see Exhibits 6 to 8.) During that year, the company organized a distribution network through independent distributors. This expanded distribution system contributed greatly to the increase in sales. Sales of Apple products to the ComputerLand retail chain accounted for 14 percent of the net sales for 1980 ($118,000). No other retail chain or store accounted for more than 3 percent of net sales.

Products were sold through 950 independent retail computer stores in the United States and Canada, and internationally through 30 independent distributors who supplied 1,300 retail stores. In 1980, however, Apple terminated independent distribution arrangements and established its own sales organization to serve retail computer stores. Apple absorbed the costs to repurchase inventory from the former distributors. Over 100,000 units had been sold by September 1980. (See Exhibit 1.)

In the late 1970s, many people still considered personal computers as something of a fad. By 1980, however, the outline of an industry had begun to take shape. Apple, Radio Shack, and Commodore were the principal manufacturers of systems retailing for less than $5,000. Apple had the second largest installed base for such systems in the United States, next to Radio Shack (a subsidiary of Tandy Corporation) which enjoyed strong market penetration due to its large number of company-owned retail stores (over 8,100 worldwide). Commodore, however, benefited from broader international retail distribution. (For an overview of the personal computer industry's products and markets, see Exhibit 2.)

EXHIBIT 1 Apple Product Shipments

APPLE II
Annual Shipments

	Year Ending				
	September 1977	September 1978	September 1979	September 1980	March 1981 (6 months)
Number sold	570	7,600	35,100	78,100	75,000

APPLE III
Monthly Shipments: Plan versus Actual

	Month		
	December 1980	January 1981	February 1981
Shipments planned	300	2,500	7,500
Shipments realized	125	500	2,500

EXHIBIT 2 Personal Computer Industry

Market Size (in millions of dollars)

	Year	
	1980	1985 (est.)
Home	120	475
School	35	145
Small business	590	2,700
Office	90	1,450
Scientific	220	1,020

Competition—An Overview of Key Competitors

Company	Product	Price*	Memory
Apple	Apple II, Apple III	$1,330 to $5,000	16K to 256K
Atari	400, 800	$400 to $1,000	16K to 48K
Commodore	VIC-20, PET	$300 to $3,000	5K to 96K
Hewlett-Packard	HP-83, HP-85	$2,250 to $3,250	16K
IBM	Personal computer	$1,600 to $6,000	16K to 256K
Radio Shack	Color computer, TRS-80	$400 to $8,000	4K to 64K
Texas Instruments	99/4	$525	16K
Xerox	SAM	$3,000	64K
Zenith	Z-89	$2,900	48K

*Suggested retail prices, varying with memory size and attachments.

SOURCE: *New York Times,* August 23, 1981.

The independent retail dealers who sold Apple computers were trained to replace and exchange most computer system components at the store. Apple required them to enter into dealer service agreements under which they could purchase service kits containing spare parts, components, manuals, and diagnostic programs. Apple typically offered a 90-day full parts and labor warranty for its products and, since January 1980, offered an extended limited warranty on the Apple II at a price of $225 for each year of coverage. Approximately 5 percent of the purchasers of Apple IIs entered into extended service agreements. About 90 percent of all repair work and diagnostic testing on the Apple II systems was provided by dealers.

Manufacturing and Personnel Policies

Manufacturing at Apple was essentially buy, assemble, and test. Most components in Apple products were purchased from outside vendors who built chips, boards, cases, and other parts to Apple specifications. Some of Apple's competitors, in contrast, manufactured many of their own components. Manufacturing facilities were maintained in Cupertino, San Jose, and Los Angeles, California; Dallas, Texas; and County Cork, Ireland.

Apple had developed production modules that could be duplicated within each plant. A module for the Apple II filled 30,000 square feet, required a crew of 70, and produced between 450 and 500 units per day. Apple utilized 90 percent of its manufacturing space capacity, operating one work shift a day, five days a week. The Cupertino plant had a special role in that it maintained at least one production module for each product. This gave the company a single location for developing new production techniques and a manufacturing location near top management.

Quality control and final system testing and inspection were performed at production facilities. In the testing process, Apple computers with special software performed diagnostic tests to isolate and identify problems. As a part of the final testing process, all systems were "burned-in" to provide assurance of electronic and mechanical functions.

Management carefully monitored sales-per-employee, which was $176,000 in 1980. In March 1981, the company employed 1,530 full-time employees, including 230 in marketing and sales, 250 in research, product development, and related engineering, 950 in manufacturing, and 100 in general management and administration. (See Exhibit 3 for an organization chart.) The company never had a work stoppage and no domestic employees were represented by labor unions.

Apple had liberal employee benefits, such as profit sharing. Virtually all professional employees owned stock, and there was an employee purchase plan in which all employees could participate. Under this plan, employees could purchase stock up to 10 percent of their salary every six months at 85 percent of the price at the beginning or end of the six months, whichever was lower. It

EXHIBIT 3 Corporate Structure

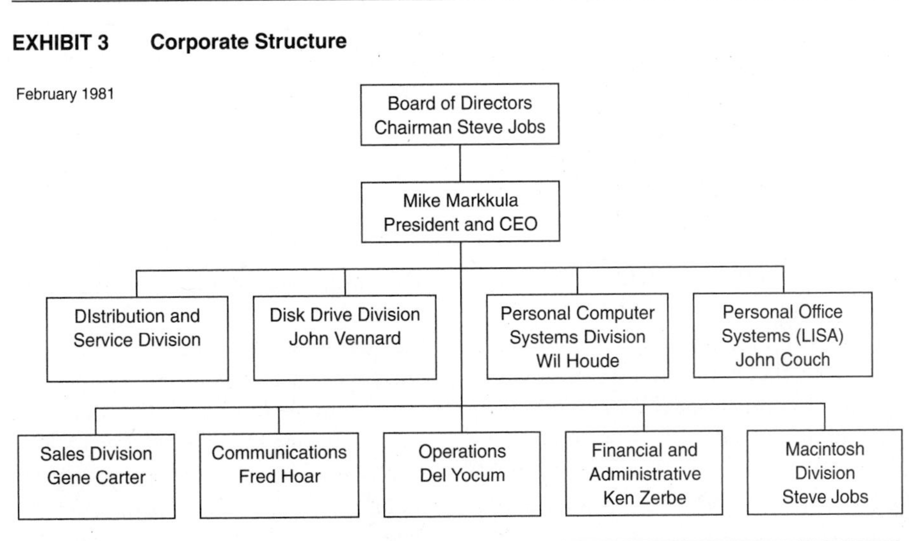

was not unusual to find workers on the assembly floor who owned Apple stock.

In December 1980, Apple Computers made its first public offering, selling 4.6 million shares at $22. The reasons for going public, as with many other things at Apple, were unconventional. Jobs recalled:

> When a company exceeds a number of shareholders (something like 500), it has to start reporting to the Securities and Exchange Commission just as if it were public. Therefore, we had the choice either to stop giving stock options to new employees or essentially to go public. It was a binary choice. Since it is Apple's philosophy that we should be an employee-owned company, the choice was simple. We went public. Every professional at Apple has a major stock option. Over 200 Apple employees have become millionaires in the past two years.

Apple also had a "loan-to-own" program through which, after one year of employment, the company gave the employee a free computer if he could demonstrate minimal computer skills. About 60 percent of the employees had an Apple computer at home. The company also paid for half of employee lunches. There were also occasional special benefits. When Apple had its first $100,000 quarter, everyone was given an extra week of vacation that year, for a total of four weeks.

The company published a set of beliefs known as "Apple Values." (See Exhibit 4.) These values helped guide decisions, policies, and procedures throughout the organization. They were designed to provide continuity and a sense of tradition as the company grew. In short, Apple Values was an attempt to delineate that which was unique to Apple. Jobs described it in this way:

> Our greatest joy is hiring people who are better at doing things than we were. Our managerial style is to hire really great people and create an environment where people can make mistakes and grow: the Apple culture. The Apple Values were, in effect, originally contained in our first business plan.

Personal Computing

Apple Computer had been an innovator in personal computers. Aside from the computers themselves, Apple's most significant innovation was the low-cost, 5¼-inch, flexible or "floppy" disk drive for the Apple II—introduced in mid-1978. The floppy disk storage replaced the less efficient cassette tape storage. It provided file memory capacity of up to 143K bytes of data, vastly increased data retrieval speed, and provided random access to stored data. These hardware enhancements increased the power and speed of the Apple II and also sped up the development of software. Over 100 independent vendors were developing Apple II software and peripheral equipment for text editing, small business accounting, and teaching.

Some of these programs were extraordinarily successful. The best seller was a financial modeling program called Visicalc, developed by two Harvard Business School students. Over 250,000 copies of Visicalc were sold at about $250 a copy. *Forbes* magazine (August 2, 1982) called it "the infant personal computer software industry's first gorilla hit."

By 1980, Apple had begun to introduce its own software, but Apple expected to write no more than 1 percent of the software that would eventually be available for its computers. Even 1 percent of these programs would be a large number, since over 100,000 were then available for the Apple II.

Apple also had introduced new peripheral devices to expand the computer's applications. Peripheral accessories manufactured by Apple included a graphics table, the floppy disk, a thermal printer, and interface circuit boards. Apple computers incorporated standard interfaces, permitting the use of peripherals designed and manufactured by others as well as those offered by Apple. These peripherals included medium-speed printers for home or business applications requiring letter-quality output; modems that provided a data communication link over telephone lines to access time-sharing services, computerized bulletin boards, or other computers; music synthesizers; portable power units; and more. The development of this software and equipment helped the growth of the personal computer business segment by increasing the variety of applications for which the computer could be used.

The Apple III

The project to build the successor to the Apple II began in late 1978 under the code name Sara, after the daughter of Wendell Sander, Apple's 16th employee, who was the designer of the new computer. Sander held a Ph.D. in electrical engineering and had worked for several years in the defense and semiconductor industries. In general, Apple was feeling a need to build a product that would eliminate the Apple II's shortcomings. "We had listened

EXHIBIT 4 Apple Bulletin

Apple Values
September 23, 1981

Apple Values are the qualities, customs, standards, and principles that the company as a whole regards as desirable. They are the basis for what we do and how we do it. Taken together, they identify Apple as a unique company.

Values are important because they determine our culture, our style. They guide our decisions, our policies, and our procedures. When they are identified and supported through management practices, they foster trust and unity, thus reducing the need for cumbersome rules and unnecessary supervision. They help Apple employees to understand the company's philosophy and objectives . . . and how they themselves contribute as individuals. Values are a compass for all. As the company grows, they provide continuity and the thread of tradition that marks Apple as different from others.

The attached list of Apple Values was created by an employee task force, based upon input from the Executive Staff. Both the Apple Values Task Force and the Executive Staff recognize that these values are GOALS. We don't always live up to them. For example, although we value teamwork, there is clearly room for improvement in the ways we work together. We should strive to live up to these values as the standard, and be looking for ways to do better. The values are guides to help us make decisions.

Identifying our values is important, but fostering them in practice is even more important. The draft of Apple Values will always be a draft, i.e., open for redefinition or affirmation. Please let us know what you think of the draft, and give us your ideas on what we can do to help Apple live up to these goals. And most of all, consider what you can do personally to support these values—to make them as alive as possible within each of us at Apple.

Thanks!!

The Apple Values Task Force

Task Force Members	*Executive Staff Members*	
Ron Boring	S. Bowers	S. Jobs
Trip Hawkins	C. Carlson	T. Lawrence
Pat Marriott	G. Carter	A. C. Markkula
Bob Montgomery	J. Couch	A. Sousan
Phil Roybal	A. Eisenstat	J. Vennard
Pat Sharp	F. Hoar	S. Wozniak
Ken Victor	R. Holt	K. Zerbe
Roy Weaver	W. Houde	

Draft: Apple Values

EMPATHY FOR OUR CUSTOMERS/USERS

One person, one computer.

We provide our dealers and users with reliable products of lasting value and dependable service. We expect our products to respond to the user's needs: To be seen as friendly, natural tools that can extend each person's analytical and imagining abilities. Most of all, we want our customers to feel that they receive more benefit from Apple than they paid for.

ACHIEVEMENT/AGGRESSIVENESS

We are going for it and we will set aggressive goals.

We are all on an adventure together.

We will continue to set high goals and high standards of performance because we realize that through meeting such challenges we will advance as a company and as individuals. We do not value risk taking for its own sake. Rather, we regard taking calculated risks as part of the adventure and the challenge of accomplishing something significant.

POSITIVE SOCIAL CONTRIBUTION

We build products we believe in.
We are here to make a positive difference in society, as well as make a profit.

Apple contributes to society by providing the power and usefulness of the computer to individual people. With this tool, people are improving the way they work, think, learn, communicate, and spend their leisure hours. As a corporate citizen of this world, we will respect our social and ethical obligations. Our profits are the result and an important measure of how well we succeed in making this contribution.

INDIVIDUAL PERFORMANCE

Each person is important; each has the opportunity and the obligation to make a difference.

The individual worth of each employee as a person is highly valued. We recognize that each member of Apple is important, that each can contribute directly to customer satisfaction. Our results come through the creativity, craftsmanship, initiative, and good work of each person as a part of a team.

TEAM SPIRIT

We are all in it together, win or lose.

EXHIBIT 4 *(concluded)*

We are enthusiastic!

We strive for a cooperative, friendly work environment that supports individual contribution as well as team effort. As a company, we know that we are all working together for a common goal. Accordingly, we want to keep our organization simple and flexible so that ideas and information can pass freely among those who need it. Indeed, our work environment serves to reflect and support all of our values.

INNOVATION/VISION

We are creative; we set the pace.

Apple was founded on the conviction that the computer could be, and should be, a personal tool. From simple beginnings, the company has accomplished in a short time what many others thought impossible. Innovation, aggressiveness, and responsible risk taking, combined with a vision of the future in which the personal computer will serve us all, will continue to motivate us.

INDIVIDUAL GROWTH/REWARD

We want everyone to enjoy the adventure we are on together.

We are committed to providing a work environment based on mutual respect and will strive to support our employees in achieving their personal objectives in line with their contribution at Apple. We encourage the growth of each individual. Sharing the tangible rewards of Apple's success as well as the challenges and satisfactions that come with it is part of our management philosophy.

QUALITY/EXCELLENCE

We care about what we do.

We take pride in our integrity and the quality of our products. We strive for absolute fairness in our dealings with customers, vendors, and competitors as well as among ourselves. In cases of dispute, we are willing to go the extra mile. The quality of our work stems directly from the care we express in all we do. It is an attitude that unites us.

GOOD MANAGEMENT

We want to create an environment in which Apple Values flourish.

We want to foster the best environment for individual initiative while maintaining the highest standards in business ethics, personal and professional integrity, and achievement.

very carefully to our customers," remembered Jobs. In fact, a great deal of marketing research had been conducted for the Apple III. Not only did this work help detail technical specifications, but it also called for a sense of urgency. "We were told that sales of the Apple II would peak around 10,000 units per month," said Houde. In order to sustain the company's growth, the Apple III had to be introduced during the "market window." As it turned out, Apple II sales charged through the 10,000 mark without a pause. Sander recalled, "We had no idea back then that the Apple II's popularity would last so long."

Heading the Personal Computer Division at this time was Tom Whitney, a Ph.D. formerly with Hewlett-Packard. His background in electrical hardware included work with the HP-35 calculator and the HP-3000 computer. The initial outline of the new product concept was largely his work.

From the very beginning, the new computer was envisioned to have an 80-character wide screen (instead of 40), upper- and lowercase capability, and a built-in disk drive. These made the new machine much closer to a full word processor—an application for which Apple II owners had been buying special plug-in cards. A built-in drive was only logical, since microcomputers were virtually useless without the programs on the floppy disks or "diskettes." At that time, the price of RAMS was dropping so the new machine gained additional internal memory. Computer memory was measured in thousand bytes, and the Apple II typically had 8 or 16K (8 or 16 thousand bytes). Whenever a pro-

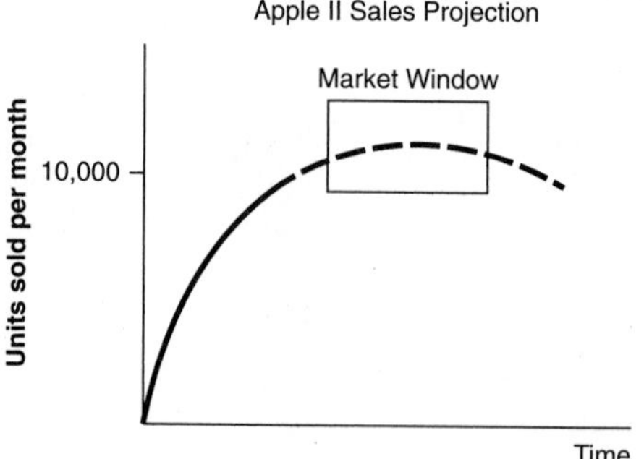

gram's memory requirements exceeded this internal quota, it had to utilize the diskettes, which had a longer access time. The common purchase of special cards by users to expand the II's internal memory pointed to this shortcoming also.

This new product, which was to become the Apple III, was envisioned to be ready in approximately one year—a short turnaround time. It would consolidate Apple's leadership role in personal computers. Although it would be far ahead of any competition, the Apple III did not presume to establish radically new standards for the industry. Indeed, some of Apple's best engineers embarked at this same time on a separate project named Lisa. Lisa would have a longer time horizon and was expected to be the company's next revolutionary product.

During the next few months, the design evolved to a product quite different from the Apple II. The new computer was to have a numeric keypad in addition to a standard typewriter keyboard. The memory was expanded considerably to 96K. An entirely new operating system, the Sophisticated Operating System (SOS, pronounced "sauce"), was created. The aluminum case was designed and cast. The hardware had been given the Apple look and feel.

SOS made the Apple III a much more versatile machine. A computer needed an operating system to create the framework in which application programs could operate. The Apple II had a comparatively inflexible system that would often call for minute changes in programs if a peripheral, say a printer, had to be changed. SOS introduced a "driver" system that allowed programs to address a "PRINTER" routine. This way, a new printer required only a new driver, not a change in every program that used it. Additionally, SOS could save files in a hierarchical framework, which was important for saving large quantities of data. SOS was also more "user friendly." The operating system was considered so advanced that Apple engineers insisted on keeping its specifications secret. However, this technical information was released a few months after the initial product introduction.

The system had made a transition from a follow-on product for the Apple II to an entirely new product. Instead of replacing the Apple II, the Apple III would coexist. (See Exhibit 5 for Apple III product illustration and data sheet.) Most significantly, the decision was made to incorporate an emulation mode so the new machine could simulate an Apple II and run software written for the II. "Essentially, emulation performs a frontal lobotomy on the machine and makes it forget that it ever was an Apple III," is how one person at Apple described it. This decision, which was hotly debated, may have added as much as 25 percent to development costs, although the additional cost per unit in hardware and labor was small. It was felt that one of the elements in Apple's success was the "cottage industry" that had sprung up to write software for the Apple II. Emulation assured the new machine access to about 90 percent of this vast resource.

Marketing

"The Apple III gave us a classic product positioning problem," said Barry Yarkoni, the product manager of the Apple III. "It originally set out to be a replacement unit for the Apple II but became much more powerful and much more expensive. We couldn't target for the same markets without losing Apple II sales and being overpriced." The new computer cost more than two times to make as did a comparable configuration of the Apple II.

It was important for maintaining sales of the II to assure the public that the III was considerably different and not a replacement. Part of Apple's solution to this problem was to suggest prices for the new computer as high as possible so different buyers would be attracted to the two computers. While the Apple II now ranged from $1,330 to $1,530, the Apple III was announced at prices ranging from $4,700 to $7,800 (depending on the configuration).

"Our strategy was to roll out the III to selected markets in a rifle shot approach, as opposed to the shotgun approach of the II," explained Yarkoni. The first market targeted was the professional user. This market had not been penetrated deeply by the Apple II, and this plan would protect the II's position in other segments, such as education, small business, and hobbyists.

This strategy led to the development of the Information Analyst package. It dictated a software "bundle" that would include a word processor, Business BASIC language, and Visicalc, the popular program for financial planning—about $700 of software. The Apple III was now positioned as a "discretionary purchase by professional people to improve their productivity."

Another marketing manager added, "In those days, it was THE computer. There were no other products competitive with it." The Apple offered far more memory, higher resolution, and a more advanced operating system than anything else on the market. The

EXHIBIT 5

The Apple III Personal Computer System

The Most Powerful Professional Computer System in Its Class

The Apple III is a powerful desktop computer system available as part of custom-tailored packages designed to solve your complex application needs. For managers, financial planners, analysts, and others who need to organize facts and figures, there's the Apple III Information Analyst System. It offers special features that make it the most powerful, easy-to-use timesaver available.

A wide variety of Apple III system configurations can be tailored to meet your specific needs. Consult your dealer for information.

Powerful Solutions for Complex Applications

The Apple III Computer System has been designed to tackle the tasks that keep you from being as productive as you'd like to be. With an Apple III, you can . . .

- Plan budgets, compare actuals with forecasts, and modify projections.
- Calculate rate-of-return, pro formas, and financial statements.
- Develop highly accurate forecasting models and pricing strategies.
- Create scientific and engineering models and study causes, effects, and trade-offs.
- Compose, revise, and print all kinds of documents—from memos and brochures to form letters and book-length manuscripts—quickly and easily.
- Maintain and update comprehensive mailing lists, sort them by name, ZIP code, or special key, and selectively print mailing labels and phone lists.
- Write complex computer programs in a variety of languages, including Apple Business BASIC and Pascal.

Professional Features for Professional Needs

In addition to its outstanding applications software, the Apple III offers a powerful operating system and all the hardware features professionals look for.

Apple III's Sophisticated Operating System (SOS)

Designed to control all of the Apple III's hardware for you, SOS handles interrupts, manages the system's memory and peripherals, provides the foundation for graphics, and performs comprehensive file management.

Apple III's Keyboard

The typewriter-style Apple III keyboard has been sculptured for maximum typing speed and accuracy. It contains 61 alpha keys and a separate 13-key numeric pad.

Four dedicated cursor control keys provide single-keystroke cursor movement; each key also fast repeats when held down, so that you can move quickly from point to point in the text. The alpha-lock key shifts only the alphabetic keys into upper case, leaving the number row unaltered. To speed numeric data entry, the layout of the numeric keypad is identical to that of a standard calculator.

Apple III's Disk Drive

A built-in, 140K-byte, flexible disk drive makes the Apple III a compact, space-saving unit. System expansion is cost effective, too, because you can add up to three external disk drives without the need for additional control hardware or software.

Apple III's Back Panel

The system's back panel (as well as most of its case) is formed of diecast aluminum. The aluminum fins on the back of the unit keep the system cool and eliminate the need for a fan.

Most peripheral devices plug directly into the Apple III's back panel connectors. Additionally, there are four large slots in the back panel for input/output connectors mounted on optional peripheral cards.

As many as three expansion floppy disk drives can be used with the Apple III. The first additional drive plugs into the "floppy disk" connector on the system's back panel; then, in "daisy chain" fashion, the second drive plugs into the first, and the third plugs into the second.

Back panel connectors are also provided for two joysticks. Application programs can be designed to take advantage of a joystick (for example, to move the cursor around the screen, or to point to displayed items). Also, one of the joystick connectors can alternately be used to connect a Silentype thermal printer to the Apple III.

The Apple III allows you to use a wide variety of video display devices. The high-resolution Monitor III connects to the system by a shielded cable, which plugs into a jack on the Apple III's back panel. Color video monitors—including NTSC (standard) color, and RGB (for exceptional color purity and resolution)—require commercially available video adaptors, which attach to the Apple III by means of a 15-pin connector that provides all the power and signals necessary.

Built into the Apple III is a two-inch speaker, which produces sound of such high quality that it can even be used to generate voice. An audio output jack located on the back panel of the Apple III also allows for connection of a separate earphone or external speaker (plugging into this jack silences the Apple III's built-in speaker).

An RS-232C connector, also located on the Apple III's back panel, provides for direct attachment of many types of "serial" input/output devices. Using a modem, for example, your Apple III can connect to other computers and data banks by phone line. Or you can quickly add a variety of high-speed or letter-quality printers—even other terminals or computers—to your system, simply by plugging them into the RS-232C connector.

Inside the Apple III

Removing the top cover reveals the peripheral card expansion section of the Apple III. Up to four different peripheral cards can be used at one time to supplement the Apple III's built-in peripheral interfaces.

For optimal computing speed, the Apple III's CPU can be "interrupted" by your system's peripheral devices whenever they require CPU control. Alternately, the CPU can also poll the devices to determine which need attention—thereby minimizing the software required for peripheral control.

The Apple III also contains many features that enhance its utility, including a number of powerful text, graphics, and color capabilities. In all text modes, for instance, the character set that appears on your monitor can be chosen from several available fonts. Special characters, graphics symbols, and even foreign language character sets can be selected quickly and easily from a diskette and used by any program on the computer.

Through the Apple III's professional display, you view 80 characters by 24 lines of easy-to-read characters. The system can also display 40 characters by 24 lines of color text on color background to add dramatic emphasis to programs.

Along with various text modes, several graphic modes are also available with the Apple III, including an ultrahigh-resolution, monochromatic mode. Up to 16 different colors are available in the high-resolution color mode, and even higher resolution color can be generated by restricting color changes slightly. On a monochromatic monitor, color is displayed as 16 different shades, making it easy for you to use shading and highlighting to enhance and emphasize your displays.

The Apple III also has an Apple II emulation mode for those users who already have an investment in Apple II software. This mode enables you to run most Integer BASIC and Applesoft programs on your Apple III. (Minor modifications may be required for Apple II programs that use the game paddles or other peripherals, however.) Because the Apple III in emulation mode behaves exactly like an Apple II Plus, the screen will display 40-character by 24-line text.

Technical Specifications

Physical dimensions:
Height: 4.8 in. (12.20 cm.)
Depth: 18.2 in. (46.22 cm.)
Width: 17.5 in. (44.45 cm.)
Weight: 26 lb. (11.8 kg.)
Cast aluminum base with molded plastic.

Processor:
Apple-designed processor utilizes 6502A as one of its major components. Other circuitry provides extended addressing capability, relocatable stack, zero page, and memory mapping.

Emulation mode:
Provides hardware emulation of 48K-byte Apple II Plus. Allows Apple II programs, with the exception of Pascal and FORTRAN, to run without modification.

Clock speed:
1.8 MHz with video off. 1.4 MHz average;
1.0 MHz in emulation mode.

Main memory:
128K (131.072) bytes of dynamic RAM memory.

ROM memory:
4K (4096) bytes used for self-test diagnostics.

Power supply:
High-voltage switching type +5, −5, −12, −12 volts.

Mass storage:
One 5.25-inch floppy disk drive built-in; 140K (143.360) bytes per diskette. Up to three additional drives can be connected by daisy-chain cable (560K bytes on-line storage).

Keyboard:
74 keys (61 on main keyboard, 13 on numeric pad):
Full 128-character, ASCII encoded;
All keys have automatic repeat;
Three special keys: SHIFT, CONTROL, ALPHA LOCK;
Two user-definable "Apple" keys;

EXHIBIT 5 *(concluded)*

Four directional arrow keys with two-speed repeat;
Four other special keys: TAB, ESCAPE, RETURN, ENTER.

Screen:
Three upper/lower case text modes:
80-column, 24-line, monochromatic;
40-column, 24-line, 16-color foreground and background;
40-column, 24-line, monochromatic;
All text modes have a software-definable, 128-character set (includes upper and lower case) with normal or inverse display.
Three graphic modes:
280 × 192, 16 colors (with some limitations);
140 × 192, monochromatic;
560 × 192, monochromatic;
plus Apple II modes

Video output:
RCA phono connector for NTSC monochromatic composite video;
DB-15 type connector for:
NTSC monochromatic composite video;
NTSC color composite video;
−5, −5, −12, −12 volt power supplies;
Four TTL outputs for generating RGB color;
Composite sync signal;
Color signals appear as 16-level grey scale on monochromatic outputs.

Audio output:
Built-in two-inch speaker;
Miniature phono jack on back panel;
Driven by six-bit digital analog converter or fixed-frequency "beep" generator.

Serial I O:
RS-232C compatible. DB-25 female connector;
Software-selectable baud rate and duplex mode.

Joysticks:
Two DB-9 connectors for two joysticks with push-buttons and switches.

Printer:
One DB-9 connector (shared with second joystick) for Apple Silentype printer.

Expansion:
Four 50-pin expansion slots inside the cabinet.

SOS:
Sophisticated Operating System handles all system I O;
SOS can be configured to handle standard or custom I O devices and peripherals by adding or deleting "device drivers";
All languages and application programs access data through the SOS file system.

Languages:
Apple Business BASIC and Pascal.

The Apple III Package

With your order for any Apple III configuration, you will receive:

- Apple III Professional Computer System with built-in disk drive, keyboard, serial (RS0232C) and Silentype printer interfaces, and 128K bytes RAM.
- Apple's Sophisticated Operating System (SOS) package, with:
  —System Owner's Guide.
  —DOS 3.3 diskettes.
  —DOS 3.3 instruction manual.
  —Standard drivers manual.
- Apple's Business BASIC programming software package with:
  —Business BASIC diskettes.
  —Instruction manual.

Plus the following (based on the configuration ordered):

Apple III Information Analyst

In addition to the basic hardware and software, with your Apple III Information Analyst order you will also receive:

- VisiCalc™ III software package with
  —VisiCalc III diskette.
  —VisiCalc III manual.
  —Toolkit sampler diskette (with prewritten VisiCalc III worksheets to help you get started).
  —Toolkit sampler manual.
- Monitor III.
- Second disk drive (Disk III—with options B and C).
- Apple III Silentype thermal printer (with option C).
- All necessary cabling, accessories, and blank diskettes to put your system to work immediately.

Apple III Information Analyst
Order No. A3P0001 (Option A)
Order No. A3P0002 (Option B)
Order No. A3P0003 (Option C).

™VisiCalc is a trademark of Personal Software, Inc.

SOURCE: Company literature.

machines that would later compete, like the IBM, were not due out until mid-1981.

Hardware and Software

The Apple III was a self-contained microcomputer with a built-in disk drive. The unit's flexibility was expanded by the inclusion of several peripheral ports in the back. These ports were simply jacks for plugs to printers, speakers, monitors, and several other "peripheral" devices. Ports were provided also for additional disk drives and, of course, joysticks for games.

The main unit of construction was an all-aluminum casing under which were attached the power supply and circuit board. This casing was the result of early concerns regarding shielding requirements that the FCC was preparing. Because the project could not wait for the new regulation, the casing had been designed to pass the most stringent of tests.

Another design problem was the printed circuit board itself. Essentially, the space allotted was insufficient for the circuitry needed, and Apple preferred not to abandon its "one-board" philosophy established with the Apple II. Nonetheless, these space limitations forced Apple to place the memory chips on a separate board that rested on top of the larger logic board like a bunk bed.

Overall styling followed the Apple II's lead with a similar color scheme and smooth lines. A matching monitor fit neatly on top of the computing unit.

User expectations were quite different for the two machines. While the hobbyist might buy an Apple II and write his own programs, an Apple III purchaser would expect a large selection of tools. The Information Analyst package was an initial approach to this demand.

The development of this software, however, was far behind hardware development. For marketing, this was a major block to selling. During the summer of 1980, nothing was available except for emulation mode and promises for the future.

Software development was understaffed and overly optimistic. "Really, no one understands how to schedule software," said Yarkoni. A shortage of reliable hardware slowed program writing still more.

Product Introduction

The National Computer Conference (NCC) was upcoming in May of 1980. The NCC was a key forum for the computer industry, and Apple decided to use the event to introduce the Apple III. This put tight time constraints on the development project. Also, word of the new computer was becoming the talk of the industry, not against Apple's wishes. "Apple leaked like a sieve. Our distributors thought they knew all about the Apple III," said one executive.

Apple treated participants of the 1980 NCC in Anaheim, California, to a great deal of fanfare, and to the new Apple III. Forced into a separate building for the amount of space it wanted, Apple provided a double-decker bus, appropriately decorated with Apple colors, to ferry people to its exhibits. In addition, the company rented Disneyland for an evening to celebrate its success. Anyone stopping by the booth could get a free ticket to the park for that evening—on Apple.

The public stock offering was also stirring up even more attention. Top management was becoming increasingly sensitive to criticism of Apple being "a single-product company." To refute this view, Apple had announced the Apple III in the prospectus. By that claim, the computer would be available by the end of 1980.

Internally, the people at Apple had an extremely difficult time getting the machine and related material ready for the show on time. Mike Scott, then Apple's president, had set the NCC deadline about eight weeks earlier, and everyone involved was racing for that milestone. With great effort, Apple engineers had produced several prototypes of the Apple III for the show. Marketing had worked to the last moment to have literature ready for the Information Analyst package. "The ink wasn't dry." Although everyone at Apple knew that a few bugs still remained to be worked out, the overall attitude at the firm towards the new product was positive.

And customers were putting down $500 deposits.

Volume Production

The transition to volume production, however, became an endless stream of problems. Engineering and production for the Apple III would later be merged into the Personal Computing System Division (PCSD), but at this point they were still separate departments. The entire production system had to be designed, and every aspect had its challenges. None of the first five or six prototypes worked.

A conflict over the internal cables was a case in point. Engineers in manufacturing had the attitude that, "The cables won't fit into the machine, which is an unmanufacturable pile of junk anyway," while their design engineers would complain back, "If you would listen to us, we would show you how to roll the cables up and slip them in." One production manager explained:

> Normally one should go through four steps in design: first, design: second, design validation; third, process design; fourth, process validation. In the case of the Apple III, we skipped both validation steps. The machine's development called for an overly ambitious schedule.

The units were burned-in for three days each. Burning-in was merely plugging in a machine (or part of a machine) and waiting to see what happened. Often units would be switched on and off or subjected to environmental tests during the burn-in to simulate actual operating conditions. Later, one participant claimed, "we needed 500 machines on (burn-in) racks for six months."

Another problem Apple had throughout this period was dealing with its tremendous growth. During 1980, sales rose from $48 million to $118 million. The number of employees increased from 240 to 670. "It seemed that every time I wanted someone, he had a new phone number," said one engineer. Production moved in September to a new facility 10 miles from the corporate offices. This 45,000-square-foot pilot plant had 100 employees and was to work out volume production methods for plants in Dallas and Ireland. Although most computers would ultimately be manufactured in these other plants, the pilot plant would always make a small volume to keep production information and experience close to the main office.

"The Apple III was the first new product Apple really had introduced. Initial volume was to be 1,000 a month, instead of 10 or 20, as with the Apple II," remembered Sander.

Reliability Problems

It was becoming painfully clear that the Apple III was fraught with problems. Design engineering had been attributing reliability failures to thermal stress induced by the completely enclosed aluminum case. Three months of temperature tests were made, cooling fins were added, holes were drilled, and the computers were still breaking down. "Weird, intermittent failures kept happening. At times, we were grasping at straws," one engineer reported.

This concern with thermal issues delayed the discovery of other sources of failure. The space constraint on the printed board had several unexpected and unwanted implications. First, the trace lines were excessively thin and sometimes didn't work. Trace lines were the copper strips on a printed circuit board that carried signals between the semiconductor devices. With great difficulty, the board was completely redesigned with wider traces. The memory board, supported over the logic board by a pair of vertical connectors, would sag in the middle—traces would break and chips would pop out of their sockets. Stiffeners were added to the board, which also helped dissipate heat. Furthermore, the first vertical connectors used were not especially good; the supplier had substituted the plating and they often lost their conductivity. This took some time to discover. They were replaced with better quality parts. One design engineer remembered with wry amusement:

> We had what we called the "in-house standard operations fix" for the Apple III. It was to pick up the front of the unit about four inches and drop it. This makes some sense because it would jolt those connectors back into action, but you couldn't very well tell a dealer to do that.

The connectors highlighted another characteristic of the Apple III's troubles—the company had several problems with suppliers. Various sources sold unreliable equipment to Apple and Apple didn't have sufficient inspection or burn-in tests to discover many of them. "We were still a small company and totally lacked things like a component evaluation group. You need a fairly sizable firm to do all that. So we just went for it."

One exciting element of the computer, for example, was the clock chip, which would run even when the machine was unplugged and track time for various programs. Unfortunately, the supplier just couldn't produce reliable chips as promised. And no second source existed because this chip was uniquely suitable for the crammed circuit board. Reliability was so low that this clock was quietly dropped from the product.

Shipments

For a few months following the NCC show, only a few Apple IIIs trickled out to dealers. Quantity shipments started in November. Mike Scott had established the 15th as the due date for 100 units to be shipped. Again, it was a deadline not easily met. Although Scott personally oversaw the production of the hardware, the software was still limited. Furthermore, packaging for the Information Analyst was squeezed out at the last moment. "You cannot believe the documentation necessary to produce six or seven booklets and a box to hold them. The specifications for the Information Analyst package made a stack several inches high," Yarkoni recalled.

Demand initially was extremely strong; however, customer reaction to the new product was not good. Because there was a certain lag time in shipping from inventory, it took a month or two for the message to become clear: The Apple III was in deep trouble. "The response was very strong," said Yarkoni. "Either they got one that worked and loved it, or they got one that didn't and hated us." Some customers were returning machines four or five times for repairs. One marketing manager recalled, "The market reputation of the III was extremely low. It didn't do any good to advertise for it because customers would go to the store only to be talked out of an Apple III by the dealer who felt he didn't need the headache."

In early 1981, Apple was considering halting the production and shipment of the Apple III. In the field, approximately 20 percent of the machines were dead-on-arrival, another 20 percent had major problems, and still more had minor bugs, such as a keyboard that would periodically "freeze." Furthermore, morale was extremely low throughout the company. Forty employees had been simultaneously let go a few weeks earlier. "Considering that we had hired something like 1,500 people in the last year," said Wil Houde, "it is actually surprising that we had only 40 'bad apples.' But it was very shocking to drop them all at once." Around this time both Mike Scott and Tom Whitney had also parted company with Apple, partly due to the Apple III. Houde, in fact, had assumed Whitney's position.

The situation prompted a *Forbes* article (April 13, 1981) entitled "Apple Loses Its Polish." *Forbes* went on to say, "Apple still has to prove that it can put together the kind of innovative products, manufacturing skills, and long-range growth that competitors like Tandy, Texas Instruments, and Hewlett-Packard have been demonstrating for years."

Explanations

Reasons given for the new product's problems were as numerous and varied as the respondents:

Design engineers

Marketing had sold the machine long before it was ready. If we could have had another six months, none of this would have happened.

The guy in charge was an "ivory tower" kind of guy who couldn't get something built.

If we had known that the Apple II was going to continue to be as successful as it has been, we would not have speeded up so much on the Apple III.

Manufacturing engineers

Design engineering just dumped the design on manufacturing and said, "Build it." They even went ahead and ordered parts for 10,000 machines.

The company's experience with the Apple II, a much simpler machine, left us totally unprepared for the Apple III.

As we were developing the III, we were also racing to keep up with Apple II demand.

Management

The Apple III was a machine that an organization had to build, not a small group of individuals.

The democratic system at Apple led to overexcitement and the premature introduction.

The Apple II had taken the world by storm. We felt we could do most anything. We got cocky.

The project was plagued by "creeping elegance," that is, never-ending improvements to the design. Once you have the idea, you should lock the visionary in the closet and build the product.

The people who put the Apple III together weren't here to learn the lessons of the Apple II. They didn't appreciate the details put into Apple II.

No one in this valley had built computers in high volume. There was nowhere to find the experience.

Alternatives

In early February 1981, Wil Houde and the rest of the PCSD management team were reassessing the Apple III. A variety of alternatives had been discussed that could be broadly encompassed by three categories: to abandon, replace, or correct the Apple III.

To abandon the machine would be quick and inexpensive, allowing reallocation of internal resources to other projects. There were approximately 6,000 units out the door, selling for about $4,000 each to the final customers. Apple could show character by publicly admitting its mistake,

EXHIBIT 6 Consolidated Balance Sheet

Assets

	September 30, 1979	September 26, 1980	March 27, 1981 (Unaudited)
Current assets:			
Cash and temporary cash investments	$ 562,800	$ 362,819	$ 74,086,000
U.S. government securities, at cost which approximates market in 1980 and at market March 27, 1981	—	2,110,710	1,800,000
Accounts receivable, net of allowance for doubtful accounts of $1,225,000 ($617,763 in 1980 and $400,000 in 1979)	9,126,010	15,814,000	34,538,000
Other receivables	52,301	1,557,000	7,887,000
Inventories:			
Raw materials and purchased parts	5,607,596	13,857,943	24,924,000
Work in process	3,727,008	9,625,234	14,838,000
Finished goods	768,113	10,708,443	13,090,000
	10,102,717	34,191,620	52,852,000
Prepaid expenses		70,066	1,989,000
Total current assets	19,843,828	54,106,215	173,152,000
Property, plant, and equipment, at cost:			
Land and buildings	—	242,851	2,084,000
Machinery, equipment, and tooling	404,127	2,688,787	6,017,000
Leasehold improvements	384,186	710,556	1,678,000
Office furniture and equipment	321,718	1,673,225	3,317,000
	1,110,031	5,315,419	13,096,000
Less: Accumulated depreciation and amortization	(209,824)	(1,311,256)	(2,808,000)
Net property, plant, and equipment	900,207	4,004,163	10,288,000
Leased equipment under capital leases, net of accumulated amortization of $572,000 ($205,358 in 1980 and $32,627 in 1979)	195,764	774,988	1,584,000
Cost in excess of net assets of purchased business, net of accumulated amortization of $39,785 ($13,193 in 1980)	—	514,592	488,000
Reacquired distribution rights, net of accumulated amortization of $782,326 ($90,022 in 1980)	—	5,311,304	4,619,000
Other assets	231,180	639,079	608,000
	$21,170,979	$65,350,341	$190,739,000

SOURCE: Company records.

and vowing never to repeat it. Or the Apple III could die a quiet, unpublicized death with no promotion from the company.

Replacing the machine with a new one begged many questions. What would be new about the Apple IV, or whatever? Furthermore, millions in development costs would have been wasted. The casting for the case itself had cost over $200,000.

Correcting the machine would entail a continuation of the "Band-Aid" approach that had been followed inconclusively for months. Every major subassembly required some change and no one knew yet how many changes were to come.

Even if Apple could correct the machine, it still had to convince the dealers and customers. Marketing estimated the cost of a reintroduction plan to be $5 million. Development of the machine itself had been only about $3 million. How should this be done? Should Apple repair old machines? Replace them? Or give dealers special upgrade kits?

Wil Houde hoped that the decision he and his colleagues were about to make at the executive committee meeting would be the right one.

EXHIBIT 6 **Consolidated Balance Sheet** (*concluded*)

Liabilities and Shareholders' Equity

	September 30, 1979	September 26, 1980	March 27, 1981 (Unaudited)
Current liabilities:			
Note payable to bank	$ —	$ 7,850,000	$ —
Note payable	—	1,250,000	1,460,000
Accounts payable	5,410,879	14,495,143	23,458,000
Accrued liabilities	1,264,459	5,241,945	10,013,000
Accrued key employee bonus	456,000	554,000	2,174,000
Income taxes payable	1,879,432	7,474,170	—
Deferred taxes on income	2,051,000	661,000	1,446,000
Current obligations under capital leases	21,823	253,870	877,000
Total current liabilities	11,083,593	37,780,128	39,428,000
Noncurrent obligations under capital leases	203,036	670,673	1,179,000
Deferred taxes on income	204,000	951,000	3,086,000
Commitments and contingencies	—	—	—
Shareholders' equity			
Common stock, no par value:			
160 million shares authorized, 55,237,000 shares issued and outstanding (48,396,928 in 1980 and 43,305,632 in 1979)	4,297,729	11,428,438	116,800,000
Common stock to be issued in business combination	—	920,210	—
Retained earnings	5,907,884	17,605,867	34,202,000
	10,205,613	29,954,515	151,002,000
Less: Notes receivable from shareholders	(525,263)	(4,005,975)	(3,956,000)
Total shareholders' equity	9,680,350	25,948,540	147,046,000
	$21,170,979	$65,350,341	$190,739,000

SOURCE: Company records.

EXHIBIT 7 Consolidated Statement of Income

	January 3, 1977 (Inception of Corporation) to September 30, 1977	Fiscal Year Ended			Six Months Ended	
		September 30, 1978	September 30, 1979	September 26, 1980	March 28, 1980	March 27, 1981
					(Unaudited)	
Revenues:						
Net sales	$ 773,977	$ 7,856,360	$47,867,186	$117,125,746	$43,090,000	$146,386,000
Interest income	—	27,126	71,795	775,797	546,000	4,178,000
	773,977	7,883,486	47,938,981	117,901,543	43,636,000	150,564,000
Costs and expenses:						
Cost of sales	403,282	3,959,959	27,450,412	67,328,954	23,813,000	82,617,000
Research and development	75,520	597,369	3,601,090	7,282,359	3,173,000	9,111,000
Marketing	162,419	1,290,562	4,097,081	12,109,498	3,478,000	16,378,000
General and administrative	76,176	485,922	2,616,365	6,819,352	1,939,000	8,519,000
Interest	5,405	2,177	69,221	209,397	13,000	737,000
	722,802	6,335,989	37,834,169	93,749,560	32,416,000	117,362,000
Income before taxes on income	51,175	1,547,497	10,104,812	24,151,983	11,220,000	33,202,000
Provision for taxes on income	9,600	754,000	5,032,000	12,454,000	5,785,000	16,606,000
Net income	$ 41,575	$ 793,497	$ 5,072,812	$ 11,697,983	$ 5,435,000	$ 16,596,000
Earnings per common and common equivalent share	$*	$.03	$.12	$.24	$.11	$.30
Common and common equivalent shares used in calculation of earnings per share	16,640,000	31,544,000	43,620,000	48,412,000	47,394,000	55,051,000

*Less than $.01.

EXHIBIT 8

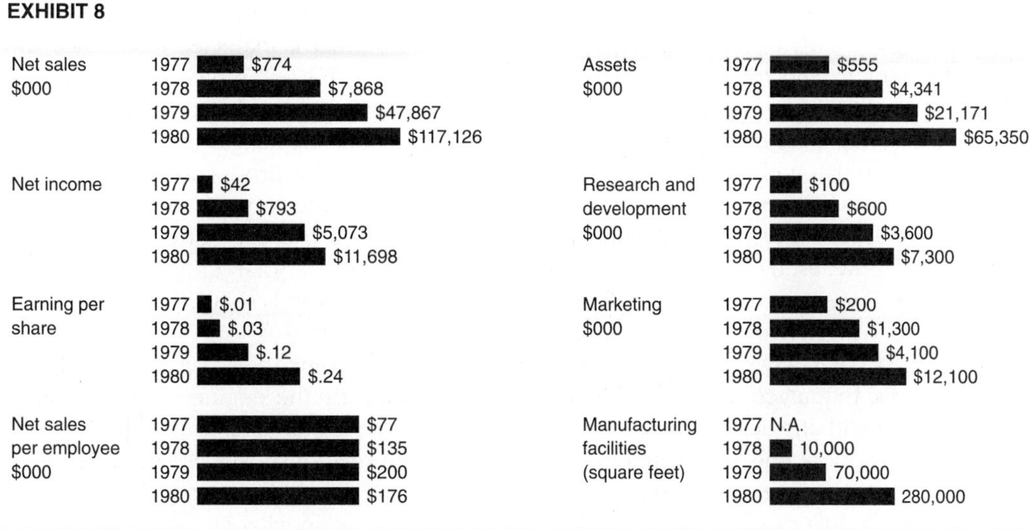

Reading IV–I
Communication between Engineering and Production: A Critical Factor

H. E. Riggs

Extensive communication between engineering and production is critical to implementing the firm's technical policy. Communication must be both formal and informal. Informal communication should be encouraged in all the ways that have become common in high-technology companies, from "beer busts" to technical symposia to off-site, multiday discussion sessions.

Regardless of the amount of informal communication, formal communication is also essential. The formal communication system between engineering and production must deal with three important, related, but distinct, challenges:

1. Introducing new products from the development laboratory to the production floor.
2. Providing the optimum—neither maximum nor minimum—level of documentation on existing products.
3. Facilitating orderly and cost-effective changes to products now in production.

Introducing New Products to Manufacturing

Handing over the new product from engineering to manufacturing tests the cooperation and communication between engineering and production personnel as does no other activity. The high-technology company that manages this transition well stands to gain timing, cost, and quality advantages that can have substantial payoffs in the marketplace.

Where departmental barriers are high and engineers are encouraged or permitted to be myopic, design engineers will attempt to maximize product performance and manufacturing engineers will try to redesign the product to reduce its cost. Such a two-step process is highly inefficient and very time consuming. Optimizing across the conflicting priorities of cost and performance—often called value engineering—must be the responsibility of everybody engaged in new product creation, including marketing managers who have a hand in setting the new product's target specifications.

Extensive communication must both precede and follow the formal transition from engineering to production. Periodic product design meetings that involve design engineers, manufacturing engineers, and material planners (and sometimes product managers from marketing and others as well) should be held monthly during the early design stage and perhaps weekly just prior to and following the "hand over" of the new product from engineering to production. In these meetings, the design staff consults with manufacturing personnel regarding design alternatives under consideration and gains insight into the issues of producibility as the product or system is being designed. Realistic tolerances are specified, and engineers are encouraged not to tighten tolerances to expedite design or to gain an additional margin of safety. (Excessively tight tolerances almost always increase manufacturing costs.) Manufacturing should share with the design team its experience with present vendors and subcontractors as engineering is selecting sources for parts or processing for the new product or system.

Both manufacturing and engineering personnel must be aware that the design process is generally not complete when manufacturing commences. Design errors that need attention may be uncovered; change requests initiated by manufacturing to facilitate fabrication or assembly must be evaluated; and operating performance that met specifications in the laboratory but cannot be replicated on the manufacturing floor must be reassessed. Proper reliance on prototype units and pilot production runs before full-scale production is attempted can reduce costly errors.

Prototype, Pilot, and Production Runs

Engineering typically produces prototypes (the first one or two units of a new product or system). The engineers and design technicians construct them at considerable cost, frequently building and rebuilding them. They use techniques appropriate to the lab but inappropriate to full-scale production—"breadboards" instead of printed circuit boards and fabricated instead of cast metal or injection-molded parts—in order to facilitate design changes and minimize tooling costs and lead times. These prototypes, which are often necessarily quite different physically from the units ultimately supplied to customers, should be both thoroughly tested in the laboratory and subjected to some field testing. The purpose of prototypes is to prove design concepts and confirm product specifications.

Once the basic design concepts have been proven in prototype and satisfactory operating specifications have been met, a pilot production run (the production of a limited quantity) should be initiated. The design used for the pilot production run should be the one that is expected to be used in full-scale production—for example, breadboards are now replaced with printed circuit boards, and substantially more investment is made in tooling. The purpose of the pilot production run is to test product producibility and to work out any bugs in the final design before the company scales up to full production. (When total anticipated volume of the product or system is small, this pilot production step can be eliminated.)

In some companies, pilot production runs are undertaken by the engineering department and, in others, by the manufacturing department. The exact reporting relationship is not particularly significant. What is important is to recognize that pilot production runs are inevitably the joint responsibility of engineering and production.

Freezing Designs

Before full-scale production is undertaken, the design must be frozen, after which time formal engineering change notices are the only mechanism for effecting changes. In the absence of a pilot production run (and sometimes even with it), the point at which design becomes final, or frozen, is often unclear. At the prototype stage, the design must be allowed to remain fluid, permitting design changes at minimum cost and documentation. But it is human nature to seek almost endlessly for small improvements and refinements. This propensity is as true for the design engineer who is a parent of the new product as it is for the artist in her sculpture or the writer in his manuscript. Just as editorial changes are expensive to effect once the manuscript has been set in type, so product design changes are expensive to effect once manufacturing has commenced.

Thus, at some point, the design of the new product must be frozen, and both manufacturing and engineering must agree upon that point. Subsequent design changes can no longer be made unilaterally by the design engineer, as they could during the prototype phase.

You can often gain important timing and cost advantages by freezing certain portions of the design before other portions. For example, in a complex computer-based system, the selection of the system's minicomputer can and should be frozen long before other portions of the system are designed, in order to provide sufficient time for the programmers to develop the necessary software and for purchasing to negotiate OEM contracts with the minicomputer supplier. Sequential freezing is appropriate: Freeze parts or components known to have long procurement lead times early; leave standard components and those parts requiring little or no tooling unfrozen until late in the design cycle. A complex design project can usefully be subjected to PERT (program evaluation and review technique) analysis to reveal the critical design concepts or components that need early freezing. This process of sequential freezing of portions of the design implies close working relationships and much communication throughout the engineering organization and between engineering and production.

Top managers of high-technology companies should see to it that procedures for freezing designs are both established and adhered to.

Using a "Skunk Works"

Some technology-based companies have successfully used an unusual organizational technique to expedite new product design and introduction. When a new product requires (1) a number of engineering disciplines, (2) careful attention to manufacturability and cost, and (3) a telescoping of the design and introduction stages, a separate task force may be created, drawing personnel from a number of functional departments in the company. When this task force is assigned separate facilities, sometimes with extra security against industrial espionage, these facilities are often referred to as the "skunk works."

The objective is to recapture the advantage of the small company: high motivation, focused purpose on a single product, system, or process, and intensive and informal communication with a minimum of organizational barriers. The task force is accorded (or assumes) high prestige in the organization, and assignment to it is eagerly sought. Extra resources are typically made available to the task force.

Arguing against the establishment of a skunk works is the fact that creating one or a series of these task forces can be disruptive to the organization. Other development projects may be interrupted and key technical personnel assigned to the task force may be unavailable for informal counsel and advice on projects to which they are not formally assigned. Acceleration of the design can also cause some loss of efficiency.

This organizational device should be used only when competitive conditions demand fast action, either to protect an existing market position or to gain a jump on anticipated competition. Although the device has proved highly effective in a number of instances, resulting in a dramatic product unveiling that left both customers and competitors in awe, its overuse reduces the opportunities for specialization, economies of scale (experience curve economies), and routinizing of procedures.

A variation on this organizational device is to assign a group of engineers to "follow" a new design through the laboratory and onto the production floor. That is, rather than turning over its design (and prototypes) to manufacturing engineering, a portion or all of the engineering design team is assigned the responsibility for moving with the product from the design engineering organization to the manufacturing engineering organization. The trade-off is that the "following" engineers will know the new product in detail, thus eliminating the need for manufacturing engineers to learn the new product, but will be less experienced and probably less capable in attacking the problems of producibility and tooling. However, a design engineer who has spent some time wrestling with new products from a manufacturing engineering viewpoint will be a more effective design engineer when he or she returns to the laboratory and another new product. Again, a type of job rotation has occurred.

Moving from Single to Multiple Products

Many emerging technical companies—that is, small but rapidly growing companies—encounter real turmoil as they move from relying on a single product to offering multiple products to the market. A small technology-based business focusing on designing and manufacturing a single product is often wonderfully efficient. It minimizes conflicting priorities because all hands are devoted to the single product. As the business grows and more product lines are added to the company's portfolio, choices must be made. The general management task suddenly becomes much more complex.

In engineering, the task of product maintenance engineering on the older products competes for attention with new product development. The need for standardization of components and subassemblies across product lines becomes evident. Compromises between standardization and optimum price/performance suddenly become necessary.

In manufacturing, quality problems that remained under control because of the undivided attention of manufacturing and engineering on the single product line now drift out of control as technical attention is diffused across many products. The existence of multiple products on the manufacturing floor complicates production scheduling. These products require both unique and common skills and often incorporate common parts or subassemblies that ought to be produced in larger lots.

The interaction between engineering and manufacturing was extensive on the company's first product line. This intimate, one-on-one communication needs to be continued on the newer products, but coordination on older products needs to be more routinized.

A key test for an emerging high-technology company is its ability to move successfully from engineering and producing a single product to engineering and producing a portfolio of product lines. The transition requires that a manufacturing engineering function be established, as well as a data base and reference system to aid in standardizing components. Task assignments in engineering must clearly recognize the dual responsibility of product maintenance and product development. A formal documentation and engineering change request system must replace the informal communication that sufficed when the company was small and produced only one product.

Engineering Documentation

Formal communication between engineering and production demands product and process documentation: drawings, bills of material (parts lists), schematics, assembly prints, software listings, and many other elements of paperwork (and now, increasingly, microfiche, computer data bases, videotapes, and other media). Most of these communication media are created by engineering and represent the detailed specification of the product to be produced or the process to be operated.

Level of Detail

A persistent dilemma facing management in high-technology companies is the decision of just how much detail to incorporate into the documentation of particular products and processes. Detailed documentation, taking the form of prints, parts lists, assembly drawing, process and assembly instructions, and sometimes audio, video, and other nonprinted media, is expensive to create, control, and update. However, skimpy documentation may be risky, allowing design changes to be effected without thorough review. Such incomplete documentation may also inhibit accurate and complete communication among the functional departments of the business.

The dilemma is resolved primarily on the basis of the relative importance the high-technology company places on manufacturing flexibility and product costs. Very detailed documentation is required when (1) production volumes are high, (2) automation and tooling are relied upon to reduce costs, and (3) less skilled manufacturing labor is to be utilized. More elaborate documentation is a prerequisite to the aggressive pursuit of learning curve economies. Such elaborate documentation is not justified, however, when volumes are small, a skilled work force can be relied upon to operate with limited instructions, and design changes are implemented at a rapid rate. As a general rule, more documentation is appropriate, justified, and necessary as one moves along the continuum from custom to standard products.

High-technology companies most frequently err on the side of too little documentation. This tendency is not surprising. In the early stages of the life of products and technologies, a minimum of documentation is appropriate. As the company, products, and technologies mature, there is a reluctance to invest engineering time and attention in paperwork on existing products rather than in designing new products. Companies that neglect documentation, however, find they are forever running to catch up with the required documentation.

General managers must strike the proper balance between too much documentation and too little. Despite protests to the contrary from most manufacturing managers, more complete and thorough documentation is not always appropriate. The right balance is a function of the overall business strategy and of the position of the particular product or product family within the product-process matrix. When the strategy is geared to a succession of new, high-technology products, skimpy documentation is both appropriate and cost effective. When the strategy depends upon achieving learning curve economies—the company is operating down and to the right on the product-process matrix—complete, up-to-date, and reliable documentation is essential.

Effects on Inventory Control

Effective inventory planning and control requires very accurate bills of material (that is, listings of individual parts, components, and subassemblies that go into a finished product). Inaccurate or incomplete bills of material preclude using sophisticated planning techniques, such as MRP. The result is that excessive raw material inventories are held in order to guard against shortages. Moreover, the omission of one or more parts from a bill of materials can cause a halt in the assembly process while the missing part is located. The result is that in-process inventories also balloon. Thus, improved inventory control in high-technology companies, an objective stressed repeatedly throughout this book, requires the active participation of engineering, as well as of the production and finance departments.

Processing Engineering Changes on Existing Products

Life in a technology-based business would be substantially simplified if all documentation, once created, could be relied upon to be both accurate and stable. Neither condition is easily achieved when both technology and product change is an ever-present fact of life. All engineering changes, whether to improve performance or to reduce costs, must be reflected in changed documentation. In addition, design errors uncovered by engineering or manufacturing personnel (and sometimes by field service personnel) must be corrected and the corrections incorporated into the documentation system.

Thus, requests for changes to existing products can—and should—emanate from all corners of the organization:

1. From engineering to take advantage of new technology or to incorporate a new product feature.
2. From the field service organization to improve reliability or to facilitate field repair.
3. From purchasing to take advantage of a new supplier or a lower price of a substitute component.
4. From marketing to improve the competitive posture of the product.
5. From manufacturing engineering to permit the use of more sophisticated tooling.
6. From production and inventory planning to permit standardization of components across product lines.
7. From production supervisors to reduce tolerances, and thereby costs, or to facilitate processing or assembly in some other way.

Just as requests for changes can emanate from all corners of the organization, so implemented changes affect all corners of the organization, including particularly purchasing, inventory control, marketing, field service, production supervision, and cost accounting. Because these organizational units will be affected by the change, they must have a hand in deciding whether the requested change should be adopted (and when), and they must be notified in a timely fashion of approved changes.

The number of change requests may be very high—in the tens for a simple product, the hundreds for a complex instrument, and the thousands for a comprehensive system. Each change is likely to have a ripple or domino effect on documentation. For example, the change of a single component may require a change in the drawing on which it first appears, on one or more bills of materials, on drawings of parts or assemblies farther up the product tree, on assembly instruction sheets, and so forth. Each change may have both obvious and not-so-obvious consequences; these need to be anticipated, evaluated, and, if appropriate, tested.

Technical companies should develop and institute formal procedures and paper flow systems to be certain that all necessary documents are changed as required, that changes do not become incorporated into the documentation before they are appropriately authorized, and that all affected individuals and groups within the organization are aware of the nature and effective date of the change in sufficient time to adapt accordingly. The process must be both rapid and thorough, but it also must be routine, if production and engineering activities are not to grind to a halt either as a result of a preoccupation with processing changes or a lack of coordination among the changes themselves.

Discipline must be built into the engineering change request system so that procedures are not short-circuited. If control of documentation is lost, the following conditions can occur:

1. Quality problems multiply as exact specifications of components become impossible to trace and unanticipated consequences arise from unauthorized design changes.
2. Inventory investments and write-offs increase as parts are made obsolete without notice and the production cycle lengthens because newly

specified parts are not planned and acquired in a timely manner.

3. Manufacturing labor costs escalate as expediting, troubleshooting, and additional setups consume both direct and indirect labor-hours.

Proper handling of engineering changes is the bugaboo of documentation methods in many high-technology companies.

Cost and Benefit Trade-Offs

All changes have both benefits and costs, even those that simply correct drawing errors. The challenge is to make the proper trade-off. Engineering changes that alter the physical specifications of particular components may render obsolete present components now in inventory and necessitate rescheduling of manufacturing work orders or purchase orders with vendors. Such obsolescence and rescheduling costs must be weighed against the advantages to be achieved from the change to decide both if and when the change should be effected. The optimum decision is often to delay the change until present inventories are depleted, until new vendors can be brought on stream, or until other conditions occur that will minimize disruption.

Some changes—for example, in computer software—must be expedited to fix a bug in a particular program, with notification rushed to various parts of the organization and to customers. Other changes in the software—changes designed to enhance capabilities or improve execution efficiencies—should be saved up and incorporated with other alterations in periodic rereleases of entirely new generations of software. Changing software documentation is expensive, and such changes typically require changes in operating, training, and service manuals as well. Batching changes may be efficient, but this advantage must be weighed against the disadvantage of delaying the introduction of an improved product to the marketplace.

The initiator of a change request may be unaware of the full ramifications of the proposed change. A change in part M may require an adaptation of part P or assembly T, expensive reworking of tooling, or a change in maintenance procedure that must be communicated to customers and the field service force. The possibility that the benefit sought from the engineering change request could be more expeditiously accomplished by an alternative change must be evaluated. For example, a problem that could be corrected by a hardware change might also be correctable by a less expensive software change.

Evaluate all changes on the basis of costs and benefits. Making the trade-offs between the costs and the benefits of change is complicated within most high-technology companies by the fact that the relevant data on both costs and benefits are not readily available to the decision maker. Manufacturing cost penalties or savings may be ascertainable (although even here most cost accounting systems do not reveal the incremental costs), but the tangible and intangible benefits or costs associated with changes in competitive position, in ease of field maintenance, or in vendor relationships are often uncertain. The costs of effecting the change—engineering time, clerical effort on documentation, renegotiation by purchasing, and possible scrapping of inventory—must be factored into the decision.

Engineering change requests must be routed for approval through each affected department: design engineering, manufacturing engineering, material planning, quality assurance, and field service. (In some companies still other departments should formally approve changes.) Each of the evaluators must be alert to the possible need to solicit input from other functions, such as marketing or finance. Checklists and rules of thumb may help streamline the process. An engineering change committee, which is responsible for making the final cost-benefit trade-off when disputes arise, should be constituted.

New Models versus Incremental Changes

I spoke earlier of the importance of freezing new product design, and now I have suggested that engineering changes may occur in large numbers. What factors should management consider in deciding how much product evolution to permit through the engineering change request mechanism?

First, saving up (or batching) engineering change requests in order to effect many changes at one time can have distinct advantages in reducing implementation costs. Disruptions in both production and engineering are minimized.

More important advantages often attend the introduction of a brand new model or line of a product.

First, the company's image in the marketplace may be enhanced when it introduces a new product or model that delivers significantly improved performance. The opportunity may exist to leapfrog the competition. A series of incremental changes may not have the same marketing impact on customers as the introduction of a new product, and competitors may be better able to react to, and sell against, a series of small improvements. When these conditions are present—as they usually are—management should restrict product evolution through small, incremental changes, even when such changes would result in some improvement in performance.

The engineering staff may benefit from an opportunity to start over on a product line, to incorporate new technology or new design concepts that cannot be utilized given the constraints of the present product. Such starting over is, of course, expensive, but new competitors entering the market are not constrained by present products. Thus, if the removal of such constraints represents an important design advantage, management should be certain that its own design engineers are not denied that advantage. For example, the full benefits of a new software language probably cannot be realized without starting over, and the maximum benefit of VLSI circuits is not realized by designing incrementally from present products.

Relatedly, new models or product lines, rather than incrementally improved present products, often permit adoption of manufacturing techniques that provide the company with significant cost and quality advantages. The use of robots in fabrication and assembly typically requires some product redesign to make optimum use of the robots' capabilities. The opportunities for automation may not be evident or, if evident, may not be economically justified if product design is accepted as a given. The concept of the product-process matrix presumes that both product design and process design are subject to changes and that the changes can and should be related.

The case should not be overstated, however. A market leader, such as IBM in mainframe computers, may need to pay particular attention to thwarting competitors' attempts to copy (often referred to as "reverse engineer") its products. A continuing series of well-planned design changes can severely complicate the process of reverse engineering and permit the leader to sustain a technological and performance edge over its competitors.

Allocation of Engineering Resources

Related to this problem of new products versus incremental changes is the inherent risk in high-technology companies that excessive engineering resources will be diverted from the truly new product to service the existing products. New products are the lifeblood of such companies; the more the company relies on technology to differentiate itself from competitors, the more this statement holds. Two sources of diversion are prevalent: product line maintenance and customer "specials."

In this paper, I have been emphasizing that continuing engineering of existing products is not unimportant, particularly as production seeks to improve product manufacturability and reduce its costs and as the need for improved documentation is realized. But such maintenance must not be permitted to consume all engineering resources.

Customers' requests for product modifications to meet their particular requirements consume precious engineering resources. The more the company accommodates such requests for specials, the more the company takes on the aspects of an engineering consulting firm rather than a manufacturing company. When important customers make such requests, they may have to be accommodated. But too often technology-based companies drift into producing increasing numbers of specials when such activity is clearly not consistent with their overall strategy.

The balanced allocation of engineering resources, assuring adequate attention to the development of truly new products, is an important challenge to general managers. When the dominant view in the councils of management is production, excessive investment in product maintenance engineering will result. When the dominant view is marketing, excessive pressure for accommodating customers' requests for specials may result—to be followed soon by dissatisfaction at the slow pace of new product development. When the dominant view in management councils is development, essential product maintenance engineering may be shortchanged and very attractive opportunities for specials may be overlooked. No such myopic views can be permitted to dominate.

■ Communication between production and engineering is particularly intense, and often necessarily nonroutine, in connection with introducing new products onto the production floor from the engineering laboratory. Prototype and pilot production runs can assist in the transfer, as can mutual agreement on timely freezing of the design. The more dependent the company is on process technology, rather than state-of-the-art product technology, the more thorough must be the product and process documentation. Because documentation is both expensive and difficult to control, high-technology companies typically underemphasize it. To maintain careful control of products, processes, quality, costs, and inventory investments, you must subject suggested changes in existing products to strict and well-defined procedures to be certain that the myriad potential ramifications of the change are fully evaluated. In formulating its engineering change policy, the high-technology company should consider the trade-off between introducing a new model and permitting product evolution by means of a series of incremental changes. The policy must also assure that engineering resources are not so committed to product maintenance and customer specials that new product development is shortchanged.

Reading IV–2
The New Product Learning Cycle

M. A. Maidique and B. J. Zirger

This paper summarizes our extensive study ($n = 158$) of new product success and failure in the electronics industry. Conventional "external factor" explanations of commercial product failure based on the state of the economy, foreign competition, and lack of funding, were found not to be major contributors to product failure in this industry. On the other hand, factors that can be strongly influenced by management such as coordination of the create, make, and market functions, the quality and frequency of customers' communications, value of the product to the customer, and the quality and efficiency of technical management explained the majority of the variance between successful and unsuccessful products. From these findings a framework for understanding and managing the new product development process that places learning and communication in the center stage was developed.

Successes and failures in our sample were strongly interrelated. The knowledge gained from failures was often instrumental in achieving subsequent successes, while success in turn often resulted in unlearning the very process that led to the original success. This observation has led us to postulate a new product "learning cycle model" in which commercial successes and failures alternate in an irregular pattern of learning and unlearning.

Research Policy, December 1985.

1. Introduction

Many factors influence product success. That much is generally agreed upon by researchers in the field. The product, the firm's organizational linkages, the competitive environment, and the market can all play important roles. On the other hand, the results of research on new product success and failure[1] is reminiscent of George Orwell's *Animal Farm* in that some factors seem to be "more equal than others." But, exactly which set of factors predominates seems to be, at least in part, a function of both the methodology and the specific population studied by the researcher.[2]

The Stanford Innovation Project (SINPRO)

In a survey of 158 products in the electronics industry, half successes and half failures, we developed our own list of major determinants of new product success.[3] The eight principal factors we identified are listed below roughly in the order of their statistical significance. Products are likely to be successful if:

1. The developing organization, through in-depth understanding of the customers and the marketplace, introduces a product with a high performance-to-cost ratio.

2. The create, make, and market functions are well coordinated and interfaced.

---

[1]R. C. Cooper, "A Process Model for Industrial New Product Development," *IEEE Transactions on Engineering Management,* EM-30, no. 1 (1983), pp. 2–11.

[2]M. A. Maidique and B. J. Zirger, "A Study of Success and Failure in Product Innovation: The Case of the U.S. Electronics Industry," *IEEE Transactions on Engineering Management,* EM-31, no. 4 (1984), pp. 192–203.

[3]Ibid.

3. The product provides a high contribution margin to the firm.

4. The new product benefits significantly from the existing technological and marketing strengths of the developing business units.

5. The developing organization is proficient in marketing and commits a significant amount of its resources to selling and promoting the product.

6. The R & D process is well planned and coordinated.

7. There is a high level of management support for the product from the product conception stage to its launch into the market.

8. The product is an early market entrant.

The study that led to these conclusions consisted of two exploratory surveys described in detail elsewhere.[4] The first survey was open ended and was divided into two sections. In the first part we asked the respondent to select a pair of innovations, one success and one failure. Successes and failures were differentiated by financial criteria. The second section of the original survey asked respondents to list in their own words the factors they believed contributed to the product's outcome. Seventy-nine senior managers of high-technology companies completed this questionnaire.

The follow-up survey was structured into 60 variables derived from three sources: (1) analysis of the results of the first survey, (2) review of the open literature, and (3) the authors' own extensive experience in high-technology product development. Each respondent, on the basis of the original two innovations identified in survey 1, was asked to determine for each variable whether it impacted the outcome of the success, failure, neither, or both. Survey 2 was completed by 59 of the original 79 managers.

The results from these two initial surveys were reported earlier.[5] To summarize, we conducted several statistical analyses for each variable and innovation type including determination of means and standard deviations, binomial significance, and clustering. Exhibit 1 shows the binomial significance for the 37 variables which differentiated between success and failure. Combining our statistical results with the content analysis of the initial survey, we derived the eight propositions listed earlier.

Using these eight factors as a starting point, we then developed a block diagram of the new product development process that focuses on the product characteristics and the functional interrelationships and competences that are most influential in determining new product success or failure (Exhibit 2). In our view, the innovation process is a constant struggle between the forces of change and the status quo. Differences in perceptions between the innovator and the customer and also between the groups that make the building blocks of the innovation process—engineering, marketing, and manufacturing—all conspire to shunt new product development or to deflect it from the path of success. Effective management attempts to integrate these constituencies and to allocate resources in a way that makes the new possible. These ideas are the basis of a model of the new product development process that we describe more fully and validate empirically in a forthcoming paper.[6]

The eight propositions resulting from our analysis were the objective "truths" that resulted from statistical analysis of our large sample of new product successes and failures. Though coincident in their salient aspects with the work of others,[7] these results, however, did not fully satisfy us. Had we missed important variables in our structured surveys? Had our respondents understood our questions? Had we failed to detect significant relations between some of the variables we identified—or between these and some yet undiscovered factors? How valid were our final generalizations? And most important, what were the underlying conceptual messages in this list of factors? In short, we were concerned that perhaps our statistical analysis might have blurred important ideas.

Reflecting on his research on the individual psyche, Carl Jung once put it this way:[8]

> The statistical method shows the facts in the light of the average, but does not give a picture of their empirical reality. While reflecting an indisputable aspect of reality, it can falsify the actual truth in a most misleading way . . . The distinctive thing about real facts, however, is their individuality. Not to put too fine a point on it, one could say that the real picture consists of nothing but exceptions to the rule, and that, in consequence, reality has predominately the characteristic of irregularity.

---

[4]Ibid.

[5]Ibid.

[6]B. J. Zirger and M. A. Maidique, (forthcoming), "Empirical Testing of a Conceptual Model of Successful New Product Development," to be submitted to *Management Science.*

[7]Cooper, "Process Model."

[8]C. G. Jung, *The Undiscovered Self* (New American Library, 1957), p. 17.

EXHIBIT 1 Significant Variables from Survey 2 Grouped by Index Variable

Successful Innovations Were:	Number of Observations	Cumulative Binomial	Significance Rating
1. Better matched with user needs.			
Better matched to customer needs.	44	8.53 E-09	+++
Developed by teams which more fully understood user needs.	44	1.27 E-05	+++
Accepted more quickly by users.	49	7.01 E-04	−−−
2. Planned more effectively and efficiently.			
Forecast more accurately (market).	43	1.25 E-07	+++
Developed with a clearer market strategy.	45	1.24 E-04	+++
Formalized on paper sooner.	45	3.30 E-03	+++
Developed with less variance between actual and budgeted expenses.	46	2.70 E-02	−−
Expected initially to be more commercially successful.			
3. Higher in benefit-to-cost.	42	8.21 E-02	+
Priced with higher profit margins.	51	6.06 E-08	+++
Allowed greater pricing flexibility.	52	1.02 E-06	+++
More significant with respect to benefit-to-cost ratio.			
4. Developed by better-coupled organizations.	43	6.86 E-03	+++
Developed by better-coupled functional divisions.	39	1.68 E-07	+++
5. More efficiently developed.			
Less plagued by after-sales problems.	35	5.84 E-05	−−−
Developed with fewer personnel changes on the project team.	28	6.27 E-03	−−−
Impacted by fewer changes during production.	41	1.38 E-02	−−
Developed with a more experienced project team.	39	2.66 E-02	++
Changed less after production commenced.	47	7.19 E-02	−
Developed on a more compressed time schedule.	39	9.98 E-02	+
6. More actively marketed and sold.			
More actively publicized and advertised.	39	4.74 E-03	+++
Promoted by a larger sales force.	28	6.27 E-03	+++
Coupled with a marketing effort to educate users.	37	1.00 E-02	++
7. Closer to the firm's areas of expertise.			
Aided more by in-house basic research.	25	7.32 E-03	+++
Required fewer new marketing channels.	25	7.32 E-03	−−−
Closer to the main business area of firm.	30	8.06 E-03	+++
More influenced by corporate reputation.	29	3.07 E-02	++
Less dependent on existing products in the market.	36	6.62 E-02	−
Required less diversification from traditional markets.	24	7.58 E-02	−
8. Introduced to the market earlier than competition.			
In the market longer before competing products introduced.	44	1.13 E-02	++
First-to-the-market type products.	39	1.19 E-02	++
More offensive innovations.	46	5.19 E-02	+
Generally not second-to-the-market.	36	6.62 E-02	−
9. Supported more by management.			
Supported more by senior management.			
Potentially more impactful on the careers of the project	31	1.66 E-03	+++
team members.	32	5.51 E-02	+
Developed with a more senior project leader.	39	9.98 E-02	+
10. Technically superior.			
Closer to the state-of-the-art technology.	36	3.26 E-02	++
More difficult for competition to copy.	45	3.62 E-02	++
More radical with respect to world technology.	42	8.21 E-02	+

EXHIBIT 2 Diagram of the Critical Elements of the New Product Development Process

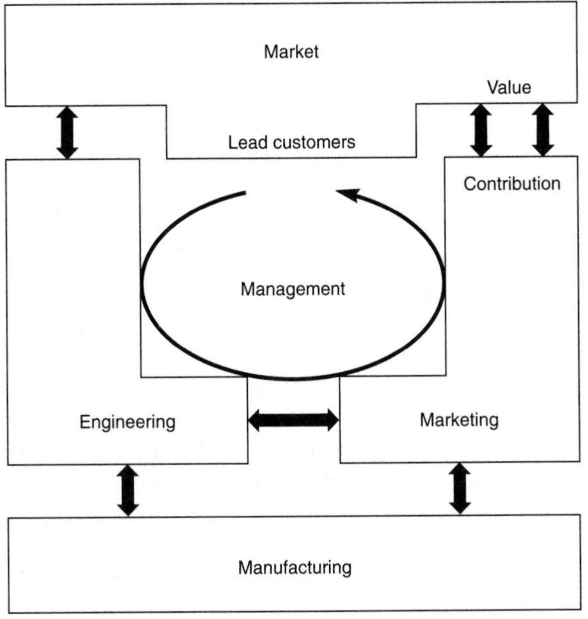

Such irregularities have caused one of the most experienced researchers in the field to wonder out loud if any fundamental commonalities exist at all in new product successes. "Perhaps," Cooper observed, "the problem is so complex, and each case so unique, that attempts to develop generalized solutions are in vain."[9]

2. Methodology

To address the concerns noted above, we prepared individual in-depth case studies for 40 of the original 158 products to search for methodological flaws or significant irregularities that might challenge the results of our statistical analysis (Exhibit 1). The case studies were prepared under the supervision of the authors by 45 graduate assistants.[10] Seventeen West Coast electronics firms which had participated in the 1982 Stanford-AEA Executive Institute and in our original two surveys served as sites for the 20 case studies. This subset of the original product pairs served as the subject of analysis for the case studies. Two or more project assistants interviewed managers and technologists and prepared written reports that included interview transcripts or summaries, background information on the firm, the competitive environment, the product development process, the characteristics of each of the two products, validation of the original survey 2, and a critical review of the factors that contributed to success or failure in each case. Overall, 101 managers and technologists were interviewed in 148 hours of interviews.

Most of the companies supplied the research teams with detailed financial, marketing, and design information regarding each one of the products, including in some cases internal memoranda that traced the products' development histories. Because of the confidentiality of this data, we must not identify any of the firms, much as we would like to thank them for their contributions to the project. In some cases, to illustrate a point, we have chosen to use examples from the public domain, or from published cases we or others have written about, and we may mention a company by name; however, the companies that collaborated with the project are either left anonymous or given fictitious names which, when first introduced, are placed in quotation marks.

This paper reports how these case studies and the associated interview transcripts enriched our earlier conclusions. In section 3, we begin to clarify the terms that we had employed in our survey, specifically *user needs* and *product value*. In section 4, we explore the meaning of success. The case studies led us to expand our concept of success and failure beyond the one-dimensional confines of financial return. Indeed, success and failure often appear to be close partners, not adversaries, in organizational and business development. Finally, in section 5, we postulate an evolutionary model of new product development, which we believe leads to a better understanding of the relationship between success and failure. For many of the propositions we present

[9]R. C. Cooper, "The Dimensions of Industrial New Product Success and Failure," *Journal of Marketing* 43 (1979), p. 102.

[10]The authors wish to express their appreciation to the following graduate students and doctoral candidates, who assisted in preparation of the individual case studies: P. Achi, G. Ananthasubramanianium, R. Angangco, C. Badger, B. Billerbeck, R. Cannon, D. Chinn, L. Christian, B. Connor, A. Dahlen, S. Demetrescu, B. Drobenko, R. Farros, H. Finger, H. Jagadish, L. Girault-Cuevas, R. Guior, T. Hardison, Y. Honda, J. Jover, C. Koo, T. Kuneida, S. Kurasaki, M. Lacayo, D. Lampaya, D. Ledakis, L. Lei, R. Ling, S. Makmuri, P. Matlock, C. Mungale, R. Oritz, B. Raschle, R. Reis, B. Russ, E. Saenger, J. Sanghani, V. Sanvido, F. Sasselli, R. Simon, P. Stamats, R. Stauffer, L. Taurel, B. Walsh, F. Zustak.

here, we lack the analytical support that underlies the eight factors identified in our original research. Nonetheless, we feel that these findings, which we hope will help to illuminate further research—including our own—are as important as our statistical results.

3. Defining "User Needs" and "Product Value"

The detailed case studies largely reinforced the principal findings of the overall study.[11] But the case studies also enriched some of the findings from structured questionnaires by providing fresh insights on several of the key variables. In this paper, we focus on the most important and perhaps the least specific variable, "understanding of the market" and "user needs" which is believed to result in products with "high value."

One of the principal findings of our large sample survey was that "user needs" and "customer and market understanding" are of central importance in predicting new product success or failure, a result that parallels the findings of the pioneering SAPPHO pairwise comparison study.[12] This result, however, does little to illuminate how a firm goes about achieving such understanding. What's more, citing user needs ex post facto as a key explicatory variable in product success can be simply disregarded as tautological. Of course, it can be argued the company "understood" user needs if the product was successful. Expanding on such criticisms, Mowery and Rosenberg have pointed out that the term *user need* is in any event vague and lacks the precision with which economists define related market variables such as demand.[13] What seems to be important, however, is to determine whether there are identifiable ex post ante actions that organizations take that develop and refine the firm's understanding of the customer's needs.

In most of the instances in which interviewees indicated a product has succeeded because of "better understanding of customer needs," they were able to support this view by citing specific actions or events. Both the experiential background of the management and developing team as well as actions taken during the development and launch process were viewed as important.

One line of argument went thus: We understood customer needs because the managers, engineers, and marketing people associated with the product were people with long-term experience in the technology and/or market. In such a situation, some executives argue, very little market research is required because the company's management has been close to the customer and to the dynamics of his changing requirements all along. As the group vice president of a major instrument manufacturer explained, "We were able to set the right design objectives, particularly cost goals, because we knew the business, *we could manage by the gut* (author's emphasis)."

This approach was evident in other firms also. When "Perfecto," a leading U.S. process equipment manufacturer, induced by a request from one of its European customers, commissioned a domestic market survey to assess potential demand for a new product that combined the functions of two of its existing products, the result was almost unanimously negative. Because of a quirk in the process flow in U.S. plants (which differed from European plants), domestic customers did not immediately see significant value in the integrated product. Notwithstanding the market survey data, Perfecto executives continued to believe that the product would prove to be highly cost effective for their worldwide customers. Buoyed by enthusiasm in Europe and a feeling of deep understanding of his customers that was the result of 13 years of experience in the numerically controlled process equipment market, Perfecto's president gave the project the go-ahead. His experience and self-confidence paid off. There was ultimately a significant demand for the new machine on both sides of the Atlantic.

These experience-based explanations, however, are only partially useful blueprints for action. The argument simply says that experienced people do better at new product development than the inexperienced, a hypothesis confirmed by our earlier research and that of others.[14]

---

[11]Maidique and Zirger, "A Study of Success."

[12]R. Rothwell, C. Freeman, A. Horley, V. I. P. Jervis, Z. B. Robertson, and J. Townsend, "SAPPHO Updated—Project SAPPHO, Phase II," *Research Policy* 3 (1974), pp. 258–91. See also C. Freeman, *The Economics of Industrial Innovation* (Harmondsworth: Penguin Books, 1974), pp. 161–97.

[13]D. Mowery and N. Rosenberg, "The Influence of Market Demand upon Innovation: A Critical Review of Some Recent Empirical Studies," *Research Policy* 8 (1979), pp. 101–53.

[14]A. C. Cooper and A. V. Bruno, "Success among High-Technology Firms," *Business Horizons* 20, no. 2 (1977), pp. 16–22.

Most of our informants, however, characterized the capture of "user needs" in action-oriented terms. For the successful product in the dyad, they described the company as having more openly, frequently, carefully, and continuously solicited and obtained customer reaction before, after, and during the initiation of the development and launch process. In some cases, the attempt to get customer reaction went to an extreme. "Electrotest," a test equipment manufacturer, conducted design reviews for a successful new product at its lead customers' plants. In general, the successful products were the result of ideas which originated with the customers, filtered by experienced managers. In one case, customers were reported to have "demanded" that an instrument manufacturer develop a new logic tester. As a rule, the development process for the successful products was characterized by frequent and in-depth customer interaction at all levels and throughout the development and launch process. While we did not find (and did not look for) what Von Hippel discovered in his careful research on electronic instruments, that users had in many cases already developed the company's next product, it was clear that, more so than any other constituency, they could point out the ideas that would result in future product successes.[15]

But when listening to customers, it's not enough to simply put in time. It is of paramount importance to listen to potential users without preconceptions or hidden agendas. Some companies become enamored with a new product concept and fail to test the idea against the reality of the marketplace. Not surprisingly, they find later that either the benefit to the customer was more obvious to the firm than to the customer himself or the product benefits were so specific that the market was limited to the original customer. For these reasons, the president of an automated test equipment manufacturer provided the following admonition: "When listening to customers, clear your mind of what you'd like to hear—Zen listening."

Unless this careful listening cascades throughout the company's organization and is continually "market"-checked, new products will not have the value to the customer that results in a significant commercial success. A predominant characteristic of the 20 successful industrial products that we examined in our case studies is that they resulted in almost immediate economic benefits to their users, not simply in terms of reduced direct manufacturing or operating costs. The successful products seemed to respond to the utility function of potential customers, which included such considerations as quality, service, reliability, ease of use, and compatibility.

Low cost or extraordinary technical performance, per se, did not result in commercial success. Unsuccessful products were often technological marvels that received technical excellence awards and were written up in prestigious journals. But typically such extraordinary technical performance comes at a high price and is often not necessary. "Very high performance, at a very high price. This is the story behind virtually every one of our new product failures," is how a general manager at "International Instruments," an instrument manufacturer with a reputation for technical excellence, described the majority of his new product disappointments.

In contrast to this phenotype, new product successes tend to have a dramatic impact on the customer's profit-and-loss account directly or indirectly. "Miltec," an electronic systems manufacturer, reported that its successful electronic counter saved its users 70 percent in labor costs and downtime. "Informatics," a computer peripheral manufacturer, developed a very successful magnetic head that was not only IBM compatible but also 20 percent cheaper and it offered a three times greater performance advantage. An integrated satellite navigation receiver developed by "Marine Technology," a communications firm, so drastically reduced on-board downtime in merchant marine ships in comparison to the older modular models that the company was overwhelmed by orders. The first 300 units paid for the $2.5 million R & D investment; overall, 7,000 units were sold. By comparison, the unsuccessful products provided little economic benefit. Not only were they usually high priced but also often they were plagued by quality and reliability problems, both of which translate into additional costs for the user.

4. How Should Product Success Be Measured?

Our original surveys used a unidimensional success taxonomy. Success was defined along a simple financial axis. Successful products produced a high return while unsuccessful products resulted in less than break-even returns. Using this measure, our population of successes and failures combined to

[15]E. A. von Hippel, "Users as Innovators," *Technology Review*, no. 5 (1976), pp. 212–39.

EXHIBIT 3 Distribution of Successes and Failures by Degree of Success/Failure for Case Studies

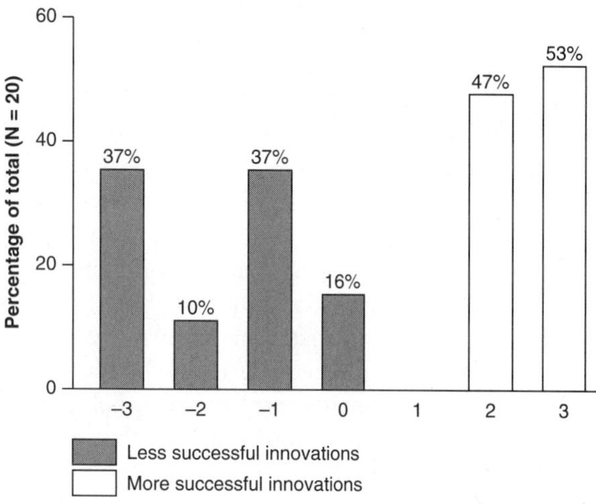

form a clearly bimodal distribution (Exhibit 3) that reinforced our assumption that we were dealing with two distinct classes of phenomena. While obtaining and plotting this type of data went beyond what most prior success-failure researchers had deemed necessary to provide, our detailed case studies lead us to conclude that this may not have been enough.

Success is defined as the achievement of something desired, planned, or attempted. While financial return is one of the most easily quantifiable industrial performance yardsticks, it is far from the only important one. New product "failures" can result in other important by-products: organizational, technological, and market development. Some of the new product failures that we studied led to dead ends and resulted in very limited organizational growth. On the other hand, many others—the majority—were important milestones in the development of the innovating firm. Some were the clear basis for major successes that followed shortly thereafter.

International Instruments, a large electronics firm, developed a new instrument based on a new semiconductor technology (diode arrays) that the firm had not yet used in one of its commercial products. The instrument, though technically excellent, was developed for a new market where the company did not have its traditionally keen sense of what value meant to the customer. Few units were sold and the product was classified as a failure. On the other hand, the experience gained with the diode array technology became the basis for enhancement of other product families based on this newly gained technical knowledge. Secondly, the organization learned about the characteristics of the new market through the diode array product, and, armed with new insights, a redesigned product was developed that was a commercial success. Was the diode array product really a failure, its developers asked?

In this and other cases we observed, the failure contributed naturally to the subsequent successes by augmenting the organization's knowledge of new markets or technologies or by building the strength of the organization itself. An example from the public domain illustrates this point. After Apple Computer had been buffeted by the manufacturing and reliability problems that plagued the Apple III launch, which caused Apple to lose its lead in the personal computer market and to yield a large slice of the market to IBM, Apple's chairman summed up the experience thus, "There is no question that the Apple III was our most maturing experience. Luckily, it happened when we were years ahead of the competition. It was a perfect time to learn."[16] As demonstrated by the manufacturing quality of the Apple IIe and IIc machines, Apple, that is the Apple II division, learned a great deal from the Apple III mishaps. Indeed, Sahal has pointed out that success in the development of new technologies is a matter of learning.[17] "There are few innovations," he points out, "without a history of lost labor. What eventually makes most techniques possible is the object lesson learned from past failures." In his classic study of technological failures, Whyte argues that most advances in engineering have been accomplished by turning failure into success.[18] To Whyte, engineering development is a process of learning from past failures.

Few would think of the Boeing Company and its suppliers as a good illustration of Sahal's and Whyte's arguments. Rosenberg, however, has pointed out that early 707s, for many years considered the safest

[16]M. A. Maidique, J. S. Gable, and S. Tylka, *"Apple Computer (A) and (B),"* Case #S-BP-229(B) (Stanford Business School Central Services, Graduate School of Business, Rm. 1, Stanford, CA, 1983). See also M. A. Maidique and C. C. Swanger, *"Apple Computer: The First Ten Years,"* Case #PS-BP-245 (Stanford Business School Central Services, Graduate School of Business, Rm. 1, Stanford, CA, 1985).

[17]D. Sahal, *Patterns of Technological Innovation* (Reading, Mass.: Addison-Wesley Publishing, 1981), p. 306.

[18]R. R. Whyte, *Engineering Progress through Trouble* (London: Institution of Mechanical Engineers, 1975).

of airplanes, went into unexplainable dives from high-altitude flights. The fan-jet turbine blades used in the jumbo jet par excellence, Boeing's famed 747, failed frequently under stress in the 1969–70 period.[19] Despite these object lessons, or perhaps because of them, Boeing makes more than half of the jet-powered commercial airliners sold outside of the Soviet bloc. According to the executive vice president of the Boeing Commercial Airplane Company, himself a preeminent jet aircraft designer, "We are good partly because we build so many airplanes. We learn from our mistakes, and each of our airplanes absorbs everything we have learned from earlier models and from other airplanes."[20]

Learning by Doing, Using, and Failing

It has long been recognized that there is a strong learning curve associated with manufacturing activity. Arrow characterized the learning that comes from developing increasing skill in manufacturing as "learning by doing."[21] Learning by doing results in lower labor costs. The concept of improvement by learning from experience has been subsequently elaborated by the Boston Consulting Group and others to include improvements in production process, management systems, distribution, sales, advertising, worker training, and motivation. This enhanced learning process, which has been shown for many products to reduce full costs by a predictable percentage every time volume doubles, is called the experience curve.[22]

Rosenberg, based on his study of the aircraft industry, has proposed a different kind of learning process, "learning by using."[23] Rosenberg distinguishes between learning that is "internal" and "external" to the production process. Internal learning results from experience with manufacturing the product, "learning by doing"; external learning is the result of what happens when users have the opportunity to use the product for extended periods of time. Under such circumstances, two types of useful knowledge may be derived by the developing organization. One kind of learning (embodied) results in design modifications that improve performance, usability, or reliability; a second kind of learning (disembodied) results in improved operation of the original or the subsequently modified product.

In our study, we found another type of external learning, a "learning by failing," which resulted in the development of new market approaches, new product concepts, and new technological alternatives based on the failure of one or more earlier attempts (Exhibit 4). When a product succeeds, user experience acts as a feedback signal to the alert manufacturer that can be converted into design or operating improvements (learning by using). For products that generate negligible sales volume, little learning by using takes place. On the other hand, products that fail act as important probes into user space that can capture important information about what it would take to make a brand new effort successful, which sometimes makes them the catalyst for major reorientations. In this sense, a new product is the ultimate market study. For truly new products it may be the only effective means of sensing market attitudes. According to one of our respondents, a vice president of engineering of "California Computer," a computer peripherals manufacturer,

EXHIBIT 4 A Model of Internal and External Learning

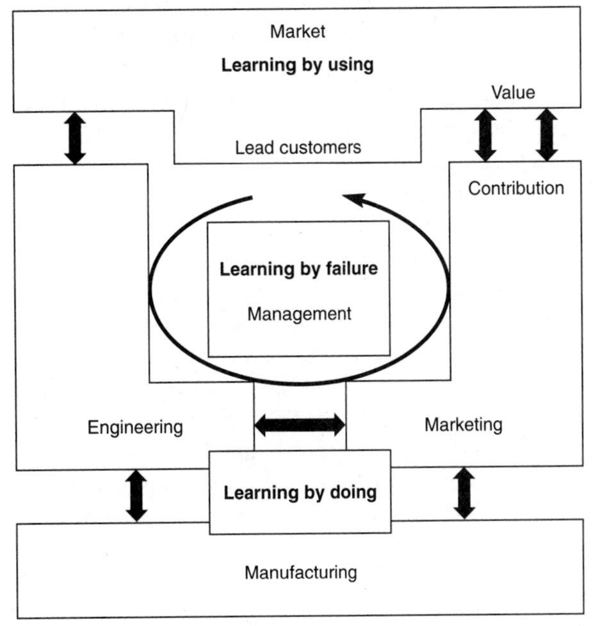

[19]N. Rosenberg, *Inside the Black Box, Technology and Economics* (Cambridge: Cambridge University Press, 1982), pp. 124–6.

[20]J. Newhouse, *The Sporty Game* (New York: Alfred A. Knopf, 1982), p. 7.

[21]K. Arrow, "The Economic Implications of Learning by Doing," *Review of Economic Studies,* June 1962.

[22]B. Henderson, *Perspectives on Experience* (Boston Consulting Group, 1968) (third printing, 1972).

[23]Arrow, "Economic Implications," pp. 120–40.

"No one really knows if a truly new product is worth anything until it has been in the market and its potential has been assessed."

Another dimension of "learning by failing" relates to organizational development. A failure helps to identify weak links in the organization and to inoculate strong parts of the organization against the same failure pattern. The aftermath of the Apple III resulted in numerous terminations at Apple Computer, from the president to the project manager of the Apple III project. Those remaining, aided by new personnel, accounted for the well-implemented Apple III redesign and reintroduction program and the highly successful Apple IIe follow-on product.[24]

When the carryover of learning from one product to another is recognized, it becomes clear that the full measure of a product's impact can only be determined by viewing it in the context of both the products that preceded it and those that followed. While useful information can be obtained by focusing on individual products or pairs of products, *the product family is a far superior unit of analysis from which to derive prescriptions for practicing managers.* The product family incorporates the interrelationship between products, the learning from failures as well as from successes. Thus, it is to product families, including false starts, not to individual products, that financial measures of success should be more appropriately applied.

Consider a triplet of communications products developed over a 10-year period by an electronics system manufacturer. For several years, Marine Technology had developed and marketed commercial and military navigation systems. These systems were composed of separate components manufactured by others, such as a receiver, teletype, and a minicomputer, none of which was specifically designed for the harsh marine environment. Additionally, this multicomponent approach, though technically satisfactory, took up a great deal of space, which is at a premium on the bridge of a ship. Each of Marine Technology's new product generations attempted to further reduce the number of components in the system. By 1975, a bulky HP minicomputer was the only outboard component.

The need for a compact, rugged, integrated navigation system had thus been abundantly clear to Marine Technology engineers and salespeople. Therefore, when microprocessors became available in the early 1970s, it was not surprising that Marine Technology's general manager initiated a program to develop a new lightweight integrated navigation system specially designed for the marine environment. The product was developed by a closely knit design team that spent six to eight months working with potential customers, and later market testing prototypes. Two years later, the company introduced the MT-1, the world's first microprocessor-based integrated navigation system. The product was an instant success. Over 7,000 units were sold at a price of $25,000 per unit. At this price, margins exceeded 50 percent.

Shortly after the success of the MT-1 was established, engineering proposed a new product (the MT-2) to Marine Technology's newly appointed president. The MT-2 was to be about one-sixth the volume of the MT-1 and substantially cheaper in price. The president was so impressed with a model of the proposed product that he directed a team, staffed in part by the original MT-1 design team members, to proceed in a top secret effort to develop the MT-2. The team worked in isolation; only a handful of upper management and marketing people were aware of the project. Three and a half years and $3.5 million later, the team had been able—by sacrificing some features—to shrink the product as promised to one-sixth the size of the MT-1 and to reduce the price to about $10,000. But almost simultaneously with the completion of the MT-2's development, a competitor had introduced an equivalent product for $6,000. Furthermore, the product's small size was not considered a major advantage. Key customers indicated the previous product was "compact enough." The company attempted to eliminate some additional features to tailor the product to the consumer navigation market, but it found that it was far too expensive for this market, yet performance and quality were too low for its traditional commercial and military markets. The product was an abject economic failure. Most of the inventory had to be sold below the cost.

A third product in the line, the MT-3, however, capitalized on the lessons of the MT-2 failure. The new MT-3 was directed specifically at the consumer market. Price, not size, was the key goal. Within two years, the MT-3 was introduced at a price of $3,000. Like the MT-1, it was a major commercial success for the company. Over 1,500 have been sold and the company had a backlog of 600 orders in 1982 when the case histories were completed.

---

[24]Maidique, Gable, and Tylka, "*Apple Computer (A) and (B).*" Also, Maidique and Swanger, "*Apple Computer: The First Ten Years.*"

At the outset of this abbreviated product family vignette, we said the family consisted of three products. In a strict sense, this is correct, but in reality there were four products, starting with what we will call the MT-0, the archaic modular system. The MT-0 was instrumental to the success of the MT-1. Through the experience with customers that it provided, it served to communicate to the company that size and reliability improvements would be highly valued by customers in the commercial and military markets in which the company operated. With the appearance of microprocessor technology, what remained was a technical challenge, usually a smaller barrier to success than deciphering how to tailor a new technology to the wants of the relevant set of customers, as the company found out through the MT-2.

The success of the MT-1 was misread by the company to mean, "the smaller, the more successful," rather than, "the better we understand what is important to the customer, the more successful." The company had implicitly made an inappropriate trade-off between performance, size, and cost. They acted as if they had the secret to success—compact size—and by shutting off its design team from its new as well as its old customers ensured that they would not learn from them the real secrets to success in the continually evolving market environment. It remained for the failure of the MT-2 to bring home to management that, by virtue of its new design, the company was now appealing to a new customer group that had different values from its traditional commercial and military customer. Equipped with this new learning, the company was now able to develop the successful MT-3.

5. The New Product Learning Cycle

There are several lessons to be learned from the history of Marine Technology's interrelated succession of products. First, their experience clearly illustrates the importance of precursors and follow-on products in assessing product success. To what extent, for instance, was the M-2 truly a failure, or, alternatively, how necessary was such a product to pave the way for the successful MT-3? With hindsight one can always argue that the company should have been able to go directly to the MT-3, but wasn't to some extent the learning experience of the MT-2 necessary? Secondly, the story illustrates once again the importance of in-depth customer understanding as well as continuous interaction with potential customers throughout the development process even at the risk of revealing some proprietary information. Whatever learning might have been possible before entering the consumer market was shunted aside by the company's secretive practices.

The product evolution pattern of "Computronics," a start-up computer systems manufacturer, reinforces these findings. One of Computronics' founders had developed a new product idea for turnkey computer inventory control systems for jobbers (small distributors) in one of the basic industries. From his experience as a jobber in this industry, he knew that it was virgin territory for a well-conceived and supported computerized system. During the development process, the company enlisted the support of the relevant industry association. Association members offered product suggestions, criticized product development, and ultimately the association endorsed the product for use by its members. The first Compu-100 system was shipped in 1973. Ten years later, largely on the strength of this product and its accessories, corporate sales had doubled several times and reached nearly $100 million, and the company dominated the jobber market.

As the company's market share increased, however, management recognized that new markets would have to be addressed if rapid growth was to continue. In early 1977, the company decided to take what seemed a very logical step to develop a system that would address the needs of the large wholesale distributors in the industry. Based on its earlier successes, the company planned to take this closely related market by storm. After a few visits to warehousing distributors, the product specifications were established and development began under the leadership of a new division established to serve the high end of the business. Since no one at Computronics had firsthand experience with this higher level segment of the distribution system, a software package was purchased from a small software company, but it took a crash program and several programmers a year to rewrite the package so that it was compatible with Computronics hardware. After testing the Compu-200 at two sites, the company hired a team of additional sales representatives and prepared for a national rollout. Ten million dollars of sales were projected for the first year.

First-year revenues, however, were minimal. Even three years after the launch, the product had yet to achieve the first year's target revenue. What had happened? The new market would appear at first glance to be a perfect fit with Computronics' skills and experience, yet a closer examination revealed considerable differences in the new customer environment which, nonetheless, were brushed away in a cavalier manner by Computronics' management, who were basking in the glow of the Compu-100's success.

As organizations in such a euphoric state often do, Computronics grossly underestimated the task at hand. The large market for warehousing distributor inventory systems was attractive to major competitors such as IBM and DEC. But only a cursory study of the new customers and their buying habits was carried out. The tacit assumption was that large warehousing distributors were simply grown-up jobbers. Yet these new customers were now much more sophisticated, had used data processing equipment for other functions, and generally required and developed their own specialized software. Increased competition and radically greater customer sophistication combined to require that Computronics be represented by a highly experienced and competent sales force. But because of the hurry to launch the product, Computronics skipped the customary training for sales representatives and launched the field sales force into a new area for the firm: the complex long-term business of selling large items ($480,000 each) to a technically knowledgeable customer. By believing that repeating past practices would reproduce past successes, Computronics had turned success into failure.

"Every victory," Carl Jung once wrote, "contains the germ of a future defeat."[25] Starbuck and his colleagues have observed that successful organizations accumulate surplus resources that allow them to loosen their connections to their environments and to achieve greater autonomy, but they explain, "This autonomy reduces the sensitivity of organizations to changing environmental conditions . . . organizations become less able to perceive what is happening so they fantasize about their environments and it may happen that reality intrudes only occasionally and marginally on these fantasies."[26] Fantasies create a myth of invincibility, yet an old Chinese proverb says, "There is no greater disaster than taking on an enemy lightly."[27]

Marine Technology's management fantasized that it had the secret of success: smaller is better. Computronics had a fantasy that similarly extrapolated its past victories: new markets will be like old markets. This is a pattern that repeats itself over and over in business. We have already alluded to one of the best publicized contemporary examples of this phenomenon: Apple Computer's Apple III on the heels of its colossally successful Apple II precursor. Even IBM is not exempt from this cycle. After taking one-third of the market with its PC (personal computer) despite its late entry, a senior executive at the IBM PC Division stated, "We can do anything."[28] "Anything" did not, as it happens, include the follow-on product to the PC, the PCjr, which—in contrast to the original PC—was not adequately test marketed to determine how consumers would react to its design features and ultimately had to be dropped from the IBM product line. IBM and Computronics, however, have both, at least temporarily, become more humble. Both are soliciting customer inputs so that they can redesign their disappointments.

The flow from success to failure, and back to success again, at Marine Technology illustrated a rhythm that we were to encounter repeatedly in our investigations. In the simplest terms, failure is the ultimate teacher. From its lessons the persistent build their successes. Success, on the other hand, often breeds complacency. Moreover, success seems to create a tendency to ignore the basics, to believe that heroics are a substitute for sound business practice. As the general manager of "Automatrix," a test equipment manufacturer, pointed out, "It's hard, very hard, to learn from your successes." Ironically, success can breed failure for firms that continue to view the future through the prism of present victories, especially in a dynamic industry environment.

These observations have led us to propose a model of new product success and failure in which successes and failures alternate with an irregular rhythm. This is not to say that for every success there must be a complementing failure. Most industrial products—about three out of five—succeed despite popular myths to the contrary.[29] For some highly successful companies, as many as three out of four new products may be commercially successful. Most com-

---

[25]C. G. Jung, *Psychological Reflections* (New York: Princeton University Press, 1970), p. 188.

[26]W. Starbuck, A. Greve, and B. L. Hedberg, "Responding to Crisis," *Journal of Business Administration,* no. 9 (1978), pp. 111–37.

[27]Lao Tzu, *Tao Te Ching* (New York: Penguin Books, 1983), p. 131.

[28]D. Le Grande, as quoted in "How IBM Made Junior an Underachiever," *Business Week,* June 25, 1984, p. 106.

[29]R. G. Cooper, "Most Products *Do* Succeed," *Research Management,* November–December 1983, pp. 20–25.

EXHIBIT 5 Learning by Moving Away from Home Base

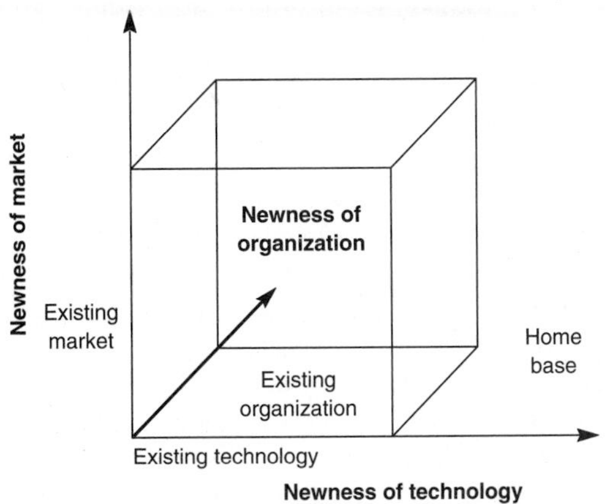

EXHIBIT 6 A Typical New Product Evolution Pattern

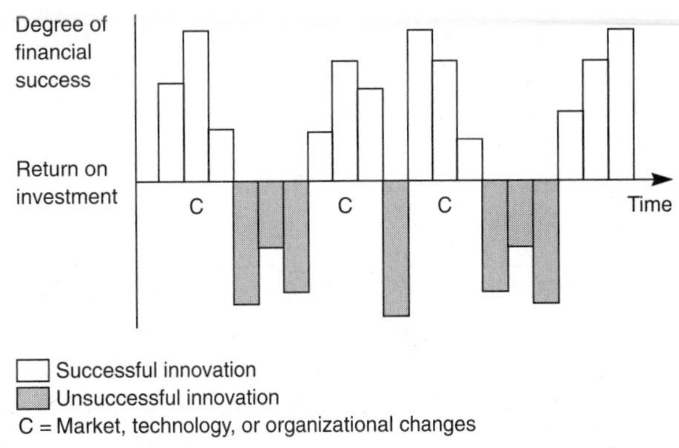

panies continuously learn by using, through their successful new products, and—as in the case of Marine Technology—they continuously develop improved designs. This is what most new product efforts are about—minor variations on existing themes.

But continued variations on a theme do not always lead to major successes. In time, further variations are no longer profitable, and the company usually decides to depart from the original theme by adopting a new technology—microprocessors, lasers, optics—or to attack a new market—consumer, industrial, government—or, alternatively, organizational changes, defections, or promotions destroy part of the memory of the organization so that the old now seems like the new. Changes in any of these three dimensions can result in an economic failure, or, in our terms, new learning about a technology, a market, or about the strengths and weaknesses of a newly formed group as shown in Exhibit 5, an extension of the familiar product–customer matrix originally proposed by Ansoff.[30] This recurrent cycle of success and failure is shown graphically in Exhibit 6.

In the model, a sequence of successes is followed by either a major organizational change, changes in product design, technology, or market directions that prompt an economic failure, which in turn spurs a new learning pattern. The model assumes a competitive marketplace, however, and is less likely to be applicable to a monopolistic situation in which a single firm dictates the relationship between customer and supplier. A second caveat is that while the pattern is roughly depicted as regular, in general it will be irregular, but the cycle of oscillation between economic success and failure, we believe, will still hold.

5.1 Success as a Stochastic Process

Success in new products is never assured. Too many uncontrolled external variables influence the outcome. Occasional or even frequent failure is a way of life for product innovations. As Addison reminds us in his Cato, "Tis not in mortals to command success."[31] But while it is not possible to assure the outcome of any one product trial, it is possible to increase the likelihood that a product or group of products will be successful. Addison goes on to add, "We'll do more, Sempronius, *we'll deserve it.*" (Authors' emphasis.) The eight factors that we identified at the outset of this article, and the cyclic model we propose, are an attempt to help managers conceptualize the new product development process so as to improve the proportion of economic successes. But on the other hand, it would be a mistake to attempt to increase the number of successes by reducing new product risk to zero by cautious, deliberate management. In the process, rewards may be also reduced to the same level.

Failure, as we have tried to argue, is part and parcel of the learning process that ultimately results in

[30] H. I. Ansoff, *Corporate Strategy* (New York: McGraw-Hill, 1965), pp. 131–33.

[31] J. Bartlett, *Bartlett's Familiar Quotations,* 14th ed. (New York: Little, Brown, 1968), p. 393.

success. Sahal sums up the process thus, "What eventually makes the development of new techniques possible is the object lesson learned from past failures . . . profit by example."[32] The important thing is to have a balance between successes and failures that results in attractive returns. Here a lesson from experienced venture capitalists, masters at the success forecasting game, is useful. As part of another research project, the authors have interviewed some of the nation's most successful and experienced venture capital investors whose portfolios have generally shown gains of 25 to 35 percent over the past 10 years. Given a large pot of opportunities, experienced venture capitalists believe they can select a group that will on the average yield an excellent return, yet few professionals are so sanguine that they believe that they can with certainty foretell any one success; they've seen too many of their dreams fail to meet expectations.

A new product developed by "Electrosystems," a military electronics company, seemed to fit a venture capitalist's dream. The company's new product, a phase-locked loop, had its origin with one of its key customers, the requisite technology was within its area of expertise, and a powerful executive championed the product throughout its development. A large market was anticipated. Thus far, a good bet, one might conclude. What's more, the resulting product was a high-quality instrument. Yet the product brought little in the way of revenues to the firm, for an alternative technology that solved the same problem in a cheaper way was simultaneously developed and introduced by a competitor.

Five years later, again spurred by a customer requirement, Electrosystems developed an electronic counter as part of a well-funded and visibly championed development program. This time, however, the product saved the customer 70 percent of his labor costs, considerably reduced his downtime, and there was no alternative technology on the horizon. This product was very successful. The point here is not that the product that ultimately produced a cost advantage to the customer was more successful. That much is self-evident. The point is that at the outset both products looked like they would provide important advantages to the customer. After all, they both originated with customers. Both projects were well managed and funded and technologically successful. Yet one met with unpredictable external competition that blunted its potential contribution. The company did not simply fail and then succeed. It succeeded because it pursued both seemingly attractive opportunities. In other words, success generally requires not one but several, sometimes numerous, well-managed trials. This realization prompted one of our wisest interviewees, the chief engineer of "Metalex," an instrument manufacturer, to sit back and say, "I've found the more diligent you are, the more luck you have."

This is the way both venture capitalists and many experienced high-technology product developers view the new product process. Venture capitalists who have compiled statistics on the process have found that only 60 percent of new ventures result in commercial success; the rest are a partial or complete loss. (Not surprisingly, this is about the same batting average that Cooper found in his study of industrial products.) About 40 to 50 percent of new venture-capital backed ventures produce reasonable returns, and only 10 to 15 percent result in outstanding investments. But it can be easily computed that such a combination of investments can produce a 25 to 30 percent return or more as a portfolio.

5.2 New Research Directions

Our research on new product success and failure has led us to reconsider our unit of analysis. Choosing the new product as the basic unit of analysis has many advantages. New products are clearly identifiable entities. This facilitates gathering research data. New products have individualized sales forecasts and return on investment criteria, and managements generally know whether these criteria are satisfied. "Successes" can be culled from "failures."

Our results, however, indicate that if financial measures of success are to be applied as criteria, a more appropriate unit of analysis is the product family. Before an individual product is classified as a failure, its contribution to organizational growth, market development, or technological advance must be gauged. New products strongly influence the performance of their successors and in turn are a function of the victories and defeats of their predecessors. Before the laurels are handed over to a winning team, an examination should be made of the market, technological, and organizational base from which the team launched its victory (Exhibit 5).

One of IBM's most notable product disasters was the Stretch computer. IBM set out to develop the world's most advanced computer, and, after spend-

[32]Sahal, *Patterns*.

ing $20 million in the 1960s for development, only a few units were sold.

On the heels of the Stretch fiasco came one of the most successful products of all time, the IBM 360 series. But when IBM set out to distribute kudos, it recognized that much of the technology in the IBM 360 was derived from work done on the Stretch computer by Stephen Dunwell, once the scapegoat for the Stretch "setback." Subsequently, Mr. Dunwell was made an IBM fellow, a very prestigious position at IBM that carries many unique perks.[33] As Newton once said, "If I have seen far it is because I stood on the shoulders of giants."[34]

We were able to gain insight into this familial product interrelationship because our success–failure dyads were often members of the same product family. But even though they were interrelated, they represented only a truncated segment of a product family. Nonetheless, in some sites, for example Marine Technology, we were able to collect data on three or four members of a product family. On the other hand, our efforts, to date, fall far short of a systematic study of product families. This is the central task of the next stage of our research.

Our limited results, however, bring into question research that focuses on the product as the unit of analysis, including our own. Consider one of our principal research findings, which is also buttressed by the findings of several prior investigators: successful products benefit from existing strengths of the developing business unit. The implication of this finding is that organizations should be wary of exploring new territories. In contrast to this result, our observations would lead us to argue just the opposite, that firms should continuously explore new territories even if the risk of failure is magnified.[35] The payoff is the learning that will come from the "failures" which will pave the way for future successes.

Careful validation of the cyclic model of product development proposed here could have other important consequences for our understanding of technology-based firms. If indeed the pattern proposed in Exhibit 6 is generalizable to firms that are continuously attempting to adapt to new markets and technologies, then there are important implications for management practice.

First, the model implies that new product development success pivots on the effectiveness of intra- and intercompany learning. This conclusion puts a premium on devising a managerial style and structure that serves to catalyze internal and external communication. Second, by implicitly taking a long-term view of the product development process, the model emphasizes the importance of long-term relationships with employees, customers, and suppliers. Out of such a view comes a high level of understanding, and therefore of tolerance for failure to achieve commercial success at any one given point in the product line trajectory. Firms need to learn that product development is a journey, not a destination. These preliminary findings are compatible with an exploratory study of new product development in five large successful Japanese companies completed by Imai and his colleagues.[36] One of the principal findings of their research was that the firms studied were characterized by an almost "fanatical devotion towards learning—both within organizational membership (sic) and with outside members of the interorganizational network." This learning, according to the authors, played a key role in facilitating successful new product development. It appears that when successful at new product development, small and large U.S. companies operate in a very similar manner to the best-managed Japanese firms.

Many key questions, however, remain to be settled. Is there an optimal balance between successes and failures? Are Japanese firms susceptible to the same oscillating pattern between success and failure as American firms? How does this balance change across industries? How can tolerance for failure be communicated without distorting the ultimate need for economic success? How can a firm learn from the failures of others? Are there characteristic success–failure patterns for a group of firms competing in the same industry? These and other related questions will occupy us in the next phase of our research.

---

[33]T. Wise, "IBM's $5B Gamble," *Fortune,* September 1966; "A Rocky Road to the Marketplace," *Fortune,* October 1966. Also, Bob Evans, personal communication (Mr. Evans was program manager for the IBM-360 system).

[34]J. Bartlett, *Bartlett's Familiar Quotations,* 13th ed. (New York: Little, Brown, 1968), p. 379.

[35]In an exploratory study of the relationship between the degree of "newness" of a firm's portfolio of products and its economic performance, the authors concluded that some "newness" results in better economic performance than "no newness." M. H. Meyer and E. B. Roberts, *New Product Strategy in Small High-Technology Firms,* WP #1428-1-84 (Sloan School of Management, Massachusetts Institute of Technology, May 1984).

[36]K. Imai, I. Nonaka, and H. Takeuchi, *Managing the New Product Development Process: How Japanese Companies Learn and Unlearn,* Institute of Business Research, Hitotsubashi University, Kunitachi (Tokyo, Japan, 1982), pp. 1–60. See also P. R. Lawrence and D. Dyer, *Renewing American Industry* (New York: The Free Press, 1983), p. 8.

Case IV–2
Texas Instruments' "Speak and Spell" Product

A. L. Jakimo and I. C. Bupp

In June 1978, the semiannual Consumer Electronics Show was held in Chicago. A few days before it opened, Gene A. Frantz, program manager for speech products at Texas Instruments' Consumer Electronics Group, was putting the finishing touches on a device that closely resembled a colorful, handheld toy radio or typewriter. It weighed about one pound and measured about 6 × 10 inches. Forty keys were arranged in 4 rows of 10 with command keys across the top and the characters arranged in alphabetical order. In spite of its toylike appearance, the product represented a major breakthrough in microelectronic technology. It was a handheld learning aid that could talk.

Its semiconductor memory was programmed with more than 200 words considered by noted educators to be among the most frequently misspelled from beginning spelling through adulthood. Words are selected at random from one of four lists of about 50 each, graduating in degree of difficulty. The selected word is "spoken" electronically—but with human inflection and fidelity—through a small speaker at the top of the case. A child using the keyboard then attempts to spell the word. As the child presses the keys, the machine speaks each letter and displays it on the LED screen. If the child fails after two tries, "Speak and Spell" says: "That is incorrect," and goes on to spell it, pronouncing each letter and the entire word. In addition, several keys are available for word games to further stimulate and encourage learning.

The "roll-out" of Speak and Spell at the June 1978 Consumer Electronics Show appeared to herald a new era of electronically synthesized speech products.

Texas Instruments Incorporated

Speak and Spell was developed by Texas Instruments Incorporated. The company was founded in 1930 as a geophysical exploration company. In the early 1950s, the company launched a determined effort to acquire proprietary expertise in the new field of semiconductor technology. This campaign met with early technical success: In 1956, TI was one of the first companies to produce an all-transistor radio. Unfortunately, the radio was unable to meet with similar success in the marketplace. The company, nonetheless, continued its thrust into the age of semiconductors. By the early 1960s, it had established itself as a leader in the manufacture of integrated circuits. From the mid-1960s through the late 1970s, the company's investments in semiconductor technology bore substantial fruit: in 1964, sales revenues stood at approximately $400 million; by 1978, this figure had grown to $2.5 billion. Recent financial statements are contained in Exhibits 1 and 2.

A major factor underlying TI's sustained growth through the 1960s and 1970s was overall expansion in the worldwide electronics market (see Exhibit 3). This expansion was very much fueled by continuing development of low-cost semiconductor products. But, more important, TI's growth was marked by its capture of dominant market shares through exploitation of learning curve economies and forward integration into end-user products. While virtually all successful semiconductor manufacturers were able, if not forced, to exploit the learning curve's declining manufacturing cost effect, only a handful were able to succeed at forward integration. At TI, forward integration was best exemplified by the company's move into handheld calculators during the early 1970s; by the late 1970s, TI was the leading manufacturer of such devices. (See Appendix I for more detail on Texas Instruments' integration strategy.)

The Learning Aids Product Line

In 1975, Ron Ritchie, later to become a vice president in the Consumer Electronics Group, was instructed by a group of influential retired TI officers to explore the use of calculators in classroom environments. In response to this directive, Ritchie and his subordinates set out to develop a program of packaged activities for demonstrating the calculator as a useful educational device. Working with universities and several schools, Ritchie's group designed a package that consisted of a TI calculator and instructional materials. Like the Scientific

EXHIBIT 1 Consolidated Financial Statements (in thousands of dollars, except per share amounts)

	For the Year Ended December 31	
	1977	1976
Income and Retained Earnings		
Net sales billed	$2,046,456	$1,658,607
Operating costs and expenses:		
Cost of goods and services sold	1,459,490	1,185,426
General, administrative, and marketing	325,978	265,889
Employees' retirement and profit sharing plans	50,151	44,666
Total	1,835,619	1,495,981
Profit from operations	210,837	162,626
Other income (net)	9,261	23,782
Interest on loans	(9,179)	(8,310)
Income before provision for income taxes	210,919	178,098
Provision for income taxes	94,281	80,678
Net income	116,638	97,420
Retained earnings at beginning of year	530,822	458,153
Cash dividends declared on common stock ($1.41 per share in 1977; $1.08 in 1976)	(32,196)	(24,751)
Retained earnings at end of year	$ 615,264	$ 530,822
Earned per common share (average outstanding during year)	$ 5.11	$ 4.25
Changes in Financial Position		
Sources of working capital:		
Net income	$ 116,638	$ 97,420
Depreciation	$ 108,063	$ 87,290
Provided from operations	224,701	184,710
Proceeds—common stock under options	110	1,263
Other	7,233	3,400
	232,044	189,373
Uses of working capital:		
Additions (net) to property, plant, and equipment	199,283	136,454
Dividends on common stock	32,196	24,751
Decrease in long-term debt	12,193	10,735
Purchase of common stock of the company for employee benefit plans	4,799	13,401
	248,471	185,341
Increase (decrease) in working capital	$ (16,427)	$ 4,032

Research Association's "SRA Reading Packages," introduced during the 1960s, the TI packages were designed to aid in classroom learning. Whereas the SRA packages focused on reading, the TI packages covered mathematics.

One of the initial problems encountered by Ritchie's group was a fear on the part of teachers that calculators would make their students lazy thinkers. The teachers thought students would come to believe that all that needed to be known to add two numbers together was the sequence of buttons to push on a calculator keyboard. TI claimed that its testing experiences proved these fears ill-conceived: Where children used calculators in the absence of any pack-

EXHIBIT 1 *(concluded)*

	December 31, 1977	December 31, 1976
Balance Sheet		
Assets		
Current assets:		
Cash and short-term investments	$ 257,131	$ 293,755
Accounts receivable	334,152	282,251
Inventories (net of progress billings)	214,278	197,647
Prepaid expenses	9,337	9,520
Total current assets	814,898	783,173
Property, plant, and equipment at cost	713,787	606,380
Less: Accumulated depreciation	319,694	303,507
Property, plant, and equipment (net)	394,093	302,873
Other assets and deferred charges	46,053	41,657
Total assets	$1,255,044	$1,127,703
Liabilities and Stockholders' Equity		
Current liabilities:		
Loans payable (international subsidiaries)	$ 38,759	$ 46,103
Accounts payable and accrued expenses	287,909	211,674
Income taxes	85,792	113,421
Accrued retirement and profit sharing contributions	34,113	30,473
Dividends payable	9,582	7,540
Current portion long-term debt	10,416	9,208
Total current liabilities	466,571	418,419
Deferred liabilities:		
Long-term debt	29,671	38,169
Incentive compensation payable in future years	14,184	10,836
Total deferred liabilities	43,855	49,005
Stockholders' equity (common shares outstanding at year-end: 1977—22,814,689; 1976—22,851,443)	744,618	660,279
Total liabilities and stockholders' equity	$1,255,044	$1,127,703

aged program, their test performance was statistically equal to that of children who had no experience with calculators. But where children used calculators as part of an organized program, their test performance was statistically better than that of children who had no experience with calculators.

Notwithstanding the apparent benefits of the TI packages, they could not be successfully marketed. Among the reasons cited for this failure was the existence of hundreds of highly autonomous and greatly politicized school districts. Setting up a sales network to market the packages to these districts was beyond TI's expertise. Moreover, the product life cycle of a typical product marketed to school districts was about three to four years; in contrast, the product life cycle for a typical TI product was about 18 to 24 months. Ritchie's attention thus turned from classroom packages containing TI calculators to products that could be marketed through the retail outlets with which TI was accustomed to doing business.

The first such product to which Ritchie turned his attention was a handheld device that could help children learn the principles of arithmetic. Unlike a calculator which is passive in that it makes

EXHIBIT 2 Financial Information

	Years Ended December 31									
	1977	1976	1975	1974	1973	1972	1971	1970	1969	1968
Summary of Operations (thousands of dollars)										
Net sales billed	$2,046,456	$1,658,607	$1,367,621	$1,572,487	$1,287,276	$943,694	$764,258	$827,641	$831,822	$671,230
Operating costs and expenses	1,835,619	1,495,981	1,252,833	1,403,105	1,141,824	860,625	705,094	773,113	769,983	621,917
Profit from operations	210,837	162,626	114,788	169,382	145,452	83,069	59,164	54,528	61,839	49,313
Other income (net)	9,261	23,782	11,971	4,159	6,746	7,178	6,840	4,529	3,936	4,258
Interest on loans	(9,179)	(8,310)	(10,822)	(10,741)	(6,654)	(5,676)	(6,526)	(7,014)	(5,474)	(3,209)
Income before provision for income taxes	210,919	178,098	115,937	162,800	145,544	84,571	59,478	52,043	60,301	50,362
Provision for income taxes	94,281	80,678	53,795	73,179	62,309	36,541	25,755	22,182	26,790	24,038
Net income	$ 116,638	$ 97,420	$ 62,142	$ 89,621	$ 83,235	$ 48,030	$ 33,723	$ 29,861	$ 33,511	$ 26,324
Earned per common share (average outstanding during year)*	$5.11	$4.25	$2.71	$3.92	$3.67	$2.17	$1.53	$1.35	$1.53	$1.21
Cash dividends paid per common share*	1.320	1.000	1.000	.920	.555	.415	.400	.400	.400	.400
Common shares (average shares outstanding during year, in thousands)*	22,842	22,933	22,920	22,854	22,691	22,139	22,085	22,072	21,919	21,819
Financial Condition (thousands of dollars)										
Working capital	$ 348,327	$ 364,754	$ 360,722	$ 314,302	$ 306,968	$ 282,049	$ 261,398	$210,957	$189,271	$157,158
Property, plant, and equipment (net)	394,093	302,873	253,709	280,449	219,941	154,992	154,954	171,436	182,377	145,835
Long-term debt, less current portion	29,671	38,169	47,530	72,755	67,690	71,373	94,778	86,801	94,595	52,927
Stockholders' equity	744,618	660,279	585,288	541,372	469,337	369,627	328,702	303,236	281,548	253,462
Employees at year-end	68,521	66,162	56,682	65,524	74,422	55,934	47,259	44,752	58,974	46,747
Stockholders of record at year-end	24,438	22,425	21,359	18,977	16,135	15,177	16,210	17,738	17,808	18,649

*Adjusted for stock split in 1973.

EXHIBIT 3 Estimates of Total Value (at the factory level) of Goods Shipped by U.S.-Based Manufacturers (in millions of dollars)

Year	Consumer Electronics*	Industrial and Commercial	Federal Electronics	Total
1973	7,014.2	19,553.0	11,929	38,496.2
1974	6,768.5	22,227.7	12,497	41,493.2
1975	7,186.8	23,603.1	12,910	43,699.9
1976	9,425.2	26,136.0	15,659	51,220.2
1977	12,135.0	30,084.7	16,638	58,857.7
1978	14,030.0	35,048.0	18,210	67,288.0
1979	15,393.6	41,037.6	19,920	76,351.2
1981	15,767.0	50,651.0	20,754	87,172.0
1982	21,402.2	59,908.2	24,460	105,770.4

*Includes domestic-made equipment, domestic-label imports, and foreign-label imports.

SOURCE: *Electronics,* January 1975; January 1978; January 4, 1979.

no inquiries to the user, the learning device was to be capable of carrying on a "dialog" with a small child. In the words of one person involved with the project, the device was to function like an "electronic flashcard machine." A product of this type would require a light-emitting diode (LED) display capable of presenting "dialog" characters, such as question marks, plus signs, and equal signs, as well as the 13 to 14 "passive" characters built into conventional calculator displays. Satisfying this requirement with 1975 LED-display technology, however, would be cost prohibitive. Not until TI achieved a breakthrough in this technology during 1976 did "dialog" characters become economically feasible. Indeed, this breakthrough allowed Ritchie to develop the "Little Professor"—a handheld device packaged in a bright yellow plastic housing and slightly larger than a conventional calculator.

While the TI mathematics packages developed a year earlier were retail priced at $100 apiece (including the calculator and the instructional materials), Little Professor was retail priced at less than $20 apiece. More significantly, whereas the packages were designed to be marketed to school districts, Little Professor was to be marketed to consumers.

Soon after commercial production of Little Professor began in August of 1976, TI quickly discovered, much to its pleasant chagrin, that it could not build the product fast enough. Production was increased by a factor of four over a demand estimate made in June of 1976.

Within a year after Little Professor was introduced, further advances in battery, integrated circuit, and display technology allowed the design of a second mathematics learning aid: "Dataman." This product incorporated all the features of Little Professor, as well as seven additional learning activities. By Christmas of 1977, TI appeared to be on the verge of a stunning success with its two learning aids.

Near the time that shipments of Little Professor began, in the fall of 1976, Paul Breedlove, a product manager working under Ron Ritchie, conceived of an idea to build a lost-cost speech synthesizer on an integrated circuit that could be incorporated in consumer products.

Synthetic speech had been around for some time. It is produced by circuits that are essentially an electronic model of the human vocal tract. Just as human speech is created by air impulses passing through the vocal cords and the vocal tract, synthetic speech is generated by processing electronic impulses through a rapidly changing electronic filter. The result is synthetically produced speech that sounds like that heard over the telephone.

Human speech generates two basic types of sounds. The vowel sounds, referred to as voiced sounds, are produced by an air impulse from the lungs passing through the open vocal cords, causing them to vibrate. As the vibrating air impulse moves up through the vocal tract, the shape of the throat, the nasal passages, the jaw, and the lips determine what the pitch of that vowel sound is to be—high or low—and thus which vowel is sounded.

Consonants are represented by unvoiced sounds that are produced by an air impulse being forced through constricted openings along the vocal tract. This generates an air turbulence resulting in such sounds as S, SH, TH, F, etc. Where the sound waves produced by voiced vowel sounds are regularly spaced low-frequency sound waves, those produced by unvoiced sounds are erratic, randomly spaced high-frequency waves.

Speech is first converted into frames of 12 digital codes each at the rate of 40 frames per second. As each frame of a motion picture film stops the action for that instant of time, each frame of speech "stops the action" of the vocal tract for that 1/40 of a second or milliseconds. This "action" is then converted into 12 codes that represent the pitch for that instant of sound, the loudness, and 10 characteristics reflecting the shape of the vocal tract at the instant.

To artificially produce speech, the microcomputer within the learning aid generates 8,000 electronic signals per second that act like the air impulses generated by the lungs. At the same time, the microcomputer recalls a speech frame from the memory. The pitch characteristic selects either a periodic pitch signal to represent a voiced sound or a random noise signal for an unvoiced sound.

This signal is combined with a loudness characteristic and then processed through a unique 10-stage lattice filter where it is combined with the 10 vocal tract characteristics. In essence, the filter acts on the electronic signals to accomplish what the vocal tract does to the air signals from the lungs. The result is passed through a digital-to-analog converter and out through a small speaker.

Breedlove had in mind a major breakthrough in electronic speech synthesis. He wanted to design a single LSI chip that, in addition to the logic circuitry needed to accomplish speech synthesis, would also include memory on the order of 256K bits and circuitry from innovative new modes of user interaction. He applied for a $25,000 "IDEA grant."

"Objectives, Strategies, and Tactics" (OST) at Texas Instruments

The organizational structure at Texas Instruments combined a traditional product-line hierarchy with an array of management systems known as "Objectives, Strategies, and Tactics" or, simply, "OST."

TI's 32 operating divisions (ranging from $50 million to $150 million each) were divided among four major groups: Digital Systems, Consumer Electronics, Equipment, and Semiconductors.

Digital Systems encompassed three major product areas: Computer Systems, Terminals and Peripherals, and Printers.

The Consumer Electronics group covered four major product areas: Specialty Products, such as handheld learning devices; Consumer Calculators; Professional Calculators; and Time Products, such as digital watches.

The Equipment group was primarily responsible for radar and other electronic hardware for military applications.

Finally, the Semiconductor group served as TI's source of integrated circuits. This group manufactured and sold its wares to TI's other groups, as well as to outside original equipment manufacturers.

Each operating division was divided into Product Customer Centers ($10 million to $100 million each). As of 1978, there were 80 such units. Roughly equivalent to the product departments of conventional product-line structured firms, many PCCs had their own engineering, manufacturing, and marketing units, although assistance was also available from corporate-level staffs. The latter included a high-powered Corporate Research Laboratory.

Overlaid across the operating hierarchy was OST. In the early 1960s, Patrick E. Haggerty, then president of TI, diagnosed the company's susceptibility to a classic business problem: In the absence of proper incentives, operating managers will concentrate on the profitability of existing products at the expense of developing products for future growth. Haggerty conceived of OST, a management system that would hopefully immunize TI to this potential malady. In the late 1960s, his successor, Mark Shephard, Jr., turned the concept into a working reality by creating a dual reporting structure. In addition to maintaining the conventional product-line operating hierarchy, a separate OST hierarchy was established.

At the bottom of the OST pyramid were specific R&D projects, called Tactical Action Programs (TAPs). Each TAP was headed by a TAP manager. Related TAPs were grouped into Strategies, which were managed by Strategy managers. In turn, groups of related Strategies formed Objectives. Each Objective was headed by an Objective manager. In 1978, OST consisted of 250 TAPs, 60 Strategies, and 12 Objectives.

In addition to creating a dual reporting structure, Shephard split TI's annual spending budget into two separate funds: an OST fund and an operating fund.

While the operating fund was managed by the conventional operating hierarchy, the OST fund was placed under the control of a corporate committee charged with the task of setting R&D spending guidelines through the use of a zero-based budgeting system. On an annual basis, each Strategy manager was required to submit a prioritized list of funding proposals for TAPs to be carried out during the following year. In March of each year, a strategic planning conference was held in Dallas. Attending this meeting were TI's 500 managers as well as the board of directors. Together, the managers and the board decided on the corporate plan and the allocation of OST funds. In March of 1979, over 400 TAPs proposals were expected. A table showing the growth of TI's R&D budget is contained in Exhibit 4.

OST was connected to the operating hierarchy in two ways. First, most TAP managers were simultaneously PCC managers. Similarly, most Strategy managers were simultaneously division heads. This link, the company contended, afforded an opportunity to avoid the classic "hands-off" problem of moving products from R&D into commercial production. Second, OST allowed a TAP to be pulled together from whatever PCCs were required, thereby affording TI a substantial amount of agility and speed for entering new businesses.

The purpose of the dual OST/operating structure was to ensure that managers would not underplay or postpone long-range strategic programs in lieu of short-range profits. Nevertheless, the OST bureaucracy had a tendency to miss ideas proposed by people deep within the corporation. In 1973, TI attempted to overcome this problem by creating IDEA—a mini-R&D program designed to avoid the massive presentation and documentation procedures required in OST. In 1978, approximately $1 million was allocated to IDEA. These funds were administered by 40 senior technical staffers; each had authority to grant up to $25,000 to employees with notions for product or process development.

EXHIBIT 4 Research and Development and Capital Expenditures at TI (in millions of dollars)

Year	R&D	Capital
1975	50.0	67.4
1976	71.7	137.0
1977	95.7	200.0
1978	113.0	300.0

SOURCE: *Business Week*, September 18, 1978, p. 66.

Development of Speak and Spell

During the fall of 1976, Breedlove received his $25,000 IDEA grant and a design team was assigned to the program: Gene Frantz as program manager and Larry Brantingham as MOS–LSI chip designer. One of their first hurdles would be gaining the support of TI's Corporate Research Laboratory, for therein worked Richard Wiggins, one of TI's experts at designing large-scale integrated (LSI) circuits for consumer products. They could not proceed with their speech synthesis concept without Wiggins' assistance.

The design team, which now included Wiggins, spent December of 1976 feeling each other out. By the end of the month, they had reached an agreement: Working together they would attempt to develop Speak and Spell, a talking device designed to help children learn how to spell. Demonstrating the technical feasibility of such a product to upper management would be their first joint task.

To establish the technical feasibility of Speak and Spell, two steps were necessary. First, the sequence of steps needed to be performed by the product's circuitry would have to be well defined. For lack of a better term, we will call such a sequence of steps a "product logic." After being well-defined, the product logic would have to be proven effective. To demonstrate the effectiveness of a product logic, the latter would have to be first incorporated in a computer program for simulation by a general-purpose computer. An important objective during the computer simulation phase of the project was designing a product logic that would produce a voice capable of being understood. As Frantz noted: "Usually, a single word pronounced out of context is hard to understand when uttered by a human being, let alone an electronic device. And this is especially true with single syllable words, which become their own context."

The second objective to be achieved during the simulation phase was setting forth a convincing case to upper management that the logic used for the computer simulation could be put into a chip set consisting of only two or three chips.

At the end of March 1977, a computer simulation of Speak and Spell was presented to upper management. The first word uttered by the TI 980 computer used for the presentation was "ovoviviparous." While the simulation's voice was sufficiently clear, the probability of being able to incorporate the logic into a small, relatively inexpensive set of integrated circuits was not. The logic employed by the Brantingham-Wiggins team required 200,000 additions and 200,000 multiplications be performed in one second. Mostly on faith, management gave Frantz the go-ahead to take the project one step further: the development of a "breadboard" system. During this next stage, the Speak and Spell product logic would be converted into a circuit logic.

Once the design of a circuit logic is completed, it must be shown to work. One way of accomplishing this would be to manufacture a system of integrated circuits that would incorporate the precise circuit logic to be proven. The fabrication of such a specific set of ICs, although the ultimate goal, would be quite expensive and time consuming. Moreover, there would be no guarantee that the initially proposed circuit logic would perform according to expectation. As a result of a need for circuit modification, a completely new set of ICs would have to be fabricated, thereby costing more in precious R&D dollars and irrecoverable engineering time. An alternative to this method of "fabricate and test" is the "breadboard" system. The development of the latter calls for putting together a group of existing ICs that contain all the necessary gates but need to be wired to each other to emulate the circuit logic. The device on which the ICs are linked to each other consists of an array of sockets that facilitate assembly and disassembly of various circuits from the group of existing ICs. This device is known by electronics engineers as a "breadboard." As characterized by Brantingham, "the gate-by-gate breadboard circuit offers the first chance to estimate the size and price of the barn."

Design to Cost

In June of 1977, the Speak and Spell project was formally transferred from the IDEA program to the OST system. At that point, Frantz was at work trying to answer two interrelated questions: First, what price could TI hope to draw from consumers for the Speak and Spell? This information had a direct impact on the design of the circuit logic, since different designs would entail varying manufacturing costs. Second, would the Speak and Spell chip system consist of two chips or three chips?

> The design-to-cost concept must be made to permeate Texas Instruments. Its application must become second nature not only to those who design, but to those who manufacture and market. It must be applied not only to high-volume products, but—in adapted form—to limited-volume products. And it must be applied not only to the products and services we sell, but to our internal functions as well. Design-to-cost principles, creatively adapted, will make a major contribution to the achievement of TI's objectives.[1]

Design-to-cost is an engineering discipline that establishes, as a primary design parameter, a timetable of unit production costs derived from a timetable of unit prices at which the product can win and retain the desired market share.

Frantz knew that three features of this statement were of special importance: First, unit cost is a primary design parameter, equal in importance to performance. Second, in the case of high-volume markets, this cost parameter takes the form of a timetable of steadily decreasing costs spanning the entire lifetime of the product. This cost timetable is established long before the product goes into production. But since experience curves are volume dependent rather than time dependent, these cost goals are subjected to continual revision as the future unfolds and as volume requirements become more predictable.

The third feature is the heart of the concept. The cost timetable is derived from a price elasticity curve. Preparation of this curve begins with an exhaustive analysis of the number of units the market will be willing to buy at specific prices during the life of the product.

Frantz also knew that while the design-to-cost concept was simple common sense, its application was uncommon. Too often in high-technology areas, design practice is merely to advance performance capabilities, total up the costs, mark these up by the normal margin, and then hand the product over to marketing with instructions to "sell it" (Appendix I). But customers are not interested in technology for technology's sake. Customers want quality, reliability, and performance at the lowest feasible price.

Normally the first step of the design-to-cost approach would be to determine basic performance requirements: What does the potential customer want the product to do? Then, when dealing with markets where the volume is elastic, it is necessary

---

[1]J. Fred Bucy, president, Texas Instruments. (See Appendix II for further remarks by Mr. Bucy.)

to try to determine price elasticity: How will the market expand as the price of the product is lowered—that is, how much are how many customers willing to pay for this product?

After this careful market study has established prices and volumes, profit margins necessary to finance growth and reward stockholders can be applied. In this way, working backwards from price, unit production cost objectives are established. The price elasticity curve also serves as a basis for determining the production volume and price at which a significant share of market can be obtained. Taken together, these estimates of performance, price, cost, and volume give a definite target for product design.

The next step is to apply experience-curve theory to determine future manufacturing costs. Working with prices and volumes from the price elasticity curve, required costs versus cumulative production are plotted. These points will rarely plot as a straight line, so the experience curve must be drawn through two important checkpoints: The cost of the first significant manufacturing run, and the required cost of the product at maturity.

Finally, the experience curve is translated into target costs by date, by estimating the market volume growth in terms of units per quarter. In this way, the experience curve becomes the cost timetable. It shows the slope down which costs must be driven. Adding gross profit margins yields a price timetable—which must also be checked against the analysis of prices the market will be willing to pay.

However, to answer the price question for Speak and Spell, Frantz was faced with an immediate problem: How would he go to the marketplace to determine the need and affordable price of a product nobody had ever seen or conceived of? He was forced to rely on a conventional TI market research tool: the focus group. A focus group consists of a panel of consumers asked to assess what they would pay for a given product. Ordinarily, focus groups were given the actual product, or a reasonable facsimile, to evaluate. But, in the case of Speak and Spell, no such product or reasonable facsimile existed. The need to convince potential consumers that the product was not another "pull-string" toy was crucial. As a substitute for the actual device, Frantz decided to use a combination of a tape recording, an artist's rendering, and an oral description for focus group presentations made during the summer of 1977. Preliminary analysis of the responses from consumers indicated that a successful retail price would lie somewhere between $40 and $50.

EXHIBIT 5 Alternative Circuit Designs for Speak and Spell

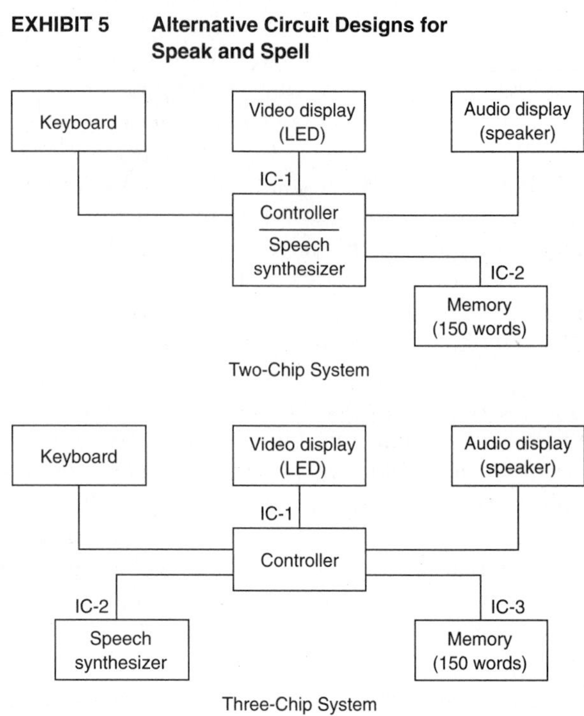

Turning to the second question, Frantz noted that he initially thought Speak and Spell would use a two-chip system: one chip for the controller and synthesizer, the other for storing the machine's vocabulary. (See Exhibit 5 for an illustration of the possible internal designs of Speak and Spell.) Some of Frantz's engineers, however, argued for separating the controller and synthesizer into two separate chips. They argued that a separate synthesizer chip could be put to use in several other applications (e.g., warning devices for automobiles and aircraft). The existence of other uses for a speech synthesis integrated circuit would allow its R&D costs to be spread over a wider base of products. Moreover, other applications would mean increased profits for TI as a whole. The probability and extent of being able to spread R&D costs and of increased returns from expanded applications of a separate speech synthesis chip had to thus be factored into the decision between a two- or three-chip system.

The advocates of the three-chip system also argued that a three-chip system would involve significantly less risk in the manufacturing process. Their contention was based on the fact that a separate controller and separate synthesizer would be easier to fabricate than a more complicated controller/synthesizer.

The only way Frantz could evaluate the argument that there would exist other demands for a speech synthesis chip was through interdivisional communication. After several months of positive feedback from other TI divisions, Frantz was convinced of the need for flexibility: a three-chip system was adopted.

By October of 1977, Frantz had the Speak and Spell breadboard system operating. The next phase would be the design and fabrication of a chip set that would incorporate the circuitry worked out on the breadboard system. This last step took six months. By late April 1978, Frantz was being congratulated as the father of a new line of voice products. With the semiannual Consumer Electronics Show only a month away, he hurried to put the finishing touches on the prototype to be rolled out at the show.

Supervoice

In developing Speak and Spell, a large part of Frantz's efforts was focused on converting TI's laboratory knowledge of speech synthesis into a marketable consumer product. Yet, in commenting on the hurdles that he and his colleagues had to surmount, Franz noted that "the real problem was never designing the product's logic and eventually incorporating it in a two- or three-chip integrated circuit set. Rather, it was finding a voice that could satisfy three basic requirements: quality, clarity, and amenability to being digitalized."

Voice quality is simply the characteristic of a voice that makes it pleasing to listen to; voice clarity is the characteristic that renders a voice easily understood in terms of pronunciation; and amenability to being digitalized is the characteristic that allows a voice to be electronically synthesized such that the least amount of information needs to be processed per unit of time. It was Franz's hope that one voice could satisfy all three requirements in an optimal way.

The search for this optimal voice (i.e., "Supervoice") began very early in the Speak and Spell development program. The search consisted of taking hundreds of tape recordings of different voices and then subjecting them to the three requirements. The search stretched from professional speakers in Dallas to the Shakespearian actor whose voice was used for the computer "HAL" in the movie *2001: A Space Odyssey*. As intuitively expected, TI's researchers learned that a normal friendly voice was most readily accepted by a small child. More important was the finding that children were indifferent to the sex of a voice. This information was warmly received by Frantz, since synthesizing a male voice required less information processing per unit of time than synthesizing a female voice.

Through trial and error, Frantz finally decided to use the voice of a Dallas disc jockey for the Speak and Spell prototype to be introduced in June 1978. This voice was also used in the fall 1978 production runs of the product. Yet, by the start of 1979, Frantz was not entirely certain that the disc jockey's voice was as close to "Supervoice" as possible. Indeed, as of January 1979, TI was still looking for voices to be used in synthesizer circuits of the future.

Educational Merchandising

As TI gained merchandising experience with its handheld calculators, it learned that the written informational materials included with its products were extremely important. *Owners Manuals* and *Programmed Learning Guides* became important tools in preventing returns of calculators thought by their owners to be faulty and in building consumer loyalty to TI. The importance of these materials was reflected in the establishment of an Education and Communication Center. Managed by Don Scharringhausen, who reported directly to Ron Ritchie, the ECC was directly responsible for preparing the consumer literature that accompanied TI's products.

In the first half of the 1970s, the consumer literature accompanying a specific product, such as a simple four-function calculator, was largely prepared after the product itself was fully developed and ready for production. The move into more sophisticated programmable calculators and learning aids, such as Little Professor, Dataman, and Speak and Spell, however, brought a change in the process. As the importance of *Owners Manuals* and *Programmed Learning Guides* increased, the drafters of this literature became more involved in the actual design of the products. For the learning aids line, a separate Product Customer Center was set up in the Education and Communication Center. This PCC, Educational Merchandising, was managed by Ralph Oliva, a Ph.D. in solid-state physics from Rensselaer Polytechnic Institute.

Oliva was responsible for the "learning factors engineering" underlying the development of TI's learning aid line. "Learning factors engineering" was the process of bringing three points to bear in the development of each learning aid: first, the operation of each learning device had to be easily understood by its potential user; second, the product itself had to be able to telescope its value to prospective purchasers viewing the item in a retail outlet; and, third, the learning procedures carried out by the device had to be educationally sound.

To achieve these three goals, it was necessary for Oliva to assert some sort of balance to the design engineers responsible for the development of the actual hardware. For example, in the case of Speak and Spell, Oliva had to take charge of the list of words that would be programmed into the memory of the device. Although this assumption of power by Oliva was by no means a major matter, it marked the transition from the era in which all product design matters were handled exclusively by the semiconductor engineers.

To assure that TI's learning aids were each educationally sound, Oliva enlisted the support of outside authorities. Using these authorities raised an important question: Should the names of education authorities be displayed anywhere in the literature included with the product or in advertisements for the product? If this question was answered affirmatively, TI would have to worry about royalty payments as well as lump-sum consulting payments. For TI's first five learning aids (Little Professor, Dataman, Speak and Spell, Spelling B, and First Watch) it was decided that the authorities consulted in the development of the products would not be mentioned in product literature or advertisements.

In addition to worrying about the role of authorities in the development and merchandising of learning aids, Oliva was confronted with two broader questions. The first covered the area of market research; the second, the area of merchandising.

As noted above, TI used several focus groups during the development of Speak and Spell to acquire a feel for the market's interest in the product. Based on this research, TI decided the retail price for Speak and Spell would initially be set at $55. At this price, however, TI discovered that it could not make Speak and Spell fast enough to keep up with demand. This fact was consistent with reports in January 1979 from manufacturers of toys employing integrated circuits that were being sold during the 1978 Christmas buying season. These manufacturers, as well as the semiconductor manufacturers of the integrated circuits being used in the toys, felt that at least a million more products could have been sold during the holiday buying season if demand had been more accurately estimated and production appropriately adjusted. To avoid a recurrence of this problem, Oliva was concerned with developing a more reliable mechanism for predicting demand for future learning aids.

Another question confronting Oliva involved the marketing of learning aids. Some observers outside TI wondered if the company would try to use the route of school textbook publishers: market the devices to school districts. TI's earlier experience with the mathematics packages, however, seemed to suggest that the school district route would not be a good one for TI's learning aids. To market to school districts, a network of sales agents would have to be set up. Oliva wondered if there was enough margin in the products to support such a system. An alternative was getting into a joint venture with a textbook publisher with a sales agent network already in place. At the start of 1979, Oliva viewed such a venture as possible, but in need of further analysis.

Production Problems

As noted above, TI's Semiconductor Group supplied its end-user product divisions with integrated circuits and other semiconductor components. This sole source of supply presented the Speak and Spell Product Customer Center with a couple of problems. First, all integrated circuits developed by any PCC in the Consumer Product Group had to meet standards set forth by the Semiconductor Group. Moreover, since any chip design modifications would entail modifications in the chip manufacturing process, all such design changes had to be approved by the Semiconductor Group. The existence of a modification/approval bureaucracy meant some reduction in the speed with which products like Speak and Spell could be developed and improved.

To some degree, the inability of the Consumer Product Group to manufacture Speak and Spell fast enough was due to an inability to get the Semiconductor Group to manufacture the needed integrated circuits fast enough. As Larry Brantingham, the principal integrated circuit design engineer for the speech synthesizer chip, stated: "To the Semiconductor Group, we (the Speak and Spell PCC) are just another customer." Indeed, the Semiconductor Group serviced hundreds of customers—end-product PCCs at TI, as well as outside original equipment manufacturers.

One way of overcoming the sole source of supply problem presented by the Semiconductor Group was backward integration by the Consumer Product Group.

Quality control presented Gene Frantz with another production problem. During most of the 1970s, the consumer products manufactured by TI were inspected by performing visual tests of the products' displays. On a typical calculator assembly line, for example, 10 percent of the people on the line would be employed at checking product displays for expected results of pushing various buttons on the calculator keyboards. Through the experience of assembling millions of items, TI learned that the vision of inspectors viewing displays for several hours will gradually grow more critical. As the inspector's vision became more critical, he or she would throw increasing numbers of good products onto the scrap heap. To counteract this "false negative" phenomenon, TI learned how to calibrate its effects into the production economics at hand.

In the late 1970s, TI began a concerted effort to automate its consumer product assembly lines. As one line manager stated: "We want to go from making one calculator in *x* seconds to *x* calculators in one second." Part of the automation effort involved the use of computerized video test systems. The latter were made possible through technological improvements in electronic optical character reading devices. A computerized video test system consisted of a video camera that watched calculator displays respond to bursts of air trained on the keyboards. The camera would feed the resulting information on the displays to a computer that could determine if the calculators were functioning properly.

Speak and Spell, of course, required audio testing in conjunction with visual testing. Therefore, TI was precluded from using the computerized test systems on the Speak and Spell devices. Instead, human inspectors had to be employed. This, however, presented TI with a problem it had never before experienced. Whereas video testing by humans would result in increasing numbers of false negatives, audio testing by humans would result in increasing numbers of false positives. The reason for the false positives was due to the fact that the human ear will acclimate itself to the same sound heard repeatedly over a period of time. Thus, as a typical day wore on, the average inspector would approve increasingly more Speak and Spell devices that, if heard at the beginning of the day, would have been rejected. With Speak and Spell, therefore, the quality control process had to be entirely recalibrated.

Future of Learning Aids and Speech Products

By the end of 1978, TI's line of learning aids consisted of five products: Little Professor, Dataman, Speak and Spell, Spelling B, and First Watch. The Spelling B product was a derivative of the Speak and Spell; it performed many of the learning games programmed into Speak and Spell, but did not include speech synthesis. First Watch, as its name suggests, was developed as a device to help children learn about time. Fortuitously, TI learned that small children enjoyed pushing the button on an LED digital watch and viewing the result. In contrast, adults very much disliked the need to have to push a button on a digital watch to learn the time. With the advent of liquid crystal displays (LCDs) for use in digital watches, the adult segment of the digital watch market rejected the LED digital watch. Instead of facing a mature, or declining, market for LED digital watches, TI was able to make use of them in the First Watch product.

After three years of growing sales in its expanding learning products line, TI was determined to increase the range and capability of such products. One way of improving the capability of such products was to increase the amount of information contained in their memory chips. Rather than increasing the number of memory chips to be simultaneously attached to a learning device controller, TI decided to develop a line of memory chips that could be plugged into the learning products and bought separately. For example, each of the memory chips in the Speak and Spell contained about 150 words. With plug-in memory chips, to be used one at a time, the vocabulary could be expanded to thousands of words. The development of a line of plug-in memory chips presented more of a marketing problem than a technological one—TI had been selling plug-in modules containing programs for use in its line of programmable calculators as early as 1977.

One of the ways by which TI hoped to expand the breadth of its speech products line was through the development of devices that could understand voices as well as synthesize them. Speech recognition, however, required five times as many calculations per unit of time as did speech synthesis. As of 1979, further development in digital speech technology and integrated circuit technology would be needed before speech recognition could become a commercial reality.

Perhaps most important, learning aids would help bridge the gap between an era of passive, handheld digital devices and an era of very sophisticated home computer systems. In the late 1970s, predictions were made that sales of home computers would reach *x* million units by the early 1980s. Some observers, however, cautioned that many of these sales would be to small businesses who viewed such devices as relatively inexpensive substitutes for the minicomputers being marketed by traditional computer mainframe manufacturers. To sell home computers to households, a long period of consumer education and familiarization as to their uses would be necessary. Some people at TI thought that learning aids would help perform this function.

APPENDIX I

Excerpts from a paper presented by Dr. Morris Chang of Texas Instruments at a conference on "Tomorrow in World Electronics," London, 1974.

Vertical Integration: Components to System

Why Do Semiconductor Manufacturers Integrate Upwards into the Systems Business?

Increased Value Added

The most important motivation is the opportunity for higher growth resulting from increased value added for products where the principal function is already performed by semiconductors. Exhibit 6 shows the semiconductor content in some of the electronic equipment. Consumer calculators have a semiconductor content of 30 percent to 35 percent. This means, of course, that if the semiconductor manufacturer sells $15 of semiconductors to a calculator manufacturer, he gets only $15 of sales, but if he makes and sells the calculator himself, he gets $45 of sales. The same magnitude of increase in value added exists in minicomputers with semiconductor memories. For data terminals, point-of-sale systems, and electronic watches, the multiplying factor is even larger. For the first five types of equipment that I have listed (Exhibit 6), semiconductors in fact constitute the heart of the end-equipment. Other technologies are undoubtedly also necessary for those five types of equipment, but the semiconductor technology is the most important and perhaps the most difficult to master among all the technologies that are required to make each of those types of equipment. For that reason, those five types of equipment are very logical candidates for the vertical integration of semiconductor manufacturers.

Item 6 of Exhibit 6 is solid-state color TV. Here, while semiconductors perform the vital signal processing functions, the present picture tube technology is not within the present semiconductor technology. In order to be successful in color TV, a semiconductor manufacturer would have to either acquire the present picture tube technology, or develop a substitute technology for picture tubes. Neither is likely in the short term. Therefore, color TV is not an easy candidate for vertical integration of semiconductor manufacturers in the near term.

Item 7 of Exhibit 6 is mainframe computers. Semiconductors perform the key function of logic, and, increasingly, the memory function. However, the expertise required in systems marketing, software, and technologies other than semiconductor constitutes great barriers to a semiconductor manufacturer attempting to integrate upward.

This list (Exhibit 6) is, of course, not intended as an all-inconclusive one for all the candidate areas that semiconductor manufacturers could integrate into. Rather, it serves to illustrate the motivation of

EXHIBIT 6 Semiconductor Content in End-Equipment (as percentage of factory selling price)

Product	Percentage Semiconductor Content
1. Consumer calculators	30–35
2. Mini and microcomputers (CPU with SC memory)	25–35
3. Data terminals	12–15
4. Point-of-sale systems	12–15
5. Electronic wristwatch (with SC display)	8–15
6. Color TV (solid state)	15
7. Mainframe computers	<10

upward integration: namely, increased value added. It also illustrates the criterion that determines whether an upward integration is likely, namely, whether semiconductor technology is the dominant technology in the end-equipment or not.

Shrinking Product Life Demands Close Coupling with End-Market

The second reason for the semiconductor manufacturers to integrate vertically is that the rapid advance of semiconductor technology has shrunk the product lifetime of the end-equipment, and this phenomenon in turn demands a close coupling between the semiconductor manufacturer and the end-market.

. . . The rapid advance of semiconductor technology demands that the design of the semiconductor components, if it can still be called a component, proceed in parallel with the design of the end-equipment in which the component will be used. This parallel development can, of course, be done between a component vendor and a systems customer, but the trade secrets and proprietary inhibitions are such that parallel development between two companies is seldom as satisfactory an arrangement as parallel development within the same company. When component development and system development do not proceed in parallel, valuable time is lost. And when you think of the average product life cycle as two years, the loss of a few months would be a serious matter.

I also want to make an additional point. As semiconductor components become more complex, the investment that the semiconductor manufacturer makes in component design and development becomes more and more substantial. And as I pointed out earlier, the rapid product obsolescence allows only a short time window in which to recover the substantial design and development investment. It becomes essential for the semiconductor manufacturer to utilize this time window to the maximum. Therefore, it is essential to have equipment using your advanced components on the market as early as possible. The only way to do it is to make and market your own equipment. I said earlier that the first reason for semiconductor manufacturers to integrate vertically is to increase value added. But really, in order to recover his investment in component design, it may become mandatory in many instances for the semiconductor manufacturer to integrate vertically and therefore to get his own equipment on the market as soon as possible.

Benefits to System Manufacturers

What are the benefits of semiconductor makers' vertical integration to traditional system manufacturers? Are they the losers? The answer is no. I can see two very clear benefits to the traditional system manufacturers.

The most important benefit is lower component prices. As you know, semiconductor prices generally follow experience curves with a slope of 70 percent to 80 percent, which means that each time the cumulative unit volume doubles, the price declines 20 percent to 30 percent. When a semiconductor manufacturer first uses his components in his own equipment, the cost of the components is high because it is at the beginning of the experience curve. As the components are made available to other equipment manufacturers, the other equipment manufacturers share the lower component cost with the semiconductor manufacturer.

Another valuable benefit of vertical integration to the traditional system manufacturer is the broadening of markets resulting from the innovative end-product and the semiconductor cost reduction.

Let us look at the worldwide market growth of three of the seven end-products I discussed earlier. In Exhibit 7, the period 1970 to 1974 has been selected because this is the period of initial impact of higher density integrated circuits. You will recall from Exhibit 6 that these products have a high semiconductor content—in the 25 percent to 35 percent range—and their performance and price are greatly influenced by semiconductor technology. Note that their annual growth rate in the past three years is in the 40 percent to 50 percent range, which is about four to five times the growth rate of the total elec-

EXHIBIT 7 Market Growth of End-Products with High Semiconductor Content

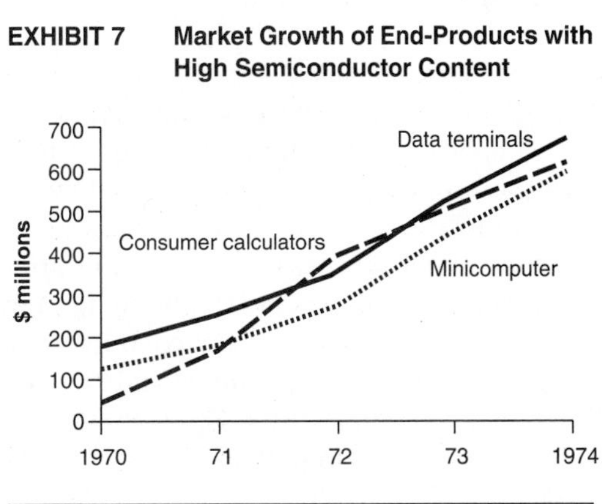

tronics market over the same period. Such explosive growth benefits all the manufacturers of those types of equipment since the market size becomes so large as to accommodate many participants.

Barriers to Downward Integration into Semiconductors

So far I have talked about semiconductor manufacturers integrating upward into the equipment business. What about the possibility of equipment manufacturers integrating downward into semiconductor components? This, of course, can happen. It has been done successfully in quite a few cases and has been attempted in even more cases. As I see it, there are two major barriers to downward integration. The first barrier is that a system manufacturer may not have semiconductor technology. Semiconductor technology has progressed to a degree of sophistication and complexity now that it will take a company not having it considerable time, investment, and talents to develop it. In this respect, a system manufacturer attempting to integrate downward into semiconductor components will have the same barrier as a semiconductor manufacturer integrating upward into such fields as TV picture tubes or large computers. The second barrier is that an equipment manufacturer must develop a large production base in semiconductors and sufficient research and development in order to remain competitive in semiconductors. The large production base is necessary because of the experience curve effect that I talked about earlier in semiconductors. The research and development is necessary because of the quick pace of advance in the semiconductor technology.

Implications of Vertical Integration

Now I want to comment on some of the implications of vertical integration. The first and perhaps most obvious implication of vertical integration is that the horizons of semiconductor companies have now broadened to extend their reach beyond the traditional component business, as a growing array of sophisticated end-equipment is now being built by what were hitherto known as semiconductor manufacturers. With vertical integration and the use of high-density components, the semiconductor producer is becoming an important practitioner of system design. Consequently, the boundary lines between component houses and system houses are becoming increasingly blurred.

Yet another important implication of vertical integration by semiconductor companies is the reduced labor content in end-equipment. Large-scale integration has simplified assembly by incorporating most of the complexity in the chip and drastically reducing the number of components needed. This tears down national or geographic barriers for the production of new equipment with a high semiconductor content. For example, a calculator can now be assembled in almost any country with relatively little difference in cost. In the near future, I can see that an electronic watch or a minicomputer can be assembled in any part of the world with relatively little difference in cost. New products with high semiconductor content could be produced indigenous to the market. This change has important ramifications for trade, industrial development, and for the growth of multinational companies.

Electronics is a dynamic industry that depends heavily on technological developments. Since semiconductor companies are at the leading edge of technology and have demonstrated their ability to introduce innovative, high-volume electronic products, they will come to play an increasingly important role in the total electronics industry. Vertical integration is not a newfangled craze but a viable way of growth for component manufacturers. Companies that develop and capitalize on the potential of new technology can achieve high rates of growth. Therefore, small companies today can become giants in just a few years. And giants today, unless they also continually develop and harness technology, can become noncompetitive and cease to grow in a short time. Vertical integration therefore has opened up possibilities for a reordering of hierarchy in the electronics industry.

APPENDIX II

Excerpts from: "Marketing in a Goal-Oriented Organization," by J. Fred Bucy, president and chief operating officer, Texas Instruments Incorporated; November 17, 1976, New York University Key Issues lecture series.

Marketing is but one leg of the "create," "make," and "market" functions of our business at Texas Instruments. Marketing strategy is a part of overall product strategy, and product strategy is derived from corporate strategy.

The "Marketing Concept" teaches that a company must focus on making what the customer wants, rather than on selling what the company makes. This is sound advice. But, like many simplistic statements, it obscures some major issues. First, there is a belief by the stronger proponents of the Marketing Concept that competitive products are essentially alike, and, therefore, success goes to the company that places the highest priority on marketing.

This belief in the supremacy of marketing over the "create" and "make" functions is based on the idea that equal technology quickly becomes available to all participants in a market through the mobility of the technical community and today's communications. If this were true, competition for market share would be won or lost based on the mechanics of bringing the product to the user, as the concept suggests. But this simply is not the case in high-technology businesses. Marketing is vitally important, but technology is still a prime determinant.

Technology encompasses the thousands of detailed steps that are necessary to develop and manufacture a product. Science gives us knowledge, but not concepts. Science may suggest what can be built, but only technology tells us how to build it. Frequently, technology alone permits us to invent new products to create markets, and new *science* is not always needed.

It's true that research findings are often made widely available—but the fruits of technology development rarely are. It's the lifeblood of competitive leadership, and successful companies guard it jealously.

In the United States, government-sponsored research accounts for 53 percent of all R&D. Except for a few areas crucial to defense, these research findings are available to all. Yet, certain companies consistently use this widely available research to produce superior products at lower prices—because they have developed their own superior technologies.

In addition to the free availability of government-sponsored research, private industry carries on active exchanges of research data through technical symposia, the publication of papers, and the like. In fact, our dissemination of this information is so free that Eastern Bloc countries have long been amazed at the ease with which they can acquire what has been so costly for us to learn. But data acquired in the course of research doesn't reveal much of the "how to" needed to design and manufacture a product.

This know-how is so crucial that, at TI, we develop and build most of our critical manufacturing systems—and we would like to build all of them. First, this permits us to keep the performance characteristics of these systems confidential. Second, advances we make in design and manufacturing technology give us an important competitive edge. When production equipment is bought on the open market, by definition your productivity is about the same as your competition's.

A company that enjoys life based on the assumption that there is no better way to design and produce a product than the currently available technology can be in for a rude awakening. It's happened time and again—in electronics, in business machines, in calculators, and now in watches, with electronic watches displacing many mechanical watches just as pin-lever movements displaced many Swiss movements a generation ago.

Technology is by no means a constant in the competitive equation. To the contrary, it is a most important variable.

The second point that the Marketing Concept tends to obscure is that create, make, and market functions must be tightly interwoven in a system of management, corporate philosophy, and the corporate purpose. None of these functions can operate effectively on a stand-alone basis.

At TI, we define a basic corporate philosophy and enunciate corporate goals that represent good citizenship in the broadest sense. These goals establish the basic purpose of the corporation, which neither we nor society should be allowed to forget. The basic purpose of corporations is to exercise wise stewardship in managing a large share of the physical assets of society. We strive to manage in a way that produces the maximum return to society—in new and better products, in creation and upgrading of jobs, in concern for the environment, and in community well-being. In short, TI's purpose is to provide a higher living standard, in both quality and quantity, at lowest cost, for TI's employees, its customers, and the community at large. Fulfilling this purpose requires that we make an adequate return on assets.

This basic philosophy is as old as TI. We formalized it in our corporate objective in 1961, and it has remained substantially unchanged. A fundamental element of this objective is a statement of corporate ethics—ethics that go further than just being within the law—and that cover situations where no law exists. We communicate these standards to all employees and tolerate no deviation. Expedient compromises may promise short-term gains, but they can grow into a corporate cancer that will destroy the institution.

In addition to providing this ethical framework, TI's corporate objective defines the corporation's business intentions and goals; the kinds of business in which it will engage; the mix of business and geography; the company's posture toward employees, stockholders, customers, vendors, governments, and politicians; its specific profit goals and growth goals; and the methodology of growth. TI has always emphasized *internal* growth.

Within the corporate objective, we define a number of "business objectives" that specify the short- and long-range goals for major groupings of our business. These goals cover the worldwide markets to be served, the products and services for these markets and how to sell them, growth goals by product and market, technology requirements, and financial goals by product. This brings us to TI's Objectives, Strategies, and Tactics system.

This system, which we call "OST," provides an organization that overlays our decentralized product-customer center structure. It cuts across conventional organizational lines, so that an objective manager often has strategy managers reporting to him from various divisions of the company. A strategy manager, in turn, may have tactical action program (TAP) managers from many areas outside his conventional functional responsibility. As a result, a TI manager's responsibility usually exceeds his line authority. It also means that strategic organizations can quickly be formed or altered to meet rapid changes in our dynamic markets. Each business objective manager, strategy manager, and tactical action program manager is responsible for achieving agreed-upon product goals.

High volumes alone do not drive costs down; they merely provide the opportunity. At TI, capitalizing on this opportunity starts with "design-to-cost." This involves deciding today what the selling price and performance of a given product must be years in the future and designing the product and the equipment for producing it to meet both cost and performance goals. Stated another way, unit cost is a primary design parameter. It is a specification equal in importance to functional performance, quality, and service. This parameter takes the form of a timetable of steadily decreasing costs over the entire lifetime of the product.

In part, the cost timetable is determined by the price elasticity curve, which is a plot of the relationship of the price of a product to its potential sales volume. Unit price is the independent variable. Volume is the dependent variable. Typically, these curves have a knee where the market growth rate in units increases rapidly once a certain price level is penetrated.

This is the kind of result used to make the critical trade-off between cost and performance that sets the final design parameters. Constructing this curve is one of the most challenging of all marketing problems. Perhaps the most effective approach for both consumer and industrial products is to segment the market carefully and then to conduct broad customer surveys within the segments you expect to penetrate. The focal point of these surveys is what price the customer is willing to pay for specific product characteristics.

The cost timetable, in addition to being a function of the elasticity curve, is also a function of how quickly the knee of the curve will be approached, how large the start-up volume will be, and how quickly the volume increases on the experience curve.

The discipline created in an organization by setting pricing for the lifetime of a product is itself a powerful tool in the management of cost reduction. At the same time, the volume-dependent nature of the experience curve means that continual review and revision of cost goals are necessary as the future unfolds and volume requirements become more predictable. Thus, the design-to-cost approach becomes a forcing function for continuous productivity improvement throughout the entire lifetime of a product.

In addition to designing and manufacturing-to-cost, we must also distribute-to-cost. It's a mistake to devote thousands of engineering hours to wringing pennies out of manufacturing costs, only to have multi-tiered distribution add back dollars to the ultimate price paid by the customer. TI feels a responsibility to be innovative in using the right distribution channels to make sure that manufacturing economies are passed through distribution to the customer. The experience curve phenomenon, which requires us to produce at continually lower costs, also requires that we distribute at continually lower costs.

One example: five years ago, the small businessman who needed a mechanical four-function calculator had little choice but to call an office equipment dealer. Since a calculator then sold for perhaps

$1,000, the dealer could justify several personal sales calls, as well as personal service after the sale. His gross margin on the sale of this product would be $400 to $450 a unit.

Today, an electronic calculator selling for less than $100 will outperform that old $1,000 machine. The margin available to the retailer who sells this product is about $35 per unit. This won't support the large sales and service organizations that previously existed. The result is that department stores now serve much of the small business market, and serve it at substantially less cost to the customer. The high level of personal service is no longer required because of the higher reliability of the electronic calculator. The business equipment dealers have reoriented their thrust toward the high end of the programmable calculator market.

Since the founding of TI, we have worked to create an organization and an institutional "culture" in which continuing productivity increases, cost reduction, and the design-to-cost approach are viewed as moral obligations to society.

There are times when companies have no choice but to raise prices. But it is morally wrong for institutions to believe that just because their labor and material costs have gone up, they are automatically entitled to raise their prices on an equivalent basis. It is just as wrong to expect wages to go up automatically, unless equal or greater gains can be made in productivity.

Price and wage increases will always be the first choice, though, unless design-to-cost and productivity improvement are implicit in the "culture" of the corporate institution. These elements must be so thoroughly built into the company's behavioral pattern that it actively, automatically, and continuously seeks to improve its mode of operation in order to give its customers more for less.

Case IV–3
Microsoft LAN Manager

K. Cross, T. J. Kosnik, B. A. Seecharan, and M. Maidique

In February of 1990, Jacob Christenson looked out a window overlooking the 240-acre Microsoft campus on a rainy day in Redmond, Washington. He had just been promoted to chief network engineer, replacing his former boss Darryl Ellis, supervising 136 programmers and testers. His promotion was, however, a mixed blessing.

Christenson had joined Microsoft in 1987 as a test manager working for Darryl Ellis. Their primary software product was LAN Manager version 1.0 (known as "1.0"), a network operating system that allowed groups of personal computers (LANs) to link together effectively.[1] LAN Manager 1.0 had introduced some ground-breaking ideas, but had lacked features which users took for granted in other network software. Therefore, in 1988 Ellis chose Christenson to lead development of LAN Manager 2.0 ("2.0"), an improved version that would supply features found in competitors' products. Simultaneously, Ellis began work on a new architecture that would be the seamless, elegant foundation for a future LAN Manager version 3.0 ("3.0") and would leapfrog the competition.

Eli Phelps was the group product manager—Jacob Christenson's counterpart on the marketing side (see Exhibit 1). Phelps was responsible for achieving the marketing goals:

> We estimate our unit market share to be about 20%. This isn't good enough, especially since our competition, the NetWare products from Novell, has 60% of the market share. By 1992, we want 40% of the network market. 1.0 is innovative, but lacks some essential features. We need 2.0 and 3.0.

But in January 1990, with 2.0 nearing release, Darryl Ellis left the network unit to direct the newly formed Application Strategy group and Jacob Christenson was promoted to Ellis's former post.

Darryl Ellis's departure left Jacob Christenson with several problems. When Jacob moved up to

---

Some data, including names of principals in the case, have been disguised. Reprinted with permission of the Graduate School of Business.

[1]LAN stands for Local Area Network, which is a group of personal computers linked together. LAN Manager, like Novell's NetWare products, ran the network operations (e.g., moving files, maintaining security) as essentially an operating system for the entire network. LANs allowed users both to use their own powerful personal computers for individual applications and to access central data and to send mail like in a mainframe or minicomputer office system. Since they linked PCs already in use at many offices, LANs could serve as an inexpensive alternative to a minicomputer.

EXHIBIT 1 Network Business Unit Organization

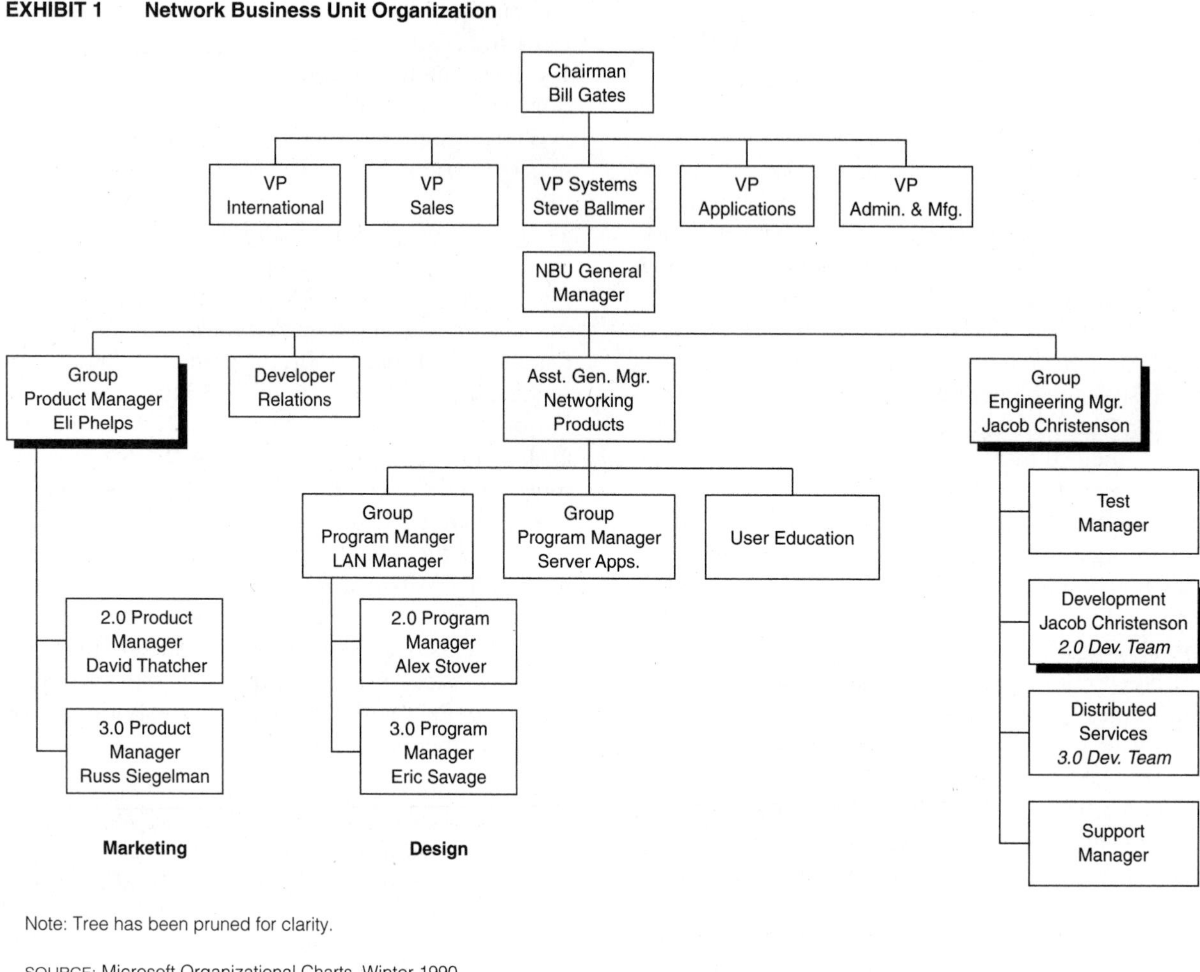

Note: Tree has been pruned for clarity.

SOURCE: Microsoft Organizational Charts, Winter 1990.

Engineer Manager, he had no one to take over 2.0. Moreover, the release date for 2.0 was slipping as final debugging dragged on (see Exhibit 2). Finally, although 3.0 was elegant on paper, Christenson knew there were serious practical issues regarding its implementation. Using Ellis's architecture, most of 3.0 would not be completed for two years, and some portions of the design might be extremely time-consuming to implement.

Christenson needed to answer three pressing questions: On which project should he focus the manpower, experience, and attention of this staff? Could he tune the development process to insure a proper balance of technical elegance and market pragmatism? How might the Network Business Unit (NBU) as a whole accelerate development of 3.0?

Microsoft Background

Market Conditions

The microcomputer software market can be broken into three components: (1) *systems,* such as MS-DOS, LAN Manager, and OS/2, which provided the operating instructions for computers and networks; (2) *applications,* like spreadsheets and word processors, which allowed computer users to accomplish specific tasks; and (3) *languages,* such as BASIC, COBOL, and C, which allowed programmers to write their own applications. Typically in this industry, the fixed costs of developing software were quite large in comparison to the standard variable costs of producing the software—diskettes,

EXHIBIT 2 LAN Manager Time Line (Approximate dates of major milestones)

Novell

January, 1983
Novell founded by Raymond Noordra to compete with IBM Token Ring and Xerox/DEC Ethernet. Its flagship product was NetWare.

September 1986
Novell ships NetWare SFT (System Fault Tolerance), a major upgrade.

September 1987
Novell ships NetWare OPT, a new version capable of supporting networks made up of different brands of hardware.

May 1989
Novell announces NetWare 386, an upgraded version, and begins OEM contracting.

September 1989
Novell ships NetWare 386 to OEMs and value-added resellers (VARs).

1983	1984	1985	1986	1987	1988	1989	1990

Microsoft

June 1984
MS-NET ships, but competes poorly with NetWare.

June 1986
Darryl Ellis hired to start NBU and 1.0.

August 1987
Jacob Christenson hired to run NBU Testing for 1.0.

August 1988
Code for 1.0 completed.

September 1988
- 1.0 ships
- Christenson's team starts coding 2.0.
- Ellis begins architecture for 3.0

September 1989
Eric Savage leaves 2.0 to write the spec for 3.0.

November 1989
Original OEM ship date for 2.0, decision finalized to sell retail, causing schedule to slip.

February 1990
Ellis leaves NBU, Jacob Christenson promoted.

Note: Because of the decision in Nov. to sell 2.0 through retail outlets rather than just OEMs, a number of enhancements were added specifically for the benefit of retail customers.

manuals, and copying. Consequently, a developer could spend millions creating a software package, provided the product could be sold to a large enough market to spread the fixed cost among thousands to millions of customers.

The growth of Microsoft and its largest competitors depended then on large markets which could offset the large development costs required in the software industry. Microsoft produced software that could be aimed to a wide customer base which enabled each customer to pay less than 1/10,000 to even 1/100,000 of the development cost. Since the typical variable costs of producing software merely represented 10–15% of the sale price, software developers could get a sizable gross profit from a software package with a retail price of $300, even allowing a 40–50 percent margin for the distribution channel if the market were large enough to recover development costs.

Exhibit 3 provides income statements for several leading hardware suppliers (Apple, Compaq, and IBM) and software suppliers (Ashton-Tate, Lotus, Microsoft, and Novell). Notwithstanding these companies' well known successes, the need to please a wide customer base with appealing *features, quickly,* and with high *quality* combined in a sometimes unforgiving marketplace to make continual success in the software industry extremely difficult. Early software pioneers such as Software Arts, Visicorp, Multimate, and Wordstar had either gone bankrupt, been swallowed up by competitors, or become paralyzed in a declining market position.

Even strong companies with good products could stumble in the software business. For exam-

EXHIBIT 3 Sample Income Statements (1989)

(In millions, except income per share and number of employees)

	Apple	Compaq	IBM	Ashton-Tate	Lotus	Microsoft	Novell
Revenues	$ 5,284	$ 2,876	$ 62,710	$ 265	$ 556	$ 804	$ 422
Cost of Revenues	2,695	1,715	27,701	66	105	204	147
Gross Profit	2,589	1,161	35,009	200	451	599	275
% Gross Profit	49.0%	40.4%	55.8%	75.5%	81.1%	74.5%	65.2%
Research & Development	$ 420	$ 132	$ 6,827	$ 69	$ 94	$ 110	$ 43
Sales & Marketing	1,207	333	21,289	92	222	219	129
Administration & General	327	211	0	77	61	24	32
Total Operating Costs	1,955	676	28,116	238	377	343	203
Operating Income	634	485	6,893	($38)	74	242	72
% Operating Income	12.0%	16.9%	11.0%	−14.3%	13.3%	30.1%	17.1%
Interest & Other Income	$ 110	$ 14	($248)	$ 6	$ 11	$ 9	$ 6
Income before Taxes	744	498	$6,645	($32)	85	251	77
Provision for Taxes	290	165	2,887	($3)	17	80	29
Net Income	454	333	3,758	($29)	68	171	49
Income per Share	3.53	7.77	6.47	($1.09)	1.61	3.03	1.46
% Net Income	8.6%	11.6%	6.0%	−10.9%	12.2%	21.3%	11.6%
Number of Employees	$14,517	9,500	383,200	1,430	3,000	5,780	2,120
Total Assets	$ 3,000	$ 2,090	$77,734	$266	$ 604	$ 721	$ 347
Stockholders' Equity	1,486	1,172	38,509	197	278	562	236
Net Income per employee	31,274	35,053	9,807	($20,280)	22,667	29,585	23,113

SOURCE: 1989 Annual Reports.

ple, Ashton-Tate, whose dBase II software had dominated the microcomputer database market from 1981 to 1985, stumbled badly in the late 1980s. Ashton-Tate experienced problems with the development of dBase IV, a powerful upgraded version of its database product. Numerous bugs delayed the launch of dBase IV until 1988, and then triggered a product recall when many customers experienced system crashes. Ashton-Tate's market share slid from 68 percent in 1985 to 45 percent in 1988, and in August of 1989, the company laid off 15 percent of its workforce.[2]

Microsoft, as well as a few successful competitors, paved a path of prosperity and growth in this turbulent market. The adoption of technical standards, such as in the extremely successful Microsoft Disk Operating System (MS-DOS), reduced risks for both producers and users. These standards enabled more developers to design programs which could interact with other software in smoother, standardized ways. Producers could then develop software compatible with software in which its customers had already invested. For example, when Microsoft introduced Excel, a spreadsheet with a graphical user interface, included features allowed users familiar with Lotus 1-2-3 commands to understand related Excel commands. This strategy made the new Excel similar to and interactive with Lotus 1-2-3, the leading spreadsheet product when Excel was introduced.

Microsoft hoped LAN Manager 2.0 and 3.0 would follow the success of its other products. These products were expected to be sold in a variety of configurations for different size networks, as LAN Manager 1.0 had been. Although development costs were higher for LM products than most Microsoft products, so were the prices. Pricing was based on the number of users supported by the network. Jacob estimated the 2.0 contribution from original equipment manufacturers (OEMs) and retail sales would be a profitable $75–$100 per supported user, similar to 1.0.

The Company

Microsoft Corporation was founded in 1975 by Paul Allen and Bill Gates with the vision to create software that would someday combine with cheap, powerful personal computers to make possible a computer on every desk and in every home. Its first product, designed by Bill Gates himself, was a BASIC intepreter for the first commercial personal computer, the Altair. For several years Microsoft created interpreter and compiler programs for use on a variety of personal computers.

In 1980, Microsoft began to develop the MS-DOS operating system for IBM. A milestone in Microsoft's history followed when IBM introduced the IBM Personal Computer in 1981 with MS-DOS as the standard operating system. Microsoft's product line expanded further in 1982 when the company introduced Multiplan, a spreadsheet package. With the introduction of Multiplan, Microsoft began to compete in all three areas of software: operating systems (with MS-DOS), applications (with Multiplan, and later Word, Excel, and Works), and languages (with BASIC and C compilers).

Sales and profits grew exponentially, and the company went public in 1986. By 1990, Microsoft dominated most of the operating systems market, and sold products successfully in the other two areas. It was listed in *Business Week* as the 68th most valuable company in the U.S.[3] With a market value of over $8 billion and with fewer than 6,000 employees, Microsoft was a remarkably productive, successful company (see Exhibit 4). In 1990 Microsoft was seeking to maintain its growth as high margins and its stellar success attracted scores of new competitors.

Position and Strategy

In 1990 Microsoft offered two of the most widely-used microcomputer operating systems: (1) MS-DOS, an operating system for older computers with less computing power and for new computers running the Windows graphical user interface, and (2) OS/2, a graphical, high-power, multi-tasking operating system. Since every computer needed an operating system, and since Microsoft products had become industry-standard for successive generations of IBM and compatible computers, these products represented a solid base for Microsoft's business. Additionally, Microsoft's reputation in systems helped establish the company in the applications market. Thus, Microsoft garnered increasing market share in many applications categories.

Microsoft applications were built to work together wherever possible. First-time users often started

[2] *Business Week*, 11/13/89, p. 102.

[3] Listing based on market value, *Business Week*, 6/16/90, p. 131.

EXHIBIT 4 Microsoft Income Statements

(in thousands)

	1986	1987	1988	1989	1990 est†
Net Revenues	$197,514	$345,890	$590,827	$803,530	$1,183,446
Cost of Revenues	40,862	73,854	148,000	204,185	252,668
Gross Profit	156,652	272,036	442,827	599,345	930,778
R&D Expenses	$ 20,523	$ 38,076	$ 69,776	$110,220	$ 180,615
Sales & Marketing	57,668	85,070	161,614	218,997	317,593
General & Admin.	17,555	22,003	23,990	278,988	39,332
Total Operating Costs	95,746	145,149	255,380	608,205	537,540
Operating Income	60,906	126,887	187,447	242,230	393,238
Non-Operating Income	$ 5,078	$ 8,638	$ 10,750	$ 16,566	$ 23,326
Stock Option Expense	$ 0	($14,187)	($14,459)	($8,000)	($6,000)
Income Before Taxes	65,984	$121,338	$183,738	250,796	410,564
Provision for Taxes	$ 26,730	$ 49,460	$ 59,830	$ 80,258	$ 131,378
Net Income	39,254	71,878	123,908	170,538	279,186
Income per share	0.78	1.30	2.22	3.03	4.68

†Microsoft's fiscal year ends June 30, 1990.

SOURCE: Annual Reports.

with the general purpose product Works,[4] which was frequently bundled with computer hardware. They could then migrate to more sophisticated, specialized, and powerful applications, like Word[5] and Excel,[6] all within the Microsoft family of products.

As systems became standardized and other competitors found it easier to reach a widening market, Microsoft increasingly met head-to-head competition on reputation, performance, features, time-to-market, and service. Although no other software company offered the same breadth, in specific niches competitors often made it to market first, sometimes with better products. For example, Microsoft's LAN Manager was playing catch-up with Novell's well-established and successful NetWare products.

A second problem was the strength of Microsoft's initial product offerings. Microsoft was sometimes criticized by industry watchers for releasing initially weak products, such as Windows 1.0. Windows was a Graphical User Interface (GUI) program for the MS-DOS operating system that allowed users to give instructions (e.g., copy this file, open that application) by pointing at icons on the screen with a mouse, rather than by typing the instructions, as was typical of command-based systems. GUI had been a central application strategy for Microsoft, with many of its products switching to this intuitive, easy-to-learn icon system. Unfortunately, initial releases of Windows were only limited successes in the market, in part because their features were incomplete and in part because the hardware of the mid-1980s did not have the power and speed needed to support complicated GUI code. Moreover, Microsoft had trouble implementing GUI features in all its applications. It was not until 1990, with the impending release of the more powerful Windows 3.0, that the market showed real interest. By then, competitors were creating their own GUI products.

Like Windows, several Microsoft products had gone through two or three upgraded versions before they were really successful. While this process of offering an *upgrade path* was familiar to software users, and while it was common practice within the software industry, it did not seem to be an ideal situation. There was considerable pressure to approach the power, performance, quality, and feature set that the customers wanted on the first try.

[4] *Works* was a computer software package that combined spreadsheet, communication, word processing, charting, graphics, and database functions in one easy-to-use, integrated package.

[5] *Word* was a specialized, sophisticated word processing software package.

[6] *Excel* was a sophisticated, graphical spreadsheet software package.

Competition for Network Products

In the early 1980s, the fledgling LAN market was highly fragmented. Competing technological approaches had been proposed by several hardware vendors including IBM, Digital Equipment Corporation (DEC), and Xerox. Interested primarily in selling their proprietary hardware, they pushed "solutions" like Ethernet (Xerox and DEC) and Token Ring (IBM). These "solutions" were combinations of proprietary hardware and software intended to win and lock in a customer, and none had emerged as an industry standard.

In 1983, Raymond Noordra founded Novell Corporation to serve the LAN market. Initially the company provided its own LAN hardware and software solutions, but with a difference. Novell's software, NetWare, was made widely compatible with non-Novell hardware (e.g., IBM, Apple, etc.). NetWare became popular because of this compatibility and flexibility. In 1988, Novell changed its strategy to be "software focused, hardware-independent" and spun off most of its hardware business.

In 1984, Microsoft entered the network operating system market with MS-Net. However, in most performance tests, NetWare was twice as fast as the competing version of MS-Net. While NetWare began to dominate the market, MS-Net sold modestly. Microsoft perceived Novell's growing superiority in a strategic market as a potential threat. In 1986, they hired Darryl Ellis to build a Network Business Unit within Microsoft to focus specifically on the network market, and to compete head-to-head with Novell. Both companies were scrambling to develop an industry standard, hardware-independent network operating system.

Developing Software

The Traditional Process

The traditional industry approach to developing software was similar in many ways to other engineering projects. Engineers gathered with representatives from other parts of the company (sales, marketing, production, etc.) to decide on the basic attributes of their software product. Once the general concept was sketched out, detailed specifications, *specs,* were written. Programmers then wrote the computer *code* needed to make the computer do the intended job. Since the code was often very long—programs could have as many lines of code as there are names in the New York phone book—projects were divided into sections for various programmers to complete individually.

Some industry observers compared writing a program to building a skyscraper; many specialized people were needed. Organizing the efforts of many specialized but interdependent people to create a single complicated skyscraper was a classic project management problem. The plumbers, welders, electricians, stonemasons, and carpenters did separate jobs under the coordination of a construction manager, working from blueprints prepared by an architect.

Traditional Problems

Historically, skyscraper architects had been far more successful than most software developers, even profitable ones like Microsoft. While skyscrapers could be planned, budgeted, and scheduled with reasonable accuracy, software projects often were not. Software development was attempted by many companies. Banks, airlines, manufacturing firms, computer hardware makers, electronics and aerospace companies, utilities, and others saw the benefits of computers in their industries, and developed proprietary software for external and internal uses.

But roughly 30 percent of all software development projects ended up as *runaways*—programs that turned into "Frankenstein monsters," disrupting the company's normal business, gobbling extra money and manpower, delaying other projects, and eventually costing twice as much time and funding as originally planned. Consulting firms specializing in straightening out runaway projects did a big business. According to *Fortune* magazine, in 1989 the market for such services was estimated at over $11 billion, over ten times the revenue of Microsoft that year, and growing by 16 percent per year.[7]

Despite overall success with many of its products, Microsoft too had experienced difficulty developing some products. For example, OS/2 was released later than expected, and Word 3.0 for the Macintosh had contained a serious bug which caused Microsoft to issue a replacement version 3.01 shortly after introduction. However, while they sometimes experienced traditional problems, Microsoft's approach to developing software was not traditional.

---

[7] 9/25/89, p. 108.

EXHIBIT 5 **Typical Microsoft Project Milestones**

(somewhat simplified)

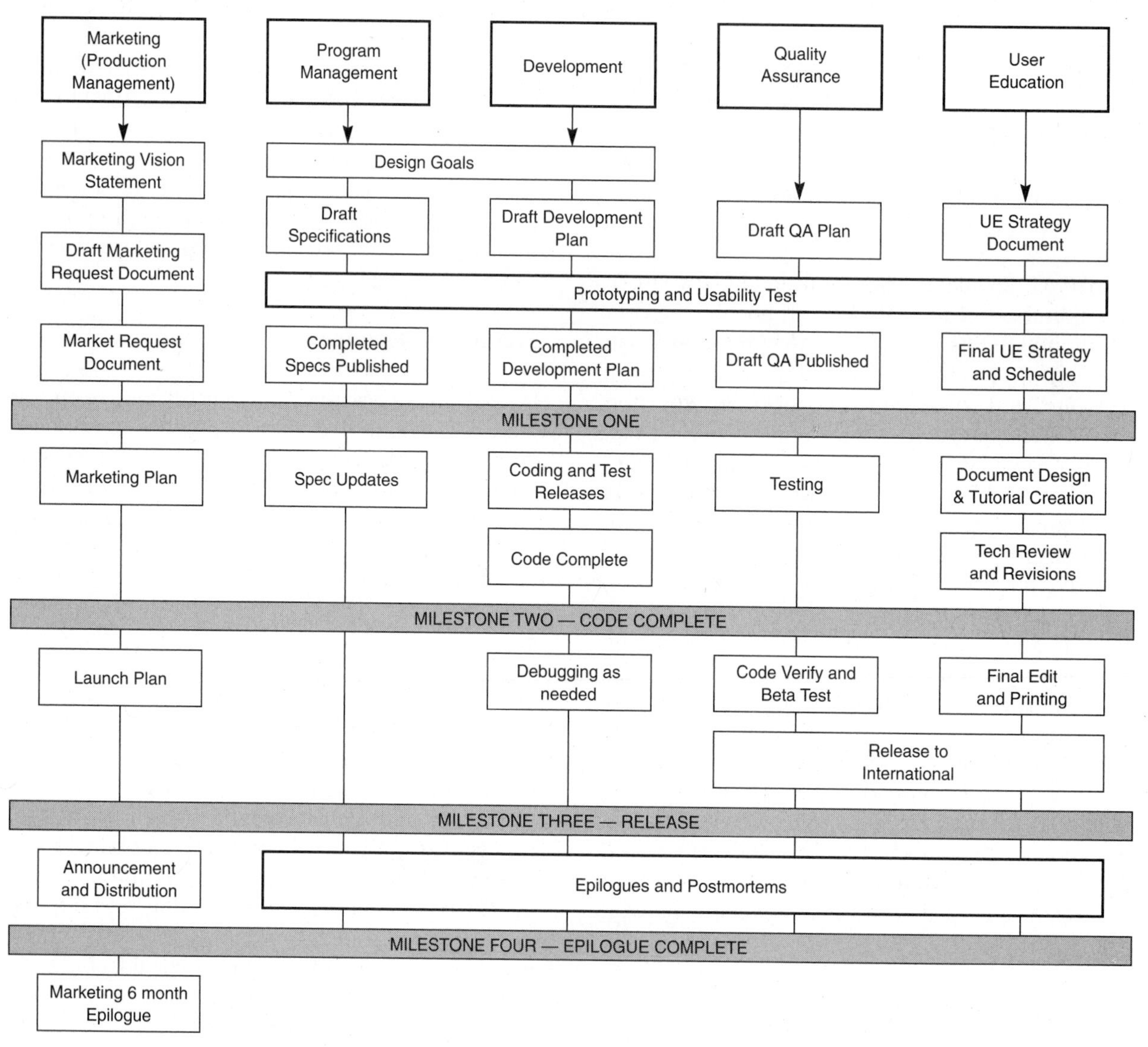

SOURCE: *Data Access Business Unit Methodology*, Feb. 1990; *Office Business Unit Guide*, Sept. 1989.

Microsoft's Development Process

Development

At Microsoft, a typical project involved the efforts of several teams working concurrently on different aspects of the new product. Generally, there were three development phases: *planning, development,* and *quality assurance*. The Data Access Business Unit (DABU) had a thirty page methodology guide, the most comprehensive *method* Microsoft had written down in fifteen years of developing software (see Exhibit 5). Several other Microsoft business units also had guidelines, all simpler, shorter, and less specific. The brevity of Microsoft's methodologies contrasted with methods used elsewhere in the industry, most of which were more detailed and far longer. For example, Anderson Consulting's popular Method/1, used for developing custom software, was thousands of pages long.

Microsoft's developers seemed to think little of methods—many had not seen the guidelines supposedly used by their own business units. Charts like Exhibit 5 were used as fallbacks, and as training for new programmers who wanted to learn about the parallel efforts of various teams. Christenson explained, "The main use of guides is to define terms, so that when I ask someone if their code is 'complete', they know exactly what I am asking."

Projects involved representatives from different functional areas. The program manager designed and modified the product specifications, and coordinated the teams' efforts. The product manager handled the creation and implementation of a marketing plan for the product. The development team wrote and rewrote the code, while user education produced the documentation and manuals. The test group took the product specifications and engineered a set of tests to verify that what the product specification said should happen actually did, and kept track of all the bugs.

The different groups used a form of *matrix organization,* with managers reporting along both functional lines (up the hierarchy) and project lines (across the hierarchy). Thus, the test manager for product X was responsible to *both* the business unit test manager *and* the product X team. Moreover, communications for project team members tended to be within their product, rather than functional, groups. Thus, the product X test manager tended to talk more with other members of the product X team than with other test managers. Communication, coordination, and liaison duties for the various teams fell to program managers, on the development side, and product managers, on the business side (see Exhibits 6A and 6B).

Developers did a *build* of the software, and then sent it to the testers as if delivering it to a customer. Testers ran tests and, when the tests failed, they wrote up a bug description of the newly found error. The bug report was entered into a database and prioritized according to severity criteria used by the developers. The development team then distributed debugging assignments. Typically, there was a new build every week, sometimes every day.

Throughout the project there were *code reviews,* during which one or more managers examined an individual programmer's work, and *milestones,* when the project as a whole was reviewed. Part of

EXHIBIT 6A Typical Software Development Team Communication

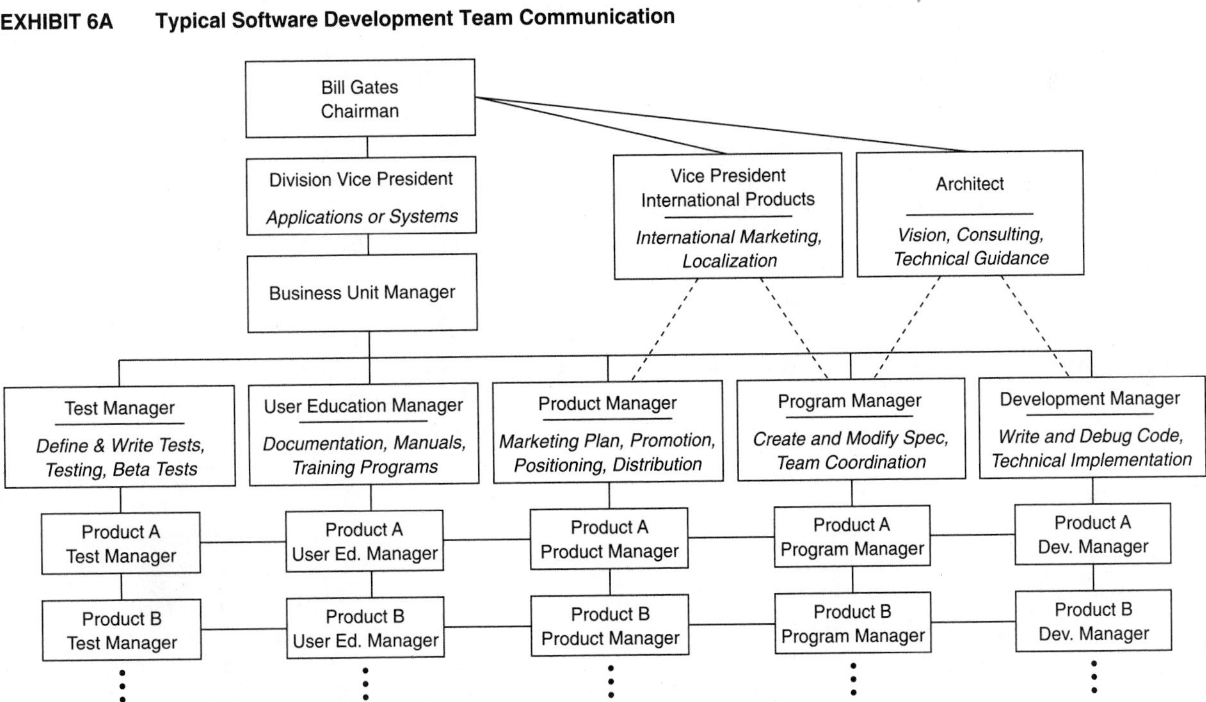

EXHIBIT 6B Typical Software Development Team Communication

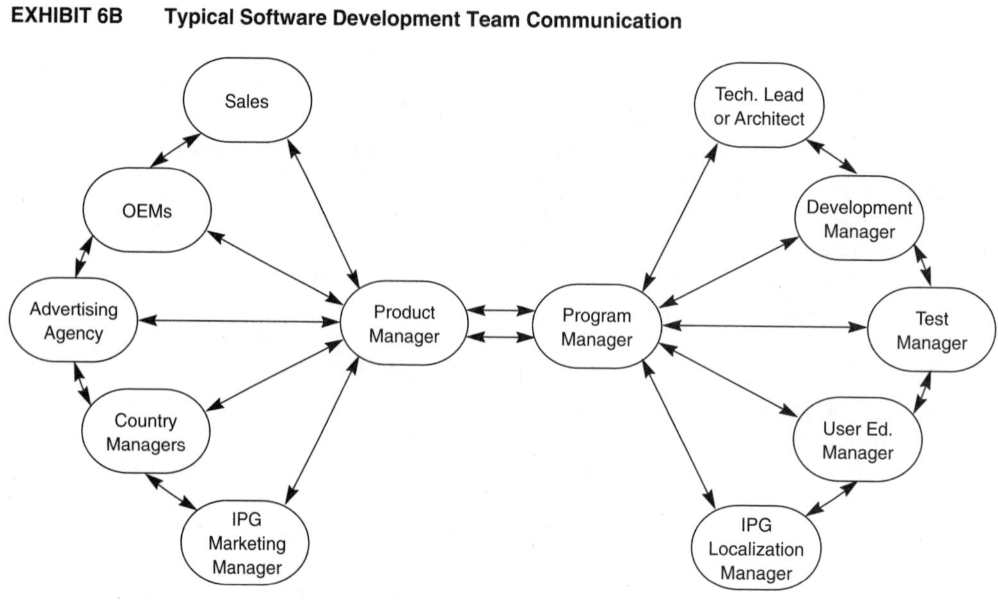

the initial planning for projects was the definition of milestone goals and criteria. At each milestone the managers had the option to change the direction of the project, or the schedule, as necessary in light of the progress of the various teams. Sometimes new features would be added to the specification along the way, as a clearer picture of the market needs and competition became available.

Development reached the *code complete* milestone by finishing all the features according to the product specifications. The only code written after that milestone was to fix software bugs. Once the test group had verified the code, it was released for *beta testing*. During beta testing it was given to actual customers on a trial basis to uncover any problems missed by the project teams. The final, beta-tested version was then released to the International Products Group, to be localized for foreign markets, and to Production where it was mass produced, bundled with manuals, and shipped to distributors, retailers, or OEMs.

Managing Projects

Views on the nuts and bolts of project management varied within Microsoft. The optimal project size, planning effort, design change flexibility, and project evaluation were openly debated issues.

Many projects had been completed by teams of fewer than 12 developers, but newer projects were becoming much larger; OS/2 had 50 and LAN Manager 2.0 had 70 developers. The trend toward larger programs meant a parallel trend in development teams. The Network Business Unit in particular felt this trend because networking systems tended to be more complicated than applications.

To plan activities, managers relied on the *functional spec*. The spec was the list of product features and sometimes included information on how they were to be implemented: a blueprint. "Up front work enhances stability later on," one programmer claimed. Some developers tried to understand the problem at hand and to plan ahead. "I usually start worrying when people say, 'Don't worry about it, it's trivial.' You end up writing code before you know if it will work," a development manager explained. However, in Christenson's opinion, project teams initially understood only 50 percent of the tasks finally needed to complete a project. He anticipated that unforeseen snags would occur and dealt with them as they came, rather than trying to eliminate them by overplanning at the start.

Design change flexibility was a key issue in project management. Bill Gates said:

> Large companies are very rigid; they freeze the specs. If, during the process, someone has a good idea we change plans to give them a chance to follow up on it. We allow for judgment to add or to drop features as the process unfolds.

This *plan-to-be-flexible* approach naturally complicated the jobs of those people actually running the projects. Christenson explained how he handled projects: "You have to get the content of the project decided first—a moving spec is no fun at all. Decide the content and get into the DCR (Design Change Request) process. During the DCR period, we try not to waffle; we either make changes, or we don't."

Project evaluation was different at Microsoft from most other companies. Managers regarded the choice of performance metrics as a subtle but potentially dangerous pitfall. For example, Microsoft kept almost no development cost data. Managers not only did not know how much their products cost to develop, they had little interest in finding out. "We prefer it this way. When we thought about it, we decided that project costing was not worthwhile, even though our competitors do it," Phelps stated. Christenson stressed, "The key numbers are not deadlines or costs, but total work, in man-months or lines of new code, and bug rates, meaning bugs found per week and bugs fixed per week." Another developer elaborated, "You have to pick your goals carefully in the software process. We ignore idealism. We don't make it perfect—we make it good."

Tools

Development tools and equipment were ubiquitous at Microsoft. On average, there were two computers per employee. Many employees' desks had both the latest version of Apple's Macintosh and a Compaq or IBM PC. Bill Gates explained, "People are never satisfied with the tools we have here, and that's good. They keep designing better test software, for example. We devote a large percentage of our resources to keeping people well equipped." One architect elaborated, "We don't bother justifying $15,000 computer purchases. Basically, we just put in a requisition. You have to be ordering a $100,000 system before someone asks you about it." NBU's testing labs had over 270 computers. Fiber optic networks linked the computers all over Microsoft's campus in Redmond, Washington.

Electronic mail, *e-mail,* expedited communication and created nearly universal access to anyone at Microsoft or its business partners. "E-mail is utterly essential to Microsoft. I get over a hundred messages a day. Also, it is very easy to include other people: you [copy] them right on the mail. If I'm discussing strategy with you, it is no cost to me to include five or ten other people in the discussion," said one architect. "It is not strictly hierarchical in the sense that anyone can send mail to Bill Gates. Having levels of management is necessary in a large organization so that you can get leverage in your management time. But if you make it a barrier to communication, it's a disaster." Its ability to use information from other computer sources, such as previously written documents or raw computer code, meant that e-mail was more useful at Microsoft than voice-mail or even telephones. One industry observer described Microsoft's e-mail system as: "The electronic equivalent of conversations in the halls."

Guidance

Bill Gates described his role in development, saying, "From my level, I worry about five key issues:

- Are project people taking enough of a long-term view in their vision of the products?
- Are they being pragmatic enough in their vision so that we'll be able to ship on a reasonable schedule?
- When and where does it make sense to share code between projects?
- Where might a competitor be likely to introduce a breakthrough product that might hurt our market share?
- What parameters should we adjust to gain market share against leading competitors?"

In addition to Bill Gates, six *architects* helped shape Microsoft's vision of the future. Gates used the term *architect* to describe those individuals who had attained Level 15, the highest rung on the software engineering ladder (see Exhibit 7). An architect was someone who could "consistently and independently design and produce world-class products." They were extremely skilled computer and software experts who served as technical resources for the company. They migrated through assignments, sometimes running whole departments, other times helping out as individual contributors on projects. In addition to the six official architects, several other top technical people also worked in architect-like roles, although not yet actually promoted to Level 15.

Microsoft's management was extremely competent technically. Gates himself wrote some of Microsoft's early software, and was an active and critical participant in code reviews. Darryl Ellis elaborated, "Unlike other companies, if you go up the

EXHIBIT 7 Technical Ladder (for Software Design Engineers)

Level 9	(Summer Intern): A person who is expected to learn the principles of software engineering on an internship basis.
Level 10	(New Hire): A person starting at Microsoft who is expected to learn the programming methods, conventions, practices and standards of the computer industry as they apply at our corporation. The person may be working under close supervision.
Level 11	A person who is familiar with corporate and industry practices and hence can work as independently as necessary and can "run with the ball." Proposed designs and approaches for review and agreement from peers and supervisor.
Level 12	A person who has some "wins" during his or her participation in all aspects of larger projects and therefore is expected to consistently render clear technical judgment and have a long-term view. This may require providing technical guidance to others.
Level 13	A champion who is expected to consider all external issues of a project and can ensure that they are handled correctly. This requires providing technical direction to others.
Level 14	(Lead Software Developer): A major technical resource to others in the company. Must be able to consistently make key decisions on the goals and structure of the project and to shape corporate practices.
Level 15	(Architect): A person who can consistently and independently design and produce world-class products.

(Note: There is a parallel ladder for Test Engineers.)

SOURCE: Microsoft internal documents.

Microsoft management ladder, you find people get more technically competent. That allows them to see the faults and merits of your ideas instantly. You can't B.S. the people two levels up around here; they're probably better at your job than you are."

Tension between technical vision and market demands guided the new product introduction process. Russ Siegelman, LAN 3.0's Product Manager explained, "In my case, development is dominated not by market realities but by people with vision, typically architects like my former boss, Darryl Ellis. Sometimes you get great but impossible visions and you have to inject some realism. But, that is tough because even our customers don't know what they will want. Product managers have to guess where the market will go, relying on gut instincts and occasional focus groups. Naturally, the product manager, with only fuzzy arguments, has a hard time changing a product's design and content." Although technical vision was particularly influential in the Systems Division, Phelps added, "We do lots of stuff just to please the market. In fact, LAN Manager 2.0 is almost entirely market-driven. Particularly when we get close to the release date, the product manager's marketing input is key."

Corporate Culture

Microsoft's culture reinforced a strong work ethic. Bill Gates and other senior managers frequently worked weekends. Every night the Microsoft parking lots stayed full past dinnertime. Staffers roamed the halls late at night sustained by enthusiasm and caffeine.[8] "Microsoft is intense but fun," claimed one developer.

Microsoft encouraged people to communicate openly, coordinate with others involved in related activities, and do whatever made sense to solve problems. "There was a party last night at Bill Gates' house for the summer interns. Bill sent e-mail out afterwards to various interns and the people who supervised them saying: 'Hey, I think there is more overlap in your groups' work than you suspect. Your summer interns seem to be doing identical things.' Now the summer interns have learned a good thing, that you should coordinate your efforts, and that the chairman of the company is interested enough in their working efficiently that he will do something about it."

Structured flexibility was a goal implicitly pursued by Microsoft's culture as a response to the complicated, intellectual task of programming, the mercurial marketplace, and the chronic short supply of good people. One architect described his view: "Any organization that is based on very fixed notions of job titles is not going to cope with the kinds of dynamic things in our market. Without

[8]Free coffee and soft drinks represented the third largest personnel-related expense, behind only salaries and health care.

good people you cannot do anything, but good people are not enough. You also have to have a good organization—otherwise, even the best people can be frustrated and brought to their knees by organizational tasks. Most of all the strategy and culture that you instill must say, 'Your common goal is more important than either people or organization'."

Challenges

At Microsoft, there were three perpetual challenges for the development teams: (1) the tension of balancing the feature set, time-to-market needs, and quality requirements, (2) the coevolution of Microsoft's products and its internal capabilities, and (3) the constant need to fine-tune management practices as products and development team size grew. Designing the development process to meet these challenges was important to create a sustainable advantage over the competition.

Features, Time, and Quality

Developing software could be a very profitable business, but there were three catches.

The first catch was providing the features, performance, and functionality needed to satisfy a wide customer base. Spending several million development dollars was fine if a developer could then sell a million copies, but disastrous if only a few hundred were sold. Unfortunately, in the rush to market, products were often "defeatured," reducing the breadth of their appeal. For LAN Manager, the task was complicated by the fact that only 5–10 percent of the users may want a given incremental feature.

The second catch was cycle time. If a firm was slow bringing a good product to market, a competitor, even an inferior one, could steal its potential customers and become the market standard. However, quality problems and complexity caused many products to be introduced much later than originally planned. McKinsey & Co., a management consulting firm, estimated for products with a five year life cycle that a six month delay could result in 33 percent less profit. Other new product researchers agreed: in high-tech industries, time-to-market was a critical element of success in the marketplace.

The third catch was product quality. Software bugs and errors in computer instructions could render a new software product useless. Hasty software design led to programs with more bugs, which took longer to fix, causing long delays and allowing competing products to jump ahead in the marketplace. Some companies sold bug-infested, unreliable software, later to recall or replace, often facing lawsuits and damaged reputations. Even minor bugs increased customer telephone support and maintenance efforts dramatically. Microsoft was certainly familiar with the costs associated with customer support. During a one-year period, Microsoft logged 1,984 customer support calls for LAN Manager 1.0 totaling 4,323 hours of direct labor and costing Microsoft an estimated $215 per call. Furthermore, one support specialist estimated that "buggy" products took twice as much telephone support and three to four times as much in total field support efforts as "non-buggy" ones, like LAN Manager 1.0. One industry adage warned: "The sweetness of meeting a release deadline never outlasts the bitter taste of a recall." Typical NBU projects had roughly two testers for every three developers. Full testing, combined with the trend towards larger programs with more features, caused many delays.

For example, one development project was planned to last 135 days, but took 420 days, due to complications in implementing new features and removing bugs. Development managers did not want to risk pushing the programmers into mistakes; one product released six weeks early with untested sections of code had crashed for 60 percent of the customers.

Furthermore, the fact that customer expectations and competing products were moving targets could make the last few months of development particularly fluid. Ellis explained why Microsoft put a premium on last minute flexibility: "It is in that time frame that you begin to get better intelligence, and realize the changes you should make. With LAN 1.0 we probably added 30 percent more functionality between the code complete and when we actually finished. Unfortunately, testing thrives on a frozen spec."

The tension among features, time, and quality was a fact of life. One architect stated, "It's cheaper to build the quality in at the start," while another architect, Ellis, argued: "It's amazing how many software battles you win just by being first to market." When asked how they resolve this tension, a third architect explained: "We decide on a case-by-case basis. There is a technological inflation rate in the market. You might get ahead of the inflation rate by selling your best technology now; you might get ahead by selling an even better technology six months from now. We estimate future conditions and decide which approach will put us farthest ahead, or least behind. It's the difference between long-term quality and short-term quality."

Co-evolution of Products and Capabilities

Improvements in hardware and software products reinforced one another. As chip makers produced faster, more powerful microprocessors, computer manufacturers built larger, more sophisticated microcomputers, and software developers designed more elaborate programs to take advantage of the hardware.

The mutually supportive evolution of chips, computers, and software experienced periodic breakthroughs (see Exhibit 8). For example, the introduction of the Intel 80386 microprocessor chip allowed IBM to introduce the 80386-based PS/2 personal computer. The PS/2 was more powerful than its predecessors and could run more sophisticated software, in part because of the 80386. Recognizing a potential market, programmers rushed to create programs to run on the PS/2. The rapid availability of software made the PS/2 more salable, which in turn created more demand for Intel's 80386.

EXHIBIT 8 Evolution in the Computer Industry

(major products by approximate introduction date)

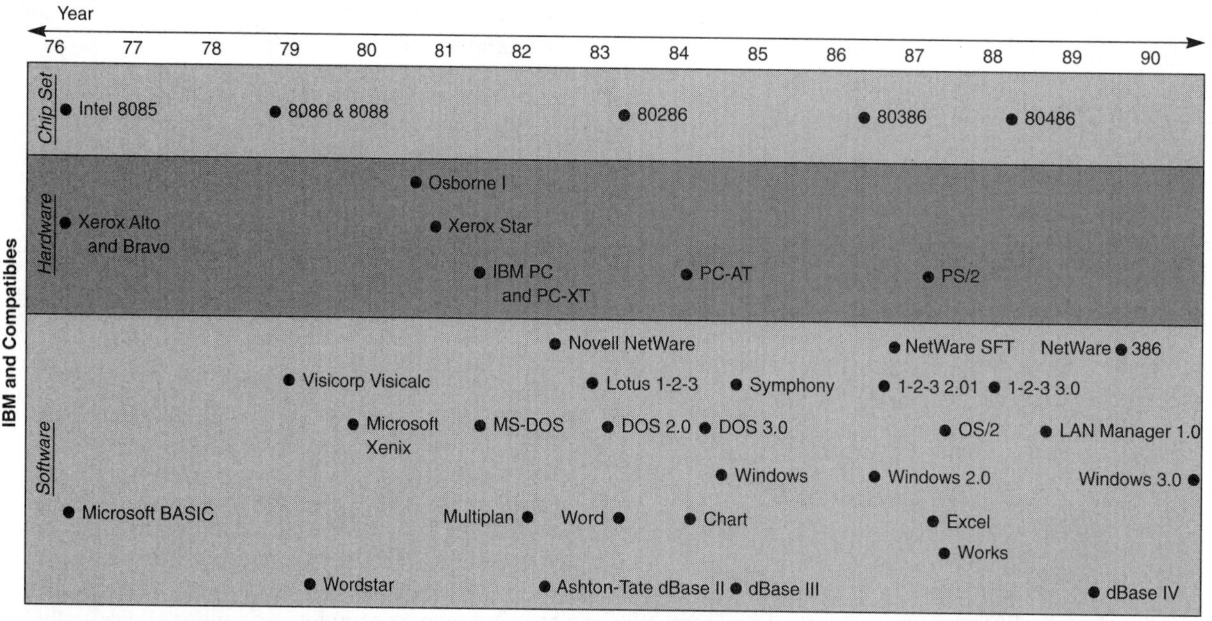

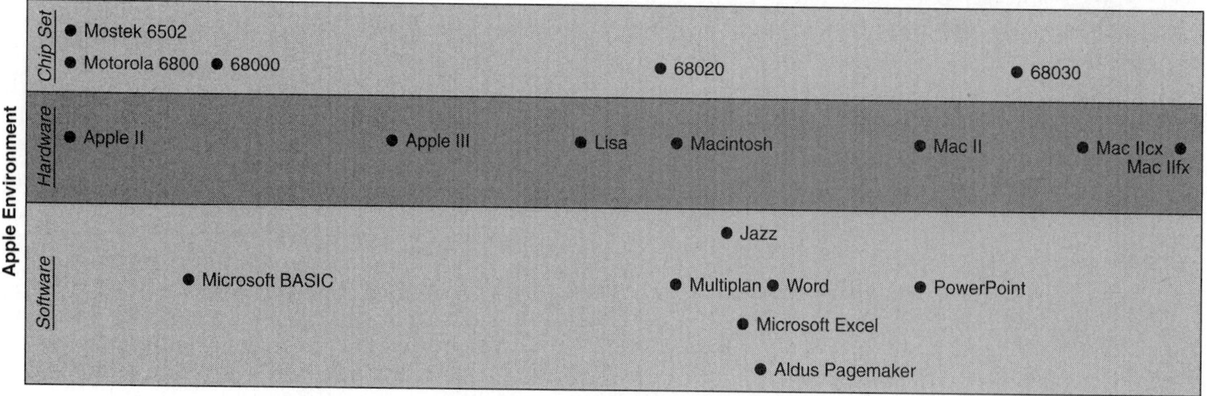

Envisioning future breakthroughs was critical. Within the Systems Division that housed the Network Business Unit, there were several cross-functional task forces focusing on different areas of technology. Each task force produced a page-long *vision statement* predicting developments and setting goals for Microsoft's product line.

Timing was important to the successful implementation of this vision. Lagging behind developments elsewhere in the industry meant lost opportunities and playing catch-up. Introducing products prematurely meant the software could end up unsupported by hardware developments, and therefore unattractive to the customer. Such had been the case for MacroMind Corporation's multimedia product, "Director," which was marketed with limited success prior to the availability of hardware with enough speed and memory to support its multimedia features. Ideally, the task forces would accurately anticipate technological breakthroughs and formulate a product strategy to keep Microsoft in step with developments elsewhere.

Microsoft faced the challenge of keeping the processes, organizations, tools, skill sets, personnel, and capabilities evolving at the same breakneck pace with which products progressed. Unfortunately, the formulation of product strategy based on evaluations of evolving technology often left the issue of process strategy unaddressed. With the expectation of periodic breakthroughs in products, Microsoft would also have to handle process changes. "No one process is going to work for everyone," said a systems developer. "We need to evolve the process to meet our needs." An architect echoed that thought: "New products need new ways of making them."

Changing Management

One trend in Microsoft's products was increasing size (see Exhibit 9). As hardware platforms became more powerful, elaborate software became possible. Earlier versions of software products were upgraded into more sophisticated, multi-featured programs. In contrast to earlier, smaller projects completed by teams of fewer than a dozen, LAN 2.0 required 70 developers and 40 testers (see Exhibit 10).

One architect described the problem: "Small teams are tremendously effective—communication is easy and the members develop a local language. But the programs are getting too big. That means you need more people to finish them on time, and that means more communication. Worse still, if the team size is *n*, the communications overhead is *n-squared.* As the teams grow, pretty soon you spend all your time in meetings, instead of writing code." Most veteran developers had experienced the phenomenon known as the *mythical man-month:*

EXHIBIT 9 Code Growth by Year and Product

(approximations, in 1,000 lines of code)

Year	BASIC	MS-DOS	Multiplan	PC-Word	Excel	OS/2	Word for Windows
1976	3						
1977	5						
1978	7						
1979	8						
1980	9						
1981	30	7					
1982	40	7	35				
1983	40	20	35	35			
1984	75	40	35	60			
1985	80	40	80	70			
1986	80	40	95	70			
1987	95	40	100	100	200	500	
1988	95	50	100	150	500	800	450

Each entry indicates how many thousands of lines of programming code were included in each Microsoft product.
For example, MS-DOS 1.0, released in 1981, included approximately 7000 lines of code. MS-DOS 2.0, released in 1983, included 20,000 lines.
"Word for Windows" was the next generation of Word designed to run on the Windows GUI system.

SOURCE: "*Software for Personal Computers,*" N. Myrvhold and W. Gates.

EXHIBIT 10 LAN Manager Labor Distribution

Number of programmers by type

Version	Developers		Testers	Total
	Regular	Experienced		
LAN Manager 2.0	62	8	40	110
LAN Manager 3.0	16	4	6	26
Subtotal	78	12	46	136

Developers are programmers assigned the duty of writing code. They are classified as regular versus experienced based on the length of their experience in writing similar code.
Testers are programmers who write code specifically to test code written by the developers.

adding more people to a project did not speed up development, and could often slow it down by diverting effort to training and coordination.[9]

This trend was troubling news for development managers at Microsoft. For example, Microsoft followed a policy of hiring primarily college graduates with little or no experience. Dozens of talented summer interns were brought in each year, and the best ones offered a chance to return as full employees after school. An architect explained this policy, "We hire new kids out of school because it's stable, predictable, and optimal for long-term growth. Programmers with vision can't be found and integrated easily, they have to be grown." While college graduates knew computer theory, they often had little understanding of practical project management. Unfortunately, the growing size of projects meant skilled project management was becoming more important to the success of a product.

Many people at Microsoft resisted the idea of importing professional management. Ellis described one of his experiences with such management elsewhere: "ROLM was a different kind of environment from Microsoft. It was death-by-management. The people managing ROLM in the mid-1980s didn't seem to have the technical breadth needed really to understand and make decisions with confidence." The VP for Advanced Technologies echoed the importance of technical people: "A large team, a large organization, a quality manual, great service, and a reputation for quality products—all those things are very, very important to making a good product. But you can have all those things and still not have something that makes people go 'WOW!'. The 'WOW!' part still comes from great technology, great design, and great code. The essence of the software development process is getting the right people and the right training and the right sort of technology environment."

Within NBU, however, project management was evolving into a specialty of its own. In particular, NBU had two program managers working on the LAN Manager line, Eric Savage and Alexis Stover. Eric wrote the initial specs, froze the spec, and started the *design change request* (DCR) process,[10] then moved on to the spec for the next product. Alexis Stover took over for Eric, ran the DCR process, identified problems, and managed the overall team effort. Alexis, LAN 2.0's program manager, clarified her role saying, "Eric finished LAN 2.0's spec before he joined the LAN 3.0 team. Now, I mostly handle the coordination and integration issues, and try to get LAN 2.0 out the door." She described herself as a *project manager,* differentiating between her role and that of Savage, whom she regarded as more focused on the software design activities of the program manager position. Elsewhere, *both* the spec writing *and* team coordination duties fell to the program manager, but NBU had found that Stover and Savage had worked successfully in separate, specialized roles through two generations of products.

The growing product line, project team size, and code length challenged Microsoft constantly to reconsider its management practices and policies, as the needs of development changed.

[9]F. P. Brooks, Jr., *The Mythical Man-Month: Essays on Software Engineering,* (Reading MA: Addison–Wesley Publishing, 1975).

[10]During the design change request process, the program manager froze the spec, but allowed other team members to make formal requests to change the spec. Such requests were proposed and defended at weekly DCR meetings. Typically, the managers would reach a consensus on if and how the spec should be changed.

EXHIBIT 11 Worldwide LAN System Software Market Projections

	1987	1988	1989	1990	1991	1992	1993	1994
Nodes† (in thousands)								
New Nodes†	1,247	2,311	3,286	4,773	4,712	5,535	5,408	6,467
Add-on Nodes‡	124	698	1,728	1,977	3,688	4,390	5,972	6,283
Total Nodes	1,371	3,009	5,014	6,750	8,400	9,925	11,380	12,750
Annual % increase		119.5%	66.6%	34.6%	24.4%	18.2%	14.7%	12.0%
Revenues (in thousands of dollars)								
New Licenses	$317	$495	$636	$ 913	$1,126	$1,292	$1,384	$1,450
Add-ons	$ 12	$ 70	$173	$ 198	$ 369	$ 439	$ 597	$ 628
Total Revenue	$329	$565	$809	$1,111	$1,495	$1,731	$1,981	$2,078
Annual % increase		71.7%	43.2%	37.3%	34.6%	15.8%	14.4%	4.9%

Figures are for worldwide market with all types of PC nodes on networks. Due to differences in hardware systems and market niche requirements, LAN Manager could not compete in the entire worldwide market. Observers estimated LAN Manager could reach 30–70% of the worldwide market, similar to NetWare. Dollar values represent final sales at retail.

†A "node" is equivalent to a single user or terminal supported by the network.
‡"Add-ons" are upgrades to existing networks to support more users.

SOURCE: International Data Corp., 1990.

LAN Manager

The Network Market

Microsoft's senior management believed networks would be increasingly important to their customers and they were willing to invest in the LAN Manager product line. The Director of Administration and Investor Relations pointed out: "NBU is ramping up people faster than revenues—technically, operating at a loss. But in this business, up-front costs are large, and when Bill Gates decides the market is going somewhere, he is willing to pay to be there when it arrives. We're investing $45 million *more* in networks over the next two years. It has to do with standard-setting, and it's *that* important."

Microsoft was experienced in operating systems and standard-setting, and had a strong reputation, a wide product line, and substantial financial resources (see Exhibit 3). However, Novell, its key competitor, had been in the LAN market longer and had developed upgraded products quicker and with more features. Novell also held an advantage in distribution through value-added resellers (VARs). VARs made their money by putting together integrated information systems for their clients. VARs were knowledgeable, but not locked in to a particular hardware type, and NetWare's compatibility made their work easier. Novell had relationships with 1,200 VARs. Microsoft traditionally sold products through retail outlets like Computerland, and to OEM hardware makers like IBM. While well-suited for other Microsoft products, these channels might be problematic for LAN Manager. Retail customers were wary of the complexity of network operating systems, and OEM hardware makers were reluctant to use software which was widely compatible with hardware from competitors.

The Network Business Unit

Eli Phelps, NBU's group product manager, was responsible for achieving NBU's marketing goals. He explained the motivation for NBU strategic efforts: "Tightly integrated applications over a network is where everyone is going to want to be. Minicomputers do that now, but with all the breakthroughs in chips, LANs are becoming cheaper and more flexible.[11] We want to make LAN Manager the standard network operating system." The importance of this market put the Phelps and Christenson team in a critical position at Microsoft (see Exhibit 11). Said Phelps, "We would like to double our market share in the next two and a half years. LAN 2.0

[11]Texas Instruments, a major electronics and chip maker, estimated that while software productivity, processing speed, number of computer users, and electronic communication would increase by tenfold during the 1990s, memory, video compression, network bandwidth, and data available over networks would increase by a hundredfold.

has innovative, neat features, but basically, it's a parity product. We won't have a technically dominant product until we introduce LAN 3.0, and that is assuming we get it soon enough."

Whether or not 3.0 could be complete in a two-year time frame was still unknown. Architecture alone for 3.0 had taken the better part of a year. Furthermore, there were disagreements between Darryl Ellis and Eric Savage, who had recently moved from the 2.0 team to become the 3.0 program manager. Savage, the 3.0 program manager who was charged with writing the 3.0 spec, said, "I don't have the feeling, studying the 3.0 architecture, that it is buildable. The 3.0 people are considering designs that universities and think-tanks haven't solved yet. Right now, my desire is to make the staff realize the practical needs of the market and to spec something that is possible." Both Phelps, the Group Product Manager, and Christenson appreciated Savage's reservations, while admiring the LAN 3.0 ambition. Said Phelps, "Even people who want desperately to kill 3.0 admit it is brilliant. If we could make it work, we would have an amazing product."

For the time being, shipping 2.0 was NBU's most pressing problem. Its OEM release date, originally intended for November of 1989, slipped to May of 1990, and even that seemed questionable. The job of Alex Stover, 2.0's program manager, had been complicated in November when Phelps, in an effort to augment his VAR and OEM strategies, finalized the decision to sell 2.0 through retail outlets in shrink-wrapped boxes. Stover explained that decision's impact: "Suddenly, trivial features became the most important. For example, OEMs care little about Microsoft's installers because they add their own, but with retail customers our installer better be user-friendly, bug-free, and compatible with everything. As a result, we have more testing, compatibility, and integration issues, so the schedule slips."

Christenson's Dilemmas

Jacob Christenson needed to make a series of decisions about how to manage the final phases of 2.0 while bringing 3.0 development on track.

Experience

That morning, Andy Held, one of Christenson's best developers, had asked to transfer to the 3.0 team, "because that is where the really interesting work is happening." Christenson could sympathize with a skilled programmer's desire to avoid the menial debugging cleanup of 2.0. He also knew that whatever gains might result from shifting a top programmer to 3.0 would only occur at a cost to 2.0. The 2.0 team had eight of Christenson's most experienced implementors (see Exhibit 10). Should he shift Held (and the others) to 3.0 now, or wait until May?

Headcount

About 70 developers were working on 2.0, and 20 on 3.0 (see Exhibit 10). By moving bodies one way or the other Christenson could change the completion dates for the projects, but moving manpower was complicated by a strong rivalry between the teams. The 2.0 team considered themselves the "moneymakers" of NBU, while regarding the 3.0 team as dreamers who had little idea what worked and had never actually built a product. Meanwhile, the 3.0 team viewed the 2.0 effort as an ugly but necessary stopgap measure put together by "seat-of-the-pants" programmers. Christenson had appreciated this rivalry as a source of motivation when running just the 2.0 team, but now that he was in charge of both, it was a headache. How much manpower should Christenson move? To which project? When?

Mindshare

One of Christenson's programmers had just sent him e-mail asking for advice on whether to spend Friday debugging a part of 2.0 (which was nominally his job) or to let it slip until the weekend and spend Friday attending a meeting to discuss the 3.0 spec. Christenson was acutely aware of this indirect drain on 2.0. Christenson's own double role of both Group Engineering Manager *and* 2.0 Development Manager worsened the problem. As 3.0 design work got down to the details, 2.0 people spent more and more *mindshare* solving 3.0 problems. What advice should he give?

Elegance vs. pragmatism

With 3.0 moving into the implementation phase under intense time-to-market pressure, Christenson worried that the 3.0 staff lacked either the will or the skill to crunch its design down to a deliverable, market-pleasing form. Since eight of the twelve experienced developers were working on 2.0 (see

Exhibit 10), Darryl Ellis had staffed 3.0 with new people who had not worked on 1.0 or 2.0. What steps could he take to balance pragmatism and timeliness with technical elegance?

Accelerating the process

To get 3.0 out the door in 1992 would require accelerating 3.0's pace. Of course, Novell would not be standing still during the next two years, so Christenson was re-examining management practices. Building a competitive advantage based on how Microsoft managed development, rather than just on the features of a particular product release, would be important to assaulting Novell's entrenched market position. For example, formalizing the project management role, although a controversial move away from the technical-generalist approach, might help Microsoft gain a development edge. Christenson sought creative, long-term improvements to NBU development both to accelerate 3.0 and to give NBU an advantage over Novell.

Jacob Christenson needed a plan that would overcome past problems, meet engineering's ongoing challenges, and provide Eli Phelps with the products he needed to accomplish Microsoft's goals.

Case IV–4
Plus Development Corporation (A) (Abridged)

Innovation starts with a belief; development transfers belief to evidence.
Joel Harrison

N. S. Langowitz and S. C. Wheelwright

In late September 1984 the Hardcard® product development project had been underway for nearly six months. The miniaturized 10-megabyte hard disk drive that plugged into the slot of an IBM PC was like no other product on the market. The Plus development team had been working with its Japanese manufacturing counterpart, Japan Electro-Mechanical Corporation (JEMCO), to get the product into the pipeline by June 1985. But the schedule had been gradually slipping as Plus and JEMCO engineers adjusted to each other's work style. Though there was daily progress, something would surely have to change to meet Hardcard's target product introduction date.

Background

The inspiration for what eventually became Hardcard came from customer conversations about what the ultimate low-cost disk drive subsystem would look like. James Patterson, president of Quantum Corporation—makers of hard disk drives—saw the solution as a "tin can surrounded by a few chips" that would be directly connected to the computer's motherboard (the main circuit board holding the microprocessor). This solution would necessitate integrating functions that were currently separate, such as the disk drive, the disk electronics, and the controller. And the disk drive would have to attach to the computer system without any cables.

Patterson shared this vision of the ultimate low-cost disk drive with Quantum's senior managers, but there were technical as well as marketing problems. On the technical side, the various hard disk drive components were too big to downsize a drive beyond the current size. Existing hard disk drives were generally larger than most personal computers. Also, the supporting electronics, in the form of integrated circuits, were not integrated enough to allow them to fit into a small space. (See Exhibit 1 for a description of hard disk drives and how they work.)

On the marketing side, there were no clear standards for how small to shrink the disk drive and controller for the personal computer market. Since any downsizing would take many months and millions of dollars, it was very important that the resulting product fit the standards that were beginning to emerge.

Quantum's strategy to date had been to stay out of the personal computer market, which it saw as highly volatile, and focus instead on providing hard disk storage to the minicomputer and technical workstation segments of the computer market. This market segment had generally accepted standards

EXHIBIT 1 How Disk Drives Work

A mass storage system, commonly called a disk drive, is comprised of three major elements: the disk, the disk drive, and the electronic controller. The combination of the disk and the disk drive is sometimes called the head disk assembly (HDA). The disk, also referred to as the "media," is where data are stored through the use of magnetics. In small capacity systems, two types of media are generally in use. Fixed, or rigid, media is a metal platter coated with a magnetic-sensitive coating. Floppy media is a plastic or mylar platter coated with magnetic-sensitive material. Data are stored in concentric rings on the disks. Hard disk drives use fixed media while "floppy" drives use floppy media.

The disk drive element has several subcomponents, including a magnetic head (containing an electromagnet), an actuator, an optical encoder, and a servo arm. The head serves to "read" or "write" data from or onto the media. "Writing" occurs when electric current passes through the head's electromagnet while the head is positioned above the spinning disk. A magnetic field is produced that orients the magnetic particles on the disk in a particular direction. In "reading," the head senses the magnetic orientation of the particles on the media and translates that pattern back into electric signals representing the data. The actuator controls the speed at which the head can "read" or "write," while the servo arm positions the heads in the appropriate position over the disk. The optical encoder serves to convert digital signals received from the computer through the electronic controller into analog signals that direct the servo arm and head. The disk drive also has a motor that rotates the disk, as well as a metal casting that holds the head disk assembly that serves as a base for the entire disk drive package.

The electronic controller functions as an intelligent interface between the head disk assembly and the computer. It interprets signals, defines data, responds to "seek" commands from the computer, and transmits data between the disk drive and the computer. The controller's electronics, a combination of integrated circuits, metal tracing (equivalent to wires), and discrete electronic components, are mounted on a printed circuit board, thus connecting all the electronic parts into a functional unit.

for size and electrical interface, and Quantum had already established a successful niche for itself.

By 1983, the personal computer market was already undergoing rapid change. Significant was IBM's introduction of the IBM PC in 1981, followed by the IBM PC-XT in 1983, which added to the PC an important feature—an internal hard disk. The addition of the PC-XT to IBM's personal computer line established the Winchester 5 1/4-inch hard disk drive as a standard technology for personal computers. The PC-XT had a 10-megabyte hard disk; an upgrade, scheduled for early in 1986, would have a 20-megabyte hard disk.

It was possible to add an existing hard disk drive to the original IBM PC, but the installation of the disk drive, the controller, the cabling, and the electronic switch settings required technical knowledge and hours of time. Both the IBM PC and PC-XT had three free "expansion slots" sized to accommodate plug-in cards, for example, to add memory or to provide communications capability by means of a modem.

IBM's entry into the personal computer segment created volume demand for personal computers and their standard components. Component technology—including electronics, integrated circuits, and peripherals—advanced at a rapid pace. One day in late 1983, when Quantum's manager of new product development opened up the case of an IBM XT, he suddenly recognized the feasibility of Patterson's idea. Joel Harrison's eyes followed the cable as it ran from the disk drive plug-in controller card to the separate hard disk drive at the front of the machine, and he realized that it didn't have to be that way. "Why couldn't the controller and the drive reside on a *single plug-in card?*" he wondered. Following up on the idea, Jim Patterson asked Stephen Berkley, then marketing vice president at Quantum, to put together a business plan for the development of a hard disk on a plug-in card for the personal computer marketplace.

In November 1983, four managers from Quantum started Plus Development Corporation, with Quantum owning 80 percent of the new venture. Berkley became president of Plus; Joel Harrison, vice president of engineering; Dave Brown, executive vice president of operations; and Dale Hiatt, vice president of manufacturing and quality. (At Quantum, Brown and Hiatt had been vice president of engineering and vice president of manufacturing, respectively.) The hard-disk-on-a-card design, which ultimately became known as Hardcard, emerged as the most promising option of the various product possibilities considered by the Plus team during its original business planning. It was to be a 10-megabyte hard disk drive integrated onto a controller card that would slide into a single IBM PC card slot. The design would radically simplify the process of installing a Winchester disk drive into a personal computer, reducing the time required from hours to minutes. The goal was to have the Hardcard provide hard disk capability identical to that of an IBM PC-XT. Dale Hiatt said, "That is our focus. We live and die that focus."

The Microcomputer Mass Storage Market

The largest group of customers for hard disk drives in late 1983 was microcomputer producers such as IBM, Apple, and Hewlett-Packard. These original equipment manufacturers (OEMs) integrated disk drives, made by third-party producers such as Tandon, Seagate, or Shugart, into their own computer systems and then offered the entire package—perhaps computer system unit, monitor, and hard disk drive—for sale to end users. In 1983 OEMs purchased approximately 830,000 internal hard disk drives with up to 30 megabyte capacity. The price for these hard disks ranged from $500 to $650. Substantial markups of three to four times the OEM price occurred in the distribution channel until, for example, the retail price that the end-user customer paid for a 10-megabyte hard disk as part of a system might be $2,400. Two things seemed likely to affect the price to the end user. First, the high distribution channel margins provided incentive to disk drive manufacturers to offer their products directly to end users. Second, learning curves of 65 to 70 percent were common in disk drive manufacturing. Existing disk drive products had experienced an average price erosion of 20 to 40 percent per year. Plus planned to have the 10-megabyte Hardcard retail for $895 in late 1985.

As personal computers began to proliferate, retail demand developed for add-on hard disk drives. Add-on sales were made through retail computer stores, such as Computerland or Businessland, to individuals and small businesses who already owned personal computers and wanted to expand their mass storage capability. Plus hoped to target this market niche. Hardcard would be aimed at customers who wanted to convert their existing IBM or IBM-compatible PCs into XTs. (Exhibit 2 shows the growth of the U.S.-installed base of IBM and IBM-compatible PCs from 1981 to 1984, and projection of the 1985 installed base of rigid [or hard] disks and PCs.)

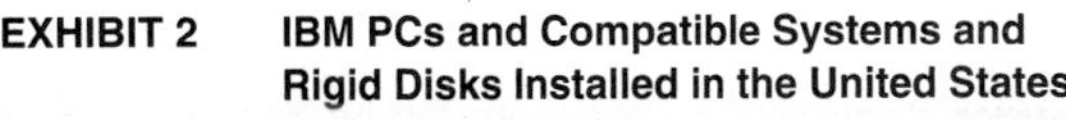

EXHIBIT 2 IBM PCs and Compatible Systems and Rigid Disks Installed in the United States

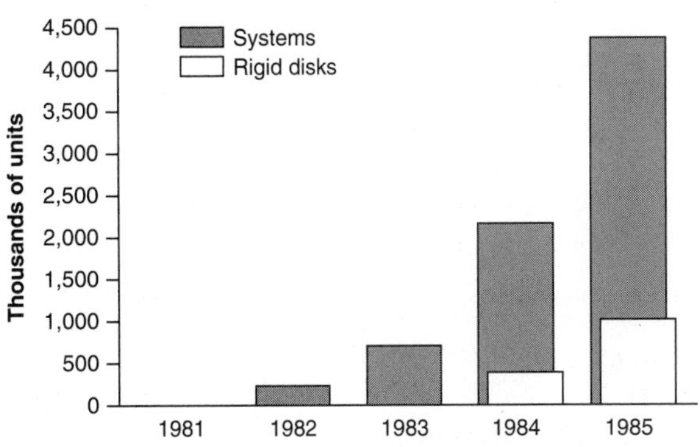

SOURCE: InfoCorp, *Segment Update: Mass Storage*, July 12, 1985.

The Development of Hardcard

Armed with their business plan, the four Plus managers began to consider the details of how to manufacture Hardcard. In early 1984, they traveled to Japan, primarily to source components for heads, disks, and motors. The Plus managers saw computers as a maturing business and foresaw a future similar to that of watches, calculators, and floppy disk drives—all industries that Japanese manufacturers had come to dominate. Plus expected that disk drives might soon go the same route.

As the Plus managers visited with Japanese manufacturers and suppliers, they found two surprises. First, electronics companies in the videotape recorder business, such as Sony, JVC, and Sanyo, were expecting and fearing saturation in the video market. This fear was heightened by the recent entry of Korean manufacturers such as Samsung into the video business. Plus found that these Japanese electronics companies were rushing to get into the computer market. The Plus managers also discovered that the companies making electronics components, such as Kyocera, NEC, and Toshiba, sought the opportunity to forward integrate into computer products. These two findings made the new managers ask themselves, "How are we going to compete with these guys?" since it seemed clear they might jump into the computer products market soon.

The Japanese tour heightened Plus' awareness that the new company had a particular need to fill. Because Hardcard would be a retail distribution product, the Plus managers believed they would need an instant ramp-up to volume production. They wanted to be able to "flick a switch" and have production reach 5,000 to 10,000 units per month, with high quality. Many of the Japanese companies they visited were capable of such a high-volume ramp, whereas Quantum, for example, took many months from product launch to achieve that output rate. The Plus managers feared that any U.S. operation they set up would be unable to achieve instant ramp-up; they knew the retail market would not allow them years to become as good as the Japanese manufacturers they had visited.

Choosing a Manufacturer

During their trip to Japan, it seemed clear to the four Plus managers that a tie-up with a Japanese company could offer Plus quality manufacturing and the achievement of instant ramp-up. Because of close relationships that often existed between Japanese manufacturers and their suppliers, a Japanese connection might also allow Plus more flexibility for future product changes. On the downside, a Japanese tie-up meant a high investment of senior management time as well as potential difficulties stemming from cultural differences.

Toward the end of their trip, the Plus managers met the senior management at JEMCO and toured its manufacturing facilities. A subsidiary of Japan Trading Corporation, JEMCO was solely a manufacturing company, receiving most of its product designs from Japan Trading's central laboratories and manufacturing for private label or for Japan Trading. JEMCO had no marketing function of its own. The company had been tremendously successful in recent years; the Plus managers talked with many Japanese executives who considered JEMCO to be the premier electromechanical manufacturer in Japan. At JEMCO's videocassette recorder plant, a new VCR rolled off the production line every few seconds. Dave Brown's reaction, after touring the JEMCO factory, was similar to the other Plus managers': "You feel insignificant. Their [JEMCO's] manufacturing expertise is beyond imagination; I've never seen anything like it in my life." Not only did JEMCO stand out in its manufacturing excellence, but also the Plus managers were confident that they could work well with JEMCO's executives, whose management style featured teamwork and open communication. On the other side, JEMCO had an incentive to work with Plus. It was interested in the opportunity to broaden its product offerings and manufacturing expertise by working with designs from companies other than Japan Trading.

The Plus managers left Japan quite excited about JEMCO. Nonetheless, they "had some gut-wrenching discussions," according to Brown, at home about whether to team up with a Japanese company. While the business reasons seemed clear, on an emotional level Plus managers were concerned about being unpatriotic and whether they were "copping out" on American manufacturers. In the end, Brown argued that they had to acknowledge JEMCO's manufacturing expertise. Berkley and Hiatt agreed. The process was set in motion to team up with JEMCO. Plus' expectation was that it would supply design and marketing expertise while JEMCO supplied manufacturing expertise.

Product Design Philosophy and Technical Choices

From the time Joel Harrison made his initial observation that a hard disk on a card might be possible, he had been tinkering with the design. The Hardcard would be Harrison's fifth hard disk drive in the last 10 years. Of the five designs to which he had contributed, only two had the same size disk. Harrison thoroughly understood hard drive technology and was well versed in the design adjustments required to build for a particular disk size. Yet it would surely be a challenge to miniaturize a drive to 3 1/2 inches for Hardcard. Further, Hardcard was Harrison's first drive for the retail market. Plus hoped to introduce Hardcard in time for Christmas 1985; this seemed critical to retail success not only because of the home market, but also because much of the business market tended to spend late in the year to use up budgeted funds. In addition, Quantum was anxious to have Plus contribute financially during calendar 1985.

Harrison recognized the vast difference between the retail and OEM disk drive markets. OEM customers frequently asked for product changes; they adapted to initial bugs and often demanded changes in features or functionality. In fact, the manufacturers came to rely on feedback from the field as they finalized a product's design. But in the retail world, customers were totally unforgiving. A manufacturer had only one chance to provide the right product. The product concept for Hardcard, Harrison said, was therefore kept simple: "convert a PC into an XT on a single board." This simple concept made it easier to determine whether a design change contributed to the goal and avoided the "creeping definitionalism" that Harrison had seen complicate and slow down other projects.

In addition to the well-defined product concept, the Hardcard project was to involve only proven technologies and proven processes. This was similar to the approach taken at Quantum. Harrison believed that what he called "focused innovation" was required for success. In new product development, Harrison maintained that the number of items the design team had never done before should be limited to five. Harrison commented: "This is an art. It's not the only way to do it."

Hardcard design involved two major subassemblies, the HDA (head/disk assembly) and the printed circuit (controller) board. (Exhibit 3 shows the final Hardcard design.) The mechanical engineers worked on the HDA, and the electrical/digital engineers were mainly responsible for the controller board. In January, the first mock-up was a "show-and-tell piece." It was a block of aluminum with a disk that didn't even spin. From that point onward, Hardcard developers progressed from prototyping the mechanicals in metal and the electronics on printed circuit boards to creating working parts and designing the electronic circuitry into custom chips.

EXHIBIT 3 The 10 Megabyte Hardcard

A. Hardcard—Shown with Exposed Head Disk Assembly

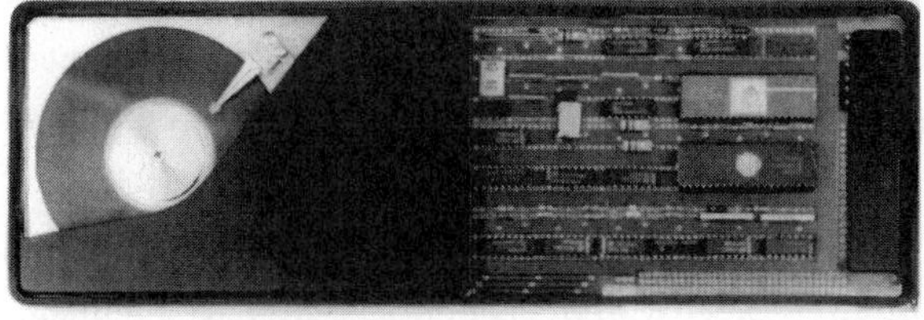

B. The Hardcard Being Inserted into a PC Expansion Slot

SOURCE: Plus Development Corporation.

The Problem of Cultural Differences

Although the business agreement with JEMCO was not finalized until August 1984, a development schedule in early spring identified June 1985 as a target date for commercial production. JEMCO engineers, under the leadership of Toshihiro Utamoro, came to Plus in April 1984 to work with the 20 Plus engineers who were already on the project. The Plus engineers included mechanical, analog, and digital design engineers, as well as quality engineers. The JEMCO engineers, who were without their families, worked a long day at Plus, coming in at 8:15 A.M. and working until 8:00 P.M. They then went to English class from 8:00 until 11:00 P.M. Plus engineers generally worked similar hours (except no English classes), although if an individual engineer was finishing a particular piece of the project, he or she would work even longer. None of the Plus engineers spoke Japanese. A translator was on hand virtually every day. The Plus engineers were responsible for product design while the JEMCO engineers addressed manufacturability.

The JEMCO engineers were assigned to remain at Plus until the project was completed. There was also a Japan-based JEMCO manufacturing group that was an integral part of the design team. Phone calls went back and forth: the phone bill was equal to the travel bill. On the phone JEMCO could veto a design, and compromise solutions often evolved as a result of these calls. JEMCO was especially influential regarding the manufacturability of the mechanical HDA subassembly. Digital design was an area in which JEMCO engineers had less experience. Most JEMCO products until this time had been analog-based audiovisual consumer products.

During the initial period when engineers from both companies were learning to cooperate with each other, Plus held special classes so that the JEMCO engineers could learn about disk drive technology and applicable digital design theory. The styles of the two groups were very different. The JEMCO engineers could not describe in abstract terms how to design Hardcard for manufacturability; they preferred to see prototypes and then give concrete suggestions of what to change. The Plus engineers, on the other hand, tended to be contemplative before drawing—let alone prototyping. Once Plus learned that the JEMCO engineers were excellent at turning prototypes around quickly, Plus engineers began using more prototypes. The use of prototypes also helped communication. The JEMCO engineers were able to point to a part of the design to identify a problem, rather than having to describe the problem in English.

Achieving Manufacturability

Plus and JEMCO engineers spent the first three months almost entirely in design meetings. The JEMCO motto was "total cost down" and its target production yield was 99 percent. At first the Plus engineers thought they were wasting their time with all these meetings. They couldn't understand why the JEMCO engineers kept demanding so many details of how the design would work. The JEMCO engineers wanted to have specifications for everything—exactly how high, thick, or wide a piece would be. For the JEMCO engineers, "less than 10 mm" was not an acceptable specification. The Plus engineers were forced to specify exactly—"9.8 mm high." Before starting production, JEMCO engineers wanted to know for sure that the product could be made easily. The Plus engineers had difficulty adapting to JEMCO's approach. Bill Moon, the project's manager of mechanical engineering, commented, "They live by specifications. The idea is that if every part meets specs, then every product assembled from those parts will work." Gradually the Plus engineers began to respect that different approach.

Frequently the JEMCO engineers called for design changes to enhance manufacturability, even if there was no great cost savings. For example, the actuator latch on the disk drive was redesigned so that it would lie against the metal curve of the disk inset in its relaxed position, allowing the disk to be easily inserted (or taken out for service). The new design saved only two yen (approximately one penny) in labor cost per unit, but it made the product more "manufacturable."

JEMCO engineers also called for the redesign of a metal plate guarding the disk drive. The original part was to be screwed into place during manufacture. JEMCO wanted each part to snap into place, so that the production worker would not have to use any judgment in aligning the part. The JEMCO engineers did not like screws, and they maintained that glue was too hard to control. This redesign required two months.

Process Philosophy and Design

JEMCO engineers designed the Hardcard production process during product design; they believed that the design of product parts and the design of the equipment that assembled those parts were inextricable. Plus senior managers had described JEMCO's automated VCR line, which they had seen in Japan, to the Plus engineers, who then assumed that JEMCO would automate Hardcard production and therefore require simple parts. But JEMCO did not equate automation with simplicity. Gradually, Plus managers realized that JEMCO did not care whether the Hardcard had simple parts; what mattered was whether the parts would meet specifications and could be *made* simply, even if a complicated tool was required. JEMCO wanted a reliable process.

JEMCO's manufacturing philosophy also called for testing at every step of the production process. In a typical U.S. plant the head arm assembly might be inserted, then the drive motor mounted, with a test done afterward. If the head arm assembly failed in test, the drive motor would have to be removed in order to fix the head arm assembly. JEMCO preferred a different assembly sequence. The head arm assembly would be inserted and tested; if the head arm assembly passed, the drive motor could then be inserted and tested. The point was to eliminate problems at each step, so that "quality of the yield on the line is the quality in the field."

Bill Moon summed up the essence of JEMCO's manufacturing excellence: "One, prove the dimensions and tolerances that are required on each part up front. Two, create appropriate assembly tools. And three, check at every step of the process." It took some time for the Plus engineers to understand all this. Plus also learned that JEMCO's approach to manufacturing had important implications not only for product development but also for vendor relations.

Vendor Management and the Single-Source Philosophy

Plus managers were committed to the ideal of Plus as a small and entrepreneurial company, excellent at design and marketing, and relying heavily on vendors for manufacturing expertise. Plus looked at vendors in this way: "Do we need to put in resources? Maybe we don't—we can rely on their [an outside company's] work." Plus wanted to focus on adding value in its own areas of expertise and to avoid trying to be the expert in everything. This implied that relationships with vendors were of critical importance.

U.S. suppliers were selected by a team that included the Plus manager most directly involved; John Aubuchon, materials manager; Dale Hiatt, vice president of manufacturing; and Bob Lyells, manager of quality and reliability. The criteria for source evaluation were: (1) trust—the potential for a good working relationship, (2) quality/monitoring, (3) the supplier's process philosophy, (4) delivery capability and timing, (5) aggressive pricing, and (6) the use of technology to back up the supplier's claims. Components were characterized as critical if the manufacturer's sudden disappearance or failure would be a major problem, or if the particular design had never been done before—some of the ICs, for instance. Noncritical components were standard off-the-shelf parts. Plus visited and evaluated U.S. suppliers of both critical and noncritical components. Plus selected Japanese suppliers of critical components on JEMCO's recommendation and relied on JEMCO's existing relationships for off-the-shelf parts sourced from Japan. Components such as the motor, off-the-shelf chips, and heads were sourced in Japan, while others, such as the media and custom-integrated circuits, were sourced in the United States.

Plus wanted vendors that were proven companies, with mature processes using proven technologies, an approach that JEMCO supported fully. John Aubuchon said, "Our objective was total cost down, without sacrificing the quality." Plus selected a single source for all critical items, following the theory that the best partnerships formed that way. They stressed the difference between a *single* source—in which case other companies could make a part, if necessary, and a *sole* source—where that source was the only supplier capable of making a part. By avoiding sole sources, Plus kept away from exclusive technologies, which fit with its focus on proven technologies.

As part of the single-source philosophy, Plus managers looked at a vendor's process closely, tried to learn it from beginning to end, and tried to understand whether the vendor had its process in control or if Plus could help it gain better control. Hiatt recalled, we "visited vendors of our vendors, three levels down" because you "can't afford somebody else's screw-up." They did their best to make sure that the vendors and JEMCO conducted up-front feasibility tests of all potential "show stoppers." On critical components Plus started by presenting the vendor with a budget: specifying a target price that might be 20 to 30 percent below the street price. Plus gave these target prices to all potential vendors, to someone as high up in the company as possible. At the same time that Plus presented its budget, it promised to single source the part—it shared its business plan without quite divulging the product—and offered to help the vendor in any way possible. (The only vendor Plus told about the whole product up front was the Japanese motor vendor; Plus needed it to understand the Hardcard design in order to determine whether the motor it had designed was possible.) Plus tried to avoid intense nose-to-nose negotiations with vendors, which Hiatt described as "demeaning to everyone." The emphasis in negotiations was to understand the vendor's process, and then either change the vendor's component or Hardcard, in order for the vendor to make money on the part.

Vendors often gasped when they saw the budgeted prices. Plus would then ask them what Plus could do to help them meet the spec and price. For example, the Hardcard had been designed to take a "wide distribution" of components—component tolerance specifications were relatively loose. Vendors would specify the range typical of "standard" output, and Plus would design to use 90 percent of it. (Accepting a wider distribution enhanced the vendor's yield so that, even at Plus' low price, the vendor could be profitable.) For example, Plus was somewhat tolerant of errors on hard disk media because it could map those errors and mark them as bad, so that Hardcard would be perceived as error-free. Any bad spots on the media would be transparent to the customer.

Market Introduction: Push Ahead or Reschedule?

By September 1984, Hardcard development was well on its way, but a variety of events had caused the projected first factory shipment date to slip from its original June 1985 goal. See Exhibit 4 for the original rough-cut engineering development schedule and Exhibit 5 for the more detailed project schedule as of late September 1984 showing work completed

EXHIBIT 4 Original Plus Project Schedule

Task	Start Date	End Date
Visit Japan	Dec. 3, 1983	Dec. 21, 1983
Hire Staff	Jan. 3, 1984	July 30, 1984
Work on Design	Jan. 4, 1984	Jan. 31, 1984
Produce Product Specs	Feb. 1, 1984	May 20, 1984
Create Mock-up	March 4, 1984	March 15, 1984
Choose Key Technologies	March 11, 1984	March 29, 1984
Select Vendors	March 4, 1984	March 29, 1984
Manufacturing Design Review	April 15, 1984	July 12, 1984
Develop Test Equipment	May 2, 1984	Aug. 2, 1984
Develop Breadboard	April 1, 1984	Sept. 19, 1984
Develop "Fatcards"	May 21, 1984	Aug. 21, 1984
Develop Software	June 26, 1984	Jan. 23, 1985
DVT	Aug. 22, 1984	Jan. 29, 1985
Develop VLSI	Aug. 22, 1984	Jan. 29, 1985
Develop HDA	April 1, 1984	Sept. 19, 1984
Motor Development	March 4, 1984	April 18, 1985
Acquire Tooling	Sept. 12, 1984	Dec. 16, 1984
Build 1st Functional Prototype	Jan. 31, 1985	Feb. 6, 1985
Design and Build 2nd Prototype	Feb. 7, 1985	May 2, 1985
Transfer Design to Factory	Feb. 7, 1985	May 9, 1985
Maturity Testing	March 3, 1985	March 28, 1985
Beta Testing and Redesign	March 31, 1985	May 20, 1985
Marketing Functions	March 4, 1984	March 13, 1985
Approve Final Design	May 21, 1985	May 28, 1985
Begin Production	May 28, 1985	

and work in progress; Exhibit 6 contains excerpts from Joel Harrison's July and August status reports.

Harrison called a meeting of the key managers. He identified two options: They could schedule a later introduction date, or they could push ahead and do a mop-up job once the product was in the market. "OK, look," said Harrison, "you've all seen my status reports. We've fallen behind. Making June is impossible unless we cut some corners; if we do, maybe we could still do it. I consider myself pretty good at schedule compression, but I've looked at every way I can imagine to resequence, regroup, and double up—even sounding out JEMCO on steps they might compress—and it's just not possible without skipping some things and cutting a few corners."

"Yeah, well you know why we're behind, Joel," Bill Moon responded. "My guys have been in constant meetings with the JEMCO folks, and I don't need to tell you how many redesigns we've done for them. The amount of detail they want is driving us crazy. In fact one reason we have so many staffing positions open is that all this interaction with JEMCO has taken a lot of time and attention that had to come from somewhere."

Dale Hiatt spoke: "Now wait a minute. Isn't some of that detail important to getting this thing manufactured right? That's why we signed them up, isn't it? We're going to need an instant ramp. So, if it's detail they need, we'd better make sure we give it to them."

"So you're saying we should reschedule, Dale?" asked Harrison.

"If that's what it'll take, I guess so. Yes," Hiatt answered. "But we need to hit the Christmas market. If there's a way to get it done on target, we need to think hard about it. We're riding on this one product, and as much as 40 percent of our business will depend on getting this product out there by the Christmas season."

"That's exactly it. We'd better get something out there soon," added Hank Chesbrough, product marketing manager. "This is going to be a terrific product. Just think of all those people waiting to upgrade their PCs. And we can be the ones to let them do it pain-free. Joel's got a staffing search on already. Why don't we just hire a few extra engineers? We're bound to recoup the $40K per hire if we hit the market right."

EXHIBIT 5 Detailed Plus Project Schedule—September 1984

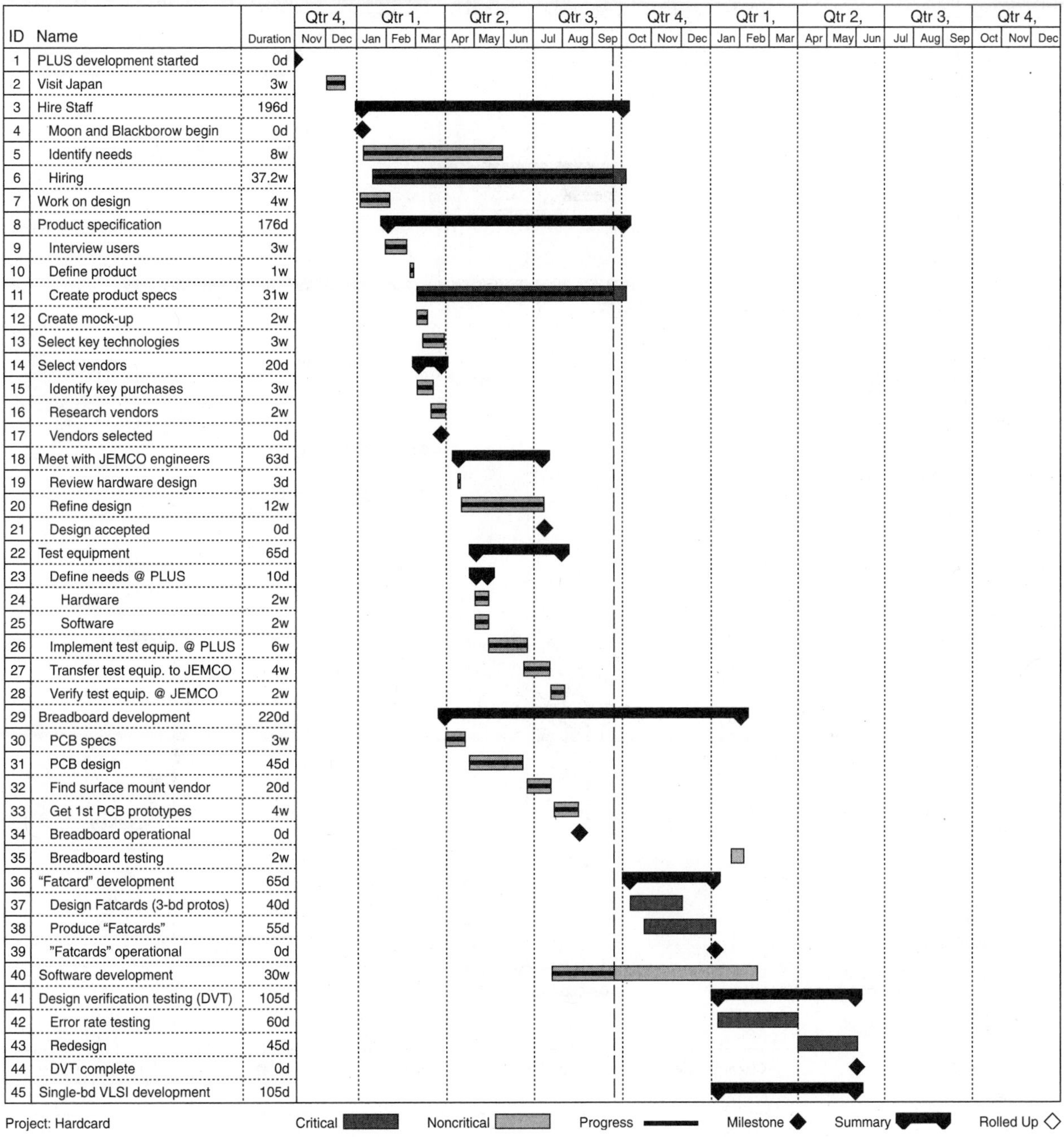

ID	Name	Duration
1	PLUS development started	0d
2	Visit Japan	3w
3	Hire Staff	196d
4	Moon and Blackborow begin	0d
5	Identify needs	8w
6	Hiring	37.2w
7	Work on design	4w
8	Product specification	176d
9	Interview users	3w
10	Define product	1w
11	Create product specs	31w
12	Create mock-up	2w
13	Select key technologies	3w
14	Select vendors	20d
15	Identify key purchases	3w
16	Research vendors	2w
17	Vendors selected	0d
18	Meet with JEMCO engineers	63d
19	Review hardware design	3d
20	Refine design	12w
21	Design accepted	0d
22	Test equipment	65d
23	Define needs @ PLUS	10d
24	Hardware	2w
25	Software	2w
26	Implement test equip. @ PLUS	6w
27	Transfer test equip. to JEMCO	4w
28	Verify test equip. @ JEMCO	2w
29	Breadboard development	220d
30	PCB specs	3w
31	PCB design	45d
32	Find surface mount vendor	20d
33	Get 1st PCB prototypes	4w
34	Breadboard operational	0d
35	Breadboard testing	2w
36	"Fatcard" development	65d
37	Design Fatcards (3-bd protos)	40d
38	Produce "Fatcards"	55d
39	"Fatcards" operational	0d
40	Software development	30w
41	Design verification testing (DVT)	105d
42	Error rate testing	60d
43	Redesign	45d
44	DVT complete	0d
45	Single-bd VLSI development	105d

Timeline: Qtr 4 (Nov, Dec); Qtr 1 (Jan, Feb, Mar); Qtr 2 (Apr, May, Jun); Qtr 3 (Jul, Aug, Sep); Qtr 4 (Oct, Nov, Dec); Qtr 1 (Jan, Feb, Mar); Qtr 2 (Apr, May, Jun); Qtr 3 (Jul, Aug, Sep); Qtr 4 (Oct, Nov, Dec)

Project: Hardcard — Critical; Noncritical; Progress; Milestone; Summary; Rolled Up

Bob Lyells was not convinced. As manager of quality and reliability, he did not look forward to mopping up after a sloppy ramp-up. "Not so fast, you guys. You know how Utamoro is. To hit the introduction target, I thought I heard Joel say we'd have to cut some corners. Utamoro would never knowingly agree to compromise the production yield, and his engineers are still going over the design with a fine-tooth comb. JEMCO insists on solving all problems up front."

Moon said, "It's not even clear extra engineers would help, Hank. JEMCO needs three months for product transfer and maturity testing. Like Bob said, they need to know it'll work before they'll flip that

EXHIBIT 5 *(concluded)*

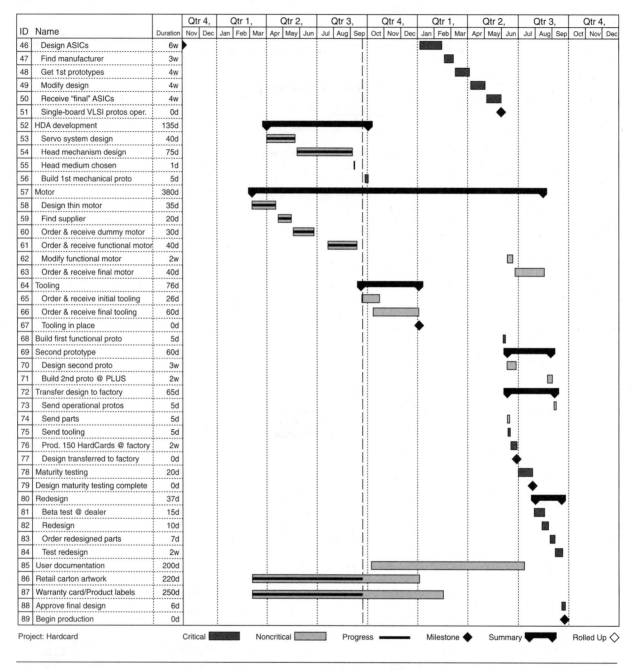

Qtr 4, Nov Dec | Qtr 1, Jan Feb Mar | Qtr 2, Apr May Jun | Qtr 3, Jul Aug Sep | Qtr 4, Oct Nov Dec | Qtr 1, Jan Feb Mar | Qtr 2, Apr May Jun | Qtr 3, Jul Aug Sep | Qtr 4, Oct Nov Dec

ID	Name	Duration
46	Design ASICs	6w
47	Find manufacturer	3w
48	Get 1st prototypes	4w
49	Modify design	4w
50	Receive "final" ASICs	4w
51	Single-board VLSI protos oper.	0d
52	HDA development	135d
53	Servo system design	40d
54	Head mechanism design	75d
55	Head medium chosen	1d
56	Build 1st mechanical proto	5d
57	Motor	380d
58	Design thin motor	35d
59	Find supplier	20d
60	Order & receive dummy motor	30d
61	Order & receive functional motor	40d
62	Modify functional motor	2w
63	Order & receive final motor	40d
64	Tooling	76d
65	Order & receive initial tooling	26d
66	Order & receive final tooling	60d
67	Tooling in place	0d
68	Build first functional proto	5d
69	Second prototype	60d
70	Design second proto	3w
71	Build 2nd proto @ PLUS	2w
72	Transfer design to factory	65d
73	Send operational protos	5d
74	Send parts	5d
75	Send tooling	5d
76	Prod. 150 HardCards @ factory	2w
77	Design transferred to factory	0d
78	Maturity testing	20d
79	Design maturity testing complete	0d
80	Redesign	37d
81	Beta test @ dealer	15d
82	Redesign	10d
83	Order redesigned parts	7d
84	Test redesign	2w
85	User documentation	200d
86	Retail carton artwork	220d
87	Warranty card/Product labels	250d
88	Approve final design	6d
89	Begin production	0d

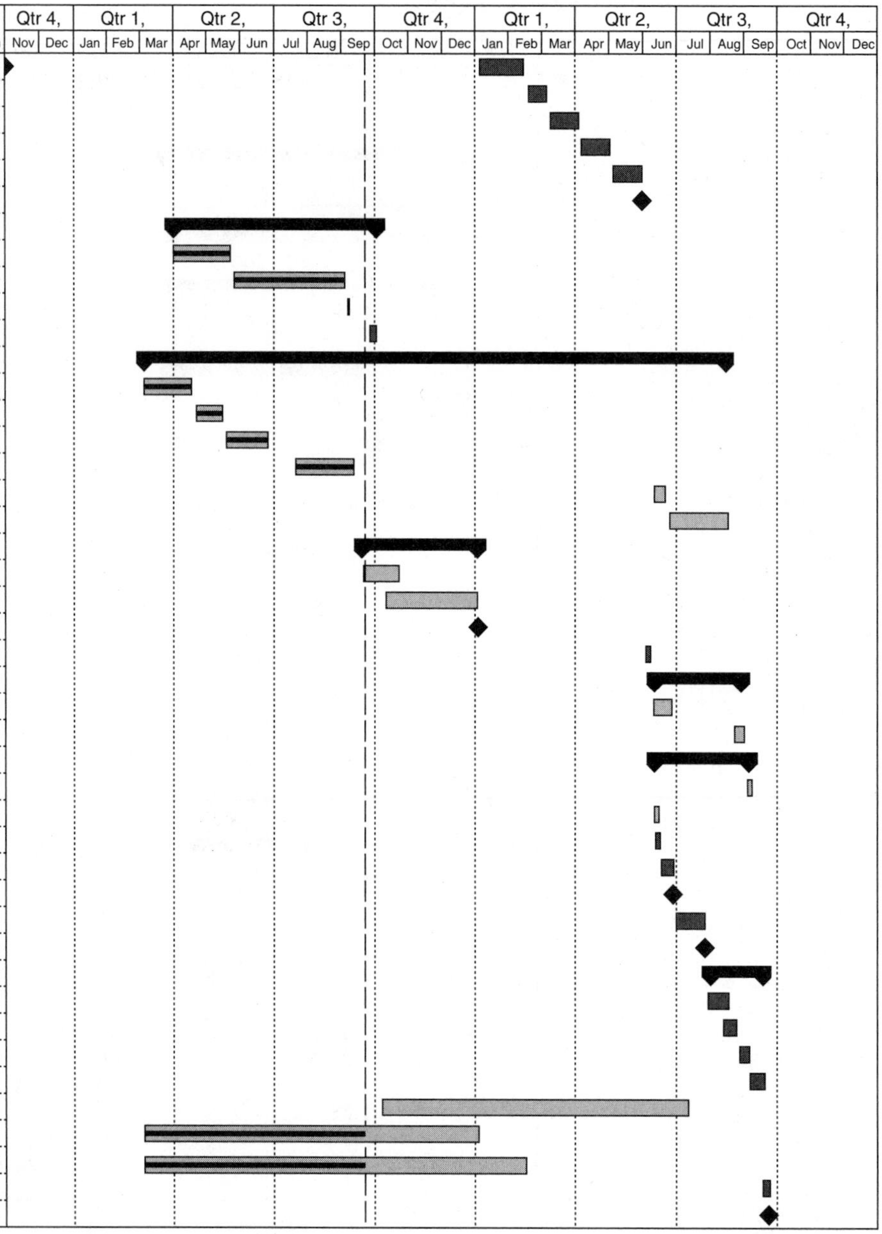

Project: Hardcard — Critical, Noncritical, Progress, Milestone ◆, Summary, Rolled Up ◇

switch in June. If we're gonna push ahead, we'd better figure out how we're going to solve JEMCO's requirements. Besides, most of JEMCO's interactions are primarily on mechanical issues. We've got a whole raft of software tasks to do ourselves and those are already as compressed as possible."

Chesbrough chimed in again at this point. "Don't forget that we're responsible for marketing as well. In our marketing approach, we're trying to create a unique image for service and reliability. That means cultivating key dealers, building a distribution network, developing a training program for dealers, and establishing policies covering pricing, margins, promotion, and service. If we're going to reschedule, we need at least six to nine months if we're serious about creating a unique image and reputation in

EXHIBIT 6 Plus Engineering Status Reports

Schedule Status:*

- The Hardcard Project is on schedule for June 1985 production.
- The following milestones are behind schedule or have been rescheduled:
  1. Mechanical Engineering Architecture based upon JEMCO input (was July 13 now due July 20). This is the critical path for mechanical engineering of Hardcard. The July 20 date just keeps the prototypes on schedule.
  2. Start Test Development has been rescheduled awaiting the hiring of our first test engineer (was July 16 now Aug. 15).
  3. The Hardcard Specification requirements are not well defined. This issue must be resolved before the specification can be finished.
- The Breadboard phase is complete.
- Several breadboard testing items have been delayed until DVT testing of the prototypes beginning in October.
- The following detailed schedules have been developed and are now being used in conjunction with the master schedule:
  - Drive/Controller firmware development schedule
  - Software development schedule including the PC BIOS and compatibility
  - Three Digital VLSI Chip development schedules
  - DVT prototype schedule and use plan

Recruiting/Staffing:†

- Recruiting needs focus.
- New employees: new Mechanical Engineer and Digital Engineer start Aug. 20 and Aug. 1, respectively.
- Seven Present Openings: There are seven openings, two with candidates. Openings are for Digital Engineer, Mechanical Engineer, Diagnostic Programmer, Computer Scientist, Engineering Technicians (2), and Test Engineer.

Schedule Status:

- Hardcard Project is on schedule for June 1985 production. *VLSI and Firmware/Software are the present critical paths.*
- The following milestones are behind schedule or have been rescheduled based upon the Engineering/Manufacturing Master Schedule:
  1. Start Test Development (was July 16 now Aug. 1). The first test equipment meeting with JEMCO will be held Aug. 1.
  2. The Hardcard Specification requirements are not well defined. This issue must be resolved before the specification can be finished.
  3. Software Quality/Reliability testing plans have not begun. Action will begin when our Quality/Reliability engineer starts.
- Motors from the vendors are the critical path for September mechanical prototypes. Commit dates have not yet been received.
- The Analog printed circuit board for September prototypes is being expedited to keep it on schedule. The Digital board is on schedule.
- Heads and disks are on schedule for September mechanical prototypes.
- Firmware is on schedule.

Staffing/Recruiting:‡

- New Manager of Software Development began this week.
- Present Openings: Nine openings with one offer extended for Analog Technician and one other candidate. Offer made for Digital Engineer was turned down, priority of this position is reduced however. Positions open are: Software Technician, Mechanical Engineer, Diagnostic Programmer, Test Engineers (3), Engineering Technicians (2), and Digital Engineer.

Schedule Status:

- The DVT Plan is behind schedule. Recovery status by Friday.
- Mechanical Engineering parts for 100 prototype units may be late due to unplanned design iterations. Exact ME parts status will be available by Friday. Great effort will be made not to slip the schedule.
- Digital and Analog VLSI chips are on schedule.
- Product Design Specifications are late; Bob Couse is now responsible for Product Specs.
- Printed circuit boards are on schedule.
- There are technical problems with Start Stop Testing; the test conditions are not under control; the media has problems that may be due to the lubricant thickness.

*SOURCE: *July 16, 1984, Plus report.*
†SOURCE: *July 30, 1984, Plus report.*
‡SOURCE: *Aug. 29, 1984, Plus report.*

the market. We don't want to be late at the 11th hour and have everyone conclude it was all just hype, that Plus is really just as unreliable and on the edge of being out of control as everyone else."

"OK, so what's it gonna be?" Dave Brown asked. I'm hearing arguments on both sides, but we need a commitment to get this project done, one way or the other."

Reading IV–3
Organizing and Leading "Heavyweight" Development Teams

Kim B. Clark and Steven C. Wheelwright

Effective product and process development requires the integration of specialized capabilities. Integrating is difficult in most circumstances, but is particularly challenging in large, mature firms with strong functional groups, extensive specialization, large numbers of people, and multiple, ongoing operating pressures. In such firms, development projects are the exception rather than the primary focus of attention. Even for people working on development projects, years of experience and the established systems—covering everything from career paths to performance evaluation, and from reporting relationships to breadth of job definitions—create both physical and organizational distance from other people in the organization. The functions themselves are organized in a way that creates further complications: the marketing organization is based on product families and market segments; engineering around functional disciplines and technical focus; and manufacturing on a mix between functional and product market structures. The result is that in large, mature firms, organizing and leading an effective development effort is a major undertaking. This is especially true for organizations whose traditionally stable markets and competitive environments are threatened by new entrants, new technologies, and rapidly changing customer demands.

This article zeros in on one type of team structure—"heavyweight" project teams—that seems particularly promising in today's fast-paced world yet is strikingly absent in many mature companies. Our research shows that when managed effectively, heavyweight teams offer improved communication, stronger identification with and commitment to a project, and a focus on cross-functional problem solving. Our research also reveals, however, that these teams are not so easily managed and contain unique issues and challenges.

Heavyweight project teams are one of four types of team structures. We begin by describing each of them briefly. We then explore heavyweight teams in detail, compare them with the alternative forms, and point out specific challenges and their solutions in managing the heavyweight team organization. We conclude with an example of the changes necessary in individual behavior for heavyweight teams to be effective. Although heavyweight teams are a different way of organizing, they are more than a new structure; they represent a fundamentally different way of working. To the extent that both the team members and the surrounding organization recognize that phenomenon, the heavyweight team begins to realize its full potential.

Types of Development Project Teams

Exhibit 1 illustrates the four dominant team structures we have observed in our studies of development projects: functional, lightweight, heavyweight, and autonomous (or tiger). These forms are described below, along with their associated project leadership roles, strengths, and weaknesses. Heavyweight teams are examined in detail in the subsequent section.

Functional Team Structure

In the traditional functional organization found in larger, more mature firms, people are grouped principally by discipline, each working under the direction of a specialized subfunction manager and a senior functional manager. The different subfunctions and functions coordinate ideas through detailed specifications all parties agree to at the outset, and through occasional meetings where issues

---

 Reprinted from the *California Management Review,* Volume 34, Number 3, Spring 1992. By permission of The Regents.

Adapted from Chapter 8 of Steven C. Wheelwright and Kim B. Clark, *Revolutionizing Product Development: Quantum Leaps in Speed, Efficiency, and Quality* (New York, NY: Free Press, 1992).

EXHIBIT 1 Types of Development Teams

A. Functional Team Structure

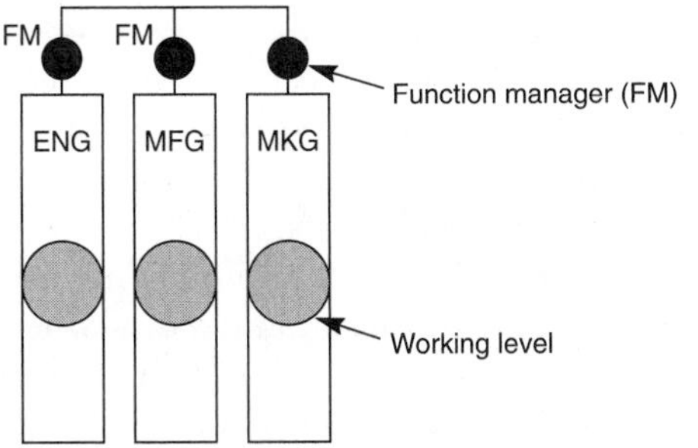

B. Lightweight Team Structure

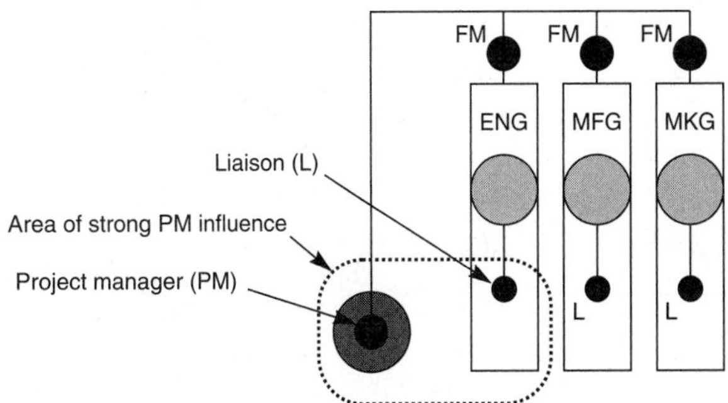

C. Heavyweight Team Structure

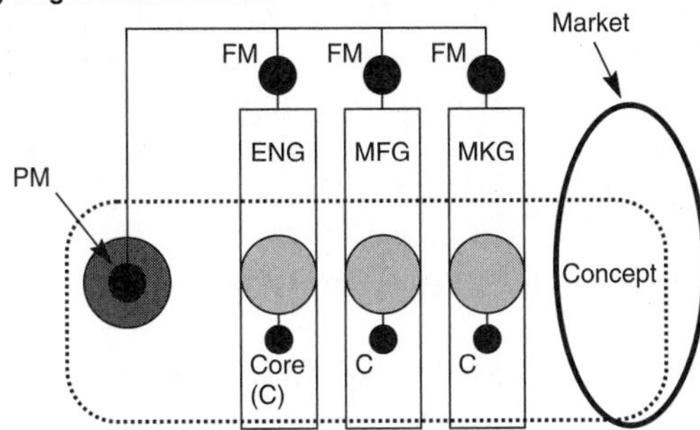

D. Autonomous Team Structure

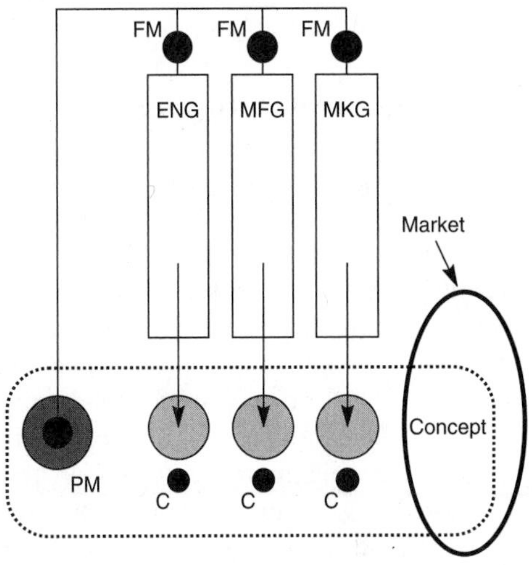

that cut across groups are discussed. Over time, primary responsibility for the project passes sequentially—although often not smoothly—from one function to the next, a transfer frequently termed *throwing it over the wall.*

The functional team structure has several advantages and associated disadvantages. One strength is that those managers who control the project's resources also control task performance in their functional area; thus, responsibility and authority are usually aligned. However, tasks must be subdivided at the project's outset (i.e., the entire development process is decomposed into separable, somewhat independent activities). But on most development efforts, not all required tasks are known at the outset, nor can they all be easily and realistically subdivided. Coordination and integration can suffer as a result.

Another major strength of this approach is that, because most career paths are functional in nature until a general management level is reached, the work done on a project is judged, evaluated, and rewarded by the same subfunction and functional managers who make the decisions about career paths. The associated disadvantage is that individual contributions to a development project tend to be judged largely independently of overall project success. The traditional tenet cited is that individuals cannot be evaluated fairly on outcomes over which they have little or no control. But as a practical matter, that often means that no one directly involved in the details of the project is responsible for the results finally achieved.

Finally, the functional project organization brings specialized expertise to bear on the key technical issues. The same person or small group of people may be responsible for the design of a particular component or subsystem over a wide range of development efforts. Thus the functions and subfunctions capture the benefits of prior experience and become the keepers of the organization's depth of knowledge while ensuring that it is systematically applied over time and across projects. The disadvantage is that every development project differs in its objectives and performance requirements, and it is unlikely that specialists developing a single component will do so very differently on one project than on another. The "best" component or subsystem is defined by technical parameters in the areas of their expertise rather than by overall system characteristics or specific customer requirements dictated by the unique market the development effort aims for.

Lightweight Team Structure

Like the functional structure, those assigned to the lightweight team reside physically in their functional areas, but each functional organization designates a liaison person to "represent" it on a project coordinating committee. These liaison representatives work with a "lightweight project manager," usually a design engineer or product marketing manager, who coordinates different functions' activities. This approach usually figures as an add-on to a traditional functional organization, with the functional liaison person having that role added to his or her other duties. The overall coordination assignment of lightweight project manager, however, tends not to be present in the traditional functional team structure.

The project manager is a "lightweight" in two important aspects. First, he or she is generally a middle- or junior-level person who, despite considerable expertise, usually has little status or influence in the organization. Such people have spent a handful of years in a function, and this assignment is seen as a "broadening experience," a chance for them to move out of that function. Second, although they are responsible for informing and coordinating the activities of the functional organizations, the key resources (including engineers on the project) remain under the control of their respective functional managers. The lightweight project manager does not have power to reassign people or reallocate resources and instead confirms schedules, updates time lines, and expedites across groups. Typically, such project leaders spend no more than 25 percent of their time on a single project.

The primary strengths and weaknesses of the lightweight project team are those of the functional project structure. But now at least one person over the course of the project looks across functions and seeks to ensure that individual tasks—especially those on the critical path—get done in a timely fashion, and that everyone is kept aware of potential cross-functional issues and what is going on elsewhere on this particular project.

Thus, improved communication and coordination are what an organization expects when moving from a functional to a lightweight team structure. Yet, because power still resides with the subfunction and functional managers, hopes for improved efficiency, speed, and project quality are seldom realized. Moreover, lightweight project leaders find themselves tolerated at best, and often ignored and even preempted. This can easily become a "no-win" situation for the individual thus assigned.

Heavyweight Team Structure

In contrast to the lightweight set-up, the heavyweight project manager has direct access to and responsibility for the work of all those involved in the project. Such leaders are "heavyweights" in two respects. First, they are senior managers within the organization; they may even outrank the functional managers. Hence, in addition to having expertise and experience, they also wield significant organizational clout. Second, heavyweight leaders have primary influence over the people working on the development effort and supervise their work directly through key functional people on the core teams. Often, the core group of people are dedicated and physically colocated with the heavyweight project leader. However, the longer-term career development of individual contributors continues to rest not with the project leader—although that heavyweight leader makes significant input to individual performance evaluations—but with the functional manager, because members are not assigned to a project team on a permanent basis.

The heavyweight team structure has a number of advantages and strengths, along with associated weaknesses. Because this team structure is observed much less frequently in practice and yet seems to have tremendous potential for a wide range of organizations, it will be discussed in detail in the next section.

Autonomous Team Structure

With the autonomous team structure, often called the "tiger team," individuals from the different functional areas are formally assigned, dedicated, and colocated to the project team. The project leader, a "heavyweight" in the organization, is given full control over the resources contributed by the different functional groups. Furthermore, that project leader becomes the sole evaluator of the contribution made by individual team members.

In essence, the autonomous team is given a "clean sheet of paper"; it is not required to follow existing organizational practices and procedures, but allowed to create its own. This includes establishing incentives and rewards as well as norms for behavior. However, the team will be held fully accountable for the final results of the project: Success or failure is its responsibility and no one else's.

The fundamental strength of the autonomous team structure is focus. Everything the individual team members and the team leader do is concentrated on making the project successful. Thus, tiger teams can excel at rapid, efficient new product and new process development. They handle cross-functional integration in a particularly effective manner, possibly because they attract and select team participants much more freely than the other project structures.

Tiger teams, however, take little or nothing as "given"; they are likely to expand the bounds of their project definition and tackle redesign of the entire product, its components, and subassemblies, rather than looking for opportunities to utilize existing materials, designs, and organizational relationships. Their solution may be unique, making it more difficult to fold the resulting product and process—and, in many cases, the team members themselves—back into the traditional organization upon project completion. As a consequence, tiger teams often become the birthplace of new business units or they experience unusually high turnover following project completion.

Senior managers often become nervous at the prospects of a tiger team because they are asked to delegate much more responsibility and control to the team and its project leader than under any of the other organization structures. Unless clear guidelines have been established in advance, it is extremely difficult during the project for senior managers to make midcourse corrections or exercise substantial influence without destroying the team. More than one team has "gotten away" from senior management and created major problems.

The Heavyweight Team Structure

The best way to begin understanding the potential of heavyweight teams is to consider an example of their success, in this case, Motorola's experience in developing its Bandit line of pagers.

The Bandit Pager Heavyweight Team

This development team within the Motorola Communications Sector was given a project charter to develop an automated, on-shore, profitable production operation for its high-volume Bravo pager line. (This is the belt-worn pager that Motorola sold from the mid-1980s into the early 1990s.) The core team consisted of a heavyweight project leader and a handful of dedicated and colocated individuals, who represented industrial engineering, robotics, process engineering, procurement, and product design/CIM. The need for these functions was dictated by the Bandit platform automation project and its focus on manufacturing technology with a minimal change in product technology. In addition, human resource and accounting/finance representatives were part of the core team. The human resource person was particularly active early on as subteam positions were defined and jobs posted throughout Motorola's Communications Sector and played an important subsequent role in training and development of operating support people. The accounting/finance person was invaluable in "costing out" different options and performing detailed analyses of options and choices identified during the course of the project.

An eighth member of the core team was a Hewlett-Packard employee. Hewlett-Packard was chosen as the vendor for the "software backplane," providing an HP 3000 computer and the integrated software communication network that linked individual automated workstations, downloaded controls and instructions during production operations, and captured quality and other operating performance data. Because HP support was vital to the project's success, it was felt essential they be represented on the core team.

The core team was housed in a corner of the Motorola Telecommunications engineering/manufacturing facility. The team chose to enclose in glass the area where the automated production line was to be set up so that others in the factory could track the progress, offer suggestions, and adopt the lessons learned from it in their own production and engineering environments. The team called their project Bandit to indicate a willingness to "take" ideas from literally anywhere.

The heavyweight project leader, Scott Shamlin, who was described by team members as "a crusader," "a renegade," and "a workaholic," became the champion for the Bandit effort. A hands-on manager, who played a major role in stimulating and facilitating communication across functions, he helped to articulate a vision of the Bandit line and to infuse it into the detailed work of the project team. His goal was to make sure the new manufacturing process worked for the pager line, but would provide real insight for many other production lines in Motorola's Communications Sector.

The Bandit core team started by creating a contract book that established the blueprint and work plan for the team's efforts and its performance expectations; all core team members and senior management signed on to the document. Initially, the team's executive sponsor—although not formally identified as such—was George Fisher, the sector executive. He made the original investment proposal to the board of directors and was an early champion and supporter, as well as direct supervisor in selecting the project leader and helping get the team underway. Subsequently, the vice president and general manager of the Paging Products division filled the role of executive sponsor.

Throughout the project, the heavyweight team took responsibility for the substance of its work, the means by which it was accomplished, and its results. The project was completed in 18 months as per the contract book, which represented about half the time of a normal project of such magnitude. Further, the automated production operation was up and running with process tolerances of five sigma (i.e., the degree of precision achieved by the manufacturing processes) at the end of 18 months. Ongoing production verified that the cost objectives (substantially reduced direct costs and improved profit margins) had indeed been met, and product reliability was even higher than the standards already achieved on the off-shore versions of the Bravo product. Finally, a variety of lessons were successfully transferred to other parts of the sector's operations, and additional heavyweight teams have proven the viability and robustness of the approach in Motorola's business and further refined its effectiveness throughout the corporation.

The Challenge of Heavyweight Teams

Motorola's experience underscores heavyweight teams' potential power, but it also makes clear that creating an effective heavyweight team capability is more than merely selecting a leader and forming a team. By their very nature—being product (or process) focused, and needing strong, independent leadership, broad skills and cross-functional perspective, and clear missions—heavyweight teams may conflict with the functional organization and raise questions about senior management's influence and control. And even the advantages of the team approach bring with them potential disadvantages that may hurt development performance if not recognized and averted.

Take, for example, the advantages of ownership and commitment, one of the most striking advantages of the heavyweight team. Identifying with the product and creating a sense of esprit de corps motivate core team members to extend themselves and do what needs to be done to help the team succeed. But such teams sometimes expand the definition of their role and the scope of the project, and they get carried away with themselves and their abilities. We have seen heavyweight teams turn into autonomous tiger teams and go off on a tangent because senior executives gave insufficient direction and the bounds of the team were only vaguely specified at the outset. And even if the team stays focused, the rest of the organization may see themselves as "second class." Although the core team may not make that distinction explicit, it happens because the team has responsibilities and authority beyond those commonly given to functional team members. Thus, such projects inadvertently can become the "haves" and other, smaller projects the "have-nots" with regard to key resources and management attention.

Support activities are particularly vulnerable to an excess of ownership and commitment. Often the heavyweight team will want the same control over secondary support activities as it has over the primary tasks performed by dedicated team members. When waiting for prototypes to be constructed, analytical tests to be performed, or quality assurance procedures to be conducted, the team's natural response is to "demand" top priority from the support organization or to be allowed to go outside and subcontract to independent groups. While these may sometimes be the appropriate choices, senior management should establish make-buy guidelines and clear priorities applicable to all projects—perhaps changing service levels provided by support groups (rather than maintaining the traditional emphasis on resource utilization)—or have support groups provide capacity and advisory technical services but let team members do more of the actual task work in those support areas. Whatever actions the organization takes, the challenge is to achieve a balance between the needs of the individual project and the needs of the broader organization.

Another advantage the heavyweight team brings is the integration and integrity it provides through a system solution to a set of customer needs. Getting all the components and subsystems to complement one another and to address effectively the fundamental requirements of the core customer segment can result in a winning platform product and/or process. The team achieves an effective system design by using generalist skills applied by broadly trained team members, with fewer specialists and, on occasion, less depth in individual component solutions and technical problem solving.

The extent of these implications is aptly illustrated by the nature of the teams Clark and Fujimoto studied in the auto industry.[1] They found that for U.S. auto firms in the mid-1980s, typical platform projects—organized under a traditional functional or lightweight team structure—entailed full-time work for several months by approximately 1,500 engineers. In contrast, a handful of Japanese platform projects—carried out by heavyweight teams—utilized only 250 engineers working full-time for several months. The implications of 250 versus 1,500 full-time equivalents (FTEs) with regard to breadth of tasks, degree of specialization, and need for coordination are significant and help explain the differences in project results as measured by product integrity, development cycle time, and engineering resource utilization.

But that lack of depth may disclose a disadvantage. Some individual components or subassemblies may not attain the same level of technical excellence they would under a more traditional functional team structure. For instance, generalists may develop a windshield wiper system that is complementary with and integrated into the total car system and its core concept. But they also may embed in their design some potential weaknesses or flaws that might have been caught by a functional team of specialists who had designed a long series of windshield wipers. To counter this potential disadvantage, many organizations order more testing of completed units to discover such possible flaws and have components and subassemblies reviewed by expert specialists. In some cases, the quality assurance function has expanded its role to make sure sufficient technical specialists review designs at appropriate points so that such weaknesses can be minimized.

Managing the Challenges of Heavyweight Teams

Problems with depth in technical solutions and allocations of support resources suggest the tension that exists between heavyweight teams and the functional groups where much of the work gets done. The problem with the teams exceeding their bounds reflects in part how teams manage themselves, in part how boundaries are set, and in part the ongoing relationship between the team and senior management. Dealing with these issues requires mechanisms and practices that reinforce the team's basic thrust—ownership, focus, system architecture, integrity—and yet improve its ability to take advantage of the strengths of the supporting functional organization—technical depth, consistency across projects, senior management direction. We have grouped the mechanisms and problems into six categories of management action: the project charter, the contract, staffing, leadership, team responsibility, and the executive sponsor.

The project charter

A heavyweight project team needs a clear mission. A way to capture that mission concisely is in an explicit, measurable project charter that sets broad performance objectives and usually is articulated even before the core team is selected. Thus, joining the core team includes accepting the charter established by senior management. A typical charter for a heavyweight project would be the following:

> The resulting product will be selected and ramped by Company X during Quarter 4 of calendar year 1991, at a minimum of a 20 percent gross margin.

[1] See Kim B. Clark and Takahiro Fujimoto, *Product Development Performance* (Boston, MA: Harvard Business School Press, 1991).

This charter is representative of an industrial products firm whose product goes into a system sold by its customers. Company X is the leading customer for a certain family of products, and this project is dedicated to developing the next generation platform offering in that family. If the heavyweight program results in that platform product being chosen by the leading customer in the segment by a certain date and at a certain gross margin, it will have demonstrated that the next generation platform is not only viable, but likely to be very successful over the next three to five years. Industries and settings where such a charter might be found would include a microprocessor being developed for a new computer system, a diesel engine for the heavy equipment industry, or a certain type of slitting and folding piece of equipment for the newspaper printing press industry. Even in a medical diagnostics business with hundreds of customers, a goal of "capturing 30 percent of market purchases in the second 12 months during which the product is offered" sets a clear charter for the team.

The contract book

Whereas a charter lays out the mission in broad terms, the contract book defines, in detail, the basic plan to achieve the stated goal. A contract book is created as soon as the core team and heavyweight project leader have been designated and given the charter by senior management. Basically, the team develops its own detailed work plan for conducting the project, estimates the resources required, and outlines the results to be achieved and against which it is willing to be evaluated. (The table of contents of a typical heavyweight team contract book is shown in Exhibit 2.) Such documents range from 25 to 100 pages, depending on the complexity of the project and level of detail desired by the team and senior management before proceeding. A common practice following negotiation and acceptance of this contract is for the individuals from the team and senior management to sign the contract book as an indication of their commitment to honor the plan and achieve those results.

The core team may take anywhere from a long week to a few months to create and complete the contract book; Motorola, for example, after several years of experience, has decided that a maximum of seven days should be allowed for this activity. Having watched other heavyweight teams—particularly in organizations with no prior experience in using such a structure—take up to several months, we can appreciate why Motorola has nicknamed this the "blitz phase" and decided that the time allowed should be kept to a minimum.

EXHIBIT 2 Heavyweight Team, Contract Book—Major Sections

- Executive summary
- Business plan and purposes
- Development plan
  - —Schedule
  - —Materials
  - —Resources
- Product design plan
- Quality plan
- Manufacturing plan
- Project deliverables
- Performance measurement and incentives

Staffing

As suggested in Exhibit 1, a heavyweight team includes a group of core cross-functional team members who are dedicated (and usually physically colocated) for the duration of the development effort. Typically there is one core team member from each primary function of the organization; for instance, in several electronics firms we have observed core teams consisting of six functional participants—design engineering, marketing, quality assurance, manufacturing, finance, and human resources. (Occasionally, design will be represented by two core team members, one each for hardware and software engineering.) Individually, core team members represent their functions and provide leadership for their functions' inputs to the project. Collectively, they constitute a management team that works under the direction of the heavyweight project manager and takes responsibility for managing the overall development effort.

While other participants—especially from design engineering early on and manufacturing later on—may frequently be dedicated to a heavyweight team for several months, they usually are not made part of the core team though they may well be colocated and, over time, develop the same level of ownership and commitment to the project as core team members. The primary difference is that the core team manages the total project and the coordination and integration of individual functional efforts, whereas other dedicated team members work primarily within a single function or subfunction.

Whether these temporarily dedicated team members are actually part of the core team is an issue firms handle in different ways, but those with considerable experience tend to distinguish between core and other dedicated (and often colocated) team members. The difference is one of management responsibility for the core group that is not shared equally by the others. Also, it is primarily the half a dozen members of the core group who will be dedicated throughout the project, with other contributors having a portion of their time reassigned before this heavyweight project is completed.

Whether physical colocation is essential is likewise questioned in such teams. We have seen it work both ways. Given the complexity of development projects, and especially the uncertainty and ambiguity often associated with those assigned to heavyweight teams, physical colocation is preferable to even the best of on-line communication approaches. Problems that arise in real time are much more likely to be addressed effectively with all of the functions represented and present than when they are separate and must either wait for a periodic meeting or use remote communication links to open up cross-functional discussions.

A final issue is whether an individual can be a core team member on more than one heavyweight team simultaneously. If the rule for a core team member is that 70 percent or more of his or her time must be spent on the heavyweight project, then the answer to this question is no. Frequently, however, a choice must be made between someone being on two core teams—for example, from the finance or human resource function—or putting a different individual on one of those teams who has neither the experience nor stature to be a full peer with the other core team members. Most experienced organizations we have seen opt to put the same person on two teams to ensure the peer relationship and level of contribution required, even though it means having one person on two teams and with two desks. They then work diligently to develop other people in the function so that multiple team assignments will not be necessary in the future.

Sometimes multiple assignments will also be justified on the basis that a function such as finance does not need a full-time person on a project. In most instances, however, a variety of potential value-adding tasks exist that are broader than finance's traditional contribution. A person largely dedicated to the core team will search for those opportunities and the project will be better because of it. The risk of allowing core team members to be assigned to multiple projects is that they are neither available when their inputs are most needed nor as committed to project success as their peers. They become secondary core team members, and the full potential of the heavyweight team structure fails to be realized.

Project leadership

Heavyweight teams require a distinctive style of leadership. A number of differences between lightweight and heavyweight project managers are highlighted in Exhibit 3. Three of those are particularly distinctive. First, a heavyweight leader manages, leads, and evaluates other members of the core team and is also the person to whom the core team reports throughout the project's duration. Another characteristic is that rather than being either neutral or a facilitator with regard to problem solving and conflict resolution, these leaders see themselves as championing the basic concept around which the platform product and/or process is being shaped. They make sure that those who work on subtasks of the project understand that concept. Thus they play a central role in ensuring the system integrity of the final product and/or process.

Finally, the heavyweight project manager carries out his or her role in a very different fashion than the lightweight project manager. Most lightweights spend the bulk of their time working at a desk, with paper. They revise schedules, get frequent updates, and encourage people to meet previously agreed upon deadlines. The heavyweight project manager spends little time at a desk, is out talking to project contributors, and makes sure that decisions are made and implemented whenever and wherever needed. Some of the ways in which the heavyweight project manager achieves project results are highlighted by the five roles illustrated in Exhibit 4 for a heavyweight project manager on a platform development project in the auto industry.

The *first role* of the heavyweight project manager is to provide for the team a direct interpretation of the market and customer needs. This involves gathering market data directly from customers, dealers, and industry shows, as well as through systematic study and contact with the firm's marketing organization. A *second role* is to become a multilingual translator, not just taking marketing information to

EXHIBIT 3 Project Manager Profile

		Lightweight (limited)	Heavyweight (extensive)
Span of coordination responsibilities			
Duration of responsibilities			
Responsible for specs, cost, layout, components			
Working level contact with engineers			
Direct contact with customers			
Multilingual/multidisciplined skills			
Role in conflict resolution			
Marketing imagination/concept champion			
Influence in:	engineering		
	marketing		
	manufacturing		

the various functions involved in the project, but being fluent in the language of each of those functions and making sure the translation and communication going on among the functions—particularly between customer needs and product specifications—are done effectively.

A *third role* is the direct engineering manager, orchestrating, directing, and coordinating the various engineering subfunctions. Given the size of many development programs and the number of types of engineering disciplines involved, the project manager must be able to work directly with each engineering subfunction on a day-to-day basis and ensure that their work will indeed integrate and support that of others, so the chosen product concept can be effectively executed.

A *fourth role* is best described as staying in motion: out of the office conducting face-to-face sessions, and highlighting and resolving potential conflicts as soon as possible. Part of this role entails energizing and pacing the overall effort and its key subparts.

A *final role* is that of concept champion. Here the heavyweight project manager becomes the guardian of the concept and not only reacts and responds to the interests of others, but also sees that the choices made are consistent and in harmony with the basic concept. This requires a careful blend of communication and teaching skills so that individual contributors and their groups understand the core concept and have sufficient conflict resolution skills to ensure that any tough issues are addressed in a timely fashion.

It should be apparent from this description that heavyweight project managers earn the respect and right to carry out these roles based on prior experience, carefully developed skills, and status earned over time, rather than simply being designated "leader" by senior management. A qualified heavyweight project manager is a prerequisite to an effective heavyweight team structure.

Team member responsibilities

Heavyweight team members have responsibilities beyond their usual functional assignment. As illustrated in Exhibit 5, these are of two primary types. Functional hat responsibilities are those accepted by the individual core team member as representative of his or her function. For example, the core team member from marketing is responsible for ensuring that appropriate marketing expertise is brought to the project, that a marketing perspective is provided on all key issues, that project subobjectives dependent on the marketing function are met in a timely fashion, and that marketing issues that impact other functions are raised proactively within the team.

EXHIBIT 4 The Heavyweight Project Manager

Role	Description
Direct market interpreter	First-hand information, dealer visits, auto shows, has own marketing budget, market study team, direct contact and discussions with customers
Multilingual translator	Fluency in language of customers, engineers, marketers, stylists; translator between customer experience/requirements and engineering specifications
Direct engineering manager	Direct contact, orchestra conductor, evangelist of conceptual integrity and coordinator of component development; direct eye-to-eye discussions with working level engineers; shows up in drafting room, looks over engineers' shoulders
Program manager "in motion"	Out of the office, not too many meetings, not too much paperwork, face-to-face communication, conflict resolution manager
Concept infuser	Concept guardian, confronts conflicts, not only reacts but implements own philosophy, ultimate decision maker, coordination of details and creation of harmony

But each core team member also wears a team hat. In addition to representing a function, each member shares responsibility with the heavyweight project manager for the procedures followed by the team, and for the overall results that those procedures deliver. The core team is accountable for the success of the project, and it can blame no one but itself if it fails to manage the project, execute the tasks, and deliver the performance agreed upon at the outset.

EXHIBIT 5 Responsibilities of Heavyweight Core Team Members

Functional Hat Accountabilities

- Ensuring functional expertise on the project
- Representing the functional perspective on the project
- Ensuring that subobjectives are met that depend on their function
- Ensuring that functional issues impacting the team are raised proactively within the team

Team Hat Accountabilities

- Sharing responsibility for team results
- Reconstituting tasks and content
- Establishing reporting and other organizational relationships
- Participating in monitoring and improving team performance
- Sharing responsibility for ensuring effective team processes
- Examining issues from an executive point of view (Answering the question, "Is this the appropriate business response for the company?")
- Understanding, recognizing, and responsibly challenging the boundaries of the project and team process

Finally, beyond being accountable for tasks in their own function, core team members are responsible for how those tasks are subdivided, organized, and accomplished. Unlike the traditional functional development structure, which takes as given the subdivision of tasks and the means by which those tasks will be conducted and completed, the core heavyweight team is given the power and responsibility to change the substance of those tasks to improve the performance of the project. Since this is a role that core team members do not play under a lightweight or functional team structure, it is often the most difficult for them to accept fully and learn to apply. It is essential, however, if the heavyweight team is to realize its full potential.

The executive sponsor

With so much more accountability delegated to the project team, establishing effective relationships with senior management requires special mechanisms. Senior management needs to retain the ability to guide the project and its leader while empowering the team to lead and act, a responsibility usually taken by an executive sponsor—typically the vice president of engineering, marketing, or manufacturing for the business unit. This sponsor becomes the coach and mentor for the heavyweight project leader and core team and seeks to maintain close, ongoing contact with the team's efforts. In addition, the executive sponsor serves as a liaison. If other members of senior management—including the functional heads—have concerns or inputs to voice, or need current information on project status, these are communicated through the executive sponsor. This reduces the number of mixed signals received by the team and clarifies for the organization the reporting and evaluation relationship between the team and senior management. It also encourages the executive sponsor to set appropriate limits and bounds on the team so that organizational surprises are avoided.

Often the executive sponsor and core team identify those areas where the team clearly has decision-making power and control, and they distinguish them from areas requiring review. An electronics firm that has used heavyweight teams for some time dedicates one meeting early on between the executive sponsor and the core team to generating a list of areas where the executive sponsor expects to provide oversight and be consulted; these areas are of great concern to the entire executive staff and team actions may well raise policy issues for the larger organization. In this firm, the executive staff wants to maintain some control over:

- Resource commitment—head count, fixed costs, and major expenses outside the approved contract book plan;
- Pricing for major customers and major accounts;
- Potential slips in major milestone dates (the executive sponsor wants early warning and recovery plans);
- Plans for transitioning from development project to operating status;
- Thorough reviews at major milestones or every three months, whichever occurs sooner;
- Review of incentive rewards that have company-wide implications for consistency and equity; and
- Cross-project issues such as resource optimization, prioritization, and balance.

Identifying such areas at the outset can help the executive sponsor and the core team better carry out their assigned responsibilities. It also helps other executives feel more comfortable working through the executive sponsor, since they know these "boundary issues" have been articulated and are jointly understood.

The Necessity of Fundamental Change

Compared to a traditional functional organization, creating a team that is "heavy"—one with effective leadership, strong problem-solving skills, and the ability to integrate across functions—requires basic changes in the way development works. But it also requires change in the fundamental behavior of engineers, designers, manufacturers, and marketers in their day-to-day work. An episode in a computer company with no previous experience with heavyweight teams illustrates the depth of change required to realize fully these teams' power.[2]

Two teams, A and B, were charged with development of a small computer system and had market introduction targets within the next 12 months. While each core team was colocated and held regular meetings, there was one overlapping core team member (from finance/accounting). Each team was charged with developing a new computer system for their individual target markets but by chance, both products were to use an identical, custom-designed microprocessor chip in addition to other unique and standard chips.

The challenge of changing behavior in creating an effective heavyweight team structure was highlighted when each team sent this identical, custom-designed chip—the "supercontroller"—to the vendor for pilot production. The vendor quoted a 20-week turnaround to both teams. At that time, the supercontroller chip was already on the critical path for Team B, with a planned turnaround of 11 weeks. Thus, every week saved on that chip would save one week in the overall project schedule, and Team B already suspected that it would be late in meeting its initial market introduction target date. When the 20-week vendor lead time issue first came up in a Team B meeting, Jim, the core team member from engineering, responded very much as he had on prior, functionally structured development efforts: Because initial prototypes were engineering's responsibility, he reported that they were working on accelerating the delivery date, but that the vendor was a large company, with which the computer man-

[2] Adapted from a description provided by Dr. Christopher Meyer, Strategic Alignment Group, Los Altos, CA.

ufacturer did substantial business, and known for its slowness. Suggestions from other core team members on how to accelerate the delivery were politely rebuffed, including one to have a senior executive contact his or her counterpart at the vendor. Jim knew the traditional approach to such issues and did not perceive a need, responsibility, or authority to alter it significantly.

For Team A, the original quote of 20-week turnaround still left a little slack, and thus initially the supercontroller chip was not on the critical path. Within a couple of weeks, however, it was, given other changes in the activities and schedule, and the issue was immediately raised at the team's weekly meeting. Fred, the core team member from manufacturing (who historically would not have been involved in an early engineering prototype), stated that he thought the turnaround time quoted was too long and that he would try to reduce it. At the next meeting, Fred brought some good news: through discussions with the vendor, he had been able to get a commitment that pulled in the delivery of the supercontroller chip by 11 weeks! Furthermore, Fred thought that the quote might be reduced even further by a phone call from one of the computer manufacturer's senior executives to a contact of his at the vendor.

Two days later, at a regular Team B meeting, the supercontroller chip again came up during the status review, and no change from the original schedule was identified. Since the finance person, Ann, served on both teams and had been present at Team A's meeting, she described Team A's success in reducing the cycle time. Jim responded that he was aware that Team A had made such efforts, but that the information was not correct, and the original 20-week delivery date still held. Furthermore, Jim indicated that Fred's efforts (from Team A) had caused some uncertainty and disruption internally, and in the future it was important that Team A not take such initiatives before coordinating with Team B. Jim stated that this was particularly true when an outside vendor was involved, and he closed the topic by saying that a meeting to clear up the situation would be held that afternoon with Fred from Team A and Team B's engineering and purchasing people.

The next afternoon, at his Team A meeting, Fred confirmed the accelerated delivery schedule for the supercontroller chip. Eleven weeks had indeed been clipped out of the schedule to the benefit of both Teams A and B. Subsequently, Jim confirmed the revised schedule would apply to his team as well, although he was displeased that Fred had abrogated "standard operating procedure" to achieve it. Curious about the differences in perspective, Ann decided to learn more about why Team A had identified an obstacle and removed it from its path, yet Team B had identified an identical obstacle and failed to move it at all.

As Fred pointed out, Jim was the engineering manager responsible for development of the supercontroller chip; he knew the chip's technical requirements, but had little experience dealing with chip vendors and their production processes. (He had long been a specialist.) Without that experience, he had a hard time pushing back against the vendor's "standard line." But Fred's manufacturing experience with several chip vendors enabled him to calibrate the vendor's dates against his best-case experience and understand what the vendor needed to do to meet a substantially earlier commitment.

Moreover, because Fred had bought into a clear team charter, whose path the delayed chip would block, and because he had relevant experience, it did not make sense to live with the vendor's initial commitment, and thus he sought to change it. In contrast, Jim—who had worked in the traditional functional organization for many years—saw vendor relations on a pilot build as part of his functional job, but did not believe that contravening standard practices to get the vendor to shorten the cycle time was his responsibility, within the range of his authority, or even in the best long-term interest of his function. He was more concerned with avoiding conflict and not roiling the water than with achieving the overarching goal of the team.

It is interesting to note that in Team B, engineering raised the issue and, while unwilling to take aggressive steps to resolve it, also blocked others' attempts. In Team A, however, while the issue came up initially through engineering, Fred in manufacturing proactively went after it. In the case of Team B, getting a prototype chip returned from a vendor was still being treated as an "engineering responsibility," whereas in the case of Team A, it was treated as a "team responsibility." Since Fred was the person best qualified to attack that issue, he did so.

Both Team A and Team B had a charter, a contract, a colocated core team staffed with generalists, a project leader, articulated responsibilities, and an executive sponsor. Yet Jim's and Fred's understanding of what these things meant for them personally and for the team at the detailed, working level was quite different. While the teams had been through similar training and team startup processes, Jim ap-parently saw the new approach as a different organizational framework within which work would get done as before. In contrast, Fred seemed to see it as an opportunity to work in a different way—to take responsibility for reconfiguring tasks, drawing on new skills, and reallocating resources, where required, for getting the job done in the best way possible.

Although both teams were "heavyweight" in theory, Fred's team was much "heavier" in its operation and impact. Our research suggests that heaviness is not just a matter of structure and mechanism, but of attitudes and behavior. Firms that try to create heavyweight teams without making the deep changes needed to realize the power in the team's structure will find this team approach problematic. Those intent on using teams for platform projects and willing to make the basic changes we have discussed here can enjoy substantial advantages of focus, integration, and effectiveness.

Reading IV–4
The Power of Product Integrity

Kim B. Clark and Takahiro Fujimoto

Some companies consistently develop products that succeed with customers. Other companies often fall short. What differentiates them is integrity. Every product reflects the organization and the development process that created it. Companies that consistently develop successful products—products with integrity—are themselves coherent and integrated. Moreover, this coherence is distinguishable not just at the level of structure and strategy but also, and more important, at the level of day-to-day work and individual understanding. Companies with organizational integrity possess a source of competitive advantage that rivals cannot easily match.

The primacy of integrity, in products and organizations alike, begins with the role new products play in industrial competition and with the difficulty of competing on performance or price alone. New products have always fascinated and excited customers, of course. Henry Ford's Model A made front-page news after near-riots erupted outside dealers' showrooms. But today, in industries ranging from cars and computers to jet engines and industrial controls, new products are the focal point of competition. Developing high-quality products faster, more efficiently, and more effectively tops the competitive agenda for senior managers around the world.

Three familiar forces explain why product development has become so important. In the last two decades, intense international competition, rapid technological advances, and sophisticated, demanding customers have made "good enough" unsatisfactory in more and more consumer and industrial markets. Yet the very same forces are also making product integrity harder and harder to achieve.

Consider what happened when Mazda and Honda each introduced four-wheel steering to the Japanese auto market in 1987. Although the two steering systems used different technologies—Mazda's was based on electronic control, while Honda's was mechanical—they were equally sophisticated, economical, and reliable. Ten years earlier, both versions probably would have met with success. No longer. A majority of Honda's customers chose to install four-wheel steering in their new cars; Mazda's system sold poorly and was widely regarded as a failure.

Why did consumers respond so differently? Product integrity. Honda put its four-wheel steering system into the Prelude, a two-door coupe with a sporty, progressive image that matched consumers' ideas about the technology. The product's concept and the new component fit together seamlessly; the car sent a coherent message to its potential purchasers. In contrast, Mazda introduced its four-wheel steering system in the 626, a five-door hatchback that consumers associated with safety and dependability. The result was a mismatch between the car's conservative, family image and its racy steering system. Too sophisticated to be swayed by technology alone (as might have been the case a decade before), Mazda's potential customers saw no reason to buy a car that did not satisfy their expectations in every respect, including "feel." (Mazda's new advertising slogan, "It just feels right," suggests the company's managers took this lesson to heart.)

Product integrity is much broader than basic functionality or technical performance. Customers who have accumulated experience with a product expect new models to balance basic functions and economy with more subtle characteristics. Consumers expect new products to harmonize with their values and lifestyles. Industrial customers expect them to mesh with existing components in a work system or a production process. The extent to which a new product achieves this balance is a measure of its integrity. (One of integrity's primary metrics is market share, which reflects how well a product attracts and satisfies customers over time.)

Product integrity has both an internal and an external dimension. Internal integrity refers to the consistency between a product's function and its structure: the parts fit smoothly, the components match and work well together, the layout maximizes the available space. Organizationally, internal integrity is achieved mainly through cross-functional coordination within the company and with suppliers. Efforts to enhance internal integrity through this kind of coordination have become standard practice among product developers in recent years.

External integrity refers to the consistency between a product's performance and customers' expectations. In turbulent markets like those in which Honda and Mazda were competing, external integrity is critical to a new product's competitiveness. Yet for the most part, external integrity is an underexploited opportunity. Companies assign responsibility for anticipating what customers will want to one or more functional groups (the product planners in marketing, for example, or the testers in product engineering). But they give little or no attention to integrating a clear sense of customer expectations into the work of the product development organization as a whole.

Of course, there are exceptions. In a six-year study of new product development (see "Focus on Development"), we found a handful of companies that consistently created products with integrity. What set these companies apart was their seamless pattern of organization and management. The way people did their jobs, the way decisions were made, the way suppliers were integrated into the company's own efforts—everything cohered and supported company strategy. If keeping the product line fresh and varied was a goal, speed and flexibility were apparent at every step in the development process, as were the habits and assumptions that accustom people and organizations to being flexible and to solving problems quickly. For example, product plans relied on large numbers of parts from suppliers who focused on meeting tight schedules and high quality standards even when designs changed late in the day. Product and process engineers jointly developed body panels and the dies to make them through informal, intense interactions that cut out unnecessary mistakes and solved problems on the spot. Production people built high-quality pro-

Focus on Development

What are the sources of superior performance in product development? What accounts for the wide differences in performance among companies in the same industry? To answer those questions, we studied 29 major development projects in 20 automobile companies around the world. (Three companies are headquartered in the United States, eight in Japan, and nine in Europe.) The projects ranged from micro-mini cars and small vans to large luxury sedans, with suggested retail prices from $4,300 to more than $40,000. Our research methods included structured and unstructured interviews, questionnaires, and statistical analysis. Throughout the study, we strove to develop a consistent set of data (including both measures of performance and patterns of organization and management) so that we could identify the constants among projects that differed greatly in scope and complexity.

We chose to concentrate on the automobile industry because it is a microcosm of the new industrial competition. In 1970, a handful of auto companies competed on a global scale with products for every market segment; today more than 20 do. Customers have grown more discerning, sophisticated, and demanding. The number of models has multiplied, even as growth has slowed, and technology is ever-more complex and diverse. In 1970, for example, the traditional V-8 engine with 3-speed automatic transmission and rear-wheel drive was the technology of choice for 80% of the cars produced in the United States. By the early 1980s, consumers could choose among 34 alternative configurations. In this environment, fast, efficient, effective product development has become the focal point of competition and managerial action.

totypes that tested the design against the realities of commercial production early in the game and so eliminated expensive delays and rework later on.

The examples we draw on in this article all come from the auto industry. We chose to look at a single industry worldwide so that we could identify the factors that separate outstanding performers from competitors making similar products for similar markets around the globe. But our basic findings apply to businesses as diverse as semiconductors, soup, and commercial construction. Wherever managers face a turbulent, intensely competitive market, product integrity—and the capacity to create it—can provide a sustainable competitive advantage.

The Power of a Product Concept

Products are tangible objects—things you can see, touch, and use. Yet the process of developing new products depends as much on the flow of information as it does on the flow of materials. Consider how a new product starts and ends.

Before a customer unpacks a new laptop computer or sets up a high-speed packaging machine, and long before a new car rolls off the showroom floor, the product (or some early version of it) begins as an idea. Next, that idea is embodied in progressively more detailed and concrete forms: Ideas turn into designs, designs into drawings, drawings into blueprints, blueprints into prototypes, and so on until a finished product emerges from the factory. When it is finally in customers' hands, the product is converted into information once again.

If this last statement sounds odd, think about what actually happens when a potential buyer test-drives a new car. Seated behind the wheel, the customer receives a barrage of messages about the vehicle's performance. Some of these messages are delivered directly by the car: the feel of the acceleration, the responsiveness of the steering system, the noise of the engine, the heft of a door. Others come indirectly: the look on people's faces as the car goes by, comments from passengers, the driver's recollection of the car's advertising campaign. All these messages influence the customer's evaluation, which will largely depend on how he or she interprets them. In essence, the customer is consuming the product *experience,* not the physical product itself.

Developing this experience—and the car that will embody it—begins with the creation of a product concept. A powerful product concept specifies how the new car's basic functions, structures, and messages will attract and satisfy its target customers. In sum, it defines the character of the product from a customer's perspective.

The phrase "pocket rocket," for example, captures the basic concept for a sporty version of a subcompact car. Small, light, and fast, a pocket rocket should also have quick, responsive handling and an aggressive design. While the car should sell at a premium compared with the base model, it should still be affordable. And the driving experience should be fun: quick at the getaway, nimble in the turns, and very fast on the straightaways. Many other design and engineering details would need definition, of course, for the car to achieve its objectives. But the basic concept of an affordable and fun-to-drive pocket rocket would be critical in guiding and focusing creative ideas and decisions.

By definition, product concepts are elusive and equivocal. So it is not surprising that when key project participants are asked to relate the concept for a new vehicle, four divergent notions of value emerge. Those for whom the product concept means *what the product does* will couch their description in terms of performance and technical functions. Others, for whom the concept means *what the product is,* will describe the car's packaging, configuration, and main component technologies. Others, for whom product concept is synonymous with *whom the product serves,* will describe target customers. Still others, reflecting their interpretation of the concept as *what the product means to customers,* will respond thematically, describing the car's character, personality, image, and feel.

The most powerful product concepts include all these dimensions. They are often presented as images or metaphors (like pocket rocket) that can evoke many different aspects of the new product's message without compromising its essential meaning. Honda Motor is one of the few auto companies that make the generation of a strong product concept the first step in their development process.

When Honda's engineers began to design the third-generation (or 1986) Accord in the early 1980s, they did not start with a sketch of a car. The engineers started with a concept—"man maximum, machine minimum"—that captured in a short, evocative phrase the way they wanted customers to feel about the car. The concept and the car have been remarkably successful: since 1982, the Accord has been one of the best-selling cars in the United States; in 1989, it was the top-selling car. Yet when it was time to design the 1990 Accord, Honda listened to the market, not to its own success. Market trends were indicating a shift away from sporty sedans toward family models. To satisfy future customers' expectations—and to reposition the Accord, moving it up-market just a bit—the 1990 model would have to send a new set of product messages.

As the first step in developing an integrated product concept, the Accord's project manager (the term Honda uses is *large product leader*) led a series of small group discussions involving close to 100 people in all. These early brainstorming sessions involved people from many parts of the organization, including body engineering, chassis engineering, interior design, and exterior design. In line with Honda tradition, the groups developed two competing concepts in parallel. The subject of the discussions was abstract: What would be expected of a family sedan in the 1990s. Participants talked frequently about "adult taste" and "fashionability" and eventually came to a consensus on the message the new model would deliver to customers—"an adult sense of reliability." The ideal family car would allow the driver to transport family and friends with confidence, whatever the weather or road conditions; passengers would always feel safe and secure.

This message was still too abstract to guide the product and process engineers who would later be making concrete choices about the new Accord's specifications, parts, and manufacturing processes. So the next step was finding an image that would personify the car's message to consumers. The image the product leader and his team emerged with was "a rugby player in a business suit." It evoked rugged, physical contact, sportsmanship, and gentlemanly behavior—disparate qualities the new car would have to convey. The image was also concrete enough to translate clearly into design details. The decision to replace the old Accord's retractable headlamps with headlights made with a pioneering technology developed by Honda's supplier, Stanley, is a good example. To the designers and engineers, the new lights' totally transparent cover glass symbolized the will of a rugby player looking into the future calmly, with clear eyes.

The next and last step in creating the Accord's product concept was to break down the rugby player image into specific attributes the new car would have to possess. Five sets of key words captured what the product leader envisioned: "open-minded," "friendly communication," "tough spirit," "stress-free," and "love forever." Individually and as a whole, these key words reinforced the car's message to consumers. "Tough spirit" in a car, for example, meant maneuverability, power, and sure handling in extreme driving conditions, while "love forever" translated into long-term reliability and customer satisfaction. Throughout the course of the project, these phrases provided a kind of shorthand to help people make coherent design and hardware choices in the face of competing demands. Moreover, they were a powerful spur to innovation.

Consider this small slice of the process. To approximate the rugby player's reliability and composure ("stress-free"), the engineers had to eliminate all unnecessary stress from the car. In technical terms, this meant improving the car's NVH, or noise, vibration, and harshness characteristics. That, in turn, depended on reducing the "three gangs of noise," engine noise, wind noise, and road noise.

To reduce engine noise, the product engineers chose a newly developed balance shaft that rotated twice as fast as the engine and offset its vibration. The shaft made the Accord's compact 4-cylinder engine as quiet as a V-6 and conserved space in the process. But since the shaft was effective only when the engine was turning over reasonably quickly, the product engineers also had to design a new electrically controlled engine mount to minimize vibration when the engine was idling.

Moreover, once the engine was quieter, other sources of noise became apparent. The engineers learned that the floor was amplifying noise from the engine, as was the roof, which resonated with the engine's vibration and created unpleasant, low-frequency booming sounds. To solve these problems, the engineers inserted paper honeycomb structures 12 to 13 millimeters thick in the roof lining—a solution that also improved the roof's structural rigidity and contributed to the car's tough spirit. They also redesigned the body floor, creating a new sandwich structure of asphalt and sheet steel, which similarly strengthened the body shell.

Multiply this example hundreds of times over and it is clear why a strong product concept is so important. At its core, the development process is a complex system for solving problems and making decisions. Product concepts like those developed at Honda give people a clear framework for finding solutions and making decisions that complement one another and ultimately contribute to product integrity.

Organizing for Integrity

When cars were designed and developed by a handful of engineers working under the direction of a Henry Ford, a Gottlieb Daimler, or a Kiichiro Toyoda, organization was not an issue. What mattered were the engineers' skills, the group's chemistry, and the master's guidance. These are still vital to product integrity; but the organizational challenge has become immeasurably more complex. Developing a new car involves hundreds (if not thousands) of people working on specialized pieces of the project in many different locations for months or even years at a time. Whether their efforts have integrity—whether the car performs superbly and delights customers—will depend on how the company organizes development and the nature of the leadership it creates.

Efforts to organize development effectively are rooted in the search for solutions to two basic problems. One is designing, building, and testing the product's parts and subsystems so that every element achieves a high level of performance. In a car, this means that the brakes hold on wet or icy roads, the suspension gives a smooth ride on rough roads, the car corners well on sharp turns, and so on. Because performance at this level is driven by expertise and deep understanding, some specialization, both for individuals and for the organization, is essential. Yet specialization is a double-edged sword. By complicating communication and coordination across the organization, it complicates the second problem that development organizations face: achieving product integrity.

When markets were relatively stable, product life cycles long, and customers concerned most with technical performance, companies could achieve product integrity through strong functional organizations. Managers could commit whatever resources and time it took to make products that worked well, and external integrity (matching the product to customer expectations) was simply a by-product of those efforts. But as competition intensified and customers' needs and wants grew harder to predict, integration became an explicit goal for most product developers. By the late 1980s, even the most resolutely functional development organizations had established formal mechanisms such as coordination committees, engineering liaisons, project managers, matrix structures, and cross-functional teams to improve product development.

Structural mechanisms like these are only a small part of achieving product integrity, however. At best—when they are reinforced and supported by the behaviors, attitudes, and skills of people in every part of the development organization—they speed problem solving and improve the quality of the solutions. But by design, they are focused inward; they do not address integrity's external dimension. So unless the company makes a deliberate effort to integrate customers into the development process, it is likely to create products that are fresh, technologically advanced, and provide good value but that often fall short with sophisticated consumers.

For this reason, external integration is the single most important task for new product development. It represents a conscious organizational effort to enhance the external integrity of the development process by matching the philosophy and details of product design to the expectations of target customers. Generating a distinctive product concept that anticipates future customers' needs and wants is the first step in external integration. Infusing this concept into drawings, plans, detailed designs, and, ultimately, the product itself is the substance of its ongoing work.

To get some sense of how thorough (and hard) this infusion process actually is, consider a few of the conflicts Honda faced during the planning stage for the third-generation Accord.

The vehicle's product concept (man maximum, machine minimum) included maximum space and visibility for the occupants, minimum space for the car's mechanisms, a wide, low body for aesthetics, superb handling and stability, and superior economy in operation. To convey a feeling of spaciousness, the design called for a low engine hood and a larger-than-usual front window. Both features increased the driver's visibility and sense of interaction with the outside world. But the window size also meant that the cabin would get uncomfortably hot on sunny days unless the car had a big air conditioner—as well as a powerful engine to run it.

A large engine—the obvious solution—was precluded by the decision to keep the hood low, since the only suspension system that would work was an expensive, double-wishbone construction that narrowed the engine chamber. And in any case, the engineers wanted the engine to be light so that the car would handle sharply.

EXHIBIT 1 **Double Wishbone Front Suspension**

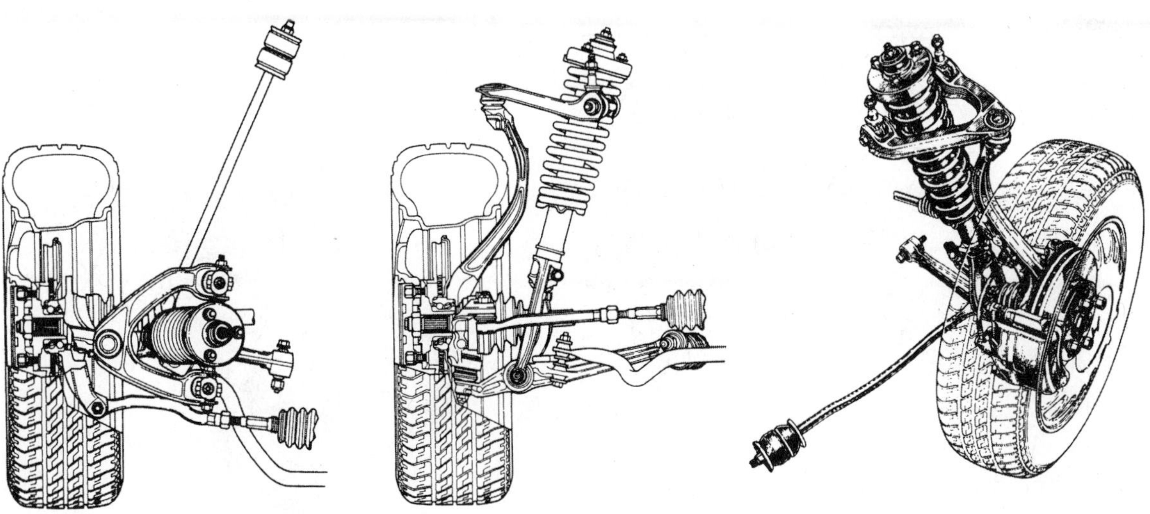

The height of the hood became a battlefield, with body, engine, and chassis engineers warring over millimeters. What made the conflict constructive—it ultimately led to the development of a new engine that was both compact and powerful—was the fact that all the combatants understood what the Accord had to achieve. Guided by the large product leader, who saw every argument as an opportunity to reinforce the car's basic concept, the engineers could see their work through future customers' eyes.

As Honda's experience indicates, external integration extends deeply into the development organization, and it involves much more than being "market oriented" or "customer driven." It begins with customers, to be sure, since the best concept developers invariably supplement the cooked information they get from marketing specialists with raw data they gather themselves. But strong product concepts also include a healthy measure of what we call "market imagination": they encompass what customers say they want and what the concept's creators *imagine* customers will want three or more years into the future. Remembering that customers know only existing products and existing technologies, they avoid the trap of being too close to customers—and designing products that will be out-of-date before they are even manufactured.

Interestingly, companies that are heavily driven by market data tend to slip on external integrity. As a rule, these companies have well-equipped marketing organizations with great expertise in formal research, and they are adept at using data from focus groups, product clinics, and the like to develop customer profiles. But these methods rarely lead to distinctive product concepts. In fact, to the extent that they limit or suppress the imaginations of product designers, they can actually harm a new product's future competitiveness.

How auto companies organize for external integration—and how much power they invest in their integrators—varies greatly. Some companies create an explicit role for an "external integrator" and assign it to people in a few functional units (testers in engineering, for example, and product planners in marketing). Others assign all their external integrators to a single specialized unit, which may be independent or organized by product. Similarly, the work of concept creation and concept realization may be broken up among different groups in the development organization or consolidated under one leader, as it is at Honda.

We have already seen how advantageous consolidating responsibility can be for enhancing external integration. This approach is equally successful in achieving internal integrity.

One of the thorniest issues in creating a strong product concept is when (and how) to involve functional specialists other than those who make up the product development team. As we saw with the

EXHIBIT 2 1990 Honda Accord Valve Train

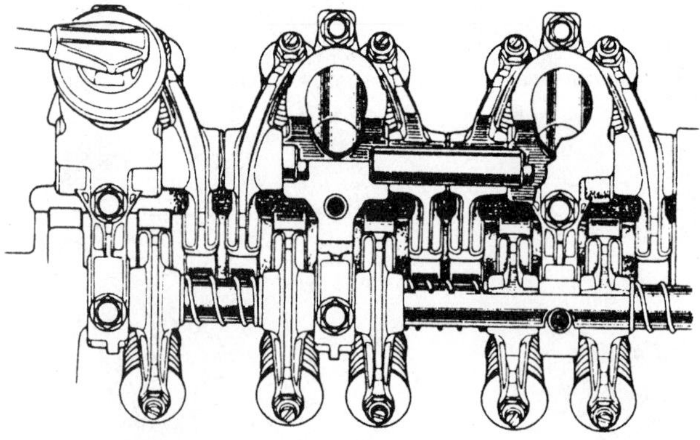

EXHIBIT 3 Second-Order Balance System

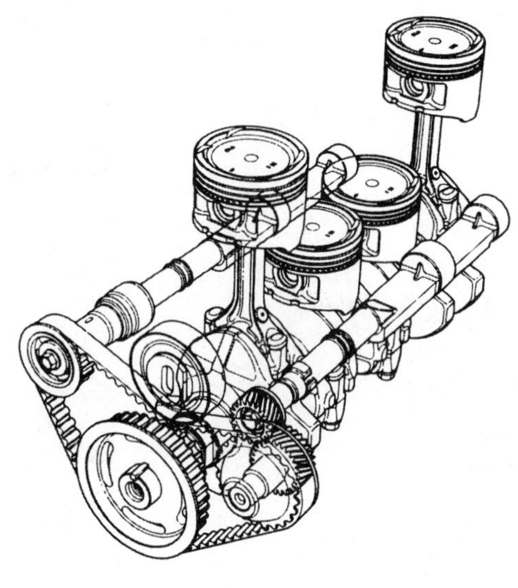

Accord, the product concept has clear repercussions for every aspect of the development process, from design and layout to cost and manufacturability. So on the one hand, front-loading input and information from specialists downstream is highly desirable. On the other hand, broad downstream involvement can easily jeopardize the distinctiveness and clarity of a product concept if (as often happens) negotiations and battles among powerful functions lead to political compromises and patchwork solutions.

The fact that working-level engineers were involved in the concept stage of the Accord's development was essential to its product integrity. Faced with tough choices about the car's front end, the engineers had not only a clear concept to guide them but also one they felt they owned. Moreover, their solution—the new engine—enhanced the Accord's internal integrity by raising its level of technical performance. At the same time, internal demands and functional constraints never compromised the Accord's basic concept. Like many of the other product managers we spoke with, the Accord's product leader knew that democracy without clear concept leadership is the archenemy of distinctive products.

There are other ways to balance downstream expertise with strong concept leadership, of course. (One of Honda's rivals also makes early cross-functional negotiations an important part of its new product development work, for example, but gives a small group of concept creators and assistants six months or so to establish the concept first, before the negotiations begin.) The important point is that integrity depends on striking a balance between the two. Companies that trade off one for the other sacrifice both product and organizational integrity. Those that place sole responsibility for the product concept with a specialized unit (often one within marketing) end up with lots of last-minute design and engineering changes. Conversely, companies that initiate senior-level, cross-functional negotiations at the very start of every project usually find themselves with undistinguished products.

The integration that leads to product integrity does not surface in organization charts alone, nor is it synonymous with the creation of cross-functional teams, the implementation of "design for manufacturing," or any other useful organizational formula for overhauling development work. Ironically, efforts to increase integration can even undermine it if the integrating mechanisms are misconstructed or if the organization is unprepared for the change. At one U.S. auto company, we found a very coherent cross-functional project team with great spirit and purpose. But the team was made up solely of liaisons and included none of the working engineers actually responsible for drawings and prototypes. So for the most part, engineers ignored the team, whose existence only masked the lack of true integration.

What distinguishes outstanding product developers is the consistency between their formal structures and the informal organization that accomplishes the real work of development. In the case of the Honda Accord, we have seen some important characteristics of such consistency: the company's preference for firsthand information and direct (sometimes conflict-full) discussion; the way specialists are respected but never deified; the constant stream of early, informal communication (even at the risk of creating confusion or inefficiencies in the short run); and, most important, the primacy of strong concept leadership.

Integrity's Champion: The Heavyweight Product Manager

The key to product integrity is leadership. Product managers in companies whose products consistently succeed accomplish two things without fail. They focus the whole development organization on customer satisfaction. And they devise processes (both formal and informal) for creating powerful product concepts and infusing them into the details of production and design. In our lexicon, they are "heavyweight" product managers, and they differ significantly from their lighter weight counterparts in other companies.

During the 1980s, product managers began to appear at more and more of the world's auto companies. In most cases, the title means relatively little. The position adds another box to the organization chart, but the organization's basic structure is still heavily functional. Product managers in these companies coordinate development activities through liaison representatives from each of the engineering departments. They have no direct access to working-level engineers, no contact with marketing, and no concept responsibility. Their positions have less status and power than the functional managers' do, and they have little influence outside of product engineering (and only limited influence within it). Their job is to collect information on the status of work, to help functional groups resolve conflicts, and to facilitate completion of the project's overall goals. They do not actually impair a product's integrity, but neither can they contribute much to it.

The contrast with the heavyweight's job could not be more striking. In a few auto companies, product managers play a role that simply does not exist in other automakers' development organizations. Like the Accord's large product leader, they are deeply involved in creating a strong product concept. Then, as the concept's guardians, they keep the concept alive and infuse it into every aspect of the new product's design. As one heavyweight product manager told us, "We listen to process engineers. We listen to plant managers. But we make the final decisions. Above all, we cannot make any compromise on the concept. The concept is the soul of the vehicle; we cannot sell it."

Guardianship like this is crucial because the product concept can get lost so easily in the complexity of actually designing, planning, and building a new car. The problems that preoccupied the Accord's product engineers were often almost imperceptibly small: a three-millimeter gap between the window glass and the body; the tiny chips on the car's sills that come from stones kicked up on the road; a minuscule gap between the hood and the body. But problems like these are the stuff of product integrity: All the magic is in the details.

Keeping track of those details, however, is no easy matter. Nor is it easy to keep the product concept fresh and clear in many people's minds during the months (and years) that development consumes. For that reason, heavyweight product managers must be a little like evangelists, with the product concept as their Bible and the work of exhorting, preaching, and reminding as their mission. To paraphrase an assistant product manager in one of the heavyweight organizations, subtle nuances such as the car's taste and character have to be built into the design by fine-tuning. They cannot be expressed completely in planning documents, no matter how detailed those may be. So the product manager has to interact continuously with the engineers to communicate his intentions and to refresh and reinforce their understanding of the product concept.

As concept guardians, heavyweight product managers draw on both personal credibility and expertise and the organizational clout that comes with the job. Themselves engineers by training, heavyweight product managers have a broad knowledge of the product and process engineering required to develop an entire vehicle. Years of experience with their companies give their words weight and increase their influence with people over whom they have no formal authority.

Product planners and engineers working on the detailed design of specific parts typically fall into this category. Yet as we have seen, the substance of their work is vital to a new car's integrity. To track design decisions and ensure that the concept is being translated accurately, heavyweight managers communicate daily with the functional engineering

EXHIBIT 4 4-Door Sedan Exterior Dimensions

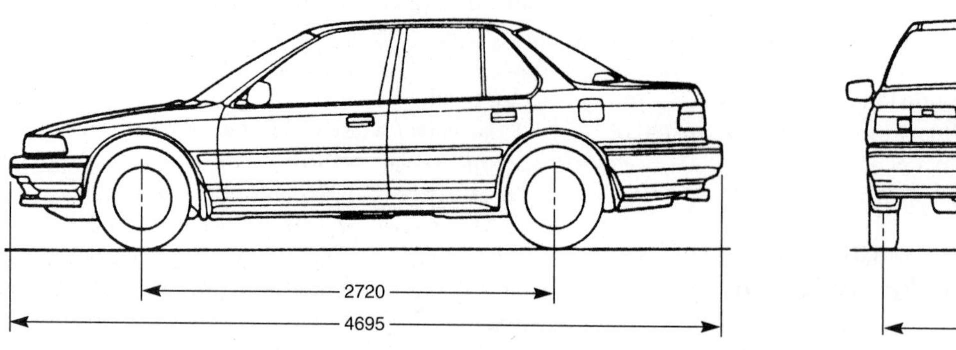

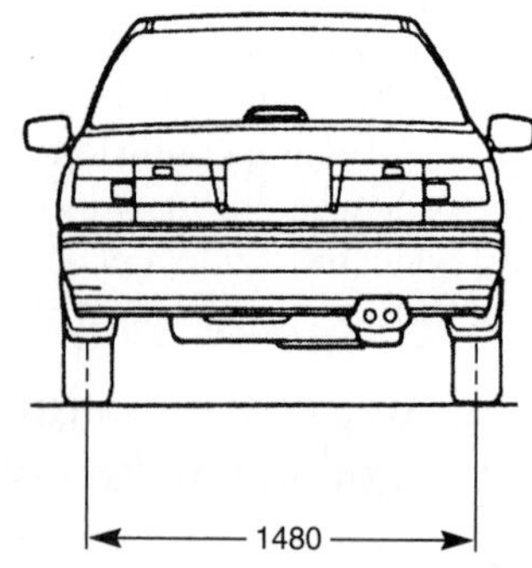

departments. They also intervene directly when decisions about parts or components that are particularly problematic or central to the product concept are being made. From a functional point of view, this is clearly a breach of organizational etiquette. But in practice, this intervention is usually readily accepted, in part because it is backed by tradition but mostly because of the product manager's credibility. When heavyweights visit bench-level engineers, they come to discuss substantive issues and their input is usually welcome. They are not making courtesy calls or engaging in morale-building exercises.

Organizationally, the heavyweight manager effectively functions as the product's general manager. In addition to concept-related duties, the responsibilities that come with the job include: coordinating production and sales as well as engineering; coordinating the entire project from concept to market; signing off on specification, cost-target, layout, and major component choices; and maintaining direct contact with existing and potential customers. Some of this work occurs through liaison representatives (although the liaisons themselves are "heavier" than they are in the lightweight organizations since they also serve as local project leaders within their functional groups). But there is no mistaking the heavyweights' clout: engineering departments typically report to them (which ones depends on the internal linkages the company wishes to emphasize). Heavyweights are also well supplied with formal procedures like design review and control of prototype scheduling that give them leverage throughout the organization.

Still, probably the best measure of a product manager's weight is the amount of time that formal meetings and paperwork consume. Lightweight product managers are much like high-level clerks. They spend most of the day reading memos, writing reports, and going to meetings. Heavyweights, in contrast, are invariably "out"—with engineers, plant people, dealers, and customers. "This job can't be done without wearing out my shoes," one experienced manager commented. "Since I'm asking other engineers for favors, I shouldn't ask them to come to me. I have to go and talk to them."

What lies behind "product managers in motion" is the central role that information plays in bringing new products to life. Take the heavyweight's interaction with customers. Talented product managers spend hours watching people on the street, observing styles, and listening to conversations. Department stores, sports arenas, museums, and discotheques are all part of their "market research" beat.

Heavyweight product managers are equally active in their relations with the test engineers. Like the product manager, test engineers stand in for the customer. When they evaluate a suspension system or test-drive a new car, they are rehearsing the experience the future customer with consume. To do this successfully, in ways that will ensure product integrity, the test engineers must know what to look for. In other words, they must be crystal clear on the product concept.

Heavyweight product managers make sure this clarity exists. They often test-drive vehicles and talk about their experiences with the test engineers. Many can and do evaluate the car's performance on the test track and show up almost daily during critical tests. They also seize every opportunity to build good communication channels and deepen their ties

EXHIBIT 5 **4-Door Sedan Interior Dimensions and 4-Door Sedan Visibility**

with younger engineers. One product manager said he welcomed disagreements among the test engineers because they gave him a good reason to go out to the proving ground and talk about product concepts with younger people with whom he would not otherwise interact.

If we reverse direction to look at how heavyweight product managers promote internal integrity, the same kind of behavior and activities come to the fore. Direct contact with product engineers and testers, for example, not only reinforces the product concept but also strengthens the links between functions, speeds up decision making and problem solving, and makes it easier to coordinate work flows. In fact, almost everything a product manager does to infuse the concept into the details makes the organization itself work better and faster. The reason is the strong customer orientation that the product concept—and product manager—convey.

The product manager's job touches every part of the new product process. Indeed, heavyweight product managers have to be "multilingual," fluent in the languages of customers, marketers, engineers, and designers. On one side, this means being able to translate an evocative concept like the pocket rocket into specific targets like "maximum speed 250 kilometers per hour" and "drag coefficient less than 0.3" that detail-oriented engineers can easily grasp. On the other side, it means being able to assess and communicate what a "0.3 drag coefficient" will mean to customers. (The fact that the translation process from customer to engineer is generally harder than that from engineer to customer explains why engineering tends to be the heavyweight product managers' native tongue.)

Because development organizations are continually involved in changing one form of information into another, face-to-face conversations and informal relationships are their life's blood. Heavyweight managers understand this and act on it. Aware that product concepts cannot be communicated in written documents alone (any more than the feel and sensibility of a new car can be captured in words alone), they travel constantly—telling stories, coining phrases, and generally making sure that nothing important gets lost in translation.

The Improvement Ethic

How a company develops new products says a great deal about what that company is and does. For most companies, the journey toward competing on integrity began during the 1980s. Quite possibly, it was inaugurated with a commitment to total quality or to reducing the lead time for developing new products. Heavyweight product management constitutes the next step on that journey. Taking it leads down one of two paths.

Some companies introduce a heavyweight product management system modestly and incrementally. A typical progression might go like this: shift from a strictly functional setup to a lightweight system, with the integrator responsible only for product engineering; expand the product manager's sphere to include new tasks such as product planning or product-process coordination; then raise the product manager's rank, appoint people with strong reputations to the job, and assign them one project rather than a few to focus their attention and expand their influence. Senior managers that face deep resistance from their functional units often choose this path.

Other companies (particularly smaller players) take a faster, more direct route. One Japanese company leapt to a strong product manager system to introduce a new model. Backed by the widespread belief that the project might well determine the company's future, senior management created an unusually heavy product manager to run it. An executive vice president with many years of experience became the product manager, with department heads from engineering, production, and planning acting as his liaisons and as project leaders within their functional groups. With these changes, management sent a clear signal that the company could no longer survive in its traditional form.

The project succeeded, and today the product is seen as the company's turnaround effort, its reentry as a competitor after years of ineffectual products. The project itself became a model for subsequent changes (including the creation of a product manager office) in the regular development organization.

How a company changes its organization and the speed with which it moves will depend on its position and the competitive threat it faces. But all successful efforts have three common themes: a unifying driver, new blood, and institutional tenacity. (See "The Case for Heavyweight Product Management," which describes Ford Motor Company's progress toward becoming a heavyweight organization.)

Just as engineers need a vision of the overall product to guide their efforts in developing a new car, the people involved in changing an organization need an objective that captures their imaginations. Where changes have taken hold, senior managers have linked them to competition and the drive for tangible advantage in the marketplace.

During the 1980s, the quest for faster development lead time was particularly powerful in driving such efforts. But lead time is not an end in itself. Rather, its pursuit leads people to do things that improve the system overall. In this respect, lead time is like inventory in a just-in-time manufacturing system: Reducing work-in-process inventory is somewhat effective, but attacking the root causes of excess inventory truly changes the system.

Companies that successfully focus on lead time generally emphasize changes in internal integration. Product integrity can drive companies to higher performance. Managed well, the drive to create products that fire the imagination gives the implementation of a heavyweight system energy and direction.

Of the many change efforts we have seen, the most successful were led by new people. Some were new to the company, but most came from within the organization. Sometimes viewed as mavericks, they saw the potential for change where others saw more of the same. A company cannot change everyone. It can, however, create new leaders and empower people who are attuned to the new direction the company has to take. It can also find nontraditional ways to identify and develop heavyweight product managers for the future, such as apprenticeship systems.

Moving to a heavier product manager structure is a process of discovery—one the U.S. auto company with the ineffectual cross-functional team we described earlier knows very well. Like many others, that company has discovered that changes in organizational structure are important but insufficient. To create a true team, greater change—particularly in the behavior of traditionally powerful functional managers—is needed.

The journey to heavyweight product management is hard, surprisingly so for many managers. Those who succeed do so because they have tenacity. Outstanding companies understand that projects end but the journey doesn't. The challenge to learn from experience and continuously improve is always there.

Yet in company after company, the same problems crop up over and over. Why do most companies learn so little from their product development projects? The explanation is simple: At the end of every project, there is pressure to move on to the next. The cost of this tunnel vision is very high. Those few companies that work at continuous improvement achieve a significant competitive edge. Moving to a more effective development organization can be the basis for instilling an ethic of continuous improvement. Companies that compete on integrity exercise that ethic every day.

Author note: We gratefully acknowledge the help of Nobuhiko Kawamoto, CEO of Honda Motor Company, and Tateomi Miyoshi, large product leader for the Honda Accord.

The Case for Heavyweight Product Management

In the early 1980s, successful products filled the Ford Motor Company's scrapbooks but not its dealers' showrooms. Its cars were widely criticized. Quality was far below competitive standards. Market share was falling. In addition, the company's financial position was woeful, and layoffs were ongoing, among white-collar staff and factory workers alike. By the end of the decade, history was repeating itself: The Ford Explorer, introduced in the spring of 1990, may prove to be Ford's most successful product introduction ever. Despite the fact that it debuted in a down market, the four-door, four-wheel-drive sport-utility vehicle has sold phenomenally well. Rugged yet refined, the Explorer gets all the important details right, from exterior styling to the components and interior design.

Behind the Explorer lay a decade of changes in Ford's management, culture, and product development organization. The changes began in the dark days of the early 1980s with the emergence of new leaders in Ford's executive offices and in design studios. Their herald was the Taurus, introduced in 1985. Designed to be a family vehicle with the styling, handling, and ride of a sophisticated European sedan, the car offered a distinctive yet integrated package in which advanced aerodynamic styling was matched with a newly developed chassis with independent rear suspension and a front-wheel-drive layout. The car's interior, which minimized the chrome and wood paneling that were traditional in American roadsters, had a definite European flavor. So did the ride and the way the car handled: The steering was much more responsive, and the ride was tighter and firmer.

The development efforts that produced the Taurus set in motion profound changes within the Ford engineering, manufacturing, and marketing organizations. Traditionally, Ford's development efforts had been driven by very strong functional managers. In developing the Taurus, however, Ford turned to the "Team Taurus," whose core included principals from all the major functions and activities involved in the creation of the new car. The team was headed by Lew Veraldi, at the time in charge of large-car programs at Ford, and it served to coordinate and integrate the development program at the senior management level.

Team Taurus was the first step on a long path of organizational, attitudinal, and procedural change. As development of the Taurus went ahead, it became clear that integrated development required more than the creation of a team and that there was more to achieving integrity than linking the functions under the direction of a single manager. So the next step in Ford's evolution was the development of the "concept to customer" process, or C to C.

The C to C process took shape during the mid-1980s, as Ford sought aggressively to cut lead time, improve quality, and continue to bring attractive products to market. Led by a handpicked group of engineers and product planners, the C to C project focused on devising a new architecture for product development: Its members identified critical milestones, decision points, criteria for decision making, and patterns of responsibility and functional involvement. This architecture was then implemented step by step, in ongoing programs as well as in new efforts.

At about the same time, in 1987, Ford formalized the "program manager" structure that had evolved out of the Taurus experience. (Program manager is the term Ford uses for the position we call product manager.) As part of this structure, senior management affirmed the centrality of cross-functional teams working under the direction of a strong program manager. Moreover, cross-functional integration was reinforced at the operating level as well as at the strategy level. The change in marketing's role is a good example: instead of adding their input through reports and memoranda, marketing people (led by the program manager) meet directly with designers and engineers to discuss concept development and key decisions about features, layout, and components. Similarly, program managers have been given responsibility for critical functions like product planning and layout, where many of the integrative decisions are made.

In successive programs, Ford has refined its approach and pushed integration further and further. The strength of the program managers has also increased. The results are visible in the products Ford developed during the latter part of the 1980s—and in their sales. Beginning with the Taurus, Ford has scored impressive market successes with a number of its new cars: the Lincoln Continental, which expanded Lincoln's share of the luxury market; the Thunderbird Super Coupe, which compares favorably with European high-performance sedans; the Probe, the result of a joint development project with Mazda and which enthusiasts generally rate higher than Mazda's own effort, the MX6; and the sport-utility Explorer.

Building Competences/Capabilities through New Product Development

Case IV–5
Braun AG: The KF 40 Coffee Machine (Abridged)

Karen Freeze

"If we're going to do it, we've got to quit stalling," exclaimed Albrecht Jestädt,[1] head of development for a new coffeemaker at Braun AG. "I've said all I can about polypropylene, and I'm convinced we can go with it," he added, taking another sip of his beer.

At the end of a day in January 1983, Jestädt and his colleagues were discussing Braun's newest design: an elegant, cylindrical coffeemaker, called the "KF 40," destined for the mid- and upper end of the mass market. To meet management's cost targets, however, they would have to use polypropylene, a much less expensive plastic than Braun's traditional material, and whether so doing would jeopardize Braun's reputation for quality was a matter of intense debate throughout the company. Unlike the very expensive polycarbonate, Braun's traditional material, polypropylene could not be molded into large, complicated parts (like the KF 40's "tank") without suffering so-called "sink" marks on surfaces that were supposed to be flawlessly even. So the designers had devised a solution that involved a major departure from the smooth, winter-white surfaces characteristic of all Braun household products. (See Exhibit 1 for a prototype.)

"The decision is obvious," claimed Gilbert Greaves, business director for household products. "We need this product *now*, and we have to stop being quite so picky."

"I think we should be picky," said Hartwig Kahlcke, the industrial designer on the project. "But we feel that the rippled design for the tank actually enhances the surface appearance, without compromise."

"Maybe," said Hartmut Stroth, recently appointed director of corporate communications. "But it's no trivial matter. It's true that if we lose a year, we might not get in the market at all. Yet *nothing* is worth losing our reputation for superior quality. Not even the mass market." Stroth, who had served for over a decade in various communications positions at Braun, was very sensitive to the importance of Braun's "visual equity" and the need for maintaining it: "Not only do we have to think hard about how this corrugated surface design would fit into the Braun 'look,' but also about what that look represents. The idea of using design to mask sink marks bothers me in principle, and it may not work in practice, especially if the stuff doesn't hold up. I'm anything but risk-averse in this business, but I need to be convinced."

"Then let's go ahead with the trial tooling," Kahlcke responded. "The chairman has already OKed it; maybe that will convince you." Not waiting for Stroth's response, Kahlcke inquired about the chairman's views to date. "I know he liked the design, and I know he wants the product. What does he think about the material at this point?"

"You tell me," answered Lorne Waxlax, chairman of the board and Braun's CEO. He would have to make the ultimate decision and had just dropped in, as was his custom, to get the latest thinking on the KF 40.

Company Background: Braun by Design

Braun AG began as a family-owned radio and small appliance business founded in 1921 by Max Braun.[2] In the 1940s, Braun developed a novelty, the electric razor, which he introduced in 1950. After Braun's death in 1951, his sons, Artur and Erwin, took over, and three years later they asked their friend, Fritz Eichler, an artist then working in the theater, to help them find a new approach to their struggling business. In 1955, looking for an architect to help build a new office building, the company hired Dieter Rams, just two years out of architecture school.

Rams became Eichler's protégé, and together they built a small, intense design department at the com-

[1]See Appendix for identification and pronunciation glossary.

[2]AG=Aktiengesellschaft (joint stock company).

EXHIBIT 1 Two Views of the KF 40

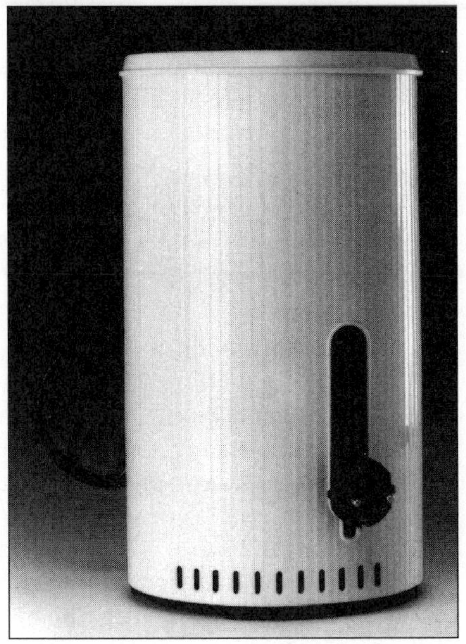

pany's headquarters in Kronberg, Germany. Convinced they could change the taste of their fellow citizens, Eichler, Rams, and colleagues set out to design and build a new kind of product. (See Exhibit 2 for Rams' 10 commandments of good design.)

EXHIBIT 2 10 Principles of Good Design

1. Good design is innovative.
2. Good design enhances the usefulness of a product.
3. Good design is aesthetic.
4. Good design displays the logical structure of a product; its form follows its function.
5. Good design is unobtrusive.
6. Good design is honest.
7. Good design is enduring.
8. Good design is consistent right down to details.
9. Good design is ecologically conscious.
10. Good design is minimal design.

"Braun has an uncompromising commitment towards the pursuit of excellence in performance-oriented design. Every product designed and manufactured by Braun must adhere to these commandments of good design. So, too, should every consumer demand such quality in the selection of a product—be it furniture, clothing, an automobile or a home appliance."

—Dieter Rams
Braun's Chief Designer

Eichler and Rams believed that their design philosophy should permeate the company, providing a recognizable identity not only in its products, but in every aspect of its relations with customers. (See Exhibit 3, "The Principles of Braun's Corporate Identity.") In Rams' view, achieving that identity required top management support of good design, and teamwork—constant interaction among disciplines. But designers also needed certain responsibilities and authority; otherwise, they would arrive, at most, at "superficial product cosmetics."

According to Rams, designers needed four things. First, they had to be responsible for configuring all elements of the product that would influence its final appearance. Second, designers needed the authority to determine the dimensions of a product (e.g., the positioning and ergonomic design of its operating functions); third, they must be the ones to decide on surface structures, colors, product labeling, and imprinting; fourth, they needed to cooperate with the engineers on construction problems (e.g., manufacturability) whenever the form of a product directly depended on the construction.

Although Rams was not without critics, his work was an effective counterweight to the popular assumption that designers merely dreamed up the external form of a product. Moreover, he adamantly

EXHIBIT 3 The Principles of Braun's Corporate Identity

"Braun regards the consumer as a *partner* in its business, not as an *object* of its strategy that is open to manipulation.

"Braun believes that consumer desires relate to genuine needs, and employs its expertise, inventiveness, know-how, etc. to satisfy these needs.

"Braun seeks to satisfy these needs in an optimal way, perhaps even better than the consumer expects.

"However, Braun refuses to persuade people to buy its products on the basis of presentation which meets—or pretends to meet—entirely different needs (which are not amenable to rational consideration) for prestige, ego-support, ostentatious consumption, cosmetic effectiveness, etc.

"Braun refuses to exploit human weaknesses to improve its results, and rejects any means of 'hidden persuasion.'

"Braun also rejects all methods involving purely superficial attraction: in place of this, it has demonstrated that firm concentration on product design which is as good and functional as possible—including external aspects—is also experienced as aesthetically satisfying."

stood by his own definition of "functional": that the purpose of good design is to fulfill the *primary function* of a product, including its need to be appealing to the user so it would be a welcome object in his or her environment.

By the mid-1970s Braun had built a thriving business, primarily in small home appliances (e.g., shavers, coffeemakers, and mixers), with additional sales in consumer electronics (e.g., cameras and hi-fi equipment). Further, the Braun design group was succeeding in its mission. One of its first products, a heavy-duty kitchen mixer (1957), was still in production and selling well. Most famous was their shaver, familiar to men all over the world. Many Braun products had won design awards; 36 of them, including Braun's first coffeemaker, had found a permanent place in New York's Museum of Modern Art.[3]

[3]A testimony to the appeal of Braun products was the emergence of a Braun Collectors Club (Braun-Design Sammler, later the FreundesKreis Braun-Design). Its members, entirely independently from the company, collected Braun products and published a newsletter.

The company's mission was carried out not only in its products, but also in its people. The company's principles had permeated its corporate consciousness and were second nature even at lower levels in the organization. Almost any employee could tell a visitor that Braun's values were embodied in its products, which had to have three characteristics: (a) first-class design; (b) superior quality; and (c) functions or features ahead of the competition. "We'll never bring out just a me-too product," echoed in every department.

The Gillette Connection

In 1967, the Braun brothers sold the company to an American consumer products giant, Gillette, well known for its mass-produced, mass-marketed products like razors, blades, and toiletries that had been marketed in Europe since the turn of the 20th century. For the first several years, Gillette left Braun's product strategy intact while infusing some of its management expertise into the organization. In fact, very few people knew that this German company *par excellence* had an American owner. But Braun soon began to expand its operations in other countries and extend its target markets beyond the opinion leaders it had originally cultivated. For example, in 1971, Lorne Waxlax, a Gillette manager since 1958, took charge of Braun's Spanish plant. He largely refocused the operation, emphasizing product development, sophisticated manufacturing, market research, and television advertising. The plant manufactured Braun's first successful mass-produced kitchen appliance, the hand blender, and served as the training ground for Braun's mass-produced appliance motors. By the early 1980s, Braun sales exceeded $400 million (see Exhibit 4).

EXHIBIT 4 Braun Group Financial Information
(*Millions of dollars*)

	1980	1981	1982
Net sales	$496.1	$451.4	$403.4
Profit from operations	23.6	22.8	33.3
Identifiable assets	384.3	325.2	301.5
Capital expenditures	21.5	23.6	20.4
Depreciation	17.3	18.9	16.6

Braun's Organization and Operations

Braun AG in 1983 was organized into three main functions: business management, technical operations, and group sales. (See organization chart in Exhibit 5.) Business management, a coordinating group established in 1976, was essentially strategic marketing. Until Gillette came along, Braun had assumed that if one made a good product, it would sell. And it generally did. But in 1975, marketing became more important, as the domestic and international marketing people came together under a single group. A director for each product group reported to the head of business management, as did the director of communications, which included packaging.

Technical Operations

Braun invested heavily in technology, and all key technically related disciplines were based at company headquarters under Dr. Thomas H. Thomsen, recently appointed director of technical operations. Previously, he had been head of engineering for Gillette in both London and Boston. Technical operations comprised four functional groups: R&D, Manufacturing, Quality Assurance, and Industrial Design.

R&D

The research and development department employed 220 people and included scientists and engineers working on advanced technology, as well as those involved in product development. R&D was headed by Dr. Peter Hexner, an American ex-army colonel who had directed Gillette's advanced technology department for 10 years. He commented on the challenge of balancing technology with the demands of design: "We have the classic conflicts. Design wants an elegant shaver a centimeter thick, and I have to knock reality into their heads: 'You can't fit a motor into a case a centimeter thick.'"

Engineering

Process development and manufacturing engineering were part of the manufacturing organization,

EXHIBIT 5 Corporate Structure

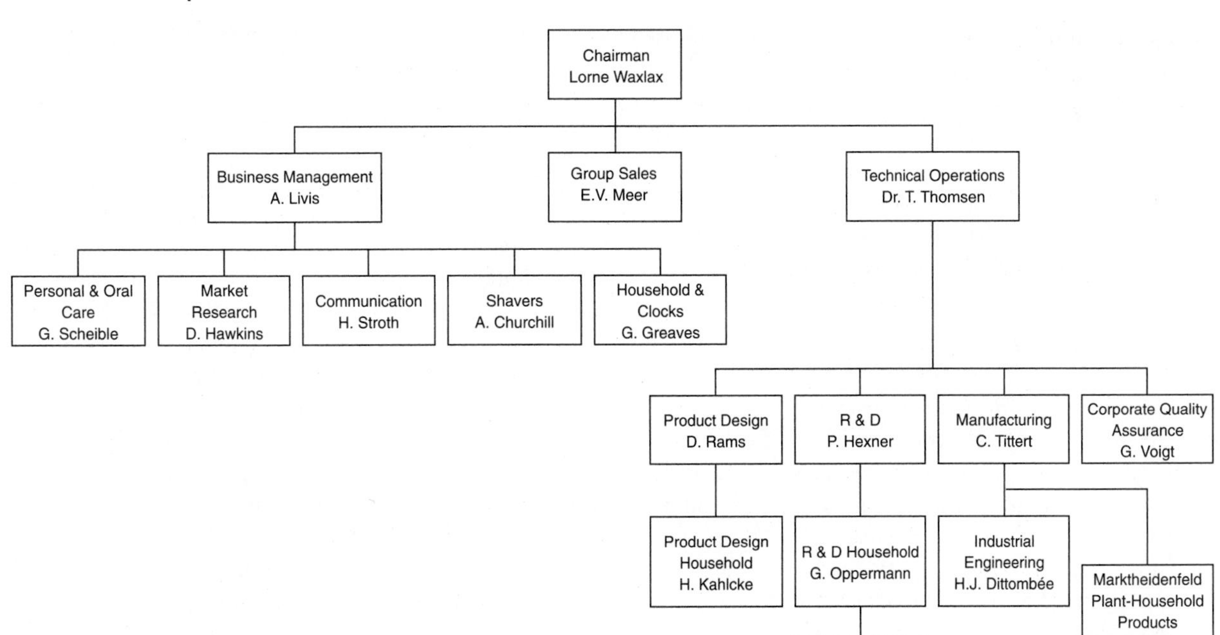

which managed Braun's component and assembly plants. Over three-quarters of Braun's manufacturing activity took place in its two large state-of-the-art plants in Walldürn and Marktheidenfeld (smaller operations were located in Spain, Ireland, Mexico, Argentina, and Brazil). Because of German labor's high cost, the manufacturing organization was continually pressured to produce efficiently, particularly in a plant like Marktheidenfeld that produced a wide variety of low-volume products including kitchen appliances. (For example, the plant produced around 700 units of the KF-35 coffeemaker per day.) While efforts to improve operations included automation, especially assembly, more challenging was designing a product so it required minimal assembly. "Anyone can make a cheap product with many parts and hire cheap labor offshore to screw them on. But not everyone can reduce as many parts as possible to one," said Bernard Wild, plant director at Marktheidenfeld. "We can prove that advanced industrial nations don't have to forfeit manufacturing just because their labor costs are high. Our resources are in our brains and imaginations—our know-how."

Quality assurance

Quality assurance was responsible for analysis of competitive offerings and rigorous testing during the product development process. Because Braun insisted that all its products be better than those of all the competition, the quality group relentlessly pursued the smallest detail with very high standards. As Werner Utsch, a quality engineer, commented, "We take them apart down to the last screw."

Industrial design

The fourth group in technical operations, industrial design, had an impact on the company far beyond its 16-member size. Indeed, Dieter Rams, head of the department, felt that small size was an important ingredient in its success. The department employed seven designers, most of whom had won the Braun Prize, a design award the firm had offered to design students since 1968. By 1983 Rams' international stature often resulted in his being equated with Braun design almost exclusively. Yet he found this star status awkward: "I constantly have to stress that I don't do everything; I'm simply the motor that drives the department. I try to give other people the credit they deserve."

Until recently, Rams had reported only to the chairman. But because of time limitations, Waxlax assigned industrial design to technical operations, where most problems could be solved. The direct line to the chairman remained, but was used only for the most important issues and impasses. Rams noted, "I've had a good understanding with every chairman I've worked with. But often designers aren't so lucky. We often educate business management people to the point where they begin to understand design and are supportive to us, but then they leave."

Product Development: The Triangle of Power—Design, Technology, Marketing

Product development had been relatively informal until 1980, when three people, representing R&D, business management, and manufacturing engineering, came together to develop procedures to make the process more operational and efficient. The result was a product development manual, introduced in 1981, that covered the responsibilities of key persons in a team (called an MTS team, for marketing-technology-strategy), definitions of elements in project development (e.g., different kinds of models), product specification guide, stages ("categories"), and signoff points in the process. (See Exhibit 6 for the project manual's table of contents.)

The "product program manager" (PPM) was responsible for maintaining these procedures; he or she chaired team meetings and represented the team vis-à-vis management, reporting directly to the head of technical operations or business management. The team itself had no formal leader. Various people took over as the stage in the product development process dictated, and stronger personalities could be influential; Jestädt, for example, first as product program manager, then as R&D manager for coffee, had quickly emerged as the de facto leader of the coffee machine project. (See Exhibit 7 for the PPM's and team's formal responsibilities.) In addition to the core team, people from other groups and disciplines—sometimes as many as 40—became involved as the project proceeded.

The team's monthly reports to the chairman had a standard format, divided into four sections:

EXHIBIT 6 Contents of Product Development Handbook

	Chapter
Project Procedures for New Products	**1**
Introduction	1.1
Goals	1.2
Assumptions	1.3
Tasks, Competence, Responsibilities	**2**
Project team	2.1
Project manager	2.2
Project team representatives	2.3
Project Development Procedure	**3**
Assumptions/principles	3.1
Implementation	3.2
Definition of terms	3.3
Exceptions	3.4
Project Profile	**4**
Explanations	4.1
Forms for project profile	4.2
Project Reporting	**5**
Project book	5.1
Reporting to the chairman	5.2
Summary	**6**
Product development flow chart	6.1

Description, Status, Further Steps, and Problems (or Risks). Although these monthly reviews were considered effective in motivating people to move toward the project goal, Waxlax did not like to use them as a threat: "The trick is to know whether the deadline is truly viable or not. It's easy for marketing to insist on a deadline—they don't have to do the work. I believe the engineers know better than I how fast the team can go, and for that reason I don't want to force it unduly."

Waxlax saw the meetings as an efficient way to keep up to date on all that was going on and to keep on top of problems and conflicts as they arose. He didn't believe in minimizing conflict, but saw it as positive for the company: "It's often the guy who is against something who forces it to become better." He also viewed the monthly meetings as "a chance for me to encourage people," he added.

The point at which a project became formal and began to adhere to the *Projektablauf* [Project Procedures] varied. If, for example, a project had proceeded informally rather far in its development before entering the formal product development process, it might simply be formalized and have product specifications delineated. In its early stages, a project like the KF 40 might have provided monthly reports to the chairman for some time before becoming a formal project. (See Exhibit 8 for the Braun product development process line.)

Industrial Design's Role

The industrial design department played a central role in development, particularly at the front end of the process. Because most key disciplines at Braun were located in the same building, much communication about development took place informally, and no one really kept track of where ideas came from and when they first got together with a colleague from another department. That design, because of its reputation, often received disproportionate credit for a product occasionally irked some engineers and scientists, whose contributions were less visible. Well aware of this problem, the company's chairman accepted the responsibility of keeping the rivalry healthy.

Industrial design's relationship to other departments varied. Within the "triangle of power" (design-technology-marketing), design felt most akin to technology. The designers kept up with new developments in such fields as materials science, for example. "We understand technology, so when we have an idea, it is not unrealistic technically. We don't come up with totally impossible ideas," explained Rams. Likewise, with manufacturing, the group knew what it meant to design a product for manufacturability; if they were having difficulties, all they had to do was to go down the hall and across the parking lot to the engineering building. Such interaction among all disciplines was daily fare at Braun.

Marketing was something else, however. Business management often had conflicts with design because, said the marketers, the latter insisted on certain principles that were not always viable in the marketplace. "The problem with designers," Greaves, director of household products, sighed, "is that they think they design for eternity. Rams will hand me a 1965 design and expect me to go for it today." Sometimes the conflicts were trivial. For example, "one time we argued with Kahlcke (an industrial designer) over the baseplate of the mixer. Because of his obsession with details, he wanted it changed. I told him that was ridiculous, since no one

EXHIBIT 7 Formal Responsibilities of the Project Manager and Project Team Members*

The Project Team

Tasks

- Collective development of the project goals and procedures (the Project Profile) on the basis of the product concept determined by the MTS team as well as the product profile.
- The assignment of functional-specific tasks to the relevant team member.
- The independent solving of problems in order to reach the goals articulated by the project profile.
- The development of alternatives when deviations from the project profile are necessary and the formulation of written proposals for changes for approval of the MTS team.

Authority

- Shortening of the planned course of product development when possible through changes in the project profile.

Responsibility

- The responsibility of the project team consists of the responsibility of the individual team members and the project manager.

The Project Manager

Tasks

- Overall coordination of the project from planning to production startup and control over fulfillment of project goals.
- Requisition of representatives from functional departments and the establishment of a project team.
- Calling and running of project meetings; preparation of meeting reports.
- Maintenance of the Project Book.
- Written records of project assignments.
- Planning and implementation of phase reviews at the end of each development category and whenever needed.
- Reports to product line manager.

Authority

- The right to direct information from team members and their superiors in the respective departments.
- The right to make necessary changes in the project profile and to submit written proposals for changes for approval by the MTS team.

Responsibility

- For coordination of
  -individual assignments in all functions.
  -project procedures.
  -information flow (including among team members).
  -supervision of costs, deadlines, and performance in accordance with the project profile.
- For the content of the project profile and project reports.
- For assuring that any changes in the product objectives set by the MTS team are made only in exceptional circumstances and only with the approval of the MTS team.

The Team Members

Tasks

- Handling of tasks in their functional area.
- Assure readiness, in cooperation with the product line supervisor, for their department's contribution to the project.
- Timely reports to the project manager about the completion of their department's tasks or deviation therefrom, in accordance with the project profile.
- Communicate information from their product line superior and other colleagues in their department.
- Nominate further representatives from their department (in agreement with the product line supervisor).

Authority

- Each team member can request that the project manager call a team meeting.
- Each team member has operating room, within the project profile, for solving problems.

Responsibility

- The team members of individual departments bear responsibility for the technical performance of their part of the work.
- The team members are responsible for ensuring the flow of information from their departments that pertains to the project.

*From *Handbuch Projektablauf von neuen Produkten,* section 2.

EXHIBIT 8 Product Development Procedures Outline and Definitions

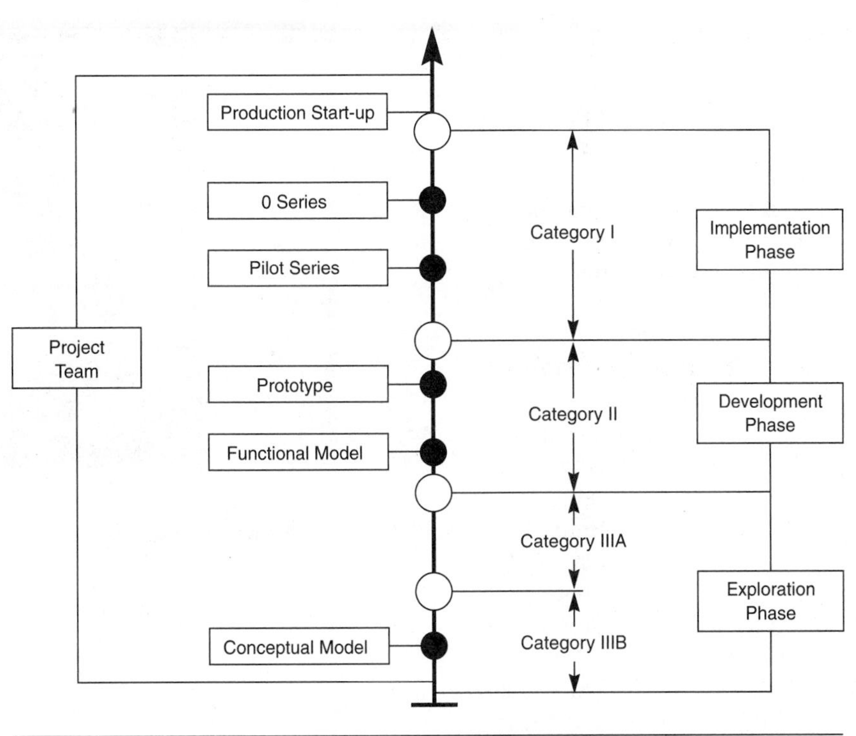

would ever see it," recounted Greaves. "The cord storage was not in the base, so there was no reason whatsoever to turn the mixer over. But Kahlcke got his way!"

People in industrial design had a different perspective. Noted Rams: "I don't mind if technology has greater influence than design; we understand each other and can work things out. But when marketing gets power, it can be bad." For example, sometimes marketing got its way with regard to color. "Why should we pay attention to color fads? Just because red cars are popular one year, why should we have a red hairdryer? It is not integral to the design."

A New Strategy

Lorne Waxlax became chairman of Braun in 1980. After his five-year stint in Spain, he had managed Braun's non-Central European export business for three years, and then headed business management for two. Waxlax had long wanted to encourage Braun to get rid of cameras and hi-fi and to focus more effectively on its core technologies in the personal care and appliance businesses. As chairman, Waxlax could proceed with this strategy.

While narrowing the product line, Waxlax also saw opportunity in six segments of the consumer appliance business: coffeemakers, irons, toasters, hairdryers, shavers, and food preparation products. They were big, and they were constant; the market for coffeemakers in Europe alone was over 9 million units per year. Even a small percentage share would make a good business, but Waxlax was "always going for a big share." Both business management and Braun's designers eagerly embraced this new strategy. Rams made very clear his philosophy: good design should be for everyone.

By 1983 Braun was well established in several product families. Electric shavers were its biggest and most widely marketed product line, accounting for half the company's revenues. In many countries Braun held first place in market share; wherever it was present, it was among the top three. The household division, whose image was represented by its classic kitchen machine, produced coffeemakers, mixers, juice presses, food processors, food choppers, and irons as well. In the personal care area, hairdryers and curling irons were the most successful, having achieved market leadership in Europe. Braun's exports were continuing to grow: In 1982 exports accounted for 75 percent of its turnover.

Waxlax and his top managers wished to focus on Braun's core products and expertise, its reputation for excellence in design, and the opportunities within grasp at the upper end of the mass market. Balancing these three dimensions of the company—technology, design, and business management—while maintaining the integrity of its corporate mission was management's key challenge.

Coffeemakers: The KF 40 Project

One August day in 1981, when half of Germany was on holiday and the other half getting ready to leave, Waxlax wrote a memo to Gilbert Greaves, asking him to check into the possibilities for Braun in coffeemakers, a key element in the new strategy. Braun had entered the coffeemaker business in 1972 with the KF 20, a novel cylindrical design that won many design awards and was enthroned in the Museum of Modern Art in New York. (See Exhibit 9.) Available in strong red and yellow, it had entered the consciousness of upper-income coffee drinkers in both Europe and the United States. It was, however, a very expensive machine, and expensive to produce, retailing at about DM 120.

EXHIBIT 9 KF 20

EXHIBIT 10 KF 35

A few years later, the company introduced the KF 35, a sleeker version of the then popular "L-shape" epitomized by Mr. Coffee. It cost about 40 percent less than the KF 20 to produce, retailing at about DM 90. The design department was not fully satisfied with it: "I always thought it looked like a chemical lab sitting on the table," declared Rams, disdainfully. (See Exhibit 10.) The unit enjoyed only average sales, about 150,000 units annually.

The Competition

Braun's major competitors in the middle-to-high-end coffee machine segment were two German companies, Krups and Rowenta. Braun's market research defined this segment in terms of price points: DM 70 retail or above. In Germany and France, two of the biggest markets for coffeemakers, half the units were sold in that range. The market researchers were confident that a new Braun coffeemaker family offered across the entire spectrum, from DM 72 to DM 136, would be competitive in Europe, where the greater part of the market (about 70 percent of 9 million units annually) was for replacements. An open question was how soon Krups and Rowenta would copy Braun's design, as was their custom.

The U.S. market was considerably less certain, yet crucial if Braun was to attain a volume permitting a tolerable return on investment. "You don't go for the small appliance business because of the margins. You have to have high volumes," remarked Waxlax. Americans had been introduced to filter coffee systems through Mr. Coffee, a low-end product. Would they be willing to pay for Braun quality? With the currency exchange rate at DM 2.40 to $1.00, it was reasonable to expect imports to the United States to grow. The market for filter coffee machines was already running at about 11 million units, and penetration was still low. Braun's distribution system in the United States was practically nonexistent, however, and Waxlax wondered if it could be sufficiently developed in time.

What the "KF 35 Successor" Has To Be

Upon receiving Waxlax's coffee machine memo in August 1981, Greaves set to work with his people and in two months came up with a rough description of a product Braun could sell:

> It should have a shortened filter, slimmer jug [than the competition]; it should come in different colors, the water tank should be opaque, the tubes should be completely covered up, the filter should be tight and compact, the thermal jug should be more elegant, lighter, handier, taller, slimmer, and presentable on the coffee table.

That idea, which marketing articulated in October 1981, evolved into a "product profile" that Greaves circulated to key people on December 2, 1981. In this memo Greaves discussed, as Waxlax had asked, the issue of the cost/volume relationship and presented the direct costs and price points in connection with assumed volumes. He also analyzed the market segments and defined those segments where Braun could realistically compete. He determined that (*a*) a range of models—at least two—would be necessary; (*b*) this range was defined so that it could be constructed on a "building block system" to "minimize tooling investments"; and (*c*) the range would enable Braun to compete in medium to high price segments, at retail prices about DM 70. This would mean that Braun had to compete with key players—Krups, Rowenta, Siemens, and AEG—on features, not price. To be profitable, it would have to cost fully one-third less in direct costs than the KF 35, or 60 percent less than the KF 20. (See Exhibit 11 for summary of Greaves' memo.)

When the document was sent to R&D for feasibility analyses, R&D's first reaction to the target costs was "Nonsense! You can't make a coffeemaker for DM 23 in this company!"[4] Nor did engineering take the idea well: "To be honest," confessed Hans-Jürgen Dittombée, manager of industrial engineering, "we thought the cost targets were impossible. We are responsible for technical planning and didn't see how we could get there."

Working with Greaves on the project was a young, energetic product program manager, Albrecht Jestädt, a mechanical engineer with experience in production and engineering. Upon hearing R&D's and Engineering's reactions, Jestädt refused to take "no" for an answer and set about looking for alternatives. If Braun can't manufacture it, at least we can sell an OEM product that we design, he reasoned. Over the next year, he explored options in and outside of Germany and managed to find a manufacturer in Switzerland who could meet the cost requirements.

The KF 40: Problem Solving in Development

In the meanwhile Jestädt and the designer for household products, Hartwig Kahlcke, teamed up and began to develop the product. Kahlcke, a quiet contrast to the ebullient Jestädt, had come to the design department 10 years earlier and worked on the KF 35. Kahlcke had also dealt extensively with the Spanish group because they did so many household products. "We share a vision," Jestädt declared, "and we're both willing to do what we must to realize it." That vision had as its starting point the KF 20 and its still novel cylindrical design. How could they use the cylinder within the cost parameters? They had to use less material and only one heating element to start with. "Our first design was really terrific—the water tank completely surrounded the filter. But then we realized that we had to think modularly, so manufacturing costs would be minimized, and so we had to drop it," Jestädt recalled.

Jestädt and Kahlcke knew that the cylindrical form not only was appealing, but it used less material than the "chemical lab," the KF 35. Going back and forth they came up with five or six blue foam models before settling on what they believed was the

[4]Direct costs [DC] at Braun included only labor and materials, not the myriad of other costs involved in producing a product, such as nonlabor manufacturing costs, development costs, capital investment, etc.

EXHIBIT 11 Excerpts from Memorandum "Product Profile—Coffee Machine Range"
(from Gilbert Greaves to G. Voigt)

December 2, 1981

Background

A key element in determining the viability of a filter-coffee machine entry is the investment/volume required. The problem is that volume depends on the range offered. [But a wide range] necessitates different tools for housings, water tanks, etc., thus increasing the investment cost for entry.

A further element determining the range is price segmentation. In Germany 52% of the unit volume is sold under DM 59; [this would require] a direct cost we cannot realistically expect from Braun.

Conclusions

1. A range of models will be needed.
2. A range has been defined which can be constructed on a "building block" system to minimize tooling investments.
3. This range will enable Braun to compete in medium to high price segment only . . . retail sales prices above 70 DM. We will have to compete on feature, not on price.

This document [based on a market survey] will serve as an input to R&D to evaluate costs, feasibility, and timing based on the [following] volume estimates.

Range

The Braun range will be differentiated from competition by the following characteristics:

1. The premium model in the range will have a thermal flask. Into this thermal flask the coffee can be filtered direct. Coffee can be held off the hot plate in the flask at 80 degrees Celsius for 45 minutes. This prevents evaporation and aroma loss.
2. All models in the Braun range will be compatible with a special "Coffee ground dispenser." This stores 500g of ground coffee in an airtight hopper and has a metering system allowing the coffee ground to be dispensed by cups into the coffee machine filter.
3. All models in the Braun range will have a laterally pivoting filter allowing the filter to be swung out of the machine and underneath the hopper so that the consumer does not need to handle the coffee ground at any time. The filter can be lifted out to dispense with the paper filter and coffee ground.

optimal configuration: a cylinder within a cylinder, operating on the same principle as the KF 35 but much more compact. The main novelty: It would be operated from the front, and thus it would take less space and look even slimmer on the kitchen counter. (See Exhibit 12 for the initial concept.)

A Single Heating Element

At the same time, other disciplines continued working on the project. R&D, after exclaiming "impossible" at the very idea, took up the challenge and looked at how to get the cost out of the heating element and many other dimensions of the machine. The cost target presupposed a single heating element for both heating the water and keeping the coffee hot, rather than the two needed for the KF 20. Within those parameters, they finally decided that they could go for aluminum rather than copper in the heating element, which would be cheaper, but it would mean different dimensions for the various parts because of differences in conductivity. Keeping the coffee temperature at 82°C was considered an absolute must by the designers and marketing alike, even though they knew it was essentially an insoluble problem because of the level of time that coffee might be held.

How to Attach a Handle Invisibly

R&D also responded to new design concepts. Kahlcke and Rams, for example, wanted to glue the handle on the pot and asked Engineering to explore adhesives. The design reasons were both aesthetic and functional: The conventional means of attaching the handle to the coffee jug was the metal band, which both interrupted the line of the jug and collected dirt. In the course of working on the adhesives, it had become clear that manufacturing engineering would have to design an automated gluing process, in order to keep the costs down. The good news by spring 1983 was that the

EXHIBIT 11 *(concluded)*

The range will consist of the following models:

	1	2	3	4	5	6	7	
Standard Features								
Cup à 125 cc	8	8	8	12	12	12	12	
Anti Drip	x	x	x	x	x	x	x	
Pivoting Filter	x	x	x	x	x	x	x	
Translucent Tank	x	x	x	x	x	x	x	
Pilot Switch	x	x	x	x	x	x	x	
Warming Plate	x	x	x	x	x	x	x	
Cord Compartment	x	x	x	x	x	x	x	
Optional Features								
Glass Jug	x	x	x	x	x	x		
Thermal Jug							x	
Coffee Dispenser			x			x	x	
Calcification Indicator			x			x	x	
Detachable Tank		x	x		x	x	x	
Fixed Tank	x			x				
Target Direct Cost	22	23	29	24	25	31	36	
Target Price Point DM	74	78	99	82	85	105	122	
Target Price Point £	18.5	19.5	24.75	20.5	21.25	26.25	30.5	
Annual Volume Assumptions (000)								**Total**
Year 1	150	50	60	50	50	40	100	500
Year 2	225	75	90	75	75	60	150	750
Year 3	300	100	120	100	100	80	200	1000

EXHIBIT 12 **KF 40—Initial Concept**

design and manufacturing process was expected to cost less than the conventional metal-band method. R&D still had not found the ideal adhesive, however, one that would hold for years under heat, impact, and moisture.

Stop That Drip!

R&D had other challenges. The marketing people had found that an anti-drip device would be very attractive for customers, but Braun wanted to go at least one step beyond the competition. The idea was to prevent drips either from the filter (when one pulls out the coffeepot) or from the water tube (when one swings the filter out). It was supposed to be a relatively easy assignment but, as Gunter Oppermann, head of R&D for household products, pointed out, "Simple is most difficult," and that was what the project was about. The drip-stop was a case in point. "It has to be dual-action (stopping the flow when either the pot *or* the filter was pulled out), and we have to go around some outside patents. We thought about toilet flushers as a model and started from there. We didn't want the device to stick, and yet it must be sturdy."

When a Coffeemaker Makes Coffee

Quality assurance was working on several aspects of the new machine, including its end product. "We found that we didn't really know anything about coffee," quality engineer Werner Utsch confessed, "so we had to analyze and test some more, and that has led us to work with the coffee producers." The tests revealed valuable information: "We have found that our competition doesn't know much about coffee either." The next step would be blind taste tests, for which they needed a functional model.

What Does the Market Tell Us?

The market researchers continued gathering data as well. In October 1982 they tested the thermal jug concept and determined that it would be an essential selling feature. The next month they tested filter systems; the swivel filter won hands down. At this time, contrary to results a year earlier, the market wanted a detachable, transparent water tank. It was "significantly preferred over a nontransparent one" and "should be included . . . if the price is not prohibitive to the customer." (See Exhibit 13 for market test results.) Jestädt and Kahlcke had, however, already developed a modular design that could not accommodate a transparent tank.

To Design Means to Think

Operating from the principle that "no parts = no assembly costs," Jestädt and Kahlcke were striving to collapse the number of parts into as few as possible. This was where Rams' motto, "To design means to think [Designarbeit ist Denkarbeit]," converged with Bernard Wild's view of Braun's know-how. Working with machine tool experts headed by Friedhelm Bau, Jestädt and Kahlcke had designed a configuration that incorporated many large and small parts that in the past would have been screwed together. The water tank was now part of the appliance housing, and the whole large piece, known simply as the "tank," was now central to their product concept, for it accounted for a good chunk of the savings in assembly costs. (See Exhibit 14.) It was, however, the largest, most complicated part ever attempted in polypropylene injection molding at Braun, and as such would be risky. (Exhibit 15 explains injection molding.)

The Manufacturing Challenge

Manufacturing and toolmaking engineers were involved from the beginning of the project. Bernard Wild had prepared an analysis of plant requirements in order to achieve the projected volumes for the new coffeemaker. As soon as polypropylene was proposed, Bau's toolmaking department started working with plastic suppliers and toolmakers in Berlin, who had experience with designing large tools for polypropylene. Bau was convinced that the large tank could be molded on the three 330-ton molding machines (presses) available at Marktheidenfelt. One machine could make 1,500 moldings (tank units) per day. With estimated volumes at 500,000 the first year, ramping up to 2,000,000 units the fourth year, the plant needed to be prepared to manufacture 10,000 units per day, given the 220 days per year that the plant operated. They were assuming a one-minute cycle time for the "tank" part, but could not be certain of it. They could start with three molds (or "tools"), one each for the 10- and 12-cup units and one for the thermal carafe, but they preferred to have the flexibility offered by five molds—two each for the 10- and 12-cup units.

If the product took off as expected, they would need four more molding machines and at least as many molds. Each machine cost about DM 500,000. The estimated cost for each tank mold was DM 250,000 and the lead time for tooling was around nine months for the large molds. Because the molds were not interchangeable for various types of plastics, the choice of plastic was crucial to engineering's planning.

Polypropylene: A Question of Braun-ness

Braun had pioneered in the use of plastics as early as the 1950s, when it rejected fake wood and overstuffed designs for its products. Its designers, engineers, and toolmakers were experienced in making both clear and opaque parts from several different kinds of plastic. For the outer housing of its appliances, the company had traditionally used polycarbonate, a dense, stable material that could be fashioned into precision parts with smooth surfaces. Polycarbonate was, however, too expensive for the new coffee machine's requirements.

EXHIBIT 13

January 10, 1983

Report on Coffee Maker Tests

Title	Date of Report *Month*	*Year*	Comments
Coffee machine group discussions	10	1981	Desired improvements of the Braun coffee machine with thermal jug: Shortened filter, slimmer jug, should come in different colors, the water tank should be opaque, the tubes should be completely covered up, the filter should be tight and compact, the thermal jug should be more elegant, lighter, handier, taller, slimmer, and presentable on the coffee table.
Thermos jug concept	10	1982	The concept of a thermos jug with aroma test protective lid is preferred by the majority of respondents over a conventional glass jug with removable hot plate. There's a theoretical potential for a detachable heating or heat protection device.
Coffee filter system	11	1982	The best filter system for our new coffee acceptance test machine would be a swivel filter and the best water tank would be a transparent one.
Coffee machine features	12	1982	BMR would recommend the following concept test features to be considered for the new coffee machine range: built-in decalcifier, jug with heat and aroma preservation, swivel filter system, transparent detachable water tank, capacity 10–12 cups.

SOURCE: Company documents.

For that reason, Jestädt had begun working with ABS, which sold for about half of polycarbonate's going rate (see Exhibit 16). Even that, as it turned out, would probably be too expensive. The alternative, polypropylene, was the material of choice for low-end producers, but had never before been considered by Braun, except for interior parts that could benefit from its lower density and other features. The amount of polypropylene needed for each KF 40 unit was estimated at 700–950 grams. The problem with polypropylene for use in injection molding was its instability during the cooling process. Having a lower specific weight than the denser plastics, it tended to shrink unevenly and fall off, or "sink," at edges and meeting points. The resultant "sink marks" marred the surface and looked "cheap." Nor

EXHIBIT 14 The KF 40 Tank

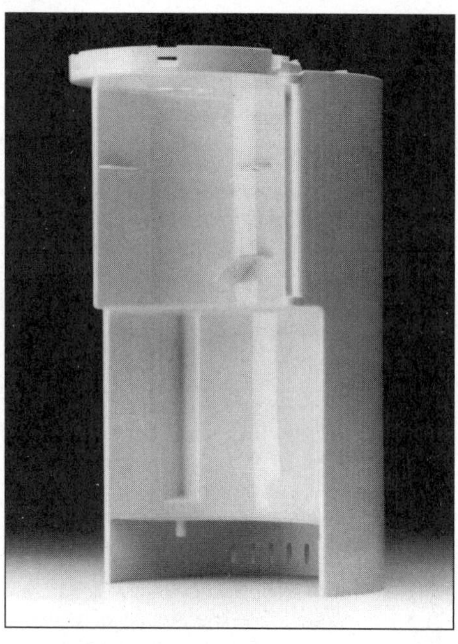

did polypropylene become as rigid as the more expensive materials, thus posing additional design challenges. Large parts were therefore especially vulnerable to a flimsy feel and had to be designed with the need to control that problem. It might mean thicker walls or a shape in the mold that would buttress the form from within.

When polypropylene was first suggested, many colleagues familiar with its problems immediately objected: It will not be a *Braun* product if we use this cheap stuff, they warned. Despite such adamant objections, Jestädt and Kahlcke began working with chemical suppliers and toolmakers to explore ways of improving the quality of polypropylene parts. In fall 1982 they achieved a breakthrough: Why not let necessity be the mother of design in this case? If we can't get a perfectly smooth surface, let's minimize the effect of the sink marks by treating the surface in some way. This inspiration led to the idea for a corrugated surface that would both mask flaws and actually enhance the design as well.

NO! said the purists, for whom Braun design was synonymous with absolutely smooth, winter-white

EXHIBIT 15 Note on Injection Molding

Injection-molding technology permits the high-speed molding of thin, often complex parts out of metal or plastic. It involves (*a*) melting the material to a liquid state; (*b*) injecting the liquid under pressure into a metal mold; (*c*) waiting a number of seconds until the liquid cools and solidifies; (*d*) opening the mold; (*e*) withdrawing the part; (*f*) closing the mold again. To be precise and consistent, the process needs computer controls and robotized handling.

The easiest form to mold in this way is the cone, because it comes out from the mold easily. As soon as there are straight sides and protruding features, the design problem is vastly more complicated. Industrial designers, engineers, and tool designers work together to develop a design that can be produced effectively. For example, the mold needs to open at some point, and a flash line, preferably a very thin one, will show. The designers need to determine where the line's effects are minimal and design the mold accordingly.

In the case of plastic injection molding, the material is not held in liquid form. Rather, it is fed to the machine in small beads, like small white beans, which are melted instantly under pressure at the nozzle. This way the temperature can be controlled and there is less waste.

An important point in the design of a mold is the cooling rate of the plastic. This rate is determined by the properties of the plastic itself and by the shape of the part—its thickness at any given point and the distance of that point from the nozzle through which the liquid is injected. Because the part cannot be removed until all of it has solidified, these problems must be taken into consideration when designing the part. Moreover, the injection temperature of the plastic and the temperature of the cooling water have to be kept constant via computer controls.

A mold may be very complicated, with more than one axis. Then the order in which the parts of the mold are opened and removed has to be carefully thought through. The "tank" part of the Braun coffee machine incorporated parts that would conventionally have been cast in at least five separate components and then screwed or snapped together. To save labor costs, the company invested in knowledge and tooling up front. This enabled them to keep production in high-wage Germany.

Some plastics are easier to cast than others. Those with low density, like polypropylene, are less stable, and this needs to be compensated for in the design of large parts. A large wall, for example, needs to be thicker or have a supporting shape built into the design. Because of the design implications of the variations in plastics, the same mold cannot be used for multiple kinds of plastic.

The quality of the molded part is determined not only by the design of the mold, but also by the interior surface finish of the mold. The quality of the metal, usually a special alloy steel, and the finishing technology used (e.g., erosion, grinding, polishing) determine how well a mold can meet its tolerances and how long it will last.

EXHIBIT 16 Properties of Plastics

	Polycarbonate	ABS	Polypropylene
Cost DM/kg (1983)	8.5 DM	3.95 DM	2.8 DM
Specific weight	1.2	1.05	0.9
Melting temp.	220°C	200°C	165°–170°C
Softening temp.	160°C	140°C	120°C
Color-fastness	yes	no	yes
Shrinkage	0.5–0.7%	0.3–0.9%	0.3–2.5% (1–2.5% unfilled)

surfaces. "It's a compromise," said Utsch, "and I don't like compromises." Utsch, head of quality assurance for the project, kept pointing to polypropylene's tendency to scratch: "It's just too soft. Even a fingernail can scratch it. And if you wipe it off with the same sponge you wiped the counter off with, you can scratch it with food particles or coffee grounds." Even Rams was skeptical at first, but eventually came to support the solution. "It is the obvious way to go, given the project requirements."

Polypropylene did have some advantages other than its price, Oppermann pointed out: "It doesn't absorb water, so it won't stain easily. And, as far as we can tell, it won't get brittle as fast as polycarbonate, so it won't chip easily."

Jestädt, ever confident, explored further. Willing to take risks, R&D director Hexner supported R&D's involvement in trying to make polypropylene work. Like everyone else, he knew that if it didn't work, it would be extremely costly. "They are talking about a *huge* and very complicated tool for the tank. If it doesn't work, we'll have to throw it away and be another year behind." But Hexner didn't see any choice: "We've been given the job of making this thing at a ridiculous cost. My people say that it's possible only with polypropylene, and I agree." To Hexner the "purists" were entirely unrealistic. "If a Braun product *has* to have a smooth surface, then you have two choices: Go with flaws, or forget it. And that is ridiculous!"

Hexner's boss, Dr. Thomsen, did not think it ridiculous to consider further choices. Nor did Waxlax. "We could make a business with, say, ABS. But it would be a different business," Thomsen contended. Waxlax was worried about the U.S. market implications: "We'd either have to drop the U.S. market, and that means low volumes, or restrict it to the higher-priced department store segment."

Jestädt and Kahlcke, meanwhile, were not insensitive to the design concerns. The ridges of the corrugated surface would have to be absolutely smooth, with no peaks or valleys, so that they would not catch any dirt. That job was turned over to the toolmakers. By the end of 1982 Bau's department was confident that the job could be done using the 330-ton molding machines at Marktheidenfeld. An outside consultant had suggested that the molding machines should be larger (500-ton) for a part the size of the tank, but that would mean an additional investment of DM 2 million for two new machines and upgrades of the old machines. Because the larger machines were much slower than the smaller ones, it would take five of them to produce the same number of units per day as the three 330-ton machines could produce.

The OEM Threat

In December 1982, Jestädt had presented his plan for a Swiss company to manufacture the new design. At the same meeting, someone brought in a cheap DM 29 coffeemaker from a supermarket and challenged those present, "If these guys can sell a coffeemaker for DM 29, you can surely make one for DM 23." As the discussion proceeded, the group realized that the new design was so special that it would be dangerous to let it out to a subcontractor; they would have to keep it inside in order to assure a competitive lead.

At that point it was proposed to take three months and build a trial tool to test the material; Waxlax approved DM 140,000 for the test and the tool, if the team chose to take that step. The proposal was, according to a project report for December 12, simply to "clarify if polypropylene is suitable for the appliance housing material." That was the point, according to Dittombée of industrial engineering. "I am confident that we can master polypropylene *technically,*" he said, "but the discussion is about whether *Braun* can—or should—use it." For the purists, such a trial was far better than ordering the production dies and finding out polypropylene wouldn't work in this design and product.

A Material Decision

Over the next four months the coffeemaker project became more intense. At the report to management at the end of January 1983, drawings for the functional model were presented, and a schedule established (see Exhibit 17). The new 10-cup coffeemaker now had a name: the KF 40. A second model, the KF 45, would have a 3–4 cup switch, costing one DM more. According to this schedule, the functional model would be ready by the end of March, with final tool drawings complete on May 16. The formal go/no-go decision would be made on May 17, followed by a "category I" signoff, which released the drawings so that tools could be ordered. Production ramp-up was estimated to begin in April of 1984, to reach 3,000 units per day within three months.

All this assumed that the KF 40 could be made with polypropylene and that all the other problems, such as the drip-stop, could be solved in time. By producing this schedule, business man-

EXHIBIT 17 Project Report, Coffee Maker KF 40

January 26, 1983

Product Description:

KF 40: 10-cup version with swinging filter, anti-drip, and cord storage
DC target: FY 1982/83: 23.50 DM

KF 45: same as the KF 40, but with switch for brewing 3–4 cups
DC target: FY 1982/83: 24.30 DM

Status:

Blueprints for the construction of a functional model have been prepared, and it is currently being built.

Further steps:

▪ Prepare drawings for parts and tools	by 28 January 1983
▪ Requisition parts and tools; produce the authorization request	by 18 March 1983
▪ Have the authorization request approved	by 29 April 1983
▪ Finish the functional model	by 25 March 1983
▪ Test the functional model by QC	by 16 May 1983
▪ Build the design model	by 30 March 1983
▪ Complete drawings for tool orders	by 16 May 1983
▪ Go or no-go decision If go, then Category I release	by 17 May 1983
▪ Planned startup of production	April 1984

Risks:

The above schedule does not include the production of prototypes. Only if the tests of the functional model reveal no major problems will it be possible to meet the planned deadlines.

Project: Coffee Makers KF 40 and KF 45 Signed: A Jestädt, Project Mgr.
Project Number: 542 Date: 26 January 1983 Version: 1

agement had already cast its vote of confidence. Waxlax knew that Greaves tended to be conservative in his forecasts, and therefore one didn't have to worry about unrealistic figures in his analyses. Neither engineering nor design wanted to be pushed, however, and that Waxlax respected. The decision was a strategic one: a big risk—but one with a big payoff if they succeeded. The risk was not so much financial, though a million DM in molds and two years in development costs would not be insignificant. Should they go ahead without trial tooling, take three months for the trial test, rethink their positioning with a more expensive plastic, or walk away from the project? What risks were they willing to take and how far should they go before modifying the business strategy? Waxlax intended to take his time in listening to all points of view.

APPENDIX IDENTIFICATION AND PRONUNCIATION GLOSSARY

Friedhelm **Bau** [Freedhelm Bow, as in "now"]	Manager, Machine Tools
Max **Braun** [Brown]	Founder, Braun AG
Artur and Erwin **Braun**	Sons and heirs of Max
Hans-Jürgen **Dittombée**	Manager, Industrial Engineering
Fritz **Eichler** [Ei as in Einstein]	Former director of design; member, board of directors
Gilbert **Greaves**	Business director, Household Products
Peter **Hexner**	Director of R&D
Albrecht **Jestädt** [Ahlbrecht *Ye*-shtet]	Mechanical engineer
Hartwig **Kahlcke** [Hartvig *Kahl*-keh]	Industrial designer, Household Products
Krups [Kroops]	Major German home appliance firm
Marktheidenfeld [Markt-*haydn*-felt]	Plant where KF 40 will be manufactured
Gunter **Oppermann** [Goonter Operman as in "open"]	Manager, R&D Household Products
Dieter **Rams** [Deeter Rahms]	Director of Design
Rowenta [Roventa]	Major German home appliance firm
Hartmut **Stroth** [Hartmoot Strote]	Director of Communications
Thomas H. **Thomsen**	Director of Technical Operations
Werner **Utsch** [Verner Ootsh]	Quality engineer, Household Products
Lorne **Waxlax**	Chairman, Braun AG
Bernard **Wild** [Bearnard Vealt]	Plant manager, Marktheidenfeld

Case IV–6
Chaparral Steel: Rapid Product and Process Development

Gil Preuss and Dorothy Leonard-Barton

In this report, we have utilized graphic depictions of how we measure up—not only against our industry, but against ourselves. They are both important, but it's how we compare to our own past performance that matters most. . . . We value trust and responsibility, risk and curiosity, knowledge and expertise, networking and information exchange, humor and humility.

1990 Annual Report

To stand still is to fall behind.

Gordon Forward, CEO

No one calls a meeting when something happens—you just go, you see what the problem is. You don't have "that's not my area," or "I don't really know that much about it." You just show up.

A Chaparral millwright

6 A.M., March 26, 1991. Lou Colatriano, a general manager and project leader, stuck his head into Gordon Forward's office. "We're starting up the near net shape cast," he shouted. Forward, Chaparral Steel's president and chief executive officer, grabbed his personalized hard hat and green work coat and headed over to the new large section mill. Looking around the quarter-mile-long building, Forward viewed Chaparral's latest achievement with pride. A combination of new internally developed technology, old purchased equipment, and a great deal of ingenuity had brought this project to life.

Gathered around in expectation, everyone waited to see the first runs on the recently completed steel caster and rolling mills for the production of large width (up to 24-inch) beams. If the process worked, Chaparral would be able to compete successfully in a large and growing segment of the steel industry. The technology had been tested, but only on a pilot caster using a different casting mold, with different equipment. For the first time the $60 million investment was going to be fully tested, and no one was certain whether the new caster would work as the operators started the process and began pouring molten steel through the caster and mold to be rolled.

The molten steel poured out of the bathtublike tundish into the mold and threaded out in two large glowing strands of steel. Suddenly, the second strand on the caster stopped. Andy Griffith, the casting machine operator, had shut it down within three seconds of detecting a possible flaw in the strand. Like all steelmakers, he feared a breakout, the horrific bursting of the molten steel's fragile "skin." The smallest malfunction—a slight warp in the caster mold, the mold's not oscillating correctly, impurities like a tiny oxygen bubble in the steel itself—could lead to white hot liquid steel cascading over the equipment—and possibly people—below. When cooled, the steel had to be painstakingly hacked off. "In casting, everything has to be perfect," explained one operator. "You can't lose water pressure, you can't lose hydraulics—or anything else. If one little thing goes wrong, the whole system goes." Such a catastrophe could only be avoided by the split-second decisions of skilled, vigilant operators.

Very carefully, the casting crew restarted the second strand. Casting continued for hours, as jubilation began spreading through the mill: The near net shape mold worked. After 48 hours straight, Colatriano could head home to bed. Once again, Chaparral had rapidly translated technology into product. Griffith was rueful, however. He felt he had reacted prematurely, shutting off the caster unnecessarily and causing two hours of wasted work. Seeing his discouragement, his supervisor went over and clapped him on the back: "Hey, everybody makes mistakes. You just fix it and keep on going."

Back in his office, Gordon Forward pondered the future. At Chaparral, growth meant individual development—and testing the limits—of technology and equipment; but growth also meant expansion. Now the company was reaching 1,000 employees. Going beyond that number risked the unique culture Chaparral had so carefully built, but given the implications of the successfully tested technology that night, expansion was inevitable. The question was how to grow. Should Chaparral attempt to "clone" itself in another plant elsewhere? *Could* Chaparral sustain its culture with 2,000 or 3,000 employees in the plant?

The U.S. Steel Industry

From 1950 to 1990 the United States' share of the world steel industry shrank from 47 percent to 11 percent. Integrated steel companies, which turned ore into pig iron and then converted the iron to steel, suffered dramatic losses during the 1980s, as producers from Brazil, Korea, Japan, and elsewhere expanded their steel exporting to the United States. Steel mills closed by the hundreds, over 200,000 workers were laid off, and whole regions of the country were economically devastated. The major mills' share of the U.S. steel market shrank from 64 percent in 1979 to about 36 percent in 1989, and to a projected 30 percent by the mid-1990s, according to a recent study by PaineWebber (see Exhibit 1 for selected data from that report).

One segment of the steel industry, however, was profitable and expanding. Minimills, using state-of-the-art technology and ferrous scrap as raw material, took over significant niches of the market, competing successfully against both domestic and foreign steel producers. Beginning with those sectors providing the greatest competitive advantage, such as reinforcement bar used in concrete construction ("rebar") and other small, simple shapes that could be cast and rolled in long production runs, as well as specialty steels, minimills expanded to produce larger width bars and beams. The only remaining sector integrated mills dominated in 1991 was flat rolled steel, which required large and expensive production equipment. By the mid-1990s industry analysts projected that minimills would claim almost a 25 percent share of the U.S. steel market. According to a 1991 PaineWebber report, however, minimills were facing an "endemic oversupply" in their traditional products of rebar and other small bar sizes.[1] This oversupply would result in only average minimill performance in the near future, except for the few pacesetters.

The PaineWebber report also noted:

> (C)urrently . . . the capacity to produce large structurals [that is, beams] in the United States is about 4.5 million tons. Moreover, imports in 1990 amounted to about 350,000 tons. In comparison, apparent consumption in 1991 is estimated at just 3.0 to 3.1 million tons—down from the peak several years ago of 4.0 million tons and the "normal" level of demand of about 3.5 million tons. We are clearly approaching a point at which some competitors will be driven from the marketplace.[2]

Minimill Technology[3]

Minimills traditionally used three important technologies to produce steel: an electric arc furnace, a continuous caster, and a rolling mill (see Exhibit 2 for a process flow diagram). For raw material, minimills used 100 percent ferrous scrap of which auto bodies were a significant portion. The initial capacity for the arc furnaces was relatively small, ranging from 50,000 to 250,000 tons per year (tpy). After the cover was swung to one side, shredded scrap was loaded into the furnace. Three electrodes were then lowered into the closed furnace to within six to eight feet above the scrap. Once the power was turned on (typically 30,000 to 50,000 megawatts), an electric arc formed between the electrodes and the scrap. The intense heat created by the electric arc caused an explosion and melted the steel. The dust from the furnace contained chromium, cadmium, and lead, which the EPA labeled hazardous waste. Chaparral contracted with a reclamation facility that recovered the metals for reuse and rendered the dust nonhazardous.[4]

When the steel in the furnace (called a "heat") was completely melted, the furnace tilted and the metal was poured into a ladle, lifted by a crane to the top of a continuous casting machine. The molten metal was then released from the ladle into a tundish, a rectangular trough-shaped receptacle with holes in the bottom corresponding to the number of strands the machine could cast—typically two to four. Through the tundish holes the metal drained down into molds that oscillated to insure a more homogeneous structure in the metal cast.

As it began to cool, the steel shrank slightly in the water-cooled mold and the strands then flowed into covered spray chambers. Next, semi-solid on the outside yet molten on the inside, the strands moved slowly through a curved track of rollers toward a horizontal plane. About 15 feet below the spray chambers, the strands solidified and continued their

---

[1]"Accelerating Change Threatens Traditional Producers," *World Steel Dynamics,* PaineWebber, June 18, 1991, p. 15.

[2]Ibid., p. 37.

[3]Material in this section is drawn from *Red River Steel (A)*, no. 685-055.

[4]Chaparral's auto shredder processed 600,000 automobiles annually, or one every 18 seconds, a rate that exceeded General Motors' rate of automobile manufacture. Chaparral's ultimate goal was to recycle the entire automobile, for example, turning the plastics into fuel.

EXHIBIT 1 Structure of the U.S. Steel Industry, 1973–1990

	1973			1979			1989			Mid-1990s (Estimate)		
	Number of Companies	Tons Shipped	Share of ASC	Number of Companies	Tons Shipped	Share of ASC	Number of Companies	Tons Shipped	Share of ASC	Number of Companies	Tons Shipped	Share of ASC
Major mills*	8	78.8	64%	8	73.4	64%	5	35	36%	5	30	30%
"Reconstituted"†	0	0	0%	0	0	0%	17	28	29%	20	24	24%
Other traditional‡	20	26.1	21%	20	17.7	15%	5	3.7	4%	4	2.7	3%
Minimills	32	5.8	5%	48	8.2	7%	33	17	17%	30	23.6	24%
Specialty§	—	0.8	1%	10	1.0	1%	9	1.3	1%	8	1.3	1%
Domestic totals	70	111.5	91%	86	100.3	87%	69	85	87%	67	81.6	81%
Steel imports		15.2	13%		17.5	15%		17.5	17%		23	23%
Steel exports		4	3%		2.8	2%		4.2	4%		3	3%
Apparent steel consumption (ASC)‖		122.7	100%		115	100%		98.3	100%		101.6	100%

*Major mills are integrated steel firms using blast furnaces.
†Reconstituted mills were owned by major mills and then were either shut down and reopened or simply spun off.
‡Other traditional mills are integrated steel firms using electric furnaces.
§Specialty steel firms are classified based on their final product.
‖Apparent steel consumption is calculated based on total domestic shipments minus exports plus imports.

SOURCE: *World Steel Dynamics*, March 1990, PaineWebber

EXHIBIT 2 Process Flow

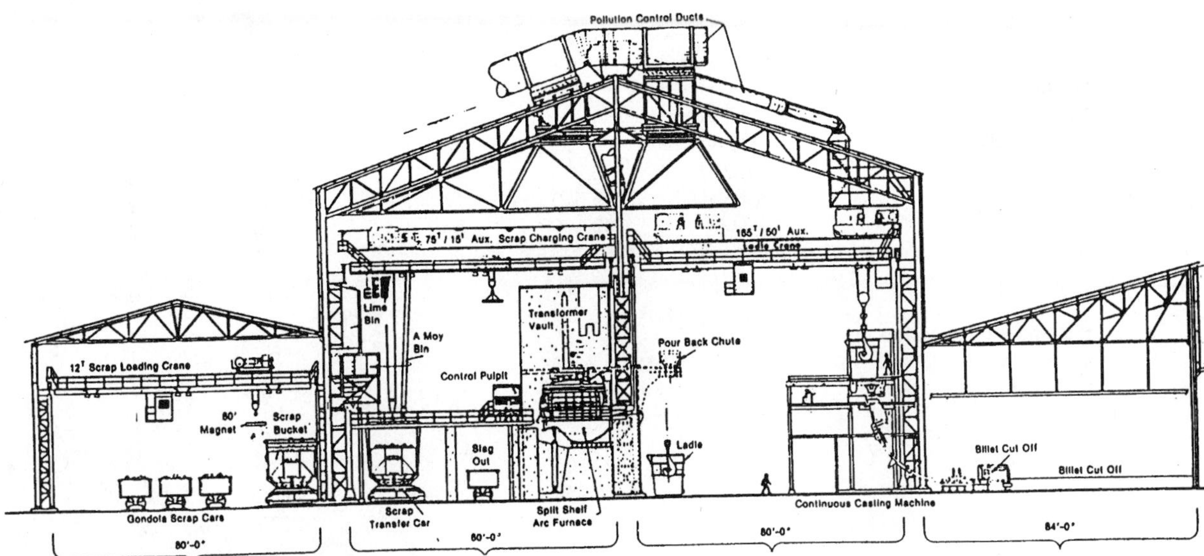

SOURCE: Company documents.

path through straighteners. Still orange and pliable, the strands were cut by an automatic torch into standard lengths called billets, typically 40 feet long. The last step was air-cooling on racks that moved and turned over each billet over a course of 250 to 300 feet. A 100-ton heat took two hours to cast.

Before they could be rolled, in most mills, the billets had to be reheated in a gas reheat furnace at the head of the rolling mill. Billets were released individually from the furnace and passed through approximately 15 rolling stands, sets of rollers weighing several tons that squeezed and stretched the hot billet into a smaller size and finally into a specific shape. During the rolling process, the initial passes altered the molecular makeup of the steel, thereby increasing its strength and tensility. An originally square billet might evolve through various shapes including round, oval, square, pentagonal as well as irregular shapes on its path toward becoming a ¾-inch round rebar. After rolling, the bars cooled on long racks and were cut for shipping.

Chaparral Steel

In 1973 the Chaparral Steel Co. was founded in Midlothian, Texas, a small rural town 30 miles south of Dallas, as a 50/50 joint venture between Texas Industries, Inc. (TXI), which produced cement and concrete products, and Co-Steel International Ltd., a Canadian corporation owning steel mills in New Jersey, Canada, and the United Kingdom. An initial employment of 235 grew to 938 by 1990. In 1985 TXI bought out Co-Steel's share of Chaparral to become sole owner and in 1988 sold approximately 20 percent of Chaparral's stock in a public offering. Through that offering, over 95 percent of Chaparral's employees became company shareholders (see Exhibit 3 for financial information).

The founders of Chaparral were dedicated steelmen determined to break all the "rules" of Big Steel. They ultimately chose the plant site on the basis of a sign managers saw at the Midlothian Chamber of Commerce: "Need money? Try working!" Chaparral began operations with a relatively homogeneous group of shopfloor workers, most of them farmworkers with no background in steel, combined with a highly skilled management team. "We were looking for bright, enthusiastic, articulate people—with a twinkle in their eyes," noted Dennis Beach, vice president of administration.

To attract such people and keep them, Chaparral management stressed both individual growth and teamwork to maximize flexibility. Only two organi-

EXHIBIT 3 Selected Financial Data (in thousands, except per-share), Chaparral Steel Company and Subsidiaries

	1990	1989	1988	1987	1986
Results of Operations					
Net sales	$404,155	$451,490	$376,398	$318,807	$297,155
Gross profit	80,188	126,771	98,250	73,708	67,432
Employee profit sharing	3,210	6,935	3,067	1,627	962
Interest expense	12,556	15,050	17,027	18,463	21,935
Income from operations	24,046	49,106	30,714	12,730	8,778
Net income	24,046	49,106	34,609	12,730	8,778
Total shipments (000 tons)	1,240	1,314	1,264	1,212	1,088
Per Share Information					
Income from operations	$ .74	$ 1.57	$ .98		
Net income	.74	1.57	1.11		
Dividends*	.13	.10	—		
For the Year					
Funds from operations	$ 41,792	$ 74,275	$ 67,989	$ 48,603	$ 38,148
Capital expenditures	36,711	28,924	22,204	14,279	7,019
Year-end Position					
Total assets	$382,621	$373,938	$323,381	$320,579	$309,924
Net working capital	87,509	89,728	63,713	58,513	42,607
Long-term debt	94,012	95,546	119,616	140,156	158,297
Stockholders' equity	181,021	162,702	108,885	94,276	81,546

*Does not include cash dividends paid to Texas Industries, Inc., previously its sole shareholder, in the amounts of $75,000,000 and $20,000,000 in 1989 and 1988, respectively.

SOURCE: Company documents.

zational levels separated the CEO and operators in the rolling mill. There were no time clocks, everyone was on salary, and every employee participated in profit sharing. Moreover, there were no staff positions at Chaparral: Everyone had line responsibilities, with decision making pushed down to the lowest possible point. According to one millwright, Chaparral's goal was "trying to go where no man had gone." But, he added, "there is always the challenge of staying one step ahead . . . and we are not going to put in new technology unless we are one step ahead to begin with." To keep "one step ahead," employees, management included, were involved in continuous training, education, and learning. Chaparral instituted a highly unusual companywide apprenticeship program, featuring 7,280 hours of on-the-job training and extensive course work in generic technical and interpersonal skills, as well as company-specific knowledge. Courses were taught by foremen who rotated from teaching duties back into the mill. Chaparral considered its plant to be a laboratory and, in fact, there was no R&D function separate from production: "Everybody is in research and development," said Forward.

An unusual practice at Chaparral was called "vicing." When a supervisor was absent for some reason, instead of having the previous shift supervisor cover for the absent person, the most senior operator was temporarily promoted to "vice" supervisor. At the same time, the previous shift's supervisor stayed on but in a subordinate position (at his or her same pay rate). Thus, the supervisor's knowledge was continuously available, while the senior operator gained experience and practiced new responsibilities.

All Chaparral employees carried business cards reading "member of the sales force." Visiting customers was integral to Chaparral's culture; in 1990, 78 people from production—including operators—visited a customer site at least once. Teams, including managers, supervisors, and technical staff traveled the world investigating new technologies and benchmarking against the best-of-class wherever they found it. "We send the people who can best tell us what's going on—whoever they are," commented Forward. Self-directed teams at Chaparral arose in 1990 in response to new technology, which required new skills. Seventy people were needed for the new mill, and Chaparral's management gave the employees a choice: Chaparral would hire the new people, or they could work leaner and find the needed people among existing employees. As a group, the workforce decided to do away with some supervisory (foreman) positions and have self-directed teams.

Dennis Beach summed up Chaparral's culture as follows:

> It is organic and technologically driven. It continues to grow with people who are comfortable with ambiguity and change. This results in a humanistic approach with a high degree of professionalism—and a fun place to work.

Chaparral was established with the goal of becoming the international low-cost supplier of quality steel. By setting such a goal, the firm accepted a moving objective that placed demands on all employees to constantly improve productivity. This was clearly expressed by a senior pulpit (control) operator: "You just take it upon yourself to roll as much steel as you can whether you are the pulpit operator, the roller, or the furnace operator. We want to do the best we possibly can." Innovation and flexibility became everyone's responsibilities. "Even though it is one company, it is flexible enough that each department pretty much handles its own policies such as who will run what equipment, how we are going to run it and what is best for us to do," explained one millwright.

In 1983, only nine years after its founding, Chaparral set a productivity record for minimills of 1.8 labor hours per ton; by 1990 it set yet another record of 1.4 labor hours per ton—compared to an average of 2.2 across all minimills and 4.6 labor hours per ton of steel produced by the Big Six U.S. integrated mills. In addition, Chaparral produced 1,449 tons/employee compared to an average of 800 tons per employee by U.S. steel manufacturers (see Exhibit 4 for a 1989 competitive benchmark summary comparing Chaparral to other minimills and to the "Big Six"). Also in 1983, Chaparral was awarded the right to use the Japanese Industrial Standard certification on its general structural products. This certification, rewarded only after years of consistent high quality, was a significant statement of Chaparral's success: Chaparral was not only the first U.S. steel company to receive this certification, but it was only the second company outside of Japan so honored.

Products, Markets, and Competitors

> We never stray far from the market in our mentality. That is what drives us.
>
> Duff Hunt
> GM of operations for special projects

To meet the changing needs of its customers, Chaparral rolled reinforcing bar (rebar), special bar quality steel, merchant shapes (small sizes), structural shapes (large sizes), and beams, primarily I and H shaped beams (see Exhibit 5 for illustrations and descriptions of Chaparral's primary steel products). The rolled steel sizes ranged from ⅜-inch reinforcement bar (rebar) to 24-inch-wide beams, resulting in the broadest range of products of any steel plant in the United States. Each product set had distinct markets, customer bases, and geographic areas. As various industry and geographic sectors of the economy cycled up and down, Chaparral adjusted to changing demands and redirected steel production to meet the markets' needs. In fact, Beach felt that "Chaparral's flexibility in diverting steel to high demand products from low demand ones is one of our strategic advantages." Because of this flexibility, Chaparral described itself as a market mill. The market determined its product mix, so that the composition of Chaparral's product mix each year likely differed significantly from the previous year. In any given year a single product's share of total products shipped might range from 0 to 40 percent (see Exhibit 6 for data on the changing product mix at Chaparral and in other U.S. steel mills).

In 1990, Chaparral shipped 95 percent of its steel to 44 states in the continental United States; the remaining 5 percent was shipped to Europe, Japan, Southeast Asia, and Mainland China, doubling the export share from the previous year. Approximately 40 percent of Chaparral's products were sold in Texas, Oklahoma, Louisiana, and Arkansas; an additional 18 percent went to the southeastern United States and 17 percent to the Midwest United States.

EXHIBIT 4 Competitive Benchmark Summary* (1989)

	Net Sales (million $)	Total Shipments (000 tons)	Operating Profit (EBIT) ($/ton shipped)	Productivity (labor hrs/ton)
Big Six				
Armco	1,715	4,036	20	5.1
Bethlehem	4,310	9,779	36	6.3
Inland	2,183	4,856	36	6.5
LTV	4,086	7,646	41	5.0
National	2,200	4,957	22	5.3
USX	5,386	11,469	37	4.3
Subtotal	19,880	42,743	(avg.) 27	(avg.) 4.6
Minimills				
Bayou	209	674	26	2.1
Birmingham	443†	1,234	58	2.7
Chaparral	452	1,314	65†	1.4
Florida	532	1,322	56	3.8
New Jersey	124	402	25	1.7
North Star	1,033	2,520	49	2.8
Nucor	1,269	1,980	49	2.7
Subtotal	4,009	9,446	(avg.) 46	(avg.) 2.2
Other integrated				
Subtotal	4,105	8,342	45	4.9
Specialty				
Subtotal	3,804	2,882	316	21.5
Grand total	31,798	63,413		4.0
Total industry	39,800			

*Data collected by AUS consultants, "Steel Briefing," January 1991, except where noted.
†Calculated from company annual reports.

Chaparral had 859 customers in all: distribution centers, original equipment manufacturers, and fabricators operating in the construction, railroad, defense, automotive, mobile home, and energy industries. As a result of its broad product mix, by 1991 Chaparral was in a position to compete directly with integrated steel companies and minimills both in the United States and abroad on the basis of price, quality, and service.

Chaparral's Technology Growth

Chaparral's basic approach to steel production was to operate its mill at full capacity in order to achieve the lowest possible unit cost of production. Chaparral's original furnace, rated initially at 250,000 tpy, was modified and improved to reach a capacity of 700,000 tpy by 1991. The second furnace, purchased in 1982, was rated by its manufacturer at 500,000 tpy. It too was significantly modified, achieving an operating capacity of 1,000,000 tpy. According to Paul Wilson, general manager of operations for production, "The basic structures were not changed, but we made it run at its real capacity through a series of projects such as a new transformer and an improved scrap feeder."

The furnace capacity increases, in turn, put pressure on all other sectors in the continuous casting operation to improve. When first purchased, the initial casting equipment was also rated at 250,000 tpy. Based on a production philosophy of never limiting the furnaces' production, the caster was improved and upgraded in step with each furnace enhancement. One operation pushed the other to reach new productivity goals and improve quality and adaptability. Chaparral's actual production level in fiscal year 1990 of 1,240,000 tpy yielded an operating level 85 percent of capacity. This rate

EXHIBIT 5 Product Description

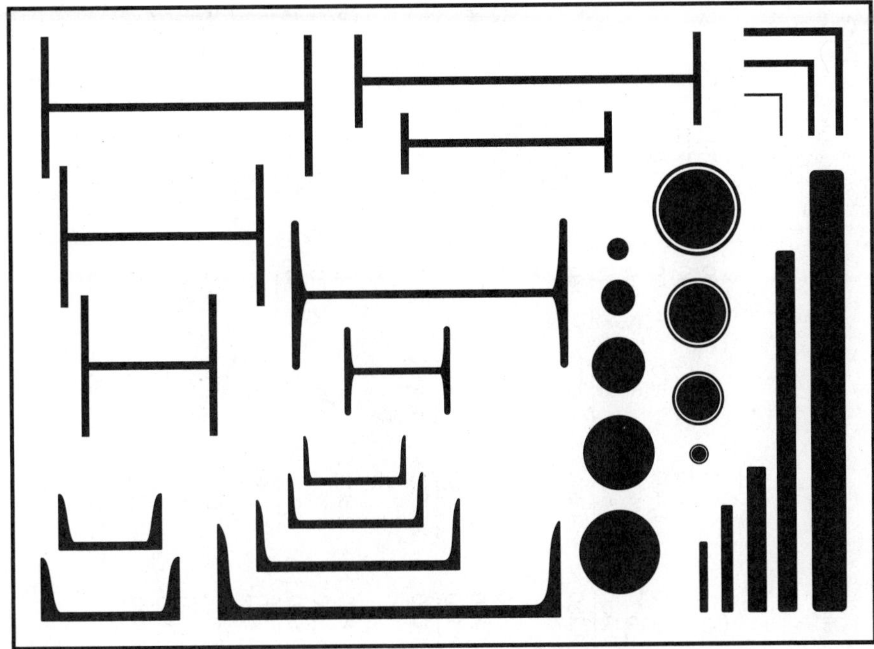

Reinforcing bar (Rebar) All commercial sizes of rebar from ⅜-inch diameter to 2¼-diameter, for use in construction.

Merchant quality rounds Cylindrical steel bars used in construction and fabrication operations.

Special bar quality rounds Produced in a large variety of carbon and alloy grades primarily for use in the forging, machining, cold drawing, and oil industries.

Beams Used in both the construction and fabrication industries and low-rise construction, they include wide-flange beams (ranging in size from 4 inches by 4 inches to 14 inches by 6½ inches) as well as certain sizes of standard "I" beams.

Merchant shapes and other products Structural channels, angles, flat bars, and narrow plates used in the equipment manufacturing and construction industries, particularly in the construction of utility toward and low-rise structures.

SOURCE: Company documents.

was roughly equivalent to the U.S. steel industry's average operating level.

Because there was no separate R&D area at Chaparral, projects were always being developed and tested in the plant. "The ideas come from just about everybody," reflected a maintenance supervisor. "From the operators on the equipment, the millwrights, and right on up to the top." A pulpit operator agreed: "You are always there, always asking questions; you are constantly trying to learn more about what you are doing, about your process." He noted that new digital controls for the furnace control pulpit had been purchased following the recommendation and persistent advocacy of a maintenance engineer. Considering all the development projects underway, "We have had some things that have failed, but not many," recalled Wilson. Hunt added: "We have a knowledge-based culture here—knowledge based on experience. Maybe we are not perfectly right, but let's get it in and get it going and learn from it."

An illustration of Hunt's point was a recent episode when the water cooling hoses on the caster began to burst. A millwright recounted the incident:

> We tried two or three kinds of hoses, and then everybody just got together and called some person they might have dealt with—vendors, experts in the field—anyone they thought would know how to fix the problems. They even pulled in one guy from the training

EXHIBIT 6 USA Shipment Matrix for Steel Products, 1989E

	Chaparral Steel					Domestic Shipments							
Product	1984	1985	1986	1987	1988	Minimills	Other EF*	Integrated Mill	Subtotal	Imports	Exports	Apparent Steel Consumption	Approximate Price per Ton (June 1989)
Rebar	259	260	301	337	245	4,900			4,900	200	100	5,000	325
Bar and light shapes													
Merchant bar						2,100	200		2,300	100	60	2,340	$345
Light shapes to 3″						1,100	100		1,200	120	50	1,270	
SQ bar-ingot route							800	800	1,600	250	50	1,800	
–CC						900	1,000	500	2,400	200	50	2,550	
Cold finished						150	300	1,050	1,500	250	30	1,720	
Total	421	425	426	340	375	4,250	2,400	2,350	9,000	920	240	9,680	
Structurals													
>3″ to 8″						2,400	300	50	2,750	600	100	3,250	$350
8″ and above						700	250	1,400	2,350	1,000	100	3,250	$400
Rails							300	150	450	300		750	
Total	174	257	361	535	644	3,100	850	1,600	5,550	1,900	200	7,250	
Wire rod													
Commodity						1,900	400	200	2,500	500	10	2,990	
Special grades						550	200	1,000	1,750	750	30	2,470	
Wire products						50	600	550	1,200	450	50	1,600	$325
Total						2,500	1,200	1,750	5,450	1,700	90	7,060	
Plate (incl. in coils)						600	900	6,100	7,600	1,600	800	8,400	$450
Tubular goods						800	1,600	2,500	4,600	2,500	500	6,600	
Semifinished						400	700	1,100	2,200	2,800	300	4,700	
Flat rolled, all other							200	42,000	42,200	7,000	2,500	46,700	$500†
Totals	854	942	1,088	1,212	1,264	16,350	7,750		81,500	18,620	4,730	95,390	

Note: Trade shipments by U.S. mills are estimated as of August 1989.
*Other domestic steel mills with electric furnaces.
†$500 per ton for cold rolled steel. Hot rolled steel cost $380 per ton, and galvanized steel cost $640 per ton.

SOURCE: All information based on the *World Steel Dynamics* report developed at PaineWebber, March 1990.

department, sat him down, and said, "Tell us what you think." Within a couple of hours, we were getting calls back, service people were showing up, and we worked the problem out.

Chaparral's creativity, experimentation, and risk-taking came together in the development of its most recent two projects: the beam blank and the near net shape programs. The company pushed technology significantly beyond any yet available in the marketplace and earned Chaparral one of its first patents.

Beam Blank and Near Net Shape Projects

Both of these projects originated from an attempt to explore new products. By 1984, Chaparral's existing products had achieved their desired market penetration, and any attempt to increase market share further would have required additional price cuts. One option for the firm was to expand further into specialty steels, typical minimill products. The alternative was to increase beam size capacity and directly challenge large integrated steel companies. Duff Hunt explained:

> There were quite a few imports in the mid-1980s, up to some 35 percent of the market in certain product groups, for example, around 16-inch beams. We knew we could knock off some of these imports. Also, there were a few segments with large steel producers acting as suppliers we could compete against as well.
>
> Overall, going up in product size made sense; it was a similar customer base and a good complementary product to the current product line. Moreover, our whole history is in long products (bars and structural shapes) as opposed to coiled flat rolled.

Rebar for construction was Chaparral's initial product. Starting in 1985, however, beams grew as a share of their total product shipped. At first, Chaparral could roll only beams up to 10 inches wide, limiting them to a small segment of the market. The constraining factor was the available horsepower in the rolling mill. Making medium and large section beams (14 and 24 inches, respectively) required too much power and replacing the mills was too expensive. Chaparral had to look elsewhere in the process for possibilities to make the large sizes inexpensively.

Beam Blank Project

Chaparral employees actively searched the world for new technologies to improve their processes. In 1984, John Beaton, a caster mold expert, and Duff Hunt went to Japan for an update on a new method: profile casting.

Early Chaparral molds cast steel into a 5.25-inch square, but modifications in the early 1980s permitted casting into 5 by 7 rectangles. From that square or rectangle, the steel was reheated and rolled into all the final shapes required. Profile casting, however, directly cast steel into shapes—such as a dog-bone—that were easier to roll and required significantly fewer rolling passes to produce beams. Fewer rolling passes meant a reduction in energy costs to produce the steel—by as much as 50 percent. Since energy comprised 25 percent of all steel production costs, the savings potential was enormous.

Profile casting technology had been initially explored in the United States and later developed by the large Japanese steel companies. The profile casting machine Beaton and Hunt observed in Japan, however, cost more than all of Chaparral's capital equipment at the time. Moreover, recalled Hunt, "It was a huge, massive piece of equipment in a complex shop and needed 30 people to operate it." The Japanese technology also cast into a very large size shape (profile) that required several additional steps and heavy rolling equipment before reaching the final product.

"We came back from Japan," Hunt explained, "realizing we could not employ that technology. It did not fit our mentality, it did not fit our company, and it did not fit our casting machine." Chaparral needed to continuously improve, but with minimal investment. It would have to invent its own technology; buying from the outside was impossible.

Once challenged, Chaparral felt confident—previous projects had generally proved fruitful. For example, the company had developed an electromagnetic stirrer for steel in the mold when no such equipment existed elsewhere. It had also designed and built the world's fastest automobile shredder and scrap handler, having searched the world in vain for this machinery. Chaparral's equipment could shred a car in 18 seconds. Profile casting, however, seemed to be an order of magnitude more complicated than these previous efforts.

The goal was clear: to produce the same results as the expensive, large Japanese equipment, only more cheaply. The challenge was also clear: success depended on creating a new mold. Irregular shapes were extremely difficult to cast; inappropriate geometry would cause the steel in the mold to bind as it solidified and shrank. Over the following two years, through extensive cut and test trials, the final shape evolved. Iterations began with a rectangular design having only a small notch cut out along the two longer sides. Eventually, the cut-out section expanded, reaching a final dog-bone shape of 10 by 8 inches, with the central section only 4 inches wide. Concurrently, Chaparral engineers, with help from a local university, built a 6/10th scale water model near the production area to mimic the flow of steel and test fluid dynamics in the mold.

To test the designs fully, one strand (out of five) on one of Chaparral's two casting machines was allocated. Overall, from 1984 to 1989, five mold designs were tried on the casting machine. Initially, an existing mold was cut into four pieces and welded back together to form the appropriate shape. Although the intense heat of molten steel disintegrated the welds, these tests of the novel design were inexpensive. Next, Chaparral ordered a simple copper mold. This lasted longer before eventually succumbing to the intense heat, thus providing engineers enough time to gather needed information. Then, after these tests, high-quality copper alloy molds were ordered.

Chapparal had long-standing relationships with its suppliers. But with the beam blank project, Hunt observed, "We had to become very aggressive with them. We told them: We are going to develop this technology—are you going to help us or not?" Suppliers were skeptical. Given their innovative design, the molds could not be produced by traditional manufacturing techniques and thus were both expensive and difficult to build. Only after seeing Chapparal's own test results were the suppliers persuaded to make the attempt.

The first mold Chaparral ordered was from a traditional supplier, a German copper firm. The supplier balked, however, when additional changes and greater flexibility were demanded of them. Chaparral continued development with an Italian firm for the next three iterations of the molds. That firm also eventually exhausted its expertise and patience, so Chaparral returned to the initial German supplier to place the order for the final beam blank mold. One of Chaparral's operators participated in this final mold development, living in Germany for several months and working on the mold's assembly. When the prototype caster was subsequently built at Chaparral, the same operator worked daily on its construction and initial operation.

The constant changes cost Chaparral $40,000 each time new toolings and molds were abandoned. The challenge with suppliers, according to Hunt, was that "we were evolving and changing the shape as they were building the tools to make the mold." Five mold designs were actually tested even though several more were designed and built. Suppliers were amazed that the company did not appear to begrudge the "wasted" money. From Chaparral's standpoint, each prototype enabled the next step in innovation.

Near Net Project

In December 1987, while the beam blank project was in full swing, ideas were already being kicked around for near net (i.e., final) shape casting. With the beam blank, Chaparral would be able to produce 14-inch I-beams; with the near net shape, however, existing capacity and flexibility could be further expanded, enabling the production of 24-inch I-beams without huge capital outlays.

The near net shape project originated at Rosie's, a nearby diner and Chaparral's informal corporate lunchroom. Daily, nearly every table would be occupied by company employees exchanging ideas and making business decisions. One such lunch hour found Lloyd Schmelzle, senior vice president of operations, sketching on a napkin the shape of steel as it appeared halfway through the rolling process of wide-section beams. If Chaparral could only cast directly into that shape, he suggested, the rolling time and cost for producing such beams would be significantly reduced.

By the end of lunch, the project itself was taking shape, as Schmelzle's napkin was passed around.[5] A somewhat startling goal was set: to produce beams for the cost of rebar, the cheapest form of steel. If it could achieve that objective, Chaparral could compete directly with integrated steel companies. "The market opportunity was there," noted Hunt, "if we could conquer the technology to produce the product." He added:

---

[5]Schmelzle had a great deal of experience in steel: prior to this project, he had already designed five *different* mills.

> We decided on those two sizes (18 and 24 inches) based on which ones would be the most technically difficult and challenging. We also felt we should not base our evaluation on only one mold size because there might be some idiosyncrasies in the process we needed to learn about. So we selected a second size based on the amount of North American consumption. We went after the most technically difficult for one size and the greatest number of tons in the marketplace for the second.

At the time Chaparral returned to its German supplier, it placed not one, but two orders. The first was for the final beam blank mold; the second was for the near net shape mold to be used on a pilot caster. Since the dog-bone shape was the most desirable, Chaparral engineers and managers designed a series of possible dog-bone shapes. In 1989 Chaparral built a full-scale, single strand pilot caster in the production area to test the near net shape ideas. Only 17 months after the initial napkin drawing, in May 1989, Chaparral cast its first steel on the pilot caster.

After the first runs, segments of steel from the pilot caster were tested for strength and quality in a small Mexican lab. A key advantage to the dog-bone was the reduced need for rolling, but a major uncertainty was whether the steel quality was high enough. Chaparral experts knew that the first several mill passes strengthened the steel and improved quality. No one could predict with certainty, however, whether reducing the number of subsequent passes would alter the steel's crystalline structure in some unacceptable way. Thus, when steel samples were sent to the lab, everyone waited anxiously. When the lab reported positive results, relief surged throughout the mill: The near net shape had excellent metallurgical properties.

The initial mold tested on the pilot caster was actually a more radical design than was necessary. Once engineers saw that their "test-the-limits" design was feasible, they decided to retreat somewhat from the extreme dog-bone shape for the first production runs and use a mold with straight rather than concave ends on the "bone" shape. The mold supplier, of course, would have to make these needed changes. The German firm had the final mold for the near net shape (in the radical design) all prepared for shipment. "They were so proud," recalled one engineer. "They had done such a good job on delivery and even wanted to know if we wanted it air freighted or shipped by sea. We told them that we didn't need it: 'Cut it apart and make it look like this,' we said. They had a heart attack!" Once again, one innovation followed so hard on the heels of the previous one that they essentially overlapped. Now, however, Chaparral engineers faced another challenge: Would the new straight-sided shape work? The process had been tested using the more radical design. The new shape should be easier to cast and to roll—but again the issue was, would steel quality suffer?

"We tested the limit because we never leave anything the same," explained Hunt. Everything up to this point had been successful, he added:

> We made the caster run and flowed the liquid into the mold. The shape came out of the casting machine without tearing itself apart. We rolled the cast shape and examined the physical properties of the product. After all that testing, the only remaining question was if we were really ready to spend the money now and build a rolling mill and production casting machine.

In fall 1989, an off-site management meeting addressed the possibility of building a second site elsewhere using the near net shape technology. In attendance were all the senior vice presidents (Marketing, Engineering, Operations, Finance) and the vice presidents (Quality Control and Sales, Raw Materials, Administration), along with CEO Gordon Forward. The group concluded that the project was still risky and they preferred to run it first in the existing plant by adding a new large section mill. Further, to meet cost objectives, a "hot-link" between the caster and that rolling mill would be necessary.

Chaparral managers once again searched the world and discovered that only one plant, in Poland, used hot-link; no such process had yet been attempted in the United States. With hot-link, steel was rolled into its final shape immediately after being cast; it did not significantly cool down as a billet before reheating and rolling. This meant, however, that steel quality could not be inspected until after its final rolling. And no one was confident that the technology could consistently meet customers' quality demands. Nevertheless, given the knowledge gained from the pilot caster, the goal of "making beams for the cost of rebar" could be achieved. The go-ahead signal was given. On March 26, 1991, the near net shape equipment was tested on the new large section mill for the first time.

Throughout the project, engineers built flexibility into the components to encourage future development and enhancement. They designed a caster that could run at 150 inches per minute even though they currently intended using it at only 120 inches/minute. They designed rolling equipment with a wider production capacity than currently needed. To improve the overall coordination of the hot-link between the caster and rolling equipment, the general manager of the rolling mill was assigned to be the manager of the casting machine as well. Thus, instead of separate teams for casting and molding, the teams now were vertically integrated, by furnace. Furnace A had a casting and rolling team, as did Furnace B.

Overall, the near net project cost approximately $60 million, including $12 million for capital equipment. The design included a caster with two bays and a separate turret, as well as new rolling equipment developed and built for the new large section mill. Chaparral succeeded in establishing a 50 percent energy advantage over its competition.

Rolling Technology

A key component of the near net shape success was the new mill's ability to accept near net shape and produce a wide variety of products. To meet Chaparral's needs new milling equipment was designed, by internal engineers and external consultants, for flexibility in rolling various products. Before the near net shape process, the rolling technology at Chaparral was "in line." In both the rebar and the medium section mills, the cold billet was reheated in a furnace and sent straight through as many as 16 successive rolling mill strands without being reversed.

To meet the cost and production objectives of the near net shape, the new large section mill used reversible rolling equipment with the hot-link technology. Since significantly fewer passes were required overall, this "old" technology of reversible equipment was more efficient. Immediately after casting from the near net shape mold, the steel was sent directly through the large section mill's first five stands. After going through stands six, seven, and eight, the rolls were adjusted and the billet was passed through those same stands again before being sent to two finishing stands. The challenge for Chaparral operators was that as one billet came out of the furnace and entered the first stand, another billet was still in the middle of the mill reversing. The timing was tricky. In most mills a billet was not released from the furnace until the previous billet had been completely rolled, but that practice, of course, limited productivity.

To protect its proprietary mold knowledge, Chaparral learned to machine its own molds; there were occasions, however, when Chaparral leased molds to a joint venture partner, then took the molds back to do the final machining internally. Since the Italian firm that was one of Chaparral's biggest suppliers of molds was also employed by NuCor and other competitors, information about Chaparral's molds did spread.

Duff Hunt summed up the thinking that had enabled Chaparral to stretch itself so successfully: "We use products to do research. We can close the feedback loop between researchers and users by using new methods and new materials within our own facility." Production manager Paul Wilson agreed: "In other companies, the word is, 'Don't rock the boat.' Here, we rock the hell out of the boat. We don't know the factory's limits. We want it to change, to evolve."

Forward's Dilemma

Even as the new large section mill began rolling steel, innovative technologies for alternative methods of steel manufacturing were developing. Forward knew that he could no longer put off the choice between further investment and growth at Chaparral's Midlothian site and the construction of a new facility; if he opted for the latter option, he would have to select a site for the new plant. Should it be located near the existing plant in Midlothian, elsewhere in the United States, or should he look to Europe or Asia? Due to the costs of transporting steel, the new site would need to be convenient to an adequate supply of scrap material and adjacent to markets for its products. Forward also had to consider whether Chaparral's culture and values could be duplicated in a new site. He had many other issues to consider. Should Chaparral expand into new steel products? Could Chaparral use its knowledge in scrap handling to develop an extensive recycling business with steel as well as other materials? Did its knowledge in producing steel enable it to successfully produce other higher margin metals such as aluminum?

Case IV–7
Associated Instruments Corporation: Analytic Instruments Division

Sandeep Dugal and
Steven C. Wheelwright

On October 1, 1985, Bob Hoffenberger, division manager for Associated Instruments Corporation's Analytic Instruments Division, felt considerable dismay as he studied the latest marketing projections for the model 77000 mass spectrometer. The 77000 was the division's hot development effort, which was scheduled to begin customer shipments in late 1986. The annual volume projections for the 77000 had been drifting steadily downward over the past few months, while the projected sales price had risen to cover increases in the projected cost of goods sold as the product's design evolved. Those cost increases had resulted from improved features added to the basic product and changes to make it more reliable.

Both division management and the design team had deemed each individual improvement a necessity, given the high priority assigned to product performance and product reliability. Yet, at a higher price than originally planned, the 77000 might fail to capture the market position envisioned when corporate approved the product development effort. By falling short of key strategic and profit goals outlined for it by management, the 77000 threatened to disrupt the smooth execution of the five-year business strategy the division had embarked on in 1983.

Hoffenberger knew that corporate management would be expecting a review and update on the 77000 project within the next week. From a passing comment made by the CEO, he knew corporate was aware of the increasing price (cost) and decreasing volume projections. He felt he should do his homework and take a position before his next review meeting, rather than wait for questions that he was not prepared to answer.

Corporate Background

The Associated Instruments Corporation (AIC) was a $200 million-plus designer, manufacturer, and marketer of precision instruments for construction firms, chemical laboratories, university research facilities, and other institutions. (See Exhibit 1 for financial statements.) The Analytic Instruments Division, one of six divisions within the company, manufactured high-quality, high-priced, fully featured mass spectrometers and related instruments. The company traditionally had been a technology leader. Recently, however, each division increasingly had been required to compete on the basis of price as the performance of competitors' equipment had improved and as industry product standards had emerged. This was particularly true in the Analytic Instruments Division, where the rate of technological change in mass spectrometry had slowed markedly. With the maturing of its base technology, the Analytic Instruments Division could no longer expect customers to pay the 25 to 50 percent premium for its equipment they had been willing to pay in the past. Thus, part of the repositioning of AIC and its divisions involved changing priorities and building the capability to develop cost-effective yet highly featured and highly reliable products. The 77000 effort was the Analytic Instruments Division's first attempt to address this new reality and operationalize this new strategy.

Mass Spectrometers and the Mass Spectrometry Industry

Mass spectrometers were powerful analytic instruments used to isolate and identify the chemical compounds or elements in a sample. Mass spectrometers were designed to work in conjunction with several pieces of associated equipment including powerful small computers, liquid and gas chromatographs, and various detector devices. Customers were moving toward more systems, although in the mid-1980s, stand-alone units still represented almost 50 percent of the market. (The building blocks for a mass spectrometer system were offered individually by the Analytic Instruments Division or in combination, linked through the division's proprietary software network.)

EXHIBIT 1 AIC Corporate Financial Statements (Fiscal year ending August 31, 1985; in 000s)

Corporate Assets		Corporate Liabilities and Equity	
Current assets		Current liabilities	
Cash	$ 11,050	Accounts payable	$ 15,944
Accounts receivable	34,190	Other accrued liabilities	53,567
Inventories	64,760	Total current liabilities	69,511
Deferred tax benefit	4,372		
Prepaid expenses	1,511	Long-term debt & equity	
Total current assets	$115,883	Long-term debt	37,030
		Deferred taxes	7,807
Property, plant, & equipment		Deferred employee benefits	9,296
Land, buildings, & improvements	60,122	Common stock	28,154
Machinery & equipment	43,666	Retained earnings	33,184
Less: Depreciation	(29,671)	Translation adjustments	5,118
Net property, plant, & equipment	74,117	Stockholders' equity	66,456
Total	$190,000	Total	$190,000

Corporate Profit and Loss

Net revenues	$201,070
Cost & expenses	
Costs of goods sold	116,977
Research & development	18,629
Selling, general, & administrative	48,941
Interest, net	4,101
Income before taxes	12,422
Provision for income taxes	5,590
Net Income	$ 6,832

In a mass spectrometer system, small quantities of the sample to be analyzed were vaporized in a low-pressure chamber. Molecules were analyzed using one of several techniques, such as electron impact or field ionization. When chemical compounds were ionized, for example, they formed unique mass/charge combinations, each of which created a different signal when accelerated using electric and magnetic fields. The nature of each element was determined by this unique "fingerprint," and the quantity was determined by the intensity of the signal. By the mid-1980s, the output of most mass spectrometers was fed directly to a small computer that used a database and sophisticated software to automatically analyze and identify the nature and quantity of the compounds in the sample.

Customers for mass spectrometers included independent chemical laboratories, such as test houses, or chemical analysis laboratories—often part of large companies—that needed to determine the composition of a sample for research, quality, or environmental protection purposes. In addition, mass spectrometers were increasingly used on production lines to monitor the chemical composition of products, by-products, and wastes. Oil, pharmaceutical, and chemical companies were some of the biggest users of mass spectrometers. Although the market had been maturing during the early 1980s, it was expected to continue to grow at 15 to 20 percent per year as environmental protection concerns required more companies to determine the quantity of certain compounds.

In addition to AIC, three U.S. firms competed in the mass spectrometer industry: Hewlett-Packard, Varian Associates, and Finnigan Corporation. All four companies were California-based. In addition, competitors from Japan, Germany, and Great Britain held viable positions in this worldwide market. (U.S. industry sales, as well as AIC's Analytic Instruments Division's market share, are shown in Exhibit 2).

EXHIBIT 2 Industry and Division Sales of Mass Spectrometers

Year	U.S. Industry Sales (000s)*	Analytic Instruments Division U.S. Sales (000s)	U.S. Market Share†
1986 (est.)	$158,000	$19,000	12.0%
1985 (est.)	126,000	17,800	14.1
1984	106,022	16,221	15.3
1983	92,871	14,952	16.1
1982	87,623	14,721	16.8
1981	96,100	17,298	18.0
1980	82,500	14,190	17.2

*U.S. sales were thought to represent about half of the total worldwide market.
†Although data were sketchy, Associated's Analytic Instruments Division thought its worldwide market share was about the same as its U.S. market share. The 1986 estimates do *not* include any sales of the 77000.

SOURCE: Division estimates.

Mass spectrometers currently were priced in the $3,000 to $10,000 range, but prices had been falling 10 to 20 percent per year. When purchased with peripherals like small computers, gas chromatographs, and software networks, they were part of a much more expensive system, priced in the $25,000 to $120,000 range. Virtually all of the major competitors sold their products as individual instruments or modules, as well as complete systems.

New equipment manufacturers' warranties in the mid-1980s ranged from 90 to 180 days. Most customers subsequently purchased a service contract that was renewable every 12 months and priced annually at 4 to 10 percent of the original unit price. Purchase decisions were based not only on reliability and price but also on the availability of such special features as automatic loading, versatile software, faster speeds, user-friendliness, and easy-to-read displays.

The Analytic Instruments Division of AIC had a reputation for being relatively high priced in comparison with its competitors but offering the latest in features and system capabilities. The division's sales force focused on sophisticated customers in research and analytical laboratories who valued performance and advanced features. As illustrated by the market share figures in Exhibit 2, the division had done extremely well with its third-generation mass spectrometer family, introduced in 1980. However, by 1984, that offering was being challenged effectively by competitors and the division expected its market position to continue to slip until the introduction of the fourth-generation 77000 in late 1986.

Analytic Instruments Division, 1983–1985

The Analytic Instruments Division historically had designed most of its products in-house but purchased many of the parts and subassemblies such as high-precision mechanical components and displays. As a result of the emphasis on technology leadership and the latest features, engineering design teams generally had functioned quite autonomously, with only minimal input from other functions. According to one division executive, "In those days, manufacturing was just trying to keep up, . . . and marketing and sales were seen as necessary evils."

In the early 1980s, the Analytic Instruments Division found itself under increasing competitive pressure on all aspects of the product—features, price, reliability, and follow-on service. For example, dead-on-arrival (DOA) rates were very high (5 to 15 percent) and the company's European subsidiary had made it a habit to reinspect every unit it received from the Analytic Instruments Division before shipping to its final customers. By late 1983, declines in market share, margins, and growth had become apparent throughout the division, and a general sense of gloom permeated most of the planning meetings in those days.

It was at this time that Bob Hoffenberger was appointed division general manager. Hoffenberger, who had come from the sales and marketing function of a strong competitor, was viewed as very bright and capable. Young and aggressive, Hoffenberger set out to develop a strategy to improve the division's competitive position and profitability. In line with the general strategy being supported by the corporate offices of AIC, Hoffenberger's long-range plan consisted of three steps or phases:

1. Cut costs to "trim the fat."
2. Upgrade manufacturing's role and capability to compete in a cost-competitive environment, and develop (in parallel) a new fourth-generation family of products.
3. Based on the success of the new product family, expand the sales force and enhance the field support group.

This entire plan was to be accomplished in a three- to four-year span and staged so that the division could remain profitable throughout that period. Under this plan, the sales force would be upgraded as the fourth-generation effort neared market introduction, but it would not be expanded until it actually had new products to sell. In turn, the design of the new product was to be done using largely existing resources (but with more marketing and manufacturing input), and the manufacturing improvements were to be largely a self-directed, self-funded effort. While this plan would stretch the division's resources significantly, it was one that everyone agreed was absolutely necessary and one to which people were willing to make a commitment.

Under Hoffenberger's strategy, the 77000 product development effort played a central role. It was not only the logical next generation for product development, as well as for the overall strategy, but it also was to provide the basis for profitably expanding the sales and field service organization and regaining the type of market leadership position the division had enjoyed in 1981.

The 77000 New Product Development Effort

Discussions of a possible fourth-generation product began in earnest in June of 1983. As a part of those discussions, the basic procedure to be used for product development was reviewed and revised. It was agreed that product development should be a business effort and should be initiated by completing three major steps:

1. Writing a feasibility proposal (referred to as a *job order*).
2. Preparing a detailed marketing-driven *product plan*.
3. Obtaining *corporate approval* of a formal new product development proposal.

During the feasibility stage (in 1983), approximately $50,000 was allocated to the study and exploration of competitors' products and features that might be included in this fourth-generation mass spectrometer effort. The *job order* was to include a brief summary of the product's unique features and its estimated cost and development schedule. The *product plan* was then to be developed by the marketing group, focusing on the market opportunity and the market needs. It was to be a comprehensive and fairly lengthy document that covered in competitive, financial, and technical terms the major aspects of the effort and its intended results. This document was to be combined with the formal product development proposal and "signed off" by several senior managers before *corporate approval* of major funding for the development effort. The official start date of the project was the date on which this corporate approval was given.

Historically, product development at the Analytic Instruments Division had been treated rather informally and had been largely under the control of the engineering group. Often development steps had been omitted or circumvented because the engineering group did not perceive them as necessary or useful or because senior management was imposing pressure on the schedule, unaware of the difficulties caused by resulting shortcuts.

However, Hoffenberger had persuaded corporate management to agree not only that the 77000 was essential to the division's strategy, but also that it should be used as an opportunity to establish a new mode for the division's product development efforts.

In June of 1983, the feasibility job order was prepared and approved, and Bill Lind, a 10-year veteran of the division's engineering group, was appointed project manager. (Lind had worked on the third-generation product family, was extremely well respected by both his technical colleagues and division management, and was regarded as someone who could work closely with the other functions.) Lind and a half-time employee spent the next nine months refining the project proposal, researching the concepts behind the new product, and working with marketing to define the market needs and opportunities. Lind focused on reducing cost, perhaps by half. A variety of ideas for cost reductions were gathered and evaluated by talking with manufacturing, marketing, customers, and field service, and by studying competitors' products. In addition, Lind determined that the product had to be significantly more reliable (greater up-time and significantly fewer dead-on-arrivals) and needed to correct or eliminate minor irritants (such as noise or unnecessarily hard-to-use features) that had prompted customer complaints.

By mid-1984, it was clear to everyone in the division that the 77000 was feasible, that it had a good shot at delivering on its primary objectives, and that it was absolutely necessary to the division's overall strategy. At this point, additional resources were committed, even though the formal new product development proposal was not yet completed and approved. (The final approval was obtained in early November of 1984.) Exhibit 3 summarizes several of the project parameters incorporated in that formal proposal and outlines the staffing that was approved and on-board as of November 1, 1984.

As had been the practice in the division in the past, the initial development project for the 77000 family was to concentrate on designing, manufacturing, and introducing the platform or core product offering. This was to be the fully featured model 77000. Subsequently (usually 6 to 18 months later), additional models and options would be developed and offered, including a stripped-down (low-cost) version and special modules aimed at specific subsegments of the market. While everyone was aware of these natural follow-ons, they were not detailed extensively in the initial job order, product plan, and corporate approval. Rather, the initial approval and resources related directly to the core product, in this case the 77000.

By the fall of 1984, Lind and his team had identified a number of potential sources of cost savings on the 77000. Those included (1) greatly reducing the number of parts to be assembled into the final unit; (2) giving the vendors more complete responsibility for the design, quality, reliability, and cost of the components or subassemblies they supplied; and (3) getting the division's own manufacturing operation up and going with just-in-time. In addition, the design team discussed the possibility of changing to injection-molded plastic for some of the key parts, rather than using the much higher variable-cost machined parts made from sand castings. While plastic molding would add substantial tooling fixed costs, the team felt that the increased reliability and the significantly lower variable costs of these injection-molded parts would be much more in keeping with the goals for the fourth-generation product. In addition, the team decided that the five circuit boards in the third-generation product could be reduced to a single board. Finally, a number of minor changes, such as purchasing the switches, fan, and other items with connecting cables trimmed to length and ready for final assembly, would further improve the cost picture on the 77000.

To build solid reliability into the product, the pump design—a major source of field failure and probably the most important subassembly from a reliability point of view—was given special attention. By December of 1984, pump design had been completed, and 10 units had been built. Beginning on January 1, 1985, these units were to be run continuously, 24 hours a day, seven days a week, for an entire year to verify and improve (as needed) their reliability.

Although initially cost had been the driving force for Lind and his design team, features became the central focus of their efforts in 1985. Lind and members of his team had visited a number of customers in late 1984 and determined that while cost was extremely important, features had to at least match (and because of the division's historical reputation, should in many cases exceed) those of competitors.

The design team made fairly good progress during the last quarter of 1984 and the first quarter of 1985. By the middle of 1985, the purchasing department was actively involved in the design effort, seeking and establishing relationships with qualified vendors. One of the goals in the product development effort was to decrease significantly the number of vendors, to increase their range of responsibility, and to select vendors on the basis of reliability and lifetime cost, not just initial component prices. All key vendors were visited by a team consisting of three members of the product development team—a design engineer, a manufacturing engineer, and a representative from purchasing. Each vendor was evaluated by the three individually as well as collectively, and any individual team member could veto approval of a particular vendor.

During the spring of 1985, as the development team sought to refine and close in on the remaining open issues of the design, it became clear that some difficult trade-offs and choices still had to be made. A low-cost display device had been selected for the 77000 in early 1985, but there was a nagging feeling

EXHIBIT 3 Initial Research and Development 77000 Project Proposal (November 1, 1984)

A. Key Project Parameters

1. Schedule (as planned, Nov. 1, 1984)

Event/Task	Date
Complete 1st engineering breadboard assembly	Aug. 1, 1984
Breadboard review	Oct. 16, 1984
Interface freeze (for networking into a system)	Nov. 15, 1984
Completion of 1st engineering prototype parts	March 15, 1985
Completion of 1st prototype engineering evaluation	June 15, 1985
Completion of 2nd prototype parts (fabricated in engineering)	Aug. 15, 1985
Completion of 2nd prototype parts (assembly & final test in manufacturing)	Sept. 15, 1985
Release package tooling	Aug. 15, 1985
Prototype review	Nov. 15, 1985
Engineering buyoff complete	Dec. 15, 1985
1st pilot run tested	April 15, 1986
1st production run (customer shipment)	July 15, 1986
Manufacturing buyoff complete	Oct. 15, 1986

2. Project investment

Design engineering expenses (excluding labor)	$1,925,000
Engineering labor	842,000
Other direct project	126,000
Total	$2,893,000

3. Annual volume projections

1986 (Startup, July 15, 1986)	250
1987	1,700
1988	2,000
1989	2,100

4. 77000 product price/cost-of-goods-sold (COGS)

Average annual unit sales	2,000
Average price/unit	$4,500
COGS—factory cost	
Material	645
Component labor	22
Direct factory labor	138
Overhead (Including Tooling)	803
Total COGS	$1,608

B. Project staffing (core group as of Nov. 1, 1984)

1—Software eng.	1—Mechanical drafting	½—Purchasing
2—Mechanical eng.	1—PCB layout	¼—Marketing
2—Electrical eng.	½—Lab technician	¼—QA
1½—Chemist	1—Manufacturing eng.	1—Project manager (Lind—Engineering)

that it was not consistent with the division's traditional quality image nor would it match the performance of competitors' products upon introduction. However, its cost was low enough to enable the 77000 to meet its primary factory cost objectives. A much better, more costly alternative display had been identified, but because of its significantly higher cost, no one on the project team wanted to champion its adoption.

In addition, a number of other small enhancements and features were identified, each representing only $5 or $10 in additional cost of goods sold, but all of which would further enhance the 77000. About this time (March 1985), the division's marketing vice president left to join another firm, and that position was empty for almost five months.

In August, a new vice president of marketing, Fred Taylor, was brought in from one of the other divisions at AIC. Within a couple of weeks, Taylor realized that the 77000 development effort was losing momentum. His investigations indicated that some tough choices needed to be made and enthusiasm rekindled. With Hoffenberger's approval, he spent the first 10 days of September doing an in-depth review of the 77000 development effort. Lind and his team welcomed this review because they saw the need for more marketing input and Taylor had a strong reputation throughout the corporation.

Reassessment and Midcourse Adjustment

After reviewing the 77000 project in detail, Taylor joined with Lind, Hoffenberger, and Jean Smith, the division's vice president of manufacturing, for an all-day offsite meeting. The group reached several conclusions that day. First, each of the small enhancements and features that had already been added to the design was appropriate and could be provided without significantly increasing the factory cost. (Manufacturing's discovery of several small incremental improvements in its process would provide savings about equal to the costs added by these features.) In fact, Taylor's investigations indicated that conflict resolution had worked well on these small issues—the knowledgeable functions had surfaced issues and options early, worked out balanced solutions, and pursued those effectively.

A second conclusion was that the much more attractive fluorescent display should be adopted in place of the cheaper unit selected in early 1985. Taylor's questioning had found virtually unanimous agreement in the division on this point, but because there was no way to offset the additional factory cost of $150 per unit, no one had wanted to make the decision to adopt it. Basically, the team had waited for someone more senior to act. However, without a marketing vice president to push for resolution and with Hoffenberger tied up in several other pressing division issues, the team simply had opted to live with its initial selection of the cheaper display unit. While Hoffenberger, Lind, Taylor, and Smith agreed and committed to the fluorescent display, they also charged Taylor with pulling together the data needed to evaluate its impact on price and volume and to suggest ways to compensate for that.

A third conclusion was that the project schedule had slipped a couple of months, in part because the fluorescent display device issue had not been resolved as rapidly as it should have. Lind was charged with developing a revised project schedule that detailed the remaining steps to market introduction and manufacturing buyoff. Because of the importance of this project to the division and its entire strategy, Hoffenberger, with the group's concurrence, decided that he should play a more active role and have the entire development team report directly to him for the duration of the project.

Following this meeting, the marketing group—with appropriate input from engineering and manufacturing—actively pursued its assignment regarding the impact and modifications required by the higher priced, higher quality fluorescent display. It concluded that one way to build volume was to pull forward the development of the stripped-down, low-cost 77100 model and ready it for introduction at the same time the 77000 was introduced. Because the 77000 and 77100 were to be a product family, the division's strength and reputation were in premium quality, a consistent image was important, and the 77100 was to be a stripped-down (defeatured) version, not an inferior quality version, the group members concluded that the more expensive display would need to be used in the 77100, as in the 77000. Their analysis also showed that in order to realize the margin goals needed for the division to maintain its profitability and meet its overall strategic commitments to the corporation, the additional $150 in cost of goods sold would translate into $600 added to the selling price. This addition to the price would have a significant impact on the product's anticipated sales volume.

At this point Taylor went back to the original marketing input to the product development effort (contained in the product plan) and updated the volume/price projections for the 77000. As shown in Exhibit 4, Taylor and his people determined that at a price of $4,500 per unit for the full-featured 77000 and $2,800 per unit for the stripped-down 77100, the division could expect to be selling 2,000 units a year by 1988.

While the division had always had a stripped-down version of its core product, that version had been viewed primarily as a line extension to be sold to good, solid customers who had applications that were extremely price-sensitive, rather than as a

EXHIBIT 4 Volume/Price Projections for the 77000 (as of 10/1/85)

	Price per Unit (77000)				
	$4,000	$4,500	$5,000	$5,100	$5,500
Annual Sales Volume (1988)*					
Featured Unit (77000)	2,000	1,800	1,600	1,500	1,300
Stripped-Down Unit (77100)	100	200	250	250	250
Total volume	2,100	2,000	1,850	1,750	1,550
Projected 77000 COGS† (Direct factory cost)	$1,560	$1,608	$1,730	$1,755	$1,910

Tooling Options:	As Originally Planned‡	Lower-Volume Option
Initial investment (One-time charge)	$160,000	$57,000
Variable cost (per unit produced)	$86.50/unit	$101.00/unit
Production process	More automated Tighter tolerances Extra 10% MTBF	Modest automation Meets specifications Meets MTBF goal

*Assumes both versions are offered and the stripped-down version is pushed with traditional AIC customers for their price-sensitive applications. The stripped-down version would be priced at about $2,800. This price was viewed by marketing as the maximum possible to still be considered competitive with low-end competitors in 1988.

†Each of these costs *would increase by $150* with the addition of the higher cost fluorescent display.

‡The projected COGS shown above includes the cost of this tooling option.

major source of revenue. In fact, the Analytic Instruments Division's sales force did not sell into the really price-sensitive market segment. The stripped-down 77100 was to have a very limited set of features so that it would not cannibalize the fully featured 77000. In addition, it was to be priced where it could make some contribution and yet be competitive with the really low-cost offerings of some of the low-end companies in the marketplace.

Originally, the direct factory costs had been targeted at $1,608 for the fully featured 77000 unit, assuming production volumes of 2,000 units per year. When eventually introduced, the stripped-down 77100 would have far fewer software features as well as limited capabilities for flow control of the sample being tested but would be produced on the same production line as the 77000. Eliminating these options on the 77100 would save only $80 or roughly 5 percent in factory costs. With the cost increase of the fluorescent display, factory cost would rise $150 to $1,758 on the 77000 and $1,678 on the 77100, assuming combined volumes of 2,000 units per year.

Taylor and his team determined that if the price of the fully featured 77000 were raised to $5,100 (as needed to maintain margin percentages and cover the additional cost of the fluorescent display), sales volume of the 77000 would drop significantly, although the stripped-down 77100 volume would increase slightly because of the bigger price gap between the two units. However, the total combined annual volume would drop to 1,750 (versus 2,000), and this drop would have major implications for the division's overall performance.

As Smith and her manufacturing team explored the options for additional cost cutting to offset some of the cost of the higher quality fluorescent display, it became clear that the significant opportunities for manufacturing cost reductions (switching to a single printed circuit board, changing to vendor parts that were fully tested and ready for final assembly, and changing to fewer parts from more reliable vendors) already had been incorporated. The best that manufacturing felt it could do using the fluorescent display was a factory cost of $1,758 for the 77000 (at 2,000 total units per year).

EXHIBIT 5 Revised Product Development Schedule (October 1, 1985)

Events/Tasks	Date
Prototype parts in manufacturing	Nov. 12, 1985
Packaging and die cast tooling release	Nov. 19, 1985
8 prototype units completed (assembly through final test)	Dec. 10, 1985
Start prototype evaluations (Marketing, Engineering, QA, Field Service, and Manufacturing)	Dec. 10, 1985
Inputs to technical publications completed	Jan. 15, 1986
All long lead time items on order	Feb. 1, 1986
Review of prototype evaluations	Feb. 11, 1986
Engineering design buyoff (complete)	March 11, 1986
Pilot run parts in-house	May 20, 1986
Pilot run completed (including shopfloor testing)	July 22, 1986
QA evaluation of pilot run units completed	Oct. 2, 1986
1st production run completed (customer shipment)	Oct. 8, 1986
Manufacturing buyoff	Jan. 15, 1986

In late September 1985, manufacturing pulled together additional information on the tooling options associated with the injection-molded parts in the new product. As originally planned, there would be a fixed cost of $160,000 for tooling, and the parts coming from that tooling would have a variable cost of $86.50 per mass spectrometer produced. Smith's group suggested that those fixed costs could be lowered substantially by changing to a less automated, more manual, injection-molded part.

Manufacturing estimated that this lower-volume option would have onetime fixed tooling costs of $57,000 and a variable cost per mass spectrometer produced of $101. However, manufacturing was quick to point out that this lower-volume option, while meeting the specifications, would not hold tolerances as tight as the higher-volume option. In addition, while it would meet the mean-time-between-failures (MTBF) goal for the 77000, manufacturing was confident that the higher fixed-cost option would exceed that goal by at least 10 percent. (These numbers are summarized in Exhibit 4.)

The analysis of the schedule done by Lind and the development team showed that indeed the project was a couple of months behind its original plan. However, test results from the prototype pumps that had been running continuously for almost nine months indicated even higher reliability than originally planned. Based on the test results, Lind estimated that product reliability was likely to be twice that experienced with the third-generation product. Lind was confident that the revised schedule his team had just completed was realistic and would deliver on the project's primary objectives. (See Exhibit 5.)

Hoffenberger's Decision

On October 1, 1985, as Hoffenberger reviewed the available data (including some estimates he had put together with Taylor's help—see Exhibit 6) and the inputs he had received from manufacturing, marketing, design, and the entire development team, he realized that he needed to commit to a detailed action plan. His choices (as he, Lind, Taylor, and Smith had outlined them on the preceding afternoon) appeared to be as follows:

1*a*. Stay with the existing plan and level of tooling and parts automation, and then, after introducing the 77000, pursue an aggressive cost-reduction effort to refine the design, develop the 77100, help key vendors, and further improve the division's own manufacturing processes. This option was attractive in that it minimized disruption to the current product development project, would initiate customer shipments in October of 1986, and yet subsequently developed a cost-reduction capability, which he felt was essential to the company and to his division. Committing to this option would make it highly likely that this capability would be developed because market and business strategy pressures would demand it. Hoffenberger was aware that Lind and his development team favored this option.

EXHIBIT 6 Additional Data Collected by Hoffenberger during September 1985

A. Cost of further delays in the 77000 introduction

1. Market share (Hoffenberger's and Taylor's estimates)

   a. By late 1986, during each month when the third-generation product was available but the fourth (the 77000) was not, the division's market share would slip by 0.2% per month (2.4% per year).
   b. Once the fourth-generation product (77000) was available, the division should see its market share gain 0.5% per month (6.0% per year) for the first year. During the second year of 77000 availability, the division should gain additional market share of 2%–3% to put it at about 20% share of market. (This assumed the division's share of market was still 10%+ at the time of 77000 introduction.)

2. Margins (Marketing's and Manufacturing's estimates)

   a. During 1986, the third-generation product was expected to deliver gross margins (Revenue − Factory Cost) of 50% on average revenues of $6,600 per unit. The pretax contribution margin (after manufacturing, marketing, and selling costs but before depreciation, interest, and G&A costs) was expected to be 25%.
   b. Within six months of introduction (and at a price of $5,100), the 77000 was expected to have a gross margin of 60%–65% and a pretax contribution margin of about 40%. (At a price of $2,800, the 77100 was expected to have a gross margin of 35% and a pretax contribution margin of 15%).

B. Cost of warranty and service

1. For the third-generation product, introduced in 1980, the following pattern had emerged:

	Full Cost as % of Initial Price	Price Charged to Customer
Months 1–3 (under full warranty)	2%	0%*
Months 4–27 (under full-service contract)	2%	4%
Months 28–39 (under full-service contract)	2%	4%
Months 40–51 (under full-service contract)	3%	6%
Months 52–63 (under full-service contract)	4% (est.)	8%

2. For the fourth-generation product (both the 77000 and the 77100), the warranty and service dollar costs per unit were expected to be no more than half of those experienced on the third generation and might be considerably less than that. The division would be in a much better position to estimate these costs on the 77000 in February of 1986, following the full evaluation of the initial 8 prototypes. (See Exhibit 5.)

* Included in purchase price.

1*b*. While sticking with the basic plan, he could accept the reality of the numbers (Exhibit 4) and switch now to smaller-volume, less-automated, lower-cost tooling. This would be the safe thing to do, and there would be substantial opportunity after the 77000 was introduced to work on refinements and cost reductions. This choice would ensure that the division could meet its margin targets, and although it would fall somewhat short of its revenue targets, he knew there were a number of other potential products that the reenergized division had identified recently that might fill that revenue shortfall. His own inclination was to take this route, because he knew the division was already extremely stretched and he wanted to be certain that the 77000 was a success. His division controller and the corporate planner were likely to be strong supporters of this option as well.

2. A second major option that had surfaced recently seemed intriguing. The division had solicited a proposal from an outside engineering consulting firm to perform a value engineering review of the 77000 project early in 1986. This review would be aimed at refining the design, scrutinizing each component and subassembly for cost-reduction opportunities, and linking the various cost elements of the product to the value those elements provided in the marketplace.

Although such value engineering was new to Associated Instruments, Hoffenberger was aware that it had been used extensively by other firms. A few more months of in-house work would be required before the consulting engineering firm could make a definitive proposal, but preliminary discussions suggested that such a value engineering review would (*a*) add three months to the development schedule (delaying product introduction until January 1987), (*b*) shave about 10 percent off the factory cost of goods sold (assuming this would be a normal project), and (*c*) cost approximately $90,000 (the price charged by the consulting firm).

This option not only would reduce factory costs and teach his management team much about value engineering, but also, by adding another short prototype cycle to the development, would ensure that the reliability and performance of the 77000 would be the best possible when it was introduced. Hoffenberger had contacted a sufficient number of the consulting firm's prior clients to feel comfortable with the firm's claims regarding improvements in factory cost, product performance, and market introduction.

3. Finally, he could accelerate development of the 77100, the stripped-down version, so that it could be introduced simultaneously with the fully featured 77000. The objective in doing so would be to obtain a significant chunk of business at the low end, in addition to the fully featured business. Relying as much on his own experience and gut feel as anything, he felt that the stripped-down version might be able to sell 400 or 500 units if it were promoted appropriately, and that it might even add another 100 to 200 units of annual sales to the 77000 version just because it would be so exciting to the marketplace. Thus, even at $5,100 for the fully featured version, if the division pursued this option, it might well realize sales of 2,100 units a year by 1988.

While this option would clearly delay the project another two or three months (until January of 1987), he had a number of ideas for how it might be pursued. From a marketing perspective, if advertised appropriately it could give the sales force a tremendous boost at introduction and provide them access to a much wider customer base, especially if the warranty period were lengthened significantly. For manufacturing, it could add needed volume to cover fixed tooling costs, but also provide the ongoing discipline to reduce costs even further since almost a quarter of the volume would be at the low end. Finally, it would give him an opportunity to make his mark on the division and particularly its new product development effort. For Hoffenberger, this option was the most exciting personally, although probably the most risky and the least well developed of the four.

As Hoffenberger reviewed these options, he also reflected on the new product development process that had brought the fourth-generation product to this point. He wondered if it were as much an improvement as he had originally thought. If it were, why had it taken so long to resolve the fluorescent display issue? Obviously the month of September 1985 had been a period of reopening the development funnel. Was that appropriate? Even now, he wondered if he had handled it well. Finally, the very fact that marketing had been able to go several months without executive input to the project suggested some shortcomings in how they viewed their role. After preparation of the initial product plan, was volume, price, and profit analysis the appropriate extent for marketing's input?

Case IV–8
Campbell Soup Company

Geoffrey K. Gill and Steven C. Wheelwright

On March 9, 1988, Jim Elsner, vice president of engineering systems at Campbell Soup Company, sighed as he began to review John Gardner's report on the status of the Plastigon program. In January 1988, Elsner had asked Gardner to evaluate the status of engineering systems' Plastigon program and to develop his best plan for getting the Plastigon production line up and running as soon as possible. The Plastigon program was Campbell's first production-scale attempt at a microwavable soup, a product area that was considered key to Campbell's future success. Although the equipment for the line had been installed in Maxton, North Carolina, one of Campbell's five regional soup plants, over a year and a half earlier, it still was nowhere near ready to be turned over to production for regular operation.

Having been hired away from General Electric less than a year earlier, Elsner knew his boss was counting on him not only to resolve Plastigon's technical problems, but also to strengthen Campbell's engineering effectiveness and efficiency. As Elsner saw it, the Plastigon program brought to light two broad issues that he and his technical group needed to address. One was the project management approach used within the engineering systems group. The Plastigon program clearly had suffered because of limits in the group's traditional approach. The second issue raised by Plastigon was what role engineering systems should take in Campbell's push into nontraditional packaging systems (such as nonmetal cans for microwavability). Elsner was not at all sure that the current organization structure and management practices of engineering systems, and its interaction and alignment with marketing and the plants, could support the variety and volume of projects already on the horizon.

Campbell Soup Company

Headquartered in Camden, New Jersey, Campbell Soup Company was a diversified food processor known for its strong brands and product quality. Its 1987 sales of $4.5 billion (75 percent U.S. and Canada and 25 percent overseas) came from soup products (where Campbell's U.S. market share was approximately 60 percent), spaghetti products (the Franco-American and Prego lines), canned vegetable juices (primarily V8 and tomato juice), frozen dinners (through Le Menu, Swanson, and Mrs. Paul's), bakery products (Pepperidge Farm), and new enterprises (food service and Godiva Chocolates). With $1.6 billion of its 1987 revenues coming from soup products, Campbell dominated two of the three primary segments of that market—condensed soups (what Campbell people referred to as "red and white," from the color of their labels) and ready-to-serve soups (which Campbell addressed through its Chunky and Home Cookin' brands). The third segment was dry soup, which included instant dry soup and the rapidly growing Ramen Noodle subsegments. The U.S. division, under Herb Baum, was further subdivided into major product categories and a functionally organized U.S. manufacturing arm. (See Exhibit 1 for details.)

The food market and Campbell's competitive response changed rapidly during the 1980s. Consumers were demanding greater quality and freshness as well as convenience (through portion control and microwavability). Hence, Campbell's customer base—direct retailers (for example, supermarket chains) and distributors (who resold Campbell's products to independent stores)—was experiencing significant change. Convenience stores were increasing their share of the total food market, and supermarket chains were focusing on the periphery of their stores, where produce, dairy, baked goods, meat, and deli departments were gaining importance. Within the interior areas of food stores, private label and generic products were competing with branded products. In addition, Campbell was also witnessing sweeping changes among its competition, such as the consolidation of small competitors and the entry of foreign food processors into the U.S. market. Japanese firms recently had created a new market segment, dry ramen noodle "soups," suggesting a low-end Japanese entry strategy into food processing not unlike that observed in many other U.S. industries.

With Gordon McGovern, Campbell's chief executive officer, as a prime driver, the Campbell Soup Company took dramatic steps in response to these new challenges. In the 1980s, McGovern decentralized the U.S. business units and sales force into five regions to strengthen links with customers and consumers. Coming from a marketing and manufacturing background (he had been a plant manager, a marketing manager, and CEO of Pepperidge Farm), he pressed for development of world-class manufacturing and strong technical expertise, bringing in additional leadership and focusing resources. McGovern also championed Campbell's move into new products and markets—especially microwavable products. While the total market for such products in the United States was only $650 million in 1987, it was expected to be over $3 billion by 1992. Although Campbell's initial push in the early 1980s was into the frozen segment of this market (with Le Menu frozen dinners), McGovern felt strongly that developing microwavable shelf-stable soups[1] was not only a major opportunity but a necessity if Campbell were to retain its leadership of the soup business.

[1]Shelf-stable products were products like canned goods, that needed no refrigeration until opened.

EXHIBIT 1 1988 Corporate and U.S. Division Organization

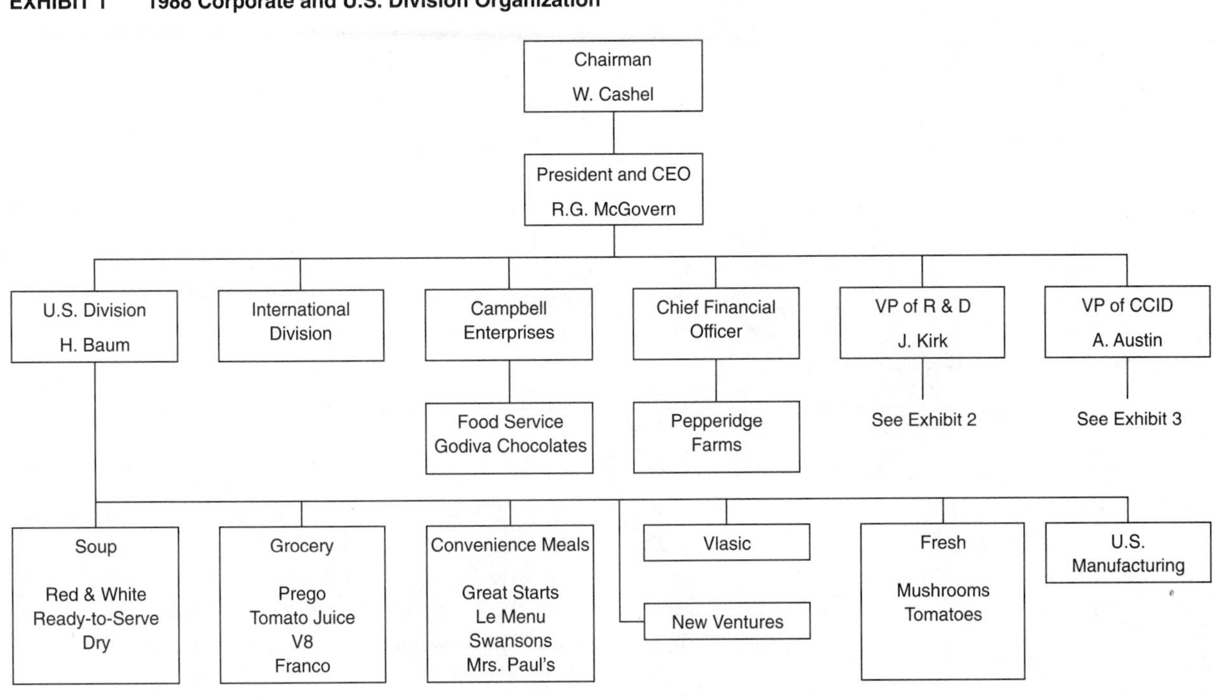

Developing and Applying Technology at Campbell

While Campbell Soup Company had always supported its business strategy of superior quality through strong technical competence, in the early 1980s McGovern saw opportunity and advantage in strengthening its technical expertise at three levels—in research and product development, in engineering and packaging, and in the factories. McGovern strengthened the factories primarily through reorganizing into regional centers that could support the market regions, develop a critical mass of supporting engineering disciplines, and integrate a broad set of activities under each of five regional manufacturing vice presidents. By having more resources available to the regional manufacturing operations, McGovern hoped to enable them to become more self-sufficient and to require less engineering support from the corporate technical functions. The corporate research and development organization comprised three groups: the Campbell Institute for Research and Technology (CIRT) and two departments under the Containers and Capital Improvements Division (CCID).

McGovern charged the senior leadership of the corporate engineering functions to use the resources that had been released from the factory support tasks to achieve significant improvements in technical capabilities. Those improvements were to be applied to differentiate further Campbell's products and processes and to add significantly to its competitive advantage.

Campbell Institute for Research and Technology (CIRT)

In 1983, Dr. Jim Kirk was recruited from the University of Florida to head the Campbell Institute for Research and Technology. At Florida, Kirk had run an extensive R&D program and was an accomplished researcher himself. At Campbell, CIRT was responsible for both long- and short-term research and product development, including process concept development. In early 1988, CIRT employed over 300 professionals, 30 percent of whom were PhDs.

CIRT was divided into three primary operating departments: agricultural research, process R&D (microbiology and the pilot plant), and product

EXHIBIT 2 1988 Campbell Institute for Research and Technology (CIRT) Organization

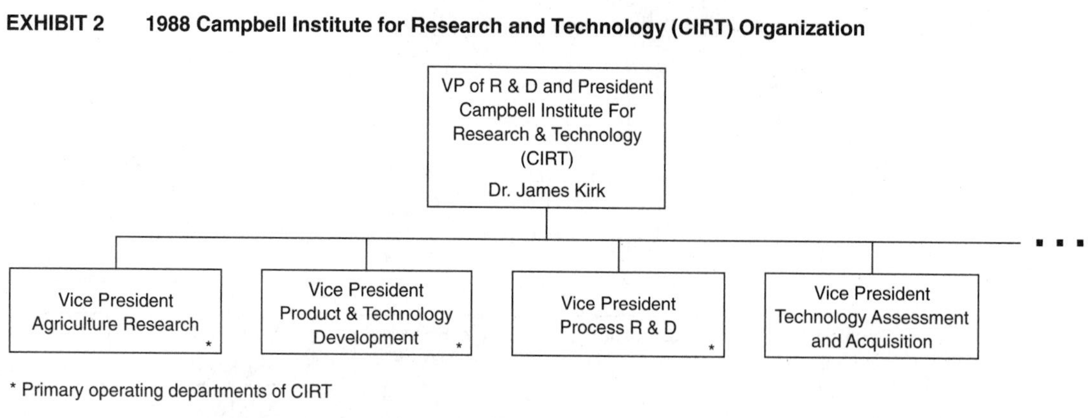

development. (See Exhibit 2 for an organization chart.) The *agricultural research department* was directed primarily toward improving key ingredients, like tomatoes, and improving Campbell's farming operations, which included poultry and mushroom production—two critical inputs to its overall business. The *process R&D department* had responsibility for microbiology—researching the causes of food spoilage and improving product safety—and doing process development. Through its pilot plant section, CIRT did the initial work on process development before turning it over to engineering systems for scale-up and installation of full plant production lines. The *product development department* employed food engineers, scientists, and chefs to create new recipes and entirely new products. In addition, this department was expending considerable efforts in developing low-salt recipes as substitutes for existing products.

Containers and Capital Improvements Division (CCID)

In 1984, McGovern had hired Al Austin to head the Containers and Capital Improvements Division. Austin's experience included several decades in the packaging industry, working with a variety of marketing, sales, and engineering disciplines. Most recently, he had been a senior executive at a major packaging firm. The focus of CCID was on engineering and packaging development across a broad range of activities. These fell naturally into three departments: real estate, packaging, and engineering systems. (See Exhibit 3 for the 1988 organization chart.) *Real estate* was responsible for the acquisition of Campbell's real estate and plant facilities.

Austin brought in Dr. Mel Druin in 1985 to manage the second department, *packaging,* which developed packaging for all of Campbell's products. While most of the group's resources historically focused on metal can technology, the emphasis had shifted in recent years to plastic containers for microwavability and other nonmetal packages. (Druin had been with Celanese, a plastics and synthetic fibers firm.) In early 1988, this group employed over 50 professionals.

Engineering systems, under Jim Elsner, consisted of over 200 engineers and was responsible for developing advanced manufacturing processes for new food products and providing more traditional efficiency improvements in existing processes for all of Campbell's divisions. It also developed and/or purchased the plant equipment for new lines and provided special engineering support to the regional manufacturing plants. Engineering systems was viewed throughout the Campbell organization as a service group—responding to requests for support and initiatives from the line functions.

Within the engineering systems department, people were organized either by disciplines or by areas of project focus. For example, the advanced engineering systems group, which represented almost a third of Elsner's department, had subgroups that focused on advanced control systems (sensors and computerized manufacturing control), in-house equipment development, entirely new processes (working closely with CIRT), next-generation plant engineering, and advanced mechanical systems (filling, closing, sterilizing, etc.). The engineering ser-

EXHIBIT 3 1988 Containers and Capital Improvements Division (CCID) Organization

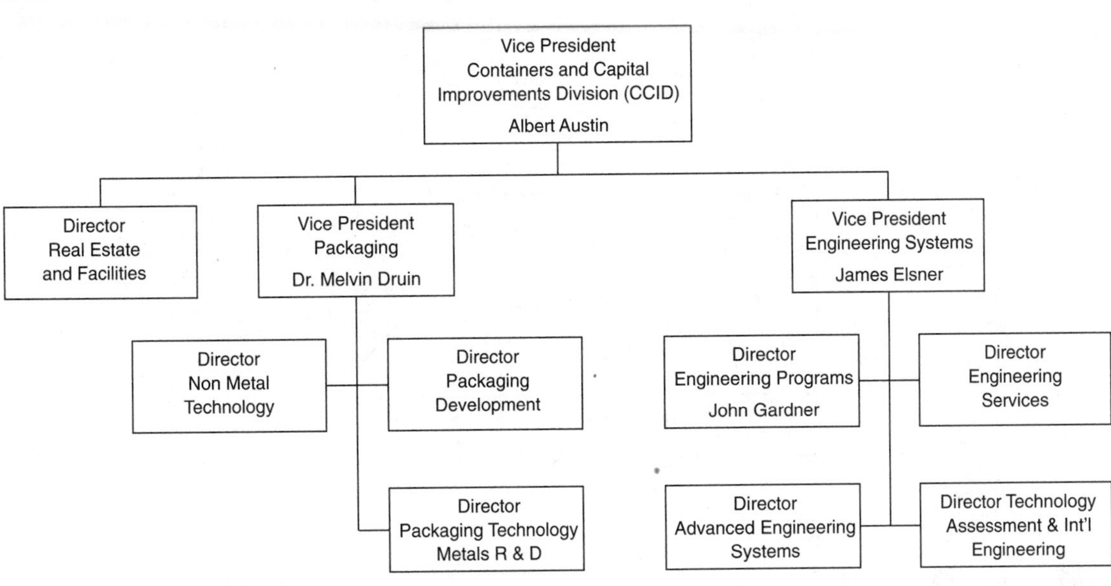

vices group provided traditional engineering services (drafting, civil, electrical, etc.) as well as environmental services.

Because of engineering systems' broad responsibilities, many diverse programs/projects were under way simultaneously (in early 1988, there were over 500). Programs (called projects if they were relatively small and could be handled largely within engineering) ranged from simple soup line extensions (taking two weeks of a single engineer's time), to long-term development efforts such as the development of new production processes or of an entirely new production line like Plastigon. Historically, the large number of simultaneous programs had meant that engineers typically divided their time among three or four projects or more during any given calendar period. Recently, Elsner had set up a special engineering programs group, which at this point included the effort Gardner was heading up in connection with Plastigon, and had responsibility for business unit liaisons and program prioritization.

The engineers in the containers and capital improvements division often worked closely with the professionals in CIRT, at senior as well as lower levels in the organization. As management liked to describe it, CIRT had primary responsibility for product, packaging had primary responsibility for the package, and engineering systems had primary responsibility for the production process. These three tasks were often referred to internally as P^3 (P-cubed).

The Management of Engineering Programs

With engineering systems as a centralized functional support group, a major management challenge was allocating that resource across a decentralized, diversified corporation. In 1988, the basic procedure had been in place for over a decade. The engineering systems department would first project aggregate demand for its services on an annual basis, and then use those projections during the budgeting cycle to negotiate modest increases to accommodate growing demands. Subsequently, those resources would be allocated on a program or project basis as individual opportunities were identified, reviewed, and approved.

A request for an engineering program or project could be initiated from anywhere within Campbell (see Exhibit 4). However, the primary sources (and those traditionally with a higher probability of success) were initiated either by the manufacturing plants or by the business units. Once a request was initiated, engineering systems would review its scope and technical content and write a brief but formal proposal. Often there was little work done at this stage on design issues or feasibility of concepts, in part because so many of the projects were simply

EXHIBIT 4 Project (and Program) Request Flowchart

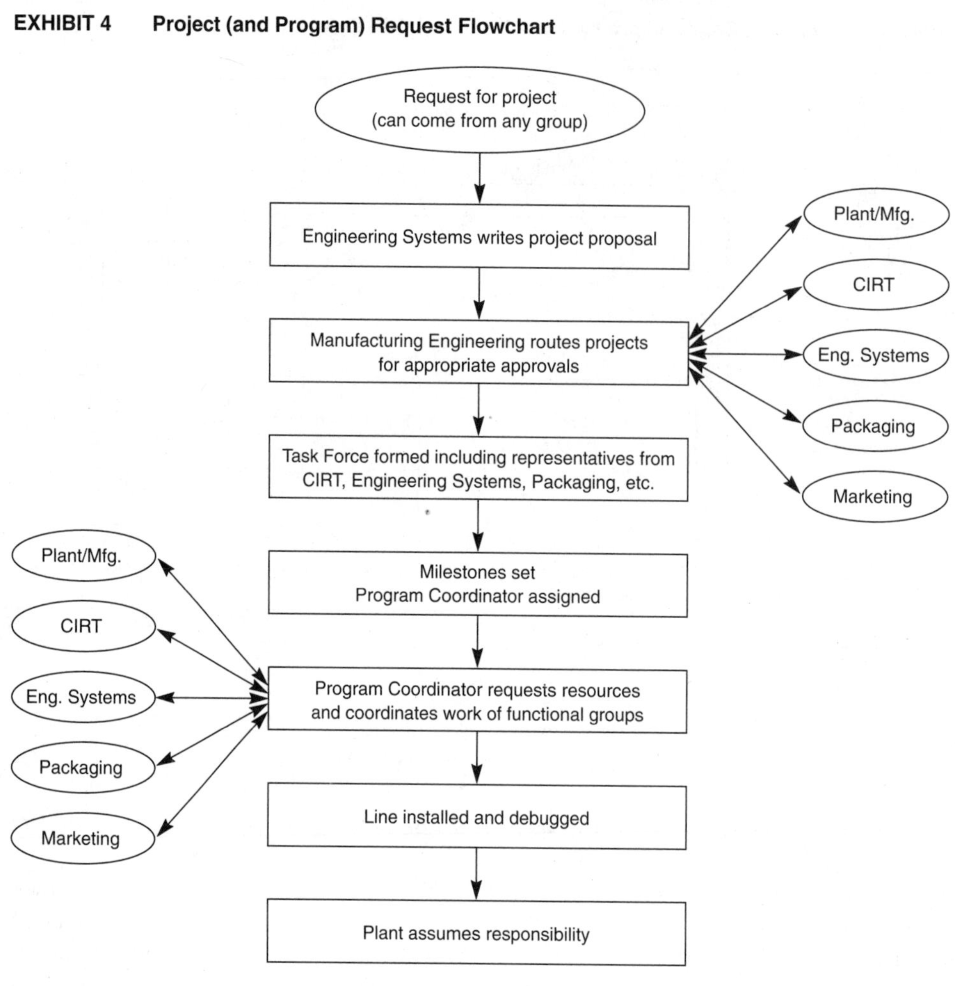

extensions or enhancements of an existing operating activity.

Once prepared, the brief proposal was sent to manufacturing engineering (a subgroup within Campbell U.S. manufacturing) for review. Following predetermined guidelines, manufacturing engineering identified the organizational units that needed to give preliminary approval. This sign-off ensured that all the parties affected by the project agreed with the project's purpose and need and were willing to support its eventual implementation. Next, resources were allocated by the appropriate engineering directors within Elsner's department. Any conflicting requests (such as for a scarce functional specialty or because of conflicting priorities) were resolved by the functional manager, if possible. If not, they were resolved by negotiating at the vice president level.

Each technical program or project within engineering systems or packaging was assigned a program coordinator. (A coordinator could have literally dozens of projects, but probably only one sizable program.) As a practical matter, if a project needed someone from packaging to do a week or two of work, the program coordinator would either talk directly with the desired engineer or with the manager of the appropriate packaging group. Generally speaking, the directors within packaging and engineering systems would determine and agree on priority, and the managers working for them would do the actual people selection and staff assignments for individual tasks and projects.

If a program could be handled primarily by engineering systems and/or packaging, then the program coordinator would take initial responsibility for the entire activity until it was handed over to one of the operating plants. If, however, a program required ongoing input from other groups—such as CIRT or marketing within a business unit, or even a manufacturing plant (because of transition issues)—then a program or project *task force* would be organized. This task force would have representatives from each of the primary organizational units involved and would meet weekly or biweekly to review the program and to make sure that technical inputs were provided and received.

Campbell had used task forces, particularly in the management of new product introductions, for a long time. The procedures, however, had become more complicated as the company grew and decentralized. As the marketing manager for red and white described it:

> We've had the task force concept for 30 or 40 years. Historically, these groups were small and centrally located because the company was small and more centralized. Thus everybody knew each other, and everybody could attend every meeting. Today, however, there are so many functional groups, which are so dispersed geographically, you need a scorecard to know who they are, and missing one of the weekly or biweekly meetings is no big deal.

When a task force was established, the leadership role generally fell to the person from the business unit (marketing), who was in some sense a customer for the new product development effort. As a practical matter, however, since those doing the bulk of the work did not report to that person, the day-to-day project leadership usually fell to a CIRT, engineering, or packaging coordinator and was passed to the manufacturing plant production line manager later on.

Pursuing Microwavable Soups[2]

In response to McGovern's mandate, several marketing groups within Campbell U.S. began exploring possible microwavable products and alternative packages. For the U.S. convenience meals group (see Exhibit 1), who had long been in the "TV dinner" business, this was simply another incremental step. Their efforts focused on developing microwavable entrées (under the Le Menu or Swanson brands) that could be prepared frozen and then cooked in the consumer's microwave oven. Since the product was stored in frozen form, the technical requirements for shelf stability were not nearly as great as they would be for a product stored at room temperature. In addition, the frozen dinners were high-value products whose ingredients were a significant proportion of their cost.

For the soup business units, microwavable shelf-stable products represented a much bigger step. In the early 1980s, the ready-to-serve (RTS) business unit responded by looking for the ideal container for such a product. Focus groups and consumer surveys revealed that the container should have several characteristics: (1) the consumer should be able to eat the soup directly from the container; (2) the top of the container should be easy to open without a can opener; (3) the container should have handles so that it could be immediately removed by the consumer without danger of getting burned; and (4) the container should have an attractive, table-ready appearance.

In addition to the consumer requirements, there were a number of technical specifications. First, the container must be sealed airtight so that the food would not go bad when stored on the shelf. Second, to be microwavable, the container could not be made of metal. Third, it had to withstand not only the heat of the microwave, but also the heat of sterilization (the container and its soup had to be heated to 250°F for 40 minutes or longer during the production process). Finally, the container should not affect the taste and quality of the food.

While some market surveys indicated that consumers might pay up to twice as much (on a per-serving basis) for a microwavable soup, it was clear that there were significant economic constraints as well as technical and consumer preference considerations. A metal can line running at 600 units per minute resulted in fixed operating costs of $.10 per unit, while the same line running at a quarter of that speed (150 per minute) would incur fixed operating costs of $.40 per unit. Microwavable soup packaging costs tended to be much higher than those for conventional soup. The containers themselves were significantly more expensive, but another major differential lay in running the production line.

With the above issues in mind, the packaging group began to search for a company that could provide an appropriate container. The first effort (1983) resulted in a package that used a "scrapless forming process" (SFP). This package consisted of a plastic bowl covered with an all-plastic peel-off lid.

[2]Cost data in this section are representative of the industry, but have been disguised to protect the proprietary interests of Campbell Soup Company.

As part of the SFP development, CIRT set up a small hand-operated pilot line with 25 people packing 12 units per minute. It quickly became evident that the cost of the container and the eventual cost of the entire production process were going to be substantial. CIRT therefore developed a premium line of ready-to-serve soups called Cookbook Classics, with top-quality ingredients, for what was to be a premium-priced product.

The output of the SFP product line was test-marketed in six stores in the Camden, New Jersey, area. While the response to the Cookbook Classic product line was excellent and to a microwavable soup was quite positive, unfortunately, the seal on the SFP package was so strong that a knife with a serrated edge had to be included to "saw" the plastic lid off. It was decided that this seal was too difficult to open and defeated one of the major benefits of microwave packaging—convenience.

As the search continued and the packaging group identified several other possible containers, marketing conducted a consumer survey to evaluate various options and to determine the most suitable one. Because differences in price were not included in the survey, most customers chose the container with the most desirable attributes—the "Plastigon" bowl. This container was a brown plastic bowl, that looked like a crockpot, with a metal foil cover. The foil could be peeled off by hand before heating, and the two "ears" protruding from the top of the bowl enabled a consumer to remove the bowl from the microwave without getting burned. (See Exhibit 5 for a photograph of the Plastigon container.)

Although the initial cost of the Plastigon container was high (28 cents per bowl), the task force decided to go ahead with it. Preliminary market tests indicated that even at a premium price (99 cents retail per unit), a sizable market for the product existed (approximately 100 million units annually). To make this price profitable, it was expected that learning curve effects would cut the cost of the Plastigon bowl by a factor of two within a three-year period.

EXHIBIT 5 Plastigon Container

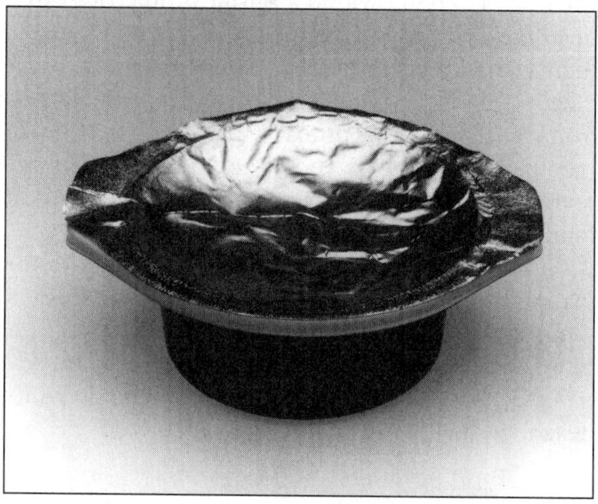

Description of Container:

- Easy peel-off foil cover
- Two ears on sides allow consumer to pick up the bowl when hot without burning his or her fingers
- Attractive, table-ready appearance
- Container cost: 28¢ per bowl
- 10-ounce size

The Engineering Program to Support Plastigon

While engineering systems was an SFP task force member in 1983, the project had never really gotten out of the hands of CIRT, packaging, and the marketing group, and thus there had been only a small formal engineering project set up. When Plastigon emerged in late 1983 as the "ideal container," engineering systems established a major program and appointed John Dalton as coordinator to move that effort from its initial development in CIRT on through to a point where it could be transferred to a manufacturing plant. From the start, Austin and Elsner's predecessor recognized that this program would be a significant challenge. While engineering had worked with the frozen food groups on developing production lines for microwavable products, those were much simpler; they did not involve cooking and sterilization, and the seals did not need the same durability and reliability to maintain an airtight shelf-stable state.

The P^3 team had already developed a small-scale Plastigon prototype line in its laboratories in Camden, but much of the work on that line was done by hand, and CIRT had difficulty getting consistent results. Because the prototype line's technologies differed significantly from those proposed by engineering for the actual production line, the role of the pilot line was unclear, and eventually it was discontinued.

The Plastigon program began in earnest in late 1983 with Dalton and a small group from engineering systems directing the preliminary design of a

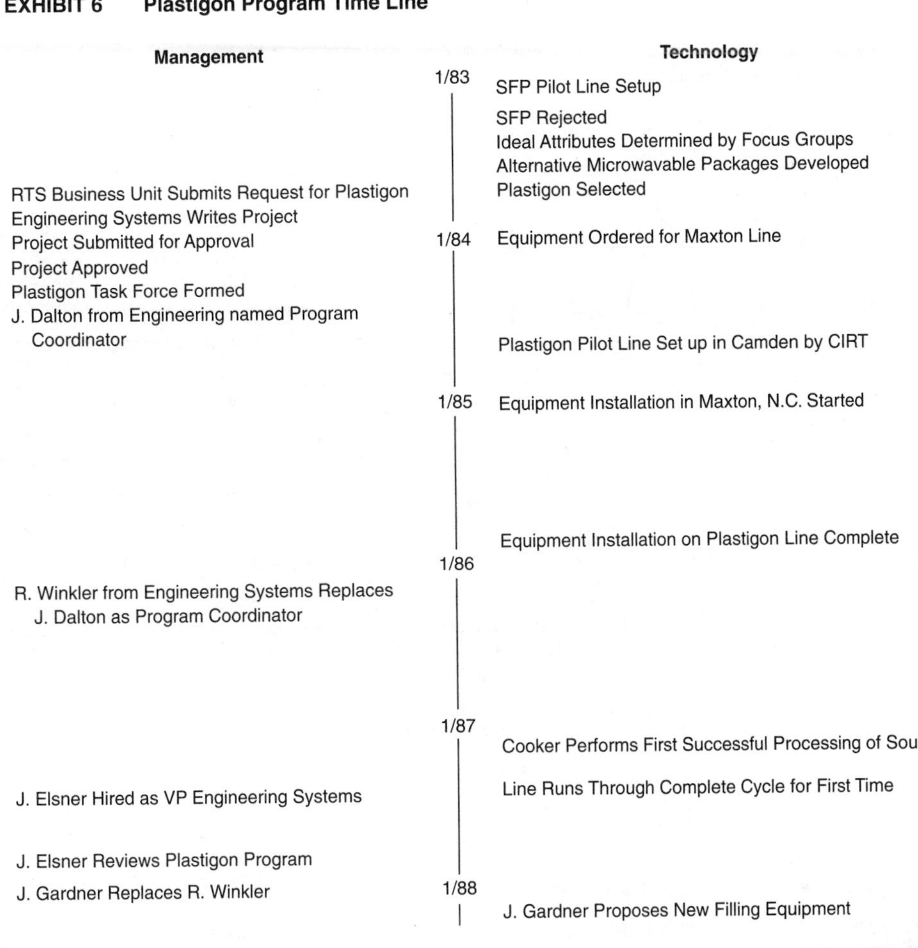

EXHIBIT 6 Plastigon Program Time Line

production line process. (See Exhibit 6 for a program time line.) While no one remembered exactly how the decision was made, it was agreed that the production line should be a continuous process operation running at a rate of 200 units per minute. Although this rate was less than the 600 cans per minute of a typical metal can soup line, the goal was considered aggressive.

The line that engineering systems designed (see Exhibit 7) was very similar to a canned soup line, broken down into six sections:

1. Blending, where the soup ingredients were mixed.
2. Filling, where the bowls were filled with soup.
3. Sealing, where the tops were placed on the bowls and sealed.
4. Cooking, where the soup was cooked and sterilized.
5. Incubation, where the bowls were tested for leaks.
6. Secondary packaging, where the bowls were individually boxed. (After secondary packaging, the bowls were placed in a case by hand.)

Each section was connected by a moving conveyor, making the line a continuous process. Despite the new shape of the containers, the conveyor system itself was fairly standard. But because each section of the line involved different technologies, different engineer(s) were assigned to them.

In late 1983, engineering systems put together a $10 million proposal to develop, acquire, install, and start up the Plastigon production line. The proposal was approved by the Campbell Board of Directors early in 1984. At that point, each of the process engineers assigned to each section of the line was given a budget by the program coordinator and immedi-

EXHIBIT 7 Plastigon Production Line

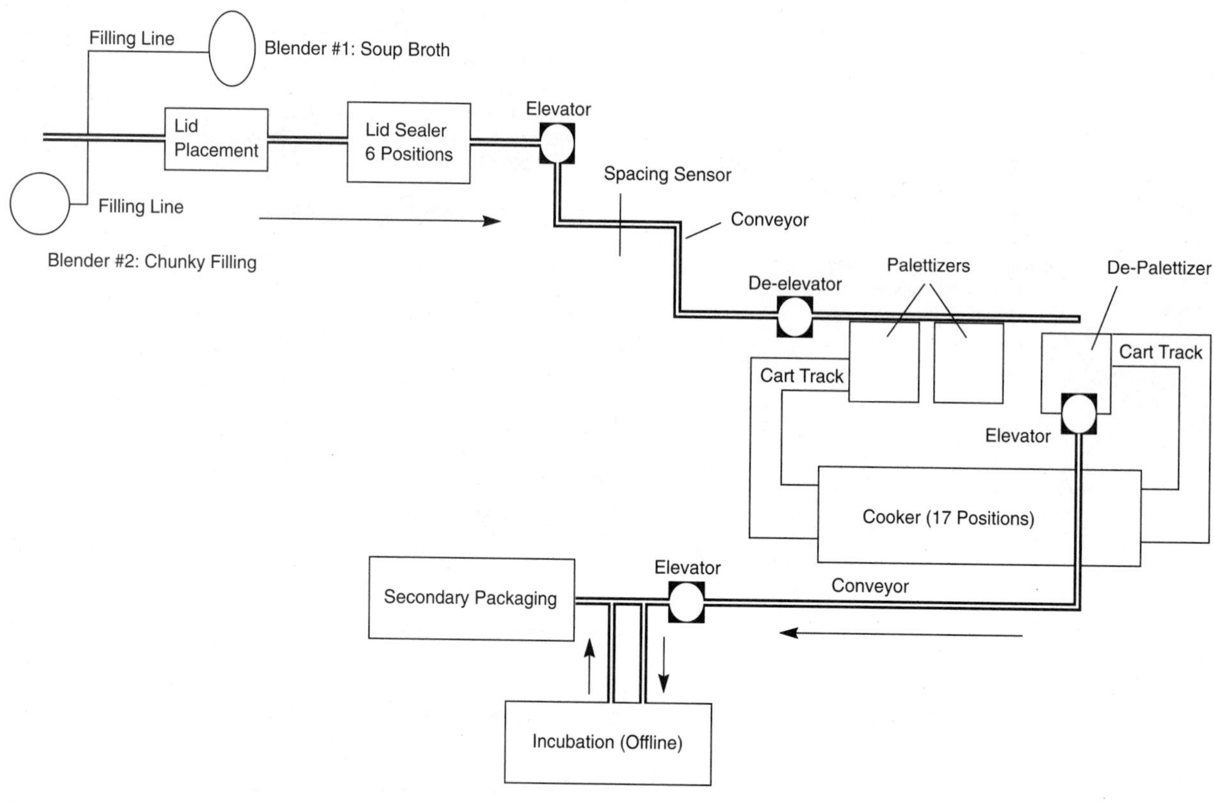

ately began to work with vendors to develop the required equipment. In parallel, a pilot scale line was ordered for Camden to test out concepts. (Frequently Campbell developed production lines without first doing a pilot of that particular production process because of its extensive experience in manufacturing food products.)

The process engineers were quite familiar with equipment procurement. They specified the characteristics (capacity, tolerances, speed, etc.) of the equipment for their section and then sought out a vendor who could provide it. In retrospect, the equipment turned out to be sufficiently different from standard soup-making equipment that in many cases the vendor could not deliver exactly what was promised. Neither the vendor nor the Campbell engineers had adequately specified the equipment to anticipate this, however. Thus virtually every piece of equipment was "first of a kind."

After several discussions among senior management, it was decided in 1984 that the new Plastigon production line should be installed in the Maxton, North Carolina, plant, one of the five regional U.S. plants making soups and other canned products. Maxton was Campbell's most efficient plant and had sufficient floor space to install the Plastigon line without expanding the building.

Over the next two and a half years, the equipment was ordered and delivered for each section of the line. When a piece of equipment arrived, the engineer(s) responsible for it would travel to Maxton to get the installation process started. Because of the large size of the equipment (the cooking chamber was a thick-walled, steel container 70 feet long and 15 feet in diameter), installation often involved major construction.

In early 1986, Bob Winkler became program coordinator for Plastigon, replacing Dalton. Winkler continued to hold regular task force meetings in Camden on a biweekly or monthly basis, and, by mid 1986, most of the equipment had been installed and the engineers were working to get each piece to run by itself without product. The engineers based in Camden, New Jersey, had to fly to Maxton to work on the equipment, sometimes as often as 30 times a year. Several of the engineers left the company or switched to other programs that required less travel.

Getting the Plastigon Line Up and Running

From mid-1986 through 1987, engineers from packaging and engineering systems worked to debug the line and get it running. In late 1986 packaging technology—nonmetal R&D—was put into a single department, which provided some additional focus from the packaging side. However, coordination between engineers from various groups was difficult because often the engineers were not at the plant at the same time. Even when some were present, they had their own tests to run and usually were not interested in running the line as a whole. Also, the engineers found themselves short of support staff to run the line because the plant did not want to devote operators and management time to something still in the "experimental" stage. As one of the engineers on the program recalled:

> For the first 18 months of the debug and start-up phase, no one at the plant was really committed to the line. In fact, as the time for turning on the production line drew closer, they actually wanted less and less to be involved. Their position was, "Wait until it's a proven process" and then we'll be ready to "accept" the line for our operation.

In part, the factory was following standard procedures by not getting involved too early. The general rule was that engineering systems and packaging took responsibility until the process had been "qualified," and then the plant took over. In addition, the Maxton plant was being stretched during this same period as it tried to run existing lines and also bring two-piece metal cans into full production. Finally, plant managers privately worried about the new lines' impact on their financial performance, since they were measured primarily on month-to-month operating results.

As the engineers sought to debug their individual sections and pieces of equipment and to begin running the line together, a number of important technical problems arose. Because the bowls had rounded bottoms and overhanging lips, they were more difficult to manage on the conveyor lines. The system also had a large number of limit switches that checked to make sure that parts were within the required range. The cooker system alone had 150 limit switches. When one of the limit switches failed to make connection, that system would be shut down. This would cause a chain reaction that might set off 30 different alarms. The engineers would then have to track down the root causes of the failure and correct them.

By late 1987, most of the mechanical problems had been straightened out and testing began on bowls filled with water. This was done to ensure that no product manufactured with the test process was shipped to customers by mistake. (Campbell had strict regulations of the procedures used when running soup through a test process.)

When the bowls filled with water were sent through the cooker they became deformed. Solving this problem was especially difficult because the engineers had to evaluate degrees of "badness" to determine whether a change had improved matters or made them worse. Eventually, after exhausting all the relevant parameters, the engineers decided it was impossible to run the cooker at the rated speed. The cooker was slowed to half its original speed, and by completing tests on the full matrix of values of all variables, the engineers were able to determine a combination of those values where the bowls went through the cooker without deformation.

The cooker was then tested on preprocessed soup and finally on the actual soup. Because the thermal properties of the soup were different from water, several additional adjustments had to be made to the production process at each stage. While the cooker was being debugged, other parts of the line were also having difficulties. When the bowls were filled, soup splashed onto the rim. Although such splashing was common on metal can lines, on the Plastigon line, it prevented the metal foil lid from sealing properly. Even when the rims of the bowls were clean, the seals were often inadequate.

Within a few months of his arrival at Campbell, Elsner arranged for a review of the Plastigon project. As Elsner recalled:

> I knew the Plastigon program was in trouble, so I asked the engineering team to develop a *detailed* program plan for solving the problems. I then went down to Maxton, North Carolina, where they were working. When I got there, they had a single overhead slide with five or six bullet points. I asked them if that was their idea of a detailed plan. There was dead silence. I thought to myself, "Oh, no . . ." Finally, one of the old-timers spoke up. He said, "I know we look like idiots, but this is new to us. We've never had to do this before."

By January 1988, soup had been produced on the Plastigon line, but the line would rarely work for more than an hour at a time and large losses of product because of bad seals or other problems were common. It was at this point that Elsner replaced Winkler with Gardner, giving him full engineering responsibility for the Plastigon engineering program and requesting that within six weeks he come back with his plan of action for completing the project. Gardner's background was well suited to this assignment because of his extensive work with frozen foods, which had experienced similar problems. In fact, Gardner considered the Plastigon line "nothing more than a frozen food line with a sterilizer instead of a freezer."

Parallel Developments in Microwavable Products

During 1986 and 1987, interest in microwavable products both inside and outside Campbell had grown significantly. While this helped to build general knowledge about what options were viable, how consumers might respond to them, and some of their basic economics, it also had served to fuel direct competition for Plastigon as the microwavable soup solution for Campbell. (See Exhibit 8 for a comparison of the economics of several types of microwavable soups to a standard Chunky can of soup.)

Competitive Introductions

Since the Plastigon program had been initiated, several of Campbell's competitors had developed shelf-stable microwavable products. (See Exhibit 9.) Hormel, for example, had developed a line of nine entrées (chili, beef stew, etc.) in a microwavable container. Hormel's container was essentially a plastic can with a metal "pop" top. The top was a standard can top commonly used in peanut or potato chip cans with a ring that could be pulled to open the can. The top was attached to the plastic can with a double seam. When the top was peeled off, the ring that sealed the top to the can remained. Despite this metal ring, the can was microwavable as long as the metal ring did not touch the edge of the microwave.

Both Chef Boyardee and Dial's DoubleTree food division also were involved in putting their products in a similar microwavable container. Chef Boyardee had test-marketed microwavable versions of some of its Italian products (for example, lasagna and ravioli), and Dial's DoubleTree food division was test-marketing three product families (entrées, pastas, and soups) that could be put in the plastic can.

General Foods also had announced its intentions to serve the microwavable shelf-stable market with a line of entrées (for example, pepper steak and chicken) in a "tray" container. The plastic tray was covered with a metal foil that was heat-sealed during production in a manner similar to Plastigon (the foil had to be removed before heating in the microwave). The tray itself, however, was not made out of a "high barrier"[3] material, so the shelf life of the General Foods container was not nearly as long as Plastigon or other competitive products.

Although none of these products was out of the test market stage as of early 1988, and only Dial was involved with a soup product, they represented competitive threats to a Plastigon-type soup container. Furthermore, because of the relatively high value of an entrée (compared with soup), these products were less affected by the high costs of the packaging. A key result of these competitive actions was that the marketing people wanted to get to market fast with soup in a microwavable container. This pressure caused them to jump from one container or form of package to another.

Developments within Campbell

Because of the delays in getting the Plastigon production line up and running, some people in packaging and marketing were starting to question the original intent of "obtaining the ultimate solution for microwavable soups in one giant step." To many, the Hormel/Chef Boyardee/Dial containers seemed to offer an interim solution to the problem.

The red and white marketing group of Campbell U.S. in late 1986 initiated its own effort to develop a microwavable soup in a container that was essentially a minor modification of the Hormel package. This effort, supported by subefforts in CIRT, engineering systems, and packaging, was referred to as the DRG program (the name was taken from the material used in the container). Everyone agreed that the DRG container was a halfway step between

[3]A high barrier material did not allow the flow of oxygen through it. In this case, approximately 20 cc of oxygen passed through the tray per year compared to approximately 2–3 cc for a high barrier material such as that used in the Plastigon container.

EXHIBIT 8 Comparisons of Economics of Different Containers

	Metal Can Chunky Soup	Plastigon	DRG	Brick Pack	Dry
Serving size	10 oz.	9.5 oz.	7.5 oz.	8 oz.	10 oz.
Cost of container	$0.07	$0.28	$0.25	$0.16	$0.27
Cost of label/secondary packaging	$0.02	$0.06	$0.03	$0.00	$0.04
Ingredients	$0.15–0.25	$0.15–0.25	$0.10–0.18	$0.07–0.10	$0.15–0.20
Fixed operating cost per hour*	$3,600	$3,000	$2,700	$2,000	$1,000
Theoretical line rate (units/minute)	600/min.	200/min.	250/min.	200/min.	500/min.
Actual line rate	600/min.	50/min.†	200/min.†	200/min.	500/min.
Operating cost per unit‡	$0.10	$1.00	$0.22	$0.17	$0.03
Total cost per unit	$0.34–0.44	$1.49–1.59	$0.60–0.68	$0.40–0.43	$0.49–0.54
Wholesale price	$0.57	$0.85	$0.60	$0.45	$0.53
Suggested retail price	$0.65	$0.99	$0.70	$0.50	$0.60
Estimated annual unit sales (millions of $)	$195	$200	$140	$40	$20
Factory investment (millions of $)	$12	$10	$7	$8	$4

Note: All figures have been disguised.

*Operating cost per hour includes overhead, utilities, labor, and depreciation. These costs are largely independent of the number of units produced.

†There were some quality problems at these rates.

‡Operating cost per unit is the operating cost per hour divided by the number of units (actual) produced in each hour.

a traditional can and the "ultimate" microwavable container (such as Plastigon) because the top was sealed with a standard double seal in a manner very similar to a metal can. However, it was also clear (given what competitors were doing) that DRG might offer red and white a way to get a microwavable soup to market even sooner than Plastigon would do so for the RTS business unit.

The DRG container had few of Plastigon's premium features—it had no easy-peel lid, it was not as attractive, and there were no special handles on the sides. Its economics were better, however (see Exhibit 8), and this product was expected to serve essentially the same market as Plastigon. Although DRG was to contain a ready-to-serve product, the red and white business unit was responsible for DRG because the product was to be taken from a red and white soup recipe and because they were the ones who initiated it.

While it was still too soon to tell what kind of start-up problems Campbell might have on the DRG production line, Elsner's engineers felt that because this container was more similar to a metal can, the problems probably could be solved within a few months. Assuming the problems were ironed out as expected, however, it still would be late 1988 before DRG would be sufficiently test-marketed and available in sufficient quantity and quality to permit a national rollout.

Other Campbell Microwavable Efforts

Another product in development was a drinkable soup in a brick pack (the foil-lined cardboard boxes often used for individual servings of juices). While this product used a well-understood technology, its market was somewhat different from Plastigon's market. Although both were convenience foods, the brick pack could contain only drinkable soups, and because it could not be microwaved in its present form (because of the foil liner), the soups had to be put into a mug to be microwaved. Efforts were under way to develop a microwavable plastic-lined brick pack; however, these were at least a year or two away from being commercially viable.

Packaging a dry soup in a microwavable bowl had also been suggested by one of the marketing groups. This product would allow the consumer to add water and then microwave the soup without having to find a container for the soup. Although dry soups were typically low-end, their convenience might make this type of product viable despite the package's high cost (27 cents).

One of the most interesting technologies with promise for microwavable soup was aseptic packaging, where the soup was sterilized independently of the packaging and then added to a sterile package. This technology separated the cooking step

EXHIBIT 9 Alternate Microwavable Containers

A. SFP Container:

- Saw top—difficult and messy to open
- No protection against burnt fingers
- Container cost: 25¢ per bowl
- 10-ounce size

B. DRG Container:

- Easy-open "pop-top"
- Foam insulated walls to prevent burns
- Can-like top should be faster and easy to seal
- Container cost: 25¢ per bowl
- 7.5-ounce size

Other Options:

C. Brick Pack

- Not yet microwavable
- Drinkable soups only
- Container cost: 16¢ per container
- Highly convenient

D. Aseptic

- Technology of the future
- Not ready for production environment
- Better taste
- More convenient?

from sterilization of the bowl. With aseptic packaging, the flavor of the soup could be improved significantly while eliminating one of the most erratic steps in the Plastigon production line process. Many people at Campbell felt that this technology was the "wave of the future." Unfortunately, because of several technical issues that remained, it looked like aseptic soup packaging was still several years away. This made it difficult to estimate the cost and market size for this technology.

In spite of these many options, and while all the technologies were useful, there were those within marketing who were not convinced. In the view of the marketing manager for red and white:

Each of the new convenience technologies has slightly different consumer attributes and addresses a different market segment. The Plastigon product is a high-end product—almost a meal. DRG might be targeted as a snack or a meal for kids. The brick pack soups are more like a beverage than a soup. The advantage of the dry soups is that the consumer can just add hot water if the microwave is not available.

While all of the technologies have attractive features, it is not clear that any of them is really necessary. A lot of the impetus to go into microwavable soups has come from McGovern rather than from solid market data. If you think about it, if we can just increase our market share in the red and white brand by one or two points, we would end up with more profit than from any reasonable sales projections for all these other segments.

Issues for Engineering Systems

In late February 1988, Elsner met with Gardner to discuss the status of the Plastigon engineering program. It was clear from Gardner's assessment that, while there had been many mistakes made along the way, the project was basically sound. Gardner was convinced that he and his engineering team could get the program on line and running over the next several months. Gardner had followed up with a memo outlining the major elements of his action plan for achieving that objective (see Exhibit 10).

As Elsner sat down to review Gardner's memo on March 8, he reflected on what he had learned about the Plastigon program over the last several months:

> When I first saw that six-bullet slide, I got a sick feeling in the pit of my stomach. But I think we've come a long way since then, and I'm anxious to see what John wants to do. I want to make sure that John is on the right track, because the project is important. We not only have to get the line running well, but we've got to build momentum behind the product in other parts of the company.

EXHIBIT 10 Action Plan

MEMORANDUM

To: J. Elsner
From: J. Gardner
Re: Near-Term Plan for Getting the Plastigon Line Up and Running
Date: 6 March 1988

Current Status

When I arrived at Maxton, the line was not running as a complete system. The eight engineers from engineering systems and the two from packaging were getting in each other's way. The engineering systems engineers wanted to run the line, but packaging would refuse to allow it because they were afraid of shipping bad product. This meant that engineering could not run tests on the whole system. Everyone was burned out.

As you know, I brought a couple of my own people down with me and we began to run the line. To get good seals, we've slowed down the sealing system and lowered the sealing temperature. With this new process, we get a good seal that a customer can open without too much effort. Because the sealer can only seal six bowls at a time, the reduced speed has limited the output of the line to 50 bowls per minute. We are currently trying to build the line up from there.

As we discussed in detail a few days ago, the current status of the Plastigon line is that we have run it for as much as four hours straight, but, in general, the line will not remain up for more than half an hour or so. I believe that it is possible to get the line running as a working production line within a six-month time frame. I'm committed to making that happen.

The key problem with the effort so far is that the line has not been run enough as a complete system. The people down at Maxton have been trying to debug each of the parts of the system separately, but most of the problems involve two or more subsystems. We need to balance the line and then run it as a system, fixing problems as they come up. I see three steps to getting a working production line:

Equipment Changes

There are a couple of equipment changes that we need to make as soon as possible. The largest is that we need to replace the filling equipment. The current filling nozzles splash the soup onto the rim of the bowl which prevents a good seal from forming. To fix this problem, I would suggest using the FEMLO filling system which has been used for years on frozen lines. In addition, I plan to remove all the limit switches that are not directly related to product safety. Currently, there are over 200 limit switches on the line which get tripped any time something moves a little out of tolerance. Most of the time, the problem is not serious, is random, and would correct itself without intervention. By eliminating the unnecessary switches, we will be able to run the line consistently and deal only with the important problems. As we get those taken care of, we can then address refinements.

Once these equipment changes are implemented, we will try to get it running consistently, debugging the line as a system and fixing problems as they come up.

Engineering Team

We need to have a dedicated team down at Maxton for the next six months that can focus on getting the system running. I will detail my exact requirements within a week, but I would like to get at least a couple more engineers with frozen food experience. (These would be in addition to myself and the eight others I have already selected.) In addition to this team, I will need some support from the plant. In particular, I will need six machine operators and a plant production manager who should start to take over supervision of the day-to-day operations and get up to speed on how the line runs.

EXHIBIT 10 *(concluded)*

Long-Term Development

In six months, we should have the system running consistently on one shift. We should be able to get some improvement in the system performance by making lots of small adjustments and we will probably be able to push the system to about 100 bowls/minute or possibly a little more by late summer. At that point, marketing is going to have to get involved and develop a rollout plan, and we will have to add a second shift.

For improvement beyond 100 bowls per minute, we need to develop a better understanding of the process. We will start to build this knowledge base over the next six months. We should then look at bringing packaging technology back in to consider material changes and other options that will improve the performance of the system, especially its running speed. It may be that we have to rethink the entire concept of the line. The current, continuous system, while theoretically more efficient than a batch system, is not very flexible. We may not be able to adjust it sufficiently to obtain adequate efficiency.

With all these projects going on in microwavable products, I've also got to make sure that we know where Plastigon fits in the overall scheme of things, and how we ought to be supporting these efforts. In a sense, the Plastigon program captures a lot of the issues that face engineering systems and Campbell as a whole in managing development. It's clear we've got to improve how we do individual programs and projects, but we've also got to do something about how we decide what the whole set of projects should be, and how we allocate resources in response to the many requests we receive. What we do about Plastigon could set a pattern for what we do with those larger issues.

Reading IV–5
Creating Project Plans to Focus Product Development

Steven C. Wheelwright and Kim B. Clark

The long-term competitiveness of any manufacturing company depends ultimately on the success of its product development capabilities. New product development holds hope for improving market position and financial performance, creating new industry standards and new niche markets, and even renewing the organization. Yet few development projects fully deliver on their early promises. The fact is, much can and does go wrong during development. In some instances, poor leadership or the absence of essential skills is to blame. But often problems arise from the way companies approach the development process. They lack what we call an "aggregate project plan."

Consider the case of a large scientific instruments company we will call PreQuip. In mid-1989, senior management became alarmed about a rash of late product development projects. For some months, the development budget had been rising even as the number of completed projects declined. And many of the projects in the development pipeline no longer seemed to reflect the needs of the market. Management was especially troubled because it had believed its annual business plan provided the guidance that the marketing and engineering departments needed to generate and schedule projects.

To get to the root of the problem, the chief executive first asked senior managers to compile a list of all the current development projects. They discovered that 30 projects were under way—far more than anticipated, and, they suspected, far more than the organization could support. Further analysis revealed that the company had two to three times more development work than it was capable of completing over its three-year development planning horizon. (See Exhibit 1.)

With such a strain on resources, delays were inevitable. When a project ran into trouble, engineers from other projects were reassigned or, more commonly, asked to add the crisis project to their already long list of active projects. The more projects they added, the more their productivity dropped. The reshuffling caused delays in other projects, and the effects cascaded. Furthermore, as deadlines slipped and development costs rose, project managers faced pressure to cut corners and compromise quality just to keep their projects moving forward.

The senior management team also discovered that the majority of PreQuip's development resources—primarily engineers and support staff—was not focused on the projects most critical to the business.

Reprinted by permission of *Harvard Business Review,* March–April 1992.

EXHIBIT 1 PreQuip's Development Predicament: Overcommitted Resources

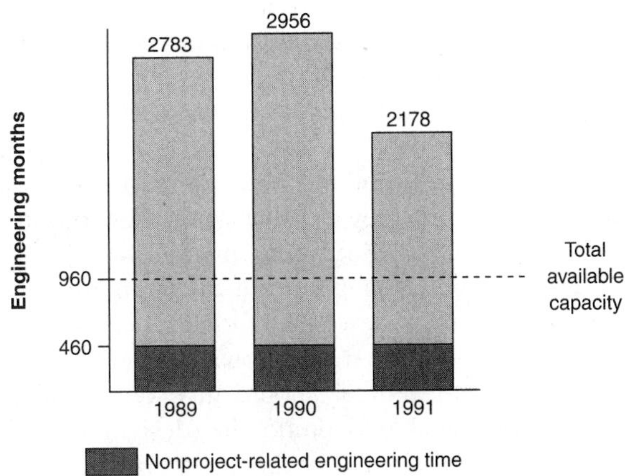

PreQuip had 960 engineering months each year to allocate to development work. But combining the time it would take to keep its current 30 projects on schedule with the time engineers spent doing nonproject development work, the company found it had overcommitted its development resources for the next three years by a factor of three.

When questioned, project leaders admitted that the strategic objectives outlined in the annual business plan had little bearing on project selection. Instead, they chose projects because engineers found the technical problems challenging or because customers or the marketing department requested them. PreQuip had no formal process for choosing among development projects. As long as there was money in the budget or the person making the request had sufficient clout, the head of the development department had no option but to accept additional project requests.

Many engineers were not only working on noncritical projects but also spending as much as 50 percent of their time on nonproject-related work. They responded to requests from manufacturing for help with problems on previous products, from field sales for help with customer problems, from quality assurance for help with reliability problems, and from purchasing for help with qualifying vendors. In addition to spending considerable time fixing problems on previously introduced products, engineers spent many hours in "information" and "update" meetings. In short, they spent too little time developing the right new products, experimenting with new technologies, or addressing new markets.

PreQuip's story is hardly unique. Most organizations we are familiar with spend their time putting out fires and pursuing projects aimed at catching up to their competitors. They have far too many projects going at once and all too often seriously overcommit their development resources. They spend too much time dealing with short-term pressures and not enough time on the strategic mission of product development.

Indeed, in most organizations, management directs all its attention to individual projects—it micromanages project development. But no single project defines a company's future or its market growth over time; the "set" of projects does. Companies need to devote more attention to managing the set and mix of projects. In particular, they should focus on how resources are allocated between projects. Management must plan how the project set evolves over time, which new projects get added when, and what role each project should play in the overall development effort.

The aggregate project plan addresses all of these issues. To create a plan, management categorizes projects based on the amount of resources they consume and on how they will contribute to the company's product line. Then, by mapping the project types, management can see where gaps exist in the development strategy and make more informed decisions about what types of projects to add and when to add them. Sequencing projects carefully, in turn, gives management greater control of resource allocation and utilization. The project map also reveals where development capabilities need to be strong. Over time, companies can focus on adding critical resources and on developing the skills of individual contributors, project leaders, and teams.

Finally, an aggregate plan will enable management to improve the way it manages the development function. Simply adding projects to the active list—a common practice at many companies—endangers the long-term health of the development process. Management needs to create a set of projects that is consistent with the company's development strategies rather than selecting individual projects from a long list of ad hoc proposals. And management must become involved in the development process *before* projects get started, even before they are fully defined. It is not appropriate to give one department—say, engineering or marketing—sole responsibility for initiating all projects because it is usually not in a position to determine every project's strategic worth.

Indeed, most companies—including PreQuip—should start the reformation process by eliminating or postponing the lion's share of their existing projects, eventually supplanting them with a new set of projects that fits the business strategy and the capacity constraints. The aggregate project plan provides a framework for addressing this difficult task.

How to Map Projects

The first step in creating an aggregate project plan is to define and map the different types of development projects; defining projects by type provides useful information about how resources should be allocated. The two dimensions we have found most useful for classifying are the degree of change in the product and the degree of change in the manufacturing process. The greater the change along either dimension, the more resources are needed.

Using this construct, we have divided projects into five types. The first three—derivative, breakthrough, and platform—are commercial development projects. The remaining two categories are research and development, which is the precursor to commercial development, and alliances and partnerships, which can be either commercial or basic research. (See Exhibit 2.)

Each of the five project types requires a unique combination of development resources and management styles. Understanding how the categories differ helps managers predict the distribution of resources accurately and allows for better planning and sequencing of projects over time. Here is a brief description of each category:

Derivative projects range from cost-reduced versions of existing products to add-ons or enhancements for an existing production process. For example, Kodak's wide-angle, single-use 35mm camera, the Stretch, was derived from the no-frills Fun Saver introduced in 1990. Designing the Stretch was primarily a matter of changing the lens.

Development work on derivative projects typically falls into three categories: incremental product changes, say, new packaging or a new feature, with little or no manufacturing process change; incremental process changes, like a lower cost manufacturing process, improved reliability, or a minor change in materials used, with little or no product change; and incremental changes on both dimensions. Because design changes are usually minor, incremental projects typically are more clearly bounded and require substantially fewer development resources than the other categories. And because derivative projects are completed in a few months, ongoing management involvement is minimal.

Breakthrough projects are at the other end of the development spectrum because they involve significant changes to existing products and processes. Successful breakthrough projects establish core products and processes that differ fundamentally from previous generations. Like compact discs and fiber-optics cable, they create a whole new product category that can define a new market.

Because breakthrough products often incorporate revolutionary new technologies or materials, they usually require revolutionary manufacturing processes. Management should give development teams considerable latitude in designing new processes, rather than force them to work with existing plant and equipment, operating techniques, or supplier networks.

Platform projects are in the middle of the development spectrum and are thus harder to define. They entail more product and/or process changes than derivatives do, but they don't introduce the untried new technologies or materials that breakthrough products do. Honda's 1990 Accord line is an example of a new platform in the auto industry: Honda introduced a number of manufacturing process and product changes but no fundamentally new technologies. In the computer market, IBM's PS/2 is a personal computer platform; in consumer products, Procter & Gamble's Liquid Tide is the platform for a whole line of Tide brand products.

Well-planned and well-executed platform products typically offer fundamental improvements in cost, quality, and performance over preceding generations. They introduce improvements across a range of performance dimensions—speed, functionality, size, weight. (Derivatives, on the other hand, usually introduce changes along only one or two dimensions.) Platforms also represent a significantly better system solution for the customer. Because of the extent of changes involved, successful platforms require considerable up-front planning and the involvement of not only engineering but also marketing, manufacturing, and senior management.

Companies target new platforms to meet the needs of a core group of customers but design them for easy modification into derivatives through the addition, substitution, or removal of features. Well-designed platforms also provide a smooth migration path between generations so neither the customer nor the distribution channel is disrupted.

EXHIBIT 2 Mapping the Five Types of Development Projects

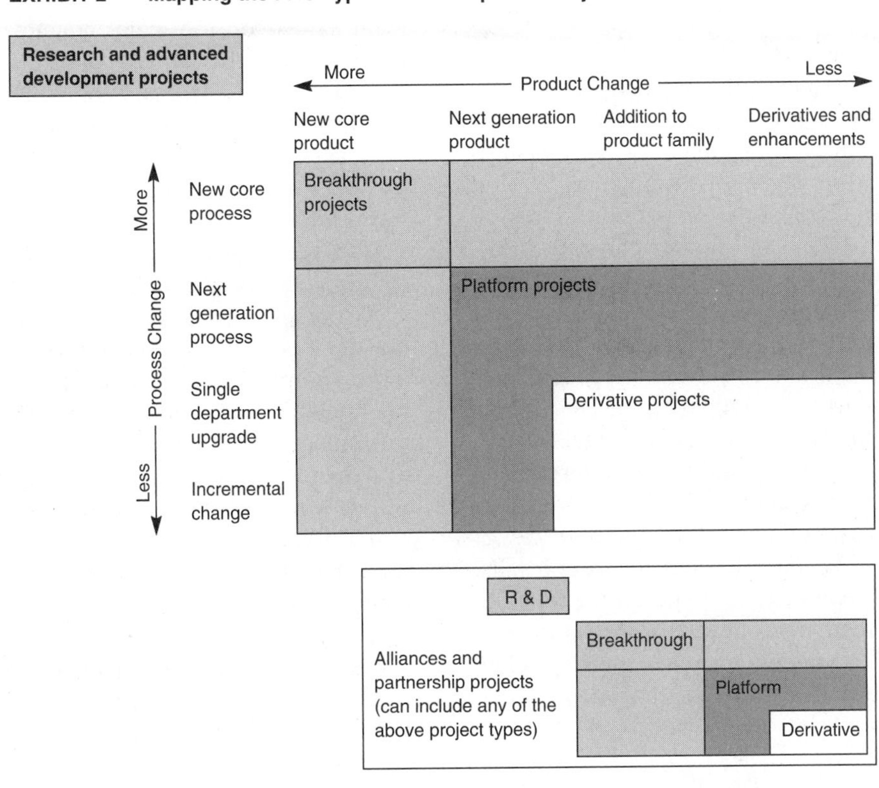

Consider Intel's 80486 microprocessor, the fourth in a series. The 486 introduced a number of performance improvements; it targeted a core customer group—the high-end PC/workstation user—but variations addressed the needs of other users; and with software compatibility between the 386 and the 486, the 486 provided an easy migration path for existing customers. Over the life of the 486 platform, Intel will introduce a host of derivative products, each offering some variation in speed, cost, and performance and each able to leverage the process and product innovations of the original platform.

Platforms offer considerable competitive leverage and the potential to increase market penetration, yet many companies systematically underinvest in them. The reasons vary, but the most common is that management lacks an awareness of the strategic value of platforms and fails to create well-thought-out platform projects. To address the problem, companies should recognize explicitly the need for platforms and develop guidelines for making them a central part of the aggregate project plan.

Research and development is the creation of the know-how and know-why of new materials and technologies that eventually translate into commercial development. Even though R&D lies outside the boundaries of commercial development, we include it here for two reasons: It is the precursor to product and process development; and, in terms of future resource allocation, employees move between basic research and commercial development. Thus R&D projects compete with commercial development projects for resources. Because R&D is a creative, high-risk process, companies have different expectations about results and different strategies for funding and managing it than they do for commercial development. These differences can indeed be great, but a close relationship between R&D and commercial development is essential to ensure an appropriate balance and a smooth conversion of ideas into products.

Alliances and partnerships, which also lie outside the boundaries of the development map, can be formed to pursue any type of project—R&D, breakthrough, platform, or derivative. As such, the amount and type of development resources and management attention needed for projects in this category can vary widely.

Even though partnerships are an integral part of the project development process, many companies fail to include them in their project planning. They often separate the management of partnerships from the rest of the development organization and fail to provide them with enough development resources. Even when the partner company takes full responsibility for a project, the acquiring company must devote in-house resources to monitor the project, capture the new knowledge being created, and prepare for the manufacturing and sales of the new product.

All five development categories are vital for creating a development organization that is responsive to the market. Each type of project plays a different role; each requires different levels and mixes of resources; and each generates very different results. Relying on only one or two categories for the bulk of the development work invariably leads to suboptimal use of resources, an unbalanced product offering, and eventually, a less than competitive market position.

PreQuip's Project Map

Using these five project types, PreQuip set about changing its project mix as the first step toward reforming the product development process. It started by matching its existing project list to the five categories. PreQuip's product line consisted of four kinds of analytic instruments—mass spectrometers, gas and liquid chromatographs, and data handling and processing equipment—that identified and isolated chemical compounds, gases, and liquids. Its customers included scientific laboratories, chemical companies, and oil refineries—users that needed to measure and test accurately the purity of raw materials, intermediate by-products, and finished products.

PreQuip's management asked some very basic questions in its attempt to delineate the categories. What exactly was a breakthrough product? Would a three-dimensional graphics display constitute a breakthrough? How was a platform defined? Was a full-featured mass spectrometer considered a platform? How about a derivative? Was a mass spectrometer with additional software a derivative?

None of these questions was easy to answer. But after much analysis and debate, the management team agreed on the major characteristics for each project type and assigned most of PreQuip's 30 projects to one of the five categories. The map revealed just how uneven the distribution of projects had become—for instance, less than 20 percent of the company's projects were classified as platforms. (See Exhibit 3.)

Management then turned its attention to those development projects that did not fit into any category. Some projects required substantial resources but did not represent breakthroughs. Others were more complicated than derivative projects but did not fall into PreQuip's definition of platforms. While frustrating, these dilemmas opened managers' eyes to the fact that some projects made little strategic sense. Why spend huge amounts of money developing products that at best would produce only incremental sales? The realization triggered a reexamination of PreQuip's customer needs in *all* product categories.

Consider mass spectrometers, instruments that identify the chemical composition of a compound. PreQuip was a top-of-the-line producer of mass spectrometers, offering a whole series of high-performance equipment with all the latest features but at a significant price premium. While this strategy had worked in the past, it no longer made sense in a maturing market; the evolution of mass spectrometer technology was predictable and well defined, and many competitors were able to offer the same capabilities, often at lower prices.

Increasingly, customers were putting greater emphasis on price in the purchasing decision. Some customers also wanted mass spectrometers that were easier to use and modular so they could be integrated into their own systems. Others demanded units with casings that could withstand harsh industrial environments. Still others required faster operating speeds, additional data storage, or self-diagnostic capabilities.

Taking all these customer requirements into account, PreQuip used the project map to rethink its mass spectrometer line. It envisaged a single platform complemented with a series of derivative products, each with a different set of options and each serving a different customer niche. By combining some new product design ideas—modularity and simplicity—with some features that were currently under development, PreQuip created the

EXHIBIT 3 Before: PreQuip's Development Process Was Chaotic . . .

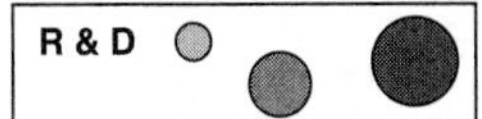

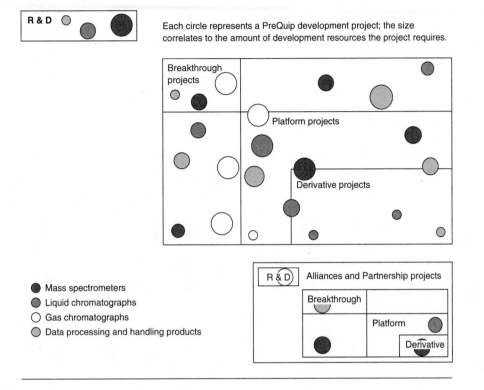

Each circle represents a PreQuip development project; the size correlates to the amount of development resources the project requires.

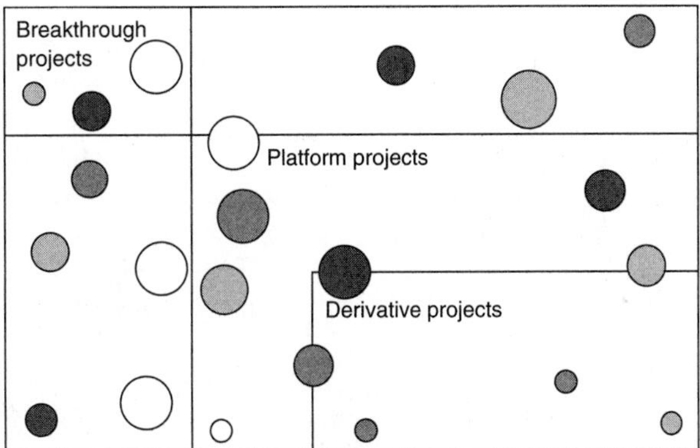

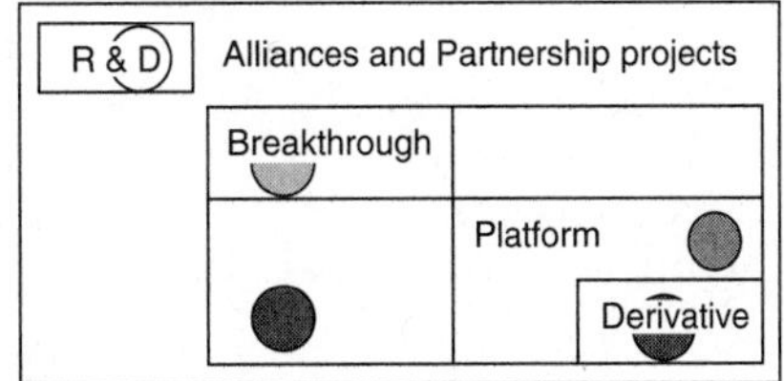

- Mass spectrometers
- Liquid chromatographs
- Gas chromatographs
- Data processing and handling products

concept of the C-101 platform, a low-priced, general-purpose mass spectrometer. In part because of its modularity, the product was designed to be simpler and cheaper to manufacture, which also helped to improve its overall quality and reliability. By adding software and a few new features, PreQuip could easily create derivatives, all of which could be assembled and tested on a single production line. In one case, a variant of the C-101 was planned for the high-end laboratory market. By strengthening the casing and eliminating some features, PreQuip also created a product for the industrial market.

Mapping out the new mass spectrometer line and the three other product lines was not painless. It took a number of months and involved a reconceptualization of the product lines, close management, and considerable customer involvement. To provide additional focus, PreQuip separated the engineering resources into three categories: basic R&D projects; existing products and customers, now a part of the manufacturing organization; and commercial product development.

To determine the number of breakthrough, platform, derivative, and partnership projects that could be sustained at any time, the company first estimated the average number of engineering months for each type of project based on past experience. It then allocated available engineering resources according to its desired mix of projects; about 50 percent to platform projects, 20 percent to derivative projects, and 10 percent each to breakthrough projects and partnerships. PreQuip then selected specific projects, confident that it would not over-allocate its resources.

In the end, PreQuip canceled more than two-thirds of its development projects, including some high-profile pet projects of senior managers. When the dust had settled in mid-1990, PreQuip had just 11 projects: three platforms, one breakthrough, three derivatives, one partnership, and three projects in basic R&D. (See Exhibit 4.)

The changes led to some impressive gains: between 1989 and 1991, PreQuip's commercial development productivity improved by a factor of three. Fewer projects meant more actual work got

EXHIBIT 4 After: PreQuip's Development Process Was Manageable

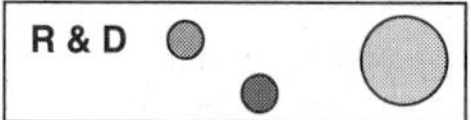

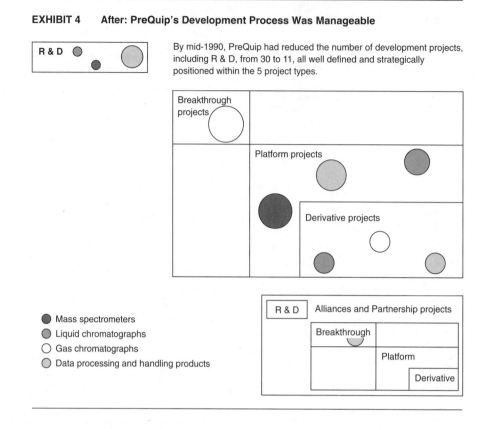

By mid-1990, PreQuip had reduced the number of development projects, including R & D, from 30 to 11, all well defined and strategically positioned within the 5 project types.

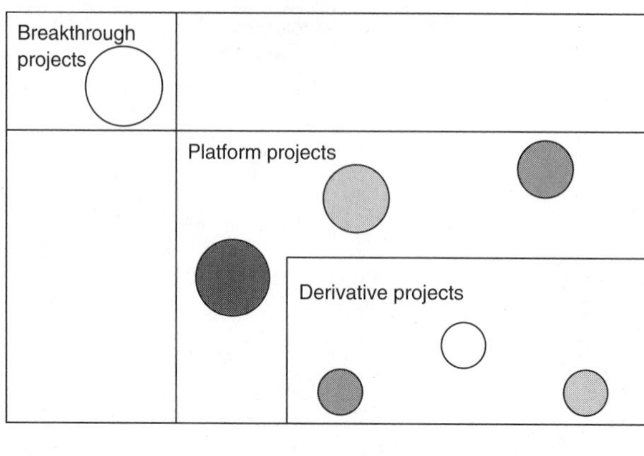

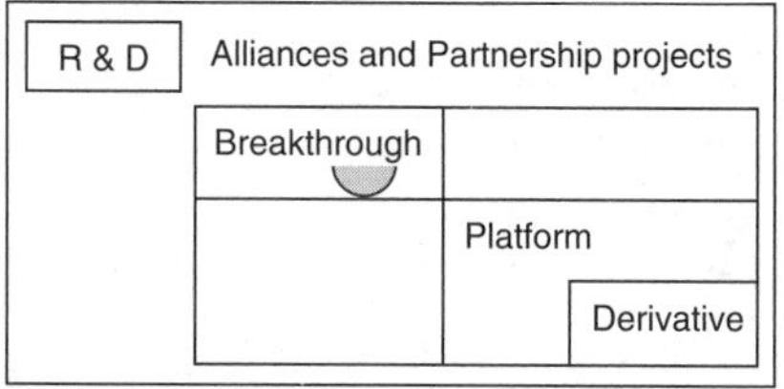

- Mass spectrometers
- Liquid chromatographs
- Gas chromatographs
- Data processing and handling products

done, and more work meant more products. To avoid overcommitting resources and to improve productivity further, the company built a "capacity cushion" into its plan. It assigned only 75 full-time-equivalent engineers out of a possible 80 to the eight commercial development projects. By leaving a small percent of development capacity uncommitted, PreQuip was better prepared to take advantage of unexpected opportunities and to deal with crises when they arose.

Focus on the Platform

PreQuip's development map served as a basis for reallocating resources and for rethinking the mix of projects. Just as important, however, PreQuip no longer thought about projects in isolation; breakthrough projects shaped the new platforms, which defined the derivatives. In all four product lines, platforms played a particularly important role in the development strategy. This was not surprising considering the maturity of PreQuip's industry. For many companies, the more mature the industry, the more important it is to focus on platform projects.

Consider the typical industry life cycle. In the early stages of growth, innovative, dynamic companies gain market position with products that have dramatically superior performance along one or two dimensions. Whether they know it or not, these companies employ a breakthrough-platform strategy. But as the industry develops and the opportunity for breakthrough products decreases—often because the technology is shared more broadly—competitors try to satisfy increasingly sophisticated customers by rapidly making incremental improvements to existing products. Consciously or not, they adopt a strategy based on derivative projects. As happened with PreQuip, this approach ultimately leads to a proliferation of product lines and overcommitment of development resources. The solution lies in developing a few well-designed platform products, on each of which a generation of products can be built.

In the hospital bed industry, for example, companies that design, manufacture, sell, and service electric beds have faced a mature market for years. They are constantly under pressure to help their customers constrain capital expenditures and operating costs. Technologies are stable and many design changes are minor. Each generation of product typically lasts 8 to 12 years, and companies spend most of their time and energy developing derivative products. As a result, companies find themselves with large and unwieldy product lines.

In the 1980s, Hill-Rom, a leading electric-bed manufacturer, sought a new product strategy to help contain costs and maintain market share. Like other bed makers, its product development process was reactive and mired in too many low-payoff derivative projects. The company would design whatever the customer—a single hospital or nursing home—wanted, even if it meant significant commitments of development resources.

The new strategy involved a dramatic shift toward leveraging development and manufacturing resources. Hill-Rom decided to focus on hospitals and largely withdraw from the nursing home segment, as well as limit the product line by developing two new platform products—the Centra and the Century. The Centra was a high-priced product with built-in electronic controls, including communications capabilities. The Century was a simpler, less complex design with fewer features. The products built off each platform shared common parts and manufacturing processes and provided the customer with a number of add-on options. By focusing development efforts on two platforms, Hill-Rom was able to introduce new technologies and new product features into the market faster and more systematically, directly affecting patient recovery and hospital staff productivity. This strategy led to a less chaotic development cycle as well as lower unit cost, higher product quality, and more satisfied customers.

For companies that must react to constant changes in fashion and consumer tastes, a different relationship between platform and derivative projects makes sense. For example, Sony has pioneered its "hyper-variety" strategy in developing the Walkman: it directs the bulk of its Walkman development efforts at creating derivatives, enhancements, hybrids, and line extensions that offer something tailored to every niche, distribution channel, and competitor's product. As a result, in 1990, Sony dominated the personal audio system market with over 200 models based on just three platforms.

Platforms are critical to any product development effort, but there is no one ideal mix of projects that fits all companies. Every company must pursue the projects that match its opportunities, business strategy, and available resources. Of course, the mix evolves over time as projects move out of development into production, as business strategies change, as new markets emerge, and as resources are enhanced. Management needs to revisit the project mix on a regular basis—in some cases every six months, in others, every year or so.

Steady Stream Sequencing: PreQuip Plans Future Development

Periodically evaluating the product mix keeps development activities on the right track. Companies must decide how to sequence projects over time, how the set of projects should evolve with the business strategy, and how to build development capabilities through such projects. The decisions about changing the mix are neither easy nor straightforward. Without an aggregate project plan, most companies cannot even begin to formulate a strategy for making those decisions.

PreQuip was no different. Before adopting an aggregate project plan, the company had no concept of project mix and no understanding of sequencing. Whenever someone with authority had an idea worth pursuing, the development department added the project to its active list. With the evolution of a project plan, PreQuip developed an initial mix and elevated the sequencing decision to a strategic responsibility of senior management. Management scheduled projects at evenly spaced intervals to ensure a "steady stream" of development projects. (See Exhibit 5.)

A representative example of PreQuip's new strategy for sequencing projects is its new mass spectrometer, or C series. Introduced into the development cycle in late-1989, the C-101 was the first platform conceived as a system built around the new modular design. Aimed at the middle to upper end of the market, it was a versatile, modular unit for the laboratory that incorporated many of the existing electromechanical features into the new software. The C-101 was scheduled to enter manufacturing prototyping in the third quarter of 1990.

PreQuip positioned the C-1/X, the first derivative of the C-101, for the industrial market. It had a rugged casing designed for extreme environments and fewer software features than the C-101. It entered the development process about the time the

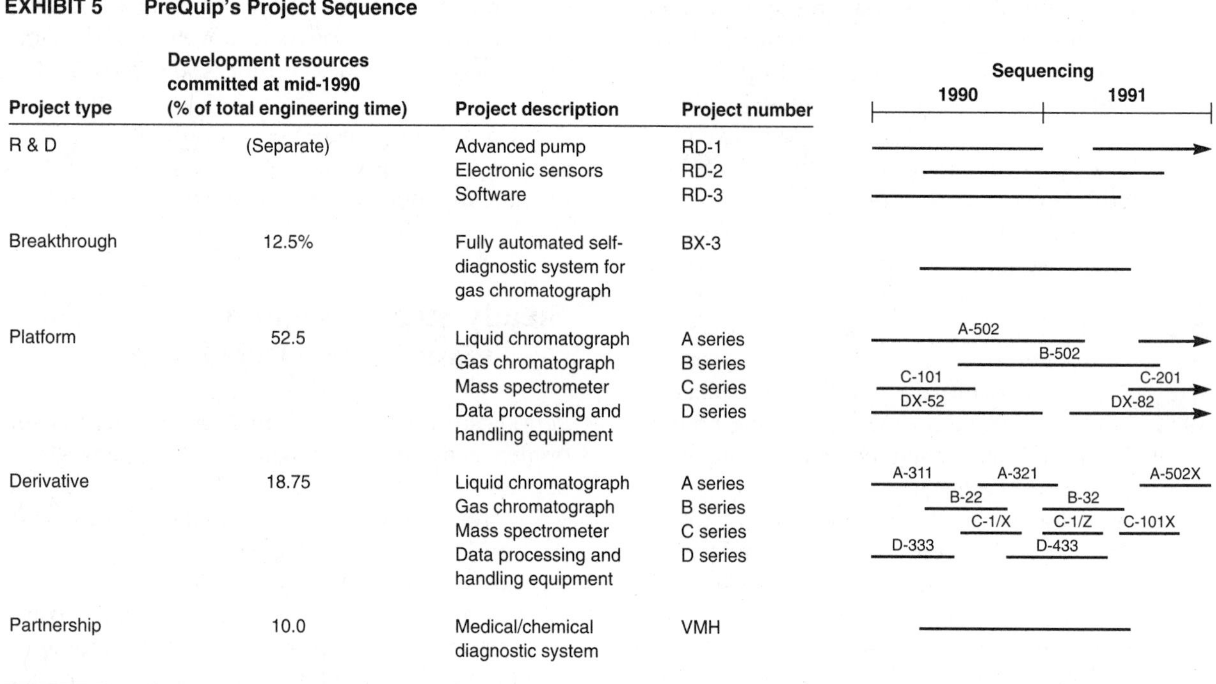

EXHIBIT 5 PreQuip's Project Sequence

Project type	Development resources committed at mid-1990 (% of total engineering time)	Project description	Project number
R & D	(Separate)	Advanced pump Electronic sensors Software	RD-1 RD-2 RD-3
Breakthrough	12.5%	Fully automated self-diagnostic system for gas chromatograph	BX-3
Platform	52.5	Liquid chromatograph Gas chromatograph Mass spectrometer Data processing and handling equipment	A series B series C series D series
Derivative	18.75	Liquid chromatograph Gas chromatograph Mass spectrometer Data processing and handling equipment	A series B series C series D series
Partnership	10.0	Medical/chemical diagnostic system	VMH

C-101 moved into manufacturing prototyping and was staffed initially with two designers whose activities on the C-101 were drawing to a close.

Very similar to the C-1/X was the C-1/Z, a unit designed for the European market; the C-1/X team was expanded to work on both the C-1/X and the C-1/Z. The C-1/Z had some unique software and a different display and packaging but the same modular design. PreQuip's marketing department scheduled the C-101 to be introduced about six months before the C-1/X and the C-1/Z, thus permitting the company to reach a number of markets quickly with new products.

To leverage accumulated knowledge and experience, senior management assigned the team that worked on the C-1/X and the C-1/Z to the C-201 project, the next-generation spectrometer scheduled to replace the C-101. It too was of a modular design but with more computer power and greater software functionality. The C-201 also incorporated a number of manufacturing process improvements gleaned from manufacturing the C-101.

To provide a smooth market transition from the C-101 to the C-201, management assigned the remainder of the C-101 team to develop the C-101X, a follow-on derivative project. The C-101X was positioned as an improvement over the C-101 to attract customers who were in the market for a low-end mass spectrometer but were unwilling to settle for the aging technology of the C-101. Just as important, the project was an ideal way to gather market data that could be used to develop the C-201.

PreQuip applied this same strategy across the other three product categories. Every other year it planned a new platform, followed by two or three derivatives spaced at appropriate intervals. Typically, when a team finished work on a platform, management assigned part of the team to derivative projects and part to other projects. A year or so later, a new team would form to work on the next platform, with some members having worked on the preceding generation and others not. This steady stream sequencing strategy worked to improve the company's overall market position while encouraging knowledge transfer and more rapid, systematic resource development.

An Alternative: Secondary Wave Planning

While the steady stream approach served PreQuip well, companies in different industries might consider alternative strategies. For instance, a "secondary wave" strategy may be more appropriate for companies that, like Hill-Rom, have multiple product lines, each with their own base platforms but with more time between succeeding generations of a particular platform.

The strategy works like this. A development team begins work on a next-generation platform. Once the company completes that project, the key people from the team start work on another platform for a different product family. Management leaves the recently introduced platform on the market for a couple of years with few derivatives introduced. As that platform begins to age and competitors' newer platforms challenge it, the company refocuses development resources on a set of derivatives in order to strengthen and extend the viability of the product line's existing platform. The wave of derivative projects extends the platform life and upgrades product offerings, but it also provides experience and feedback to the people working on the product line and prepares them for the next-generation platform development. They receive feedback from the market on the previous platform, information on competitors' platform offerings, and information on emerging market needs. Key people then bring that information together to define the next platform and the cycle begins again, built around a team, many of whose members have just completed the wave of derivative products.

A variation on the secondary wave strategy, one used with considerable success by Kodak, involves compressing the time between market introduction of major platforms. Rather than going off to work on another product family's platform following one platform's introduction, the majority of the development team goes to work immediately on a set of derivative products. This requires a more compressed and careful assessment of the market's response to the just-introduced platform and much shorter feedback loops regarding competitors' products. If done right, however, companies can build momentum and capture significant incremental market share. Once the flurry of derivative products has passed, the team goes to work on the next-generation platform project for the same product family.

Before 1987, Kodak conducted a series of advanced development projects to explore alternative single-use 35mm cameras—a roll of film packaged in an inexpensive camera. Once used, the film is processed and the camera discarded or recycled. During 1987, a group of Kodak development engineers worked on the first platform project, which resulted in the market introduction and volume production of the Fling 35mm camera in January 1988. (The product was later renamed the Fun Saver.) As the platform neared completion, management reassigned the front-end development staff to two derivative projects: the Stretch, a panoramic, double-wide image version of the Fling, and the Weekend, a waterproof version.

By the end of 1988, Kodak had introduced both derivative cameras and was shipping them in volume. True to the definition of a derivative, both the Stretch and the Weekend took far fewer development resources and far less time than the Fling. They also required less new tooling and process engineering since they leveraged the existing automation and manufacturing process. The development team then went to work on the next-generation platform product—a Fun Saver with a built-in flash.

No matter which strategy a company uses to plan its platform-derivative mix—steady stream or secondary wave—it must have well-defined platforms. The most advanced companies further improve their competitive position by speeding up the rate at which they introduce new platforms. Indeed, in a number of industries we've studied, the companies that introduced new platforms at the fastest rate were usually able to capture the greatest market share over time.

In the auto industry, for example, different companies follow quite different sequencing schedules, with markedly different results. According to data collected in the late 1980s, European car companies changed the platform for a given product, on average, every 12 years, U.S. companies every 8 years, and Japanese companies every 4 years. A number of factors explain the differences in platform development cycles—historical and cultural differences, longer development lead times, and differences in development productivity.[1]

In both Europe and the United States, the engineering hours and tooling costs of new products were much higher than in Japan. This translated into lower development costs for Japanese car makers, which allowed faster payback and shorter economic lives for all models. As a consequence, the Japanese could profitably conduct more projects and make

---

[1]Based on research by Kim B. Clark and Takahiro Fujimoto. See their article, "The Power of Product Integrity," *Harvard Business Review*, November–December 1990, p. 107.

more frequent and more extensive changes than both their European and U.S. competitors and thus were better positioned to satisfy customers' needs and capture market share.

The Long-Term Goal: Building Critical Capabilities

Possibly the greatest value of an aggregate project plan over the long-term is its ability to shape and build development capabilities, both individual and organizational. It provides a vehicle for training development engineers, marketers, and manufacturing people in the different skill sets needed by the company. For instance, some less experienced engineers initially may be better suited to work on derivative projects, while others might have technical skills more suited for breakthrough projects. The aggregate project plan lets companies play to employees' strengths and broaden their careers and abilities over time. (See Exhibit 6)

Thinking about skill development in terms of the aggregate project plan is most important for developing competent team leaders. Take, for instance, an engineer with five years of experience moving to become a project leader. Management might assign her to lead a derivative project first. It is an ideal training ground because derivative projects are the best defined, the least complex, and usually the shortest in duration of all project types. After the project is completed successfully, she might get promoted to lead a larger derivative project and then a platform project. And if she distinguishes herself there and has the other required skills, she might be given the opportunity to work on a breakthrough project.

EXHIBIT 6 Eight Steps of an Aggregate Project Plan

1. Define project types as either breakthrough, platform, derivative, R&D, or partnered projects.
2. Identify existing projects and classify by project type.
3. Estimate the average time and resources needed for each project type based on past experience.
4. Identify existing resource capacity.
5. Determine the desired mix of projects.
6. Estimate the number of projects that existing resources can support.
7. Decide which specific projects to pursue.
8. Work to improve development capabilities.

In addition to creating a formal career path within the sphere of development activities, companies should also focus on moving key engineers and other development participants between advanced research and commercial development. This is necessary to keep the transfer of technology fresh and creative and to reward engineers who keep their R&D efforts focused on commercial developments.

Honda is one company that delineates clearly between advanced research and product development—the two kinds of projects are managed and organized differently and are approached with very different expectations. Development engineers tend to have broader skills, while researchers' are usually more specialized. However, Honda encourages its engineers to move from one type of project to another if they demonstrate an idea that management believes may result in a commercially viable innovation. For example, Honda's new lean-burning engine, introduced in the 1992 Civic, began as an advanced research project headed by Hideyo Miyano. As the project moved from research to commercial development, Miyano moved too, playing the role of project champion throughout the entire development process.

Besides improving people's skills, the aggregate project plan can be used to identify weaknesses in capabilities, improve development processes, and incorporate new tools and techniques into the development environment. The project plan helps identify where companies need to make changes and how those changes are connected to product and process development.

As PreQuip developed an aggregate project plan, for example, it identified a number of gaps in its capabilities. In the case of the mass spectrometer, the demand for more software functionality meant PreQuip had to develop an expertise in software development. And with an emphasis on cost, modularity, and reliability, PreQuip also had to focus on improving its industrial design skills.

As part of its strategy to improve design skills, the company introduced a new computer-aided design system into its engineering department, using the aggregate project plan as its guide. Management knew that one of the platform project teams was particularly adept with computer applications, so it chose that project as the pilot for the new CAD system. Over the life of the project, the team's proficiency with the new system grew. When the project ended, management dispersed team members to other projects so they could train other engineers in using the new CAD system.

As PreQuip discovered, developing an aggregate project plan involves a relatively simple and straightforward procedure. But carrying it out—moving from a poorly managed collection of ad hoc projects to a robust set that matches and reinforces the business strategy—requires hard choices and discipline.

At all the companies we have studied, the difficulty of those choices makes imperative strong leadership and early involvement from senior management. Without management's active participation and direction, organizations find it next to impossible to kill or postpone projects and to resist the short-term pressures that drive them to spend most of their time and resources fighting fires.

Getting to an aggregate project plan is not easy, but working through the process is a crucial part of creating a sustainable development strategy. Indeed, while the specific plan is extremely important, the planning process itself is even more so. The plan will change as events unfold and managers make adjustments. But choosing the mix, determining the number of projects the resources can support, defining the sequence, and picking the right projects raise crucial questions about how product and process development ought to be linked to the company's competitive opportunities. Creating an aggregate project plan gives direction and clarity to the overall development effort and helps lay the foundation for outstanding performance.

Reading IV–6
The New Product Development Map

Steven C. Wheelwright and W. Earl Sasser, Jr.

No business activity is more heralded for its promise and approached with more justified optimism than the development and manufacture of new products. Whether in mature businesses like automobiles and electrical appliances, or more dynamic ones like computers, managers correctly view new products as a chance to get a jump on the competition.

Ideally, a successful new product can set industry standards—standards that become another company's barrier to entry—or open up crucial new markets. Think of the Sony Walkman. New products are good for the organization. They tend to exploit as yet untapped R&D discoveries and revitalize the engineering corps. New product campaigns offer top managers opportunities to reorganize and to get more out of a sales force, factory, or field service network, for example. New products capitalize on old investments.

Perhaps the most exciting benefit, though, is the most intangible: corporate renewal and redirection. The excitement, imagination, and growth associated with the introduction of a new product invigorate the company's best people and enhance the company's ability to recruit new forces. New products build confidence and momentum.

Unfortunately, these great promises of new product development are seldom fully realized. Products half make it; people burn out. To understand why, let's look at some of the more obvious pitfalls.

1. *The moving target.* Too often the basic product concept misses a shifting market. Or companies may make assumptions about channels of distribution that just don't hold up. Sometimes the project gets into trouble because of inconsistencies in focus; you start building a stripped-down version and wind up with a load of options. The project time lengthens, and longer projects invariably drift more and more from their initial target. Classic market misses include the Ford Edsel in the mid-1950s and Texas Instruments' home computer in the late 1970s. Even very successful products like Apple's Macintosh line of personal computers can have a rocky beginning.

2. *Lack of product distinctiveness.* This risk is high when designers fail to consider a full range of alternatives to meet customer needs. If the organization gets locked into a concept too quickly, it may not bring differing perspectives to the analysis. The market may dry up, or the critical technologies may be sufficiently widespread that imitators appear out of nowhere. Plus Development introduced Hardcard,® a hard disk that fits into a PC expansion slot, after a year and a half of development work. The company

thought it had a unique product with at least a nine-month lead on competitors. But by the fifth day of the industry show where Hardcard® was introduced, a competitor was showing a prototype of a competing version. And within three months, the competitor was shipping its new product.

3. *Unexpected technical problems.* Delays and cost overruns can often be traced to overestimates of the company's technical capabilities or simply to its lack of depth and resources. Projects can suffer delays and stall midcourse if essential inventions are not completed and drawn into the designers' repertoire before the product development project starts. An industrial controls company we know encountered both problems: It changed a part from metal to plastic only to discover that its manufacturing processes could not hold the required tolerances and also that its supplier could not provide raw material of consistent quality.

4. *Mismatches between functions.* Often one part of the organization will have unrealistic or even impossible expectations of another. Engineering may design a product that the company's factories cannot produce, for example, or at least not consistently at low cost and with high quality. Similarly, engineering may design features into products that marketing's established distribution channels or selling approach cannot exploit. In planning its requirements, manufacturing may assume an unchanging mix of new products, while marketing mistakenly assumes that manufacturing can alter its mix dramatically on short notice. One of the most startling mismatches we've encountered was created by an aerospace company whose manufacturing group built an assembly plant too small to accommodate the wing-span of the plane it ultimately had to produce.

Thus new products often fail because companies misunderstand the most promising markets and channels of distribution and because they misapprehend their own technological strengths or the product's technological challenges. Nothing can eliminate all the risks, but clearly the most important thing to do early on when developing a new product is to get all contributors to the process communicating: marketing with manufacturing, R&D with both. Products fail from a lack of planning; planning fails from a lack of information.

Developing a new generation of products is a lot like taking a journey into the wilderness. Who would dream of setting off without a map? Of course, you would try to clarify the purpose of the journey and make sure that needed equipment is available and in order. But once committed to the trip, you need a map of the terrain, something everybody can study—the focus for discussion, the basis for planning alternative courses. Knowing where you've come from and where you are is essential to knowing how to get where you want to go.

Mapping Existing Products

We have often used this analogy of a map with corporate managers involved in product development, and gradually it became clear to us that an actual map is needed, not just an analogy. Managers need a way to see the evolution of a company's product lines—the "where we are"—in order to expose the markets and technologies that have been driving the evolution—the "where we've come from." Such a map presents the evolution of current product lines in a summary yet strikingly clear way so that all functional areas in the organization can respond to a common vision. The map provides a basis for sharing information. And by enabling managers to compare the assumptions underlying current product lines with the ideal assumptions of new research, it points to new market opportunities and technological challenges. Why, for example, should an organization build for department stores when specialty discount outlets are the emerging channels of distribution? Why bend metals when you can mold ceramics?

Exhibit 1 illustrates a generic map that indicates how the product offerings in one generation may be related to each other. These relations are the building blocks that allow us to track the evolution of product families from one generation to another.

The map categorizes product offerings (and the development efforts they entail) as "core" and "leveraged" products, and divides leveraged products into "enhanced," "customized," "cost reduced," and "hybrid" products. (These designations seem to cover most cases, but managers should feel free to add whatever other categories they need.) A core product is the engineering platform, providing the basis for further enhancements. The core product is the initial, standard product introduced. It changes little from year to year and is often the benchmark against which consumers compare the rest of the product line.

EXHIBIT 1 Generic Product Development Map

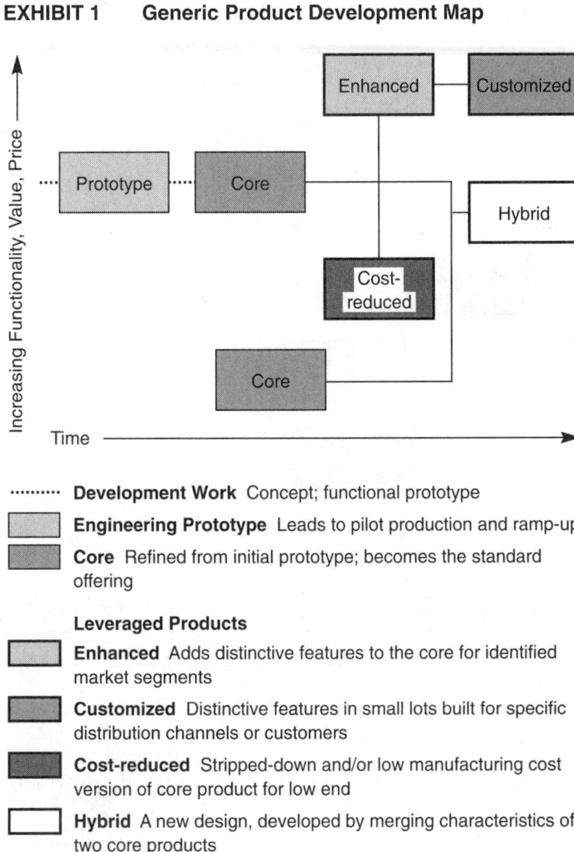
Increasing Functionality, Value, Price
Prototype
Core
Enhanced
Customized
Hybrid
Cost-reduced
Core
Time
Development Work Concept; functional prototype
Engineering Prototype Leads to pilot production and ramp-up
Core Refined from initial prototype; becomes the standard offering
Leveraged Products
Enhanced Adds distinctive features to the core for identified market segments
Customized Distinctive features in small lots built for specific distribution channels or customers
Cost-reduced Stripped-down and/or low manufacturing cost version of core product for low end
Hybrid A new design, developed by merging characteristics of two core products

Enhanced products are developed from the core design; distinctive features are added for various, more discriminating markets. Enhanced products are the first products leveraged from the capabilities put in place to produce the core and the first aimed at new or extended market opportunities. Often companies even identify them as enhanced versions, for example, IBM's DisplayWrite 3.1 is an enhanced version of DisplayWrite 3. But a leveraged product isn't necessarily more costly: The idea is simply to get more out of a fixed process—more "bang for the buck." As companies leverage high-end products, they may customize them in smaller lots for specific channels or to give consumers more choice. The cost-reduced model starts with essentially the same technology and design as the core product but is a stripped-down version, often with less expensive materials and lower factory costs, aimed at a price-sensitive market. (Think of the old Chevrolet Biscayne, which was many times the vehicle of choice for taxicabs and business fleets.)

Finally, there is the hybrid product, developed out of two cores. The initial two-stage thermostat products—accommodating a daytime and nighttime temperature setting—were hybrids of a traditional thermostat product and high-end, programmable thermostat lines.

On the generic map, from left to right is calendar time, and from bottom to top designates lower to higher added value or functionality, which usually also means a shift from cheaper to more expensive products.

These distinctions—core, hybrid, and the others—are immediately useful because they give managers a way of thinking about their products more rigorously and less anecdotally. But the various turns on the product map—the various "leverage points"—also serve as crucial indicators of previous management assumptions about the corporate strengths and market forces shaping product evolutions.

A map that shows a proliferation of enhanced products toward the high end, for example, says something important about the market opportunities managers identified after they had introduced the core. A map's configuration raises necessary questions about dominant channels of distribution—then and now. That products could have been leveraged in particular ways, moreover, says something important about in-house technological and manufacturing capabilities—capabilities that may still exist or may need changing. The map generates the right discussions. When managers know how and why they have leveraged products in the past, they know better how to leverage the company in the present.

The First Generation

How can managers plan, develop, and position a set of products—that is, how do they build a dynamic map? With the generic map in mind, let us track offerings from generation to generation, as shown in Exhibit 2. Imagine a very simple line of vacuum cleaners, Coolidge Corporation's "Stratovac," introduced, say, in 1952. The core product, the Stratovac, was a canister-type appliance with a 2.5 horsepower motor. Constructed mainly from cut and stamped metals, it was distributed through department stores and hardware chains.

The following year, reaching for the somewhat more affluent suburban household, Coolidge

EXHIBIT 2 The First Generation of Coolidge Vacuum Cleaner (1952–1968)

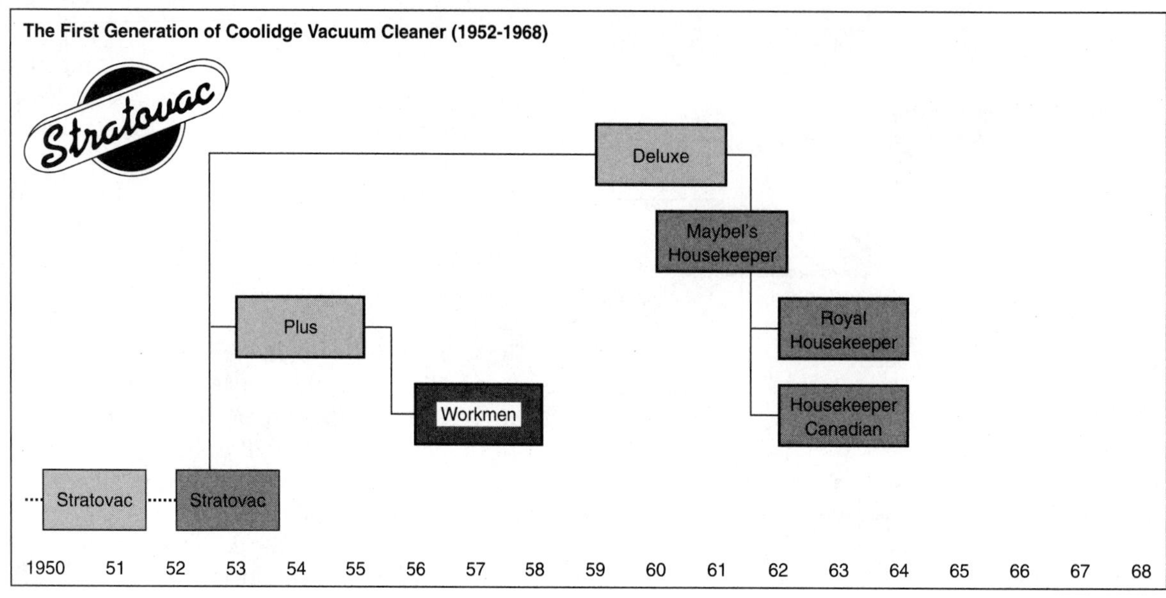

brought out the "Stratovac Plus," an enhanced Stratovac delivered in a choice of three colors, with a 4 horsepower motor and a recoiling cord. In 1959, the company introduced the "Stratovac Deluxe"—a Stratovac Plus with a vacuum resistance sensor (which cut off the power when the bag was full) and a power head with a rotating brush for deep pile or shag carpeting. By 1959, the basic Stratovac cost $89, the Stratovac Plus, $109, and the Stratovac Deluxe, $159.

To reach the industrial market at $79, Coolidge had decided to offer the "Stratovac Workman," a stripped-down Plus model—one color, no recoiling cord. That was introduced in 1956. And when Deluxe sales rocketed, Coolidge offered Maybel's department store chain a customized version of it, the Stratovac "Maybel's Housekeeper." This came out in 1960, in Maybel's blue gray, with the power head. The price was "only" $129. (Coolidge eventually customized the "Housekeeper Canadian" for the Simpton's chain in Canada and the "Royal Housekeeper" for the Mid-Lakes chain in England.)

Again, this is a simple product line, but even so, the map raises interesting questions, especially for younger managers who came after this era. Why the Stratovac Plus? Why a proliferation of products toward the high end?

In fact, during the 1950s, most companies marketed home appliances through department stores with product families visibly shaped by the distribution channels. Products stood side by side in the stores, to be demonstrated by a salesperson. The markup was similar for each product on the floor.

What differentiated products in product families at the time was an appliance manufacturer's reach to satisfy more or less obvious customer segments—customers differentiated by factors like income and marital status. (In the 1950s, most vacuum cleaner purchasers were women, with more or less money, time, and patience.)

How Coolidge leveraged its products also points to certain fixed—and not especially unique—manufacturing capabilities. During the 1950s, company engineers designed appliances for manual assembly and traditional notions of economies of scale. By the end of the 1950s, Coolidge acquired new vacuum sensor innovations from the auto industry. It also learned certain flexible manufacturing techniques, making different colors and options possible.

EXHIBIT 3 The First Generation of Coolidge Vacuum Cleaner (1952–1968)

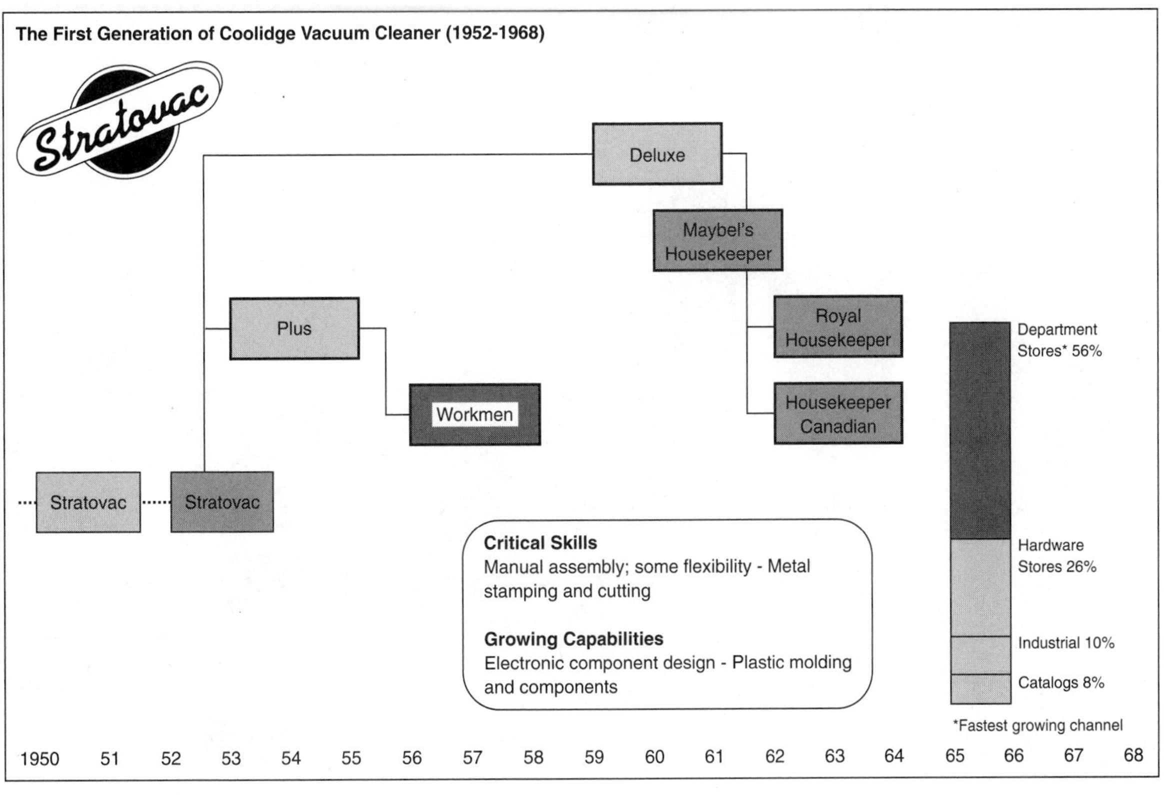

By 1958, Coolidge had solved most of the technical problems of the Stratovac line and had recruited a number of ambitious design engineers to integrate vacuum sensor and power heads into the line. The life cycle of the product—including development time, which stretched back to 1949—was typical for core products of that time: 10 to 15 years. Demand for the Stratovac remained strong throughout the 1950s, and Coolidge sold to department stores in roughly the same proportion as its competition, except for companies organized around the door-to-door trade.

The company's increased (and not fully utilized) technical competence and the steadiness of its key distribution channels are crucial pieces of information to add to the map (see Exhibit 3). The map summarizes technical competence in the oval beneath the product lines and Coolidge's gross sales by distribution channel in the box graph. The fastest growing distribution channel in the industry—in this case, department stores—is shaded for emphasis.

The Second Generation

With so much technical talent in-house, and a society growing increasingly affluent, Coolidge could not be expected to rest on the Stratovac's success indefinitely. Sales were steady, but by the mid-1960s customers assumed there would be some innovations. The age of plastics was dawning; the vanguard of the baby boom was taking apartments; it was the "new and improved" era.

Moreover, marketing people at Coolidge began to detect a new potential market at the low end. People who had relied on their Stratovacs for a decade were looking around for a second, lighter weight appliance for quick cleanups or for the workroom or garage. Lighter weight and cheaper naturally meant more reliance on plastic components.

In the early 1960s, Coolidge managers decided on two product families, each with its own core product (see Exhibit 4). The design team that had brought out the old core Stratovac would handle the

EXHIBIT 4 The First Generation of Coolidge Vacuum Cleaner (1952–1968)

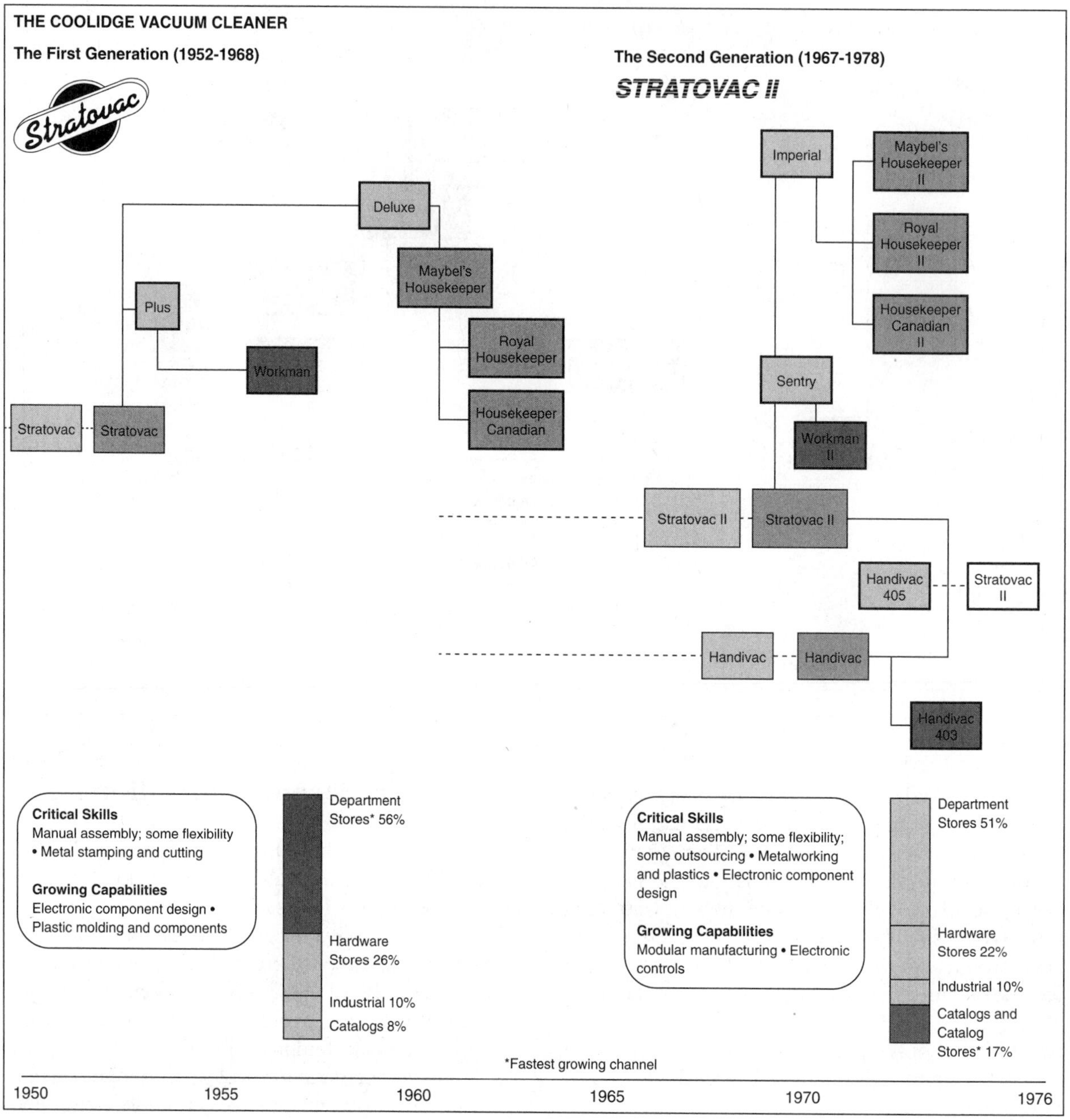

THE COOLIDGE VACUUM CLEANER

The First Generation (1952-1968)

Stratovac

Deluxe

Maybel's Housekeeper

Plus

Royal Housekeeper

Workman

Housekeeper Canadian

Stratovac

Stratovac

The Second Generation (1967-1978)

STRATOVAC II

Imperial

Maybel's Housekeeper II

Royal Housekeeper II

Housekeeper Canadian II

Sentry

Workman II

Stratovac II

Stratovac II

Handivac 405

Stratovac II

Handivac

Handivac

Handivac 403

Critical Skills
Manual assembly; some flexibility • Metal stamping and cutting

Growing Capabilities
Electronic component design • Plastic molding and components

Department Stores* 56%

Hardware Stores 26%

Industrial 10%

Catalogs 8%

Critical Skills
Manual assembly; some flexibility; some outsourcing • Metalworking and plastics • Electronic component design

Growing Capabilities
Modular manufacturing • Electronic controls

Department Stores 51%

Hardware Stores 22%

Industrial 10%

Catalogs and Catalog Stores* 17%

*Fastest growing channel

1950 1955 1960 1965 1970 1976

"Stratovac II," and company new hires would design a second line, the all-plastic, mass-produced "Handivac" ("any color, so long as it's beige").

The Stratovac II, introduced in 1968, was heavier and had a 4.3 horsepower motor, resulting in a slightly noisier operation, "jet noise," which the marketing people reasoned would actually increase respect for its power. Half of the case was now plastic for a "streamlined" appearance. The core Stratovac II boasted a new dust-bag system, which virtually eliminated the need for handling dust. A retractable cord was also standard.

The Stratovac II "Sentry," an enhanced version of the core, included electronic controls for variable speed and came in many colors. The Stratovac II "Imperial," like the old Deluxe model, came with the power head. The Stratovac II Workman continued to sell steadily to the light industrial market, as did the Stratovac II Housekeeper line to the department store chains that still sold the vast majority of units.

Most notable about the Stratovac II was how little changed it was, certainly on the manufacturing end. Assembly was still chiefly manual, along the lines of the 1950s—no priority given to modularity, design for manufacturability, or any of the considerations that would drive designers later on. There was some outsourcing of components to Mexico and Taiwan but no real attention to automation. The only significant change in the Stratovac II came in 1973, when inflationary pressures pushed management to develop a fully plastic casing and critical plastic components—in effect, a hybrid developed by merging technologies of the high-end vacuum cleaner with the low-end Handivac.

Handivac, the second core product, introduced in 1969, was something of a disappointment—mostly because of the inexperience of the team managing its development. Reliability was a problem, given Handivac's almost complete dependence on plastic components, components subjected to higher than expected temperatures from an old, slightly updated 2.5 horsepower motor. Weight was also a problem: It was not as light as promised. Mass-production lines, which were partially automated, were considered a success when they were finally debugged.

Perhaps the greatest problem with the Handivac, however, was the fact that, like the Stratovac II, it was sold mainly through department stores and hardware chains, where markups were too large to permit it a significant advantage over the more expensive core product. Handivac sold for $79, while the Stratovac II sold for $99. Handivac managers tried to cut costs by going to an overseas supplier for a lighter weight, somewhat less powerful motor—over the vehement objections of Stratovac II designers, who had depended on Handivac's participation in their motor plant to keep their own costs in line.

Eventually, Handivac introduced a cost-reduced "Handivac 403," which sold for $69, importing a 3.0 horsepower motor and cord subassembly from Japan. The enhanced "405" sold for $83. Handivac engineers began at this time to interact with Japanese manufacturing managers. But there were still no distribution channels where Handivac could enjoy the "price busting" opportunity it needed. The most promising channel, though hardly dominant, was the growing chains of catalog stores, which sold the Handivac 403 for $63, a 10 percent reduction in the department store price.

The Third Generation

During 1976 and 1977, a number of external and internal pressures led to a redesign of the entire product line. Department stores were still the major source of revenue, but competitors were proliferating and the Stratovac II group felt the need to offer an increasing number of more enhanced and more customized products to maintain demand at the profitable high end. Consumers would pay a premium, marketing people believed, only if the company could produce so many versions that all customers felt they were getting the right color with the right options. Moreover, Coolidge had canvassed Stratovac II customers, who hadn't appreciated the "jet sound," as designers had assumed. Bulk was also a problem, as was the vacuum's unattractive look.

Inside the company, Coolidge's two design teams had become more cooperative, particularly as the advantages of molded plastic became obvious to everyone. The hybrid Stratovac II, which had been redesigned in plastic wherever possible, was something of a victory for the young Handivac designers over the more traditional group. Flexibility and cost were the keys to satisfying many markets, and plastics answered both needs. Eventually the more traditional designers also came to see the advantage of going to Japan for a smaller, lighter, more reliable motor—and for a number of subassemblies critical to the company's goal of offering arrays of options.

Concurrently in the mid-1970s, the Handivac designers were pressing for a complete merging of the design engineering teams and for studying Japanese manufacturing techniques. They argued that if flexibility, cost, and quality were going to be crucial, the manufacturing people would have to become more involved in product design. The young guard also believed that Coolidge could produce motors domestically—at required levels of quality—if it adopted certain innovations in machine tool and winding automation and instituted statistical process control at its existing motor plant.

Where the younger design group still lacked credibility, however, was on the bottom line. Top management was reluctant to give up on a two-track approach when the Handivac group had failed to deliver an appliance that made even as much as the Housekeeper line. The number of catalog stores was growing, and newer discount appliance chains were springing up in big cities, but the Handivac faced intense competition. Could the younger designers hope to come in with enough products, offering enough features, and at low enough costs to meet this competition?

In the end, Coolidge management decided to develop two core product families in its third generation (see Exhibit 4). The Stratovac II team redesigned the high-end vacuum cleaner in six models, the "Challenger 6000" series. All appliances in this series came with a power head and a new bag system. By steps—6001, 6002, and upward—consumers could buy increasingly sophisticated electronic controls. And they could order the 6004 and 6005 in an array of colors.

The 6000 series was constructed almost entirely of molded plastic. Manufacturing came up with an automated way of applying hot sealant to critical seams, and the Challenger's motor was quieter. Top management agreed with the younger engineers that a more advanced motor factory could be constructed in the United States. The design teams didn't merge, but they found themselves working more closely together and increasingly with manufacturing.

The traditional design group simultaneously came out with the "Pioneer 4000" series. This was a middle-range product, somewhat smaller than the Challenger 6000, and not offering a power head. The marketing people felt that department stores would want a cost-reduced model to compete with the proliferating "economy" products that discount chains were now offering. (The 4001, 4002, and 4003 were distinguished, again, by electronic controls.) The Pioneer 4000 series was leveraged largely from the Challenger 6000 as a cost-reduced version.

Since both series offered stripped-down models, Coolidge did not introduce a specific industrial product and eliminated the Workman. Coolidge executives also believed that it was no longer worthwhile to customize models for particular department stores where margins were shrinking, so they eliminated the Housekeeper line.

A year after they introduced the Challenger 6000, the Handivac team brought out its new series of products, the "Helpmate." With minor modifications, Helpmate was customized as "Helpmate SE," targeted at different low-end market segments—college students, apartment dwellers, do-it-yourselfers, and the industrial market. The cleaner was lightweight. Attachments varied, as did graphic design: The company expected a Spartan gray color and a longer hose to appeal to commercial customers and bright pastels and different size brushes to appeal to women college students.

The key to the Helpmate line, however, was its manufacturing. The motor was no longer outsourced, and designers worked with manufacturing engineers on modular components and subassemblies. Top management agreed to set aside manufacturing space in the assembly plants for cellular construction of the Helpmate so that the company could respond quickly to demand for particular models. And Helpmate came in at two-thirds the price of the Pioneer 4000.

There was still some debate among Helpmate's product development team members about most likely channels. Some saw it designed only for discount chains and catalog stores, which by 1978 had pretty much eclipsed hardware stores. Others saw the Helpmate as a low-end product for department stores too. In the end, Helpmate was a smash in the discount stores and all but disappeared from department stores.

The Next Generation?

Imagine that Coolidge managers are gathered in 1985 to consider the company's future. Their three-generation map has simplified a great deal of information—information the managers might intuitively understand but could not have looked at so clearly before. Where can they go from here?

Looking at their map, it's clear that Coolidge's product offerings are not appropriately matched to the new environment. They have aimed most of their products at department stores, and now discount chains are growing at a tremendous rate. They had devoted too much attention to figuring out how to leverage products at the high end, when the big battle was shaping up at the low end. Now Coolidge's managers wonder how long it will be before power options and accessories show up on cheaper, sturdier import lines distributed to high-volume outlets.

More growth in the company's manufacturing capabilities is obviously very important now. The map indicates the growing reciprocity between design and manufacturing engineers, owing largely to the initiatives of the younger design group. It would not be hard to imagine a merging of all engineering groups and the use of temporary dedicated development teams at this point. Product life cycles have obviously been shrinking; designers have to think fast now and cooperate across functional lines. To bring out a new line of inexpensive products that are both reliable and varied in options, Coolidge will need automated, flexible manufacturing systems. This development means bringing all parts of the company together—designers with marketing, manufacturing with both. It means, interestingly enough, a need for even clearer, more complete new product development maps.

The finished product development map presented in Exhibit 5 may appear elementary, but managers who have mapped their products' evolution have experienced substantial payoff in several areas. First, the map can be extremely useful to product development efforts. It helps focus development projects and limit their scope, making them more manageable. The map helps set specifications and targets for individual projects, provides a context for relating concurrent projects to one another, and indicates how the sequence of projects capitalizes on the company's previous investments. These benefits do much to minimize the likelihood of encountering two of the pitfalls we identified at the outset of this article, the moving target and the lack of product distinctiveness.

A second important benefit is the motivation the map provides the various functional groups—all with a stake in effective product development—to develop their own complementary strategies. As illustrated in the Coolidge Corporation example, the product development map raises a number of issues regarding distribution channels, product technology, and manufacturing approaches that must be answered in all parts of the company if the map is to represent the organization's agreed-on direction.

This point brings up the need for "submaps" in each functional area. In the Coolidge case, the first couple of product generations may not have shown the need for a more careful distribution channel map, but by the third the need is painfully clear. Capturing other strategic marketing variables in, say, a price map, a competitive product positioning map, and a customer map would enable the marketing function to identify and present important trends in the marketplace, define targets for future product offerings, and provide guidance for developing and committing sales and marketing resources.

Equally apparent by the third generation is the need for supporting maps in design engineering. A set of design engineering submaps can produce a clearer sense of the mix of engineering talent the company requires, how it should be organized and focused, and the rate at which the company should bring new technologies into future product generations. These maps would not only help managers integrate design resources with product development efforts but would also ensure that they hire and train new employees in a timely and effective manner and that they focus new project tools (such as computer-aided engineering) on pressing product development needs. The key is achieving technical agreement in advance of product development.

Toward the end of the third generation at Coolidge, the map reveals the need for more detailed manufacturing functional maps to bring out issues raised in the "critical skills" oval. Such maps would focus on strategic issues relating to manufacturing facilities, vendor relationships, and automation technology.

Again, the development of such functional submaps not only benefits manufacturing but also helps the company maximize the return on new product development resources. The most interesting and useful benefits will come out of debates about what to put in the submaps.

Submaps capture the essence of the functional strategies, and when integrated with the new product development map, serve to tie those functional strategies together and provide both a foundation and a process for achieving a company's business strategy. The whole process facilitates the cross-functional discussion and resolution of strategic issues. How often have well-intentioned functional managers met to discuss their various substrategies only to have those from other functions tune out within the first two minutes, as the discussion becomes too technical, too detailed, or simply too parochial to comprehend?

Mapping provides a process for planning that avoids too much detail (like budgeting) and too much parochialism (like traditional functional strategy sessions). Managers will inevitably develop linkages across the organization by going through the steps of selecting the resources or factors to develop into a map, identifying the key dimensions

EXHIBIT 5 The Coolidge Vacuum Cleaner

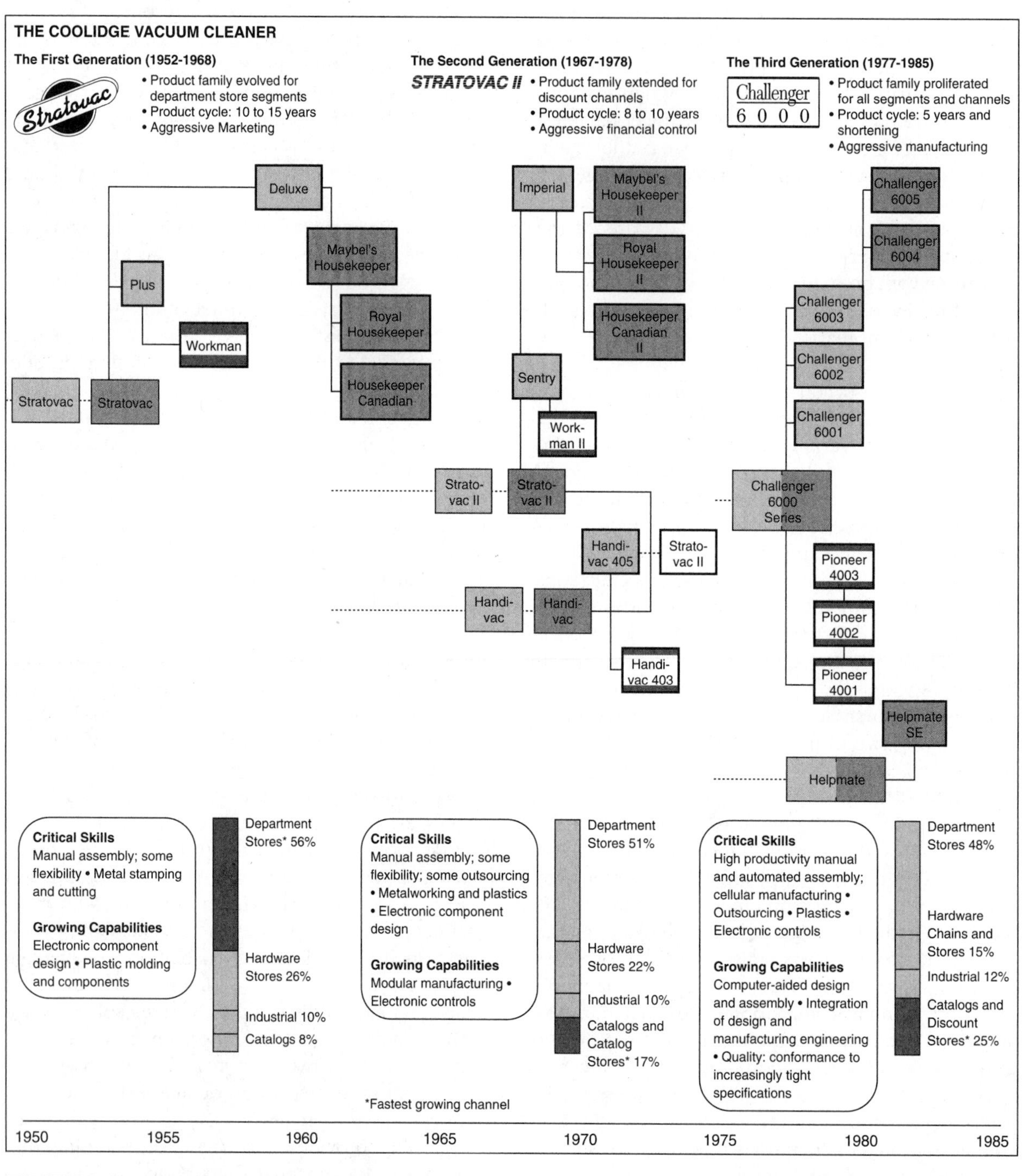

to capture in the map, reviewing historical data to understand the relationships of those dimensions, and examining what is likely to drive future versions of the map. Functions can share their maps to communicate, refine, and agree on important product strategy choices. It is the sharing of functional capabilities—capabilities applied in a systematic, repetitive fashion to product development opportunities—that will become the company's competitive advantage.

Reading IV–7
Accelerating the Design-Build-Test Cycle for Effective Product Development[1]

Steven C. Wheelwright and Kim B. Clark

Perhaps no topic has gained such widespread attention among managers in recent years as effective product development. Rapid, high-quality, on-target product development is central to competition in industries ranging from consumer packaged goods to electronics, from appliances to pharmaceuticals, and from automobiles to steel. Firms that consistently define, resource, and execute new product development projects significantly more effectively and efficiently than their competitors are rewarded by significant strategic advantage.

Speed is at the heart of that advantage. But it must be speed born of enduring capability. Indeed, the themes that characterize outstanding development projects—clarity of objectives, focus on time to market, integration inside and out, high-quality prototypes, and strong leadership, to name a few—reflect capabilities that allow the firm to move quickly and efficiently to develop attractive products and manufacturing processes. The power of such capabilities lies in the competitive leverage they provide. A firm that develops high-quality products rapidly may pursue several competitive options. It may start a new product development project at the same time as competitors, but introduce the product to the market much sooner. Alternatively, it may delay the beginning of a new development project in order to acquire better information about market developments, customer requirements, or critical technologies, introducing its product at the same time as its competitors but bringing to market a product much better suited to the needs of its customers. Furthermore, it may use its resources to develop additional products that more closely meet the demands of specific customer niches. Whatever the mix of customer targeting, speed to market, and product breadth a firm chooses to pursue, its advantages in fundamental capabilities provide a competitive edge.

The advantage of such capability has been widely recognized in the worldwide auto industry. By the late 1980s, leading Japanese auto firms (most notably Toyota and Honda) were developing major new cars (or "platforms") in 36 months and replacing existing product generations every four years. European and U.S. auto firms were taking approximately 60 months to develop similar projects, expending considerably more resources, and replacing existing product generations every eight-plus years.[2] This rapid development gave the leading Japanese firms significant advantages in forecasting customer preferences and offering newer designs (on average), faster paybacks, and more innovative products incorporating newer technologies. The evident power of development led Chrysler, Ford, and General Motors, as well as many European firms, to launch major efforts to revamp their approach to product development.

Competitive advantage results in large part from the way work gets done during the process of development. Especially important is the way in which engineering (both design and manufacturing process) and marketing combine technical detail—specific dimensions, parts parameters, materials, and components—into a coherent whole that more than meets customer expectations, even when such expectations are difficult to identify.

The magic in a winning new product or a superior process is in the details. Understanding how individuals, work groups, and organizations carry out problem solving in product and process engineering, field service, and manufacturing is central to accelerated product development. In this context a "problem" occurs when developers encounter a gap between the current design (or plan, process, or prototype) and customer requirements. For example, in the development of a medical diagnostic instrument, prototype testing and interaction with customers might reveal that nurses and technicians experience a glare on the display that makes it difficult to read. The customers' experience signals the existence of a problem, but does not define it precisely. Excessive glare could be the result of an inappropriate display angle, inappropriate materials, the absence of control in the manufacturing process, or any number of underlying causes. Although there may be a team member responsible for the display, solving excessive glare is likely to involve issues that extend beyond that narrow functional domain. Thus, the problem cuts across disciplines and perhaps even functions.

---

[1]Adapted from Steven C. Wheelwright and Kim B. Clark, *Revolutionizing Product Development* (New York: Free Press, 1992).

Reprinted by permission of *International Marketing Review* 11 (1994), pp. 32–46.

[2]See Kim B. Clark and Takahiro Fujimoto, *Product Development Performance* (Boston: HBS Press, 1991).

How the development team takes action to close such a gap—the way it frames and defines the problem, generates alternatives, organizes and conducts tasks, and implements solutions—determines the speed, efficiency, and effectiveness of problem solving. Where such problems are critical to overall system performance, drive program lead time, involve significant resources, or have decisive influence on a customer's perception of the product or process as a whole, the effectiveness of problem solving at the detailed local level can have a powerful influence on the overall performance of the development process. Effective problem solving at the working level is not a sufficient condition for overall success, but in our experience, it is a critical and necessary part of an outstanding development process.

An understanding of effective problem solving in development is essential for everyone involved in development teams, and particularly crucial for general managers. Our research and experience have led us to conclude that the role of the general manager is to build capability and create effective processes in the organization. Carrying out that role requires an in-depth understanding of the problem-solving process at the working level. General managers need to understand the process not only because changes often provide significant leverage for improving development, but also because such an understanding can be an important guide in making investment decisions about processes and capabilities. Furthermore, deep understanding may be useful as general managers make decisions about specific projects. With a framework for thinking about detailed problem solving and an understanding of modern methods and systems, general managers will be in a much better position to evaluate the potential and progress of specific products or processes under development. Finally, such understanding can enable a general manager to assess and strengthen existing development capabilities so that accelerated product development can become a source of competitive advantage.

In the next section, we examine in detail the design-build-test cycle that, for most development projects for manufactured products, is the fundamental building block of effective and efficient problem solving. We include a description of alternative modes of problem solving and their implications for organizational skills and capabilities. Next we examine how superior capabilities at conducting the design-build-test cycle can be used to make dramatic improvements in individual product development efforts. Utilizing faster rates of organizational learning is at the heart of such improvements.

Having examined how the effectiveness of an individual development project benefits from such basic problem-solving capability, in the final section we consider how a firm can leverage that ability into a competitive advantage across a series of projects. Throughout the paper we use a number of examples from our research to illustrate key concepts and ideas. While each situation is unique, our hope is to show how managers in a wide range of development settings may develop and apply effective patterns of problem solving.

A. Problem Solving in New Product Development

Solving problems during development is a learning process. No matter how much an engineer, a marketer, or a manufacturer may know about a given problem, there are always aspects of a new system that must be understood before an effective design can be developed. Except for the easiest of problems, developers are unlikely to come up with a complete design in a single iteration. Instead, developers go through several iterations, learning a little more about the problem and alternative solutions each time before converging to a final design and detailed specifications.

The Design-Build-Test Cycle

Each iteration or problem-solving cycle consists of the three phases illustrated in Exhibit 1. In the *design phase,* a developer frames the problem and establishes goals for the problem-solving process. Problem framing is crucial, since the apparent gaps in performance that we observe are often caused by underlying conditions that are difficult to observe and characterize. A problem with noise in the winding mechanism of a 35mm camera, for example, may be caused by the type of material, gear width, or a variety of other design parameters, including the precision of the manufacturing process. The frame put on a problem also depends on how objectives are defined. In the case of noise, for example, it may be apparent because of customer feedback that the old design had undesirable noise characteristics. A clear objective of the new system could be, therefore, to reduce noise below a given threshold

EXHIBIT 1 The Design-Build-Test Cycle in Product Development Problem Solving

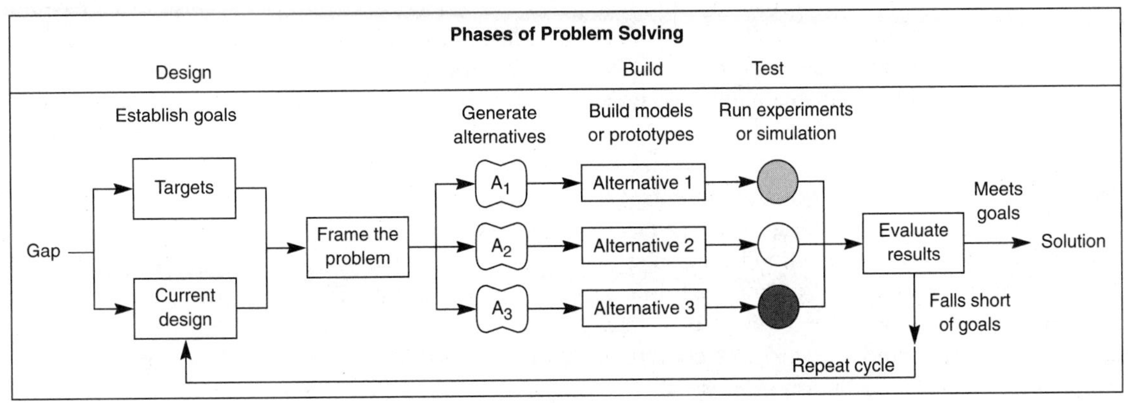

level. A deeper understanding of the problem, however, may suggest that customers like to hear the rewind system working. Thus, the objective may not be simply to reduce noise below some threshold, but rather to create the right kind of sound—a sound that is distinct but soft and nonabrasive.

Once the developer has framed the problem, the next step in the design phase is to generate alternatives. Based on the developer's understanding of the relationship between design parameters and customer attributes, several designs for physical models may be appropriate. The purpose of the alternative designs may be to explore the relationship between design parameters and specific customer attributes. If the particular design cycle under discussion comes at a later stage of development, the purpose of the alternative designs may be to refine an established concept.

In the second or *build phase* of the problem-solving cycle, working models of the design alternatives are built that allow for testing. Depending upon what a developer is trying to learn, the working models may take several forms. At an early stage of gear development on a 35mm camera, for example, a developer may implement alternatives electronically in a computer-aided design (CAD) workstation, using the computer to display graphically and visually the gears' characteristics. For some purposes it may be useful to take the build phase one step further, creating alternatives using easy-to-work-with materials such as plastic or soft metals. While computer simulation may provide sufficient information to arrive at effective solutions, later-stage testing and development may require building physical prototypes using materials and production processes reasonably close to those used in a commercial process.

In the third or *test phase* of the problem-solving cycle, working models, prototypes, or computer-generated images are tested. Depending upon the purposes of the problem-solving cycle, the tests may focus on a particular dimension or may involve full-scale system evaluation. In the case of gear noise, for example, an early testing scheme may examine the decibel level generated by alternative designs. Such a test could be run in a testing laboratory and the results used to generate an understanding of the connection between different design parameters and the overall noise level. Subsequently, given designs may be implemented with prototype parts and tested with potential customers.

Although conducting tests appears relatively straightforward, in practice getting good information out of the testing phase requires careful forethought and skillful execution of a test plan. In a laboratory setting, test engineers worry about things such as accuracy, precision, and the ability to calibrate measurements. In addition, tests are subject to random variation caused by fluctuations in the environment that have not been accounted for or controlled. In order to cope with such randomness from vibration, temperature, humidity, and even stray magnetic fields, engineers often repeat tests to identify the amount of noise in the testing process. But even when engineers have well-designed procedures to deal with random variation and have established instruments and processes to ensure accurate and precise measurement, there is still the problem of fidelity. Fidelity refers to the extent to which the test being conducted reflects the actual case of interest. With respect to gears in the film rewind system, for example, will a laboratory test of decibel levels reflect the way customers will perceive noise when using the camera? Are customers involved in the field tests representative of the customers they are trying to reach? Are test conditions effectively representative of the mode in which the camera will be used?

A single design-build-test cycle generates insight and information about the connection between specific design parameters and customer attributes. That information becomes the basis for a new design-build-test cycle and the process continues until developers arrive at a solution—a design—that meets requirements. Thus, the effectiveness of problem solving in development depends not only on the speed, productivity, and quality of each individual step in the cycle, but also on the number of cycles required to achieve a solution. The number of cycles depends directly on the extent to which activities at each of the problem-solving steps are linked and integrated.

The challenge in effective problem solving, therefore, is both to execute individual elements of the cycle (and individual cycles) rapidly and well and to link individual cycles so that solutions are coherent. As pressure for improved performance in lead time, cost, and quality has increased, firms have adopted a variety of methods to improve the execution and linkage of problem-solving cycles. At first glance, many of these methods appear to be little more than applied common sense—plan your work, think before you act, consider the consequences, and do it right the first time. While common sense is an all-too-rare commodity, there is more to structured methods—such as quality function deployment (QFD), design for manufacturability (DFM), and computer-aided engineering (CAE)—than a straightforward application of what everyone already knows. The difficulty is in finding a method and logic that works where people, information, objectives, and capabilities interact in a complex system.

Methods of Communication in Problem Solving

At the heart of such methods, and indeed underlying any design-build-test cycle, is the extent to which problem solving is truly integrated. This shows up most forcibly in relationships between individuals or engineering groups where the output of one's problem-solving cycle is the input for the other's. Consider, for example, the relationship between a design group responsible for designing a plastic part and a process engineering group responsible for designing the mold that will be used to produce it. The upstream group—in this case, the part designers—solves its design problem by establishing the part's physical dimensions, how it will interface with other parts in the system, its surface characteristics, and the particular material to be used in its construction. All these solutions—dimensions, tolerances, interfaces, surface characteristics, and materials—become inputs into the downstream organization's design problem—in this case, the design of molds to be used in the production of the part. The mold designer's problem is to create a mold (or set of molds, particularly if the part is to be produced in volume) that will give the part its shape and surface characteristics, but will also be sufficiently durable, cost effective, and operational that the part can be manufactured in volume (can withstand repeated use without breaking or sticking) reliably at low cost. How these two engineering groups work together determines the extent of integration in the design and development of the part and its associated mold and directly impacts the effectiveness of their joint design-build-test cycle in achieving development objectives.

The choices firms make about communication between upstream and downstream groups and how to link the actual work in time shape the nature of cross-functional integration. The key issue is the extent to which work is done in parallel. Exhibit 2 puts the communication patterns together with different approaches to parallel activity to create four modes of upstream-downstream interaction.

The first panel depicts what we call the *serial mode* of interaction. This is a classic relationship in which the downstream group waits to begin its work until the upstream group has completely finished its design. The completed design is transmitted to the downstream group in a one-shot transmission of information. This one-way, "batch" style of communication may not convey all of the important nuances and background to the final design, nor does it necessarily comprehend the strengths and opportunities afforded by the downstream group. In that sense, the problem solving that lies behind the design of the product and that will produce the design of the mold is not integrated.

The second mode—what we call *early start in the dark*—links the upstream and downstream groups

EXHIBIT 2 Four Modes of Upstream-Downstream Interaction

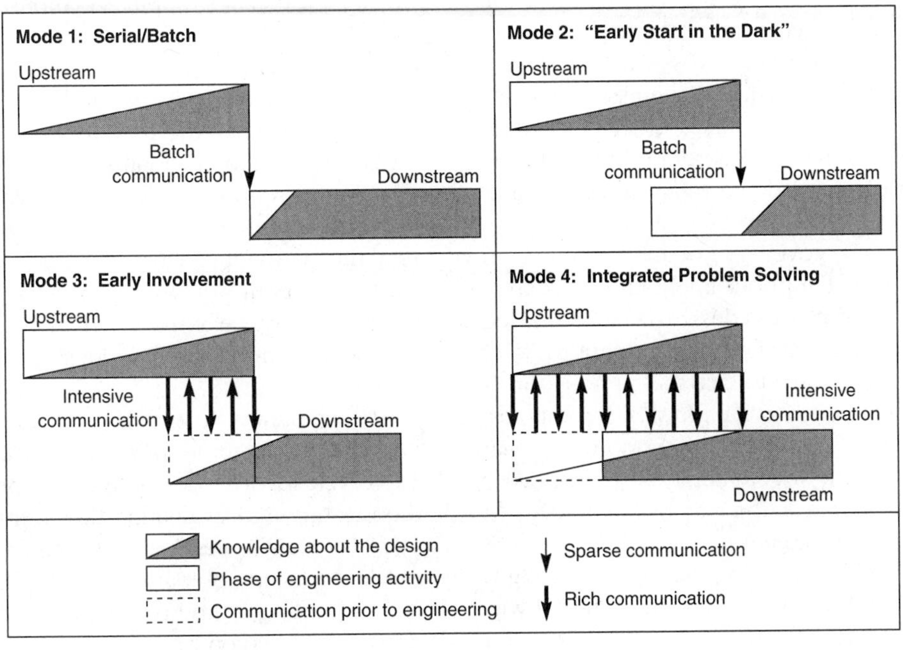

in time, but continues to employ a batch style of communication. This mode of interaction often occurs where the downstream group faces a deadline that it feels cannot be met without an early start on the project. But the upstream group communicates only at the end of its work, so the downstream group in effect has to begin in the dark. When the completed upstream design arrives, the downstream group may be surprised by the design and experience a period of confusion as it tries to adjust its work. While the net result may be some reduction in overall lead time, the extent of the surprise and confusion can often be sufficient to make the process longer than the process in mode one. Although the downstream and upstream groups work in parallel, and in this sense are "concurrent," in actuality they operate without information and the problem-solving cycles in the two organizations are not linked.

The third mode—what we call the *early involvement mode*—begins to move toward real integration. In this mode the upstream and downstream players engage in two-way communication of preliminary, fragmentary information, although the upstream group is still involved in the design of the part well before the downstream group begins its work. Thus, while the downstream group develops insight about the emerging design and participates through feedback and interaction in the design process, it waits until the design is complete before undertaking problem solving in its own domain. The downstream group benefits from early involvement in two ways. First, the part design reflects a much better understanding of the issues confronting the process engineers than was true in either modes one or two. Second, the mold designers themselves have a much better sense of the issues and objectives embodied in the design. The net effect is that they are able to complete their work with fewer delays and downstream changes. In this sense, problem solving in the downstream and upstream groups is much more integrated.

The last mode in Exhibit 2—what we call *integrated problem solving*—links the upstream and downstream groups in time and in the pattern of communication. In this mode, downstream engineers not only participate in ongoing dialogue with their upstream counterparts, but use that information and insight to get a flying start on their own work. This changes the content of the downstream work in the early phases of upstream design and is also likely to change fundamentally the content of communication between the two groups. Whereas in mode three the content of feedback from downstream engineers had to rely on past practice, theoretical knowledge, and engineering judgment, under integrated problem solving that feedback will also reflect actual practice in attempting to implement the upstream design.

Communication that is rich, bilateral, and intense is an important, even essential, element of integrated problem solving. Where problem solving between upstream and downstream groups is intimately connected, the practice of "throwing the design (blueprints) over the wall"—inherent in mode one—will not support timely mutual adaptation of product and process design. What is needed to capture the nuance and detail important for joint problem solving is face-to-face discussion, direct observation, interaction with physical prototypes, and computer-based representations. Moreover, that intimate, rich pattern of communication must occur in a timely way so that action may be taken to avoid costly mistakes downstream.

Integrated problem solving during the design-build-test cycle relies on early action by the downstream group, dense, rich dialogue between upstream and downstream participants, and a style of problem solving that is broader and more comprehensive than one experiences in the more narrow functional focus inherent in mode one. Indeed, effective integration places heavy demands on the organization. The engineering process must link problem-solving cycles in time; communication must be rich, precise, and intense; and the relationship between upstream and downstream groups must support and reinforce early and frequent exchange of constraints, ideas, and objectives. Moreover, because problem solving across traditional functional boundaries occurs in real time, the capacity for quick and effective action is critical. Thus, effective integration relies on a specific set of capabilities, attitudes, and relationships that management must enhance and build over time.

B. Utilizing Superior Design-Build-Test Capabilities to Achieve Rapid New Product Development

During the course of a product development project, the major design-build-test cycles involve the creation of prototypes or the testing of the production process in a pilot plant. Carrying out prototype or pilot production cycles well can have a decisive impact on the overall development effort. Consider, for example, prototyping data gathered from three firms in the major appliance industry during the mid-1980s. These data, and the design-build-test cycles they reflect, are summarized in Exhibit 3.

Differences in lead time among these firms are striking. A major new product development effort ranges from 12 to 22 months and 14 to 20 months at Companies A and B, respectively, whereas at Company C, it takes 36 months. Looking at where that total time is spent reveals a very different pattern for the two faster firms than for Company C. The source of that difference is reflected in the number and duration of the design-build-test cycles needed by each firm.

At Companies A and B, a major development effort requires three primary prototyping cycles. Each cycle involves design, building prototypes, and then testing and evaluating those units. The initial cycle for Companies A and B consists of taking the product concept, preparing sample drawings, building and testing a prototype unit based on the initial drawings, and then revising the design to complete the final drawings. While there are undoubtedly some small subcycles, the allocation of calendar time suggests they must be relatively minor if this first cycle takes from 7 to 14 months. Subsequently, these two companies do a second cycle which takes three to six months and involves preparing tooling for the factory, producing samples from that tooling, assembling units from such sample parts (as part of a prepilot production run), and complete testing of the resulting units. Finally, these firms engage in a third cycle of one to three months—the pilot production run—where revisions from the second cycle are incorporated into the final product and process designs, and the entire system is tested by building pilot production units. Customers evaluate those units, final revisions are made, and plans for volume production of the new product are approved. Market rollout and production ramp-up then follow.

In stark contrast, Company C engages in five separate design-build-test cycles. The first cycle, planned to take 10 months, is analogous to the first cycle at Companies A and B, but ends without completion of a fully functional prototype unit. A second cycle of six months is required to refine the design geometry, tolerances, and physical relationship of the subassemblies. The results of those two cycles then are combined into a third cycle, which takes five months and builds a handful of final engineering models that can be tested and evaluated. The

EXHIBIT 3 Prototype Cycles and Design Timetables (in months): Major Appliances

Event/Activity	Companies A & B Design-Build-Test (Prototyping) Cycles	Company A	Company B	Company C	Company C Design-Build-Test (Prototyping) Cycles
Prefeasibility scoping	Cycle (1)	1–3	2–6	3	Cycle (1)
Drawing for feasibility, sample		1–2	1–2	1	
Build sample		1–2	1	1	
Test sample		2–5	2	3	
Drawings for design geometry		design frozen		2	Cycle (2)
Build design geometry				2	
Test design geometry				3	
Complete drawings for issue		2	2	1	
Build evaluation models				2	Cycle (3)
Test evaluation models (drawing release)				3	
Tool release	Cycle (2)		2		Cycle (4)
Tooling time		2–4	2–3	6	
Inspect samples				2	
Prepare and conduct prepilot run				1	
Testing of product		1	1	2	
Prepare and conduct pilot run	Cycle (3)			1	Cycle (5)
Prepare for production		2–3	1	3	
Total Development Project Cycle Time		12–22 months	14–20 months	36 months	

output of that third cycle is a set of final revisions to the engineering drawings.

Company C's fourth cycle is analogous to the second cycle at Companies A and B, but requires 11 months versus the 3 to 6 required by the other two firms. Its aim at all three companies is to procure and test the tooling and to plan and carry out a prepilot production run. The prototypes built during the prepilot run are then tested thoroughly, and final revisions are made to the design of the product and its manufacturing process. Finally, Company C engages in a fifth prototyping and test cycle—pilot production—that is analogous to the third cycle pursued at Companies A and B. However, Company C requires four months rather than the one to three months required by Companies A and B.

It is instructive to contrast the substantive differences between Companies A and B and Company C. One difference is that activity and cycle durations in the first two firms generally are anticipated to vary from project to project, whereas Company C anticipates that the planned duration of each cycle will be the same on every project. An even more striking difference is Company C's sequence of five design-build-test cycles. Companies A and B have compressed the time from concept to preproduction, while Company C has subdivided project steps to reduce complexity and "level of concurrency." Their intent has been to reduce what they perceive as the risks of costly mistakes. However, Company C, like Companies A and B, would claim that it is pushing hard to reduce its product development cycle time. So why does it use five cycles instead of three?

The explanation for the number and duration of the cycles at Company C lies in how rapidly their organization solves problems, learns, and converges to a final design. Because of poor communication, a narrow technical focus, and an excessively segmented process, Company C needs five cycles to reach a final design that can be produced in volume. Furthermore, because of the way Company C handles the sequence of individual activities and the way it structures and manages the project, it also needs more time to complete each cycle. If management arbitrarily were to cut that time or eliminate one or two cycles, many issues would go unresolved, leading to serious problems in production and the field.

Conceptually, any development project can be thought of (and usually is, at least implicitly) as a sequence of design-build-test cycles. Within each cycle, the prototype serves as a focal point for problem-solving, testing, communication, and conflict resolution. Furthermore, it forces specificity in design, provides feedback about the choices made thus far, and highlights remaining unresolved issues. By creating a physical embodiment of the design's current state, engineers are able to study critical issues of functionality, marketing can test and explore customer needs and reactions, and manufacturing can determine the feasibility and options it has for producing the product in volume.

But in spite of prototyping's substantial potential and leverage, Company C treats it as a technical and tactical concern. Even after reviewing the data in Exhibit 3, management at Company C did not conceive of prototyping as a management tool. They did not grasp the nature of the process and its potential role in making development work more effectively. The same seems to hold true even for industries where new product development is the basis of competition, and the speed of development and resulting product performance is the focus of the firm's stated strategy. For example, in the engineering workstation segment of the computer industry, where firms such as Sun Microsystems, DEC, Hewlett-Packard, and IBM compete for a large, growing market, recent studies reveal differences in the number and duration of such cycles even greater than in major appliances—from as few as 3 cycles with durations as short as 100 days each, to as many as 11 cycles with durations as long as 200 days each.[3] Furthermore, the variety of ways in which prototyping cycles are managed and linked to the product development effort itself are as numerous as the number of firms in the industry.

C. Turning Rapid Product Development Capability into Competitive Advantage

Rapidly executing design-build-test cycles may allow a firm to shorten its lead time on a particular project, but competitive advantage derives from the ability to consistently execute rapid development in a series of projects over time. With that capability, the firm may not only get to market more effectively, but in fact change the rules of the game. The interaction between two consumer electronics firms—firms we will call Northern and Southern—illustrates how such a competitive advantage might take shape and influence the nature of competition over repeated generations of product development activity.

Northern and Southern Electronics competed head-to-head in the compact stereo market. Until 1985, both Northern and Southern followed standard industry cycles in new product development, pricing, and manufacturing costs. With a product development cycle of 18 to 20 months, both firms introduced new generations of product every two years. Between major generation changes in products there were frequent model upgrades and price declines as the cost of key components and manufacturing fell with increasing volume. Thus, until the mid-1980s, both Southern and Northern had prices and costs that tracked each other closely, and both mirrored industry averages (see Exhibit 4A).

In the early 1980s, stimulated by the efforts of its new vice president of engineering, Southern embarked on a concerted effort to reduce its product development lead time. Without compromising quality, the entire organization began to develop the skills and characteristics associated with rapid, on-target design-build-test cycles. Stronger leadership, more effective cross-functional integration, greater attention to issues of manufacturability and design, more effective prototyping, and a revamped development process gradually led to a reduction in development lead time from 18 to 12 months.

As Exhibit 4B suggests, Southern began to make competitive use of its new development capability in early 1986. At that point it broke with industry tradition and introduced its next generation of stereo product about six months sooner than expected. With a more advanced system and superior performance, Southern was able to command a premium price in the marketplace. Although Northern followed six months later on a standard cycle, its next generation stereo was unable to command its traditional market share. As a result, Northern's volume increased more slowly than expected and its cost position began to erode slightly relative to Southern.

Southern Electronics introduced its next generation product 18 months later in the fall of 1987. Once again the product achieved a premium price in the market. However, Southern did not fully exploit its

[3]For additional information on prototyping in the workstation industry, see David Ellison and Steven C. Wheelwright, "The Prototyping of PCBs in Engineering Workstation Development Projects," Harvard Business School Working Paper, 1991.

EXHIBIT 4A Standard Competitive Patterns for the Compact Stereo Market

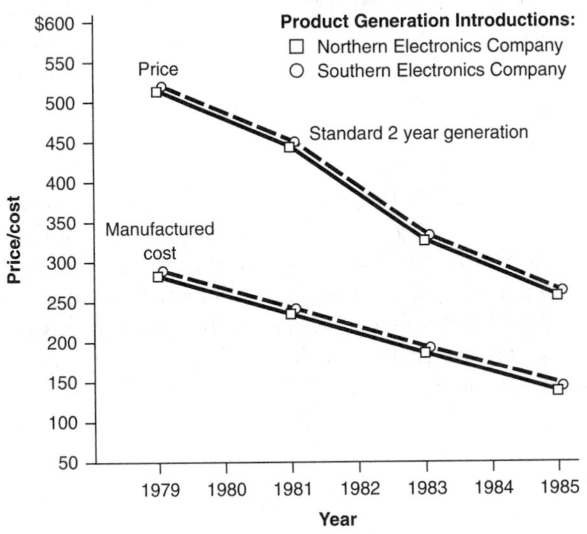

EXHIBIT 4B Competition on Rapid Development Capabilities in the Compact Stereo Market

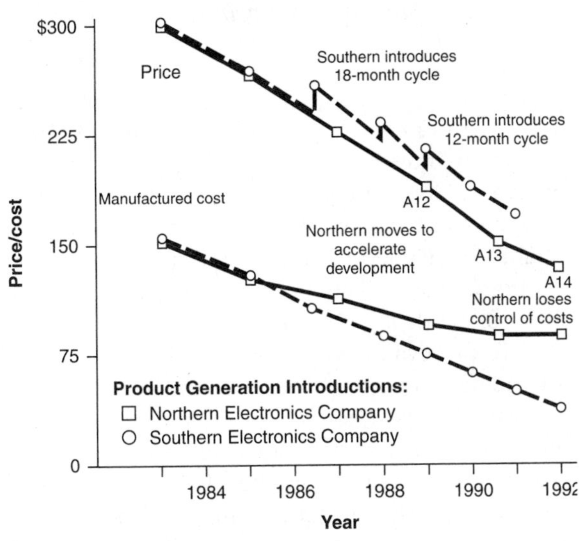

premium pricing opportunity. Instead, it lowered prices somewhat to increase further its market share. At that point, not only was Northern behind in product features and technology, but Southern's aggressive pricing posture put even more pressure on Northern's sales volume and margins. Although Northern fought back with price discounts, increased advertising, and promotions to dealers, it was unable to stem the erosion of its historical market position. The result was an even greater disparity in the cost positions of Northern and Southern Electronics.

In late 1988, Northern introduced its next generation stereo system, the A12. Developed under the motto "beat Southern," Northern's executives felt that the A12 would be the product to regain its former competitive position in the market. Much to their surprise, however, the rollout of the A12 in early 1989 was met by Southern's introduction of its next generation stereo system: Southern had moved to a 12-month product introduction cycle in late 1988. At that point Northern was a full generation of technology behind Southern in its market offerings. Northern's management determined that the only course of action open was to accelerate development of the next generation system, the A13. They thus embarked on a crash development effort to bring the A13 to market in early 1990. At the same time, Northern began development of the A14, which was targeted for the Christmas 1990 selling season. The A14 was to get back into the competitive ball game on solid footing—a "close the gap" strategy.

While Northern's strategic intent was to catch up to Southern with accelerated product development, the reality was much different. Northern brought the A13 to market in early 1990, but the development process was so hectic and the ramp-up in manufacturing so strained that the company effectively lost control of its costs. The product came to market but was much more expensive and less effective than the company had planned. Because of its many problems, scarce development resources that were to have been moved to the A14 in early 1990 were focused instead on correcting problems and cleaning up the A13's design. To make matters worse, Southern continued to follow its 12-month introduction cycle and actually beat Northern to the market with its next generation product. The result for Northern was a further erosion in margins and market position.

Without making fundamental changes in its development process, which Northern management considered neither necessary nor within the charter of those working on the A14, Northern's attempt to push ahead with the A14 for the 1990 Christmas season was a dismal failure. The A14 product had so many problems in the field and was so expensive to manufacture that the product line became a serious financial drain on the company.

The key to Southern's success in the compact stereo market was its consistent ability to bring excellent products to market before its competitors. This ability was rooted in fundamental changes management had made in its development process. These included obtaining broad-based organizational and individual buy-in to key project goals at the onset and empowering and encouraging development teams to modify the development process. Teaching the organization the skills and attitudes needed for integrated problem solving, and then reconfiguring the design-build-test cycles to utilize fully that newfound problem-solving skill, was central to Southern's improved development capability. In addition it harnessed that capability to a marketing and pricing strategy that was well targeted at Northern's weaknesses. In effect, Southern changed the nature of competition in the industry; Northern was forced to play a game for which it was ill suited—a game Northern never fully comprehended until it was years behind in capability.

Southern Electronics' ability to bring a competitive product to market more rapidly than its chief rivals created three potential sources of advantage:

- *Quality of design*—more timely, on-target product offerings.
- *Performance*—more rapid use of emerging technologies.
- *Market share and margins*—more flexibility in pricing and share goals.

We have observed such advantages in a number of fast-cycle competitors in a wide range of industries. Firms such as Honda in automobiles, Applied Materials in semiconductor production equipment, ACS in angioplasty, Sony in audio products, Matsushita in VCRs, Philips in computer monitors, Hill-Rom in hospital beds, and Quantum in disk drives have made the ability to bring outstanding products to market rapidly a central feature of their competitive strategy. Once achieved, and subsequently maintained as the organization grows, an advantage built around fast-cycle capability founded on superior design-build-test skills seems to be strong and enduring.

Perhaps the most powerful effect of such capability is its leverage in changing the nature of competition. By improving development productivity and shortening the time between product generations, a firm such as Southern strengthened its own position and made painfully clear the weaknesses of its rival's approach to product development. Although Northern may have faced competitive difficulties no matter how it responded to the Southern challenge, by attempting accelerated development in the context of its traditional systems, Northern created internal confusion, strained its resources, and reduced the effectiveness of its development organization. In addition, previously enthusiastic, capable, and hard-working product managers became frustrated and disappointed.

This is what has happened in the auto industry and is currently under way in many other industries. It is what makes the acceleration of design-build-test cycles through fundamental change in the problem-solving process such a strategic advantage and a matter of utmost concern for senior management.

Reading IV–8
How to Integrate Work and Deepen Expertise

Dorothy Leonard-Barton, H. Kent Bowen, Kim B. Clark, Charles A. Holloway, and Steven C. Wheelwright

To be a leader in global manufacturing in the 1990s, a company must excel in two seemingly contradictory ways. First, it must constantly build and refresh its individual areas of expertise so it has the critical capabilities needed to stay ahead of the pack. And second, it must get its ever-changing mix of disciplines to work together in the ever-changing way needed to prevail in the ever-changing competitive environment. In other words, a company must find the way that best enables it at a given point in time both to come up with a product that meets customer needs better than the competition's *and* to create that product faster and more efficiently than competitors.

Most manufacturers, especially those companies that have reorganized themselves by cross-functional processes, have already discovered how difficult it is to integrate various disciplines and still maintain functional excellence. "Is it even possible to achieve both things?" executive after executive laments. There is a solution. It lies in the creative use of development projects.

As the critical juncture where functional groups meet, development projects are the true test of an organization's integrative abilities. More important, development projects can be used as a tool for strengthening the relationship among functions, while still giving them the room they need to advance their own expertise. To attain this leverage, though, executives must approach development projects with those goals in mind and must take into account how their company's strengths and weaknesses will help or hinder the project in trying to attain those goals.

Eastman Kodak learned this lesson when it developed its FunSaver camera in the late 1980s. Although the project was not all smooth sailing, it had a happy ending and, overall, superbly illustrates how a company can get functions to work together effectively, enhance functional expertise, and create a winning product to boot.

Looking to expand the company's product line, Kodak's technical-development group in the mid-1980s proposed an intriguing new product: a disposable camera. Film would be packaged in a simple, inexpensive, sealed plastic camera. Once the pictures had been taken, the consumer would hand the camera to a photofinisher, who would extract the film and discard the camera. (Later on, the company developed a system to recycle the used cameras.) Marketing would target this "single-use" camera at people who suddenly found themselves without their camera or who needed a camera for outdoor activities like boating or a beach outing, where they might be nervous about bringing an expensive camera. The disposable camera would be sold at convenience outlets and at major tourist attractions such as Disney World.

Initially, senior managers placed the project under the direction of the film division because they envisioned the FunSaver more as a premium film product than as a camera, but that proved to be a mistake. The project languished for months because the film division thought the camera would be a low-margin business that would cannibalize sales of film, a very high-margin business.

In the meantime, the camera division lobbied Kodak executives to take over the project, pointing out that Fuji intended to market a single-use camera in the United States that it had already introduced in Japan. The camera division also promised to structure the camera's costs and pricing so that its per-unit profit margin would match or exceed the company's current margin on a roll of film. Management gave the nod.

The project then took off. In a bid to streamline decision making, design the camera rapidly and efficiently, and ensure that its design would make it easy to manufacture, the camera division's development team decided to take several steps. It placed design and manufacturing, which traditionally were separate functional groups at Kodak, under one project leader. And it created a small, dedicated team of engineering, manufacturing, and marketing people, who shared the same work space. While this approach was new for Kodak, the team members believed it was essential to complete the project rapidly.

The project leader also strongly believed that computer-aided design and computer-aided manufacturing (CAD/CAM) could make a huge difference in designing the camera and optimizing its manufacturability. Kodak had used CAD/CAM systems in other projects, but they had been technical engineering systems used by specialists. The project leader wanted a CAD/CAM system that could do more—one that could help integrate the work of the entire team—and persuaded senior managers to buy into his vision of using the project to create this new capability. So, at the outset of the project, the team had three explicit goals: to produce the camera quickly; to create new methods for integration; and to develop new CAD/CAM technology that would enable Kodak to develop high-quality, easy-to-manufacture products faster and more efficiently.

Team members customized the new CAD/CAM system to make it easy for them to share information and get immediate feedback from one another. Each designer of a component, system, mold, or manufacturing subsystem would work on his or her part, then insert an updated drawing into the master schematic for the whole camera and/or the manufacturing process. Then each morning, a new composite design would be downloaded so that all engineers could see the effects of their combined efforts. Although only the original designer could alter the drawing of his or her part, anyone could critique any drawing and request changes. In addition, manufacturing engineers used the system to generate simulations of prototypes of the manufacturing process, which enabled them to work out kinks that would have shown up in the actual manufacturing system. As a result, they were able to reach full production much faster when actual manufacturing began.

Kodak introduced the FunSaver in 1988, just as Fuji's camera was hitting the U.S. market. But, aided by aggressive advertising, the FunSaver immediately grabbed the lead, and it has held on to it. Kodak quickly introduced two follow-on products, the Weekend, a waterproof camera, and the Panoramic, a camera with a wide-angle lens. These products contributed greatly to the overall success of the FunSaver: more than 100 million have been sold. Kodak was able to develop the Weekend and the Panoramic in record time by using not only the same basic product design and manufacturing process but also the same people, the same project-management procedures, and the same CAD/CAM system.

Besides creating a successful product, the FunSaver project proved to the company that integrating functions was possible and highly advantageous. In this case, the CAD/CAM technology fostered a significant degree of interaction among the design, tooling, and manufacturing engineers within engineering as well as between engineering and marketing. In addition, the CAD/CAM system provided discipline and a common set of principles for achieving the desired integration. Subsequent development teams at Kodak organized their work in a similar manner, and leaders of the FunSaver project implemented the new principles for achieving integration elsewhere, when they moved on to other projects.

The FunSaver project also gave Kodak a new technical capability: CAD/CAM. Rather than try to introduce this emerging technology on a companywide or divisional scale, Kodak—thanks to the inspiration of the project manager—gave it a test run on a manageable scale. Afterward, the company went on to widen its use of the CAD/CAM system, again by means of development projects, charging each team with customizing the system to best serve its needs.

The project also provided Kodak with a path leading away from a tradition that had become a major problem for the company: the autonomy of each functional group. Before the FunSaver, development projects had proceeded in sequential fashion, with one functional department completing its work and passing the results to the next in the chain. While this approach resulted in high performance and quality, it slowed decision making and meant that an extensive amount of rework typically had to be conducted during the development process in order to get all the components and subsystems of a product or process to mesh. In the new time-sensitive competitive environment, Kodak's design-engineering process, once a core capability, had become a rigidity.

Finally, the shaky beginning of the project provided a valuable lesson about development teams. It demonstrated that a project must fit the objectives of the organization that is responsible for carrying it out. The film division did not fully support the project. The camera division, however, got right behind it and refined its definition so that it would meet Kodak's profitability goals, advance companywide learning, and develop new capabilities.

Leveraging Capabilities, Breaking Rigidities

Core capabilities are not just technologies and workforce skills. They are a capacity for action. They are the essence of what makes an organization unique in its ability to provide value to customers over a long period of time. But this is hardly a revelation.

What many managers do not yet understand about capabilities, however, is that each consists of four elements whose interaction determines how effectively the organization can exploit it. Those elements are: *knowledge and skills*—technical know-how and personal "know-who," including ties to important groups such as government regulatory bodies or the scientific community; *managerial systems*—tailored incentive systems, in-house educational programs, or methodologies that embody procedural knowledge; *physical systems*—plant, equipment, tooling, and engineering work systems that have been developed over the years, and production lines and information systems that constitute compilations of knowledge; and *values*—the attitudes, behaviors, and norms that dominate in a corporation.

An interesting example of a core capability that encompasses several of these elements is networking at Digital Equipment. Workstations or terminals are on virtually everyone's desk and are connected with sophisticated software so that any employee around the world can reach any other. The physical system supports a very horizontal, networked style of management. Because individual freedom and responsibility are the values that DEC employees prize the most, any requests for action are more likely to be met, and met more quickly, if they are sent through the horizontal chain of the informal network than if they are passed through the vertical chain of command. This networking approach permeates the company's routines and culture and fosters a task-force approach to most issues.

Take DEC's CDA software project to develop a computer architecture for linking desktop-publishing products. During this project, which started in late 1986, DEC employees were asked to field-test prototype software sent to them over the network. Some 150 reviewers provided their feedback in an electronic notes file. The on-line file provided "living specs" that enabled the team to perfect the software code continually. Later, the team members estimated that 90 percent of the bugs in the software were found by this method. DEC's networking capability clearly enhanced the project's success.

DEC's networking system is also a reason why project ideas often originate in the ranks. Development teams are authorized to initiate projects off-line, which give rise to multiple, ongoing experiments, some of which became full-fledged projects. Corporate strategy evolves as much from these projects as from top-management direction. Such empowerment of employees engenders a tremendous sense of project ownership and spurs team members to make remarkable achievements, often in the face of great odds. Development teams charge ahead with little supervision, believing they will be able to alter the direction of their group significantly and turn the course of their mammoth corporation a critical degree or two.

The downside of a core capability, as we have pointed out, is that it can become a rigidity. A strength can become a weakness. The very reason for a company's traditional success can become an obstacle to developing new capabilities or maintaining the right balance of capabilities. This was most obvious in the technology-intensive companies that the Manufacturing Vision Group studied.

Consider the DECstation 3100 effort, which was undertaken in 1988 to develop DEC's first workstation based on reduced-instruction-set computing (RISC) technology. In this project, the internal field-testing capability that had served DEC so well in the past proved to be a liability. The project team recruited an internal "wrecking crew" of DEC volunteers to evaluate the prototype product and rewarded employees who found the most bugs with prototype workstations.

But both the DEC engineers designing the workstation and the volunteers who tested it focused almost exclusively on the machine's performance—on building a "hot box" of excellent hardware—rather than on the amount of applications software that could run on it. In hindsight, that is not surprising. DEC had become a giant in the computer industry as a result of its machines that shared DEC's proprietary VAX architecture and VMS operating system. A plethora of applications software was available for these machines. As a result, DEC engineers designing new machines typically did not worry about software availability. But the DECstation 3100 was aimed at giving DEC a foothold in the market dominated by RISC-based machines with UNIX operating systems.

Though the workstation was a technical gem and benefited from the wrecking crew's suggestions, it had difficulty penetrating the market because only 20 application programs had been developed by the time DEC introduced the product. Potential customers chose competing workstations, even though they were less advanced, because they had many more application programs (more than 500 in some cases). The team members naïvely believed that the DEC volunteers provided a good test market, that a hot box would sell simply on its performance, and that users would develop their own applications. DEC's engineers might have been happy to do so, but potential customers clearly were not.

The Dark Side of Values

Of the four elements that determine the effectiveness of a core capability, the one most overlooked and most misunderstood—and most difficult to change—is also the one that is the most powerful when aligned with the other three. This element is values.

A project undertaken in the early 1980s at Hewlett-Packard to develop the company's first personal computer illustrates how values can trip up a project. In this case, HP consciously pitted the project against one of its core values, the fierce autonomy of its divisions, but underestimated how hard it would be to change that core value. Each HP division traditionally focused on specific product lines and had its own marketing, manufacturing, engineering, finance, and personnel functions. Division managers were expected to make a profit, and if one division developed a component for another, it would "sell" it at full price. This approach made a lot of sense when the challenge was attacking sev-

Prototypes: Tools for Learning and Integrating

Effective development teams build prototypes often and early to learn rapidly, minimize mistakes, and successfully integrate the work of the many functions and support groups involved in the project. Prototypes can provide a common language and a focal point for people from a wide variety of disciplines. They help each group understand how its work affects the work of other groups and enable the team to spot problems that require cross-functional solutions. By doing so, prototypes not only enable products to be developed and launched more quickly but also result in products that are both higher-quality and more effective in fulfilling their intended purpose in the marketplace.

By prototypes, we do not mean merely the physical embodiments of the nearly final products made by craftspeople before production begins. We mean a series of representations, including early mock-ups, computer simulations, subsystem models, and models featuring system-level engineering, as well as production prototypes.

The most successful teams studied by the Manufacturing Vision Group frequently and regularly built a variety of prototypes; started creating prototypes of the entire system very early in the development process; and made each successive model more closely approach the desired final product in terms of form, content, and the customer experience it provoked. This process provided each team with an invaluable progress report on its success in dealing with unresolved issues and in meeting its schedule.

The most successful teams also built multiple copies of each prototype so that everyone involved in the development and eventual production, sale, use, and servicing of the product (including suppliers, prospective customers, and dealers) could rapidly evaluate it and offer feedback. Indeed, the best use of prototypes enabled companies to test regularly during the development process:

- The degree to which the decisions made about factors like design, specifications, and materials were executing faithfully *the intent* of the design.
- The cost and ease with which the manufacturing system—including production processes, purchasing, and test routines—could deliver the product.
- The extent to which the critical aspects of the unfolding product—including the functionality of individual subsystems and the way the subsystems work together—were satisfying the targeted customers' stated desires and latent needs (qualities or features they seem to want but have trouble articulating).

But the projects that exploited prototypes in this manner were the exception. Indeed, most of the projects studied by the Manufacturing Vision Group failed to create enough prototypes. And often the prototypes they did build (1) were not created early enough to solve problems that took more time and resources to solve later; (2) focused on only one or two components and not on the entire system; (3) were not used to test the manufacturing processes that would produce the final product; and (4) were not widely tested in the field, meaning that an opportunity to glean potentially invaluable reactions from customers was missed.

Building prototypes early is critical for companies because decisions affecting about 85 percent of the ultimate total cost of the product (including its manufacture, use, maintenance, and disposal) are typically made during the first 15 percent of a development project. Changes that are made late in the project invariably upset the sought-after balance among product features, cost, and quality, and therefore cause subsequent delays and suboptimal solutions. Conversely, if needed changes in, say, one subsystem can be spotted early or proposed changes for improving performance can be tested and acted on early, the ripple effect—the impact on and changes that need to be made in other subsystems—can be minimized.

For example, when Ford was developing its 1991 Crown Victoria/Grand Marquis in the late 1980s, it had its plant in St. Thomas, Ontario, build full-scale prototypes of the car on the same line producing the current model. As a result, line workers could suggest numerous ways to improve the manufacturability of the car relatively early in the project. This not only enabled the development team to alter designs without greatly disrupting the project but also gave plant employees in-depth information about the product that enabled them to move to full production relatively quickly when actual manufacturing began.

A process of building prototypes, testing and evaluating them internally and in the field, and then incorporating what is learned into the next prototype is a powerful mechanism for focusing a development team's efforts. These cycles also provide milestones, when management can review progress, assess what remains to be done, and consider whether alternative paths should be taken to complete the effort.

Companies can and should use prototypes in this way for the development of processes as well as products. At Chaparral Steel, for example, a team developing a new process will typically make small batches of steel using a prototype of the process, then refine the process, make more batches, refine the process more, and so on, gradually increasing the scale until the process reaches full-production levels. Chaparral also

Prototypes: Tools for Learning and Integrating (*concluded*)

typically puts prototypes on the shop floor from the outset of a project. That approach has enabled the company to push a given new process's performance level 15 percent to 20 percent beyond what would have been possible had it taken the traditional approach of conducting most of the development work off-site.

All in all, the extensive use of prototypes provides a structure, discipline, and approach that significantly enhance the rate of learning and integration in development projects. It gives both the project team and senior managers a powerful tool for effectively monitoring, guiding, and improving the development effort.

eral distinctly separate, fast-growing markets at the same time and the key to success was to be able to respond quickly to the demands of disparate customers. HP's phenomenal growth was proof of that. But in the PC project, it certainly was not a plus.

HP senior managers decided to attack the fledgling PC market by coordinating the efforts of four divisions. While integrating the technologies of several divisions seemed logical, the company had virtually no mechanism for getting them to work closely together. HP senior managers also did not make integration an explicit project goal; they, like the division leaders, assumed that the traditional practice of divisions selling components to one another would suffice.

HP assigned the main responsibility for the PC to a team that had just started work on a new terminal for the HP 3000 minicomputer at HP's minicomputer division in Cupertino, California. Corporate executives reasoned that the team could squeeze enough computing power into the terminal, known as the HP 150, to enable it to perform as a PC.

The job of developing the keyboard was originally given to the desktop computer division in Fort Collins, Colorado. The HP 150 team required that the keyboard cost only $25. The existing Fort Collins keyboard, designed for big computers, cost $100, and the general manager of the division did not believe that the team's request for a $25 keyboard was a high priority. Keyboard design rapidly became a bottleneck. Finally, the work was brought back to the team in Cupertino for a "crash" effort that ended up taking six months.

The responsibility for the HP 150's disk drive fell to the disk-drive division in Greeley, Colorado. Rather than developing a new cost-effective drive, it simply modified an existing one. And following HP custom, the division's leaders priced the drive so that they could make a profit on the "contract." This made it harder for the team to achieve the targeted margins. In retrospect, the team would have been much better off had it turned to outside suppliers to develop the keyboard and disk drive.

As a terminal, the HP 150 did well. Customers liked it, and the division made a profit on the sales. As a personal computer, however, the HP 150 never became profitable and was unable to gain significant market share.

One value that often affects development projects is the status that companies accord different disciplines. The dominance of a given discipline can create powerful capabilities, but it can also result in dangerous rigidities. That was particularly evident at DEC and at Hewlett-Packard, where the belief that design engineering was the most critical function caused design engineers to become the elite. This status enabled both companies to grow very strong in design, which became a strategic core capability and led to the creation of a stream of sophisticated products. But it also led to an arrogance in that group that eventually turned this capability into a rigidity. The attitude at HP and at DEC was that marketing and manufacturing were less valuable than design. As a result, designers began to assume that they knew better than customers what product features and attributes were best.

The pervasive perception that manufacturing people and their concerns were relatively less important eventually became a significant problem at both companies. As a result, manufacturing problems were tackled only late in projects, causing delays, rework, and higher expenses. And because of manufacturing's perceived lower status, fewer skilled people were attracted to the function. That left manufacturing less able to solve difficult problems, which further convinced everyone that the lower status was deserved. In the United States, this problem persists in many industries, which helps explain this country's persistent weakness in manufacturing engineering and process-equipment development.

This problem was a big one in HP's Hornet project, which developed an inexpensive spectrum-analyzer instrument for testing and analyzing radio-frequency and microwave signals, that HP introduced in the mid-1980s. The manufacturing engineers on the project were assigned to it only part-time and were not added to the team until the testing phase had already begun. As a result, there was almost no thought given to manufacturability in designing the product, and the ramp-up to full production was long, complicated, and stressful for the people working in the plant.

Overcoming Rigidities

HP's DeskJet project for developing a low-cost computer printer shows how a company can use a development project to overcome a rigidity. HP executives purposely designed the project to break the negative cycle that had sapped its strength in manufacturing and to get the company to start looking to other functions besides design engineering for creative solutions. Manufacturing was strongly represented from the beginning because the project involved—for HP—novel products, markets, and customers and, as a result, novel manufacturing cost and volume requirements. Once the project team was established, managers moved the manufacturing engineers to the R&D site and insisted that the R&D engineers consult with them continually regarding the design. Eventually, the manufacturing engineers became such valuable team members that the designers even lobbied for more of them.

Sure, the chief motive for initiating this new approach was to benefit the DeskJet project. But HP executives also wanted it to signal to the rest of the company that their view of the traditional status of design and manufacturing was changing. The project was a model for teamwork, and subsequent projects were organized along similar lines. Moreover, as the status of manufacturing engineers rose, the company began to attract stronger, broader, and more senior people to manufacturing.

Managing Development to Build Capabilities

In the wide range of products it studied, the Manufacturing Vision Group discovered several essential principles that can help companies correct conflicts and imbalances and build core capabilities. They are: an incremental approach to improving and expanding capabilities; a focus on process as well as product; innovative ways to challenge conventional thinking; and coherent vision, leadership, and organization.

Incremental Advances

Companies must strive to "push the envelope" steadily and avoid reliance on great leaps. And to avoid overwhelming their development teams, they also must be careful not to push on too many fronts at the same time. For example, a Kodak team that sought to develop the "factory of the future" failed in part because it tried to push the envelope on too many fronts.

Chaparral Steel's failure to develop an electric-arc saw for cutting steel in 1985 to 1987 shows that even the best can succumb to the temptation to try to make a leap that is just too far. Chaparral wanted to find a faster and more efficient way to cut the steel it produced and discovered that the aerospace industry was using an intensely hot electric arc to cut stainless steel. But the aerospace industry had tried neither to cut sections thicker than eight inches nor to cut through high volumes of material with this process, which is what Chaparral wanted it to do. But Chaparral employees, who time and again had figured out how to get equipment to perform in ways never intended, were undeterred. They discovered, however, that they lacked the knowledge of physics and electromagnetics necessary for the project to succeed. Even with the help of an outside consultant versed in the required physics, the project was beyond Chaparral's ken.

Focus on Manufacturing Process

U.S. companies have tended to push new products but not manufacturing processes. The conventional wisdom is that efforts to develop superior product features, functionality, and ease of use, and to lower costs will create demand for new processes. But in this paradigm, process will always lag product, which can severely handicap a company because the lead time needed to develop a new process typically exceeds that for a new product.

As a company in a process industry, Chaparral naturally focuses on production processes. But the internal capability that it has developed, which enables it to obtain feedback on processes from customers, suppliers, and competitors, and to revise processes continually in almost real time is nonetheless extraordinary. Furthermore, Chaparral does this frequently *in advance of* specific product requirements, thereby creating additional new-product opportunities. With the exception of Kodak and Chaparral, the other companies that the Manufacturing Vision Group studied rarely made processes the primary target of a development project. And in the handful of instances when they did, it was virtually always in response to a desire to create specific new products.

DEC's RA90 project to develop a high-density disk drive in the 1980s is a good example. While the project did not achieve many of the original product goals, DEC viewed it as a success because it achieved a major strategic goal set at the beginning: to lay a strong foundation for future high-density storage products. DEC executives were willing to invest heavily—to the tune of $1 billion, including a new manufacturing plant—in the development of skills, market position, and critical manufacturing processes. Team members were inspired to redefine the state of the art, which would put DEC in a strong competitive position in the long run.

This view may constitute a bit of Monday-morning quarterbacking on the part of DEC managers. But, as we discussed, it is important to realize that a development project can result in a less-than-successful product and still create a strategically crucial new process.

Something similar happened with Chaparral's Microtuff 10 steel project to develop new high-quality forging steels. Although sales of the end product were limited, hardly yielding enough revenues to justify the investment, the Microtuff 10 extended the company's product line. And the fact that Chaparral, a minimill, could even produce the kind of high-quality product that only large, integrated steel companies previously could make, burnished Chaparral's reputation as a high-tech company and gave it a big advantage over other minimills.

Of course, the best projects to improve processes are those that also result in product successes, which was the case with Kodak's efforts to improve its antistatic coating process. For years, Kodak had been a leading manufacturer of micrographic films, which include the film used in microfiche machines in libraries. Studies showed that some users—the main customers are banks and insurance companies—thought that the images on Kodak films were less sharp than those on competitors' films. Kodak determined that the problem wasn't clarity; it was darkness. The images on its films appeared a bit darker because of a coating placed on the film to reduce the buildup of static electricity, which attracts dust.

The project team charged with developing a clearer antistatic coating spotted a recent process invention made by a Kodak unit in France and used it to develop quickly a new manufacturing process. New films reached the streets within a year—a feat that enabled Kodak not merely to maintain its market share but also to increase it.

"Out-of-the-Box" Thinking

A third ingredient for building capabilities and breaking rigidities is an ability to challenge conventional thinking. The Manufacturing Vision Group found several effective ways to create the out-of-the-box thinking needed to do this.

One method is the clever use of benchmarking. Most companies benchmark products or processes to find out what competitors are doing so that they can match the best or go them one better. But there are creative ways a company can use benchmarking to attain a sustainable leadership position. Chaparral demonstrated such creative thinking when it looked at practices outside its industry to develop the horizontal caster, a project we described earlier.

Another way to challenge conventional thinking—and stay ahead of competitors—is to be more resourceful and industrious in tapping the best minds in the field. When Chaparral began the Microtuff 10 project, it approached the Colorado School of Mines about cosponsoring a technical conference on forging steel, and the school agreed. The conference attracted technical papers and brought together experts who otherwise would not have convened. Chaparral employees learned enough to create new formulas for forging steel as well as related production processes.

Breaking the conventional flow of information is yet another way to challenge conventional thinking. Often, this can help a company alter its basic values so they help rather than hinder it in adapting to changes in its competitive environment. During HP's DeskJet printer project, marketing people conducted studies in shopping malls and brought back 24 suggestions for changes that they believed would ensure market acceptance. But design engineers heeded only five, discounting the others largely as a "marketing wish list." The people from marketing and the project leaders were so convinced of the important nature of the information, however, that they insisted that the design engineers go to the malls to hear for themselves what test customers were saying. Grudgingly, the engineers went, listened, and then did an about-face and made 17 more changes.

In DEC's LAN Bridge 200 project to develop a communications product for linking computer networks, the marketing people discovered early on several important features that users wanted. However, they lacked the stature and self-confidence to persuade the design engineers to include the features. Not until two senior DEC technologists gathered the same information from customers was it actually used. By the time the new information had been incorporated into the design, however, the project schedule had slipped four months.

In subsequent projects at both HP and DEC, development teams made greater efforts to ensure that designers heard what customers were demanding and heeded it. In other words, the companies had learned.

Vision, Leadership, and Organization

While constantly striving to make incremental advances, focusing on process, and generating creative thinking are important, three things are even more crucial. More than anything, a project's success—and the success of a company's range of projects—in enhancing competitiveness and generating knowledge depends on a coherent vision, strong leadership, and organization. A clear vision enables projects to take off from the start. Then, when a project faces seemingly impossible odds or hits a point where failure seems inevitable, the right kind of leadership can pull it through.

There is no one right way to organize and lead a project. Companies that master the art of picking the best for each project will end up with more than a system for managing development projects effectively. They will end up with a system that cultivates leaders who excel in getting functions to work together and advance their knowledge. Such managers will enable manufacturers not merely to attain the lead but to keep it.

PART V Conclusion

We began this book by addressing the question of how general managers should integrate technology and innovation in their firm's strategy. Within the framework of an evolutionary theoretical perspective, Part II provided insights into the substance and enactment of a comprehensive and integrated technology strategy. In Parts III and IV, we examined the ways in which technology strategy is enacted in practice. We end the book by recapitulating some of its major themes in terms of key innovation challenges faced by the top management of established firms.

Innovation Challenges in Established Firms

Throughout this book, we have posited that the innovation challenges facing established firms exist at a number of levels. One challenge entails exploiting a firm's existing opportunities to the fullest; relatively few are available, and they vanish if not seized. The materials on using product development to augment and renew a firm's capabilities provide useful tools to help the general manager meet this challenge. But this is not enough; existing opportunities will eventually be exhausted, and today's success is no guarantee for tomorrow's. Thus a second challenge involves generating entirely new opportunities, as discussed in the materials on corporate research, entrepreneurship, and innovation.

A third challenge involves balancing the portfolio of existing and new opportunities over time. This task is particularly difficult for two reasons: Resources at any given time are limited; and new and existing innovation opportunities require that conflicting management approaches be exercised simultaneously. As noted in the chapter on designing and managing systems for corporate innovation (Part III), most companies are more comfortable pursuing these challenges in sequence. Notable exceptions, however, exist: The 3M company has, for decades, continued to reinvent itself from within; Intel Corporation has transformed itself from a memory to a microcomputer company; and Hewlett-Packard Company has evolved twice—from an instrument into a computer company and, more recently, into the world's leading laser and inkjet printer company.

It seems appropriate to conclude this book with a case study that offers a window on how the key innovation challenges are managed in one of the world's leading high-technology companies. "Reshaping Apple Computer's Destiny 1992" examines the firm from its inception through John Sculley's attempts at visionary technological leadership in the computer industry. The case offers the opportunity to revisit, in some depth, many of the themes that make studying the materials in this book worthwhile.

Case V–1
Reshaping Apple Computer's Destiny 1992

Johanna M. Hurstak and David B. Yoffie

In 1992, Apple Computer was going through its second revolution in only a decade. The first came in 1984, when Apple made the transition from the Apple II computer to the Macintosh (Mac). Apple emerged from that experience as the most profitable personal computer company in the world. But now the $80 billion PC industry was in crisis, and John Sculley, Apple's chairman and CEO, was again confronted with the task of reshaping the corporation. Sculley's first steps were to launch a new, ambitious strategy to gain market share and diversify into related technologies. In the process, Sculley broke all the old rules at Apple: he cut perks, brought in new senior managers, introduced formal quality and performance systems, entered alliances with former enemies, and started pulling resources away from Apple's core Macintosh business.

Through the summer of 1992, Apple's implementation had been almost flawless: Market share was up, profits were up, and new products were coming to market as fast as any major competitor. But Sculley was fighting against time: Cutthroat pricing in the PC industry was squeezing Apple's margins; one slip in execution could be disastrous. Sculley summed up his dilemma:

> We are running as fast we can, but we still have gaps between our human resource needs, our organization, and our strategy. We have also gotten so lean at the top, we lack bench strength. In addition, Apple seems to be one of the toughest organizations in the world to change. Our culture revolves around the Macintosh and building great products that will change the world. This culture is not only strong, it's like a religion—a theology. And this theology is so deeply rooted, I worry about how the organization will react to more systems, more cuts, and less resources. How can I engineer a revolution that will make Apple one of the best professionally managed companies in the world, while keeping up the pressure, keeping up the innovation, and keeping the key people at Apple?

Sculley Takes Charge

John Sculley seemed an unlikely candidate to run the world's second largest PC company. Sculley held an MBA from Wharton Business School and a degree in architectural design from Brown University. Although nontechnical by training, he tinkered in electronics as a youth, even filing a patent application for a TV picture tube. As one of the first MBAs hired by Pepsi, he began his climb to the presidency by driving delivery trucks. Rising rapidly in the firm, Sculley left his position as head of U.S. sales and marketing to take over PepsiCo's floundering international operations in 1973. He returned to Pepsi-Cola as president four years later, after transforming the unprofitable business into an efficient revenue generator.

During his six years as Pepsi-Cola's president (1976–1983), Sculley instilled a sense of accountability and discipline without dismantling Pepsi's existing, decentralized corporate structure. He was praised for building the infrastructure of Pepsi's fragmented independent chain of bottlers by establishing regional chain trading areas to manage distribution, sales promotion, and cost accounting. Sculley also masterminded the highly successful "Pepsi Challenge" and "Pepsi Generation" advertising campaigns. By 1983, many believed that Sculley was on the fast track to succeed Donald Kendall as PepsiCo's next chairman.

In April 1983, Apple's cofounder, Steve Jobs, lured Sculley from PepsiCo to take on the presidency at Apple. Sculley's challenge was to bring organizational and marketing discipline to Apple without sacrificing creativity and spirit. However, tensions mounted between Sculley and Jobs soon thereafter. Eventually Jobs resigned after a well-publicized dispute with Sculley and the board of directors in 1985.

The 1985 Reorganization

To solidify his control over Apple's fractious organization, Sculley reorganized Apple in June 1985. He combined the Apple II and Mac divisions into a single Product Operations Group, consolidated manufacturing, and reduced the workforce by 20 percent (1,200) in Apple's first major layoff. Sculley's key decision, however, was to move Apple out of the home computer market and into the mainstream of business. Said Sculley, "We had to move away from building what engineers wanted to what the market wanted . . . We went after business because that's the biggest market with the highest profit and the fastest growth in the PC industry." Sculley focused Apple on a unique niche—desktop publishing. The Mac was particularly well suited to this task because of its sophisticated graphics and inherent ease of use.

In order to bring discipline to the organization, Sculley put in stronger financial controls and focused on key financial expenses. Apple's financial model was based on Sculley's "50-50-50" rule: sell 50,000 Macs a month, with a gross margin of 50 percent, to achieve a $50 stock price. To Sculley, the company's most important "number" was the gross margin. When he came to Apple in 1983, that figure was roughly 42 percent. By 1988, Sculley increased gross margin to 52 percent, the highest in the PC industry. However, below-the-line expenditures ballooned. There were few controls on R&D and little direct accountability. In addition, Sculley spent heavily on advertising to define Apple as an industry innovator.

People and Culture

Sculley came to a company renowned for its exciting and countercultural work environment, where employees often wore T-shirts that proclaimed "working 90 hours a week and loving it." Sculley described Apple as "the Ellis Island of American business because it intentionally attracted the dissidents who wouldn't fit into corporate America." Employees believed that they were the power of Apple and that management's role was to create an environment in which they could do wonderful things. People tended to garner influence by their charismatic personalities and leadership of successful technical projects. Employees dubbed this "the star system" and "management by celebrities."

Another aspect of the Apple culture was that technology was not just the product; it permeated everything that was done in the organization. All employees had Macintoshes at work, and all were linked electronically. Apple offered employees generous discounts and "loan-to-own" programs on its products. Computers were used in all facets of work, and the style of the Macintosh was reflected in the style of work at Apple. A marketing manager described this phenomenon:

> Here's the most interesting thing about our culture—we are what we make. I've never seen an organization where the personality of the organization is so intertwined with the personality of the product—individualistic, pure, uncompromised, ahead of everyone else, so elegant it can't fail. We *are* the Macintosh here.

Sculley was determined to preserve the positive elements of this culture and later recalled, "In 1985, I consciously did everything not to change the work environment. Rather than reaching for experienced managers, I promoted people in the company who were closely identified with either the culture or the values or were regarded as prophets of the vision." He institutionalized the Silicon Valley traditions of off-site meetings and beer busts, and made them "a fundamental way of doing business at Apple." One of Sculley's first attempts to alter Apple's direction was a 1986 speech calling for investment in computer networking technology. However, he quickly backed down when his office was besieged by a group of angry engineers. Sculley commented, "I made a mistake in not realizing how truly deep the company's link to its vision really was. They all really believed in the machine for the individual. When I first started pushing in the area of networking, I was stopped. I was simply pushing too far too fast."

Sculley likened joining Apple to pursuing a graduate degree at a university: "You select Apple because you think it can offer you an incredible, life-growing experience. Indeed, we seem to have become one of the country's most elite 'higher education' institutions, because there tend to be more than 50 applications for virtually every unadvertised job. People gravitate to us with the idea of staying three to five years and then going off to start their own companies." In return for asking people to "pour a part of [them]self into the success of the company," Sculley believed that Apple owed its employees "a chance to realize their quest to grow, to achieve, and to make a difference in the world." They were also rewarded handsomely, with salaries and benefits "in the 90th percentile."[1]

The company had a very open environment. All employees were connected on a worldwide computer network called *Applelink.* Applelink provided many services. A primary use was as an electronic mail system. It had a central library of company information and a database of old presentations Apple employees had made. Apple's current stock price was available. Workers could access many systems, including benefits information, and could update the system with desired changes. Applelink included *Hotlinks,* an informal employee informa-

---

[1]"Wherefore Art Thou, Apple?" *Upside,* October 1991, p. 46.

tion service. Employees also used Hotlinks to access *Can We Talk?*, an employee conferencing system. Can We Talk? consisted of many ongoing, often free-wheeling, employee debates of current events, social issues, or corporate issues.

Technology enabled executives to take the opinion pulse of the organization and employees to make their feelings known. Personnel were accustomed to going directly to top management to express their opinions about corporate strategy or other issues, using Applelink. Moreover, they expected to receive prompt responses. Applelink was designed so that both recipients and senders could forward copies of links to any other employees as desired. It was not unusual for links to be forwarded over and over again until dozens (and occasionally hundreds or even thousands) of employees received a copy. This was especially the case with links that addressed controversial issues, such as strategy or career mobility for women.

Hotlinks often resulted in grassroots campaigns within Apple. One example was a discussion about wasting paper, which culminated in a companywide recycling program. Another was the employee profit-sharing plan. In the spring of 1990, Apple executives changed the profit-sharing formula to reflect the strategic goal of greater market share. The new formula set revenue goals rather than just profit goals, raised the threshold for profit sharing to kick in, and strengthened the relationship between the goal and the share given to employees. This was done, however, at about the same time as several key executives were awarded large bonuses, and Sculley had talked about slowing revenue growth in an external speech. These items were discussed heatedly on Hotlinks, and ultimately the collective resistance that came through Hotlinks caused management to change the formula.

The 1988 Reorganization

As Mac sales exploded, Sculley announced yet another reorganization in 1988 (see Exhibit 1). He established three regional sales divisions: Apple Education and the Pacific; Europe; and U.S.A. In addition, he created Apple Products division. It was responsible for integrating and coordinating the process of bringing products to market and included all manufacturing, product development, product marketing, and the Advanced Technologies Group (ATG). ATG was created to explore revolutionary ideas and high-risk technologies. Apple Products was headed by Jean-Louis Gassee, a charismatic Frenchman who became famous in the industry for his personality (and his diamond earring). Gassee had built Apple's French market as director of French marketing. One person familiar with Gassee stated:

> He was a very bright man. He created creativity and pride within the engineering organization. He brought a strong French engineering tradition to Apple Products. The French engineering tradition emphasizes creativity and uniqueness as what engineers do.

Another Apple employee observed:

> Gassee felt that it was more art than science, and that you didn't design products for specific markets, but that you built elegant PCs at whatever cost.

EXHIBIT 1 Apple Computer Organization Chart, 1988

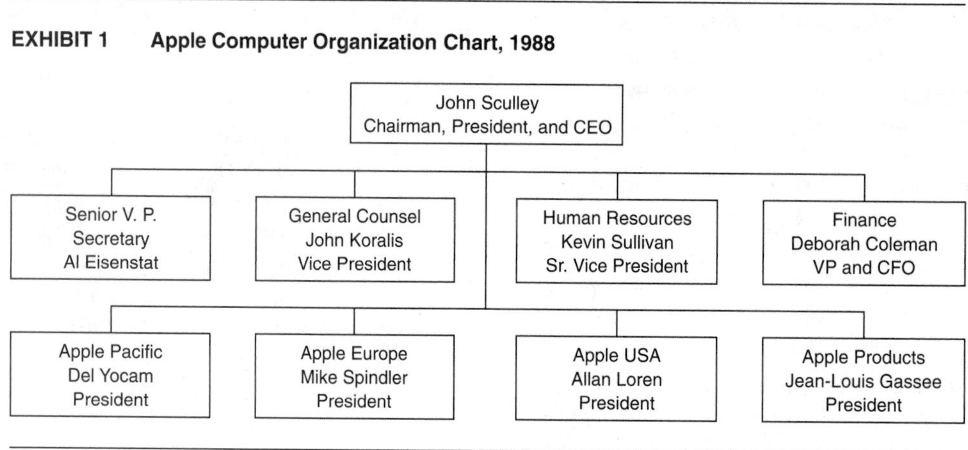

One of Sculley's greatest frustrations in the late 1980s was that his proposals for new directions in technology were often rebuffed by Gassee. Gassee strongly believed that Apple should sell single-user, proprietary systems that had very high margins with premium prices. Indeed, under Gassee's direction, Apple raised the Mac's average selling price more than 60 percent between 1988 and 1990.

During this time, Sculley brought in experienced managers from other computer companies, including Allan Loren from Cigna Information as president of Apple USA, and Kevin Sullivan from DEC as vice president of human resources. Sculley also hired more managers at operational levels—over 3,000 new employees during 1988—bringing the total to more than 9,000, only 75 of whom had been with the company at its inception. Yet the dedication to Apple values remained intact. Within six months, even former IBM and DEC employees would wholeheartedly embrace the Apple culture.

At the worldwide managers' meeting in 1990, Sculley and Spindler told the managers,

> Apple faces some incredible challenges in FY91, but we also have extraordinary strength on which to build. That strength is our employees. They're by far the most talented, enthusiastic, and productive group of people that either of us have seen in any organization. They're proud to work at Apple and ready to do whatever it takes to make Apple successful. Given this resource, and your leadership, we are confident that we can meet the challenges we face.

Apple's Competitive Position

Apple held a peculiar position in the computer industry as it entered the 1990s. It was the only real alternative hardware and software standard for PCs other than the IBM standard. (See the Appendix for background on the PC industry.) It was also more vertically and horizontally integrated than any other PC company, with the exception of IBM. Apple designed its products, usually from scratch, specifying unique chips, disk drives, monitors, and even unusual shapes for its chassis. It assembled most of its own products in state-of-the-art factories, considered among the most automated and modern in the industry. In addition, Apple developed its own operating systems software for the Mac, some of its applications software, and many of its peripherals. Indeed, almost one-third of Apple's business was imaging products, like printers and scanners designed exclusively to support Macintosh computers. About half of Apple's revenues came from overseas, and roughly half the U.S. sales were to education, where Apple had more than 50 percent of the market.

Apple's products needed to be easier to use, easier to network, and more versatile than comparable IBM machines. In many core software technologies like multimedia (integrating video, sound, and data), Apple had a two-year lead on vendors such as Microsoft. Since Apple controlled all aspects of the computer, from board design to software, it could offer a better computer "system," where all the parts—software, hardware, and peripherals—interacted in a coherent way. Unlike IBM and its clones, Apple gave customers a complete desktop solution. This made Apple's customers the most loyal in the industry. As one analyst commented, "The majority of IBM users 'put up' with their machines, but Apple's customers 'love' their Macs."

Trouble started brewing, however, in early 1990. While Gassee was raising prices, IBM PCs and clone prices fell precipitously. And that was not the only issue, according to Sculley:

> We were increasingly viewed as the "BMW" of the computer industry. Our Macintoshes were almost exclusively high-end, premium-priced computers that would continue to have limited success in penetrating the corporate marketplace. Without lower prices, we would be stuck selling to our installed base. We were also so insular that we could not manufacture a product to sell for under $3,000. We constantly fell into the trap of "creeping elegance" with not-invented-here mentality. We spent more than two years, for instance, designing a portable computer that had to be "perfect." But in the end, it was a disaster—it was 18 months late and 10 pounds too heavy.

Apple was also plagued with severe morale problems. An employee survey in 1990 indicated that most employees were still proud to work at Apple, but a majority thought that Apple lacked direction and that management was unaware of the challenges faced by employees. Many blamed Apple USA President Allan Loren, who would tell employees at communications meetings they were "stupid." And Apple's CFO, Joe Graziano, was quoted as saying, "We had a fundamental problem. Our own employees, even management, were complaining, 'What's the direction of the company?' "[2] There was

[2] *Upside,* October 1991, p. 37.

EXHIBIT 2 Applelink Sent to John Sculley

To: SCULLEY From: XXXXXX

Item forwarded by SCULLEY to SULLIVAN6 SPINDLER

Item 6795575 25-Sept-90 10: 58PDT

John:

The results of the recent employee survey were presented in our communications meeting yesterday. in my almost ten years with Apple I have never been more concerned about the health of our company than I am now.

I want to express directly to you the problem that our company is experiencing and, as I see it, the solution. I refer to "the problem" because I do think that there is one basic problem which is responsible for the serious weaknesses which were dramatically brought before us by the survey.

THE PROBLEM:
Apple has become a company that is too preoccupied with management and groups rather than great new products. Most of our potentially creative energy is wasted in management identity, culture, and politics. Managerial role-playing does not create great new products. In short, the mainstream culture of Apple has become the culture of the meeting room instead of the culture of the computer product studio/workshop.

THE SOLUTION:
Integrate the job of doing management into the studio/workshop culture of the company. This means:

1. the compensation for management work should be on a par with creative design and engineering work;

2. we should have known better than to allow a work environment where managers sit in closed offices and non-managers sit in less attractive cube-spaces (this is presently happening all over the company)—put managers in the same type of office as everybody else (for the first 10 years of the company everybody, managers and non-managers, had the same kind of work space);

3. everyone at Apple should know that they are working in direct support of the concept/design/engineering/manufacturing/marketing process that the company should be about—define that process, make internal videos about it, make sure everybody knows what it is.

We must first be willing to integrate our disciplines and culture into the product and market creation process before we can really manage anything. We need to mature past the "I am a manager so I am special" syndrome and grow into the realization that, at Apple, each individual contributor to the creative process is absolutely, indispensably special.

also expressed concern about the development of management hierarchy. (Exhibit 2 shows an Applelink sent to Sculley in 1990.)

Sculley Builds a New Apple

While the company was still profitable and before a real crisis emerged, Sculley sought to redefine Apple. One of his first moves was to clean house. By February 1990, Sculley put a new executive team in place (see Exhibits 3 and 6). Loren resigned, Gassee resigned, and Sculley promoted Michael Spindler, a German and the former president of Apple's highly profitable European division, to be president and chief operating officer. This was an emotional transition because Gassee represented part of the old core of Apple—a charismatic manager dedicated to developing cutting-edge products. Perhaps most important, Sculley realized that he would continue to have difficulty shifting the company's direction unless he had a deeper understanding of the technical issues and how the bowels of the organization worked. He therefore appointed himself chief technology officer (CTO) and began to oversee R&D and product development. This last move was especially controversial, but Sculley saw no choice. He said, "The CTO does not have to be the chief scientist, but does have to make decisions on technology. Apple is a technology company and the most important business decisions are technology/product decisions." To bring himself up to

EXHIBIT 3 Apple Computer Organization Chart, May 1992

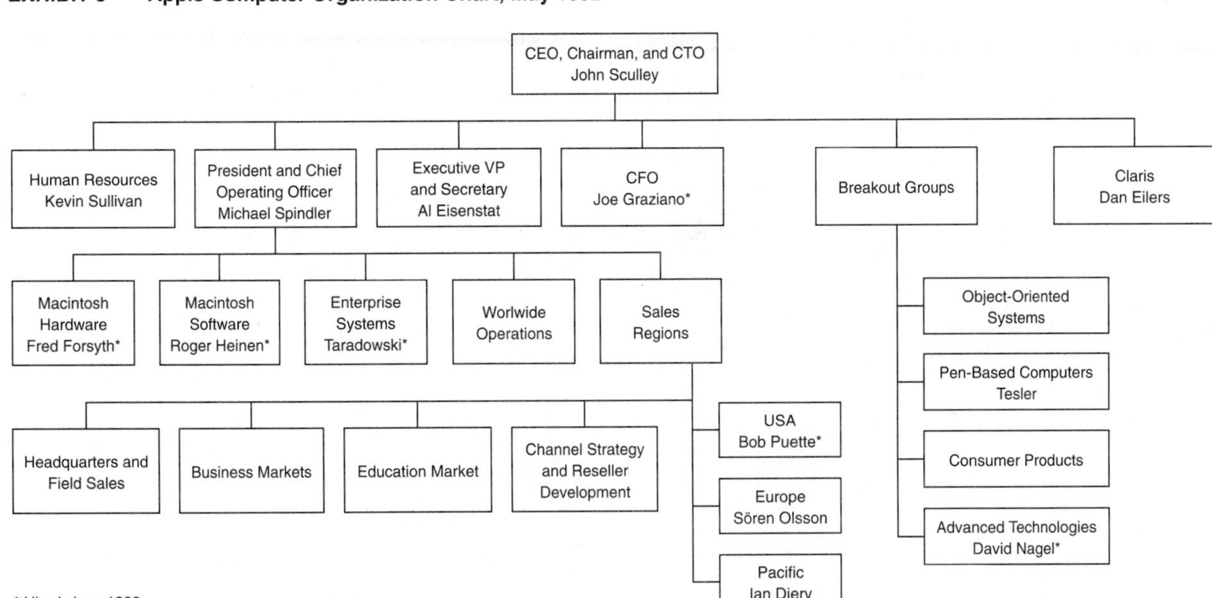

speed, he met daily with engineers to discuss product plans and technology issues whenever he was not traveling. He said he did not want executive summaries—he wanted to learn the technology and become involved in technology choices.

Agreeing that high margins and proprietary technology were no longer part of a sustainable long-term strategy, the new team worked together to plan Apple's course. Four principles would drive the corporation into the 1990s: (1) get customer input upfront; (2) time-to-market was critical. Bonuses would be tied to meeting specific milestones. If people miss, they won't get fired, but they will no longer get extra compensation; (3) innovate at the lowest possible price point versus the old philosophy of create great technology (usually at the high end); and (4) no sacred cows—everything must be questioned. Moreover, the driving force behind Apple's new approach would be maximizing shareholder value. The financial markets were pricing computer hardware companies at roughly 10 to 12 times earnings, and software companies at 20 to 40 times earnings. Apple's stock had a PE of roughly 10 and Sculley was committed to getting Apple's PE closer to companies like Microsoft (PE of ~45) and Novell (PE of ~50).

To execute this philosophy, Sculley gave the CFO, Graziano, responsibility for developing a new financial model, and gave Spindler day-to-day operations. Sculley focused on new product development and technologies. Unlike prior management teams, this new executive staff maintained close personal ties; Spindler and Sculley, in particular, kept each other informed about their strategies and the actions, working in locked-step on every major issue.

New Financial Discipline

To regain market share and compete with the clone companies, Spindler and Graziano overhauled Apple's financial strategy to target gross margins in the low 40 percent range—with the same hoped-for pretax profits. According to Graziano: "We had the highest expense structure in the industry. If you look at the cost structure of Apple and its resellers, marketing and distribution costs more than production. If Apple was to survive, we had to get into a crisis mode." (See Exhibit 4 for financials.)

To steer Apple toward lower gross margins, Graziano cut perks such as company cars and lavish parties—perks that had disappeared in the rest of Silicon Valley by the mid-1980s. Other symbolic cost-cutting measures included reducing subsidies to the company cafeterias and fitness center. By 1992, the joke was that everyone would have to

EXHIBIT 4 Apple Financials over Selected Years

	Q1 1992*	Q1 1991	1991	1990	1989	1988	1987	1985	1983	1981
Total revenues ($ millions)	$1,863	$1,676	$6,309	$5,558	$5,284	$4,071	$2,661	$1,918	$983	$334
Cost of sales	1,049	815	3,314	2,606	2,695	1,991	1,296	1,118	506	170
Research and development	131	140	583	478	421	273	192	72.5	60	21
Marketing and distribution			1,740	1,556	1,340	908	655	478	230	55
General and administrative	420	492	224	207	195	180	146	110	57	22
Operating income	263	228	447	712	634	620	371	103	130	66
Net income	166	151	310	475	454	400	218	61.3	77	39
Property, plant, equipment and other			275	321	284	186	121	66	64	NA
Depreciation and amortization			204	202	124	77	70	41	22	NA
Cash dividends paid			56	53	50	39	15	—	—	NA
Cash and temporary cash investment	988	984	893	997	809	546	565	337	143	73
Accounts receivable	973	853	907	762	793	639	406	220	136	42
Inventories	643	409	672	356	475	461	226	167	142	104
Property, plant, and equipment	456	436	448	398	334	207	130	176	110	31
Total assets	3,745	3,157	3,494	2,976	2,744	2,082	1,478	936	557	255
Total current liabilities	1,271	1,072	1,217	1,027	895	827	479	90	129	70
Total shareholders' equity	1,923	1,545	1,767	1,447	1,486	1,003	837	550	378	177
Permanent employees			12,386	12,307	12,068	9,536	6,236	4,326	4,645	2,456
International sales/sales (%)	45	45	45	42	36	32	27	22	22	27
Gross margin/sales (%)	44	51	47	53	49	51	51	42	49	49
R&D/sales (%)	7	8	9	9	8	7	7	4	6	6
ROS† (%)	8.91	9.01	4.91	8.55	8.59	9.83	8.19	3.20	7.83	11.68
ROA‡ (%)	4.43	4.78	8.87	15.96	16.55	19.21	14.75	6.55	13.82	15.29
Return on equity (%)	9	10	19	32	36	44	28	12	24	44
Stock price range	53.5–59.5‖		40.5–73.3	24.3–47.8	32.5–50.4	35.5–47.75	20.3–59.8	7.3–15.6	8.6–31.6	6.8–7.3
P/E ratio	20.31#		12.9	10.5	12.9	13.6	20.3	22.1	30.6	24.3
Market value§	6,522		6,751	4,150	5,166	5,033	4,914	1,360	2,368	1,320

*Quarter ending Dec. 27, 1991
†ROS = net income/total revenues
‡ROA = net income/total assets
§Year-end stock price times the number of shares outstanding
‖Week ending June 4, 1992
#For 12 months ending March 1992
SOURCE: Apple annual reports and *Value Line*.

time-share the vacuum cleaner to clean around their cubicles, because janitors would be the next to go. Apple's pay scales were also brought down from the 90th percentile to slightly above average for Silicon Valley.

To improve the return on Apple's R&D expenditures, Graziano tightened the R&D allocation process and established formal project reviews. R&D, which had no accountability by project, was restructured to track revenues on a project basis with bonuses tied to specific milestones. Graziano strove to push profit and loss responsibility as far down the company as possible. He expected corporate services to justify their existence and compete with outside vendors. Even after-sales support services, which had traditionally been handled through dealers and toll-free 800 numbers, were put on a profit and loss basis, and customers had to pay for telephone advice after 90 days through the use of 900 numbers.

While Graziano revamped the financial model, Spindler worked to improve operations and build accountability into the organization. Spindler, nicknamed "Diesel" by his colleagues for his tenacious management style, recalled the situation in early 1990: "The whole organization was built on abundance; there were no limits on resources. We had to explain why it's a dynamic, ruthless world." Spindler commanded universal respect among his direct reports. Unlike Gassee's staff meetings, which were filled with theological discussions about computers, Spindler kept a tight focus on the issues at hand. He met weekly with 6 to 10 critical people, where he continually stressed time-to-market issues and sought to resolve any operational conflicts.

To maintain operational discipline, Spindler reconfigured domestic operations to give profit and loss responsibility to smaller groups. He developed a new budgeting process with Graziano that laid out key operational goals and established accountability measures, through departmental budgets, marketing initiatives, and product calendars. Spindler noted that people were loyal to the product, not the company. He said, "We need to realign people to work for the company, not themselves." He made Apple's largely salaried compensation structure more commission based and created performance-related incentives to reward good management. Spindler also selected the most experienced managers and established strong management teams at the operating level. In the Mac core, he created a team of five managers (three geographic heads—U.S., Asia Pacific, and Europe—along with manufacturing and software) with increased responsibility.

The clearest indication of Spindler's success came from the testimony of a manager in the advanced technology group: "A few years ago," he noted, "there were more projects than people and no clear responsibility. Projects used to take on a life of their own; if management tried to cut one, engineers would simply rename it and carry on. Now, one person is in charge of each project, and there is an annual review process emphasizing measurable outcomes."

The New Strategy

Sculley, Spindler, and Graziano formulated a new strategy in 1990 and 1991 that had three key components: (1) reinvigorate the Mac business with a strategy to gain market share; (2) expand the Mac business into the world of enterprise computing (i.e., large corporations) through greater openness and less emphasis on proprietary systems; and (3) diversify Apple into new technologies that leveraged Apple's strengths in software.

The strategy of gaining market share required Apple to do two critical things: lower prices *and* costs to attract a larger number of users; and reduce cycle time radically. By lowering prices, Apple would match the competition. Apple also cut its workforce in a major layoff. However, Sculley noted that lower costs and higher volumes were not enough: Apple also had to bring out "hit products" through the first half of the 1990s (i.e., new Macs and derivations of older products that could be produced every 6 to 12 months). The competition was becoming so intense, Sculley believed, Apple's best chance to keep the Mac profitable was to give customers more and more options, faster. The first hit product was the Powerbook, an aggressively priced notebook computer that Apple introduced in October 1991. The Powerbook was a spectacular success, predicted to generate $1 billion in revenue within 12 months of its introduction.

The second part of the strategy was to make Apple more "open"—both technically and organizationally. On the technical side, Apple would start to offer solutions that would work with other firms' computers. On the organizational side, Sculley believed that scale economies in key technologies were simply too great in the 1990s for any one firm to control them all in-house. A new operating system, for instance, could take five years to develop and cost $500 million in R&D. He therefore concluded that Apple should build a "federation" of alliances with partners that could help leverage Apple's strengths, especially in software. He said, 'We have to have partners; we have to become more open; we have to penetrate a broader market or our application developers will abandon us; we have to license technologies in and be willing to license technologies out." However, Apple shocked the world when it chose its first significant alliance partner—its longtime nemesis, IBM.

During the summer of 1991, IBM and Apple formed two joint ventures. The underlying concept of the IBM-Apple relationship was that both companies could share costs underlying the risks of developing new technologies, but ultimately, the parent companies would still compete in computers. The JVs would operate independently, shipping their software products to both parents at agreed upon transfer prices. IBM would provide the semiconductor technology while Apple would provide most of the software and personnel.

The third leg of Sculley's strategy was to move beyond desktop and portable computers to a whole new generation of products. Sculley wanted Apple to participate in broader markets, including the mass consumer market. At the Consumer Electronics Show in January 1992, Sculley announced that Apple would create a new era of "personal electronics" with "personal digital assistants" (PDAs). PDAs would utilize Apple's most advanced software technologies. For instance, the first announced product was called Newton—a one-pound device the size of a videocassette. Newton would use a pen for data entry and combined the features of a notepad, calendar, and fax machine. Even more important, it had "intelligence"; the machine could understand and interpret everyday language, like "schedule lunch with Bob next Tuesday." The operational challenges for Apple, however, were significant. For these products to be big hits, research suggested that they must sell for $500 or less. In addition, consumers needed to be educated about the new technology, and Apple would have to sell PDA through entirely new channels. To solve these problems, Sculley enlisted the help of Japanese consumer electronics giants, particularly Sharp, Toshiba, and Sony. Although the relationship differed with each firm, Apple typically asked its Japanese partner to manufacture the hardware, while the partner got a license for Apple's software with the rights to sell the final product under its own brand name.

Organization

When Sculley described his vision of Apple in the 1990s as a federation, he saw the Mac forming the mature and profitable core while other businesses, such as the IBM and Japanese joint ventures, grew around it. Each business had its own management with profit and loss responsibility. Where in the past, Mac had dominated the entire organization, Sculley hoped that the new structure would give both independence and visibility to the new areas of growth. He envisaged that the Mac core would constitute the bulk of Apple's revenues for at least five years, generating the cash resources needed to invest in the new businesses. Sculley explained, "We will push resources out from the center to the new businesses. At the corporate level, we will only keep the smallest possible staff."

This was a dramatic blueprint for a company characterized by a traditionally amorphous and fluid structure. Indeed, some parts of the company had no organization charts in early 1992. According to one senior executive, "This is still run like a baby company. Decision making is kept simple. A core group of people gets together frequently, and that's what really holds this company together." A senior executive explained, "We have to see Mac as *a* business, not *the* business. When Mac was the center of the business, there was no objective way to consider the other parts on their own terms."

Resource Allocation

Sculley hoped that the new structure would help make resource allocation more explicit. According to Graziano, "The Mac group has to operate now under tighter financial controls in order to free up funding for the new product areas." Sculley emphasized, however, that investment in new product areas would not be entirely at the expense of the Mac. Apple wanted its partners to share the cost. In 1992, roughly 80 percent of R&D went to the Mac core and 20 percent to the new businesses. To improve Apple's productivity on R&D, Sculley and Spindler both started giving product development engineers very specific goals with shortened time horizons. The initial results had been very impressive. After numerous slips of the late 1980s, many analysts were once again touting Apple's technology leadership. Particularly in software, Apple brought to market in 1992 several key innovations, like making it easy to give voice commands to a computer.

Sculley's dilemma was how to fund the new businesses that would be critical to Apple in the late 1990s. The ongoing price war in the IBM PC world was leading companies like Compaq to drop prices as much as 50 percent every six months. While the Mac could command a premium in the marketplace, that premium was shrinking, putting enormous pressure on Apple's margin. Moreover, Sculley continued to feel that future resource decisions would be constrained by the need to keep the Mac business highly profitable. "There's little sympathy," remarked Sculley, "in the investment community if we can't make the core business support itself. If it doesn't, our shareholder value will plunge overnight. And since most of our prized employees are compensated with stock options, I constantly worry that a falling stock price will lead to a large-scale exodus."

Apple Management in 1992

Apple headed into 1992 with a strong, cohesive executive team and a small but very active board. According to Sculley, "Our team is now very pragmatic, very operational." One longtime board member agreed, "Apple management is a lot better today. Its people now are very good, and there is much less politics." A senior manager explained:

> Before it was Sculley and the warlords—Loren and Gassee—and there was lots of destructive energy internally. Now, for the first time, Sculley has a cohesive executive team that is communicating a clear vision. When Spindler took charge, he made people more accountable. Spindler provides strong leadership; he understands most aspects of the business. Sculley is a great intellect—he's always excited about the next initiative. And Spindler helps make these happen.

John Sculley

Sculley generally worked 12- to 14-hour days over seven-day weeks and was described by colleagues as "very intense" and "without much of a sense of humor." He typically rose by 4 A.M. to catch the latest economic news from Japan and Europe, before a run, workout, and 7 A.M. staff meeting (see Exhibit 5 for schedule of a typical Sculley day). Sculley read an enormous amount of material, including a daily customized electronic newspaper that tracked product reviews, and industry trade publications. In addition, either Sculley or his assistant reviewed his electronic mail messages, often numbering over 100, each day. As one board member described:

> John is one of the hardest working and brightest chief executives I know. He grasps things quickly and is very open to new ideas. He may be the least arrogant CEO I've seen. He doesn't put people down . . . His strength is his ability to see where the industry is going. He has gained a real understanding by immersing himself in the technology in recent years. In the past he was dependent on techies who gave him bad information; in addition, he used to get sold quickly on bad people . . . He's much better today.

Sculley's new hands-on approach, which evolved from his role as CTO, gave him many more opportunities to impact product development. While he could not write computer code or design a chip, he worked with technical people to define how the system would be presented to the end user. He was instrumental, for instance, in getting engineers to include key features in the Powerbook that greatly enhanced the product's functionality and user-friendliness.[3]

This attentiveness to details also made him much more responsive to problems. Despite the great success of Apple's new notebook computer in 1992, for example, its low-end model (the Powerbook 100) ran into immediate problems. Literally within a few weeks of inventory starting to build, Sculley was closely monitoring the product. His assistant tracked the product's sales and gave Sculley weekly reports on inventory. Within a month, he and Spindler jointly decided to start selling at a discount to avoid a costly write-off. Sculley noted, "We clearly made a mistake with Powerbook 100—it was somewhat underpowered compared to competitive offerings—but we very successfully kept it from becoming a crisis."

Sculley divided his time evenly between the Mac core and the new businesses, developing both internal and external relationships in each area. He sat on no outside boards other than a committee involved in education—a core Apple franchise. He hoped eventually to "get someone to run the entire Mac business" so that he could focus on Apple's new businesses.

---

[3]One example mentioned by Sculley of prodding his engineers to find better solutions was Remote Access, user-friendly software that allows the user to connect to his/her desktop in the office and access his/her files from any location.

EXHIBIT 5 John Sculley Representative Calendar, Fall 1991

MONDAY

7:00–8:00	Meeting with staff assistants
9:00–9:30	Conference call with Sony executives
10:00–11:00	General Magic Board meeting (an Apple spinoff; Apple holds minority share)
12:00–3:00	EMT meeting, including lunch
4:00–6:00	Meeting and update with Spindler

TUESDAY

7:00–7:30	Meeting with staff assistants
7:30–8:00	R&D update meeting
8:00–8:30	Human resources update meeting
8:30–10:00	IBM conference call
10:00–11:00	Meeting with Pacific PR re. conference in Japan
11:00–11:30	Apple International internal meeting
11:30–12:00	Lunch
12:00–1:00	Meeting with outside PR—review upcoming interviews
1:00–1:30	Meeting with Finance staff
2:00–2:30	Update with IS&T
3:30–5:00	Patent Award meeting and gathering
6:00	Dinner with Board member

WEDNESDAY

7:00–7:30	Meeting with staff assistants
7:30–8:00	Advanced technology update meeting
8:00–10:30	Dress rehearsal for Product Introduction speech
10:30–11:30	Meeting with Bank of Boston
11:30–12:00	Conference call with General Magic executives
1:00–3:00	Meeting re. new products
4:00–6:00	Claris Corp. Board of Directors meeting (Apple's wholly-owned software subsidiary)
6:00	Dinner w/Claris BOD members

THURSDAY

7:00–7:30	Meeting with staff assistants
7:30–8:00	R&D meeting
8:00–10:00	IBM update meetings (internal)
10:30–11:00	Interview/*Fortune* Magazine
11:00–12:00	Review Analysts Meeting speech
12:00–1:00	Lunch
1:00–3:00	Attend COO staff meeting
4:00–5:00	Conference call International Foundation

FRIDAY

7:00–7:30	Meeting with staff assistants
7:30–8:00	R&D update
8:00–10:00	Technology staff meeting
10:00–11:30	Review speeches for Sales meeting and Employee Communications meeting
11:30–12:00	Lunch
12:00–3:00	EMT Strategy meeting
3:00–4:00	CSPP conference call
4:00–4:30	Interview/Editor, *Wall Street Journal*
4:30–6:00	Final review of Product Introduction speech

Sculley was the ultimate idea-driven manager. He was constantly thinking of new ways to grow the company, reconfigure the product line, and diversify into related technology. In 1990, he focused heavily on building volume in the low-end computer market; in early 1991, he was exploring new semiconductor technologies and ways to deepen Apple's presence in large corporations; in late 1991 and early 1992, he was aggressively seeking partners for PDAs; in mid-1992, he was exploring how to leverage Apple's imaging (printer, scanner, etc.) technology. One member of Sculley's staff noted, "John announces publicly where the company will be, then leaves us to fill in the details." Another observed, "John believes that a good company should constantly be stretching. Just when you think you want to put your feet up and say, 'There, we've done it,' he comes in and provokes change." A third senior manager concurred: "Sculley is like the elder statesman of technology. He absorbs and effectively communicates a vision that comes collectively from outside and inside Apple. He articulates a farsighted vision very broadly, at a 50,000-foot level. We then have to figure out how to turn that vision into concrete plans."

Managing for the 1990s

Sculley noted with pride that "Apple now has a strong team of managers that can help lead us into the 1990s." At the highest level, the most significant decisions were made by the executive management team (EMT) that included Sculley, Spindler, Graziano, Kevin Sullivan, Albert Eisenstat, and, since April 1992, Edward Nagel (see Exhibit 6 for biographies). Below the EMT, there were several layers of managers, most of whom had been with Apple only two to three years by 1992. Apple had traditionally acquired senior management talent by hiring it from the outside. Hiring and promotion patterns showed that 50 percent of the EMT and their direct reports were either hired directly into their current job or assumed their position within a year of joining Apple. Apple's senior managers (directors and above) averaged 43 years of age and had been with the company for 5.5 years.[4] Operating in a structure of autonomous divisions, Apple managers were often functionally and geographically specialized with little lateral mobility.

Sculley also noted that the work environment was improving. Apple remained a very pleasant place to work: Its offices were bright, modern, high-tech buildings. The atmosphere was still casual, reflecting the California lifestyle of many of the employees—55 percent of whom were situated in Silicon Valley. And the company's historically strong, individualistic culture was reinforced by Apple's own technology. All employees were connected on a worldwide computer network called *Applelink,* which included *Can We Talk?,* an employee conferencing system. This electronic bulletin board featured many ongoing (and sometimes intense) employee debates of current events, social issues, and corporate issues.

Yet one senior manager observed: "The work environment is leaner and moves faster, but it's not enough. People love the work environment, but they don't like the work." People were being pushed to the limits; long hours and limited resources were leading to more "burnouts." The new financial model also left workers with only average pay and no pension benefits, so it was less attractive for some employees to stay. Another manager commented, "John is reengineering the future. Michael is relentlessly trying to extract value from the Mac at the same time as reducing expenses. That's a tough thing to do. I worry that we haven't dropped anything. People are simply working harder with less resources. We haven't fundamentally reengineered anything. This cannot continue; people are going to run out of gas." A 1992 survey also suggested that the vast majority of employees perceived that the company did not "invest" in its workforce and that executive management was not concerned about career opportunities. Even more disturbing was the 1992 survey showing no improvement over the previous year, with most employees still believing that the best people were passed over for promotion. Of course, this was nothing new: Because of rapid growth, Apple employees had constantly been stretched in their jobs and were often promoted with little time to develop appropriate management skills. However, one industry analyst commented that there continued to be "a lot of entrenched managers at Apple whose employees think (they) are incompetent."

A big question for Sculley and Spindler was whether Apple could retain its relatively informal style as the company grew bigger and more far-

[4]In contrast to senior management statistics, the average Apple employee was 36 years of age (up from 29 years in 1987) with 3.8 years' tenure in the company.

EXHIBIT 6 Biographies of Apple's Executive Management Team

John Sculley, chairman of the board, chief executive officer, and chief technology officer (age 52). He joined Apple as president and CEO and a director in May 1983 and was named chairman in January 1986. In November 1991, he was elected to the additional position of CTO.

Michael H. Spindler, president and chief operating officer (age 49). He joined Apple as European marketing manager in September 1980, was promoted to VP, Europe, in January 1984, was named VP, International, in February 1985, and was promoted to senior VP, International Sales and Marketing in November 1986. Spindler was appointed senior VP, International in January 1988, senior VP, Apple Europe Division in April 1988, and was promoted to senior VP and president, Apple Europe Division in August 1988. In January 1990, Spindler was promoted to COO and executive VP and in November 1990 he was elected president. In January 1991, he was elected a member of Apple's board of directors.

Albert A. Eisenstat, executive vice president and secretary (age 61). Eisenstat joined Apple in July 1980 as VP, general counsel and secretary. In November 1985, he was promoted to senior VP and was appointed a member of the board of directors. Eisenstat served as general counsel until January 1987 and as acting general counsel from April 1989 to June 1989. He also served as acting CFO from January 1989 to June 1989. In November 1990, Eisenstat was elected executive VP. In 1992, Eisenstat was also a director of Commercial Metals Company and Sungard Data Systems.

Joseph A. Graziano, executive vice president and chief financial officer (age 48). Graziano joined Apple in June 1989 as senior VP and CFO. In November 1990, he was elected executive VP. Before joining Apple, Graziano was CFO for Sun Microsystems from June 1987 to June 1989. Graziano also served as a director of ShareData and IntelliCorp in 1992.

Kevin J. Sullivan, senior vice president, Human Resources (age 50). Sullivan joined Apple in April 1987 as VP, Human Resources and was promoted to senior VP, Human Resources in October 1988. Before joining Apple, Sullivan was employed by DEC from 1980 to 1987, serving most recently as corporate personnel manager.

David C. Nagel, senior vice president, Advanced Technology Group (age 46). Dr. Nagel joined Apple in June 1988 as manager of applications technology within the Advanced Technology Group (ATG). Between June 1988 and May 1990, he was promoted to manager of user technologies, director of user technologies, and VP of ATG in May 1990. In November 1991, Dr. Nagel was promoted to senior VP, ATG. Previously, Dr. Nagel was employed by NASA Ames Research Center from 1973 to 1988 and most recently served as chief of the Aerospace Human Factors Research Division.

flung. Work was still done largely through committees, meetings, and consensus. One employee observed, "We are low on systems and high on the human side. There are very few formal rules or processes." Another remarked, "There is no consistent process; every time we do something we do it a different way." The informal approach to management meant that influence tended to be the primary way of achieving one's objectives. An HR manager said, "Apple is highly relationship and network oriented. If you know the right people you can get things done—there are lots of inner circles." The same was true for organization. One manager commented, "Apple is fluid and volatile. We use reorgs to make changes. Reorganization is inherent in our organizational structure."

Sculley told employees in the spring of 1992, "As we make this transition to a company with lots of technology that wants to turn them into lots of businesses, the only way we will implement it successfully is to get people working together." While Spindler believed that progress had been made in establishing more accountability and fact-based management, he acknowledged, "We're probably still more technology-rich than we are field-effective."

To bring the organization in line with the new strategy, Sculley and Spindler began to spend a significant amount of time simply communicating their vision of the new Apple to the organization. In May 1992, for example, they held a meeting for 5,000 Apple employees at the San Jose Convention Center, which was broadcast live around the world to all Apple locations. At this session, Sculley and Spindler explained their long-term vision for the company, the present operating plans, and took questions from the audience on topics ranging from strategy to ethics. Sculley also communicated to employees through announcements and internal videos of discussions between him and Spindler. In addition, forums were held each quarter during which 12 to 15 employees drawn by lottery spent a day together and a day with Sculley and Spindler. According to Sculley, these videotaped forums indicated a "much greater appreciation that management is not a dirty word."

Beginning in 1991, the EMT also held executive forums with senior management, facilitated by Apple University, to discuss how they could improve the speed and effectiveness throughout Apple. Some senior managers perceived that Apple lacked highly focused, actionable strategies. According to one executive, strategic priorities were either overly "cosmic" or else highly product-specific. Out of these meetings came several new initiatives, including Executive Readiness, the rollout of Apple Quality Management, Apple Critical Performance Indicator metrics, and a restructuring of the marketing organization. All of these programs were designed to create better operational systems and clearer organizational structures at Apple.

Executive Readiness

> Capable leadership is essential to Apple's immediate and long-term success. Thoughtful planning and execution of executive capabilities will be a strategic edge for Apple as we move forward.[5]

To strengthen management bench strength and build a more flexible organization, the EMT initiated a companywide planning process for reviewing and developing senior managers. The Executive Readiness program, launched in early 1992, aimed to develop critical leadership resources through a disciplined organizational review process that assessed Apple's management strength.

The first round of organizational review meetings in April 1992 involved a two-way discussion of the EMT with each general manager or president. In these informal and confidential meetings, the EMT strove to promote a "helpful" climate conducive to an honest appraisal of leadership talent. Executive Readiness was not conceived as a onetime event, but rather as an important annual management process. By June 1992, the EMT had met with senior managers in Mac Hardware and Worldwide Operations, Advanced Products Group (Newton), Advanced Technology Group, and Apple USA. An EMT review meeting was planned at the end of that month to evaluate the success of the first series of reviews.

There was skepticism within Apple about this process and concern about closed-door discussions. People were already stretched. Some questioned whether senior management viewed Executive Readiness as a long-term investment in people or a short-term fix to immediate business needs. Another issue was whether it was reasonable or desirable to develop people across divisional lines, given the way Apple was organized. Others questioned if the company could afford to be unable to move individuals quickly to fill unexpected gaps in leadership. One longtime Apple University manager asserted, "There is no slack in the system and no clear rotation paths."

There were indications that this was changing, however. By May 1992, the Apple University manager in charge of Executive Readiness had sat down with each general manager and created a "list" of the core competencies needed in that division. One surprising result was that all operational divisions identified customer focus as a key capability—"that would never have happened before. What started as a top-down process is now percolating back up."

Apple Quality Management

Seeking a tool to help them build better products faster and in a more cost-effective way, Apple's Worldwide Manufacturing organization began employing total quality management techniques. In August, Spindler commissioned a cross-functional steering committee to develop a plan for using total quality management throughout Apple. In February 1991, the EMT approved their proposal for an Apple Quality Management (AQM) program.

Beyond improving production processes and product quality, AQM stressed focusing on customers and using data to make decisions. Spindler, who defined quality as "the organizational performance of the entire corporation," viewed AQM as a way to "get real focus and discipline into the way each of us works." He argued, "We have to change organizational behavior by focusing on process. We've got to be more systematic now. In a sense it means losing our innocence and working a lot more professionally." The corporate AQM director added, "When we were a high-growth, high-profit company, we could always fix a problem by throwing more money or people at it. Moreover, Apple has had a history of everyone doing their own agendas. Now that the industry has flattened out, the practices of the past that were OK are no longer acceptable." (See Exhibit 7 for AQM process.)

The AQM steering committee developed a plan to implement AQM in four simultaneous phases:

[5]"Executive Readiness" Position Paper, Apple University, April 14, 1992.

EXHIBIT 7 Implementing Apple Critical Performance Measures

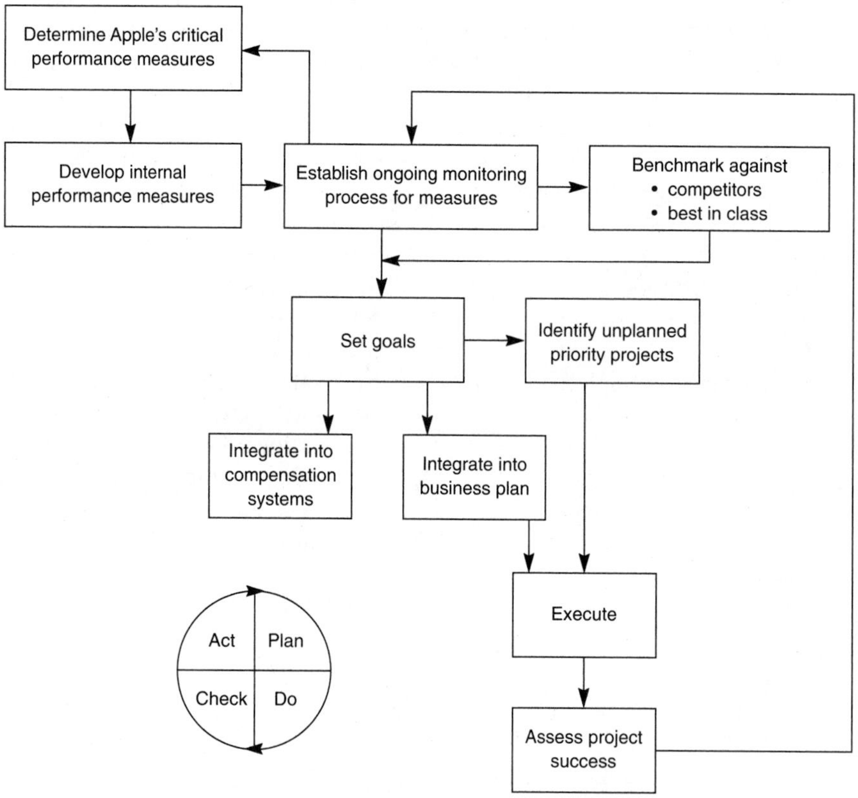

SOURCE: Company documents.

(1) education and leadership (getting the senior management on board); (2) functional process improvement (training and small PDCA[6] projects); (3) integrating systems (cross-functional process improvement and large PDCA projects); (4) policy deployment (linking long-term corporate objectives with department policy and activity plans). The AQM director explained the decision to do all four phases in parallel instead of serially: "We can't wait 3 to 10 years to get results. We won't be alive if we wait that long. Moreover, if we don't demonstrate quick wins, Apple people won't buy it. This is a really skeptical company with the attitude, 'Prove it. I'm the designer; I know best.' So we're trying to demonstrate at various levels in various departments how these tools and techniques make sense." A 16-person steering committee set 90 percent of the strategy—10 percent was done with the EMT—as well as the tactical implementation within each division. Most members were part-time and represented their respective divisions. AQM training was accomplished through AQM "101" and "102" courses given by Apple University and was also incorporated into established employee training programs.

AQM began attracting companywide attention—both positive and negative—in 1992. Management commitment to AQM was tested after the EMT announced a reorganization in March 1992. Employees queried the EMT on whether it had used the AQM process in making its decision. Sculley's admission over Applelink that the EMT did not formally use AQM made many employees cynical. Nonetheless, by May, 32 percent of the company had completed AQM orientation and 20 percent of the managers had completed AQM Integration (against goals of 50 percent for both areas in 1992).

[6]AQM was based on the Plan-Do-Check-Act (PDCA) model of process improvement used by many total quality companies worldwide, such as Komatsu.

Over 100 functional projects were in process in Apple worldwide, including Apple Assistance Center (which reduced written response time from six weeks to one day); Apple France (which cut the expense statement cycle from four weeks to five days). AQM had also contributed to more complex, phase (3) successes. For example, a cross-functional effort to redesign product packaging using new "brown boxes" addressed environmental, marketing, manufacturing, and distribution issues and saved Apple $3.1 million in 1992.

Reactions to AQM varied. One senior manager noted that the "EMT lost credibility when they espoused AQM for the masses but not for themselves." Another senior executive and longtime employee dubbed AQM "the strategy du jour." One of the biggest debates, however, was whether AQM should be an education process and state of mind, or whether it should be a formal system of measurements. According to one senior software manager, "AQM is a great idea as long as it's an educational tool. Let's make sure everyone understands what quality means. But it would be a disaster for us to hire directors of quality, appoint a vice president of quality, and then move to a 'six-sigma' like system. Such a formalized system just can't work in an organization that emphasizes creativity." The AQM corporate director acknowledged that "we've met resistance in engineering. We're starting to be successful, but we still have to break though the mind-set 'I'm creative; I don't need a process.' " Some employees were irritated by reading materials distributed in AQM classes that detailed TQM applications in other companies, protesting "we don't want to be like 'them.' " Some AQM classes were canceled because of low sign-up rates.

Apple Critical Performance Indicators

The fourth phase in implementing AQM—policy deployment—involved tying all the process improvement activities into the company's long-term objectives. In order to make process improvements in areas that truly impacted Apple, the EMT set goals and measurements around five Apple Critical Performance Indicators (ACPIs): employee alignment and commitment, core competencies, shareholder value, market share, and customer satisfaction. The EMT then put together cross-functional teams to establish these metrics in each of the 16 divisions. For example, shareholder value was being integrated into the business plan, put into the compensation system, and measured on how it impacted the bottom line (see Exhibit 8). An executive noted, "This is radically different from two years ago." Spindler added, "Metrics don't take away intuition. ACPIs just add another dimension of managing the company that is more fact-based."

Shareholder value was one of the first ACPIs to be integrated into Apple's operations. The EMT began broad training through Apple University of operating and planning managers in early 1992 to incorporate a shareholder value framework into decision-making processes. Maximizing shareholder value was included as an important goal in the 1993 business plan, and executive compensation was based on shareholder value-creating behavior.

ACPIs were being written into the performance reviews and bonuses of many divisions in 1992, as Spindler strove to have everyone measured against them by 1994. ACPIs were anchored in the performance criteria of Spindler's direct reports, in terms specifically relating to his or her job. Spindler noted that 50 percent of his compensation in 1993 depended upon the execution of ACPIs. For example, when the company did not meet its shareholder value goal in 1992, Spindler and other senior and middle managers did not receive that portion of their bonus. In Worldwide Operations, quality improvement goals were decided as a team. One engineer explained, "The whole group said, 'This is what our customer needs; this is what we're going to do to get there. Here's our target; that's what we're going to get bonuses against.' "

The debate on ACPIs was how far down should management push this system into the organization. A manager who worked for Spindler noted, "ACPIs are fine for Spindler and they're fine for me, but what about my direct reports? And that person's direct reports? Does it make sense for someone three or four levels down in the organization to be rewarded on shareholder value, even though they have little ability to impact the share price directly? If we are not careful at Apple, we will move from a company that clearly lacked adequate systems to a big bureaucracy that tries to measure everything."

Further Reorganization

In order to better align Apple's operational execution, the EMT added a market-based overlay to the way it planned and managed Apple. Agreeing that a generic approach to reaching customers had become outdated, they focused on four key mar-

EXHIBIT 8 Example of Deployment of an Apple Critical Performance Indicator

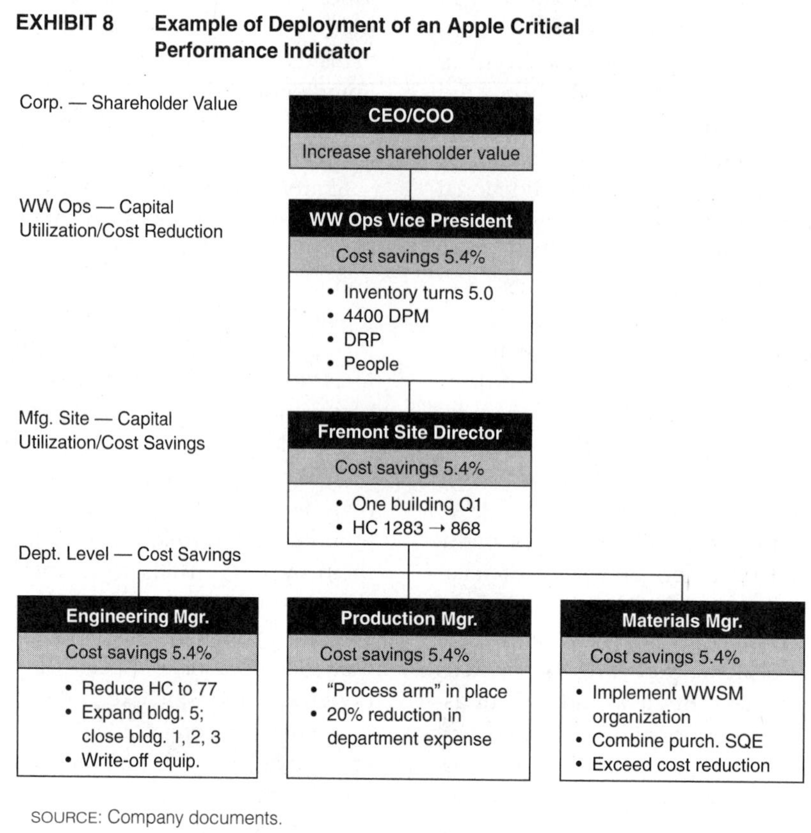

SOURCE: Company documents.

kets: K-12 education; institutional such as the government, large businesses, and higher education; consumers; and small and medium businesses. Spindler explained the intent at an employee communications meeting:

> Most PC companies in the 1970s were organized around territories. That isn't necessarily the right model for the 1990s. We have to get much closer to the customer. . . . Our most important U.S. franchise is K-12, in which we have a 60 percent market share. We have people in front of the customer, understanding what they want and using a channel which helps us to sell to them. We'd like to do this in other markets. So we're restructuring organizations that deal with the consumer market and crafting channels that help us get to the user, not the other way around. We can't be held hostage by the channel in place.

When asked at an employee communications meeting in May if he was satisfied with the pace of progress in the Apple USA reorganization, Spindler responded that he was not. Sculley added that they had to develop new market segments faster, and align with the right channels in these markets earlier than the competition. For example, every computer company except Apple offered mail order in May 1992. In addition, Apple was moving into mass merchandiser channels, but it was late. "So," Sculley stressed, "we must get even more aggressive in opening up these markets and channels and realigning people because the only way our business proposition works is if we can get high growth. So we have to go faster."

Leading the Next Generation

Sculley knew that Apple was venturing into uncharted territories. There was a lot to implement, given scarce resources, perishable technology, lack of management bench strength, and a culture that resisted greater use of systems. Yet he knew that Apple's success would depend upon how they resolved these issues. It was one thing to run a start-up with creative people doing creative things. But

Apple was now a $7 billion business exploring multiple markets with multiple technologies.

As Sculley reflected on Apple's situation in the summer of 1992, he commented:

> We have done an extraordinary job in the last two years. Our gains in market share, profitability, etc., are more than anyone should have expected. But we are in such a tough industry, I am constantly worried about how to maintain the level of performance. Everyone in the company is feeling pressure that we are cutting their funding. But I think we have to move faster and change faster. We can cut more expenses out of the organization. I also think it is better to get people to work harder rather than cutting out projects. There is deep resistance within management to cutting resources in the Macintosh division. But if we can rebalance our resources—put more money into the new technologies—we could be one of the dominant technology companies in the world by the end of the decade. I think that as early as the second half of 1993, the results will be clear to the employees and the financial markets. In some ways we have a great dilemma—we have more great technology that we can turn into great products than anyone in the world.
>
> What I have learned in the last 10 years is that I should have been involved in the technology [as CTO] much earlier; we should have moved much faster to gain market share and become a more open systems computer company; and we should have exploited more aggressively our broad technology base in software, networking, imaging, and user-interface. In the coming years, I want to move Apple in the direction of corporations like Pepsi, where you can have an aggressive firm with deep management, flexible systems, and a great deal of autonomy across diverse divisions. As we go forward, I would like the EMT to become more of a portfolio manager and create the same kind of depth, breadth, and professionalism at Apple.

*APPENDIX THE EVOLVING PERSONAL COMPUTER INDUSTRY 1976–1992**

In some ways, the personal computer was a very simple device. Most PCs were composed of five widely available components: memory storage, a microprocessor (the brains of the PC), a main circuit board called a mother board, a disk drive, and peripherals (e.g., display, keyboard, mouse, printer, etc.). Most manufacturers also bundled their PC hardware with critical software packages, especially an operating system (the software required to run applications). But from the beginning, PCs have been available in almost infinite variety. They could vary in speed, storage, physical size, weight, functionality, and so on.

During the early years of the industry, venture capital in the United States encouraged the entry of new firms, which offered products in every conceivable shape and size. By 1980, new entrants flooded the market, promoting distinct standards and unique technical features. Virtually every firm had a different configuration of hardware and software, making communication or sharing applications between machines virtually impossible. The first PCs introduced by Commodore and Apple had relatively little speed or memory. However, even these early computers allowed managers to perform tasks that were either very time consuming or reserved for expensive ($50,000 to >$1 million), multi-user mini and mainframe computers. For under $5,000, anyone could now do spreadsheet analysis and word processing.

Before IBM entered the market in 1981, most products were considered "closed" or proprietary systems. A closed system, like mainframes, minicomputers, and Apple's PCs, could not be copied or cloned because it was protected by patents or copyrights. However, closed systems typically rendered the computer incompatible with competitors' products. IBM's entry in 1981 changed the playing field by offering an "open" system. IBM released the specifications of its PC, allowing independent hardware companies to make compatible machines and independent software vendors (ISVs) to write applications that would run on different brands. Open systems had a big advantage for customers because they were no longer locked into a particular vendor's product, and they could mix and match hardware and software from different competitors to get the lowest system price. And as long as manufacturers could buy the key components, particularly Microsoft's DOS (disk operating system) and Intel's X86 family of microprocessors, they could manufacture a product that could piggyback on IBM's coattails. Between 1982 and 1986, the majority of the industry consolidated around IBM's MS-DOS/Intel X86 microprocessor standard. Among the various proprietary PC systems, which had included names like DEC, Xerox, and Wang, only Apple thrived.

Although IBM had created an open system that fostered imitators, few firms were capable of com-

---

*This Appendix is drawn from "Apple Computer 1992," HBS Case No. 782–081.

peting head to head with IBM. On the strength of its brand name and product quality, IBM captured almost 70 percent of the Fortune 1000 business market during its first four years. In addition, the personal computer was still a relatively new machine through the mid-1980s, and users were uncertain about quality, compatibility, service, and reliability. Concerns over the bankruptcies of companies, like Osborne and Leading Edge, as well as the occasional incompatible machine, led the majority of corporate buyers to buy brand-name computers through respected, high-service retail channels, such as ComputerLand. Most retailers, however, only had space on their shelves for four or five major brands. In the mid-1980s, the typical retailer carried three core, premium brands: Apple, which was the leader in user-friendliness and applications like desktop publishing; IBM, which was the premium priced, industry standard; and Compaq, which built IBM-compatible machines with a strong reputation for quality and high performance. The multitude of smaller clone companies had to compete for the remaining one or two spaces on the retailer's shelf.

The early growth in PCs was built partly on rapidly changing innovative hardware and partly on exciting software applications. In its first five years, IBM and compatibles went through four major hardware product generations—the PC (based on Intel 8088), PC XT (based on 8086 and a hard drive), PC AT (based on Intel 80286), and 80386 PCs; in the meantime, Apple went from the Apple II to Macintosh—a major breakthrough in user-friendliness and functionality. The PC explosion was also fueled by software applications. Programs like Lotus 1-2-3 and WordPerfect were nicknamed "killer apps" because they were so powerful compared to their predecessors, everyone wanted them. Most of the best programs for business applications were written for the IBM standard, while Apple dominated educational applications and graphics.

The late 1980s saw revolution turn into evolution in both hardware and software. On one front, IBM faltered, losing almost half its market share. A new generation of PC clones manufacturers such as Dell and Gateway stole share, particularly when most customers found they could no longer distinguish between low-priced and premium brands. The most significant shift was that the greatest differentiation in the industry had been between standards—IBM versus Apple. However, when Microsoft introduced its "Windows" 3.0 graphical user interface in 1990, the differences in user-friendliness between IBM machines and Macs narrowed significantly.

By 1992, the personal computer was a $50 billion hardware business, with another $30 billion in software and peripherals. The installed base of PCs approached 100 million units. However, the business had changed from a high-growth industry to an industry with a few high-growth segments. In addition, cutthroat pricing was the rule in the mainstream products. New products, like notebook computers, and traditional products sold through new channels, like direct mail, continued to sell at double-digit growth rates. But fierce competition was driving down margins for leaders and followers alike.

Name Index

Subject Index